NEW
DICTIONARY OF
AMERICAN FAMILY NAMES

NEW
DICTIONARY
OF AMERICAN
FAMILY NAMES

ELSDON C. SMITH

HARPER & ROW, PUBLISHERS
New York, Evanston, San Francisco, London

Portions of this book appeared in the *Ladies' Home Journal*.

STANDARD BOOK NUMBER: 06-013933-1

LIBRARY OF CONGRESS CATALOG CARD NUMBER: 72-79693

3BUH0000098844

To My Wife
CLARE

CONTENTS

PREFACE TO ENLARGED EDITION

When a new edition is prepared and made about three times as large as the first edition some additional explanatory comments may be expected and it is important that they be made.

Some may repeat the criticism of the first edition, that the author has failed to list references, roots, the etymological origins, and the early forms of the words from which the surnames were derived, and they do have a valid point. But to list early forms, variant spellings, sources, and all the pertinent evidence supporting the explanation of each name would have made the work unwieldy and—let's recognize it—no publisher could print it with any hope of profit. Decision was therefore made to emphasize the explanations of surnames, the meaning of the words and the way they were used to evolve into hereditary family names, rather than the technical etymology of the words from which the names were derived. Such is ample to answer the question of the man who wonders how his surname originated.

In the first edition every effort was made to include all the common surnames found in America. In adding names considerable attention has been given to those next most often found in this country. The problem of selection became much more difficult. A name might be quite common in one city or locality and quite rare elsewhere. Complete investigation of the frequency of relatively uncommon names in the country would entail endless labor. An accurate count could be made by machine in the Social Security lists, but this has not been done, except for the approximately 2180 most common surnames and these have been carefully included.

In adding the more common as well as some not so common but interesting names, a larger proportion from European and Asiatic countries other than the British Isles was necessarily included. Which is the way it should be. The United States is the home of peoples from throughout the world.

As names derived from almost every country which has contributed to the citizenship of America are here included, help had to be obtained from many of the most authoritative onomastic scholars. And the author is most happy to relate that they have freely given of their knowledge of names. The author needed more than "just a little help from my friends," and they responded.

Sincere thanks and appreciation must be given to: Grace Alvarez de Altman, L. R. N. Ashley, Morton Benson, Robert W. Buechley, Enrique Chelminsky L., Patricia Anne Davis, Geart B. Droege, Olof von Feilitzen, Joseph G. Fucilla, Demetrius J. Georgacas, Zbigniew Golab, David L. Gold, Peter D. Haikalis, Eric P. Hamp, Haakon Hamre, Douglas P. Hinkle, Jacob P. Hursky, Assar Janzen, Gillian Fellows Jensen, Kostas Kazazis, Antonas Klimas, Aziz E. La Verdi, Atsuko Levy, Johann Lyons, Ernest Maass, Gerald M. Moser, Hildegard

Must, Samuel G. T. Naparstek, W. S. W. Nowak, Larissa Onyshkevych, Ladislas Országh, Louis Palanca, Henry A. Person, Emilio Peruzzi, Jaroslav Bohdan Rudnyćkyj, Lester Sellinger, Alfred Senn, Yar Slavutych, Sterling Stoudemire, and Wolodymyr T. Zyla.

These authorities may not be credited with the many errors of commission and omission which may be found. For these only the author is responsible.

There is one other person whose contribution to the successful completion of the enlarged edition must be recognized. That is the author's wife, Clare I. Smith, who has done a great deal of detailed work in checking directories, alphabetizing, reading proofs, etc. Without her many hours of careful labor the work would be much less valuable.

ELSDON C. SMITH

PREFACE

In this vast melting pot of the world, which we call the United States of America, live the peoples of many lands. Here, side by side, they dwell, bound together by similar ideals, blood ties, common interests and enjoyment of the American way of life. Each family carries a distinctive label, a gift from medieval times, allied with its own identity and never forgotten—the family name. Since it has been a commonplace, in the possession of the family for generations, even for many centuries, it is taken for granted. Now and then one pauses to wonder how that particular family name came to identify one's ancestors.

To answer that question is the purpose of this dictionary. Some rare names originated as a result of particular actions or circumstances, the exact nature and origin of which are now probably forever lost. Others can be investigated and their origin discovered, especially the common ones that arose in many different places at about the same time. All of the common names in this country, with some of their variant forms, are here included. Many of the names have taken on a flavor or tinge that is American, the exact form not being found elsewhere, although they have been identified by the country or countries of origin.

A dictionary of this type, involving, as it does, many diverse languages and dialects, not only as spoken at the present time, but including forms used in medieval times, cannot be compiled without assistance and advice from many scholars learned in onomastics.

The American Name Society was organized some years ago to promote the study of names, and this organization has brought together practically all the scholars in this country interested in onomatology. The membership of this Society has been the principal source from which advice could be sought in connection with the many problems that arose in regard to particular family names.

With great pleasure the author therefore acknowledges his indebtedness to the following very able and learned scholars: Samuel H. Abramson, Timothy M. Bishop, Samuel L. Brown, Albert J. Carnoy, Charles Collins, Joseph N. Corcoran, Jack Autrey Dabbs, Geart B. Droege, Gösta Frantzen, Peter Fu, Joseph G. Fucilla, Demetrius J. Georgacas, Erwin G. Gudde, E. Gustav Johnson, Ellen Johnson, Aneale L. Kushmar, J. J. Lamberts, Werner F. Leopold, Alexander McQueen, Max Markrich, P. J. Meertens, James A. Morrison, Merle Morrison, Jens Nyholm, Ernst Pulgram, Jaroslav Bohdan Rudnyćkyj, Alfred Senn, Mary Florence Steiner, John P. Sydoruk, and Gutierre Tibón.

However, none of the errors can be charged against any of these erudite and competent scholars. Let's face it: the instances of bad judgment and errors are due entirely to the ignorance of the author.

Much of the completeness and accuracy of the work can be credited to the careful help and support from Clare I. Smith, my wife, who spent countless hours, days and weeks in studies of the relative frequency of American family names, and in checking and cross-checking for accuracy and completeness in the explanations. Without her steady help and encouragement this work would have taken many months longer.

To list the works consulted would serve little purpose here, since works in English on personal names are listed in *Personal Names: A Bibliography,* compiled by the author and published by the New York Public Library in 1952. Many later works have been listed by the author in bibliographies published by *Names, Journal of the American Name Society.* A select list of the more important works on personal names has been listed in Chapter XIV of *The Story of Our Names,* by the present author, published by Harper & Brothers in 1950. Of course, various works on personal names in other languages have been consulted as well as numerous standard reference works.

ELSDON C. SMITH

INTRODUCTION

After the Crusades in Europe, people began, perhaps unconsciously, to feel the need of a family name, or at least a name in addition to the simple one that had been possessed from birth. The nobles and upper classes, especially those who went on the Crusades, observed the prestige and practical value of an added name and were quick to take a surname, usually the name of the lands they owned. When the Crusaders returned from the wars, the upper classes who had stayed at home soon followed suit.

When the clerks who kept the records in the manors and on the feudal lands of the nobles and the great landowners noted the payment of fines and amercements by the vassals, they needed an additional description in order to distinguish one Robert or Leofric from another. The inclination to ridicule or compliment a neighbor or acquaintance by applying a nickname contributed to the rise of surnames.

It would do no good for the lord's clerk to ask the peasant what additional name he possessed. He didn't have any other name and hadn't thought about the matter. Therefore, when the clerk noted the vassal's name in the manor records he added, on his own initiative, a brief description. It was likely that the vassal was not known among his neighbors by the description put down by the scribe. The very earliest bynames were not names by which those so described were known, except in isolated instances.

The early forms of most descriptive bynames were with prepositions, as *atte Hill* (at the hill), *on Mylatune* (from Milton), *de Bedeford* (from Bedford), *of Boclande* (of Buckland), *buta Port* (outside the gate), *del Boys* (at the wood), *Cole sunu* (son of Cole), *filius Alann* (son of Allan), and *the Clerec* (the clerk or clergyman). Early documents were written in Latin in many countries and the names took Latin forms although the man would be known generally by the descriptive word in the common tongue, and so the family names are, in England, for example, English and not Latin. English surnames have generally dropped the prepositions, except a few names like *Atterbury, Bywater* and *Underwood.* Many French and Italian names have retained the preposition or article, as *Dupont* and *Lo Bello.*

Surnames are not just words or sounds. They originated as descriptions of the person for reasons of better identification. These early additional names were bynames and not family names. They described one individual and not his whole family.

A byname, that is, a name in addition to the Christian name and not necessarily a family name, was at first not hereditary. As long as it was descriptive of the person to whom it was applied, it was not handed down from father to son, although in some cases the same name might be borne by both father and son, as when both had red hair or both followed the same occupation. It was only gradually, over several centuries, that bynames or surnames became hereditary family names. Just as a nickname need be appropriate only for an instant, a by-name which became a family name need be descriptive only for a short time.

In England, by the end of the fourteenth century, surnames were generally hereditary; in France the process evolved a little earlier and in Germany a little later. In Italy the patricians of Venice adopted a hereditary surname system during the tenth and eleventh centuries, and they were the first in Europe. On the other hand, many family names became hereditary in very recent times in Norway, Sweden, Turkey, the mountainous districts of Wales and Scotland and among the Germanic and Slavic Jews.

Names first became hereditary, in most countries, among the nobles and land-owners. Since so many of their names were the names of the lands they held, when the son inherited the land it was only natural that he inherit the name. Among the lower classes, since the son generally learned and followed the trade of his father, the same occupational name was applied, not because it was in-herited, but because it applied to the son as well as the father. The occupational name could be said to be inherited only when the son followed another trade but was known by the same surname as the father.

Even today if one had to identify another whose name was not known, it would likely be done in one of four ways: (1) the place where the man now lived or had previously lived would be mentioned, as at the sign of the bell, or by the hill or stream, or from the manor of Newton; or (2) by the man's oc-cupation, as the smith or the carter; or (3) by referring to the father's name, as the son of John or Rob; or (4) by noting the man's most prominent character-istic, as short, fat, red (hair), or crooked mouth.

Practically all of the European family names were thus derived in one or another of the following four ways:

    I. From the man's place of residence, either present or past;
    II. From the man's occupation;
    III. From the father's name;
    IV. From a descriptive nickname.

From the man's place of residence.

Almost every city, town or village extant in the Middle Ages has served to name one or more families. While a man lived in the town or village he would not be known by its name, as that would be no means of identification—all in the village would then be so named. But when a man left his birthplace or vil-lage where he had been known, and went elsewhere, people would likely refer to him by the name of his former residence or by the name of the land which he owned. In many cases, the surname is the form of the place name current at the time the surname arose, and thus not easily recognizable on modern maps. In other cases, the place name which gave rise to the family name cannot be found on maps because the place no longer exists. It is curious to note, however, that the spelling of the surname changed along with the spelling of the town name in most cases.

Some had the name of a manor or village because they were lords of that manor or village and owned it. However, of people today who have a place name as a surname, a very small minority descended from the lord of that manor. The majority descended from vassals or freemen who once lived in the village or manor.

One might acquire a place name as a surname by living at or near the place. This is particularly true of topographical features. When people lived close to the soil, as they did in the Middle Ages, they were acutely conscious of every local variation in landscape and countryside. Every field or plot of land was identified in normal conversation by a descriptive term. If a man lived on, or near, a hill or mountain, he might receive the word as a family name. Every country had hills and mountains and living on, or near, them gave many people names, as Mr. *Maki,* from Finland, Mr. *Dumont* and Mr. *Depew,* from France, Mr. *Zola,* from Italy, Mr. *Jurek,* from Poland, Mr. *Kopecky,* from Czechoslovakia, and the ubiquitous Mr. *Hill.*

Dwelling at, or near, a lake, brook or river would distinguish one from others who lived further from the water, and such names were quite common in almost every country. Lakes gave rise to *Jarvi* (Finland), *Kuhl* (Germany), *Loch* (Scotland), and *Pond, Pool, Leake, Lynn* and *Lake* (England), while streams produced *Strom* (Sweden), *Potocki* (Poland), *Joki* (Finland), *Rio* and *Rivera* (Spain), *Klink* (Holland and Germany), and *Brooks* and *Rivers* (England), to list only a few of the most common names. Many other names include a suffix after the word to designate the man who lived at or near the lake or stream.

Identifying the origin and meaning of place names from which certain surnames are derived presents many problems. Village names are often so old that onomatologists cannot agree on their derivation. Take, for example, Elsdon, an old and pleasant village in the North of England, in Northumberland to be more exact. Perhaps the best signification is that it refers to Ellis's valley or hill. But it has also been explained as the dene or vale of Ellers, that is, Alders; or from Saxon *elde* old and *dun,* a hill, that is, old hill; or a hill or fort upon a hill referring to the Mote Hills of the Romans; in addition there is the legend of Ella, the Giant, roaming in the wooded valley or den terrifying the residents.

When a family name derives from the name of a town where the original bearer once resided, a brief explanation or translation of the town name is given in parentheses wherever possible. When more than one meaning of a place name is given, the reason often is that there are several villages with exactly the same name with reference to present-day spelling, although they were derived in different ways. For example, *Broughton* is a very common English place name. Certain villages of that name in Buckinghamshire, Cumberland, Derbyshire, Huntingdonshire, Lancashire, Leicestershire, Nottinghamshire, Oxfordshire, Wiltshire, Warwickshire, Worcestershire and Yorkshire referred to "a homestead on a brook," while other villages named Broughton, in Lancashire, Lincolnshire, Northamptonshire, Shropshire, Staffordshire and Sussex, designated "a homestead by a fortified place," and Broughton, in Hampshire and Lincolnshire, originally meant "a homestead on a hill or barrow." Many place names in Europe are of great antiquity; the meanings are so obscure that it would serve little purpose to give them without a lengthy discussion of the reasons for accepting that explanation.

Woods, stones, fields, plains, swamps, enclosures, or fenced-in places and trees are natural objects in all the Old World countries and have served to name the people living on, in or near them. Now we pay little attention to small features of the landscape, but one has only to visit a European country to appreciate the attention people paid to hills and valleys, woods and fields, buildings and bridges which became names of the people who lived by or in conjunction with them. Fords were common at a time when there were few bridges. Many of these names that appear to be from a topographical term are really from a definite town, village or field name that cannot be identified at the present time. Today we live in cities and towns where streets are named and houses are numbered so we have little occasion to use topographical terms.

To ascertain properly the meaning of the different elements in a name is not always easy. This is especially true of the common elements and more particularly true of those which make up place names, such as the English *ham, thorp, wic* and *worth.* Take the simple element *hope,* found in so many place names which have been taken as family names. It meant, among other meanings, "a piece of enclosed land in the midst of fens," "a small, enclosed valley, a blind valley," "a valley." Take again, for example, the Old English *leah,* generally found as *-ley,* a terminal element in a great many English place names and consequently an element in numerous family names. It meant "an open place in a wood, a glade, a spot where grass grew," "meadow or pasture land," "open, arable land," or "a wood, grove or forest," some of these definitions being in direct apposition. In some instances the exact meaning can be ascertained, in others it can only be guessed. The most common English place name element is *-ton,* meaning "an enclosure," "a homestead," "a village," "a town," at various times and in different parts of England. Similar difficulties occur in names from languages other than English. Most elements now meaning town or city started out meaning "a place or a settlement," often a place where only one family resided.

An important source of family names arises from residence in a house or inn identified by a signboard. In some countries, in very early times, inns and public houses were required by law to display a sign. Since few people could read, pictorial signs, rather than the written signs we have today, were the almost invariable rule. Even the early Greeks and Romans identified their public places by distinctive signs. One public house might display the picture of a white horse, another a goblet, while another might have a bush over its door. One of the commonest was a bell; others were ball, cock and swan. Animals, birds and fishes of all kinds were popular. Some of these signs were wooden or stone images, others were merely painted pictures. In later times more elaborate signs were common, and in London there were the *Angel and Glove,* the *Three Kings, Adam and Eve,* the *Whistling Oyster* and many others.

When a man lived or worked in a building identified by a pictorial sign it was only natural to refer to him by reference to his distinctive place of residence. In medieval times most people also lived where they worked. There can be little doubt that the ancient signboards provide explanation of many otherwise inexplicable family names, but the direct evidence is scanty because of the disappearance of the very early signboards. Every conceivable object, both animate and inanimate, became the subject of signboards in various countries, and influenced family names.

With regard to family names from signboards a note of caution is necessary. In later times many tradespeople adopted punning signs which helped the customers to remember their names, although such signs may have had little to do with the derivation of their names. Some went to extremes. Thus, in England, Mr. Chester exhibited a chest with a star on it; Mr. Lionel had a lion with *L* on its head; John Handcock used a hand and a cock, while John Drinkwater imitated his name with a fountain. In other European countries the same practice prevailed. Tavern, inn and shop signs continued after house signs fell into disuse.

From the man's occupation.

To describe one by reference to his occupation or profession is most natural. The most common occupational surnames are not necessarily those of the occupations followed by the most men in the Middle Ages. Where everybody was a fisherman or where everybody tilled the soil, the occupation would not serve to describe the bearer. If the fisherman moved inland or the tiller of the soil worked among sheep raisers, their occupation would become a means of identification to set them apart from others in the neighborhood.

Most of the occupations or professions reflected in our family names are those known in the small villages in Europe, or those followed in a king's, or important noble's, household, or in some large religious house or monastery. During the Middle Ages much of Europe was composed of small villages. Even the larger cities would be regarded as comparatively small today. Every village, no matter how small, would need the services of one who could work and fashion objects out of iron or other metals and thus the smith is found in every country. Bulgaria surnames him *Kovac,* the Danes use *Smed,* the Hungarians say *Kovars,* the French call him *Lefevre* and *Faure,* the Germans say *Schmidt* or *Smidt,* in Italy it is *Ferraro,* the Russians refer to *Kuznetzov,* and the Poles to *Kowal.*

Every village required the services of a *Carpenter* to build houses of wood and of a *Miller* to grind the grain. The *Bakers* and *Cooks* prepared the bread from the ground grain. *Taylors* made the clothing while the *Shoemakers* shod the people. Where the inhabitants all tilled the soil, they needed men to take care of the animals. The *Shepherds* tended the sheep. *Haywards* saw that fences or hedges were kept in repair to keep the animals from the growing crops. The *Bailiff* and the *Steward* had charge of the lord's affairs, and the *Parker* tended the lord's parks. All these common occupations and many others are repeated in the family nomenclature of every country.

Priests were always present in large numbers to nurture the religious life of the people. The clergy were not all required to lead a celibate life. The minor clergy had privileges not possessed by the common man. As the clergy were about the only ones with any education, when one desired to prove that he was a member of the clergy, about all he needed to do was to prove that he could read. In the case of one accused of crime the status of clergy was important. The clergy were tried in the church courts, which were more lenient than the judges in the secular courts, so that when one who could read was charged with a crime, he could plead "benefit of clergy," and prove it by reading the passage pointed out to him in the Bible and thus be tried in the less severe clerical courts. All this stimulated the origin of surnames referring to the many religious offices.

Occupations which were looked up to and respected were more likely to produce permanent family names than those which called attention to servile status. The *Stewards, Sargents and Franklins* surnamed many more people in proportion to their numbers than the *Vassals or Cotters*.

From the father's name.

The patronymical name, that is, the surname derived from the name of the father, is very common in all countries, and each common given name takes many forms in all countries. As children were growing up, it was natural to refer to them by the name of their paternal parent. It is easy to ascertain what Christian names and what forms of them were popular during the surname period by examining the family names derived from them. In some cases where the mother came from a more important family, or was a widow, the children might acquire their mother's name. Among Jews it was common practice to take the name of the mother, and, in a few cases, of one's wife. A boy apprenticed to learn a trade who lived with the master's family often was known by the forename or surname of the master rather than that of his father, he having grown to manhood and having become known to others in association with his master rather than his parents.

Some family names derived from the father's name use exactly the same form as the father's forename, such as *George* and *Thomas*. Many German names follow this principle. But the greater number in the western countries have some patronymical ending or beginning. With English names it is the termination *-son.* Other endings, indicating "son" are the Danish and Norwegian *-sen,* the Armenian *-ian,* the Finnish *-nen,* the Greek *-poulos,* the Polish *-wicz* and the Spanish *-ez.* Prefixes denoting "son" are the Scotch and Irish *Mac-,* the Norman *Fitz-* and the Welsh *Ap-.* The Irish *O'* means "grandson." Many of these prefixes have been dropped, especially among the Irish. In this dictionary, names which originally had the prefix are explained as "the son of . . ." or "grandson of . . ."

Other important terminations of family names are the diminutive endings. These are particularly numerous among the French, German, Irish, Italian and Spanish names. Children and older people were often referred to by hypocoristic forms, that is, an endearing or shortened form of the Christian name, such as *Dick* for Richard or *Clem* for Clement, described in the dictionary as "pet names." They are the accented syllable and may be the first part of the name as *Abe* from Abraham or *Dan* from Daniel; the middle part, as *Hans* from Johannes and *Zeke* from Ezekiel; or the last part, as *Mass* from Thomas or *Zander* and *Sander* from Alexander.

European family names which embody a Christian name include all the important Bible names in their different national forms. As an example, John, in its various national forms, produces common surnames in all countries. There are *Johnson* and *Jackson* in England, *Johns* and *Jones* in Wales, *Jensen, Jansen* and *Hansen* in Denmark, *Jonsson* and *Johanson* in Sweden, *Janowicz* in Poland, *Ivanov* in Russia and Bulgaria, *Ianson* in Scotland, *Janosfi* in Hungary, *Jantzen* in Holland, and *MacEoin* in Ireland, all referring to the son of John. *Peter, Paul, James, Simon, Michael* and *Thomas,* in their various national forms, are also exceedingly common in every country where the Bible is known.

A brief translation or explanation of the personal name from which the family name arose is generally given in parentheses. Many names which appear to be from common words are really rare old forenames which have dropped from ordinary usage. *Gold,* for example, is from the Old English *Gold* or *Golda,* a not uncommon early personal name.

It will be noted that many surnames are from the old Teutonic names, most of which are dithematic in form, that is, they consist of two elements; and translations, separated by a comma, of the two elements only are given. Certain name-themes were in use, and almost any two of them could be combined to make a name with little or no attention being given to the meaning of the combined name. Thus *William,* from *vilja* "resolution" and *helma* "helmet," means "resolution, helmet" and not "the resolute helmet" or "helmet of resolution." There is no relationship between the two elements; they are merely combined to make a new concept, a man's name. *Robert* is from two name-themes, *hrode* meaning "fame," and *beorht* meaning "bright," and there is no semantic connection between the two elements. Many name-themes are found either at the beginning or end of the name. There is *Wulfgar* and *Garulf,* and there is *Wulfsige* and *Sigewulf.* "Wolf" is a very common name-theme. Some name-themes are found usually at the beginning, others only at the end.

From a descriptive nickname.

If a man were unusually tall, or short, or fat, or slim, or slow, or fast, or long-legged, the fact would be observed and he would be nicknamed accordingly. Today, even strangers will quickly call a red-haired man "Red." Such a descriptive nickname would be added to his forename and might become a surname. *Red,* under its various forms, is a common family name in many countries. *Reid, Reed,* and *Read* are very common in England where also are found *Ruff, Russ, Russel,* and *Ruddy.* In France it would be *Rousseau, Rouse,* or *Larouse,* in Italy, *Purpura* and *Rossi,* the Czecho-Slovakians would call him *Cervenka* or *Cerveny,* the Hungarians say *Voros,* the Germans, *Roth,* the Grecian form would be *Cokinos* or *Pyrrhos,* and the Irish *Flynn.*

Names calling attention to light or dark complexion are common throughout the world. Light complexion is designated by words meaning white or pale. Thus we find *Bianco* (Italy), *Le Blanc* (France), *Labno* (Poland), *Lichter* (Germany and Holland), *Weiss* (Germany), *Bialas* (Poland), *Bily* and *Bilek* (Czecho-Slovakia), and, of course, *White* and *Light* (England). Dark-complexioned people are named by words meaning brown, dark or black. Thus, *Brown, Brun* and *Braun* come from England, France and Germany, respectively. Mr.

Black is well known; Mr. *Schwartz* comes from Germany, Mr. *Morin* from France, Messrs. *Karas, Karras* and *Melas* speak Greek, Mr. *Fekete* is a Hungarian, Mr. *Cherney* hails from Czecho-Slovakia, while the Russians would call him *Chernoff* and the Hebrews, *Pincus;* Mr. *Fosco* comes from Italy, and Mr. *Czernik* from Poland, to name only a few who end up in America.

Small or short men are so named everywhere. Italy calls them *Basso* or *Curcio.* Germany refers to them as *Klein, Kurtz, Stutz* and *Wenig.* The Poles say *Niziolek* and the Hungarians mention *Kiss.* In France it is *Lacour.* Russia names them *Malek,* and Poland knows them as *Malek* and *Malecki,* while in Lithuania it is *Mazeika* and in Czecho-Slovakia *Maly.* Besides *Small* and *Short,* England has named many of them *Litt* and *Lytle,* while the Scotch form is *Smail.* Tall or big men, likewise, stand out throughout the world. There is *Le Grand* and *Grande* from France; and *Nagy* from Hungary. It is *Longo* in Italy, *Groot* from Holland, *Feltz, Hoch, Homan,* and *Lang* in Germany, *Large, Long* and *Lang,* as well as *Longfellow* in England. The fat man is often distinguished from the large man. Germany calls him *Dick, Gross* and *Groth,* France says *Gras.* In Ukraine it is *Waskey.* The absence of "Fat" or a synonym of that word as a very common name in England draws attention to the gaunt bodies of the English.

Among some peoples the more opprobrious nicknames seem to be accepted with equanimity. One might be called Thief, Cuckold or Bastard. Other names referring to sex and parts of the body are not uncommon, as proved by early records. Among the English and most Americans this type of surname has all but disappeared. Such nicknames tend to be altered into inoffensive or meaningless words. Indeed, many milder nicknames, once so common, have gone into the discard.

Family names originating from nicknames can easily be mistaken for names in other classifications. A man who tilled the soil for a livelihood might make his own shoes in the evening and might thus receive the nickname of *Shoemaker,* though that was not his occupation. He might have made only one pair of shoes in his lifetime. Another might be nicknamed with a place name because he had once made a trip to that place. One who made a trip to Paris and bored others by continually talking about it might be so nicknamed. *Palmer* was the palm-bearing pilgrim who had returned from the Holy Land. A man might be referred to as *Hansen* merely from some close relationship with an older man named *Hans,* although not kin to him. There is a semantic relationship between topographical terms and bodily shape; a short, lumpish person, for example, might be referred to as a hillock or mound, a tall, thin man, or one with a pointed head, might be likened to a pointed hill. Indeed, any word could be used as a nickname and might become a surname.

Animal names are found as common surnames in all European countries. Every familiar animal, bird or fish has entered into some family name. The bear was the king of beasts in the north of Europe and has been much used in the formation of names. Such names are derived from a nickname applied by a man's neighbors, from some real or fancied resemblance to the animal. One noted for speed or an awkward stride might be called *Hare, Haas* or *Cooney.* A cunning or crafty person might be called *Fox, Fuchs, Voss, Todd, Liska, Liss,*

Volpe, Colfax or some other name, depending on the language or dialect spoken where he lived; a dirty or filthy person, *Hogg;* a vain man, *Poe;* an excellent swimmer, *Fish.* Color, voice, temperament and bodily shape tend to originate these animal nicknames. A dark man might be called *Crow,* one with a pleasant voice might be likened to a *Lark,* the quiet man to a *Dove* and the long-legged man would call to mind a *Crane, Heron* or *Stork.*

Another source of animal names is the house, shop or inn signs previously explained. However, all of these names must be carefully examined as the origin may be some word corrupted into the name of a familiar animal. *Badger,* for example, generally does not refer to the animal, but is one who buys commodities and transports them in a bag elsewhere for sale, or who comes from Badger, in Shropshire. Mr. *Beaver,* in many cases, came from Beauvoir, in France. Many animal surnames were first applied as forenames and are thus patronymics. One reason for the frequency of names of animals is that they were popular and common terms among the people of all parts of Europe, and since they entered into numerous dialects, we have many different names for each familiar animal, bird or fish.

These four classes of names explain the overwhelming majority of family names of Europe. Indeed, one should say that practically all surnames (except those few consciously adopted) belong to one or another of these four classes. Names in European countries are uniform in their meanings. The difference is only in the language from which they are derived. This uniformity in Europe in regard to the origin of family names might be stressed by considering the compound name, *Drinkwater,* an English name, not at all unknown. In France, the same name arose and the French spelled it *Boileau.* The Italians observed the phenomena and labeled the man *Bevilacqua.* Among the Germans the name is rather rare, but some do bear the name of *Trinkwasser,* while *Waterdrinker* is a Dutch version.

In some countries one class of names is emphasized more than others. Among the Welsh, Scotch, Irish, Danes, Swedes and Norwegians, patronymical names (surnames derived from the fathers' names) predominate, and they are very popular among the Germans and Poles; many descriptive nicknames are found among the Italians and Irish; place names are common with the English and Germans.

Corruption of family names.

Before spelling became frozen by the universal use of dictionaries and the spread of education, family names were in a constant state of flux in all countries. Names like the Scotch *Ogilvie,* the German *Baer* and the Irish *Shaughnessy,* have almost an infinite number of forms and spellings. The component parts of a name may change in form. For example, the ubiquitous *-ham* may be altered to *-am, -um, -om, -man, -nam, -num, -son* and *-hem.* As the languages and dialects changed in spelling, so did many of the names. Some retained archaic spellings, however, and thus their simple meaning became lost to the person not learned in onomatology. Various laws in the different European countries, particularly military rules and regulations, have, in this century, tended to restrict the alteration of family names.

As surnames have undergone various corruptions and changes in the countries where they arose, it is not surprising that this process of corruption and change was greatly accelerated when brought to America. For the unlettered pioneer, names of all nationalities took on a roughly phonetic spelling. There was, and still is, a strong propensity to alter an unfamiliar name into a familiar name or word with a similar sound. The Dutch *Roggenfelder* became the American *Rockefeller;* the German *Dietz* became *Deeds* in America. The number of alterations of this kind is endless. Many names that appear to be English are really derived from other tongues. The longer, more awkward or unpronounceable ones are shortened and simplified, generally with the idea of making them more like English names or at least easier on the eye and ear familiar with the English tongue. Some are deliberately translated into the more popular names. Thus, people of other nationalities than the ones mentioned in this dictionary can be found for almost every name. Many English *Miller*s are really German *Mueller*s; many English *Smith*s are really German *Schmidt*s.

In numerous instances the spelling of foreign names is altered to make their pronunciation more agreeable to American ears. Even among common English names this principle produces mutation. The terminal *-s* in many cases has no meaning other than to give a certain ease in enunciation, as *Stubbs* and *Brooks.* In other names, such as the Welsh *Edwards* and *Williams,* the final *-s* definitely designates the patronymic; in some cases it merely indicates the possessive and in others the plural, while in still others it is only the remaining evidence of an old case ending. Names without the terminal *-s* exist alongside of those where it has been added. In some instances the form with the final *-s* is more common than without it, while in other names the opposite is true. Another common alteration brought about by pronunciation is the medial *p,* as in *Thompson* and *Simpson.* The common *-sson* termination of Swedish patronymical names commonly drops one *s* in this country, *Petersson* quickly becomes *Peterson.* Many names have a terminal *-e* or *-d* or *-t,* or not, according to the fancy of present or past bearers. There are many other common corruptions and substitutions of consonants. It would take a large book to explain all of them. Each vowel may change to any other vowel. Variations in names tend to follow certain definite rules and many difficult names can be explained after the correct principle is applied.

Nationality.

In many cases, designating the proper nationality has presented difficulties. The nationality, or nationalities, given after each name merely designates the country from which most of the persons bearing that name came, and is not meant in any way to denote the language from which the word or root giving rise to the name comes. Many strictly English surnames are derived from French words or places. Many French and Italian names come from Teutonic words, Dutch includes Frisian; German includes Yiddish; Russian includes Byelorussian.

Separating nationalities within a family of languages poses problems. In the Scandinavian countries many names are common to two or more countries. Thus

Nelson and *Larson* are found commonly in both Norway and Sweden. The Celtic countries have names popular in all of them. It has been impractical to attempt to distinguish carefully between the various Soviet Socialist Republics. The Ukrainians have been identified separately, but the Byelorussians, or White Russians, have generally been included under Russians. The Slavic countries have many names in common. The Teutonic languages have provided family names which have the same form and meaning in different countries, but are more common in some nations than in others. The Romance countries have presented fewer difficulties than most of the language families.

In designating nationality the troublesome question arises as to how long a name must be resident in a country to be considered native to that country. A French name that came over to England with the Conqueror, in 1066, and has resided ever since then in England, can surely be considered an English name, especially if the name, even though French in appearance, is not common in that form in France. Roger de Beaumont, for example, is listed in *Domesday Book* (1086) as one of the Dorsetshire landowners; he took his name from Beaumont in Normandy, and the name has become common in England and the United States.

But what about the French Huguenots who went to England, Switzerland and Germany during the seventeenth century? No hard and fast rule can be set up, especially in those cases where it is difficult to find out just how long a name has been current in a country. Consistency is neither possible nor always desirable when dealing with all languages and dialects in each language, as well as archaic terms and provincial usage. To some extent the classification is arbitrary. A name may have been a rare name in a country for hundreds of years until its numbers were bolstered by another name, exactly the same in spelling but entirely different in origin. The nationality given would then be that of the later arrival.

Names may have been altered by being resident for a time in another country, but still may not have attained the nationality of that country through which it came. For example, a Polish name may have emigrated to Germany, and in the course of a hundred years the name may have been altered to look like a German name. However, upon becoming current in the United States, it might still be a Polish name and indicate Polish nationality. Thus *Bieschke* came to the United States from Poland by way of Germany. Some of the difficulties attendant upon designating nationality could have been avoided by merely noting the language from which the name was derived. However, this would not have satisfied many who wished to learn about their names and their national origin. To say that a name resident in England since the Conquest was derived from Erse, Gaelic, Breton, Cornish, Swedish, Norwegian, Icelandic, French, Dutch, Old High German or some other language, would not tell the bearer much. It might also be traced back to the Latin, Greek, Hebrew or Sanskrit, but that would be the work of the philologist, not the onomatologist.

The same name with the same spelling may be derived independently from two or more different languages and have entirely different explanations which are sometimes given under one entry. For example, the name *Brody*, sometimes spelled *Brodie,* is found in Ireland, Scotland, Germany and Russia. In Ireland it was originally *MacBruaideadha,* that is, the son of Bruaideadh (fragment, or morsel). The Scotch derived it from the barony of Brodie, in Moray, meaning a muddy place, while in Germany it referred to a man with a large or unusual beard. The Russians with that name came from Brody, in Russia. In the dictionary variant forms of the name may also be given, and the explanations may not apply equally to all forms. Thus among the Germans and Russians the form is usually *Brody* and not *Brodie.* This is an incongruity that must be accepted because of limitations of space. Whether names are grouped together or separated depends to some extent on the degree of difference in meaning and the importance of the different forms from the point of view of numbers.

Names from one language frequently spill over into another language, especially into the language current in the country where the bearer lives. If a dozen people in America have a name marked as German, for example, one can be very sure that at least one or two among them will not be a German. He may be a Frenchman, Belgian, Russian or Pole, whose name originally was so near to the German name in spelling or sound that it gradually changed to the German form. If a dozen people have a common English name, possibly three of them are of a nationality other than English, whose names have gradually adapted themselves in this country to a familiar English form. Part of them may have deliberately altered them to the English form. When two or more nationalities have substantially contributed to a certain name, more than one nationality has been credited even though in one of them there has been a slight change. Diligent search might even turn up a dozen origins for a single name; only the more important ones are listed in this dictionary because of space limitations.

Jewish names.

Jewish family names have presented unusual problems since many of them are of comparatively recent origin and artificial in nature due to their conscious adoption. In Europe, particularly outside of Spain and Portugal, many Jews did not have surnames until compelled to assume them by laws promulgated in the latter part of the eighteenth and early part of the nineteenth centuries. While a great many Jews accepted as surnames the names of the cities or villages where they were born or from whence they came and others were known or identified by the name of their father, it is clear that some knowingly adopted unusual or fanciful names. The only explanation that can be given of names like *Rosenblum* and *Greenblatt* is a translation into English. Jews living in crowded, airless and sunless ghettos frequently adopted names which alluded to green woods and fields. Some who were slow in accepting a surname were arbitrarily assigned names by the governing authorities. Some of these were of a ridiculous or startling nature. However, most of these odd and unusual names were quickly dropped or altered, especially upon arrival in the United States.

No attempt has been made to identify Jewish family names as such. Some names are borne only by Jews, others are borne by both Jews and Gentiles. Assigning nationalities to some of these Jewish names has brought forth complications. However, all of these Jewish names have been identified by nationality except a few, such as *Cohen* and *Levy,* which have been designated merely as Hebrew. It must be remembered, however, that many Eastern European Jews, upon coming to the United States, adopted German family names because at that time the German Jewish names were the aristocratic names among the Jews.

A curious practice found among the Jews has been that of adopting surnames formed from abbreviations or contractions of a man's own name added to the Hebrew titles and names of his father, or of the father's Hebrew names. Descendants of Ben Rabbi Judah Lowe became *Brill;* Rabbi David, the Hazan, produced *Bardah;* Sabbatai Cohen originated the surname *Schach.* Sheliah Tzibbur (minister of the congregation) gave rise to the name *Schatz,* while Segan Leviyyah, literally "assistant of the Leviteship," became *Segal, Segel* and the like.

Often Jews have assimilated their Jewish names with non-Jewish names current in the countries where they lived. They change to a similar-sounding name, generally one beginning with the same initial as their Jewish name. *Rabbin* becomes *Robin* and *Rabbinowitch* becomes *Robinson.* Other names are loosely translated into names current among the non-Jewish majority.

Mortal man is forever reaching for better things, and toward what he views as noble, genteel or aristocratic; and certain names, from time to time, are regarded as socially acceptable and others as plebeian. Names in Poland terminating in *-ski* were held in high esteem; a larger proportion of Poles in America bear such names than in Poland! If a degree of prestige can be obtained by the use of such a name, the element could be easily attached to occupy one's time while crossing the ocean. Certain farm names carried prestige among Norwegians, and what was to prevent them from adopting such names upon emigrating to America? In the same way many Swedes looked back and adopted the distinctive soldier name of a grandfather.

These soldier names in Sweden were an unusual feature of their permanent family names. When a young man of the peasant class was inducted into the army, he frequently adopted another name for use during his military career. Perhaps his family name was too common to identify him properly when associated with many others. These soldier names were usually of one syllable, a common Swedish word, as *Alm* (oak), *Bjork* (birch), *Hjelm* (helmet), *Quist* (twig), *Rask* (quick) or *Varg* (wolf) and the like, and might be changed when the soldier was assigned to another post. When the soldier returned to civilian life he usually discarded his soldier name and re-assumed his old family name. The soldier name was perpetuated as a hereditary family name when it was adopted by the soldier's descendants.

Common in many European countries was the custom, after one graduated from a university, to adopt a new surname, usually a translation into a Greek or Latin form of a word, or name, bearing some relationship to the bearer. If the name of one's old home was *Skog* (forest), he might adopt *Sylvander;* if the patronymic was *Karlsson,* it might be altered to *Carolus.* Linnaeus, the Swedish botanist, Latinized his original surname, *von Linné,* after he had completed his formal education. Philipp Schwarzert, the German scholar, made a translation to *Melanchthon.* Wilhelm Holtzmann, the sixteenth-century classical scholar, translated his surname to *Xylander.*

In all countries very few people have consciously selected their family names. They have merely acquiesced, generally unconsciously, in a name by which they have become known. Even those who deliberately change their name are strongly influenced by the name they seek to discard. Most of the people who change their name merely shorten the name they bear, alter its spelling to simplify it, or translate it into the language current in the place where they live. Few deliberately choose an entirely different name unless adopted into another family.

Among some of the early Swedes and Norwegians the surname changed with each generation. Thus Lars the son of Swen Olesson was not Lars Olesson but Lars Swensson, and his son would bear the surname of Larson.

To get away from the ordinary patronymical name in Sweden the government encouraged its citizens to adopt nature names, that is, names composed of two elements, usually words for trees, plants, flowers or topographical terms, without regard to meanings, and without any, or very little, relationship to the person adopting the name. Therefore, in this dictionary, such Swedish names as *Bergstrom, Almquist, Sandstrom* and *Stromkvist* can only be translated into English.

Because of the extreme age of some of the Chinese family names, only a translation has been attempted in most instances. The Chinese were the first to have hereditary family names, having had them for more than two thousand years. As the Chinese family names were greatly limited in number, the Chinese have more of the common names than their numbers in this country would seem to warrant. Japanese names usually consist of two common words with no apparent connection between them, and therefore can only be translated into English.

Scotch and Irish names beginning with *Mac* are spelled *Mac* or *Mc* in accordance with the spelling under which the greater number of any particular name are found, but they are all listed together as if spelled *Mac*. Both Irish and Scotch purists complain that the contraction to *Mc* is "wrong." In America, however, most people contract the prefix to *Mc,* the tendency being slightly stronger among the Irish. Most Irish names may take the *O'* prefix meaning "grandson." With respect to capitals in the middle of names, there is no uniformity; the prevailing practice as to a particular name is followed in this dictionary. There is usually little or no difference in nationality or meaning whether the name appears as *Du Pre* or *Dupre*.

In Italy, names beginning with a preposition or article are always written with a space between the two words, as *De Leo, La Guardia* and *Dal Santo*. The American custom of closing the space is probably due to the influence of the Gaelic *Mac* names, which are usually written without any space between the prefix and the name. In this dictionary all names are entered in the form in which they are current in America.

French and Italian names, especially the latter, besides many German and some Slavic names, are notable for the decapitation of the baptismal names. Thus the French reduce *Thomas* to *Massie, Masset, Massin, Masson* and the like, while the Germans use *Mass,* and the Italians, *Massa* and *Masso*. Various names beginning with *Cob-* and *Kob-* are aphetic forms of *Jacob* or *Jakob*. The Italian *Como* is from *Giacomo* (James), while *Zola* and *Cozzi* are from *Franzola* and *Francescozzi,* respectively.

In this *New Dictionary of American Family Names* all the common surnames found in the United States are included. American family names consist of the family names of the entire world, with the European names predominating since most of the American population are descended from European nationals. Counts have been made in many large city telephone and other directories to insure the inclusion of the most common names in the United States. Where several forms of a name are given, the most common form is given first, except possibly in a few dozen cases where two forms were so close together in point of number that it could not be known for sure which form was in most common use. In addition, the family names of many famous Americans are explained as well as some with curious or interesting names. People with odd or unusual names are prone to alter them and thus avoid the constant comment about them.

Whether a name is given as a main entry or as a variant of another name depends on how many people bear the name in America and also how far away it is, alphabetically, from the more popular name. *I* and *y* are both found, yet *Bird* is not given as a variant of *Byrd,* the more common form, as they are too far apart in the alphabet. This does not apply to *Jacobi* and *Jacoby,* and they are grouped together. *Harrison,* a very common name, is given with *Harris,* the more common one, because it would otherwise come next in alphabetical order and the explanation is the same. *Johns,* on the other hand, is separate from *Johnson* because of difference in nationality. Famous names are given more attention than their numbers warrant.

When variants of the names are listed, it must be understood that, in general, the explanations refer principally to the first form. There may, of course, be other minor explanations for some of the variants. This method was adopted in order to provide as much information as possible in the limited space available. A complete discussion of a name and its variants and cross-explanations would consume several pages for almost every entry and much would be repetitious.

Attention in this dictionary is given to the way in which the family name originated, and its meaning from an onomastic viewpoint. The philologist and the linguist are interested only in the word root, or stem, from which a name is derived, while many people are interested in the way their family name developed into its present form. Besides the exact word which formed the name, the customs and habits of many peoples must be studied. Without a feeling for the origin of family names and an understanding of how they gradually arose in various countries, the philologists are sometimes led astray in suggesting that a name is derived from a certain word or root when an understanding of the process by which names originated would cause them to reject that word and search further. A word meaning the same in another language may not be defined in exactly the same way since the root word may have affected the name differently in the other language. To be absolutely sure of the meaning and derivation of any particular family name, it would have to be traced genealogically back to its origin and the circumstances of the origin studied. This is impossible, of course, but we know that the large majority of the common names, as contained herein, arose exactly in the way explained in the dictionary.

In arriving at an explanation of a surname, it must be remembered that the meaning of the word or stem from which the surname is derived is not the dictionary meaning at the present day, but the meaning of the word at the time and in the place where the family name came into existence. Over the years words sometimes change radically in meaning; sometimes they change only slightly. *Seeley* once referred to the happy or prosperous one, then, the good, simple, innocent man. The word later changed in meaning to the silly, foolish or stupid person. As a surname it carried, chiefly, the earlier and more felicitous connotations. Thus the meaning of the surname is different from the meaning of the word today.

In the Middle Ages a word may have had different meanings or different shades of meanings in different parts of the country. At a time when dictionaries were scarce or non-existent, words were often used with little regard for the finer shades of meaning. For this reason, it will be found that in the following list an element in a name may be defined with one meaning or shade of meaning in one name and with a different meaning in another name.

Too much emphasis cannot be placed on the fact that a family name may have more than one origin, although only the most important ones are listed in this dictionary. Many names are common simply because they are derived from several different sources. *Barnes* designates the dweller near the barn or grain-storage building in some instances, while in others it is the bairn, or child, or young person of a prominent family; some with the name are descendants of Beorn (nobleman) or of Barn, a pet form of Barnabas (son of prophecy), while still others came from Barnes, the name of villages in both England and Scotland. Infrequently, it is also the Polish shortening from Bernhard and a German pet form for Berinhard. All of these origins combine to make the name very common. Indeed, most of the very common names are common because they owe their existence to several different origins. In this dictionary different derivations or origins have been separated by semicolons. Because of the limitations of space, only the more important derivations are included.

In this book the diacritical marks of the various languages are disregarded because they are not customarily used in American family names. A true "American" name does not have an accent, a tilde, an umlaut, a circumflex, a cedilla or any of the numerous other signs or marks used in the various languages. Americans just refuse to take the time to add such marks, and the foreigner soon ceases to insist upon it and he, himself, ignores the diacritical mark.

This is not a failure to recognize the difficulty in explaining many European names. For example, there is the Finnish *Saari,* designating a "dweller on an island," and the Finnish *Sääri,* meaning "dweller on, or near, a ridge." When Mr. Sääri comes to America and quickly drops the diacritical marks, one cannot later be sure of the meaning of his name. However, this difficulty is always present in any other name that has more than one origin. Names that come from languages using other than the Latin alphabet present their difficulties; not all have used the same system of transliteration.

LIST OF ABBREVIATIONS

Arab.	Arabian	**Jap.**	Japanese
Arm.	Armenian	**Kor.**	Korean
Bel.	Belgian	**Lat.**	Latvian
Bulg.	Bulgarian	**Lith.**	Lithuanian
Chin.	Chinese	**Mx.**	Manx
Cz.	Czech	**Nor.**	Norwegian
Cz.-Sl.	Czecho-Slovakian	**Pers.**	Persian
Dan.	Danish	**Pol.**	Polish
dim.	diminutive	**Port.**	Portuguese
Du.	Dutch	**q.v.**	which see
Eng.	English	**Rom.**	Romanian
Est.	Estonian	**Rus.**	Russian
Finn.	Finnish	**Scot.**	Scottish
Fr.	French	**Sl.**	Slovakian
Ger.	German	**Sp.**	Spanish
Gr.	Greek	**Sw.**	Swedish
Heb.	Hebrew	**Swis.**	Swiss
Hindi	Hindi	**Syr.**	Syrian
Hun.	Hungarian	**Tur.**	Turkish
Ice.	Icelandic	**Ukr.**	Ukrainian
i.e.	that is	**Wel.**	Welsh
Ir.	Irish	**Yu.-Sl.**	Yugoslavian
It.	Italian		

Different origins or meanings are separated by a semicolon. Different meanings of place names, the sources of the surname, separated by a semicolon are sometimes the different origins of separate place names with the same modern spelling. The first surname form listed is generally the most common.

NEW
DICTIONARY OF
AMERICAN FAMILY NAMES

Aaberg (Sw.) River mountain.

Aagaard, Aagard (Nor.) Dweller in the yard or farm by the river.

Aamodt (Nor.) Dweller near the confluence of two streams.

Aardsma (Du.) Descendant of Aard, a pet form of Hartwig (hard, combat).

Aaron, Aaronson, Aarons (Eng.) Descendant of Aaron (lofty mountain).

Aarsen (Du.) The son of Arthur (valorous; noble; Thor's eagle; bear man).

Aas (Nor.) Dweller on a ridge.

Aasgaard (Nor.) Dweller on the farm on a ridge.

Abadia (Fr., Sp.) Descendant of Obadiah (servant of God; worshiper of God); one who came from Abadia (home of the priest), in Spain.

Abadie (Fr.) Dweller near, or worker in, the abbey or monastery.

Abbate, Abbati, Abate (It.) One who was a member of an abbot's entourage.

Abbatemarco (It.) Descendant of the abbot called Marco, Italian form of Mark (belonging to the god Mars).

Abbe (Fr.) A member of an abbot's entourage.

Abbell (Eng.) Descendant of Abel (breath or vanity).

Abbey, Abbie (Scot.) Variants of Abbott, q.v.

Abbinanti, Abbinante (It.) One who came from Abbinanti, in Italy.

Abbink (Du.) Son of Abbe (noble).

Abbott, Abbot (Eng.) A member of an abbot's entourage; sometimes the lay abbot of a monastery who inherited his office; son of little Abb, a pet form of Abraham (father of multitudes); descendant of Abet or Abot, pet forms for Abel (breath or vanity).

Abdullah, Abdulla, Abdallah (Arab., Tur.) The servant of Allah.

Abe (Jap.) Depend, volume.

Abel, Abell, Abeles, Abele (Eng.) Descendant of Abel (breath or vanity).

Abelman (Eng.) One who was a servant to Abel (breath or vanity).

Abelson (Eng.) The son of Abel (breath or vanity).

Abelwhite (Eng.) A variant of Applewhite, q.v.

Abendroth (Ger.) One who came from Abbenrode (Eben's clearing), in Germany; evening red.

Abercrombie, Abercromby (Scot.) One who came from the barony of Abercrombie (crooked marsh), in Fife.

Aberdeen (Scot.) One who came from Aberdeen (mouth of the river Dee or Don), a county in Scotland.

Aberman (Heb., Scot.) Descendant of Aberman, an endearing form of Abraham (father of a multitude); one who came from Aber, a hamlet in the parish of Kilmaronock in Dumbartonshire.

Abernathy, Abernethy (Scot.) One who came from Abernathy (at the narrow opening), in Perthshire.

Abeyta (Sp.) Dweller near the hard wood or pine tree.

Abingdon (Eng.) One who came from Abingdon (Aebba's or Aebbe's hill).

Abington, Abbington (Eng.) One who came from Abington (the place of Abba's people), the name of several towns in England.

Ablin (Eng.) Descendant of little Abel (breath or vanity).

Abnee, Abney (Eng.) One who came from Abney (Abba's Island), in Derbyshire.

Abner (Eng.) Descendant of Abner (father is light).

Aborn (Eng.) Dweller at the stream.

Abplanalp (Swis.) Dweller on a flat mountain; or flat place on a mountain.

Abraham, Abrahams, Abrahamson (Eng.) Descendant of Abraham (father of a multitude).

Abramic (Yu.-Sl.) The son of Abram, Serbo-Croatian form of Abraham (father of a multitude).

Abramovich, Abramovitz, Abramowitz (Rus., Yu.-Sl., Pol.) The son of Abram (high father).

Abrams, Abram, Abramson (Eng.) Descendant of Abram (high father).

1

Abreu (*Sp.*) One who came from Abreu, in Spain.

Abruzzo, Abruzzi, Abruzzese (*It.*) One who came from Abruzzi, a region in Italy.

Abson (*Eng.*) One who came from Abson (the abbot's manor), in Gloucestershire.

Abston (*Eng.*) One who came from Abson (the abbot's manor), in Gloucestershire.

Abt (*Ger.*) A member of an abbot's entourage; sometimes the lay abbot of a monastery who inherited his office.

Abusharif (*Arab.*) Father of Sharif (honorable).

Accardi, Accardo (*It.*) Dweller where thistles grew.

Accetta (*It.*) Descendant of Accetta, a shortened form of Bonaccetta.

Accettura, Accetturo, Acceturo (*It.*) One who came from Accettura, in Italy.

Acevedo (*Sp.*) Dweller, or worker, in a plantation of holly trees.

Achenbach (*Ger.*) One who came from Achenbach (water brook), in Hesse.

Acheson (*Eng.*) The son of Ache (sword); or of Adam (red earth).

Achey (*Eng.*) Descendant of little Ache or Acha (sword).

Achilles (*Ger.*) Descendant of Achilles (without lips).

Acker (*Eng.*) One who lived on a homestead of one acre, a piece of arable land that a yoke of oxen could plow in one day.

Ackerman, Ackermann, Acreman (*Ger., Eng.*) One who plowed the lord's land and tended his plow teams.

Ackland (*Eng.*) One who came from Ackland (land where oaks grew; Aca's lane), in Devonshire.

Ackles (*Eng.*) Dweller in the oak grove.

Ackley (*Eng.*) One who came from Acle (oak wood), in Norfolk; dweller in the oak grove.

Acklin (*Eng.*) One who came from Aclam (oak wood), the name of towns in both the North and the East Ridings of Yorkshire.

Ackroyd (*Eng.*) Dweller at the oak clearing.

Ackwood (*Eng.*) Dweller in, or near, the oak wood.

Acland, Ackland (*Eng.*) One who came from Acland (Aca's lane), in Devonshire.

Acorn (*Ger.*) One who came from Eichhorn (place where squirrels abound), in Germany; dweller at the sign of the squirrel; dweller at the forest corner.

Acosta (*Sp.*) One who came from Acosta (long coast), the name of a town in Spain; dweller on the seacoast.

Acquaviva (*Fr.*) Water of life, perhaps calling to mind the quality of the man so named.

Acree, Acre, Acres (*Eng.*) Dweller in the open country or field; or by a plot of arable land; one who came from Acre (field) in Norfolk.

Acridge (*Eng.*) Dweller on a range of hills where oaks grew.

Acton (*Eng.*) One who came from Acton (homestead by the oaks or, in some cases, Aca's homestead), the name of many places in England.

Adair (*Scot., Ir.*) Descendant of Edzear or Edgar (rich, spear); dweller near the oak tree ford; grandson of Daire, an old Irish name.

Adamczyk (*Pol.*) Descendant of little Adam (man of red earth; red).

Adamek, Adamik (*Cz.-Sl.*) Descendant of little Adam (man of red earth; red).

Adamowicz (*Pol.*) The son of Adam (man of red earth; red).

Adamowski, Adamoski (*Pol.*) One who came from Adamowo (Adam's village), in Poland.

Adams, Adamson, Addams, Adam (*Wel., Eng.*) The son of Adam (man of red earth; red).

Adamski (*Pol.*) The son of Adam (man of red earth; red).

Adcock (*Eng.*) Descendant of little Ad, a pet form of Adam (man of red earth; red).

Adderley, Adderly (*Eng.*) One who came from Adderley (Aldred's grove), in Shropshire.

Addington (*Eng.*) One who came from Addington (the village of Eadda's people), the name of several places in England.

Addison, Addis, Addie (*Eng., Scot., Wel.*) The son of Addie, a pet form of Adam (red earth); the son of Ada or Adda (noble cheer).

Adducci, Adduci (*It.*) Descendant of little Adamo, Italian form of Adam (man of red earth; red).

Ade, Ades (*Eng.*) Descendant of Ade, a pet form of Adam (man of red earth; red).

Adell, Adel (*Eng.*) One who came from Adel (filthy place), in the West Riding of Yorkshire.

Adelman, Adelmann (*Eng., Ger.*) The servant of Adal or Edel (noble).

Adelson (*Eng.*) The son of Adal (noble).

Adger, Adgerson (*Eng.*) Descendant of Adger, a corruption of Edgar (rich spear).

Adham (*Eng.*) Variant of Adams, q.v.

Adkins, Adkinson, Adkin (*Eng.*) The son of little Ade, a pet form of Adam (red earth; red).

Adler (*Ger.*) Dweller at the sign of the eagle.

Adolph, Adolf, Adolfson, Adolphson (*Ger., Eng., Sw.*) Descendant of Adolf or Athalwolf (noble, wolf).

Adomaitis (*Lith.*) The son of Adom, Lithuanian form of Adam (red earth; red).

Adrian, Adrien (*Eng.*) Descendant of Adrian (from the city of Adria, which derives from Latin *ater*, black).

Adshead (*Eng.*) Dweller on, or near, Ad's headland.

Adside (*Eng.*) One who came from Adsett (Aeddi's fold), in Gloucestershire.

Aers (*Eng.*) One who was the heir of another.

Affatato (*It.*) Nickname for one thought to be bewitched.

Affleck (*Scot.*) One who came from the barony of Auchinleck (field of the flat stone), in Ayrshire; or from Affleck, in Angus.

Afton (*Eng.*) One who came from Afton (Aeffa's homestead), in Wight.

Agar, Agars (*Eng., Hun.*) Descendant of Algar (old, spear); or of Aelfgar (elf, spear); dweller at the sign of the greyhound.

Agassiz, Agassie (*Swiss*) Dweller at the sign of the magpie.

Agate (*Eng.*) Dweller at the gate or gap in a chain of hills.

Agee (*Eng., Fr.*) Descendant of Aggie, pet form of Agnes (pure); dweller near the hedge or hedgerow.

Ager, Agers (*Eng.*) Descendant of Algar (old, spear); or of Aelfgar (elf, spear).

Agnew (*Eng.*) Dweller at the sign of the lamb; one who was angelic or lamblike.

Agnos (*Gr.*) Descendant of an ecclesiastical acolyte.

Agostini, Agostino (*It.*) Descendant of Agostino, Italian form of Augustine (exalted or majestic).

Agosto (*It.*) Descendant of Agosto, Italian form of August (exalted or majestic).

Aguila (*Sp., Eng.*) Dweller at the sign of the eagle; one who made and sold needles.

Aguilar, Aguilera (*Sp.*) One who came from Aguilas (eagles), in Spain.

Aguirre (*Sp.*) Dweller on a high place; one who came from Aguirre (high place), in Spain.

Ahern, Ahearn, Aherne (*Ir.*) Grandson of Eachthighearna (horse owner).

Ahlberg (*Sw.*) Alder hill.

Ahlers (*Ger.*) Descendant of Ahlers, a form of Adelhard (noble, hard).

Ahlgren (*Sw.*) Alder branch.

Ahlquist (*Sw.*) Alder twig.

Ahlschwede (*Ger.*) Variant of Alswede, q.v.; dweller at a swamp in the forest that could be crossed by fording.

Ahlstrom (*Sw.*) Alder stream.

3

Ahmed, Ahmet, Ahmad (*Tur.*) Shortened form of Muhammed, q.v.

Ahrens (*Du.*) Dweller at the sign of the eagle.

Ahven (*Est.*) One who fished for, or sold, perch.

Aiello (*It.*) One who experienced bad luck.

Aigner (*Ger.*) Variant of Eigner, q.v.

Aiken, Aikens, Aikin (*Eng.*) Descendant of little Ad, a pet form of Adam (man of red earth; red); descendant of Acen (oaken).

Ailsworth (*Eng.*) One who came from Ailsworth (Aegel's homestead), in Northamptonshire.

Ainsley, Ainslie (*Eng., Scot.*) One who came from Annesley (An's wood), in Nottinghamshire, or from Ansley (wood with a hermitage), in Warwickshire.

Ainsworth (*Eng.*) One who came from Ainsworth (Aegen's homestead), in Lancashire.

Aird, Ard (*Scot.*) One who came from Aird (height or cape of the meadow), the name of several places in Scotland.

Airey (*Scot.*) One who came from Airie in Scotland.

Airth (*Scot.*) One who came from the barony of Airth (level green among hills), in Stirlingshire.

Aisenstein (*Ger.*) Variant of Eisenstein, q.v.

Aiso (*Jap.*) Countenance, foundation.

Aitchison (*Scot., Eng.*) The son of Ache (sword); or of Adam (man of red earth; red).

Aitken, Aitkins (*Eng., Scot.*) Descendant of little Ad, a pet form of Adam (man of red earth; red).

Akahoshi (*Jap.*) Red star.

Akaishi (*Jap.*) Red stone.

Akehurst (*Eng.*) Dweller in, or near, Aca's wood or hill.

Akeley (*Eng.*) One who came from Akeley (oak wood), in Buckinghamshire.

Akerman (*Eng.*) One who plowed the lord's land and tended his plow teams.

Akers, Aker (*Eng.*) One who lived in the cultivated field; one who farmed one acre.

Akins, Akin (*Eng., Scot.*) Variant of Aiken, q.v.; dweller near Akin, a strait in Scotland named after King Hakon of Norway.

Akiyama (*Jap.*) Autumn, mountain.

Akkerman, Akkermans (*Du.*) One who plowed the lord's land and tended his plow teams.

Akridge, Akrigg (*Eng.*) Dweller on, or near, the ridge where oak trees grew.

Akyuz (*Tur.*) One with a light complexion.

Alagna (*It.*) One who came from Alagna, in Italy.

Alaniz, Alanis (*Sp.*) The son of Alano, Spanish form of Alan (comely or fair).

Alba (*It.*) Descendant of Alba, a name sometimes given to one born at break of day.

Albanese (*It.*) One who came from Albania (hill; white).

Albano (*It.*) One who came from Albano (white), in Italy.

Albany (*Eng.*) One who came from Albania (hill; white), the kingdom of the Picts.

Albaugh, Albach (*Ger.*) One who came from Albach (swampy stream), the name of three places in Germany.

Albee, Allbee, Alby (*Eng.*) One who came from Alby (Ali's homestead), in Norfolk.

Albers, Alber (*Ger., Du.*) Descendant of Albert (noble, bright).

Albert, Alberts, Albertson (*Eng.*) The descendant, or son, of Albert (noble, bright).

Alberti, Albertini (*It.*) Descendant of Alberto (noble, bright).

Albin, Albinson (*Eng.*) Descendant of Albin (white).

Albion (*Eng.*) One who came from Albion (white island), an old name of Great Britain.

4

Albrecht, Albrect (*Ger.*) Descendant of Albrecht (noble, bright).

Albright (*Eng.*) One who came from Albright (Eadbeorht's homestead), in Shropshire.

Albrighton (*Eng.*) One who came from Albrighton (Aldbeorht's or Alubeorht's homestead), in Shropshire.

Albritton, Allbritton (*Eng.*) Variant of Albrighton, q.v.

Alburger (*Ger.*) One who came from Alburg, in Germany.

Alcala (*Sp.*) One who came from Alcala (outpost fort), the name of several places in Spain; dweller near, or worker in, the castle.

Alcantara, Alcantar (*Port., Sp.*) One who came from Alcantara (the bridge), in Spain.

Alcaraz (*Sp.*) One who came from Alcaraz (cherry tree), in Spain.

Alcazar (*Sp.*) One who came from Alcazar (the castle), in Spain; dweller near a fortress.

Alcock, Alcox (*Eng.*) Descendant or son of little Al, a pet form of Alan or Allen (comely or fair; harmony).

Alcorn (*Eng.*) One who came from Alchorne, a manor in Sussex.

Alcott (*Eng.*) Dweller in the old cottage; descendant of Alcot or Algot (noble, god).

Aldana (*It.*) Dweller near a black alder tree.

Alden, Aldine, Aldin (*Eng.*) Descendant of Ealdwine (old friend), or of Halfdan (half Dane).

Alder (*Eng.*) The older man; dweller by the alder trees.

Alderman (*Eng.*) One who was a city officer or magistrate; governor of a guild.

Aldersmith (*Eng.*) The older smith, a name probably first used to designate the parent or grandparent, the head of the family; the smith who lived by the alder tree.

Alderson (*Eng.*) Son of Aldred (old, counsel).

Aldis (*Eng.*) Descendant of Aldis or Aldous (old).

Aldred (*Eng.*) Descendant of Aldred (old, counsel).

Aldrich (*Eng.*) Descendant of Alderich (noble, ruler); sometimes a variant of Aldridge, q.v.

Aldridge, Aldredge (*Eng.*) One who came from Aldridge (village among alders), in Staffordshire.

Aldrin (*Eng.*) Dweller among the alder trees.

Alegretti (*It.*) The happy, gay, glad person.

Aleksandravicius (*Lith.*) Descendant of Aleksandras, Lithuanian form of Alexander (helper of mankind).

Aleman (*Sp., Eng.*) One who came from Germany, a German; descendant of Aleman (German).

Alessi, Alesi, Alessia, Alessio (*It.*) Descendant of Alessio, Italian form of Alex (helper of mankind).

Alex (*Eng.*) Descendant of Alex, a pet form of Alexander (helper of mankind).

Alexander (*Scot., Eng.*) Descendant of Alexander (helper of mankind).

Alexopoulos (*Gr.*) The son of Alexis, a pet form of Alexandros (helper of mankind).

Alexy (*Eng.*) Descendant of little Alex, a pet form of Alexander (helper of mankind).

Alfano (*It.*) One thought to be strong as a horse.

Alfonso (*Sp.*) Descendant of Alfonso, a Spanish form of Alphonso (noble, ready); one who came from Alfonso, in Spain.

Alford (*Eng.*) One who came from Alford (the alder ford; the ford of Ealdgyth), villages in Lincolnshire and Somerset.

Alfred, Alfredson (*Eng.*) Descendant of Alfred (elf, counsel).

Alger, Algar (*Eng.*) Descendant of Aldgar (old, spear), Aelfgar (elf, spear), or Athelgar (noble, spear).

Ali (*Arab.*) Descendant of Ali (exalted).

Alice (*Scot., Eng.*) Descendant of Alice (noble, kind). Alice was also a masculine name in the Middle Ages.

5

Alicea (*Sp.*) Descendant of Alicea (noble, kind).

Alicoate (*Eng.*) Dweller in the old cottage.

Alker (*Eng.*) Descendant of Ealhhere (temple, army).

Alkins, Alkin (*Eng.*) Descendant of little Al, a pet form of names beginning with Al, as Allen and Alexander.

Allanbrook (*Eng.*) Dweller near the white brook.

Allard (*Eng.*) Descendant of Alard (noble, hard).

Allardyce, Allardice (*Scot.*) One who came from the barony of Allardyce, in Kincardineshire.

Allaway (*Eng., Scot.*) Descendant of Aedelwig (noble, war), or of Aelfwig (elf, war), or of Ealdwig (old, war).

Allegretti (*It.*) Variant of Alegretti, q.v.

Alleman, Allemand (*Fr.*) One who came from Germany, a German.

Allen, Allan, Alan (*Eng., Scot.*) Descendant of Alan (a very old name of obscure origin); dweller near the Allen (green plain), the name of rivers in Cornwall, Dorset, Northumberland, and Stirlingshire.

Allenby (*Eng.*) One who came from Allonby (Aleyn's homestead), in Cumberland.

Allensworth (*Eng.*) Dweller near Alan's homestead.

Aller (*Eng.*) One who came from Aller (alder), the name of places in Devonshire and Somerset.

Allerton (*Eng.*) One who came from Allerton (the alder settlement; Ælfweard's estate), the name of several places in England.

Alles (*Eng.*) Descendant of Alis, an early form of Alice (noble, kind).

Alley, Allie (*Eng.*) Descendant of Ally, found as Alli in early records; dweller at a narrow passage; descendant of little Al, a pet form of Alan or Alexander, q.q.v.

Alleyne, Allain, Allyn (*Eng.*) Descendant of Alleyne, early form of Allen, q.v.

Allgood (*Eng.*) Descendant of Algod (elf, good; noble, good).

Allison, Alison (*Scot., Eng.*) The son of Ellis (God is salvation); corruption of Allanson, q.v.; the son of Alis, a pet form of Alister or Alexander (helper of mankind); the son of Alice (noble, kind), occasionally a masculine name.

Allman, Alleman, Allemang (*Eng., Fr.*) One who came from Alemaigne (all men), in Germany; a name generally applied to anyone from the Baltic states or from Holland.

Allmark (*Eng.*) Nickname for one fond of hallmarks, that is, a half-mark or one-third of a pound.

Allmond (*Eng.*) Variant of Almond, q.v.

Allred, Alred (*Eng.*) Descendant of Aldred (noble, counsel), or of Ealdred (old, counsel).

Allston (*Eng.*) Variant of Alston, q.v.

Allswang (*Dan.*) One who came from Alsovang, in Denmark.

Allums, Allum (*Eng., Scot.*) One who came from Alnham (home on the Aln river), in Northumberland; a curtailed form of McCallum, q.v.

Alm (*Ger., Sw.*) Descendant of Alm, a pet form of Alhelm and Adelhelm (noble, helmet); elm.

Almaguer (*Sp.*) Dweller on reddish-colored ground; one with red hair or a ruddy complexion.

Almanza (*Sp.*) One who came from Almanza (many waters; midway point), in Spain.

Almanzar (*Sp.*) Descendant of Almanzor (the victorious); the name is also a title given to warriors.

Almazan (*Sp.*) One who came from Almazan (fortified place), in Spain.

Almeda (*Sp.*) One who came from Almeda (sweet gum tree), in Spain.

Almeida (*Port., Sp.*) One who came from Almeida (flat land), in Portugal.

Almgren (*Sw.*) Elm branch.

Almond, Almon (*Eng.*) Descendant of Aleman (German); the man from Germany.

Almquist, Almkuist (*Sw.*) Elm twig.

Almy (*Eng.*) Dweller at the elm island.

Alonso, Alonzo (*Sp.*) Descendant of Alonso, a Spanish form of Alphonso (noble, ready).

Alper (*Ger.*) Descendant of Alber (noble, bear).

Alpern, Alperin (*Ger.*) One who came from Heilbronn (swampy spring), in Germany.

Alperstein (*Ger.*) Mountain stone.

Alpert, Alport, Allport (*Eng.*) One who came from Alport (old town), in Derbyshire.

Alsdorf (*Ger.*) One who came from Alsdorf (swampy village), the name of four places in Germany.

Alsop, Alsup, Alsip (*Eng.*) One who came from Alsop en le Dale, listed as Aleshop in 1241 (Aelle's valley), in Derbyshire.

Alston (*Eng.*) One who came from Alston (the village of one whose name began with Al), the name of several places in England.

Alswede (*Ger.*) One who came from Alswede (swampy forest), in Germany.

Alt (*Ger.*) One who was older than another with whom he was associated; descendant of Aldo, a pet form of names beginning with Alt (old), as Aldhard, Altraban, and Alderich.

Alter (*Ger.*) The old man; descendant of Althar (old, army); dweller at, or near, a poplar tree.

Altergott (*Ger.*) A nickname, the old god.

Altgeld, Altgelt (*Ger.*) One who deals in old gold; one who lives miserably to increase his hoard, a miser.

Althaus, Althouse (*Ger.*) Dweller in, or near, the old house.

Althoff, Althof (*Du.*) Dweller in, or near, the old courtyard.

Altman, Altmann (*Ger.*) The old servant; descendant of Aldman (old, man).

Alton, Alten, Altone (*Eng.*) One who came from Alton (the old village; the village at the source of the river), the name of several places in England.

Altschuh (*Ger.*) One who repaired old shoes, a cobbler.

Altschuler, Altshuler, Altschul, Altshul (*Cz.-Sl., Ger.*) One who came from the old school, the Old Synagogue of Prague; descendant of the old teacher.

Alvarado, Alvara (*Sp.*) Dweller near a white hill, or on dry terrain; one who came from Albarado (whitened place), in Spain.

Alvarez, Alvaroz (*Sp.*) The son of Alvaro (prudent).

Alvin, Alven (*Eng.*) Descendant of Ealdwine (old, friend); or of Aedelwine (noble, friend); or of Aelfwine (elf, friend).

Alvord, Alward (*Eng.*) Variants of Alford, q.v.

Amador (*Sp.*) One who is a lover, sweetheart, or suitor.

Aman, Amann (*Eng.*) Descendant of Amand (worthy of love).

Amano (*Jap.*) Heaven, field.

Amaro (*Sp.*) Dweller near where common clary, a mint of Southern Europe, grew.

Amato (*It.*) Descendant of Amato (beloved).

Amber (*Eng.*) Dweller on, or near, the Amber, a river in Derbyshire.

Amberg, Amberger (*Sw., Dan.*) Elm hill; dweller on, or near, a large hill or mountain.

Ambler (*Eng.*) One who came from Amble (Anna's promontory), in Northumberland.

Ambrose (*Eng.*) Descendant of Ambrose (immortal).

Amedeo, Amedio (*It.*) Descendant of Amedeo (love of God).

Amelio (*It.*) Descendant of Amelio (the worker).

Amend (*Ger.*) Dweller at the end of the street or row of houses.

Ames, Amis (*Eng.*) The son of Ame or Amis (friend), descendant of Ame, a pet form of Amery (work, rule); variants of Eames, q.v.

Amici, Amico (*It.*) One who was a friend to others.

Amir (*Arab.*) Descendant of the Amir, a title given to the descendants of Mohammed through his daughter Fatima.

Amirault, Amerault (*Fr.*) The highest ranking naval officer, a surname sometimes applied in derision.

Ammons, Ammon, Ammonds (*Eng.*) Descendant of Ammons (terror, protector).

Amodeo, Amodei (*It.*) Variant of Amedeo, q.v.

Amore (*Eng.*) Dweller in, or near, the marsh.

Amoroso, Amorosi, Amorose (*It.*) The lovable man; the ardent, affectionate man.

Amory, Amery (*Eng.*) Descendant of Amery (work, rule).

Amos (*Eng.*) Descendant of Amos (burden-bearer); a variant of Ames, q.v.

Ampere (*Sp.*) One who came from Ampuero (hot fountain), in Spain.

Amrein, Amrhein, Amrhine (*Ger.*) Dweller at the Rhine river.

Amsel (*Ger.*) Dweller at the sign of the black bird, a sign sometimes chosen because of the resemblance of the word to the name Anselm (divine, helmet).

Amstadt, Amstadter (*Ger.*) Dweller in the town.

Amsterdam (*Du.*) One who came from Amsterdam (dam on the Amstel river), in Holland.

Amundsen, Amundson (*Nor., Ice.*) The son of Amund (protector, forever).

Anagnos, Anagnost (*Gr.*) Descendant of an ecclesiastical acolyte.

Anagnostopolous (*Gr.*) Son of an ecclesiastical acolyte.

Analitis (*Gr.*) One who makes analyses or investigations.

Anast, Anastos (*Gr.*) Descendant of Anastasius (resurrection).

Anaya (*Fr.*) Descendant of a friar or brother, a member of a men's religious order preparing for holy orders.

Ancell, Ancel (*Eng.*) Descendant of Anselm (god, helmet).

Anchorsmith (*Eng.*) The man who made anchors.

Anda (*Sp.*) One who came from Anda (ambulate), in Spain.

Andalman, Andelman (*Ger.*) Descendant of the tradesman or shopkeeper.

Andel (*Cz.-Sl.*) One who played the part of an angel in play or pageant.

Andersen, Anders (*Nor., Dan.*) The son of Andrew (manly).

Anderson, Andrews, Andrew (*Eng., Scot.*) The son of Andrew (manly).

Andersson (*Sw.*) The son of Andrew (manly).

Andino (*Sp.*) One who came from Andino (the Andes) in Spain.

Andjelich, Andjelic (*Yu.-Sl.*) The son of Andjel, Serbo-Croatian form of Angel (messenger; angelic).

Ando (*Jap.*) Peaceful, wisteria.

Andrade (*Sp., Port.*) One who came from Andrade (road of the women), in Spain; descendant of Andres, Spanish form of Andrew (manly).

Andras (*Hun.*) Descendant of Andras, Hungarian form of Andrew (manly).

Andre, Andres (*Fr.*) Descendant of Andre (manly).

Andreasen, Andreassen, Andreason (*Nor., Dan., Sw.*) The son of Andreas, Scandinavian form of Andrew (manly).

Andreassian (*Arm.*) The son of Andreas, an Armenian form of Andrew (manly).

Andrejevic (*Yu.-Sl.*) Descendant of Andrej, Slavic form of Andrew (manly).

Andres, Andress (*Eng., Fr.*) The son of Andre, a French form of Andrew (manly).

Andresen (*Nor.*) The son of Andre, Norwegian form of Andrew (manly).

Andrews, Andrew (*Scot.*) Descendant of Andrew (manly).

Andrich (*Ger.*) Descendant of Andrich, a Wendish form of Andrew (manly).

Andrijenko (*Ukr.*) The son of Andriy, Ukrainian form of Andrew (manly).

Andros, Andrulis (*Gr.*) Descendant of Andreas, Greek form of Andrew (manly).

Andrysiak, Andrzejak (*Pol.*) Descendant of Andrezej, Polish form of Andrew (manly).

Andrzejewski (*Pol.*) The son of Andrzej, Polish form of Andrew (manly).

Angel, Angell (*Eng.*) One who acted as a religious messenger or as a messenger from God; a nickname for an angelic person; descendant of Angel, a man's name in England; variants of Angle, q.v.

Angelo, Angeli, Angele (*It.*) Descendant of Angelo (an angel).

Angelopoulos (*Gr.*) The son of Angelo (an angel).

Anger, Angier (*Fr., Eng.*) Descendant of Ansgeri (Ans, a god, spear); dweller on, or near, a pasture or grassland.

Angland (*Eng.*) Dweller on the meadow land.

Angle (*Eng.*) Dweller at, or near, the angle, nook or corner.

Anglin, Angline (*Ir.*) Grandson of Anglonn (hero; champion).

Angone (*It.*) Nickname, the strangler.

Angove (*Eng.*) One who worked in metal, a smith.

Angus (*Scot.*) Descendant of Angus (one choice); one who came from the district of Angus (said to be named after Angus, king of the Picts), the ancient name of Forfarshire.

Anhaeuser (*Ger.*) One who came from Anhausen (at the houses), in Germany.

Anhalt (*Ger.*) One who came from Anholt (at the wood), in Germany.

Annis (*Eng.*) The son of Annis, the popular pronunciation of Agnes (pure), one of the commonest feminine names in the 12th to 16th centuries.

Anschel (*Fr.*) Descendant of Anselm (divine, helmet).

Ansell, Ansel (*Eng.*) Descendant of Anselm (divine, helmet).

Anselmo, Anzelmo (*Sp., Port., It.*) Descendant of Anselmo, Spanish and

Portuguese form of Anselm (divine, helmet).

Ansley (*Eng.*) One who came from Ansley (wood with a hermitage) in Warwickshire.

Anslow (*Eng.*) One who came from Anslow (hermitage, meadow) in Staffordshire.

Anson, Ansons (*Eng.*) The son of Ann (grace); variant of Hansen, q.v.

Anspacher (*Ger.*) One who came from Ansbach (swampy brook), the name of two places in Germany.

Anstett, Ansted, Anstaedt, Anstadt (*Ger.*) One who came from Anstedt (town by the swamp), in Germany.

Anstey (*Eng.*) One who came from Anstey (narrow footpath, especially one up a hill), the name of six places in England.

Anstruther (*Scot.*) One who came from Anstruther (marshy meadow), in Fife.

Antanaitis (*Lith.*) The son of Antan, a Lithuanian form of Anthony (inestimable).

Antczak (*Pol.*) Descendant of little Ant, a pet form of Antoni, Polish form of Anthony (inestimable).

Anthony (*Wel.*) Descendant of Anthony (inestimable).

Antman (*Eng.*) The servant of Ant, a pet form of Anthony (inestimable).

Anton (*Ger.*) Descendant of Anton (inestimable).

Antonelli, Antonello (*It.*) Descendant of little Anton (inestimable).

Antonescu (*Rom.*) Descendant, or follower, of Anton (inestimable).

Antonopoulos (*Gr.*) The son of Antonos, Greek form of Anthony (inestimable).

Antonovych, Antonovich (*Rus., Yu.-Sl.*) The son of Anton, a Slavic form of Antony (inestimable).

Antonson, Antonsen (*Sw., Nor.*) The son of Anton (inestimable).

Antos (*Gr.*) The son of Antonis, Greek form of Antony (inestimable).

Antosz (*Pol.*) Descendant of Antosz,

9

Polish form of Anthony (inestimable).

Antunes (*Port.*) The son of Anton, Portuguese form of Anthony (inestimable).

Anzalone, Anzelone (*It.*) Descendant of big Anzal, a pet form of Anselmo, Italian form of Anselm (divine, helmet).

Aoki (*Jap.*) Blue, well.

Aouste, Aoust (*Fr.*) Descendant of Aoust, a pet form of Augustin (majestic).

Aparicio (*Sp.*) One who came from Aparicio (phantom), in Spain; one so emaciated as to look like an apparition or ghost.

Apelian (*Arm.*) Descendant of Abel (breath or vanity).

Apfelberg (*Ger.*) One who came from Eifelberg (chain of mountains), in Germany.

Apley (*Eng.*) One who came from Apley (meadow of apple trees), the name of several towns in England.

Aponte (*Sp.*) Dweller by the bridge.

Apostol, Apostolos, Apostolou, Apostal, Apostle (*Gr.*) Descendant of the apostle or disciple.

Apostolopoulos (*Gr.*) The son of the apostle or disciple.

Appel, Appell, Apple, Apfel (*Ger., Eng.*) Dweller near an apple tree; descendant of Adel, a short form of Adalbert (noble, bright).

Appelhans (*Ger.*) Apple John, possibly a nickname for one named Hans who had something to do with apples.

Applebaum, Appelbaum, Apfelbaum (*Ger.*) Dweller near an apple tree.

Appleberry (*Eng.*) Dweller on, or near, a hill or fortified place where apples grew.

Appleby (*Eng.*) One who came from Appleby (homestead where apples grew), the name of several places in England.

Applegarth (*Scot., Eng.*) One who came from Applegarth (apple orchard), in Scotland; or from Applegarth, in the North Riding of Yorkshire.

Applegate (*Eng.*) Dweller at the gate or entrance to the apple orchard.

Appleseed (*Eng.*) An American invention adopted by John Chapman.

Appleton (*Eng.*) One who came from Appleton (place where apples grew), the name of various places in England.

Applewhite, Applewhaite (*Eng.*) One who came from Applethwaite (clearing where apples grew), the name of places in Cumberland and Westmorland.

Appleyard (*Eng.*) Dweller at the apple orchard.

Appling, Applin (*Eng.*) Descendant of very little Ab, a pet form of Abel (breath or vanity).

Applington (*Eng.*) One who came from Appleton (place where apples grew), the name of various places in England.

Apter (*Fr.*) One who came from Apt in France.

Aquino (*It.*) One who came from Aquino, in Italy.

Arado (*It.*) One who came from Aradeo, in Italy.

Aragon (*Sp.*) Dweller on, or near, the arable land.

Arai (*Jap.*) Rough, well.

Arakawa (*Jap.*) Rough, river.

Arbogast (*Ger.*) Descendant of Arbogast (heir, stranger).

Arbuckle (*Scot.*) One who came from Arbuckle (height of the shepherd), in Scotland.

Arcaro, Arcara, Arcari (*It.*) One who made bows, i.e. weapons.

Arce (*Sp.*) One who came from Arce (maples), in Spain.

Arch, Arche (*Eng.*) Descendant of Arch, a short form of Archambault (simple, bold).

Archambault, Archambealt, Archambeau (*Fr.*) Descendant of Aircanbald (natural, bold).

Archer (*Eng.*) A fighting man armed with bow and arrows.

Archibald, Archie (*Eng., Scot.*) Descendant of Archibald (simple, bold). Archie is the pet form.

Ard, Aird (*Scot.*) One who came from the Aird, a district in the Vale of Beauty, in Scotland.

Arden (*Eng.*) One who came from Arden (dwelling house), the name of several places in England.

Ardley (*Eng.*) One who came from Ardley (Eardwulf's grove), in Oxfordshire; or from Ardleigh (dwelling in a grove), in Essex.

Ardrey (*Eng.*) Descendant of Audrey, a pet form of Etheldreda (noble, strength).

Arehart (*Ger.*) Descendant of Erhart (honor, brave).

Arellano (*Sp.*) One who came from Arellano (sieve), in Spain.

Arends, Arend (*Ger., Du.*) Descendant of Arend (eagle, rule).

Arendt (*Nor.*) Descendant of Arend (eagle, rule).

Arensberg (*Ger.*) One who came from Arensberg (sandy village), in Germany.

Arenson, Arens (*Nor.*) The son of Aren (eagle, rule).

Arenz, Arentz (*Dan.*) Descendant of Arenz (eagle, rule).

Ares (*Sp.*) One who came from Ares (Greek god of war), the name of two places in Spain.

Argiris, Argires (*Gr.*) One who deals in silver; or makes and sells silver jewelry; one with a silvery complexion.

Argos (*Gr.*) The light-complexioned or white-haired man.

Arguello (*Sp.*) One who came from Arquello (small bow or bend), in Spain.

Arias (*Sp.*) One who came from Arias (songs), in Spain.

Arita (*Jap.*) Have, rice field.

Arkema (*Du.*) The son of Harke.

Arkin, Arkins (*Nor.*) Descendant of little Arke or Erke (ever, king).

Arkwright (*Eng.*) One who made arks or chests.

Arlington (*Eng.*) One who came from Arlington (the village of Aelffrith's

or Aelfred's people, or of the people of the earl), the name of towns in Devonshire, Gloucestershire, and Sussex.

Armand, Arman (*Fr., Du.*) Descendant of Armand (strong man).

Armato (*It.*) One engaged in military life, a warrior.

Armbruster, Armbrust (*Ger.*) Fighter armed with a crossbow; one who made and sold crossbows.

Armfield (*Eng.*) Dweller on, or near, the poor open country.

Armijo (*Sp.*) Descendant of Armillo, a pet form of Hermenegildo (one who protects by his strength; one who distributes to the soldiers).

Armitage (*Eng.*) Dweller at, or near, the habitation of a hermit.

Armon, Armond (*Eng.*) Descendant of Armon, a pet form of names beginning with Ermen (large; eminent), as Ermenald and Ermenbert.

Armour, Armor (*Eng.*) One who made defensive armor for the body.

Armstead, Armistead (*Eng., Ger.*) Dweller at the hermit's dairy farm; one who came from Armstedt, in Germany.

Armstrong (*Eng., Scot.*) The strong-armed man.

Armwood (*Eng.*) One who came from Arnwood (eagle wood), in Hampshire.

Arndt, Arndtsen (*Dan.*) Descendant of Arndt (eagle, rule).

Arne (*Eng.*) One who came from Arne (house), in Dorset.

Arneberg (*Nor.*) One who came from Arneberg (Arni's hill), in Norway.

Arneson, Arnesen, Arnesson (*Nor., Dan.*) The son of Arne (eagle).

Arnett, Arney, Arnet, Arnette (*Eng.*) Descendant of little Arnold (eagle, rule).

Arnheim (*Du.*) One who came from Arnheim, in Holland.

Arno (*It.*) Dweller near the Arno, a river in Italy.

Arnold, Arnolde (*Eng.*) Descendant of Arnold (eagle, rule); one who came from Arnold (corner frequented by eagles), in Nottinghamshire.

Arnott, Arnot (*Scot., Eng.*) One who came from Arnot (earth nut), in Scotland, or from Arnold (corner frequented by eagles) in Nottinghamshire; descendant of Arnold (eagle, rule).

Arnstein (*Ger.*) One who came from Arnstein (stony waterway) in Germany.

Aronoff (*Rus.*) The son of Aron, Slavic form of Aaron (lofty mountain).

Aronsohn (*Ger.*) The son of Aron, German form of Aaron (lofty mountain).

Aronson, Arons, Aron (*Sw.*) The son or descendant of Aron, a Swedish form of Aaron (lofty mountain).

Aronstein (*Heb., Ger.*) Lofty mountain, stone.

Arquette (*Fr.*) One who fought with a small bow, an archer; one who made and sold bows.

Arquilla (*Sp.*) One who operated a kiln.

Arredondo (*Sp.*) One who came from Arredondo (round), in Spain.

Arriaga, Arriago (*Sp.*) One who came from Arriaga (stony incline), in Spain.

Arrington (*Eng.*) One who came from Arrington (the homestead of Erna's people), a village in Cambridgeshire.

Arrowsmith, Arrasmith (*Eng.*) One who made arrows, especially arrowheads.

Arroyo (*Sp.*) Dweller by a small stream.

Arsenault, Arseneau, Arceneaux (*Fr.*) One who had charge of the arsenal where weapons were stored.

Arslan (*Tur.*) Modern name meaning "lion."

Arsmith (*Eng.*) One who worked in brass; contraction of Arrowsmith, q.v.

Arteaga (*Sp.*) One who came from Arteaga (place of the huts), in Spain.

Arterberry (*Eng.*) Variant of Atterberry, q.v.

Arterburn (*Eng.*) One who came from Otterburn (otter stream), the name

of places in Northumberland and the West Riding of Yorkshire.

Arthur (*Eng., Wel.*) Descendant of Arthur (Thor's eagle; valorous, noble; bear, man).

Artis, Artos, Artus (*Eng., Fr.*) Descendant of Arthur (valorous, noble; bear, man; Thor's eagle); or of the French form Arthus; one who came from Arthes, in France.

Artley (*Eng.*) One who came from Hartley (wood near fork of river), in Westmorland.

Arundel, Arundal (*Eng., Fr.*) One who came from Arundel (hoarhound valley), in Sussex; dweller at the sign of the little swallow; one thought to possess the characteristics of a little swallow.

Arvanitis (*Gr.*) One who came from Albania (highland).

Arvia, Arvio (*It.*) Dweller on, or near, the plowed land.

Arvidson, Arvidsson (*Sw.*) The son of Arvid (man of the people).

Arzt (*Ger.*) One who practiced medicine, a doctor; one who cures by charms or conjurations.

Asato (*Jap.*) Rest, village.

Asbiornsen (*Nor.*) The son of Asbiorn (divine, bear).

Asbury, Asberry, Asbery (*Eng.*) One who came from Ashbury (Aesc's fort; fort near ash trees), the name of villages in Berkshire and Devonshire; or from Astbury (eastern fort), in Cheshire.

Aschenbrenner, Aschenbrener (*Ger., Eng.*) One who made potash, an ashburner.

Ascher, Asher, Asch (*Ger.*) Dweller near an ash tree; descendant of Ascher (ash, army); one who came from Asch, in Germany.

Aschkenasy, Aschkenasi (*Heb.*) Variant of Ashkenazi, q.v.

Ash, Ashe (*Eng.*) Dweller near an ash tree.

Ashbaugh (*Ger.*) One who came from Aschbach (muddy brook), the name of six places in Germany.

Ashbrook (*Eng.*) One who came from

Ashbrook (eastern brook), in Gloucestershire.

Ashburn, Ashburne (*Eng.*) Dweller near the Ashburn (ash tree brook), a river in Sussex.

Ashburner (*Eng.*) One who made potash by burning ashes.

Ashby (*Eng.*) One who came from Ashby (the village where ash trees grew), the name of various places in England.

Ashcom (*Eng.*) One who came from Ashcombe (ash tree valley), in Devonshire.

Ashcraft, Ashcroft (*Eng.*) Dweller on the small field where ash trees grew.

Asher (*Eng.*) Descendant of Asher (spear, army).

Ashford (*Eng.*) One who came from Ashford (the ford where ash trees grew), the name of various places in England.

Ashkenazi, Ashkenazy, Ashkenasi, Ashkinazi (*Heb.*) Descendant of Ashchenaz (the As race; fire that spreads); one who came from Ashkenaz, a kingdom near Armenia. Ashkenazi is a term now applied to Jews who were resident in the Middle Ages in Germany and France and to their descendants as distinguished from the Sephardim, the Jews of Spain and Portugal.

Ashley (*Eng.*) One who came from Ashley (the wood where ash trees grew), the name of various places in England.

Ashmore (*Eng.*) One who came from Ashmore (lake where ash trees grew; Aesca's boundary line), in Dorset.

Ashton (*Eng.*) One who came from Ashton (the village or homestead where ash trees grew), the name of various places in England.

Ashwood (*Eng.*) One who came from Ashwood (wood of ash trees), in Staffordshire.

Ashworth (*Eng.*) One who came from Ashworth (homestead among ash trees); in Lancashire.

Askeland (*Nor.*) Dweller on the ash tree farm, a farm name.

Askew (*Eng.*) One who came from Aiskew (oak wood), in the North Riding of Yorkshire.

Askin, Askins (*Eng.*) Descendant of little Aesc (ash; spear; ship).

Askwith (*Eng.*) One who came from Askwith (ash forest), in the West Riding of Yorkshire.

Aspan, Aspen (*Eng.*) Dweller in the place overgrown with aspens.

Aspergren (*Sw.*) Aspen tree, branch.

Aspinwall, Aspinall, Aspenwall (*Eng.*) Dweller near the aspen tree, stream or spring.

Asplund (*Sw.*) Aspen grove; dweller in an aspen grove.

Asquith (*Eng.*) One who came from Askwith (ash wood), in Yorkshire.

Astle (*Eng.*) One who came from Astle (eastern hill), in Cheshire.

Aston, Astin, Astone (*Eng.*) One who came from Aston (the village to the east), the name of many places in England.

Astor (*Eng., It.*) Descendant of Easter (name given to a child born at Eastertide); dweller at the sign of the hawk.

Astrup (*Nor.*) Dweller at the outlying farm; or on a ridge.

Asztalos (*Hun.*) The worker in wood, a carpenter.

Atamian (*Arm.*) Descendant of Atam, an Armenian form of Adam (red earth).

Atchison (*Scot., Eng.*) The son of Adkin, a pet form of Adam (red earth).

Atchley (*Eng.*) Dweller in, or near, an oak grove.

Atencio (*Sp.*) Descendant of Atanosio, Spanish form of Athanasius (immortal).

Athanas, Athans, Athanasopoulos, Athens (*Gr.*) Descendant of Athanasios, Greek form of Athanasius (immortal).

Athersmith (*Eng.*) The man "at ther smethe" or level field; corruption of Arrowsmith, q.v.

13

Atherton (*Eng.*) One who came from Atherton (Ethelhere's homestead), in Lancashire.

Athey, Athy (*Eng.*) Dweller at the enclosure.

Atkins, Atkinson, Atkin (*Eng.*) The son of little Ad, a pet form of Adam (red earth).

Atlas, Atlass (*Eng.*) Descendant of Edel or Eidel (noble), corrupted through Edlin and Eidles which became Atlas; an acronym from the first Hebrew words of Psalm 73, "Truly God is good to Israel."

Attaway (*Eng.*) Dweller by the road.

Atterberry, Atterbury, Attebery, Attyberry (*Eng.*) One who came from Attenborough (the fort of Eada's people; or of Edda), in Nottinghamshire; or from Adderbury (Eadburg's fortified place), in Oxfordshire.

Atterton (*Eng.*) One who came from Atterton (Eadred's homestead), the name of places in Kent and Leicestershire.

Attlee (*Eng.*) Dweller by the wood or in the clearing.

Attree (*Eng.*) Dweller near a tree; dweller by a stream or on low-lying land.

Attridge (*Eng.*) Dweller at, or near, a ridge or range of hills.

Atwater, Attwater (*Eng.*) Dweller at a stream or lake.

Atwell, Atwill, Attwell (*Eng.*) Dweller at a well, spring, or stream.

Atwood, Attwood (*Eng.*) Dweller at, or near, a wood.

Aubert, Auber (*Fr., Eng.*) Descendant of Auber, a variant of Albert (noble, bright).

Aubin (*Fr., Eng.*) Descendant of Albin (white).

Aubry, Aubrey (*Fr., Eng.*) Descendant of Alberic (noble, bright).

Auckland (*Eng.*) One who came from Auckland (the cliff on the Clyde; additional land), in Durham.

Aucoin (*Fr.*) Descendant of Alcuin (temple, friend).

Aucott (*Eng.*) Variant of Alcott, q.v.

Audubon (*Fr.*) Literally French for "of the good," probably a shortened form of a longer name or description.

Auer (*Ger.*) Dweller in, or near, a marsh; dweller at the sign of the bison; one who came from Aue (pasture), the name of many small places in Germany.

Auerbach (*Ger.*) One who came from Auerbach (marshy stream), in Germany.

Aufderheide (*Ger.*) Dweller on the unimproved or wild land or heath.

Auger, Auge (*Fr.*) Descendant of Adalgar (noble, spear).

Augustine, August, Augustin, Augustyn (*Eng.*) Descendant of Augustine (majestic).

Augustson (*Nor., Sw.*) The son of August (majestic).

Augustus (*Eng.*) Descendant of August (majestic).

Augustyniak, Augustiniak (*Pol., Ukr.*) Descendant of Augustyn, Slavic form of Augustine (majestic).

Auld (*Scot.*) Descendant of Ealda (old); the elderly person.

Aulie (*Nor.*) Dweller in, or near, the gravel land.

Ault (*Ger.*) Americanized form of Alt, q.v.

Aumann, Auman (*Ger.*) Dweller on the water meadow or pasture.

Aune (*Fr., Nor.*) Dweller near the alder tree; one who came from Aune (deserted place), in Norway.

Auslander (*Ger.*) One who came from another country, a foreigner.

Austin, Austen (*Eng., Scot.*) Descendant of Austin, a variant of Augustine (majestic).

Autry, Autrey (*Fr.*) Descendant of Aldric (old, powerful).

Avant, Avent (*Eng.*) One who was handsome or comely.

Averett, Averitt (*Eng.*) Descendant of Everard (boar, hard).

Averill (*Eng.*) Descendant of Averil (boar, battle); one who came from Haverhill (hill where oats were grown), in Suffolk.

Avers (*Eng.*) Descendant of Ever, a pet form of Everard (boar, hard).

Avery (*Eng.*) Descendant of Aelfric (elf, ruler), or Everard (boar, hard); one who came from Evreux, in France.

Avila (*Sp., Port.*) One who came from Avila, a province and city in Spain.

Aviles (*Sp.*) One who came from Aviles, in Spain; the insolent or audacious man.

Avramovich (*Rus.*) The son of Avram, a Russian form of Abram (high father).

Awerbach, Awerbuch (*Ger.*) Variant of Auerbach, q.v.

Axe (*Eng.*) One who lived on, or near, the Axe, the name of two rivers in England.

Axelrod, Axelrood, Axelrad (*Eng.*) Dweller at the clearing by the ash trees; one who made wheel axles.

Axelson, Axell, Axel (*Sw.*) The son of Axel (divine reward).

Axley (*Eng.*) One who came from Ashling (Aescla's people), in Sussex; or from Ashley (ash wood), the name of several villages in England.

Axsmith (*Eng.*) One who made axes. The old battle-ax was widely used in warfare in the fourteenth and fifteenth centuries.

Ayala (*Sp.*) One who came from Ayala, in Spain.

Ayers, Ayer (*Eng.*) Descendant of the heir, i.e., the person in whom the fee of the real property of an intestate is vested at his death.

Aylward (*Eng.*) Descendant of Aylward (noble, guardian).

Ayyoub, Ayyub (*Arab.*) Descendant of Ayyub, Arabian form of Job (desire; persecuted).

Aziz (*Arab., Pers., Tur.*) Descendant of Aziz (beloved).

Azzarello, Azzaretti (*It.*) Descendant of little Azzo, a pet form of Galeazzo.

Baacke (*Dan., Nor.*) Dweller on a hill or slope.

Baade, Baader (*Nor.*) Dweller at the sign of the boat; one who worked on a boat or ship.

Baadsgaard (*Dan.*) One who came from Baadsgaard (Barth's farm), in Denmark.

Baan (*Du.*) Dweller near the path or road; descendant of Bane or Baan (command); or of Baan, a pet form of Urbaan, Dutch form of Urban (of the town).

Baar (*Du., Ger.*) Dweller at the sign of the bear; or near a bay or gulf; one who came from Baar (bear), in Germany.

Baas (*Du.*) The overseer or head man.

Baba (*Jap., Cz.-Sl., Pol.*) Horse, space; the man with the characteristics of an old woman.

Babani (*It.*) The crab louse, a nickname.

Babb, Babbe, Babbs (*Eng.*) Descendant of Babba (baby); or of Babb, a pet form of Barbara (stranger); or of Bab, a pet form of Baptist (baptizer).

Babbington (*Eng.*) One who came from Babington (the settlement of Babba's people), in Somerset.

Babbitt (*Eng.*) Descendant of little Babb or Babba. See Babb.

Babcock (*Eng.*) The son of Babb or Bab. See Babb.

Babczak (*Pol.*) Descendant of the old woman.

Babiak (*Ukr.*) One with the appearance or manner of an old woman.

Babiarz, Babiar (*Pol., Sl.*) One who likes women.

Babich, Babick, Babicz, Babic, Babij (*Ukr., Yu.-Sl.*) One with the characteristics of a woman; one who loved women, a casanova; descendant of Baba (grandmother; father).

Babin (*Ukr., Pol.*) One with the characteristics of an old woman.

Babka (*Pol.*) One with the bearing or characteristics of an old woman.

Babson (*Eng.*) The son of Babb or Babba. See Babb.

Babu (*Hindi*) A clerk or writer.

Babusch, Babuskow (*Rus.*) Descendant of the old woman.

Baby (*Eng.*) Descendant of little Bab, a pet form of Barbara (stranger).

Baca (*It., Cz.-Sl., Pol.*) Descendant of Baca, a pet form of Iabaca, a variant of Giacomo, Italian form of Jacob (may God protect; the supplanter); one who took care of sheep, a shepherd; the head shepherd.

Bacarella (*It.*) One who took care of calves, a calfherd.

Bacchi, Bacci (*It.*) Dweller near stepping stones in a stream; or near any stone emerging from water.

Bacchus (*Eng.*) Dweller in, or near, the backhouse; worker or dweller in or near a bakehouse.

Baccus (*Eng.*) One who worked in a bakehouse or bakery.

Bach, Bache (*Ger., Eng., Wel.*) Dweller in the stream valley; one who came from Bache (valley of a stream), the name of several places in England; the small man.

Bachelor, Bachelder, Bacheller (*Eng.*) The holder, or tenant, of a small farm; an officer or servant who has care of the door in a large household; the young person, or young knight.

Bacher (*Ger.*) Dweller by a brook; one who came from Bach (brook), the name of several places in Germany.

Bachman, Bachmann (*Ger.*) Dweller at, or near, a brook or stream.

Bachmeier, Bachmeyer (*Ger.*) The farmer or head servant who lived by the brook.

Bachrach, Bacharach (*Ger.*) One who came from Bacharach (swampy estate), in Germany.

Bachynsky (*Ukr.*) One who came from Bachka (view), in the Ukraine.

Back, Backe (*Eng., Wel.*) Dweller by a brook; variants of Bach, q.v.

Backer (*Nor., Dan., Ger., Du.*) Dweller on a hill or slope; one who came from Bakker (hills), the name of several places in Norway; one who made bread, a baker.

Backhaus (*Ger.*) The man who lived near, or who worked in, the bakehouse.

Backley (*Eng.*) Dweller in, or near, Bacca's grove.

Backlund (*Sw.*) Hill grove.

Backman, Backmann, Backmon (*Ger.*) Dweller at, or near, a brook or stream.

Backstrom (*Sw.*) Hill stream.

Backup (*Eng.*) One who came from Bacup (valley by a ridge), in Lancashire.

Backus (*Eng.*) Dweller in, or near, the bakehouse.

Bacon (*Eng.*) A swineherd or peasant, from the nickname, Bacon; a bacon or lard dealer; dweller at the sign of the pig, at a time when bacon meant the live pig.

Badalamenti (*It.*) One who continually laments or complains.

Bade (*Ger.*) Descendant of Bodo (commander); or of Badu (fight); or of Bode, a pet form of names with this termination, such as Segebade and Garbode.

Baden, Bading (*Ger.*) Descendant of Bode or Bodo (ruler), often a pet form of names terminating in -bode such as Segebode and Gerbode.

Badenoch (*Scot.*) Dweller on marshy land; or at a bushy place.

Bader (*Ger.*) One who practiced surgery, a barber surgeon; one who came from Baden, in Germany; descendant of Bathari (combat, army).

Badescu (*Rom.*) The son of the elder brother or friend.

Badger, Badgers (*Eng.*) Variants of Bagger, q.v.; one who came from Badger (Bacga's shore) in Shropshire.

Badham (*Wel.*) The son of Adam (red earth).

Badillo (*Sp.*) One who came from Badillo (small ford), in Spain.

Badke (*Ger.*) Descendant of Badu (fight); or of Bode, a pet form of names with this ending such as Sigebode (victory, commander) and Garbade.

Baer, Baehr (*Ger.*) Dweller at the sign of the bear; one thought to possess bearlike qualities. The bear was the king of beasts in the north of Europe.

Baerman, Baermann (*Ger.*) The small-holder or farmer, a peasant.

Baez, Baeza (*Sp.*) Nickname for one of black or swarthy complexion; variant of Paez, q.v.

Baffa (*It.*) One with a prominent beard or mustache.

Bagby (*Eng.*) One who came from Bagby (Baggi's homestead), in the North Riding of Yorkshire.

Bagdon, Bagden (*Eng.*) One who came from Bagendon (valley of Baecga's people), in Gloucestershire; dweller in, or near, Baggi's hill pasture.

Bagdonas (*Lith.*) Descendant of Bogdan (gift of God).

Bagelman (*Ger.*) One who made and sold bagels, a leavened doughnut-shaped, hard roll.

Bagge, Bagg (*Eng.*) Metonymic for a Bagger, q.v.

Bagger (*Eng.*) One who made and sold bags; the peddler who carried his wares from place to place in a bag.

Baggett, Baggott, Baggot (*Eng.*) Descendant of little Baga or Bacga (the fat one).

Baggio (*It.*) The toad, a nickname for a lean man.

Baggs, Bagge, Bagg (*Eng.*) Descendant of Baga or Bacga (the fat one).

Baginski (*Pol.*) Dweller near a swamp or marsh.

Bagley (*Eng.*) One who came from Bagley (the rams' or pigs' woodland), the name of various places in England.

Baglivo (*It.*) A chief officer or magistrate.

Bagnall, Bagnell (*Eng.*) One who came from Bagnall (Badeca's wood or corner), in Staffordshire.

Bagshaw (*Eng.*) One who came from Bagshaw (Bacga's wood), in Derbyshire.

Bagshot (*Eng.*) One who came from Bagshot (wood where rams or pigs are found), in Surrey.

Bagthorpe (*Eng.*) One who came from Bagthorpe (Bakki's or Bacca's farm), in Norfolk.

Bagwell, Bagwill (*Eng.*) Dweller at, or near, Bagga's spring.

Bahlenhorst (*Ger.*) Dweller in, or near, a swampy thicket.

Bahnson, Bahnsen (*Ger.*) Descendant of Panno, a pet form of names beginning with Ban (precept), as Banager and Banhart.

Bahr (*Ger.*) Variant of Baer, q.v.

Baich (*Ger.*) One who came from Beich, in Germany.

Baier, Bair (*Ger.*) One who came from Bavaria.

Bail (*Fr., Eng.*) The commanding officer of a fortified position; a guardian or tutor of a minor; dweller near the wall of the outer court of the castle.

Baile (*Fr.*) One who acted as a bailiff, magistrate or judge, sometimes ironically applied.

Bailer (*Ger.*) One who inspects, measures or weighs materials.

Bailey, Baillie, Bailie, Baily (*Eng., Scot.*) One charged with public administrative authority in a certain district by the king or a lord; one who acted as agent for the lord in the management of the affairs of the manor; one who came from Bailey (clearing where berries grew), in Lancashire.

Bailiff (*Eng.*) One who acted as agent for the lord in the management of the affairs of the manor; the public administrator of a district; the chief officer of a hundred.

Bailly, Bally, Bayle (*Fr.*) French form of Bailey, q.v.

Baim, Baime (*Ger.*) One who came from Bohemia.

Bain, Baine (*Eng., Scot.*) Dweller near the Bain (straight), the name of rivers in Lincolnshire and Yorkshire; one so thin that his bones protruded.

Bainbridge (*Eng.*) One who came from Bainbridge (bridge on the Bain, i.e., straight, river), in Yorkshire.

Baines, Baynes, Banes (*Scot.*) The fair, or light-complexioned man.

Bainton (*Eng.*) One who came from Bainton (village of Bada's people; or of Baga's people), the name of places in Northamptonshire, Oxfordshire, and the East Riding of Yorkshire.

Baio (*It.*) The bay horse, possibly designating a dweller at the sign of the bay horse; one with reddish-brown hair or complexion.

Baiocchi (*It.*) From a coin worth only two cents, and thus a nickname for a worthless fellow.

Baird (*Scot.*) Descendant of the poet or bard; one who came from Bard, in Scotland.

Bairstow (*Eng.*) One who came from Bairstow (place where berries grew), the name of two places in the West Riding of Yorkshire; variant of Barstow, q.v.

Baity (*Eng.*) Variant of Batty, q.v.

Bajak (*Pol.*) One who talks nonsense; a jester.

Bajerski (*Pol.*) Dweller by the slough or muddy place.

Bajko, Bajkowski (*Pol.*) Descendant of the story teller.

Bajo (*Sp.*) One who came from Bajo (below; town in a declivity), in Spain; dweller in a low place.

Bajoras (*Lith.*) Descendant of a boyar, a member of a Russian aristocratic order abolished by Peter the Great.

Bajorek (*Pol.*) Dweller by the slough or muddy place.

Bajt (*Yu.-Sl.*) Dweller in the hut.

Bak (*Eng.*) Dweller by a brook.

Baker (*Eng., Wel.*) One who made bread.

Bakewell (*Eng.*) One who came from Bakewell (Badeca's spring), in Derbyshire.

Bakke, Bakken (*Nor.*) Dweller at, or near, a hill.

Bakker (*Du.*) One who made bread, a baker.

Balaban, Baliban (*Ukr., Rom.*) Dweller at the sign of the falcon; one who hunts with, breeds, or trains falcons.

Balance, Ballance (*Eng.*) Dweller at the sign of the balance, usually designating a scale-maker.

Balanoff, Balanow (*Rus.*) The son of Balan.

Balas, Balash, Balaskovits (*Pol.*) Descendant, or son, of the tall thin person.

Balazs (*Hun.*) Descendant of Balazs, Hungarian form of Blasius (babbler), a fourth century saint.

Balcer, Balcerak, Balcerzak (*Pol.*) Descendant of Balcer, a short form of Balthasar (Baal has formed a king).

Balch (*Eng.*) The bald man.

Balchunas, Balciunas (*Lith.*) Descendant of Baltramiejus, Lithuanian form of Bartholomew (son of Talmai, furrow).

Balcom, Balcombe (*Eng.*) One who came from Balcombe (Baegloc's hollow), in Sussex.

Bald (*Eng.*) One who was bald-headed; the fat or corpulent man; descendant of Bald, a short form of Baldwin (bold, friend).

Baldacci, Baldaccini (*It.*) Descendant of little Baldo (bold).

Baldauf (*Ger.*) Descendant of Baldolf (bold, wolf).

Balder, Balderson (*Eng.*) Descendant of Bealdhere (bold, army).

Balderston (*Eng.*) One who came from Balderston (Baldhere's homestead), in Lancashire.

Balderton (*Eng.*) One who came from Balderton (Baldhere's enclosure), in Cheshire.

Baldi, Baldini, Baldino (*It.*) Descendant of Baldo, a pet form of Garibaldo (spear, bold).

Balding (*Eng.*) The son of Beald (bold); variant of Baldwin, q.v.

Baldridge (*Eng.*) Dweller on a ridge bare of trees and vegetation.

Baldus (*Ger.*) Descendant of Baldus, a pet form of Balthasar (Baal has formed a king).

Baldwin (*Eng.*) Descendant of Baldwin (bold, friend).

Bales, Bale (*Eng.*) Dweller near the wall of the outer court of a feudal castle; the guardian of the courts, a bailward.

Balestra, Balestri (*Fr., It.*) One who fought with the crossbow; one who made crossbows.

Baley (*Eng.*) Variant of Bailey, q.v.

Balfanz (*Ger.*) One who came from Balfanz, in Pomerania.

Balfe (*Ir.*) One who stammered.

Balfour (*Scot.*) One who came from Balfour (village by pasture land), in Fifeshire.

Balice (*Pol.*) One who came from Balice (place of timber), in Poland.

Balicki, Balick, Balich (*Cz.-Sl.*) The awkward or clumsy fellow.

Balik, Balikov (*Cz.-Sl., Rus.*) The awkward or clumsy fellow.

Balint (*Hun.*) Descendant of Balint, Hungarian form of Valentine (valorous or healthy).

Balismith (*Eng.*) The smith who used a pair of bellows in his work.

Balk, Balke (*Eng.*) Dweller near the balk or ridge; one who came from Balk (ridge formed in plowing), in the North Riding of Yorkshire.

Ball, Balle, Baller (*Eng.*) Descendant of Ball, a pet form of Baldwin (bold, friend); dweller at the sign of the ball; the bald-headed man.

Ballantine, Ballantyne, Ballentine, Balentine (*Scot.*) One who came from Ballindean (village by the hill), in Fifeshire; or from the lands of Bellenden, in Roxburghshire.

Ballard (*Eng.*) The bald-headed man.

Ballin (*Ger.*) One in charge of the baths.

Balling (*Eng.*) Descendant of little Ball, a pet form of Baldwin (bold, friend).

Ballinger, Ballenger (*Eng.*) One who made bread, a baker.

Ballingham (*Eng.*) One who came from Ballingham (Badela's people), in Herefordshire.

Ballman, Balman (*Eng.*) Descendant of Bealdmann (bold, man).

Ballou (*Fr.*) One who came from Bellou (water-cress), in France.

Balmer (*Eng.*) One who dealt in balme, an aromatic substance thought to possess medicinal qualities; dealer in spices and ointments.

Balogh, Balog (*Hun.*) One who was left-handed; one who shod horses.

Balsamo (*It.*) One who made and sold balm, or perfumes and ointments.

Balsham (*Eng.*) One who came from Balsham (Baelli's estate), in Cambridgeshire.

Balswick (*Eng.*) Dweller in, or near, Baelli's dairy farm.

Baltazar, Balthaser (*Ger.*) Descendant of Balthasar (Baal has formed a king), one of the three wise men who greeted the birth of Christ.

Balter (*Ger.*) Descendant of Balter, a Tyrolean form of Walthari (rule, army).

Baltimore (*Eng.*) From Baltimore or Balintimore (town of the great house), in County Cork.

Baltsen (*Dan.*) The son of Balte (bald); or of Balt, a pet form of Balthasar (Baal has formed a king).

Balzac (*Fr.*) One who came from Balsac, in France.

Balzer, Balthazar, Balthaser (*Ger.*) Descendant of Balthasar (Baal has formed a king).

Bambach (*Ger.*) Dweller near the swampy brook; one who came from Baumbach (swampy brook), the name of two places in Germany.

Bamberger, Bamberg (*Ger.*) One who came from Bamberg (Bab's hill), in Bavaria.

Bambrick (*Eng.*) Dweller at a foot-bridge, i.e., a single log across a stream.

Bambury (*Eng.*) One who came from Bamborough or Bamburgh (Bebbe's fort), in Northumberland; one who came from Banbury (Bana's fort), in Oxfordshire.

Bamford (*Eng.*) One who came from Bamford (ford with a footbridge), the name of places in Derbyshire and Lancashire.

Bampton (*Eng.*) One who came from Bampton (the place of the dwellers at a bath or hot spring), in Devonshire.

Ban (*Yu.-Sl., Hun., Jap.*) One who governs, a governor; the governor of a province; accompany.

Banach (*Pol.*) Descendant of Banach, a

pet form of Benedykt, Polish form of Benedict (blessed).

Banahan (*Ir.*) Grandson of little Beannach (pointed; horned).

Banas (*Hun.*) The lord, or head, of the household; the lord's servant; nickname given to one assuming superior rank.

Banasiak, Banasik, Banaszak (*Pol.*) One who was round or fat.

Banaszkiewicz (*Pol.*) The son of little Banach, a pet form of Benedykt, Polish form of Benedict (blessed).

Banbury (*Eng.*) One who came from Banbury (Bana's fortified place), in Oxfordshire.

Banby (*Eng.*) Dweller in, or near, Bana's homestead.

Bancroft (*Eng.*) Dweller at an enclosure, or yard, where beans grew.

Band (*Ger.*) One who cut barrel hoops, a hooper.

Bandema (*Du.*) Descendant of Bane (command).

Bandera (*It.*) One who carried the flag.

Bandstra (*Du.*) Dweller near the road.

Bane, Banes (*Scot., Eng.*) The fair or light-complexioned man; the straight, hospitable man; one who came from Bains, Baines, or Baynes (bath), the names of places in France.

Banffy (*Hun.*) Son of the governor of a province.

Banfield (*Eng.*) Dweller at a field where beans grew.

Bangert, Bangart (*Ger.*) Dweller in, or near, an orchard or tree nursery.

Bangor (*Scot.*) One who came from Bangour (hill of goats), in West Lothian.

Bangs, Bang (*Eng., Nor., Dan.*) Dweller near a mound or embankment; one who came from Bagn, in Norway.

Banham (*Eng.*) One who came from Banham (homestead where beans were grown), in Norfolk.

Banich, Banicki, Banik (*Rus., Pol.*) One who had been exiled or banished.

Bankhead (*Scot.*) One who came from Bankhead (end of the ridge), the

name of several small places in Scotland.

Bankowski (*Pol.*) Dweller in the village.

Banks, Bank, Banker (*Eng.*) Dweller near a mound or embankment.

Banner, Bannerman (*Scot.*) A standard-bearer for king or important noble.

Bannett (*Eng., Fr.*) Descendant of little Bana (slayer); one who made and sold baskets and hampers.

Banning (*Eng.*) Son of Bana or Banna (slayer).

Banningham (*Eng.*) One who came from Banningham (homestead of Bana's people), in Norfolk.

Bannister, Banister (*Eng.*) One who made and sold baskets; one who fought with a crossbow.

Bannon (*Ir.*) Grandson of Banain (little white one).

Bansley (*Eng.*) Dweller in, or near, a grove where beans were grown.

Banson (*Eng.*) The son of Bana (slayer).

Banting, Bantin (*Eng.*) The son of little Bana (slayer).

Banwell (*Eng.*) One who came from Banwell (Bana's stream; murderer's spring), in Somerset.

Banyard (*Eng.*) Descendant of Baynard (willing, strong); dweller at the bean garden.

Baptiste, Baptist (*Fr.*) Descendant of Jean-Baptiste (St. John the Baptist). Baptiste (one who baptizes) is a common given name in Roman Catholic countries.

Bara (*Fr.*) One who is deceitful or fraudulent.

Barabas, Barabasz, Barabash (*Pol., Fr.*) Descendant of Barabbas (son of his father).

Barak (*Pol., Ukr.*) Dweller in a small hut.

Baran, Baren (*Eng., Pol., Heb.*) Variant of Baron, q.v.; descendant of Baran (ram); acronymic name commemorating Ben Rabbi Nachman.

Baranowski (*Pol.*) One who came from Barano(w) or Baranowice (Baran's settlement), in Poland.

Baranowsky (*Ukr.*) One who came from

Baranovychi (place of rams), in Ukraine.

Baranski (*Pol.*) The son of Baran (ram).

Barash (*Heb.*) Descendant of Ben Rabbi Baran, an acronymic name.

Baratta (*It.*) One who is contentious or quarrelsome.

Barba (*Sp.*) One with hair on his chin, a beard; one who came from Barba (beard), in Spain.

Barbaro (*It.*) The rude, uncivilized man; descendant of Barbaro (the stranger).

Barbarossa (*It.*) The man with a red beard.

Barbeau, Barbeauld (*Fr.*) One who caught and sold barbel, a fish.

Barbee, Barby (*Eng., Fr.*) One who came from Barby (homestead in the hills), in Northamptonshire; the bearded man.

Barber (*Eng.*) The hairdresser; one who practiced surgery, i.e., acted as a blood-letter.

Barbier (*Fr.*) One who dressed hair, a barber.

Barbieri (*It.*) One who cut and styled hair, a barber.

Barbon (*Eng.*) One who came from Barbon (stream of the bear), in Westmorland.

Barbosa, Barboza (*Port., Sp.*) One who came from Barbosa, the name of many places in Portugal; one with a beard.

Barbour, Barbor (*Eng.*) Variant of Barber, q.v.

Barbourne (*Eng.*) One who came from Barbourne (beaver stream), in Worcestershire.

Barby (*Eng.*) One who came from Barby (village on the hill), in Northamptonshire.

Barcelona, Barcellona (*It., Sp.*) One who came from Barcelona or Barcellona (the lightning), the names of places in Spain and Italy.

Barcenas (*Lith.*) Descendant of Barcenas, a short form of Bartholomew (son of Talmai, furrow).

Barclay (*Eng.*) Variant of Berkley, q.v.

Barcroft (*Eng.*) Dweller on the piece of enclosed land where barley grew.

Barcus (*Eng.*) Shortened form of Barkhouse, q.v.

Barczak, Barczuk, Barczyk (*Pol.*) One who took care of the beehives, a bee keeper.

Bard (*Eng.*) Descendant of Bard or Bart, pet forms of Bartholomew (son of Talmai, furrow); descendant of the poet or bard.

Bardavid (*Heb., Sp.*) The son of David (commander, beloved, friend).

Barden, Bardon, Bardin (*Eng.*) One who came from Barden (valley where barley grew), in Yorkshire.

Bardney (*Eng.*) One who came from Bardney (Bearda's island), in Lincolnshire.

Bardo (*It.*) Descendant of Bardo, a pet form of Bernardo, Italian form of Bernard (bear, hard).

Bardon (*Eng.*) Dweller on Bardon Hill (barrow hill hill), in Leicestershire.

Bardsley (*Eng.*) One who came from Bardsley (Beornred's wood; clearing in the wood), in Lancashire.

Bardwell (*Eng.*) One who came from Bardwell (Bearda's spring), in Suffolk.

Bardwick (*Eng.*) Descendant of Beorhtric (bright, rule); variant of Barwick, q.v.

Bare (*Eng.*) The unarmed, defenseless, or indigent man; one who came from Bare (grove), in Lancashire; dweller in, or near, a grove.

Barefoot (*Eng.*) One who had the habit of going about barefoot; persons sent to a holy place as a penance were often ordered to go barefoot; one who came from Barford (barley ford; ford of the bear; birch ford), the name of several places in England.

Barelli, Barella (*It.*) Descendant of little Bar, a pet form of Barbaro (the stranger).

Barenbaum (*Ger.*) Dweller near a pear tree.

Barends, Barendse (*Du.*) Descendant of

Barend, a form of Bernhard (bear, hard).

Barendsen (*Dan.*) The son of Barend (bear, commander).

Barfield, Barefield (*Eng.*) One who came from Bardfield (border field), in Essex.

Barfoot (*Eng.*) A variant of Barefoot, q.v.; and of Barford, q.v.

Barford (*Eng.*) One who came from Barford (barley ford; ford of the bear; birch ford), the name of several villages in England.

Barg (*Ger.*) One who came from Barg (mountain), in Germany.

Bargas (*Lith.*) One who gave credit in some way.

Barger, Bargar (*Ger., Eng.*) One who worked on a small boat or small sailing vessel, a sailor; American variant of Berger, q.v.

Barham (*Eng.*) One who came from Barham (homestead on the hill), the name of several places in England.

Baringer (*Ger.*) One who came from Behringen (Behring's place), in Germany.

Barish (*Ger.*) Descendant of Behrisch, a pet form of Beroslaw (bear, glory).

Bark, Barke (*Eng., Ger.*) Dweller near a birch tree.

Barker (*Eng.*) One who prepared leather with bark, a tanner.

Barkey (*Eng.*) Dweller on the birch island; or on Berica's island.

Barkhouse, Barkus (*Eng.*) Dweller in a house made of birch wood; dweller near the building where bark was stored for tanning purposes.

Barkin (*Eng.*) One who came from Barking (Berica's people), in Essex.

Barkley (*Eng.*) One who came from Berkeley (birch wood), in Gloucestershire; or from Berkley (birch wood), in Somerset.

Barkowiak (*Pol.*) Descendant of Bark, a pet form of Bartlomiej, a Polish form of Bartholomew (son of Talmai, furrow).

Barksdale, Barksdalle (*Eng.*) One who

lived at, or near, the valley of the birch trees.

Barkworth (*Eng.*) Dweller at the homestead where birch trees grew.

Barley, Barlee (*Eng.*) One who made and sold barley-bread; one who came from Barley (Beora's clearing; boar wood or clearing; barley clearing), the names of hamlets in Hertfordshire, Lancashire, and the West Riding of Yorkshire.

Barlieau (*Fr.*) One who came from Barlieu (high place), in France.

Barlow (*Eng.*) One who came from Barlow (barley hill or clearing), the name of places in Derbyshire and Lancashire.

Barna (*It.*) Descendant of Barna, a pet form of Barnaba, Italian form of Barnabas (son of prophecy or consolation).

Barnaby (*Eng.*) One who came from Barnaby (Beornwald's homestead), in Yorkshire; descendant of Barnabas (son of prophecy or consolation).

Barnard (*Eng.*) Descendant of Bernard (bear, firm).

Barnas (*Pol., Heb.*) Descendant of Bernhard (bear, firm), or of Barnutz or Barnitzki; a name made up by prefixing Bar (son) to the initials of the father's name.

Barndt (*Ger.*) Descendant of Barndt, a pet form of Berinhard (bear, hard).

Barnes, Barns (*Eng., Scot.*) Dweller near the barn, or grain storage building; the bairn or child, often a young person of a prominent family; descendant of Beorn (nobleman); one who came from Barnes in Surrey and Aberdeenshire; descendant of Barn, a pet form of Barnabas (son of prophecy or consolation).

Barnett, Barnette, Barnet (*Eng.*) Descendant of little Bernard (bear, hard); one who came from Barnet (place cleared by burning), in Middlesex.

Barney (*Ir.*) Descendant of Barney, a pet form of Barnabas (son of prophecy or consolation).

Barnham (*Eng.*) One who came from

Barnham (Beorna's enclosure), in Sussex.

Barnhart, Barnhardt, Barnhard (*Ger.*) Descendant of Berinhard (bear, strong).

Barnhill (*Eng.*) One who came from Barnhill (Beorn's hill), in Yorkshire.

Barnicle (*Eng.*) One who came from Barnacle (barn slope), in Warwickshire.

Barnicoat, Barnecut (*Eng.*) Dweller at the upper end of the wood.

Barnshaw (*Eng.*) One who came from Barnshaw (Beornwulf's wood), in Cheshire.

Barnsley (*Eng.*) One who came from Barnsley (Beornheard's, Beornmod's, Beornfrith's or Beorn's grove), the name of four places in England all named after men with different names.

Barnstable (*Eng.*) One who came from Barnstaple (Bearda's staple or post), in Devonshire.

Barnum (*Eng.*) Variant of Barnham, q.v.

Barnwell (*Eng.*) One who came from Barnwell (Beorna's spring; stream by the burial-mound), places in Cambridgeshire and Northamptonshire.

Barnwood (*Eng.*) One who came from Barnwood (the warrior's wood), in Gloucestershire.

Baron, Barone (*Eng., Scot., Ir.*) The landowner who held his land of the king; one who fomented strife; descendant of Baron (baron).

Barr, Barre (*Scot.*) One who came from Barr (height), in Ayrshire and Renfrewshire; dweller at the top of the hill.

Barragan (*Ir.*) Descendant of little Barr, a pet form of Barrfionn (fair head).

Barranco (*Sp.*) One who came from Barranco (gorge or ravine); dweller near a gorge or ravine.

Barre (*Fr.*) Dweller near a bar or thin pole, perhaps a barrier; one who wore a striped or variegated vestment.

Barrera (*Sp.*) One who came from Bar-

rera (clay pit where clay for pottery is obtained), in Spain.

Barrett, Barrette, Barratt (*Eng., Fr.*) Descendant of Barret (bear, rule); one who made and sold caps or narrow bands.

Barrick (*Eng.*) One who came from Berwick (grain farm), the name of several villages in England; dweller in, or near, where grain was grown in an outlying part of an estate.

Barricklow (*Eng.*) Dweller at the grain farm on the hill.

Barrier (*Fr.*) The keeper of a gate to a town or castle; one who collected tolls at a toll-gate.

Barringer (*Eng., Ger.*) Descendant of Beringar (bear, spear); American variant of Behringer, q.v.

Barrington (*Eng.*) One who came from Barrington (the homestead of Bara's people), in Somerset; or from Barrington (the homestead of Beorn's people), in Gloucestershire.

Barrios (*Sp.*) One who came from Barrios (district; suburb), the name of many places in Spain.

Barrish (*Ger.*) Variant of Barish, q.v.

Barron (*Eng., Scot., Ir.*) Variant of Baron, q.v.

Barros (*Sp.*) Dweller in a damp place; or on land which is newly cultivated.

Barrow, Barrows (*Eng.*) One who came from Barrow (wood, or hill), the name of many places in England.

Barrowcliff (*Eng.*) Dweller in a grove near a cliff or steep, rocky ascent; or possibly one who came from a village (unidentified) with that name. See Barrowclough.

Barrowclough, Barraclough (*Eng.*) One who came from Barraclough (grove in the dell), an unidentified place probably in the West Riding of Yorkshire as the name is found there.

Barrowman (*Scot.*) The townsman, citizen, or burgess; one who helps to carry a handbarrow.

Barry, Barrie (*Scot., Ir.*) One who came from Barry (height on the isle), in

Angus; one who was diligent; descendant of Barry (spear).

Barrymore (*Eng.*) Dweller at the woodland marsh.

Barski, Barsky (*Rus.*) Nickname for one with a lordly manner.

Barsley (*Eng.*) Dweller near the grove where boars were kept.

Barstow (*Eng.*) Dweller at, or near, the place where grain wás stored.

Bart (*Eng.*) Descendant of Bart, a pet form of Bartholomew (son of Talmai, furrow).

Barta, Bartos (*Cz.-Sl., Hun.*) Descendant of Bartos, a pet form of Bartholomew (son of Talmai, furrow).

Bartels, Bartel, Bartell (*Eng.*) Descendant of little Bart, a pet form of Bartholomew (son of Talmai, furrow).

Barth (*Ger., Eng.*) The man with the beard; descendant of Barth, a pet abbreviation of Bartholomew (son of Talmai, furrow).

Barthold, Barthol (*Ger.*) Descendant of Berchtwald (bright, forest).

Bartholomew, Bartholomay, Bartholomae, Bartholmey (*Eng.*) Descendant of Bartholomew (son of Talmai, furrow).

Bartie, Barty (*Scot.*) Descendant of little Bart, a pet form of Bartholomew (son of Talmai, furrow).

Bartke (*Ger.*) Descendant of little Bart, a pet form of Bartholomaus, German form of Bartholomew (son of Talmai, furrow).

Bartkowicz, Bartkiewicz (*Rus., Pol.*) The son of Bartko, a pet form of Bartholomew (son of Talmai, furrow).

Bartkowski (*Pol.*) Descendant of Bart, a pet form of Bartlomiej, a Polish form of Bartholomew (son of Talmai, furrow).

Bartkus (*Lith.*) Descendant of little Bart, a pet form of Bartholomew (son of Talmai, furrow).

Bartlett, Bartle, Bartlet (*Eng.*) Descendant of little Bart, a pet form of Bartholomew (son of Talmai, furrow).

Bartley (*Eng.*) One who came from

Bartley (birch wood), the name of places in Hampshire and Warwickshire.

Bartling (*Eng.*) Descendant of little Bart, a pet form of Bartholomew (son of Talmai, furrow).

Bartlow (*Eng.*) One who came from Bartlow (mound covered with birch trees), in Cambridgeshire.

Bartman (*Eng.*) The servant of Bart, an abbreviation of Bartholomew (son of Talmai, furrow).

Bartnick, Bartnicki, Bartnik (*Pol.*) One who came from Bartnik (place of bee keepers).

Barto (*Hun.*) Descendant of Bart, a pet form of Bartholomew (son of Talmai, furrow).

Bartok (*Hun.*) Descendant of Bartok, pet form of Bertalan, Hungarian form of Bartholomew (son of Talmai, furrow).

Bartolini (*It.*) Descendant of little Bartolo, Italian form of Bartholomew (son of Talmai, furrow).

Bartolomeo (*It.*) Descendant of Bartolomeo, Italian form of Bartholomew (son of Talmai, furrow).

Barton (*Eng.*) One who came from Barton (grain farm); the name of various places in England.

Bartos, Bartosek, Bartosiak, Bartosik, Bartosz, Bartoszek (*Pol.*) Descendant of Bartos, a pet form of Bartlomiej, Polish form of Bartholomew (son of Talmai, furrow).

Bartsch, Bartosch (*Ger.*) Descendant of Bartsch, a pet form of Bartholomaus, German form of Bartholomew (son of Talmai, furrow); American variant of Bertsch, q.v.

Bartz, Barz (*Ger.*) Dweller at the sign of the bear; one with some bearlike characteristic; descendant of Barz or Bartz, a pet form of names beginning with Bar (bear) as Berulf, Berowin and Bernhelm; dweller near tree stumps; variant of Bartsch, q.v.

Baruch, Baruck (*Ger.*) Descendant of Baruch (blessed).

Barwick (*Eng.*) One who came from Barwick (barley farm), in Norfolk; descendant of Beriwick (bear, farm).

Barwig (*Ger.*) Descendant of Barwig (bear, battle).

Bas (*Fr.*) The man with short legs.

Bascom, Bascomb, Bascombe (*Eng.*) One who came from Boscombe (box tree valley; valley where bristles grew), in Wiltshire; dweller in Basa's valley.

Base (*Eng.*) Descendant of Bass (short; fat).

Baseman (*Eng.*) The short, fat man.

Basemore, Bazemore (*Eng.*) Dweller on, or near, a moor or waste land on which there was a cowshed.

Basford, Bashford (*Eng.*) One who came from Basford (birch ford; Basa's ford), the name of places in Cheshire, Nottinghamshire, and Staffordshire.

Bash (*Eng.*) Dweller in a stream valley; one who came from Bache (valley of a stream), the name of several places in England.

Basham (*Eng.*) One who came from Barsham (Bar's homestead), the name of villages in Norfolk and Suffolk.

Bashaw (*Tur.*) A magnate or grandee, early title of honor formerly given to officers of high rank in Turkey.

Bashfield, Bashfull (*Eng.*) Dweller in the open country near a stream.

Bashley (*Eng.*) One who came from Bashley (Baegloc's grove), in Hampshire.

Bashton, Baston (*Eng.*) One who came from Baston (Bak's farmstead), in Lincolnshire.

Basic, Basich, Basik (*Pol.*) Descendant of Baz, a pet form of Bazek, Polish form of Basil (kingly).

Basile, Basil (*Eng., It.*) Descendant of Basil or Basilio (kingly).

Baskerville (*Eng.*) One who came from Bacqueville (Bassac's estate), in Normandy; or from Boscherville, in France.

Basket, Baskette (*Fr.*) Descendant of little Basque (man).

Baskin (*Eng.*) Descendant of little Bass or Bassa (short).

Basley (*Eng.*) One who came from Bashley (Baegloc's grove), in Hampshire.

Bass, Basse (*Eng.*) The short or fat person; descendant of Bass (short).

Bassett, Bassette, Basset (*Eng., Fr.*) Descendant of little Bass or Bassa (short); the short man.

Bassin (*Fr.*) One who made and sold basins, pans, and cups.

Bassler, Basler (*Ger., Swis.*) One who came from Basel, in Switzerland.

Basso (*It.*) The small, short man; dweller on the low land; descendant of Basso, a pet form of Giacobasso (may God protect; the supplanter).

Basson (*Fr.*) The little, short, fat man; one who made and sold bowls and cups.

Bast, Basten (*Ger.*) Descendant of Bast, a pet form of Sebastian (venerable).

Basta, Bastek (*Pol.*) Dweller in, or near, a tower.

Bastian, Bastien (*Du., Eng., Fr.*) Descendant of Bastian, a pet form of Sebastian (venerable).

Bataille (*Fr.*) Surname applied to the fighting, quarrelsome, pugnacious man.

Batchelor, Batcheller, Batcheler, Batchelder (*Scot.*) The holder, or tenant, of a small farm; an officer or servant who has care of the door, a door keeper.

Bateman, Batman (*Eng.*) The servant of Bate, a pet form of Bartholomew (son of Talmai, furrow); the man who baited bears kept for amusement; one who worked on a boat, a boatman.

Bater (*Eng.*) One who beats, such as a beater of cloth, a fuller, or beater of metal, a coppersmith.

Bates, Bate, Batts, Batt, Bat (*Eng.*) The son of Bate, a pet form of Bartholomew (son of Talmai, furrow); one of stout, heavy appearance.

Bateson, Batson (*Eng.*) The son of Bate, a pet form of Bartholomew (son of Talmai, furrow).

Bath (*Eng.*) One who came from Bath

(referring to the Roman baths), in Somerset.

Bathrick (*Eng.*) One who came from Bastwick (dairy farm in a lime grove), in Norfolk.

Batista (*Sp., It.*) Variant of Battista, q.v.

Battaglia (*It.*) A combatant, one engaged in war.

Batten, Battan (*Eng.*) Descendant of little Bat, a pet form of Bartholomew (son of Talmai, furrow).

Battersby (*Eng.*) One who came from Battersby (Bothvarr's town), in the North Riding of Yorkshire.

Battershall (*Eng.*) Dweller at Bothvarr's corner.

Batterson, Battison, Batteson (*Eng.*) Variants of Bateson, q.v.

Battiest (*Fr.*) Descendant of Batiste, a French form of Baptist (baptizer).

Battista (*It.*) Descendant of Battista (Baptist, from St. John the Baptist).

Battle, Battles (*Eng.*) One who came from Battle (named after the Battle of Hastings), in England; descendant of Bartle, a pet form of Bartholomew (son of Talmai, furrow).

Batty, Baty, Battie, Battey, Batey, Battee (*Eng.*) Descendant of little Batt, a pet form of Bartholomew (son of Talmai, furrow).

Bauch (*Ger.*) One with a large paunch or belly.

Bauche (*Fr.*) Dweller on mire or clayey earth; or in the woods.

Bauer, Baur (*Ger., Sl.*) One who tilled the land, a farmer.

Baugh, Baughan, Baugher, Baughman (*Wel., Ger., Scot.*) The small man; one who tilled the land, a farmer; dweller near the brook; the shabby or poor man.

Baum, Baumel, Baumer, Baumler (*Ger.*) Dweller near a tree; dweller at the barrier placed across roads by the toll collector.

Baumann, Bauman (*Ger.*) One who tilled the land, a farmer.

Baumgartner, Baumgart, Baumgarten (*Ger.*) The tree gardener, nursery-

man or orchard-grower; dweller in, or near, an orchard.

Baursmith (*Ger.*) The smith from the country.

Bausch, Bauschke (*Ger.*) Dweller on, or near, a small mound.

Bautista (*Sp.*) Descendant of Bautista, Spanish form of Baptist (the baptizer).

Bavaro (*It.*) One who came from Bavaria (land of the Boii), in Germany.

Bavier, Baver (*Fr.*) One who came from Bavaria (land of the Boii), in Germany.

Baxendale (*Eng.*) One who came from Baxenden (valley where bakestones, that is, stones on which cakes are baked, were found), in Lancashire.

Baxley (*Eng.*) One who came from Bexley (box grove) in Kent; or from Bixley (box grove), the name of villages in Norfolk and Suffolk.

Baxter (*Eng., Wel.*) One who made bread. Although the name seems to be feminine it is used chiefly of men.

Bay (*Eng.*) One with reddish-brown hair; dweller near a bay or pool.

Bayard (*Eng., Fr.*) One with reddish-brown hair or complexion; one with a proud, haughty, or reckless disposition.

Bayer, Bayr (*Ger.*) One who came from Bavaria, in Germany.

Bayfield (*Eng.*) One who came from Bayfield (Baega's open country), in Norfolk.

Bayham (*Eng.*) One who came from Bayham (Baega's homestead), in Sussex.

Baylie, Bayley, Bayly (*Eng.*) Variants of Bailey, q.v.

Bayliss, Bayless, Bayles, Baylis (*Eng.*) The son of the bailiff. See Bailey.

Baylock (*Scot.*) One who came from Balloch (pass), in Dumbartonshire.

Baylor (*Ger.*) One who handles a gauge or standard in his work.

Baymon, Bayman (*Scot., Eng.*) The man with reddish-brown hair; one who kept bees, a bee keeper.

Baynes, Bayne (*Eng.*) The fair or light-complexioned man; one who acted as an attendant at the public baths.

Baynham (*Wel.*) The son of Einion (anvil or upright).

Bays, Bayes (*Eng.*) The son of Bay (reddish-brown).

Bazel, Bazell, Bazelewski (*Pol., Ukr.*) Descendant of Bazyli, Polish form of Basil (kingly).

Bazile, Bazil (*Fr.*) Descendant of Basil (kingly).

Beach (*Eng.*) Dweller at, or near, a beech tree or brook.

Beacham, Beachem (*Eng.*) One who came from Beauchamps (beautiful plain), the name of several places in France.

Beacom (*Eng.*) One who came from Bicham (Bicca's homestead), now Beechamwell, in Norfolk; dweller in a deep hollow where gadflies were troublesome.

Beadell, Beadle, Beadles (*Eng.*) The crier, or usher, in a court; town crier; a constable.

Beagley (*Eng.*) One who came from Bagley (the rams' or pigs' woodland), the name of various places in England.

Beaird (*Scot.*) Variant of Baird, q.v.

Beal, Beale, Beall, Beals (*Eng.*) One who came from Beal (bee hill; Beaga's corner), the name of places in Northumberland and Yorkshire.

Beam (*Eng.*) One who lived by a tree; dweller at the foot bridge, a tree trunk lying across a stream.

Beamer (*Eng.*) Variant of Beemer, q.v.

Beamish (*Eng.*) One who came from Beamish (beautiful mansion), in Durham.

Beamon, Beaman (*Eng.*) Variant of Beeman, q.v.

Beamsley (*Eng.*) One who came from Beamsley (valley grove), in the West Riding of Yorkshire.

Bean, Beane, Beans (*Eng., Scot.*) Descendant of Ben, a pet form of Benjamin (son of my right hand), or of Benedict (blessed); the light-complexioned man.

Bear (*Eng., Fr.*) Dweller at the sign of the bear; one thought to possess bearlike qualities; dweller in, or near, a wood; the industrious hard-working man.

Beard (*Eng.*) One who came from Beard (bank), in Derbyshire; one who had an unusually hairy chin.

Bearden (*Eng.*) Dweller on the bare hill; or on the hill where wood was obtained.

Beardshear (*Eng.*) Variant of Berkshire, q.v.

Beardsley, Beardslee (*Eng.*) One who came from Bardsley (Beornred's wood), in Lancashire.

Beardsworth (*Eng.*) One who came from Beardwood (Bearda's homestead), in Lancashire.

Beardwood (*Eng.*) One who came from Beardwood (Bearda's homestead), in Lancashire.

Bearl, Bearle (*Eng.*) One who came from Bearl (barley hill), in Northumberland.

Bearley (*Eng.*) One who came from Bearley (grove by, or belonging to, a fortified place), in Warwickshire.

Bearse, Bearce (*Wel.*) The son of Piers (rock).

Beary (*Eng.*) Dweller in, or near, a grove or wood.

Beasley, Beesley (*Eng.*) Dweller in, or near, the meadow or wood where bees were found.

Beason (*Eng.*) Variant of Beeson, q.v.

Beata (*It.*) The saintly, devout person; descendant of Beata (blessed), a Spanish saint.

Beath (*Scot.*) One who came from Beath (birch), in Fife.

Beaton, Beton (*Scot., Eng.*) Descendant of Bate, a pet form of Bartholomew (son of Talmai, furrow); or of Bete or Beat, pet forms of Beatrice and Beatrix (she who blesses).

Beatrice (*It.*) Descendant of Beatrice (she who blesses).

Beatty, Beattie, Beaty (*Scot., Eng.*) Descendant of little Bate or Baty, pet forms of Bartholomew (son of Talmai, furrow); or of Bete or Beat, pet forms of Beatrice and Beatrix (she who blesses).

Beaucaire (*Fr.*) One who came from Beaucaire (beautiful mound), in France.

Beauchamp (*Fr.*) One who came from Beauchamps (beautiful plain), in France.

Beaudoin (*Fr.*) Descendant of Baudouin or Baldavin (bold, friend).

Beaudry (*Fr.*) One with a fine presence or martial bearing, beautiful, upright.

Beauford (*Eng.*) One who came from Beeford (ford where bees were found), in the East Riding of Yorkshire; dweller at the beautiful river crossing.

Beaufort (*Fr.*) Dweller near the beautiful fortification; one who came from Beaufort (beautiful fort), the name of three places in France.

Beaulieu (*Eng.*) One who came from Beaulieu (beautiful place), in Hampshire.

Beaumont (*Eng., Fr.*) One who came from Beaumont (beautiful mountain), the name of five places in Normandy, as well as several places in England.

Beaupré (*Fr.*) Dweller in, or near, the beautiful meadow.

Beauregard (*Fr.*) The handsome, or good-looking man, a name sometimes applied in an ironical manner; one who came from Beauregard (beautiful place), the name of several places in France.

Beauworth (*Eng.*) One who came from Beauworth (bee farm), in Hampshire.

Beaver, Beavers (*Eng., Wel.*) Dweller at the sign of the beaver; one who came from Beauvoir (fair view), in western France; the son of Ivor (lord).

Beazley (*Eng.*) Dweller in the meadow where bees were found; one who came from Beesley, in Lancashire.

Bebb (*Wel.*) Descendant of Bebb; descendant of Babb, a pet form of Barbara (the stranger).

Bechtel, Bechtell (*Ger.*) Descendant of Betto, a pet form of names beginning with Bercht (bright or famous), as Berhtari, Berahtram, and Berhtolf.

Bechtold, Bechtolt (*Ger.*) Descendant of Berchtwald (bright, forest).

Beck, Bech (*Nor., Eng., Ger., Sw., Ice.*) Dweller at, or near, the brook or stream; brook.

Becker (*Eng., Ger.*) Dweller at a brook; one who made bread, a baker.

Beckett, Becket, Beckette (*Eng.*) Dweller at the head of the stream; one who came from Beckett (bee, or Bicca's, cottage), the name of places in Berkshire and Devonshire.

Beckford (*Eng.*) One who came from Beckford (Becca's place by the river crossing), in Gloucestershire.

Beckham, Beckum (*Eng.*) One who came from Beckham (Becca's homestead), in Norfolk.

Becking (*Eng.*) The son of Becca (mattock).

Beckingham (*Eng.*) One who came from Beckingham (homestead of Becca's people), the name of places in Lincolnshire and Nottinghamshire.

Beckington (*Eng.*) One who came from Beckington (the village of Becca's people), in Somerset.

Beckles (*Eng.*) One who came from Beccles (pasture on the stream), in Suffolk.

Beckley (*Eng.*) One who came from Beckley (Beocca's meadow), the name of places in Kent, Oxford, and Sussex.

Beckman, Beckmann (*Eng., Ger.*) Dweller at a brook; one who made bread, a baker.

Beckwith (*Eng.*) One who came from Beckwith (beech wood), in Yorkshire.

Becraft (*Eng.*) Variant of Beecroft, q.v.

Becton, Beckton (*Eng.*) One who came from Beckton (village in a valley), in Hampshire.

Becvar (*Cz.-Sl., Pol.*) One who made and sold casks, buckets, and tubs, a cooper; the awkward, clumsy man.

Bedding, Beddings (*Eng.*) One who came from Beddingham or Beddington (the homestead or village of Beadda's people), in Sussex and Surrey respectively.

Beddoes (*Eng.*) The son of Beado (battle, war).

Beddow (*Eng.*) Descendant of Beado (battle, war).

Bedell (*Eng.*) The crier or usher in a court; town crier; a constable.

Bedenfield (*Eng.*) One who came from Bedingfield (the open country of Beadda's people), in Suffolk.

Bedford (*Eng.*) One who came from Bedford (Beda's ford), in Bedfordshire.

Bedgood (*Eng.*) Descendant of Beadgod (battle, good); one who habitually uses the phrase "pray God," or who frequently prays.

Bedloe (*Eng.*) One who commands love.

Bednar (*Pol., Cz.-Sl.*) One who made and sold casks and tubs, a cooper.

Bednarczyk (*Pol., Cz.-Sl.*) Little son of the maker of casks and barrels.

Bednarek, Bednarik (*Pol., Cz.-Sl.*) Son of the cooper, or maker of casks and barrels.

Bednarski (*Pol.*) One who made casks or barrels, a cooper.

Bednarz (*Pol., Cz.-Sl.*) One who made and sold casks and tubs, a cooper.

Bedrosian (*Arm.*) Descendant of Bedros, an Armenian form of Peter (a rock).

Bedstone (*Eng.*) One who came from Bedstone (Bedgeat's homestead), in Shropshire.

Bedwell (*Eng.*) One who came from Bedwell (stream in a valley), in Hertfordshire.

Beebe, Beeby (*Eng.*) Dweller at the bee farm or apiary.

Beecham, Beacham (*Eng.*) One who came from Beechamwell, originally Bicham (Bicca's homestead), in Norfolk; a corruption of Beauchamp, q.v.

Beecher, Beech (*Eng.*) Dweller at, or near, a beech tree.

Beecroft (*Eng.*) Dweller in an enclosure where bees swarmed.

Beed, Beede (*Eng.*) Descendant of Bede or Beda.

Beedle, Beedel (*Eng.*) The crier or usher in a court; town crier; a constable.

Beegan, Beegun (*Ir., Eng.*) Descendant of little Beach (bee); variant of Biggin, q.v.

Beekman (*Du.*) Dweller at, or near, the brook or stream.

Beeks, Beek (*Du.*) Dweller near a brook.

Beeler (*Ger.*) Dweller on, or near, a hill.

Beeley (*Eng.*) One who came from Beeley (Beage's grove), in Derbyshire; or from Beeleigh (wood where bees were found), in Essex.

Beem (*Du.*) Dweller in, or near, a wet, lush meadow.

Beeman (*Eng.*) One who kept bees, a bee keeper.

Beemer (*Eng.*) One who played the trumpet, a trumpeter.

Beemster (*Du.*) One who came from Beemster, Holland.

Beemsterboer (*Du.*) The farmer who came from Beemster, in Holland.

Been, Beene, Beenes (*Eng., Du.*) Descendant of Been or Ben, pet forms of Benjamin (son of my right hand); one with a short or crippled leg.

Beers, Beer (*Eng., Du.*) Dweller at, or in, the wood or grove; dweller at the sign of the bear; one who came from Beer (grove; pasture), the name of several places in England.

Beery (*Eng.*) Dweller in, or near, a grove or wood.

Beese (*Ger.*) Dweller where sedge grew.

Beeson (*Eng.*) The son of Bee (nickname from the bee); one who came from Beeston (homestead where reed or rush grew), the name of several places in England.

Beetham (*Eng.*) One who came from Beetham (flat area), in Westmorland.

Beethoven (*Ger.*) Dweller on, or near, the farm where beets were grown.

Beetle (*Eng.*) One who came from Beetley (wood where wooden mallets were obtained), in Norfolk.

Befort (*Fr.*) Variant of Beaufort, q.v.

Beggerow (*Ger.*) One who came from Beggerow, in Germany.

Beggs, Begg (*Scot.*) Descendant of Begg (little).

Begin (*Eng.*) Variant of Biggin, q.v.

Begley (*Ir., Eng.*) Grandson of the little poet; a variant of Beckley, q.v.

Begonia (*Sp.*) One who came from Begona (hill; large dark place), in Spain.

Begue (*Fr.*) One who governed a province.

Begun (*Ir.*) Descendant of little Beag (little).

Behan (*Ir.*) Descendant of Beachain (bee).

Behar (*Ger.*) Variant of Behr, q.v.

Behenna (*Eng.*) Dweller in, or near, Hanna's homestead.

Behling (*Ger.*) One who came from Behlingen, in Germany.

Behm, Behmer (*Ger.*) One who came from Bohemia (home of the Boii).

Behnke (*Ger.*) Dweller at the sign of the little bear.

Behr (*Ger.*) One who lived at the sign of the bear; one with some characteristic of the bear; descendant of Bero, a pet form of names beginning with Bar (bear), as Beroward, Beriwick, and Berulf.

Behrens, Behrendt, Behrends, Behrend, Behrent, Behren (*Ger.*) Dweller at the sign of the bear; descendant of Behren, a pet form of Bernhard (bear, hard).

Behringer (*Ger.*) One who came from Behringen, in Germany.

Beilfuss, Beilfus (*Ger.*) Descendant of Bilifuns (sword, quick).

Beilke (*Ger.*) Descendant of little Bilo, a pet form of names beginning with Bil (sword) such as Bilihar and Belimar.

Beilstein (*Ger.*) One who came from Beilstein (hatchet; helve), the name of several places in Germany.

Bein (*Ger.*) One with a deformed or crooked leg.

Beirne (*Ir.*) Grandson of Biorn (bear).

Beisner, Beiser (*Ger.*) One who hunts with trained falcons, a falconer.

Beith (*Scot.*) One who came from Beith (birch), in Ayrshire.

Beja (*Port.*) One who came from Beja (the Peace of Julius), in Portugal.

Bekker, Bekkers (*Du.*) One who made bread, a baker.

Belanger, Bellanger (*Fr.*) One who came from beautiful Anger (ancient name combining *Ans,* a divinity, and *gari,* spear); one who came from Angre or Angres, in France; variants of Boulanger, q.v.

Belasco (*Sp.*) Dweller at the sign of the raven or crow; one who took care of sheep, a shepherd; one who came from Velasco (raven), in Spain. See Velasco.

Belcaster, Belcastro (*It.*) Dweller in, or near, a beautiful castle or fortress.

Belcher (*Eng., Fr.*) Descendant of the beautiful, beloved person; the patriarch or elderly man of the family.

Belden, Belding (*Eng.*) Dweller at, or near, a beautiful hill.

Belfield (*Eng., Scot.*) Dweller in, or near, the fine piece of open land; one who came from Bellfield (nice land), the name of many small places in Scotland.

Belfiore (*It.*) Descendant of Belfiore (beautiful flower).

Belford (*Eng.*) One who came from Belford, in Northumberland.

Belfry (*Eng.*) Dweller in, or near, a tower with a bell; or in the room where there was a bell.

Belgrad, Belgrade (*Eng.*) One who came from Belgrade (white fortress), in Yugoslavia.

Belgrave (*Eng.*) One who came from Belgrave (fine grove, but originally filthy grove), in Leicestershire.

Belinsky (*Rus.*) The white or fair-complexioned man; one with white hair.

Belk (*Eng.*) One who came from Belloc (fair place), in France; dweller by a hill or ridge.

Belke, Belka (*Ger.*) One who came from Belkau (swampy meadow), in Germany; descendant of Belke, a dim. of Bele (beautiful).

Belkin, Belkind (*Rus., Ukr., Ger.*) Descendant of Belke, a dim. of Bele (beautiful).

Belknap (*Eng.*) Dweller on the top of the hill.

Bell, Belle (*Eng.*) Dweller at the sign of the bell; the handsome one; descendant of Bel, a pet form of Isabel (oath to Baal); and of Arabella (eagle, heroine).

Bella (*It.*) The handsome man.

Bellafiore (*It.*) One who cultivated beautiful flowers; dweller among beautiful flowers.

Bellagamba (*It.*) One with handsome or shapely legs; an idle person.

Bellamy (*Fr.*) The beautiful friend, an epithet often applied ironically.

Bellavia (*It.*) Dweller on the beautiful way or road.

Belleau (*Eng., Fr.*) One who came from Belleau (beautiful water) in Lincolnshire; or from Belleau (beautiful water), in France.

Beller (*Eng.*) One who made and sold bells.

Belleville (*Fr.*) One who came from Belleville (beautiful homestead), in France.

Bellew (*Eng., Scot.*) Variant of Belleau, q.v.

Bellinger, Belling (*Ger.*) One who came from Bellingen, the name of two places in Germany.

Bellino, Bellini (*It.*) Descendant of little Bell or Bella, pet forms of Arabella and Isabella.

Bellis (*Wel.*) The son of Elias (Jehovah is my God), or Elisha (God of Salvation); also sometimes from the old Welsh *Elissed* or *Helised* (charitable; benevolent).

Belliveau (*Fr.*) Dweller in a beautiful valley.

Bellman, Belman (*Eng.*) One employed to go around the streets of a town with a bell to make public announcements, a town-crier; one who came from Belman or Bellman, in Westmorland.

Bellmont, Belmonte (*Fr.*) One who came from Belmont (fair hill), the name of various lordships in France.

Bellou (*Fr.*) One who came from Bellou (place where water cress grew), in France.

Bellows, Bellew (*Eng.*) One who came from Bellou (place where water cress grew) or Belleau (fair water), in France; one who came from Belleau (Helgi's meadow; holy meadow), in Lincolnshire.

Belluomini (*It.*) The fair or handsome man.

Belly (*Fr.*) One who came from Bellay (wood of birch trees), in France.

Belofsky (*Rus., Pol.*) The light or fair-complexioned man.

Belohlav (*Cz.*) The man with white hair; the whitehead.

Belpedio (*It.*) One with handsome or well-formed feet or legs.

Belser (*Ger.*) One who came from Belsen (swamp), in Germany.

Belshaw (*Eng.*) Dweller in a beautiful, small wood or thicket.

Belsky, Belski (*Ukr.*) One who came from Belz, in Ukraine.

Belson, Bellson (*Eng.*) The son of Bele (beautiful) or of Belle (beautiful); sometimes a pet form of Isabel (oath to Baal) or a variant form of Elizabeth.

Belt, Belter (*Eng., Ger.*) One who made and sold belts and girdles.

Belton (*Eng.*) One who came from Belton (space in a settlement), the name of several places in England.

Beltran (*Sp.*) Descendant of Beltran, Spanish form of Bertram (bright, raven).

Beltz (*Ger.*) One who buys and sell furs, a furrier.

Belvedere, Belvidere (*Eng.*) Dweller near a beautiful view.

Belz (*Ger.*) One who came from Belz, in Austria.

Belzer (*Pol.*) Descendant of Belzer, a shortened form of Baltazar, Polish form of Balthasar (Baal has formed a king).

Beman, Beeman, Beaman (*Eng.*) One who kept bees, a bee keeper.

Bemis, Bemiss (*Eng.*) One who came from Beaumetz (beautiful rural cultivation), in Normandy.

Bemont (*Eng., Fr.*) Variant of Beaumont, q.v.

Benak, Benek (*Pol.*) Descendant of Benek, a pet form of Bernard (bear, hard).

Benavides, Benavidez (*Sp.*) One who came from Benavides (son of Abidis), in Spain.

Benbrook (*Eng.*) One who came from Binbrook (Bynna's stream), in Lincolnshire.

Bence (*Eng.*) Dweller by the ledge or river bank.

Bench, Benche (*Eng.*) One who lived at the ledge or terrace.

Benchly (*Eng.*) Dweller in the pasture land by the terrace, ledge, or streambank.

Benda (*Ger.*) Descendant of Benda, a pet form of Benedictus (blessed).

Bendel, Bendle, Bentall (*Eng.*) One who came from Benhall (bean corner), in Suffolk.

Bender (*Ger.*) One who made casks, a cooper.

Bendik (*Nor.*) Descendant of Bendik, Norwegian form of Benedict (blessed).

Bendix, Benedix (*Eng.*) Descendant of Benedict (blessed).

Bendoraitis (*Lith.*) The son of the cooper.

Bendt (*Sw., Ger.*) Descendant of Bernt, a shortened form of Bernhardt (bear, hard).

Benedek (*Hun.*) Descendant of Benedek, Hungarian form of Benedict (blessed).

Benedetto, Benedetti (*It.*) Descendant of Benedetto, Italian form of Benedict (blessed).

Benedict, Benedick (*Eng.*) Descendant of Benedict (blessed).

Benefield (*Eng.*) One who came from Benefield (open country of Bera's people), in Northamptonshire.

Beneke (*Du.*) Descendant of little Ben, a pet form of Benedict (blessed).

Benes (*Cz.-Sl.*) Descendant of Benes, a form of Benedict (blessed).

Benet (*Fr.*) The blessed one, a term expressing religious value; variant of Benoit, q.v.

Benfield (*Eng.*) Dweller in, or near, a field where beans were grown; one who came from Binfield (bent grass field), in Berkshire.

Benford (*Eng.*) Dweller near a river crossing where there was a tree trunk or beam used as a foot bridge.

Bengough (*Wel.*) One with red hair or livid complexion.

Bengson (*Eng.*) Variant of Bengston, q.v.

Bengston (*Eng.*) One who came from Bynna's homestead; one who came from Bensington (the village of the Benesingas), in Oxfordshire.

Bengtson, Bengtsen (*Sw., Dan.*) The son of Bengt, Swedish form of Benedict (blessed).

Benhall (*Eng.*) One who came from Benhall (bean corner), in Suffolk.

Benham (*Eng., Scot.*) One who came from Benham (Benna's homestead), in Berkshire; one who came from the lands of Benholm in Angus.

Benigno, Benigni (*It.*) The gentle, benign man; descendant of Benigno (benign), a sixth century French saint.

Beninato (*It.*) One who was well-born, of high birth.

Benion (*Wel.*) The son of Einion (anvil; upright).

Benish (*Ger.*) Variant of Bennish, q.v.

Benison (*Eng.*) The son of Ben, a pet form of Benedict (blessed), probably not relating to Benjamin.

Benitez, Benites, Benitiz (*Sp., Port.*) The son of Benito, Spanish form of Benedict (blessed).

Benjamin (*Eng.*) Descendant of Benjamin (son of my right hand).

Benker (*Ger.*) One who came from Benk, in Germany.

Benko (*Ukr.*) Descendant of little Ben, a pet form of Benedykt, Ukrainian form of Benedict (blessed).

Benkovich (*Rus., Ukr.*) The son of little Ben or Benko, pet forms of Benedict (blessed).

Benkowsky, Benkowski (*Pol.*) Descendant of Benko, a pet form of Benedykt, Polish form of Benedict (blessed).

Benn, Benne (*Eng., Ger.*) Descendant of Benne (plump one); or of Ben, a pet form of Benedict (blessed); descendant of Benn, a short form of Bernhard (bear, firm).

Bennecke, Bennek (*Ger.*) Descendant of little Benn, a pet form of Bernhard (bear, firm).

Bennema (*Du.*) The son of Benne, a pet form of Bernhard (bear, firm).

Benner (*Eng.*) One who grew and sold beans; one who made baskets.

Bennett, Bennet (*Eng.*) Descendant of little Benne, a pet form of Benedict (blessed).

Bennington (*Eng.*) One who came from Bennington (the village of the dwellers on the Beane river; the village of Beonna's people), the name of places in Hertfordshire and Lincolnshire.

Bennion (*Wel.*) The son of Einion (anvil; upright).

Bennish, Bennis (*Ger., Cz.*) Descendant of Benesch, a form of Benedikt, German form of Benedict (blessed).

Benny, Bennie (*Scot.*) One who came from Bennie, in Scotland; descendant of Ben, a pet form of Benedict (blessed).

Benoit, Benoist (*Fr.*) Descendant of Benoit, French form of Benedict (blessed).

Benridge (*Eng.*) One who came from Benridge (ridge where beans were grown), in Northumberland.

Bensinger (*Ger.*) Variant of Benzinger, q.v.

Bensley (*Eng.*) Dweller in a grove where beans were grown.

Benson, Bensen (*Eng., Dan.*) One who came from Benson (Benesa's homestead), in Oxfordshire; the son of Ben, a pet form of Benedict (blessed), rather than of Benjamin.

Bent, Bente (*Eng.*) Dweller at an unenclosed pasture, moor or heath; dweller where bent grass grew.

Bentley, Bently (*Eng.*) One who came from Bentley (clearing overgrown with bent grass), the name of many places in England.

Benton (*Eng.*) One who came from Benton (place where bent grass grew), in Northumberland.

Bentsen (*Dan.*) The son of Bent, a Danish form of Benedict (blessed).

Benz, Bentz (*Ger.*) Dweller at the sign of the little bear; descendants of Benz, a pet form of Benedictus (blessed); one who came from Benz, in Germany.

Benziger (*Ger.*) One who came from Benzingen (place overgrown with rushes), in Wurttemberg.

Benzinger, Benzing (*Ger.*) One who came from Benzingen (place overgrown with rushes), in Germany.

Benzon (*Sw., Nor., Dan.*) The son of Bendik or Benedikt, Scandinavian forms of Benedict (blessed).

Beoley (*Eng.*) One who came from Beoley (bee wood), in Worcestershire.

Beran, Beranek, Beranich (*Pol., Bul.*) Dweller at the sign of the lamb; one who cared for the lambs.

Beranek, Beran (*Ger.*) Dweller at the sign of the lamb; one with gentle, lamblike characteristics.

Berardi, Berardino (*It.*) Descendant of Berardo, a form of Bernardo (bear, hard).

Berce (*Eng.*) Dweller by a birch tree.

Bercher, Berch (*Eng.*) Dweller at a birch tree or in a birch grove; one who had the care of sheep, a shepherd.

Berck (*Du.*) Dweller near a birch tree.

Bercovitz, Bercovitch (*Pol.*) The son of Berko, a pet form of Baruch (blessed).

Berdell, Berdelle, Berdel (*Ger.*) One who came from Berdel (swampy low ground), in Germany.

Berek (*Pol.*) Descendant of Berek or little Ber; or of Berek, a pet form of Baruch (blessed).

Berenbaum (*Ger.*) Dweller near a pear tree.

Berendt, Berent, Berend (*Ger.*) Descendant of Berinhard (bear, firm); one who came from Berend (bear), in Germany.

Berens, Berenson (*Nor., Sw.*) The son of Beren, a pet form of Bernhard (bear, hard).

Berenyi (*Hun.*) One who came from Bereny, in Hungary.

Beres (*Eng.*) Dweller where barley or other grain was grown.

Beresford (*Eng.*) One who came from Barford (barley ford, perhaps ford used at the time of harvest), the name of several places in England.

Bereskin, Beroskin (*Ukr.*) Dweller near a birch tree.

Berg (*Nor., Sw., Dan., Du.*) Dweller near, or on, the hill or mountain. See also Burg.

Bergby (*Sw., Nor.,*) One who came from Bergby, the name of several places in Sweden; hill farm.

Berge (*Nor., Du., Fr.*) Dweller at, or near, a rocky mountain; or bank of river.

Bergen, Bergan, Bergin (*Nor., Du.*) Dweller on the mountain; or on the hill farm; one who came from Bergen, in Holland.

Berger, Bergeret, Bergeron (*Fr., Ger.*) One who took care of a flock, a shepherd; dweller on, or near, a mountain.

Bergersen (*Nor.*) The son of Birger (help; salvage).

Bergesen (*Nor.*) The son of Berg, possibly a short form of Birger (help; salvage).

Berggren, Bergren (*Sw.*) Mountain branch.

Bergh (*Eng.*) Dweller on, or near, the hill.

Berghoff, Berghofer (*Ger.*) One who came from Berghof (mountain farm), the name of several places in Germany.

Bergholt (*Eng.*) One who came from Bergholt (copse by a hill), in Essex.

Bergkamp (*Du.*) Dweller in an enclosure on the hill.

Berglund (*Sw.*) Mountain grove.

Bergman, Bergmann (*Ger., Sw.*) Dweller in the mountains.

Bergquist, Berquist (*Sw.*) Mountain twig.

Bergsma (*Du.*) The son of Berg (hill).

Bergson, Bergsohn (*Ger.*) The son of Berek or Berko, pet forms of Baruch (blessed).

Bergstein (*Ger.*) One who came from Bergstein (stone mountain), in Germany.

Bergstresser, Bergstrasser (*Ger.*) Dweller on a mountain road.

Bergstrom (*Sw.*) Mountain stream.

Berhorst (*Ger.*) Dweller in, or near, a thicket on a hill; or in a wood frequented by bears.

Beringer, Berringer, Bering (*Ger.*) Descendant of Beringar (bear, spear).

Beringsmith (*Eng.*) A name brought about by the intermarriage of two families—the Berings and the Smiths.

Berish (*Ger.*) Variant of Barish, q.v.

Berk, Berke, Berks (*Pol.*) Descendant of Berek or Berko, pet forms of Baruch (blessed).

Berkcy (*Eng.*) Dweller on the island where birch trees grew.

Berkhout (*Du.*) Dweller in, or near, a birch wood.

Berkley, Berkeley (*Eng.*) One who came from Berkeley (birch wood), in Gloucestershire, or Berkley, in Somerset; dweller in, or near, a birch wood.

Berkman (*Eng., Ger.*) Dweller near a birch tree; servant of Berk, a pet form of Baruch (blessed).

Berkowitz, Berkovitz, Berkowicz (*Pol., Ukr.*) The son of Berek or Berko, pet forms of Baruch (blessed).

Berkshire (*Eng.*) One who came from Berkshire (hill forest), a county in England.

Berkson (*Eng., Ger.*) The son of Berk, a pet form of Baruch (blessed); the son of Baer or Ber (bear).

Berkswell (*Eng.*) One who came from Berkswell (Beorcol's spring), in Warwickshire.

Berland, Berlander (*Ger., Eng., Nor.*) Dweller on, or near, the field where barley was grown; one who came from Berland (bear land), in Norway.

Berlet (*Fr.*) One who cultivates berle, an aquatic plant.

Berlin, Berliner, Berlinger (*Ger., Du.*) One who came from Berlin (uncultivated field), in Germany; descendant of Ber or Berl (bear).

Berlioz (*Fr.*) Dweller near where water cress grew.

Berlow, Berlowitz (*Pol.*) Descendant of Berl, a pet form of Ber (bear).

Berlt (*Ger.*) Descendant of Berlt, a contracted form of Berthold (bright, wolf).

Berman (*Eng., Ger.*) One who owned a bear and led it about for public exhibition of its tricks; descendant of Berman (bear, man); sometimes a pet form of names beginning with Ber, as Berold and Bernhard.

Bermingham (*Eng.*) One who came from Birmingham (the village of Beornmund's people), in Warwickshire.

Bermont (*Fr.*) One who came from Bermont (beautiful mountain), in France.

Bermudez (*Sp.*) The son of Bermudo, Spanish form of Bermund (bear, protection).

Bern, Berne (*Eng., Swis.*) One who came from Berne (barn) in Dorset; one who came from Bern (bush; forest; bear), in Switzerland.

Bernabe (*Fr.*) Descendant of Barnabe, French form of Barnabas (son of prophecy; consolation).

Bernacchi (*It.*) Dweller on, or near, a small hill.

Bernacki (*Pol., Ukr.*) Descendant of Bernard (bear, firm).

Bernal (*Cz.-Sl.*) Descendant of Bernal, a pet form of Bernard (bear, firm).

Bernard (*Fr., Eng.*) Descendant of Bernard (bear, firm).

Bernas (*Lith.*) Descendant of Bernas, a short form of Bernardas, Lithuanian form of Bernard (bear, firm).

Bernat (*Pol., Sl., Ukr.*) Variant of Biernat, q.v.

Bernath (*Ger.*) Descendant of Berinhard (bear, firm).

Bernau, Bernauer (*Ger.*) One who came from Bernau, in Germany.

Bernbaum (*Ger.*) Dweller near a pear tree.

Bernberg (*Ger.*) One who came from Bernburg (bear mountain), in Germany.

Berndt, Bernd (*Ger.*) Descendant of Berndt (bear, firm).

Berner (*Eng., Swis.*) One who burnt brick or charcoal; a keeper of hounds; one who came from Berne (place where bears abounded), in Switzerland.

Bernett, Bernet (*Eng.*) One who came from Burnett (place cleared by burning), in Somerset; dweller on a field cleared of trees and brush by burning.

Berney (*Scot.*) Variant of Birney, q.v.

Bernham (*Eng.*) One who came from Burnham (enclosure by a stream), the name of several villages in England.

Bernhardt, Bernhard (*Ger.*) Descendant of Berinhard (bear, firm).

Bernier (*Fr., Eng.*) A keeper of hounds; descendant of Bernard (bear, firm); or of Bernhari (bear, army).

Berns, Bern, Bernes (*Eng., Swis., Ger.*) One who came from Bernes (bear), in Normandy; or from Bern (place where bears abounded), a city and canton in Switzerland; or from Bern, in Germany.

Bernson (*Sw.*) The son of Bern (bear).

Bernstein, Bernstine (*Ger.*) One who came from Bernstein (amber), now in Poland; one who dealt in amber.

Berntsen (*Nor.*) The son of Bernt, a shortened form of Bernard (bear, hard).

Beron (*Fr.*) Descendant of Beron or Bero (bear).

Berquist (*Sw.*) Mountain twig.

Berra (*It.*) One who dwelt in a hovel or hut.

35

Berrier (*Eng., Fr.*) One who came from Berrier (hut on a hill), in Cumberland; descendant of Berry, a pet form of Barius.

Berrios, Berrio (*Sp.*) Variant of Barrios, q.v.

Berry, Berryman (*Eng.*) Dweller at, or near, a hill; dweller at, or near, a stronghold or fortified place; servant at the manor house.

Berrycloth (*Eng.*) Dweller in a grove near a cliff or steep, rocky ascent.

Berryhill (*Scot.*) One who came from Berryhill, the name of several villages in Scotland.

Berson (*Sw.*) The son of Ber, a pet form of names beginning with Ber (bear), such as Bernhard and Bernard.

Bert, Berth (*Eng.*) Descendant of Beorht (bright); or of Bert, a pet form of names beginning or ending with this element, as Herbert or Bertram.

Bertell, Bertel (*Nor., Dan.*) Descendant of Bertel (bright).

Bertelsen (*Nor., Dan.*) The son of Bertel (bright).

Bertha (*Fr., Ger.*) Descendant of Bertha (bright), an eighth century French saint.

Berthelsen (*Nor., Dan.*) The son of Berthel (bright).

Berthlein (*Ger.*) Descendant of little Berth, a pet form of Berthold (bright, wolf).

Berthold (*Ger.*) Descendant of Berthold (bright, wolf).

Berti (*It.*) Descendant of Berto, a pet form of names terminating in -berto, as Alberto, Umberto and Gilberto.

Bertini, Bertino (*It.*) Descendant of little Berto. See Berti.

Bertok (*Hun., Pol.*) Descendant of Bertok, Hungarian form of Bertram (bright, raven); or of Bertok, Polish pet form of Bertold (bright, wolf).

Bertolini, Bertolino, Bertolotti, Bertolozzi, Bertolucci (*It.*) Descendant of little Bertoldo (bright, firm).

Bertram (*Eng.*) Descendant of Bertram (bright, raven).

Bertrand, Bertran (*Fr.*) Descendant of Bertrand (bright, raven).

Bertsch, Bertsche (*Ger.*) Descendant of Berthold (bright, wolf).

Bertucci (*It.*) Descendant of little Berto, a pet form of Alberto, Italian form of Albert (noble, bright).

Berube (*Fr.*) Dweller on, or near, marshy land.

Berwick (*Eng.*) One who came from Berwick (grain farm), the name of several towns in England.

Berwin (*Eng.*) Descendant of Bernwin (bear, friend).

Besant (*Eng.*) One who produced gold coins of a kind first minted at Byzantium; one who came from Byzantium (Constantinople/Istanbul).

Besenhofer (*Ger.*) Dweller in the country estate where broom grew.

Besley (*Eng.*) One who came from Bisley (Byssa's or Bise's grove), the name of places in Gloucestershire and Surrey.

Besse, Bess (*Fr.*) Dweller near a cluster of birch trees.

Bessemer (*Ger.*) One who makes and sells brooms.

Besser, Besserer (*Dan., Ger.*) One who came from Besser (better place), in Denmark; one who collects fines.

Bessette, Bessett (*Fr.*) Dweller in, or near, a small grove of birch trees.

Bessey (*Fr.*) One who came from Bessey (Bassius' estate), in France; dweller in, or near, a grove of birch trees.

Bessie, Besse, Bess (*Fr.*) Dweller near, or in, a birch tree grove.

Bessinger (*Ger.*) One who came from Bessingen (marshy place), the name of two places in Germany.

Bessler (*Ger., Swis.*) One who came from Basel (founded by Basilus who served in Gaul under Julius Caesar), a city in Switzerland.

Besson (*Fr.*) One born at the same time as another, a twin.

Best, Beste (*Eng.*) Dweller at the sign of the beast; one with the qualities of a beast, probably not in an uncomplimentary sense.

Bester, Bestar (*Eng.*) One who took care of the beasts, a herdsman.

Besterfield (*Eng.*) Dweller in, or near, the open land of the herdsman.

Beston (*Eng.*) One who came from Beeston (homestead where reed or rush grew), the name of several places in England.

Bestwall (*Eng.*) One who came from Bestwall (place east of the wall), in Dorset.

Beswick (*Eng.*) One who came from Beswick (Beac's dairy farm; Basa's dairy farm), the name of places in Lancashire and the East Riding of Yorkshire.

Betancourt (*Fr.*) Variant of Bettencourt, q.v.

Betchworth (*Eng.*) One who came from Betchworth (Becci's homestead), in Surrey.

Bethany (*Fr.*) One who came from Betheny (Betto's estate), in France.

Bethea (*Scot.*) Descendant of Bethea (daughter, i.e., servant of Jehovah).

Bethel (*Wel.*) The son of Ithel (generous lord).

Bethke (*Ger.*) Descendant of little Beth, a German pet form of Bertram (bright, raven).

Bethune (*Eng.*) One who came from Bethune (Bettun's residence), in France.

Betka (*Rus., Pol.*) Descendant of Betka, a pet form of Elizabetka, a Slavic form of Elizabeth (oath of God).

Betley (*Eng.*) One who came from Betley (Bette's grove), in Staffordshire.

Bettelheim (*Ger.*) One who came from Bettelheim (trashy home), in Germany.

Betten (*Ger.*) Dweller near a channel.

Bettencourt (*Fr.*) One who came from Bettencourt (Betto's estate), the name of two places in France.

Bettendorf (*Ger.*) One who came from Bettendorf (Betto's village), the name of three places in Germany.

Bettenhausen (*Ger.*) One who came from Bettenhausen (muddy settlement), in Germany.

Betterley (*Eng.*) One who came from Bitterley (glade where butter was made), in Shropshire.

Betterton (*Eng.*) One who came from Betterton (Beaduthryth's homestead), in Berkshire.

Bettis, Bettison (*Eng.*) Descendant of Bett, sometimes a pet form of Beatrice (she who blesses), but also found as a masculine name.

Betton (*Eng.*) One who came from Bethune (Bettun's residence), in France.

Bettridge (*Eng.*) Descendant of Beaduric (battle, powerful).

Betts, Betz (*Eng., Ger.*) Descendant of Beatrice (one who blesses); descendant of Bezzo, a pet form of names beginning with Baer (bear), Bercht (shining; famous), or Bad (fight).

Beucher (*Ger.*) One who came from Beuchen, in Germany; descendant of Beuchert (necklace, army).

Beukema (*Du.*) The son of Beuke.

Beutler, Beutel (*Ger.*) One who made and sold purses and pouches.

Bevan, Bevans (*Wel.*) The son of Evan (gracious gift of Jehovah).

Beveridge (*Eng., Scot.*) Dweller at a farm, or ridge, frequented by beavers; one who made a practice of giving a free drink to clinch a bargain.

Beverley, Beverly (*Eng.*) One who came from Beverley (beaver stream), in Yorkshire.

Bevilacqua (*It.*) One known as a teetotaler, i.e., one who drank water.

Beville, Bevill, Bevil (*Eng.*) One who came from Beuville, in Calvados; or from Bouville, in Seine-Inferieure.

Bevington (*Eng.*) One who came from Bevington (Beofa's homestead), in Warwickshire.

Bevins, Bevan, Bevans (*Wel.*) The son of Evan, Welsh form of John (gracious gift of Jehovah).

Bevlaqua (*It.*) One known as a teetotaler, i.e., one who drank water.

Bewcastle (*Eng.*) One who came from Bewcastle (sheep shelter at an old Roman fort), in Cumberland.

Bewerley (*Eng.*) One who came from Bewerley (clearing where beavers were found), in the West Riding of Yorkshire.

Bewley (*Eng.*) One who came from Bewley (beautiful place), in Durham.

Bey (*Scot., Eng., Du.*) The son of Bheatha (life); dweller at the curve or bend in the river; or in, or near, a town.

Beyer, Beier (*Ger., Du.*) One who came from Bavaria, in Germany; dweller near a cattle shelter or shed.

Beynon (*Wel.*) The son of Eynon or Einion (anvil or upright).

Bezak, Bezark (*Pol.*) Dweller by an elder tree.

Biagi, Biagini, Biagioni (*It.*) Descendant of little Biagio (blaze).

Bialas, Bialy (*Pol.*) The light-complexioned or white-haired man.

Bialek (*Pol.*) The small, light-complexioned or white-haired man.

Bialka, Bialko (*Pol.*) The light or fair-complexioned man; one with white hair.

Bialoruski (*Pol.*) One who came from Byelorussia, a White Russian.

Biamonte (*It.*) One who came from Biamonti, in Italy.

Biancalana (*It.*) One who habitually dressed in white wool; one who cleaned and sold white wool.

Bianco, Bianchi (*It.*) The light-complexioned or white-haired man.

Bibbs, Bibb (*Eng.*) Descendant of Bibb, a pet form of Isabel (oath to Baal; also a variant of Elizabeth).

Bible (*Eng.*) Descendant of little Bibb, a pet name for Isabel (oath to Baal).

Bibro (*Pol.*) Dweller at the sign of the beaver; one who trapped beavers.

Bicek (*Cz., Pol.*) One who raised and sold bull calves.

Bichl (*Ger.*) One who came from Bichl (hill), the name of many places in Germany.

Bick, Bickel (*Ger., Wel., Eng.*) Dweller at the sign of the pickaxe; one who worked with a pickaxe; the small man; descendant of Bica.

Bickershaw (*Eng.*) One who came from Bickershaw (the grove of the bee-keepers), in Lancashire.

Bickerstaff (*Eng.*) One who came from Bickerstaffe (the landing place of the bee keeper), in Lancashire.

Bickerton (*Eng.*) One who came from Bickerton (village of the bee keepers), the name of several villages in England.

Bickett (*Eng.*) One who came from Beckett (bee shelter; Bicca's cottage), the name of villages in Berkshire and Devonshire.

Bickford, Beckford (*Eng.*) One who came from Bickford (Bica's ford), a village in Staffordshire; or from Beckford (Becca's ford), in Gloucestershire.

Bickham, Bickhem (*Eng.*) Variants of Beckham, q.v.

Bickler (*Ger.*) Dweller near a mound or knoll.

Bickley, Bickle (*Eng.*) One who came from Bickleigh (Bicca's homestead), the name of several places in England.

Bicknell (*Eng.*) Dweller at Bica's hill or corner; one who came from Bickenhill (Bica's hill), in Warwickshire.

Bickness (*Eng.*) Dweller on Bica's promontory or headland.

Bicknor (*Eng.*) One who came from Bicknor (Bica's ridge), the name of places in Gloucestershire and Herefordshire.

Bidault (*Fr.*) Descendant of Bid, a short form of names beginning with Bid (hope), such as Bidhard and Bidwald.

Biddick (*Eng.*) Descendant of Buddic (victorious one).

Biddle (*Eng.*) A variant of Bedell, q.v.

Biddlecombe (*Eng.*) One who came from Bittiscombe (Bitel's valley), in Somerset.

Bidwell, Bidwill (*Eng., Wel.*) One who came from Bidwell (stream in a valley), in Bedfordshire; the son of Idwal (lord, wall).

Biebel (*Ger.*) Descendant of Bibo, a pet

form of Bitbert (endure or desire, bright).

Bieber (*Ger.*) One who came from Bieber (beaver's place), in Germany.

Biedenweg (*Ger.*) One who lived "by the way" or street.

Biedermann, Biederman (*Ger.*) The upright, honest servant or vassal.

Biedrzycki (*Pol.*) One thought to possess the characteristics of a ladybug.

Biegel, Biegler (*Ger.*) Dweller on, or near, a hill.

Biel, Biehl, Biehler (*Ger.*) One who came from Buhl or Buhler (small hill), in Germany.

Bielarz (*Pol.*) One who bleaches or whitens cloth.

Bielawa, Bielawski (*Pol.*) One who came from Bielawa, in Poland.

Bielecki (*Pol.*) One who wears a white garment.

Bieler (*Ger.*) One who came from Bielau or Bielen, the names of places in Germany.

Bielinski (*Rus.*) One who came from Bielin (white), in Russia.

Bielski (*Pol.*) One who came from Bielsk (white), in Poland.

Bien, Bieniek, Bienik (*Pol.*) Descendant of Bien, a pet form of Benjamin (son of my right hand).

Bienenfeld (*Ger.*) Dweller on, or near, the field where bees swarmed.

Bienenstock (*Ger.*) Dweller near a tree trunk where bees swarmed.

Bienville (*Fr.*) One who came from Bienville (Bodin's village), in France.

Bier, Biers (*Eng.*) Dweller near, or worker at, the cow barn.

Bierce (*Eng.*) Dweller near the birch tree.

Biernat (*Pol., Sl.*) Descendant of Berinhard (bear, brave).

Bierstadt (*Ger.*) One who came from Bierstadt (quagmire or morass), in Germany.

Bies, Biese (*Ger.*) Dweller on land overgrown with sedge or bent grass.

Bieschke (*Pol.*) Descendant of little Piotr, Polish form of Peter (a rock).

Bigbee, Bigby (*Eng.*) One who came

from Bigby (Bekki's homestead or village), in Lincolnshire.

Bigbury (*Eng.*) One who came from Bigbury (Bicca's fort), in Devonshire.

Bigden (*Eng.*) Dweller on the large hill.

Bigelow, Biglow (*Eng.*) Dweller on, or near, the barley hill; one who came from Baguley (ram's woodland), the name of several places in England.

Biggers, Bigger, Biggar (*Eng., Scot.*) One who buys, a purchaser; one who came from Biggar (barley field), in Lanarkshire.

Biggerstaff (*Eng.*) One who came from Bickerstaffe (landing place of the bee keepers), in Lancashire.

Biggin, Biggins (*Eng.*) Dweller in a building or house, from Middle English *bigging* (building), a common place name in England; dweller in an outbuilding as distinguished from a house.

Biggles (*Eng.*) Descendant of little Bicca (thick or big).

Biggs, Bigg, Bigges (*Wel., Eng.*) The large, tall, bulky or proud man; the mighty, powerful man; descendant of Bicca (thick or big).

Bigham, Biggam (*Scot., Eng.*) One who came from the lands of Bigholme in Scotland; dweller in the big enclosure.

Bigley (*Ir.*) A variant of Begley, q.v.

Bignall, Bignal, Bignell (*Eng.*) Dweller at Biga's corner.

Bigott, Bigot (*Eng., Fr.*) Nickname given to one by reason of the excessive use of the oath, "by God"; a hypercritical or intolerant person.

Bigwood (*Eng.*) Dweller in, or near, the large group of trees.

Bihler (*Ger.*) Dweller on, or near, a hill.

Bihun (*Eng.*) One who came from Bighton (the village of Bica's people), in Hampshire.

Bilbey, Bilbee, Bilby (*Eng.*) One who came from Bilby (Bille's homestead), in Nottinghamshire.

Bilbrey, Bilbrew (*Eng.*) One who came

from Bilborough (Billa's fort), in Nottinghamshire.

Bilbrook (*Eng.*) One who came from Bilbrook (stream where water cress grew), the name of places in Somerset and Staffordshire.

Bilder (*Eng.*) Variant of Biller, q.v.

Bilek, Bilko (*Cz.-Sl.*) The light-complexioned or white-haired man.

Bilham (*Eng.*) One who came from Bilham (Billa's homestead), in the West Riding of Yorkshire.

Bill, Bille (*Ger., Eng.*) Descendant of Bilo, a pet form of names beginning with Bil (sword), as Bilihar and Biligarda; descendant of Bil (sword). Not from Bill, a relatively late pet form of William.

Biller (*Eng.*) One who made bills, weapons consisting of a long staff terminating in a hook-shaped blade.

Billeter (*Eng.*) One who cast bells, a bell founder.

Billig (*Ger.*) One who came from Billig (plain), in Germany.

Billinger (*Sw.*) One who came from Billinge, in Sweden.

Billingham (*Eng.*) One who came from Billingham (village of the Billingas), in Durham.

Billings, Billing (*Eng., Ger., Sw.*) One who came from Billing (Billa's people), in Northamptonshire; or from Billinge (sword), in Lancashire; the son of Bill (sword); one who came from Billings, in Germany; one born at the same time as another, a twin.

Billingsley, Billingslea, Billingsly (*Eng.*) One who came from Billingsley (Bylga's or Bylgi's grove), in Shropshire.

Billington (*Eng.*) One who came from Billington (Billa's hill or homestead; the ridge of the Billingas), the name of villages in Bedfordshire, Lancashire, and Staffordshire.

Billis, Billish (*Wel.*) Variant of Bellis, q.v.

Billo, Billow (*Eng., Fr.*) One who operates a bellows, a smith's assistant;

descendant of Bili, a pet form of Biliwulf (agreeable, wolf).

Billsmith (*Eng.*) One who made bills, the warrior's battle-ax.

Billups (*Ger.*) Descendant of Billup, a German variant of Phillip (lover of horses).

Billy, Billie (*Scot.*) One who came from Billie or Bellie (village; farm), in Scotland.

Bilous (*Ukr.*) One who had a white mustache.

Bilouscenko (*Ukr.*) Son of the man with the white mustache.

Bilsborrow (*Eng.*) One who came from Bilsborough (Bill's fort), in Lancashire.

Bilsdale (*Eng.*) One who came from Bilsdale (Bild's valley), in the North Riding of Yorkshire.

Bilski, Bilsky (*Pol., Ukr.*) One who came from Bilsk, in Poland.

Bilton (*Eng.*) One who came from Bilton (Billa's homestead or homestead where henbane grew), the name of villages in Northumberland and Warwickshire.

Bily (*Cz.-Sl.*) The light-complexioned or white-haired man.

Binam (*Eng.*) One who came from Binham (Bynna's homestead), in Norfolk.

Binbrook (*Eng.*) One who came from Binbrook (Bynna's stream), in Lincolnshire.

Binchester (*Eng.*) One who came from Binchester (shelter for cattle), in Durham.

Binder (*Eng., Ger.*) One who binds, a bookbinder; one who bound sheaves behind the reapers; one who made and sold casks, buckets, and tubs, a cooper.

Bindon (*Eng.*) One who came from Bindon (place on the hill), in Dorset.

Binegar (*Eng.*) One who came from Binegar (slope where beans grew), in Somerset.

Binford (*Eng.*) Dweller at a river crossing near where beans grew.

Bing, Bingen (*Ger.*) One who came from

Bingen (swampy meadow land), in Germany.

Bingaman, Bingeman (*Ger.*) One who came from Bingen (swampy meadow land), the name of two places in Germany.

Bingham (*Eng.*) One who came from Bingham (Bynna's estate), in Nottinghamshire.

Bingley (*Eng.*) One who came from Bingley (Bynna's grove), in the West Riding of Yorkshire.

Binion, Binyon (*Wel.*) The son of Einion (anvil or upright).

Binkley (*Eng.*) One who came from Bingley (hill grove), in the West Riding of Yorkshire.

Binnie, Binney (*Eng., Scot.*) Descendant of Bynni; dweller on an island in a stream; one who came from Binney, in West Lothian.

Binns (*Scot., Eng.*) One who came from Binns, in West Lothian; descendant of Binn or Bynna.

Binsey (*Eng.*) One who came from Binsey (Byni's island), in Oxfordshire.

Binsfeld (*Eng.*) Dweller in, or near, Bynna's field or land.

Binstead (*Eng.*) One who came from Binstead (place where beans were grown), the name of villages in Wight and Sussex.

Binstock (*Eng.*) Dweller at a place where beans grew.

Bintree (*Eng.*) One who came from Bintree (Bynna's tree), in Norfolk.

Bintz (*Ger.*) Variant of Benz, q.v.; descendant of Binzo.

Biondo, Biondi (*It.*) The light-complexioned or blond man.

Birch, Birchet (*Eng.*) Dweller at, or near, the birch tree or birch tree grove; one who came from Birch (newly cultivated land), in Essex.

Bircham (*Eng.*) One who came from Bircham (newly cultivated homestead), in Norfolk.

Bircher (*Eng.*) One who came from Bircher (ridge with birch trees), in Herefordshire.

Birchfield (*Eng.*) Dweller in the open country where birch trees grew.

Birchington (*Eng.*) One who came from Birchington (homestead surrounded by birch trees), in Kent.

Birchwood (*Eng.*) Dweller in, or near, a grove of birch trees.

Bird (*Eng.*) Dweller at the sign of the bird; one with birdlike characteristics.

Birden (*Eng.*) Variant of Burden, q.v.

Birdham (*Eng.*) One who came from Birdham (meadow frequented by birds), in Sussex.

Birdsall, Birdsell (*Eng.*) One who came from Birdsall (Bridd's corner), in the East Riding of Yorkshire.

Birdseye, Birdsey (*Eng.*) Dweller on an island frequented by birds.

Birdsong (*Ger.*) Translation of Vogelsanger, q.v.

Birdwell (*Eng.*) Dweller near a spring or stream frequented by birds.

Birely (*Eng.*) One who came from Birley (cowshed in a grove; grove by a fortified place), the name of several places in England.

Bires (*Ger.*) Variant of Beyer, q.v.

Birge (*Nor., Du., Fr.*) Variant of Berge, q.v.

Birk, Birks, Birke (*Eng.*) Dweller near the birch trees.

Birkby (*Eng.*) One who came from Birkby (village of the Britons), the name of places in Cumberland and the North and West Ridings of Yorkshire.

Birkdale (*Eng.*) One who came from Birkdale (birch valley), in Lancashire.

Birkeland (*Nor.*) Dweller on the farm where birch trees grew.

Birkelund (*Nor.*) Dweller in, or near, the grove of birch trees.

Birkenshaw, Birkinshaw (*Eng.*) One who came from Birkenshaw (birch grove), in the West Riding of Yorkshire.

Birker (*Eng.*) One who came from Birker (hut in a birch grove), in Cumberland.

Birkett (*Eng.*) Dweller on, or near, the headland where birch trees grew.

Birkholz (*Eng.*) One who came from Birkholt (birch wood), in Kent.

Birks (*Eng.*) Dweller by the birches.

Birmingham (*Eng.*) One who came from Birmingham (the village of Beornmund's people), a city in Warwickshire.

Birnbaum, Bernbaum, Bernbom (*Ger.*) Dweller near the pear tree; one who came from Birnbaum, now in Poland.

Birndorf (*Ger.*) One who came from Birndorf (village of pear trees), in Germany.

Birney, Birnie (*Scot.*) One who came from Birnie (moist, oozy place; pretty place), in Scotland.

Biro (*Hun., Fr.*) One who occupied the office of judge; the head or mayor of a village; descendant of Biro, a pet form of Pierre, French form of Peter (a rock).

Biron, Birong (*Eng.*) One who came from Byram (cowshed), in the West Riding of Yorkshire.

Birrell (*Eng.*) One who came from Burrill (fort hill), in the North Riding of Yorkshire.

Birstal, Birstall (*Eng.*) One who came from Birstal or Birstall (site of a fort), the names of places in the West Riding of Yorkshire and Leicestershire.

Birt, Birth (*Eng.*) Variant of Bert, q.v.

Birtley (*Eng.*) One who came from Birtley (bright grove), the name of places in Durham and Northumberland.

Birtwell (*Eng.*) Dweller near a spring where birches grew; or near a bright spring.

Birtwhistle, Birtwisle (*Eng.*) One who came from Birtwisle (now no longer in existence), in Lancashire.

Bis (*Fr.*) One with a dark gray complexion; or who wore dark gray clothing.

Bisbee (*Eng.*) One who came from Beesby (Besy's homestead), in Lincolnshire.

Bisceglie, Bisceglia (*It.*) One who came from Bisceglie (maple tree), in Italy; dweller near a maple tree.

Bischoff, Bischof, Bishoff, Bischoffer (*Ger.*) Member of a bishop's entourage or household; one who came from Bischof, in Germany; one playing the part of a bishop in play or pageant.

Bishampton (*Eng.*) One who came from Bishampton (the bishop's village proper, that is, in contradistinction to the outlying parts), in Worcestershire.

Bishop, Bishopp (*Eng.*) A member of a bishop's entourage or household; descendant of Biscop (bishop); one playing the part of a bishop in play or pageant.

Bishton (*Eng.*) One who came from Bishton (the bishop's manor), the name of several villages in England.

Biskup, Biskupski (*Pol.*) Member of a bishop's entourage; servant of the bishop.

Bisley (*Eng.*) One who came from Bisley (Bise's or Byssa's grove), the name of places in Gloucestershire and Surrey.

Bismark (*Ger.*) One who came from Bismarck (bishop's boundary), in Germany; dweller near the bishop's boundary.

Bison, Bisone (*Eng.*) The little brownish or dark gray man.

Biss (*Eng.*) One with a brownish or dark gray complexion; dweller near a biss, a tributary stream.

Bissell (*Eng.*) One who made and sold baskets holding a bushel; one who measured grain in bushels.

Bissett, Bissette (*Eng., Scot.*) The little brown, or dark-complexioned, man.

Bissing, Bisson (*Eng.*) The little man with the brownish or dark gray complexion.

Bisson, Bissonnette (*Fr.*) Dweller in, or near, a thicket, bush or brake; one who sold flax.

Bittenbinder (*Ger.*) One who made and sold casks, buckets and tubs, a cooper.

Bitter, Bitterman, Bittermann (*Ger.*) One who gathered alms in the town; one who worked for another on a farm.

Bittle, Bittler (*Ger., Eng.*) A constable, crier, or usher in a court; a jailer.

Bittner (*Ger.*) One who made casks or barrels, a cooper.

Bivens (*Wel.*) The son of Evan, Welsh form of John (gracious gift of Jehovah).

Bix (*Eng.*) Dweller near the box tree; one who came from Bix (box wood), in Oxfordshire.

Bixby (*Eng.*) One who came from Bigby (Bekki's homestead), in Lincolnshire.

Bixler (*Ger.*) One who makes and sells canisters.

Bizet (*Fr.*) The small man with dark gray complexion; or who wore dark gray clothing.

Bjerke (*Nor.*) Dweller near a birch tree.

Bjork (*Sw.*) Birch.

Bjorklund (*Sw.*) Birch grove.

Bjorkman (*Sw.*) Birch man.

Bjorkquist (*Sw.*) Birch twig.

Bjornby, Bjorneby (*Sw., Nor.*) One who came from Bjornby (bear village), the name of a couple of places in Sweden; bear village.

Bjorndal (*Nor.*) Dweller in Bjorn's valley.

Bjornrud (*Nor.*) Dweller in Bjorn's clearing.

Bjornson, Bjornsen (*Nor.*) The son of Bjorn (bear).

Bjornstad (*Nor.*) One who came from the farm belonging to Bjorn (bear), a farm name; one who came from Bjornstad (Bjorn's farm), the name of many places in Norway.

Bjurstrom (*Sw.*) Dweller near the beaver river.

Blaan (*Scot.*) Descendant of Blaan (yellow); one with light-colored complexion.

Blaauw, Blauw (*Du.*) One who was light-complexioned or blond; one wearing some article colored blue.

Blache (*Fr.*) Dweller in, or near, a grove of oak or chestnut trees.

Blacher (*Eng.*) One with white or pale complexion; one who came from Blacker (dark marsh), in the West Riding of Yorkshire.

Blachley, Blackley (*Eng.*) One who came from Blackley (dark wood), in Lancashire.

Black (*Eng.*) One with a dark or swarthy complexion; descendant of Blaec or Blac (black or pale). Note: Old English *blaec* is black, whereas Old English *blác* is white or pale, and the two words are inextricably confused in names.

Blackburn (*Eng., Scot.*) One who came from Blackburn (dark-colored stream), a town in Lancashire; or from Blackburn, the name of several places in Scotland. See note under Black.

Blackdown (*Eng.*) One who came from Blackdown (dark hill), the name of places in Dorset and Warwickshire.

Blacker (*Eng.*) Dweller in, or near, a black or dark marsh.

Blackford (*Eng.*) One who came from Blackford (dark river crossing), the name of two places in Somerset.

Blackie (*Eng.*) One who had a black eye; dweller in, or near, the dark land or enclosure.

Blackington (*Eng.*) One who came from Blatchington (the village of Blaecca's people), in Sussex.

Blackledge, Blacklidge (*Eng.*) Dweller at a black pool.

Blackman, Blackmon, Blackmun (*Eng.*) Descendant of Blaecman or Blacman (dark man), a not uncommon Early English name. See note under Black.

Blackmore, Blackmer (*Eng.*) One who came from Blackmoor (dark marsh or lake), the name of places in Dorset, Hampshire, and Hertfordshire; descendant of Blaecmaer.

Blacknard (*Eng.*) Dweller near where black nard grew; one who dealt in nard or made it from the plant.

Blackshire, Blackshaw (*Eng.*) One who came from Blackshaw (black grove), in the West Riding of Yorkshire.

Blacksley (*Eng.*) One who came from Blakesley (wood of the black wolf), in Northamptonshire.

Blacksmith (*Eng.*) One who worked in iron, the black metal.

Blackstone (*Eng., Scot.*) The man from Blackstone (black boundary stone), the name of several places in both England and Scotland; descendant of Blaecstan (black stone). See note under Black.

Blackwell, Blackwall, (*Eng.*) Dweller at, or near, the dark stream. See note under Black.

Blackwood (*Scot., Eng.*) The man from Blackwood (dark wood), the name of lands in Lanarkshire and Dumfriesshire; or from Blackwood (black wood), in the West Riding of Yorkshire.

Blade, Blades, Blaydes (*Eng.*) One who made blades and knives.

Bladesmith, Bladsmith (*Eng.*) One who made tools, swords, or blades.

Blagdon (*Eng.*) One who came from Blagdon (black hill or valley), the name of several places in England; dweller in a dark valley or on a black hill.

Blagg (*Eng.*) One with a dark or swarthy complexion.

Blaha (*Cz.-Sl.*) The blithesome or happy person; one with good fortune.

Blahut (*Cz.-Sl.*) Descendant of Blahut (good fortune).

Blaikie (*Scot.*) Descendant of little Blake. See note under Black.

Blaine, Blain (*Scot.*) The son of the disciple of Blaan (yellow) or Blane (the lean), an early Scottish saint.

Blair (*Scot.*) Dweller on a plain, one who came from Blair (plain), the name of several places in Scotland.

Blais (*Fr.*) Descendant of Blasius (babbler).

Blaisdell (*Eng.*) One who came from Bleasdale (bare spot on a hillside), in Lancashire.

Blake (*Eng.*) One with a swarthy complexion; descendant of Blaec, meaning either black or pale. See note under Black.

Blakeley, Blakely (*Eng.*) One who came from Blackley (black wood), in Lancashire.

Blakeman (*Eng.*) Same as Blackman, q.v.

Blakemore (*Eng.*) One who came from Blackmore (black wasteland), the name of several places in England.

Blakes (*Eng.*) Descendant of Blaec (black or pale).

Blakeslee, Blakesley (*Eng.*) One who came from Blakesley (wood of the black wolf), in Northamptonshire.

Blakesmyth (*Eng.*) Variant of Blacksmith, q.v.

Blakey (*Eng.*) One who came from Blakey or Blakehow (black hill), in the North Riding of Yorkshire; dweller in, or near, the dark land or enclosure; one who had a black eye; dweller at the white island.

Blakly (*Eng.*) One who came from Blackley (the black wood or clearing), in Lancashire.

Blamey (*Eng.*) Cornish form of Bellamy, q.v.

Blanc, Blanchet, Blanchon (*Fr.*) The light-complexioned or white-haired man.

Blanchard, Blancard (*Fr., Eng.*) Descendant of Blanchard (white, hard); dweller at the sign of the blanchard (white horse); the light-complexioned or white-haired man.

Blanchfield (*Eng.*) Dweller in, or near, a white field.

Bland (*Eng.*) One who came from Bland, in Yorkshire; the light-complexioned man.

Blandford, Blanford (*Eng.*) One who came from Blandford (ford where gudgeons abound), in Dorset.

Blaney, Blayney, Blayne (*Wel., Ir., Eng.*) The thin, lean man; dweller at the head of a valley.

Blank, Blanks, Blanke (*Eng., Du.*) One with a fair, or light, complexion; one who had white hair.

Blankenheim (*Ger.*) Dweller in, or near, the white house.

Blankenship, Blankensop (*Eng.*) One who came from Blenkinsopp (top valley), in Northumberland.

Blankenstein, Blankstein (*Ger.*) One who came from Blankenstein (shining stone), in Germany.

Blanton (*Eng.*) Dweller at a homestead at the end or on a point; or at the horse farm.

Blas (*Sp.*) Descendant of Blas, Spanish form of Blaze (brand).

Blasco, Blascovich (*Pol., Cz.*) Descendant, or son, of Blasius (babbler; brand).

Blase (*Eng.*) The son of Blea (livid); one who lisps or stammers.

Blaser, Blazer (*Du.*) One who played a wind instrument, a trumpeter.

Blasingame, Blassingame (*Eng.*) One who came from Bessingham (village of the Basingas), in Norfolk.

Blasquez (*Sp.*) The son of Blasius (babbler; brand).

Blaszak, Blaszczyk, Blasczyk (*Pol.*) Descendant of little Blase (babbler; brand).

Blatchford (*Eng.*) One who came from Blackford (black ford), in Somerset.

Blatchley (*Eng.*) One who came from Bletchley (Blecca's grove), the name of villages in Buckinghamshire and Shropshire.

Blatherwick (*Eng.*) One who came from Blatherwycke (blackthorn dairy farm), in Northamptonshire.

Blatt (*Ger.*) Leaf.

Blau (*Ger., Du.*) One who was light-complexioned or blond; one who wore blue clothing.

Blaul (*Ger.*) Dweller near the crushing mill.

Blaustein (*Ger.*) Dweller at the blue stone farmstead.

Blauvelt (*Du.*) One who lived at, or near, the blue field, referring to the flax field.

Blaylock, Blalock (*Eng.*) One who had lead-colored hair.

Blazek (*Cz.-Sl., Pol.*) Descendant of Blazek, a pet form of Blasius (babbler; brand).

Blazick, Blazic (*Pol.*) Descendant of Blaze (brand).

Blazowski (*Pol.*) One who came from Blazowa, in Poland.

Bleaden, Bleadon (*Eng.*) One who came from Bleadon (colored hill), in Somerset.

Bleakley (*Eng.*) One who came from Blackley (dark wood or clearing), in Lancashire.

Blecha (*Cz.-Sl.*) One with the characteristics of a flea; the small, inconsequential man.

Blecher (*Ger.*) One who worked with tin, a tinsmith.

Blechman (*Ger.*) One who worked with tin, a tinsmith.

Blecksmith (*Ger.*) Anglicized form of German Blechschmidt, a tinsmith or worker in tin.

Bledsoe (*Eng.*) One who came from Bletsoe (Blaecci's hill), in Bedfordshire.

Bleeker, Bleecker (*Du.*) One who bleaches or whitens cloth, a fuller.

Bleicher (*Ger.*) Descendant of Bleichert (shining, hard); one who bleached cloth.

Bleier (*Ger.*) One who smelts lead.

Bleiweiss (*Ger.*) One who works with white lead.

Blencow, Blencowe, Blenko, Blinco (*Eng.*) One who came from Blencow (hilltop), in Cumberland.

Blennerhassett (*Eng.*) One who came from Blennerhasset (hay hut on a hill), in Cumberland.

Bleriot (*Fr.*) One who hunted or trapped badgers; one with the characteristics of a badger, crafty and sly.

Blessing (*Eng.*) One who took the personified part of "Blessing" in the morality plays.

Blessington (*Eng.*) One who came from Bletchingdon (Blecces' hill), in Oxfordshire.

Blevins, Blevin (*Wel.*) The son of Plethyn or Plevin; the son of Bleddyn (little wolf).

Blewbury (*Eng.*) One who came from Blewbury (colored fort), in Berkshire.

Blewitt, Blewett (*Eng.*) The little man of blue or livid complexion.

Bley (*Eng.*) One with a livid complexion.

45

Blick (*Eng.*) Descendant of Blickla; one with a dark or swarthy complexion.

Blievernicht (*Ger.*) One who frequently changes his home, a wanderer.

Blindauer (*Ger.*) One who came from Blindau (wet meadowland), in Germany.

Blinder (*Ger., Heb.*) One who could not see, a blind person.

Bliss (*Eng.*) One with a blithesome or happy disposition.

Blissitt, Blissett, Blissit (*Eng.*) The happy, fortunate, blessed man; descendant of Blissot (blessed).

Blitstein, Blitzstein, Blitsten (*Ger.*) Lightning stone.

Blitz (*Ger.*) One who came from Blitze (flash of lightning), now called Bitze, in Germany; the lightning-fast man; perhaps one with a quick, fiery temper.

Blixt, Blix (*Ger.*) Variant of Blitz, q.v.; descendant of Blic (splendor).

Blizzard (*Eng.*) One who was extremely joyful or happy.

Block, Bloch (*Ger., Eng.*) The foreign man; one who lived at the sign of the block or cube; the short, stumpy, or stupid, man.

Blocker (*Ger.*) One who came from Blocken, the name of two places in Germany.

Bloden (*Eng., Ger.*) One who came from Blaydon (blue hill), in Durham; dweller near a flowering thorn tree.

Blodgett (*Wel.*) The son of little Lloyd (gray).

Blohm (*Ger.*) Dweller in, or near, the flowering meadow.

Blom (*Sw., Du.*) Flower; dweller where flowers grew.

Blomberg, Bloomberg (*Sw.*) Flower mountain.

Blomer, Bloomer (*Eng.*) One who made blooms, an iron-worker.

Blomgren, Bloomgren (*Sw.*) Flower branch.

Blommaert (*Du.*) One who cultivated and dealt in flowers, a florist.

Blomquist, Bloomquist (*Sw.*) Flower twig.

Blond, Blonde (*Fr.*) One with fair or flaxen hair or complexion.

Blondell, Blondel (*Fr., Eng.*) The little blond one; light of hair or complexion.

Blonski, Blonsky (*Pol., Ukr.*) Dweller on a plain, or level ground; or at the village green.

Blood (*Wel.*) The son of Lloyd (gray).

Bloodgood (*Ger.*) Dweller near a flower garden.

Bloodsaw (*Eng.*) One who came from Bletsoe (Bleecci's hill), in Bedfordshire.

Bloodworth (*Eng.*) Dweller in, or near, the blood-red enclosure; one who came from Blidworth (Bleath's enclosure), in Nottinghamshire.

Bloom (*Sw.*) Flower.

Bloomenthal (*Ger.*) One who came from Blumenthal (flower valley), the name of seven places in Germany.

Bloomer (*Eng.*) One who worked with wrought iron; one who worked in a bloomery.

Bloomfield (*Eng.*) Dweller in, or near, the flower field.

Bloor, Blore (*Eng.*) One who came from Blore (hill; bare spot), in Staffordshire.

Bloss (*Eng.*) One who came from Blois (barren), in France.

Blossomgame (*Eng.*) Variant of Blasingame, q.v.

Blough (*Wel.*) The short or small man.

Blount, Blunt (*Eng.*) The fair or light-complexioned man.

Blowers, Blower (*Eng.*) The bellows-blower who helped the smith at the forge.

Bloxham, Bloxom (*Eng.*) One who came from Bloxham (Blocc's homestead), in Oxfordshire.

Bloxin (*Rus.*) One with the characteristics of a flea; the small, inconsequential man.

Bloxton (*Eng.*) Dweller at Blocc's homestead.

Blubaugh (*Ger.*) One who came from Blaubach (stream stream), the name of two places in Germany.

Blucher (*Ger.*) One who came from Blucher, in Mecklenburg.

Blue (*Eng.*) One with a livid complexion; one who dressed in blue.

Bluefarb (*Ger.*) One with a blue or livid complexion; one dressed in blue.

Bluestein, Bluestone (*Ger.*) Anglicization of Blaustein, q.v.

Bluett, Bluitt (*Eng.*) The little man with the blue or livid complexion.

Blum, Blume, Bluhm (*Ger.*) Flower; dweller at the sign of the flower; one who came from Blume (flower), the name of two places in Germany.

Blumberg (*Ger.*) One who came from Blumberg (flower mountain), the name of two places in Germany.

Blumenfeld (*Ger.*) Dweller near a field or open country where flowers grew in abundance.

Blumenthal (*Ger.*) One who came from Blumenthal (flower valley), the name of seven towns in Germany.

Blumer (*Eng.*) One who made blooms or ingots of iron, an iron worker.

Blustein (*Ger.*) Dweller near a blue stone.

Bly, Blye (*Eng.*) Variant of Blyth, q.v.

Blyth, Blythe (*Eng.*) One who came from Blyth (gentle or merry), in Northumberland; dweller near the Blyth or Blythe, rivers in England; one with a gay or pleasant disposition.

Boal, Boals (*Eng.*) Dweller in a bowl-shaped valley; one who made and sold wooden bowls and dishes.

Board, Bord (*Eng.*) Dweller at a cottage or small farm.

Boardman (*Eng.*) One who hewed boards; dweller at a small farm.

Boas, Boaz (*Eng.*) Descendant of Boaz (in Him is strength).

Boatley (*Eng.*) One who came from Botley (Bota's grove), the name of several places in England; dweller in the grove where villagers could take timber for repairs or firewood.

Boatman, Boatner, Boater (*Eng.*) One who worked on a boat; one who operated a ferry.

Boatwright, Boatright (*Eng.*) One who built boats.

Boba, Bobak (*Pol.*) One who trapped marmots; dweller at the sign of the marmot.

Bobb, Bobbe, Bobber (*Eng.*) Dweller near a thicket or clump of brushwood; descendant of Bobba (a lall name).

Bobbin, Bobbins (*Eng.*) Descendant of Bobin, a pet form of Bobardt.

Bobbitt, Bobbett (*Fr.*) A haughty person who made a show of pomp; one who stammered or stuttered.

Bobek (*Pol., Cz., Sw., Dan.*) Dweller near a laurel tree; one who came from Bobacken (brook dwelling), the name of three places in Sweden.

Bober (*Cz.-Sl.*) Dweller at the sign of the beaver; one with the characteristics of a beaver.

Boberg (*Ger.*) One who came from Boberg, the name of two places in Germany.

Bobiak (*Ukr.*) Metonymic for one who raised and sold beans.

Bobinski, Bobinsky, Bobin (*Pol.*) One who raised and sold small beans.

Bobka, Bobko, Bobkowski (*Pol.*) Dweller by the laurel tree.

Boblak (*Ukr.*) Descendant of the poor, landless peasant.

Bobo, Bobowski (*Pol.*) The fat, chubby man.

Bobrick, Bobrich (*Pol.*) Dweller at the sign of the beaver; one who trapped beavers.

Bobroff, Bobrow, Bobrowski (*Pol.*) Dweller near the Bobr (beaver), a river in Poland.

Bocanegra (*Sp.*) Nickname for one with a black mouth; one who used intemperate language.

Boccaccio (*It.*) One with an ugly mouth.

Bocek (*Cz.*) One who sold bacon.

Bochantin (*Cz.-Sl.*) The wealthy or rich man.

Bochenek (*Pol.*) Dweller at the sign of the loaf of bread.

Bochnik, Bochniak (*Pol.*) One who made and sold bread, a baker.

Bocian (*Pol.*) Dweller at the sign of the stork.

Bock (*Ger.*) Dweller at the sign of the

buck; one thought to have some of the qualities of a male goat; descendant of Burgio, a pet form of names commencing with Burg (stronghold), as Burghard and Burgoald.

Bockenholt (*Ger.*) Dweller in, or near, the grove of beech trees.

Bode (*Du., Ger.*) An officer of the court, town crier, or constable; descendant of Bode, a pet form of names beginning with Bod (messenger), as Bodewig and Butulf.

Bodell, Bodel (*Scot.*) One who came from Bothel (dwelling house) in Cumberland.

Boden (*Eng.*) Same as Bodine, q.v.

Bodendorfer (*Ger.*) One who came from Bodendorf (Boda's village), the name of two places in West Germany.

Bodenham (*Eng.*) One who came from Bodenham (Bota's or Boda's homestead or enclosure), the name of villages in Herefordshire and Wiltshire.

Bodenheimer, Bodenheim (*Ger.*) One who came from Bodenheim (Bodin's homestead; homestead with good soil), in Germany.

Bodenstein (*Ger.*) One who came from Bodenstein (nether millstone), the name of two places in Germany.

Bodfish (*Eng.*) Dweller at the sign of the flat fish; seller of flat fish, such as the halibut.

Bodine, Bodin, Bodinet (*Eng.*) Descendant of Bodin or Baudin, French forms of Baldwin (bold, friend).

Bodkin, Bodkins (*Eng.*) Descendant of little Baud, a pet form of Baldwin (bold, friend).

Bodley (*Eng.*) Same as Botley, q.v.

Bodmer (*Ger.*) One who came from Bodmen, in Germany.

Bodnar, Bodnarchuk, Bodnarczuk (*Pol., Ukr.*) One who made and sold casks and tubs, a cooper.

Bodner (*Eng.*) One who delivered messages; a herald.

Bodtke (*Ger.*) Descendant of little Bodo, a pet form of names beginning with

Bod (messenger) as Bodomar and Butolf.

Body (*Hun.*) One who came from Bod (meadow), in Hungary.

Boe (*Nor.*) One who had lived on the Boe (farm), a farm name.

Boeck, Boecher (*Ger.*) One who makes bread, a baker.

Boedeker (*Ger.*) One who made and sold tubs and barrels, a cooper.

Boegner (*Ger.*) Soldier armed with bow and arrows.

Boehm, Boehme, Boehmer (*Ger.*) One who came from Bohemia (home of the Boii).

Boeing (*Ger.*) Descendant of Bodo, a pet form of names beginning with Bod (messenger), as Bodomar and Butolf.

Boelter (*Ger.*) Descendant of Baldher (bold, army).

Boening, Boenke (*Ger.*) Descendant of little Bon (alarm).

Boenisch (*Ger.*) Descendant of Boenisch, a pet form of Benedikt, German form of Benedict (blessed).

Boer (*Du.*) One who tilled the land, a farmer.

Boersma, Boerema (*Du.*) Descendant, or servant, of the farmer.

Boettcher, Boettger, Boetticher, Boettiger (*Ger.*) One who made or sold barrels or casks, a cooper.

Bogacz, Bogacki, Bogaczyk (*Pol.*) The rich or wealthy man.

Bogan, Boggan (*Ir.*) Grandson of Bogan (dim. of soft or tender).

Bogard, Bogart, Bogaart, Bogaert (*Du.*) One who worked in an orchard; dweller in, or near, the orchard.

Bogda (*Pol., Ukr.*) Descendant of Bogda, shortened form of Bogdan (gift of God).

Bogdan (*Rus., Pol.*) Descendant of Bogdan (gift of God).

Bogdanovich, Bogdanovic, Bogdanowicz, Bogdanski, Bogdanoff (*Rus., Pol., Bulg.*) The son of Bogdan (gift of God).

Bogen (*Ir., Eng., Ger.*) Descendant of Bogan, a pet form of Bog (soft, tender); dweller in the bog or marsh; or at the bend or corner.

Boger (*Nor.*) One who came from Boger (bend; winding), the name of two places in Norway.

Boggs, Bogg, Boggis, Bogges (*Eng.*) Dweller at, or near, a bog or marsh; the son of Boge or Boga (bow).

Boghosian, Bogosian (*Arm.*) Descendant of Boghos, Armenian form of Paul (small).

Bogie, Bogy (*Eng.*) Descendant of little Bogue, Boge or Boga (bow); dweller by the bend.

Bogner (*Eng., Ger.*) One who made and sold bows; an archer or crossbowman; variant of Boegner, q.v.

Bogren (*Sw.*) Farm branch.

Bogucki (*Pol.*) One who fears God.

Bogue, Boag (*Scot., Eng.*) One who came from Bogue (soft, moist), in Kirkcudbrightshire; descendant of Boge or Boga (bow).

Bogumil, Bogumill, Bogmil (*Ukr., Pol., Rus.*) Descendant of Bogumil (beloved of God).

Bogus, Boggus, Bogusz (*Pol.*) Descendant of Bogus, a shortened form of Boguslaw (God be praised).

Boguslaw, Boguslawski (*Pol., Rus.*) Descendant of Boguslaw (God be praised); one who came from Boguslaw, in Russia.

Bohac (*Cz.-Sl.*) The rich, wealthy man.

Bohachevsky (*Ukr.*) One who came from Bahachi (wealth), in the Ukraine; the wealthy man.

Bohan, Bohanan, Bohannan, Bohannon, Bohanon (*Ir.*) Grandson of little Buadhach (victorious).

Bohl, Bohle, Bohling, Bohlig, Bohlmann, Bohlman (*Ger.*) The bold or brave man; one who came from Bohl, in Germany.

Bohlander (*Ger.*) One who came from Bohland, in Germany.

Bohmann, Bohman, Bohm (*Ger.*) One who came from Bohemia (home of the Boii).

Bohn, Bohne, Bohnen (*Ger.*) Descendant of Bono, a pet form of names beginning with Bon (demand), as Bonard and Bonuald; one who grew and sold beans; one who came from Bohne, in Germany.

Bohnenberger (*Ger.*) One who came from Bohnenburg (bean fortress), the name of two places in Germany.

Bohnenkamp (*Ger.*) Dweller in or near the enclosure where beans were grown.

Bohren, Bohrer (*Ger.*) Dweller in, or near, the pine woods.

Boike, Boyke, Boyk (*Ger.*) Descendant of little Boye, a short form of Boethius (ennobling); descendant of the Boj (fight), an old Celtic tribe.

Boileau, Boilleau, Boileve (*Fr.*) One who drank water, an early nickname for a teetotaler.

Boinski (*Pol.*) One who worked with buoys.

Bois (*Fr.*) Dweller near, or in, a wood.

Boisvert (*Fr.*) Dweller in, or near, the green wood.

Boit (*Fr.*) One who made and sold boxes.

Bojan (*Yu.-Sl.*) Descendant of Bojana (fearful).

Bojczuk (*Pol.*) The timid or frightened man.

Bojko (*Ukr.*) One who came from the uplands in Western Ukrainia.

Bok (*Du.*) Descendant of Bok, a pet form of Burghard (castle, hard); one who took care of goats, a goatherd.

Boland, Bolan (*Eng.*) One who came from Bowland (land by the bend of the river), in Lancashire and the West Riding of Yorkshire.

Bolden (*Eng.*) One who came from Boldon (hill with a homestead), in Durham.

Boldt, Bold, Bolds (*Ger., Eng., Scot.*) Descendant of Baldo, a pet form of names beginning with Bald (bold or daring), as Baldhart, Baldher, and Baldawin; the bold or fierce man; dweller at a hall or mansion; a short, heavy man; one who came from Bold (dwelling), in Peeblesshire.

Bolek (*Pol.*) Descendant of Bolek, a pet form of Boleslaw (great fame).

Boleman, Boler (*Eng.*) One who made and sold wooden bowls and dishes.

Bolen, Bollen (*Eng.*) One who came from Boulogne (town), in France.

Boles, Bole (*Eng.*) One who came from Bole (tree trunk), in Nottinghamshire; or Bolas (wood where bows were obtained), in Shropshire; dweller at the sign of the bull; one with bullish characteristics; one who made and sold concave vessels or bowls.

Bolger, Bolgar (*Eng., Ir.*) One who made leather wallets or bags; the light-complexioned man.

Bolin, Bolen, Bollin (*Eng.*) Dweller near the Bollin, a river in Cheshire.

Bolingbroke (*Eng.*) One who came from Bolingbroke (the stream of the people of Bulla), in Lincolnshire.

Bolivar (*Wel.*) The son of Oliver (the olive; ancestor).

Boller (*Eng.*) One who made or sold bowls.

Bollinger, Bolling (*Ger., Swis.*) One who came from Bollingen, on Lake Zurich in Switzerland.

Bolotin (*Rus.*) Dweller on, or near, a marsh.

Bolster (*Eng.*) One who sifted meal; one who made bolts or arrows.

Bolt, Bolte (*Ger., Eng.*) Variant of Boldt, q.v.; one who made and sold bolts.

Bolter, Boulter (*Eng.*) One who made and sold bolts; one who sifts meal.

Boltinghouse (*Eng.*) Dweller near the building where meal was sifted.

Bolton, Boltin (*Eng., Scot.*) One who came from Bolton (dwelling enclosure), the name of various places in England and one in Scotland. In some instances it referred to one in the village proper in contradistinction to the outlying parts.

Boman (*Sw.*) Farm man.

Bombard (*It.*) The good man named Bard, a pet form of Bernardo, Italian form of Bernard (bear, hard).

Bonafede (*It.*) Descendant of Bonafede (good faith); the good, faithful man.

Bonaguro (*It.*) One who wished others well.

Bonamy (*Fr., Eng.*) One who was a good friend to others.

Bonanno (*It.*) One in the habit of wishing others a good year; one who had a good year.

Bonaparte, Bonapart (*It., Fr.*) Descendant of Bonaparte (good share).

Bonato (*It.*) Descendant of Buonatto (good act); one who performed some especially good act.

Bond, Bonde, Bonds (*Eng., Ice.*) A householder or a tiller of the soil; a peasant proprietor.

Bondar (*Ukr., Yu.-Sl.*) One who made and sold hoops, a hooper.

Bondarenko (*Ukr.*) The son of the hooper.

Bonder (*Eng.*) The kind, gentle man.

Bondi (*It.*) "Good day," perhaps a nickname of one who habitually used this salutation.

Bondurant (*Fr., It.*) The good man named Durand (lasting).

Bondy (*Eng.*) The husbandman or peasant.

Bone (*Eng.*) Descendant of Bone (the good).

Bonebrake (*Eng.*) Dweller in, or near, a good or pleasant thicket.

Bonehill (*Eng.*) One who came from Bonehill (hill of the bullock), in Staffordshire.

Bonelli, Bonello (*It.*) The small, good man.

Bones (*Eng.*) One so thin that his bones protruded; one who came from Bowness (rounded headland or bulls' headland), the name of places in Cumberland and Westmorland.

Boney (*Fr.*) The good, brave man.

Bonfield (*It.*) Englished variant of Bonfiglio, q.v.

Bonfiglio, Bonfilio, Bonfigli (*It.*) The good child.

Bongart, Bongard, Bongartz (*Ger.*) Dweller in, or near, an orchard or tree nursery.

Bongate, Bondgate (*Eng.*) One who came from Bongate (street of the bondmen or villeins), in Westmorland.

Bongiorno (*It.*) One in the habit of wishing others a good day; one born on an auspicious day.

Bongiovanni (*It.*) The good man named Giovanni, Italian form of John (gracious gift of Jehovah).

Bonham (*Eng.*) Nickname, the good man.

Boniface, Bonniface (*Eng.*) The fortunate man; descendant of Boniface (doer of good).

Bonifant (*Eng.*) The good child.

Bonifield (*Eng.*) Dweller near Buna's land.

Bonilla (*Sp.*) One who came from Bonilla (good), in Spain.

Bonk (*Pol.*) One having the characteristics of a horsefly.

Bonn (*Ger.*) One who came from Bonn (town) in Germany; descendant of Bone (the good).

Bonnamy (*Fr.*) Variant of Bonamy, q.v.

Bonneau (*Fr.*) Descendant of Bonwald (good, forest).

Bonnell (*Scot., Ger.*) One who came from Bonhill (house by the stream), in Scotland; descendant of little Bono, a pet form of names beginning with Bon (demand), as Bonard and Bonuald.

Bonnema (*Du.*) The son of Bonne, a Frisian pet form of Bonifacius (doer of good).

Bonner (*Eng., Wel., Ger.*) The kind, gentle person; the son of Ynyr (honor); one who came from Bonn (town), in Germany.

Bonnet, Bonnett, Bonnette (*Fr., Eng.*) Descendant of little Bonne, French form of Bonitus (goodly), an eighth century French saint; one who made and sold bonnets.

Bonney, Bonny (*Eng.*) The good, kind person.

Bonniwell (*Eng.*) One who came from Bonneville (the good village; Bunno's village), the name of several villages in France.

Bono, Buono (*It.*) The good, generally a shortened form of some compound name.

Bonomo, Bonomi (*It.*) The good man, or good-natured fellow; a simpleton.

Bonow (*Rus., Pol.*) Descendant of the nursery governess.

Bonseigneur (*Fr.*) One who was a good or respected lord of the manor.

Bonwit (*Eng.*) One who came from Bonwick (Buna's dairy farm), in the East Riding of Yorkshire.

Bonzani (*It.*) The attractive or good Zani, a pet form of Giovanni, Italian form of John (gracious gift of Jehovah).

Bood, Boode (*Du.*) Descendant of Bote (order).

Boodberg (*Sw.*) Booth mountain.

Boodell, Boodle (*Du.*) One employed as an usher or sheriff's officer, also as an executioner.

Booker, Book (*Eng., Ger.*) One who copies books; one who bleaches or whitens cloth; dweller at, or near, a beech tree.

Bookham (*Eng.*) One who came from Bookham (village by beeches), in Surrey.

Bookman, Booker (*Eng.*) One who wrote books, a scribe.

Boom (*Du.*) Dweller near a tree.

Boone, Boon, Bowne (*Eng., Wel.*) One who came from Bohon, in France; the son of Owen (young warrior; well-born).

Boonstra (*Du.*) Dweller near a spring or fountain.

Boord (*Du.*) Dweller near the border or boundary; or on the river bank.

Boose, Boos (*Du., Eng.*) Same as Booz, q.v.

Boot, Boote, Boots (*Du., Eng.*) Descendant of Bote (order); one who made and sold boots and shoes; the son of Bote (messenger).

Booth (*Eng.*) Dweller at a hut or stall, especially a herdsman's hut.

Boothby (*Eng.*) One who came from Boothby (village with huts or stalls), in Lincolnshire.

Boothroyd (*Eng.*) One who came from

51

Boothroyd (hut in a clearing; Bud's clearing), in the West Riding of Yorkshire.

Booz, Booze, Boozer (*Du., Eng.*) The angry, or cross, man; descendant of Boaz (in Him is strength); dweller near the cattle stall.

Bopp (*Ger.*) Descendant of Bube (lad), but usually a lall name.

Borak (*Pol.*) One who grew and sold beets.

Borchardt, Borchert, Borchering (*Ger.*) Descendant of Burghard (castle, strong).

Borde (*Fr.*) Dweller in a house made of planks or boards; one who operated a small farm on lease.

Bordeau, Bordeaux (*Fr.*) Dweller on the little farm; one who came from Bordeaux (little farm), in France.

Borden (*Eng.*) One who came from Borden (swine pasture hill), in Kent.

Borders, Bordner, Border (*Eng.*) One who held a cottage in the English manor, at his lord's pleasure, for which he rendered menial service.

Borek (*Pol., Cz.-Sl.*) One who came from Borek, the name of two places in Poland, and several places in Czechoslovakia.

Borg, Borge, Borgen (*Sw., Nor., Ger.*) Dweller in, or near, a fortified castle; one who came from Borg (stronghold), the name of several places in Germany.

Borgardt, Borgard, Borgert (*Ger.*) Descendant of Burghard (castle, strong).

Borgersen (*Nor.*) The son of Borger (defender).

Borglum (*Dan.*) One who came from Borglum (stronghold way), in Denmark.

Borgman, Borgmann (*Ger., Du.*) One who borrows or lends money or goods; descendant of Burgman (castle, man).

Boris (*Hun., Cz.-Sl.*) Descendant of Boris (stranger).

Bork (*Pol.*) An abbreviated form of Borowski, q.v.

Borland (*Scot.*) One who came from

Borland (home farm), the name of several places in Scotland.

Borlàse (*Eng.*) Dweller on the green bank or shore.

Born, Borne (*Eng., Ger.*) Dweller at the brook or spring.

Bornstein (*Ger.*) Dweller near a stony spring.

Borodin (*Ukr.*) The son of the man with the long beard.

Boros (*Hun.*) One who fermented and sold wine.

Borowski, Borkowski (*Pol.*) Dweller in a small wood.

Borrelli, Borrello (*It.*) A hangman or executioner; one who made collars or horse collars.

Borromeo (*It.*) One who has made a pilgrimage.

Borrows, Borroughs (*Eng.*) Dweller in, or near, a stronghold or fortified place; dweller on, or near, a hill.

Borsody (*Hun.*) One who came from the county of Borsod.

Borst (*Ger.*) One who had bristly hair.

Borucki (*Pol.*) One who came from Boruty (Boruta's place), a village in Poland.

Bos, Bose (*Fr., Du., Ger.*) Dweller in, or near, the woods; the quarrelsome man; descendant of Boso (wicked).

Bosanko (*Eng.*) Dweller in the wood.

Bosch (*Ger., Du.*) Dweller at the wood or woodland; or near a bush.

Bosco (*It.*) Dweller in, or near, a woods.

Boscombe (*Eng.*) One who came from Boscombe (bristle valley), in Wiltshire.

Bosher (*Eng.*) One who sold wood, a woodmonger.

Boskey, Bosky, Boski (*Pol.*) The godlike or divine man; one accepted by God.

Bosley (*Eng.*) One who came from Bosley (Bosa's wood), in Cheshire.

Bosman (*Du.*) The official in charge of the forest; one who worked, or lived, in the woods.

Boss, Bosse (*Eng.*) Dweller at a wood; a fat person.

Bosshart (*Eng.*) Dweller in, or near, a

wood where harts or stags were found.

Bost (*Eng.*) One addicted to boasting and bragging.

Bostick, Bostic (*Eng.*) One who came from Bostock (Bota's cell), in Cheshire.

Boston (*Eng.*) One who came from Boston (St. Botulf's stone), a village in Lincolnshire.

Bostrom (*Sw.*) Farm stream.

Boswell (*Eng.*) One who came from Bosville (wood town), a village in Normandy.

Bostwick, Boswick, Bostock (*Eng.*) One who came from Bostock (Bota's cell), in Cheshire.

Bosworth (*Eng.*) One who came from Bosworth (Bar's or Bosa's homestead), in Leicestershire.

Both, Bothe (*Eng.*) Variants of Booth, q.v.

Botham (*Eng.*) Dweller in the valley.

Bothfield, Bothfeld (*Eng.*) Dweller in the hut in the open field.

Bothwell (*Scot.*) One who came from Bothwell (booth by the fish pool), in Lanarkshire.

Botley (*Eng.*) One who came from Botley (Bota's grove), the name of several places in England; dweller in the grove where villagers could take timber for repairs or firewood.

Botsford (*Eng.*) One who came from Bottesford (house by the river crossing), the name of places in Leicestershire and Lincolnshire.

Botsmith (*Eng.*) One who made metal fittings on boats, perhaps a boatbuilder.

Bott, Botte, Botts (*Eng.*) Descendant of Bota, Botta, Boto or Bote (messenger); one thought to resemble a toad.

Botticelli (*It.*) One who made small barrels or casks; descendant of little Botto, a pet form of Giacobotto, variant of Giacomo, Italian form of James (may God protect; the supplanter).

Bottom, Bottome, Bottoms, Bottum (*Eng.*) Dweller in the valley.

Bottomley (*Eng.*) Dweller in the valley grove.

Botwell (*Eng.*) One who came from Botwell (healing spring), in Middlesex.

Boucher, Bouchier, Boucharin (*Fr.*) One who cut and sold meats, a butcher.

Boudreau (*Fr.*) Descendant of Botthar (messenger, army).

Bouffard (*Fr.*) The man who overeats, the glutton or gourmand.

Boughey (*Eng.*) Dweller by an enclosed bog or swamp.

Boughton (*Eng.*) One who came from Boughton (homestead where beeches grew; Bucca's homestead), the name of several places in England.

Bouknight (*Ger.*) The servant who uses the plow, a plowman.

Boulanger (*Fr.*) One who made bread, a baker.

Boulden, Bouldin, Bouldon (*Eng.*) One who came from Bouldon (Bula's or Bulla's hill; Bula's people), in Shropshire.

Boulton (*Eng.*) One who came from Boulton (Bola's homestead), in Derbyshire.

Boulware (*Fr., Eng.*) One who came from Boulois (birch tree); dweller near where birch trees grew; or near the weir or dam where bullocks were kept.

Bounds, Bound, Boundy (*Eng.*) A householder or a tiller of the soil; a peasant proprietor.

Bourgeois (*Fr.*) Dweller in the town, a townsman, a citizen.

Bourke, Bourk (*Ir.*) Dweller at, or near, a stronghold or fortified place.

Bourne, Bourn (*Eng.*) Dweller near the brook or stream.

Boutet (*Fr.*) Descendant of little Boto (messenger).

Boutwell (*Eng.*) Same as Bothwell, q.v.; dweller at a hall or mansion.

Bouvier, Bouyer (*Fr.*) One who took care of cattle.

Bova (*It.*) Descendant of Bova or Bovo (ox). Bova was the seventh century Virgin Martyr, daughter of King Sigibert of Austrasia.

Bove (*Ger.*) The boy or young servant, a nickname given usually in contempt.

Bovenkerk (*Du.*) Dweller, or worker, at the high or upper church.

Bovey (*Eng.*) One who came from Bovey, on the Bovey river in Devonshire.

Bovino (*It.*) One who was like an ox, sluggish and dull.

Bow, Bowe (*Eng.*) Dweller by the arched bridge; one who came from Bow (arched bridge), in Devonshire; descendant of Boga (bow).

Bowcock (*Eng.*) Descendant of little Bald, a pet form of names beginning with Bald (bold), as Baldwin and Baldric.

Bowden (*Eng., Scot.*) One who came from Bowden (Bucge's pasture), the name of several places in England; or from Bowden (house on the hill), in Scotland.

Bowditch, Bowdish (*Eng.*) One who came from Bowditch (arched bridge ditch), in Dorsetshire.

Bowdoin (*Fr.*) A partially Englished variant of Beaudoin, q.v.

Bowen (*Wel.*) The son of Owen, Welsh form of Eugene (well-born).

Bower, Bowers (*Eng., Scot.*) Dweller in a cottage or chamber; one who came from Bower (house), in Peeblesshire; one who built houses; one who made and sold bows.

Bowes (*Eng.*) One who came from Bowes (bows, probably referring to an arched bridge), in Yorkshire; descendant of Boga (bow).

Bowie (*Ir., Scot.*) Grandson of little Buadhach or Buagh (victorious); one who had yellow, or fair, hair.

Bowker (*Eng.*) A variant of Booker, q.v.; one who had charge of money; one who cut and sold meat, a butcher.

Bowland, Bowlan (*Eng.*) One who came from Bowland (land by the bend of the river), in Lancashire and the West Riding of Yorkshire.

Bowles, Bowler (*Eng., Wel.*) One who made or sold concave vessels or bowls; the son of Howel (eminent).

Bowling, Bowlin (*Eng.*) One who came from Bowling (dip in ground near a hill), in the West Riding of Yorkshire; dweller in, or near, the bull pasture.

Bowman (*Eng., Scot.*) A fighting man armed with a bow; one who made bows; the servant in charge of the cattle.

Bowser (*Fr.*) One who made and sold purses.

Bowsmith (*Eng.*) One who made bows; the later ones, especially the strong crossbows, were made of steel.

Bowthorpe (*Eng.*) One who came from Bowthorpe (Bo's farm, Bula's farm) the name of places in Norfolk and the East Riding of Yorkshire.

Bowyer (*Eng.*) One who made or sold bows.

Box (*Eng.*) Dweller near the box-tree.

Boxford (*Eng.*) One who came from Boxford (ford or shore where box grew), the name of places in Berkshire and Suffolk.

Boxley (*Eng.*) One who came from Boxley (box wood) in Kent.

Boxton (*Eng.*) Dweller at a homestead where box grew.

Boxwell (*Eng.*) One who came from Boxwell (stream where box grew), in Gloucestershire.

Boy, Boye (*Eng., Fr.*) Dweller near, or in, the wood.

Boyajian, Boyadjian (*Arm.*) One who colored cloth, a dyer.

Boyce, Boece (*Fr.*) Dweller near, or in, a wood.

Boycott (*Eng.*) One who came from Boycott (Boia's cottage; shelter for sheep), in Buckinghamshire.

Boyd (*Ir., Eng.*) One who had yellow hair; dweller by the Boyd river, in Gloucestershire.

Boyer (*Eng., Fr.*) One who made and sold bows; one who took care of, or drove, cattle.

Boyersmith (*Eng.*) One who made bows. See Bowsmith.

Boykin, Boykins (*Eng., Du.*) Descendant

of the little boy, usually a nickname for a small, mild man.

Boylan, Boyland (*Eng.*) One who came from Boyland (Boia's grove), in Norfolk.

Boyle, Boyles, Boyell, Boyll, Boyl (*Ir., Scot.*) Grandson of Baoigheall (vain pledge); one who came from Beauville, the name of two places in France.

Boynton (*Eng.*) One who came from Boynton (village of Bofa's people), in Yorkshire.

Boys, Boyes (*Fr.*) Variant of Bois, q.v.

Boysen (*Ger.*) The son of Boye or Boje (fight).

Bozek (*Pol.*) Dweller at the sign of the heathen god.

Bozeman, Boze (*Eng.*) One who took care of cows.

Bozich, Bozic (*Yu.-Sl.*) The servant of God, literally God's son.

Braasch (*Ger.*) The noisy, blustering, rowdy man; the coarse, rude, uncouth person.

Brabant, Braband, Brabandt, Brabazon (*Eng., Fr., Du., Bel.*) One who came from Brabant (uncultivated land), an old duchy in Holland and a province in Belgium.

Brabbs (*Eng.*) Dweller in the fallow, uncultivated field or district; one who came from Brabant (Flanders).

Brabec (*Cz.*) Dweller at the sign of the sparrow.

Braben, Brabin, Brabon (*Eng.*) Same as Brabant, q.v.

Brace (*Wel., Eng.*) The thick, bulky, strong man; dweller at the sign of the arm; one who made bracing-girdles, a kind of belt.

Bracewell (*Eng.*) One who came from Bracewell (Braegd's or Breith's spring), in the West Riding of Yorkshire.

Bracey, Bracy (*Eng.*) One who came from Brassy or Brécy, in France.

Brach, Brachman (*Ger.*) Dweller on, or near, the fallow land.

Brack, Bracke (*Fr., Eng.*) Metonymic for one in charge of the hounds that hunt by scent; descendant of Bracca; dweller on a strip of untilled land.

Bracken, Brackin (*Eng.*) One who came from Bracken (fern), in Yorkshire.

Brackenridge (*Scot., Eng.*) Dweller at the fern ridge; one who came from Brackenrig in the old barony of Avondale in Lanarkshire.

Brackett (*Eng.*) Dweller at the sign of the little hunting dog.

Brackley (*Eng.*) One who came from Brackley (Bracca's grove), in Northamptonshire.

Brackney (*Eng.*) Dweller on the island where bracken grew; one who came from Bradney (broad island), in Somerset.

Bradac (*Eng.*) Dweller at the large oak.

Bradbrook (*Eng.*) Dweller near the broad stream.

Bradburn (*Eng.*) One who came from Bradbourne (wide stream), in Derbyshire.

Bradbury, Bradberry (*Eng.*) One who came from Bradbury (fort built of boards), in Durham.

Braddock (*Eng.*) One who came from Braddock or Broadoak (broad oak), the name of a village in Cornwall.

Braden, Braddan, Bradeen (*Eng.*) One who came from Bradden (broad valley), in Northamptonshire, or Bradon or Braydon, in Somerset and Wiltshire, respectively.

Bradfield (*Eng.*) One who came from Bradfield (wide plain), the name of several villages in England.

Bradfish (*Eng.*) One who caught and sold broad or flat fish.

Bradford (*Eng.*) One who came from Bradford (wide ford), the name of various places in England.

Bradham (*Eng.*) Dweller in the big homestead or manor house.

Bradley (*Eng.*) One who came from Bradley (wide meadow), the name of many places in England.

Bradshaw (*Eng.*) One who came from Bradshaw (extensive grove), in Derbyshire; dweller in, or near, the big woods.

55

Bradstreet (*Eng.*) Dweller on the broad paved way.

Bradtke, Bratke (*Cz.-Sl., Pol., Ger.*) Descendant of the little brother; or of little Brado (brother); dweller at the sign of the little bear.

Bradwell (*Eng.*) One who came from Bradwell or Broadwell (wide stream), the names of several places in England.

Brady, Bradie (*Ir., Eng.*) The son of Bradach (spirited); dweller on the broad island.

Bragg, Braggs (*Eng.*) Descendant of Brego (chief).

Braham, Brayham (*Eng.*) One who came from Braham (broom enclosure), in the West Riding of Yorkshire; descendant of Braham, a shortened form of Abraham (father of a multitude).

Brahill (*Eng.*) Dweller on, or near, the Bre Hill. Bre is a Welsh and Cornish word meaning a hill, so this name really translates as hill hill.

Brahm (*Ger.*) Dweller in, or near, a marshy copse or thicket.

Brahms (*Ger.*) Descendant of Brahm, a pet form of Abraham (father of a multitude).

Braidman (*Eng.*) The large or broad man.

Braidwood (*Eng., Scot.*) Dweller at the wide wood or forest; one who came from Braidwood (broad wood), in Lanarkshire.

Brailey, Braley (*Eng.*) Dweller at the grove on the hill-slope.

Brain, Brayne, Braine (*Eng., Ir.*) Descendant of Bregen (prince); grandson of Bran (raven); one who came from Brain, in France.

Brainerd, Brainard (*Eng.*) Descendant of Brandhard (sword, hard).

Braithwaite, Brathwaite, Breathwaite (*Eng.*) One who came from Braithwaite (broad clearing), the name of places in Cumberland and Yorkshire.

Brake, Brakes (*Eng.*) Dweller in a copse or thicket.

Brakewood (*Eng.*) Dweller in, or near, a wood where brake or brushwood grew.

Bram, Brame (*Eng.*) Same as Braham, q.v.

Bramhall, Bramall (*Eng.*) One who came from Bramhall (broom corner), in Cheshire.

Bramlett, Bramlette, Bramlatt (*Eng.*) Descendant of little Bram, a shortened form of Abraham (father of a multitude.

Bramley (*Eng.*) One who came from Bramley (clearing overgrown with broom), the name of several places in England.

Brammer, Bramah (*Eng.*) Dweller in the broom-covered corner.

Bramson (*Ger.*) The son of Bram, a shortened form of Abraham (father of a multitude).

Bramwell (*Eng.*) Dweller near the spring where bramble grew.

Bran (*Eng., Heb.*) Variant of Brand, q.v.; an acronym for Ben Rabbi Nachman.

Branch, Branche (*Eng., Fr.*) One who came from Branche (bow), in Normandy; descendant of Branca or Brancher (ruler), names of two early saints; a name referring to the "day of branches," i.e., Palm Sunday.

Brand (*Eng.*) Descendant of Brand (firebrand; sword).

Brandeis, Brandes (*Ger., Cz.-Sl.*) Dweller on a burnt clearing; one who came from Brandeis, the name of three places in Bohemia.

Brandenburg, Brandenburger (*Ger.*) One who came from Brandenburg, a district in northern Germany.

Brandford (*Eng.*) Dweller near a river crossing where ravens congregated.

Brandon, Brandin (*Eng., Fr.*) One who came from Brandon (broom hill), the name of several villages in England; descendant of little Brand (sword); one who carried the firebrand or torch.

Brandt, Brant (*Ger., Eng.*) Dweller on a farm cleared by burning; dweller near the Brant (steep), a river in Lincolnshire.

Brandy (*Du., Fr.*) Descendant of Brand (firebrand; flaming sword; sword).

Branham, Brannam (*Eng.*) One who came from Brantham (Branta's homestead), in Suffolk.

Branick (*Cz.-Sl.*) Descendant of the captive.

Braniff (*Ir.*) Grandson of Branduibh (black raven).

Brann, Bran (*Eng., Sp.*) Descendant of Bran (raven); or of Berardo (man, valiant).

Brannigan, Branigan (*Ir.*) Grandson of little Bran (raven).

Brannon, Brannan (*Eng., Ir.*) Descendant of little Bran (raven).

Branscomb, Branscombe, Branscom (*Eng.*) One who came from Branscombe (Branoc's valley), in Devonshire.

Bransfield (*Eng.*) One who came from Bramfield (steep field; Brant's field), in Hertfordshire.

Bransky (*Pol.*) One taken into captivity, a prisoner.

Branson (*Eng.*) The son of Brand (sword).

Brantley, Brantly (*Eng.*) One who lived at, or near, the meadow where broom grew; one who came from Bramley (clearing overgrown with broom), the name of various places in England.

Brashear, Brashears, Brasher (*Eng.*) One who worked with brass.

Brasseur (*Fr.*) One who brewed beer or ale.

Brassington (*Eng.*) One who came from Brassington (homestead by the steep path), in Derbyshire.

Braswell (*Eng.*) One who came from Braithwell (broad stream), in the West Riding of Yorkshire.

Bratcher, Bracher (*Ger.*) Dweller on, or near, unplowed land.

Bratt (*Eng.*) One who came from Brittany, a Breton; dweller on a steep place or hillside.

Bratton (*Eng.*) One who came from Brat-

ton (newly cultivated homestead), the name of four places in England.

Braude, Braud (*Fr.*) Descendant of Braud, a contracted form of Berwald (bear, rule); the rough, uncouth man; dweller in a muddy place.

Brauer, Brower (*Ger., Du.*) One who brewed beer.

Braun, Brauneis, Braune (*Ger., Cz.*) One with a dark-brown complexion.

Braunschweiger, Braunschweig (*Ger.*) One who came from Braunschweig (Bruno's country), a city and former state in Germany.

Braunsdorf (*Ger.*) Dweller at the brown settlement.

Braunstein (*Ger.*) Dweller at the brown stone.

Brautigam (*Ger.*) One who is betrothed, a fiancé; the recent bridegroom.

Braverman, Braver (*Ger.*) One who brews beer and ale.

Bravo (*It., Sp.*) The good, honest, courageous man.

Brawley (*Scot.*) Dweller on the broad meadow.

Brawner (*Ger.*) Descendant of Brunheri (brown, army).

Braxley (*Eng.*) One who came from Brackley (Bracca's meadow), in Northamptonshire.

Braxton (*Eng.*) One who lived at, or near, Bracca's boundary mark.

Bray, Braye (*Eng.*) One who came from Bray (brow of a hill), the name of places in Berkshire and Devonshire; one who came from Bray (muddy place), the name of several places in France; the brave man; dweller on a hill.

Braydon (*Eng.*) One who came from Braydon, in Wiltshire.

Brayshaw (*Eng.*) One who came from Bradshaw (broad wood), in the West Riding of Yorkshire; dweller in the copse on the hillside.

Brazelton (*Eng.*) Dweller at a place where sulphate of iron, or a red dyewood, was worked.

Brazier, Brasier (*Eng., Fr.*) One who worked in brass.

Brazley (*Eng.*) One who came from Brisley (gadfly-infested grove), in Norfolk.

Breadman (*Eng.*) The large, broad man; one with broad shoulders.

Breadon (*Eng.*) Variant of Breeden, q.v.

Breakey (*Eng.*) Dweller on an island where brake grew.

Brearley (*Eng.*) Dweller at the briar wood; one who came from Brierly (homestead where briars grew), in the West Riding of Yorkshire.

Breault (*Fr.*) Dweller in an enclosed wood.

Breckenridge, Breckinridge (*Scot.*) Dweller at the fern ridge or hill; one who came from the lands of Brackenrig (ridge overgrown with bracken), in Lanarkshire.

Breden, Bredine, Bredon (*Eng.*) One who came from Bredon (hill hill) in Worcestershire. Both elements of this name mean "hill."

Bredfield (*Eng.*) One who came from Bredfield (broad strip of cultivated land), in Suffolk.

Breece (*Wel.*) The son of Rhys (ardor, a rush).

Breed, Breede, Brede (*Eng., Du.*) One who came from Brede (flat expanse), in Sussex; dweller on the plain; the large broad-shouldered man.

Breeden, Breeding, Breedon (*Eng.*) One who came from Breedon (hill hill), in Leicestershire. Both elements of this name mean "hill."

Breedlove (*Eng.*) Dweller near a wide pool.

Breen (*Ir.*) Grandson of Braon (sorrow); variant of O'Brien, q.v.

Breese, Breeze (*Wel.*) The son of Rhys (ardor, a rush).

Brefford (*Eng.*) One who came from Bretford (ford provided with planks), in Warwickshire.

Breger, Bregar, Bregger (*Ger.*) Dweller on the bank of a river; one who begs for alms.

Bregman (*Du., Eng.*) Dweller near the bridge; the keeper of a bridge; dweller on the brow of a hill.

Bregstone (*Eng.*) One who came from Brighstone (Beorhtwig's homestead), in Wight.

Brehm (*Ger.*) The restless man, a gadfly.

Breidenbach (*Ger.*) One who came from Breidenbach, in Germany.

Breier, Briar (*Eng.*) Dweller in the briar bushes.

Breit (*Ger.*) Dweller at the broad or wide place.

Breitbart, Breitbarth (*Ger.*) One who had a broad beard.

Breitenbach (*Swis., Ger.*) One who came from Breitenbach (settlement by a wide brook), in Switzerland; or from Breitenbach (broad stream), the name of several places in Germany; dweller near a wide stream; one with a big stomach.

Breland (*Eng.*) Dweller on the brow of a hill.

Brelsford, Brellisford (*Eng.*) One who came from Brailesford (burial place by the ford), in Derbyshire.

Bremer, Bremen (*Ger.*) One who came from Bremen (by the seashore), in Germany.

Bremhill (*Eng.*) One who came from Bremhill (bramble), in Wiltshire.

Brendel, Brendle (*Eng.*) One who came from Brindle (hill by a stream), in Lancashire.

Brenna (*Nor.*) Dweller on land cleared by burning.

Brennan, Brennen (*Ir.*) Grandson of little Bran (raven).

Brenneman (*Ger.*) Dweller near a spring.

Brenner (*Eng.*) One who burned brick or charcoal, a burner.

Brennock, Brenock (*Scot.*) One who came from Brechnock, in Wales.

Brent (*Eng.*) One who came from Brent (high place), in Devonshire; dweller near the Brent river in Middlesex.

Brentano (*It., Ger.*) One who came from Brenta (bowl), in Italy; dweller near the Brenta river, in Italy.

Brentford (*Eng.*) One who came from Brentford (hill ford; holy river ford), the name of places in Buckinghamshire and Middlesex.

Brenton (*Eng.*) One who came from Brinton (Bryni's homestead), in Norfolk.

Brereton (*Eng.*) One who came from Brereton (homestead where briars grew; briar hill), the name of places in Cheshire and Staffordshire.

Breshers, Breshears (*Eng.*) Variant of Brashear, q.v.

Bresingham, Bressingham (*Eng.*) One who came from Bressingham (the village of Briosa's people), in Norfolk.

Breslin, Bresland (*Ir.*) Descendant of little Breasal (strife; war).

Bresnahan, Bresnihan (*Ir.*) Variants of Brosnahan, q.v.

Bressler, Bresler, Breslau, Breslauer (*Ger.*) One who came from Breslau (named after King Vratislaw), in Silesia.

Bretford (*Eng.*) One who came from Bretford (ford provided with planks), in Warwickshire.

Breton, Bretton (*Eng.*) One who came from Bretton (newly cultivated enclosure), the name of places in Derbyshire and the West Riding of Yorkshire.

Brett, Bret (*Fr., Ger.*) One who came from Brette, the name of two places in France; one who came from Bretagne or Brittany, in France; descendant of Briddo (bridle).

Bretz (*Ger.*) Descendant of Briddo (bridle).

Brew (*Eng.*) Dweller at the brow of the hill.

Brewer, Brewster (*Eng.*) One who brewed beer or ale.

Brewerton (*Eng.*) Dweller at the brewer's enclosure.

Brewington (*Eng.*) One who came from Breinton (the village of Bryni's people), in Herefordshire.

Breyer, Breier, Breuer (*Ger.*) One who brewed beer; one who came from Brey, in Germany.

Brezina (*Cz.-Sl.*) One who came from Brezina (place of birch trees), the name of many places in Czechoslovakia.

Briand (*Fr.*) The erect, eminent, dignified man.

Brice (*Wel., Ir.*) The son of Rhys (ardor, a rush); descendant of Brice (speedy).

Brick, Bricks, Bricker (*Eng.*) Dweller in, or near, the heath or fallowland; dweller on a strip of newly cultivated land.

Brickett (*Eng.*) One who came from Bricett (place infested by horseflies), in Suffolk.

Brickley (*Eng.*) Dweller at, or on, the meadow newly broken up for cultivation.

Brickman (*Eng.*) Dweller near a bridge; dweller on a heath or on fallow land.

Briden (*Eng.*) Same as Breden, q.v.

Bridgeforth, Bridgeford, Bridgforth (*Eng.*) One who came from Bridgford (ford with a footbridge), the name of several places in England.

Bridgeman, Bridgman, Briggeman (*Eng.*) The keeper of a bridge; dweller near a bridge.

Bridger, Bridgers (*Eng.*) Dweller by, or keeper of, a bridge.

Bridges, Bridge (*Eng.*) Dweller at, or near, a bridge. Repair of bridges was regarded as among the "three necessary duties" of all landowners.

Bridgewater (*Eng.*) One who came from Bridgwater (the bridge), in Somerset, originally being the bridge belonging to Walter de Dowai.

Brien (*Eng.*) Descendant of Brian (strong).

Briercliffe (*Eng.*) One who came from Briercliffe (steep place where briars grew), in Lancashire.

Brierly, Brierley (*Eng.*) One who came from Brierly (glade where briars grew), in the West Riding of Yorkshire.

Brieschke, Brieske (*Ger.*) Dweller in, or near, the birch trees.

Briggins (*Eng.*) Dweller at the end of the bridge.

Briggle (*Eng.*) One who came from Brigsley (grove by a bridge), in Lincolnshire.

Briggs, Brigg (*Scot., Eng.*) Dweller neai a bridge.

Brigham (*Eng.*) One who came from Brigham (homestead by the bridge), the name of places in Cumberland and Yorkshire.

Bright, Breit, Brite (*Eng., Ger.*) Descendant of Beorht (bright); the big, broad man.

Brightly (*Eng.*) One who came from Brightley, in Devonshire.

Brighton (*Eng.*) One who came from Brighton (Beorhthelm's homestead), in Sussex.

Brightwell (*Eng.*) One who came from Brightwell (bright spring), the name of several places in England.

Briley, Brilley (*Eng.*) One who came from Brilley (burnt clearing), in Herefordshire.

Brill, Brille (*Eng., Du., Ger., Heb.*) One who came from Brill (hill), in Buckinghamshire; one who came from The Brille, in Holland; one who made, or wore, spectacles; one who came from Brill, the name of four places in Germany; an abbreviation of Ben Rabbi Judah Lowe.

Brim, Brimm (*Eng.*) Dweller on rough, rugged ground.

Brimage (*Eng.*) One who came from Bromwich (farm where broom grew), the name of places in Staffordshire and Warwickshire.

Brimfield (*Eng.*) One who came from Brimfield (bramble field), in Herefordshire.

Brimley (*Eng.*) Dweller at Bream's grove.

Brimmer (*Eng., Ger.*) Descendant of Beorhtmaer (fair, famous); Americanization of Brummer, q.v.

Brimson (*Eng.*) One who came from Briençun, in Normandy; the son of Bream.

Brinchman (*Nor., Sw., Dan.*) Dweller on a slope or side of a hill.

Brindell, Brindel, Brindle (*Eng.*) One who came from Brindle (hill by a stream), in Lancashire.

Brindise, Brindisi (*It.*) One who came from Brindisi (a toast, a drink in honor of someone), in Italy.

Brindley, Brindle (*Eng.*) One who came from Brindley (burnt wood), in Cheshire, or from Brindle (hill by a stream), in Lancashire.

Brink (*Eng., Du.*) Dweller at the edge or slope of a hill; dweller near the grassy place or hill.

Brinkley (*Eng.*) Dweller at the edge of the grove.

Brinkman, Brink, Brinkmann, Brinker (*Ger., Du.*) Dweller on, or near, the grassy hill; or by the village green.

Brinkworth (*Eng.*) One who came from Brinkworth (Brynca's homestead), in Wiltshire.

Brinsden (*Eng.*) Dweller in, or near, Brun's woodland pasture.

Brinson (*Eng.*) One who came from Briençun, in Normandy.

Brinton, Brinston (*Eng.*) One who came from Brinton (the village of Bryni's people), in Norfolk.

Brisbane, Brisben (*Eng., Scot.*) Nickname for the official torturer who broke bones.

Briscoe, Brisco (*Eng.*) One who came from Briscoe (birch wood), the name of places in Cumberland and Yorkshire.

Brison (*Eng.*) Variant of Bryson, q.v.

Bristol, Bristow, Bristoe, Bristle (*Eng.*) One who came from Bristol (the site of the bridge), in Gloucestershire.

Britt (*Eng.*) One who came from Brit (the port or borough belonging to Bredy), in Dorset.

Brittenham (*Eng.*) One who came from Brettenham (Bretta's homestead; the Britons' village), in Norfolk.

Britteridge (*Eng.*) Dweller at a steep ridge; on newly-plowed land on a ridge; descendant of Brictric (bright, rule).

Britton, Brittain, Briton, Britten, Brittin (*Eng.*) One who came from Brittany (figure picture), a region in France.

Bro (*Sw., Nor.*) Bridge; dweller near a bridge.

Broach, Broatch (*Scot.*) One who came from Broats, in Scotland.

Broadbent (*Eng.*) Dweller on, or near, the wide grassy plain.

Broadfoot (*Scot., Eng.*) One who came from Bradfute (foot of hill place), a lost place name formerly either in Ayrshire or Dumfriesshire; one who came from Bradford (wide river crossing), the name of several places in England.

Broadford (*Eng.*) Dweller near a wide stream crossing; or a wide way across a stream.

Broadhead, Brodhead (*Eng.*) One who had a big head; dweller at the wide headland.

Broadway (*Eng.*) One who came from Broadway (wide road), the name of places in Somerset and Worcestershire.

Broadwell (*Eng.*) One who came from Broadwell (wide stream), the name of places in Gloucestershire, Oxfordshire, and Warwickshire.

Broady (*Scot.*) One who came from Brodie (muddy place; little ditch), in Moray.

Broberg (*Sw.*) Bridge mountain.

Brock, Brocker, Brocks (*Eng., Heb.*) Dweller on the newly cleared and enclosed land; dweller near the stream or marsh land; dweller at the sign of the badger; one who lived near the Brock river, in Lancashire; abbreviation of Ben Rabbi Kalman.

Brockington (*Eng.*) One who came from Brockington (the village of the dwellers on the brook), in Dorset.

Brockley (*Eng.*) One who came from Brockley (grove by the brook), the name of several villages in England.

Brockman, Brockmann (*Eng.*) Dweller at a brook.

Brockway (*Eng.*) Dweller by the road along the brook.

Brockwell (*Eng.*) Dweller at the stream frequented by badgers.

Brod, Broda (*Pol., Ger., Cz.-Sl.*) One who had an unusual beard; one who came from Broda, in Mecklenburg; dweller at a ford.

Broder (*Nor., Sw., Eng.*) Descendant of the brother; a brother or kinsman.

Broderick (*Wel.*) The son of Rhodri (circle, rule), or Roderick (famous, rule).

Brodkorb (*Ger.*) One who sold bread; dweller at the sign of the bread basket.

Brodny (*Rus.*) One who lived near a shallow stream crossing.

Brodsky (*Cz., Ukr., Rus.*) One who came from Brody (ford), in the Ukraine; one with an unusual beard.

Brody, Brodie (*Ir., Scot., Ger., Rus.*) The son of Bruaideadh (fragment); one who came from the barony of Brodie (muddy place; little ditch), in Moray; one who had an unusual beard; one who came from Brody (ford; swamp), in Russia.

Broeker, Broecker (*Du.*) Dweller in the marsh or wet meadow.

Broekhuizen (*Du.*) One who came from Broekhuizen (house on a marsh), in Holland.

Broemel (*Eng., Ger.*) One who came from Bremhill (bramble hill), in Wiltshire; dweller near a bramble or blackberry bush; descendant of Broemel, a variant of Brumo, a pet form of names beginning with Brun (brown), as Brunold and Brunomund.

Brogan (*Ir.*) Grandson of little Brog (sorrowful).

Brogsdale (*Eng.*) Dweller in the valley by the brook.

Brokenshire, Brokenshaw (*Eng.*) One who came from Birkenshaw (birch grove), in the West Riding of Yorkshire.

Broker (*Eng.*) One who sells goods, a retailer; one who lived at the brook or stream.

Broman, Bromann (*Eng., Sw., Ger.*) The brown-complexioned man; dweller on the moor.

Bromberg (*Ger.*) Dweller on a brown mountain; one who came from Bromberg (brown mountain), in Austria;

or from Bromberg, now Bydgoszcz, a city in Poland.

Bromfield, Broomfield (*Eng.*) One who came from Bromfield or Broomfield (broom-covered field), the names of several places in England.

Bromley (*Eng.*) One who came from Bromley (clearing where broom grew), the name of several places in England.

Broms, Brom, Brome (*Eng.*) One who came from Brome, Broom or Broome (place where broom grew), the names of several places in England; dweller near where broom grew.

Bron (*Du.*) Dweller near the well or spring.

Brondyke (*Du.*) Dweller on, or near, Bronno's dike.

Bronkema (*Du.*) Descendant of Bronke, a pet form of Bruno (brown).

Bronson, Brons (*Eng.*) The son of Brun (brown).

Bronstein, Bronston, Bronstine (*Ger.*) Dweller near a brown stone, usually a boundary mark.

Brookbank, Brooksbank (*Eng.*) Dweller on the bank of the brook.

Brooker (*Eng.*) Dweller at the brook or stream; one who sells goods, a retailer.

Brookins, Brookens (*Du.*) Descendant of Broeke, a pet name for Broer (brother).

Brookland (*Eng.*) Dweller in the marshy land.

Brooks, Brookes, Brook, Brookman, Brooke (*Eng.*) Dweller near the spring or brook, sometimes marsh.

Brookshire (*Eng.*) Dweller in the grove by the brook.

Brooksmith (*Eng.*) The smith who lived or worked by the brook.

Broomall (*Eng.*) Variant of Broomhall, q.v.

Broome, Broom, Broomes (*Eng.*) One who came from Broome or Broom (place where broom grew), the names of several places in England.

Broomell (*Eng.*) Variant of Broomhill, q.v.

Broomfield (*Eng.*) One who came from Broomfield (broom-covered field), the name of several villages in England.

Broomhall (*Eng.*) One who came from Broomhall (corner where broom grew), in Cheshire.

Broomhill (*Eng.*) One who came from Broomhill (broom-covered hill), in Kent.

Brophy (*Ir.*) Grandson of Brogh or Broha.

Brose (*Fr., Ger.*) One who drove a two-wheeled cart; one who made two-wheeled carts; descendant of Brose, a pet form of Ambrose (immortal).

Broshears (*Eng.*) Variant of Brashear, q.v.

Brosier (*Fr.*) One who worked at a fire of live coals or glowing embers.

Brosius (*Sw.*) Descendant of Brosius, a shortened form of Ambrosius, Swedish form of Ambrose (immortal).

Brosnan, Brosnahan, Brosnihan (*Ir.*) One who came from Brosna in Kerry; dweller near the Brosna river.

Bross (*Fr.*) Dweller in, or near, brushwood; one who came from Brosse (brushwood), the name of several small places in France; one who made and sold brushes; one who made or used small wagons with two wheels.

Brossard (*Fr.*) Dweller among, or near, brushwood.

Brosseau (*Fr.*) Dweller in, or near, the brush.

Brothers (*Eng.*) Descendant of a lay brother, a member of a men's religious group preparing for holy orders; descendant of Brother (brother); fellow member of a guild or corporation.

Brotherson (*Eng.*) The son of the brother, a cousin; the son of the monk; the son of Brother, a personal name.

Brotherton (*Eng.*) One who came from Brotherton (Brodor's or Brother's homestead), in Suffolk.

Broude, Broud (*Nor.*) Dweller on the slope or side of the hill.

Brough (*Eng.*) One who came from Brough (Roman camp), the name of eight villages in England.

Brougham (*Eng.*) One who came from Brougham (the manor by the fort), in Westmorland.

Broughton (*Eng.*) One who came from Broughton (homestead on a brook; homestead by a fortified place; homestead by a hill or barrow), the name of many places in England.

Brouillet, Brouillette, Brouillete (*Fr.*) Dweller in, or near, a small, swampy wood; one who came from Breuil (swampy wood), in France.

Broun (*Eng., Scot.*) Variant of Brown, q.v.

Broussard (*Fr.*) One with shaggy, unkempt hair; a pejorative term for a countryman; dweller near the brushwood.

Browder (*Ir.*) Grandson of Bruadar (brother).

Brower, Brouwer, Browar (*Du.*) One who brewed beer, a brewer.

Brown, Browne (*Eng., Scot.*) One with a dark complexion; descendant of Brun (brown).

Brownback (*Ger.*) One who came from Brunbeck, in Germany.

Brownell (*Eng.*) Descendant of little Brun (brown).

Brownfield (*Scot.*) One who came from Brounfield (Brun's field), in Scotland.

Browning (*Eng.*) The son of Brun (brown); descendant of Bruning (brown, friend).

Brownlee, Brownley, Brownlie (*Eng.*) Dweller at the brown meadow.

Brownlow (*Eng.*) Dweller at the brown hill or burial mound.

Brownsmith (*Eng.*) One who did the bright or burnished work; the smith who worked in copper or brass.

Brownstein (*Ger.*) Dweller near a brown stone, usually a boundary mark.

Brownwell (*Eng.*) Dweller near the brown spring; or at the brown slope or corner.

Brubacher, Brubach (*Ger.*) One who came from Brubach or Brubbach (stream with lye or alkaline water; the sudsy, frothy stream), the names of places in Germany.

Brubaker (*Swis., Ger.*) One who came from Brubach in Switzerland; Americanized form of Brubacher, q.v.

Bruce, Bruse (*Scot.*) One who came from Braose (now Brieuse), in Normandy; or from Bruis (brushwood), in France.

Bruch (*Ger.*) Dweller in the marshy land or wet meadow.

Bruchhauser (*Ger.*) Dweller in the house in the marshy land or wet meadow.

Bruckner, Brucker, Bruck (*Ger.*) Dweller at, or near, a bridge.

Bruckshaw (*Eng.*) Dweller by the brook in the small wood.

Brugger, Brugman, Bruggeman (*Ger., Eng.*) Dweller by, or keeper of, a bridge.

Bruhn (*Ger.*) The dark-complexioned man.

Bruin (*Du.*) Dweller at the sign of the bear; descendant of Bruin (brown); one with a dark brown complexion.

Brumback (*Ger.*) One who came from Brombach (swampy brook), the name of seven places in Germany.

Brumfield (*Eng.*) One who came from Broomfield or Bromfield (broom-covered field), the names of various places in England.

Brumley (*Eng.*) One who came from Bromley (grove where broom grew; or where brambles grew), the name of several villages in England.

Brummell, Brummel (*Eng.*) Dweller on the hill where broom grew; variant of Broomhill, q.v.; and of Broomhall, q.v.

Brummer (*Ger.*) One who grumbles, howls, and screams.

Brun (*Ger., Fr.*) Descendant of Brun (brown); one with a dark complexion.

Brundage (*Eng.*) One who came from Brundish (Edisc on the stream), in Suffolk; or from Brownedge (brown hill), in Lancashire.

Bruner (*Ger.*) One who dug wells; descendant of Brunheri (brown, army); dweller near a spring.

Brunet, Brunetti (*Fr.*) One with brown hair or dark complexion; descendant of little Bruno (dark-complexioned; brown).

Bruni (*It.*) The dark-complexioned man; descendant of Bruno (brown); dweller near a plum tree.

Brunke, Brunk (*Ger.*) Descendant of little Brun (brown); or of Bruno, a pet form of names beginning with Brun (brown), as Brunwig and Brunolf.

Brunner, Bruner (*Ger.*) One who dug wells; descendant of Brunheri (brown, army); dweller near a spring.

Bruno (*Ger., Cz.-Sl.*) Descendant of Bruno (brown). Bruno is also a pet form of names beginning with Brun (brown), as Brunrat and Brunwart.

Bruns, Brune, Brun (*Ger., Fr., Eng.*) Descendant of Brun (brown).

Brunsdale (*Eng.*) Dweller at Brun's valley.

Brunson (*Nor., Eng.*) The son of Brun (brown).

Brunswick (*Ger.*) One who came from Brunschweig (Bruno's country), a city and former state in Germany.

Brunt (*Eng.*) Descendant of Brand (sword).

Brunton (*Eng.*) One who came from Brunton (homestead by the stream), in Northumberland.

Brush (*Eng.*) Dweller in, or near, broom or heather.

Bruton (*Eng.*) One who came from Bruton (homestead on the Brue river), the name of villages in Somerset and Wiltshire.

Bruu (*Nor.*) One who came from Bru (bridge); dweller near a bridge.

Bruun (*Sw., Nor., Dan.*) One with a dark brown complexion.

Bryant, Bryan (*Ir.*) Descendant of Bryan (strong).

Bryce (*Wel.*) The son of Rhys (ardor, a rush); descendant of Brice (speedy).

Brydon (*Eng.*) Same as Breden, q.v.

Bryson (*Eng.*) The son of Bryce (speedy).

Brzezinski, Brzozowski (*Pol.*) Dweller near a birch tree; one who came from Brzozow (place of birch trees), in Poland.

Brzostek (*Pol.*) One who came from Brzostek (place of elm trees), in Poland; dweller near an elm tree.

Buchanan (*Scot.*) One who came from Both-Chanain (the Cannon's seat), in Stirlingshire.

Buchbinder (*Ger.*) One who bound books.

Bucher, Bucker (*Ger.*) One who copied books.

Buchholz, Buchholtz, Bucholz (*Ger.*) Dweller in, or near, a beech grove; one who came from Buchholz (beech grove), the name of many places in Germany.

Buchler (*Ger.*) One who pressed oil from beechnuts; one who came from Buchel, in Germany.

Buchman, Buchmann (*Ger.*) Dweller at, or near, the beech trees.

Buchner (*Ger.*) Dweller near a beech tree; one who came from Buchen (beech tree), in Germany.

Buchta (*Cz.*) One who made and sold buchtas, a national cake made with yeast.

Buchwald, Buckwalder (*Ger.*) One who lived near the beechwood; one who came from Buchwald (beech wood), the name of several places in Germany.

Buck, Bucke (*Eng.*) Dweller at the sign of the male deer.

Buckingham (*Eng.*) One who came from Buckingham (the homestead of Bucca's people), in Buckinghamshire.

Buckland (*Eng.*) One who came from Buckland (land held by charter), the name of many places in the south of England.

Buckler (*Eng.*) One who made and sold buckles; or who made and sold shields with a boss.

Buckles (*Eng.*) One who came from Bucknall (Bucca's corner); or from Bucknell (Bucca's hill); each the name of two villages in England.

Bucklesmith (*Eng.*) One who made buckles or shields with a boss.

Buckley, Buckle, Buckly (*Eng.*) One who came from Bulkeley (bullock pasture), in Cheshire; the handsome cleric or scholar.

Bucknam, Bucknum (*Eng.*) One who came from Buckenham (Bucca's manor), the name of three places in Norfolk.

Bucknell (*Eng.*) One who came from Bucknell (Bucca's hill), the name of places in Oxfordshire and Shropshire.

Buckner (*Ger.*) Dweller at, or near, a beech tree; descendant of Burghar (stronghold, army).

Buckstead (*Nor., Dan.*) One who came from Bokstad (goat farm), in Norway; dweller at a goat farm.

Buckwalt, Buckwalter (*Ger.*) Americanized form of Buchwald, q.v.

Buda (*Hun.*) One who came from Buda (Buda's town), in Hungary.

Budd, Bud (*Eng.*) Descendant of Buda (messenger); or of Bud, a pet form of Baldwin (bold, friend) and of Botolf (command, wolf); the foolish, stupid man.

Budge (*Wel.*) The son of Hugh (spirit; mind).

Budz (*Pol.*) Descendant of Budz, a pet form of Budzimir or Budzislaw; one who came from Budzyn (the huts), in Poland.

Budzinski, Budzynski, Budzyn (*Pol.*) One who came from Budzyn (the huts), in Poland.

Buechley (*Ger.*) Dweller in, or near, a wood of beech trees.

Buehler, Buhl, Buehl, Buhler (*Ger.*) One who lived on, or near, a hill.

Buell (*Eng.*) One who came from Bueil (field infested by crows), in France.

Buelow, Bulow (*Ger., Dan., Sw.*) One who came from Bulow, in Germany.

Buerger, Buerker (*Ger.*) Dweller in a town; descendant of Burghar (stronghold, army).

Buettner, Buttner (*Ger.*) One who made and sold casks, a cooper.

Buff (*Ger.*) One who pushes or shoves.

Buffa (*It.*) One with the characteristics of a horned owl or a frog; the clown.

Buffington (*Eng.*) One who came from Bovington (the homestead of Bofa's people), in Dorset.

Bufford (*Eng.*) One in the habit of often puffing and blowing or swelling up with anger.

Buford, Bueford (*Eng.*) One who came from Beeford (ford at which bees were found), in Yorkshire.

Bugajski, Bugajsky (*Pol., Rus.*) One who took care of steers; one who made cloaks and capes, a tailor.

Bugbee, Bugby (*Eng.*) Dweller in, or near, Bucca's or Bucge's homestead.

Bugg, Buggs, Bugge (*Eng., Ger.*) Descendant of Buga or Bugga (to stoop); descendant of Burgio, a pet form of names beginning with Burg (castle), as Burgmar and Burcward.

Buggie, Buggy, Bugay, Bugee (*Eng.*) Descendant of Buga or Bugga (to stoop); one who came from Bugey, in France.

Buhajenko (*Ukr.*) Dweller at the sign of the bull.

Buhl, Buhle, Buhler (*Ger.*) One who came from Buhl, Buhle, or Buhler (all meaning "hill"), the names of many places in Germany.

Buick, Buyck (*Du.*) One who had a large stomach or paunch.

Buie (*Scot., Eng.*) The yellow or fair-haired man.

Buikema (*Du.*) Descendant of Buike, a pet form of Boye (boy; young hero).

Bukovic, Bukovich (*Cz.-Sl.*) One who came from Bukova (place of beech trees), the name of many villages in Czechoslovakia.

Bukowski (*Pol.*) Dweller near a beech tree; one who came from Bukow(o), the name of many places in Poland, Ukraine and Byelorussia.

Bulfin (*Eng.*) One who came from Bulphan (fen belonging to the fortified place), in Essex.

Bulganin (*Rus.*) One whose actions gave rise to scandal.

Bulger (*Eng., Ir.*) One who made leather wallets or bags; the light-complexioned man.

Bulkeley, Bulkley (*Eng.*) One who came from Bulkeley (bullock pasture), in Cheshire.

Bull (*Eng.*) Dweller at the sign of the bull; one thought to possess some characteristic of a bull, such as strength or firmness.

Bullard (*Eng.*) One who kept, or tended, bulls.

Bullen, Bullent, Bulleyn (*Eng.*) One who came from Boulogne (town), the name of several places in France.

Bullett, Bullitt, Bullit (*Eng.*) Dweller at the sign of the bull's head; one with a bull-shaped head.

Bullinger (*Eng.*) One who made bread, a baker.

Bullington (*Eng.*) One who came from Bullington (the homestead of Bula's people; or Bula's hill), the name of villages in Hampshire and Lincolnshire.

Bullis, Bullas (*Eng.*) One who worked at, or dwelt near, the bull-house.

Bullock, Bullocks (*Eng.*) Dweller at the sign of the young bull; one with some quality of a young bull.

Bullwinkel (*Ger.*) Dweller at the corner where bulls were kept.

Bulter (*Eng.*) One who sifted meal; one who made and sold bolts.

Bulthuis (*Ger.*) Dweller in the house on the hill.

Bumgardner (*Ger.*) Variant of Baumgartner, q.v.

Bumpus, Bumpers (*Eng.*) From Old French *bon pas* (good pace), probably a nickname for a messenger.

Bumstead, Bumsted (*Eng.*) One who came from Bumpstead (reedy place), in Essex.

Bunce (*Eng.*) The son of Bunn (good).

Bunch, Bunche (*Eng.*) Descendant of Bunn (good), one with a hump on the back, a hunchback.

Bundley (*Eng.*) One who came from Bondleigh (Bola's clearing), in Devonshire.

Bundy, Bunde (*Eng.*) Descendant of Bondig (householder; free man).

Bunge (*Ger.*) One who beat a drum, a drummer.

Bunin (*Ger.*) The good man.

Bunker (*Fr.*) The good hearted man; one who came from Boncourt (good farm), in France.

Bunnell (*Eng.*) The little, alert man; the good, kind man; one who came from Bunwell (reed stream), in Norfolk.

Bunney (*Wel.*) The son of Eynon (anvil); or of Ynyr (honor).

Bunting (*Eng.*) Descendant of Bunting (the good little pet), a term of endearment for children; dweller at the sign of the bunting (finch).

Bunton, Bunten, Buntine (*Scot.*) The good, kind person.

Buntrock (*Ger.*) One who made and sold fur coats, a furrier.

Bunyan (*Eng., Wel.*) One disfigured by a knob or hump; the son of Einion (anvil); or of Eniawn (upright).

Bunyard (*Eng.*) Descendant of Baynard (willing, strong).

Bunyea (*Eng.*) One who came from Bungay (island where Buna's people lived), in Suffolk.

Buonaguidi (*It.*) The good man named Guido (sensible; life; wood).

Buongiorno (*It.*) Nickname for one in the habit of wishing others a good day.

Buonomo (*It.*) Variant of Bonomo, q.v.

Burak, Burack (*Ukr., Pol.*) One who grew and sold beets.

Burbank (*Eng.*) Dweller at the cottage on the mound or embankment.

Burbery (*Eng.*) Dweller in a cottage at a fortified place.

Burbidge, Burbage (*Eng.*) One who came from Burbage (brook or valley of the fortified place), the name of four places in England.

Burbridge (*Eng.*) Dweller in the house by the bridge.

Burce (*Eng.*) Dweller near a birch tree.

Burch, Burcher (*Eng.*) Dweller at the birch tree or grove.

Burcham (*Eng.*) One who came from

Bircham (newly cultivated homestead), in Norfolk.

Burchard (*Eng.*) Descendant of Burgheard (fortress, hard); or of Burghard (fortress, hard).

Burchett, Burchette (*Eng.*) Descendant of little Burchard (castle, firm); dweller at the head or end of the birch grove.

Burchfield (*Eng.*) Dweller in the field where birches grew.

Burchill, Burchell (*Eng.*) Dweller at, or on, the hill of birch trees.

Burcot, Burcott (*Eng.*) One who came from Burcot (Bryda's cottage; cottage belonging to the fort), the name of places in Oxfordshire and Worcestershire; or from Burcott (cottage belonging to the fort), in Buckinghamshire.

Burd (*Eng.*) Variant of Bird, q.v.

Burda (*Cz.-Sl., Pol.*) The brawling or pugnacious man.

Burden, Burdon (*Eng.*) One who came from Burdon (valley with a cow barn; hill with a fort), the name of several places in England.

Burdett, Burdette, Burditt (*Eng., Fr.*) Descendant of Bordet (little shield); dweller near the border; dweller on a rented farm.

Burdick (*Eng.*) Descendant of little Borda (shield); one who came from Bourdic, the name of two places in France.

Burdine (*Eng.*) One who came from Burdon (valley shed), in Durham.

Burel, Burell (*Eng.*) Variant of Burrell, q.v.

Buren (*Du.*) Dweller in the neighborhood.

Bures (*Eng.*) One who came from Bures (cottage), the name of places in Essex and Suffolk.

Burford (*Eng.*) One who came from Burford (ford by a hill; ford by the fort), the name of places in Oxfordshire and Shropshire.

Burg, Burge, Burgh (*Eng., Ger.*) Dweller at the fort or fortified place; one who came from Burgh (fort), the name of many places in England; one who came from Burg (stronghold), the name of various places in Germany. See also Berg.

Burger (*Ger., Du.*) One who came from Burg (fort or stronghold), the name of places in Germany and Switzerland; one who lived in a borough, a citizen; variant of Buerger, q.v.

Burgess, Burges, Burgis (*Eng.*) A citizen or freeman of a borough who owed special duties to the king and had certain privileges.

Burgett (*Eng.*) Dweller by the castle or city gate.

Burghardt, Burghard (*Ger.*) Descendant of Burghardt (fortress, hard).

Burgin, Burgins (*Nor., Du.*) Variant of Bergen, q.v.

Burgner (*Ger.*) One who came from Burgen, in Switzerland.

Burgos (*Sp.*) One who came from Burgos (castle or stronghold), the name of several places in Spain.

Burgoyne (*Eng.*) One who came from Burgundy (dwellers in fortified places), a region mostly in France.

Burham (*Eng.*) One who came from Burham (homestead by the fortified place), in Kent.

Burhans (*Ger.*) The peasant named Hans, a pet form of Johannes (gracious gift of Jehovah).

Burian (*Ukr.*) Dweller among, or near, weeds.

Burke, Burk, Berk, Birk, Berke (*Ir.*) Dweller at, or near, the burgh or stronghold.

Burkett, Burkitt (*Eng.*) Dweller at the little stronghold; one who came from Bourguet or Bourget, in France; dweller by the headland covered with birches; descendant of Burgheard or Bourcart (fortress, hard).

Burkhardt, Burkhart, Burchardt, Burckhard, Burghart, Burghardt (*Ger.*) One who lived in a strong castle or fortress.

Burks, Burkes (*Eng., Ir.*) Dweller at, or near, the stronghold or fortified place; dweller by the birches.

Burleson, Burlison (*Eng.*) The son of the cupbearer or butler.

Burley, Burleigh (*Eng.*) One who came from Burley (grove belonging to a fortified place), the name of several places in England.

Burling (*Eng.*) The son of the cupbearer or butler.

Burlingame (*Eng.*) One who came from Burlingham (the village of Baerla's people), in Norfolk.

Burlington (*Eng.*) Dweller in the homestead of Byrla's people.

Burman, Burmann (*Eng.*) Dweller in a cottage; servant of the peasant.

Burmeister, Burmester (*Ger.*) One who tilled the land, a farmer.

Burnell (*Fr.*) The dark or brown-complexioned man.

Burness (*Scot.*) One who came from Burness (fair wind point), in Scotland.

Burnett, Burnette (*Eng.*) One who came from Burnett (place cleared by burning), in Somerset; the small, brown-complexioned one.

Burney (*Scot.*) One who came from Birnie (wet place), in Elginshire.

Burnham, Burnam (*Eng.*) One who came from Burnham (estate on a stream), the name of various places in England.

Burnley (*Eng.*) One who came from Burnley (grove by the stream), in Lancashire.

Burns, Burnes (*Eng.*) Dweller at a brook.

Burnside (*Eng.*) One who came from Burnside (Brunwulf's headland), in Westmorland.

Burnstein, Burnstine (*Ger.*) Amber.

Burr (*Eng.*) One who came from, or worked at, the fortress.

Burrage (*Eng.*) Descendant of Burgric (castle, rule).

Burrell, Burrel, Burrill (*Eng.*) One who came from Burrill (hill of the fort), in the North Riding of Yorkshire; one who made or wore burel, a coarse, brown, woolen cloth.

Burris, Burress, Burres (*Eng.*) Dweller near a stronghold or fortified place; a corruption of Burrows, q.v.

Burrows, Burroughs (*Eng.*) One who came from Burrow or Burroughs (fort or hill), the names of several villages in England; dweller near a stronghold or fortified place.

Burry (*Eng.*) One who came from Bury (fort; town), the name of several towns in England.

Burt, Burtt (*Eng.*) Descendant of Bert (bright).

Burton, Burtin (*Eng.*) One who came from Burton (village by a fort; fortified manor), the name of many villages in England; dweller near a fort enclosure.

Burwell (*Eng.*) One who came from Burwell (fort by a spring), the name of places in Cambridgeshire and Lincolnshire.

Burwick (*Eng.*) Variant of Berwick, q.v.

Bury (*Eng.*) One who came from Bury (fort; town), the name of four places in England.

Busby, Busbey (*Eng., Scot.*) One who came from Busby (shrub, homestead), in Yorkshire; one who came from the lands of Busby (bush village), in Renfrewshire.

Buscemi (*It.*) One who came from Buscemi, in Sicily.

Busch, Busche (*Ger.*) Dweller at the sign of the bush (usually a wine merchant); one who dwelt near a bush.

Buschman (*Ger.*) Dweller by, or in, the bushes.

Bush (*Eng.*) Dweller at the sign of the bush (usually a wine merchant); one who dwelt near a bush.

Bushell, Bushelle (*Eng.*) Dweller at the slope or corner overgrown with bushes; variant of Bussell, q.v.

Bushnell (*Eng.*) Dweller at the bushy slope or corner.

Busse, Buss (*Fr., Eng., Ger.*) One who came from Bus (wood), in France; dweller at a wood or thicket; descendant of Burgio, a pet form of names beginning with Burg (place of protection), as Burghard and Burgmar.

Bussell (*Eng.*) Dweller at, or near, a thicket or small wood; one who came from Boissel (small wood), in France.

Bussey, Bussie (*Eng.*) One who came from Bussy or Boissy (little wood), in Normandy; dweller at a small wood; one who came from Bushey (a thicket), in Hertfordshire.

Bustamente (*Sp.*) One who came from Bustamente (covered sepulcher), in Spain.

Buswell (*Eng.*) A variant of Boswell, q.v.

Butcher (*Eng.*) One who cut and sold meat.

Butera (*It.*) One who came from Butera, in Italy.

Butkus (*Lith.*) Descendant of Butkintas; one who occupied an apartment or quarters in some building.

Butler, Buttler (*Eng.*) One who made, or had charge of, bottles; one in charge of the butts or casks of wine.

Butt, Butte (*Eng.*) The short, stumpy man; dweller at a butt or mound; descendant of Butta.

Butterfield (*Eng.*) Dweller in, or near, a good pasture providing food for cows.

Buttermilch (*Ger.*) One who sold buttermilk.

Buttermore (*Eng.*) One who came from Buttermere (lake near where butter was produced), the name of places in Cumberland and Wiltshire.

Butters (*Eng.*) Descendant of Botthar or Bothere (messenger, army).

Butterwick (*Eng.*) One who came from Butterwick (farm where butter was produced), the name of several places in England.

Butterworth (*Eng.*) One who came from Butterworth (butter farm), in Lancashire.

Button (*Eng.*) One who came from Bitton (homestead on Boyd river), in Gloucestershire; one who made buttons.

Buttram (*Eng.*) Descendant of Bartram (bright, raven).

Buttrick, Butterick (*Eng.*) One who came from Butterwick (butter farm), the name of several places in England.

Butts, Butz (*Ger., Eng.*) One who oversees and gives commands; descendant of Bucco, a pet form of names beginning with Burg (castle), as Burghard, Burghar, and Burcward; dweller near the archery butts.

Butzen (*Ger.*) Dweller near a spring or fountain.

Buxbaum (*Ger.*) Dweller near the beech tree.

Buxton (*Eng.*) One who came from Buxton (rocking stone), in Derbyshire.

Buyer (*Eng.*) Dweller by the cowhouse.

Buzzard, Buzard (*Eng.*) Nickname for a stupid, ignorant person; one thought to possess the characteristics of a buzzard, an inferior kind of hawk, not usable in falconry.

Buzzell, Buzzelli (*It.*) Descendant of Buzzelli, a pet form of Giacobuzzi (may God protect; the supplanter).

Byas (*Eng.*) Dweller at the house on the bend or corner; or by the manor house.

Byczek (*Pol.*) One who took care of young bulls.

Bye (*Nor., Eng.*) Dweller on the farmstead; or in, or near, the town; or in a corner; one who came from Bayeux (great conquerors; fair-haired), in Normandy.

Byerly (*Eng.*) One who came from Bierley (grove by the fort), in the West Riding of Yorkshire.

Byers, Byer (*Eng.*) Dweller near a cattle shed; dweller at a land corner; one who purchased merchandise to sell to others.

Byfield (*Eng.*) One who came from Byfield (field in the bend [of the river]), in Northamptonshire.

Bygott (*Eng., Fr.*) Variant of Bigott, q.v.

Bykowski (*Pol.*) One who took care of bulls.

Bynum (*Eng.*) One who came from Binham (Bynna's homestead), in Norfolk; the dweller in the village or town.

Byrd (*Eng.*) Dweller at the sign of the bird; one with birdlike characteristics.

Byrne, Byrnes (*Ir.*) Grandson of Bran (raven); or of Biorn or Bjorn (bear).

Byron, Byram, Byrum (*Eng.*) Descendant of Byron (from the cottage); one who came from Byram (tumulus or cowshed), in the West Riding of Yorkshire.

Bysshe (*Eng.*) Dweller at the thicket or brushwood.

Bystrom (*Nor.*) Dweller at the farm on the stream.

Bystryk (*Pol.*) Nickname for one noted for his quick, rapid movements.

Bythewood (*Eng.*) Dweller by the wood.

Bywater (*Eng.*) Dweller near the water.

Caballero (*Sp.*) One who came from Caballero (horsemen), in Spain; one who rode a horse; a knight.

Caban, Cabana (*Sp.*) Dweller in a small hut.

Cabell, Cabel, Cable (*Scot., Eng.*) Descendant of Cubold.

Cabot (*Fr.*) One with a small head; dweller at the sign of the miller's-thumb, a fresh-water fish.

Cabrera (*Sp.*) One who takes care of goats, a goatherd.

Caccamo (*It.*) One who came from Caccamo, in Sicily.

Cacciatore (*It.*) One who hunts game, a hunter.

Cacioppo (*It.*) Lame dog, possibly a nickname for a lame person.

Cadbury (*Eng.*) One who came from Cadbury (Cada's fortress), the name of places in Devonshire and Somerset.

Cadby (*Eng.*) One who came from Cadby (Kati's village), the name of places in Leicestershire and the West Riding of Yorkshire.

Caddell (*Eng.*) Variant of Cadwell, q.v.

Caddick (*Eng.*) The infirm, frail man.

Cade, Cadd (*Eng.*) The big, lumpish person; descendant of Cada (large or lumpish).

Cadenhead, Caddenhead (*Scot.*) Dweller at the head of Cadon Water in Selkirkshire.

Cadieux (*Fr.*) Nickname for one who frequently used the oath, God's head.

Cadigan, Cadogan (*Ir., Wel.*) Grandson of little Ceadach (possessing hundreds); descendant of Cadwgan (small battle).

Cadiz (*Sp.*) One who came from Cadiz (walled place), in Spain.

Cadman (*Eng.*) The servant of Cada; one who came from Cadnam (Cada's homestead), in Hampshire.

Cadwallader (*Wel.*) Descendant of Cadwaladr (battle arranger).

Cadwell (*Eng.*) One who came from Cadwell (wild cat valley; Cada's spring), the name of places in Lincolnshire and Oxfordshire; one who came from Caldwell (cold stream), in the North Riding of Yorkshire.

Cady (*Scot.*) Descendant of little Cadda (battle).

Caesar (*It., Eng.*) Descendant of Caesar (hairy; blue-eyed); one who had long hair or a bushy head.

Cafferty (*Ir.*) The son of Eachmharcaigh (horse rider).

Caffrey, Caffray (*Ir.*) Descendant of Gafraidh, a Gaelic form of Godfrey (God's peace).

Cage (*Eng.*) Dweller near, or worker at, a prison.

Cagle (*Ger.*) Americanized form of Kegel, q.v.; or of Kagel, q.v.; one who made mantles with a cowl.

Cagney (*Ir.*) Descendant of Caingean (business; compact; dispute).

Cahill, Cahall (*Ir.*) Grandson of Cathal (battle; powerful).

Cahn (*Ger.*) Variant of Cohen, q.v.

Cahoon, Cahoone (*Ir., Scot.*) Variant of Calhoun, q.v.

Cain, Caine (*Ir., Eng.*) Descendant of Cathan (warrior); one who came from Caen (field of combat), in France; descendant of Cana (reed; of mature judgment).

Caird (*Scot.*) One who worked in brass,

a craftsman, later a travelling tinker; one who repaired pots and kettles.

Cairncross (*Scot.*) One who came from Cairncross (heap of stones with a cross), in Angus.

Cairns (*Eng., Scot.*) Dweller near a rocky place or natural pile of rocks; one who came from Cairns (rocky place), in Midlothian.

Cairo, Caire (*It.*) One who came from Cairo (victorious), in Italy; perhaps, in a few cases, one who came from Cairo (victorious), in Egypt.

Calabrese (*It.*) One who came from Calabrese, in Italy.

Calahan (*Ir.*) Variant of Callahan, q.v.

Calandra, Calandrino (*It.*) Dweller at the sign of the lark. Calandrino sometimes refers to a stupid man.

Calbert (*Eng.*) Descendant of Calbert (herdsman).

Caldcott (*Eng.*) One who came from Caldecott (cold huts), the name of various places in England.

Caldecot, Caldecott, Caldicot, Caldicott (*Eng.*) One who came from Caldecote (cold huts), the name of ten villages in England; or from Caldicot (cold huts), in Monmouthshire.

Calder (*Eng.*) One who lived near the Calder (violent stream), the name of several rivers in England.

Calderon (*Eng., Sp.*) One who made and sold large kettles or boilers.

Calderone, Caldrone (*It.*) Same as Calderon, q.v.

Calderwood (*Eng.*) Dweller at the wood by the Calder (violent stream), the name of several rivers in England.

Caldwell (*Eng.*) One who came from Caldwell (cold stream), in Yorkshire.

Caleb (*Eng.*) Descendant of Caleb (dog; bold).

Caley (*Mx., Scot., Eng.*) Descendant of Caoladh (slender); the slender man; one who came from Cailly (forest), in Normandy; one who came from Cayley, in Lancashire.

Calhoun, Calhoon, Calhoune (*Ir., Scot.*) Grandson of Cathluan (battle hero; battle joyful); contraction of Colquhoun, q.v.

Caliendo (*It.*) One with some characteristic of a lark.

Calkins, Calkin (*Eng.*) Descendant of little Cal, a pet form of Caleb (dog).

Call (*Scot., Ir., Eng.*) Descendant of Cathal (battle mighty); one noted for wearing a woman's close fitting cap.

Callahan, Callaghan (*Ir.*) Grandson of little Ceallach (contention).

Callan, Callen (*Ir.*) Grandson of little Cathal (battle mighty).

Callas (*Gr.*) One who coated the inside of pots and pans.

Callender, Callander, Calendar (*Eng., Scot.*) One who calenders cloth, that is, smooths it by passing it between rollers; one who came from Callander (hard wood), the name of places in Falkirk and Perthshire.

Calley (*Scot.*) Contraction of McCauley, q.v.; variant of Caley, q.v.

Callham (*Eng.*) One who came from Kelham (at the ridges), in Nottinghamshire.

Callicot, Callicott, Callicotte, Callacot (*Eng.*) One who came from Caldecote (cold huts), the name of ten villages in England.

Callin (*Mx.*) The son of Cathalan (valor).

Callis, Calliss (*Eng.*) One who came from Calais (inlet or strait), in France.

Callister (*Ir.*) The son of Alastar, Gaelic form of Alexander (helper of mankind).

Callow, Calow (*Eng.*) One who came from Callow (cold hill or bare hill), the name of villages in Derbyshire, Herefordshire, and Somerset; one who came from Calow (bare hill), in Derbyshire.

Calloway, Callaway (*Eng.*) Descendant of Calewa (bald); one who came from Galloway (stranger Gael), in Scotland.

Callum (*Eng.*) Variant of Callham, q.v.

71

Caloger (*Gr.*) American respelling of Kalogeras, q.v.

Calvano, Calvani (*It.*) One who came from Calvana, in Italy.

Calvert (*Eng.*) One who tended calves, a calfherd.

Calvin (*Eng., Fr.*) Descendant of Calvin (bald).

Calzaretta (*It.*) One who made and sold small, tightly fitting top boots or shoes.

Cam, Camm (*Wel.*) The crooked or bent man, a cripple.

Camacho (*Sp.*) One who came from Camacho in Granada; one who had a hunchback, or was otherwise crippled.

Camber, Cammer, Camb (*Eng.*) One who made combs.

Camberis (*Gr.*) Variant of Kamberos, q.v.

Cambridge (*Eng.*) One who came from Cambridge, early Grentebrige (bridge over the Granta river), in Cambridgeshire. As Granta gradually changed to Cam, it was thought that Cambridge was the bridge across the Cam so that about the sixteenth century the Granta was renamed Cam. Also one who came from Cambridge (bridge over the Cam river), in Gloucestershire.

Camden (*Eng.*) One who came from Campden (valley with enclosures), in Gloucestershire.

Camel (*Scot.*) American pronunciation variant of Campbell, q.v.

Camero (*Sp.*) Dweller in a hall or apartment.

Cameron (*Scot.*) The man with a crooked or wry nose; one who came from Cameron (crooked hill), the name of three places in Scotland.

Camillo (*It.*) Descendant of Camillo (attendant at religious ceremonies).

Camp (*Eng., Fr.*) Dweller in, or near, a field, usually an enclosed piece of land.

Campagna (*It.*) Dweller in, or near, a field or meadow.

Campana (*It.*) One who was deaf; dweller near the bell; or at the sign of the bell.

Campanella, Campanino (*It.*) One who lived near the bells, or belfry; one who lived at the sign of the bell.

Campbell (*Scot.*) One with a wry mouth, or, perhaps, arched lips. It has been suggested that the epithet was applied by neighboring clans on account of moral, rather than physical, defects.

Camper (*Ger.*) Americanized variant of Kamper, q.v.

Campfield (*Scot.*) One who came from Campfield (battlefield), in Scotland.

Campion, Campione (*Fr., Eng.*) Same as Champion, q.v.

Campo (*It., Sp.*) Dweller in, or near, a field.

Campos (*Sp.*) Dweller in the fields; one who came from Campos, the name of several places in Spain.

Campsall (*Eng.*) One who came from Campsall (river bend corner), in the West Riding of Yorkshire.

Campton (*Eng.*) One who came from Campton (crooked stream homestead), in Bedfordshire.

Canada (*Sp.*) One who came from Canada (small canal), the name of several places in Spain; dweller in a dell or ravine; or near a cattle path.

Canady, Canaday, Cannady (*Scot., Ir.*) Variant of Kennedy, q.v.

Canales, Canale (*Sp., Fr.*) One who came from Canales (watercourse), the name of several places in Spain; dweller near the canal, an artificial channel filled with water.

Canary (*Pol.*) Dweller at the sign of the canary.

Canavan (*Ir.*) Descendant of Ceanndubhan (little black head).

Cancel, Cancela (*Sp.*) One who came from Cancela (screen of open ironwork), in Spain; one who made the wooden screen at the doors of churches.

Candelaria, Candelario (*Sp.*) Descendant of Candelari, a name given to celebrate the feast of the Purification of the Virgin.

Candelier, Candeliez (*Fr.*) One who made and sold candles and small wax images for ecclesiastical offerings.

Candler (*Eng.*) Same as Chandler, q.v.

Candover (*Eng.*) One who came from Candover (beautiful stream), in Hampshire.

Cane (*Eng.*) Descendant of Cana (reed; of mature judgment); one who is slender as a reed.

Canfield (*Eng.*) One who came from Canfield (Cana's field), in Essex.

Canino (*It.*) One who came from Canino, in Italy.

Canmore (*Scot.*) The man with the big head.

Cann, Can (*Eng.*) One who came from Cann (deep valley), in Dorset.

Cannamore (*Scot.*) One with a big head.

Cannell (*Mx.*) Descendant of Conall's son.

Cannella, Cannello (*It.*) Dweller where bent grass grew.

Canning (*Eng., Ir.*) One who came from Cannings (Cana's people), in Wiltshire; a corruption of Cannon, q.v.; grandson of Canan (little wolf cub).

Cannon, Canon, Canning (*Eng., Ir.*) A clergyman on the staff of a cathedral or important church; a member of a canon's entourage; descendant of Canan (little wolf cub).

Cannova (*It.*) Dweller near where hemp grew; one who worked in a wine cellar.

Cantalupo (*It.*) One who came from Cantalupo, in Italy.

Canter (*Eng.*) Variant of Cantor, q.v.

Canterbury, Canteberry (*Eng.*) One who came from Canterbury (the town or fort of the people of Kent), in Kent.

Canterton (*Eng.*) One who came from Canterton (village of the Kentishmen), in Hampshire.

Cantley, Cantlie (*Eng.*) One who came from Cantley (Canta's grove), the name of villages in Norfolk and the West Riding of Yorkshire.

Canton (*Fr.*) Dweller in a corner.

Cantor, Cantore (*Eng., It.*) The soloist who sang liturgical music in the synagogue; one who leads the singing in a cathedral.

Cantrell, Cantrall (*Fr., Eng.*) One who likes to sing; the little singer.

Cantu (*Sp., It.*) Dweller near a circular stone; or rolling stone; or near a rocky peak; one who came from Cantu (singing), in Italy.

Cantwell (*Eng.*) One who came from Canwell (Cana's spring), in Staffordshire.

Canty (*Ir.*) Descendant of Cainteach (satirist).

Cap (*Fr.*) Dweller at the head or end of something.

Capablanca (*Sp.*) One who wore a white cloak.

Cape (*Eng.*) One who made the long cloak or cape.

Capehart (*Ger.*) Variant of Gebhardt, q.v.

Capek (*Cz.-Sl.*) Dweller at the sign of the little stork; one thought to possess the qualities of a little stork.

Capella, Capelli (*It.*) Dweller near a chapel; one who made and sold caps; one who cared for she-goats.

Caplan, Caplin (*Ger., Pol.*) An Anglicization of Kaplan, q.v.

Caplenko (*Ukr.*) Dweller at the sign of the heron.

Capone, Caponi (*It.*) Same as Caputo, q.v.

Caporale (*It.*) One who was a corporal in the army; one who took care of animals, a herdsman; one who helped in the kitchen; one who was bold or audacious.

Caporelli (*It.*) One with a large or prominent chest.

Capote (*Sp.*) One who wore a capote, a short cloak without hood, of bright color, used by bull-fighters; one who wore a short cloak with sleeves to keep off rain.

Capozzi, Capozzo (*It.*) One with a small head; one who raised and sold cabbages; descendant of Capozzi, a pet

73

form of Iacapo, an Italian form of James (may God protect; the supplanter).

Capp (*Eng.*) A nickname for a monk in a hood; one who made and sold caps.

Capparelli (*It.*) One who is untidy; dweller near where mushrooms grew.

Cappello, Cappetta (*It.*) One who wore an unusual cap or other headgear.

Capper, Capps (*Eng.*) One who made and sold caps.

Capra, Capri, Caprio (*It.*) Dweller at the sign of the goat; one with the characteristics of a goat.

Capre (*Swis.*) Dweller near the priest's house.

Capron (*Fr.*) One who made and sold hoods or coverings for the head.

Caputo (*It.*) One with a large or unusual head; one who was stubborn or dullwitted.

Caraballo (*Sp.*) One who came from Carballo, in Spain.

Caras (*Gr.*) Variant of Karas, q.v.

Caraway (*Scot.*) One who came from Carloway (Karl's bay), in Lewis in the Outer Hebrides.

Carberry, Carbery (*Ir.*) Grandson of Cairbre (charioteer).

Carbis (*Eng.*) Dweller near the hill fort, or earthwork.

Carbonaro, Carbonara (*It.*) One who mined and sold coal.

Carbone, Carboni (*It.*) One who mined coal or burnt charcoal.

Card, Carde (*Eng., Fr.*) One who cards or combs wool.

Cardella, Cardelli, Cardello (*It.*) Dweller at the sign of the gold finch.

Carden, Cardon, Cardin (*Eng.*) One who came from Carden (rocky homestead), in Cheshire.

Cardenas (*Sp., Lith.*) The dark-complexioned or bluish man; one who came from Cardenas, in Spain; descendant of Kardas (sword).

Cardew (*Eng.*) Dweller at the black fort; one who came from Cardew (black fort or castle), in Cumberland.

Cardiff (*Eng.*) One who came from

Cardiff (fort of Didius; Taff river fort), in Wales.

Cardinale, Cardinali (*It.*) One connected in some way with a cardinal's establishment; dweller at the sign of the cardinal (bird).

Cardington (*Eng.*) One who came from Cardington (village of Cenred's people), in Bedfordshire.

Cardon (*Eng.*) Dweller by thistles; one who came from Carden (rock enclosure), in Cheshire.

Cardona, Cardone (*It.*) Dweller among thistles.

Cardozo, Cardoso (*Sp., Port.*) One who came from Cardoso (place where thistles grew), in Spain.

Cardwell (*Eng.*) One who came from Cardonville (Chardo's village), in Normandy.

Cardy (*Eng.*) Variant of Cardew, q.v.

Careless, Carless (*Eng.*) The man free from care; the unconcerned man.

Carew (*Eng.*) One who came from Carew (fort), in Pembrokeshire.

Carey (*Ir.*) Grandson of the dark-complexioned man.

Cargill, Cargile, Cargle (*Scot.*) One who came from Cargill (fort or rock of the wager; white fort), in Perthshire.

Cargo (*Eng.*) One who came from Cargo (rock hill), in Cumberland.

Carham (*Eng.*) One who came from Carham (the rocks), in Northumberland.

Carhart, Carhartt (*Eng.*) Descendant of Gerhart (spear, hard).

Carhill (*Eng.*) Dweller on, or near, a rocky hill.

Carini (*It.*) The little, dear man.

Carl, Carle (*Eng.*) The husbandman or countryman; descendant of Carl (man).

Carlberg (*Sw.*) One who came from Carlberg (man mountain), in Sweden.

Carlbury (*Eng.*) One who came from Carlbury (fort of the free peasants), in Durham.

Carlby (*Eng.*) One who came from

Carlby (the village of the free peasants), in Lincolnshire.

Carli, Carlo (*It.*) Descendant of Carlo, Italian form of Charles (man).

Carlin, Carling, Carlan (*Ir., Fr.*) Descendant of Caireallan; descendant of little Carl (man).

Carlington (*Eng.*) One who came from Carleton (the homestead of the free peasants), the name of many places in England.

Carlisle (*Eng.*) One who came from Carlisle (wall of the god Lugus), in Cumberland.

Carlow, Carlough (*Scot.*) One who came from Carlowrie (speaking rock), in Scotland.

Carlsmith (*Eng.*) This is a coalescing of the forename *Carl* with the surname *Smith.*

Carlson, Carlsen (*Nor., Sw., Dan.*) The son of Carl (man).

Carlstrom (*Sw.*) One who came from Carlstrom (Carl's stream), in Sweden.

Carlton, Carleton (*Eng.*) One who came from Carleton (the homestead of the free peasants), the name of many places in England.

Carlyle, Carlile (*Eng.*) Variant of Carlisle, q.v.

Carman, Carmon (*Eng.*) Descendant of Carlman or Carman (male, man); one who drove a cart.

Carmichael, Carmichel, Carmickle (*Scot.*) One who came from Carmichael (castle of St. Michael), in Lanarkshire; dweller near the big rock.

Carmody (*Ir.*) Grandson of Cearmaid (black hunting dog).

Carmony (*Fr.*) One who came from Carmona, in France.

Carnegie (*Scot.*) One who lived in the lands of Carryneggy, in Angus.

Carnell, Carnall (*Eng.*) A fighter whose post was at the crenels of the battlement or the walls.

Carnes, Carne, Carn (*Eng.*) Dweller near a natural pile of rocks; one who came from Carn, the name of various small places in Cornwall.

Carney, Carny (*Ir., Wel.*) Grandson of Cearnach (victorious); dweller on a high and barren hill.

Carnforth (*Eng.*) One who came from Carnforth (crane's ford), in Lancashire.

Carnoy (*Fr., Bel.*) One who came from Carnoy (forest of hornbeam trees), the name of places in Belgium and France.

Caro (*Fr., It.*) Dweller at the sign of the stag or hart; the dear, beloved person.

Carolan, Carollan (*Ir.*) Descendant of little Cearbhall (stag).

Carollo (*It.*) Descendant of little Carlo (manly).

Caron (*Eng., Fr.*) One who came from Cairon (Carius' estate), the name of two places in France.

Carone, Caronia (*It.*) Descendant of the youngest child.

Carpenter, Carpentier (*Eng., Fr.*) One who worked with wood.

Carpintero (*Sp.*) One who worked with wood.

Carr (*Eng., Ir., Scot.*) Dweller at, or near, a rock; or marsh; or an enclosed place; grandson of Carra (spear).

Carrasquillo, Carrasquilla (*Sp.*) Dweller near a buckthorn tree.

Carre (*Fr.*) The thick, squat, dumpy man; the man with a stocky, square body; dweller on, or near, the square; or on some square plot of land.

Carrea (*Sp.*) One who came from Santa Maria de Carrea, a parish in Spain.

Carreira (*Port.*) One who came from Carriera (road), in Portugal.

Carrell, Carrel (*Fr.*) One who made square-headed bolts or arrows for the crossbow.

Carrera, Carrero (*Sp.*) One who came from Carrero (road), the name of several places in Spain.

Carrick (*Eng., Scot.*) Dweller near a craig or rock; one who came from

Carrick (sea cliff or rock), in Ayrshire.

Carrie (*Eng.*) One who came from Carew or Carey, names of places in Somerset, derived from British river names.

Carrier (*Fr.*) One who worked in a quarry.

Carrigan, Carrogan (*Ir.*) Variant of Corrigan, q.v.

Carrillo (*Sp.*) One with an unusual or prominent cheek.

Carrington (*Eng.*) One who came from Carrington (the homestead of Curra's people), the name of villages in Cheshire and Lincolnshire.

Carrion (*Sp.*) One who came from Carrion (brushwood; town), the name of several places in Spain.

Carroll, Carol (*Ir.*) Grandson of Cearbhall (stag).

Carruthers, Carrothers, Carothers (*Scot.*) One who came from Carruthers (fort of Rydderch), in Dumfriesshire.

Carry (*Eng.*) Same as Carey, q.v.

Carson (*Scot., Eng., Mx.*) Dweller in, or near, a marsh; the garçon or servant; the son of Car, a pet form of names beginning with Car, as Carmichael.

Carstairs (*Scot.*) One who came from Carstairs (castle of Tarres), in Lanarkshire.

Carswell (*Eng., Scot.*) One who came from Carswell (spring where watercress grew), in Berkshire; or from Carswell, the name of places in Lanarkshire and Roxburghshire; or from Carsewell (low land near a spring), in Renfrewshire.

Cartagena (*It.*) One who came from Cartagena (new town), in Spain.

Carter, Cartter (*Eng.*) One who drove a cart.

Carthew (*Eng.*) Same as Cardew, q.v.

Cartlidge, Cartledge (*Eng.*) Dweller near a lake in rocky ground.

Cartmel, Cartmall (*Eng.*) One who came from Cartmel (rocky ground near a sandbank), in Lancashire.

Cartworth (*Eng.*) One who came from

Cartworth (Certa's homestead), in the West Riding of Yorkshire.

Cartwright (*Eng.*) One who made carts, usually small two-wheeled vehicles.

Carty (*Ir.*) Grandson of Carthach (loving).

Caruso (*It.*) One with shorn or close cut hair; one who worked in the sulphur pits.

Caruthers (*Scot.*) Same as Carruthers, q.v.

Carvalho (*Port.*) One who came from Carvalho (oak tree), in Portugal.

Carver (*Eng.*) The wood-carver, or cutter.

Carveth (*Eng.*) Dweller near the castle burying place.

Carwardine (*Eng.*) One who came from Carden (rocky homestead), in Cheshire. An early form of the village name was Cawardyn.

Cary (*Ir.*) Variant of Carey, q.v.

Casa (*Sp.*) Dweller in, or near, some particular house.

Casals (*Sp.*) Dweller in, or near, the country house of an ancient family.

Casanova, Casanovas (*It., Sp.*) Dweller in, or near, the new or recently constructed house; one who came from Casanova (new house), in Spain.

Cascio (*It.*) Descendant of Cassius (vain).

Case (*Eng.*) One who came from Case, in France; dweller at a manorial farm.

Casella (*Sp.*) Dweller in the little house.

Casey (*Ir.*) Grandson of Cathasach (vigilant, or watchful).

Cash (*Eng.*) An English variant of Cass, q.v.

Cashin, Cashen (*Ir.*) Grandson of Casan (little, curly-haired one).

Cashman (*Ir., Eng.*) Grandson of Casan (little, curly-haired one); an officer whose duty was to make arrests.

Casino (*Sp.*) One who came from Casino (small house), in Spain.

Caskey (*Scot.*) Son of Ascaidh, a pet form of Askell (kettle of the gods).

Caspari (*It.*) Descendant of Caspari (treasure; horseman).

Casper (*Ger., Eng.*) Descendant of Caspar or Kaspar (treasure; horseman).

Cass (*Fr., Eng.*) Dweller at, or near, an oak tree or forest; or at a hedged enclosure; one who made and sold copper pots; the son of Cass, a pet form of Cassandra (helper of men).

Cassano (*It.*) One who came from Cassano, in Italy.

Cassell, Cassel, Cassal (*Fr., Eng.*) One who came from Cassell (castle), in France; variant of Castle, q.v.

Casserly (*Ir.*) The son of Casarlach.

Cassidy, Cassiday (*Ir.*) Grandson of Caiside (curly-headed).

Casson, Cason (*Eng.*) Descendant of little Cass or Cassius (vain); descendant of Cassandra (helper of men).

Castagna (*It.*) Dweller near a chestnut tree.

Castaneda (*Sp.*) One who came from Castaneda (chestnut trees), the name of several places in Spain.

Castello, Castelo (*Port.*) Dweller near, or worker in, the castle; one who came from Castelo (castle), in Portugal.

Caster (*Eng.*) One who came from Caister (Roman camp), the name of villages in Norfolk and Lincolnshire.

Casterton (*Eng.*) One who came from Casterton (homestead by a Roman fort), the name of places in Rutland and Westmorland.

Castillo (*Sp.*) Dweller near, or worker in, the castle or fortress; one who came from Castillo (fortress), in Spain.

Castle (*Eng.*) Dweller in, or near, the large fortified building; worker in the castle.

Castleberry (*Eng.*) Dweller in, or near, the castle near the fortified place.

Castleton (*Eng., Scot.*) One who came from Castleton (homestead by the castle or fortified place), the name of several places in England and Scotland.

Caston (*Eng.*) One who came from Caston (Catt's homestead), in Norfolk.

Castro (*Sp., Port.*) One who lived at, or near, the castle or fortress; one who came from Castro (fortress), in Spain.

Castronovo (*Sp.*) Dweller in, or near, the newly-constructed castle or fortress.

Castroverde (*Sp.*) Dweller in, or near, the green castle or fortress.

Casutt (*Swis.*) Dweller in the lower house.

Caswell (*Eng.*) One who came from Caswell (spring or stream where watercress grew), the name of several places in England.

Caswick (*Eng.*) One who came from Keswick (cheese farm), the name of several places in England.

Catalano, Catalani (*It.*) One who came from Catalan, in Spain.

Catcher, Catch (*Eng.*) One who chases game, a huntsman.

Catchings, Catching (*Eng.*) One who worked in a kitchen.

Cates, Cate (*Eng.*) The son of Cate, a pet form of Cato (cautious); one who had charge of provisions.

Catford (*Eng.*) One who came from Catford (wild cat ford), in Kent.

Cathcart (*Scot.*) One who came from the lands of Cathcart (battle on the Cart river), in Renfrewshire.

Cather (*Scot.*) One who came from Cather (fort), in Dumbartonshire.

Cathey, Cathie (*Scot.*) A shortening of Maccathay (son of Cathan).

Catlett (*Eng.*) Dweller at the sign of the small wild cat; descendant of Catlett (small cat).

Catlin (*Fr.*) Descendant of little Catherine (pure).

Catron (*Fr.*) Descendant of Catron, a pet form of Catherine (pure).

Cattenhead (*Eng.*) Possibly one who came from Cattenhall (Catta's corner), in Cheshire.

Catterson (*Eng.*) The son of Catlin, a pet form of Catherine (pure).

Catterton (*Eng.*) One who came from Catterton (hill fort settlement), in the West Riding of Yorkshire.

Catworth (*Eng.*) One who came from

Catworth (Catt's homestead), in Huntingdonshire.

Cauble (*Ger.*) One who came from Kabel (cable), the name of several places in Germany.

Caudle, Caudill, Caudel (*Eng.*) One who came from Caudle (cold stream), now Caudle Green in Gloucestershire; one who could not hold his liquor, from Middle English *caudel* (a hot drink), given to sick people.

Caulcutt, Caulcott (*Eng.*) One who came from Caulcott (cold cottage), in Oxfordshire.

Cauley (*Eng.*) One who came from Caughley (daw wood), in Shropshire.

Caulfield (*Scot., Eng.*) One who came from Cauldfield (cold field), in Dumfriesshire; dweller at a cabbage field; or at a cold or bleak field.

Caulkins (*Eng.*) Variant of Calkins, q.v.

Causey (*Eng.*) One who came from Causey (paved way), the name of villages in Northumberland and Cumberland; dweller near a causeway.

Cavallo, Cavallaro (*It.*) One who had charge of the horses; dweller at the sign of the horse; one who came from Cavalla (horse), in Italy.

Cavanaugh, Cavanagh (*Ir.*) Grandson of little Caomh (comely), or Caomhan, the names of fifteen Irish saints.

Cavell, Cavel (*Eng., Fr.*) The little, bold, active man.

Cavendish (*Eng.*) One who came from Cavendish (Cafna's pasture), in Suffolk.

Caver (*Eng.*) Descendant of Cafa, or possibly Cafhere.

Caverly (*Eng.*) One who came from Calverley (pasture for calves), in the West Riding of Yorkshire.

Cavett (*Fr.*) Dweller in, or near, a small hollow or sunken road.

Cavey (*Ir.*) Contraction of Mac Daibhidh, that is, son of David (commander; beloved; friend).

Cavil (*Eng.*) One who came from Caville

or Cavil (jackdaw field), in the East Riding of Yorkshire.

Caviness, Cavness (*Eng.*) Abbreviated form of Cavendish, q.v.

Cawley (*Eng.*) One who came from Caughley (daw wood), in Shropshire.

Cawood (*Eng.*) One who came from Cawood (jackdaw wood), the name of places in Lancashire and the West Riding of Yorkshire.

Cawthon, Cawthorn, Cawthorne (*Eng.*) One who came from Cawthorn (bare thorn bush), in the North Riding of Yorkshire; or from Cawthorne in the West Riding of Yorkshire; one who made and sold cauldrons.

Cayton (*Eng.*) One who came from Cayton (Caega's homestead), the name of places in the North Riding and the West Riding of Yorkshire.

Caywood (*Eng.*) One who came from Cawood (wood where jackdaws were seen), the name of places in Lancashire and the West Riding of Yorkshire.

Cazeau (*Fr.*) Dweller near, or in, an unusual house.

Ceaser (*Eng.*) Descendant of Cesario (the hairy one).

Cech (*Pol.*) One who belonged to the guild or association.

Cecil (*Eng., Wel.*) Descendant of Cecil or Cecilius (blind); Anglicized form of Seissyllt (sixth).

Cedarbaum (*Ger.*) Dweller near a cedar tree.

Cedarblade (*Sw.*) Cedar leaf.

Cedarleaf (*Sw.*) Cedar leaf, an Americanized form.

Cedergren, Cedergreen (*Sw.*) Cedar branch.

Cederholm (*Sw.*) Cedar river island.

Cederlund (*Sw.*) Cedar grove; dweller in a grove of cedar trees.

Cegielski (*Pol.*) Dweller near, or worker in, a place where bricks were baked.

Celestini, Celestino, Celestine (*It.*) Descendant of Celestino (heavenly). Celestine was the name of five popes.

Cella (*It.*) Dweller in a cell, probably in some religious house.

Cellini (*It.*) Dweller at the sign of the little bird.

Celmer (*Eng.*) Descendant of Celmar.

Centanni, Centanne (*It.*) Nickname for one in the habit of proposing a toast in which the words "hundred years" were used.

Centeno (*Sp.*) One who came from Centeno (rye), in Spain.

Cepeda (*Sp.*) One who came from Cepeda (exposed roots; spot where heath abounds), in Spain; one who makes and employs traps for catching wild animals.

Cephas, Cephus (*Eng.*) Descendant of Cephas (a stone).

Cerda (*Sp.*) One who came from Cerda (place of swine), in Spain.

Cerejeira (*Port.*) Dweller near a cherry tree.

Cerf (*Fr.*) Dweller at the sign of the hart, Jewish emblem of Naphtali.

Cermak (*Cz.-Sl.*) One with the qualities of a robin; dweller at the sign of the robin.

Cernak (*Cz.-Sl.*) One who came from Cerna (black), the name of several villages in Czechoslovakia.

Cerne (*Yu.-Sl.*) The dark-complexioned or swarthy man, black.

Cernoch (*Cz.-Sl.*) One who was black, a Negro.

Cerny (*Cz.-Sl.*) One with a swarthy complexion, black.

Cervantes, Cervantez (*Sp.*) One who came from Cervantes, in Spain; descendant of Cervanto.

Cervenka (*Cz.-Sl.*) The ruddy or red-haired man; dweller at the sign of the robin.

Cerveny (*Cz.-Sl.*) The red-haired, or ruddy, man.

Cesario, Cesare, Cesaro (*It.*) Descendant of Cesario (the hairy one); dweller at, or near, a fruit grove or flower garden.

Cesna, Cessna (*Cz.-Sl.*) The upright or honorable man.

Cezanne (*Fr.*) One who came from Cezan (Cassius' home), in France.

Chabad (*Heb.*) Acronymic combination of three words *chochma, binah, deah* (wisdom, understanding, knowledge).

Chacon (*Fr.*) The egotistical man; one who thinks only of himself; one who came from Chacun, in France.

Chadbourne (*Eng.*) One who came from Chatburn (Ceatta's stream), in Lancashire.

Chadd (*Eng.*) Descendant of Ceadd or Ceadda (defense; war).

Chadderton (*Eng.*) One who came from Chadderton (homestead near the hill fort), in Lancashire.

Chaddock (*Eng.*) Descendant of little Chad (defense; war).

Chadwell (*Eng.*) One who came from Chadwell (cold spring; St. Chad's spring), the name of villages in Essex and Leicestershire.

Chadwick (*Eng.*) One who came from Chadwick (Ceadda's farm), the names of places in Lancashire and Warwickshire.

Chaffee, Chaffe (*Eng.*) One with a bald head.

Chaffin (*Eng.*) Descendant of the little bald one.

Chagall (*Fr., Ger.*) One who cultivated rye; a variant of Segal, q.v.

Chagford (*Eng.*) One who came from Chagford (ford where broom grew), in Devonshire.

Chaiken, Chaikin, Chaikind (*Rus.*) Dweller at the sign of the gull; descendant of Khayke, a dim. of Khaye.

Chaikovsky, Chaikivsky (*Pol., Ukr.*) One who came from Chaikivtsi (place frequented by seagulls), in the Ukraine.

Chaillier (*Fr.*) One who breaks stones into smaller pieces.

Chaimowitz (*Ger.*) Descendant of Chaim, Yiddish form of Hyman (life).

Chait, Chaitkin, Chaitlen (*Heb.*) One who made outer garments, a tailor.

Chalfant, Chalfont (*Eng.*) One who came

from Chalfont (Ceadel's spring), in Buckinghamshire.

Chalfen, Chalfin (*Heb.*) One who changed money.

Chalifoux (*Fr.*) Dweller near the hot oven; metonymic for the lime burner.

Chalkley (*Eng.*) One who came from Chawleigh (calf pasture), in Devonshire.

Chalmers (*Scot.*) Officer in charge of the private household of a king or nobleman; one who served as a chamber attendant.

Chalupa (*Pol.*) Dweller in a peasant's cottage.

Chalupka, Chaloupka (*Cz.*) Dweller in a small cottage.

Chamberlain, Chamberlin (*Eng., Fr.*) The officer in charge of the private household of a king or important nobleman.

Chambers (*Eng.*) The officer in charge of the private household of a king or important nobleman; one who worked in the chamber, sometimes the reception room of an important household.

Chamblis, Chambliss (*Fr.*) One who came from Chambles (curve or bend), in France.

Chambord (*Fr.*) One with long legs.

Chambre (*Fr.*) One who came from Chambre (room), the name of several places in France.

Champ (*Fr.*) Dweller in, or near, the field.

Champagne (*Fr.*) One who came from the Champagne (level country), a region in France.

Champion (*Fr., Eng.*) One who engaged in combat, a champion, usually one engaged to fight for another.

Champlain (*Fr.*) Englished variant of Champagne, q.v.

Champley (*Fr.*) One who came from Chambly (Camillius' estate), in France.

Champlin (*Eng.*) Variant of Chamberlain, q.v.

Champness (*Eng.*) One who came from

Champagne (level country), a region in France.

Champney (*Fr.*) One who came from Champagne (the plain), a town in France.

Chan (*Chin.*) Old.

Chance (*Fr., Eng.*) One who came from Chance (Cantius' estate), in France; nickname for one having good luck.

Chancellor (*Eng., Scot.*) One who held the office of chancellor, an official who kept registers of an order of knighthood; or an ecclesiastical judge; one who was an official secretary.

Chandler (*Eng.*) One who made or sold candles and small wax images for ecclesiastical offerings.

Chaney (*Eng.*) A variant of Cheney, q.v.

Chang (*Chin., Kor.*) Draw-bow; open; mountain; constantly.

Channell (*Eng.*) Dweller near the canal.

Channing (*Eng., Ir.*) Palatal form of Canning, q.v.

Chapa (*Sp.*) One noted for wearing an unusual cloak.

Chapin (*Fr.*) One who made and sold low shoes.

Chaplin (*Eng.*) A clergyman who has a chapel, a chaplain.

Chapman, Chipman, Chepman (*Eng.*) The merchant or tradesman, a peddler.

Chapp (*Eng.*) A shortening of Chapman, q.v.; one who made and sold chapes, churchmen's vestments.

Chappell, Chapel, Chapple, Chapell, Chappelle (*Eng.*) Dweller near a chapel or sanctuary.

Chaput (*Fr.*) One attired in a cope, a long enveloping ecclesiastical vestment; one who came from Chapet (cope), in France; one who worked in wood, a carpenter.

Charbonneau, Charboneau (*Fr.*) One who made and sold charcoal.

Charet (*Fr.*) One who worked with, or sold, hand carts or barrows.

Charles (*Eng., Fr.*) Descendant of Charles (man); one who came from

Charles (rock palace), in Devonshire.

Charlesworth (*Eng.*) One who came from Charlesworth (Ceofl's homestead), in Derbyshire.

Charlet, Charlot (*Fr.*) Descendant of little Charles (man).

Charley (*Eng.*) One who came from Charley (rock woods), in Leicestershire.

Charlock (*Eng.*) One who came from Charlock (cold stream), in Northamptonshire.

Charlton, Charleston (*Eng.*) One who came from Charlton (village of the free peasants), the name of many places in England.

Charlwood (*Eng.*) One who came from Charlwood (the peasant's wood), in Surrey.

Charman (*Eng.*) One who drove a cart; one who worked in a quarry.

Charney (*Eng.*) One who came from Charney (island in the Charn river), in Berkshire.

Charpentier (*Fr.*) One who worked with wood, a carpenter.

Charter, Chartier (*Eng., Fr.*) One who drove a cart, a carter.

Chartley (*Eng.*) One who came from Chartley (rough, open place in a wood), in Staffordshire.

Chartridge (*Eng.*) One who came from Chartridge (rough open place in a wood in a range of hills), in Buckinghamshire.

Charvat (*Fr.*) The bald-headed man.

Chase, Chace (*Eng., Fr.*) Dweller at the hunting ground or woods; dweller in a small cabin.

Chasen, Chasin (*Fr.*) One who made and sold door and window frames.

Chasseur (*Fr.*) One who hunted game, a huntsman.

Chastain, Chasteen (*Eng.*) The governor or keeper of a castle.

Chatburn (*Eng.*) One who came from Chatburn (Ceatta's brook), in Lancashire.

Chateaubriand, Chateaubriant (*Fr.*) One who came from Chateaubriant (for-

tress of Brientius or Bryan), in France.

Chatelaine, Chatelain (*Eng.*) One who served as governor or constable of a castle; or as warden of a prison.

Chatfield (*Eng.*) One who came from Catfield (field frequented by wild cats), in Norfolk.

Chatham (*Eng.*) One who came from Chatham (homestead by a forest), in Essex.

Chatman, Chatmon (*Eng.*) Variant of Chapman, q.v.

Chatterton (*Eng.*) Variant of Chadderton, q.v.

Chaucer (*Eng.*) One who made, or sold, pantaloons or tight coverings for the legs and feet.

Chauncy, Chauncey (*Eng.*) One who came from Chancey or Chançay (Cantius' estate), in France.

Chauvet, Chauvin (*Fr.*) Descendant of the little bald man.

Chavarria (*Sp.*) One who came from Chavarri, in Spain; shortened form of Echevarria, q.v.

Chavez, Chaves (*Sp.*) Descendant of Jaime, a Spanish form of Jacobus (may God protect; the supplanter); or of Isabel (oath to Baal), a Spanish male name.

Chavin (*Fr.*) One who came from Chavin (Cavannus' estate), in France.

Chavis (*Fr.*) One who came from Chavois (hollow), in France.

Chazin, Chazen (*Heb.*) The soloist who sang liturgical music in the synagogue.

Cheatham, Cheetham, Cheathem, Cheetam, Cheatum (*Eng.*) One who came from Cheetham (homestead by a forest), in Lancashire.

Cheatley (*Eng.*) One who came from Chatley (Ceatta's grove), in Essex.

Chedsey (*Eng.*) One who came from Chedzoy (Cedd's island), in Somerset.

Chedworth (*Eng.*) One who came from Chedworth (Cedda's homestead), in Gloucestershire.

Cheedle (*Eng.*) Dweller in a grove in a narrow valley.

Cheek, Cheeks, Cheke (*Eng.*) One with a prominent jaw; a pet name of endearment meaning chick or little chicken.

Cheers (*Eng.*) The dear, beloved man.

Cheesebourough (*Eng.*) One who came from Cheseburgh, now Cheeseburn (gravel fort), in Northumberland.

Cheeseman (*Eng.*) One who made, or sold, cheese.

Cheever, Cheevers (*Eng.*) Dweller at the sign of the goat; one who cared for goats.

Chelford (*Eng.*) One who came from Chelford (Ceolla's ford), in Cheshire.

Chelius (*Ger.*) One who made and sold boxes or coffers.

Chellberg (*Eng.*) One who came from Chelborough (chalk hill), in Dorset.

Chellew (*Eng.*) Dweller in the house by the pool.

Chelminsky, Chelminski (*Rus., Pol.*) One who came from Chelm (hillock), the name of several places in Poland and Russia.

Cheltenham (*Eng.*) One who came from Cheltenham (hill enclosure), in Gloucestershire.

Chelton (*Eng.*) Variant of Chilton, q.v.

Chemitt (*Ger.*) Variant of the German Schmidt, found among the Creoles in Louisiana.

Chen (*Chin.*) Attend to, arrange.

Chenault (*Fr.*) Dweller near the irrigation canal.

Cheney, Cheyne (*Eng.*) One who came from Quesney, Cheney or Chenay (oak grove), in France; dweller near the chain, or barrier, used to close a street at night.

Cheng (*Chin.*) Journey; to complete.

Chennell (*Eng.*) One who came from Chenal (canal), in France; dweller near the small oak tree.

Chenoweth (*Eng.*) Dweller in the new or recently constructed house; one who came from Chenowath (new house), in Cornwall.

Cherington, Cherrington (*Eng.*) One who came from Cherrington (church enclosure), in Gloucestershire.

Cherne (*Cz.*) One with a dark or swarthy complexion, black.

Cherney (*Cz.-Sl.*) The dark-complexioned man.

Chernich, Chernick (*Yu.-Sl., Rus.*) One with a dark complexion.

Chernoff (*Rus.*) The dark-complexioned person.

Cherry, Cherrie, Cherrey (*Eng.*) Dweller at, or near, a cherry tree; a beloved person.

Chesham (*Eng.*) One who came from Chesham (enclosure by a heap of stones), in Buckinghamshire.

Cheshire, Chesher, Chesshire (*Eng.*) One who came from Cheshire (Roman fortification district), a county in England.

Chesler, Chessler (*Eng.*) One who made and sold cheese.

Chesley (*Eng.*) One who came from Chearsley (Ceolred's meadow), in Buckinghamshire.

Chesnay, Chesney (*Eng.*) Same as Cheyne, q.v.

Chess, Chessman (*Eng.*) One who made and sold cheese.

Chesser, Chessor (*Eng.*) One who came from Cheshire (Roman fortification district), a county in England.

Chessick (*Eng.*) One who came from Cheswick (cheese farm), in Northumberland.

Chessington (*Eng.*) One who came from Chessington (Cissa's hill), in Surrey.

Chessor, Chesser (*Eng.*) A variant of Cheshire, q.v.

Chester (*Eng.*) One who came from Chester (walled town), the name of several places in England; dweller near an old Roman fort or camp.

Chestleigh (*Eng.*) One who came from Chearsley (Ceolred's grove), in Buckinghamshire.

Chestnut, Chesnutt, Chesnut (*Eng.*) Dweller near the chestnut tree.

Chetham (*Eng.*) Variant of Cheatham, q.v.

Chetwood, Chetwode (*Eng.*) One who came from Chetwode (wood wood, from *cet*, a British name for a wood to which was later added an explanatory Old English *wudu*), in Buckinghamshire.

Cheung (*Chin.*) Sedate.

Cheval (*Fr.*) Dweller at the sign of the horse.

Chevalier, Chevallier (*Fr.*) One who acted as a military servant to the king, a knight; one who held his land of the king in exchange for military service; member of a legion of honor.

Chevallo (*It.*) Nickname given because of some horselike quality; dweller at the sign of the horse.

Chevrier (*Fr.*) One who took care of goats, a goatherd.

Chevrolet (*Fr.*) Dweller at the sign of the little goat.

Chew (*Eng., Chin.*) One who came from Chew (river of the chickens); dweller near the river Chew, in England; one who came from Chew, a province in China; hill.

Cheyne, Cheyney (*Eng., Scot.*) One who came from Chenay, Cheney, Le Quesnay, or Quesnay (oak grove), in France; dweller at an oak grove.

Chez (*Fr.*) Dweller in an isolated house.

Chi (*Chin.*) Lucky; young; record.

Chiappe (*It.*) Descendant of Ciappa, a pet form of Giacomo, Italian form of James (may God protect; the supplanter).

Chiappetta, Chiappetti, Chiapetta (*It.*) Descendant of little Ciapo, a pet form of Giacomo (may God protect; the supplanter).

Chiaro, Chiarello (*It.*) One with a clear or light complexion.

Chichester (*Eng.*) One who came from Chichester (Cissi's fortification; Roman fort on a bog), in Sussex.

Chichton (*Eng.*) Dweller in, or near, Cicca's homestead.

Chick (*Eng.*) A pet name of endearment from the chicken; dweller at the sign of the chick.

Chicken (*Fr.*) The little, poor man.

Chicoine (*Fr.*) One frequently engaged in lawsuits; or who haggles or quibbles over small matters.

Chidester (*Eng.*) Variant of Chichester, q.v.

Chidley, Chidlow (*Eng.*) One who came from Chidlow (Cidda's tumulus), in Cheshire.

Chidsey (*Eng.*) Variant of Chedsey, q.v.

Chiero (*It.*) The cleric or wandering scholar.

Chiesa (*It.*) Dweller near, or worker in, a church.

Chilcote (*Eng.*) One who came from Chilcote (the children's cottage), in Leicestershire; or from Chilcote (cot of the retainers), in Northamptonshire.

Childers, Childer (*Eng.*) Of obscure origin, but possibly a descendant of Chilbert (cauldron, bright); or possibly referring to one who has had a child; might be a contraction of childer-house, and thus designate one who operated such a place.

Childerston (*Eng.*) One who came from Cholderton (Ceolweard's homestead; village of Ceolhere's people), the name of places in Hampshire and Wiltshire; or from Chilson in Oxfordshire or Chilston in Kent, both formerly spelled Childeston (homestead of the young nobleman).

Childress (*Eng.*) A variant of Childers, q.v.

Childs, Child, Childe (*Eng.*) An attendant, a young man or young knight, sometimes the youngest son; descendant of Cilda (child).

Chiles, Chillis (*Eng.*) Variant of Childs, q.v.

Chilson, Chillson (*Eng.*) One who came from Chilson (homestead of the young nobleman), in Oxfordshire.

Chilton (*Eng.*) One who came from Chilton (the noble youth's homestead), the name of several villages in England.

Chin (*Chin., Kor.*) Increase; true; to grasp.

Ching (*Eng.*) An old spelling of King, q.v.

Chinn (*Eng.*) One with a prominent or large chin.

Chinnock (*Eng.*) One who came from Chinnock (small ravine), in Somerset.

Chiodo, Chiodini (*It.*) One who made and sold nails.

Chionis, Chionos (*Gr.*) One who came from Chios (snow), an island, also chief town, in the Aegean Sea.

Chiovari, Chiovare (*It.*) One who came from Chiavari, in Italy; one who made and sold keys.

Chipchase (*Eng.*) One who came from Chipchase (heap of logs), in Northumberland.

Chipley (*Eng.*) One who came from Chipley (wood where logs were obtained; Cippa's grove), the name of villages in Suffolk and Somerset.

Chipman (*Eng.*) Variant of Chapman, q.v.

Chippindale (*Eng.*) One who came from Chippendale (the valley with the market place), in Lancashire.

Chipps (*Eng.*) Descendant of Cippa (trader).

Chisby (*Eng.*) One who came from Chisbury (Cissa's fortified place), in Wiltshire.

Chisholm, Chisholme, Chisolm (*Scot.*) One who came from Chisholm (waterside meadow where cheese was made), in Roxburghshire.

Chism, Chisum, Chisom (*Scot., Eng.*) Abbreviated form of Chisholm, q.v.

Chittenden (*Eng.*) One who came from Chittenden (Citta's valley), in Kent.

Chittick, Chittock (*Eng.*) Descendant of little Chit (child).

Chitty (*Eng.*) Descendant of little Citta.

Chitwood (*Eng.*) Variant of Chetwood, q.v.

Chiu (*Chin.*) Mound; to teach.

Chivington (*Eng.*) One who came from Chevington (homestead of Ceofa's people; Ceofa's homestead), the name of places in Northumberland and Suffolk.

Chmelar (*Cz.*) One who grew and sold hops.

Chmid (*Du.*) Variant of Dutch Smid found among the Creoles in Louisiana.

Chmiel (*Pol.*) One who grew hops.

Chmielewski (*Pol.*) The son of the hop grower.

Chmura (*Pol.*) Possibly a nickname for one so light-colored or white as a cloud.

Cho (*Chin., Kor.*) To establish; to draw a bow.

Choate, Choat (*Eng.*) The fat or chubby person.

Choi, Choy (*Chin.*) Tortoise.

Chojnacki (*Pol.*) One who came from Chojnacki (pine trees), in Poland.

Cholewa (*Pol., Ukr.*) One who made boots.

Cholmondeley, Cholmeley (*Eng.*) One who came from Cholmondeley (Ceolmund's grove), in Cheshire. The village name and the surname are often pronounced Chumley.

Chong (*Chin.*) Hanging bell.

Chopwell (*Eng.*) One who came from Chopwell (merchant's spring), in Durham.

Chorley (*Eng.*) One who came from Chorley (the peasant's grove), the name of places in Cheshire, Lancashire, and Staffordshire.

Chorlton (*Eng.*) One who came from Chorlton (settlement of the free peasants; Ceolfrith's homestead), the name of several places in England.

Chorvat (*Ukr., Pol., Sl.*) One who came from Croatia, a Croat.

Chou, Chow (*Chin.*) Everywhere.

Chouinard (*Fr.*) One who baked white bread.

Christ, Chrest (*Eng.*) Descendant of Christ, a pet form of Christian (follower of Christ); or of Christopher (Christ-bearer).

Christensen, Christenson (*Dan.*) The son of Christian (follower of Christ).

Christian (*Eng., Ger.*) Descendant of Christian (follower of Christ); one who came from Krystan, in Germany.

Christiano, Christiani (*It., Port., Sp.*) Descendant of Christiano (follower of Christ).

Christiansen, Christianson (*Nor., Dan.*) The son of Christian (follower of Christ).

Christie, Christy (*Scot., Eng.*) Descendant of Christie or Christy, pet forms of Christian (follower of Christ) and Christopher (Christ-bearer).

Christl, Christal (*Scot.*) Descendant of Christal, a pet form of Christopher (Christ-bearer).

Christman, Christmann, Chrisman (*Ger.*) Descendant of Christianus (follower of Christ); the servant of Christian.

Christmas (*Eng.*) Descendant of Christmas, a name given to a child born on that day.

Christopher (*Eng., Scot.*) Descendant of Christopher (Christ-bearer); dweller at the sign of St. Christopher.

Christophersen, Christoffersen (*Dan., Nor., Sw.*) The son of Christopher (Christ-bearer).

Christopherson (*Eng.*) The son of Christopher (Christ-bearer).

Chrobak (*Ukr.*) Dweller at the sign of the worm; one with wormlike characteristics.

Chronis, Chrones, Chronos (*Gr.*) Descendant of Chronis, a pet form of Polychronis (he who may live many years; an old man); or of Chronos (time), known also as Saturn, the Greek god of time.

Chruscinski (*Pol.*) Dweller among, or near, brushwood.

Chrysler (*Ger.*) Americanized spelling of Kreisler, q.v.

Chrystal (*Scot.*) Descendant of Chrystal, a pet form of Christopher (Christ-bearer).

Chrzanowski (*Pol.*) One who came from Chrzanow (horse radish), in Poland.

Chu (*Chin.*) Vermilion; to bless; bamboo; every.

Chubaty (*Ukr.*) One with a prominent tuft.

Chubb (*Eng.*) The thick, fat man.

Chudak (*Cz.-Sl.*) A poor man, one who owned little in material goods.

Chudy (*Pol.*) The tall, lean, lanky man.

Chumley, Chumbley, Chumlea (*Eng.*) One who came from Chulmleigh (Ceolmund's grove), in Devonshire; popular pronunciation of Cholmondeley, q.v.

Chung (*Chin.*) Hanging bell.

Church (*Eng.*) Dweller near, or worker in, a building used for Christian worship; one who came from Church (the church), in Lancashire.

Churchill, Churchull (*Eng.*) Dweller on, or near, the church hill; one who came from Churchill (church hill), the name of several places in England.

Churchwell (*Eng.*) Dweller at the spring by the church.

Chute (*Eng.*) One who came from Chute (forest), in Wiltshire.

Ciaccio, Ciaccia (*It.*) The large or fat man.

Ciampa, Ciampi (*It.*) One who was left-handed.

Cibulka, Cibula (*Cz.*) One who raised and sold onions.

Ciccolo, Ciccola (*It.*) Descendant of Cicco, a pet form of Francisco (the free).

Ciccone (*It.*) Descendant of big Cicco, a pet form of Francisco (the free).

Cicero (*It.*) Descendant of Cicero (chick pea or vetch); one who raised and sold chick peas.

Cichocki (*Pol.*) The quiet, silent man.

Cichon, Cichy (*Pol.*) The quiet or calm person.

Ciecko (*Pol.*) The young person or child.

Cielak (*Pol.*) One who took care of calves.

Cierniak, Cierny (*Cz.-Sl.*) The dark or swarthy man.

Cieslak, Ciesla (*Pol.*) The worker in wood, a carpenter.

Cihlar (*Cz.*) One who made, or built with, bricks.

Cimino (*It.*) One who grew cumin or caraway, a plant of the carrot family; dweller near where cumin or caraway grew.

Cinquegrani (*It.*) Nickname after a coin weighing five grains.

Cintron (*Port., Sp.*) One who came from Cintra (curvature of a bow), in Portugal.

Cipolla (*It.*) One who cultivated and sold onions.

Cipriani, Cipriano (*It.*) Descendant of Cipriano, Italian form of Cyprian (island of the tree); one who came from Cyprus (tree island).

Cirone (*It.*) The ugly, chubby man.

Cirrincione (*It.*) Dweller at the sign of the greenfinch.

Cisek, Ciske (*Pol.*) Dweller near a small yew tree.

Cisneros (*Sp.*) One who came from Cisneros (swan roost), in Spain.

Ciszewski (*Pol.*) One who came from Ciszewo, in Poland; the quiet man.

Citron, Citrone (*Fr.*) One who raised and sold lemons.

Ciucci, Ciucio (*It.*) Dweller at the sign of the donkey; one thought to possess the characteristics of a donkey.

Ciura (*Fr.*) One who raised and sold chick peas.

Claesson, Claessens, Claeson (*Sw., Nor.*) The son of Claes, a pet form of Nikolaus (people's victory).

Claffey, Claffy (*Ir.*) Son of Flaitheamh (ruler; lord).

Clafford (*Eng.*) Variant of Clifford, q.v.

Clagett, Claggett (*Eng.*) One who came from Claygate (entrance to the clayey district), in Surrey.

Clagg (*Eng.*) One who came from Clegg (haystack), in Lancashire; dweller on clayey soil.

Claghorn (*Scot.*) One who came from Cleghorn (clay house), in Lanarkshire.

Claiborne (*Eng.*) Variant of Clayborn, q.v.

Clair, Claire (*Eng., Fr.*) Descendant of Clair (illustrious), a man's name; the light-complexioned man; one who came from Clare (clayey slope), the name of several places in England;

one who came from St. Clare or St. Clair, the names of various places in France.

Clampitt (*Eng.*) Dweller near the clay pit.

Clancy, Clancey (*Ir.*) The son of Flannchadh (ruddy warrior).

Clanfield (*Eng.*) One who came from Clanfield (clean open field), the name of places in Hampshire and Oxfordshire.

Clanton (*Eng.*) One who came from Clandon (hill free of weeds), in Surrey.

Clapham (*Eng.*) One who came from Clapham (homestead on a hill), the name of places in Bedfordshire, Surrey, and Sussex.

Clapp (*Eng.*) Descendant of Clapa (chatter).

Clapper (*Eng.*) Dweller near the rough or natural bridge across a stream, or stepping stones.

Clapshaw (*Eng.*) Dweller in, or near, a grove on a hill.

Clapton (*Eng.*) One who came from Clapton (homestead on a hill), the name of places in Berkshire and Cambridgeshire.

Clare (*Eng., Ir.*) One who came from Clare (clayey hillside; gentle or bright), the name of villages in Oxfordshire and Suffolk; one who came from St. Clair or St. Clare (bright or clear) the names of various places in France; or from Clare (a plain), the name of several villages and a county in Ireland.

Clarewood (*Eng.*) One who came from Clarewood (clover enclosure), in Northumberland.

Claridge (*Eng.*) Descendant of Clarice (bright).

Claris (*Eng.*) Descendant of Claris (bright).

Clark, Clarke (*Eng.*) A clergyman, scholar, scribe or recorder (British pronunciation of clerk).

Clarkston (*Scot.*) One who came from Clarkston (clerk's homestead), in Scotland.

Clasby (*Eng.*) One who came from Cleasby (Klepp's homestead), in the North Riding of Yorkshire.

Clason, Clayson, Classon (*Scot., Eng.*) The son of Clas, a pet form of Nicholas (people's victory).

Class (*Eng.*) Descendant of Clas, a pet form of Nicholas (people's victory).

Classen, Clasen, Claassen (*Sw., Nor.*) The son of Clas, a pet form of Nicholas (people's victory).

Clatt (*Scot.*) One who came from Clatt (rocky pillar or cliff), in Aberdeenshire.

Claudio (*It., Sp.*) Descendant of Claudio, Italian and Spanish form of Claude (lame).

Clausen, Claussen, Clauson (*Nor., Dan., Eng.*) The son of Claus, a pet form of Nicholas (people's victory).

Claver (*Eng.*) One who tended a gate; or had charge of the keys of a door or prison.

Clawson (*Eng.*) One who came from Clawson (Clac's homestead), in Leicestershire; the son of Claus, a pet form of Nicholas (people's victory).

Claxton (*Eng.*) One who came from Claxton (Clac's homestead), the name of several places in England.

Clay, Claye (*Eng.*) Dweller at the clayey place.

Clayborn, Clayborne (*Eng.*) Dweller near the stream with clay banks.

Claybrook, Claybrooks (*Eng.*) One who came from Claybrooke (clayey stream), in Leicestershire; dweller near the brook with clayey shores.

Clayburn (*Eng.*) Variant of Clayborn, q.v.

Claycombe, Claycomb (*Eng.*) Dweller in the clayey, narrow valley.

Clayman (*Eng.*) One who prepares the clay in brickmaking.

Claypole, Claypool (*Eng.*) One who came from Claypole (clayey pool), in Lincolnshire.

Clayton (*Eng.*) One who came from Clayton (village on clayey soil), the name of several towns in England.

Clear (*Eng., Ir.*) Variant of Clare, q.v.; one who came from Clere (gentle; lukewarm; bright), in Hampshire.

Clearwater (*Eng.*) Dweller near a gentle or lukewarm stream; or by a bright lake or stream.

Cleary (*Ir.*) Grandson of Cleireach (cleric or clerk).

Cleator (*Eng.*) One who came from Cleator (hut by a rock or cliff), in Cumberland.

Cleaver, Clever (*Eng.*) Dweller near a cliff; one who cut or split wood for laths.

Cleaves, Cleve, Cleave (*Eng.*) Dweller at the cliff; or rock; or steep descent; or at the bank of a river.

Clegg, Cleggs, Cleggett (*Eng., Nor.*) Dweller on clayey soil; one who came from Clegg (haystack), in Lancashire; dweller near a large haystack, probably referring to a farm name.

Cleghorn (*Scot.*) One who came from Cleghorn (clay house), in Lanarkshire.

Cleinesmith (*Ger.*) Anglicization of Kleinschmidt, q.v.

Cleland, Clelland (*Scot.*) One who came from Cleland (clay land), in Lanarkshire.

Clem (*Eng.*) Descendant of Clem, a pet form of Clement (merciful).

Clemenceau (*Fr.*) Descendant of little Clement (merciful).

Clemens, Clemons, Clemmons (*Scot., Ger.*) Descendant of Clement (merciful).

Clemenson, Clemensen, Clemmensen (*Dan.*) The son of Clement (merciful).

Clemente, Clementi, Clemento (*It.*) Descendant of Clement (merciful).

Clements, Clement (*Scot., Fr.*) Descendant of Clement (merciful).

Clemo, Climo (*Eng.*) Dweller on the slope or hillside.

Clendening, Clendenin, Clendenen (*Scot.*) One who came from Glendinning (glen of the fair hill), in Westerkirk, Dumfriesshire.

Clerc, Clerq (*Fr.*) The clergyman; a learned man or scholar.

Clerie, Clery (*Ir.*) Variant of Cleary, q.v.

Clerkenwell (*Eng.*) One who came from Clerkenwell (the spring of the clerks or clerics), in Middlesex.

Clerkin, Clerken (*Eng.*) A clerk; one who performed sacerdotal functions.

Clettenberg (*Ger.*) One who came from Klettenberg, in Germany.

Clevedon (*Eng.*) One who came from Clevedon (hill with a cliff), in Somerset.

Cleveland, Cleaveland (*Eng.*) One who came from Cleveland (hilly district), in Yorkshire.

Clevett (*Eng.*) Dweller near a small cliff.

Clew, Clewes (*Eng.*) Dweller at a hollow or ravine.

Clewlow (*Eng.*) One who came from Clulow (tumulus at a hollow or ravine), in Cheshire.

Cleworth (*Eng.*) One who came from Clayworth (homestead in a river fork), in Nottinghamshire.

Cliburn, Cliborn (*Eng.*) One who came from Cliburn (cliff stream), in Westmorland.

Cliff, Cliffe (*Eng.*) Dweller near a steep descent or slope; or near a steep rock.

Clifford (*Eng.*) One who came from Clifford (ford at a cliff), the name of several places in England; dweller at the shallow river crossing with the steep bank.

Clifton (*Eng.*) One who came from Clifton (homestead on hill slope or bank of river), the name of various places in England.

Clinch (*Eng.*) Dweller by the hill; one who came from Clinch or Clench (lump), in Wiltshire.

Cline (*Ger.*) An Anglicization of the German, Klein, q.v.

Clinesmith (*Ger.*) Englished spelling of Kleinschmidt, q.v.

Clinkscales, Clinkscale (*Eng.*) One who

made armor by clinching the scales of metal to leather or heavy linen.

Clinton (*Eng.*) Dweller at the hill enclosure.

Clithero (*Eng.*) One who came from Clitheroe (song-thrush hill), in Lancashire.

Clive (*Eng.*) One who came from Clive (cliff), the name of places in Cheshire and Shropshire.

Cloder (*Eng.*) One who harrowed or rolled land to free it of clods.

Cloford (*Eng.*) One who came from Cloford (river crossing where burdock grew), in Somerset.

Clopton (*Eng.*) One who came from Clapton or Clopton (homestead by a lump or hill), the names of several places in England.

Close (*Eng.*) Dweller at an enclosure or fenced yard.

Clothier (*Eng.*) One who made and sold cloth.

Cloud (*Eng., Scot.*) Dweller near the rock or mass of stone; the son of Leod (ugly).

Clough (*Eng., Wel.*) Dweller at a hollow or ravine; or near a crag or rocky hillock.

Clougherty, Cloherty (*Ir.*) Dweller at, or near, a stone.

Clousing (*Ger.*) The son of Klaus, a pet form of Nicolaus, German form of Nicholas (people's victory).

Clouston (*Scot.*) One who came from Clouston (cleft homestead), in Orkney.

Cloutier, Cloutrier (*Fr.*) One who made and sold nails.

Clow (*Eng.*) Dweller at a hollow or ravine.

Clucas (*Mx.*) A condensation of MacLucas, the son of Luke (light).

Cluff (*Eng.*) Dweller at a hollow or ravine.

Clugston (*Eng.*) One who came from Cloughton (homestead in a ravine), in the North Riding of Yorkshire.

Cluny, Clunie, Cluney (*Eng., Scot.*) One who came from Cluny (Clunius' farm), in France; or from Clunie (slope near the reef), in Perthshire.

Clutter (*Fr.*) Variant of Cloutier, q.v.

Clutterbuck (*Eng.*) Dweller near a noisy brook; a loud person, a roisterer.

Clyne, Clynes (*Scot.*) One who came from Clyne (a slope), the name of two places in Scotland.

Cnota (*Pol.*) The good, virtuous man.

Coachman (*Eng.*) One who drove a carriage or handled a coach; one who made couches.

Coade (*Eng.*) Dweller in the wood.

Coady (*Eng.*) Dweller at, or near, a wood.

Coakley, Cokeley, Cokely (*Eng.*) Dweller in, or near, a wood frequented by wild birds.

Coan (*Ir.*) Grandson of Comhghan (twin); variant of Coyne, q.v.

Coates, Coats, Coate (*Eng.*) Descendant of one who occupied a cottage and tilled ten acres or less; one who came from Coates or Cotes (cottage or shelter), the names of several places in England.

Coatsworth (*Eng.*) Dweller at the cottage enclosure.

Cobb, Cobbe (*Eng.*) One who came from Cobb (round reef; semicircular pier), in Dorset; dweller near the roundish mass or lump; descendant of Cobb, a pet form of Jacob (may God protect; the supplanter).

Coblentz, Coblens (*Fr.*) One who came from Koblenz (confluence), in Germany.

Coburn (*Eng.*) One who came from Colburn (cool stream), in Yorkshire; dweller at a stream frequented by game birds.

Coccia (*It.*) One with a large or unusual head.

Cocco, Cocci, Cocca (*It.*) Descendant of Cocci, a diminutive suffix, a pet form of such names as Francoccio and Domenicocci.

Cochran, Cochrane (*Ir., Scot.*) Grandson of little Cogar (confident); one who came from Cochran (red brook) in Renfrewshire.

Cock, Cocks (*Eng.*) Descendant of Cock (boy; wild bird); one who strutted like a cock; the watchman or leader.

Cockburn (*Scot.*) One who came from Cockburn (red stream), in Scotland.

Cockcroft (*Eng.*) Dweller in, or near, an enclosed piece of land where cocks were kept.

Cocker (*Eng.*) Dweller near the Cocker (crooked), the name of rivers in Cumberland and Lancashire.

Cockerham (*Eng.*) One who came from Cockerham (homestead on the Cocker river), in Lancashire.

Cockfield (*Eng.*) One who came from Cockfield (Cocca's open land), in Durham.

Cockle (*Eng.*) Dweller near Old English *coccel*, a weed common in the fields; one who made head coverings for women.

Cockram, Cockrum (*Eng.*) Condensed form of Cockerham, q.v.

Cockrell, Cockerill (*Eng.*) One who raised and sold young cocks, a poultry dealer.

Cockson (*Eng.*) The son of Cock (boy).

Codd (*Eng.*) Metonymic for a maker of leather bags; nickname for a stupid man; one with a protruding stomach.

Codding (*Eng.*) The son of Codda (a bag).

Coddington (*Eng.*) One who came from Coddington (village of Cotta's people; Codda's homestead), the name of four places in England.

Codman (*Eng.*) One who carried, and sold goods from, a bag or pouch.

Cody (*Ir.*) The helper or assistant; the son of Odo or Otho (wealthy); grandson of Cuidightheach (helper).

Coe (*Eng.*) Dweller at the sign of the jackdaw.

Coelho (*Port.*) One who hunted rabbits; dweller at the sign of the rabbit.

Coen (*Ir.*) Grandson of Comhghan (twin); variant of Coyne, q.v.; the son of Eoghan (well-born).

Coffer, Cofer, Cofferer (*Eng.*) One who made coffers, boxes and chests; one who kept the treasure box; a treasurer; one who made and sold coifs, a kind of close-fitting cap for both sexes.

Coffey, Coffee (*Ir.*) Grandson of Cobhthach (victorious).

Coffin (*Eng., Fr.*) The bald man; one who sold baskets.

Coffman (*Ger.*) The merchant or tradesman, an Anglicization of Kaufmann.

Cogan, Coggan, Cogen (*Eng.*) One who came from Cogan (bowl), in South Wales; dweller in a bowl-shaped valley; a corruption of Kogan, q.v.

Cogburn (*Scot.*) Variant of Cockburn, q.v

Cogger (*Eng.*) One who built boats; one who worked on a boat; a sailor.

Coggeshall, Cogshell (*Eng.*) One who came from Coggeshall (Cogg's corner or hill), in Essex; one who came from Cogshall (Cogg's corner or hill), in Cheshire.

Coggins (*Eng.*) Descendant of Coggin (little cock); dweller at the sign of the little cock.

Coggs (*Eng.*) One who came from Cogges (hill), in Oxfordshire.

Coghill (*Eng.*) Dweller on, or near, the hill frequented by wild birds.

Coglianese (*It.*) One who came from Cogliano, in Italy; dweller on the Coglians, a peak on the Austrian-Italian border.

Cogman (*Eng.*) One who worked on a boat, a sailor.

Cognac (*Fr.*) One who came from Cognac (Connius' estate), in France.

Cogswell (*Eng.*) Dweller at a spring frequented by game birds; one who came from Cogshall (Cogg's hill), in Cheshire.

Cohen, Cohn, Cohan (*Heb.*) The priest. This name indicates a family claiming descent from Aaron, the high priest.

Cohoon (*Ir., Scot.*) Variant of Calhoun, q.v.

Coke (*Eng.*) Variant of Cook, q.v.

Coker (*Eng.*) One who came from Coker (water), in Somerset; one who put

up hay in cocks, a hayworker; the fighter or cockfighter; a reaper.

Cokinos (*Gr.*) The ruddy-complexioned or red-haired man.

Cokley (*Eng.*) One who came from Cockley (clayey soil), in Norfolk.

Colangelo (*It.*) Descendant of Colangelo, a combination of Col from Nicola (people's victory), and Angelo (messenger).

Colantonio (*It.*) Descendant of Colantoni, a combination of Col from Nicola (people's victory) and Antonio, Italian form of Anthony (inestimable).

Colbert (*Eng.*) Descendant of Colbert (cool, bright).

Colburn, Colborne (*Eng.*) One who came from Colburn (cool stream), in Yorkshire; dweller near a cold stream.

Colby (*Eng.*) One who came from Colby (Koli's homestead), the name of places in Norfolk and Westmorland.

Colclough (*Eng.*) Dweller in the cold hollow or ravine.

Coldiron (*Eng., Sp.*) Variant of Calderon, q.v.

Coldren (*Eng.*) Variant of Calderon, q.v.

Coldwater (*Eng.*) Dweller near a cold body of water.

Coldwell (*Eng.*) One who came from Coldwell (cool spring), in Northumberland; variant of Caldwell, q.v.

Cole, Coles (*Eng.*) Descendant of Cole, a pet form of Nicholas (people's victory).

Colebrook (*Eng.*) One who came from Colebrook (cool stream), the name of several villages in England.

Colegate, Colgate (*Eng.*) Dweller at a cool gap in a chain of hills.

Colegrove (*Eng.*) Dweller at the dark grove.

Coleman, Colman (*Eng., Ir.*) Servant of Cole, pet form of Nicholas (people's victory); descendant of Coleman or Colman (little dove); or of Coelmund.

Colerick (*Eng.*) Sharpened form of Coleridge, q.v.

Coleridge (*Eng.*) One who came from Coldridge (ridge where charcoal was produced), in Devonshire; dweller at the black ridge; or at the cold ridge; or on the range of hills where hazels grew.

Colestock (*Eng.*) Dweller near the black monastery; or near the black tree trunk.

Colesworthy (*Eng.*) Dweller in, or near, Col's homestead.

Colewell (*Eng.*) One who came from Coldwell (cool spring), in Northumberland; variant of Colwell, q.v.

Coley (*Eng.*) Descendant of little Cole, a pet form of Nicholas (people's victory).

Colfax, Colfox (*Eng.*) Dweller at the sign of the black fox; a crafty person; one with black hair.

Colgan (*Ir.*) Grandson, or son, of Colga.

Colin (*Eng.*) Descendant of little Cole, a pet form of Nicholas (people's victory).

Collado (*Sp.*) One who came from Collado (narrow pass), the name of several places in Spain.

Collar, Coller (*Eng.*) One who made and sold charcoal.

Collard (*Eng.*) Descendant of Collard, a pet form of Nicholas (people's victory).

Colledge, Collidge (*Eng.*) One who came from Coldridge (ridge where charcoal was made), in Devonshire.

Collen (*Ir.*) Variant of Cullen, q.v.

Collender (*Eng.*) Variant of Callender, q.v.

Collett, Collette, Collet (*Eng., Fr.*) Descendant of little Cole, a pet form of Nicholas (people's victory).

Colletti (*It.*) Dweller on, or near, a hill; descendant of little Cola, a pet form of Nicola (people's victory).

Colley, Collie (*Wel., Eng.*) Descendant of little Coll, a pet form of Nicholas (people's victory).

Collier, Colier (*Eng.*) One who worked, or dealt in, coal, a coal miner; one who made wood charcoal; one who

worked in, or came from the village of Caulieres, in France.

Collinge (*Eng.*) Descendant of Colin, a pet form of Nicholas (people's victory); the son of Cole, pet form of Nicholas (people's victory).

Collins, Collinson, Collings, Colling (*Eng.*) Son of little Cole, a pet form of Nicholas (people's victory).

Collinsworth (*Eng.*) One who came from Colworth, early form, Colingwurth (the homestead of Coling's people), in Bedfordshire; or of Collingwood (wood of disputed ownership), in Staffordshire.

Collison (*Eng.*) The son of Coll or Cole, a pet form of Nicholas (people's victory).

Collister (*Scot.*) Contraction of McAllister, q.v.

Collum (*Eng.*) One who came from Colham (Cola's enclosure), in Middlesex.

Collyer (*Eng.*) Variant of Collier, q.v.

Colomb, Colombe (*Fr.*) One who raised doves; descendant of Colomb (dove).

Colombo, Colombani, Colombini (*It.*) One who raised doves; descendant of Colomb (dove).

Colon (*Sp.*) Descendant of Colon, Spanish form of Columbus (dove); one who raised and sold doves.

Colonna (*It.*) Descendant of little Cola, a pet form of Nicola (people's victory).

Colquhoun (*Scot.*) One who formerly resided on the lands of Colquhoun (narrow corner or wood), in Dumbartonshire.

Colquitt, Colquite (*Eng.*) Dweller in the narrow wood.

Colson, Coleson (*Eng.*) The son of Cole, a pet form of Nicholas (people's victory).

Colston (*Eng.*) One who came from Colston (Kol's homestead), in Nottinghamshire.

Colt (*Eng.*) One who took care of colts; one who was frisky and lively.

Colter (*Eng.*) One who took care of colts, a colt-herd.

Colthard, Coltard (*Eng.*) One who herded colts.

Colton (*Eng.*) One who came from Colton (Cola's homestead; homestead on the Cole river), the name of several places in England.

Columbus (*Eng.*) Descendant of Columba (dove).

Colville, Colvill (*Eng., Scot.*) One who came from Colleville (Col's farm), in Normandy.

Colvin (*Eng., Scot., Ir.*) Descendant of Calvin (bald); son of Anluan (great hero); one who came from Colleville (Col's farm), in Normandy; descendant of Ceolwine (ship, friend).

Colwell (*Eng.*) One who came from Colwell (cool stream), the name of villages in Devonshire and Northumberland.

Combs, Combe, Combes, Comb (*Eng.*) Dweller at the deep hollow or valley; one who came from Combs (crest of hill), the name of places in Derbyshire and Suffolk.

Comeaux, Comeau (*Fr.*) Dweller in a dry valley.

Comer (*Eng.*) One who made and sold combs.

Comerford (*Eng.*) One who came from Comberford (Combra's ford), in Staffordshire.

Comfort (*Eng.*) One who comforts, supports, helps, or encourages others; one who is a source of strength.

Comiskey (*Ir.*) The son of Cumascach (confuser).

Como (*It.*) Descendant of Como, a pet form of Giacomo (may God protect; the supplanter).

Compton (*Eng.*) One who came from Compton (hollow estate), the name of many places in England.

Comstock (*Eng.*) Dweller in a deep valley; one who came from Comstock (monastery in a narrow valley), in England.

Conant, Conan (*Ir.*) Grandson of Conan (little hound).

Conaway (*Wel.*) Variant of Conway, q.v.

Conboy (*Ir.*) Grandson of Cubuidhe (yellow hound).

Concannon (*Ir.*) Grandson of Cucheanainn (fair-headed hound).

Concepcion (*Sp.*) Descendant of Concepcion, a name given in religious devotion to the Immaculate Conception of the Virgin Mary.

Condicot, Condicote (*Eng.*) One who came from Condicote (Cunda's cottage), in Gloucestershire.

Condit, Conditt (*Fr.*) Merchant of pickled foods.

Condon (*Ir.*) Grandson of Cudubhan; one who came from Canton, in Glamorganshire, Wales.

Cone (*Ger.*) American variant of Kohn, q.v.

Conerly (*Ir.*) Variant of Connelly, q.v.

Coney, Cony (*Eng.*) One thought to possess the timidity or other characteristics of a rabbit; dweller at the sign of a rabbit; one who dealt in rabbitskins, a furrier.

Conforti (*It.*) One who enjoyed comfort.

Congdon (*Eng.*) One who came from Congdon (king's hill), in Cornwall.

Conger (*Eng.*) Descendant of Congar (bold, spear).

Congleton (*Eng.*) One who came from Congleton (homestead at the bend), in Cheshire.

Congram (*Eng.*) One who came from Congham (village at the bend), in Norfolk.

Congrave, Congreve (*Eng.*) One who came from Congreve (grove in a valley), in Staffordshire.

Conington (*Eng.*) One who came from Conington (king's manor), the name of villages in Cambridgeshire and Huntingdonshire.

Conklin, Conkling, Concklin (*Du.*) From Dutch *konkelen*, designating one who plots or conspires; descendant of the petty king or chieftain.

Conley, Conly (*Ir.*) Grandson of Conghalach (valorous).

Conlon, Conlin, Conlan (*Ir.*) Grandson of little Conall (high or powerful).

Conn (*Ir.*) Descendant of Conn, a pet form of Constantine (constant).

Connaghty, Conaty (*Ir.*) One who came from the province of Connacht, in Ireland.

Connell, Connal (*Ir.*) Grandson of Conall (high or powerful).

Connelly, Connolly, Connally (*Ir.*) Grandson of Conghal or Conghalach (valorous), the name of seven Irish saints.

Conners, Conner (*Ir.*) Variant of Connors, q.v.

Connery, Conrey (*Ir.*) Grandson of Conaire (dog keeper).

Connors, Connor (*Ir.*) Grandson of Concobair (meddlesome); or of Conchor (high-will or desire).

Conoscenti, Conosenti (*It.*) One who was known, an acquaintance.

Conover (*Du.*) Extreme Americanized corruption of Kouwenhoven, q.v.

Conrad, Conrath (*Ger.*) Descendant of Conrad (bold, counsel).

Conrick (*Ir.*) Son of Annrac.

Conroy, Conry (*Ir.*) The son of Cu-raoi (hound of the plain).

Considine (*Eng.*) Descendant of Constantine (constant or firm of purpose).

Constable (*Eng.*) Originally count of the stable, later a military or civil officer; governor of a royal fortress.

Constantine (*Eng.*) Descendant of Constantine (constant or firm of purpose).

Constantinescu (*Rom.*) The son of Constantine (constant or firm of purpose).

Constantopoulos, Constantopulos (*Gr.*) The son of Constantine (constant or firm of purpose).

Conti, Conte (*It.*) A nobleman; the count; one in the service of a count.

Contreras (*Sp.*) One who came from Contreras, in Castile.

Converse (*Eng., Fr.*) One who has been converted (to the Christian religion); one converted to a religious life as an adult.

Conway (*Ir., Scot., Wel.*) Grandson of Connmhach; dweller at the sign of the yellow hunting dog; one who came from Conway (noisy or stormy), in Scotland; or from Conway, in Wales.

Conwell (*Ir.*) Son of Conmhaol (high chief).

Conybear (*Eng.*) Dweller at a grove where there were many rabbits.

Conyers (*Eng.*) One who coined money, a minter; one who came from Coignieres or Cogners (places where quince trees grew), the names of places in France.

Conyngham, Coningham (*Scot.*) Variant of Cunningham, q.v.

Cooch (*Eng.*) Variant of Couch, q.v.

Coogan, Cogan (*Ir.*) Son of Cogain (contention or strife).

Cook, Cooke (*Eng.*) One who prepared food.

Cooksey, Cooksie (*Eng.*) One who came from Cooksey (Cucu's island), in Worcestershire.

Cool (*Eng.*) One who came from Coole (cows' hill), in Cheshire.

Cooley (*Ir., Eng.*) The son of the servant of St. Mochuille; descendant of little Cole, a pet form of Nicholas (people's victory).

Coolidge, Cooledge (*Eng.*) Dweller near a pool of cold water; one who came from Cowlinge (Cul's or Cula's people), in Suffolk; or from Cookridge (Cuca's stream), in the West Riding of Yorkshire.

Coombs, Coombes (*Eng.*) One who came from Coombes (valleys), in Sussex; dweller in a narrow valley.

Coon, Coons (*Ger.*) An Anglicization of the German Kuhn, q.v.

Cooney (*Eng.*) Dweller at the sign of the rabbit; one thought to possess the characteristics of a rabbit.

Cooper, Couper, Cowper (*Eng.*) One who made and sold casks, buckets, and tubs.

Cooperman (*Eng.*) The servant or helper of one who made casks, buckets, and tubs.

Coopersmith (*Eng.*) The smith who made tubs and casks; variant of Coppersmith, q.v.

Coots, Cootes, Coote (*Eng.*) One who occupied a cottage and tilled ten acres or less; one thought to have the characteristics of a coot, such as stupidity.

Cope (*Eng.*) One who made the long cloak or cape.

Copeland (*Eng.*) One who came from Copeland (bought land), in Cumberland.

Copenhaver (*Ger.*) Americanized form of Kopenhofer, a corrupted German surname.

Copland (*Scot., Eng.*) One who came from Coupland, in Scotland; or from Coupland (bought land), in Northumberland.

Copley, Copely (*Eng.*) Dweller at the meadow on top of the hill.

Copp, Coppe (*Eng., Ger.*) Dweller at the top or summit of a hill; English form of Kopf, q.v.

Coppage, Coppedge (*Eng.*) Dweller at the top of the ridge or steep hill.

Copper (*Eng.*) One who made and sold wooden casks, buckets, and tubs.

Coppersmith, Copersmith (*Eng., Ger.*) One who worked in copper and brass.

Coppinger (*Eng.*) Dweller at the hilltop meadow.

Copple (*Eng.*) One who came from Coppull (peaked hill), in Lancashire; or from Cople (Cocca's pool), in Bedfordshire.

Coppola (*It.*) One who made and sold caps; descendant of Coppola, a shortened form of Jacoppola, variant of Iacoppo, an Italian form of Jacob (may God protect; the supplanter).

Coquelin (*Fr.*) The small man who prepared and cooked food.

Corbally (*Ir.*) One who came from Corbally, in County Louth.

Corbell, Corble (*Eng.*) One who made and sold baskets.

Corbett, Corbet (*Eng., Fr., Ir.*) Dweller at the sign of the raven; the son of Corbet (raven).

Corbin, Corbyn, Corban (*Eng., Fr., Ir.*) Dweller at the sign of the raven; descendant of Coirbin (little chariot).

Corboy (*Ir.*) The son of Corrbuidhe (yellow crane).

Corby (*Scot.*) One who came from Corby (Cor's homestead), in Roxburgh.

Corcoran, Corcrane, Corkran (*Ir.*) Grandson of Corcran (dim. of Corcair, purple).

Cordeiro, Cordeira (*Port.*) One who took care of the lambs.

Cordell, Cordill (*Fr.*) One who made and sold light rope.

Corder, Cordier, Cord (*Eng.*) One who made and sold cords or rope.

Cordero (*Sp.*) One who made strings for guitars and violas; one who had charge of sheep, a shepherd; the meek, gentle man.

Cordes (*Fr.*) One who came from Cordes (ropes), in France; one who made rope.

Cordiner, Cordner, Cordon (*Eng.*) One who worked in leather; a shoemaker.

Cordingley (*Eng.*) Dweller at Cordin's grove.

Cordova, Cordoba (*Sp.*) One who came from the city or province of Cordoba in Spain.

Corey (*Ir.*) Dweller in, or by, a hollow; grandson of Corradh or Corra (spear).

Corfield (*Eng.*) Dweller in, or near, the field infested by ravens.

Corkery (*Ir.*) Grandson of Corcair (purple).

Corkill, Corkhill (*Mx.*) Son of Thorketill (the cauldron of Thor).

Corkin (*Ir.*) Son or grandson of Corcan.

Corley (*Eng.*) One who came from Coreley (grove frequented by cranes), in Shropshire; or from Corley in Warwickshire.

Corliss, Corlis (*Eng.*) The cheerful or merry person.

Cormac, Cormack (*Ir.*) Grandson of

Cormac (son of Corb; son of chariot, a charioteer).

Corman, Cormann (*Ger.*) One who raises, or deals in, grain.

Cormier (*Fr.*) Dweller at, or near, a sorb tree.

Cornbrook (*Eng.*) One who came from Cornbrook (crane's stream), in Lancashire.

Cornelius (*Eng.*) Descendant of Cornelius (hornlike).

Cornell, Cornel (*Eng.*) Descendant of Cornelius (hornlike); dweller at the dogwood tree hill.

Corner (*Eng.*) Dweller at a nook or angle of land; a coroner or crown officer charged with the care of the private property of the king.

Cornett, Cornet (*Eng.*) One who played the cornet, a wind instrument made of horn or resembling a horn.

Corney (*Eng., Ukr.*) One who came from Corney (grain or crane island), the name of places in Cumberland and Hertfordshire; one with a dark or swarthy complexion.

Cornforth (*Eng.*) One who came from Cornforth (crane's ford), in Durham.

Cornhill (*Eng.*) One who came from Cornhill (grain hill), in Middlesex.

Cornish (*Eng.*) One who came from Cornwall (the Welsh in Cornavia), a county in England.

Cornstubble (*Eng.*) Dweller on land where the stumps of wheat or other grain were left in the ground after reaping.

Cornthwaite (*Eng.*) Dweller in a forest clearing where grain was grown; or in a cleared meadow frequented by cranes.

Cornwall, Cornwallis (*Eng.*) One who came from the county of Cornwall (the Welsh in Cornavia).

Cornwell (*Eng.*) One who came from Cornwell (crane's stream), in Oxfordshire; a variant of Cornwall, q.v.

Corona (*It.*) One who played the part of a king in the pageants and festivals; dweller at the sign of the crown.

Coronado (*Sp.*) Possibly a nickname for one resembling a clergyman who has received the tonsure.

Corot (*Fr.*) Dweller in the corner or angle.

Corrado (*It.*) Descendant of Corrado, Italian form of Conrad (bold, counsel).

Corral (*Sp.*) One who came from Corral (courtyard), the name of several places in Spain.

Correa (*Sp.*) One who came from Correa (belt of leather), in Spain.

Corriero (*It.*) One who carries messages, a courier; an attendant on travelers who arranges lodging at inns on the way.

Corrigan (*Ir.*) Grandson of Corragan, a dim. of Corra (spear).

Corso (*It.*) Descendant of Corso, a pet form of Bonaccorso.

Corson (*Eng., Fr.*) One who came from Coursan or Courson, the names of several places in France; one who made and sold tight-fitting vestments.

Cort, Corte (*Fr.*) Dweller near the court; one who frequents the court of a prince; or is a worker therein.

Cortes (*Port.*) One who came from Cortes (court or town), the name of several places in Spain; the polite, courteous man.

Cortese (*It.*) The polite, courteous man.

Cortez (*Sp.*) One who came from Cortes (court or town), the name of several places in Spain.

Corwin (*Eng.*) Dweller near the white enclosure or castle.

Cory, Corry (*Ir.*) Variant of Corey, q.v.

Cosby (*Eng.*) One who came from Cosby (Cossa's village), in Leicestershire.

Cosentino, Cosenza (*It.*) One who came from Cosenza; or the northern section of Calabria, in Italy.

Cosey, Cossey (*Eng.*) Dweller at the causey or paved way.

Cosgrave (*Ir.*) Grandson of Coscrach (victorious).

Cosgriff (*Ir., Eng.*) Variant of Cosgrave, q.v.; variant of Cosgrove, q.v.

Cosgrove (*Eng., Ir.*) One who came from Cosgrove (Cofa's wood), in Northamptonshire; variant of Cosgrave, q.v.

Cosley, Coseley (*Eng.*) One who came from Coseley (charcoal burner's grove), in Staffordshire.

Coss (*Eng.*) One who came from Corse (bog), in Gloucestershire; dweller in, or near, a bog or fen.

Cosson (*Fr.*) A retailer or middleman, later a specialist as a retailer of lace; descendant of little Cosse (husk or pod).

Cost, Coste, Costard (*Eng.*) Descendant of Coste, a pet form of Constantine (constant or firm of purpose).

Costa (*It., Port., Sp.*) Dweller on a hillside; or on the shore or coast; one who came from Costa, the name of several places in Spain.

Costabile (*It.*) One who acted as a military officer or constable.

Costain (*Eng.*) Descendant of Constantine (constant or firm of purpose).

Costantino, Costantini (*It.*) Descendant of Costantino, Italian form of Constantine (constant or firm of purpose).

Costanzo, Costanza (*It.*) Descendant of Costanzo (constant or firm of purpose).

Costello, Costelloe (*Ir.*) The son of Oisdealbh; one who is like a fawn or deer.

Coster, Costner (*Du.*) The sexton. See Koster.

Costin, Coston, Costen (*Eng.*) Descendant of Costin, a pet form of Constantine (constant or firm of purpose).

Cote, Cott (*Eng.*) Dweller at a cottage, a manor inhabitant who tilled only ten acres or less.

Cotgrave (*Eng.*) One who came from Cotgrave (Cotta's grove), in Nottinghamshire.

Cotley (*Eng.*) One who came from Cotleigh (Cotta's grove), in Devonshire.

Cotness (*Eng.*) One who came from Cotness (headland with cottages), in the East Riding of Yorkshire.

Coton (*Fr.*) Descendant of little Cot, a pet form of Nicolas (people's victory).

Cottenham (*Eng.*) One who came from Cottenham (Cotta's manor), in Cambridgeshire.

Cotter (*Eng.*) A cottager who tilled only five or ten acres in a manor, and occupied a small cottage.

Cotterell, Cotterill (*Eng.*) The small cottager; one who occupied a small cot or cottage; an under tenant who held land in absolute villenage.

Cottingham (*Eng.*) One who came from Cottingham (homestead of Cotta's people), the name of places in Northamptonshire and the East Riding of Yorkshire.

Cottle (*Eng., Fr.*) One who tilled only five or ten acres and occupied a small cottage; one who came from Cotleigh (Cotta's grove), in Devonshire; or from Cotehele (wood by the estuary), in Cornwall; one who made or dealt in armor.

Cotto (*It.*) Descendant of Cotto, a pet form of names with this ending, as Francescotto and Domenicotto.

Cotton, Cotten, Coton (*Eng.*) One who came from Coton or Cotton, the names of various places in England; dweller at the cottages.

Cottrell, Cottrill (*Eng.*) Dweller in a small cottage.

Coty, Cotey (*Fr.*) Descendant of Cautius (careful).

Couch, Couchman (*Eng.*) One who couches and carpets, an upholsterer; one who had red hair.

Coughlin, Coughlan, Coghlan, Caughlin (*Ir.*) Grandson of Cochlan (dim. of cochal, a hooded cloak).

Coulon, Colon (*Fr.*) A variant of Colomb, q.v.

Coulson, Coulsen (*Eng.*) Son of Cole, a

pet form of Nicholas (people's victory).

Coulter (*Eng.*) One who tended colts, a colt-herd.

Coulthard (*Scot.*) One who took care of colts.

Council, Councill (*Eng.*) Descendant of Council (counselor); an official adviser or counselor; member of a council, a councilor.

Counts, Count, Counter, Countiss (*Eng.*) One who counts, an accountant or treasurer.

Coupe (*Eng.*) Variant of Copp, q.v.

Coursey (*Eng.*) One who came from Courcy (Curtius' estate), in Calvados.

Courtland (*Eng.*) Dweller on, or near, the land belonging to the castle or manor house.

Courtman (*Eng.*) Dweller in, or near, the castle or large house; servant at the castle.

Courtney, Courtenay (*Ir., Fr.*) Descendant of Cuirnin (little horn or drinking cup); one who came from Courtenay (Curtius' estate), the name of two places in France.

Courtright (*Eng.*) Variant of Cartwright, q.v.

Courts, Court (*Eng.*) Dweller or employee at a castle, large house or mansion; the short, small man.

Cousins, Cousin (*Fr.*) The cousin or kinsman.

Cousland (*Scot.*) One who came from Cousland (cow's pastureland), in Midlothian.

Coutts (*Eng.*) Dweller at the sign of the coot; variant of Coots, q.v.

Cove (*Eng.*) One who came from Cove (valley among hills; an inlet or creek), the name of several small places in England.

Covell, Covel (*Eng.*) Dweller in a small chamber or cave; one who came from Colville (Col's farm), in Normandy.

Covelli, Covello (*It.*) Descendant of Covelli, a shortened form of Iacovelli, a variant of Giacomo, Italian

form of James (may God protect; the supplanter); one who came from Montecovello, a mountain in Italy.

Coven (*Eng., Ger.*) One who came from Coven (valley among hills), in Staffordshire; variant of Koven, q.v.

Coveney, Coveny (*Eng.*) One who came from Coveney (bay or lake island), in Cambridgeshire.

Coventry (*Eng.*) One who came from Coventry (Cofa's tree), in Warwickshire.

Covey (*Ir.*) Descendant of Cobhthach (victorious).

Coviello (*It.*) Descendant of Coviello, a shortened form of Iacovelli, variant of Giacomo, Italian form of James (may God protect; the supplanter).

Covier (*Fr.*) One who made barrels, a cooper.

Covington (*Eng.*) One who came from Covington (homestead of Cufa's people), in Huntingdonshire.

Cowall, Cowal (*Scot.*) One who came from Cowal, in Argyllshire.

Cowan, Cowen (*Ir., Scot.*) Dweller at a hollow; worker in metal, a smith; a corruption of Colquhoun, q.v.; grandson of Comhghan (a twin).

Coward, Cowart (*Eng.*) One who tended cows.

Cowden (*Eng.*) One who came from Cowden (cow pasture), in Kent.

Cowdery (*Eng.*) Variant of Cowdrey, q.v.

Cowdrey, Cowdry, Cowdray (*Eng.*) One who came from Cowdray (hazel copse), in Sussex.

Cowell, Cowhill (*Eng.*) One who came from Cowhill (cow's hill), in Gloucestershire.

Cowgill (*Nor.*) Dweller in the ravine where cows were kept.

Cowherd (*Eng.*) One who tended cows.

Cowhey (*Ir., Scot.*) Variant of Cowie, q.v.

Cowie (*Ir., Eng., Scot.*) Grandson of Cobhthach (victorious); dweller on the island where cows grazed; one who came from Cowie (wood), the name of several places in Scotland.

Cowles (*Eng.*) The son of Cole, a pet form of Nicholas (people's victory).

Cowley (*Eng.*) One who came from Cowley (Cufa's meadow; cow meadow; clearing where charcoal was burnt), the name of several places in England.

Cowling, Cowing (*Eng.*) One who came from Cowling (hill) or Cowlinge (Cula's people), villages in the West Riding of Yorkshire and in Suffolk, respectively.

Cowlishaw (*Eng.*) One who came from Cowlishaw (wood grimy with coal dust), in Lancashire.

Cowman (*Eng.*) One who took care of the cows, a cowherd.

Cowper (*Eng.*) One who made and sold casks, buckets, and tubs.

Cowperthwait, Cowperthwaite (*Eng.*) Dweller in, or near, the cooper's clearing in the wood.

Cowton (*Eng.*) One who came from Cowton (Cuda's homestead), in the North Riding of Yorkshire.

Cox, Coxe (*Eng.*) Dweller at the sign of the cock, a common signboard; dweller near a small hill or clump of trees; variants of Cook, q.v.

Coxon, Coxen (*Eng.*) Variant of Cockson, q.v.

Coxwell (*Eng.*) One who came from Coxwell (wild bird spring; hill spring), in Berkshire.

Coy, Coye (*Eng.*) The quiet, shy man.

Coyle (*Ir.*) The son of Dubhghall (the black stranger).

Coyne (*Ir.*) Grandson of Conn (reason; a freeman); or of Cadhain (wild goose); shortened form of Kilcoyne, q.v.

Cozzi, Cozza, Cozzo (*It.*) Descendant of Cozzi, a pet form of names ending in -cozzo, as Francescozzo (little Francesco) and Domenicozzo (little Domenico); one with an unusual head.

Crabb, Crabbe (*Eng.*) Nickname for the ill-natured, fractious man; one thought to walk or act like a crab; dweller near a crabtree.

Crabtree (*Eng.*) Dweller at, or near, a crab-apple tree.

Crackston (*Eng.*) One from Crafton, early form Croxton, (place where wild saffron grew), in Buckinghamshire.

Cracraft (*Eng.*) Dweller in, or near, the pasture frequented by crows.

Craddock (*Eng.*) One who came from Craddock (gentle stream), in Devonshire.

Craft (*Eng.*) Dweller in the small, enclosed field.

Crafton (*Eng.*) One who came from Crafton (homestead where wild saffron grew), in Buckinghamshire.

Craig, Cragg, Craige (*Scot., Eng.*) Dweller at, or near, a rock or crag.

Craighead (*Scot.*) One who came from Craighead (end of the rock), the name of several places in Scotland.

Craigie (*Scot.*) One who came from Craigie (at the rock), the name of several places in Scotland.

Crain, Craine (*Eng.*) Variant of Crane, q.v.

Cram, Cramb (*Eng., Scot.*) One who came from Crambe (the bends), in Yorkshire; one who came from Crombie (crooked place), in Banffshire.

Cramer, Creamer (*Ger.*) The shopkeeper or tradesman; one who traveled through the country buying butter, hens, and eggs which he carried to the market in a cram, or pack, on his back.

Crampton, Cramton (*Eng.*) One who came from Cronton (homestead frequented by crows), in Lancashire.

Crandall, Crandell, Crandle (*Eng.*) One who came from Crondall (a hollow), in Hampshire; dweller in a valley frequented by cranes.

Crandon, Cranden (*Eng.*) One who came from Crandon (green hill; crane's hill), in Somerset.

Crane, Cran (*Eng.*) Dweller at the sign of the crane; one who lived near the Crane river in England.

Cranford (*Eng.*) One who came from

Cranford (crane's ford), in Middlesex.

Cransford (*Eng.*) One who came from Cransford (ford frequented by cranes), in Suffolk.

Cranshaw (*Scot.*) One who came from Cranshaws (wood frequented by cranes), in Scotland.

Cranston (*Scot.*) One who came from the barony of Cranston (homestead of Cran), in Midlothian.

Crapper (*Eng.*) Variant of Cropper, q.v.

Crater (*Eng.*) One who packs goods in a crate.

Craven, Cravens, Cravener (*Eng.*) One who came from Craven (garlic), in Yorkshire.

Crawford (*Scot., Eng.*) One who came from Crawford (crows' pass), in Lanarkshire; dweller near a river crossing where crows were seen.

Crawley (*Eng.*) One who came from Crawley (crows' wood or hill), the name of several places in England.

Cray (*Eng.*) Dweller near the Cray (fresh; clean), a river in Kent.

Crayton (*Eng.*) One who came from Creaton (rocky homestead), in Northamptonshire, or from Creighton (rocky homestead), in Staffordshire.

Creagh (*Ir.*) Descendant of Craobh (branch).

Creasy, Creasey (*Eng.*) One who came from Cressy (Crixsius' farm), in France.

Crebo (*Eng.*) Dweller near a ridge of rocks.

Creech (*Scot., Eng.*) One who came from Creich (boundary), in Fifeshire; one who came from Creech (hill), the name of places in Dorset and Somerset; dweller by the creek.

Creed (*Eng.*) One who came from Creed (church of St. Creda), in Cornwall; descendant of Creda (creed).

Creedon, Creeden, Creaton (*Eng., Ir.*) One who came from Creeton (Craeta's homestead), in Lincolnshire; grandson of Criodan; one who

came from Creaton (rocky homestead), in Northamptonshire.

Creekmore (*Eng.*) Dweller near the stream in the marsh or wasteland.

Creely, Creeley (*Ir.*) Son of Raghailleach (counsel, power).

Crehan (*Ir.*) Grandson of little Creach (blind); or of the small person.

Creighton, Cregan, Creighan (*Eng., Ir.*) One who came from Creaton (rocky homestead), in Northamptonshire; or from Creighton (rocky homestead), in Staffordshire; grandson of Criochan (little blind one; small person).

Cremona (*It.*) One who came from Cremona, in Italy.

Crenshaw (*Eng.*) One who lived near the grove frequented by cranes; variant of Cranshaw, q.v.

Crerar (*Scot.*) One who made sieves; one who helped the miller, a sifter.

Crespo, Crespa (*Sp.*) One with wavy or curly hair.

Cress (*Eng.*) Dweller near where water cress grew.

Creswell (*Eng.*) One who came from Cresswell (spring where water cress grew), in Derbyshire.

Crewe, Crew (*Eng.*) One who came from Crewe (stepping stones across a stream), in Cheshire; dweller at, or worker near, a cattle pen; a shortened form of Carew, q.v.

Crews, Crewes (*Eng.*) Variant of Cruse, q.v.

Crichlow (*Eng.*) Dweller on, or near, the hill or mound on which there was a cross; dweller on a hill, from British *cruc* "hill" to which was added an explanatory Old English *hlaw* "hill."

Crichton, Crichten (*Scot.*) One who came from the old barony of Crichton (village on the border), in Midlothian.

Crick (*Eng.*) One who came from Crick (hill), in Derbyshire.

Crider (*Ger.*) Americanized form of Kreiter, q.v.

Crigler (*Ger.*) Americanized form of Kriegler, q.v.

Crigley, Criggley (*Ir.*) The son of Raghallach.

Crilly, Crilley (*Ir.*) The son of Raghailleach.

Crim (*Eng.*) Dweller near a small pond or pool.

Crimmons, Crimmins, Crimmings (*Ir.*) Grandson of Cruimin (little bent one).

Cripps (*Eng.*) One with curly hair.

Crisp (*Eng.*) The man with curly hair; descendant of Crisp, a pet form of Crispin (curly).

Crispin (*Eng., Fr.*) One with curly hair.

Crispino, Crispi (*It.*) One with curly hair.

Crist, Criss (*Eng.*) Descendant of Crist, a pet form of Christian (follower of Christ) and Christopher (Christbearer).

Criswell (*Eng.*) One who came from Cresswell (stream where water cress grew), in Derbyshire. There were parishes named Cresswell in Northumberland and Staffordshire also.

Critchell (*Eng.*) One who came from Crichel, from British *cruc* (hill) to which was added an explanatory Old English *hyll* (hill).

Critchett (*Eng.*) The little crooked or bent person.

Critchfield (*Eng.*) Dweller in, or near, the open place on a hill.

Critchlow (*Eng.*) Variant of Crichlow, q.v.

Crites, Crite (*Ger.*) One who came from Kreitz, in Germany, an Americanized form.

Crittenden, Crittendon (*Eng.*) One who came from Criddon, formerly Critendone (Cridela's hill), in Shropshire.

Crnich (*Yu.-Sl.*) One with a dark or swarthy complexion, black.

Crocker (*Eng.*) One who made earthen pots, a potter.

Crockett, Crocket (*Eng.*) The little, crooked or deformed person.

Crocomb, Crocombe (*Eng.*) One who came from Crowcombe (crow valley), in Somerset.

Crofford (*Scot., Eng.*) Variant of Crawford, q.v.

Croft, Crofts (*Eng.*) One who came from Croft (enclosure), the name of several places in England; dweller at the small, enclosed field.

Crofter (*Eng.*) Dweller on a piece of enclosed land.

Crofton (*Eng.*) One who came from Crofton (homestead with an enclosure; homestead by a hill), the name of several places in England.

Crofutt (*Eng.*) Variant of Crawford, q.v.

Croissant (*Heb., Fr.*) The young Jew of rapid growth; the young man who grows up quickly.

Croke, Croak, Croake (*Eng.*) Dweller at a nook or bend in a river; variants of Crook, q.v.

Cromartie (*Scot.*) One who came from Cromarty (crooked height), in Ross and Cromarty; or from Cromarty, a county, now Ross and Cromarty.

Cromie, Crombie (*Scot.*) One who came from Crombie (crooked place), in Scotland.

Crompton (*Eng.*) One who came from Crompton (homestead in the bend of a river), in Lancashire.

Cromwell (*Eng.*) One who came from Cromwell (winding stream), in Nottinghamshire.

Cronin, Cronen (*Ir.*) Descendant of the little brown-complexioned or swarthy man.

Cronkhite (*Ger., Du.*) One who was ill, an invalid, an American corruption of the German name, Krankheit.

Crook, Crooks, Crooke (*Eng., Scot.*) One who came from Crook (hill; bend of a river), the name of several places in England and Scotland; same as Croke, q.v.

Crooker (*Eng.*) Dweller at a nook or bend; variant of Crocker, q.v.

Crookham (*Eng.*) One who came from Crookham (homestead at the corner or bend), the name of places in

Berkshire, Hampshire, and Northumberland.

Crookshank, Crookshanks (*Eng.*) The bowlegged man; one with a crooked leg.

Crookston (*Scot.*) One who came from Crookston (homestead on the hill), in Renfrew.

Croom, Croome (*Eng.*) One who came from Croom (narrow valley), in the East Riding of Yorkshire; or from Croome (winding stream), in Worcestershire.

Cropley (*Eng.*) One who came from Cropredy, spelled Cropelie in Domesday Book (hill by a brook).

Cropper (*Eng.*) One who crops or reaps the grain, a farm laborer.

Cropsey (*Eng.*) Dweller on Croppa's island.

Cropton (*Eng.*) One who came from Cropton (hill homestead), in the North Riding of Yorkshire.

Crosby, Crosbie, Crossby (*Eng., Scot.*) One who came from Crosby (village at the cross), the name of several villages in England and Scotland.

Crosier, Croser (*Eng.*) One who bore the bishop's staff or the cross at a monastery; one who made and sold crosses; dweller near a cross.

Cross, Crosse (*Eng.*) One who lived near a cross at a roadside dedicated to some saint, it often serving as a marker or guide post.

Crossland, Crosland (*Eng.*) One who came from Crosland (land by the cross), in the West Riding of Yorkshire.

Crossley, Crosley (*Eng.*) One who lived at the glade, or meadow, by the cross.

Crossman (*Eng.*) Dweller near the cross.

Crosson (*Eng.*) One who came from Crossens (headland with crosses), in Lancashire; dweller near the small market cross.

Crosswhite, Crosswhy, Crosswaith (*Eng.*) Variant of Crosthwaite, q.v.

Crosthwaite, Crosthwait (*Eng.*) One who came from Crossthwaite (clearing by a cross), the name of places in Cumberland, Westmorland, and the North Riding of Yorkshire.

Croston (*Eng.*) One who came from Croston (homestead by a cross), in Lancashire. The cross may have been a market cross.

Croswell (*Eng.*) Dweller at the spring where a cross had been erected.

Crotchett (*Fr.*) One who worked with a hook.

Crothers (*Eng.*) Variant of Carruthers, q.v.

Crotty (*Ir.*) Grandson of Crotach (hunchbacked).

Crouch, Croucher (*Eng.*) Dweller near a cross; one who came from Crouch (cross), now Crouch End, in Middlesex.

Croughton (*Eng.*) One who came from Croughton (homestead in the narrow valley), in Cheshire; or from Croughton (homestead in a river fork), in Northamptonshire.

Crouse (*Eng.*) The bold, audacious, lively man; one who made and sold mugs or pots.

Crowder, Crowther (*Eng.*) One who played a crowd, an ancient Celtic stringed instrument.

Crowe, Crow (*Eng.*) Dweller at the sign of the crow; one thought to possess the characteristics of a crow.

Crowell, Crowel (*Eng.*) One who came from Crowell (crows' stream), in Oxfordshire.

Crowford, Crowfoot (*Eng.*) Variant of Crawford, q.v.

Crowland (*Eng.*) One who came from Crowland (land by the bend), in Lincolnshire.

Crowles (*Wel.*) Descendant of one who came from Crowle (winding), villages in Worcestershire and Lincolnshire.

Crowlesmith (*Eng.*) The smith who worked or dwelt by the crow-lea, the meadow infested by crows.

Crowley, Crolley (*Ir.*) The son of Roghallach; grandson of Cruadhlaoch (tough hero).

Crown (*Eng.*) Dweller at the sign of the crown.

Crowner (*Eng.*) One who made crowns.

Crowninshield (*Eng.*) Dweller at the sign of the crown and shield.

Croxton (*Eng.*) One who came from Croxton (Croc's homestead), the name of eight villages in England.

Croy (*Scot.*) One who came from Croy (hard, firm ground), in Inverness.

Croydon, Croyden (*Eng.*) One who came from Croydon (valley where saffron grew), in Surrey.

Crozier (*Eng.*) One who bears a cross, or has something to do with a cross; the bearer of a bishop's crook or pastoral staff.

Cruce (*Eng.*) Variant of Cross, q.v.

Cruickshank, Cruckshank, Cruikshank (*Scot.*) Dweller at, or near, the crooked projecting point of a hill; a person with bow legs.

Crum, Crume (*Eng.*) The crooked, or deformed person.

Crumble (*Eng.*) One who came from Cromwell (winding stream), in Nottinghamshire; or from Crumble, now The Crumbles (small piece of land), in Sussex.

Crumley (*Eng.*) One who came from Crumble, now The Crumbles (small piece of land), in Sussex.

Crummie, Crummy (*Scot.*) Dweller on the lands of Crummy which belonged to the Abbey of Culross.

Crump, Crumb (*Eng.*) The crooked, maimed, or deformed person.

Crumpton (*Eng.*) One who came from Crompton (homestead at the bend), in Lancashire.

Cruse, Cruise (*Eng.*) Dweller near a cattle pen; the nimble or lively person; dweller at, or near, a cross.

Crusoe (*Eng.*) Dweller near the Krusau river in Schleswig-Holstein.

Crutch (*Eng.*) Dweller near a cross.

Crutcher (*Eng.*) Dweller at a cross; one who came from Crutch (hill), in Worcestershire.

Crutchfield (*Eng.*) Dweller at, or in, the field on the hill; one who came from Cruchfield (hill field), in Berkshire.

Crutchley (*Eng.*) Dweller in the grove with the cross.

Cruxton (*Eng.*) One who came from Cruxton (Croc's homestead), in Dorset.

Cruz (*Sp., Port.*) Dweller at, or near, a cross.

Cryer, Crier (*Eng.*) One appointed to make public announcements in the village.

Cryfield (*Eng.*) One who came from Cryfield (field at a river fork), in Warwickshire.

Crystal (*Scot.*) Descendant of Crystal, a pet form of Christopher (Christbearer).

Csillag (*Hun.*) Dweller at the sign of the star.

Cudahy, Cuddihy, Cuddahy (*Ir.*) Grandson of Cuidighthigh (helper).

Cuddy, Cuddie (*Eng., Scot.*) Descendant of Cuddy, a pet form of Cuthbert (famous, bright).

Cudlip (*Eng.*) Nickname for one with a cut or cleft lip.

Cudmore (*Eng.*) Dweller at the cut or divided marsh or waste land.

Cudney (*Eng.*) Dweller on Cuda's island.

Cudworth (*Eng.*) One who came from Cudworth (Cuda's or Cutha's homestead), the name of places in Somerset and the West Riding of Yorkshire.

Cuevas (*Sp.*) One who came from Cuevas (caves), in Spain.

Cuff, Cuffe (*Eng.*) Descendant of Cuffa or Cufa (rounded top).

Culbert (*Eng.*) Descendant of Culbert (cool, bright).

Culbertson, Culberson (*Eng.*) The son of Culbert or Colbert (cool, bright).

Culford (*Eng.*) One who came from Culford (Cula's ford), in Suffolk.

Culham (*Eng.*) One who came from Culham (Cula's meadow), in Oxfordshire.

Culhane (*Ir.*) Descendant of little Cathal (battle mighty).

Culkin, Culkeen (*Ir.*) Son of Wilkin, a

pet form of William (resolution, helmet).

Cull (*Eng.*) Descendant of Culla; descendant of Cole, a pet form of Nicholas (people's victory).

Cullen, Cullens, Cullins (*Ir., Eng., Scot.*) Grandson of Cuileann (holly); a cub or puppy, an affectionate term; the handsome person; dweller in, or near, a small wood; dweller near a holly tree; one who came from Cullen (little nook), in Scotland.

Cullerton (*Eng.*) One who came from Culkerton (enclosure of the giants; dwarf's retreat), in Gloucestershire.

Culligan (*Ir.*) Descendant of Colgan.

Cullinan, Cullinane (*Ir.*) Grandson of little Cuileann (holly).

Cullingworth (*Eng.*) One who came from Cullingworth (the homestead of Cula's people), in the West Riding of Yorkshire.

Cullison (*Eng.*) The son of Culla.

Cullom, Cullum (*Eng.*) Same as Culham, q.v.

Cullyford (*Eng.*) One who came from Culford (Cula's ford), in Suffolk.

Culp (*Ger., Scot.*) Dweller at the sign of the calf; one who cared for the calves; one who came from Colp (cow; heifer), in Aberdeenshire.

Culpepper (*Eng.*) One who gathered and sold pepper, a spicer.

Culross (*Scot.*) One who came from Culross (holly wood), in Perthshire.

Culver (*Eng.*) Dweller at the sign of the culver or dove.

Culwell (*Eng.*) Variant of Colwell, q.v.

Culworth (*Eng.*) One who came from Culworth (Cula's homestead), in Northamptonshire.

Cumberland, Cumberlander (*Eng.*) One who came from Cumberland (land of the Cumbrians or Britons), a county in England.

Cummersdale (*Eng.*) One who came from Cummersdale (valley of the Cumbrians or Britons), in Cumberland.

Cummings, Cummins, Cumming, Cumine (*Scot., Eng., Ir.*) One who came from Comines (Commios' estate), in France; grandson or descendant of Cuimin (little bent one).

Cunard (*Eng.*) Descendant of Cynehard (royal, hard).

Cundall (*Eng.*) One who came from Cundall (valley valley), from Old English *cumb* meaning "valley" to which the Scandinavians added their own explanatory *dalr* (valley). The village is in the North Riding of Yorkshire.

Cundey, Cundy (*Eng.*) Dweller near the dog-man's house.

Cundiff (*Eng.*) Dweller at a cliff in a valley.

Cuneo (*It.*) One who came from Cuneo (wedge), a province in Italy.

Cunha (*Port.*) One who came from Cunha, in Portugal.

Cunliffe, Cunliff (*Eng.*) One who came from Cunliffe (cliff of Gunhildr), in Lancashire; descendant of Cynelaf (kingly heritage); or of Gunleif (war, heritage).

Cunniff, Cunniffe, Conniff (*Ir.*) The son of Cudubh (black hound).

Cunningham (*Scot.*) One who came from Cunningham (rabbit farm), in Ayrshire; one who came from a royal manor.

Curcio, Curcione (*It.*) One of low stature; one who tended goats; dweller at the sign of the goat.

Cureton (*Eng.*) Dweller in a homestead where there were dogs.

Curie (*Fr.*) One who came from Curey (Curius' estate), in France.

Curington (*Eng.*) One who came from Cortington (the village of Cort's people), in Wiltshire.

Curley, Curly, Curle (*Scot.*) Dweller near Curley (bend or turn in the road), in Scotland; one who came from Curley (Curilla's estate), in France; one who had curly hair.

Curnow (*Eng.*) One who came from Cornwall, a Cornishman.

Curran, Corran (*Ir.*) Grandson of Corran (dim. of Corradh, spear).

Currier (*Eng.*) One who dressed leather.

Curry, Currie (*Ir., Eng.*) Grandson of Corra (spear); one who came from Curry, the name of several places in England.

Curtin (*Ir.*) Grandson of Cartan; the son of the hunchbacked man.

Curtis, Curtiss (*Eng.*) One with court-like, or elegant, manners, well-bred.

Curtright (*Eng.*) Variant of Cartwright, q.v.

Cusack, Cusick, Cusac (*Ir., Eng., Ukr.*) One who came from Cussac (Cotius' place), in France; one who was a member of a cavalry troop on the Russian steppes, a Cossack.

Cushing (*Eng.*) Descendant of little Cuss, a pet form of Custance or Constance (constant or firm of purpose).

Cushman (*Eng.*) One who made cuish or thigh armor.

Custer (*Eng.*) One who made feather beds and cushions.

Cutbirth (*Scot.*) Descendant of Cuthbert (famous, bright).

Cutcombe (*Eng.*) One who came from Cutcombe (Cuda's valley), in Somerset.

Cuthair (*Eng.*) One who cut hair, a barber. Phrases often became nicknames.

Cuthbertson (*Eng., Scot.*) The son of Cuthbert (famous, bright).

Cutler (*Eng.*) One who made, repaired or sold knives and other cutting instruments.

Cutone (*It.*) One who dealt in cotton.

Cutright, Cutwright (*Eng.*) One who made carts, usually small two-wheeled vehicles, a cartwright.

Cutshall (*Eng.*) Dweller in, or near, Cod's corner.

Cutshaw (*Eng.*) Dweller in, or near, Cuda's shaw or thicket; or at the divided wood.

Cutter (*Eng.*) One who cut cloth.

Cutting (*Eng.*) The son or family of Cutha (famous); a corrupt form of the French *Cotin* or *Cottin* which are the diminutives of the terminal syllable of Jacquot and Nicot.

Cuttle (*Eng.*) Dweller at the cottage on the hill; metonymic for one who made coats of mail; one who made and sold short knives or daggers, a cutler; descendant of little Cutt, a pet form of Cuthbert (famous, bright).

Cutts (*Eng.*) Descendant of Cutt, a pet form of Cuthbert (famous, bright).

Cuvier (*Fr.*) One who makes and sells wash tubs; one who came from Cuvier (Cuperius' place), in France.

Cuxham (*Eng.*) One who came from Cuxham (Cuc's meadow), in Oxfordshire.

Cuxton (*Eng.*) One who came from Cuxton (Cuola's stone), in Kent.

Cuyler (*Du.*) An archer or crossbowman.

Cwik (*Pol.*) A cunning fellow.

Cygan (*Pol.*) One of a wandering Caucasian race, a gypsy.

Cyr (*Fr.*) Descendant of Cyr (teacher); one who came from St. Cyr, in France.

Cyrus (*Eng.*) Descendant of Cyrus (the sun; throne).

Czaja (*Pol.*) Dweller at the sign of the large lapwing; one with some of the characteristics of a large lapwing.

Czajka (*Pol., Ukr., Rus.*) One with some of the characteristics of a small lapwing or gull; one who operated a small boat.

Czajkowski (*Pol., Ukr.*) One who came from Czajkow(o) (the gull's settlement), the name of many places in Poland and Ukraine.

Czapka (*Pol.*) One who made and sold caps.

Czapla (*Pol.*) Dweller at the sign of the heron; one with the characteristics of a heron, such as long neck or long legs.

Czarnecki (*Pol.*) One who came from Czarny (black), the name of several places in Poland; one with a dark or swarthy complexion.

Czarnik (*Pol.*) One who came from Czarnik (black), in Poland; the little, swarthy or dark-complexioned man.

Czech (*Ger.*) One who came from Bohemia (home of the Boii).

Czerniak (*Pol.*) One who came from Czernia (black), a village in Poland; dweller near the Czernia river; the dark-complexioned man.

Czernocky (*Cz.-Sl.*) The black-eyed man.

Czerwinski (*Pol.*) One who came from Czerwien (red dye), in the Ukraine; one with a scarlet or crimson complexion.

Czerwonka (*Pol.*) One with red hair or a ruddy complexion.

Czijka (*Pol.*) Dweller at the sign of the lapwing; one thought to possess the shrill wailing voice or the flapping gait of the lapwing.

Czuba, Czub (*Pol.*) One with a tuft or unusual head of hair.

Czubak, Czubek (*Pol.*) One with an unusual tuft or crest; one with a prominent head of hair.

Czyz (*Pol.*) Dweller at the sign of the green or yellow finch; one thought to possess some of the characteristics of the finch.

Czyzewski (*Pol.*) One with yellow or canary-colored hair; one who raised and sold canaries.

Dabbs (*Eng.*) The son of Dabb, a pet form of Robert (fame, bright).

Dabney (*Eng.*) One who came from St. Martin d'Aubigny (Albinius' estate), in La Manche; or from St. Aubin d'Aubigny, in Ille-et-Vilaine.

Dabrowski (*Pol.*) One who came from Dabrowa (oak grove), the name of several places in Poland; dweller in, or near, an oak grove.

Dace, Dacey, Dacy (*Eng., Ir., Fr.*) Dweller near the Dacy (now Aire), a river in England; one who came from the South; one who came from Acy (Accius' estate), the name of several places in France.

Da Costa (*Port.*) Dweller on the shore or coast.

Dade (*Eng.*) Descendant of Daddo (deed, exploit).

Dadford (*Eng.*) One who came from Dadford (Dodda's ford), in Buckinghamshire.

Dafoe (*Fr.*) Variant of De Foe, q.v.

Dagg (*Eng.*) One who habitually carried a dagger; one who made and sold daggers.

Dagger, Daggers, Daggar (*Eng.*) One who habitually carried a dagger.

Daggett (*Eng.*) Descendant of little Dagr (day), or of Daegga (day).

Dagley (*Eng.*) Dweller in, or near, Daegga's grove.

Daglish (*Eng., Scot.*) One who came from Dawlish (black stream), in Devonshire; variant of Dalgleish, q.v.

Dagnall, Dagnell (*Eng.*) One who came from Dagnall (Daecca's corner), in Buckinghamshire.

D'Agostino, Dagostino (*It.*) Descendant of Agostino, Italian form of Augustine (exalted or majestic).

Dagwell (*Eng.*) Dweller at, or near, Daegga's spring.

Dahl, Dahle (*Nor., Ger.*) Dweller in the valley.

Dahlberg (*Sw.*) Valley mountain.

Dahlen (*Nor., Sw.*) Dweller in the valley; one who came from Dalen (valley), in Sweden.

Dahlgren (*Nor., Sw.*) Valley branch.

Dahlheimer (*Ger.*) One who came from Dahlheim (valley homestead), in Germany.

Dahlin (*Sw.*) One who came from the valley or dale.

Dahlke (*Ger.*) Descendant of little Dahl, a pet form of names beginning with Dal (gift), as Dalibor and Dalimir.

Dahlman, Dallman (*Sw., Ger.*) Valley man; dweller in a dale or valley.

Dahlquist (*Sw.*) Valley twig.

Dahlstrom (*Sw.*) Valley stream.

Dahm, Dahms, Dahme (*Ger.*) One who came from Dahme (dam), in Germany; descendant of Dahm, a pet form of Adam (red earth).

Daigle (*Ger.*) Descendant of Dago, a pet form of names beginning with Tag (the day), as Dagobald, Dagwart and Dagomar.

Dailey, Daily (*Ir.*) Grandson of Dalach (frequenting assemblies).

Dailide (*Lith.*) One who worked with wood, a carpenter.

Dakin (*Eng.*) Descendant of little Day, a pet form of David (commander; beloved; friend).

Dale, Dales (*Eng.*) Dweller in the valley.

D'Alessandro, Dalessandro (*It.*) The son of Alessandro, Italian form of Alexander (helper of mankind).

Daley (*Ir.*) Variant of Daly, q.v.

Dalgleish, Dalglish (*Scot.*) One who came from the lands of Dalgleish, in Selkirkshire.

Dalham (*Eng.*) One who came from Dalham (meadow in a valley), the name of villages in Kent and Suffolk.

Dalke (*Ger.*) Variant of Dahlke, q.v.

Dall (*Eng.*) Dweller in the valley.

Dallas (*Scot.*) One who came from the old barony of Dallas (place on the plain), in Moray.

Dally (*Eng., Ir.*) One who came from Dawley (grove in a valley; grove of Dealla's people), the name of places in Middlesex and Shropshire; grandson of Dalach (frequenting assemblies).

Dalrymple (*Scot.*) One who came from the lands of Dalrymple (field on the curving stream), in Ayrshire.

Dal Santo (*It.*) Descendant of Santo (the saint).

Dalstrom (*Sw.*) Valley stream.

Dalton (*Eng.*) One who came from Dalton (village in the valley), the name of several places in England.

Dalwood (*Eng.*) One who came from Dalwood (wood in a valley), in Devonshire.

Daly (*Ir.*) Grandson of Dalach (frequenting assemblies).

Dalzell (*Scot.*) Present pronunciation of Dalziel, q.v.

Dalziel (*Scot.*) One who came from Dalziel (white field), in Lanarkshire.

Damato, D'Amato (*It.*) Descendant of Amato (beloved).

D'Ambrosio (*It.*) The son of Ambrosio, Italian form of Ambrose (immortal).

Dameron, Damron (*Fr.*) Nickname for a small, young man, one of little virility.

Damewood (*Eng.*) Dweller in, or near, the wood belonging to the dame, a lady of station or authority.

Damico, D'Amico (*It.*) The son of Amico (friend).

Damien, Damian (*Fr., Bel.*) Descendant of Damian (taming), an Arabian saint.

Damitz, Damit (*Ger.*) One who came from Damitz, in Germany.

Damm, Dammer, Dammann (*Eng., Ger.*) Dweller or worker at the dam or dike; one who came from Damm (dike), the name of several places in Germany.

Dammeson (*Eng.*) The son of Dame (lady), an old given name.

Damon, Damond (*Fr.*) One who came from up the river or the upper waters.

D'Amore, Damore (*It.*) Descendant of Amore (love, or, sometimes, a child of love).

Dampier, Dampeer (*Eng.*) One who came from Dampierre (St. Peter), the name of numerous places in France.

Damson (*Eng.*) Shortened form of Dammeson, q.v.; the son of the mistress of the household.

Dana (*Eng., Fr.*) One who came from Denmark; descendant of Daniel (judged of God).

Danaher, Danagher, Dannaher (*Ir.*) Descendant of Duineachar (man loving).

Danahy, Danehy, Dannahy (*Ir.*) Grandson of Duineachaidh (humane).

Danbury (*Eng.*) One who came from Danbury (fort of Dene's people), in Essex.

Danby (*Eng.*) Dweller at the Dane's homestead.

Dancer (*Eng.*) One who danced at fair and festival.

D'Ancona (*It.*) One who came from the province or city of Ancona (elbow), in Italy.

Dancy, Dancey (*Eng.*) One who came from Anisy, in Calvados; one who came from Dauntsey (Domgeat's island), in Wiltshire.

Dandison (*Scot.*) The son of Dand or Dandie, pet forms of Daniel (judged of God).

D'Andrea (*It.*) The son of Andrea, Italian form of Andrew (manly).

Dandridge (*Eng.*) One who came from Tandridge (ridge with swine pasture), in Surrey. The original form was probably Dennhrycg.

Dandy, Dandie (*Eng.*) Descendant of Dandy, a pet form of Andrew (manly), or of Daniel (judged of God).

Dane, Dain (*Eng.*) One who came from Denmark (forest of the Danes); dweller near the Dane river, in Cheshire.

Danek (*Pol., Ger.*) Descendant of Danek, pet form of Bogdan (gift of God); one who came from Denmark (forest of the Danes).

Danfield (*Eng.*) One who came from Tanfield (field with willows or branches), in the North Riding of Yorkshire.

Danford, Danforth (*Eng.*) One who came from Darnford (concealed ford), in Suffolk; or from Denford (ford in a valley), in Berkshire.

D'Angelo, Dangelo (*It.*) The son of Angelo (an angel).

Dangerfield (*Eng.*) One who came from Angerville (Anger's estate), in Normandy.

Dangles (*Fr.*) Dweller in the house on the corner.

Dangleterre (*Fr.*) One who came from England, an Englishman.

Danielewicz (*Pol.*) The son of Daniel (judged of God).

Daniels, Danielson, Daniel (*Wel., Eng., Sw.*) The son of Daniel (judged of God); the son of the Welsh Deiniol (attractive).

Danilevicius (*Lith.*) The son of Danil, a Lithuanian form of Daniel (judged of God).

Danilovic, Danilovich (*Bulg.*) The son of

Danil, Bulgarian form of Daniel (judged of God).

Dankert (*Ger.*) Descendant of Thanchard (idea, bold).

Dankin (*Eng.*) Descendant of little Dan, a short form of Daniel (judged of God).

Danko (*Ukr.*) Descendant of Danko, a pet form of Bogdan (gift of God).

Danks (*Eng.*) Descendant of Dankin, a pet form of Daniel (judged of God).

Danley (*Eng.*) Dweller in, or near, the Dane's grove.

Dann, Dan (*Scot.*) Descendant of Dan, a pet form of Daniel (judged of God).

Danna, D'Anna (*It.*) The son of Anna (grace).

Dannenberg (*Ger.*) One who came from Dannenberg (pine tree-covered mountain), the name of three places in Germany.

Danner (*Ger.*) Dweller at, or near, a fir tree.

Dansby (*Sw.*) One who came from Dansby (Dan's farm), in Sweden.

Danson (*Eng.*) The son of Dan, a pet form of Daniel (judged of God).

Dante (*It.*) Descendant of Durand (lasting).

Dantzer (*Ger.*) One who danced; a dancing partner.

Danylenko, Danyluk (*Ukr.*) The son of Danyl, Ukrainian form of Daniel (judged of God).

Danziger, Danzig (*Ger.*) One who came from Danzig (place of the Goths; Dane's town), in Poland.

Da Prato (*It.*) One who came from Prato (meadow), in Italy.

Darby (*Eng., Ir.*) One who came from Darby or Derby (both names meaning place frequented by wild animals), the names of several places in England; grandson of Diarmaid (free man).

Darcy (*Fr.*) One who came from Arcy (Arsius' estate), in France.

Darden, Dardon (*Eng.*) One who came from Darton (animal enclosure), in the West Riding of Yorkshire.

Dare, Dares (*Eng.*) Descendant of Deor (brave; bold).

Darfield (*Eng.*) One who came from Darfield (open country frequented by wild animals), in the West Riding of Yorkshire.

Dargan (*Ir.*) Grandson of little Dearg (red).

Dargis (*Lith.*) One who works in rainy or misty weather; one with a morose or gloomy temperament.

Darke, Dark, Darks (*Eng., Fr.*) The dark-complexioned swarthy man; one who fought with bow and arrow, an archer; one who came from Arc (arch), the name of several places in France.

Darkwood (*Eng.*) Dweller in, or near, the dark or gloomy wood.

Darland (*Fr.*) Descendant of Arland (looter).

Darley (*Eng.*) One who came from Darley (grove frequented by wild animals), the name of several places in England.

Darling (*Eng.*) Descendant of Deorling (beloved); one who was dearly loved; the son of a nobleman, usually the eldest son.

Darlington (*Eng.*) One who came from Darlington (village of Deornoth's people), in Durham.

Darnell, Darnall (*Eng.*) One who came from Darnall (hidden nook), in Yorkshire.

Darrell, Darrett (*Eng.*) Descendant of little Deor (brave; bold).

Darrow, Darrough, Darrah, Darragh (*Ir.*) The son of Dubhdarach (black man of the oak).

Darsy, Darsey, Darsie (*Eng., Scot.*) One who came from Arsy (Arcius' estate), the name of several places in France; one who came from the lands of Dairsie (oak of fornication), in Fife.

Dart (*Eng.*) Dweller near the Dart (river where oaks grew), a river in Devonshire.

Dartford (*Eng.*) One who came from Dartford (Darent river crossing), in Kent.

Darton (*Eng.*) One who came from Darton (wild animal enclosure), in the West Riding of Yorkshire.

Darville, Darvel (*Scot.*) One who came from Darvel (oakwood by the settlement), in Ayrshire.

Darwin (*Eng.*) Dweller near the Darwen (clear water), a river in Lancashire; descendant of Deorwine (dear, friend).

da Santa Maria (*Port.*) A name adopted to express devotion to the Virgin Mary.

Dase, Dasey (*Eng., Ir., Ger.*) Variant of Dace, q.v.; one who caresses another.

Dash, Dasche, Dashe (*Eng.*) One who came from Ash (ash tree), the name of various places in England; dweller at the sign of the badger; one who worked at a tavern drawing the ale.

Dasilva (*Port.*) Dweller in the wood or thicket.

Daskal (*Gr.*) One who instructed others, a teacher.

Dassow (*Rus., Pol.*) The son of Dass, a pet form of Bogdan (gift of God); one who came from Daszewo, in Poland.

Dattilo, Dattolo, Dattalo (*It.*) Dweller near a date palm tree.

Dauber, Daube, Daub (*Eng., Ger.*) One who plastered buildings or whitewashed walls; dweller at the sign of the pigeon; one who raised and sold pigeons.

Dauchy, Dauche (*Fr.*) One who came from Auchy (Alcius' estate), in France.

Dauer (*Ger.*) One who prepares Cordovan leather; one who is useful.

Daugherty (*Ir.*) Grandson of Dochartach (unfortunate).

Daukus, Daukaus (*Lith.*) Descendant of Daukas, a short form of Daukantas.

Daum, Daume (*Ger., Fr.*) One with a large or unusual thumb; also possibly shortened from Daumler, i.e., one who squeezed the thumb during an inquisition, a torturer.

Daun (*Scot., Eng.*) Variant of Don, q.v.

Davalle, Da Valle (*Port.*) Dweller in the valley.

Davenport (*Eng.*) One who came from Davenport (town on the Dane river), in Cheshire.

Davey (*Scot.*) Descendant of little David (commander; beloved; friend).

Davidson, Davids, David (*Scot., Wel.*) The son of David (commander; beloved; friend).

Davila (*Sp.*) One who came from Avila, in Spain.

Davis, Davies (*Eng., Wel.*) The son of Davie, a pet form of David (commander; beloved; friend).

Davison (*Eng.*) The son of Davy or Davie, pet forms of David (commander; beloved; friend).

Daviston (*Eng.*) Dweller near David's homestead.

Davy, Davie, Davi (*Scot., Eng.*) Descendant of Davie or Davy, pet forms of David (commander; beloved; friend).

Dawes, Dawe, Daw (*Wel.*) Descendant of Daw, a pet form of David (commander; beloved; friend); dweller at the sign of the jackdaw; one lacking in wits, a simpleton.

Dawkins (*Eng.*) Descendant of little Dawe, a pet form of David (commander; beloved; friend).

Dawley (*Eng.*) One who came from Dawley (valley grove), in Middlesex or from Dawley (grove of Dalla's people), in Shropshire.

Dawlish (*Eng.*) One who came from Dawlish (black stream), in Devonshire.

Dawson (*Eng.*) The son of Daw, a pet form of David (commander; beloved; friend).

Day, Dey, Daye (*Eng., Wel.*) The dairy worker; kneader of bread; female servant, but the term was used later of men; descendant of Dai, a pet form of Dafydd, Welsh form of David (commander; beloved; friend).

Dayan (*Heb.*) The rabbinic judge.

Daykin (*Eng.*) Descendant of little Day,

a pet form of David (commander; beloved; friend).

Daylie (*Eng., Ir.*) One who came from Ouilly (Olius' estate), the name of several places in France; variant of Dailey, q.v.

Days (*Wel.*) Descendant of Dai, a pet form of Dafydd, Welsh form of David (commander; beloved; friend).

Dayton (*Eng.*) One who came from Deighton (homestead surrounded by a ditch or moat), the name of several places in Yorkshire.

Deacon, Dekan (*Eng.*) One who assisted priest or minister.

Deacy, Deasy, Deasey (*Ir.*) One who came from the Decies (people) of Waterford, in Munster.

Deadman, Deadmon (*Eng.*) One who came from Debenham (deep river homestead), in Suffolk.

Deady (*Ir.*) Grandson of Deadach (tooth).

Deak (*Eng.*) Descendant of Deak, a pet form of David (commander; beloved; friend).

Deakins (*Wel.*) The son of little Deak, a pet form of David (commander; beloved; friend).

Deal, Deale, Deals (*Eng., Ger.*) One who came from Deal (valley), in Kent; dweller on the allotted land; Americanization of Diehl, q.v.

Dean, Deane (*Eng.*) Dweller at the valley or woodland pasture; one who was the head of a body of canons of a cathedral church; a member of a dean's entourage.

De Angelis (*Sp.*) Descendant of Angel (messenger; angelic).

Dear, Deare (*Eng.*) Descendant of Deora (beloved); nickname for the beloved person; or for the bold, brave man.

Dearborn (*Eng.*) Dweller near a stream frequented by wild animals.

Dearden (*Eng.*) Dweller in the valley frequented by wild animals.

Dearing (*Eng.*) The son of Deora (beloved).

Dearman (*Eng.*) The servant of Deora

(beloved); one who had something to do with deer or wild animals.

Dearnley, Dearnaley (*Eng.*) One who came from Dearnley (hidden clearing), in Lancashire.

Dearson (*Eng.*) The son of Deora (beloved).

Deas (*Eng.*) One who made bread, a baker; one who worked in a dairy, usually a woman.

Deasson, Desson (*Scot.*) The son of Deas, a pet form of David (commander; beloved; friend).

Deasy, Deacy, Deasey (*Ir.*) One who came from the Decies (people) of Waterford, in Munster.

Death, Deth, Deeth (*Eng.*) One who came from Ath in Belgium; one who played the part of Death in the pageants and plays.

Deatherage, Deathridge (*Eng.*) Dweller at a range of hills where tinder was obtained.

Deaton (*Eng.*) Variant of Deighton, q.v.; one who came from Ditton (homestead of Dudda's people), in Shropshire.

Deaver (*Ir.*) Variant of Dever, q.v.

De Bartolo (*It.*) Descendant of Bartolo, a shortened form of Bartolomeo, Italian form of Bartholomew (son of Talmai, furrow).

De Bat (*Fr.*) Dweller in the valley.

Debeer (*Du.*) Dweller at the sign of the bear.

De Bellis (*It.*) Descendant of the handsome man.

De Berry (*Fr.*) One who came from Berry (Barius' estate), in France.

De Biase, De Bias (*Fr.*) One who came from Bias, in France.

De Boer (*Du.*) One who tilled the soil, a farmer; one who rose from the peasant class.

De Bold, De Bolt (*Du.*) One who came from Bolt, in Holland.

De Bruin, De Bruyn, De Brown (*Du.*) One with a dark or brown complexion.

Debs, Debes (*Ger.*) Descendant of Debes,

a pet form of Matthebus, a form of Mathias (gift of Jehovah).

Debussy (*Fr.*) One who came from Busy (Busius' estate), in France.

De Caluwe (*Bel.*) One with horny or callous skin.

De Camp, De Camps (*Fr.*) Dweller in the field.

De Carlo, De Carli (*It.*) The son of Carlo, Italian form of Charles (man).

De Caro (*Fr.*) One who came from Caro (Caroth's place; small thicket), the name of two places in France.

Decatur (*Bel.*) Dweller at the sign of the cat.

Dechambre (*Fr.*) An attendant on a king or lord in his bedroom.

De Chatelet, Dechatelets (*Fr.*) Dweller near the small castle or fortified place.

De Christo (*Port.*) A religious name expressing devotion to Christ.

De Cicco (*It.*) The son of Cicco, a pet form of Francesco, Italian form of Francis (free).

Decker, Dekker, Deckert (*Ger., Du.*) One who covered roofs with tile, straw, or slate; one who came from Deck or Decker, the names of places in Germany.

De Clerck, De Clerk (*Bel., Du.*) The clerk or administrator; the clergyman, scholar or scribe.

De Cola (*It.*) The son of Cola, a pet form of Nicola, Italian form of Nicholas (people's victory).

De Coster (*Fr., Du.*) The officer in charge of the sacristy, a sacristan.

De Courcey, De Courcy (*Fr.*) One who came from, or who owned, the fief of Courcey (passageway).

De Cristoforo (*It.*) The son of Cristoforo, Italian form of Christopher (Christbearer).

De Decker, Dedecker (*Du.*) One who covers roofs with tile, straw, or slate; the roofer.

Dedic (*Yu.-Sl.*) Nickname for an old man or grandfather.

Dedina (*It.*) The son of Dina, Italian form of Dinah (judgment).

Dedmond, Dedman (*Eng.*) One who came from Debenham (homestead in a deep valley), in Suffolk.

Dee, Dea (*Ir., Wel.*) Grandson of Deaghadh (good luck); dweller near the Dee river; one with a dark or swarthy complexion.

Deeds, Deede, Deed (*Eng.*) Descendant of Deda (deed).

Deegan, Degan, Deagan, Deagon (*Ir.*) Grandson of Dubhceann (black head).

Deemer (*Eng.*) One who occupied the office of judge.

Deer, Deere (*Scot.*) One who came from Deer (forest), in Aberdeenshire.

Deerfield (*Eng.*) Dweller in the open country frequented by wild animals.

Deering, Dearing (*Eng.*) Descendant of Deoring (beloved).

De Falco (*It.*) The son of Falco (hawk).

De Felice (*It.*) The son of Felice, Italian form of Felix (happy or fortunate).

De Feo (*It.*) The son of Feo, a pet form of Maffeo, Italian form of Matthew (gift of Jehovah).

Deffenbaugh (*Ger.*) One who came from Diffenbach, a farm in Germany; or from Tiefenbach (deep brook), the name of many small places in Germany.

De Filippo, De Filippis (*It.*) The son of Filippo, Italian form of Philip (lover of horses).

De Foe (*Fr.*) Dweller at the beech tree.

De Fontaine (*Fr.*) Dweller near the spring or pool of running water.

De Forest (*Fr.*) Dweller in the forest.

De Francesco, De Francisco (*It.*) The son of Francesco, Italian form of Francis (free).

De Franco (*It.*) The son of Franco, a pet form of Francesco, Italian form of Francis (free).

De Frank (*Fr.*) Descendant of Frank (free).

De Frenza (*It.*) One who came from Firenze (flourishing), the city we call Florence, in Italy.

De Fries, Defrees (*Du.*) One who came from Frisia, a Frisian.

Degas (*Fr.*) Dweller in, or near, a forest.

De Gaulle (*Fr.*) Dweller near the rampart or protective barrier.

Degen, Degener, Degner (*Ger.*) One who made rapiers; descendant of Thegan, a pet form of names commencing with Degen (young warrior), as Deganhart and Theganbert; the young warrior or follower; descendant of Degenher (young warrior, army).

De George, De Giorgio (*It.*) The son of George (farmer), the former being an Anglicized form.

De Giulio (*It.*) The son of Giulio, Italian form of Julius (downy-bearded or youthful).

Degnan, Degmon, Degman (*Eng., Ir.*) The servant who worked in a dairy; variant of Dignan, q.v.

De Graff, de Graaf, De Graaff, De Graf (*Ger., Du.*) The count, or, in England, an earl.

De Grazia, De Grazio (*It.*) The son of Grazia (grace).

De Gregorio (*It.*) The son of Gregorio, Italian form of Gregory (watchful).

de Groot, De Groote (*Du.*) The big, or tall, man; one who came from Groot (large place), in Holland.

de Haan (*Du.*) Dweller at the sign of the cock.

Dehn, Dehne, Dehnel (*Ger.*) Descendant of Dehn, a pet form of names beginning with Degen (young warrior), as Deganhart, Theganbald, and Degenher; descendant of Dano, a pet form of names beginning with Dane (the Dane), as Danaold and Danafrid.

Deibler (*Ger.*) One who raised pigeons, a pigeon fancier; or who sold pigeons.

Deighton (*Eng.*) One who came from Deighton (homestead surrounded by a ditch or moat), the name of several places in Yorkshire.

Deitch, Deitz, Deitsch (*Ger.*) One who came from Germany, a Yiddish form of Deutsch, q.v.

Dejean (*Fr.*) The son of Jean, French form of John (gracious gift of Jehovah).

111

De Jesus (*Port.*) A substituted religious name, expressing devotion to Jesus.

De John (*It.*) The son of Gian, short form of Giovanni, Italian form of John (gracious gift of Jehovah), an Anglicized Italian name.

De Jong, De Jonge, De Jonghe (*Du.*) The young man; one younger than another with whom he was associated; the younger son.

De Julio (*Sp.*) Descendant of Julio, Spanish form of Julius (downy-bearded or youthful).

Dekker (*Du.*) One who covered roofs with tile, straw, or slate.

De Koker (*Ger., Du.*) One who prepared food, the cook.

De Koven (*Ger., Du.*) One who came from Koven, in Germany; or from Odekoven (ancestral manor), in Germany.

Delaby (*Fr.*) One who came from Laby, in France.

Delacroix (*Fr.*) Dweller near the cross. See Cross.

De La Cruz (*Sp.*) Dweller near the cross. See Cross.

De Lacy (*Eng., Fr.*) One who came from Lassy (Lascius' estate), in France.

Delafield (*Eng.*) Dweller in the open country or land free of trees.

Delage (*Fr.*) One who had charge of the hedges or fences.

Delahanty, Delahunty (*Ir.*) Grandson of Dulchaointeach (plaintive satirist).

Delahay, Delahaye (*Eng., Fr.*) Dweller by the enclosure, or hedged enclosure.

Delamar, De Lamar, De La Mar (*Eng.*) One who came from La Mare (the pool), the name of several places in France.

Delancey (*Fr.*) One who came from Lanchy or Lancie (Lancius' estate), the names of places in France.

Deland (*Eng.*) Dweller on the land in the valley.

Delaney, Delany (*Ir.*) Descendant of the challenger; grandson of Dubslaine or Dubhslainge (black of the Slaney).

Delano (*Fr.*) One who came from La Noe

(the wet land), the name of several places in France; dweller in, or near, a marsh.

Delanty (*Ir.*) Descendant of Dulchaointeach (plaintive satirist).

De La Rosa, Delarosa (*Sp., It.*) Dweller where roses grew; or at the sign of the rose.

De Larue, Delarue (*Fr.*) Dweller on the street or paved way.

Delashaw (*Eng.*) Dweller in, or near, the small wood or thicket.

De LaTorre, Dela Torre, Delatorre (*Sp.*) Dweller near the tower.

Delatre, Delattre (*Fr.*) Dweller in a house containing a tiled hearth.

Delavigne (*Fr.*) Dweller in, or near, the vineyard.

Del Boccio (*It.*) Dweller near where thorny shrubs grew.

Delbridge (*Eng.*) Dweller on, or by, the bridge.

Del Castillo (*Sp.*) Dweller near, or worker in, the castle.

Del Corso (*It.*) Dweller near the highway.

Delcourt (*Fr.*) One employed at the court, usually of a king or prince.

Deleeuw (*Du.*) Dweller at the sign of the lion.

De Leo, Deleo (*It.*) The son of Leo (lion).

De Leon (*Sp.*) One who came from Leon (lion), a region and ancient kingdom in Spain; descendant of Leon (lion).

De Leonardis (*It.*) The son of Leonardo (lion, hard).

Delfin (*Sp.*) Dweller at the sign of the dolphin; one who aped the bearing of a prince.

Delfino, Delfini (*It.*) Dweller at the sign of the dolphin; nickname for an expert swimmer.

Delfosse (*Fr.*) Dweller near the ditch or trench.

Delgado (*Sp.*) The crippled or deformed person; the thin man.

Del Giorno (*It.*) One who worked or did something by the day.

Delhaye (*Fr.*) Dweller near the hedge.

Deligiannis, Deligianes (*Gr.*) Descendant

of crazy or mad Giannis, Greek form of John (gracious gift of Jehovah).

Delisi (*It.*) The son of Lisi, a pet form of Elizabeth (oath of God).

De Lisle, Delisle (*Fr.*) Dweller on the island.

Dell (*Eng.*) Dweller at the deep hollow or vale.

Dellacqua (*It.*) Dweller near the water.

Dellert, Deller (*Eng.*) Dweller in the dell or vale.

Dellinger (*Ger.*) One who came from Delling (cove), the name of two places in Germany.

Dello Iacono, Delloiacono (*It.*) Descendant of the deacon.

Dell'Orfano (*It.*) One without parents, an orphan, usually one born out of wedlock.

Delman (*Eng.*) Dweller in the dell or vale.

Delmar (*Sp.*) Dweller near the sea.

Delmonico (*It.*) Descendant of the monk, a male member of a religious order.

Del Monte (*Sp.*) Dweller on the mountain.

Deloney (*Ir.*) Variant of Delaney, q.v.

De Long, De Longe (*Fr.*) One who came from Long (large place), the name of several places in France; the tall man.

De Lorenzo (*Sp.*) Descendant of Lorenzo, Spanish form of Lawrence (the laurel, symbol of victory).

Delorey (*Fr.*) Dweller at, or near, a granary.

Delorme (*Fr.*) One who came from Lorme (elm tree), the name of several places in France; dweller near the elm tree.

Del Principe (*It.*) Descendant of the prince.

Del Rio (*Sp.*) Dweller near the river.

Delson (*Eng.*) The son of Del, a pet form of names beginning with Adel (noble), as Adelbert and Adelard.

De Luca (*It.*) The son of Luca, Italian form of Luke (light).

Del Valle (*Sp.*) Dweller in the valley.

Del Vecchio (*It.*) Descendant of the old man.

Delves (*Eng.*) Dweller by the ditch or quarry.

De Maio (*It.*) Descendant of Maio, one named from birth in the month of May.

Demakis, Demas (*Gr.*) Descendant of Dhimos, a pet form of Dhimosthenis, a Greek form of Demosthenes (strong with people).

Deman (*Eng.*) Variant of Doman, q.v.

De Mar, Demar, De Mars (*Sp.*) Dweller near the sea.

De Marchi (*It.*) The son of Marchi, pet form of Melchiorre, Italian form of Melchior (king).

De Marco (*It.*) The son of Marco (belonging to Mars, the god of war).

Demaree (*Fr.*) Dweller near the sea.

De Martini, De Martino (*It.*) Descendant of Martini, a name given to one born on Tuesday.

Demas (*Fr.*) Dweller in, or near, the small house.

De Matteo (*It.*) The son of Matteo, Italian form of Matthew (gift of Jehovah).

Dembinski (*Pol.*) Dweller in, or near, an oak wood.

Dembo (*Pol.*) Dweller near an oak tree.

Dembowski, Dembski (*Pol.*) Dweller near an oak tree.

De Meester (*Du.*) The master workman or teacher.

De Meo (*It.*) Descendant of Meo, a pet form of names so ending, as Bartolomeo and Tomeo; also a pet form of Matteo, Italian form of Mathias (gift of Jehovah).

Demers (*Eng.*) One who built dams.

Demeter (*Eng., Cz.-Sl., Hun.*) Descendant of Demeter (goddess of fertility and harvests).

De Meyer (*Fr.*) Descendant of the steward, farmer, or head servant.

De Michael, De Michele (*Fr., It.*) Descendant of Michael (who is like God).

De Mille (*Fr.*) Descendant of Mile, a pet form of Emile, French form of Emil (work).

Deming, Demming (*Eng.*) Son of

Demma (damage; injury); one who came from Migny or Migne (Magnius' estate), the names of towns in France.

Demircloglu (*Tur.*) The son of the smith.

Demko, Demkowicz (*Pol.*) Descendant, or son, of Demko, a pet form of Demjan.

Demma, Demme (*Eng.*) Descendant of Demma (damage; injury).

De Monte (*Fr., Sp.*) Dweller on, or near, a hill.

Demopoulos, Demopulos (*Gr.*) The son of Demos, a pet form of Demosthenes (strong with people), or of Demetrius (of Demeter, the goddess of fertility and harvests).

Demos (*Gr.*) Descendant of Demos, a pet form of Demosthenes (strong with people); or of Demetrius (of Demeter, the goddess of fertility and harvests).

Dempsey (*Ir.*) Grandson of Diomasach (proud).

Dempster (*Scot., Mx.*) One who held court, a judge.

Demski (*Pol.*) Dweller at, or near, an oak tree.

Demus (*Ger.*) Descendant of Demus, a pet form of Nikodemus, a German form of Nicodemus (victory of the people).

De Muth, Demuth (*Ger.*) Descendant of Muth (humility; modesty); the humble or modest man.

De Napoli (*It.*) One who came from Naples, Italian Napoli (new city), in Italy.

Denard (*Fr.*) Descendant of Nard, a pet form of Bernard (bear, hard) and Leonard (lion, hard).

De Nardo, De Nardi (*It.*) Descendant of Nardo (hard), a pet form of Bernardo and Leonardo.

Denberg (*Eng.*) One who came from Denbury (the fort of the Devon people), in Devonshire.

Dendtler (*Ger.*) One who dealt in second-hand goods.

Deneen (*Ir.*) Variant of Dineen, q.v.

Denenberg, Denenburg (*Ger.*) Variants of Dannenberg, q.v.

Denenholz (*Du.*) Dweller in, or by, a grove of fir trees.

Denes (*Hun.*) Descendant of Denes, Hungarian form of Dennis (belonging to Dionysus, Grecian god of wine; judge of men).

De Neve (*Fr.*) One who came from Neve (a place in water) in France.

Dengler (*Eng.*) Dweller in a deep dell or narrow valley.

Denham, Denman (*Eng.*) One who came from Denham (homestead in a valley; the hill of Dunn's people), the name of several places in England, dweller in a valley.

Denis, Deny (*Fr.*) Descendant of Denis (belonging to Dionysus, the Grecian god of wine).

Deniz (*Tur.*) Dweller near the sea.

Dennehy, Denehy (*Ir.*) Grandson of Duineachaidh (humane).

Dennen (*Ir.*) Grandson of Doineannach (stormy or tempestuous).

Denning (*Eng.*) The son of Dene (the Dane).

Dennis (*Eng., Ir.*) Descendant of Denis (belonging to Dionysus, Grecian god of wine); descendant of the brown fighter or warrior.

Dennison, Denison, Denson (*Eng., Ir.*) Son of Denis (belonging to Dionysus, Grecian god of wine); son of the brown fighter or warrior.

Denny, Denney, Dennie (*Scot., Eng.*) One who came from Denny (wet land), a town and parish in Stirlingshire; or from Denny (Dane's island), in Cambridgeshire; pet form of Dennis, q.v.

Denovan (*Scot.*) One who came from Denovan (fort by the river), in Stirlingshire.

Densford (*Eng.*) One who came from Denford (river crossing in a valley), in Berkshire.

Densham (*Eng.*) One who came from Denham (homestead in a valley; hill of Dunn's people), the name of several places in England.

Denslow (*Eng.*) Dweller at the Dane's hill.

Densmore (*Eng.*) Variant of Dinsmore, q.v.

Denson (*Eng.*) The son of the dean; the son of the Dane; the son of Den, a short form of Denis (belonging to Dionysus, Grecian god of wine).

Dent (*Eng.*) One who came from Dent (hill), in the West Riding of Yorkshire.

Denton, Denten (*Eng.*) One who came from Denton (homestead in a valley), the name of many places in England.

D'Entremont (*Fr., Swis.*) Dweller between the mountains; one who came from Entremont, in Switzerland.

Denver (*Eng.*) One who came from Denver (Dane's passage), in Norfolk.

Denwood (*Eng.*) Dweller at a hollow in the woods; or at a swine pasture in the woods.

De Nys, De Nye, Denye (*Fr.*) Descendant of Denys, French form of Dennis (belonging to Dionysus, the Grecian god of wine).

Denz, Densel, Denzer (*Ger.*) The dancer, troubadour, or minstrel who performed at fair or festival.

De Pasquale (*It.*) Descendant of Pasquale, Italian form of Pascal (sufferings; child born during Jewish Passover or Christian Easter).

De Paul, De Pauw (*Fr.*) Descendant of Paul (small).

Depew, Depue, Dupuy (*Fr.*) Dweller on, or near, a hill.

De Pietro, Depietri (*It.*) The son of Pietro, Italian form of Peter (a rock).

De Pinto (*Port., Sp.*) One who came from Pinto (colored), in Portugal.

Depner (*Ger.*) One who made utensils of earthenware or metal, a potter.

Deppe (*Ger.*) Descendant of Deppe, a pet form of Detburn (folk, bear).

Depperschmidt (*Ger.*) The smith or artisan who made utensils of earthenware or metal, a potter.

De Pre, Depre, De Pree (*Fr.*) Dweller in the meadow.

De Priest (*Du., Eng., Fr.*) The priest or pastor; one who was a member of a priest's household; descendant of the priest.

Derby (*Eng.*) One who came from Derby (homestead frequented by wild animals), in Derbyshire.

Derbyshire (*Eng.*) One who came from Derbyshire (homestead in district frequented by wild animals), a county in England.

Derden (*Eng.*) Dweller in the valley where animals roamed.

Dering (*Eng.*) The son of Deora (beloved).

Derington (*Eng.*) One who came from Derrington (homestead of Dudda's people), in Staffordshire.

Derk (*Dan.*) Descendant of Derk, a pet form of Diederik (people, rule).

Derksen (*Dan.*) The son of Derk, a pet form of Diederik (people, rule).

Derman (*Eng.*) Descendant of Deormann (the beloved man).

Dermody (*Ir.*) Descendant of Diarmard (freeman).

Dern, Derner (*Ger.*) One who came from Derne (muddy place), the name of two places in Germany; or from Dehrn in Germany.

Dernbach (*Ger.*) One who came from Dernbach (muddy stream), the name of four places in Germany.

Dernburg (*Ger.*) One who came from Derneburg (fortress in a swamp), in Germany.

De Roche, De Rocher (*Fr.*) Dweller near the rock or cliff.

De Roeck (*Du.*) Dweller at the sign of the rook.

De Rosa, De Rose (*It.*) The son of Rosa or Rose (rose).

Derr (*Fr., Ger.*) Variant of Durr, q.v.

Derrick, Derricks, Derrickson (*Eng.*) Descendant of Derrick, a pet form of Theodoric (people, rule).

Derricote, Derricoate (*Eng.*) Dweller near the enclosure or shelter for deer or wild beasts.

Derritt (*Eng.*) Variant of Derrick, q.v.

115

Derry, Deery (*Ir.*) Descendant of Doireidh.

Dersham (*Eng.*) One who came from Dersingham (homestead of Deorsige's people), in Norfolk.

Derwent (*Eng.*) One who came from Derwent (river through oak trees), in Yorkshire; dweller by the Derwent, the name of several streams in England.

Derwinski (*Pol.*) One who came from Derwince, in Poland.

Desai (*Hindi*) A district officer; descendant of the Desai, a Hindi title with no English equivalent.

De Salvo (*It.*) The son of Salvo (salvation).

De Santis (*Port., Sp.*) The holy or sanctified man; one who came from Dos Santos, the name of places in Portugal and Spain.

De Santo (*Sp., It.*) The holy or sanctified man; descendant of the saint; or of the maker of saintly images.

Descartes (*Fr.*) Dweller in the outskirts of a town, a suburbanite.

Desch, Descher (*Ger.*) One who made and sold purses, pouches, and handbags.

Deschamps, Descamps (*Fr.*) Dweller in, or near, the cultivated lands or fields.

Deschatelets (*Fr.*) Dweller near the small castles; one who came from Chatelet (small castle), the name of several places in France.

De Simone (*It.*) The son of Simone, Italian form of Simon (gracious hearing; hearkening; snub-nosed).

De Sitter (*Du.*) The shoemaker, one who made and sold shoes.

Desjardins, Des Jardins (*Fr.*) Dweller in, or near, the gardens; one who cultivated a garden.

Desmarais (*Fr.*) Dweller in, or near, the marsh.

De Smet, De Smedt, De Smidt (*Du.*) The worker in metal, the smith.

Des Moineaux (*Fr.*) Dweller at the sign of the sparrow; one with the characteristics of a sparrow, i.e., lively, quick, fleet.

Desmond (*Ir.*) One who came from South Munster.

Desmoulins (*Fr.*) Dweller near the mill.

De Sousa, De Souza (*Port.*) One who came from Sousa or Souza (salty place), the names of several places in Portugal.

Despagne (*Fr.*) One who came from Spain, a Spaniard.

Despota, Despot (*It.*) The head of a household; the master or lord.

De Stefano, De Stefani (*It.*) The son of Stefano, Italian form of Stephen (crown or garland).

Determann, Deterding, Deters (*Ger.*) Descendant of Dethard (people, hard).

Dethloff, Detloff (*Ger.*) Descendant of Dethloff (people, wolf).

Detmer, Dettmer (*Ger.*) Descendant of Detmar, a form of Theudemar (people, fame).

Detrick (*Ger.*) Variant of Dietrich, q.v.

Dettloff (*Ger.*) Variant of Dethloff, q.v.

Dettmann, Dettman (*Ger.*) Descendant of Teutman (people, man).

Detweiler, Detwiler (*Swis., Ger.*) One who came from Datweil, in Canton Zurich.

Deubel, Deuble (*Ger.*) One who raised and sold pigeons.

Deuter (*Eng.*) One who was unduly hesitant or timid.

Deutsch, Deutscher, Deutch, Deutschmann, Deutschman, Deutsche (*Ger., Du.*) One who came from Germany, a German.

Deval (*Fr.*) Dweller in the valley.

De Valera (*Sp.*) One who came from Valero (fortification), in Spain.

Devaney, Devanie (*Ir.*) Descendant of the cormorant, or diving sea bird; descendant of Dubheannaigh (Black of Eanach).

De Vaughn (*Du.*) One who carried the flag or banner.

Deveaux, Deveau (*Fr.*) Dweller in a valley.

Deveney, Devenny (*Ir.*) Descendant of Dubheannaigh (Black of Eanach).

Devens, Devins (*Ir.*) Grandson of the little poet.

Dever (*Ir.*) Descendant of the successful one; grandson of Dubhodhar (black Odhar).

Devereaux, Devereux (*Fr.*) One who came from Evreux, in France.

Devery (*Fr.*) Irish variant of Devereaux, q.v.

De Vilbiss (*Ger.*) One who is bold enough to bite the devil, from German *Teufelbeiss* (devil bite).

De Ville (*Fr., Eng.*) One who came from Ville (town), the name of many places in France; dweller in the town; a fanciful spelling for one who played the part of the devil in play and pageant.

Devine (*Ir., Fr., Eng.*) Descendant of the little poet; one who came from Vins, in France; a man of more than ordinary excellence.

De Vito (*It.*) The son of Vito (life).

Devitt (*Ir.*) The son of little David (commander; beloved; friend).

Devlin (*Ir.*) Descendant of the plasterer or dauber; one who came from Dublin (black pool); grandson of Doibhilin.

De Vos (*Du., Eng.*) Dweller at the sign of the fox; nickname for a crafty, cunning man.

De Voto (*It.*) The saintly, devout man; descendant of Voto, a pet form of Iacovoto, an Italian pet form of Jacob (may God protect; the supplanter).

De Voy (*Fr.*) Dweller in the house by the road.

De Vriendt (*Du., Bel.*) One who was a friend, an esteemed person.

de Vries (*Du.*) The Frisian, i.e., one who came from the province of Friesland (curled hair; free).

Dew (*Eng., Wel.*) One with black or dark complexion; descendant of Dew, a pet form of David (commander; beloved; friend); the large or fat man.

Dewar, Dewer (*Scot.*) One who came from Dewar (dark plowed land), in Midlothian; an official who had custody of the relic of a saint.

Dewberry, Deuberry (*Eng., Fr.*) One who came from Dewsbury (David's fort), in Yorkshire; one who lived at the edge of town, a variant of the French, Dubarry.

Dewey (*Wel., Scot.*) Descendant of Dewi, a Welsh form of David (commander; beloved; friend), or of little Dew, a pet form of David.

De Witt, De Wit, De Witte (*Du.*) The light-complexioned or white-haired man.

De Wolf, De Wolfe, De Wulf (*Du.*) Dweller at the sign of the wolf; one with the characteristics of a wolf.

Dewsnap (*Eng.*) One who came from Dewsnap (Dew's hillock), in Cheshire.

Dexter (*Eng.*) One who dyed cloth.

De Young (*Du.*) Partial Anglicization of De Jong, q.v.

De Zutter (*Bel.*) One who made and sold shoes, a shoemaker.

Diachenko, Diaczenko (*Ukr.*) The son of the cantor.

Diakoumis, Diakoumakos (*Gr.*) Descendant of little Iakobos, Greek form of Jacob (may God protect; the supplanter).

Di Ambrosio (*Sp.*) Descendant of Ambrosio, Spanish form of Ambrose (immortal).

Diamond (*Eng.*) Descendant of Daymond (day, protection); dealer in diamonds.

Diana (*Eng., It.*) Descendant of Diana (bright as day), the Roman moon-goddess.

Di Angelo (*It.*) The son of Angelo (messenger).

Dianovsky (*Ukr.*) Descendant of Dian (given).

Diaz, Dias (*Sp., Port.*) The son of Diago, corrupted form of Diego, Spanish form of Jacob (may God protect; the supplanter).

Dibble (*Eng.*) Descendant of little Dibb, a pet form of Dibald from Tibald or Theobald (people, bold).

Di Benedetto (*It.*) The son of Benedetto, Italian form of Benedict (blessed).

117

Di Bernardo (*It.*) The son of Bernardo, Italian form of Bernard (bear, hard).

Di Bonaventura (*It.*) The son of Bonaventura (good fortune).

Di Bruno (*It., Sp.*) The son of Bruno (brown).

Di Camillo (*It.*) The son of Camillo (attendant at religious ceremonies).

Di Canio (*It.*) The son of Canio (gray).

Di Carlo (*It.*) The son of Carlo, Italian form of Charles (man).

Di Cesare, Di Cesari (*It.*) The son of Cesare (the hairy one).

Di Cianni (*It.*) The son of Cianni, a pet form of Giacomo, Italian form of James (may God protect; the supplanter).

Di Cicco (*It.*) The son of Cicco, a pet form of Francesco, Italian form of Francis (free).

Dick, Dicke, Dicks, Dickes (*Ger., Eng.*) The large or fat man; descendant of Dick, a pet form of Richard (rule, hard).

Dickens, Dicken, Dickins (*Eng.*) The son of little Dick, a pet form of Richard (rule, hard).

Dicker, Dickerman (*Eng.*) One who made dikes or ditches.

Dickerson (*Eng.*) The son of the maker of dikes or ditches.

Dickey, Dickie (*Eng.*) Descendant of little Dick, a pet form of Richard (rule, hard).

Dickinson (*Eng.*) The son of little Dick, a pet form of Richard (rule, hard).

Dickman, Dickmann (*Ger.*) The big, or fat, man.

Dickson (*Eng.*) The son of Dick, a pet form of Richard (rule, hard).

Dickstein (*Ger.*) Dweller near the large stone.

Di Cosola, Di Cosolo (*It.*) The son of Cosola (little name).

Di Crescenzo (*It.*) The son of Crescenzio (growing; coming forth).

Di Cristofano (*It.*) The son of Cristofano, an Italian form of Christopher (Christ-bearer).

Didenko (*Ukr.*) The son of the grandfather.

Didier (*Fr.*) Descendant of Didier (beloved).

Di Dio (*It.*) The son of Dio (God), a pet form of such names as Diodoro, Diogene, and Diomede.

Di Domenico (*It.*) The son of Domenico, Italian form of Dominic (the Lord's day).

Diduch (*Ukr.*) One likened to a good, helping gnome in Ukrainian demonology; descendant of the grandfather.

Dieball, Diebel (*Ger.*) Variant of Diebold, q.v.

Diebold (*Ger.*) Descendant of Diebald, a variant of Theobald (people, bold).

Dieckhaus (*Ger.*) One who came from Dieckhaus (dike house), in Germany; dweller in a house on the dike.

Dieckmann, Dieckman, Diecker (*Ger.*) Dweller on, or near, a dike; one who worked on the dike.

Dieffenbach, Diefenbach, Diefenbacher, Dieffenbacher, Diefenbaker (*Ger.*) One who came from Diefenbach (boggy brook), the name of three places in Germany.

Diehl (*Ger.*) Descendant of Diehl, from Dudo, a pet form of names beginning with Diet (people), as Theudoricus, Teuduin, and Theudulf.

Diemer (*Ger.*) One who came from Diehmen, in Germany.

Diener, Dienner (*Ger.*) One who served others, a servant.

Diengott (*Ger.*) One who served God; a clergyman.

Dienhart (*Ger.*) Descendant of Deganhart (warrior, hard).

Dienst (*Ger.*) One who served others, a servant.

Dienstag (*Ger.*) One who worked or performed some service on Tuesdays; descendant of Dienstag, a name given to one born on Tuesday.

Dierkes, Dierking (*Ger.*) Descendant of Theudoricus (people, rule).

Diesel (*Ger.*) Descendant of Diesel, a pet form of Mattheisel, a German form of Matthew (gift of Jehovah); or of Teuzo (people).

Diessel (*Ger.*) Dweller near where thistles grew.

Dieter (*Ger.*) Descendant of Diether (people, army); sometimes from Dietrich, q.v.

Dietrich, Diedrich, Diederich, Dietrick, Dieterich (*Ger.*) Descendant of Dietrich, a German form of Theodoric (people, rule).

Dietz, Dietsch, Dietze, Dietzel, Dietzen (*Ger.*) Descendant of Teuzo, a pet form of names beginning with Diet (people), as Dietrich, Theudoald, and Theotwig; one who came from Dietz, also called Diez (people), in Germany.

Diffenbaugh (*Ger.*) Variant of Dieffenbach, q.v.

Diffy, Diffay (*Fr.*) One who came from Defay (communal grazing land), in France; dweller in, or near, a place enclosed by a hedge.

Di Filippo (*It.*) The son of Filippo, Italian form of Philip (lover of horses).

Di Fiore (*It.*) The son of Fiore (flower).

Di Gangi (*It.*) The son of Gangi, a pet form of Gangolf (going, wolf).

Digby (*Eng.*) One who came from Digby (settlement by a ditch or drain), in Lincolnshire.

Diggins (*Eng.*) The son of little Digg or Dick, pet forms of Richard (rule, hard).

Diggs (*Eng.*) Descendant of Digg, a pet form of Richard (rule, hard).

Di Giacomo (*It.*) The son of Giacomo, Italian form of James (may God protect; the supplanter).

Di Giovanni (*It.*) The son of Giovanni, Italian form of John (gracious gift of Jehovah).

Dignan, Dignum, Digman (*Ir.*) Grandson of little Dubhceann (black head).

Di Grazia (*It.*) Descendant of Grazia (grace).

Di Gregorio (*It.*) The son of Gregorio, Italian form of Gregory (watchful).

Dilday, Dildy (*Ger.*) Dweller on, or near, a wet place; overseer of the annual church festival.

Dilger (*Eng.*) Possibly one who came

from Dilicar (dill field), in Westmorland.

Dill, Dille (*Eng.*) Descendant of Dill or Dila (the dull one).

Dillard, Dillards (*Eng.*) Descendant of little Dill (the dull one).

Dillashaw (*Eng.*) Dweller by the wood or thicket; or in Dylla's wood or shaw.

Diller (*Eng.*) Dweller near a field of dill; one who grew and sold dill, a commonly cultivated plant in the Middle Ages.

Dilling (*Eng.*) The son of Dila (the dull one).

Dillingham (*Eng.*) One who came from Dullingham (the village of Dulla's people), in Cambridgeshire.

Dillman (*Eng.*) One who grew and sold dill.

Dillon (*Ir.*) Descendant of little Dill or Dillo (the dull one).

Dilworth, Dillworth (*Eng.*) One who came from Dilworth (homestead where dill was grown), in Lancashire.

Di Maggio (*It.*) Descendant of Maggio (name given to one born in the month of May).

Di Marco, Di Marca (*It.*) The son of Marco, Italian form of Mark (belonging to the god Mars).

Di Maria (*It.*) The son of Maria (bitterness; wished for child; rebellion).

Di Martino (*It.*) The son of Martino, Italian form of Martin (belonging to the god Mars).

Di Maso (*It.*) The son of Maso, a pet form of Tommaso, Italian form of Thomas (a twin).

Di Meo (*It.*) The son of Meo, a pet form of Matteo, Italian form of Matthew (gift of Jehovah).

Di Michele, Di Miceli (*It.*) The son of Michele, Italian form of Michael (who is like God).

Dimick, Dimmick (*Eng.*) One who came from Dymock (pigsty), in Gloucestershire.

Dimitrakopoulos (*Gr.*) The son of little Dimitris (of Demeter, the goddess of fertility and harvests).

Dimitrov, Dimitroff (*Bulg.*) The son of

Dimitur, Bulgarian form of Demetrius (of Demeter the goddess of fertility and harvests).

Dimmick, Dimock, Dimmack (*Eng.*) One who came from Dymock (pigsty), in Gloucestershire.

Dimopoulos (*Gr.*) The son of little Dimosthenis, the Greek form of Demosthenes (strong with people).

Dimsdale (*Eng.*) One who came from Dimsdale (possibly both parts mean a small valley), in Staffordshire.

Di Napoli (*It.*) Variant of De Napoli, q.v.

Di Natale (*It.*) The son of Natale, Italian form of Natalie (birthday).

Dineen, Dinneen (*Ir.*) Grandson of little Donn (brown).

Dingels (*Eng.*) One who came from Dingle (deep hollow), in Lancashire; dweller near a deep hollow.

Dinges, Dingess (*Ger.*) Descendant of Dionys, short form of Dionysios, German form of Dionysus (Grecian god of wine; judge of men).

Dingle (*Eng.*) Dweller in a deep dell or narrow valley; one who came from Dingle, in Lancashire.

Dingman (*Eng.*) Dweller at a deep hollow or narrow valley.

Dingsdale (*Eng.*) One who came from Dinsdale (corner belonging to Deighton), the name of places in Durham and the North Riding of Yorkshire.

Dingus (*Eng.*) Dweller in a house in a narrow valley.

Dingwall, Dingwell (*Scot.*) One who formerly lived on the lands of Dingwall (meeting of the local council), in Ross and Cromarty.

Dini, Dino (*It.*) Descendant of Dini or Dino, pet forms of names with these endings, as Orlandini, Bernardini, Corradino, and Rinaldino.

Dinkelman, Dinkel (*Ger.*) One who dealt in spelt, a kind of wheat.

Dinning (*Eng.*) The son of Dinn, a pet form of Denis (belonging to Dionysus; judge of men); descendant of Dunn (dark brown).

Di Novo, Dinovo (*It.*) Descendant of Novo (new).

Dinse (*Ger.*) Variant of Dinges, q.v.

Dinsmore, Dinsmoor (*Eng.*) One who came from Dinmore (great hill), in Herefordshire.

Dinter (*Ger.*) One who made and sold ink.

Dinwiddie, Dinwoodie (*Scot.*) One who came from the lands of Dinwoodie (hill with the shrubs), in Dumfriesshire.

Dion, Dionne (*Fr.*) Descendant of Dion (Grecian god of wine; judge of men); one who came from Dionne, in Burgundy.

Diorio, Di Orio (*It.*) The son of Iorio or Orio, pet forms of Onorio (honor).

Di Paolo (*It.*) The son of Paolo, Italian form of Paul (small).

Di Pasquale (*It.*) The son of Pasquale, Italian form of Pascal (sufferings).

Di Pietro (*It.*) The son of Pietro, Italian form of Peter (a rock).

Di Pinto (*It.*) The son of Pinto (the painted one).

Dipple (*Eng., Scot.*) Descendant of Dibald, a corruption of Theobald (people, bold); one who came from Dipple (dark stream), in Scotland.

Dippold (*Eng.*) Descendant of Dibald, a variant of Tibald, a form of Theobald (people, bold).

Di Prima (*It.*) The son of Primo (the first).

Director (*Ger.*) The manager or master.

Dirksen (*Dan.*) The son of Dirk, a pet form of Diederik (people, rule).

Di Salvo (*It.*) The son of Salvo, a pet form of Salvatore (savior).

Di Santo, Di Santi (*It.*) The son of Sante (saint).

Disch, Discher (*Ger.*) One who made cabinets, a joiner.

Dishman, Dishmon, Disher (*Eng.*) One who made and sold dishes.

Di Silvestro (*It.*) The son of Silvestro, Italian form of Silvester (forest dweller).

Di Silvio (*It.*) The son of Silvio, Italian masculine form of Silvia (forest).

Diskin, Diskind (*Ir.*) Descendant of Discin, a diminutive of *diosc*, "barren person."

Disley (*Eng.*) One who came from Disley, in Cheshire.

Dismore (*Eng.*) One who possessed ten marks.

Disney (*Eng.*) One who came from Isigny (Isina's estate), in Calvados.

Dispensa, Dispenza (*It.*) Descendant of Dispensa (dispensation).

Disraeli (*Fr.*) One who came from Israel (prevailing with God).

Disselhorst (*Ger.*) Dweller near a thicket of thistles.

Dissen (*Ger.*) One who came from Dissen, the name of two places in Germany.

Di Stasio (*It.*) The son of Stasio, a pet form of Anastasio, Italian form of Anastasius (one who shall rise again; resurrection).

Di Stefano, Distefano (*It.*) The son of Stefano, Italian form of Stephen (crown or garland).

Distel (*Ger., Fr.*) Dweller near where thistles grew.

Ditch, Ditchman (*Eng.*) Dweller by the ditch or dike.

Dithmar, Dithmer (*Ger.*) Variant of Dittmer, q.v.

Ditkowsky (*Ukr.*) Descendant of the old man or grandfather.

Ditlove, Ditlow (*Ger.*) Variant of Dethloff, q.v.

Ditter (*Ger., Eng.*) Variant of Dieter, q.v.; one who composes pieces; a public crier.

Ditteridge (*Eng.*) One who came from Ditteridge (ridge along a dike or ditch), in Wiltshire.

Dittmann, Dittman (*Ger.*) Descendant of Teutman (people, man).

Dittmer, Dittmar (*Ger.*) Descendant of Theudemar (people, fame).

Di Turi, Dituri (*It.*) The son of Turi, a pet form of Turiddu (savior).

Divane (*Ir.*) Descendant of little Dubh (black).

Di Venere (*It.*) The son of Venus (goddess of love).

Divens (*Ir.*) Variant of Devens, q.v.

Diver, Divers (*Eng.*) Dweller at the sign of the dive, that is, any one of several species of diving birds, such as a loon.

Di Vincenzo (*It.*) The son of Vincenzo, Italian form of Vincent (conquering).

Divine (*Eng.*) Nickname for a man of more than ordinary excellence.

Di Vito, Di Vita, Divita (*It.*) The son of Vito (life) or Vita.

Di Vittorio (*It.*) The son of Vittorio, Italian form of Victor (the victorious).

Divizio (*It.*) One with bad habits; addicted to vice.

Dix (*Eng.*) Descendant of Dick, a pet form of Richard (rule, hard).

Dixie, Dixey (*Eng.*) Descendant of little Dick, a pet form of Richard (rule, hard).

Dixon (*Eng.*) The son of Dick, a pet form of Richard (rule, hard).

Djordjevic, Djordjevich (*Yu.-Sl.*) The son of Djordje, Serbo-Croatian form of George (farmer).

Djuric (*Sl.*) Descendant of Djurik, a Slovakian form of George (farmer).

Dlouhy (*Cz.-Sl.*) The tall man.

Dlugopolski (*Pol.*) Dweller near a long field.

Dluhy (*Cz.*) The long or tall man.

Dmytrenko (*Ukr.*) The son of Dmytro, a Ukrainian form of Demetrius (of Demeter, the goddess of fertility and harvests).

Doak (*Scot.*) Variant of Doig, q.v.

Doane, Doan, Done (*Eng., Ir.*) Dweller at, or near, the slope of a hill; grandson of Duban (black).

Dobbie (*Eng.*) Descendant of little Dobb, a pet form of Robert (fame, bright).

Dobbins, Dobbin, Dobyne, Dobynes, Dobbyn (*Eng.*) Descendant of little Dob, a pet form of Robert (fame, bright).

Dobbs, Dobb (*Eng.*) The son of Dobb or Dob, pet forms of Robert (fame, bright).

Dobeck, Dobecki, Dobek (*Pol.*) Dweller near a little oak tree.

121

Dober (*Eng.*) One who did whitewashing or plastering.

Dobie, Dobies (*Eng., Scot.*) Descendant of little Dobb, a pet form of Robert (fame, bright).

Dobkin (*Eng.*) Descendant of little Dobb, a pet form of Robert (fame, bright).

Doble, Double (*Eng.*) Descendant of little Dob, a pet form of Robert (fame, bright).

Dobler (*Ger.*) One who lived in the wooded valley or ravine; one who came from Dobler (wooded valley), in Germany.

Dobner (*Ger.*) One who came from Dobeneck, in Germany.

Dobosz (*Pol.*) One who beats a drum, a drummer.

Dobrick, Dobrik (*Ger.*) One who came from Dobrikau (good meadow), in Austria; or from Dobra (good place), the name of various places in Germany; descendant of Dobrslaw (good, glory).

Dobrin, Dobrinski (*Rus., Pol.*) The good person.

Dobrovits, Dobrovitz (*Pol.*) The son of the good man.

Dobrowolski (*Rus.*) Descendant of the volunteer.

Dobrowski (*Pol.*) Descendant of the good man.

Dobry (*Pol., Cz.*) The good man.

Dobrzynski (*Pol.*) One who came from Dobrzyn, the name of two places in Poland.

Dobson (*Eng.*) The son of Dob, a pet form of Robert (fame, bright).

Doby, Dobey (*Eng., Scot.*) Descendant of little Dobb, a pet form of Robert (fame, bright).

Dobyne, Dobynes (*Eng.*) Variants of Doby, q.v.

Dochtermann, Dockterman (*Ger.*) One who married the daughter, a son-in-law.

Dockendorf (*Ger.*) One who came from Dockendorf (doll's village), in Germany.

Dockery (*Eng.*) One who came from Dockray (hollow), in Cumberland.

Docking (*Eng.*) One who came from Docking (place where dock, a troublesome weed, grew), in Norfolk.

Dockstader (*Ger.*) Dweller by the dock landing place.

Doctor (*Scot., Ger.*) One who practiced medicine; one who was highly educated, generally a teacher.

Dodd, Dodds, Dod, Dods (*Eng., Scot.*) Descendant of Dod (rounded summit); or of Dod, a Scottish pet form of George (farmer); dweller on Great Dodd, the name of a hill in Cumberland.

Dodford (*Eng.*) One who came from Dodford (Dodda's ford), in Northamptonshire.

Dodge (*Eng.*) Descendant of Dodge, a pet form of Roger (fame, spear).

Dodgen, Dodgin, Dodgion (*Eng., Scot.*) Descendant of little Dogg, from Dodge, a pet form of Roger (fame, spear).

Dodgson, Dodgshon (*Eng.*) The son of Dodge, a pet form of Roger (fame, spear).

Dodson (*Eng., Scot.*) The son of Dod (rounded summit); or of Dod, a Scottish pet form of George (farmer).

Dodwell (*Eng.*) One who came from Dodwell (Dodda's spring), in Warwickshire.

Doe (*Eng.*) Dweller at the sign of the doe or female deer.

Doerfler (*Ger.*) One who came from Dorfl or Dorfle (village), the names of places in Germany.

Doering (*Ger.*) One who came from Thuringia, in Germany.

Doerner, Doern (*Ger.*) One who came from Dorn (place where thornbushes grew), the name of two places in Germany.

Doerr, Dorr (*Ger.*) Descendant of Dorr, a pet form of Isidorus (gift of Isis); descendant of Dioro, a pet form of names beginning with Teuer (dear), as Diurard and Deorovald.

Doetsch (*Ger.*) The fat or plump man.

Doggett (*Eng.*) Descendant of little

Docca; one thought to possess a head like a dog.

Doheny, Dohenny (*Ir.*) Descendant of Dubhchonna (black Conna).

Doherty (*Ir.*) Grandson of Dochartach (hurtful or unfortunate).

Dohm (*Ger.*) One who came from Dohm (the spring), the name of two places in Germany; dweller near the cathedral.

Dohner (*Ger.*) Descendant of Dohnert (free man, hard); one who came from Dohna (place where a bird snare was set), in Germany; one who snares birds.

Dohrmann, Dohrman (*Ger.*) Dweller at the gate.

Dohs, Dohse (*Ger.*) Descendant of Dose, a pet form of Teuzo (people); dweller near a boggy brook.

Doi (*Jap.*) Soil or ground, well.

Doig (*Scot.*) Descendant of the servant of Dog, a pet form of St. Cadoc (warlike).

Dolan (*Ir.*) One with a dark complexion or black hair; a variant of Doolin, q.v.

Dolansky (*Pol.*) One who came from Dolany (valley), in Poland.

Dolasinski (*Pol.*) Dweller in, or near, the forest.

Dolby (*Eng.*) One who came from Dalby (settlement in a valley), the name of several places in England.

Dolce, Dolci (*It.*) The kind, sweet person.

Dolder, Dold (*Eng.*) Dweller near the allotment of land; or near the boundary mark.

Dole (*Eng.*) One who was entitled to a share of the common field; dweller on the share of the common field; or at the division of land or boundary mark.

Dolehide (*Eng.*) One who shared a hide of land, an amount necessary for the support of a free family and its dependents.

Dolezal (*Cz.*) One who ended his grief.

Dolgin, Dolgins (*Rus.*) The tall man.

Dolin, Dolins (*Fr.*) One who worked with a plane.

Dolina (*Rus.*) Dweller in the valley.

Dolinka, Dolinko (*Cz.-Sl., Pol.*) Dweller in the valley.

Doll, Dolle (*Eng., Ger.*) Dweller at a division of land or boundary mark; descendant of Doll, a pet form of names beginning with Dult (patience), as Dultwic and Duldfrid.

Dollar (*Scot.*) The man from Dollar (dale of plowed land), in Clackmannanshire.

Dollarhide (*Eng.*) One who owned and tilled a hide of land (about 120 acres).

Dolley, Doley (*Eng.*) One who came from Ouilly (Olius' farm), the name of five places in Normandy.

Dolnick (*Cz.-Sl.*) Dweller in the lower place.

Dolph (*Eng.*) Descendant of Dolph, a pet form of Adolph (noble, wolf); or of Rudolph (fame, wolf).

Dolphin, Dolfin (*Eng.*) Descendant of Dolgfinnr.

Dolsby (*Eng.*) One who came from Dalby (homestead in a valley), the name of several places in England.

Dolton (*Eng.*) One who came from Dolton (homestead frequented by doves), in Devonshire.

Domagala, Domagalski (*Pol.*) Descendant of the exacting or critical man.

Doman, Dooman (*Eng.*) One who pronounces the verdict or doom, a judge.

Domanski (*Pol.*) One who deceives, tricks, or cheats.

Domaracki (*Pol.*) One who loves his home.

Domas (*Lith.*) Descendant of Domas, pet form of Dominikas, Lithuanian form of Dominick (the Lord's day).

Domash, Domashewicz (*Pol.*) Descendant of Thomas (a twin).

Dombeck, Dombek (*Dan.*) One who came from Dombaek (silent stream), in Denmark.

Dombkowski (*Pol.*) One who came from Dombkowo, in Poland.

Dombrowski, Dombroski (*Pol.*) Dweller in, or near, the oak grove.

Domek (*Pol.*) Dweller in the small house.

Domin (*Eng.*) Variant of Doman, q.v.

Domingo (*Sp.*) Descendant of Domingo, Spanish form of Dominick (the Lord's day).

Domingues (*Port.*) The son of Domingo, Portuguese form of Dominick (the Lord's day).

Dominguez, Dominguiz (*Sp.*) The son of Domingo, Spanish form of Dominick (the Lord's day).

Dominiak (*Pol.*) Descendant of Dominik, Polish form of Dominick (the Lord's day).

Dominick, Domenico, Domenick, Dominic (*It.*) Descendant of Dominick (the Lord's day), a name sometimes given to one born on Sunday.

Domino (*It.*) Descendant of the little, good man.

Dominique (*Fr.*) Descendant of Dominique, French form of Dominick (the Lord's day).

Domke, Dompke (*Ger.*) Descendant of little Dom (judgment); dweller in a small house.

Domovich (*Yu.-Sl.*) Dweller in the house or home; the son of Dom, a pet form of Dominik, Yugoslavian form of Dominick (the Lord's day).

Don (*Scot., Eng.*) Dweller near the Don (a god), a river in Aberdeenshire; descendant of Donn (brown); the dark, swarthy man; descendant of Don, a pet form of Donald (brown-haired stranger; world-ruler).

Donahue, Donohue, Donaghue, Donoghue, Donohoe (*Ir.*) Descendant of Donough (brown battler).

Donaldson, Donald, Donalds (*Scot., Eng.*) The son of Donald (dark or brown-haired stranger; world-ruler).

Donat (*Fr., Eng.*) Descendant of Donatus (given), a fourth century saint.

Donath (*Ger.*) Descendant of Donatus (given).

Donato, Donati, Donat (*It.*) Descendant of Donato (given).

Donegan, Dongan (*Ir.*) Descendant of the little brown man; grandson of little Donn (brown).

Donelson (*Scot.*) The son of Donal or Donel (world-mighty).

Dones, Donis (*Eng.*) Dweller on, or near, the hill or hill pasture.

Doney (*Eng.*) Variant of Downey, q.v.

Donk (*Du.*) One who came from Donk (knoll in a swamp), in Brabant.

Donker (*Du.*) The dark, gloomy man.

Donlan, Donlon, Donlin (*Ir.*) Grandson of little Domhnall (world-mighty).

Donnat, Donnet, Donney (*Fr., Scot.*) Descendant of Donat (given), the name of several saints.

Donnellan, Donelan, Donelon, Donelin (*Ir.*) Grandson of Domhnall (world-mighty).

Donnelly, Donnelley, Donley (*Ir.*) Grandson of Donnghal (brown valor); descendant of the dark-complexioned, valiant man.

Donner (*Ger.*) Descendant of Donner (Thunar, the god of thunder).

Donnersberger (*Ger.*) Dweller on the Donnersberg (thunder mountain).

Donofrio, D'Onofrio (*It.*) The son of Onofrio (supporter of peace).

Donovan (*Ir.*) Grandson of Donndubhan (brown Dubhan); grandson of Donndamhan (little, brown poet).

Doody (*Ir.*) One with dark complexion or black hair; grandson of Dubhda (black).

Dooley (*Ir.*) Grandson of Dubhlaoch (black hero); descendant of the dark warrior.

Doolin, Doolan, Dooling, Doolen (*Ir.*) Grandson of Dubhfhlann (black Flann); the defiant man.

Doolittle (*Eng.*) From the French *de l'hotel* referring to one who lived in the mansion house or palace; a loafer or idle person.

Dooman, Doman (*Eng.*) One who occupied the office of judge, a doom-man.

Doon (*Ir.*) Grandson of Dubhan (little black one).

Doonan (*Ir.*) Grandson of Little Donn (brown).

Doornbos, Dorenbos (*Du.*) Dweller by,

or among, the thorn trees or bramble bushes.

Dopp (*Ger.*) One who made pots and jars, a potter.

Doppelt (*Ger.*) One who was a double or twin.

Doran, Dorran (*Ir.*) The alien or foreigner.

Dorband (*Ger.*) One who made door hinges and other iron fittings for doors.

Dore, Dorat (*Fr.*) One who gilds, a gilder; descendant of Dore, a pet form of Isadore (gift of Isis).

Dorencz (*Pol.*) Sentence nickname, verbal imperative, "put it in his hand."

Dorf, Dorff (*Ger.*) One who came from Dorf (village), the name of many places in Germany; or from Dorff (village), in Germany; dweller in the village.

Dorfman, Dorfmann (*Ger.*) One who formerly lived in the village.

Dorgan (*Ir.*) Variant of Dargan, q.v.

Doris (*Ir.*) Descendant of Dubhros (black Ros).

Dority (*Ir.*) Descendant of black Artach (noble bear).

Dorman, Dormand (*Eng.*) The beloved, or dear, man; one who had charge of the door or gate; descendant of Deormund (dear, protection).

Dorn, Dorner, Dorne (*Eng., Ger.*) One who came from Dorn (stronghold), in Worcestershire; one who came from Dorn (thorn), the name of two places in Germany.

Dorociak, Dorocke (*Pol.*) Descendant of Dorociak, pet form of Teodor, Slavic form of Theodore (gift of God); or of Dorota, Polish form of Dorothy (gift of God).

Dorr (*Eng.*) Dweller near a gate or a narrowing valley.

Dorram (*Eng.*) One who came from Dereham (enclosure for wild animals), in Norfolk.

Dorrance (*Eng.*) Variant of Durrand, q.v.

Dorris (*Ir.*) Variant of Doris, q.v.

Dorsch (*Ger.*) One who lived at the sign of the small codfish; one who grew and sold parsnips or cabbages.

Dorsett, Dorset (*Eng.*) One who came from Dorset, a county in England.

Dorsey (*Ir., Fr.*) Grandson of Dorchaidhe (dark man); one who came from Arcy (stronghold), in France.

Dorton (*Eng.*) One who came from Dorton (homestead in a pass), in Buckinghamshire.

Dorward (*Scot., Eng.*) Variant of Durward, q.v.

Dory (*Eng.*) One who had golden hair.

Dose (*Ger., Eng.*) Dweller near the Dose (muddy brook), a tributary of the Em; the dizzy, stupid, foolish man. See also Doss.

Dosen (*Nor.*) One who came from Dosen (heap of stones), in Norway.

dos Passos (*Port.*) A name adopted to express devotion to the passion of Christ.

Doss, Dose (*Ger.*) Descendant of Doss or Dose, forms of Teuzo, pet forms of names beginning with Diet (people), as Theudoricus and Theudoald.

Dost, Doster (*Ger.*) Dweller near where wild thyme grew; one who gathered herbs, an herbalist.

Dotey (*Eng.*) The brave, strong man.

Dotson (*Eng.*) The son of Dudd (fat, clumsy person); or of Dot (lazy, listless person).

Dott (*Scot., Eng.*) Sharpened form of Dodd, q.v.; the little person.

Dotton (*Eng.*) One who came from Dotton (homestead of Dodda's people), in Devonshire.

Doty, Doughty (*Eng.*) The brave, strong man.

Doubek (*Cz.-Sl.*) Dweller near a small oak tree.

Doubleday (*Eng.*) The servant of Dobb, a pet form of Robert (fame, bright), or of Dobel (twin).

Doucette, Doucet, Doucett (*Fr.*) The sweet person, a name given an amiable person, sometimes ironically, however.

Doudy (*Ir., Scot.*) Variant of Dowdy, q.v.

Dougall, Dougal (*Scot.*) The dark arrival; the black stranger.

Dougan, Doughan (*Ir., Scot.*) Descendant of Dubhagan (little black one).

Dougherty (*Ir.*) Variant of Doherty, q.v.

Douglas, Douglass (*Scot.*) Dweller at the black water or stream; one who came from Douglas (dark stream), in Lanarkshire.

Doukas (*Lith.*) Variant of Daukus, q.v.

Dour (*Eng.*) Dweller near the water.

Dove (*Eng.*) Dweller near the Dove (black or dark), the name of several rivers in England; one thought to possess the gentle characteristics of a dove.

Dover (*Eng.*) One who came from Dover (the waters), a village in Kent.

Dow (*Ir.*) One with a dark complexion or black hair.

Dowd, Doud, Dowds (*Ir.*) One with a swarthy complexion, black; grandson of Dubhda (black).

Dowdell, Dowdall (*Eng.*) One who came from Dowdale (valley frequented by doves or does).

Dowdy, Dowdie (*Ir., Scot.*) Grandson of Dubhda (black).

Dowell, Dowel (*Ir.*) Grandson of Dubhghall (black foreigner); descendant of the dark foreigner.

Dower, Dowers (*Eng.*) One who made dough, a baker.

Dowie (*Scot.*) Shortened form of MacIldowie (son of the black lad).

Dowling (*Ir.*) Grandson of Dunlang, an ancient Irish name; grandson of Dubhfhlann (black Flann).

Downer (*Eng.*) Dweller on, or near, the hillock.

Downey, Downie (*Scot., Ir.*) One who came from Downie, the name of several places in Scotland; dweller at the little hill; the brown-haired man; grandson of Dunadhach (belonging to a fort).

Downing, Downings (*Eng.*) Descendant of Dunn (dark brown); dweller at the hill or hill pasture.

Downs, Downes, Down (*Eng.*) Dweller on, or near, the hill or hill pasture.

Dowrich (*Eng.*) Dweller in a wet or marshy place.

Doyle (*Ir., Eng.*) Grandson of Dubhghall (black foreigner); the swarthy stranger or foreigner; one who came from Ouilly (Olius' farm), the name of five places in Normandy.

Doyley, D'Oyley (*Eng.*) One who came from Ouilly (Olius' farm), the name of five places in Normandy.

Dozier (*Fr.*) Dweller in, or near, a water willow grove.

Drabik, Drabek (*Cz.-Sl.*) The loafer, ruffian or hoodlum.

Draeger (*Ger.*) One who carried goods, a porter.

Drag (*Pol.*) Dweller near a pole; one who used a long staff for support.

Drager (*Ger.*) Variant of Draeger, q.v.

Dragisic, Dragic (*Yu.-Sl.*) Descendant of Dragi, a pet form of names beginning with Drag (love), as Dragomir and Dragoslav.

Drago (*It.*) Dweller at the sign of the dragon.

Dragon (*Eng.*) Dweller at the sign of the dragon; metonymic for Old French *dragonier* (standard-bearer); nickname for one resembling a dragon; one who bore a standard emblazoned with a dragon either in battle or in pageants and processions.

Dragovich (*Yu.-Sl.*) The son of Drago (beloved).

Drain, Draine (*Ir., Eng.*) Grandson of Drean (wren); dweller at, or near, the drain.

Drake, Drakes (*Eng.*) Dweller at the sign of the dragon; one so nicknamed because of a dragon in his coat of arms; one with the qualities of a male duck; one who played the part of a dragon in the mysteries and miracle plays.

Drane (*Eng.*) Dweller at a drain; one considered to be a drone, a lazy man.

Draper, Drapier (*Eng., Fr.*) One who made, or sold, woolen or other cloth.

Draye, Dray, Drey (*Eng.*) Descendant of Drew, Dru or Drogo (carrier).

Drayer (*Du.*) One who fashioned objects on a lathe, a turner.

Drayster (*Eng.*) One who dried cloth by stretching it on tenters.

Drayton (*Eng.*) One who came from Drayton (homestead near a portage, or on a narrow strip of land), the name of many places in England.

Drechsel, Drechsler (*Ger.*) One who fashioned objects on a lathe, a turner.

Dreger (*Ger.*) Variant of Dreyer, q.v.

Dreher (*Ger.*) Variant of Dreyer, q.v.

Dreis, Dreiser (*Ger.*) Descendant of Dreis, a pet form of Andreas, German form of Andrew (manly); one who came from Dreis (swampy spring), the name of two places in Germany.

Drell (*Rus.*) Dweller at the sign of the arrow.

Drennan, Drennen (*Ir.*) Grandson of Draighnean (blackthorn).

Drescher (*Ger.*) One who threshes grain with a flail.

Dresner, Dressner, Dresdner, Dresden (*Ger.*) One who came from Dresden (at the ferry; wharf), in Saxony.

Dressler, Dresser, Dressel (*Eng.*) One who finishes textile fabrics to give them a nap or smooth surface.

Drew, Drews, Drewes (*Eng.*) Descendant of Drew, Dru or Drogo (carrier); or of Drew, a pet form of Andrew (manly).

Drewniak (*Pol.*) One who made lattice-work of wood.

Drexel, Drexler (*Ger.*) One who turned a lathe, a turner.

Dreyer, Dryer, Dreier (*Ger.*) One who fashioned objects on a lathe, a turner.

Dreyfus, Dreyfuss, Dreifuss, Dreifus (*Ger.*) One who made trivets; three feet; one who came from Treves or Trier (place of the tribe of the Treviri), in Germany.

Drezner (*Ger.*) Variant of Dresner, q.v.

Dribin (*Rus.*) The quick, fast walker; one who drove a cart used for hauling sheaves of grain.

Drinan, Drinane (*Ir.*) Descendant of Draighnean (blackthorn).

Drinkale, Drinkall (*Eng.*) One in the habit of replying to a pledge in drinking with the phrase *drinc hail*, that is, drink good health or good luck; one who drank ale immoderately.

Drinkard (*Eng.*) One who drank too much, a drunkard.

Drinkwater (*Eng.*) One known as a teetotaller, i.e., one who drank water; one so poor as to be able to drink only water.

Driscoll (*Ir.*) Grandson of Eidirsceol (interpreter).

Drish, Drisch (*Ger.*) Dweller in, or near, the uncultivated field or meadow.

Driskell, Driskill (*Ir.*) Grandson of Eidirsceol (interpreter).

Driver (*Eng.*) One who drove a herd of cattle, especially to distant markets; same as Carter, q.v.; one who drives a vehicle.

Drobny (*Pol.*) The small, thin man.

Droege (*Ger.*) Dweller on dry land; a droll person.

Drone, Dron, Drown (*Scot.*) One who came from Dron (hill ridge), in Perthshire; dweller at the rump or hill ridge.

Drooker (*Ger.*) One who prints, a printer; one who pressed cloth.

Droski (*Rus.*) One who drove a coach, a coachman.

Drost, Droste (*Ger., Du.*) The high bailiff or chief magistrate.

Drover (*Eng.*) One who drives domestic animals to market; one who deals in cattle.

Drower (*Eng.*) One who draws something, such as a cart.

Drozd (*Pol., Ukr.*) One with some characteristic of a thrush; dweller at the sign of the thrush.

Drucker, Druckman, Druck (*Ger., Du.*) A printer; one who pressed cloth.

Drukker (*Du.*) One who prints or works as a compositor or a pressman.

Druktenis, Druktanis (*Lith.*) The strong man.

Drumgoole, Drumgold (*Ir.*) One who came from Druimgabhail, in Ireland.

Drumm, Drum (*Ger., Scot.*) One who was stumpy, ungainly in appearance; one who was boorish, rude, or coarse; one who came from Drum (the back; hill-ridge), the name of many places in Scotland.

Drummer (*Ger.*) One who beat a drum, a drummer.

Drummey, Drummy (*Ir.*) Grandson of Druim (black); descendant of the black person.

Drummond (*Scot.*) One who came from the barony of Drummond or Drymen (a ridge), in Scotland.

Drunken (*Sw.*) Descendant of Drucken (drunken), a Swedish soldier name.

Drury (*Eng.*) A sweetheart or lover.

Drwal (*Pol.*) One who bought and sold timber.

Dryden (*Scot.*) One who came from Dryden (dry valley), in Edinburgh.

Drye, Dry (*Eng.*) The crafty, cunning man.

Drymalski (*Ukr.*) The lazy, sleepy man.

Drypool (*Eng.*) One who came from Drypool (dirty pool), in the East Riding of Yorkshire.

Drysdale (*Scot.*) One who came from Dryfesdale, pronounced Drysdale (valley of the river Dryfe), in Scotland.

Drzewicki (*Pol.*) One who fought with a spear.

Duane (*Ir.*) Descendant of the fisherman; grandson of Dubhan (little black person).

Duarte (*Port., Sp.*) Descendant of Duarte, a Portuguese form of Edward (rich, guardian).

Dub (*Cz-Sl.*) Dweller by the oak tree.

Dubbs, Dubb (*Eng.*) Dweller near a pool.

Dube, Dub, Duba (*Fr.*) One who raised and sold feather-legged pigeons; dweller at the sign of the feather-legged pigeon.

Dubeau (*Fr.*) The handsome one.

Dubek, Dubec (*Cz.*) Dweller near an oak tree.

Dubicki (*Pol.*) Dweller on, or near, a field covered with clods.

Dubiel (*Cz.-Sl., Pol., Ukr.*) One who was strong as an oak.

Dubin (*Rus.*) Dweller near an oak tree.

Dubinski, Dubinsky (*Pol., Rus.*) Dweller in, or near, the oak wood; one who came from Dubno, in Russia.

Dublinski, Dublin (*Ukr., Pol., Ir.*) Dweller near the oak tree; one who came from Dublin (oak tree), in the Ukraine; or from Dublin (black pool), in Ireland.

Dubofsky, Dubowsky (*Rus., Ukr., Cz.-Sl., Pol.*) Descendant of Dub (oak), dweller near an oak tree.

Du Bois, Dubosc, Duboscq (*Fr.*) Dweller in, or near, a small wood.

Du Bose (*Fr.*) Americanized variant of Du Bois, q.v.

Dubovik, Dubowski (*Ukr., Pol.*) One who rowed a boat made of oak, an oarsman.

Dubow, Du Bow (*Rus., Ukr., Cz.-Sl.*) The son of Dub (oak).

Dubreuil (*Fr.*) Dweller in, or near, a damp wood; or an enclosed wood.

Du Brock (*Fr.*) Dweller on, or near, a rocky place; one who came from Broc (rocky place), in France.

Dubsky (*Pol., Rus.*) Dweller near an oak tree.

Dubuc (*Fr.*) Dweller near a tree stump.

Dubuisson (*Fr.*) Dweller near a bush; one who lived at the sign of the bush.

Duc (*Fr.*) Dweller at the sign of the owl; one with the characteristics of an owl.

Ducey (*Ir.*) Grandson of Dubhghur (black choice).

Ducharme, Du Charme (*Fr.*) Dweller near the hornbeam or yoke-elm tree.

Du Chene, Duchesne (*Fr.*) Dweller near an oak tree.

Duck (*Eng.*) Dweller at the sign of the duck; one thought to possess some characteristic of a duck; descendant of Docca; descendant of Duck, a pet form of Marmaduke (sea leader; steward).

Duckert (*Ger.*) Descendant of Tuchard (worth, brave).

Duckett (*Eng.*) Descendant of little Duke,

a pet form of Marmaduke (sea leader; steward).

Duckham (*Eng.*) Dweller at the duck homestead.

Ducksworth, Duckworth (*Eng.*) One who came from Duckworth (Docca's homestead), in Lancashire.

Duclos (*Fr.*) Dweller in, or near, the enclosed vineyard.

Duda (*Pol., Ukr.*) One who played a bagpipe.

Dudak (*Pol.*) One who played the pipe.

Dudas (*Lith.*) One who played a trumpet or brass instrument.

Dudden (*Eng.*) One who came from Duddon (Dudda's hill), in Cheshire.

Duddles, Duddleson (*Eng.*) The son of little Dudda.

Duddleston (*Eng.*) One who came from Dudleston (Duddel's homestead), in Shropshire.

Duddy (*Ir., Eng.*) Grandson of Dubhda (black); dweller near Dudda's place.

Dude (*Ger.*) Descendant of Dudy (bagpipe); metonymic for a bagpiper.

Dudek (*Cz.-Sl., Pol.*) One who played a bagpipe; dweller at the sign of the hoopoe; one with the characteristics of a hoopoe.

Dudgeon (*Scot.*) The son of Dodge, a pet form of Roger (fame, spear).

Dudle, Dudel, Duddle (*Eng.*) Descendant of little Dudda (fat, clumsy person).

Dudley (*Eng.*) One who came from Dudley (Dudda's meadow), in Worcestershire.

Dudstone (*Eng.*) One who came from Dudstone (Dudd's homestead), in Shropshire.

Dudzik (*Pol.*) One who came from Dudki, or Dudy (settlement of the Dudki family), in Poland; one who played the bagpipe.

Dudzinski (*Pol.*) One who played the shawm, a wind instrument of the oboe class.

Duerr, Duer (*Eng., Ger.*) Dweller near a gate or pass between hills; the thin, lean man.

Duff (*Ir.*) Grandson of Dubh (black);

one with a swarthy complexion, black.

Duffield (*Eng.*) One who came from Duffield (place frequented by doves), the names of villages in Derbyshire and the East Riding of Yorkshire.

Duffin (*Ir.*) The little person with a dark complexion; descendant of Dolphin or Dolfin (Delphian); grandson of Dubhfionn (black Fionn).

Duffus (*Scot., Eng.*) One who came from Duffus (dark water), in Moray; dweller near the dovecot; the servant in charge of the dove house.

Duffy, Duffey (*Ir.*) Grandson of Dubhthach (black).

Dufort (*Fr.*) The strong man; one who came from Fort (stronghold), the name of several small places in France.

Dufour (*Fr.*) The official who operated the public oven, a baker.

Dufresne, Du Fresne (*Fr.*) Dweller in the ash grove.

Dugan (*Ir., Wel.*) Variant of Duggan, q.v.

Dugas (*Fr.*) Dweller on, or near, a tract of uncultivated land.

Dugdale (*Eng.*) Dweller in the valley where ducks were raised.

Duggan, Duigan (*Ir., Wel.*) Grandson of Dubhagan (little black one); descendant of little Dug, a Welsh pet form of Richard (rule, hard).

Dugger, Duggar (*Ger.*) Descendant of Duggert, a form of Tuchard (worth, hard).

Duggleby (*Eng.*) One who came from Duggleby (Dufgall's settlement), in the East Riding of Yorkshire.

Dugmore (*Eng.*) Dweller in the wet waste ground where ducks were found.

Dugo (*It.*) The son of Ugo (spirit).

Duguid (*Scot.*) One who does good, a phrase name.

Duhamel (*Fr.*) The man from the hamlet, possibly the countryman.

Duignan, Duigenan (*Ir.*) Descendant of Dubhceann (black head).

Duke, Dukes (*Eng.*) Descendant of Duke,

a pet form of Marmaduke (sea leader; steward).

Dul, Dulak (*Pol.*) The round, fat man.

Dulaney (*Ir.*) Variant of Delaney, q.v.

Dull, Duller (*Scot.*) The man who came from Dull (a plain), a village and parish in Perthshire.

Dullard (*Eng.*) The dull or stupid man.

Dulles (*Eng.*) One who came from the village of Dulas (dark river), in Herefordshire; dweller near the Dulas river, in England.

Dulski, Dulsky (*Pol.*) One who raised and sold pears.

Dumas (*Fr.*) Dweller on the little farm; or in the small farmhouse.

Dumelle, Du Melle (*Fr.*) One who came from Melle (ring), in France.

Dumitru, Dumitriu (*Rom.*) Descendant of Dumitru, Romanian form of Demetrius (of Demeter, the goddess of fertility and harvests).

Dumm, Dummer (*Eng.*) Dweller near, or on, a *dun* (hill).

Dumont, Du Mont (*Fr.*) One who lived on, or near, a hill.

Dumper (*Eng.*) One who came from Dummer (lake by a hill), in Hampshire.

Dunagan, Dunigan, Duneghan, Dunican (*Ir.*) Descendant of little Donn (brown).

Dunaj, Dunajski (*Pol.*) Dweller near the Dunaj, that is, the Danube river.

Dunams, Dunhums (*Eng.*) One who came from Dunham (homestead on a hill), the name of places in Cheshire and Norfolk; or from Dunham (Dunna's homestead), in Nottinghamshire.

Dunaway (*Eng.*) Dweller on the road or way to the hill.

Dunbar (*Scot.*) One who lived on the lands of Dunbar (fort on the heights), in Scotland.

Duncan, Duncanson (*Ir., Scot.*) Descendant of Donnchad (brown warrior).

Dundas (*Eng., Scot.*) Dweller on, or near, the south hill; one who came from Dundas (south hill), in Scotland.

Dundee (*Scot.*) One who came from Dundee (hill of God), in Angus.

Dundon (*Eng.*) One who came from Dundon (valley by the hill), in Somerset.

Dungee, Dungey (*Eng.*) Dweller by the hill fort.

Dunham (*Eng.*) One who came from Dunham (the homestead on the hill), the name of several places in England.

Dunhill (*Eng.*) Dweller on, or near, the dark brown hill.

Dunkel, Dunkle (*Scot.*) One who came from Dunkeld (wood of Celidon), in Perthshire.

Dunker (*Ger.*) The dark, dusky, gloomy man; one who whitewashes buildings.

Dunkerley (*Eng.*) Variant of Dunkley, q.v.

Dunkin, Dunkins (*Ir., Scot.*) Grandson of Donncheann (brown head); descendant of Donnchad (brown warrior).

Dunkirk (*Eng.*) One who came from Dunkerque (church on the sandhill), in France.

Dunkley, Dunklee (*Eng.*) One who came from Dinckley (fort by a wood in a wood; two of the elements refer to a wood or grove), in Lancashire.

Dunklin (*Eng.*) The little short, fat man.

Dunlap, Dunlop (*Scot.*) One who came from the lands of Dunlop (hill at the bend), in Ayrshire.

Dunleavy, Dunlevy (*Ir.*) Descendant of Donnshleibhe (Brown of the mountain).

Dunmars (*Eng.*) Dweller on brown, marshy land.

Dunmore (*Scot.*) One who came from Dunmore (big hill), the name of several places in Scotland.

Dunn, Dunne (*Ir.*) The dark-brown-complexioned one; grandson of Donn (brown).

Dunning (*Scot., Ir.*) One who came from Dunning (little hill or fort), in Perthshire; the little brown-haired man; grandson of little Donn (brown).

Dunnington (*Eng.*) One who came from Dunnington (homestead of Dudda's or Dunna's people), in the East Riding of Yorkshire.

Dunphy, Dunfey (*Ir.*) Grandson of Donnchadh (brown warrior).

Dunscomb, Dunscombe (*Eng.*) One who came from Dunscomb (Dunn's valley), in Devonshire.

Dunsmoor, Dunsmore (*Eng.*) One who came from Dunsmore (Dunn's marsh or high wasteland), in Warwickshire.

Dunsmuir (*Scot.*) One who came from the lands of Dundemore, in Fife.

Dunson (*Eng.*) The son of Dunn (dark brown).

Dunstan, Dunstane (*Eng.*) One who came from Dunstan (stone on a hill), in Northumberland.

Dunston, Dunstone (*Eng.*) One who came from Dunston (Dunn's stone), in Derbyshire; or from Dunston (Dunn's homestead), the name of several places in England; or from Dunstone (Dunstan's homestead), in Devonshire.

Dunton (*Eng.*) One who came from Dunton (village on a hill), the name of several places in England.

Dunville (*Eng.*) One who came from Dunville (hill estate), or Donville (Dono's estate), the names of places in France.

Dunwell (*Eng.*) Dweller near a spring on a hill.

Dunwich (*Eng.*) One who came from Dunwich (port with deep water), in Suffolk.

Dunwoody, Dunwoodie (*Scot.*) One who came from the lands of Dinwoodie (hill with the shrubs), in Dumfriesshire.

Dunworth (*Ir.*) Descendant of Donndubhartach (brown Dubhartach).

Duparcq, Duparc, du Parcq (*Eng., Fr.*) Dweller near the enclosure stocked with animals for the use of hunters.

Dupee (*Fr.*) Dweller in the house on the hill; or at the top of the hill.

Duplessis, Du Plessis (*Fr.*) Dweller in the enclosure formed by interlacing branches.

Dupont (*Fr.*) One who lived near a bridge.

Dupree, Du Pree, Dupre (*Fr.*) Dweller in a meadow, literally "of the meadow."

Dupuis (*Fr.*) Dweller near a well or a pit.

Dupuy (*Fr.*) Dweller on the height; or on the elevated place; or on a hill or mound.

Duque (*Sp.*) One connected in some way with a duke's household. A Duque was a nobleman in charge of a province.

Duran, Durand (*Fr.*) Descendant of Durand (lasting).

Durante, Durant, Durrant (*It.*) Descendant of Durante (lasting).

Durbin (*Eng.*) One who came from Durban, in France.

Duren, Duran (*Eng.*) Descendant of Durand (lasting).

Durer (*Ger.*) One who came from Duren (water), the name of three places in Germany.

Durham (*Eng.*) One who came from Durham (island with a hill), in Durham.

Durkee (*Rus., Ukr.*) The stupid or dull man.

Durkin, Durkan (*Ir.*) The son of Duarcan (the gloomy one).

Durkovic (*Yu.-Sl., Rus.*) The son of Durko (the stupid one).

Durling (*Eng.*) Descendant of Deorling (beloved); one who was dearly loved.

Durocher (*Fr.*) Dweller near the crags or rocks.

Durr (*Fr., Ger.*) Dweller on dry soil; the thin, lean man.

Durrand, Durrant, Durrance (*Eng.*) Descendant of Durand (lasting).

Durrell, Durell (*Eng.*) The little, stern, severe man.

Durrett (*Eng.*) Corruption of Durward, q.v.

Dursey (*Eng.*) Descendant of Deorsige.

Durso, D'Urso (*It.*) One with the characteristics of a bear; one who entertained with a trained bear.

Durst (*Ger.*) The bold or daring man.

Durston (*Eng.*) One who came from

Durston (Deor's homestead), in Somerset.

Durward, (*Scot., Eng.*) One who occupied the position of door-ward or door keeper to the king, a hereditary office; one in charge of a door at a monastery or religious house.

Duse (*Fr.*) The clever, skillful, expert man.

Dusek (*Pol.*) Descendant of Dusek (little ghost or spirit).

Dusenbury, Dusenberry, Dusenbery (*Du.*) One who came from Doesburg, in Holland; one who lived on the Dusen hill, in Germany.

Dushkin, Duskind, Duskin (*Rus.*) Descendant of Dushe, a pet form of Devorah, a Jewish form of Deborah (bee).

Dussault (*Fr.*) Dweller near the waterfall.

Dust (*Eng.*) Descendant of Dust, a pet form of Thurstan (Thor's stone); one with a dust-colored complexion.

Duster (*Ger.*) The gloomy, mournful man.

Dustin (*Eng.*) One who came from Duston (dusty homestead), in Northamptonshire.

Duszynski (*Pol.*) One who came from Durzyn or Duzyn, the name of villages in Poland.

Duthie (*Scot.*) Descendant of Dubhthach (black-jointed).

Dutka (*Pol., Ukr., Rus.*) One who played the pipe or flute; one who used a quill pen.

Dutson (*Eng.*) The son of Dudd or Dudda.

Dutton (*Eng.*) One who came from Dutton (Dudda's homestead), in Cheshire.

Duty (*It.*) Descendant of Duti, a short form of names beginning with Diot (God), as Diotajuti, Diotallevi, and Diotiguardi.

Duvall, Duval (*Fr.*) Dweller in the valley.

Duwe (*Ger.*) One who raised and sold pigeons.

Duwell (*Ger.*) One who played the part of the devil in plays and pageants.

Duxbury (*Eng.*) One who came from Duxbury (Deowuc's fortified place), in Lancashire.

Dvorak (*Cz.-Sl.*) One who belonged to the lord's estate, a vassal; a courtier or attendant at the court of a prince.

Dwan (*Ir.*) Descendant of little Dubh (black).

Dwight (*Eng.*) Descendant of Dwight or Diot, possibly pet forms of Dionysus (Greek god of wine; judge of men); the light-complexioned person.

Dwinell (*Fr.*) Descendant of little Douin, a pet form of Hardouin (hard, friend).

Dworak (*Ger.*) One who is in attendance at the court of a prince, a courtier.

Dworkin (*Rus.*) One who worked in the court or yard, a yardman; descendant of Dvorke, a dim. of Dvoyre.

Dwyer, Dwyar (*Ir.*) Descendant of the dark, tawny man; grandson of Dubhodhar (black Odhar).

Dyas (*Wel.*) Descendant of Deyo or Deio, pet forms of David (commander; beloved; friend).

Dybas (*Pol., Ukr.*) One who fights by lurking or lying in ambush; a foundling.

Dybdahl (*Nor., Dan.*) One who came from Dybdahl (deep valley); dweller in a deep valley.

Dye (*Eng.*) Descendant of Dye, a pet form of Dionysus (Greek god of wine; judge of men).

Dyer, Deyer, Dier, Dyers (*Eng.*) One who dyes cloth.

Dykas (*Lith.*) The idle, vain, useless person.

Dyke, Dykes (*Eng.*) Dweller on, or near, a dike or embankment.

Dykhuizen (*Du.*) Dweller in the house on the dike.

Dykstra (*Du.*) Dweller on, or near, a dike or embankment.

Dynan (*Ir.*) Grandson of Daghnan.

Dyson (*Eng.*) The son of Dy or Dye, pet

forms of Dionysus (Grecian god of wine; judge of men).

Dziadosz, Dziadus (*Pol.*) The old man or grandfather.

Dzialo (*Pol.*) Dweller at the sign of the cannon; one who fought with a cannon or gun.

Dziedzic, Dziedzik (*Pol.*) One who rented land to another, a landlord.

Dzierzanowski (*Pol.*) One who came from Dzierzanowo, in Poland.

Dzierzawski (*Pol.*) One who leased and operated a farm.

Dzik, Dzikowski (*Pol.*) The wild, savage man.

Dziuba, Dziubczynski (*Pol., Ukr., Rus.*) Bird's beak, a nickname.

Each (*Eng.*) One who came from Each (oak), in Kent.

Eacott (*Eng.*) Dweller in the cottage by the water.

Eades, Eads, Eadie, Eady (*Eng.*) Descendant of Ead, a pet form of Anglo-Saxon names such as Eadweard, Eadmund, Eadwine, and Eadgyth.

Eagan (*Ir.*) The son of little Aodh (fire).

Eager (*Ir.*) Descendant of Edgar (rich, spear).

Eagle, Eagles (*Eng.*) Descendant of Aegel (noble); dweller at the sign of the eagle; one who came from Eagle (oak wood), in Lincolnshire.

Eagleston (*Eng.*) One who came from Eggleston (Ecgel's homestead), in Durham.

Eaglin (*Eng.*) Descendant of Agilina (noble).

Eaker (*Eng.*) Dweller at the cultivated field; one who farmed one acre.

Eakins, Eakin (*Eng.*) Descendant of little Ead, a pet form of names beginning with Ead, such as Eadward and Eadwine.

Ealy, Ealey (*Eng.*) One who came from Ely (eel district), in Cambridgeshire.

Eames (*Eng.*) The son of the uncle.

Earhart, Earhardt (*Ger.*) American variant of Ehrhardt, q.v.

Earl, Earle, Earles, Earls (*Eng.*) Descendant of an earl; one connected in some way with an earl's household; one who came from Earle (hill with an enclosure), in Northumberland; one who acquired the nickname from acting the part in play or pageant.

Early, Earley (*Eng.*) One who came from Earley (eagle wood), in Berkshire; dweller by the earl's meadow.

Earnest (*Ger.*) An Americanization of Ernst, q.v.; one who made and sold harness and suits of mail.

Earnshaw (*Eng.*) Dweller in, or near, the grove frequented by eagles; one who came from Earnshaw (eagle grove), in Lancashire.

Earp (*Eng.*) The dark, swarthy man.

Earskin, Earskines (*Scot.*) One who came from Erskine (green ascent), in Renfrewshire.

Earth, Earthman (*Eng.*) One who worked in the earth, a farmer.

Earwaker (*Eng.*) Descendant of Eoforwacer (boar, watchman).

Easdale (*Scot.*) One who came from Easdale (east valley), in Argyllshire.

Easley (*Eng.*) One who came from Eastleigh or Astley (the eastern wood; clearing in a wood), the names of several places in England.

Eason (*Eng., Scot.*) The son of Ea or Aythe, pet forms of Adam (red earth).

East (*Eng.*) One who came from an easterly place; dweller at the east end of the village.

Easter (*Eng.*) One who came from Easter (sheepfold), in Essex; dweller near a sheepfold.

Easterling (*Eng.*) A merchant who came from the shores of the Baltic having a reputation for honest dealings, giving rise to the word "sterling."

Easterwood (*Eng.*) One who came from Eastwood (eastern wood; eastern meadow), the name of places in Essex and Nottinghamshire; dweller east of the wood.

Eastham (*Eng.*) One who came from Eastham (the eastern homestead), the name of places in Cheshire, Somerset, and Worcestershire.

Easthope (*Eng.*) One who came from Easthope (eastern valley), in Shropshire.

Eastin (*Scot.*) One who came from Easton (the eastern homestead), the name of places in Peeblesshire and West Lothian.

Eastman (*Eng.*) One who came from the east; descendant of Eastmund or Estmunt (east, protection); one who came from the Baltic countries.

Easton (*Eng.*) One who came from Easton (the eastern homestead), the name of several places in England.

Eatherton (*Eng.*) One who came from Atherton (Aethelhere's homestead), in Lancashire.

Eatmon, Eatman, Eatmonds (*Eng.*) Descendant of Edmund (rich, protection).

Eaton (*Eng.*) One who came from Eaton (homestead on a river, or island), the name of various places in England.

Eaves (*Eng.*) Dweller by the edge or border; descendant of Eaf, a pet form of names beginning with Eofor (wild boar), as Eburhard and Eburwulf.

Ebel, Eble, Ebell (*Ger., Du., Fr.*) Descendant of Ebilo or Eble (boar), or of Ebulo (wild boar); or of Abel (breath or vanity).

Ebling (*Ger.*) The son of Ebel (noble, bright; wild boar).

Eben, Ebbens (*Eng.*) Descendant of Eben (the rock).

Eber, Ebers (*Ger., Heb.*) Dweller at the sign of the boar; descendant of Eber, a pet form of names beginning with Eber (boar), as Eberhard and Eberwin; one who came from the other side, that is, a foreigner.

Eberhardt, Eberhart, Eberhard (*Ger.*) Descendant of Eberhard (boar, strong).

Eberle, Eberlein, Eberling (*Fr., Ger.*) Descendant of little Ebilo (boar), or

of little Eber, a shortened form of Eberhard (boar, strong).

Eberly (*Ger.*) Descendant of Eberli, a pet form of Eberhard (boar, strong).

Ebersole (*Ger., Swis.*) One who came from Ebersol (wild boar slough), in Switzerland.

Eberspacher (*Ger.*) One who came from Ebersbach (dirty brook), the name of many places in Germany.

Ebert (*Ger.*) Descendant of Ebert, a pet form of Eberhard (boar, strong).

Ebinger (*Ger.*) One who came from Ebing (watery place), the name of two places in Germany; or from Ebingen, in Germany.

Ebner (*Ger.*) Dweller in the lowlands; one who came from Eben (level land; plain), the name of various places in Germany.

Ebsen (*Dan.*) The son of Eb, a pet form of Eberhard (boar, strong).

Ebstein (*Ger.*) Variant of Epstein, q.v.

Eby, Ebey (*Eng., Swis.*) Descendant of Eby, a pet form of Ebbe or Ebba (boar).

Eccles (*Eng., Scot.*) One who formerly lived in the village of Eccles (church), there being two of that name in Scotland and three in England; dweller near a church.

Echeles (*Eng.*) Dweller on land added to an estate.

Echevarria, Echavarria, Echeverria, Echaverria, Echevaria (*Sp.*) One who came from Echevarria (new house), in Spain; dweller in the recently constructed house.

Echols, Echoles (*Eng., Scot.*) Dweller near the church; one who came from Eccles (church), the name of several places in England and Scotland.

Eck, Ecke (*Ger.*) One who lived at the corner; dweller at a steep slope.

Eckberg (*Sw.*) Oak mountain.

Eckdahl (*Sw.*) Oak valley; dweller in an oak valley.

Eckel (*Ger.*) Descendant of Eckel, a short form of Eckehard (sword edge, brave).

Eckenroth (*Ger.*) One who came from Eckenroth, in Germany.

Ecker, Eckmann, Eckerman (*Ger.*) Dweller on a farm located on a steep slope.

Eckerling (*Ger.*) Descendant of little Ecke, a pet form of Eckhardt (sword edge, brave).

Eckersall (*Eng.*) One who came from Ecclesall (Eccles' corner), in the West Riding of Yorkshire.

Eckert, Eckardt, Eckart, Eckhart, Eckard (*Ger.*) Descendant of Agihard (sword edge, brave).

Eckhaus, Eckhouse (*Ger.*) Dweller at the corner house.

Eckholm (*Sw.*) Oak river island.

Eckl (*Ger.*) Descendant of Eckl, a pet form of Eckehard (sword edge, brave).

Eckland (*Sw.*) Variant of Ecklund, q.v.

Eckles (*Eng.*) One who came from Eccles (oak pasture), in Kent; or from Eccles (church), the name of several places in England.

Ecklund (*Sw.*) Oak grove.

Eckmayer (*Ger.*) The farmer who lived at the corner.

Eckner (*Ger.*) Dweller at the angle or corner.

Eckrich (*Ger.*) Descendant of Eckrich (sword edge, rule); one who fed mast or pannage to animals.

Eckstein (*Ger.*) Dweller at the corner or boundary stone.

Eckstrom (*Sw.*) Oak stream.

Eckwald, Eckwall (*Sw.*) Dweller in the oak forest.

Economopoulos (*Gr.*) The son of Oikonomos, a title of merit; or of the steward.

Economos (*Gr.*) One who managed a large household, a steward.

Economou, Economu (*Gr.*) Variant of Economos, q.v.

Eddings, Eddins (*Eng.*) Descendant of little Ead or Ede (rich).

Eddington (*Eng.*) One who came from Eddington (Eadgifu's homestead), in Berkshire.

Eddis (*Eng.*) The son of Ead or Ede (rich).

Eddleman, Eddlemon (*Eng.*) The servant of Edel (noble).

Eddy, Eadie, Eady, Eddie (*Eng.*) Descendant of little Ead or Ede (rich), pet forms of names beginning with Ead, such as Edward, Edmund, and Edgar.

Eddystone (*Eng.*) One who came from Eddistone (Ecghere's homestead), in Devonshire.

Edel, Edele (*Eng.*) Descendant of Edel (noble); the nobleman.

Edelberg (*Sw.*) One who came from Edelberg, in Sweden.

Edelheit (*Ger.*) Descendant of Adalhaid (noble, heath).

Edelman, Edelmann (*Ger., Du.*) The nobleman; a noble or good man; the husband of Edel or Adele (noble).

Edelson (*Eng.*) The son of Edel or Adel (noble).

Edelstein, Edelstone (*Ger.*) Noble stone; one who dealt in precious stones.

Eden, Edens (*Eng.*) Descendant of little Ede or Ead (prosperity).

Eder, Ederer (*Ger.*) One who lived near the Eder river, in West Germany.

Edfeldt (*Sw.*) Tongue of land, field.

Edfors (*Sw.*) Tongue of land, waterfall.

Edgar (*Eng.*) Descendant of Edgar (rich, spear).

Edge (*Eng.*) One who came from Edge (edge or hillside), the name of places in Cheshire and Shropshire.

Edgecombe, Edgecomb (*Eng.*) Dweller at the edge or border of the valley.

Edgefield (*Eng.*) One who came from Edgefield (pasture, open country), in Norfolk.

Edgell (*Eng.*) Descendant of Ecgel (little sword); dweller at the ridge hill.

Edgerly, Edgerley (*Eng.*) One who came from Edgerley (Ecgheard's meadow), in Shropshire.

Edgerson (*Sw., Nor.*) The son of Edgar (rich, spear).

Edgerton (*Eng.*) One who came from Egerton (Ecghere's homestead; vil-

135

lage of Ecgheard's people), the name of places in Cheshire and Kent.

Edgeston (*Eng.*) One who came from Edgton (hill with an edge), in Shropshire; or from Eddistone (Ecghere's homestead), in Devonshire.

Edgett (*Eng.*) Descendant of little Ecga (sword).

Edgeworth (*Eng.*) One who came from Edgeworth (homestead by the hillside), the name of places in Gloucestershire and Lancashire.

Edgren (*Sw.*) Heath branch.

Edie (*Scot.*) Same as Eddy, q.v.

Edingburg, Edinburg (*Scot.*) One who came from Edinburgh (fortress of Eadwine; hill-slope fort), in Scotland.

Edinger (*Ger.*) One who came from Edingen (swamp), the name of three places in Germany.

Edington (*Eng., Scot.*) One who came from Edington (homestead of Ida's people; Eadwine's homestead; uncultivated hill), the name of places in Northumberland, Somerset, and Wiltshire; or from Edington (Hading's village), in Berwickshire.

Edison, Edson (*Eng.*) The son of Edie or Eadie, pet forms of Edmund (rich, protector), Edward (rich, guardian), Edwin (rich, friend), etc.

Edler, Edlen (*Ger.*) The nobleman; a noble or good man.

Edlin, Edling (*Eng.*) Descendant of Edelina (noble, serpent); descendant of little Ead or Ede (rich), pet forms of names beginning with Ead, as Eadwine and Eadmond.

Edlind (*Sw.*) Heath linden tree.

Edlund (*Sw.*) Heath grove.

Edman (*Eng.*) Descendant of Edmond (rich, protector); or of Eadmann (rich, man).

Edmett (*Eng.*) Descendant of Edmond (rich, protector).

Edmiston (*Scot.*) One who came from Edmonstone (Eadmund's homestead), in Midlothian.

Edmonds, Edmunds, Edmond (*Wel.*) The son of Edmond or Edmund (rich, protection).

Edmondson (*Scot.*) The son of Edmond (rich, protection).

Ednam (*Scot.*) One who came from Ednam (village of Aedan or Aidan), in Roxburghshire.

Edom (*Scot.*) Descendant of Adam (red earth).

Edstrand (*Sw.*) Heath shore.

Edstrom (*Sw.*) Heath stream.

Edvardsen (*Nor.*) The son of Edvard, Norwegian form of Edward (rich, guardian).

Edwards, Edward (*Wel.*) The son of Edward (rich, guardian).

Edwin, Edwins, Edwinson (*Eng.*) Descendant of Eadwine (rich, friend).

Eenigenburg (*Du.*) One who came from Eenigenburg, in Holland.

Effertz, Effert (*Ger.*) Descendant of Evert (boar).

Effinger (*Swis., Ger.*) One who came from Effingen, in Switzerland.

Efron, Effron (*Heb.*) Variant of Ephron, q.v.

Efrussy, Efrusy (*Heb.*) One who came from Ephratah, a locality probably identified with Bethlehem.

Egan (*Ir.*) The son of little Aodh (fire).

Egebrecht, Eggebrecht (*Ger.*) Descendant of Agabert (sword, bright).

Egel, Egell (*Eng.*) Descendant of Egel (noble).

Egeland (*Dan., Nor.*) Dweller on land where oaks grew; or on the farm on the ridge.

Egert (*Ger.*) Variant of Eggert, q.v.

Egger, Eger (*Ger., Eng.*) One who came from Egg, Egge, or Eggen (harrow), the names of many places in Germany; descendant of Agar (awe, spear); or of Edgar (rich, spear).

Eggert, Eggers (*Ger.*) Descendant of Agihard (sword edge, brave).

Eggerud (*Nor.*) Dweller on the ridge farm, a farm name.

Eggleston, Egleston, Egelston (*Eng.*) One who came from Eggleston, in Durham, or Egglestone, in Yorkshire, both meaning Ecgel's home-stead.

Egloff (*Ger.*) Descendant of Agilolf (swordpoint, wolf).

Ehardt (*Ger.*) Shortened form of Ehrhardt, q.v.

Ehlen (*Ger.*) One who came from Ehlen (swamp), the name of two places in Germany.

Ehlert, Ehlers (*Ger.*) Descendant of Adalhard (noble, brave); or of Adalhari (noble, army).

Ehling, Ehlinger (*Ger.*) One who came from Ehlingen, the name of two places in Germany.

Ehlmann, Ehlman (*Ger.*) Descendant of Ehlman or Agilman (sword point, man).

Ehmann, Ehman (*Ger.*) One who was married, a husband.

Ehrenberg (*Ger.*) One who came from Ehrenberg (honor mountain), the name of three places in Germany.

Ehrenreich (*Ger.*) One with a good reputation.

Ehrensperger (*Ger.*) One who came from Ehrensperg (hill of honor), the name of three places in Germany.

Ehrhardt, Ehrhard, Ehrhart, Ehret (*Ger.*) Descendant of Ehrhart (honor, hard).

Ehrlich (*Ger.*) The honest man.

Ehrmann, Ehrman (*Ger.*) A man of honor, a gentleman.

Eiberg (*Ger.*) One who came from Eiberg (yew tree mountain), the name of three places in Germany.

Eibert (*Du., Ger.*) Descendant of Eibert, a contracted form of Agilbert (sword, bright).

Eich, Eicher, Eichler, Eichner, Eichmann (*Ger.*) Dweller near an oak tree.

Eichberger, Eichberg (*Ger.*) One who came from Eichberg (mountain with oak trees), the name of several places in Germany.

Eichelberger, Eichelberg (*Ger.*) One who came from Eichelberg (mountain with oak trees), the name of several places in Germany; dweller on a hill where oak trees grew.

Eichenbaum, Eichelbaum (*Ger.*) Dweller near an oak tree.

Eichenberger, Eichenberg (*Ger.*) One who came from Eichenberg (oak mountain), the name of several places in Germany.

Eichenstein (*Ger.*) One who came from Eichenstein (oak stone), in Germany.

Eichholz (*Ger.*) One who came from Eichholz (oak forest), the name of many places in Germany.

Eichhorn, Eichorn (*Ger.*) Dweller at the sign of the squirrel.

Eichinger (*Ger.*) One who came from Eiching (place of oaks), in Germany.

Eichorst (*Ger.*) Dweller near an oak aerie.

Eichstaedt, Eichstadt (*Ger.*) One who came from Eichstaedt (place where oaks grew), in Germany.

Eide, Eiden, Eidson (*Ger.*) Descendant of Eden (rich).

Eiermann, Eierman, Eier (*Ger.*) One who buys and sells eggs.

Eifel, Eifler (*Ger.*) One who came from, or who dwelt in, a mountainous district.

Eigenbauer (*Ger.*) The peasant who holds land on feudal tenure.

Eigner (*Ger.*) The peasant with a freehold, that is, land on which he did not pay rent.

Eiland (*Eng.*) Dweller on an island.

Eiler, Eilers, Eilert (*Ger.*) Descendant of Eilert, a form of Agilbert (sword point, bright).

Eimer, Eime (*Ger.*) Descendant of Aginmar (sword point, fame).

Einhorn (*Ger.*) Dweller at the sign of the unicorn; one thought to possess the characteristics of a one-horned animal.

Einig (*Ger.*) One who came from Einig (united place; swamp), in Germany.

Einstein (*Ger.*) One who lines, or encloses, with stone, a mason; dweller in a stone enclosure.

Eirich (*Ger.*) Descendant of Eirich, a pet form of Hir (sword).

137

Eisele, Eisel (*Ger.*) One who dealt in iron, an ironmonger.

Eiseman, Eisman, Eismann, Eisemann, Eissman (*Ger.*) One who works with, or deals in, iron; descendant of Isanman (iron, man); an alteration from Isaac (he who laughs).

Eisen (*Ger.*) One who worked with iron; one who came from Eisen (horseshoe), the name of two places in Germany.

Eisenberg, Eisenberger (*Ger.*) One who came from Eisenberg (iron mountain), in Thuringia.

Eisenhower, Eisenhauer (*Ger.*) The iron cutter, or iron miner; maker of eisenhauers, a saber or sword blade capable of shearing an iron nail.

Eisenhut, Eisenhuth (*Ger.*) Dweller near iron-works or a forge; one who made helmets of sheet iron.

Eisenmann, Eisenman (*Ger.*) One who works with, or deals in, iron; descendant of Eisenmann (iron man).

Eisensmith (*Ger.*) The smith who worked in iron, a blacksmith.

Eisenstadt, Eisenstaedt (*Ger.*) One who came from Eisenstaedt (iron place), the name of a village in Austria.

Eisenstein (*Ger.*) One who came from Eisenstein (iron stone), in Germany.

Eiserer (*Ger.*) One who dwells beyond or outside some particular area.

Eiserman (*Ger.*) Variant of Eisenmann, q.v.

Eisner, Eisler (*Ger.*) One who deals in ironware.

Eitel (*Ger.*) Descendant of little Eid (fire; burn; hearth), a pet form of names beginning with Eid, as Eitar and Aitrich.

Eizenga (*Du.*) The son of Eise (sword).

Ek (*Sw.*) Dweller near an oak tree.

Ekberg, Ekeberg, Ekenberg (*Nor.*) Dweller on the hill where oak trees grew.

Ekblad, Ekeblad (*Sw.*) Oak leaf.

Ekdahl, Ekendahl (*Sw.*) Oak valley; dweller in the valley where oak trees grew.

Ekholm (*Sw.*) Oak river island.

Eklund (*Sw.*) Oak grove.

Ekman, Ekner (*Sw.*) Dweller by oak trees.

Ekstrand (*Sw.*) Oak shore.

Ekstrom (*Sw.*) Oak stream.

Ekwall, Ekvall (*Sw.*) Oak grassy ground.

Elam (*Eng.*) Dweller by the elm tree; one who came from Elham (homestead by a heathen temple), in Kent.

Eland, Elander (*Eng.*) Dweller on an island.

Elbaum (*Fr., Ger.*) Dweller near an aldertree.

Elbe (*Ger.*) Dweller near the Elbe (water), the name of two rivers in Germany.

Elbert (*Eng., Ger.*) Descendant of Albert (noble, bright); or of Elbracht.

Elden, Eldean (*Eng.*) One who came from Elden (elf valley), in Suffolk.

Elder (*Eng.*) One who is older than another with whom he is associated; dweller at, or near, an elder tree.

Elderson (*Eng.*) The son of the older man; the older son.

Eldon (*Eng.*) One who came from Eldon (Ella's hill), in Durham.

Eldred (*Eng.*) Descendant of Aldred (old, counsel).

Eldridge, Eldredge (*Eng.*) One who came from Elbridge (plank bridge), in Kent.

Elefant, Elefante (*Ger.*) Dweller at the sign of the elephant. House signs have been found showing that what was called "elephant" was represented by the picture of a camel.

Eleftheriou, Eleftherio (*Gr.*) The son of Eleftherios, a Greek form of Theodore (gift of God).

Elerby, Ellerby (*Eng.*) One who came from Ellerby (Aelfweard's homestead), in the East Riding of Yorkshire.

Eley (*Eng.*) One who came from Ely (eel district), in Cambridgeshire.

Elfenbaum, Elfanbaum (*Ger.*) Dweller near the elf's tree.

Elfenbein (*Ger.*) One who cut ivory, a turner.

Elfman (*Ger.*) Descendant of Alfwin (noble, friend).

Elford (*Eng.*) One who came from El-ford (Ella's ford; the elder ford), in Northumberland.

Elg (*Sw., Nor.*) Elk; dweller near the heathen altar or sanctuary.

Elgar (*Eng.*) Descendant of Aelfgar (elf, spear); or of Ealdgar (old, spear); or of Aethelgar (noble, spear).

Elia (*Sp., It.*) One who came from Elia (the sun), in Spain; descendant of Elia, Italian form of Elias (Jehovah is my God).

Elias (*Eng.*) Descendant of Elias (Jehovah is my God).

Eliason, Eliasen (*Eng., Sw., Nor.*) The son of Elias (Jehovah is my God).

Eliopoulos (*Gr.*) The son of Eli, a Greek pet form of Ellis (God is salvation).

Eliot (*Eng.*) Variant of Elliott, q.v.

Elish, Elisha (*Eng.*) Descendant of Elisha (God is salvation).

Elizalde (*Sp.*) Descendant of Elizalde, a Basque form of Elizabeth (oath of God).

Elizondo (*Sp.*) One who came from Elizondo (adjacent to the church), in Spain.

Elke, Elkes (*Ger.*) Descendant of Elke, a pet form of Elkihard (temple, hard).

Elkin, Elkins (*Eng.*) Descendant of little Elie, a form of Elias (Jehovah is my God).

Ellard (*Eng.*) Descendant of Alward or Elward (elf guardian), or of Eliard (little Elias).

Ellaway (*Wel.*) Descendant of Elwy (gain).

Ellefson, Ellefsen (*Nor.*) The son of Eilif (always life).

Ellen (*Eng., Ger.*) Dweller at, or near, the Ellen, a river in Cumberland; dweller near an elder tree; one who came from Ellen (elbow), the name of three places in Germany.

Eller (*Ger.*) Dweller at, or near, an alder tree; one who came from Ellen (elbow), the name of three places in Germany, or from Eller, the name of five places in Germany.

Ellerton (*Eng.*) One who came from Ellerton (Aethelheard's homestead; the alder homestead), the name of several places in England.

Ellick (*Eng.*) One who came from Elwick (Ella's dairy farm), the name of places in Durham and Northumberland.

Ellickson (*Eng.*) The son of Ellis (God is salvation).

Ellicott (*Eng.*) One who came from Elcot (Ella's cottage), in Berkshire; dweller in the old cottage.

Elligan (*Ir.*) Descendant of little Faoilleach (joyful).

Ellin, Elin (*Eng.*) Variant of Ellen, q.v.

Ellinger, Elling (*Ger.*) One who came from Ellingen, the name of three places in Germany.

Ellingham (*Eng.*) One who came from Ellingham (village of Ella's people), the name of four places in England.

Ellingson, Ellingsen (*Nor.*) The son of Erling (chief descendant).

Ellingswood (*Eng.*) Dweller near the wood of Ella's people, possibly a lost place name.

Ellington (*Eng.*) One who came from Ellington (the homestead of Ella's people), in Huntingdonshire.

Elliott, Elliot (*Eng.*) Descendant of little Elijah or Elias (Jehovah is my God).

Ellis, Ellison (*Eng.*) Descendant of Ellis (God is salvation).

Elliston (*Eng.*) One who came from Ellastone (Eadlac's homestead), in Staffordshire.

Ellithorpe (*Eng.*) One who came from Ellenthorpe (the village of the *Aetheling*), in the North Riding of Yorkshire.

Ellman, Ellmann (*Ger.*) Descendant of Hellmann, a German Jewish synonym for Samuel (God hath heard); one who came from Germany, a German.

Ellswood (*Eng.*) Dweller in, or near, the wood belonging to Elli.

Ellsworth (*Eng.*) One who came from Elsworth (Elli's homestead), in Cambridgeshire.

Ellwanger (*Ger.*) One who came from Ellwangen (boggy meadow slopes), the name of two places in Germany.

Ellyson (*Eng.*) The son of Ellis (God is salvation).

Elm, Elman (*Eng.*) Dweller near an elm tree; one who came from Elm (elm), in Cambridgeshire.

Elmer (*Eng.*) Descendant of Aylmer (noble, famous).

Elmore (*Eng.*) One who came from Elmore (shore where elms grew), in Gloucestershire.

Elms (*Eng.*) Dweller near one or more elm trees.

Eloy (*Fr.*) Descendant of Eloy (worthy of choice), the seventh century French saint, patron saint of metal workers.

Elrick (*Eng.*) Descendant of Alderich (noble, ruler); or of Aelfric (elf, ruler).

Elridge (*Eng.*) One who came from Aldridge (dairy farm among alders), in Staffordshire.

Elrod (*Eng., Heb.*) Descendant of Aelred (temple, counsel); or of Elrawd (God is the ruler).

Elsdon (*Eng.*) One who came from Elsdon (Ellis's valley or hill), in Northumberland.

Else, Elsen, Elser, Elsner (*Ger., Du.*) Dweller at, or near, the alder tree; one who came from Elsen (alder), in Germany.

Elsea, Elsey (*Eng.*) Descendant of Aelfsige, (elf, victory).

Elsham (*Eng.*) One who came from Elsham (Elli's homestead), in Lincolnshire.

Elsholz (*Ger.*) Dweller in, or near, the wood where alders grew; one who came from Elsholz (alder wood), in Germany.

Elson, Elsen (*Eng., Dan.*) The son of Ell, a pet form of Ellis (God is salvation), and Elias (Jehovah is my God); one who came from Elson

(Elli's homestead or hill), in Shropshire.

Elster (*Ger.*) Dweller at the sign of the magpie; dweller on the Elster river.

Elston (*Eng.*) One who came from Elston (the homestead of Ethelsige or Aelfwig or Elias), the name of three manors in England.

Elting (*Ger.*) One who came from Eltingen, in Germany.

Elton (*Eng.*) One who came from Elton (Ella's homestead; village of Aethelheah's people), the name of eight villages in England.

Elvidge (*Eng.*) Descendant of Alfwig (elf, war).

Elward, Elwart, Elwardt (*Eng., Ger.*) Descendant of Aylward (noble or awe or elf, guard).

Elwell (*Eng.*) One who came from Elwell (the wishing well), in Dorset.

Elwood, Ellwood (*Eng.*) Descendant of Aelfweald (elf, ruler).

Ely (*Eng.*) One who came from Ely (eel district), in Cambridgeshire; descendant of Elie, an English form of Elias (Jehovah is my God).

Elzie, Elzey, Elzy (*Ger.*) One who came from Elz or Elze (bog), the names of places in Germany.

Elzinga (*Du.*) Descendant of Eise (sword).

Emanuel, Emanuelson (*Eng.*) Descendant of Emanuel (God is with us).

Embery, Embrey, Embry, Embree (*Eng.*) One who came from Emborough (smooth hill), in Somerset; or from Henbury (the monks' fort), in Dorset; descendant of Emery (work, rule).

Embleton (*Eng.*) One who came from Embleton (Eanbeorht's or Eanbald's homestead; Aemele's hill; elm valley), the name of four villages in England, all with different derivations.

Emde (*Ger.*) One who came from Emde (water), in Germany.

Emden (*Ger.*) One who came from Emden, in Germany.

Eme, Emm (*Scot.*) Descendant of Emma

(nurse); or of Em, a pet form of Emory (work, rule).

Emerich, Emerick (*Ger.*) Descendant of Emerich, a German form of Amalric (work, rule).

Emerson, Emmerson (*Eng.*) The son of Emery (work, rule).

Emery, Emory (*Eng.*) Descendant of Emery (work, rule).

Emig (*Ger.*) Descendant of Emig, a pet form of Emery (work, rule).

Eminger (*Ger.*) One who came from Emmingen (water place), the name of two places in Germany.

Emlund (*Sw.*) Elm grove.

Emmel, Emmell (*Ger.*) Descendant of Emmel, a pet form of Amalric (work, rule).

Emmerich, Emmerick (*Ger.*) Descendant of Emmerich, a German form of Amalric (work, rule).

Emmering (*Ger.*) One who came from Emmering (watery place), the name of three places in Germany.

Emmett, Emmet (*Eng.*) Descendant of little Emery (work, rule).

Emmons (*Eng.*) Descendant of little Emery (work, rule).

Emody (*Hun.*) One who came from Emod, in Hungary.

Emond, Emonds (*Eng.*) Descendant of Emeno; or of Edmond (rich, protector).

Emrich, Emrick (*Eng.*) Descendant of Emery (work, rule).

Emslie, Emsley (*Eng.*) Dweller at the elm grove; one who came from Helmsley (Helm's wood or island), in Yorkshire.

Endacott (*Eng.*) Dweller in the end cottage.

Ende, End (*Eng., Ger.*) Dweller at the boundary or end of a row; one who came from End or Ende, the names of several places in Germany.

Ender, Enders (*Ger., Nor.*) Descendant of Ender, a pet form of Andreas, German form of Andrew (manly); one who came from End or Ende, the names of several places in Germany.

Enderle (*Eng., Ger.*) One who came from Enderby (Eindrithi's homestead), the name of four villages in England; descendant of little Ander or Andrew (manly).

Enderlin (*Ger.*) Descendant of little Ender, a pet form of Andreas, German form of Andrew (manly).

Endicott (*Eng.*) Dweller at the end cottage.

Endler (*Ger.*) Descendant of Endel, a pet form of Andreas, German form of Andrew (manly).

Endo (*Jap.*) Far, wisteria.

Endon (*Eng.*) One who came from Endon (hill where lambs were kept), in Staffordshire.

Endre, Endres (*Hun., Fr.*) Descendant of Endre, Hungarian form of Andrew (manly); or of André, French form of Andrew.

Eng, Enge (*Nor., Du., Chin.*) Dweller in, or near, the meadow; dweller at the lane or narrow street; one who came from Eng, a district in China.

Engberg (*Sw.*) Meadow mountain.

Engdahl, Engdall (*Sw.*) Meadow valley.

Engebretson, Engebretsen (*Sw., Nor.*) The son of Engebret, Scandinavian form of Engelbert (angel, bright).

Engel, Engels (*Ger., Du.*) The man from England; one who lived in the meadow or grassland.

Engelbert, Engelbrecht (*Ger.*) Descendant of Engelbrecht (angel, bright).

Engelbretsen (*Nor.*) The son of Engelbret (angel, bright).

Engelhardt, Engelhard, Engelhart, Englehart, Englehardt (*Ger.*) Descendant of Engelhard (angel, hard).

Engelland (*Nor., Du.*) One who came from Engeland (meadow land), in Norway; one who came from England, an Englishman.

Engelmann, Engelman, Engelsman (*Ger.*) The servant of Engel, a short form of names beginning with Engel such as Engelhard and Engelbert; one who came from England, an Englishman; dweller at the sign of the angel.

Engelthaler (*Ger.*) Dweller in, or near, Engel's valley; one who came from Engenthal (narrow valley), in Germany.

Enger, Engen, Engert (*Nor., Ger.*) Dweller in the meadows; or on the meadow; one who came from Engen or Enge (wet meadow; narrow place), in Germany.

Engerman, Engermann (*Ger.*) Dweller in the meadow.

Engh (*Sw., Nor., Dan.*) Meadow; dweller in a meadow.

England, Englund (*Eng.*) Dweller at the ing-land or meadow land; one who came from England (land of the Angles), a name acquired elsewhere and kept on return to the native land.

Englander (*Ger.*) One who came from England, an Englishman.

Engle, Engles (*Ger., Du.*) Variant of Engel, q.v.

Englefield (*Eng.*) One who came from Englefield (Ingweald's open land), in Surrey.

Engler (*Ger.*) Descendant of Engelher (angel, army); one who came from Engeln (angel), the name of three places in Germany.

English (*Eng.*) An Englishman. Possibly the name was acquired while outside of England and brought back.

Englund (*Sw., Nor.*) Meadow grove; dweller at the meadow grove.

Engquist (*Sw.*) Meadow twig.

Engram (*Eng.*) Variant of Ingram, q.v.

Engstrom (*Sw.*) Meadow stream.

Enion, Ennion (*Wel.*) Descendant of Einion (anvil).

Enis, Enish (*Eng., Ir.*) Dweller at the island or secluded spot; grandson of Aonghus (one choice).

Enk, Enke (*Ger.*) One who works for another, a servant.

Enlow, Enloe (*Eng.*) Dweller on the hill.

Ennes (*Port.*) The son of Eann, early Portuguese form of John (gracious gift of Jehovah).

Ennis, Ennes (*Eng., Ir.*) Dweller at the island or secluded place; grandson of Aonghus (one choice).

Eno (*Eng.*) Descendant of Eno, a pet form of Eginhard (awe, hard).

Enoch, Enochs (*Eng.*) Descendant of Enoch (dedicated; trained).

Enomoto (*Jap.*) Hackberry, base.

Enos (*Eng., Fr.*) Descendant of Enos (mortal man).

Enright, Enwright (*Ir.*) The son of Innreachtach or Ionnrachtach (unlawful).

Enriquez, Enriquiz (*Sp.*) The son of Enrique, Spanish form of Henry (home, rule).

Ensley (*Eng.*) One who came from Ansley (grove with a hermitage), in Warwickshire.

Enslow (*Eng.*) One who came from Anslow (grove with a hermitage), in Staffordshire.

Ensor (*Eng.*) One who came from Edensor (Eden's bank), in Derbyshire.

Enstone (*Eng.*) One who came from Enstone (Enna's stone), in Oxfordshire.

Enstrom (*Sw.*) Variant of Engstrom, q.v.

Ensworth (*Eng.*) One who came from Emsworth (Aemele's homestead), in Hampshire.

Entin, Entinger, Entner (*Ger.*) One who came from Entingen, in Germany.

Enville (*Eng.*) One who came from Enville (smooth open country), in Staffordshire.

Enwell, Enwill (*Eng.*) One who came from Enville (smooth open country), in Staffordshire.

Entwhistle, Entwistle, Entwisle (*Eng.*) One who came from Entwisle (Enna's tongue of land in a river fork; ducks in a river fork), in Lancashire.

Eorio (*It.*) One who came from the east.

Ephraim (*Heb.*) Descendant of Ephraim (twin fruit; increasing).

Ephron (*Heb.*) Descendant of Ephron (large young hind; fawn-like).

Episcopo (*It.*) Descendant of a bishop; a member of a bishop's entourage.

Epley (*Eng.*) One who came from Apley (apple wood), the name of places in Lincolnshire and Wight; or from Ipley (wood by a hill), in Hampshire.

Eppenstein (*Ger.*) Dweller near Eppert's stone.

Epperson (*Eng.*) One who came from Epperstone (Eophere's stone), in Nottinghamshire.

Epps, Epp (*Ger.*) Descendant of Epp, a pet form of names beginning with Eber (boar), as Eburhard and Eburwin.

Epstein, Eppstein (*Ger.*) One who came from Eppstein (Eppo's stone), in Germany; one who came from Ebstein, a place no longer in existence, in Austria.

Erazmus (*Eng.*) Descendant of Erasmus (amiable; lovable).

Erb, Erbe (*Ger.*) Descendant of Arpus, a pet form of names beginning with Erbe (inheritance), as Erbhart and Arbrich; one who inherited property.

Erbach, Erbacher (*Ger.*) One who came from Erbach (swampy brook), the name of many places in Germany.

Erber (*Ger.*) One who inherited an estate.

Erby (*Sw.*) Gravel homestead.

Erdelyi, Erdely (*Hun.*) One who came from the province of Erdely (Transylvania), in Romania.

Erdmann, Erdman (*Ger.*) The land worker or farmer.

Erdos (*Hun.*) Dweller in, or near, the forest or wooded land.

Erenberg (*Ger.*) One who came from Ehrenberg, in Germany.

Erhardt, Erhard, Erhart (*Ger.*) Descendant of Erhart (honor, brave).

Erickson, Ericsson, Ericksen, Ericson (*Nor., Sw.*) The son of Eric (ever king).

Erikson, Eriksen (*Dan., Nor., Sw.*) The son of Erik (ever king).

Erkert, Erker (*Ger.*) Dweller in the alcove or corner.

Erl (*Eng.*) Same as Earl, q.v.

Erlandson (*Sw., Nor.*) Son of Erland (foreigner).

Erlanger (*Ger.*) One who came from Erlangen, in Germany.

Erlich (*Ger.*) Variant of Ehrlich, q.v.

Erman, Ermann (*Ger.*) Variant of Ehrmann, q.v.

Ernst, Ernest (*Ger.*) Descendant of Ernust (earnestness); the sincere, earnest man.

Ernstein (*Ger.*) Descendant of Ernsting, a form of Ernst (grave or serious); one who came from Ernsting (Ernst's stone), the name of several places in Germany.

Errington (*Eng.*) One who came from Errington (bright stream homestead), in Northumberland.

Erskine (*Scot.*) One who came from Erskine (green ascent), in Renfrewshire.

Ertel, Ertl, Ertell (*Ger.*) Descendant of little Ert or Ort (point of sword), a pet form of names beginning with Ort, such as Ortoff, Ortwin, and Ortlib.

Ervin, Erwin (*Eng., Ger.*) Descendant of Erwinne or Eorwine (sea, friend).

Erwinski (*Pol.*) Descendant of Erwin (sea, friend).

Esau (*Eng.*) Descendant of Esau (hairy).

Escamilla, Escamillia (*Sp.*) One who came from Escamilla (small bench), in Spain.

Esch, Esche (*Du., Ger.*) Dweller near an ash tree; one who came from Esch (ash), the name of several places in Germany.

Eschbacher, Eschbach (*Ger.*) One who came from Eschbach (ash brook), the name of many places in Germany; dweller near the brook where ash trees grew.

Escobar (*Sp.*) One who came from Escobar (place where broom grows), in Spain; dweller near where broom grew; or in an area of dense undergrowth.

Escobedo (*Sp.*) One who came from Escobedo (place where broom is sold), in Spain.

Escott, Escot (*Eng.*) One who came from Escot (eastern cottage), in Devonshire; dweller in the eastern cottage.

Escudier (*Fr.*) One of gentle birth, attendant upon a knight; one who made and sold shields.

Esh (*Eng.*) One who came from Esh (ash tree), in Durham.

Eskenazi (*Heb.*) Variant of Ashkenazi, q.v.

Eskridge (*Eng.*) One who came from Askrigg (narrow corner of land), in Yorkshire.

Esmite (*Sp.*) A Spanish or Mexican variation of English Smith, q.v.

Esmond, Esmonde (*Eng.*) Descendant of Eastmund (grace, protection).

Esparza (*Sp.*) One who came from Esparza (barren; place where feather grass grew), in Spain.

Espenschied, Espenshade (*Ger.*) Dweller near the boundary marked by aspen trees.

Esper, Espersen (*Nor.*) The son of Esper (Os, a god, bear; divine man).

Espinal (*Sp.*) One who came from Espinal (place of thorns), in Spain.

Espino (*Sp.*) One who came from Espinoza (thorny place), the name of many places in Spain; dweller near a thorn tree.

Espinosa, Espinoza (*Sp.*) One who came from Espinosa (thorny thicket), in Spain.

Esposito (*It.*) Descendant of Esposito (exposed), a name sometimes given to a foundling.

Espy (*Scot.*) One who came from Esbie (hamlet at the ash tree), in Scotland.

Esquivel (*Sp.*) One who came from Esquivel (grassy place; hideout), in Spain.

Essen (*Ger.*) One who came from Essen (standing water), the name of several places in Germany.

Esser, Esserman (*Ger.*) One who made wheels or carts, a wheelwright or cartwright; one who came from Essen (standing water), the name of several places in Germany; one who is a big eater.

Essex (*Eng.*) One who came from Essex (east Saxons), a county in England.

Essig (*Ger.*) One who produces and sells vinegar.

Essington (*Eng.*) One who came from Essington (the village of Esne's people), in Staffordshire.

Estabrook, Estabrooke, Estabrooks, Esterbrook (*Eng.*) Dweller at the easterly stream.

Estelle, Estell, Estall (*Eng., Fr.*) Dweller at the east hall; descendant of Estelle (star).

Estep, Estepp (*Sp.*) Descendant of Estep, a variant of Estevan, Spanish form of Stephen (crown or garland).

Ester (*Eng.*) One who came from Easter (sheepfold), in Essex.

Esterle, Esterly (*Eng.*) One who came from Asterleigh (eastern grove), in Oxfordshire; or from Asterley (eastern grove), in Shropshire.

Esterman (*Eng., Ger.*) One who came from the east; the husband of Esther (a star).

Esters, Esterson (*Sw.*) The son of Ester, Swedish form of Esther (star).

Estes (*Eng.*) The son of East (easterly), or of Est (gracious).

Esteves (*Port.*) The son of Estevao, Portuguese form of Stephen (crown or garland).

Estevez (*Sp.*) The son of Esteve, a pet form of Esteban, Spanish form of Stephen (crown or garland).

Estey, Esty (*Eng.*) Dweller at the east island; or the east enclosure.

Eston (*Eng.*) One who came from Eston (the east village) in the North Riding of Yorkshire.

Estrada (*Sp.*) One who came from Estrada (paved road), in Spain; dweller near a paved road.

Estridge, Estrigg (*Eng.*) Dweller on, or near, the east ridge.

Estrin, Estrine (*Ger.*) Descendant of Ester, a variant of Esther (star).

Estwick (*Eng.*) One who came from Eastwick (the eastern dairy), the name of places in Hertfordshire and the West Riding of Yorkshire.

Etchegoyhen, Etchegoyen (*Fr.*) Dweller in a house situated in the forest.

Etchells (*Eng.*) One who came from Etchells (added land), in Cheshire.

Etchingham (*Eng.*) One who came from Etchingham (meadow of Ecci's people), in Sussex.

Etchison (*Eng.*) The son of Aecce or Ecci or Ecga (sword).

Etheridge, Etheredge, Ethridge, Etteridge (*Eng.*) Descendant of Aethelric (noble, rule).

Etherton (*Eng.*) One who came from Atherton (Aethelhere's homestead), in Lancashire.

Ethington (*Eng.*) One who came from Atherington (village of Eadhere's people), in Devonshire.

Etienne (*Fr.*) Descendant of Etienne, French form of Stephen (crown or garland).

Ettelson (*Eng.*) The son of Ettel, a form of Ethel (noble).

Ettema (*Du.*) The son of Ette, a pet form of names beginning with Edel (noble), as Edelbold and Edelhard.

Etter (*Eng.*) Descendant of Etard, a French form of Eidhart (rich, hard).

Ettinger, Etting (*Ger.*) One who came from Oettingen, in Bavaria.

Ettlinger (*Ger.*) One who came from Ettlingen (dirty water), in Germany.

Eubanks, Eubank (*Eng.*) Dweller on the ridge where yew trees grew.

Euell (*Ger.*) Variant of Eul, q.v.

Eugene (*Fr.*) Descendant of Eugene (well-born).

Eul, Eule (*Ger.*) Dweller at the sign of the owl.

Eulenberg (*Ger.*) One who came from Eulenberg (owl mountain), in Germany.

Euler (*Ger.*) One who made utensils of earthenware or metal, a potter; one who came from Eulen, in Germany; dweller in, or near, a small meadow.

Eustice, Eustace, Eustis (*Eng.*) Descendant of Eustace (steadfast).

Evangelista (*Sp.*) One who chants the gospels in the church.

Evanoff, Evanow (*Rus.*) The son of Evan (gracious gift of Jehovah).

Evans, Evan (*Wel.*) The son of Evan, Welsh form of John (gracious gift of Jehovah).

Even (*Sw., Fr.*) Descendant of Even, a Swedish form of John (gracious gift of Jehovah); descendant of Even, a French saint.

Evenden (*Eng.*) Dweller in the level valley; one who came from Eafa's valley.

Evenhouse (*Eng.*) Dweller in the level house.

Evensen, Evenson (*Sw.*) The son of Even, a Swedish form of John (gracious gift of Jehovah).

Everett, Everette, Everitt, Everard (*Eng.*) Descendant of Everard (boar, hard).

Everhart, Everhard (*Eng., Ger.*) Descendant of Eburhard (boar, hard), also spelled Eberhard.

Everingham (*Eng.*) One who came from Everingham (the village of Eofor's people), in the East Riding of Yorkshire.

Everly (*Eng.*) One who came from Everley (boar, grove), the name of places in Wiltshire and the North Riding of Yorkshire.

Evers, Everson (*Eng.*) The son of Ever, a pet form of Everard (boar, hard).

Evert, Everts, Evertsen (*Sw.*) Descendant, or son, of Evert (boar, hard).

Evett, Evitt, Evitts (*Fr.*) Descendant of little Eve (life); nickname for one thought to have the characteristics of a bee.

Evon (*Wel.*) Variant of Evans, q.v.

Evoy (*Ir.*) The son of the yellow-haired lad.

Ewald, Ewaldt, Ewalt (*Ger.*) Descendant of Ewald (eternity, power); one who advised as to the law.

Ewart (*Eng.*) One who came from Ewart (river homestead), in Northumberland.

Ewell (*Eng.*) One who came from Ewell (river source), in Kent.

145

Ewers, Ewer (*Eng.*) The servant or household officer who supplied guests at the table with water to wash their hands, etc.; a water-bearer.

Ewert, Ewart (*Eng.*) One who came from Ewart (homestead on a stream), in Northumberland; one who tended ewes.

Ewing, Ewen, Ewins (*Eng.*) Descendant of Ewen (well-born).

Exman (*Eng., Ger.*) One who made and sold axes; dweller in a nook or corner.

Exner (*Ger.*) One who took care of the oxen and bullocks.

Exson (*Eng.*) The son of Acke or Acca.

Exton, Exon (*Eng.*) One who came from Exton (town of the East Saxons; ox farm), the name of places in Hampshire and Rutland.

Eyer, Eyers (*Eng.*) Variant of Ayers, q.v.

Eyerly (*Eng.*) Dweller near the heir's grove.

Eyre, Eyres (*Eng.*) Same as Ayers, q.v.

Ezard (*Eng.*) Descendant of Ishild (ice, battle).

Ezell, Ezelle (*Eng.*) One who came from Isell (Isa's corner), in Cumberland.

Faas (*Ger.*) Descendant of Faas or Vas, pet forms of Gervais, a German form of Jervis (spear, servant).

Faasen, Faassen (*Nor.*) One who came from Faasen (pasture by a waterfall), in Norway.

Fabbri, Fabbrini (*It.*) One who worked in metals, a smith.

Faber, Fabre (*Fr.*) The worker in metals, a smith.

Faberson (*Eng.*) The son of the smith, the worker in metal.

Fabian, Fabyan (*Eng.*) Descendant of Fabian (bean-grower).

Fabiano, Fabbiano (*It.*) Descendant of Fabiano, Italian form of Fabian (bean grower).

Fabis, Fabish (*Ger.*) Descendant of Phoebe (bright).

Fabri, Fabricius, Fabrie (*Fr.*) The worker in metals, a smith.

Fabrique (*Fr.*) One who worked at the forge with metal, a smith.

Fabry (*Fr.*) Variant of Faber, q.v.

Fachet (*Fr.*) Dweller in a wood.

Fackler (*Ger.*) One who gathers hemp or flax.

Factor, Facktor, Facter (*Ger.*) One who managed a business or estate for another.

Fadden (*Ir.*) The son of Paden, a pet form of Patrick (noble or patrician).

Faden (*Ger.*) Thread, a nickname for one who makes clothing, a tailor.

Fagan, Fagen, Fagin (*Ir.*) Descendant of Pagan (the rustic).

Fagel, Fagelson (*Sw.*) Descendant, or son, of Fagel (bird).

Fager, Fagerman (*Ger.*) One who came from Vagen (slimy or muddy place), in Germany.

Fagerstrom (*Sw.*) Dweller near a stream frequented by birds; fair river.

Fagiano (*It.*) Dweller at the sign of the pheasant; one who bred and sold pheasants.

Fagone (*It.*) Dweller near a large beech tree.

Fagot (*Fr.*) One who gathers and sells bundles of firewood.

Faherty (*Ir.*) Descendant of Fathartach.

Fahey, Fahy (*Ir.*) Descendant of the reasonable man; grandson of Fathadh (foundation).

Fahlberg (*Sw.*) Plain mountain; gray mountain.

Fahlstrom (*Sw.*) Plain stream; gray stream.

Fahndrich (*Ger.*) One who bore the standard or banner, an especially trusted man expected to protect the flag in battle.

Fahnestock (*Ger.*) One who embroidered flags.

Fahrbach, Fahrenbach (*Ger.*) One who came from Fahrenbach (muddy brook), the name of three places in Germany.

Fahrenkrog (*Ger.*) One who came from Fahrenkrog, in Germany.

Fahrner, Fahrer, Fahrmann (*Ger.*) One who operated a ferry, a ferryman.

Faidley (*Eng.*) One who came from Faddiley (Fadda's grove), in Cheshire.

Fail, Failing, Fails (*Eng.*) Descendant of Fagel (glad).

Fain, Faine (*Fr.*) One who came from Fain (pagan temple), the name of several places in France; dweller near a pagan temple.

Fair, Fayer, Faires (*Eng.*) The light-complexioned or handsome man; one who lived or worked at the fair or market; descendant of Fair (beautiful).

Fairbairn (*Eng.*) The beautiful or handsome child.

Fairbanks, Fairbank (*Eng.*) Dweller on, or near, the ridge where bulls or sheep were confined; or by the beautiful banks or shore.

Fairbrother (*Eng.*) The brother of Fair (handsome); the father's brother, i.e., uncle.

Fairchild (*Eng.*) The handsome youth; the son-in-law.

Fairclough, Faircloth, Faircliff (*Eng.*) Dweller in the beautiful hollow or ravine.

Fairfax (*Eng.*) One who had blond hair.

Fairfield (*Eng.*) One who came from Fairfield (beautiful field; hog field), the name of places in Derbyshire and Worcestershire.

Fairhurst (*Eng.*) Dweller in, or near, the beautiful wood.

Fairless (*Eng.*) Dweller near the bull meadow; one who traveled alone, i.e., without a companion or equal.

Fairley, Fairleigh, Fairlie (*Eng.*) One who came from Fairlee (beautiful glade), in Wight, or from Fairley (fern clearing), in Shropshire.

Fairman (*Eng.*) Descendant of Farman (traveler); the handsome man.

Fairstead (*Eng.*) One who came from Fairstead (beautiful place), in Essex.

Fairweather, Fayerweather (*Eng.*) One who worked only in good weather; one with a happy disposition; one who came from Faweather (many-colored heather), in Yorkshire.

Faison (*Fr.*) One who breeds and sells pheasants.

Fake (*Eng.*) Descendant of Fauke, a variant of Fulk (people).

Fala, Falla (*Scot.*) One who came from Fala (pale hill), in Midlothian.

Falbo (*It.*) Descendant of Flavio (blond).

Falck (*Sw.*) One who took care of the falcons or hawks; one who hunted with falcons.

Falco, Falcone (*It.*) Dweller at the sign of the hawk or falcon; a bold, keen-eyed or nimble person; dweller near, or on, the Falco mountain, in Italy; one who came from Falcone (falcon), in Sicily.

Falconer (*Eng.*) One who kept and trained falcons or hawks to hunt game.

Falduto (*It.*) One who made capes and coats.

Fales (*Eng.*) The son of Fagel (glad).

Falk, Falke (*Ger., Nor., Sw.*) One who took care of the falcons or hawks; one who hunted with falcons; dweller at the sign of the falcon.

Falkenberg (*Sw.*) One who came from Falkenberg (falcon mountain), a city in Sweden.

Falkenthal (*Ger.*) One who came from Falkenthal (valley frequented by falcons), in Germany.

Falkingham (*Eng.*) One who came from Falkenham (Falta's homestead), in Suffolk.

Falkner, Falknor (*Ger., Eng.*) One who kept and trained falcons or hawks to hunt game.

Fall (*Eng.*) Dweller at, or near, the Fal, a river in Cornwall; dweller near the waterfall; or on the slope.

Faller, Fallert (*Eng., Ger.*) Dweller at the slope or waterfall; one who came from Fall (waterfall), in Germany.

Fallon, Falloon, Fallin, Fallen (*Ir.*) Grandson of Fallamhan (ruler).

Falls (*Eng.*) Dweller on the slope; or near the waterfall.

Faloona, Faloon (*Ir.*) Grandson of Fallamhan (ruler).

Falsey (*Ir.*) Descendant of Faolchadh (wolf warrior).

Falstein (*Sw.*) Plain stone; gray stone.

Falstone (*Eng.*) One who came from Falstone (multicolored stone), in Northumberland.

Faltum (*Eng.*) One who came from Feltham (meadow where hay was obtained; homestead in open country), the name of places in Middlesex and Somerset.

Falvey (*Ir.*) Grandson of Failbhe (lively).

Falzone (*It.*) One who made, or worked with, scythes or sickles.

Fambro (*It.*) One who worked in metal, a smith.

Familar, Familiar, Famillar (*Sp.*) One who was a domestic servant, especially of the clergy.

Fancher (*Eng.*) Variant of Fincher, q.v.

Fane (*Eng., Wel.*) The glad, joyful, well-disposed man; descendant of Fane; the slender man.

Fanelli, Fanella (*It.*) Dweller at the sign of the linnet, a common small finch; descendant of Fano, a pet form of Cristofano, a variant of Cristoforo, Italian form of Christopher (Christ-bearer).

Fang (*Chin.*) Square.

Fanger, Fangmann (*Ger.*) One who captured game; one who came from Fang (place where game were found), in Germany.

Fann, Fanner (*Eng.*) Dweller in, or near, the marsh or fen; one who made winnowing fans.

Fanning, Fannon, Fannin (*Ir.*) Descendant of the little blond man; grandson of little Fionn (fair).

Fano (*Sp.*) One who came from Fano (sacred place), in Spain.

Fanshaw, Fanshawe (*Eng.*) Dweller in the grove frequented by young animals; or at the grove by the winnowing fan; or by the fen or marsh. Fanshaw Gate in Derbyshire was named after the Fanshaw family.

Fant (*Eng.*) The immature person, one with the characteristics of a child.

Fantasia (*It.*) Imagination, a name to describe an eccentric or insane person.

Fanti (*Fr., It.*) Nickname for a small or childish man; one engaged in military service, a foot soldier.

Fantozzi (*It.*) One with the characteristics of a small child.

Fanucchi, Fanucci (*It., Fr.*) Descendant of little Fano, pet form of Cristofano, Italian variant of Christopher (Christ-bearer).

Farabee (*Eng.*) One who came from Ferriby (homestead at the ferry), the name of places in Lincolnshire and the East Riding of Yorkshire.

Faraday (*Ir.*) Descendant of Feradach (illustrious man).

Farago (*Hun.*) One who carved objects from wood, a woodcarver.

Farber (*Ger.*) One who dyed cloth.

Farcroft (*Eng.*) Dweller in the beautiful, enclosed land.

Farewell (*Eng.*) One who came from Farewell (beautiful spring), in Staffordshire.

Fargo (*Fr.*) Descendant of Fargeau (of iron).

Faria (*Port.*) One who came from Faria, in Portugal.

Farias (*Sp., Port.*) One who came from Feria (place of the fair), in Spain; or from Faria (place of the fair), in Portugal.

Farina, Farino (*It.*) One who ground grain, a miller.

Farinella (*It.*) One who conveyed flour from the mill to the home.

Farkas, Farkash, Farkis (*Hun.*) Descendant of Farkas (tailed beast; wolf); dweller at the sign of the wolf; one with wolflike characteristics.

Farland (*Eng.*) Dweller on the fair or fine land.

Farley, Farleigh (*Eng., Ir.*) The man who came from Farley or Farleigh (fern-covered clearing), the names of several places in England; grandson of Faircheallach (super-war).

Farlow (*Eng.*) One who came from Farlow (hill covered with ferns), in Shropshire.

Farmer, Farmar (*Scot.*) One who farmed the revenue, a tax collector.

Farnan (*Eng.*) Descendant of Farman (traveler).

Farndel (*Eng.*) Dweller in a valley where ferns grew.

Farnell, Farnall (*Eng.*) Dweller at the corner or hill overgrown with ferns; one who came from Farnhill (fern covered hill), in the West Riding of Yorkshire.

Farner (*Ger.*) One who came from Fahrnau (swampy place), in Germany.

Farneti (*It.*) Dweller among orach, a weed; and by metaphor, a fool.

Farnham, Farnum (*Eng.*) One who came from Farnham (homestead where ferns or thorns grew), the name of various places in England.

Farnsworth, Farnworth (*Eng.*) One who came from Farnworth (homestead where ferns grew), in Lancashire.

Faro (*Eng.*) Variant of Farrow, q.v.

Faron (*Fr.*) One who made and sold candles; descendant of Faron or Faro, the name of a seventh century Burgundian saint.

Farquhar, Farquharson (*Scot.*) The son of Farquhar (friendly).

Farr (*Eng., Scot.*) Dweller at the sign of the bull or boar; one who came from Farr (passage), in Sutherland.

Farragut (*Scot.*) A nickname, the good traveler.

Farrand, Ferrand (*Eng., Fr.*) Descendant of Ferrand, a contraction of Ferdinand (journey, venture); one who had iron-gray, or graying, hair.

Farrar (*Scot.*) A corruption of Farquhar (friendly).

Farrell, Farrall (*Ir.*) Grandson of Fearghal (super valor).

Farren, Farrin (*Ir.*) Grandson of Arachan.

Farrington (*Eng.*) One who came from Farrington (manor where ferns grew), in Somerset.

Farris, Faris (*Ir.*) Grandson of Fearghur (better choice).

Farrow (*Eng.*) Dweller at the sign of the boar or pig.

Farry, Fary, Farey (*Eng.*) Dweller on the beautiful island.

Farson (*Eng.*) The fair or handsome son.

Farthing (*Eng.*) One who paid rent of a farthing, the fourth of a penny; one who occupied a quarter of a virgate which is about seven or eight acres.

Farwell (*Eng.*) One who came from Farewell (beautiful stream), in Staffordshire.

Farwick (*Eng.*) Dweller in a beautiful building; descendant of Farwig (travel, battle).

Fasano (*It.*) The pheasant, a nickname given to a dullard.

Fasel (*Ger.*) Dweller at the sign of the bull or boar; one who took care of the domestic animals used for breeding purposes.

Fashing (*Ger.*) The gay, exuberant, vivacious man; one who celebrated Shrove Tuesday.

Fashingbauer (*Ger.*) The peasant who settles his accounts at Shrovetide, the time for confession preparatory to Lent; the exuberant farmer who celebrates Shrove Tuesday.

Fasse (*Ger.*) Descendant of Fasse, a pet form of Servatius (to save).

Fassett, Fasset (*Eng.*) One who came from Fawcett (multicolored hillside), in Westmorland; or from Forcett (fold by a ford), in the North Riding of Yorkshire.

Fasso, Fasse (*It.*) Dweller at the sign of the pigeon; one thought to possess some characteristic of a pigeon.

Fastwolf (*Ger.*) Descendant of Fastwolf (strong, wolf).

Fata (*Rom.*) The effeminate man.

Fath, Fathman (*Ger.*) One who had charge of a household, a steward; one who acted as an overseer or magistrate.

Fattore (*It.*) One who managed a farm or household for another, a steward.

Fatz (*Ger.*) One who teases or irritates others.

149

Faubus (*Ger.*) From Phoebus (bright), a name taken by Jews as equivalent to Me'ir and Uriboth with the same meaning.

Faucher (*Fr.*) One who cut grass or grain or harvested crops; descendant of Falchari (falcon, army).

Faul, Faull (*Eng.*) Dweller by the slope, or waterfall.

Faulcon (*Eng.*) Variant of Falconer, q.v.; one thought to possess some characteristics of a falcon.

Faulhaber (*Ger.*) One whose land produced foul or bad oats.

Faulk (*Eng.*) Descendant of Fulk (people).

Faulkenham, Faulkingham (*Eng.*) One who came from Falkenham (Falta's homestead), in Suffolk.

Faulkner (*Eng.*) The falconer, i.e., one who keeps and trains falcons or hawks to hunt game.

Faunt (*Eng.*) One with the characteristics or habits of a child.

Fauntleroy (*Eng.*) The son of the king, in some cases his attendant or nurse.

Faure, Faur (*Fr.*) One who worked in metal, a smith.

Faust (*Ger.*) Descendant of Faustus (fortunate); the lucky, auspicious man; dweller at the sign of the closed fist.

Fava, Favela (*It., Port.*) One who raised and sold beans.

Favaro (*It.*) One who raises and sells beans.

Faversham (*Eng.*) One who came from Faversham (the smith's village), in Kent.

Faverty (*Ir.*) Variant of Faherty, q.v.

Favorite, Favoriti (*It.*) One who is regarded with particular affection or esteem, the favorite one.

Fawcett, Faucett (*Eng.*) One who came from Fawcett (multicolored hillside), in Westmorland.

Fawell (*Eng.*) One with fallow-colored or tawny hair.

Fawkes, Fawke (*Eng.*) Descendant of Fulk or Fulco or Fawke (people), an Old Germanic name found in various spellings.

Fay, Faye (*Eng., Fr., Ir.*) One who came from Fay or Faye (beech tree), in France; descendant of the reasonable man; grandson of Fathadh (foundation).

Fayson (*Fr.*) Variant of Faison, q.v.

Fazekas (*Hun., Sl.*) One who made and sold utensils of earthenware, a potter.

Fazio, Fazzi, Fazzio (*It.*) One who acted as a watchman or sentinel; dweller by a beech tree.

Feagins, Feagan (*Ir.*) Descendant of little Aodh (fire).

Fearing (*Eng.*) One who came from Feering (fit for service), in Essex.

Fearn (*Eng., Scot.*) Dweller among ferns; one who came from Fearn (alder), in Rossshire.

Fearnley (*Eng.*) Variant of Fernley, q.v.

Fearon, Feron (*Eng., Fr.*) One who dealt in iron goods, a smith.

Fears, Feare, Fear (*Eng.*) One who was a companion or friend to another.

Feaster (*Ger.*) American variant of Pfister, q.v.

Feather, Featherman (*Eng.*) Dweller at the sign of the feather; a dealer in feathers.

Feathers (*Scot.*) One who came from Fetters, in Fifeshire.

Featherstone, Featherston (*Eng.*) One who came from Featherstone (a tetralith, i.e., three upright stones and a headstone), the name of places in Northumberland and Yorkshire.

Fechner (*Ger.*) One who deals with spotted or colored furs.

Feddersen (*Dan.*) The son of Fedder, a pet form of Frederik, Danish form of Frederick (peace, rule).

Feddor (*Rus., Pol.*) Descendant of Fedor, a Slavic form of Theodore (gift of God).

Fedele, Fedelle (*It.*) The faithful man.

Feder, Fedder (*Ger.*) Dweller at the sign of the feather; one who bought and sold feathers.

Federici, Federico, Federighi (*It.*) Descendant of Federico, Italian form of Frederick (peace, rule).

Federinko, Federowski (*Ukr.*) Descendant of Fedir, Ukrainian form of Theodore (gift of God).

Federman (*Ger.*) One who bought and sold feathers.

Fedor, Fedorow (*Rus.*) Descendant of Fedor, a Russian form of Theodore (gift of God).

Fedorenko, Fedorchuk, Fedoruk (*Ukr.*) The son of Feodor, Ukrainian form of Theodore (gift of God).

Fee (*Ir.*) Grandson of Fiaich (raven).

Feehan (*Ir.*) Descendant of little Fiaich (raven).

Feeley, Feely (*Ir.*) Grandson of Fitcheallach (chess player).

Feeney, Feeny (*Ir.*) Descendant of the soldier.

Feffer, Fefferman, Feferman (*Ger.*) Variant of Pfeffer, q.v.

Fegan (*Ir.*) Variant of Fagan, q.v.

Fegley (*Eng.*) One who came from Faddiley (Fadda's grove), in Cheshire.

Feher (*Hun.*) The white-haired or light-complexioned man.

Fehl, Fehlman (*Ger.*) Dweller in, or near, a swamp.

Fehlhaber (*Ger.*) One who grew large crops of oats; the wealthy oat grower.

Fehling (*Ger.*) One who came from Fehling (plain; field), in Germany.

Fehrmann, Fehr (*Ger.*) One who operated a ferry, a ferryman.

Feicht, Feichter (*Ger.*) Dweller by, or in, the spruce woods.

Feig, Feige, Feigen (*Ger.*) One who is timid or fearful; one who is unlucky, near to death.

Feigel (*Ger.*) Violet; dark-colored man.

Feigenbaum (*Ger.*) Dweller near a fig tree.

Feigl (*Ger.*) Dweller near where violets grew.

Feikema (*Du.*) The son of Feike, Frisian form of Frederick (peace, rule).

Feil, Feiler (*Ger.*) One who was mercenary; one who came from Feil, in Pfalz.

Fein (*Ger.*) The refined, courtly, aristocratic man.

Feinberg (*Ger.*) Dweller on, or near, the Feinberg (fair mountain), in Austria.

Feinglass (*Ger.*) Fine glass.

Feingold (*Ger.*) Fine gold.

Feinman (*Ger.*) The refined, distinguished, aristocratic man.

Feinsmith (*Ger.*) The smith who made small metal objects.

Feinstein (*Ger., Fr.*) Fine stone; one who dealt in gold and silver ornaments and precious stones, a jeweler.

Feist (*Ger.*) The fat, stout, corpulent man.

Feit, Feiter, Feith (*Ger.*) One who had charge of a household, an overseer; a warden; descendant of Feit, a German short form of Vitus (animated).

Feiwell (*Heb.*) Descendant of Feiwel, a sound-imitating form of Greek Phoibos, the sun god; translation of Hebrew Uri, "my light."

Fekete (*Hun., Sl.*) One with a swarthy complexion, or black hair.

Felber (*Ger.*) Dweller in the pasture or meadow; one who came from Felben (white willow), in Germany.

Feld, Felde (*Eng., Ger.*) Dweller on land free from trees, a field; one who came from Felde (field), the name of four places in Germany.

Feldgreber, Feldgraber (*Ger.*) Dweller near the ditch or stream in open country.

Feldhaus (*Ger.*) One who came from Feldhaus (field house), in Germany; dweller in the house in the open country.

Feldheim (*Ger.*) Dweller in the home or cottage in the field; one who came from Feldheim (field home), in Germany.

Feldkamp (*Ger.*) One who came from Feldkamp (field enclosure), in Germany.

Feldman, Feldmann, Feltman, Feltmann (*Ger., Eng.*) The worker in the field or open country.

Feldmar (*Ger.*) Dweller near the boundary of the field.

Feldon (*Eng.*) One who came from Feldom (fields), in the North Riding of Yorkshire.

Feldstein (*Ger.*) Field stone; dweller on the Feldstein, a hill in Germany.

Felgenhauer (*Ger.*) One who made wheels by cutting the wooden wheel rims.

Felice (*Fr.*) Descendant of Felix (happy or fortunate).

Feliciano (*Sp.*) Descendant of Feliciano, Spanish form of Felician (happiness); the happy, fortunate, lucky man.

Felicitas (*Sp.*) The pleasant, happy person.

Felix (*Eng.*) Descendant of Felix (happy).

Fell, Fells, Fels (*Eng., Ger.*) Dweller on, or near, the rocky mountain; one who dealt in hides or furs.

Feller, Felman, Fellerman (*Ger.*) One who dealt in furs, a furrier.

Fellinger, Fellin (*Ger.*) One who came from Felling (moor), in Germany.

Fellner (*Ger.*) One who came from Velden (field; swamp), the name of two places in Germany; one who deals in skins, a furrier.

Fellows, Fellowes (*Eng.*) One who was a partner or associate of another; dweller near the newly cultivated land.

Felsenthal (*Ger.*) Dweller in a rocky valley.

Felske, Felski (*Ger., Pol.*) Descendant of Feliks, Polish form of Felix (happy or fortunate).

Felt, Felte, Feldt (*Ger.*) Dweller in the field or open country.

Feltes (*Bel.*) Descendant of Felt, a pet form of Philibert (love, bright).

Feltham (*Eng.*) One who came from Feltham (homestead in open country; meadow where hay was obtained), the name of places in Middlesex and Somerset.

Felthouse (*Eng.*) Dweller in, or near, the house where felt was made.

Feltinton (*Eng.*) One who came from Felkington (hill of Feoluca's people), in Northumberland.

Felton, Felten (*Eng.*) One who came from Felton (homestead in open country), the name of several places in England.

Feltwell (*Eng.*) One who came from Feltwell (spring where felte grew), in Norfolk.

Feltz, Felz (*Du., Ger.*) Descendant of Felz or Volz, short forms of names beginning with Volk (people), as Volkold and Fulculf; the tall, large man.

Feminella (*It.*) One with womanish characteristics.

Fenberg (*Nor.*) Dweller on Finnr's hill.

Fencl, Fenchel, Fencel, Fencil (*Ger.*) One who buys and sells spices; one who grows and sells fennel, an herb cultivated for the aromatic flavor of its seeds.

Fender (*Scot., Eng.*) One who came from Fender (clear stream), in Scotland; one who defends others.

Fendley (*Scot.*) Variant of Finley, q.v.

Fenemore (*Eng.*) One who came from Fennymere (musty lake), in Shropshire; one who was dearly loved, from Old French *fin amour* (dear love).

Feng (*Chin.*) Fruitful; to mount.

Fenger (*Ger.*) Variant of Finger, q.v.

Fenimore (*Eng.*) Variant of Fenemore, q.v.

Fenn, Fenne (*Eng.*) Dweller at the marsh, or fen.

Fennell (*Eng.*) Dweller at, or near, the corner of the marsh.

Fennelly (*Ir.*) Grandson of Fionnghalach (fair or valorous).

Fenner (*Eng.*) Variant of Venner, q.v.; dweller at the marsh or fen.

Fennessey, Fennessy (*Ir.*) Grandson of Fionnghus (fair choice).

Fenning (*Eng.*) The son of Faegen (fain); dweller at the fen meadow.

Fenske, Fensch (*Ger.*) Descendant of Wenzeslav (wreath, glory).

Fenster, Fenstermacher, Fenstermaker (*Ger.*) One who made and sold windows and window glass.

Fenton (*Eng.*) One who came from Fenton (homestead in a marsh), the name of several places in England; dweller by the spring.

Fentress (*Eng.*) One inclined to venturous or hazardous undertakings.

Fenwick (*Eng., Scot.*) One who came from Fenwick (farm by a marsh), the name of places in Northumberland and Yorkshire; or from Fenwick (dwelling in a fen), in Ayrshire.

Fenzel (*Ger.*) Descendant of Fenzel, a dialectic form of Wenzel, a short form of Wenzelaus (wreath, fame); one employed by another, a servant.

Ferber (*Ger.*) A painter or stainer.

Ferdinand (*Eng.*) Descendant of Ferdinand (journey, venture; adventuring life).

Ferdman (*Ger.*) One who dealt in horses; or who cared for them.

Ferenc, Ference (*Hun.*) Descendant of Ferenc, the Hungarian form of Francis (free).

Ferencz, Ferenczy, Ferenzi (*Hun.*) Variant of Ferenc, q.v.; the son of Ferenc.

Feret, Ferret, Ferreter, Ferriter (*Eng.*) One who hunts rabbits and small game with a ferret.

Ferguson, Fergus (*Scot.*) The son of Fergus (manly strength; super choice).

Ferina, Ferino (*Sp.*) One who is like a wild beast.

Ferm (*Sw.*) The smart, clever man, a soldier name.

Ferme (*Fr.*) One who has a steady character; dweller in a fortified or enclosed place.

Fermi, Fermo (*It.*) One who came from Fermo (firm), in Italy; descendant of Fermo (firm).

Fern, Fearn (*Scot.*) One who came from Fearn (alder tree), in Scotland; dweller by an alder tree.

Fernald (*Fr.*) The worker in iron, or one who dealt in iron, a dim. form.

Fernander (*Sw.*) Dweller at a distance.

Fernandez, Fernandes, Fernando (*Sp., Port.*) Son of Fernando (journey, venture).

Fernbach (*Ger.*) Dweller at the distant stream; or at the swampy stream.

Fernell (*Eng.*) One who came from Farnhill (fern covered hill), in the the West Riding of Yorkshire.

Fernley (*Eng.*) Dweller in, or near, a grove where ferns grew.

Fernstrom (*Sw.*) Distant stream; dweller at the stream near where ferns or brackens grew.

Ferone (*It.*) One who was in charge of the money box, a cashier.

Ferrante (*It.*) Descendant of Ferrante, an Italian form of Ferdinand (journey, venture; adventuring life).

Ferrara, Ferrera (*It.*) One who came from Ferrara (Forum Allieni), a province in Italy.

Ferraro, Ferrari, Ferrero, Ferreri, Ferrario (*It.*) A worker in metals, a smith.

Ferreira (*Port.*) One who came from Ferreira (iron mine or workshop), the name of numerous places in Portugal; dweller near a smith's shop.

Ferrell, Ferrall, Ferrill (*Ir.*) Grandson of Fearghal (super valor).

Ferrer (*Sp.*) The worker in metals, a smith.

Ferri (*It.*) Nickname for one with ironlike characteristics.

Ferrick (*Ir., Fr.*) The son of little Pier (rock); one who had large ankle bones.

Ferrier (*Eng., Fr.*) One who operated a ferry; one who worked in iron, a blacksmith; one who made horseshoes.

Ferring (*Eng.*) One who came from Ferring (fit for service), in Sussex.

Ferrington (*Eng.*) One who came from Farrington (homestead where ferns grew), in Somerset.

Ferrini, Ferroli (*It.*) One who makes small tools, or small iron objects.

Ferris, Ferrise (*Ir., Fr.*) Variant of Farris, q.v.; one who shoes horses or works with iron.

Ferriter (*Eng.*) One who searches for rabbits with a ferret.

Ferro, Ferrone, Ferroni (*It.*) Dweller near where iron was mined.

Ferry (*Eng., Fr.*) Dweller at, or near, a ferry; one who operated a ferry; descendant of Ferry, a pet form of Frederic (peace, rule).

Ferryman (*Eng.*) One who operated a ferry.

Ferstel (*Ger.*) One in charge of the forest possessions of the manor; illegitimate descendant of a prince; one in the service of a prince.

Fertig (*Ger.*) One who was prepared, fit, and able to perform a task.

Fessler (*Ger.*) One who made and sold small wooden kegs and tubs.

Festa (*It.*) The glad, joyous, gay man.

Fetherston (*Eng.*) Variant of Featherstone, q.v.

Fetridge (*Scot.*) Son of Peadrus (rock), a shortened form of MacFetridge.

Fett, Fette, Fettig, Fetting (*Ger.*) Descendant of Fett (the corpulent one).

Fetter, Fetters (*Ger.*) An uncle, that is, the father's brother; the cousin or kinsman.

Fetzer, Fetzner (*Ger.*) Dweller in, or near, a reedy swamp or moss-grown place.

Feuer (*Eng., Ger.*) One who worked in metals, a smith.

Feuerstadt (*Ger.*) Dweller at a place where a forge was located.

Feuerstein, Feuerstine (*Ger.*) One who worked with flint.

Feuillet, Feuillette (*Fr.*) Dweller at the sign of a leaf, used generally to represent a wine merchant.

Feulner (*Ger.*) One who made files.

Feurer (*Ger.*) One who tends a fire, a fireman.

Fevre (*Fr.*) The worker in metals, a smith.

Few, Feu (*Eng., Fr.*) Dweller near a beech tree.

Fewer (*Eng., Ger.*) Variant of Feuer, q.v.

Fewkes (*Eng.*) The son of Fulk (people).

Fewsmith (*Eng.*) One who made the wooden framework of the saddletree, a fewster.

Fey, Feye (*Eng., Ger.*) One who came from Fay (beech), in France; dweller at the beech tree; descendant of Fey, a short form of Sophie (wisdom).

Feyerer (*Ger.*) Variant of Feurer, q.v.

Ffoulkes, Ffoulke (*Eng.*) Variant of Foulkes, q.v. An early form of a capital *F* was ff.

Ffrench (*Eng.*) One who came from France, a Frenchman. An early form of a capital *F* was ff.

Ffulke (*Eng.*) Descendant of Fulk (people).

Fiala (*Ukr.*) One who made and sold goblets.

Fialkowski (*Pol.*) Dweller near where violets grew.

Ficarelli, Ficarella (*It.*) Dweller near a fig tree.

Ficht, Fichter, Fichtner (*Ger.*) Dweller at, or near, a fir tree.

Fick, Ficke, Fickes (*Eng.*) Descendant of Fech, or Feche (fated to die).

Fickett (*Eng.*) One who works with a small iron-pointed implement; one who fought with a spear or other pointed weapon; descendant of little Fech (fated to die).

Fico (*It.*) Dweller near a fig tree; one who raised and sold figs.

Fidanze, Fidanzia, Fidanza (*It.*) The faithful man.

Fiddelke (*Ger.*) One who played the little fiddle or stringed instrument.

Fiddle (*Eng.*) Metonymic for one who played the fiddle.

Fidler, Fiedler, Fiddler (*Eng., Ger.*) One who played a fiddle or stringed instrument.

Fiduccia (*It.*) The trustworthy man.

Fiebig (*Ger.*) Dweller near the cattle path.

Fiedor, Fiedorczuk, Fiedorowicz (*Rus.*) Descendant of Feodor, Russian form of Theodore (gift of God).

Fiegel, Fiegelman (*Ger.*) One who made utensils of earthenware or metal, a potter; one who played a fiddle or stringed instrument.

Fielding (*Eng.*) Dweller near the fields or the meadow of the open country.

Fieldman (*Eng.*) One who worked in the open country.

Fields, Field (*Eng.*) Dweller in an open tract of arable land, or open country, land free of trees, usually not fenced.

Fier, Fierer (*Ger.*) One of four; soldier of the fourth regiment.

Fierstein, Fiersten, Fierston (*Ger.*) One who used a feuerstein or flint to start a fire; firestone.

Fifer, Fife (*Scot.*) One who came from Fife. See Fyfe.

Fifield (*Eng.*) One who came from Fifield (an estate of five hides, i.e., as much land as could be tilled by five plows), the name of several places in England.

Figaro (*It.*) One who cultivated and sold figs; dweller near fig trees.

Figg, Figgs, Figge, Figgers (*Ger., Eng.*) Descendant of Fey, pet form of Sophie (wisdom); or from Figge, a pet form of Fridulf (peace, wolf); one who worked with an iron-pointed instrument.

Fight (*Eng.*) Dweller on riverside grassland.

Figiel, Figlewicz (*Pol.*) Descendant of the cunning, crafty man.

Figueiredo (*Port.*) Dweller in, or near, a grove of fig trees.

Figueroa (*Sp.*) One who came from Figueroa (fig tree), the name of several towns in Spain; one who made and sold statuettes.

Figura (*Sp., It.*) One with an unusual face or appearance.

Figurski (*Pol.*) One with a good figure or stature.

Figus (*Cz.-Sl., Pol., Ukr.*) Dweller near a fig tree; one who grew and sold figs.

Fike, Fikes (*Du.*) Descendant of Feike (peace).

Fikret (*Tur.*) Descendant of Fikret (mind).

Filar, Filarski (*Pol.*) Dweller near the pillar or column.

Filbert (*Eng.*) Descendant of Filbert (very bright).

Filbey, Filby, Filbee (*Eng.*) One who came from Filby (Fili's homestead), in Norfolk.

Filbin (*Ir.*) The son of Fhilibin (plover); or of Philpin, dim. of Philip (lover of horses).

Filc (*Pol., Cz.*) One who made and sold felt cloth.

Filer, Filerman (*Eng.*) One who files, smooths or polishes; one who made and sold files; one who spun wool or yarn, a spinner.

Files (*Eng.*) Dweller on the level field or plain; one who came from The Fylde (level field), in Lancashire.

Filiatreault (*Fr.*) The son-in-law; son of the sister, a nephew.

Filip (*Eng., Nor., Sw., Pol., Yu.-Sl.*) Dweller at a hayfield or plot of newly cultivated land; descendant of Filip, Slavic and Scandinavian form of Philip (lover of horses).

Filipiak, Filipek (*Pol.*) Descendant of little Filip, Slavic form of Philip (lover of horses).

Filipovic, Filipovich (*Yu.-Sl.*) The son of Filip, Slavic form of Philip (lover of horses).

Filipowicz (*Pol.*) The son of Philip (lover of horses).

Filippi, Filippini (*It.*) Descendant of Filippo, Italian form of Philip (lover of horses).

Filkins (*Eng.*) Descendant of little Phil, a pet form of Philip (lover of horses); one who came from Filkins (Filica's people), in Oxfordshire.

Filler (*Ger.*) One who removed and prepared hides, a skinner.

Fillipp, Fillip (*Eng.*) Descendant of Philip (lover of horses).

Fillmore, Filmore (*Eng.*) Descendant of Filimar or Filomor (very famous).

Fillpot (*Eng.*) Descendant of little Phil, a pet form of Philip (lover of horses).

Filpi (*It.*) Descendant of Filpi, a pet form of Filippo, Italian form of Philip (lover of horses).

155

Filson (*Eng.*) The son of Phil, a pet form of Philip (lover of horses).

Finan, Finnan (*Ir., Scot.*) Descendant of little Fionn (fair).

Finch (*Eng.*) Dweller at the sign of the finch; the simple-minded person.

Fincher (*Eng.*) One who trapped and sold finches.

Finchum (*Eng.*) One who came from Fincham (homestead frequented by finches), in Norfolk.

Findeisen (*Ger.*) A worker who has learned smith handicraft, a journeyman smith.

Finder (*Ger.*) One who discovered things or invented new processes.

Findlater, Findlator (*Scot.*) One who came from Findlater (white, clear hillside), in Banffshire.

Findlay, Findley (*Scot.*) Sharpened form of Finley, q.v.; one who came from Findlay (clear calf), in Scotland.

Findon (*Scot., Eng.*) One who came from Findon (clear, white hill), in Scotland; or from Findon (hill with heap of wood), in Sussex.

Fine (*Eng., Ger.*) The fine or elegant person; a clever man.

Fineberg (*Ger.*) Variant of Feinberg, q.v.

Finegan, Finigan (*Ir.*) Grandson of little Fionn (fair).

Finegold, Fingold (*Ger.*) Fine gold.

Fineman, Finerman (*Ger.*) The cultivated, refined, courtly, aristocratic man.

Finerty (*Ir.*) Grandson of Fionnachta (beautiful snow).

Finfer (*Ger.*) The official who was one of five governing a group.

Fingall (*Scot.*) The white stranger; one who came from the Hebrides.

Finger, Fingar (*Ger.*) One with a peculiar or unusual finger; one who came from a place using this word in some transferred sense; descendant of one at the sign of the ring, a goldsmith.

Fingerhood (*Ger.*) American translation of Fingerhut, q.v.

Fingerhut (*Ger.*) One who made and sold thimbles; one who used a thimble, making garments, a tailor.

Fingerman (*Ger.*) One who made and sold finger rings.

Fini, Fino (*It.*) Descendant of Fini or Fino, a pet form of names with this termination, as Serafino and Ruffino.

Fink, Finke, Finck, Fincke (*Ger.*) Dweller at the sign of the finch.

Finkel, Finkle (*Ger.*) Dweller at the sign of the little bird; descendant of Finkel (little bird), a popular woman's name in the Middle Ages.

Finkelstein, Finklestein (*Ger.*) Pyrites; descendant of Finkel (little bird), with the addition of "stein" (stone) to give the name a German look and sound. See Finkel.

Finkler (*Ger.*) One who caught and sold birds.

Finkley (*Eng.*) One who came from Finkley (grove frequented by finches), in Hampshire.

Finkston (*Eng.*) Dweller in a homestead where finches were found.

Finley, Finlay (*Scot.*) Descendant of Fionnla (fair hero); one who came from Findlay (clear calf), in Scotland.

Finmere (*Eng.*) One who came from Finmere (lake frequented by woodpeckers), in Oxfordshire.

Finn, Finne (*Ir.*) Grandson of Fionn (fair).

Finnegan, Finnigan (*Ir.*) Grandson of little Fionn (fair).

Finnerty (*Ir.*) Grandson of Fionnachta (beautiful snow).

Finney (*Ir.*) Descendant of the soldier.

Finocchio (*It.*) One who cultivated and sold fennel, a perennial European herb prized for the aromatic flavor of its seeds; descendant of Fino, a pet form of Serafino (serpent; luminous), and Ruffino (red).

Finseth (*Nor.*) One who came from Finset (Finn's dwelling), in Norway.

Finstad (*Nor., Eng.*) One who came from Finstad (Finnr's homestead; the Lapp's town), in Norway; or from Fenstead (heap of wood), in Suffolk.

Finstock (*Eng.*) One who came from

Finstock (place frequented by wood-peckers), in Oxfordshire.

Finston (*Eng.*) Dweller in, or near, Finn's homestead.

Finstrom (*Sw., Finn.*) One who came from Finstrom, in Finland.

Finton (*Eng.*) One who came from Fenton (homestead by a fen), the name of seven places in England.

Finucane (*Ir.*) Descendant of Fionnmhacan (fair little son).

Fiore, Fiori (*It.*) Dweller at, or near, a place where flowers are grown.

Fiorella, Fiorelli, Fiorello (*It.*) Variant of Fiorito, q.v.

Fiorentino (*It.*) One who came from Firenze (Florence, city of flowers), in Italy.

Fioretto, Fioretta, Fioretti (*It.*) Variant of Fiorito, q.v.

Fiorito, Fiorita (*It.*) Descendant of Fiorita (flowers); one who cultivated flowers; dweller at the sign of the flower; one who came from Fiorita (flowers), in Italy.

Fireman (*Eng.*) A variant of Fairman (handsome man).

Firestone, Firestein (*Ger.*) American translation of Feuerstein, q.v.

Firman, Firmin (*Eng.*) The firm, strong man.

First (*Ger.*) Variant of Furst, q.v.

Firth (*Scot.*) One who came from Firth (bay), in Roxburghshire; or from Firth (bay), in Orkney.

Fischer (*Ger.*) One who caught or sold fish.

Fischl, Fischel (*Ger.*) Dweller at the sign of the little fish; the little dealer in fish.

Fish, Fisch (*Eng., Ger.*) A fisherman or dealer in fish; dweller at the sign of the fish.

Fishburn (*Eng.*) One who came from Fishburn (stream with plenty of fish), in Durham.

Fisher (*Eng.*) One who caught or sold fish.

Fishleigh, Fishley (*Eng.*) One who came from Fishley (the fisherman's grove), in Norfolk.

Fishman (*Eng.*) A fisherman or seller of fish.

Fisk, Fiske (*Sw.*) A fisherman; often a Swedish soldier name.

Fitch (*Eng.*) One who came from Fitz (Fita's spur of land), in Shropshire; dweller at the sign of the fitch, the European polecat; one with the characteristics of a polecat; one who fought, or worked with, a pointed instrument.

Fithian (*Eng.*) Descendant of Fithian, a variant of Vivian (alive).

Fitts, Fitt, Fitte (*Eng.*) Variant of Fitz, q.v.

Fitz, Fitze (*Eng.*) Son, one who was the son of his father with whom he was associated. Sometimes it is merely the shortened form of one of the many surnames commencing with this prefix.

Fitzer (*Ger.*) One who was a skillful pattern weaver.

Fitzgerald, Fitz Gerald (*Eng., Fr., Ir.*) The son of Gerald (firm, spear).

Fitzgibbons, Fitzgibbon (*Eng., Ir.*) The son of Gibbon or Gib, a pet form of Gilbert (pledge, bright).

Fitzhenry (*Eng., Ir.*) The son of Henry (home ruler).

Fitzhugh (*Eng., Ir.*) The son of Hugh (spirit; mind).

Fitzmaurice, Fitzmorris (*Eng., Ir.*) The son of Maurice or Morris (moorish or dark-skinned).

Fitzner (*Ger.*) Dweller at, or near, a pool.

Fitzpatrick (*Ir., Eng.*) The son of Patrick (noble or patrician).

Fitzsimmons, Fitzsimons (*Ir., Eng.*) The son of Simon (gracious hearing; hearkening; snub-nosed).

Fitzwater, Fitzwalter (*Eng.*) The son of Walter (rule, folk or army).

Fiveash (*Eng.*) Dweller near five ash trees.

Fix (*Ger.*) Descendant of Fix, a pet form of Vitus (animated).

Fixler, Fixman (*Ger.*) Descendant of Friede, a short form of Fridulf (peace, wolf).

Fjeld (*Nor.*) Dweller on the hill or mountain.

Fjeldstad (*Nor.*) Dweller on the mountain farm.

Fjellman (*Nor., Sw.*) Dweller on the mountain.

Flack, Flach (*Ger.*) Dweller at the plain or level field.

Flagg, Flagge (*Eng.*) One who came from Flagg (sod, turf), in Derbyshire.

Flagler (*Ger., Eng.*) One who makes and sells plows; one who plows the fields; one who paved with flat stones.

Flagstad (*Nor.*) One who came from Flagstad (windy place), in Norway.

Flaherty (*Ir.*) Grandson of Flaithbheartach (bright ruler).

Flakes, Flake (*Ger.*) Dweller on a flat, level field.

Flakus (*Pol., Ukr.*) One who sold tripe.

Flamm, Flam, Flamme (*Ger.*) Dweller at the sign of the flame; one who works with a flame such as a smith.

Flanagan, Flanigan, Flannigan, Flannagan (*Ir.*) The little ruddy man; grandson of little Flann (red).

Flanders (*Eng.*) One who came from Flanders (plain), a medieval county extending along the coast of the low countries.

Flannery, Flanery (*Ir.*) Grandson of Flannabhra (red eyebrows).

Flasch, Flesch, Flaschen (*Ger.*) Dweller at the sign of the flask or bottle, generally designating a tavern.

Flashman (*Eng.*) Dweller by the pool or bog.

Flaska (*Pol.*) One who made and sold small bottles and flasks.

Flatley (*Eng., Ir.*) Dweller in a grove on flat, level ground; grandson of Flaitile (prince; poet).

Flatt (*Eng.*) Dweller on the level ground.

Flattery (*Ir.*) Grandson of Flaitre (prince; poet).

Flaubert (*Fr.*) Descendant of Flobert (glory, bright).

Flauter (*Eng.*) One who played a flute.

Flavin (*Ir.*) Grandson of little Flaitheamh (lord).

Flaws (*Scot.*) One who came from Flawis, in the Orkney Islands.

Flaxman, Flaxer, Flax (*Eng.*) One who dealt in flax or who produced linen from flax.

Flebbe (*Ger.*) One with a wide or big mouth.

Fleche (*Fr.*) The archer; one who made and sold arrows.

Fleck (*Eng., Ger.*) One with a disfiguring spot or mark; dweller on a small plot of land.

Fleckenstein (*Ger.*) Dweller on stony ground.

Fleet (*Eng.*) One who came from Fleet (stream), the name of six places in England.

Fleetwood (*Eng.*) Dweller in, or near, a wood by a stream.

Flegel, Flegle (*Ger.*) One who threshes or flails grain.

Fleig, Fleigel, Fleigle (*Ger.*) The fly, a nickname for a small, insignificant man.

Fleischer, Fleisher (*Ger.*) One who cut and sold meats, a butcher.

Fleischhauer (*Ger.*) The hewer, or cutter, of meat, a butcher.

Fleischman, Fleischmann, Fleishman (*Eng., Ger.*) One who sold meat, a butcher.

Fleming, Flemming (*Eng.*) One who came from Flanders, a medieval county extending along the coast of the Low Countries.

Flescher, Flesch (*Ger.*) Dweller at the sign of the flask or bottle, generally designating a tavern; one who made and sold flasks.

Fletcher, Flecher (*Eng.*) One who made, or sold, arrows, and sometimes bows as well.

Flexman (*Eng.*) Variant of Flaxman, q.v.

Flick (*Eng., Ger.*) A variant of Fleck, q.v.

Flickinger (*Ger.*) One who patches or repairs things; one who came from Flickingen (repair place), in Germany.

Flieger (*Ger.*) One who plows the soil, a plowman.

Flight (*Eng.*) One who fought with the

longbow; the contentious man, one engaged in strife.

Flinchum (*Eng.*) One who came from Flintham (homestead where flints were found), in Nottinghamshire.

Flink, Flinker (*Du., Ger.*) The sturdy, stalwart man; the quick, active man.

Flint (*Eng.*) Descendant of Flint (rock or flint); one who came from Flint, a town and county in Wales.

Flodin, Floden, Flodeen (*Sw.*) One who came from Floda, in Sweden.

Flodstrom (*Sw.*) River stream.

Flom (*Nor.*) Dweller on land subject to flooding.

Flood (*Eng.*) Dweller at, or near, the place where a stream often overflows; descendant of Floyd (gray).

Florczak (*Pol.*) Descendant of little Florek, a pet form of Florian (flowering or blooming).

Florek (*Pol.*) Descendant of little Flor, a pet form of Florian (flowering or blooming).

Florence (*Eng.*) Descendant of Florence (flourishing), a name used by both men and women in the Middle Ages; one who came from Florence (flourishing), in Italy.

Flores (*Sp.*) Dweller near where flowers grew.

Florian (*Eng.*) Descendant of Florian (flowering or blooming).

Florio (*It.*) Dweller, or worker, among flowers.

Floros (*Gr.*) Dweller at the sign of the green finch or linnet.

Florsheim (*Ger.*) One who came from Florsheim (swampy habitation), in Germany.

Flory, Fleury (*Fr.*) One who came from Fleury (place where flowers grew), the name of several places in France; descendant of Flory, a pet form of Florence, Flora and Florian (blooming or flowering).

Flosi (*It.*) The soft, weak, flabby person.

Floss, Flossman (*Ger.*) One who floats timber on a raft.

Flournoy (*Fr.*) Dweller in the place of flowers.

Flowers, Flower (*Eng., Wel.*) One who made arrows; descendant of Flower or Flour (flower); or of Llywarch (chief).

Floyd (*Wel.*) Descendant of Lloyd (gray).

Flucker, Flucke, Fluck (*Scot.*) Descendant of Fluckart, a variant of Folkard (people, hard).

Fluder (*Ger.*) Dweller in, or near, a swamp.

Fluke (*Eng.*) Descendant of Folc or Fulke (people).

Fluker (*Scot.*) Variant of Folker, q.v.

Fly, Flye (*Eng.*) One thought to possess some characteristic of a fly.

Flyer (*Ger.*) One who is a refugee, fugitive, or deserter.

Flynn, Flinn (*Ir.*) The red-haired or ruddy-complexioned man.

Fobes, Fobbs, Fobb, Fobs (*Eng.*) Descendant of Fobba.

Foch (*Fr.*) One who came from Foix, in France.

Focht (*Ger.*) One who fights, a soldier.

Fodor (*Hun., Bulg., Pol., Rus., Ukr.*) One with curly hair; descendant of Feodor, Slavic form of Theodore (gift of God).

Foeller (*Ger.*) One who shares a residence with another.

Foelsch (*Ger.*) Descendant of Fulco, a pet form of names beginning with Volk (people), as Folcman and Fulkerich.

Foerster, Foerstner (*Ger.*) A forest warden or game keeper.

Fogarty, Fogerty (*Ir.*) Descendant of the exiled man.

Fogel, Fogle (*Ger., Du.*) Dweller at the sign of the bird; one with birdlike characteristics.

Fogg (*Eng.*) Descendant of Fogg, a pet form of Fulcher (people, army).

Fohrman (*Ger.*) Variant of Fuhrmann, q.v.

Folan (*Ir.*) The son of little Faol (wolf).

Foldes (*Hun.*) One who owned land.

Folds (*Eng.*) Dweller, or worker, at the fold or cattle pen.

Foley, Foly (*Ir.*) Grandson of Foghlaidh (plunderer).

Folger, Folgers (*Ger.*) A follower or vassal; descendant of Folcger (folk, spear).

Foljambe (*Eng.*) One with a useless or maimed leg.

Folk, Folkes (*Eng.*) Descendant of Fulk (people); or of Folk, a pet form of names beginning with Volk (people), as Folcger and Folcmar.

Folker, Folkers (*Ger., Eng.*) Descendant of Folcger (people, spear); or of Fulcher (people, army).

Folkman, Folkmann (*Ger.*) Descendant of Folcman (people, man).

Folland (*Nor.*) One who came from Folland (beach where it is difficult to land), in Norway.

Follansbee, Follensbee (*Eng.*) One who came from Follingsby in Durham.

Follett, Follette (*Fr.*) The little foolish person.

Folliard (*Fr.*) The silly or foolish man.

Follmann, Follman (*Ger.*) Variant of Folkman, q.v.

Follmer, Folmer (*Eng., Ger.*) One who came from Fulmer (lake frequented by birds), in Buckinghamshire; or from Falmer (pleasant lake), in Sussex; descendant of Folcmar (people, fame).

Folsom (*Eng.*) One who came from Foulsham (Foghel's homestead), in Norfolk.

Folstaff (*Eng.*) Descendant of Fastolf (firm, wolf).

Folton (*Eng., Scot.*) One who came from Fulton (fowl enclosure), in Roxburghshire.

Foltz, Folz (*Ger.*) Descendant of Foltz, a short form of names beginning with Volk (people), as Fulcger, Fulcmar, and Fulculf.

Fomby (*Eng.*) One who came from Formby (Forni's homestead), in Lancashire.

Fonseca (*Port., Sp.*) Dweller near a dry well or dry spring; one who came from Fonseca (dry spring), in Spain.

Font (*Fr.*) Dweller at the spring.

Fontaine (*Fr., Eng.*) One who came from Fontaine (spring), in France; dweller near a spouting spring or pool.

Fontana, Fontano, Fontanetta (*It.*) Dweller at, or near, a spring.

Fontanez (*Sp.*) The son of Fontan (fountain).

Fonte, Font (*Port., It., Eng.*) One who came from Fonte (spring), the name of places in Portugal and Italy; dweller near the fountain or spring; dweller near the Font, a river in Northumberland.

Fontenot, Fontenay, Fonteneau (*Fr.*) Dweller near the small springs; one who came from one of the many villages in France with similar spellings, and derivations.

Fonville (*Fr.*) One who came from Fonville, in France.

Foote, Foot (*Eng.*) Dweller at the lower part of the hill.

Foraker (*Eng.*) Dweller at the four acre enclosure.

Foran (*Ir.*) Descendant of the little, cold man.

Forberg (*Nor., Sw.*) One who came from Forberg (protruding ledge of a hill; hill where pines grew), the name of eight places in Norway; pine tree mountain; fodder hill.

Forbes, Forbis (*Scot.*) One who came from Forbes (field place), in Aberdeenshire.

Forcett (*Eng.*) One who came from Forcett (cattle pen by a ford), in the North Riding of Yorkshire.

Ford, Forde, Forder (*Eng.*) Dweller, or worker, at a stream crossing; one who came from Ford (shallow river crossing), the name of six places in England.

Fordham (*Eng.*) One who came from Fordham (homestead by a river crossing), the name of several places in England.

Fordyce (*Scot.*) One who came from Fordyce (south woodland), in Banffshire.

Foreman, Forman (*Eng.*) One who tended pigs; one who supervises the

work of others, an overseer; dweller
by a ford.

Forester (*Eng.*) Dweller, or worker, in
the forest; a woodman.

Forgan (*Scot., Wel.*) One who came
from Forgan, in Fife; Welsh variant
of Morgan, q.v.

Forgeron (*Fr.*) One who worked in iron,
a blacksmith.

Forget, Forgett (*Fr.*) Descendant of
Fargeau (of iron), a variant of
Ferreolus; dweller, or worker, at the
little forge.

Forgue (*Fr.*) One who worked in metals,
usually iron, a blacksmith.

Forman (*Eng.*) One in charge of the pigs,
a swineherd.

Formanski (*Pol.*) One who attended on a
coach, a coachman.

Formund (*Eng., Scot.*) Descendant of
Farmund (kindred, protection); one
who came from the lands of For-
mond, in Fife.

Fornaciari (*It.*) One who worked at a
furnace; one who worked in metal.

Fornek (*Pol.*) One who drove a wagon or
cart, a carter.

Fornell, Fornall (*Fr.*) The man who had
charge of the oven, a baker.

Forner (*Ger.*) Dweller on, or near, a
meadow where ferns grew.

Forness (*Eng.*) Variant of Furness, q.v.

Forney (*Ice.*) Descendant of Forni
(ancient one).

Fornier (*Fr.*) Variant of Fournier, q.v.

Forrest, Forest (*Eng.*) Dweller at, or in,
a large wood or forest.

Forrester (*Eng.*) An officer in charge of
the forest for a king or lord; the
worker in the forest.

Forristall, Forrestall (*Ir.*) Custodian of
the forest, a gamekeeper.

Fors (*Sw.*) Waterfall.

Forsberg (*Sw.*) Waterfall mountain.

Forshaw (*Eng.*) Dweller in, or near, the
fore or front wood.

Forslund (*Sw.*) Waterfall grove.

Forsman (*Sw.*) Dweller near a waterfall.

Forst, Forste, Forstner (*Ger.*) Dweller in,
or near, a forest.

Forster, Forester (*Eng.*) A forest warden,
or game keeper, a manor official.

Forsyth, Forsythe (*Scot.*) One who came
from Forsyth, in Scotland; descendant of Fearsithe (man of peace).

Fort, Forte (*Eng., It., Fr.*) Descendant
of Fort (strong); the strong man.

Fortenberry, Fortenbery, Fortenbury
(*Ger.*) One who came from Fur-
tenbach, in Germany.

Fortgang (*Ger.*) Dweller at the path or
way leading to the gate.

Forth, Forthman (*Eng.*) Dweller at the
shallow river crossing.

Fortier (*Fr.*) One employed at a fortress; one who made and sold gim-
lets.

Fortin (*Eng., Fr.*) One who came from
Forton (homestead by a ford), the
name of several places in England;
dweller near the little fort; descendant of little Fort (strong).

Fortino (*Sp.*) Dweller near a small fortified place; one with little strength, a
weakling.

Fortman (*Eng.*) The man with strong
hands.

Fortner (*Ger.*) Dweller near the ford or
river crossing; one who had charge
of the door or gate.

Fortson (*Eng.*) The son of the strong
man.

Fortuna (*It.*) Descendant of Fortuna
(good fortune), a name sometimes
given to foundlings.

Fortunato (*It.*) The fortunate person.

Fortune (*Eng., Scot.*) The fortunate or
lucky person; one who came from
the lands of Fortune, in East Lothian.

Forward (*Eng.*) One who took care of
pigs, a swineherd.

Fosco (*It.*) One with a dark complexion.

Fosdick, Fosdike, Fosdyke (*Eng.*) One
who came from Fosdyke (Fot's
ditch), in Lincolnshire.

Foss, Fosse (*Ger., Eng., Fr., Nor.*)
Dweller at the sign of the fox; one
with the qualities of a fox; dweller
near a waterfall; dweller near a ditch
or trench.

Fossen, Fossum (*Nor.*) One who came from Fossen (pasture by a waterfall), the name of several places in Norway.

Fossett (*Eng.*) Dweller by the small ditch.

Foster (*Eng.*) One in charge of a forest, a forest warden; a gamekeeper, a manor official.

Foston (*Eng.*) One who came from Foston (Fot's homestead), the name of five places in England.

Fothergill (*Eng.*) Dweller in Fother's ravine.

Fotopoulos, Fotopulos (*Gr.*) The son of Photes (light).

Foucher, Fouche, Fouch (*Fr.*) Descendant of Folchari (people, army); one who mows or reaps crops.

Foulkes, Foulke, Foulk, Foulks (*Wel., Eng.*) Descendant of Foulk or Fulk (people).

Fountain, Fountaine (*Fr.*) Dweller at, or near, a spouting spring.

Fournier (*Fr.*) One who baked bread, a baker.

Fowkes, Fowke (*Eng.*) Descendant of Foulk or Fulk (people).

Fowle (*Eng.*) Dweller at the sign of the bird, especially a game bird.

Fowler (*Eng.*) The bird-catcher or gamekeeper.

Fowlkes (*Eng.*) Descendant of Foulk or Fulk (people).

Fox, Foxx (*Eng.*) Dweller at the sign of the fox; one with some of the qualities of a fox.

Foxboro, Foxborough (*Eng.*) Dweller near a fox burrow.

Foxton (*Eng.*) One who came from Foxton (village frequented by foxes; valley of the foxes), the name of five places in England.

Foxworth, Foxworthy (*Eng.*) Dweller at the homestead infested by foxes.

Foy, Foye (*Eng., Ir.*) One who came from Foy (the church of St. Mwy), in Herefordshire; the reasonable man; grandson of Fiaich (raven).

Foyer (*Scot.*) One who came from Foyers (terraced slope), in Inverness.

Fracassi (*It.*) The braggadocio, a loud bully.

Fradin (*Fr.*) The bad, wicked man.

Fraerman (*Ger.*) The free man, one not under obligation of service to a lord.

Fraga (*Fr.*) Dweller near a thicket of brambles; one who gathered and sold raspberries.

Frahm, Frahmke (*Ger.*) Descendant of Frumold (first, bold).

Frain, Frane, Frayne, Frayn (*Eng.*) Dweller by an ash tree.

Frale, Fraile (*Eng.*) The frail, weak man.

Fraley, Frailey (*Ger.*) American variant of Froelich, q.v.

Frame, Frames (*Eng.*) The vigorous, bold man.

Frampton (*Eng.*) One who came from Frampton (homestead on the Frome river; Freola's people's village), the name of several places in Dorset and Gloucestershire.

France, Francia (*Eng., Scot.*) One who came from France (land of the Franks or freemen); descendant of France, a pet form of Francis (free).

Franceschi, Francesconi (*It.*) Descendant of Francesco, Italian form of Francis (free).

Franceschini, Franceschina (*It.*) Descendant of Franceschini, an Italian variant of Francesco (free).

Franchi, Franchini, Franchina (*It.*) Descendant of Francesco, Italian form of Francis (free).

Francis (*Wel., Eng., Fr.*) Descendant of Francis (free).

Francisco, Francesco (*Sp., It.*) Descendant of Francisco or Francesco, Spanish and Italian forms of Francis (free).

Franck (*Ger.*) Descendant of Franck, German form of Frank (free).

Franckowiak (*Pol.*) Descendant of Franck, German form of Frank (the free).

Franco (*Sp., Port., It.*) One who came from Franco (free) in Spain; descendant of Franco, Spanish and Italian form of Frank (free).

Francois (*Fr.*) Descendant of Francois, a French form of Francis (free).

Francuz (*Pol.*) One who came from France, a Frenchman.

Franczak, Franczyk (*Pol.*) Descendant of Franciszek, Polish form of Francis (free).

Frandsen (*Dan., Sw.*) The son of Frands, a form of Francis (free).

Frangella, Frangello (*It.*) Dweller at the sign of the finch.

Frangos (*Gr.*) Descendant of Frangos, a shortened form of Frankiskos, Greek form of Frank (free); one who came from West Europe.

Frank, Franks, Franke, Franck, Francke, Franken (*Ger.*) One who came from Franconia, in central Germany; the free man; descendant of Frank (the free).

Frankel, Frankle (*Ger., Fr.*) Descendant of little Frank (free); one who came from France; one who came from Franken, the German form of Franconia, an old duchy in south central Germany.

Frankenberger, Frankenberg (*Ger.*) One who came from Frankenberg (the hill of the Franks), in Saxony.

Frankenstein (*Ger.*) One who came from Frankenstein (the Frank's stone), the name of several places in Germany. The name has been impaired by the monster created by Frankenstein in the tale by Mary W. Shelley.

Frankfort, Frankfurt, Frankfurter (*Ger.*) One who came from Frankfort or Frankfurt (ford of the Franks), in Germany.

Franklin, Franklyn (*Eng.*) A freeholder who held substantial land for which he paid only a small rent and who rendered little or no service to the lord.

Frankovich (*Rus.*) The son of Frank (the free).

Frankowiak (*Pol.*) Descendant of Franek, a pet form of Franciszek (free).

Frankton (*Eng.*) One who came from Frankton (Franca's homestead), in Warwickshire.

Fransen, Franson (*Sw., Nor., Du.*) The son of Frans (free).

Franz, Frantz, Franze (*Ger.*) Descendant of Franz, German form of Francis (free).

Franzen (*Sw.*) The son of Franz (free).

Frase, Fraze (*Fr.*) One who raised and sold strawberries.

Fraser, Frasier, Frasher (*Scot., Ir.*) Variant of Frazier, q.v.

Fratto (*It.*) Dweller near a briar patch.

Frauenhoffer (*Ger.*) One who came from Frauenhof or Frauenhofen (the woman's homestead), the names of places in Germany.

Frawley (*Ir.*) Grandson of Fergal or Farrell (super-valor).

Frazier, Frazer, Fraizer (*Scot., Ir.*) One who came from Friesland, a Frisian.

Frear (*Eng.*) Descendant of the friar.

Frearson (*Eng.*) The son of the friar.

Frech, Freake (*Ger.*) The bold man.

Frechette, Freche (*Fr.*) One who came from Frechet or Freche (ash trees), the names of several places in France.

Freckelton (*Eng.*) One who came from Freckleton (Frecla's homestead), in Lancashire.

Freda (*It.*) Descendant of Freda, a pet form of Friderico, a variant of Frederick (peace, rule).

Frederick, Fredrick, Fredericks, Fredricks (*Ger., Eng.*) Descendant of Frederick (peace, rule).

Frederickson, Fredricksen, Fredriksen, Fredrikson (*Sw., Nor., Dan.*) The son of Fredrik, Scandinavian form of Frederick (peace, rule).

Free (*Eng.*) The free-born man; one who held land for which he paid little or no rent and rendered no service to the lord.

Freeberg, Freeburg (*Ger.*) Variant of Freiberg, q.v.

Freeborn, Freeburn (*Eng.*) One born free; descendant of Freobeorn (peace, warrior).

Freed, Frid (*Sw.*) Peace (of mind or soul), a Swedish soldier name.

Freedberg, Fredberg (*Sw.*) One who came from Fredberg (peaceful mountain), in Sweden.

Freedman (*Ger.*) Variant of Friedman, q.v.

Freel (*Eng.*) The frail, weak man.

Freeland (*Eng.*) Dweller, or worker, on land held without obligation of rent or service.

Freeling, Freehling (*Ger.*) One who came from Frieling or Frielingen (freed men), in Germany; one born in the spring; or prematurely born.

Freelove (*Eng.*) Descendant of Frithulaf (peace, survivor).

Freely (*Ir.*) Grandson of Fearghal (super-valor).

Freeman (*Eng.*) The free man, one whose status was just above that of a serf; one who owned land but was not of noble birth.

Freemantle (*Eng.*) One who came from Freemantle (cold cloak), in Hampshire.

Freemark, Freimark (*Ger.*) Dweller in, or near, a market town or place with special priorities or privileges.

Freemond, Freemon (*Fr., Eng.*) Descendant of Fremond (peace, protection); variant of Freeman, q.v.

Freeney, Freeny (*Eng.*) Dweller near an ash tree; one who came from Fraisnes (ash), in France; or from one of the similarly spelled French villages.

Freer (*Eng.*) Descendant of the friar.

Freese (*Eng., Ger.*) One who came from Friesland, in Holland.

Freeston (*Eng.*) One who came from Freston (the Frisian's homestead), in Suffolk.

Frei (*Ger.*) The free man, one whose status was above that of a serf.

Freiberg, Freiberger (*Ger.*) One who came from Freiberg (free mountain), in Saxony.

Freid, Freiden, Freides (*Ger.*) Descendant of Friede, a pet form of Friederich, German form of Frederick (peace, rule).

Freidheim (*Ger.*) One who came from Friedheim (peaceful homestead), in Germany.

Freidhof (*Ger.*) Dweller near the cemetery or churchyard.

Freidin, Freidinger (*Ger.*) The faithless, flighty, refractory person.

Freilich (*Ger.*) The freed or enfranchised man.

Freiman, Freimann (*Ger.*) The free man, one whose status was just above that of a serf; one who owned land but was not of noble birth.

Freimark (*Ger.*) Dweller at a boundary of a settlement having special privileges.

Freimiller, Freimuller (*Ger.*) The miller who was free from the control of the lord.

Freimuth (*Ger.*) One with a noble disposition.

Freiser (*Ger.*) One who is unjustly severe, a ruthless tyrant or blood-thirsty villain; a pirate.

Freisinger (*Ger.*) One who came from Freising, in Germany.

Freitag, Freytag (*Ger.*) Descendant of Freitag, the name sometimes given to one born on Friday.

Freitas (*Port.*) One who came from Freitas, in Portugal.

Freiwald (*Ger.*) Dweller in, or near, the free woods, that is, the place where peasants could freely take branches and logs.

Frelich, Frelix (*Ger.*) Variant of Froelich, q.v.

Fremling (*Sw.*) The stranger or recent arrival.

Fremont (*Fr.*) Descendant of Fremond (peace, protection).

French (*Eng., Scot.*) One who came from France, a Frenchman.

Frenette (*Fr.*) Dweller near ash trees.

Frenkel (*Ger.*) Variant of Frankel, q.v.

Frenz, Frenzel (*Ger.*) Descendant of Frenz, a pet form of Franziscus, German form of Francis (free).

Freres, Frere (*Eng.*) Descendant of the friar; a member of a religious order, a friar. At the Reformation many of the friars renounced their vows of chastity and married.

Frese (*Ger.*) One who came from Friesland, a Frisian.

Freshwater (*Eng.*) One who came from

Freshwater (river with fresh water), in Wight.

Fresno (*Sp.*) One who came from Fresno (ash trees), in Spain; dweller near an ash tree.

Frett, Fretter (*Eng.*) One who made and sold interlaced work consisting of jewels or flowers in a network used as an ornament usually for the hair.

Fretwell (*Eng.*) One who came from Fritwell (wishing spring), in Oxfordshire.

Freud (*Ger.*) The gay or joyful man.

Freudenberg (*Ger.*) One who came from Freudenberg (pleasure mountain), the name of four places in Germany.

Freudenthal (*Ger.*) One who came from Freudenthal (pleasure valley), the name of two places in Germany.

Freund, Freundt (*Ger.*) An esteemed person, a friend.

Freundlich (*Ger.*) The pleasant, friendly man.

Frew (*Eng., Scot.*) Variant of Free, q.v.; one who came from Frew (stream), in Perthshire.

Frey (*Nor., Ger.*) One who worshiped Frey, the Norse god of love, marriage and fruitfulness; variant of Frei, q.v.

Freyer, Friar (*Eng.*) A member of a religious order, a friar or brother; descendant of the friar. At the Reformation many friars renounced their vows of chastity and married. Nickname for a guildsman.

Friberg (*Ger., Sw.*) Variant of Freiberg, q.v.; free mountain.

Fricano (*It.*) One who had been to Africa and returned; the black-haired, dark-complexioned man.

Frick, Fricke (*Eng., Swis., Ger.*) The bold or brave man; one who came from Frick, in Switzerland; descendant of Frick, a pet form of Friedrich, German form of Frederick (peace, rule).

Fricot (*Fr.*) Descendant of Fricard (bold, strong).

Fridell, Friddle (*Fr.*) The peaceful man.

Fried, Friede (*Ger.*) Descendant of Fried, a pet form of Friedrich (peace, rule).

Friedberg (*Ger.*) One who came from Friedberg (peaceful mountain), the name of three places in Germany.

Frieder (*Ger.*) Descendant of Friederich (peace, rule).

Friedhoff, Friedhof (*Ger.*) Dweller near the cemetery.

Friedl, Friedel, Friedle (*Ger.*) Descendant of Friedl, a pet form of Friedilo (peaceful); or of Friedrich (peace, rule).

Friedlander, Friedland (*Ger.*) One who came from Friedland (peaceful country), the name of towns in Brandenburg and Mecklenburg, Germany.

Friedlund (*Sw., Ger.*) Peace grove; one who came from Friedland (quiet place), in Germany.

Friedman, Friedmann (*Ger.*) Descendant of Friduman (peace or security, man); a Germanized form of the name Solomon (peaceful), a form adopted by Jews.

Friedrich, Friedrichs (*Ger.*) Descendant of Friedrich (peace, rule).

Friel (*Ger.*) Descendant of Friel, a variant of Fride (peace).

Frieling (*Eng.*) Son of Frithel (weak).

Friend (*Ger., Eng.*) An esteemed person, a friend.

Frierson (*Eng.*) The son of the friar.

Fries, Friese, Friesen, Friess (*Ger.*) One who came from Frisia, in northern Germany.

Friesenhahn (*Ger.*) One who came from Friesenhagen, in Germany.

Friesleben (*Ger.*) One who leads a free life.

Frighetto (*It.*) One who made and sold small frying pans.

Frigo (*It.*) One who came from Friesland.

Friis (*Dan., Nor., Sw.*) One who came from Friesland, a Frisian.

Frink, Frinkle (*Eng.*) Descendant of Frank (free).

Fript (*Eng.*) Dweller at the village.

Frisbie, Frisby, Frisbee, Frisbey (*Eng.*) One who came from Frisby (the

165

Frisian's village), the name of two places in Leicestershire.

Frisk (*Sw.*) Sound; healthy.

Frison (*Fr.*) One who gathered and sold wild cherries; or who dealt in frise, a wool material; one who came from Frizon (Friso's village), in France.

Fritsch, Fritsche, Fritscher (*Ger.*) Descendant of Fritz, a pet form of Friedrich, German form of Frederick (peace, rule).

Fritschi (*Swis.*) Variant of Fritsch, q.v.

Fritz, Fritze (*Ger.*) Descendant of Fritz, a pet form of Friedrich (peace, rule).

Frizzell, Frissell, Frizell (*Scot.*) Early forms of Frazier, q.v.

Froberg (*Ger.*) One who came from Frohberg (pleasant mountain), in Germany.

Frobisher (*Eng.*) One who furbishes or polishes armor or weapons.

Froebel (*Ger.*) Dweller near a willow tree.

Froehlich, Froelich, Frohlich, Fralick (*Ger.*) The merry or cheerful person; the wise person.

Froggatt (*Eng.*) One who came from Froggatt, in Derbyshire.

Frogner (*Nor.*) One who came from Frogner, the name of several places in Norway.

Frohmann, Frohman (*Ger.*) The pious, devout, religious man; the gay, happy man.

Froid (*Sw.*) Joy; delight.

Fromm, From, Frome, Froom (*Ger., Eng.*) The quiet, pious, or devout man; one who came from Frome (from the Frome river), the name of several places in England.

Fronczak, Fronczyk, Frontczak, Frontzak (*Pol., Ger.*) Descendant of little Franz, a German form of Francis (free).

Frosch, Froschle (*Ger.*) Dweller at the sign of the frog.

Froseth (*Nor.*) One who came from Froset (Freyr's, the god's, dwelling), in Norway.

Frost (*Eng., Wel.*) Descendant of Frost

(one born at the time of frost); a contraction of Forrest, q.v.; one cold in behavior or temperament.

Frothingham (*Eng.*) One who came from Frodingham (the settlement of Froda's people), the name of places in Lancashire and Yorkshire.

Fruchter (*Ger.*) One who came from Frucht (place where fruit was produced), in Germany.

Frueh, Fruh (*Ger.*) One in the habit of rising early in the morning.

Fruehauf, Fruhauf (*Ger.*) One born before marriage of parents; one in the habit of rising early in the morning.

Fruendt (*Ger.*) One who was a friend or companion.

Frugoli (*It.*) One who made rockets; nickname for an active, lively man.

Fruhstuck (*Ger.*) One who prepared breakfast.

Fruhwirth (*Ger.*) Dweller in, or keeper of, the inn where breakfast was served.

Frumkin (*Rus.*) Descendant of Frumke, a dim. of Fruma (pious).

Fry, Frye (*Eng.*) The free man, i.e., free of obligations to the lord of the manor.

Fryc (*Pol.*) Descendant of Fryc, pet form of Fryderyka, Polish form of Frederick (peace, rule).

Frydenberg (*Dan., Nor.*) One who came from Frydenberg, the name of places in Denmark and Norway.

Frydenlund (*Nor.*) One who came from Frydenlund, the name of three places in Norway.

Frydman (*Sw.*) Descendant of Fridmund (peace, protection).

Frydrych (*Pol.*) Descendant of Frydrych, a Polish form of Frederick (peace, rule).

Fryer (*Eng.*) Variant of Freyer, q.v.

Frystak, Frystack (*Pol.*) Descendant of Frys, a pet form of Franciszek (free), and of Fryderyk (peace, rule).

Fu (*Chin.*) Teacher.

Fuad (*Arab.*) Descendant of Fuad (heart).

Fuchs (*Ger.*) One who lived at the sign

of the fox; one with foxlike characteristics; one who came from Fuchs (fox), in Germany.

Fuentes, Fuente (*Sp.*) One who came from Fuentes or Fuente (fountain; spring), the name of many places in Spain; dweller near a spring.

Fuertes (*Sp.*) One who came from Fuertes (fortification), in Spain; descendant of Fuertes, a variant of Fortunio (fortune).

Fugate (*Eng.*) Dweller at the fowl gate.

Fuggiti (*It.*) One who has run away or escaped.

Fuglsang (*Ger.*) Dweller in field where birds sang; dweller in a place cleared by fire frequented by birds.

Fugman (*Eng.*) The servant of Fuge, a pet form of Fulcher (people, army).

Fuhrmann, Fuhrman, Fuhrer, Fuhr (*Ger.*) One who drove a wagon or cart, a carter.

Fuhs (*Ger.*) Dweller near a stream.

Fujii (*Jap.*) Wisteria, well.

Fujikawa (*Jap.*) Wisteria, river.

Fujimoto (*Jap.*) Wisteria, base.

Fujioka (*Jap.*) Wisteria, hill.

Fujita (*Jap.*) Wisteria, rice field.

Fukuda (*Jap.*) Good luck, rice field.

Fukumoto (*Jap.*) Good luck, base.

Fulbright (*Eng.*) Descendant of Fulbeorht (people, bright).

Fulcher (*Eng.*) Descendant of Fulcher (people, army).

Fulford (*Eng.*) One who came from Fulford (dirty river crossing), the name of several places in England.

Fulgham, Fulghum, Fulgiam, Fulgium (*Eng.*) One who came from Foulsham (Fugol's homestead), in Norfolk; dweller in a foul or dirty place; or in a place frequented by wild birds.

Fulham, Fullam (*Eng.*) One who came from Fulham (Fulla's homestead), in Middlesex.

Fulk (*Eng.*) Descendant of Fulk (people).

Fulkerson, Fulcher (*Eng.*) The son of Fulker (people, guard), or of Fulk (people).

Fuller (*Eng.*) One who cleaned and thickened cloth.

Fullerton (*Eng.*) One who came from Fullerton (the village of the bird-catchers), in Hampshire.

Fullilove, Fullalove (*Eng.*) One who is "full of love," a nickname for one with a passionate affection for one of the opposite sex.

Fullington (*Eng.*) One who came from Folkington (the village of Fulca's people), in Sussex.

Fulljames (*Eng.*) One who had a useless or maimed leg.

Fullman (*Eng.*) The foul or dirty man; descendant of Folcman (people, man).

Fulmer, Fullmer, Fulmore, Fullmore (*Eng., Ger.*) One who came from Fulmer (lake frequented by birds), in Buckinghamshire; descendant of Folcmar (people, fame).

Fulop (*Hun.*) Descendant of Fulop, Hungarian form of Philip (lover of horses).

Fulsang (*Ger.*) Variant of Fuglsang, q.v.

Fulson (*Eng.*) One who came from Foulsham (homestead frequented by birds).

Fulton (*Scot.*) One who came from Fulton (fowl enclosure), in Roxburghshire.

Fultz (*Ger.*) Descendant of Fulco, a short form of names beginning with Volk (people), as Folcward and Fulculf.

Fulwood, Fullwood (*Eng.*) One who came from Fulwood (dirty wood), in Lancashire.

Fumo, Fumi (*It.*) The haughty or vain man.

Fung (*Chin.*) To mount.

Funk, Funke, Funck (*Ger.*) The sparkling or animated person.

Funkhouser (*Ger.*) Dweller near the house where there was a smith's forge; one who came from Funkenhausen (spark house), in Germany.

Funo (*Jap.*) Cloth, field.

Funston (*Eng.*) Dweller at the homestead by the spring or fountain.

Fuqua (*Fr.*) Descendant of Folc (people); or of Fulcward (people, guardian).

Furber, Furbur (*Eng., Scot.*) One who furbishes or polishes armor or weapons.

Furey (*Ir.*) Grandson of Fiodhabhra (bushy eyebrows).

Furguson (*Scot.*) Variant of Ferguson, q.v.

Furlong (*Eng., Ir.*) Dweller at, or near, the furlong, a designation of an area rectangular in shape, and as long as the distance the plow went without turning.

Furlough, Furlow (*Eng.*) One given permission to be absent; variant of Farlow, q.v.

Furman, Fuhrman, Fuhrmann (*Ger.*) One who conveyed passengers by boat across a stream, a ferryman; one who drove a wagon or cart, a carter.

Furmanek, Furmaniak, Furmanski (*Pol.*) One who drove a coach, a coachman.

Furnace (*Eng., Fr., Scot.*) Variant of Furness, q.v.; one who came from Furnace (a furnace), in Scotland.

Furnald (*Fr.*) Variant of Fernald, q.v.

Furnell (*Eng.*) One who came from Fournels or Fournols, in France.

Furness, Furniss (*Eng., Fr., Scot.*) One who came from Furness (podex headland), in Lancashire; one who came from Furneaux (furnaces), in France; or from Furness in Ross and Cromarty.

Furnish (*Eng., Fr.*) One who came from Furness (podex headland) in Lancashire, or from Furneaux (furnaces) in France.

Furnival (*Eng.*) One who came from Fournival (Furnus' domain), in France.

Furr (*Eng.*) One who made or sold garments of fur or garments so trimmed.

Furry, Furrey, Furey, Fury (*Ir., Scot.*) Grandson of Fiodhabhra (bushy eyebrows).

Furst, Fuerst (*Ger.*) One who acted the part of a prince in play or pageant; member of a prince's entourage.

Furtado (*Port.*) One who robs others.

Further, Furth (*Ger.*) One who came from Furth (ford), a Jewish suburb of Nurnberg, in Germany.

Furuta (*Jap.*) Old rice field.

Fury (*Fr.*) One who is inquisitive or nosy.

Fus (*Rom.*) Metonymic for one who made and sold spindles.

Fusco (*It.*) One with a dark or swarthy complexion; one of a disagreeable or antisocial nature.

Fuss (*Ger.*) One with a crippled or deformed foot.

Fussel (*Ger.*) One with a small foot.

Futrell (*Fr.*) One who came from Foutreau, in France.

Futterman, Futterer, Futter (*Ger.*) One who raised and sold fodder or feed for animals.

Fuzzey (*Fr.*) One who made and sold steel used to ignite combustibles.

Fyfe, Fyffe (*Scot.*) One who came from Fife or Fifeshire (named after Fib, one of the sons of Cruithne, legendary father of the Picts), in Scotland.

Gaal (*Du.*) Descendant of Gale (gay or lively).

Gaardbo (*Sw.*) Farm dwelling.

Gabay, Gabbay (*Heb.*) Treasurer of the congregation.

Gabe (*Eng.*) Descendant of Gabe, a pet form of Gabriel (strong man of God).

Gabel, Gable, Gabl, Gaebel (*Ger., Eng.*) One who made and sold agricultural implements, such as pitchforks; dweller by a fork in the road; one who came from Gabel (fork), in Germany; descendant of little Gabe, a pet form of Gabriel (strong man of God).

Gabler (*Eng.*) One who collected taxes.

Gabor (*Hun., Sl.*) Descendant of Gabor, Hungarian form of Gabriel (strong man of God).

Gabriel (*Eng., Fr.*) Descendant of Gabriel (strong man of God).

Gabrielsen, Gabrielson (*Dan., Nor.*) The son of Gabriel (strong man of God).

Gabrys, Gabrysiak, Gabryszak (*Pol.*) Descendant of Gabryel, Polish form of Gabriel (strong man of God).

Gac (*Pol.*) One engaged in fascine work.

Gach, Gache (*Pol.*) One who is fond of women, a ladies' man.

Gacki, Gacke, Gacek, Gaca (*Pol.*) One who worked with fascine, probably in protecting house walls for winter.

Gadberry, Gadbury (*Eng.*) Dweller near Gadd's fortified place.

Gadbois, Gadbaw (*Fr.*) Dweller at the sign of the woodcock.

Gaddis (*Eng.*) The son of Gadd (comrade).

Gaddy, Gaddey, Gaddie (*Eng.*) Descendant of little Gadd (comrade).

Gade, Gadson (*Eng.*) Descendant, or son, of Gade or Gad (comrade).

Gaden (*Ger.*) Dweller in a hut with one room.

Gadie (*Scot.*) One who came from Gadie (twig or branch), in Aberdeenshire.

Gadsden (*Eng.*) One who came from Gaddesden (Gaete's valley), in Hertfordshire.

Gadson (*Eng.*) Variant of Gadsden, q.v.; the son of Gadd (comrade).

Gadwell, Gadwill (*Eng.*) One who came from Gabwell (Gabba's spring), in Devonshire.

Gadzala (*Pol.*) One who conciliates or reconciles others, a peacemaker.

Gadzinski (*Pol.*) Dweller at the sign of the reptile; one thought to have the characteristics of a reptile.

Gaeding, Gaede, Gaedke (*Ger.*) Descendant of Gaddo, a pet form of Gadafrid (comrade, peace).

Gaertig (*Ger.*) Descendant of Gard, a pet form of names beginning with Gart (farmstead), as Gartlieb and Gardulf.

Gaetano, Gaeto (*It.*) One who came from Gaetano, in Italy.

Gaff (*Ir.*) The son of Eochaidh (rich in cattle).

Gaffen, Gaffin (*Scot., Ir., Fr.*) Sharpened form of Gavin, q.v.

Gaffey (*Ir.*) The son of Eochaidh (rich in cattle).

Gaffney, Gafeney (*Ir.*) Descendant of Gawain (calf).

Gafford (*Eng.*) Variant of Gifford, q.v.

Gage (*Eng.*) One who acted as pledge for another in the courts; one who measured or tested things.

Gagle, Gagler (*Ger.*) Dweller in, or near, a myrtle bog.

Gagliano (*It.*) Variant of Gallo, q.v.

Gagliardi, Gagliardo (*It.*) The strong, vigorous man; one who dances.

Gaglione (*It.*) One who raised and sold chickens; nickname for a man of large stature.

Gagne (*Fr.*) One who came from Gagne (Gannus' estate), in France; one who farmed land for which he paid rent.

Gagnon (*Fr.*) One who cultivated a plot of land, a peasant farmer.

Gahagan (*Ir.*) The son of little Eochaidh (rich in cattle).

Gahan (*Ir.*) Descendant of Gaoithin, a pet form of Maolghaoithe (chief of the wind).

Gail, Gaile (*Eng.*) Descendant of Gail (gay or lively); the gay or lively man.

Gailey (*Eng.*) One who came from Gailey (grove overgrown with bog myrtle), in Staffordshire.

Gaillard, Gailard (*Eng.*) The gay, lively man.

Gaines, Gaynes (*Eng.*) Descendant of Gegn (straight).

Gainsboro, Gainsborough (*Eng.*) One who came from Gainsborough (Gegn's fort), in Lincolnshire.

Gair (*Scot.*) The short man.

Gaither, Gaiter, Gaiters, Gaitor (*Eng.*) One who took care of goats, a goatherd.

Gaitskill (*Eng.*) One who came from Gatesgill (goat shelter), in Cumberland.

Gaizutis (*Lith.*) The bitter, sour person.

Gajda (*Rus., Cz.-Sl.*) One in the habit of using *gajda,* meaning "hi," or "hey" in exclamations; dweller in, or near, a wood.

Gajewski (*Pol.*) Dweller in, or near, a wood.

Gal (*Fr., Hun.*) Dweller at the sign of the rooster; the strutting, well-dressed man; descendant of Gal, a French form of Gall, a seventh century saint; dweller in the woods; one who came from Gal, in Hungary.

Galanis (*Gr.*) One with blue eyes.

Galanopoulos (*Gr.*) The son of the blue-eyed man.

Galante, Galanti (*It.*) The courteous man; the gallant, lady's man.

Galantiere (*Bel.*) The playful, sprightly man.

Galarza (*Sp.*) One who came from Galarza (stone mound), in Spain.

Galas, Gallas (*Fr.*) The elegant, gay, playful man.

Galasso, Galassi, Galassini (*It.*) Dweller at the sign of the large rooster; descendant of Galassi, an Italian form of Galahad (valorous); one who raised and sold chickens.

Galati, Galatti (*It.*) One who came from Galati, in Sicily.

Galban (*Sp., Fr.*) One who came from Galbe (curve), in France.

Galbraith, Galbreath, Galbreth (*Scot.*) A stranger or foreigner, especially the foreign Briton.

Gale (*Wel., Eng.*) Dweller near a jail; a gay or lively person.

Galecki, Galeckas, Galec, Galic (*Pol.*) Dweller at the sign of the crow; one who possessed the characteristics of a crow.

Galen, Galan (*Fr., Sl.*) The elegant, gay man; one who cultivated women, a boy friend or suitor.

Galer (*Eng.*) A jail keeper or turnkey.

Gales (*Eng.*) One who came from Wales, a Welshman.

Galey (*Eng.*) One who worked on a galley, the vessel propelled by both oars and sails.

Galicia (*Sp.*) One who came from Galicia (land of the Gallaici), a region in Spain.

Galindo, Galindez (*Sp.*) Descendant of Galindo, a form of Garin (spear, friend); one who came from Galindo (place of chickens), in Spain.

Galinski, Galinsky (*Ukr., Rus.*) One who raised and sold first grade grain.

Galioto, Galiotto (*It.*) A base, dishonest fellow, a rascal.

Galitz (*Ukr.*) One who came from Halyc, in the Ukraine.

Galka, Galkiewicz, Galkowski (*Pol.*) Dweller at the sign of the ball; or near a rounded hill.

Gall, Galle, Gahl (*Scot.*) The stranger or foreigner.

Gallacher, Gallaher (*Ir., Scot.*) Grandson of Gallchobhar (valorous victor; foreign help).

Gallagher, Gallegher, Gallaher, Galliger, Galligher (*Ir.*) The foreign helper or assistant; grandson of Gallchobhar (valorous victor; foreign help).

Gallant, Galante, Galland (*Eng., Fr.*) The gay, polite, brave person; one in gay or fine attire.

Gallardo (*Sp., It.*) Gallardo is a word originally used after a name to distinguish between others of the same name which eventually developed into a surname. It means "elegant, graceful." In Italy the name refers to a descendant of Gallardo, Italian form of Walhard (foreign, hard).

Gallas (*Fr.*) A variant of Gallant, q.v.

Gallego, Gallegos (*Sp.*) One who came from Gallego or Gallegos (Galicia, an ancient Spanish kingdom), the names of places in Spain.

Galler (*Ger.*) Descendant of Gall (stranger).

Gallery (*Scot., Ir.*) One who came from Gallery (stranger Gael), in Angus; descendant of the gray youth.

Gallet (*Fr.*) The merry, joyous companion.

Galletly (*Scot., Eng.*) Variant of Golightly, q.v.

Galley, Gally (*Eng.*) One who worked on

a galley, the large, low vessel used in the Middle Ages to transport merchandise; dweller near, or keeper of, the galilee, the porch or chapel at the entrance to a church.

Galli (*Fr.*) Variant of Gal, q.v.

Gallichio, Gallicchio (*It.*) Dweller at the sign of the small rooster.

Gallien (*Fr.*) Descendant of Gallien (sea calm). Gallienus was a Roman emperor; also a Greek philosopher and physician had the name of Gallien.

Galligan (*Ir.*) Grandson of Gealagan (little white one).

Gallik (*Pol.*) One who serves others, a servant.

Gallimore (*Eng.*) Dweller at, or near, the foreigner's moor or waste land.

Gallina (*It.*) One who raised and sold chickens; the timid man.

Gallinaro (*It.*) One who dealt in poultry.

Gallivan (*Ir.*) Grandson of Gealbhan (bright, white).

Gallo, Galli (*It.*) Nickname given because of some resemblance to a rooster, possibly strutting like one; dweller at the sign of the rooster; descendant of Gallo (stranger). Gallo was a seventh century Irish missionary saint.

Gallon (*Scot., Eng.*) One who came from Gallon (standing stone), in Scotland; descendant of little Gale (pleasant; merry).

Galloway, Gallaway (*Scot.*) One who came from Galloway (white hillface; the stranger Gael), a district in Scotland comprising Wigtown and Kirkcudbright counties.

Gallup, Galup, Galut, Gallop (*Fr.*) A flat-bottomed boat used to load and unload ships, the surname being applied to the crew members.

Galluzzi, Galluzzo (*It.*) Descendant of little Gallo (cock).

Galowitch, Galowich, Galowitsch, Galowitsh (*Pol.*) One with a big head; dweller near a small rounded hill.

Galpin (*Fr.*) The galloper, indicating a messenger.

Galston (*Scot.*) One who came from Galston (stranger's village), in Ayrshire.

Galsworthy (*Eng.*) One who came from Galsworthy (slope where bog myrtle grew), in Devonshire.

Galt (*Scot., Eng.*) The stranger or foreigner; one thought to possess some characteristic of a boar or hog.

Galton (*Eng.*) One who came from Galton (homestead overgrown with bog myrtle; village subject to tax), in Dorset.

Galus, Galusha (*Pol., Cz.*) One who is loud or noisy.

Galuszka (*Ukr., Rus.*) One who cooked and sold small boiled dumplings.

Galvan, Galvin (*Sp., Ir.*) Descendant of Gawain (hawk of battle; white hawk); grandson of Gealbhan (bright, white).

Galvez (*Sp.*) One who came from Galvez (white falcon), in Spain.

Gamage (*Eng.*) One who came from Gamaches, in France.

Gambale (*It.*) One who made and sold leggings.

Gamble, Gambell, Gambill (*Eng.*) Descendant of Gamel (old).

Gamboa (*Sp.*) One who came from Gamboa (quince), in Spain.

Gamboney (*Fr.*) One with a small or short leg.

Game, Games (*Eng.*) The man fond of, or good at, playing games; the man with the short or deformed leg; one who frequently won the gamen, the prize in the foot-race.

Gamlin (*Eng.*) Descendant of little Gamel (old); the little, old man.

Gammell, Gammill (*Eng.*) Descendant of Gamel (old).

Gammon, Gammons (*Eng.*) One with a short leg.

Gamson (*Eng.*) The son of Gam, a pet form of Gamel (old).

Gancarz (*Pol.*) One who made utensils of earthenware or metal, a potter.

Gandel, Gandell (*Ger.*) Dweller near a

slag heap; descendant of little Gand (charm).

Gandolfi, Gandolfo (*It.*) Descendant of Gandolfo (charm, wolf).

Gandy (*Eng.*) One who took care of small ganders; the servant of Game (game).

Ganey (*Fr.*) Descendant of little Wano (hope).

Gang (*Ger.*) The hale, hearty, vigorous man.

Gangi (*It.*) Dweller at the sign of the prairie hen.

Gangler (*Ger.*) An itinerant dealer; one who buys and sells in gross.

Ganja (*Hindi*) Dweller by the river.

Ganley (*Ir.*) The son of the old hero.

Gannet (*Eng.*) One who came from Gannat (Waddin's estate), a town in central France.

Gannon (*Ir.*) Descendant of the fair-haired man.

Gans, Ganz, Gantz, Gansz (*Ger.*) One who lived at the sign of the goose; one with the qualities of a goose.

Gansauer (*Ger.*) One who came from Gansau (goose meadow), in Germany.

Ganschow, Ganschaw, Ganshaw (*Ger.*) One who came from Ganschow, in Germany.

Ganser (*Ger.*) One with the characteristics of a gander; one who took care of, or dealt in, geese.

Gant, Gantt (*Fr.*) One who made and sold gloves.

Gantner (*Ger.*) One who sells to the highest bidder, an auctioneer.

Ganzer (*Ger.*) Variant of Ganser, q.v.

Garabedian (*Arm.*) Descendant of Garabed (forerunner, referring to John the Baptist); one who held the office of a herald.

Garand (*Fr.*) One who guarantees the debt of another; one who is a surety or provides bail for another.

Garay (*Sp.*) One who came from Garay (storehouse for grain), in Spain.

Garbe, Garb (*Ger., Pol.*) Descendant of Gerbo, a pet form of names beginning with Ger (spear), as Gerbert and Gerbrand; one who had a humpback.

Garber, Garbrecht, Garbers (*Ger.*) Descendant of Garber, a variant of Garibert (spear, bright).

Garbutt, Garbett (*Eng.*) Descendant of Gerbold (spear, bold); or of Gerbod (spear, herald).

Garcia (*Sp., Port.*) Descendant of Garcia, Spanish form of Gerald (spear, firm); one who came from Garcia, in Spain.

Gard (*Eng.*) The guard, keeper, or watchman.

Garden (*Scot., Eng.*) One who came from the barony of Gardyne (garden); one who tended a garden.

Garding (*Eng.*) Dweller near a garden.

Gardley (*Scot.*) One who came from Gartly (thicket on the hill), in Aberdeenshire.

Gardner, Gardiner (*Eng., Fr.*) One who tended a garden, cultivating flowers and vegetables.

Garfield (*Eng.*) Dweller on the grassy land or pasture.

Garfinkel, Garfinkle, Garfunkel (*Ger.*) Carbuncle, a red precious stone, the garnet cut cabochon, probably one who dealt in these stones.

Garforth (*Eng.*) One who came from Garforth (Gaera's ford), in the West Riding of Yorkshire.

Gargano (*It.*) Dweller at the sign of the frog; one with the characteristics of a frog.

Garibaldi (*It.*) Descendant of Garibaldi (spear, bold).

Garibay (*Sp.*) One who came from Garibay (abundance of wheat), in Spain.

Garite, Gariti (*Fr.*) One who guards or watches, especially from a sentry box, turret or hut.

Garland (*Eng.*) Descendant of Gaerland (spear, land); dweller at the triangular field; dweller at the sign of the garland.

Garlic, Garlich, Garlick (*Ger., Eng.*) Descendant of Gerlach (spear, tournament); dweller at the sign of the garlic; one who raised and sold garlic.

Garling (*Eng.*) One who came from Garlinge (green hill), in Kent.

Garlington (*Eng.*) One who came from Girlington (village of youth).

Garlovsky (*Cz.*) Variant of Karlovsky, q.v.

Garman, Garmon (*Eng.*) Descendant of Garmund (spear, protection).

Garner, Garnier (*Eng.*) Descendant of Garner or Warner (protection, warrior).

Garnett, Garnet (*Eng.*) Descendant of little Guarin, or Garnet (protection, friend).

Garnon, Garnham (*Eng.*) The man with the mustache.

Garofalo, Garofolo, Garofala, Garafolo (*It.*) Dweller near where soapwort (Bouncing Bet) was grown; dweller near a clove tree.

Garon (*Fr.*) Descendant of little Garo (spear).

Garr (*Eng.*) Dweller at the top of the hill; descendant of Gar, a pet form of names beginning with Gar (spear), as Garwine and Gardulf.

Garraway (*Eng.*) One who came from Garway (Guoruoe's church), in Herefordshire.

Garreau (*Fr.*) Dweller near, or worker at, the sheep fold or cattle pen.

Garren, Garron (*Eng.*) Dweller by the Garren (crane), a river in Herefordshire.

Garretson (*Eng.*) The son of Gerald (spear, rule); or of Gerard (spear, hard).

Garrett, Garratt (*Eng.*) Descendant of little Gerard (spear, hard).

Garrick (*Eng.*) One who came from Garrick (Gara's dwelling), in Lincolnshire.

Garriga (*Sp.*) One who came from Garriga (place where dyeweed grew; oak forest), in Spain.

Garrigan (*Ir.*) Descendant of little Gears (fierce).

Garris, Garrish (*Eng.*) The wild wavering, wayward man.

Garrison (*Wel., Eng.*) The son of Garry, a pet form of Garrath (spear, hard).

Garrity, Garity (*Ir.*) The son of Aireachtach (member of a court or assembly).

Garrod (*Eng.*) Descendant of Gerard (spear, hard); or of Garaud (spear, rule).

Garrou (*Fr.*) Dweller on uncultivated land; descendant of Garaud, French form of Gerald (spear, rule).

Garrow (*Scot., Ir.*) The rough, stout, brawny man.

Garroway, Garraway (*Eng.*) Descendant of Garwig (spear, war); one who came from Garway (Guoruoe's church), in Herefordshire.

Garry (*Ir.*) The son of Fearadhach (manly); grandson of Gadhra (mastiff).

Garside (*Eng.*) Dweller at the side of the yard or garden.

Garson (*Eng., Fr.*) One who attends another; a manservant; the small young man.

Garstka, Garstki (*Pol.*) Handful, a nickname of some sort.

Garston (*Eng.*) One who came from Garston (Esgar's homestead; grazing farm; big stone), the name of four places in England.

Garth, Garthe (*Eng.*) Dweller in an enclosed yard; or on a farm.

Gartland (*Nor.*) One who came from Gartland, in Norway.

Gartley (*Scot.*) One who came from Gartly (thicket on the hill), in Aberdeenshire.

Gartner, Gaertner (*Ger.*) One who tended a garden, cultivating flowers and vegetables.

Garton, Garten (*Eng.*) One who came from Garton (homestead enclosed by a fence), in the East Riding of Yorkshire.

Garver (*Ger.*) Variant of Garber, q.v.; or of Gerber, q.v.

Garvey, Garvie (*Ir., Scot.*) Descendant of Gairbhit (rough peace); the rough, rude man.

Garvin, Garven, Garvan (*Ir.*) Grandson of little Garbh (rough).

Garwood (*Eng.*) Dweller among the fir trees.

Gary (*Ir.*) Variant of Garry, q.v.

Garza (*Sp.*) Dweller at the sign of the heron or dove. Garza also has the general meaning of bird.

Gascon (*Eng.*) One who came from Gascony (land of the Vasks or Basques).

Gasior, Gasiorowski (*Pol.*) One who raised and sold ganders; dweller at the sign of the gander; one thought to possess the characteristics of a gander.

Gaskill, Gaskell (*Eng.*) One who came from Gaisgill (wild goose valley), the name of places in Westmorland and Yorkshire.

Gaskin, Gaskins, Gasking (*Eng.*) One who came from Gascony (land of the Basques), a region in southwest France.

Gasner (*Ger.*) Variant of Gassner, q.v.

Gaspard (*Fr.*) Descendant of Gaspard, French form of Gaspar (master of the treasure).

Gasparro, Gaspari, Gasparini (*It.*) Descendant of Gaspare, Italian form of Gaspar (master of the treasure).

Gasper, Gaspar (*Eng.*) Descendant of Gaspar or Jasper (master of the treasure). See Kaspar.

Gasperec (*Cz.-Sl., Yu.-Sl.*) Descendant of Gaspar (master of the treasure).

Gass, Gassmann (*Ger.*) Dweller on a lane or street.

Gassen (*Ger.*) One who came from Gassen (streets), in Germany.

Gassensmith (*Ger.*) The smith who had his shop on the street.

Gasser, Gasse, Gass (*Ger.*) One who lived on an alley, that is, the avenue.

Gassin (*Fr.*) Dweller among oak trees; one who came from Cassen (place of oak trees), in France.

Gassmann, Gassman (*Ger., Eng.*) One who lived, or worked, on the street; the servant of Gass or Wace (watchful).

Gassner (*Ger.*) Dweller on the village street.

Gast (*Fr., Ger., Du.*) Dweller near an uncultivated field; one who came from a distance, a stranger.

Gasteier (*Ger.*) Dweller near a stile or steep path up a hill.

Gastel (*Fr.*) One who made and sold cakes and tarts.

Gaston (*Eng., Scot.*) One who came from Gascony, in France.

Gately (*Eng.*) One who came from Gateley (clearing where goats were kept), in Norfolk.

Gatenby (*Eng.*) One who came from Gatenby (Gaithan's homestead), in the North Riding of Yorkshire.

Gaters, Gater (*Eng.*) One who took care of goats, a goatherd; dweller by the road, or by the gate.

Gates (*Eng.*) One who lived in, or near, the gate or gap in a chain of hills.

Gatesgill (*Eng.*) One who came from Gatesgill (shelter for goats), in Cumberland.

Gateward (*Eng.*) One who took care of goats, a goatherd; one who guarded a gate or door; a gate keeper.

Gatewood, Gatwood (*Eng.*) Dweller in, or by, the wood frequented by goats; dweller at the entrance to the wood.

Gathercoal, Gathercole (*Eng.*) One who gathered coal, possibly an old man whose blood was thought to become cold making him weak; one who gathered charcoal.

Gathers (*Eng.*) One who collects dues from the guild members or collects rents or tithes.

Gathings, Gathing (*Wel.*) The rough, ugly man.

Gathman (*Ger.*) Dweller near a narrow opening or gate.

Gatley (*Eng.*) One who came from Gatley (goat's cliff; goat's grove), the name of places in Cheshire and Herefordshire.

Gatlin, Gatling, Gattling (*Eng.*) The fellow or companion; later, a wandering, idle man.

Gatson (*Eng.*) The son of Gadd (comrade).

Gatter, Gatterman (*Ger.*) Dweller near the town gate or entrance; one in charge of the gate.

Gatterdam (*Ger.*) Dweller at the sluice gate.

Gatto, Gattone, Gatti (*It.*) Dweller at the sign of the cat; one thought to possess some of the qualities of a cat.

Gatton (*Eng.*) One who came from Gatton (enclosure where goats were kept), in Surrey.

Gatz, Gatsch, Gatzke (*Ger.*) Descendant of Gato, a pet form of Gadafrid (comrade, peace).

Gau (*Ger.*) Dweller on land, the country in contrast to the city; descendant of Gau, a pet form of names beginning with Gau (district), as Gawiman and Gavioald; the quick, crafty, cunning man.

Gauche, Gaucher (*Fr.*) One who was left-handed; the awkward, clumsy person.

Gauden, Gaudin (*Fr.*) Descendant of little Gaud (ruler), a French form of Waldo.

Gaudet, Gaudette (*Fr.*) Descendant of little Gaud (ruler).

Gaudio (*It.*) The happy, glad, pleased man.

Gauer (*Ger.*) One who came from Gaue (district), in Germany.

Gauger (*Ger.*) One who entertains by tricks, a juggler, clown, or buffoon.

Gaughan, Gaughen (*Ir.*) Descendant of little Gaibhteach (plaintive).

Gaulke (*Ger.*) One dressed in worn shabby clothing, threadbare; the little, naked, bare person.

Gault, Gaul, Gauler (*Scot.*) The stranger or foreigner.

Gaunt, Gauntt (*Eng.*) The tall, thin, angular man; one who made and sold gloves; one who came from Ghent (rock), in Belgium.

Gauntlett (*Eng.*) One who made small gloves, especially strong ones to defend the hand from wounds in combat.

Gauss, Gaus, Gause (*Ger.*) Dweller at the sign of the goose; one with some characteristic of a goose.

Gausselin (*Eng.*) Descendant of Joscelin (the just).

Gautier, Gauthier (*Fr.*) Descendant of Gautier (rule, army).

Gavagan, Gavaghan, Gavigan (*Ir.*) Descendant of little Gaibhteach (plaintive); the son of little Eochaidh (rich in cattle).

Gavert (*Ger.*) Descendant of Gevert, a form of Gebhard (gift, brave).

Gavilan (*Sp.*) Dweller at the sign of the sparrow hawk; one who used an iron hook in his work.

Gavin, Gavan (*Scot., Ir., Fr.*) Descendant of Gavin, Scottish form of Gawain (hawk of battle); grandson of little Gabhadh (want; danger); one with the characteristics of a gull; dweller at the sign of the gull.

Gavreau (*Fr.*) Descendant of little Gauvain, French form of Gawain (hawk of battle).

Gavrick (*Ukr.*) Descendant of Havryk, a pet form of Havrylo, Ukrainian form of Gabriel (strong man of God).

Gavril (*Gr.*) Descendant of Gavril, pet form of Gavrilis, Greek form of Gabriel (strong man of God).

Gaw (*Eng., Scot.*) The foreigner or stranger.

Gawin (*Scot.*) Variant of Gavin, q.v.

Gawlik (*Pol.*) One who came from Gawlik, in Poland; descendant of little Gawel (God is my strength).

Gawne (*Eng.*) Dweller in, or near, the field frequented by hawks.

Gawron, Gawronski (*Pol.*) One known for gaping or staring.

Gay, Gaye (*Eng.*) The merry or blithe person; one in the habit of wearing colorful apparel.

Gayden (*Eng.*) One who came from Gaydon (Gaega's hill), in Warwickshire.

Gayer (*Ger.*) Variant of Geier, q.v.

Gayford (*Eng.*) A gutturalized form of Heyford (ford used during the hay harvest), designating one who came from one of the villages of that name in England.

Gayhart, Gayheart (*Eng.*) The merry, blithe man.

Gayles, Gayle (*Eng.*) One who came from Gayles (ravine), in the North Riding of Yorkshire; the light, pleasant, merry man.

Gaylor, Gayler (*Eng.*) Variant of Galer, q.v.

Gaylord, Gaillard (*Eng.*) The gay or blithe person; descendant of Gaillard (gay).

Gaynor, Gainer (*Ir.*) Son of the light-complexioned or white-haired man.

Gayten, Gayton (*Eng.*) One who came from Gayton (Gaega's homestead; goat enclosure), the name of several villages in England.

Gazda, Gazdziak (*Sl., Yu.-Sl.*) One who rented houses, a landlord; one who controls others.

Gbur, Gburek (*Pol.*) The peasant or small landowner.

Geanes (*Ir.*) Descendant of the fettered prisoner.

Gear, Geare (*Eng.*) The wild, changeful man; dweller near the fish trap; or near the hill fort or earthwork.

Gearhart (*Ger.*) Variant of Gerhardt, q.v.

Gearon, Gearen (*Eng.*) Descendant of Gerin (spear).

Gearring, Gearing (*Eng.*) Descendant of the villain, possibly derived from appearance in play or pageant.

Geary (*Ir.*) Grandson of Gadhra (hound or hunting dog).

Gebauer (*Ger.*) The peasant or tiller of the soil in the village.

Gebbie (*Scot.*) Descendant of little Gib, a pet form of Gilbert (pledge, bright).

Gebel (*Ger.*) Descendant of Gabel, a pet form of names beginning with Geben (gift), as Gebald and Gebolf.

Gebhardt, Gebhart, Gebhard, Gebert (*Ger.*) Descendant of Gebahard (gift, brave); the generous person,

one who gladly and freely gave of his goods or wealth.

Gecht, Gechter (*Ger.*) The sudden, fierce, blustering, violent person.

Geddes, Geddis (*Scot.*) One who came from Geddes (place of the ridge), in Nairnshire.

Geddy, Geddie, Gedde (*Eng., Scot.*) One possessed of an evil spirit; the mad, insane person.

Gedelei, Gedelley (*Hun.*) One who came from Godollo, in Hungary.

Gedraitis (*Lith.*) Variant of Giedraitis, q.v.

Gedvilas, Gedvila (*Lith.*) One inclined to mourning, sad; one who hopes, an optimistic person.

Gee (*Eng., Chin.*) The crooked or deformed person; well-mannered.

Geers, Geer (*Eng.*) Variant of Gear, q.v.

Geert, Geerts (*Du.*) Descendant of Geert, a sharp form of Gerrard (spear, hard).

Geffen, Geffin (*Eng., Du.*) Descendant of Geff, a pet form of Geoffrey (God's peace; land, peace); one who came from Geffen, in Holland.

Gehl, Gehle (*Ger.*) Descendant of Gehl, a pet form of Gehlhardt (mischievous, hard).

Gehm (*Ger.*) Descendant of Gehm, a pet form of Geminianus, a fourth century saint; or of Gehm, a form of Gamm (joy).

Gehr (*Ger.*) Descendant of Gehr, a pet form of names beginning with Ger (javelin), such as Gerwig and Gerulf.

Gehrig (*Ger.*) Descendant of Gerwig (javelin, battle).

Gehring (*Ger.*) One who came from Gehring (wedge-shaped place), the name of two places in Germany; descendant of Gehring, a pet form of Gerulf (javelin, wolf).

Gehrke, Gehrkens (*Ger.*) Descendant of little Gero, a pet form of names beginning with Ger (spear), as Gerhard and Gerwald.

Geib, Geibel (*Ger.*) Dweller in the muddy or dirty place.

Geier (*Ger.*) Dweller at the sign of the

vulture or hawk; one with the characteristics of a vulture or hawk; one who came from Geyen (place of vultures), in Germany.

Geiger (*Ger.*) One who played a violin.

Geimer (*Ger.*) One who exercised control, an overseer or taskmaster.

Geis, Geiser, Geiss, Geisser, Geise (*Swis.*) One who came from Geiss (place where goats graze), in Switzerland; descendant of Geiss, a variant of Giso, a pet form of names beginning with Gis (spear), as Gisulf and Gisher.

Geisler, Geissler, Gessler (*Ger.*) Descendant of Gisalhar (spear, army); one who was a vassal or feudal tenant; one who beat another; one who butchered goats and small animals; one who came from Geislar or Geisler, the names of places in Germany.

Geist (*Ger.*) Descendant of Geist (spirit); one who came from Geistingen (Geist's settlement), in Germany.

Gelb (*Ger.*) The yellow-haired or blond man; descendant of Gelb, a pet form of Gilbert (pledge, bright).

Gelbart, Gelbort (*Ger.*) One with a yellow beard.

Gelber (*Ger.*) The yellow-haired or blond man.

Gelderman, Geldermann, Gellerman (*Du.*) One who came from Gelders, a province in Holland.

Gelfand, Gelfond (*Pol., Ger.*) One who loaned money on the security of personal property pledged in his keeping, a pawnbroker; variant of Helfand, q.v.

Gellatly, Gillatly (*Scot., Eng.*) Variant of Golightly, q.v.

Geller, Gellar (*Ger.*) Descendant of Gelther (sacrifice, army); one who is known for shrieking; one who came from Geldern, in Prussia.

Gellert (*Ger.*) Descendant of Gildard (pledge, hard).

Gelman, Gellman (*Ger.*) The money man, perhaps a money changer.

Gelsomino (*It.*) Dweller near jasmine; or near lilacs or mock orange.

Geltner (*Ger.*) One who made and sold buckets.

Gembala (*Pol.*) One with a big mouth.

Gemeinhardt (*Ger.*) Dweller in, or near, the community woods.

Gemignani (*It.*) One who came from Gemignani, in Italy.

Gemmell, Gemmel, Gemmill (*Scot., Nor.*) Descendant of Gamel (old); one born at the same time as another, a twin.

Gemskie (*Pol., Ger.*) One with a big mouth.

Gendel, Gendill (*Ger.*) Descendant of Gendel, a short form of Gandalhart (werewolf, hard).

Gendreau (*Fr.*) The son-in-law who inherits the house from the father-in-law.

Genge (*Ger.*) The healthy, hearty man.

Gengler (*Ger.*) Variant of Gangler, q.v.

Genius, Geniusz (*Pol.*) One with extraordinary endowment or talent.

Gennarelli, Gennaro (*It.*) Descendant of Gennaro, Italian form of Januarius (sacred to Janus, the Latin deity), the fourth century patron saint of Naples.

Gennett (*Eng.*) Variant of Gannet, q.v.

Genova (*It.*) One who came from Genova, Italian form of Genoa (mouth), the Italian seaport.

Genovese (*It.*) One who came from Genova (head of the water), a province in Italy.

Genson (*Eng.*) The son of Gen, a pet form of Gentius (family); or of Jean, the French form of John (gracious gift of Jehovah).

Genteman, Gent (*Eng.*) The noble, graceful, wellborn man.

Genter (*Ger.*) One who came from Ghent (rock), in Belgium.

Genther (*Ger.*) Variant of Guenther, q.v.

Gentile, Gentle (*It., Eng.*) One with polished, well-bred manners; or of a gentle or benign character; one of noble birth; originally one not a Christian.

Gentili (*It.*) Variant of Gentile, q.v.

Gentleman (*Eng., Scot.*) The man of

gentle or noble birth; one who was an officer in a king's or noble's household.

Gentner (*Ger.*) One who sells at auction, an auctioneer.

Gentry (*Eng.*) A courteous person; one of noble birth.

Gentzen, Gentz (*Ger.*) The son of Johannes, German form of John (gracious gift of Jehovah).

Genutis (*Lith.*) Descendant of Genute, a pet form of Gene; dweller at the sign of the woodpecker.

Genys (*Lith.*) Dweller at the sign of the woodpecker; one thought to possess the characteristics of a woodpecker.

Geocaris (*Gr.*) Descendant of Georgios, Greek form of George (farmer).

Geoghegan, Gegan (*Ir.*) The son of little Eochaidh (rich in cattle).

Georgacas, Georgakas (*Gr.*) Descendant of big or fat Georgios (farmer).

Georgacopoulos (*Gr.*) The son of Georgios, Greek form of George (farmer).

Georgas (*Gr.*) Descendant of Georgis, a Greek form of George (farmer).

George (*Wel., Fr.*) Descendant of George (farmer); dweller at the sign of St. George.

Georgelos (*Gr.*) Descendant of Georgios, a Greek form of George (farmer).

Georges, Georget (*Fr.*) Descendant of Georges, French form of George (farmer).

Georgescu (*Rom.*) Descendant, or follower of, George (farmer).

Georgeson (*Eng., Scot.*) The son of George (farmer).

Georgevich (*Rus.*) The son of George (farmer).

Georgi (*Bulg.*) Descendant of Georgi, Bulgarian form of George (farmer).

Georgieff, Georgiev (*Bulg.*) The son of Georgi, Bulgarian form of George (farmer).

Georgion (*Gr.*) Descendant of George (farmer).

Georgis (*Gr.*) Descendant of Giorgis, a Greek form of George (farmer).

Georgopoulos, Georgopulos (*Gr.*) The son of Georgios, Greek form of George (farmer).

Georgoulis, Georgulis (*Gr.*) Descendant of Georgios, Greek form of George (farmer).

Gepford (*Eng.*) Descendant of Giffard (gift, brave).

Gephart, Gephardt (*Ger.*) Variant of Gebhardt, q.v.

Geppert (*Ger.*) Descendant of Godafrid (God, peace).

Geraci, Gerace (*It.*) One who came from Gerace, in Italy.

Geraghty, Geraty, Gerraughty (*Ir.*) The son of the assemblyman.

Geraldi, Gerali (*It.*) Descendant of Geraldo, Italian form of Gerald (spear, rule).

Gerald, Geralds (*Eng.*) Descendant of Gerald (spear, rule).

Gerard (*Eng.*) Descendant of Gerard or Gerald (spear, firm).

Gerardi, Gerardy (*It.*) Descendant of Gerardo, Italian form of Gerard (spear, hard).

Geraud, Gerault (*Fr.*) Descendant of Gerard (spear, firm).

Gerber (*Ger.*) One who prepared leather, a tanner or currier.

Gerdes (*Du.*) Descendant of Gerd, a pet form of Gerard (spear, hard).

Gerding (*Ger.*) Son of Gerd, a pet form of Gerhard (spear, hard).

Gergans, Gergen, Gergens (*Ir.*) Grandson of little Gearg (fierce).

Gergely (*Hun.*) Descendant of Gergely, Hungarian form of Gregory (watchful).

Gerhardt, Gerhard, Gerhart (*Ger.*) Descendant of Gerhard (spear, hard).

Gerich, Gerick, Gericke, Gerig (*Ger.*) Descendant of Gero, a pet form of names beginning with Ger (spear), such as Gerhard, Germund, and Gerulf.

Gering, Geringer (*Ger.*) One who came from Gering, in Germany; descendant of Gero, a pet form of names beginning with Ger (spear), as Gerhard and Gerland.

Gerke, Gerk, Gerken (*Ger.*) Descendant

of little Gero, a pet form of names beginning with Ger (spear), as Gerlach and Geremar.

Gerlach (*Ger.*) Descendant of Gerlach or Gerolah (spear, tournament).

Gerlich (*Ger.*) Descendant of Gerlach (spear, tournament).

Gerling, Gerlinger (*Ger.*) One who came from Gerling, in Germany; variant of Gering, q.v.

Germain, Germaine (*Fr.*) Descendant of Germain (spear, people); one who was a full brother to another.

German, Germann (*Eng., Ger.*) The man from Germany; descendant of German (a German); or of Germund (spear, protection).

Germano (*It.*) One related to another, a brother or cousin; descendant of Germano, Italian form of Germain (spear, people).

Gerner, Gernert (*Ger.*) One who came from Gern (muddy place), in Germany.

Gernon (*Eng.*) The man with the mustache.

Gerold (*Eng.*) Descendant of Gerold (spear, rule).

Gerome (*Fr.*) Descendant of Gerome, a French form of Jerome (holy name).

Geron (*Fr.*) Descendant of little Gero (spear).

Geroulis (*Lith., Gr.*) Variant of Gerulis, q.v.

Gerrard (*Eng.*) Descendant of Gerard (spear, hard).

Gerrick (*Eng.*) Variant of Garrick, q.v.

Gerrish, Gerish (*Wel., Eng.*) The showy or resplendent person.

Gerritsen, Gerrits (*Nor., Dan., Du.*) The son of little Gert, a pet form of Gerhard (spear, hard).

Gerritsma (*Du.*) The son of Gerrit, a Dutch form of Gerhard (spear, hard).

Gerrity (*Ir.*) The son of Oireachtach (member of an assembly).

Gerry, Gerrie (*Eng.*) Descendant of Gari (spear); the changeable, giddy, person.

Gersch, Gersh, Gershman (*Ger.*) One who raised and sold barley.

Gershman (*Heb., Ger.*) An endearing form of Gershon, q.v.; variant of Hershman, q.v.

Gershon, Gerson (*Heb.*) Descendant of Gershon or Gershom (violent expulsion); one who lived in a foreign land.

Gerstein, Gersten (*Ger.*) Dweller at, or in, the barley field; one who came from Gersten (barley field), in Germany.

Gerstenberg, Gerstenberger (*Ger.*) One who came from Gerstenberg (barley mountain), in Germany.

Gerster, Gerstner (*Ger.*) One who grew barley.

Gerstung (*Ger.*) One who came from Gerstungen (barley field village), in Thuringia.

Gerth (*Ger.*) Descendant of Gehrt, a short form of Gerhart (spear, hard).

Gertz, Goertz, Gertsch, Gerz (*Ger.*) Descendant of Goertz, a pet form of Gerhard (spear, hard); also of other names commencing with Ger, as Geremar, Geribald, and Germund.

Gerulis, Gerullis, Gerules (*Lith., Gr.*) The little, good or pleasant man; the healthy man.

Gervais (*Eng.*) Descendant of Gervais or Gervase (spear, servant).

Gervasi, Gervasio (*It.*) Descendant of Gervasio, Italian form of Gervase (spear, servant).

Gerwig (*Ger.*) Descendant of Gerwig (spear, battle).

Geschke (*Ger.*) Descendant of Geschke, a pet form of Johannes (gracious gift of Jehovah).

Geschwent, Geschwindt, Geschwendt (*Ger.*) The rapid, swift, impetuous man or worker; one who came from Geschwend (place cleared by fire), the name of two places in Germany; dweller in a place burnt out.

Gesell, Gessell (*Ger.*) One who was a companion or friend; dweller near a hall or assembly room; one bound by an agreement to serve another in learning an art or trade, an apprentice.

Geske, Gesky (*Ger.*) Variant of Geschke, q.v.

Gess, Gesse (*Fr.*) One who raised and sold peas.

Gessler, Gessner (*Ger.*) Variant of Gassner, q.v.

Gestautas, Gestaut (*Lith.*) Descendant of Gestautas.

Getchell, Gatchell (*Eng.*) One who came from Gatesgill (shelter for goats), in Cumberland.

Geter (*Ger.*) One who produces objects by casting or molding them, a molder; dweller in a place overgrown with weeds.

Gettinger (*Ger.*) One who came from Gottingen, the name of three places in Germany.

Gettleman, Gettelman (*Ger.*) The man or servant of God.

Getty (*Ir., Scot., Ger.*) The son of Eiteach; one who came from Dalgetty (windy field), in Fife; one who was a godfather to another.

Getz (*Ger., Heb.*) Descendant of Getz, a short form of names beginning with Gote (Goth), or Gott (god), or God (good), as Gozbert, Gozhart, Godeman, Goteleib, and Gozwin; abbreviation from the initials of Gabbai Shel Tsedeka (Treasurer of Charity).

Geyer, Gey (*Ger.*) One who came from Gey or Geyen (place of vultures), the names of places in Germany; variant of Geier, q.v.

Gfroerer, Gfrorer (*Ger.*) One to whom soldiers came for superstitious protection in battle.

Ghent (*Du., Eng.*) One who came from Ghent (rock), in Belgium.

Gherardi (*It.*) Variant of Gerardi, q.v.

Ghilardi (*It.*) Variant of Gilardi, q.v.

Ghilarducci (*It.*) Descendant of little Gilardo (pledge, hard).

Ghiotto (*It.*) One who enjoys eating, a gormandizer.

Gholston (*Eng.*) Dweller near the stone where ghouls were seen.

Ghoston, Ghosten (*Eng.*) Dweller in, or near, the homestead haunted by a ghost.

Giacchetti (*It.*) Descendant of little Giachi, a pet form of Giacomo, Italian form of James (may God protect; the supplanter); one who wore an unusual jacket.

Giacomini (*It.*) Descendant of little Giacomo, Italian form of James (may God protect; the supplanter).

Gialamas (*Gr.*) One who erases.

Giammarco (*It.*) Descendant of Giovanni (John) Marco (Mark).

Giammaria (*It.*) Descendant of Giovanni (John) Maria (Mary).

Giampietro (*It.*) Descendant of Giovanni (John) Pietro (Peter).

Gianakakis, Gianakas (*Gr.*) The son of Giannes, a pet form of Ioannes, Greek form of John (gracious gift of Jehovah).

Gianaras, Gianaris (*Gr.*) Descendant of Giannes, a pet form of Ioannes, (gracious gift of Jehovah).

Giancola (*It.*) Combination of Gian, Italian form of John (gracious gift of Jehovah), and Cola, pet form of Nicola, Italian form of Nicholas (people's victory).

Gianfrancesco, Gianfrancisco (*It.*) Descendant of Giovanni (John) Francesco (Francis).

Giangrande (*It.*) Descendant of big Gian, a pet form of Giovanni, Italian form of John (gracious gift of Jehovah).

Giangrasso (*It.*) Descendant of fat Giovanni, Italian form of John (gracious gift of Jehovah).

Giannakopoulos, Gianakopoulos (*Gr.*) The son of Giannes, a pet form of John (gracious gift of Jehovah).

Giannelli, Gianeschi (*It.*) Variant of Giannetti, q.v.

Giannetti, Giannini (*It.*) Descendant of little Gianni, a pet form of Giovanni, Italian form of John (gracious gift of Jehovah).

Giannola (*It.*) Variant of Giancola, q.v.

Giannone, Giannoni (*It.*) Descendant of

Gianni, a pet form of Giovanni, Italian form of John (gracious gift of Jehovah).

Giannopulos, Giannopoulos, Gianopolus (*Gr.*) The son of Giannos, Greek form of John (gracious gift of Jehovah).

Giardini, Giardina (*It.*) Dweller near, or one who cultivates, a garden.

Gibbons, Gibbon, Gibons, Gibbins (*Eng.*) Descendant of little Gib, a pet form of Gilbert (pledge, bright).

Gibbonson (*Scot.*) The son of little Gib, a pet form of Gilbert (pledge, bright).

Gibbs, Gibs, Gibb (*Eng.*) Descendant of Gib, a pet form of Gilbert (pledge, bright).

Giberson (*Eng.*) The son of Gilbert (pledge, bright).

Giblin (*Eng.*) Descendant of little Gib, a pet form of Gilbert (pledge, bright).

Gibson (*Eng.*) The son of Gib, a pet form of Gilbert (pledge, bright).

Gibula (*Pol.*) The mobile, active person.

Giddens (*Eng.*) The son of Gidd, a short form of Gideon (great warrior; tree-feller).

Giddings (*Eng.*) One who came from Gidding (Gydda's people), in Huntingdonshire; or from Gedding (Gydda's people), in Suffolk.

Gideon (*Eng.*) Descendant of Gideon (great warrior; tree-feller).

Gidley (*Eng.*) One who came from Gidleigh (Gydda's grove), in Devonshire.

Giedraitis (*Lith.*) Descendant of Giedrius (cheerful); the fair, clear, serene person, a nickname.

Gielarowski (*Pol.*) One who came from Gielaron (Gielar's settlement), in Poland.

Gielow (*Ger.*) One who came from Gielow, in Germany.

Gier (*Ger.*) The greedy, covetous man; variant of Geier, q.v.

Gierhahn (*Ger.*) Descendant of Gierhahn, a Slavic form of George (farmer).

Gierke (*Ger.*) Variant of Gehrke, q.v.

Gierman (*Ger.*) One who was greedy; one who had charge of the hawks; descendant of Gereman (spear, man).

Giersch (*Ger.*) Descendant of Gerisch, a pet form of Gertrude (spear, strength).

Giertz (*Ger.*) Variant of Gehrke, q.v.

Giese, Gies, Giess (*Ger.*) Descendant of Giso, pet form of names beginning with Gis (spear), as Gisbert, Gisher, and Gissold.

Giesel, Gieselmann (*Ger.*) Descendant of Gisilo, a pet form of names beginning with Geisel (rod), as Gisalfrid and Gisalhart.

Giesler (*Ger.*) Descendant of Gisilhar (rod, army).

Giff, Giffey, Giffin (*Eng.*) Descendant of Giff, a pet form of Gifford (gift, hard); or of Giffy, a pet form of Geoffrey (God's peace; land, peace).

Giffen (*Scot.*) One who came from Giffen (ridge), in Ayrshire.

Gifford, Giffard (*Eng., Scot.*) Descendant of Giffard (gift, hard); one with fat cheeks.

Gigante, Giganti (*It.*) The very large man, a giant.

Giglio, Gigli (*It.*) Dweller where lilies grew; dweller on the peak.

Gignac (*Pol.*) Descendant of Jignac, a pet form of Ignatius (fiery).

Gil (*Sp.*) Descendant of Gil, Spanish form of Giles (shield bearer; kid); one who came from Gil (protected one), in Spain.

Gilard (*Fr.*) Descendant of Gilard (pledge, hard).

Gilardi (*It.*) Descendant of Gilardo (pledge, hard).

Gilberg (*Nor.*) One who came from Gilberg (mountain with a ravine), in Norway; dweller on a hill with a gully.

Gilbert, Gilbertson, Gilberts (*Eng.*) Descendant of Gilbert (pledge, bright).

Gilberto (*It.*) Descendant of Gilberto (pledge, bright).

Gilbreth, Gilbraith (*Scot.*) Variant of Galbraith, q.v.

Gilbride (*Scot., Ir.*) Descendant of the devotee of St. Brigid (strength).

Gilby, Gilbey (*Eng.*) One who came from Gilby (Gilli's village), in Lincolnshire.

Gilchrist, Gilchriest, Gilcrest (*Scot.*) The servant of Christ.

Gildea (*Ir.*) The servant or disciple of God.

Gildemeister (*Ger.*) The head of the guild.

Gilden (*Eng.*) The golden man, probably the one with golden hair.

Gilderman (*Eng.*) Dweller, or worker, at the guildhall; one who gilds, a gilder.

Gildersleeve (*Eng.*) Dweller at the sign of the gilded sleeve; one with a golden sleeve.

Gildhaus (*Ger.*) Dweller in, or near, the guild house, the meeting place of the members.

Gildon (*Fr.*) Descendant of little Gild, a pet form of Gilard (pledge, hard).

Gildsmith (*Eng.*) One who gilds, a gilder; variant of Goldsmith, q.v.

Giles, Gile (*Eng.*) Descendant of Giles (shield bearer).

Gilfeather (*Ir.*) Son of the servant of St. Peter.

Gilfillan (*Ir.*) The son of the devotee of St. Faolan.

Gilfoyle, Gilfoy, Gilfoil (*Ir.*) The son of the servant, or devotee, of St. Paul.

Gilgan, Gilgen (*Ir.*) Descendant of the little servant or youth.

Gilhooly, Gilhooley (*Ir.*) The son of the youthful glutton; or of the servant of the glutton.

Gilkerson, Gilkes, Gilkison, Gilkeson (*Eng.*) The son of Gilk, a shortened form of Gilchrist (servant of Christ); or of Gilkin, a diminutive form of Gill, a form of Julius (downy-bearded or youthful).

Gill (*Ir.*) The son of the foreigner.

Gillard, Gillarde (*Eng.*) The gay or blithe person; descendant of Gaillard (gay).

Gillen, Gillan, Gillon (*Ir.*) Descendant of the little servant or youth.

Gillespie (*Scot., Ir.*) The servant of the bishop.

Gillette, Gillett, Gillet (*Fr.*) Descendant of little Giles, Gilles or Gille, a variant of the Latin, Aegidius (shield or protection).

Gilley (*Scot.*) Variant of Gillie, q.v.

Gillham (*Eng.*) Variant of Gilliam, q.v.

Gilliam, Gilliams, Guilliams, Guillam (*Eng.*) Descendant of Guilliam (resolution, helmet), the name of William as influenced by the French Guillaume.

Gillian (*Eng.*) Descendant of Julian (downy-bearded or youthful).

Gilliand (*Scot., Ir.*) Variant of Gilliland, q.v.

Gilliard, Gillyard (*Eng.*) Variant of Gillard, q.v.

Gillick (*Ir.*) The son of Ulick, a pet form of William (resolution, helmet).

Gillie, Gillies (*Scot., Ir.*) Descendant of the servant of Iosa (Jesus).

Gilligan (*Ir.*) Descendant of the little servant or youth.

Gilliland, Gilleland (*Scot., Ir.*) The son of the devotee of St. Faolan.

Gillin, Gilling (*Eng.*) One who came from Gilling (Getla's people), in the North Riding of Yorkshire.

Gillingham (*Eng.*) One who came from Gillingham (the village of Gylla's people), the name of several places in England.

Gillis, Gilles (*Scot., Ir.*) The servant or disciple of Jesus.

Gillogly (*Ir.*) The son of the gluttonous lad.

Gills (*Eng.*) Descendant of Gill, a pet form of Gillian or Julius (downy-bearded or youthful).

Gillum (*Eng.*) Descendant of Guilliam (resolution, helmet), a French form of William.

Gilman, Gillman (*Eng.*) The servant of Gill, a pet form of Gilbert (pledge, bright), and of Gillian (downy-bearded or youthful).

Gilmartin (*Ir.*) The son of the servant of St. Martin.

Gilmore, Gilmour, Gilmer (*Ir.*) The son of the servant or devotee of Mary, that is, the Virgin.

Gilpin (*Eng.*) Descendant of little Gil, a pet form of Gilbert (pledge, bright).

Gilroy (*Ir.*) The son of the red youth.

Gilruth (*Ir.*) The servant of Ruth (red).

Gilski (*Pol.*) Dweller at the sign of the bullfinch or redfinch.

Gilson (*Eng.*) The son of Gill, a pet form of Julian (downy-bearded or youthful) and several other names; one who came from Gilson (Gydel's hill), in Warwickshire.

Giltnane (*Ir.*) The son of the servant of St. Senan.

Gimbel, Gimble, Gimpel (*Ger., Eng.*) Dweller at the sign of the bullfinch; descendant of Gundbald (combat, bold); or of Gumbel, a pet form of Gumbert (combat, bright); a blockhead or dunce.

Ginger (*Eng.*) One who prepared and sold ginger and other condiments.

Gingle, Gingold (*Ger.*) Descendant of Gingel, from Gingo, a short form of names beginning with *gang* (walk), as Gangrich, Gengerich, and Gangbert.

Ginley (*Ir.*) The son of Fionnghal (fair valor).

Ginn, Genn (*Eng., Ir.*) Descendant of Ginn or Genn, pet forms of Guinevere (fair lady) or of Eugene (well-born); one with a fair complexion.

Ginocchio (*It.*) Nickname for one with an unusual or lame knee.

Ginoza (*Jap.*) Silver, seat.

Ginsberg, Ginsburg (*Ger.*) One who came from Gunzburg (Gunz's stronghold), in Bavaria.

Ginther, Ginter (*Ger.*) Variant of Gunther, q.v.

Ginty (*Ir.*) Descendant of Fionnachta (beautiful snow).

Gintz (*Ger.*) Descendant of Gunz, a pet form of Gunzo (war).

Ginza (*Jap.*) Silver, seat.

Gioia, Gioioso (*It.*) One who expresses gladness and joy.

Giordano (*It.*) Descendant of Giordano (flowing down), a name given to one baptized in the River Jordan.

Giovannetti, Giovannini (*It.*) Descendant of little Giovanni, Italian form of John (gracious gift of Jehovah).

Giovenco (*It.*) Dweller at the sign of the calf or bullock; one who took care of calves.

Gipson, Gipp, Gips (*Eng.*) The son of Gip, a pet form of Gilbert (pledge, bright).

Giragosian (*Arm.*) Descendant of Giragos, Armenian form of George (farmer).

Giraldi, Giraldo (*It.*) Descendant of Giraldo (spear, rule).

Girard, Giraud (*Fr.*) Descendant of Girard (spear, firm).

Girardi (*It.*) Variant of Gerardi, q.v.

Girardin (*Fr.*) Descendant of little Girard (spear, firm).

Girdauskas (*Lith.*) Descendant of Gird, a pet name for names beginning with this stem, as Girdene, Girdute, and Girdvainis.

Girdvainis, Girdwain (*Lith.*) Descendant of Girdvainis.

Girod (*Fr.*) Descendant of Gerard (spear, firm).

Giron (*Fr.*) Variant of Geron, q.v.

Giroux (*Fr.*) Descendant of Giroux (old man); or of Girulf (spear, wolf).

Girsch (*Ger.*) Descendant of Giersch, a pet form of Gertrude (spear, strength).

Girten, Girton (*Eng.*) One who came from Girton (homestead on gravelly soil), the name of places in Cambridgeshire and Nottinghamshire.

Girtly (*Eng.*) Dweller in, or near, a thin wood on gravelly soil.

Gish (*Ger.*) Descendant of Gies (scion; pledge; hostage), a short form of such names as Giesebrecht and Gisulf.

Gist (*Eng.*) Middle English form of

Guest, q.v.; descendant of Gest or Gist (guest).

Gittelson, Gitelson, Gittelsohn (*Ger.*) The son of Gittel (good).

Gittins, Gittings (*Wel.*) The rough or unkempt man.

Giudice, Giudici (*It.*) One who occupied the office of judge; one who acted the part of a judge in a play or pageant.

Giuliano, Giuliani (*It.*) Descendant of Giuliano, Italian form of Julian (downy-bearded or youthful); one who came from Giugliano, in Italy.

Giunta, Giunti, Giuntoli (*It.*) Descendant of Giunta (safe arrival).

Giustino (*It.*) Descendant of Giustino, Italian form of Justin (just or upright).

Givens, Givans (*Scot., Eng.*) Descendant of little Gib, a pet form of Gilbert (pledge, bright).

Givhan (*Ir.*) The son of Duibhin, a dim. of Dubh (black).

Givin, Given (*Ir., Scot.*) The son of little Dubh (black).

Gjertsen (*Nor., Dan.*) The son of Gjert, a form of Gerhard (spear, hard).

Glab, Glabe (*Pol.*) Dweller in, or near, the deep hole or ravine.

Glabman (*Eng.*) Dweller in the glade or grassy open space in the forest.

Glad, Gladd (*Eng.*) One who dwelt in the glade; descendant of Glad, a pet form of Gladwin (kind, friend).

Gladden, Gladding (*Eng.*) Descendant of Gladwin (kind, friend).

Glade, Glader (*Eng.*) Dweller in the grassy open space in the wood.

Gladhill (*Eng.*) Dweller at the hill frequented by gledes (kites or hawks).

Gladish, Gladis (*Ger.*) Dweller on the smooth, flat ground.

Gladney, Gladny (*Eng., Pol.*) Dweller at the narrow enclosure; the gaunt or hungry man.

Gladstein (*Scot.*) Variant of Gladstone, q.v.

Gladstone (*Scot.*) One who came from Gledstanes (kite's rock), in Lanarkshire.

Gladwell (*Eng.*) Dweller at the clear spring.

Gladwin (*Eng.*) Descendant of Gladwin (kind, friend).

Glancy, Glancey (*Ir.*) The son of Flannchadh (ruddy warrior).

Glandon (*Eng.*) One who came from Clandon (hill free of weeds), in Surrey.

Glantz, Glanz, Glanzner (*Ger.*) One who polishes or brightens material.

Glanville (*Eng.*) One who came from Glanville (Gland's town), in Calvados.

Glascott (*Eng.*) Dweller in, or near, the glass worker's shop; one who came from Glascote (glass worker's hut), in Warwickshire.

Glasebrook (*Eng.*) One who came from Glazebrook (blue, green, gray stream), in Lancashire.

Glasener, Glasner (*Ger.*) One who made and sold glass.

Glasgow, Glasco, Glasgoe (*Scot.*) One who came from Glasgow (gray hound; black brook; gray wood), in Lanarkshire.

Glass, Glasser, Glaser (*Eng.*) One who made or sold glassware; descendant of Glas (gray).

Glassman, Glassmann (*Ger., Eng.*) One who dealt in glass.

Glasson (*Eng.*) One who came from Glasson (bright spot), in Lancashire.

Glatt, Glatter (*Ger.*) One with smooth, glossy hair; dweller at the flat place; one who came from Glatt (smooth, flat place), in Germany; or from Glatten (smooth), in Germany.

Glatthaar (*Ger.*) One with smooth hair.

Glatz, Glatzel (*Ger.*) The man with a bald head.

Glatzer (*Ger.*) One who came from Glatz (bald spot), in Germany.

Glavin (*Ir.*) Grandson of Glaimhin (glutton).

Glaze (*Eng.*) One with a pale or gray complexion.

Glazer, Glazier, Glazar (*Eng.*) One who made and sold glass.

Glazewski (*Pol.*) Dweller at a rocky or stony place.

Glazner (*Ger.*) Variant of Glasener, q.v.

Gleason, Gleeson (*Ir.*) The descendant of the little green man, possibly referring to the color of his clothes.

Gleavy (*Ir.*) The son of Flaitheamh (ruler; lord).

Gledhill (*Eng.*) One who came from Gledhill (hill frequented by kites), in the West Riding of Yorkshire.

Gleghorn (*Scot.*) One who came from Cleghorn (clay house), in Lanarkshire.

Gleich, Gleicher (*Ger.*) One who came from Gleichen (slippery place), in Germany; one who is good looking or handsome; one who works with sheet metal.

Glenday, Glendy (*Scot.*) One who came from Glenday, a district in Angus.

Glendenning, Glendinning (*Scot.*) One who came from Glendinning (glen of the fair hill), in Dumfriesshire.

Glendon (*Eng.*) One who came from Glendon (hill free of weeds), in Northamptonshire.

Glenn, Glen (*Wel.*) Dweller in the glen or valley.

Glennon (*Ir., Eng.*) The son of Lennan (small coat); one who came from Glendon (clean hill), in Northamptonshire.

Gley (*Ger.*) Descendant of Gley, pet form of Elegius (the chosen), patron saint of metal workers.

Glick, Glickman, Glicker, Glickerman (*Ger.*) The lucky or fortunate man. English forms.

Glickstein (*Ger.*) Lucky stone.

Glidden (*Eng.*) A variant of Gladwin, q.v.

Glinka, Glink (*Pol.*) Dweller on clayey soil.

Glinski (*Pol.*) Dweller on clay ground.

Glispie, Glespie (*Scot.*) A shortened form of Gillespie, q.v.

Glogowski (*Pol.*) Dweller near hawthorns; one who came from Glogow (hawthorn), the name of two places in Poland.

Glomb, Glombicki (*Pol.*) The wise or learned man.

Gloria (*Sp.*) Descendant of Gloria (fame; glory).

Glorioso (*It.*) The famous, illustrious, glorious man.

Gloss, Glos, Gloser (*Eng.*) Dweller at the enclosure.

Glossop (*Eng.*) One who came from Glossop (Glott's small, enclosed valley), in Derbyshire.

Gloster, Glouster (*Eng.*) One who came from Gloucestershire (bright Roman fort), a county in England.

Glotzer (*Ger.*) The coarse, awkward, clumsy fellow.

Glover (*Eng.*) One who made or sold gloves.

Glowa, Glowacki (*Pol.*) One with a large or unusual head.

Glowicki, Glowinski, Glowski (*Pol.*) Dweller near the head or upper end; one with an unusual or misshapen head.

Gluck, Gluckman, Glueck (*Ger.*) The lucky person; the happy man.

Gluckstein, Glueckstein (*Ger.*) Lucky stone.

Gluesing (*Ger.*) One who came from Glusing (swamp), the name of three places in Germany.

Glumac (*Yu.-Sl.*) One who performs in the theater, an actor.

Glynn (*Wel.*) Dweller in the narrow valley.

Gnadt, Gnat, Gnatek, Gnatczynski, Gnatt (*Pol.*) Descendant of Gnat, a pet form of Ignacy, Polish form of Ignatius (fiery).

Gniadek, Gniady (*Pol.*) One in charge of the bay horses.

Gniewek (*Pol.*) The little, angry or indignant man.

Gnojek (*Pol.*) The dirty, nasty person.

Goadsmith (*Eng.*) Variant of Goodsmith, q.v.

Goatley (*Eng.*) One who came from Godley (Goda's grove), in Cheshire; dweller in a grove where goats were raised.

Gobel, Goble (*Ger.*) Descendant of

Gobel, a variant of Godebold (God, bold).

Gober (*Ger.*) Descendant of Gober, a pet form of Gabriel (God is my strength).

Goc, Gocek, Goch (*Pol.*) Descendant of Goc, a pet form of Goclaw and Godzislaw.

Godawa, Godawski (*Pol.*) The joyous, gay, festive man.

Godbehere, Godbeer, Godbeher (*Eng.*) Nickname acquired through frequent use of the phrase "[may] God be here [in this house]."

Godbert, Godburt (*Eng.*) Descendant of Godebert (God, bright).

Godbey, Godby (*Eng.*) One who came from Goadby (Gouti's village), in Lincolnshire.

Godbold, Godbolt (*Eng.*) Descendant of Godebald (God, bold).

Goddard (*Eng.*) Descendant of Goddard (God, hard).

Godden (*Eng.*) Variant of Godwin, q.v.

Godeau (*Fr.*) Descendant of Godaud (God, ruler); or of Godard (God, hard); one who worked in a vineyard.

Godesmith (*Eng.*) Variant of Goodsmith, q.v.

Godfrey, Godfree, Godfray (*Eng., Scot.*) Descendant of Godfrey or Godefrid (God's peace).

Godhelp (*Eng.*) Possibly a nickname acquired through repeated use of the exclamation, "God help [us]."

Godin (*Eng.*) Descendant of little God, a pet form of names beginning with this element, such as Godwin and Godfrey.

Godinez (*Sp.*) The son of Gunta (battle).

Godlewski (*Pol.*) One who displayed a coat-of-arms.

Godley, Godlee (*Eng.*) One who came from Godley (Goda's grove), in Cheshire.

Godlove (*Eng.*) One addicted to the expression "God love [it, you, or him]."

Godmund (*Eng.*) Descendant of Godmund (God, protection).

Godsafe, Godsave (*Eng.*) Nickname acquired through repeated use of the phrase, "on God's half," that is, in God's name or for God's sake.

Godsal, Godsall (*Eng.*) One who came from Godshill (God's hill), in Hampshire; the well-regarded man, the good soul.

Godshalk, Godshall (*Ger.*) Variant of Gottschalk, q.v.

Godsmark (*Eng.*) One who bore God's mark, that is, the sign of the plague.

Godson (*Eng.*) The son of Gode or Goda (God or good); the son of God, a pet form of names beginning with this element, such as Godric and Godbert; one sponsored at baptism.

Godwin, Godwyn (*Eng.*) Descendant of Godwine (dear, friend; God's friend).

Godzicki (*Pol.*) One who conciliates or reconciles others, a go-between.

Goebel (*Ger.*) Descendant of Godbeald (God, brave).

Goede (*Ger.*) Descendant of Godo, a pet form of names beginning with Gott (God), as Godaberht and Godeman.

Goedert (*Ger.*) Descendant of Gotahard (good, stern).

Goellner (*Ger.*) Variant of Goldner, q.v.

Goelz, Goeltz (*Ger.*) Variant of Golz, q.v.; one who gelded swine.

Goens (*Fr.*) Variant of Goins, q.v.

Goepp, Goeppner (*Ger.*) Descendant of Gobbo, a pet form of Godaberht (God, bright).

Goering (*Ger.*) The son of Gero, a pet form of names beginning with Ger (spear), as Germund and Gerwin; one who came from Goring, in Germany.

Goes (*Ger.*) One who raises and sells geese.

Goethals (*Du.*) Descendant of little Goethe, a pet form of names beginning with Gott (God), as Godabert and Godfrey.

Goethe (*Ger.*) An abbreviation or pet form of one of the old German names beginning with Gott (God), as Gottfried (Godfrey), or Gotthardt (Goddard).

Goettert (*Ger.*) Descendant of Godehard (God, stern).

Goettler (*Ger.*) Descendant of Goettler, a pet form of Gottfried (God's peace).

Goetz, Goettsche (*Ger.*) Descendant of Goetz, a pet form of Godizo (God); the beautiful person.

Goff (*Ir.*) The worker in metals; the ruddy or red-haired man; son of Eochaidh (rich in cattle).

Goforth (*Eng.*) Nickname for a messenger ordered to start out for his destination.

Goggin, Goggins, Gogins, Goggans (*Ir.*) One who came from Cogan, a parish in Glamorganshire.

Gohr, Gohrke (*Ger.*) Dweller in, or near, a swamp.

Going (*Ir., Fr.*) The worker in metal, a smith; variant of Goins, q.v.

Goins, Goines, Goinges, Goin (*Fr.*) Descendant of Gudin (God's friend).

Golab (*Pol.*) Dweller at the sign of the pigeon; metonymic for one who raised and sold pigeons.

Golan, Goland, Golant (*Pol.*) The naked or bare man; one who wears little clothing.

Golas (*Rus.*) Nickname for one who had a loud or unusual voice.

Golby, Golbey (*Sw.*) One who came from Golby, in Sweden.

Gold, Golde (*Eng.*) Descendant of Gold or Golda, Old English personal names derived from the precious metal.

Goldberg, Goldberger (*Ger.*) One who came from Goldberg (gold mountain), the name of five places in Germany.

Goldblatt (*Ger.*) Gold leaf.

Goldbourn, Golborn, Golbourn (*Eng.*) One who came from Golborne (stream where marigold grew), the name of places in Cheshire and Lancashire.

Golden, Golding, Goulding (*Eng.*) Descendant of Goldwin (gold, friend); one who had golden hair.

Goldenberg (*Ger.*) One who came from

Goldenberg (gold mountain), in Germany.

Goldfarb (*Ger.*) Gold color; one with golden hair.

Goldfinch (*Eng.*) Dweller at the sign of the goldfinch.

Goldfine, Goldfein (*Ger.*) Gold fine.

Goldfinger (*Ger.*) One who made and sold gold rings.

Goldie (*Scot.*) Descendant of little Gold (gold, the metal).

Goldin, Golding (*Eng.*) Descendant of Golding (son of Gold); one with golden hair.

Goldman (*Eng.*) The servant of Gold or Golda (gold); one who worked in gold.

Goldner (*Ger.*) One who works with gold, a gilder.

Goldrick, Goldrich (*Eng.*) Descendant of Goldric (gold, rule).

Goldsberry, Goldsbury, Goldsborough (*Eng.*) One who came from Goldsborough (Godhelm's or Golda's fort), the name of several places in England.

Goldsby (*Eng.*) One who came from Goulceby (Kolk's settlement), in Lancashire.

Goldsmith, Goldschmidt, Gouldsmith (*Eng., Ger.*) One who made or sold gold articles, a jeweler, later a banker.

Goldstein (*Ger.*) Gold stone; one who used a goldstein, a touchstone used by a goldsmith to test gold; dweller at the sign of the gollstein, a topaz emblematic of the goldsmith's shop.

Goldstone, Goldston (*Eng.*) One who came from Goldstone (Goldstan's grove; Golda's stone), the name of places in Kent and Shropshire.

Goldsworthy (*Eng.*) One who came from, or worked on, Gold's farm; one who came from Galsworthy (slope where bog myrtle grew), in Devonshire.

Goldthorp, Goldthrip (*Eng.*) One who came from Goldthorpe (Golda's farm), in the West Riding of Yorkshire.

Goldthwait, Goldthwaite (*Eng.*) One who came from Gold's clearing.

Goldwasser, Goldwater (*Ger.*) Gold water.

Goldworm, Goldwurm (*Ger.*) Descendant of Goldwurm (gold, worm), apparently a personal name.

Goldwyn, Goldwin (*Eng.*) Descendant of Goldwine (gold, friend).

Goldyn (*Eng.*) Descendant of Goldwine (gold, friend).

Golebiowski (*Pol.*) One who came from Golebiow (dove), in Poland.

Golec, Golecki (*Pol.*) The naked man; the poor wretch.

Golembiecki (*Pol.*) One with the qualities or characteristics of a dove.

Golembiewski (*Pol.*) Dweller at the sign of the pigeon; one who raises and sells pigeons.

Golenpaul (*Rus.*) Dweller in, or near, an open field.

Golightly (*Eng.*) A messenger or runner who was fleet of foot.

Golik, Golinski (*Pol.*) The poor or naked man.

Goll (*Scot., Eng.*) Variant of Gall, q.v.; descendant of Goll, a pet form of Goliath (giant; fat).

Golliday, Golladay (*Eng.*) Variants of Galloway, q.v.

Gollob, Gollub (*Rus.*) Dweller at the sign of the pigeon or dove.

Golly, Gollay, Golley (*Eng.*) Descendant of little Goll, a pet form of Golias or Goliath (giant; fat).

Golman (*Eng.*) Variant of Goldman, q.v.

Golomb (*Pol.*) Dweller at the sign of the dove; one who raised and sold pigeons.

Golonka (*Pol.*) One who made and sold lace.

Golosinec (*Ukr., Pol.*) One with a strong voice.

Golson (*Eng.*) The son of Gold or Golda (gold, the metal).

Golston (*Eng.*) Variant of Goldstone, q.v.

Golub (*Rus., Pol.*) Dweller at the sign of the pigeon or dove; one who came from Golub (pigeon), in Poland.

Golz, Goltz (*Ger.*) One without a beard, a boyish man.

Gomberg (*Rus., Ger.*) One who came from Homburg (high fortified place); or from Homberg (high mountain), the names of several places in Germany.

Gombert (*Ger.*) Descendant of Gombert (war, bright).

Gomes (*Port.*) The son of Gomo, a pet form of Gumesindo or Gumersindo (man, path).

Gomez (*Sp.*) The son of Gomo, a pet form of Gomesano (man, path).

Gomolka, Gomulka (*Pol.*) One who made and sold whey cheese; one who came from Gomolka, in Poland.

Gompers (*Ger.*) Descendant of Gundberht (war, bright).

Goncalves (*Port.*) The son of Goncalo (battle, elf).

Gonciarz (*Pol.*) One who made and sold pots.

Gonda (*Swis.*) Dweller at the stony slope.

Gonnella (*It.*) Descendant of little Goni, a pet form of Francesconi (free), and of Domenicone (the Lord's day); one who wore an unusual skirt.

Gonnigan (*Ir.*) The son of Donnagain (little brown one).

Gonsalves, Gonsalvez (*It., Sp.*) The son of Consalvo (battle, elf).

Gonska, Gonsky, Gonski (*Rus.*) One who carries messages, a messenger.

Gonzalez, Gonzales (*Sp.*) The son of Gonzalo (battle, elf). Gonzales was a twelfth century Spanish saint.

Gooch (*Wel., Ir.*) The red-haired or ruddy man; son of Eochaidh (rich in cattle).

Good, Goode (*Eng.*) Descendant of Goda or Gode (good), which is also the first element in many names such as Godmund, Godric, and Godwine. In these names it often refers to God; occasionally it refers to the good man.

Goodal, Goodall (*Eng., Scot.*) One who came from Gowdall (corner overgrown with marigold), in the West Riding of Yorkshire.

Goodale (*Eng.*) A nickname meaning "good ale," given to a brewer who made good ale; variant of Goodall, q.v.; one who brewed and sold godale, a kind of beer.

Gooday, Goodday (*Eng.*) The good or efficient servant; one in the habit of using the phrase on meeting or parting: "God give you a good day" or "Have a good day."

Goodbody (*Eng.*) The good person, used as an epithet of courteous address.

Goodchild (*Eng.*) The good, approved child, that is attendant, young knight, or member of the lower nobility; the man for whom another was sponsor at baptism.

Goodell (*Eng.*) One who came from Gowdall, formerly Goodall (corner overgrown with marigold), in the West Riding of Yorkshire.

Goodenough, Goodnough, Goodnow, Goodenow (*Eng.*) Said to be a nickname for one who was sufficient or satisfactory in some sense; sometimes a corruption of *god cnafa* (good child).

Goodfellow (*Eng., Scot.*) The man of companionable qualities; a jolly person.

Goodfriend (*Eng.*) The aimable or pleasant companion.

Goodgame (*Eng.*) One proficient at games; the good sport.

Goodhart, Goodheart (*Eng.*) The pleasant, agreeable, good-hearted man.

Goodhue, Goodhugh (*Eng.*) One who was an able and competent servant; one with a good color or complexion; the good man named Hugh (spirit; mind).

Gooding (*Eng.*) Descendant of Goding; or sometimes of Godwin (God's friend).

Goodjohn (*Eng.*) The good companion; the pleasant, agreeable man named John (gracious gift of Jehovah).

Goodkin, Goodkind (*Eng.*) The divine, godly man; the good, obedient child.

Goodloe, Goodlow (*Eng.*) One who came from Goodleigh (Goda's grove), in Devonshire; dweller at Goda's hill.

Goodman, Goodmon (*Eng., Scot.*) Descendant of Godmann (good man); or of Gudmund (war, protection); a landowner who held as a subtenant; the husband or head of the house.

Goodmiller (*Eng.*) The able, efficient grinder of grain.

Goodness, Goodniss (*Eng.*) Dweller on a pleasant headland or cape.

Goodnight (*Ger.*) Perversion of Gutknecht, q.v.

Goodrich, Goodrick (*Eng.*) One who came from Goodrich (Godric's castle), in Herefordshire; descendant of Godric (God's rule).

Goodridge (*Eng.*) Descendant of Godric (God's rule); one who came from Goodrich (Godric's castle), in Herefordshire.

Goodrum (*Eng.*) Descendant of Guthorm (combat, dragon).

Goodsell (*Eng.*) Variant of Godsal, q.v.

Goodsmith (*Eng.*) An able and competent worker in metals.

Goodson (*Eng.*) The son of Gode or Goda (good); or of God, a short form of names beginning with God (good), as Godric and Godwin; the good son; the man of God; the godson, that is, one who has been sponsored in baptism by another.

Goodspeed (*Eng.*) A wish of success, probably a nickname for one who frequently exclaimed "God speed [you]."

Goodstein, Goodstone (*Ger., Eng.*) Good stone; one who came from Godstone (God's or Cod's homestead), in Surrey.

Goodwick (*Eng.*) One who came from Godwick (Goda's dwelling), in Norfolk.

Goodwillie (*Scot., Eng.*) Nickname for the liberal, cordial man; the pleasant, agreeable man named Willie, a pet form of William (resolution, helmet).

Goodwin, Goodwine, Goodwyn (*Eng.*)

Descendant of Godwin (God's friend).

Goody (*Eng.*) Descendant of little Goda or Gode (good).

Goodyear (*Eng.*) One in the habit of wishing others a good year, as in a new year's greeting; or wishing another a good harvest; descendant of Godhere (good, army).

Goold (*Eng.*) Variant of Gold, q.v.

Goolsby (*Scot.*) One who came from Golspie (Gold's dwelling), in Sutherland.

Goosby (*Nor., Sw.*) One who came from Gaaseby (Gasi's homestead), in Norway; goose village.

Gootnick (*Ger.*) Respelling of Gutknecht, q.v.

Gora (*Pol., Rus.*) Dweller on, or near, a mountain.

Goral, Goralka, Goralski, Gorall (*Pol.*) One who dwelt in the mountains, a mountaineer.

Goralczyk (*Pol.*) The little mountaineer.

Goran, Goranson (*Sw.*) Descendant of Goran, Swedish form of George (farmer).

Gorczyca (*Pol.*) One who raised and prepared mustard.

Gordon, Gorden, Gordan (*Scot., Eng., Rus.*) One who came from Gordon (spacious hill), in Berwickshire; one who lived on, or near, a three-cornered hill or wedge-shaped piece of land; one who came from Grodno (fortified place), in Byelorussia.

Gordy (*Scot.*) One who came from Gourdie (dregs; an arm), in Scotland.

Gore, Gorr (*Eng.*) One who lived near, or on, the triangular piece of land; one who tilled such a piece; one who came from Gore (triangular land), in Kent.

Gorecki (*Pol.*) One who lived on, or near, the mountain.

Goreham (*Eng.*) Variant of Gorham, q.v.

Gorell, Gorill (*Eng.*) Variants of Gorrell, q.v.

Goren, Gorens (*Sw.*) Variant of Goran, q.v.

Gorey, Gory (*Ir.*) Descendant of Guaire (noble).

Gorfinkle, Gorfinkel (*Ger.*) Variant of Garfinkel, q.v.

Gorges (*Fr.*) One who came from Gorges (pass; defile), in France; dweller near a defile or ravine.

Gorham (*Eng.*) Dweller on the triangular homestead.

Gorin, Goron (*Fr., Sw., Rus.*) Dweller at the sign of the little pig; one who raised pigs; variant of Goran, q.v.; dweller on the mountain.

Gorka (*Pol.*) Dweller on, or near, the little hill.

Gorlach (*Ger.*) Variant of Gerlach, q.v.

Gorman (*Ir.*) The descendant of the little blue man, possibly referring to the color of his clothes; the son of Gormain, dim. form of Gorm (blue).

Gorme (*Scot.*) One with a livid complexion; one dressed in blue.

Gormley (*Ir.*) Grandson of Goirmghialla (blue hostage), Goirmghiolla (blue servant), or Goirmrhleaghach (blue spearman).

Gorniak, Gornick (*Pol.*) One who works in a mine, a miner.

Gorny, Gorney (*Fr., Rus.*) One who came from Gournay (swampy place; Gordus' estate), in France; dweller on the mountain.

Gorrell (*Eng.*) The man with the fat stomach; descendant of Garwulf (spear, wolf).

Gorrie, Gorry (*Scot., Ir.*) Descendant of Goraidh, Scottish form of Godfrey (God's peace); variant of Gorey, q.v.

Gorse, Gorss, Gorst (*Fr., Eng.*) Dweller near a hedge of thorn bushes; or among gorse or furze, a low, prickly evergreen shrub with spinelike leaves and yellow flowers growing in the moors.

Gorski, Gorska, Gorske (*Pol.*) Dweller on, or near, a mountain.

Gorton (*Eng.*) One who came from Gorton (dirty homestead), in Lancashire.

Gory (*Pol.*) Dweller on, or near, a hill.

Gosch, Gosh, Gosche (*Ger.*) Descendant of Gosch, a pet form of names beginning with Gos (God), as Goschalk and Godwin.

Gosciniak (*Pol.*) One who operated an inn or public house.

Gose (*Fr., Eng.*) Variant of Goss, q.v.

Gosfield (*Eng.*) One who came from Gosfield (open country where wild geese were found), in Essex.

Gosling (*Eng.*) Descendant of Jocelyn or Gocelin (just).

Gosnell (*Eng.*) Dweller at Gosa's corner.

Goss, Gosse (*Eng., Ger., Fr., Hung.*) Dweller in, or near, a moor or wood; a Goth; a shortened form of names beginning with the element *god;* dweller near a hedge of thorns; dweller at the sign of the goose; one who came from the former town of Goss, in Austria.

Gossage (*Eng.*) One who came from Gosfordsich in Lancashire.

Gosselin, Goslin (*Fr., Eng.*) Descendant of Goselin or Jocelin (just).

Gossett (*Eng.*) Descendant of little Goss or Joss (Goth).

Gosstrom (*Sw.*) Goose stream.

Gosswiller (*Ger.*) One who came from Gersweiler, the name of two places in Germany.

Gostomski (*Pol.*) One who came from Gostom, in Poland.

Gotham (*Eng.*) One who came from Gotham (estate where goats were kept), in Nottinghamshire.

Gothard (*Eng.*) One who took care of goats, a goatherd; descendant of Gotthard (God, firm).

Goto (*Jap.*) Rear, wisteria.

Gotsch (*Ger.*) Descendant of Gotsch, a pet form of Gottfried (God's peace).

Gotsis (*Hun.*) Variant of Kocsis, q.v.

Gott (*Ger., Eng.*) Descendant of Gott, a shortened form of names beginning with Gott (God), as Godabald, Godaberht, and Godafrid; dweller near a watercourse or channel.

Gottdiener (*Ger.*) The servant of God, a priest.

Gotter (*Ger.*) One who came from Gottern, in Germany.

Gottesman (*Ger.*) The pious man of God; God's servant.

Gottfried (*Ger.*) Descendant of Gottfried (God's peace).

Gotthelf, Gotthilf, Gothelf (*Ger.*) Descendant of Gotthelf (aid of God).

Gottlieb (*Ger.*) Descendant of Gottlieb (God, love).

Gottschalk, Gottschall (*Ger.*) Descendant of Gotesscalc (God's servant).

Gotz (*Ger.*) Descendant of Gotz, a pet form of Gottfried (God's peace).

Goudeau, Goudeaux (*Fr.*) Variant of Godeau, q.v.

Goudsmit (*Du.*) Dutch form of Goldsmith, q.v.

Goudy, Goudie, Gowdy (*Scot.*) Descendant of little Gold or Golda (gold).

Gough (*Eng., Ir.*) The ruddy or red-haired man; son of Eochaidh (rich in cattle).

Gould (*Eng.*) Descendant of Gold or Golda, Old English personal names derived from the metal.

Goulden (*Eng.*) Variant of Golden, q.v.

Goulding (*Eng.*) The son of Gold or Golda (gold).

Goulet (*Fr.*) Dweller on a narrow piece of land; or on a narrow stream; one who came from Goulet (gorge; mountain pass), in France.

Gounod (*Fr.*) Descendant of little Gon, a pet form of Hugon, French variant of Hugh (spirit, mind).

Gourley, Gourlay (*Ir.*) The son of Toirdealbhach (shaped like a god).

Gouwens (*Ir.*) Variant of Gowens, q.v.

Govan (*Scot.*) One who came from the lands of Govan (dear rock), in Lanarkshire.

Gove (*Scot., Ir.*) Variant of Gow, q.v.

Governale, Governile (*It.*) Descendant of Governale, the name of the attendant of Sir Tristram de Liones in the Breton cycle of romances.

Gow, Gowan, Gove (*Scot., Ir.*) The worker in metals, a smith; one who came from Govan (small school house; dear rock), in Lanarkshire.

Gowens, Gowen (*Ir.*) One who worked in metal, a smith.

Gower, Gowar, Gowers (*Eng., Wel.*) One who came from Gohier (Godehar's estate), in France; or from Goelle, anciently Gohiere, in France; descendant of Godehar (good, army); one who came from Gower (Gwyr), a peninsula in Glamorganshire.

Gowing, Gowin (*Ir.*) The son of the smith.

Goya (*Sp., Jap.*) One who came from Goya, in Spain; five, dwelling.

Goyer (*Fr.*) One who made and sold billhooks.

Goyette (*Fr.*) One who used a small billhook in his work.

Graan (*Du.*) One who raised or ground grain.

Grab, Grabbe, Grabb (*Ger., Pol.*) Dweller near a grave; dweller near a yoke-elm or hornbeam tree.

Grabarek, Grabarczyk (*Pol.*) One who plunders or pillages, a robber.

Grabe, Graben, Grabemann (*Ger.*) Dweller near a ditch, moat, or dike; one who came from Graben (ditch), the name of many small places in Germany.

Graber, Grabner (*Ger.*) One who came from Graben (ditch), the name of many small places in Germany; or from Grab, in Germany; one who dug in the ground, a digger.

Grabiner (*Ger.*) One who came from Graben (ditch), the name of many small places in Germany.

Grabinski (*Pol.*) Dweller near an elm tree.

Grable, Grabl, Grabel, Grabell, Grabill (*Ger.*) Dweller near a ditch or gully.

Grabow, Grabower (*Ger.*) One who came from Grabow (place where beech trees grew), in Germany.

Grabowski, Grabowsky (*Pol.*) One who came from Grabow (yoke-elm place), the name of three places in Poland.

Grace (*Eng.*) The large or fat person. See also Gras.

Gracia (*Sp.*) Descendant of Gracia, Spanish form of Grace (thanksgiving).

Gracz (*Pol.*) One who played games; one who gambled.

Graczyk (*Pol.*) The little man who played a musical instrument, a musician.

Grad, Grader (*Ger.*) Dweller in the castle or town; one who came from Grad (town), in Germany.

Gradl, Gradle, Gradman (*Ger.*) Dweller on, or near, a tract of arable land.

Gradolph, Gradolf (*Ger.*) One who came from Kradolf (dirty town), in Germany.

Grady, Gradie (*Ir.*) Grandson of Grada (noble, illustrious).

Graeber (*Ger.*) One who digs graves.

Graef, Graefe, Graeff, Graefen (*Ger.*) Variant of Graf, q.v.

Graf, Graff (*Ger., Fr., Eng.*) The earl or count; overseer in a lord's establishment; one who acted as a public scribe.

Graffy (*Eng.*) One who wielded a pen, a public scribe.

Grafham (*Eng.*) One who came from Grafham (homestead in the grove), in Huntingdonshire; or from Graffham (homestead in the grove), in Sussex.

Grafton (*Eng.*) One who came from Grafton (homestead by a grove), the name of several places in England.

Grage, Gragg, Graggs (*Ger.*) One with grizzled hair or gray complexion.

Graham, Grahame (*Eng., Scot.*) Dweller at the gray homestead; one who came from Grantham (Granta's homestead), spelled Graham in Domesday Book, in Lincolnshire.

Grahn (*Ger.*) One who came from Grano (place of grain), in Germany.

Grain (*Eng.*) One who came from the Isle of Grain (sandy shore), in Kent.

Grais (*Fr.*) One who came from Grais (sandstone), in France; dweller on, or near, sandstone.

Grajek, Grajewski (*Pol.*) One who played the violin.

Gramm, Gram, Grams (*Ger., Fr.*) The displeased, annoyed, angry man; the sad or melancholy man.

Grammer, Gramer (*Eng.*) The grammarian or scholar.

Gran (*Nor.*) Dweller near the spruce tree.

Granados, Granado, Granada (*Sp.*) One who came from Granada (pomegranate), in Spain.

Granahan (*Ir.*) The son of Reannachain (sharp, pointed).

Granara (*It.*) One who dealt in grain; dweller by a granary.

Granat, Granath (*Sw.*) One who raised and sold pomegranates.

Granata, Granatelli (*It.*) Dweller by a pomegranate tree; one who came from Granada (place where pomegranates grew), in Spain.

Granato (*It.*) One who wore a garnet.

Granberg (*Nor.*) Dweller on the hill where spruce trees grew.

Granby (*Eng.*) One who came from Granby (Grani's homestead), in Nottinghamshire.

Grandberry, Granberry, Granbery (*Eng.*) One who came from Grandborough (green hill), the name of places in Buckinghamshire and Warwickshire.

Grandclement (*Fr.*) Descendant of big or tall Clement (merciful).

Grande, Grand (*Fr.*) The large or fat man.

Granderson (*Eng.*) Variant of Grandison, q.v.

Grandfield (*Eng.*) Corruption of Granville, q.v.

Grandinetti (*It.*) One who was somewhat large; or almost grown up.

Grandison (*Eng., Swis.*) The big or tall son; one who came from Granson, in Switzerland.

Grandolfo, Grandolph (*It.*) Variant of Gandolfi, q.v.

Grand Pre, Grandpre (*Fr.*) Dweller on, or near, the large meadow.

Grandy, Grandys (*Fr., Nor.*) The tall man; one who came from Grande (dry land close to water), in Norway.

Granger, Grange, Grainger (*Eng., Scot., Fr.*) One who was in charge of a farmhouse with outbuildings; one who came from Grange (farm), the name of many places in Scotland; the tenant farmer.

Grankowski (*Pol.*) One who came from Grankow, in Poland.

Granley (*Eng.*) One who came from Cranleigh (cranes' wood), in Surrey; or from Cranley (cranes' wood), in Suffolk.

Granlund (*Sw., Nor.*) Spruce grove; dweller in, or near, a spruce or pine grove.

Grannan, Grannon (*Ir.*) Descendant of little Granach (pleasant).

Granquist (*Sw.*) Pine twig.

Gransby (*Eng.*) One who came from Grainsby (Grein's homestead), in Lincolnshire.

Granstrom (*Sw., Nor.*) Pine stream; dweller near a stream where spruce trees grew.

Grant (*Eng., Fr., Scot.*) The large or fat man.

Grantham (*Eng.*) One who came from Grantham (Granta's grove), in Lincolnshire.

Granthom (*Fr.*) The large or tall man.

Granton (*Scot.*) One who came from Granton (green hill), in Midlothian.

Granville (*Eng.*) One who came from Granville or Grandville (big estate), the names of several places in France.

Gras, Grass (*Fr., Eng.*) One who came from Grasse or Gras, in France; the large or fat person; dweller on the grass or village green.

Grassi, Grasso (*It.*) The fat, fleshy man.

Grater (*Eng.*) One who brightens or furbishes things.

Grattan (*Ir.*) The son of Neachtan (the pure one).

Gratton (*Eng.*) One who came from Gratton (great hill), the name of several places in England.

Gratz (*Ger.*) Descendant of Gratz, a pet form of Grad (greedy or covetous;

castle or town); one who came from Gratz, now Graz, in Austria.

Graubart, Graubard (*Ger.*) The man with the gray beard; the old man.

Grauer, Grau (*Ger.*) The gray man, probably referring to an old gray-haired man.

Grauman, Graumann (*Ger.*) The man with gray hair or hoary complexion.

Graupe (*Ger.*) One who dealt in hulled grain or groats.

Gravel, Gravell (*Eng., Fr.*) Descendant of the little reeve or bailiff; dweller in the small grove.

Gravely (*Eng.*) One who came from Graveley (brushwood grove), the name of places in Cambridgeshire and Hertfordshire.

Graver (*Eng.*) One who engraved or carved wood, stone, metal or the like; one who digs in the ground.

Graves, Greaves (*Eng.*) Descendant of the grave, a minor official appointed by the lord of the manor to supervise his tenants' work; dweller in, or near, a grove.

Gray, Graye (*Eng., Fr.*) The gray-haired man; one who came from Gray (Gradus' estate), in France.

Graydon (*Eng.*) Dweller on, or near, the gray hill.

Grayer (*Ger.*) One who came from Kray (crow), in Germany.

Grays (*Mx.*) Dweller at the grove.

Grayson (*Eng.*) The son of Greve (earl), or of the grave. See Graves.

Graziano, Graziani, Grazian (*It.*) The polite, gracious man.

Grbic (*Yu.-Sl.*) One with a hunchback.

Greaney (*Ir.*) Grandson of Grainne, a woman's name.

Grear (*Scot.*) Contraction of MacGregor, q.v.

Greasham, Gresham (*Eng.*) One who came from Gresham (grazing homestead), in Norfolk.

Greasley (*Eng.*) One who came from Greasley (gravelly wood), in Nottinghamshire.

Greathead (*Scot.*) The man with the large head.

Greathouse (*Eng.*) Dweller near, or worker in, the big house.

Greb, Grebe, Grebb (*Ger.*) Variant of Graff, q.v.

Greco, Grego (*It.*) One who came from Greece, a Greek.

Greeff (*Du.*) The headman in the village, a mayor.

Greeley (*Eng., Ir.*) Dweller at the gray grove; the son of Raghallach.

Green, Greene (*Eng.*) Dweller at, or near, the village green, or grassy ground.

Greenbaum (*Ger.*) Dweller at the sign of the green tree.

Greenberg, Greenburg (*Ger.*) One who came from Grunberg (green mountain), in Hesse, Germany.

Greenblatt (*Ger.*) Green leaf. See Greenleaf.

Greenfield (*Eng.*) Dweller at the verdant field or pasture; one who came from Greenfield (grassy place), in Lincolnshire.

Greenfogel (*Ger.*) Dweller at the sign of the green bird.

Greengard (*Eng.*) One who came from Greenodd (green promontory), in Lancashire.

Greengrass, Greengras, Greengus (*Eng.*) Dweller at the green, grassy place.

Greenhalgh (*Eng.*) One who came from Greenhalgh (green hollow), in Lancashire.

Greenhead (*Eng.*) One who wore a green hood.

Greenhill (*Eng.*) One who came from Greenhill (hill haunted by a ghost or spectre), in Worcestershire; dweller on the green-covered hill.

Greenholt, Greenholdt (*Eng.*) Dweller in a green wood or copse.

Greenhouse (*Eng.*) Dweller in the house on the village green.

Greenhut (*Eng., Ger.*) Dweller in the green hut, hovel, or small cottage; one who wore a green hat.

Greenidge (*Eng.*) Dweller on, or near, the green ridge; one who came from Greenriggs (green ridge), in Westmorland.

Greenland (*Eng.*) Dweller on the green land or glade.

Greenlaw (*Scot., Eng.*) One who came from Greenlaw (verdant hill), the name of several places in Scotland; dweller on the green hill or mound.

Greenleaf (*Eng.*) One who played the part of a wild man in public pageants, dressed in green leaves.

Greenlee, Greenleigh, Greenly, Greenley (*Eng.*) Dweller in the verdant wood or glade.

Greenman (*Eng.*) Dweller at the sign of the green man; a forest warden (who dressed in green); one who enacted that part in plays and pageants.

Greenough (*Eng.*) One who came from Greenhaugh (green enclosure), in Northumberland.

Greenquist (*Sw.*) Branch, twig.

Greensmith (*Eng.*) One who worked in lead; the smith who lived or worked on the village green.

Greenspan, Greenspon, Greenspahn (*Ger.*) One who made and used or sold verdigris, a substance much used in early chemical arts.

Greenstein, Greenstone (*Ger.*) Green stone.

Greenstreet (*Eng.*) Dweller by the green paved road.

Greenup (*Eng.*) Dweller in the green hollow or valley.

Greenwald (*Ger.*) Dweller in the green forest.

Greenway, Greenaway (*Eng., Wel.*) Dweller at the green road or path; descendant of Goronwy (hero; crown).

Greenwell (*Eng.*) Dweller near a green (grassy) spring.

Greenwich (*Eng.*) One who came from Greenwich (green dwelling), in Kent.

Greenwood (*Eng.*) Dweller in the verdant wood or forest.

Greer (*Scot.*) A contraction of MacGregor, q.v.

Greet, Grete (*Eng.*) The great or large person; dweller near the Greet river (gravelly stream), in Nottingham-shire; one who came from Greet (gravel), the name of several villages in England.

Grega (*Cz.-Sl.*) Descendant of Grega, a Czech form of Gregory (watchful).

Gregersen (*Nor., Dan.*) The son of Gregor, Norwegian and Danish form of Gregory (watchful).

Gregg, Greg, Greggs (*Eng.*) Descendant of Greg, a pet form of Gregory (watchful).

Gregoire, Gregori (*Fr.*) Descendant of Gregoire, French form of Gregory (watchful).

Gregorich (*Yu.-Sl.*) The son of Gregor, Yugoslavian form of Gregory (watchful).

Gregorio (*It.*) Descendant of Gregorio, Italian form of Gregory (watchful).

Gregorson (*Eng., Scot.*) The son of Gregor (watchful).

Gregory, Gregor (*Eng., Scot.*) Descendant of Gregory (watchful).

Gregson (*Eng., Scot.*) The son of Greg, a pet form of Gregory (watchful).

Greif, Greiff (*Scot., Eng.*) The overseer, manager, or head workman on a farm.

Greig (*Scot.*) Descendant of Greg, a pet form of Gregory (watchful).

Greiner, Grein, Greinke (*Ger.*) The unpleasant, quarrelsome person.

Grek (*Rus.*) One who came from Greece, a Greek.

Grelle, Greller, Grell (*Ger.*) The irate or angry man.

Grellner (*Ger.*) One who made spears.

Gremley (*Eng.*) One who came from Grimley (wood haunted by a ghost), in Worcestershire.

Grenier (*Fr.*) One who operated a granary.

Grennan, Grennon (*Eng., Ir.*) The man with the mustache; grandson of little Grianach (sunny; pleasant).

Grennell (*Eng.*) Dweller at the green hill; one who came from Greenhill (hill haunted by a ghost), in Worcestershire.

Grenon (*Fr.*) One with a mustache.

195

Grenz, Grens (*Ger.*) Dweller near the boundary or frontier.

Grenzebach (*Ger.*) Dweller at the boundary stream; or at the Grenzebach (slippery or boggy brook), the name of several streams in Germany.

Gresey (*Eng.*) One who came from Gresty (Graega's path), in Cheshire.

Gresham, Grisham (*Eng.*) One who came from Gresham (grazing farm), in Norfolk.

Gress (*Fr., Ger.*) Dweller on a pebbly or sandstone piece of land; one who came from Gris (sandstone), in France; or from Gresse (grassy ground), in Germany; the fat man.

Grether (*Ger.*) Descendant of Grete, a pet form of Margarete, German form of Margaret (pearl).

Greve (*Scot.*) Same as Grieve, q.v.

Grevin (*Ir.*) Grandson of little Griobhtha (griffinlike warrior).

Grewe, Grew (*Eng.*) Dweller at the sign of the crane; one with some characteristic of a crane.

Grey, Greye (*Eng.*) The man with gray hair. Grey is the usual spelling in England.

Greystone (*Eng.*) Dweller near a gray stone or rock.

Gribbin, Gribben, Gribbon (*Ir.*) Grandson of Gribin; the son of Robin, pet form of Robert (fame, bright).

Gribble (*Eng.*) Corrupt form of Grimbald, q.v.

Grice, Grise (*Eng.*) One thought to have the characteristics of a pig; one who took care of pigs.

Gricus, Gricius (*Eng.*) One with gray hair; dweller at the sign of the pig; one who took care of the pigs.

Grider (*Ger.*) American pronunciation variant of Kreiter, q.v.

Gridley (*Eng.*) Dweller in, or near, Grida's wood.

Griebel, Griebell, Griebler (*Ger.*) Dweller in, or near, the small depression or excavation; one who digs, especially graves.

Grieco (*It.*) One who came from Greece, a Greek.

Grief, Grieff (*Scot.*) Variants of Grieve, q.v.

Grieger (*Ger.*) Descendant of Grieger, a form of Gregorius (watchful).

Grier, Grierson (*Scot.*) Descendant of Grier, a shortened form of Gregor (watchful).

Gries, Griese, Griesel (*Ger.*) One who came from Gries (gray or sandy place), the name of several places in Germany; dweller on the sand or sandy shore.

Grieshaber (*Ger.*) One who raises and sells oats, especially the groats or oat kernels.

Griesmann, Griesman (*Ger.*) The gray-haired or old man.

Grieve, Grieves (*Scot.*) A minor official appointed by the lord of the manor to supervise his tenants' work; descendant of Greifi (count; earl).

Griff, Grife (*Eng., Wel.*) One who came from Griff (hollow), in Warwickshire; or from Griffe (hollow), in Derbyshire; descendant of Griff, a short form of Griffith (fierce lord).

Griffee, Griffey, Griffy (*Wel.*) Descendants of little Griff, a pet form of Griffith (fierce lord).

Griffin, Griffen (*Eng.*) Dweller at the sign of the griffin, a fabulous monster, half lion and half eagle; one with a ruddy complexion; descendant of Griffin or Gryffyn (fierce lord).

Griffith, Griffiths (*Wel.*) Descendant of Griffith (fierce lord).

Grigaitis, Grigaitas (*Lith.*) The son of Grigas, a pet form of Grigalius, Lithuanian form of Gregory (watchful).

Grigaliunas (*Lith.*) Descendant of Grigalius (watchful).

Grigas (*Lith.*) Descendant of Grigas, a short form of Grigalius, Lithuanian form of Gregory (watchful).

Griggs, Grigg (*Eng.*) Descendant of Greg, a pet form of Gregory (watchful).

Grigonis (*Lith.*) Descendant of Grigas, q.v.

Grigorian (*Arm.*) Descendant of Grigor,

Armenian form of Gregory (watchful).

Grigsby (*Eng.*) Dweller at the homestead belonging to Grig, a pet form of Gregory (watchful).

Grill, Grille (*Ger.*) One who came from Grill, the name of several places in Germany and Austria; dweller at the sign of the cricket.

Grilli, Grillo (*It.*) Nickname for one thought to possess the characteristics of a cricket; the small, young man.

Grimaldi, Grimaldo (*It.*) Descendant of Grimaldi (mask, bold).

Grimbald (*Eng.*) Descendant of Grimbald (mask, bold).

Grimble (*Eng.*) One who came from Grimley (grove haunted by a ghost), in Worcestershire; descendant of Grimbald (mask, bold).

Grimes, Grimson (*Eng.*) Descendant of Grim (mask). See Grimm.

Grimley (*Eng., Ir.*) One who came from Grimley (grove haunted by a ghost), in Worcestershire; descendant of Goirmshteaghach (blue-spearman).

Grimm, Grim, Grime, Grimme (*Eng., Ger.*) Descendant of Grim (mask), the first element of names like Grimbald, Grimkell and Grimulf; the fierce, savage person.

Grimman (*Scot.*) Descendant of Hromund (fame, protection).

Grimmett (*Eng.*) Descendant of little Grim (mask).

Grimsby (*Eng.*) One who came from Grimsby (Grim's village), in Lincolnshire.

Grimsell (*Eng.*) One who came from Greenhill, earlier, Grimeshyll (hill haunted by a ghost), in Worcestershire.

Grimshaw (*Eng.*) Dweller in a copse haunted by a ghost; one who came from Grimshaw (Grim's wood), in Lancashire.

Grimsley (*Eng.*) Dweller in, or near, Grim's grove.

Grimwood (*Eng.*) Dweller in a wood haunted by a ghost.

Grindale, Grindal, Grindel (*Eng.*) One who came from Grindale (green valley), in the East Riding of Yorkshire.

Grinder, Grindler (*Eng.*) One who ground grain, a miller; one who sharpened iron tools on a grindstone.

Griner (*Eng.*) One who ground grain, a miller.

Grinnage (*Eng.*) One who came from Greenwich (green dairy farm), in Kent.

Grinnell, Grindle, Grindel (*Eng.*) One who came from Grindle (green hill), in Shropshire; dweller on, or near, a green hill.

Grinstead, Grinsted (*Eng.*) One who came from Grinstead (green site), in Sussex.

Grinton (*Eng.*) One who came from Grinton (green grove), in the North Riding of Yorkshire.

Grisby (*Eng.*) One who came from Greasby (fort with a trench), in Cheshire.

Grisdale (*Eng.*) One who came from Grisedale (pig's valley), in Cumberland.

Grisin (*Rus.*) Descendant of Grisa, a pet form of Gregorij, Russian form of Gregory (watchful).

Grissom, Grisson, Grison (*Eng.*) The gray-haired man, often in reference merely to an old man.

Grist (*Eng.*) The gray-haired man; sharpened form of Grice, q.v.

Griswold (*Eng.*) Dweller at a wood frequented by pigs.

Gritzenbach (*Ger.*) Dweller at the stream where groats were produced.

Gritzmacher (*Ger.*) One who made and sold groats.

Grizzard (*Fr.*) One with gray hair or grizzled appearance.

Grizzle, Grizely (*Eng.*) One who came from Greasley (gravelly grove), in Nottinghamshire.

Groark (*Ir.*) The son of Ruarc, a Celtic form of Roderick (fame, rule).

Groat (*Du.*) The large tall man.

Grob, Grobe (*Ger.*) The coarse, uncouth, rough man; the big thick man.

Grobelny (*Pol.*) Dweller on, or near, the dike.

Grober (*Ger.*) One who came from Groben (swamp), in Germany.

Groble, Grobl (*Ger.*) Descendant of Grobel, a pet form of names beginning with Hrod (fame), as Hrotbald and Hrodobert; one who digs, a gravedigger.

Grobstein (*Ger.*) Dweller by the big, thick stone.

Groch, Grochocki, Grochowiak, Grochowski, Grochowsky (*Pol.*) One who raised and sold peas.

Grod, Grodsky (*Pol.*) Dweller, or worker, in the castle or fortified town.

Grodecki, Grodinsky (*Pol., Rus.*) Dweller in the castle or fortified town.

Grodnitzky (*Rus.*) One who came from Grodno (fortified place), in Byelorussia.

Grodzicki (*Pol.*) Dweller near, or worker in, the castle.

Grodzins (*Lith., Lat.*) Dweller in, or near, a hedged in place.

Groebe, Groeber (*Ger.*) One who came from Groben (swamp), in Germany.

Groeger (*Ger.*) Descendant of Gregor, a German form of Gregory (watchful).

Groeller (*Ger.*) One who came from Groll (grassy, swampy area), in Germany; the angry, irate man.

Groen, Groene (*Du.*) The young, inexperienced, vigorous person; one who wore green clothing.

Groenendijk (*Du.*) One who came from Groenendijk (green embankment), the name of two places in Holland.

Groeneveld (*Du.*) Dweller on, or near, the green field; one who came from Groeneveld (green field), in Holland.

Groenewold, Groenwald (*Ger., Du.*) Dweller in, or near, the green wood.

Groesbeck (*Du.*) One who came from Groesbeek (large brook), in Holland.

Groetsema (*Du.*) The son of Groetse (greetings).

Groetzinga (*Pol.*) One who came from Grodziega (enclosure), in Poland.

Groff, Groffman, Grofman (*Ger., Du.*) Variant of Grob, q.v.

Grogan (*Ir.*) Grandson of little Gruag (hair of the head); or of little Grug (fierceness).

Groh, Grohe, Grohman, Grohmann (*Ger.*) The gray-haired man.

Groll (*Ger.*) One who came from Groll (grassy, swampy area), in Germany; the angry, irate man.

Groller, Grollinger (*Ger.*) One with a bad temper or rough personality.

Grom, Groman (*Eng.*) The serving man or manservant, especially one in charge of animals.

Grombacher (*Ger.*) One who came from Grombach (crooked stream), in Germany.

Gromek (*Pol.*) A nickname meaning "little thunderbolt."

Gromer, Gromar (*Fr.*) Descendant of Gronmar (green, fame).

Gromyko (*Rus.*) Thunder, an adopted name.

Gron (*Sw.*) Green.

Gronberg (*Sw.*) Green mountain.

Gronek (*Pol., Ukr., Rus.*) Dweller near a small cluster of something, such as trees.

Groner, Groener (*Ger.*) One who came from Grone (green), in West Germany; descendant of Gronhari (green, army).

Gronholm (*Sw.*) Green island.

Gronke (*Ger.*) Thunder, possibly a nickname for a loud voiced person.

Gronlund (*Sw.*) Green grove.

Gronski, Gronsky (*Pol.*) One who belongs to the group, an associate.

Groombridge (*Eng.*) One who came from Groombridge (the boy servant's bridge), in Kent.

Grooms, Groom, Groomes (*Eng.*) A serving-man, a manservant, sometimes a boy servant; one who took care of sheep, a shepherd.

Groot, Groote (*Du.*) The big, or tall, man; one who came from Groot (large place), in Holland.

Groothuis (*Du.*) Dweller in, or near, the big house; worker in the manor house.

Grootstadt (*Du.*) One who came from the big city.

Groppi, Groppo (*It.*) Dweller on a hillside.

Gros (*Fr.*) The large, fat man.

Grosch, Grosche (*Ger.*) One who coined groschen, an old gold or silver monetary unit.

Grose (*Eng.*) The large, stout man.

Groseclose (*Ger.*) Variant of Grosklaus, q.v.

Grosjean (*Fr., Du.*) Descendant of big Jean, a French and Dutch form of John (gracious gift of Jehovah).

Grosklaus (*Ger.*) Big Klaus, a pet form of Nikolaus (people's victory).

Gross (*Ger.*) The large, or fat, person.

Grosscup (*Ger.*) Americanized form of Grosskopf, q.v.

Grosser, Groser (*Eng.*) The merchant in gross, a wholesaler.

Grosshans (*Ger.*) The large man named Hans, a pet form of Johannes (gracious gift of Jehovah).

Grossklas (*Ger.*) The large man named Klaus, a pet form of Nikolaus (people's victory).

Grosskopf (*Ger.*) One with a fat or thick head.

Grossman, Grossmann (*Ger.*) The large, or fat, man.

Grosso, Grossi (*It.*) The fat, fleshy man.

Grosschmidt (*Ger.*) One who made heavy iron articles; the large or stout smith.

Grosvenor (*Eng.*) The chief, or royal, huntsman.

Groszek (*Pol.*) One who raised and sold green peas.

Grote (*Du., Ger.*) The big or tall man.

Groth, Grothe (*Ger.*) The large, or fat, man.

Grothaus (*Ger.*) Dweller in, or near, the big house.

Grotto, Grotta (*It.*) Dweller in a cavern.

Grout (*Du.*) Variant of Groot, q.v.

Grover (*Eng.*) Dweller in, or near, a grove.

Groves, Grove (*Eng.*) One who lived in, or by, the small wood.

Growley (*Eng.*) One who came from Grovely Wood (ditch grove), in Wiltshire; or from Graveley (grove with brushwood), the name of places in Cambridgeshire and Hertfordshire.

Grubb, Grubbs, Grubbe (*Eng.*) The short, dwarfish man; the coarse, unpolished man.

Gruber, Grube, Grubman, Grubner (*Ger.*) Dweller near a mine, ditch or quarry.

Grudzien, Grudzinski (*Pol.*) One who was born or acted in some way in December.

Gruel (*Fr.*) One who grinds and sells wheat flour.

Gruen, Gruener (*Ger.*) Dweller in a green place; or in the country; one who came from Grun, Gruna, or Grunau (green meadow), the names of various places in Germany; the young, inexperienced, vigorous person.

Gruenberg (*Ger.*) Dweller on, or near, the green hill or mountain.

Gruenther (*Ger.*) The gentleman who had an estate in land, an aristocrat.

Gruhlke (*Ger.*) Descendant of little Gruhl, a pet form of Hruodilo.

Gruhn (*Ger.*) Variant of Gruen, q.v.

Grumbacher, Grumbach (*Ger.*) One who came from Grumbach (dirty stream), in Germany.

Grumbecker (*Ger.*) Variant of Grumbacher, q.v.

Grumbley (*Eng.*) One who came from Grimley (grove haunted by a ghost), in Worcestershire; descendant of Grimbald (mask, bold).

Grummel (*Eng.*) Descendant of Grimbald (mask, bold).

Grun, Grune (*Ger.*) One who came from Grun (green meadow), in Germany; one dressed in green.

Grunberg, Grunberger (*Ger.*) One who came from Grunberg (green mountain), the name of several places in Germany.

Grund, Grundman, Grundmann (*Ger.*) One who dwelt in the valley or bottom land.

Grundler (*Ger.*) One who came from Grundl (ground), in Germany; one who possessed land.

Grundstrom (*Sw.*) Ground stream.

Grundy (*Eng.*) Descendant of Gundric (war, rule); or of Gundred (war, counsel).

Grunenwald (*Ger.*) Dweller near a green forest.

Gruner (*Ger.*) Variant of Gruen, q.v.; descendant of Gronhari (green, army).

Grunewald, Gruenewald, Gruenwald (*Ger.*) One who came from Grunewald (green forest), the name of several places in Germany; descendant of Gronwald (green forest); dweller in, or near, the green wood.

Grunwald (*Pol., Ger.*) One who came from Grunwald (green forest), in Poland; variant of Grunewald, q.v.

Gruodis (*Lith.*) The roundish, ball-like man.

Gruszka (*Pol.*) Dweller near the pear tree.

Grzegorczyk, Grzegorski (*Pol.*) Descendant of Grzegorz, Polish form of Gregory (watchful).

Grzegorzak (*Pol.*) Descendant of Grzegorzok, a Polish form of Gregory (watchful).

Grzegorzewski (*Pol.*) One who came from Grzegorzewo (Gregory's place), in Poland.

Grzelak (*Pol.*) Descendant of Grzelak, a pet form of Grzegorz, Polish form of Gregory (watchful).

Grzyb, Grzybek (*Pol.*) One who gathered and sold mushrooms; dweller near where mushrooms grew.

Grzybowski (*Pol.*) One who came from Grzybow (place where mushrooms were found), in Poland.

Grzywacz (*Pol.*) One who raised and sold ringdoves.

Gschwind, Gschwindt, Gschwend (*Ger., Fr.*) The quick, blustering, furious, violent person; the rapid, swift worker.

Guagliardo (*It.*) Variant of Gagliardo, q.v.

Gualano (*It.*) One who breaks up the soil, a plowman.

Guard (*Eng.*) One who worked as a guard or watchman.

Guardino (*It.*) One who acted as warden in a jail; or who was a keeper in a noble's household; one who had charge of domestic animals, a herdsman; the superior in a convent.

Guardiola (*It., Sp.*) Dweller near a guardhouse or sentry box.

Guarino (*It., Sp.*) Descendant of Guarino, Italian and Spanish form of Garwin (spear, friend).

Gubbins, Gubbin (*Eng.*) Descendant of little Gibb, a pet form of Gilbert (pledge, bright); or of little Guba.

Gucciardo (*It.*) Dweller at the sign of the lark; the stubborn, obstinate man.

Gudaitis (*Lith.*) The son of the White Russian.

Gudas (*Lith.*) One who came from Byelorussia, a White Russian; sometimes a nickname for a stupid foreigner.

Gudde (*Ger.*) Dweller in the bush or woodlands; descendant of Gode, a pet form of names beginning with Gott (God; good), as Godehard and Godafrid.

Gude (*Eng.*) Descendant of Goda (good; God); variant of Good, q.v.

Guderian (*Ger.*) The good man named John (gracious gift of Jehovah).

Gudermuth (*Ger.*) One in the habit of wishing others, "Good Courage."

Guderyahn, Guderjan (*Ger.*) The good man named Yahn, or Jan, German forms of John (gracious gift of Jehovah).

Gudgeon, Gudgin (*Eng.*) The greedy man; the credulous, gullible man; dweller at the sign of the gudgeon.

Gudger (*Eng.*) Late development of Goodyear, q.v.

Gudmundson (*Sw.*) The son of Gudmund (good, protection).

Guendling (*Ger.*) Descendant of Gundel, a pet form of Gundlach (combat, jump; tournament).

Guenther, Guenthner (*Ger.*) Descendant of Guntard (war, bold).

Guercio (*It.*) One who is cross-eyed or walleyed.

Guerin (*Fr., Ir.*) Descendant of Guerin, French form of Warren (protection, friend); grandson of little Gear (sharp).

Guerino (*It.*) Descendant of Guerino. Guerino was the hero of a romance of the Middle Ages.

Guernsey (*Eng.*) One who came from the isle of Guernsey, in the English Channel.

Guerra (*Sp.*) Nickname for one active in military operations. Such activity by Count Pedro Fernandez de Castro caused him to become known as Don Pedro de la Guerra.

Guerrera, Guerrero, Guerrieri (*Sp., It.*) One who engaged in combat, a warrior.

Guess (*Eng.*) Softened form of Guest, q.v.

Guest (*Eng.*) The accepted stranger, a newcomer or guest.

Guetzlaff, Guetzloff (*Ger.*) Descendant of Godislav (beauty, fame).

Guevara, Guevarra (*Sp.*) One who came from Guevara (place overgrown with ferns), in Spain.

Guffey (*Scot., Ir.*) The son of Cobhthaigh (victorious).

Guggenheim, Gugenheim (*Ger.*) One who came from Jugenheim, in Germany.

Guglielmi, Guglielmo (*It.*) Descendant of Guglielmo, Italian form of William (resolution, helmet).

Gugliuzza (*It.*) Descendant of little Gugli, pet form of Guglielmo, Italian form of William (resolution, helmet).

Guice (*Eng.*) One who came from Guise (Wiso's place), in France; son of Guy (sensible; life; wood).

Guidice, Guidici (*It.*) Descendant of little Guido, Italian form of Guy (sensible; life; wood).

Guido, Guidi, Guida (*It., Sp.*) Descendant of Guido, Italian and Spanish form of Guy (sensible; life; wood).

Guiffra, Guiffre (*Fr.*) Descendant of Guiffre, French form of Giffard (gift, hard).

Guilbault, Guilbeau (*Fr.*) Descendant of Guilard, French form of Willard (resolution, brave).

Guild (*Scot.*) A variant of Gold, q.v.

Guilford (*Eng.*) One who came from Guildford (river crossing where marigolds grew), in Surrey.

Guilfoyle, Guilfoy (*Ir.*) The son of the servant, or devotee, of St. Paul.

Guillemin (*Fr.*) Descendant of little Guillaume, French form of William (resolution, helmet).

Guillen (*Fr.*) Descendant of little Guill, a pet form of Guillaume, French form of William (resolution, helmet).

Guillotin, Guillemet, Guillet, Guilotte (*Fr.*) Descendant of little Guillaume (resolution, helmet).

Guillotte (*Fr.*) Descendant of little Guill, pet form of Guillaume, French form of William (resolution, helmet).

Guinan, Guinane (*Ir.*) Grandson of Cuinean.

Guinand (*Fr.*) Descendant of little Guin, French form of Wine (friend); or of Wignand (combat, venture).

Guiney (*Ir.*) Descendant of the prisoner.

Guinn (*Ir.*) Shortened form of McQuinn, q.v.

Guinness (*Ir.*) The son of Aonghus (onechoice).

Guinsberg (*Ger.*) Variant of Ginsberg, q.v.

Gulbrandsen, Gulbransen (*Nor.*) The son of Gulbrand (war, sword).

Gulick, Gulik (*Eng.*) Descendant of Guthlac (war, play).

Gullatt, Gullatte, Gullett (*Fr.*) Descendant of Guillet, a dim. form of Guillaume, French form of William (resolution, helmet).

Gullen, Gullan, Gullane (*Scot.*) One who came from Gullane (sword guard), in East Lothian.

Gulley, Gully (*Eng.*) Dweller at the sign

of the little gull; dweller by a water channel.

Gulli, Gullo (*It.*) One in charge of the goats, a goatherd.

Gulliford (*Eng.*) One who came from Guildford (river crossing where marigolds grew), in Surrey.

Gulliver, Gullifer (*Eng.*) One who eats voraciously, a glutton; descendant of Wulfhere (wolf, army).

Gulyas (*Eng.*) Descendant of Golias, a softened form of Goliath (great or fat).

Gum (*Eng.*) Descendant of the man, from Old English *guma* (man).

Gumbiner, Gumbinger (*Ger.*) One who came from Gumping, the name of two places in Germany.

Gumbleton (*Ir., Eng.*) One who came from Comberton (Cumbra's homestead), the name of places in Cambridgeshire and Worcestershire.

Gumm (*Eng.*) Descendant of Guma (man).

Gump, Gumps (*Eng.*) Dweller on, or near, the flat place.

Gumpert, Gumprecht (*Ger.*) Descendant of Gundobert (war, bright).

Gunby (*Eng.*) One who came from Gunby (Gunni's or Gunhild's village), the name of places in Lincolnshire and the East Riding of Yorkshire.

Gundel (*Ger.*) Descendant of Gundulf (war, wolf).

Gundelfinger (*Ger.*) One who came from Gundelfingen, the name of three places in Germany.

Gunder, Gunderman (*Ger.*) Descendant of Gundhari (war, army).

Gunderson, Gundersen (*Nor.*) The son of Gunder (war).

Gundlach (*Ger.*) Descendant of Gundlach (war, tournament).

Gundrum (*Ger.*) Descendant of Gundram (war, raven).

Gundy, Gundry (*Eng.*) Descendant of Gundric (war, rule); or of Gundred (war, counsel).

Gunia (*Pol.*) One who made and sold smocks and frocks.

Gunkel (*Ger.*) One who made and sold spindles.

Gunn (*Scot.*) Descendant of Gunn (war); also an abridged form of many longer names, like Gunnar, Gunulf, Gunnhildr, etc.

Gunnar, Gunnarson (*Sw., Ice.*) Descendant of Gunnarr (war, battle).

Gunnell (*Eng.*) Descendant of Gundwulf (war, wolf); or of Gunnhild (war, battle).

Gunnersen, Gunnerson (*Nor.*) Softened form of Gunderson, q.v.

Gunning (*Nor., Eng.*) Descendant of Gunning or Gunnic (war or strife); the son of Gunn (war).

Gunshaw (*Eng.*) Dweller near Gunni's copse or thicket.

Gunter, Gunther (*Ger., Eng.*) Descendant of Gunter (war, bold).

Gunthorpe, Gunthorp, Gunthrop (*Eng.*) One who came from Gunthorpe (Gunnhild's or Gunni's farm), the name of five places in England.

Gunzburg (*Ger.*) One who came from Gunzburg (Gunz's stronghold), in Bavaria.

Guptill (*Scot.*) Dweller at the sign of the fox; one with foxlike characteristics.

Gura, Gurak (*Pol.*) Dweller on, or near, a hill.

Gurevitz, Gurewitz (*Pol.*) Dweller on the mountain.

Gurka, Gurko, Gurke (*Pol.*) Dweller near, or on, a small hill.

Gurley (*Mx.*) The son of Toirdealbhach (shaped like the god Thor).

Gurney, Gurnee, Gurnea (*Fr.*) One who came from Gournay (Gornus' estate), in France.

Gurry (*Fr.*) Descendant of Gurie or Guris (rich, powerful).

Gurski, Gursky (*Pol.*) Dweller on the mountain.

Gurvey (*Ir.*) Variant of Garvey, q.v.

Gurvitz (*Pol.*) Dweller in the mountains.

Guscott (*Eng.*) One who came from Goscote (shelter for geese; hut among gorse), the name of places in Leicestershire and Staffordshire.

Guse, Gusek (*Pol., Ger.*) Dweller at the

sign of the goose; one who raised and sold geese; one who came from Gusen, in Germany.

Guss (*Ger.*) Dweller at the sign of the goose; one who took care of geese.

Gust (*Sw.*) Descendant of Gust, a pet form of Gustaf (Goth's staff).

Gustafson, Gustavson (*Sw.*) The son of Gustav (Goth's staff).

Gustavsen (*Nor.*) The son of Gustav (Goth's staff).

Gustin (*Sw.*) Descendant of Gusten (god, stone).

Gustis, Gustison (*Sw.*) Descendant, or son, of Gust, a pet form of Gustaf (Goth's staff).

Guston (*Eng.*) One who came from Guston (Guthsige's grove), in Kent.

Gut, Gutt (*Ger.*) The free tenant; the very good man.

Gutekunst (*Ger.*) One with good skill and dexterity.

Gutenberg (*Ger.*) One who came from Gutenberg (farm hill; pleasant mountain), the name of several places in Germany.

Gutfreund (*Ger.*) The good friend.

Guth (*Ger.*) The good, stout-hearted or agreeable man; descendant of Godo, a pet form of names beginning with Gott (God), as Goteleib, Godulf, and Godelmar.

Guthman, Guthmann (*Ger.*) Descendant of Guthmund (combat, protection).

Guthridge (*Eng.*) Descendant of Godrich (good or God, rule); one who came from Goodrich (Godric's castle), in Herefordshire.

Guthrie (*Scot.*) One who came from the barony of Guthrie (windy place), in Angus.

Gutierrez (*Sp.*) The son of Gutierre, Spanish form of Walter (rule, folk or army).

Gutjahr, Guthjahr (*Ger.*) One in the habit of wishing others "a good year"; one who gave new year's presents.

Gutkin (*Ger.*) The good child.

Gutknecht (*Ger.*) The good, or able, servant; God's servant; one devoted to God.

Gutman, Gutmann (*Ger.*) Descendant of Guthmund (combat, protection); the good man.

Gutowski, Gutow (*Pol.*) One who came from Guty, in Silesia.

Gutrich (*Ger.*) Descendant of Gutrich (good, rule).

Gutstadt (*Ger.*) One who came from the pleasant town.

Gutstein (*Ger.*) Good stone.

Gutt, Gutter, Gutterman (*Fr., Ger.*) One who owns a substantial amount of land; one who came from Guttau or Gutter (muddy place), the names of places in Germany.

Guttenberg, Guttenberger (*Ger.*) One who came from Guttenberg (pleasant mountain), the name of three places in Germany.

Guttendag (*Ger.*) One in the habit of wishing others "a pleasant day."

Guttman, Guttmann (*Ger.*) Descendant of Gudmund (war, protection); the able or efficient servant.

Gutweiler (*Ger.*) One who came from Gutweil (pleasant village), in Germany.

Gutwillig (*Ger.*) Descendant of good Willig, a shortened from of Wilhelm, German form of William (resolution, helmet).

Gutwirth (*Ger.*) One who was a good innkeeper; or a good landlord; or a good husband.

Gutzman, Gutzmann (*Ger.*) Descendant of Godeman (God, man); one who came from Gutz, in Germany; the good, upright man; one in the service of God.

Gutzwiller (*Ger.*) One who came from Gutweiler (pleasant hamlet), in Germany.

Guy, Guye (*Eng.*) Descendant of Guy (sensible; life; wood).

Guyer (*Eng.*) The man who acted as a guide.

Guyon (*Eng.*) Descendant of little Guy (sensible; life; wood).

Guyton (*Fr.*) Descendant of little Guit, short form of Guitard (wood, hard).

Guzik, Guzek (*Pol.*) The little button, a nickname, usually for a small, insignificant man.

Guzman (*Sp.*) Descendant of Guzman (good man); a lord or nobleman.

Guzowski (*Pol.*) One who came from Guzow, in Poland.

Guzy (*Pol.*) Dweller near a mound or bump.

Guzzo, Guzzi (*It.*) Descendant of Guzzo or Guzzi, pet forms of Francesguzzi, Domenicuzzi and the like.

Gwatkin (*Wel.*) Descendant of Gwatcyn, Welsh form of Watkin. See Watkins.

Gwiasda, Gwiazdonik (*Pol.*) Dweller at the sign of the star.

Gwilliam (*Wel.*) Descendant of Gwilliam, a Welsh form of William (resolution, helmet).

Gwin, Gwinn (*Wel.*) Variant of Gwynn, q.v.

Gwizdala, Gwizdalski, Gwizdak (*Pol.*) One who whistled or blew a whistle.

Gwozdz (*Pol.*) One who made and sold nails.

Gwynett (*Wel.*) One who came from Gwynedd, an ancient province of Northwest Wales.

Gwynn, Gwyn, Gwynne (*Wel.*) The light-complexioned person.

Gyllstrom (*Sw.*) Golden stream.

Gyorgy (*Hun.*) Descendant of Gyorgy, Hungarian form of George (farmer).

Gyure (*Eng.*) One who acted as a guide.

Haack, Haak, Haake (*Du.*) Dweller at the bend or hook in the river.

Haag (*Du.*) Dweller in, or near, the hedged enclosure; keeper of the hedges or fences; one who came from The Hague (the hedge), in Holland.

Haak, Haake (*Du.*) One who prepares and sells food.

Haaker (*Du.*) One who hangs herring up to smoke them.

Haan (*Du.*) Dweller at the sign of the cock.

Haanstra (*Du.*) Dweller in a nook or corner.

Haar, Haarman, Haarmann (*Ger.*) Dweller in, or near, the moor or swamp; or on an eminence or high place.

Haas, Haase, Hase (*Du., Ger.*) Dweller at the sign of the hare; one thought to possess some of the characteristics of a hare.

Habbishaw (*Scot.*) One who came from Habbieshowe (Halbert's hollow), in Ayrshire.

Habel (*Ger., Cz.*) Descendant of Habel, a form of Gallus (the Gaul).

Habenicht (*Ger.*) One who had nothing, a man without resources.

Haber, Hafer, Haberkorn (*Ger.*) One who grew oats; dweller near where oats grew.

Haberland (*Ger.*) Dweller near the oat field.

Haberle, Haberly (*Eng.*) One who came from Habberley (Heathuburg's grove), the name of villages in Shropshire and Worcestershire.

Haberman (*Ger.*) One who grew and sold oats.

Haberstroh (*Ger.*) Oats and straw, a nickname for a grain farmer.

Habib (*Arab.*) The dear, beloved person.

Habich, Habig (*Ger.*) Dweller at the sign of the hawk; one who hunts with hawks.

Hachmeister (*Ger.*) The master of the hawks in falconry; the servant in charge of the hedges and fences and their repair.

Hack (*Eng.*) Dweller at the gate, or entrance, to a forest; descendant of Hake, a pet form of Hakon (high kin).

Hackbarth, Hackbert, Hackbart (*Ger.*) Descendant of Hagabert (enclosed place, bright).

Hackel, Hackl (*Ger.*) One who draws flax or wool through a set of bristles; the coarse, rude, rough man.

Hacker (*Eng.*) One who cultivates the soil with a hoe or hack; a maker of hacks.

Hackett (*Eng.*) Descendant of little Hack or Hache (hook).

Hackins (*Eng.*) Variant of Hawkins, q.v.

Hackler, Hackner (*Ger.*) One who cut wood or used a pickax or mattock; one who uses a hand tool; one who cut meat, a butcher.

Hackman, Hackmann (*Ger., Eng.*) One who keeps a shop; a huckster; one who cuts or hacks wood.

Hackney (*Eng.*) One who came from Hackney (Haca's island), in Middlesex; one who took care of the ambling horses or mares used by ladies.

Hackshaw (*Eng.*) Dweller in, or near, an oak grove.

Hackworth (*Eng.*) One who came from Hackworth (Haca's homestead), in Devonshire; or from Ackworth (Acca's homestead), in the West Riding of Yorkshire.

Hadaway (*Eng.*) Variant of Hathaway, q.v.

Haddad, Hadad (*Syr., Arab.*) One who worked in metal, a smith.

Hadden, Haddon, Haden (*Eng.*) One who came from Haddon (heather-covered hill), the name of several places in England.

Haddix (*Eng.*) Variant of Haddock, q.v.

Haddock, Haddox (*Eng.*) Dweller at the sign of the haddock; one who caught and sold haddocks; one who came from Haycock (barley farm), in Lancashire.

Haderlein (*Ger.*) Descendant of Haderlein, a form of Hadheri (fight, army); one who quarrels.

Haderly (*Eng.*) One who came from Hatherley (hawthorn wood), in Gloucestershire.

Hadesman (*Ger.*) Husband of Hadassah (a myrtle).

Hadfield (*Eng.*) One who came from Hadfield (heather-covered open country), in Derbyshire.

Hadge (*Ger.*) Descendant of Hadge, a shortened form of Heidenreich (mighty over the heathen).

Hadjepetris (*Arab., Gr.*) One named Petris who had made a pilgrimage to Mecca or the Holy Land. Petris is the Greek form of Peter (a rock).

Hadley (*Eng.*) One who came from Hadleigh (heather-covered clearing), the name of several places in England; or from Hadley (Headda's clearing), in Worcestershire.

Hadlock (*Eng.*) One who came from Hadlow (heather-covered hill), in Kent.

Hadlow (*Eng.*) One who came from Hadlow (heather-covered hill), in Kent.

Hadsock, Hadstock (*Eng.*) One who came from Hadstock (Hada's place), in Essex.

Haduch (*Sl.*) One who acted as armor bearer for a nobleman; one who fought on foot, a foot soldier.

Haefner (*Ger.*) Variant of Hafner, q.v.

Haeger, Haegele (*Ger.*) Variant of Hagler, q.v.

Haerle (*Ger.*) One with smooth, glossy hair.

Haertel (*Ger.*) Variant of Hertel, q.v.

Haffey (*Ir.*) Grandson of Eachaidh (rich in cattle).

Hafford (*Eng.*) One who came from Halford (crossing in a narrow valley), the name of places in Devonshire and Warwickshire.

Hafner, Haffner (*Ger.*) One who made utensils of earthenware, a potter.

Hagan (*Ir., Ger., Eng.*) Grandson of Ogan (young); or of little Aodh (fire); descendant of Hagano (forest man).

Hagberg (*Sw.*) Pasture, or willow, mountain.

Hage (*Ger.*) Dweller near the hedge or fence.

Hagedorn (*Du.*) Dweller near a hawthorn tree.

Hagele (*Ger.*) Variant of Hagler, q.v.

Hageman, Hagemann, Hagerman (*Ger.*) One who repaired and maintained the village hedges; dweller in a hedged enclosure; one in charge of a forest, a forest keeper.

Hagemeyer (*Ger.*) One who repaired the hedges or fences, and kept the animals from straying; dweller near, or in, the enclosure.

Hagen (*Ger., Ir.*) One who came from Hagen (enclosure), the name of many small places in Germany; dweller at, or near, the thorn fence; descendant of Hagano (forest man); dweller in a grove.

Hagenauer (*Ger.*) One who came from Hagenau (hedged meadow), the name of several places in Germany.

Hagendorf (*Ger.*) One who came from Hagendorf (hedged hamlet), the name of three places in Germany.

Hager, Hagar (*Eng.*) The tall, slender man; descendant of Hagar (flight; stranger).

Hagerup (*Dan., Nor.*) One who came from Hagerup (enclosed habitation), in Denmark.

Haggard, Haggart (*Eng.*) The wild, untamed man.

Haggerty, Hagerty, Hagarty, Haggarty (*Ir.*) Grandson of Eigceartach (unjust).

Haggins, Hagins (*Ir.*) Grandson of little Og (young).

Hagler (*Eng.*) Dweller at a hedged enclosure.

Haglund, Hagglund (*Sw.*) Pasture, or willow, grove; hedge grove.

Hagman, Haggman (*Eng.*) Dweller at the hedged enclosure; descendant of Hagmund (skilful, protection).

Hagnauer (*Ger.*) One who came from Hagnau (hedged meadow), in Germany.

Hagner (*Ger.*) One who came from Hagen (enclosure), the name of numerous places in Germany.

Hagopian (*Arm.*) Descendant of Hagop, Armenian form of Jacob (may God protect; the supplanter).

Hagstrom, Haggstrom (*Sw.*) Pasture, or willow, stream; hedge stream.

Hague (*Eng.*) Dweller by the hedged enclosure.

Hagy (*Swis., Ger.*) Dweller on a plot of land surrounded by a hedge.

Hahn, Hahne (*Ger.*) One who lived, or worked, at the sign of the cock.

Haight, Haigh, Haig (*Eng.*) One who came from Haigh (enclosure), the name of places in Lancashire and Yorkshire; dweller at a hedged enclosure.

Hailes, Haile (*Eng., Scot.*) One who came from Hailes, in Gloucestershire; or from Hailes (hall), in Midlothian.

Hailey (*Eng.*) One who came from Hailey (hay clearing), in Oxfordshire.

Hain, Haine (*Eng., Ger.*) Dweller at the hedged enclosure; or in the grove.

Hainault (*Fr.*) One who came from Hainaut, a medieval county in Belgium and Northern France; descendant of little Hain, a pet form of names beginning with Hain (enclosed place), as Hainwald and Hainfrid.

Haines (*Eng.*) One who came from Haynes (enclosures), in Bedfordshire; dweller near the hedged enclosures.

Hainsworth (*Eng.*) One who came from Hainworth (Hagena's enclosure), in the West Riding of Yorkshire.

Hair, Haire (*Ir., Scot., Eng.*) Descendant of Ir (sharp); dweller at the sign of the hare; one with unusual hair.

Hairgrove (*Eng.*) Variant of Hargrave, q.v.

Hairston (*Scot., Eng.*) One who came from Hairstones (standing stones), in Peeblesshire; variant of Harston, q.v.

Haithcox (*Eng.*) One who hunted the heathcock, the black grouse.

Hajduk (*Ukr., Pol.*) A footman in Hussar or Cossack uniform; a messenger; a running footman.

Hajek (*Cz.-Sl.*) Dweller in, or near, a small wood or grove; one who came from Hajek (grove), the name of many villages in Czechoslovakia.

Hajyousif (*Arab.*) Descendant of the man named Joseph who has made a pilgrimage to Mecca.

Hakala (*Finn.*) Dweller on the pasture land.

Hakanson (*Sw.*) The son of Hakan, a

Swedish form of Haakon (high, kin).

Hake, Hakes (*Eng.*) Descendant of Hake, a short form of Hakon (high, kin).

Hakin (*Arab.*) The learned, scholarly man; one who practiced medicine, a doctor.

Halaburt (*Eng.*) Variant of Halbert, q.v.

Halama (*Du.*) One who came from Hallum, in Holland.

Halas (*Pol., Ukr.*) One who makes a lot of noise or bustle.

Halasz (*Hun.*) One who caught or sold fish, a fisher.

Halbe, Halb (*Ger.*) One who came from Halbau (half meadow), in Germany.

Halberstam (*Ger.*) Dweller near a tree stump.

Halbert (*Eng.*) Descendant of Halbert (noble, bright).

Halbrook (*Eng.*) Variant of Holbrook, q.v.

Haldane, Haldean (*Eng.*) Descendant of Healfdane (half Dane); one who was half Danish.

Haldemann, Haldeman, Halde (*Ger.*) Dweller on the mountain-side; one who came from Halden, a common place name in Switzerland.

Hale, Hail (*Wel., Eng.*) Dweller at the corner, nook, small hollow, or secret place; one who came from Hale (nook) or Hales (corners), the names of several places in England.

Halevy, Halevi (*Heb.*) The Levite, a man from the tribe of Levy; one pledged for a debt or vow; the priest's assistant.

Haley (*Eng.*) Dweller at the way, or passage, leading to the hall.

Halfacre (*Eng.*) Dweller on a homestead consisting of half an acre; one who tilled only half an acre.

Halfhill (*Eng.*) One who lived halfway up the hill.

Halfknight (*Eng., Scot.*) One who held his land of the lord of the manor paying half a knight's fee.

Halfmann (*Ger.*) One who worked at a seaport; a seaman.

Halford (*Eng.*) One who came from

Halford (ford in a narrow valley; hawkers' ford), the name of places in Devonshire and Shropshire.

Halfpenny, Halpenny (*Ir., Eng.*) Grandson of Ailpin (little, stout person); one who held land at a rental of half a penny.

Halfyard (*Eng.*) Dweller at half a yardland, or homestead consisting of half a yardland (about fifteen acres); one who tilled half a yardland.

Haliburton, Halliburton (*Scot.*) One who came from Halyburton (village by the holy enclosure), in Berwickshire.

Halicki, Halick, Halik (*Pol.*) One who came from Galicia in East Central Europe, a Galician.

Halil (*Arab.*) One who was a friend.

Halinski (*Pol.*) Dweller in the pasture or meadow.

Hall, Halle (*Eng., Ger.*) Dweller in, or near, the manor house; or in, or near, a stone house; servant in the principal room of the manor house; dweller at the rock or stone, generally a boundary marker; one who came from Hall or Halle (salt-works), the names of places in Germany.

Hallahan (*Ir.*) Grandson of little Aille (handsome; beautiful).

Hallam, Hallum (*Eng.*) One who came from Hallam or Halam (corner; remote valley), the names of several places in England.

Hallas (*Pol.*) The noisy, bustling man.

Hallberg (*Sw.*) Boulder mountain.

Halleck, Hallock (*Eng.*) Variant of Haluch, q.v.

Hallen, Hallin (*Eng.*) The servant in the hall or manor house.

Hallenbeck (*Sw.*) Raspberry brook; rock brook.

Haller, Halle (*Ger., Eng.*) One who came from Halle (salt-works), in Germany; same as Hall, q.v.

Halleran (*Ir.*) Descendant of Allmhuran (stranger from beyond the sea); variant of Holleran, q.v.

Hallett (*Eng.*) Descendant of little Hal,

207

a pet form of Harry or Henry (home rule).

Halley (*Eng.*) Dweller at the hall in the grove or open place in a wood.

Hallford, Halford (*Eng.*) One who came from Halford (ford in a narrow valley; hawkers' ford), the name of several places in England.

Hallgren (*Sw.*) Boulder branch.

Halliday (*Eng.*) Descendant of Halliday, a name sometimes given to a child born on a Sunday or other holy day.

Halligan, Hallagan, Hallighan, Hallaghan (*Ir.*) Grandson of little Aille (handsome or beautiful); descendant of the little handsome man; variant of Hallihan, q.v.

Hallihan, Hallahan (*Ir.*) Descendant of little Aille (handsome).

Hallinan (*Ir.*) Grandson of Aigheanain (noble offspring).

Halling, Hallin (*Eng.*) One who came from Halling (Heall's people), in Kent; the servant in the hall or manor house.

Hallingsworth (*Eng.*) One who came from Hollingworth (holly homestead), in Cheshire.

Hallisey, Hallissey, Hallisy (*Eng.*) One who came from Hollesley (hollow meadow), in Suffolk.

Halliwell, Hallawell (*Eng.*) Dweller near the holy well or spring; one who came from Haliwell (holy spring), in Middlesex; or from Halliwell (holy spring), in Lancashire.

Hallman, Hallmann (*Eng., Ger.*) The servant in the hall or manor house.

Hallmark (*Eng.*) Nickname, Half-a-mark, that is, one-third of a pound, possibly for one who paid a coin of that denomination annually as rent for his land; dweller on, or near, the hill field.

Hallom, Hallam (*Eng.*) One who came from Hallam (remote valley), the name of places in Derbyshire and the West Riding of Yorkshire; or from Halam (corner), in Nottinghamshire; or from Hollym (village of the

Hollym people), in the East Riding of Yorkshire.

Halloran (*Ir.*) Grandson of Allmhuran (stranger from beyond the sea).

Halloway (*Eng.*) One who came from Holloway (sunken road), in Middlesex.

Hallowell (*Eng.*) One who came from Haliwell, in Middlesex, or Halliwell, in Lancashire, both meaning holy spring.

Hallquist (*Sw.*) Boulder twig.

Hallstrom (*Sw.*) Boulder stream; dweller near stream with many boulders.

Hallworth (*Eng.*) Descendant of Haluarthr (gem, guard); dweller at, or near, Hal's enclosure.

Halm (*Eng.*) Shortened form of Hallom, q.v.

Halper (*Heb., Ger.*) Variant of Halperin, q.v.

Halperin, Halpern, Halprin (*Heb., Ger.*) A money-changer; one who came from Heilbronn (holy well) in Wurttemberg.

Halpin (*Ir., Fr.*) Grandson of Ailpin (little, stout person); a money-changer.

Halsey, Halse (*Eng.*) One who came from Halse (neck of land), the name of places in Northamptonshire and Somerset.

Halsted, Halstead (*Eng.*) One who came from Halstead (place of the hall; shelter for cattle), the name of places in Essex, Kent, and Leicestershire.

Halter, Halterman (*Eng.*) One who made and sold halters.

Halton (*Eng.*) One who came from Halton (homestead in a corner; look-out hill), the name of various villages in England.

Haluch (*Eng.*) Dweller in a shed or hovel; or in a hollow or depression in the ground.

Haluska, Halushka (*Ukr.*) One who resembled a dumpling, a short, fat, dumpy person.

Halvorsen, Halverson (*Nor.*) The son of Halvor (firm, prudence).

Halyckyj (*Ukr.*) One who came from

Halycyna, that is, Galicia, a region in Ukraine.

Ham (*Eng.*) One who came from Ham (meadow on a stream), the name of many places in England. See also Hamm.

Hamacher (*Ger.*) One who made harness, especially neck harness for draft horses.

Hamada (*Jap., Arab.*) Beach, rice field; dweller on a stony desert.

Hamann, Hamman (*Ger.*) Descendant of Hamann, a variant of Johannes (gracious gift of Jehovah); one who came from Hamm, in Germany.

Hamasaki (*Jap.*) Beach, headland.

Hambleton (*Eng.*) One who came from Hambleton (Hamela's homestead), the name of places in Lancashire and the West Riding of Yorkshire.

Hamblin, Hamblen, Hamblet (*Eng.*) Descendant of little Hamo or Hamon (home).

Hambly (*Eng.*) One who came from Hamble (crooked), in Hampshire.

Hambrick, Hambric (*Ger.*) Descendant of Heimbrecht (home, bright).

Hambright, Hambrite (*Ger.*) Descendant of Heimbrecht (home, bright).

Hamburg, Hamburger (*Ger.*) One who came from Hamburg (forest fortress), in Germany.

Hamby (*Eng.*) One who came from Hanby (Hundi's homestead), in Lincolnshire.

Hamdan (*Tur.*) Descendant of Hamdan (praise).

Hameetman (*Du.*) One who surveys or inspects the dikes.

Hamelen, Hamelin (*Eng.*) Variants of Hamlin, q.v.

Hamen (*Eng.*) Abbreviated form of Hammond, q.v.

Hamer (*Eng.*) One who came from Hamer (rock or cliff), in Lancashire.

Hamernik, Hamernick (*Pol.*) One who works in metal with a hammer.

Hames, Hammes (*Eng.*) The son of Ham or Hamo (home); one who came from Hames, in Cumberland.

Hamid (*Arab.*) One who believed in God.

Hamill, Hamel, Hamil (*Eng.*) One who came from Hammill (Hamela's wood), in Kent; descendant of little Hamo or Hamon (home).

Hamilton (*Eng., Scot.*) One who came from Hambleton (bare or treeless hill), the name of several villages in England; one who lived at Hamela's farm or enclosure.

Hamlin, Hamlet, Hamling, Hamlett, Hamlyn (*Eng.*) Descendant of little Hamo or Hamon (home).

Hamm (*Eng., Ger.*) One who lived on, or near, the enclosed plot of land; descendant of Hamo (home); dweller at the low, wet meadow; one who came from Hamm, the name of several places in Germany.

Hammad (*Arab.*) Dweller on a stony desert.

Hamman, Hammann (*Ger.*) Descendant of Hans, a pet form of Johannes (gracious gift of Jehovah).

Hammarlund (*Sw.*) Hammer grove.

Hammarquist (*Sw.*) Hammer twig.

Hammarskjold (*Sw.*) Hammer shield.

Hammer, Hammar, Hamer (*Ger., Sw., Eng., Wel.*) One who worked with metal, a smith; one who came from Hamm, Hamme, or Hammer (woodland; pasture), the name of many places in Germany; dweller on, or near, a steep, rocky hill; dweller on flat land by a stream; one who came from Hanmer (on the pool), in Flintshire.

Hammerberg (*Ger., Sw.*) One who came from Hammerberg (woodland mountain), the name of three places in Germany; hammer mountain.

Hammergren (*Sw.*) Hammer branch.

Hammerlund (*Sw.*) Hammer grove.

Hammerman (*Ger.*) One who shaped metal at a forge with a hammer, a smith.

Hammermeister (*Ger.*) One who worked in a foundry or ironworks.

Hammersley (*Eng.*) One who came from

Hamersley (rocky grove); dweller near a grove by a cliff or large rock.

Hammersmith, Hammerschmidt (*Eng., Ger.*) One who came from Hammersmith (blacksmith's shop; the hammersmith's smithy), now a part of London, in Middlesex; the smith who worked with a hammer.

Hammerstein (*Ger.*) One who came from Hammerstein (stronghold; stone homestead), the name of four places in Germany.

Hammett, Hammitt (*Eng.*) Descendant of little Hamo (home).

Hammill, Hammell (*Eng.*) One who came from Hammill (Hamela's wood), in Kent; the scarred or mutilated man.

Hammock, Hammoc (*Eng.*) Dweller near the oak tree on the low-lying pasture land.

Hammond, Hammons, Hammonds, Hammon, Hamond, Hamon (*Eng.*) Descendant of Hamo or Hamon (home); descendant of Heahmund (chief; protector).

Hamnett (*Eng.*) Descendant of little Hamo (home).

Hamp, Hampe (*Eng., Ger.*) One who came from Hamm or Ham (flat, low-lying meadow; enclosure), the name of numerous places in England; descendant of Hampo, a pet form of names beginning with Hag (thorn bush), as Haginbald and Heinprecht; or of Hamp, a pet form of Hamprecht (hedge, bright).

Hampden (*Eng.*) One who came from Hampden (village in a valley), in Buckinghamshire.

Hampel, Hample (*Eng.*) One who came from Hamble (crooked), in Hampshire.

Hamper (*Eng.*) One who made and sold goblets, cups and bowls.

Hampshire, Hamsher, Hamshire (*Eng.*) One who came from Hampshire (high homestead; Hamtun district), the name of a county in England.

Hampstead (*Eng.*) One who came from Hampstead (homestead; manor),

the name of several places in England.

Hampton (*Eng.*) One who came from Hampton (enclosure in a village; high village), the name of several places in England.

Hamre, Hamrin, Hamren (*Nor.*) Dweller on, or by, a cliff.

Hamson, Hampson (*Eng.*) The son of Ham or Hamo (home).

Han (*Chin.*) Fence.

Hanaford (*Eng.*) Dweller near a river crossing frequented by wild birds.

Hanahan, Hanagan (*Ir.*) Descendant of little Annadh (delay).

Hanauer, Hanau (*Ger.*) One who came from Hanau (muddy meadow), in Germany.

Hanbury (*Eng.*) One who came from Hanbury (high fortified place), the name of villages in Staffordshire and Worcestershire.

Hanby (*Eng.*) One who came from Hanby (Hundi's village), in Lincolnshire.

Hance (*Eng.*) Descendant of Hans, a pet form of John (gracious gift of Jehovah); dweller at the sign of the hand.

Hancock, Handcock, Hancox, Handcox (*Eng.*) Descendant of little Hane, a pet form of John (gracious gift of Jehovah).

Hand (*Eng., Ger.*) Dweller at the sign of the hand; one with a peculiar or misshapen hand.

Handel, Handell (*Ger.*) Descendant of little Hand or Hanto, pet forms of names beginning with Hand (hand), as Hantbert and Hantwin; descendant of Handolf (hand, wolf); one who peddled goods or engaged in trade, a tradesman.

Handelman, Handelsman, Handleman (*Ger.*) The merchant or shopkeeper.

Handler, Haendler (*Ger.*) One who bought and sold goods, a dealer or trader.

Handley (*Eng., Scot.*) One who came from Handley (high grove), the name of several places in England; descendant of Ainle (warrior).

Handloser (*Ger.*) One who occupied land for which he paid rent.

Handmacher, Handmaker (*Ger.*) One who made things by hand.

Hands (*Ger.*) Sharpened form of Hans, q.v.

Handschuh, Handschu, Handschug (*Ger.*) Dweller at the sign of the glove; one who made and sold gloves.

Handshaker (*Eng.*) One who came from Handsacre (Hand's field), in Staffordshire.

Handwerker (*Ger.*) A skilled worker; one who performs engineering work.

Handy (*Eng.*) The polite, courteous man; one who came from Hanby (Handi's stream; Hundi's village), the name of two places in Lincolnshire; descendant of Handi.

Hane (*Eng.*) Variant of Hayne, q.v.

Hanek (*Ger.*) Descendant of little Hann, a pet form of Johannes (gracious gift of Jehovah).

Haney, Hanney, Hannay (*Eng., Ir.*) One who came from Hanney (island frequented by wild cocks), in Berkshire; grandson of Eanna (bird).

Hanford (*Eng.*) One who came from Hanford (stone ford; Hana's ford), the name of places in Dorset and Staffordshire.

Hanger (*Ger.*) Dweller on a slope or incline.

Hanifin, Hanifen, Hanifan, Hanefan, Hanafan, Hanafin (*Ir.*) Descendant of little Ainbhioth (storm).

Hanik, Hanick, Hanicke (*Cz.-Sl.*) Descendant of little Hann, a pet form of Jan, Czech form of John (gracious gift of Jehovah).

Hanisch, Hanish (*Ger.*) Descendant of little Hann, a pet form of Johannes, German form of John (gracious gift of Jehovah).

Hankey (*Ger.*) Descendant of little Hank, a pet form of Heinrich (home, rule).

Hankins, Hankinson, Hankin (*Eng.*) The

son of little Hane, a pet form of John (gracious gift of Jehovah).

Hanko, Hankosky (*Pol.*) Descendant of Hanka, a Polish form of Anna (grace).

Hanks, Hank, Hanke, Hankes, Hanko (*Ger.*) Descendant of Hanke, a pet form of Heinrich (home, rule).

Hanley, Handley, Hanly (*Eng., Ir.*) One who came from Hanley (high meadow), in Staffordshire, or from Handley, with the same meaning, the name of several places in England; grandson of Ainte (beauty; hero or warrior).

Hanlon (*Ir.*) Grandson of Anluan (great hero or warrior).

Hann (*Eng.*) Descendant of Hann, a short form of Johann (gracious gift of Jehovah); or a pet form of Randolph (shield, wolf); or a pet form of Henry (home, rule).

Hanna, Hannah, Hannay (*Scot., Eng.*) Descendant of Senach (old, wise); or of Annan (grace); one who came from Hannah (Hanna's island), a parish in Lincolnshire.

Hannaford (*Eng.*) One who came from Handforth or Hanford (cock's ford), the names of several places in England.

Hannan (*Ir.*) Grandson of Ainnin; or of Aincin (unborn); or of little Annadh (delay).

Hannaway (*Ir.*) Variant of Hanvey, q.v.

Hannemann, Hanneman (*Ger.*) Descendant of Hannemann, a pet form of Johannes (gracious gift of Jehovah).

Hannett (*Eng.*) Descendant of little Hann, q.v.

Hannibal (*Eng.*) Descendant of Anabel (lovable). This name has no connection with the Carthaginian general.

Hannig (*Ger.*) Dialectal form of Hennig, q.v.

Hannigan, Hanigan, Hanihan (*Ir.*) Grandson of little Annadh (delay); descendant of the little slow man; variant of Hanahan, q.v.

Hanninen (*Finn.*) The son of Hannu, a

Finnish short form of John (gracious gift of Jehovah).

Hanning (*Eng.*) The son of Hann. See Hann.

Hannington (*Eng.*) One who came from Hannington (Hana's hill; cock's hill), in Wiltshire.

Hanniwell, Hanwell (*Eng.*) One who came from Hanwell (Hana's road), in Oxfordshire.

Hannon (*Ir.*) Grandson of little Annadh (delay).

Hannum (*Eng.*) One who came from Hanham (cock or stone meadow), in Gloucestershire.

Hanover (*Ger.*) One who came from Hannover (high shore), in Prussia.

Hanrahan (*Ir.*) Grandson of the little Anradh (warrior; champion).

Hanratty (*Ir.*) Descendant of Hanrachtaigh (illegal).

Hans (*Ger.*) Descendant of Hans, a pet form of Johannes, German form of John (gracious gift of Jehovah).

Hansberry (*Eng.*) One who came from Hanbury (high fortress), the name of places in Staffordshire and Worcestershire.

Hansbrough, Hansbro, Hansbury (*Eng.*) Dweller in, or near, Hama's or Hana's fortified place.

Hanschmidt (*Ger.*) The worker in metals named Hans, a pet form of Johannes, German form of John (gracious gift of Jehovah).

Hanscom, Hanscomb (*Eng.*) One who came from Hascomb (witches' valley), in Surrey.

Hansel, Hansell, Hanselman (*Ger., Eng.*) Descendant of little Hans, a pet form of Johannes (gracious gift of Jehovah); descendant of Anselm (divine, helmet).

Hansen, Hanson, Hanssen (*Dan., Sw., Nor.*) The son of Hans, a pet form of Johannes, Scandinavian form of John (gracious gift of Jehovah).

Hanus, Hanysz (*Pol.*) Descendant of Hanna, a form of Anna (grace).

Hanvey (*Ir.*) Grandson of Ainbhioth (storm).

Hanway (*Eng.*) One who came from Hanwey (Hana's road), now called Hanwell, in Oxfordshire.

Hanwell (*Eng.*) One who came from Hanwell (Hana's spring), in Middlesex. See Hanway.

Hanzel, Hanzl, Hanzlik (*Cz.-Sl.*) Descendant of little Hann, a pet form of Jan, Czechoslovakian form of John (gracious gift of Jehovah).

Happ, Happe (*Eng., Ger.*) The suitable, relevant man; descendant of Haep (proper); one who made vinedresser's knives and sickles; descendant of Happ, a pet form of Happrecht (fight, bright).

Happs (*Eng.*) Dweller by the aspen tree.

Hara (*Jap., Ir.*) Field; grandson of Eaghra.

Haraburda, Haraburd (*Pol.*) One who brawls or bullies others.

Haracz (*Pol.*) One who collected taxes or tribute; one who has been ransomed.

Harada (*Jap.*) Field, rice field.

Haralson (*Sw.*) The son of Harald, Swedish form of Harold (army, power).

Haran (*Ir.*) Descendant of little Earadh (fear); or of Anradh (warrior).

Harasym, Harasymenko (*Ukr.*) Descendant of Harasym.

Haraway (*Eng.*) Dweller near the road or path where hares abounded.

Harbaugh, Harbach (*Ger.*) One who came from Harbach, in Germany.

Harbeck, Harbecke (*Sw., Nor.*) Rabbit brook; one who came from Harebak (rabbit stream), in Norway.

Harbin, Harbinson, Harbison (*Eng.*) Descendant of little Harb, a pet form of Herbert (army, bright).

Harbor, Harbour, Harber (*Eng.*) Dweller near, or worker in, a shelter, lodging house or inn.

Harbro (*Eng.*) One who came from Harborough (hill where oats grew; hill where the herd grazed), the name of places in Leicestershire and Warwickshire.

212

Harbut, Harbot, Harbud (*Eng.*) Descendant of Herbert (army, bright).

Harcourt (*Eng.*) One who came from Harcourt (hawker's cottage), in Shropshire, or from Harcourt, (Hariulf's domain), in France.

Hard (*Eng., Ger.*) Descendant of Hard (bold), a pet form of names terminating in -hard, such as Eberhardt and Bernhard; dweller at the sign of the red deer; or on the hard, firm land.

Hardaway (*Eng.*) Dweller at the path used by the herd.

Hardcastle (*Eng.*) One who came from Hardcastle (cheerless dwelling), in the West Riding of Yorkshire; dweller at the earthwork-enclosure where sheep were kept.

Hardeman, Hardemon (*Eng.*) The servant of Hardy (bold); descendant of Hardiman (bold, man).

Harden (*Eng., Scot.*) One who came from Harden (high enclosure; hare valley), the name of places in Staffordshire and the West Riding of Yorkshire; one who came from Harden (higher hill), in Roxburghshire.

Harder, Harders (*Eng., Ger.*) Dweller at, or near, the hard or firm embankment; one who took care of animals, a herder.

Hardesty, Hardisty (*Eng.*) Dweller at the pen where the herd was kept.

Hardgrave (*Eng.*) Sharpened form of Hargrave, q.v.

Hardiman (*Eng.*) The servant of Hardy (bold).

Harding, Hardin (*Eng.*) Descendant of Hardwin or Harding (firm, friend); the son of Hard (firm).

Hardman, Hardmon (*Eng.*) One who took care of the herd (cattle, sheep, etc.).

Hardrick (*Eng.*) Variant of Hardwick, q.v.

Hardt (*Ger.*) Dweller in, or near, the willow wood; one who came from Hardt (willow wood), the name of many places in Germany; one who took care of animals, a herdsman;

dweller in, or near, a wood; variant of Hard, q.v.

Hardwick, Hardwicke (*Eng.*) One who came from Hardwick (sheep pasture), the name of several places in England.

Hardy, Hardie (*Fr., Scot., Eng.*) Descendant of Hardi, a short form of Hardouin (bold, friend); one who came from Hardy (Hard's island), in Lancashire.

Hare (*Eng.*) Dweller at the sign of the hare; one thought to possess some of the characteristics of a hare; dweller near a rock or heap of stones.

Harewood (*Eng.*) One who came from Harewood (gray wood; hare's wood), the name of three places in England.

Harfield, Harfeld (*Eng.*) One who came from Harefield (army field), in Middlesex.

Harger (*Eng.*) Descendant of Harger (army, spear).

Hargrave, Hargraves, Hargreaves (*Eng.*) One who came from Hargrave (hare's grove), the name of several places in England.

Hargrett, Hargett, Harget, Hargitt (*Ger.*) Variant of Hergott, q.v.

Hargrove, Hardgrove (*Eng.*) Variant of Hargrave, q.v.

Harig (*Ger.*) Descendant of Haro, a pet form of names beginning with Heer (army), as Harihard and Hariger.

Haring (*Ger., Eng.*) Dweller at the sign of the herring; one who netted and sold herring.

Haritos (*Gr.*) The gracious, attractive, charming man.

Harke, Hark (*Ger., Est.*) Descendant of Haro, a pet form of names beginning with Heer (army), as Haribald and Harmar; dweller at a fork in the road; or near where two streams came together.

Harkenrider (*Du.*) One who raked or cleared off reeds.

Harker (*Eng.*) One who keeps and trains hawks to hunt game; one who sells wares from place to place, a peddler.

Harkins, Harkin (*Ir., Eng.*) Descendant

213

of Ercan (red, speckled); or of little Har, a pet form of Harry or Henry (home rule).

Harkness (*Eng., Scot.*) Dweller near the (heathen) temple, or on, or near, the cape or headland.

Harlan, Harland (*Eng., Nor.*) Dweller on the land infested with hares; one who came from Haerland, in Norway.

Harley (*Eng.*) One who came from Harley (hare's wood), the name of places in Shropshire and Yorkshire.

Harlin, Harling (*Eng.*) One who came from Harling (Herela's people), in Norfolk.

Harlow (*Eng.*) One who came from Harlow (meeting place), the name of places in Essex and Northumberland.

Harmening (*Ger.*) The son of Harmen (army, man).

Harmer (*Eng.*) Descendant of Hermar (army, fame).

Harmon, Harman, Harmen (*Eng.*) Descendant of Herman (army, man).

Harms (*Ger., Du.*) Descendant of Hariman or Herman (army, man); one who came from Harms, in Germany.

Harmston (*Eng.*) One who came from Armston (Earnmund's homestead), in Northamptonshire.

Harnack (*Ger.*) The hard-necked or obstinate person.

Harnden (*Eng.*) One who came from Horndon (hill where thorns grew; horn-like hill), the name of several places in England.

Harness, Harnish (*Eng.*) One who made armor and harness.

Harnett (*Eng.*) Descendant of little Arnald (eagle, rule).

Harney, Hartney (*Ir.*) Grandson of Athairne (fatherly).

Harnisch (*Ger.*) One who made and sold armor.

Harold, Harrold, Harroldson (*Eng.*) Descendant of Harold (army, power); one who came from Harrold (gray wood) in Bedfordshire; occasionally from the office of herald, i.e., one

who bore messages from rulers or commanders or acted as heralds in tourneys.

Haroutunian (*Arm.*) Descendant of Haroutyoun (resurrection).

Harp (*Eng.*) Dweller at the sign of the harp; metonym for one who made harps or played the harp.

Harper (*Eng., Scot.*) One who played the harp at fair and festival; or for an important lord, often a hereditary official.

Harr, Harre (*Ger.*) Descendant of Harro, a pet form of names beginning with Heer (army), as Haribald and Herman.

Harrar (*Arab.*) One who embroiders silk.

Harrell, Harrel (*Eng.*) One who came from Harel, in Normandy; descendant of little Harry, an English pet form of Henry (home rule).

Harrer (*Ger.*) One who grew or sold flax.

Harrett (*Ir.*) Descendant of Harold (army, power).

Harridge (*Eng.*) Descendant of Hereric (army, rule); dweller on the ridge frequented by hares.

Harries (*Eng.*) The son of Harry, an English pet form of Henry (home rule).

Harrigan (*Ir.*) Grandson of little Anradh (champion).

Harriman (*Eng.*) The servant to Harry (home rule).

Harrington (*Eng., Ir.*) One who came from Harrington (the heath-dwellers' enclosure), in Northamptonshire; grandson of the tall or powerful man.

Harris, Harrison, Harries (*Wel., Eng.*) The son of Harry, the English version of Henry (home rule).

Harriston (*Eng.*) Variant of Harston, q.v.

Harrity (*Ir.*) Descendant of Aireachtach (member of an assembly).

Harrod (*Eng.*) Variant of Harold, q.v.

Harrop (*Eng.*) One who came from Harrop (hares' valley), in the West Riding of Yorkshire.

Harrow (*Eng.*) One who came from Harrow (Guma's people), in Middlesex.

Harrower (*Eng.*) One who pulverizes and smooths the soil, a harrower.

Harrum (*Eng.*) One who came from Harome (stone), in the North Riding of Yorkshire.

Harry (*Wel.*) Descendant of Harry, a pet form of Henry (home rule).

Harston (*Eng.*) One who came from Harston (Heoruwulf's homestead; gray boundary stone), the name of places in Cambridgeshire and Leicestershire.

Hart, Harte (*Eng.*) Dweller at the sign of the hart or stag, the adult male of the red deer; one who came from Hart (stag island), in Durham.

Hartel, Hartle, Hartl (*Eng.*) One who came from Harthill (hill where stags were seen), the name of places in Cheshire, Derbyshire, and the West Riding of Yorkshire.

Harter (*Ger.*) One who came from Hart (willow wood), the name of many small places in Germany; one who took care of animals, a herder.

Hartfield, Hartsfield (*Eng.*) One who came from Hartfield (open land frequented by stags), in Sussex.

Hartford (*Eng.*) One who came from Hartford (stag ford), or Hereford (army ford), the names of several places in England.

Hartig (*Du.*) The strong, robust man.

Hartigan (*Ir.*) Grandson of little Art (stone; bear).

Hartke, Hartzke (*Ger.*) Descendant of Hartke, a pet form of Hartwig (hard, battle).

Hartley (*Eng.*) One who came from Hartley (stag clearing), the name of several places in England.

Hartlove, Hartlieb (*Ger.*) Descendant of Hartlieb (hard, beloved).

Hartman, Hartmann (*Ger.*) Descendant of Hartmann (strong, man).

Hartness (*Eng.*) One who came from Hartness (the district subject to Hart), in Durham.

Hartnett, Harnett (*Ir.*) Grandson of Artneada (battle bear).

Hartney (*Ir.*) Grandson of Athairne (fatherly).

Harton (*Eng.*) One who came from Harton (stag's hill; gray homestead), the name of places in Durham and the North Riding of Yorkshire.

Hartrich, Hartridge (*Eng.*) Dweller at the ridge frequented by stags.

Hartry (*Scot.*) One who came from Hartree (old tree), in Scotland.

Hartshorn, Hartshorne (*Eng.*) One who came from Hartshorne (stag's headland), in Derbyshire.

Hartstone, Hartstein (*Ger.*) Dweller on a rough, stony terrain; one who came from Hartenstein (rough, stony place) in Germany.

Hartung, Hardung, Harting (*Ger.*) The son of Hart (strong); descendant of Harto, a pet form of names beginning with Hart, as Hardher and Hardmod.

Hartwell (*Eng.*) One who came from Hartwell (stags' spring or stream), the name of places in Buckinghamshire, Northamptonshire, and Staffordshire.

Hartwig, Hartwich, Hartweg, Hartewig (*Ger.*) Descendant of Harduwich (hard, battle).

Harty (*Eng.*) One who came from the Isle of Harty (stag island), in Kent.

Hartz (*Ger.*) American variant of Hertz, q.v.

Hartzell, Hartzel (*Eng., Ger.*) One who came from Hartshill (Heardred's hill), in Warwickshire; dweller at the sign of the little red deer; one with heart or feeling.

Hartzog (*Ger.*) Variant of Herzog, q.v.

Harunoglu (*Tur.*) The son of Harun, Turkish form of Aaron (lofty mountain).

Harvard (*Eng.*) Descendant of Hereward (army, protection).

Harvell, Harville (*Eng.*) Variant of Harwell, q.v.

Harvey (*Eng.*) Descendant of Harvey (bitter; carnage-worthy).

Harwell (*Eng.*) One who came from Harwell (pleasant stream; stream flowing from the hill), the name of places in Berkshire and Nottinghamshire.

Harwich (*Eng.*) One who came from Harwich (camp), in Essex.

Harwood, Harewood (*Eng.*) One who came from Harwood or Harewood (gray wood; hare's wood), the names of several places in England.

Hascall, Hascal (*Ger.*) Variant of Haskell, q.v.

Hasegawa (*Jap.*) Long, valley, river.

Haseltine, Haseldine, Haseldene (*Eng.*) One who came from Hesleden (hazel valley), in Durham; or from Haslingden (hazel valley), in Lancashire; or from Hazleton (homestead where hazels grew), in Gloucestershire; dweller in a valley where hazels grew.

Hasenfang (*Ger.*) One who hunts and captures hares.

Hasenjaeger (*Ger.*) One who hunts hares.

Hash (*Eng.*) Dweller at the ash tree.

Hashimoto (*Jap.*) Bridge, base.

Hasim (*Tur., Arab.*) The gentle or handsome man.

Haske (*Ger.*) Descendant of Haschke, a pet form of Johannes, German form of John (gracious gift of Jehovah).

Haskell, Haskel (*Ger.*) Descendant of Ezekiel (God is powerful), from a Yiddish form.

Haskett, Haslett (*Eng.*) Dweller at the headland where hazel trees grew.

Haskew, Haskow, Haskey (*Eng.*) One who came from Aiskew (oak wood), in the North Riding of Yorkshire.

Haskins, Haskin (*Eng.*) Descendant of little Aesc (ash; spear; ship).

Haslam, Haslem (*Eng.*) One who came from Haslam (hazel land), in Lancashire; or from Hasland (hazel grove), in Derbyshire.

Hasler, Hassler (*Eng., Ger.*) One who came from Haselor (hazel slope), in Warwickshire; or from Haselour (hazel slope), in Staffordshire; or from Hassel, the name of many places in Germany; or from Hasel, in Germany.

Hasley (*Eng.*) One who came from Haseley (hazel wood), the name of places in Oxfordshire, Warwickshire, and Wight.

Haslop, Haslup, Haslip (*Eng.*) Dweller in the valley where hazels grew.

Haspel (*Ger.*) One who made reels for the storage of yarn.

Hass, Hasse (*Ger.*) Descendant of Hazzo (combat); variant of Haas, q.v.

Hassan, Hasan (*Arab., Eng.*) Descendant of Hassan (the beautiful); one who came from Hazon (end of the hedge), in Northumberland.

Hassel, Hassell, Hassall, Hasselman, Hasselmann (*Ger., Eng.*) One who came from Hassel (place where hazel trees grew), the name of many places in Germany; one who came from Hassall (witches' corner), in Cheshire; dweller near a hazel tree.

Hassett, Hassey (*Eng., Ir.*) Variant of Haskett, q.v.; grandson of Aisidh (strife).

Hassid (*Heb.*) The pious, reverent man.

Hasson (*Sw.*) The son of Hasse, a pet form of Hans, shortened form of Johannes (gracious gift of Jehovah).

Hastie, Hastey, Hasty (*Scot., Ir.*) The impatient, violent person; the son of Hodge, a pet form of Roger (fame, spear).

Hastings (*Eng.*) One who came from Hastings (Haesta's people), in Sussex; descendant of Hasting or Haesten (violence).

Hata (*Jap.*) Farm.

Hatch (*Eng.*) Dweller by the gate or entrance to a forest; one who came from Hatch (gate), the name of several places in England.

Hatcher (*Eng.*) Dweller near the gate, or entrance, to a forest.

Hatchett (*Eng.*) One who made small axes; one who fought with the hatchet or small ax.

Hatfield (*Eng.*) One who came from Hatfield (heather field), the name of various places in England.

Hathaway, Hatheway (*Eng.*) Dweller at the heath road, or way through the heath.

Hathcoat, Hathcoate (*Eng.*) One who came from Heathcote (cottage on the heath), in Derbyshire; dweller in the cottage on the heath or tract of uncultivated land.

Hathcock (*Eng.*) Dweller at the sign of the heathcock, the black grouse; one with the characteristics of a heathcock.

Hatherley (*Eng.*) One who came from Hatherleigh or Hatherley (hawthorn wood), the names of places in Devonshire and Gloucestershire respectively.

Hathorne, Hathorn (*Eng.*) Variants of Hawthorne, q.v.

Hatley (*Eng.*) One who came from Hatley (Haetta's grove), the name of places in Bedfordshire and Cambridgeshire.

Hatridge (*Eng.*) Variant of Hattrick, q.v.

Hatt (*Eng.*) One who made head coverings; dweller near a clump of trees; dweller at the sign of the hat.

Hatten (*Ger.*) One who came from Hatten (swamp), in Germany; dweller in, or near, a swamp or bog.

Hattenbach (*Ger.*) One who came from Hattenbach (swampy brook), in Germany.

Hatter (*Eng.*) One who made and sold hats and caps.

Hattis (*Eng.*) One who made and sold hats; dweller on, or near, a hill.

Hatton, Hattan, Haton (*Eng.*) One who came from Hatton (homestead on a heath), the name of nine places in England.

Hattori (*Hun.*) One who came from Hattor, in Hungary.

Hattrick (*Eng.*) Descendant of Heathoric (war, rule).

Hatz, Hatzell (*Ger.*) Dweller at the sign of the magpie, or little magpie; one with some characteristic of a magpie.

Hatzenbuehler (*Ger.*) One who came from Hatzenbuhl (hill of the chase), in Germany.

Hatzis (*Gr.*) One who had made a pilgrimage to the holy land.

Hauber (*Ger.*) One who made and sold hoods and bonnets.

Haubert (*Ger.*) Descendant of Hugubert (mind, bright).

Hauck, Hauk, Hauke (*Ger.*) Descendant of Hauck, a pet form of Hugo (spirit; mind).

Hauer (*Ger.*) One who makes hay; one who cuts wood, grass, or meat, a cutter; one who came from Haue (pickax) or Hauen, the names of places in Germany; one who used a pick, a miner.

Hauf, Haufe, Hauff (*Ger.*) Dweller by a heap or pile.

Haug, Haugen, Hauge (*Nor., Ger.*) Dweller on, or near, a pasture; dweller near a small hill or burial mound; descendant of Haug, a pet form of Hugo (spirit; mind).

Hauger (*Ger.*) Descendant of Hucger (mind, spear).

Haugh, Haughey (*Ir.*) Grandson of Eachaidh (rich in cattle).

Haughney (*Ir.*) The son of Facthna, the name of four Irish saints.

Haughton (*Eng.*) One who came from Haughton (settlement in a corner; or on a ridge), the name of ten places in England.

Haugland (*Nor.*) Dweller at a farm on a hill or mound.

Haumann (*Ger.*) One who came from Hau (place where wood is felled), the name of two places in Germany; one who cut and sold hay or wood.

Haun (*Ger.*) Descendant of Hun, a pet form of Hunold (high, power); one who came from Haun (mire), in Germany.

Haupert (*Ger.*) Variant of Hubert, q.v.

Haupt (*Ger.*) One with a large or unusual head; dweller at the top of the hill or mountain; dweller at the sign of the head.

Hauptmann, Hauptman (*Ger.*) The district captain or leader; the head man in a borough.

Hauschild, Hauschildt (*Ger.*) A trooper,

217

mercenary or professional soldier; a blustering, browbeating man, a bully or braggart.

Hauser (*Ger.*) Dweller in a house for which a money rent is paid; descendant of Hauser, a pet form of Balthasar (Bel has formed a king); one who came from Hausen (houses), the name of many small places in Germany.

Hausknecht (*Ger.*) The servant in the house, a domestic servant; general servant; farm hand; man servant; steward or head servant.

Hausler (*Ger.*) Dweller in a house with little or no arable land; one who makes his living as a daily wage earner.

Hausman, Hausmann (*Ger.*) Dweller in a house; servant in the house.

Hausner (*Ger.*) One who came from Hausen (houses), the name of many places in Germany.

Haussmann, Haussman (*Ger., Fr.*) The house servant.

Hauswirth (*Ger.*) The owner of a house; head of the family.

Hautigan (*Ir.*) Variant of Hartigan, q.v.

Havas (*Hun.*) The white-haired or very light-complexioned man; dweller on, or near, snow-covered land.

Havel, Havill (*Ger., Eng.*) Dweller near the Havel, a river in Germany; one who came from Hauteville (high town), the name of several places in France.

Havelka (*Cz.-Sl.*) Descendant of little Pavel, Slavic form of Paul (small).

Havemeyer (*Ger.*) One employed as a judge or magistrate.

Havens, Haven (*Eng.*) Dweller by the harbor.

Haver (*Eng.*) Dweller at the sign of the buck or male goat; one thought to possess some characteristic of a billy goat.

Havercroft (*Eng.*) One who came from Havercroft (oat field), in the West Riding of Yorkshire.

Haverfield (*Eng.*) Dweller by, or in, the oat field.

Haverhill (*Eng.*) One who came from Haverhill (hill where oats were grown), in Suffolk.

Haversham (*Eng.*) One who came from Haversham (goat homestead), in Buckinghamshire.

Haverstick, Haverstock (*Eng.*) Dweller in a place where oats were grown.

Havey (*Ir.*) Variant of Heavey, q.v.

Havighurst (*Ger.*) One who came from Havekost (wood where hawks were seen), the name of four places in Germany; dweller in the wood frequented by hawks.

Haviland, Haverland (*Fr., Ger., Eng.*) Dweller on, or near, an oat field; one who came from Havelland (oat land), in Germany; one who came from Haveringland (land of Haefer's people), in Norfolk.

Havis (*Eng.*) Descendant of Avis (bird).

Havlik, Havlick, Havlicek (*Cz.-Sl., Ukr.*) Descendant of Havlik, a pet form of Gabriel (strong man of God).

Havoc (*Eng.*) Dweller at the sign of the hawk; one with the characteristics of a hawk.

Havranek (*Cz.-Sl.*) One who worked on a farm; the owner or manager of a farm.

Hawerbier (*Ger.*) One who brewed and sold beer or ale made from oats.

Hawes, Haws, Haw (*Eng.*) Dweller at the hedged enclosure; descendant of Haw or Hal, pet forms of Harry or Henry (home, rule).

Hawk, Hawke, Hawkes (*Eng.*) Dweller at the sign of the hawk; one with the characteristics of a hawk; descendant of Haw or Hal, pet forms of Harry or Henry (home, rule).

Hawkins, Hawkinson, Hawkings (*Eng.*) The son of little Haw or Hal, pet forms of Harry or Henry (home, rule).

Hawkshaw (*Eng.*) One who came from Hawkshaw (wood frequented by hawks), in Lancashire.

Hawksworth (*Eng.*) One who came from Hawksworth (Hoc's homestead; Hafoc's homestead), the name of places in Nottinghamshire and the West Riding of Yorkshire.

Hawley (*Eng.*) One who came from Hawley (hall in the wood or clearing), in Hampshire; or from Hawley (holy glade), in Kent.

Hawn (*Ger.*) American pronunciation variant of Hahn, q.v.

Haworth (*Eng.*) One who came from Haworth (hawthorn enclosure), in Yorkshire; variant of Hayward, q.v.

Hawryluk (*Ukr.*) The son of Havrylo, Ukrainian form of Gabriel (strong man of God).

Hawrysz (*Ukr.*) Descendant of Havrylo, Ukrainian form of Gabriel (strong man of God).

Hawthorne, Hawthorn (*Eng.*) One who came from Hawthorn (hawthorn tree), a village in Durham; dweller near a hawthorn tree.

Hay (*Eng.*) Dweller in, or near, a hedged enclosure; one who came from Hay (enclosure), in Herefordshire; dweller in a forest fenced off for hunting. See also Hayes.

Hayashi (*Jap.*) Forest.

Haycock, Haycox (*Eng.*) Dweller at the sign of the hedge cock; one thought to possess some characteristic of a hedge fowl; dweller by the small enclosure.

Haycraft (*Eng.*) Dweller by the hay field.

Hayden, Haydin, Haydon (*Ir., Eng.*) Descendant of the armored man; one who came from Heydon (hay valley or hill), the name of places in Cambridgeshire and Norfolk.

Haydn (*Ger.*) Dweller on, or near, the heath; one who took part in a crusade.

Hayes (*Eng.*) Dweller at the hedge or hedged enclosure; keeper of the hedges or fences; one who came from Hayes (enclosure), a common name of minor places in England.

Hayford (*Eng.*) One who came from Heyford (ford used when harvesting hay), the name of places in Northamptonshire and Oxfordshire.

Haygood, Hagood (*Eng.*) The wild, untamed man.

Hayhurst (*Eng.*) Dweller in the hedged enclosure near the wooded hill.

Hayley (*Eng.*) Dweller on the high clearing.

Haymaker (*Eng.*) One who made and repaired hedges or hedged enclosures.

Hayman, Haymon, Haymond (*Eng.*) One who made, repaired or trimmed hedges.

Hayne, Hayn, Hain (*Eng.*) One who came from Hayne (hedges), the name of many minor places in England; keeper of the hedges or fences.

Haynes (*Eng.*) One who came from Haynes (enclosures), in Bedfordshire; dweller near the hedged enclosures.

Haynie, Hainey (*Eng., Ir.*) One who came from Hanney (island frequented by wild cocks), in Berkshire; grandson of Eanna, an old Irish saint.

Haynsworth (*Eng.*) One who came from Ainsworth (Aegen's homestead), in Lancashire.

Hays (*Eng.*) Variant of Hayes, q.v.

Hayslett, Hayslet, Hayzlett (*Eng.*) Variants of Hazlett, q.v.

Haythorne, Haythorn (*Eng.*) Variants of Hawthorne, q.v.

Hayton (*Eng.*) One who came from Hayton (hay homestead), the name of several places in England.

Hayward (*Eng.*) The manorial official who had charge of the hedges and was guardian of the cultivated land to protect it from straying cattle.

Haywood (*Eng.*) One who came from Haywood (enclosed wood), the name of several places in England.

Hayworth, Haywarth (*Eng.*) Variant of Haworth, q.v.

Hazard, Hazzard (*Fr.*) One who played games of chance, a gambler.

Hazel, Hazle, Hazell (*Eng.*) Dweller at, or near, the hazel bushes.

Hazelip (*Eng.*) Dweller in the hazel valley.

219

Hazeltine, Hazeldean (*Eng.*) Dweller in a valley where hazels grew.

Hazelton (*Eng.*) One who came from Hazleton (homestead with hazel bushes), in Gloucestershire.

Hazelwood, Hazlewood (*Eng.*) One who came from Hazlewood (wood where hazel bushes grew), the name of several places in England.

Hazely, Hazeley (*Eng.*) One who came from Hazeley (hill enclosure), in Hampshire.

Hazen, Hazan (*Eng., Sp.*) One who came from Hazon (enclosed sandy meadow), in Northumberland; one who served as cantor in the synagogue.

Hazlett, Hazlitt, Hezlitt (*Eng.*) Dweller at the hazel copse or wood.

Hazley, Hazeley (*Eng.*) One who came from Hazeley (hill enclosure), in Hampshire; one who came from Hazeleigh (Haegel's grove), in Essex.

Heacock (*Eng.*) Variant of Hathcock, q.v.

Head (*Eng.*) Dweller at the upper end of some natural feature such as wood, land, valley and the like; one with a large or peculiar head; one who came from Hythe (landing place), in Kent.

Headen, Headon (*Eng.*) One who came from Headon (hill where heather grew), the name of places in Nottinghamshire and Wight.

Headland (*Eng.*) Dweller at, or near, the headland, the area reserved at the end of the field for the turning of the plows, and for access by the villagers to the different ridges or plots.

Headley (*Eng.*) One who came from Headley (clearing overgrown with heather), the name of several places in England.

Headrick (*Scot.*) Dweller at the ridge of land at the end of a field or open country.

Heald (*Eng.*) Dweller on a slope or bend.

Healy, Healey, Hely (*Eng., Ir.*) One who came from Healaugh (high clearing

or wood), the name of several places in England; or from Heeley (high clearing or wood), in the West Riding of Yorkshire; grandson of the skilful or learned man.

Heaney, Heany (*Ir.*) Grandson of Eanna, an early Irish saint.

Heap, Heaps (*Eng.*) Dweller at, or near, a heap, i.e., hill; one who came from Heap (hill), in Lancashire.

Heard (*Eng.*) One who tended domestic animals, a herdsman.

Hearn, Herne, Hearne (*Ir., Eng.*) Descendant of the little fearful or distrustful one; grandson of Eachthigheirn (horse-lord); dweller at the corner; one who came from Herne (stone), in Bedfordshire; or from Herne (corner), the name of places in Cheshire and Kent.

Hearon (*Eng.*) Dweller in a nook or corner; variant of Heron, q.v.

Hearst (*Eng.*) Dweller on, or near, a copse or wooded eminence.

Heart, Hearts (*Eng.*) Dweller at the sign of the hart or stag; one thought to have some characteristic of the hart.

Heasley (*Eng.*) Variant of Hazley, q.v.

Heaston (*Eng.*) One who came from Haston (head stone), in Shropshire.

Heater, Heatter, Heeter (*Eng.*) One who came from Haytor (rocky peak where ivy grew), in Devonshire.

Heath, Heth (*Eng.*) One who came from Heath (waste land with low shrubs), the name of several places in England.

Heathcott, Heathcoat, Heathcote (*Eng.*) One who came from Heathcote (cottage on the heath or waste land), the name of places in Derbyshire and Warwickshire.

Heatherly (*Eng.*) Dweller in the thin wood where low shrubs or heather grew; one who came from Hatherleigh (hawthorn wood), in Devonshire; or from Hatherly (hawthorn wood), in Gloucestershire.

Heathershaw (*Eng.*) One who came from Heatherslaw (stag hill), in Northumberland; dweller in the thicket where heather grew.

Heatherwick (*Scot.*) One who came from the lands of Haddirvyk or Hathirvyk, in Angus; one who came from Heatherwick or Hedderwick (dairy farm among heather; heath bay), in East Lothian.

Heathington (*Eng.*) One who came from Heighington (the village of Heca's people), in Durham.

Heatley (*Eng.*) One who came from Heatley (meadow covered with heath or low shrubs), in Cheshire.

Heaton (*Eng.*) One who came from Heaton (homestead on high land), the name of several places in England.

Heavens, Heaven (*Wel.*) Descendant of Evan, the Welsh form of John (gracious gift of Jehovah).

Heavey (*Ir.*) Grandson of Eimheach (swift).

Hebbard, Hebard, Hebberd (*Eng.*) Descendant of Hibbert (high, bright).

Hebble (*Eng.*) Dweller near a hebble (narrow plank bridge).

Hebblethwaite, Hebblewhite (*Eng.*) One who came from Hebblethwaite (clearing by a plank bridge), in the West Riding of Yorkshire.

Hebel, Hebele (*Nor., Ger.*) Descendant of Hebald (high, strong).

Heber (*Ger.*) One who worked as a laborer in lifting or hoisting materials.

Heberer (*Ger.*) One who raised, or dealt in, hay.

Hebert (*Ger.*) Descendant of Hebert (combat, bright).

Hebron (*Eng.*) One who came from Hebron (high mound), in Northumberland.

Hechavarria (*Sp.*) An aspirate form of Echevarria, q.v.

Hecht, Hechter (*Ger.*) Dweller at the sign of the pike (fish); one who fished for, or sold, pike.

Heck, Hecker, Hecke (*Eng., Ger.*) Dweller near the gate, or entrance, to a forest; one who came from

Heck (gate), in the West Riding of Yorkshire; dweller near a fence or hedge.

Heckel (*Eng., Ger.*) Dweller near the small gate; one who cuts or chops (flesh or wood).

Heckenbach (*Ger.*) One who came from Heckenbeck (stream at the edge), in Germany; dweller at the brook by the hedge or brushwood.

Hecker (*Ger.*) One who chops; one who cultivates vines, a vinegrower.

Heckler (*Eng.*) One who dressed hemp or flax.

Heckmann, Heckman, Hecktman (*Ger.*) One who took care of the hedges or fences.

Hecox (*Eng.*) Abbreviated form of Hickcox, q.v.

Hector (*Ger., Scot.*) Descendant of Hector (defender).

Hedberg (*Sw.*) Heath mountain.

Hedderman (*Eng.*) Dweller on a heath.

Hedeen (*Fr.*) Descendant of Haido; one who came from Hesdin (shelter for animals and people), in France.

Hedemark, Hedmark (*Nor.*) One who came from Hedmark (heath boundary), a county in Norway.

Hedgecock (*Eng.*) Variant of Hitchcock, q.v.

Hedges, Hedge, Hedger (*Eng.*) Dweller by a hedge.

Hedgley, Hedgeley (*Eng.*) One who came from Hedgeley (Hiddi's grove), in Northumberland.

Hedin, Hedon (*Eng.*) One who came from Hedon (heather hill), in the East Riding of Yorkshire.

Hedlund (*Sw.*) Heath grove.

Hedman (*Sw.*) Dweller on the heath.

Hedrick, Hedrich (*Ger.*) Descendant of Haidrich (heath, rule).

Hedstrom (*Sw.*) Heath stream.

Heelan (*Ir.*) Grandson of Faolan (little wolf).

Heemstra (*Du.*) Dweller in a farmstead surrounded by a fence or moat.

Heenan (*Ir.*) Grandson of little Eidhean (ivy).

Heeney (*Ir.*) Descendant of Eanna.

221

Heep (*Eng.*) Variant of Heap, q.v.

Heer (*Du.*) One who lets land, a landlord; a gentleman or lord; one who apes the manners of a lord.

Heerema (*Du.*) The son of Heare, a Frisian form of Hare (army).

Heermann, Heermans (*Ger.*) Descendant of Herman (army, man).

Heersema (*Du.*) Descendant of little Heer, a form of Hare (army).

Heether (*Eng.*) One who came from Heather (waste land; a heath), in Leicestershire.

Hefferan (*Eng., Ir.*) One who took care of the heifers; variant of Heffernan, q.v.

Heffernan, Hefferren, Heffern (*Ir.*) Grandson of Ifearnan.

Heffner (*Ger.*) One who fashioned utensils of earthenware, a potter.

Heffron (*Ir.*) Grandson of little Eimhear; grandson of little Amhra (prosperous or eminent).

Hefler, Hefner (*Ger.*) One who made utensils of earthenware or metal, a potter.

Heflin (*Ger., Fr.*) One who bought and sold oats.

Hefner (*Ger.*) Variant of Hafner, q.v.

Heftel, Heft (*Ger.*) One who made hooks and eyes; or buckles.

Hefter (*Ger.*) One who made and sold bracelets, brooches, and buckles.

Hegarty (*Ir.*) Variant of Haggerty, q.v.

Hegedus (*Hun.*) One who played a fiddle or stringed instrument, a fiddler.

Hegel (*Ger.*) Dweller near a hedge or hedged enclosure.

Heger (*Eng.*) One who made hedges or fences; one in charge of a park or forest.

Hegg, Hegge (*Eng.*) One who lived near the hedged or fenced enclosure.

Heglund, Hegland (*Dan., Sw., Nor.*) One who came from Hegelund (bird-cherry grove), in Denmark; dweller at the enclosed or hedged grove; hedge grove.

Hegstrom (*Sw.*) Hedge stream.

Hegwood, Hegward (*Eng.*) Dweller in an enclosed wood; manorial official in

charge of the hedges. See Hayward.

Hegy, Hegyi (*Hun.*) One who lived on, or near, a mountain.

Hehl (*Ger.*) Descendant of Hehl, a pet form of names beginning with Hag (enclosed place), as Hagiman and Hagiwolf; or of Heilwig (good fortune, battle); or of Johannes (gracious gift of Jehovah).

Hehn (*Ger.*) Descendant of Hagano, a pet form of names beginning with Hag (hedged place), as Haganrich and Haginold.

Heiberger (*Ger.*) Dweller on, or near, a clearing, an area of felled trees.

Heidegger, Heidecker (*Swis.*) One who came from the fortress of Heidegg in the Canton of Zurich.

Heidelberg, Heidelberger (*Ger.*) One who came from Heidelberg (bilberry hill), in Baden.

Heidemann, Heideman, Heide, Heid (*Ger.*) Dweller on, or near, the unimproved or wild land; or on the heath.

Heiden, Heider, Heidinger (*Ger., Du.*) Dweller on, or near, uncultivated land covered by coarse grass and low bushes; the rustic or countryman.

Heidenreich (*Ger.*) Descendant of Heidenreich (mighty over the heathen), a name promoted during the time of the Crusades.

Heidkamp (*Ger.*) Dweller at the enclosure on the heath.

Heidorn (*Ger.*) Dweller near an enclosure of thorn bushes.

Heidrich (*Ger.*) Contracted form of Heidenreich, q.v.; descendant of Haidrich (heath, rule).

Heidt, Heidtman (*Du.*) Dweller in a place where heather grew.

Heifetz (*Rus., Heb.*) Descendant of Chaifetz (desire; gift); one who came from Haifa, in Israel.

Height (*Eng.*) Dweller at the height or top of the hill.

Heil, Heile, Heyl (*Ger.*) Descendant of Heilo, a pet form of names beginning with Heil (salvation or holy), as Heilker and Hailwich.

Heiland (*Ger.*) One who heals or saves; one who skins animals.

Heilbronn, Heilbronner, Heilbron (*Ger.*) One who came from Heilbronn (safe spring; holy spring), the name of five places in Germany; variant of Halperin, q.v.

Heilbrunn (*Ger.*) One who came from Heilbrunn (safe spring; holy spring), in Germany.

Heilemann (*Ger.*) Variant of Heilman, q.v.

Heilgeist (*Ger.*) Dweller near the hospital of the Holy Ghost.

Heilig (*Ger.*) One who carved holy images; dweller near a holy place; one who performed sacerdotal functions.

Heilman, Heilmann (*Ger.*) The sound or healthy man; descendant of Hellmann, a German Jewish synonym for Samuel (God hath heard); descendant of Heilman (salvation, man).

Heim (*Ger.*) Descendant of Heimo (home), a pet form of names beginning with Heim, as Heimard, Heimrich and Heimoald.

Heiman, Heimann (*Ger., Heb.*) Descendant of Hagiman (enclosed place, man); one who came from Hagen (enclosed place), in Germany; descendant of Hyam (life).

Heimbach (*Ger.*) One who came from Heimbach (swampy brook), the name of many small places in Germany.

Heimberg, Heimberger (*Ger.*) One who came from Heimberg (home mountain), the name of four places in Germany.

Heimerdinger (*Ger.*) One who came from Heimerdingen (swampy settlement), in Germany.

Heimlich (*Ger.*) Dweller at the private or secluded home.

Heimonen (*Finn.*) One related to another, a member of the tribe.

Heimsoth, Heimsath (*Ger.*) One who came from Heimsath (swampy place), in Germany.

Hein, Heine, Heinen (*Ger.*) Descendant of Heino, a pet form of names beginning with Hein (home; protection), such as Heinfrid, Heinrich, and Heinhard; or beginning with Hag (hedged place), as Haganrich and Haginold.

Heinberg (*Ger.*) Dweller in the grove on the hill.

Heinemann, Heineman (*Ger.*) The servant to Hagano (forest, man), a pet form of names beginning with Hag (hedged place; home), as Haganrich and Haginold; caretaker of a wood or forest.

Heiner (*Ger.*) One who came from Heine, the name of two places in Germany.

Heinisch (*Ger.*) Descendant of Heino, a pet form of names beginning with Hagin (home; hedged place), as Haganrich and Haginold.

Heinke, Heinkel (*Ger.*) Descendant of little Hein, a pet form of Heinrich, German form of Henry (home, rule).

Heinlein, Heinlen (*Ger.*) Descendant of little Hein, a pet form of Heinrich (home, rule).

Heinold (*Ger.*) Descendant of Haginold (home, bold).

Heinonen (*Finn.*) The son of Heino, a pet form of names beginning with Hagin (home).

Heinrich, Heinrichs (*Ger.*) Descendant of Heinrich, German form of Henry (home, rule).

Heinsohn, Heinsen (*Ger.*) The son of Hein, q.v.

Heintzleman, Heinzelman (*Ger.*) Variant of Heinemann, q.v.

Heinz, Heintz, Heinze, Heins (*Ger.*) Descendant of Heinz, a contraction of Heinrich, German form of Henry (home, rule).

Heise (*Ger.*) Descendant of Heise, a pet form of Heidenrich (heath, rule; mighty over the heathen).

Heiser (*Ger.*) Dweller on, or near, uncultivated land covered by coarse

223

grass and low bushes; one who came from Hausen (houses), the name of many small places in Germany.

Heisler, Heissler (*Ger.*) One who worked by the day, a day laborer.

Heiss, Heisse (*Ger.*) The lively, vigorous, cheerful person; the bold, audacious man.

Heitman, Heitmann (*Ger.*) Dweller in, or near, the heath.

Heitsmith, Heitschmidt (*Ger.*) The smith who lived, or worked, by the heath or open, uncultivated field.

Heitz (*Ger.*) Descendant of Heizo, a pet form of Heinrich (home, rule); also a pet form of names beginning with Heid (heath), as Haidrich and Haidulf.

Helberg (*Sw., Nor., Dan.*) Dweller on, or near, the holy hill or mountain; or on, or near, the hill of Hel, the old Scandinavian goddess of death.

Helbig, Helbing (*Ger.*) Descendant of Heilwig (prosperity, battle).

Helbraun (*Fr.*) One who came from Heilbronn (safe spring; holy spring), in France.

Held, Heldt, Helt (*Ger., Du., Eng.*) The hero or champion; one who lived on the slope or declivity.

Helfand, Helfant (*Ger.*) One who came from Helfand, in Saarburg; dweller at the sign of the elephant.

Helfenbein (*Ger.*) One who carved ivory figurines.

Helfer (*Ger.*) One who assists or helps another; one who came from Helfe, in Germany.

Helfert (*Ger.*) Descendant of Hildifrid (battle, peace).

Helfgot, Helfgott (*Ger.*) One who helped God.

Helford (*Eng.*) One who came from Helford (ford over Hayle river), in Cornwall.

Helfrich, Helfrick, Helfridge (*Ger.*) Descendant of Helfen (help, rule).

Helgeson, Helgesen, Helgason (*Sw., Nor.*) The son of Helgi (holy).

Helland (*Eng.*) One who came from Helland (old church), in Cornwall.

Hellberg (*Sw.*) Boulder mountain.

Heller, Helle, Hellerman (*Ger., Eng.*) One who came from Halle or Hall (house; salt house) in Germany; one nicknamed after the old heller, an obsolete copper coin worth about a fourth of a cent; dweller on the hill.

Helliwell (*Eng.*) One who came from Haliwell (holy spring), in Middlesex; dweller at the holy well or spring.

Hellman, Hellmann (*Eng., Ger.*) Dweller in a deep, wide valley; one who settled on communal land; descendant of Hellmann, a German-Jewish synonym for Samuel (God hath heard).

Hellstrom, Helstrom (*Sw.*) Boulder stream.

Hellyer, Hellier, Helliar (*Eng.*) One who covered roofs with thatch, slate, or tile, a roofer.

Helm, Helme (*Eng., Du., Ger., Sw.*) Dweller near the roofed shelter for cattle; dweller at the elm tree; descendant of Helmo, a pet form of names beginning with Helm, as Helmhart, Helmold, and Helmarich; descendant of Helm (helmet); helmet.

Helman (*Ger.*) One who attempted to heal others.

Helmbold, Helmboldt (*Ger.*) Descendant of Helmbald (helmet, bold).

Helmer, Hellmer (*Ger.*) Variant of Hilmer, q.v.

Helmholtz (*Ger.*) Descendant of Helmold (helmet, rule).

Helmick, Helmich (*Ger.*) Descendant of Helmwig (helmet, battle).

Helminski (*Pol.*) Dweller at the sign of the helmet.

Helmold (*Ger.*) Descendant of Helmold (helmet, rule).

Helms (*Eng.*) Dweller at the elm trees.

Helperin (*Heb., Ger.*) Variant of Halperin, q.v.

Helphrey (*Eng.*) Descendant of Helphrey (aid, peace).

Helseth (*Nor.*) One who came from

Helseth (Helgi's shieling; holy shieling), in Norway.

Helton (*Eng.*) One who came from Helton (the homestead by the slope), the name of several places in England.

Helwig, Hellwig, Hellweg, Helwich (*Ger.*) Descendant of Haluig (man, fight); dweller at, or near, a military road; one who came from Hellweg (army road), in Germany; descendant of Hiltiwic (fight, fight); descendant of Hailwich (holy, fight).

Heman (*Eng.*) Descendant of Heahmund (high, protection); or of little Hamo (dress); dweller at the hedged enclosure.

Hembree, Hembry (*Eng.*) One who came from Emborough (smooth hill), in Somerset; or from Henbury (Hemede's fortified place), in Cheshire.

Hemelstrand (*Sw., Nor.*) Sky shore.

Hemenway, Hemingway (*Eng.*) Dweller at the road to Heming's estate, or to Hemma's people.

Hemmer, Hemm, Hemme (*Eng.*) Dweller near the border; one who came from The Hem (the border), in Shropshire.

Hemming, Hemmings (*Eng.*) The son of Hemming (covering; dress).

Hemmrich (*Ger.*) One who came from Hemmerich, in Germany.

Hempel, Hemphill, Hemple (*Eng., Ger.*) One who came from Hempshill (Hemede's hill), in Nottinghamshire; descendant of Haginbald (hedged place, bold).

Hempstead (*Eng.*) One who came from Hempstead (homestead; high homestead; place where hemp grew), the name of several places in England.

Hemstreet (*Eng.*) Dweller on, or near, the high, or main, paved road.

Hemsworth (*Eng.*) One who came from Hemsworth (Hemede's homestead; Hymel's homestead), the name of places in Dorset and the West Riding of Yorkshire.

Hemwall (*Sw.*) Home; grassy field.

Hench, Henche (*Ger.*) Descendant of Hink, a pet form of names beginning with Hagin (hedged place), as Haginbald, Haginher, and Haganrich.

Hendee, Hendy, Hendyman (*Eng.*) The polite, courteous man.

Hendel, Hendell, Hendelman (*Ger.*) One who bought and sold goods, a dealer or trader.

Hender (*Eng.*) Dweller in the old homestead.

Henderson, Henryson (*Eng., Scot.*) The son of Henry (home, rule).

Hendle (*Fr.*) One who quarrels over business.

Hendler (*Ger.*) Variant of Handler, q.v.

Hendley (*Eng.*) One who came from Henley (high wood; hen grove), the name of several places in England.

Hendon, Henden (*Eng.*) One who came from Hendon (valley where hinds were kept; high hill), the name of places in Gloucestershire and Durham.

Hendricks, Hendrick, Hendrich, Hendrix (*Ger.*) Descendant of Heinrich, German form of Henry (home, rule).

Hendrickson, Hendricksen (*Sw., Dan.*) The son of Hendrick, Scandinavian form of Henry (home, rule).

Hendriks, Hendrikse (*Du.*) The son of Hendrik, Dutch form of Henry (home, rule).

Hendry, Hendrie, Hendries (*Eng.*) Descendant of Henry (home, rule).

Heneghan, Henehan, Henaghan, Henahan, Hennegan (*Ir.*) Grandson of Eidhneachan.

Hengehold (*Ger.*) Dweller in a swampy wood.

Hengst, Hengster (*Eng.*) Descendant of Hengest (stallion); one who took care of stallions.

Henke, Henkel, Henk, Hencke, Henkes (*Ger.*) Descendant of Hagano or Heino (hedged place), a pet form of names so beginning, such as Haginold, Haginwarth and Haganrich.

Henkin, Henken (*Eng.*) Descendant of little Henry (home, rule).

225

Henley (*Eng.*) One who came from Henley (high wood; clearing; wood frequented by wild birds), the name of several places in England.

Henn, Henne (*Eng.*) Descendant of Henn, a pet form of Henry (home, rule); dweller at the sign of the hen or wild bird.

Henneberry (*Eng.*) One who came from Henbury (high fort), in Gloucestershire.

Hennelly (*Ir.*) Variant of Fennelly, q.v.

Henneman (*Eng.*) The servant in charge of the hens.

Henner (*Ger.*) Descendant of Henne, a pet form of Johannes (gracious gift of Jehovah); or of Heino, a pet form of Heinrich (home, rule).

Hennessy, Hennessey, Hensy (*Ir.*) Grandson of Aonghus (one-choice).

Henney, Henny (*Eng.*) One who came from Henny (island frequented by wild birds), in Essex.

Hennig (*Ger.*) Descendant of Hann, a pet form of Johann, German form of John (gracious gift of Jehovah); or of Heinrich, German form of Henry (home, rule).

Hennigan, Heneghan (*Ir.*) Descendant of Eidhneachan.

Henning, Hennings (*Eng., Ger.*) Dweller at the meadow frequented by wild birds, such as moorhens or partridges; descendant of Hann, a pet form of Johannes (gracious gift of Jehovah).

Henningsen (*Nor., Dan.*) The son of Henning (dexterous).

Hennis (*Eng.*) Variant of Ennis, q.v.

Henrich, Henrichs (*Ger.*) Descendant of Heinrich, German form of Henry (home, rule).

Henrici (*It., Ger.*) Descendant of little Henry (home, rule).

Henricks, Henrickson (*Sw.*) Descendant of Henrick, a Scandinavian form of Henry (home, rule).

Henriksen, Henrikson (*Dan., Sw., Nor.*) The son of Henrik, Scandinavian form of Henry (home, rule).

Henriques (*Port.*) The son of Henrique, Portuguese form of Henry (home, rule).

Henry, Henri (*Eng., Fr.*) Descendant of Henry (home, rule).

Hensel, Henschel, Hentschel, Henzel, Hensle (*Ger.*) Descendant of little Hans, a pet form of Johannes (gracious gift of Jehovah).

Henshall (*Eng.*) One who came from Hensall (Hethin's corner), in the West Riding of Yorkshire.

Henshaw (*Eng.*) Dweller in, or near, the grove frequented by wild birds, as moorhens, partridges, etc.; one who came from Henshaw (Hethin's enclosure), in Northumberland.

Hensley (*Eng.*) Dweller in the wood frequented by wild birds.

Henson, Hensen (*Nor.*) The son of Hens, a pet form of Johannes (gracious gift of Jehovah).

Henthorne, Henthorn (*Eng.*) One who came from Henthorn (thicket frequented by wild birds), in Lancashire.

Henton (*Eng.*) One who came from Henton (high homestead; homestead where hens were kept), the name of places in Oxfordshire and Somerset.

Hentschel, Hentsch (*Ger.*) Descendant of Hentschel, a pet form of Johannes (gracious gift of Jehovah).

Hentz, Hentzel, Henz, Henzel (*Ger.*) Descendant of Hentz or Henz, pet forms of Heinrich (home, rule).

Henwood (*Eng.*) Dweller in the wood where hens were kept; one who came from Henwood (the nun's wood), in Warwickshire.

Heotis (*Gr.*) One who came from the island of Chios.

Hepburn (*Eng., Scot.*) One who came from Hepburn (high tumulus), in Northumberland; one who lived by the dog-rose tree at the brook.

Hepp, Heppe (*Ger.*) Dweller at the sign of the goat; one who works with a sickle or vinedresser's knife; one who prunes or cares for grapevines.

Hepple (*Eng.*) One who came from

Hepple (corner where hips grew) in Northumberland.

Hepplewhite (*Eng.*) Variant of Hebblethwaite, q.v.

Heppner, Hepner (*Ger.*) One who grew hops.

Hepworth (*Eng.*) One who came from Hepworth (homestead where hips grew), in Suffolk.

Herald (*Eng.*) One who held the office of herald and delivered formal messages or proclamations from a sovereign or general, later charged with duties concerning armorial bearings and questions of precedence; a variant of Harold, q.v.

Heraty (*Ir.*) Grandson of Oireachtach (frequenting assemblies).

Herb (*Ger., Eng.*) Descendant of Herb, a pet form of Herbert (army, bright).

Herbert, Herberts (*Wel., Eng.*) Descendant of Herbert (army, bright).

Herbig (*Ger.*) Descendant of Herwig (army, battle).

Herbold (*Eng.*) Descendant of Herbald (army, bold).

Herbst, Herbster (*Ger.*) One who harvests crops in the autumn.

Herd, Herde (*Eng.*) One who took care of domestic animals; a shepherd.

Herda (*Cz.-Sl.*) The haughty, proud man.

Herdman (*Eng.*) One employed to herd cattle, sheep or other animals.

Herdrich, Hertrich (*Ger.*) Descendant of Hertrich (brave, rule).

Heredia (*Sp.*) One who came from Heredia (the inheritors), in Spain; one who inherits from another, an heir.

Hereford (*Eng.*) One who came from Hereford (army ford), in Herefordshire.

Herendy (*Hun.*) One who came from Herend, in Hungary.

Herenyi (*Hun.*) One who came from Hereny, in Hungary.

Herforth, Herford (*Eng.*) Variant of Hereford, q.v.

Hergott, Herigodt, Herget, Hergert (*Ger.*) Descendant of Heregod

(army, Goth), or of Hariger (army, spear).

Herhold (*Ger.*) One who announces messages, a herald or messenger. See Herald.

Heriot, Herriot, Herriott (*Scot.*) One who came from Heriot (army equipment; fee paid to lord on death of tenant), in Midlothian; descendant of little Henry (home, rule).

Herkel (*Ger.*) Descendant of little Herk, a pet form of Haruc (holy place).

Herkert (*Ger.*) Descendant of Hercrat (holy place, counsel).

Herkimer (*Ger.*) One who came from Herkheim (muddy homestead), in Germany.

Herlihy, Herlihey (*Ir.*) Descendant of the under lord.

Herlinger, Herling, Herlin (*Ger.*) One who came from Herrlingen, in Germany; descendant of Herilo, a pet form of names beginning with Heer (army), as Herman and Hariulf.

Herman, Hermann, Hermanns (*Eng., Ger., Du.*) Descendant of Herman (army, man).

Hermanson, Hermansen (*Eng., Sw., Dan., Nor.*) The son of Herman (army, man).

Hermes (*Gr.*) Descendant of Hermes (the lordly), the messenger of the gods.

Hernandez (*Sp.*) Son of Hernando (journey, venture).

Herndon (*Eng.*) Dweller in a nook, or corner, by a hill.

Herne, Hern (*Eng., Ir.*) One who came from Herne (stone), in Bedfordshire; or from Herne (corner), the name of places in Cheshire and Kent; variant of Hearn, q.v.

Hernon (*Ir.*) Grandson of Iarnain.

Herold, Herrold (*Eng.*) Variant of Herald and Harold, q.v.

Herr, Herre (*Ger., Fr.*) One in the service of a lord or noble; in some instances a lord or noble.

Herrell (*Fr.*) One who came from Herelle (hunting place).

Herrera, Herrero (*Sp.*) The worker in iron, a smith.

Herrick (*Eng.*) Descendant of Hereric (army, rule).

Herring, Hering (*Ger., Eng., Scot.*) Descendant of Hering (son of Here, army); one who fished for, and sold, herring, an important article of food in medieval England; dweller at the sign of the herring.

Herrington (*Eng.*) One who came from Herrington (village of Here's people), in Durham.

Herriot, Herriott (*Fr.*) Descendant of little Henry (home, rule).

Herrmann, Herrman, Heerman, Heermann (*Ger.*) One who served in the army; descendant of Hariman (army, man).

Herron, Heron (*Eng.*) Dweller at the sign of the heron; one with the appearance of a heron, i.e., thin, with long legs.

Hersam, Hersham (*Eng.*) One who came from Hersham (Haeferic's estate), in Surrey.

Herschel (*Ger., Cz.*) Dweller at the sign of the stag or red deer; descendant of little Hersch, a pet form of Herman (army, man).

Hersey (*Eng.*) One who came from Herse (railed place), the name of several hamlets in France.

Hersh, Hershey, Hersch, Herrscher (*Ger., Swis.*) Dweller at the sign of the red deer; one with some characteristic of a deer.

Hershberger (*Ger.*) One who came from Herschberg (red deer mountain), in Germany.

Hershenson (*Ger.*) The son of little Hersh, a Yiddish form of Harry (home, rule).

Hershman (*Heb., Ger.*) Dweller at the sign of the hind or red deer, a name favored by Jews through the blessing of Jacob in Genesis 49:21.

Herskovitz, Herskowitz, Herskovits (*Pol., Rus.*) Descendant of Hersk (hind), a name favored by Jews through supposed reference to the blessing of Jacob in Genesis 49:21.

Herson (*Ger.*) The son of Hersh (red deer).

Herst (*Eng.*) Variant of Hirst, q.v.

Herstein (*Nor.*) Descendant of Herstein (army, stone).

Hert (*Ger.*) Descendant of Hert, a pet form of names beginning with Hart (hard), as Hartman and Hardulf.

Hertel, Hertle (*Fr., Ger.*) Descendant of little Hart (strong), or of little Hert, a pet form of Hertrich (strong, powerful).

Hertelendy, Hertelendi (*Hun.*) One who came from Hertelend, in Hungary.

Herter (*Du., Ger.*) One who took care of domestic animals, a herdsman or shepherd.

Hertlein, Hertline, Hertling (*Ger.*) Descendant of little Hert, a pet form of names beginning with Hart (hard), as Hartman and Hardulf.

Hertz, Herz (*Ger.*) Dweller at the sign of the heart; a courageous man; dweller at the sign of the hart.

Hervey (*Eng.*) Descendant of Herwig (army, war); variant of Harvey, q.v.

Herweg (*Eng.*) Descendant of Herwig (army, war); dweller by the army road.

Herzberg (*Ger.*) One who came from Herzberg (red deer mountain), the name of two towns in West Germany.

Herzfeld (*Ger.*) One who came from Herzfeld, in Germany.

Herzl (*Ger.*) Dweller at the sign of the little heart.

Herzog (*Ger.*) One who led an army; a duke.

Hesek (*Ger.*) Descendant of Hesek, a pet form of Hesekiel, German form of Ezekiel (strength of God).

Heseltine, Hesseltine (*Eng.*) Same as Haseltine, q.v.

Hesket, Heskett (*Eng.*) One who came from Hesket (race course; ash tree hill; at the head of some feature), the name of two places in Cumberland.

Hesketh (*Eng.*) One who came from Hesketh (race course), the name of places in Lancashire and the North Riding of Yorkshire.

Hesleden (*Eng.*) One who came from Hesleden (hazel valley), in Durham.

Hesler (*Eng.*) The servant in the kitchen who turned the spit and roasted the meat.

Heslop, Heslip, Heslup, Heslep (*Eng.*) Dweller in the hazel valley.

Hespen (*Eng.*) Dweller near the aspen tree.

Hess, Hesse (*Ger.*) One who came from Hesse (the hooded people), in Germany.

Hesser (*Ger.*) One who came from Hessen (hill country interlaced with swamps), in Germany.

Hession (*Ir.*) Grandson of Oisin (little animal).

Hessle, Hessel (*Eng.*) One who came from Hessle (hazel grove), villages in both the East and the West Ridings of Yorkshire.

Hessler (*Ger.*) One who came from Hesel (place where hazels grew), the name of three places in Germany.

Hesslich (*Du.*) The ugly person.

Hester (*Ger.*) Dweller at, or near, a young tree, especially a beech tree.

Heston (*Eng.*) One who came from Heston (homestead in the brushwood), in Middlesex.

Hethcote (*Eng.*) Variant of Heathcott, q.v.

Hetherington (*Eng.*) One who came from Hetherington (village of the dwellers on a heath), in Northumberland.

Hetland (*Nor.*) One who came from Hetland (place where hazel trees grew), in Norway.

Hetman (*Ger.*) Variant of Hauptman, q.v.

Hett (*Eng., Ger.*) One who came from Hett (hat, used to indicate the shape of the hill), in Durham; descendant of Hett, a pet form of names beginning with Hader (fight), as Hathowulf and Hadedeus.

Hetterley (*Eng.*) One who came from Hatherley or Hatherleigh (hawthorn wood), the names of places in Gloucestershire and Devonshire respectively.

Hettinger (*Ger.*) One who came from Hettingen (swamp settlement), in Germany.

Hetton (*Eng.*) One who came from Hetton (hill where hips grew; homestead on a heath), the name of places in Durham and Northumberland.

Hetzel (*Ger.*) Descendant of Hetzel, a pet form of Hermann (army, man).

Heuberger (*Ger.*) One who came from Heuberg (hill where hay was produced), the name of many places in Germany.

Heuer (*Ger.*) One who tilled a piece of land on which he paid rent; one who mowed hay.

Heumann, Heuman (*Ger.*) The peasant who made and sold hay; descendant of Hagiman (enclosed place, man).

Heuser (*Ger.*) One who came from Hausen (houses), the name of many small places in Germany.

Heverly (*Eng.*) One who came from Everley (boar wood), the name of places in Wiltshire and the North Riding of Yorkshire.

Hewes, Hewson (*Eng.*) The son of Hew, a variant spelling of Hugh (spirit; mind); or of one who was a servant.

Hewitt, Hewett, Hewlett (*Eng.*) Descendant of little Hew, a variant of Hugh (spirit; mind).

Hextor (*Eng.*) One who came from Exeter (the Roman fort on the Exe river), in Devonshire.

Hey (*Eng.*) Dweller at the hedge or hedged enclosure; the tall man.

Heyden (*Eng.*) One who came from Heydon (hay valley), in Cambridgeshire.

Heyer (*Eng., Scot.*) Descendant of the heir, i.e., the person in whom the fee of the real property of an intestate is vested at his death; one who came from Ayr (beach island), in Ayrshire.

Heyerdahl (*Nor.*) Heath valley.

Heyes, Heys (*Eng.*) Variant of Hayes, q.v.

Heylin (*Wel.*) Descendant of Heilyn (cup-bearer).

Heyman, Heymann (*Ger.*) Descendant of Hagimar (hedged place, famous); variant of Heiman, q.v.

Heyn, Heyne (*Ger.*) Descendant of Heino or Hagano, pet forms of names beginning with Hag (hedged place), as Heinpreht and Haginold.

Heyward (*Eng.*) Variant of Hayward, q.v.

Heywood (*Eng.*) One who came from Heywood (high or enclosed wood), the name of places in Lancashire and Wiltshire; dweller in, or near, an enclosed wood.

Hiatt (*Eng.*) Dweller at the high gate or gap in a chain of hills.

Hibbard, Hibbert, Hibberd (*Eng.*) Descendant of Hibbert (high, bright).

Hibbeler, Hibbler, Hibler (*Ger.*) Dweller on a hillock.

Hibbott (*Eng.*) Descendant of Hibbert (high, bright).

Hibbs (*Eng.*) Descendant of Hibb, a short form of Hibbert (high, bright); or of Ibb, a pet form of Isabel (oath to Baal).

Hibdon (*Eng.*) One who came from Hebden (hip valley), in the West Riding of Yorkshire.

Hick, Hicken (*Eng.*) Descendant of Hick (from Rick), a pet form of Richard (rule, hard).

Hickcox, Hickcocks, Hickock (*Eng.*) Descendant of little Hick, a pet form of Richard (rule, hard); descendant of little Heah (high or exalted).

Hickel (*Eng., Ger.*) Descendant of little Hick, a pet form of Richard (rule, hard); or of Hicel; dweller at the sign of the woodpecker; descendant of Hickel, a pet form of names beginning with Hug (spirit; mind), as Hugold and Hugiwulf.

Hickenbottom, Hickinbotham (*Eng.*) Variant of Higginbotham, q.v.

Hickenlooper (*Du.*) The battle runner or messenger.

Hickerson (*Eng.*) The son of Hicker, a rhymed form of Ricker, q.v.

Hickey, Hicklin, Hickok, Hickox (*Eng.*) Descendant of little Hick, a pet form of Richard (rule, hard).

Hickman (*Eng.*) The servant of Hick, a pet form of Richard (rule, hard).

Hicks, Hickson (*Eng.*) The son of Hick, pet form of Richard (rule, hard); the son of Hicca (courage).

Hidalgo (*Sp.*) One of noble descent, a lord; one who apes the manners or appearance of the nobility.

Hiddleson (*Eng.*) One who came from Huddleston (Hudel's homestead), in the West Riding of Yorkshire.

Hides, Hide (*Eng.*) One who held a hide of land, i.e., as much land as could be tilled with one plow during the year.

Hiebel (*Ger.*) Dweller on a hillock.

Hieber (*Ger.*) Variant of Huber, q.v.

Hietala (*Finn.*) Dweller in a sandy place.

Higa (*Jap.*) Ratio, good.

Higashi (*Jap.*) East.

Higbee, Higby, Higbie, Higbe (*Eng.*) One who came from Hyge's settlement.

Higdon (*Eng.*) Dweller on, or near, the high hill.

Higginbotham, Higginbothan, Higginbottom, Higginbothom, Higganbotham (*Eng.*) Dweller in, or near, the valley owned by Higgin; dweller in the valley of oak trees; or in the low place enclosed by a hedge.

Higgins, Higgin, Higginson, Higgens, Higgs (*Eng., Ir.*) The son of little Higg or Hick, pet forms of Richard (rule, hard); descendant of Uige (knowledge).

High (*Eng.*) Dweller on the high place, such as an eminence or hill.

Higham (*Eng.*) One who came from Higham (high homestead; enclosure on an island), the name of numerous places in England.

Highley (*Eng.*) One who came from Highley (Hugga's grove), in Shropshire.

Highsmith (*Eng.*) The tall worker in metals; the smith on the higher place.

Hight (*Eng.*) Dweller at the height or top of the hill.

Highton (*Eng.*) Dweller at the upper homestead.

Hightower (*Eng.*) Dweller in, or near, the tall tower.

Hilaire (*Fr.*) Descendant of Hilary (cheerful).

Hilary, Hillary (*Eng.*) Descendant of Hilary (cheerful); the cheerful, gay person.

Hilbert (*Eng.*) Descendant of Hildebert (battle, bright).

Hilborn, Hilbourn, Hilburn (*Eng.*) Dweller near a small stream issuing from a cavelike recess.

Hild (*Ger., Fr.*) Descendant of Hild (battle), a short form of names beginning with this element, as Hildeman, Hildewig, and Hildebrand.

Hildebrand, Hildebrandt, Hildebrant, Hildenbrand, Hilderbrand (*Eng., Ger.*) Descendant of Hildebrand (battle, sword).

Hilditch (*Eng.*) Dweller at the ditch or dyke by a ridge or hill.

Hildreth (*Eng.*) Descendant of Hildefrith (war, peace).

Hiley (*Scot.*) One who came from Hillie, in Scotland.

Hilgart (*Eng.*) Descendant of Hildegar (battle, spear).

Hilger, Hilgers, Hilgert (*Eng.*) Descendant of Hildegar (battle, spear).

Hilker, Hilk (*Ger.*) Descendant of Hildegar (battle, spear).

Hilkevitch, Hilkin (*Ukr.*) Nickname for one with long arms.

Hill, Hills (*Eng.*) Dweller at, or near, a hill, or on rising ground; one who came from Hill (hill), the name of various places in England.

Hillebrand, Hillebrandt, Hillenbrand (*Ger.*) Variant of Hildebrand, q.v.

Hiller (*Eng.*) Dweller on, or near, a hill; one who constructed slate roofs.

Hillery (*Eng.*) Variant of Hilary, q.v.

Hillesheim (*Ger.*) One who came from Hildesheim (swampy homestead), in Germany.

Hillhouse (*Scot., Eng.*) One who came from Hillhouse (house on the hill), the name of several places in Ayrshire; dweller at the house on the hill.

Hilliard (*Eng.*) Dweller at the hill enclosure; descendant of Hildyard (war, enclosure).

Hillier (*Eng., Fr.*) Variant of Hiller, q.v.; or of Hilaire, q.v.

Hillinger (*Ger.*) One who came from Hilling (Hild's farmstead), the name of two places in Germany.

Hillis (*Scot., Eng.*) Shortened form of Hillhouse, q.v.

Hillison (*Eng.*) The son of Hild (battle).

Hillman (*Eng.*) Dweller on, or near, a hill; the servant of Hild (battle).

Hillock (*Scot.*) Dweller near the oak tree on the hill.

Hillsman (*Eng.*) The servant of Hild (battle).

Hillson (*Eng.*) The son of Hild (battle).

Hillstone, Hilston (*Eng.*) One who came from Hilston (Hildulf's homestead), in the East Riding of Yorkshire.

Hillstrom (*Sw.*) Boulder stream.

Hillyard, Hildyard (*Eng.*) Descendant of Hildegard (battle, stronghold); dweller at the hill yard or enclosure.

Hillyer (*Eng.*) Variant of Hellyer, q.v.

Hilmer (*Ger.*) Descendant of Hildimar (fight, fame).

Hilson (*Eng., Scot.*) The son of Hild (battle).

Hilt (*Ger.*) Descendant of Hilt or Hild (battle), a pet form of names beginning with Hilde, such as Hildebrand and Hildebrecht.

Hilton (*Eng.*) One who came from Hilton (homestead on the hill), the name of several places in England.

Himes (*Eng.*) The son of Hyam (life).

Himmel, Himmler, Himel (*Ger.*) Dweller

231

at the sign of the heavens or sky; or in, or near, a field so named.

Himmelblau, Himelblau (*Ger.*) One who lived in a place colored a heavenly blue; or who dressed in such a color.

Himmelfarb (*Ger.*) One dressed in a heavenly color, i.e., blue.

Himmelhoch (*Ger.*) Heaven high.

Himmelreicher, Himmelreich (*Ger.*) One who came from Himmelreich (kingdom of heaven), the name of three places in Germany.

Himmelstein (*Ger.*) Heaven stone.

Himpelmann (*Ger.*) One who prances about, a jumping Jack; descendant of Haginbald (hedged enclosure, bold).

Hinchcliffe, Hinchcliff, Hinchliffe, Hinchliff, Hinchsliff (*Eng.*) Dweller near an overhanging cliff.

Hinchey (*Ir.*) Grandson of Aonghus (one-choice).

Hinckley, Hinkley (*Eng.*) One who came from Hinckley (Hynca's homestead), in Leicestershire.

Hincks, Hinkes (*Ger.*) Descendant of Hinck, a pet form of Heinrich, German form of Henry (home, rule).

Hinderer, Hinderman (*Ger.*) Dweller in the back or further part of the village.

Hindesmith (*Eng.*) The worker in metal who was a servant to another.

Hindley, Hindle (*Eng.*) One who came from Hindley (wood frequented by hinds, the female of the hart), in Lancashire.

Hindman, Hindmon (*Eng.*) One who took care of the hinds or deer; the servant of the peasant.

Hindmarch, Hindmarsh (*Eng.*) Dweller on, or near, the low, wet land where deer were found.

Hines, Hinds, Hine, Hindes (*Eng.*) One who was a domestic servant; one who was timid as a hind.

Hingst (*Eng.*) Variant of Hengst, q.v.

Hinkle, Hinkel, Hinkler (*Ger.*) Dweller at the sign of the little chicken; an affectionate name for a friend; descendant of Hinkel, a pet form of

Heinrich, German form of Henry (home, rule).

Hinley (*Eng.*) Variant of Hindley, q.v.

Hinman (*Eng.*) Variant of Hindman, q.v.

Hinojosa (*Sp.*) One who came from Hinojosa (fennel grove), in Spain.

Hinrichs, Hinrichsen (*Dan.*) The son of Heinrich, a Danish form of Henry (home, rule).

Hinsch (*Ger.*) Descendant of Hinsch, a pet form of Haganrich or Hinrich (hedged enclosure, rule).

Hinshaw, Hindshaw (*Eng.*) Dweller at the copse or wood frequented by the female of the red deer.

Hinson (*Eng.*) The son of the hind or servant.

Hinterhauser (*Ger.*) Dweller in the rear house.

Hinton (*Eng.*) One who came from Hinton (homestead on high land; the monk's homestead), the name of many places in England.

Hintz, Hintze, Hinsch, Hinz, Hinze (*Ger.*) Descendant of Heino (hedged place), a pet form of names beginning with Hag, as Haginold, Heinarad, and Haginher.

Hipple (*Eng.*) One who came from Hepple (corner where hips grew), in Northumberland.

Hipps (*Eng.*) Descendant of Hipp; or of Hibb, a short form of Hibbert (high, bright).

Hipsley (*Eng.*) One who came from Ipsley (grove on a hill), in Warwickshire.

Hirata (*Jap.*) Flat, rice field.

Hird (*Scot.*) One who took care of domestic animals, a herdsman.

Hirn, Hirniak (*Ukr.*) One who worked in a mine, a miner.

Hirsch, Hirsh (*Ger.*) Dweller at the sign of the hart; one thought to possess some characteristic of a hart; name adopted by Jews as the emblem of Naphtali (a hind let loose); descendant of Hirsh, a Yiddish form of Harry (home, rule).

Hirschauer (*Ger.*) One who came from

Hirschau (red deer meadow), in Germany.

Hirschberg (*Ger.*) One who came from Hirschberg (red deer mountain), the name of two towns in Germany and one in Lower Silesia.

Hirschel (*Ger.*) Dweller at the sign of the little hart.

Hirschfeld, Hirschfield, Hirshfield, Hirshfeld (*Ger.*) One who came from Hirschfeld (open country where red deer were seen), the name of three places in Germany.

Hirschkopf (*Ger.*) Dweller at the sign of the hart's head.

Hirschmann, Hirschman, Hirshman (*Heb., Ger.*) Dweller at the sign of the hind or red deer, a name favored by Jews through the blessing of Jacob in Genesis 49:21.

Hirschtritt (*Ger.*) Dweller near where red deer were in the habit of passing.

Hirsley (*Eng.*) One who came from Hursley (horse pasture), the name of places in Hampshire and Wiltshire.

Hirst (*Eng.*) One who came from Hirst (wooded hill), the name of places in Northumberland and the West Riding of Yorkshire; dweller at the wood or hill.

Hirt, Hirth (*Eng.*) One who took care of domestic animals, a herdsman.

Hirtle (*Ger.*) Descendant of Herto, a pet form of names commencing with Hart (strong), as Hardolt, Hardulf, and Hardwin.

Hirtz, Hirz (*Ger.*) Variant of Hirsch, q.v.

Hiscock, Hiscox (*Eng.*) Descendant of little Hick, a pet form of Richard (rule, hard).

Hiser (*Ger.*) Variant of Heiser, q.v.

Hislop (*Eng.*) Dweller in the enclosed land in a marsh where hazel trees grew.

Hisson (*Ir.*) Descendant of Oisin (wild animal).

Hitchcock, Hitchcox (*Eng.*) Descendant of little Hitch, a pet form of Richard (rule, hard).

Hitchings, Hitchins, Hitchens, Hitchen

(*Eng.*) One who came from Hitchin (the Hicce tribe), in Hertfordshire; the son of little Hitch or Hick, pet forms of Richard (rule, hard).

Hitchman (*Eng.*) The servant of Hitch or Hich, pet forms of Richard (rule, hard).

Hite, Hites (*Eng.*) Dweller at the height or top of the hill.

Hitler, Hittler (*Ger.*) One who supervised the salt works.

Hitz (*Ger.*) Descendant of Hitz, a pet form of names beginning with Hild (battle), as Hildibert and Hildulf.

Hixson, Hixon, Hix (*Eng.*) The son of Hick, a pet form of Richard (rule, hard); one who came from Hixon (Hyht's hill), in Staffordshire.

Hjelm (*Sw.*) Helmet.

Hjorth, Hjort (*Sw.*) Red deer; hart.

Hlad, Hladko (*Ukr.*) The smooth fat man.

Hladik, Hladek, Hladky (*Cz.-Sl.*) The large or fat man.

Hlavacek, Hlavaty, Hlavac (*Cz.-Sl.*) One with a large or distinctive head.

Hlinko (*Ukr., Rus.*) Dweller on clay soil.

Hnatek, Hnatuk, Hnatusko (*Cz.-Sl., Ukr., Rus.*) Descendant of Hnat, a pet form of Ignatiy, Slavic form of Ignatius (fiery).

Hnatko, Hnatt, Hnat (*Ukr., Rus.*) Descendant of Hnat, a Slavic form of Ignatius (fiery).

Ho (*Chin.*) What; to congratulate.

Hoadley (*Eng.*) One who came from Hoathly (heather-covered clearing), in Sussex.

Hoag (*Nor., Ger.*) The tall man; variant of Haug, q.v.

Hoagland (*Nor.*) Dweller on the high or upper land.

Hoaglund (*Nor.*) Dweller at the high or upper grove.

Hoard (*Eng.*) Keeper of the hoard or treasure; contraction of Howard, q.v.

Hoare, Hoar (*Eng.*) The hoary or gray-haired man.

Hoban, Hobin (*Ir.*) Grandson of Uban.

Hobart, Hobert (*Eng.*) Corruption of Hubert (mind, bright).

Hobbs (*Eng.*) Descendant of Hobb, a pet form of Robert (fame, bright).

Hobin (*Eng.*) Descendant of little Hob, a pet form of Robert (fame, bright).

Hobkirk (*Scot.*) One who came from Hobkirk (church on the enclosed land), in Roxburghshire.

Hobson (*Eng.*) The son of Hob, a pet form of Robert (fame, bright).

Hoch, Hoche (*Ger., Fr.*) The high, or tall, man; descendant of Hoch, a pet form of names beginning with Hoch (high), as Hochbert and Hochmuot.

Hochbaum (*Ger.*) Dweller near a tall tree.

Hochberg, Hochberger (*Ger.*) One who came from Hochberg (high mountain), the name of numerous places in Germany.

Hochfelder, Hochfeld (*Ger.*) One who came from Hochfeld (high open country), the name of several places in Germany.

Hochhauser (*Ger.*) One who came from Hochhausen (tall houses), the name of three places in Germany.

Hochman (*Ger.*) The tall man.

Hochstadter, Hochstadt (*Ger.*) One who came from Hochstadt (lofty town), the name of several places in Germany.

Hochstatter, Hochstetter (*Ger.*) One who came from Hochstatt (lofty place), the name of two places in Germany.

Hochstein (*Ger.*) One who came from Hochstein (high rock), the name of two places in Germany.

Hochwert (*Ger.*) The honored, highly esteemed man.

Hock, Hocker (*Ger.*) Dweller near a knob or protuberance; one who peddles or hawks goods.

Hockaday (*Eng.*) Descendant of Hockaday (one born the fifteenth day after Easter).

Hockenhull, Hockinghull (*Eng.*) One who came from Hockenhull (Hoca's hill), in Cheshire.

Hockensmith (*Ger.*) One who made hoes or hatchets.

Hocker (*Ger.*) The shopkeeper, huckster, or tradesman.

Hockersmith (*Eng., Ger.*) The worker in metal who lived or worked on a hill.

Hockett (*Fr.*) One who carried the bishop's crozier.

Hockin (*Eng.*) The tall, proud man.

Hocking, Hockings (*Eng.*) The son of Hoc (hook).

Hockinson (*Eng.*) The son of little Hodge, a pet form of Roger (fame, spear).

Hockley (*Eng.*) One who came from Hockley (Hocca's grove), in Essex.

Hodder (*Eng.*) One who made and sold head coverings or hoods.

Hodes (*Eng., Ger., Heb.*) Descendant of Hod (hood); or of Hodge, a pet form of Roger (fame, spear); shortened form of Hadassah (myrtle; bride).

Hodgdon (*Eng.*) One who came from Hoddesdon (Hod's hill), in Hertfordshire.

Hodges, Hodge, Hodgson (*Wel., Eng.*) Descendant of Hodge, a pet form of Roger (fame, spear).

Hodgkins, Hodgkinson, Hodgkin, Hodgin, Hodgins (*Eng.*) The son of little Hodge, a pet form of Roger (fame, spear).

Hodgman (*Eng.*) The servant of Hodge, a pet form of Roger (fame, spear).

Hodson (*Eng.*) The son of Hod (hood); or of Hudde, a pet form of Richard (rule, hard), and of Hugh (spirit; mind).

Hodur (*Cz.-Sl.*) The good worthy man.

Hoe (*Eng.*) One who came from Hoe (spur of hill), the name of places in Hampshire and Norfolk.

Hoefer, Hoeffer (*Ger.*) One who owned, or worked, a farm; one who came from Hof (farm), or Hofen (farm), the names of many small places in Germany.

Hoeffner (*Ger.*) Variant of Hoffner, q.v.

Hoefle, Hoefferle (*Ger.*) One who came from Hofle (small manor), in Germany; dweller on a small farm.

Hoeft (*Ger.*) One with a peculiar or

unusual head; dweller at the summit or peak; or at the sign of the head.

Hoegh, Hoeh (*Dan.*) Dweller on a spur of land.

Hoehn, Hoehne (*Ger.*) The slanderous, scornful, sarcastic man.

Hoeksema, Hoeks (*Du.*) Descendant of little Hoek, a Frisian form of Hugo (spirit; mind).

Hoekstra (*Du.*) Dweller at the corner place; or on a hook of land.

Hoel, Hoell, Hoelle (*Eng.*) Descendant of Hoel (eminent).

Hoellen, Hoeller (*Ger.*) One who came from Hollen (at the fens; deep valley), the name of several places in Germany.

Hoelscher (*Ger.*) One who made and sold wooden shoes or clogs.

Hoeltzer, Hoelzer (*Ger.*) One who came from Holz (grove), the name of many places in Germany; dweller in the grove or wood.

Hoen, Hoene (*Du.*) Dweller at the sign of the hen; one who raised and sold chickens.

Hoenig, Hoening (*Ger.*) Descendant of Hoenig, a pet form of Heinrich (home, rule); one who came from Honig (place where honey was found), in Germany.

Hoeper (*Ger.*) One who came from Hope (raised land in a marsh), the name of three places in Germany.

Hoeppner (*Ger.*) One who raised and sold hops.

Hoerner (*Ger.*) One who came from Horne (crescent), in Germany; one who fashioned articles from horn; player on a wind instrument; one who made wind instruments.

Hoey (*Ir.*) Grandson of Eochaidh (rich in cattle).

Hofbauer (*Ger.*) One who worked a farm.

Hofeld, Hoffelt (*Ger.*) One who came from Hofeld or Hoffeld (settlement on open country), the names of several places in Germany.

Hofer, Hofert (*Ger.*) One who owned, or worked, a farm; one who came

from Hof (farm) or Hofen (farm), the names of many small places in Germany.

Hoff, Hof (*Ger., Eng.*) Dweller in a courtyard or fenced-in place; one who came from Hof (farm), the name of many small places in Germany; or from Hoff (heathen temple), in Westmorland.

Hoffberg Hoffenberg (*Nor., Ger.*) Dweller near a court on the hill or mountain.

Hoffer, Hoffert (*Ger.*) One who came from Hof, Hofen, or Hoffen (farm), the names of many small places in Germany; the peasant or small landowner; one who owned a manor or country estate.

Hoffman, Hoffmann (*Ger.*) One who worked a large farm either as owner or manager; the farm, or manor, servant.

Hoffner (*Ger.*) One who worked, or resided, on a hof, that is, manor or farm; variant of Hoffer, q.v.

Hoffstadter, Hofstadter, Hoffstad, Hofsteadter (*Ger.*) One who came from Hofstadt (farm town), in Germany.

Hofmann, Hofman (*Ger.*) Variant of Hoffman, q.v.

Hofmeister, Hoffmeister (*Ger.*) The steward or head-servant.

Hofstetter, Hostetter (*Ger., Swis.*) One who came from Hofstetten, the name of several villages in Germany and Switzerland.

Hofstra (*Du.*) Dweller in, or near, a courtyard.

Hogan (*Ir.*) Grandson of little Og (young).

Hogarth, Hoggarth (*Eng.*) Dweller at the high enclosure; or at the pen for young sheep; one who took care of swine.

Hogben, Hogbin (*Eng.*) The bent, deformed man; dweller near the pen for young sheep.

Hogberg (*Sw.*) Dweller on, or near, a high mountain.

Hoge (*Ger.*) Dweller at the height, or top of a hill or mountain.

Hogebaum (*Ger.*) Dweller near the tall tree.

Hogeboom (*Du.*) Dweller near a tall tree.

Hogeland (*Ger.*) Dweller on the high land.

Hoger (*Du.*) Dweller at the higher place.

Hogg, Hogge, Hoggs (*Eng.*) Dweller at the sign of the hog or young sheep; descendant of Hoga (careful or prudent); a nickname applied to a coarse, self-indulgent, gluttonous, or filthy person; descendant of Hodge, a pet form of Roger (fame, spear); dweller near a portion of wood marked off for clearing.

Hoglind, Hoglin (*Sw.*) High linden tree.

Hoglund (*Sw.*) High grove.

Hogstedt (*Sw.*) Dweller on, or near, a high place.

Hogston (*Scot.*) One who came from Hogston (Hoga's homestead), in Scotland.

Hogstrom (*Sw.*) High stream.

Hogue (*Eng.*) Dweller at the sign of the hog (pig); one with the characteristics of a pig; dweller at a hillock or barrow; or near the enclosure where young sheep were kept; one who cared for pigs.

Hohenberger (*Ger.*) One who came from Hohenberg (high mountain), the name of many places in Germany.

Hohensee (*Ger.*) One who came from Hohensee (high lake), in Germany.

Hohenstein (*Ger.*) One who came from Hohenstein (high stone), the name of several places in Germany.

Hohenzy (*Ger.*) Dweller near an open lake; variant of Hohensee, q.v.

Hohl, Hohlen (*Ger.*) Dweller in, or near, a cave or cavern; or hollow place.

Hohmann, Hohman (*Ger.*) Dweller on a high place; the high, haughty, aristocratic man; descendant of Hohmann (high man).

Hohmeier (*Ger.*) The meier who lived in a high place. See Meier.

Hohn, Hohne (*Ger.*) One who raised and sold hens or birds.

Hohner (*Ger.*) One who abuses, reviles, and slanders others; one who comes from Hohn (place of birds), the name of several places in Germany.

Hohol, Hoholl (*Nor.*) Dweller near the hill where hay is grown; or on the rounded or isolated hill.

Hoisington (*Eng.*) One who came from Horsington (village of Horsa's people), in Lincolnshire.

Hoit (*Du., Ir.*) Variant of Hoyt, q.v.

Hojnacki (*Pol.*) Dweller near a pine tree.

Hokanson (*Sw.*) The son of Haakon (useful).

Hoke, Hoker (*Eng.*) Dweller near the spur, bend, or corner, referring to some natural feature.

Hokinson (*Sw.*) Americanized spelling of Hokanson, q.v.

Holbach (*Ger.*) One who came from Holbach (crooked stream; valley stream), in Germany.

Holbein (*Ger.*) One with a crooked leg.

Holbert (*Eng.*) Variant of Hulbert, q.v.

Holbrook, Holbrooks (*Eng.*) One who came from Holbrook (stream in a deep ravine), the name of several places in England.

Holcomb, Holcombe, Holcum (*Eng.*) One who came from Holcombe (deep ravine), the name of several places in England.

Hold (*Eng., Dan.*) The man of high rank, a nobleman, in the Danelaw.

Holdaway, Hollaway (*Eng.*) One who came from Holloway (sunken road), in Middlesex.

Holdcroft (*Eng.*) One who came from Holcroft (small piece of enclosed arable land in a ravine or valley), in Lancashire.

Holden, Holdener (*Eng., Ger.*) One who came from Holden (deep valley), in Yorkshire; or from Holden, in Germany.

Holder (*Eng.*) One who was a tenant or occupier of land.

Holderby (*Eng.*) One who came from Holdenby (Halfdan's homestead), in Northamptonshire.

Holderness (*Eng.*) One who came from Holderness (headland or low marshy ground .of the hold, a man of high rank in the Danelaw), in the East Riding of Yorkshire.

Holdorf (*Ger.*) One who came from Holdorf (woodland village), in Germany.

Holdsworth (*Eng.*) One who came from Holdsworth (Halda's homestead), in the West Riding of Yorkshire.

Holdt (*Ger.*) Dweller in, or near, the woods.

Hole, Holl (*Eng.*) Dweller at the hollow, or low land.

Holebeck (*Eng.*) One who came from Holbeck (deep stream), in Nottinghamshire.

Holec, Holecek (*Cz.-Sl., Ukr.*) The naked or poor man.

Holeman (*Eng.*) Dweller in the hollow.

Holen (*Nor.*) One who came from Holen (rounded hill; isolated hill), the name of several places in Norway.

Holford (*Eng.*) One who came from Holford (ford in a deep valley), in Somerset.

Holgate (*Eng.*) One who came from Holgate (hollow road), in the West Riding of Yorkshire.

Holic, Holich (*Cz.-Sl.*) One who cut hair, a barber.

Holifield, Hollifield, Hollyfield (*Eng.*) One who came from Holifield (holy field), in Oxfordshire.

Holinger (*Ger.*) One who came from Holingen, in Germany.

Holl, Holle (*Ger., Eng.*) Dweller in a low, wet, swampy area; or in the hollow or valley.

Holland, Hollander (*Eng., Scot., Ger., Nor.*) Dweller on the low land; one who came from Holland (land on a projecting ridge of land), the name of several places in England and in Scotland; one who came from the Netherlands; dweller on the rounded hill farm.

Hollandsworth (*Eng.*) One who came from Hollingworth (holly homestead), the name of places in Cheshire and Lancashire.

Hollatz (*Ger.*) One who has a bald head.

Holleb, Hollub, Holub (*Ger., Pol.*) Dweller at the sign of the dove; one with dovelike characteristics.

Hollen, Hollin (*Scot., Du.*) Dweller in, or near, the hollies; descendant of Holle (loyalty).

Hollenbach, Hollenback (*Ger.*) One who came from Hollenbach (brook in low, swampy land), the name of several places in Germany.

Hollenbeck (*Ger.*) One who came from Hollenbek (swampy stream), the name of several places in Germany.

Hollender (*Eng., Ger.*) One who came from Holland. See Holland.

Holler (*Ger.*) Dweller near the elder tree; or in a low, uncultivated valley.

Holleran, Holloran (*Ir.*) Descendant of the stranger from beyond the sea.

Hollerway (*Eng.*) One who came from Holloway (sunken road), in Middlesex; dweller by a depressed road.

Holley, Holly, Hollie (*Eng.*) Dweller at, or near, a holly tree.

Holliday, Holiday (*Eng.*) Descendant of Halliday or Haliday (name given to one born on Sunday or other holy day).

Holliman, Holloman (*Eng.*) Same as Holyman, q.v.

Hollinger (*Ger.*) One who came from Hollingen (boggy homestead), the name of two places in Germany; or from Holling, the name of three places in Germany.

Hollingsworth (*Eng.*) One from Hollingworth (holly enclosure), the name of places in Cheshire and Lancashire.

Hollins, Hollin, Hollen (*Eng.*) Dweller near the holly trees.

Hollis, Hollister (*Eng.*) Dweller at, or near, the holly trees.

Hollman (*Eng.*) Dweller in the hollow.

Holloway (*Eng.*) One who came from Holloway (hollow or sunken road), in Middlesex; dweller near a wide ditch. A wide ditch was often dug out as a boundary between two estates.

Hollowell, Holliwell (*Eng.*) One who came from Hollowell (deep stream),

237

in Northamptonshire; dweller near the holy spring.

Hollum (*Eng.*) One who came from Hollym (settlement of the Hollym people), in the East Riding of Yorkshire.

Holm, Holme (*Dan., Sw., Eng., Nor.*) Dweller at, or near, the holly tree; dweller on, or near, the hill; one who came from Holme (island), the name of many places in England; dweller on the small island, or on the spot of dry land in a fen; island.

Holman, Holmen (*Nor.*) Dweller on the island.

Holmberg (*Sw., Nor.*) River island mountain; dweller near, or on, a hill on the island, or dry land in a fen.

Holmer (*Eng.*) One who came from Holmer (pool in a hollow), the name of places in Buckinghamshire and Herefordshire.

Holmes (*Eng.*) Dweller at, or near, the holly tree; or on a river island; or on, or near, a hill; dweller on a piece of dry land in a fen.

Holmgren (*Sw.*) River island branch.

Holmquist (*Sw.*) River island twig.

Holmstedt (*Sw.*) Dweller at the island homestead.

Holmstrom (*Sw.*) River island stream.

Holovatenko (*Ukr.*) The son of a man with a big head.

Holowicki (*Ukr.*) One with a large or unusual head.

Holsey (*Eng.*) One who came from Halse (necklike point of land), the name of places in Northamptonshire and Somerset.

Holst, Holste (*Ger.*) Dweller in a forest.

Holstein (*Ger.*) One who came from Holsten (forest), the name of three places in Germany.

Holston (*Eng.*) One who came from Halston (stone in a corner), in Shropshire.

Holstrom (*Sw.*) Hill stream.

Holt, Holte, Holts (*Eng.*) Dweller by the wood or copse; one who came from Holt (wood), the name of various places in England.

Holter (*Eng.*) Dweller by the wood.

Holton (*Eng.*) One who came from Holton (homestead on a spur of land; or in a remote valley; or by a hollow; or belonging to Hola), the name of various places in England, with these different meanings.

Holtz, Holz (*Ger.*) Dweller in, or near, a grove; one who came from Holz or Holzen (grove), the names of many places in Germany.

Holtzman, Holzman, Holzmann (*Ger.*) One who cut wood in the forest; dweller in the forest.

Holub (*Cz.-Sl., Ukr.*) Dweller at the sign of the pigeon; one who trapped pigeons for food.

Holy (*Cz.-Sl.*) One without clothing, bare.

Holyman (*Eng.*) One who performed sacerdotal functions, a priest, monk, or anchorite; one thought to be very pious; a nickname often applied in an ironic manner.

Holyoke (*Eng.*) Dweller at the sacred oak.

Holzapfel, Holtsapple (*Ger.*) Dweller near the crab apple tree.

Holzer, Holtzer, Holzner (*Ger.*) One who cut wood; dealer in lumber; one who worked with wood, a carpenter; one who came from Holz or Holzen (grove), the names of many places in Germany.

Holzhauer (*Ger.*) One who cuts wood or fells trees.

Holzhausen (*Ger.*) One who came from Holzhausen (wood houses), the name of many places in Germany.

Holzinger (*Ger.*) One who came from Holzingen (forest farmstead), in Germany.

Holzkamp, Holzkamper (*Ger.*) One who came from Holzkamp (woods enclosure or preserve), in Germany; the owner of an estate in land.

Holzrichter (*Ger.*) Custodian, guardian, or warden of a wood.

Holzwarth (*Ger.*) Same as Holzrichter, q.v.

Homan, Homann (*Ger.*) The high or tall

man; descendant of Homan (high, man).

Homer (*Eng.*) Dweller at the small island or land partially surrounded by streams; dweller on a spot of dry land in a marsh; variant of Holmer, q.v.

Homewood (*Eng.*) One who came from Holmwood (wood in a low-lying river land), in Surrey.

Homfray (*Eng.*) Descendant of Humphrey (giant, peace).

Homolka (*Cz.*) One with long legs.

Honaker (*Nor., Sw.*) Hen, cultivated field.

Honan (*Ir.*) Grandson of little Eoghan.

Honda (*Jap.*) Base, rice field.

Hondros (*Gr.*) The thick, fat man.

Honer (*Eng.*) One who sharpened tools on a whetstone, a grinder or honer.

Honesty, Honest, Hones (*Eng.*) One with an honorable position, respectable.

Honey (*Eng.*) Descendant of Honey, a pet name used as a term of endearment.

Honeycutt (*Eng.*) One who came from Huncoat (Huna's cottage), in Lancashire; or from Huncote (Huna's cottage), in Leicestershire. Early spellings are Hunnecotes and Hunecote.

Honeyman (*Eng.*) One who kept bees to produce honey; descendant of Hunman (young bear, man).

Honeywell (*Eng.*) Dweller at, or near, a spring or well where honey was found.

Honeywood (*Eng.*) Dweller in, or near, the group of trees where honey was found.

Hong (*Chin.*) From the dynasty of that name.

Honig, Honigmann (*Ger.*) One who produced and sold honey; variant of Hoenig, q.v.

Honkisz (*Sl.*) Descendant of Hankis, a form of Hanna, dialectal for Anna (grace).

Honorable (*Eng.*) The man worthy of respect, esteem, or reverence.

Honore, Honor (*Fr.*) Descendant of

Honore, French form of Honoria (honor; honorable).

Hood (*Eng.*) One who made head coverings or hoods; one who came from Hood (shelter), the name of places in Devonshire and Yorkshire; descendant of Hood or Hud, a pet form of Richard (rule, hard), and of Hugh (spirit, mind).

Hoog, Hooge (*Du.*) The tall man.

Hoogakker (*Du.*) Dweller in, or near, the high field.

Hoogenboom (*Du.*) Dweller near the tall tree.

Hoogendoorn (*Du.*) Dweller near the high thorns.

Hoogland, Hooglant (*Du.*) Dweller on the high land.

Hooker, Hooks, Hook, Hooke (*Eng.*) One who lived near the spur, river bend, or corner, referring to some natural feature; one who came from Hook (hook; corner; headland; hill), the name of various places in England.

Hoole, Hooley (*Eng.*) One who came from Hoole (hollow; hovel), the name of places in Cheshire and Lancashire.

Hooper, Hoopes, Hoops, Hoper (*Eng.*) One who made hoops, a cooper; one who lived on the hop, a piece of enclosed land in a marsh.

Hoopersmith (*Eng.*) One who made hoops of iron for barrels, casks, tubs, etc.

Hooton, Hooten (*Eng.*) One who came from Hooton (homestead on the spur of a hill), the name of several places in England.

Hoover (*Swis., Ger.*) Feudal tenant of a German hide of land (about 120 acres).

Hope (*Eng.*) Dweller on the raised or enclosed land in the midst of a marsh or waste land; dweller in a small, enclosed valley, especially a smaller one branching out from the main valley; dweller in a hollow among the hills.

Hopewell (*Eng.*) One who came from

Hopwell (spring in a valley), in Derbyshire.

Hopgood (*Eng.*) Descendant of Habgood.

Hopkins, Hopkinson, Hopkin (*Wel., Eng.*) The son of little Hob, a variant of Rob, pet forms of Robert (fame, bright).

Hoppe, Hopp (*Eng.*) Descendant of Hop or Hob, pet forms of Robert (fame, bright).

Hoppenrath (*Ger.*) One who came from Hoppenrade (swampy clearing), in Germany.

Hoppensteadt, Hoppenstedt (*Ger.*) One who came from Hoppenstedt (market place), in Germany.

Hopper, Hoppers (*Eng.*) One who danced at fair and festival; one who lived on the raised or enclosed land in the midst of a marsh.

Hopson (*Eng.*) The son of Hop or Hob, pet forms of Robert (fame, bright).

Hopwood (*Eng.*) One who came from Hopwood (wooded valley), the name of several places in England.

Horace (*Eng.*) One who came from Harras (altar on a heap of stones), in Cumberland; descendant of Horace (keeper of the hours; punctual).

Horak (*Cz.*) Dweller in the mountains.

Horan (*Ir.*) Descendant of the belligerent or warlike one; grandson of little Anradh (warrior or champion); grandson of Odhar (dark gray).

Horbach (*Ger.*) One who came from Horbach (swampy, muddy stream), the name of several places in Germany.

Horberg (*Ger., Nor.*) One who came from Horburg, in Germany; one who came from Haarberg (ring hill; gray stream hill), the name of two places in Norway.

Horder (*Eng.*) One who kept the hoard, a treasurer.

Hori (*Jap.*) Moat.

Horka (*Cz.-Sl.*) One who came from Horka, the name of many villages in Czechoslovakia.

Horky, Horkay (*Hun.*) One who came from Horka, in Hungary.

Horman, Hormann (*Ger.*) Dweller near a hornlike projection; or at a nook or corner.

Horn, Horne (*Eng., Ger.*) One who lived near the horn-like projection, probably a projecting hill or spur of land; dweller at a nook or corner.

Hornbach, Hornback, Hornbaker (*Ger.*) One who came from Hornbach (muddy brook), the name of two places in Germany.

Hornberger, Hornberg (*Ger.*) One who came from Hornberg (horn-shaped mountain), the name of several places in Germany.

Hornblower, Hornblow (*Eng.*) One who sounded the horn to call the workmen to their work for the lord of the manor.

Hornbostel (*Ger.*) One who came from Hornbostel (corner settlement), in Germany.

Hornburg (*Ger.*) One who came from Hornburg (mountain fortress), the name of twelve places in Germany.

Hornby (*Eng.*) One who came from Hornby (Horni's homestead; Hornbothi's homestead), the name of places in Lancashire, Westmorland, and the North Riding of Yorkshire.

Horner (*Eng., Ger.*) One who made horn spoons, combs, etc.; one who blows a horn, a trumpeter; descendant of Hornher (horn, army); one who came from Horn (crescent), the name of several places in Germany.

Hornick (*Cz.-Sl.*) Dweller on a mountain.

Hornik (*Cz.*) One who worked in a mine, a miner.

Hornsby (*Eng.*) One who came from Hornsby (Orm's homestead), in Cumberland.

Hornstein (*Ger.*) One who came from Hornstein (horn stronghold), the name of two places in Germany.

Hornung, Horning (*Ger., Eng.*) Descendant of Hornung (February); one born out of wedlock, a love son or bastard; descendant of Horno, a pet form of names beginning with Horn (horn), as Hornhardt and Hornulf.

Horobenko (*Ukr.*) Dweller at the sign of the sparrow.

Horowitz, Horowicz (*Cz.-Sl., Rus.*) Variant of Horwitz, q.v.

Horrell (*Eng.*) One who came from Horrel (dirty hollow), in Devonshire.

Horridge (*Eng.*) One who came from Horwich (gray wych-elms), in Lancashire.

Horrigan, Horrogan, Horagan (*Ir.*) Descendant of little Anradh (warrior).

Horrocks, Horrox, Horrock (*Eng.*) Dweller near the hoar oak or gray oak.

Horsey (*Eng.*) One who came from Horsey (horse island), the name of places in Norfolk and Suffolk.

Horsham (*Eng.*) One who came from Horsham (enclosure where horses were kept), the name of places in Norfolk and Sussex.

Horsley (*Eng.*) One who came from Horsley (pasture for horses), the name of several places in England.

Horst, Horstman, Horstmann (*Ger.*) Dweller in a thicket or near shrubbery; one who came from Horst (woodland), the name of many places in Germany.

Horton (*Eng.*) One who came from Horton (village on muddy land), the name of various places in England.

Horvath, Horvat, Horwath (*Hun.*) One who came from Croatia, a Croatian.

Horwich, Horwitch (*Eng.*) One who came from Horwich (gray wych-elms), in Lancashire.

Horwitz, Horvitz (*Cz.-Sl., Rus.*) One who came from Horice or Horitz (mountainous place), in Bohemia; the son of the mountaineer.

Hosch (*Ger.*) The ugly person; one who jokes, the joker.

Hosek (*Cz.*) One with the characteristics of a little boy.

Hoselton (*Eng.*) One who came from

Hazleton (homestead where hazels grew), in Gloucestershire.

Hosfield (*Eng.*) One who came from Hasfield (open land where hazel bushes grew), in Gloucestershire.

Hosford (*Eng.*) One who came from Horsford (horse ford), in Norfolk.

Hoshell (*Eng.*) One who came from Horsell (muddy shelter for animals), in Surrey.

Hoshizaki (*Jap.*) Star, headland.

Hoskins, Hoskin, Hoskings, Hosking (*Eng., Wel.*) Descendant of little Os or Hos, pet forms of Osbert, Osgood, Osmund and similar names; sometimes a corruption of Hodgkin, q.v.; dweller near a sedge marsh.

Hoskinson, Hoskison (*Eng.*) The son of little Os, a pet form of names beginning with Os (a god), as Osborn and Oscar.

Hosman (*Eng.*) Variant of Houseman, q.v.

Hosmer (*Eng.*) Descendant of Osmer (Os [a god], fame).

Host, Hoste, Hoster (*Eng.*) One who kept a public place of lodging, the landlord of an inn.

Hostetler, Hostetter (*Ger.*) One who came from Hofstadt, Hofstatt, or Hofstetten (place of the farms or manors), the names of many small places in Germany.

Hostler (*Eng.*) One who accepts and entertains wayfarers, especially at a monastery; one who keeps an inn.

Hosty (*Cz.-Sl.*) One who entertains another, a host.

Hoswell (*Eng.*) One who came from Haswell (spring where hazels grew), the name of places in Durham and Somerset.

Hotchkiss, Hotchkins, Hotchkin (*Eng.*) The son of little Hodge, a pet form of Rodger or Roger (fame, spear).

Hotchner (*Scot., Eng.*) One who drove cattle.

Hoth (*Eng.*) Dweller at a heath or waste land.

Hottinger (*Ger.*) One who came from Hottingen (farmstead on the moor),

241

the name of several places in Germany.

Hotton (*Eng.*) One who came from Hoton (homestead on a spur of hill), in Leicestershire.

Hotz (*Ger.*) Descendant of Hotz, a pet form of names beginning with Hug (spirit; mind), as Hugwin and Hugiwulf.

Houchins, Houtchens (*Eng.*) Variant of Hutchins, q.v.

Houck, Houk (*Eng., Ger.*) Descendant of Huc, a form of Hugo (spirit, mind).

Houdek (*Cz.*) One who expressed himself in hoots or derisive shouts.

Hough (*Eng.*) One who came from Hough (spur of hill), in Cheshire; dweller on the spur of a hill.

Houghton (*Eng.*) One who came from Houghton (homestead on the spur of a hill), the name of various places in England.

Houle (*Eng.*) Dweller in the hollow or valley.

Houlette (*Fr.*) One who carried a shepherd's crook or a bishop's cross.

Houlihan, Houlahan (*Ir.*) Grandson of little Uallach (proud).

Hourihan, Hourihane, Hourigan (*Ir.*) Descendant of little Anradh (warrior; champion).

House (*Eng.*) Dweller near, or in, an unusual house, perhaps a religious house or convent; servant in such a house; the son of How, a variant of Hugh (spirit; mind).

Householder (*Eng.*) One who occupies a house with his family as his own dwelling; one qualified to vote by reason of his occupancy of a house.

Houseman (*Eng.*) The servant who worked in the house, probably a religious house.

Houser, Hooser (*Eng.*) One who made, or dealt in, hose, i.e., stockings or socks; one who built houses.

Housewright (*Eng.*) One who built houses, especially of timber.

Housley (*Eng.*) One who came from Houseley (house in a grove), in the West Riding of Yorkshire.

Houston (*Scot.*) One who came from Houston (Hugh's town), in Scotland.

Houtsma (*Du.*) The son of little Hout, a Frisian form of Hugo (spirit; mind).

Houze, Houzz (*Fr.*) One who made and sold boots; dweller at the sign of the boot.

Hovanec, Hovaniec, Howaniec (*Cz.*) The pupil or foster child.

Hovde (*Nor.*) Descendant of the headman or chief; dweller on a ridge; or near a shrine or altar.

Hove (*Eng.*) One who came from Hove (hood, probably used in the sense of shed), in Sussex.

Hoversen (*Dan.*) The son of Haavard (look-out hill).

Hovey (*Eng.*) One who came from Havys (Elavus' homestead), in France.

Hoving (*Du.*) The son of Hove.

Hovland, Hoveland (*Nor.*) One who came from Hovland (land with heathen temple), in Norway.

Hovorka (*Cz.-Sl.*) One who was overly talkative, garrulous.

Hovsepian (*Arm.*) Descendant of Hovsep, Armenian form of Joseph (He shall add).

Howalt (*Ger.*) Descendant of Hugold (spirit, rule).

Howard (*Eng.*) Descendant of Howard (high, warden; eweherd; heart, protection); a corruption of Hayward, q.v.

Howarth (*Eng.*) One who came from Howarth (ford by hill), in Lancashire; descendant of Howard (high warden; eweherd; heart, protection).

Howden (*Eng.*) One who came from Howden (deep valley; head valley), the name of places in Northumberland and the East Riding of Yorkshire.

Howe, Howes, How (*Eng.*) Descendant of How, a variant of Hugh (spirit; mind); dweller on, or near, a projecting ridge of land, a promontory; one who came from Howe (hill), the name of places in Norfolk and the North Riding of Yorkshire.

Howell, Howells, Howel (*Eng., Wel.*) Descendant of Howell (eminent); descendant of little How, a variant of Hugh (spirit; mind).

Howie, Howey (*Scot.*) Descendant of little How, a variant of Hugh (spirit; mind).

Howkins, Howkinson (*Eng.*) Descendants of little How, a pet form of Hugh (spirit; mind).

Howland (*Eng.*) Dweller at, or near, a hillock.

Howlett (*Eng.*) Descendant of little How, a pet form of Hugh (spirit; mind).

Howley (*Eng., Ir.*) One who came from Howle (hill), in Shropshire; grandson of Uallach (proud).

Howorth (*Eng.*) One who came from Haworth (hawthorn enclosure), in the West Riding of Yorkshire; descendant of Howard (high warden; eweherd; heart, protection).

Howson (*Eng.*) The son of Hugh (spirit; mind).

Howze (*Eng.*) Descendant of How, a variant of Hugh (spirit; mind); variant of House, q.v.

Hoxsey (*Scot.*) One who came from Hoxay (mound on an island), in Scotland.

Hoy, Hoye (*Scot., Eng., Ir., Chin.*) One who came from Hoy (high isle), in the Orkney Islands; dweller at a bluff or hill; grandson of Eochaidh (rich in cattle); sea.

Hoyer, Hoier (*Ger.*) One who makes hay; one who came from Hannover, a city and province in Germany; descendant of Hucger (spirit, spear).

Hoyle (*Eng.*) Dweller in, or near, a hollow or low land.

Hoyne (*Ir.*) Grandson of Eoghan (well-born).

Hoyt, Hoyte (*Du., Ir.*) Descendant of Hoyte (spirit; mind); grandson of Ud.

Hrabe (*Cz.*) Descendant of a count; one connected in some way with a count's household; dweller near an elm tree.

Hradek (*Cz.*) Dweller in, or near, a small castle.

Hrajnoha (*Ukr.*) One who keeps time with his foot by tapping.

Hrbacek, Hrback, Hrbek (*Cz.*) One with a hump on his back, a hunchback.

Hrdlicka (*Cz.-Sl.*) A timid person; one thought to possess the characteristics of a turtledove; dweller at the sign of a turtledove; an affectionate name for a friend.

Hribar (*Yu.-Sl.*) Dweller on the hill.

Hrncir (*Cz.-Sl.*) One who made earthen utensils, a potter.

Hromada (*Cz.-Sl.*) Dweller in the community, a neighbor; or near a heap or pile.

Hruby, Hrubec (*Cz.-Sl.*) One with a gruff or low voice.

Hruska (*Cz.-Sl.*) Dweller near a pear tree.

Hrycaj, Hrycyk (*Ukr.*) Descendant of Hryhoriy, Slavic form of Gregory (watchful).

Hryhorczuk, Hryhorij (*Ukr.*) Descendant of Hryhor, a pet form of Grigor, Ukrainian form of Gregory (watchful).

Hrynko (*Rus., Ukr.*) Descendant of little Hryn or Hrynko, a pet form of Grigorij, Russian form of Gregory and of Grigor, Ukrainian form of Gregory (watchful).

Hsia (*Chin.*) Why; feast.

Hsu (*Chin.*) To promise; composed.

Huang (*Chin.*) Yellow; supreme.

Hubacek, Hubachek (*Cz.-Sl.*) One with thick lips.

Hubbard, Hubbart (*Eng.*) Descendant of Hubert (mind, bright).

Hubbell, Hubble (*Eng.*) Descendant of Hubbald or Hubald (mind, bold).

Hubel, Hubble (*Ger.*) Dweller on, or near, a small hill.

Huber (*Ger., Swis.*) Feudal tenant of a German hide of land (about 120 acres); one who came from Hub (hide of land), the name of many small places in Germany.

Hubert, Hubbert, Hubberts (*Eng.*) Descendant of Hubert (mind, bright).

243

Hubner (*Ger.*) Variant of Huebner, q.v.

Hubrich (*Ger.*) One who came from Hohberg (high mountain), in Germany.

Hubsch, Huebsch (*Ger.*) The handsome man.

Huck (*Fr.*) Descendant of Huc, a pet form of Hugo (spirit; mind).

Huckins (*Eng.*) Descendant of little Huck, a pet form of Hugo, the modern German form of Hugh (spirit; mind).

Hudak, Hudek, Hudec, Hudik (*Cz.-Sl.*) One who played an instrument, a musician; the red-haired or ruddy man.

Huddleston, Huddlestun (*Eng.*) One who came from Huddleston (Huda's homestead), in the West Riding of Yorkshire.

Hudgins, Hudgin, Hudgens (*Eng.*) Descendant of little Hudd, a pet form of both Hugh (spirit; mind) and Richard (rule, hard).

Hudley (*Eng.*) Dweller in, or near, Hudd's grove.

Hudnall (*Eng.*) One who came from Hucknall (Hucca's valley), in Derbyshire.

Hudson (*Eng.*) The son of Hudde, a pet form of Richard (rule, hard); and of Hugh (spirit; mind).

Huebner (*Ger.*) One who worked a hube, a plot of land of about 120 acres.

Huegel (*Ger.*) Dweller on, or near, a mound or hill; descendant of little Hugo (spirit; mind).

Huels, Huelsman (*Ger.*) One who came from Huls (swampy land; holly), the name of three places in Germany; dweller on land where hollies grew.

Huemmer (*Ger.*) Variant of Hummer, q.v.

Huening (*Ger.*) One who came from Huning (dirty water), in Germany; descendant of Huno, a pet form of names beginning with Hunne (young bear), as Hunrich and Hunwald.

Huerta (*Sp.*) Dweller near an enclosed place, a garden or orchard.

Huerter (*Ger.*) One who came from Hurth (barred gate; town), the name of two places in Germany; one who made and sold baskets.

Huetson (*Eng.*) Son of little Hugh (spirit; mind).

Huey (*Eng., Ir.*) Descendant of little Hugh (spirit; mind); variant of Hoey, q.v.

Huff, Huf, Huffer (*Ger., Eng., Wel.*) Dweller or worker on a hube, a farm of about 120 acres; dweller on, or by, a bluff or hill or hollow; one who came from Huffen, in Germany; descendant of Hwfa.

Huffman (*Ger.*) Worker on a hube, a farm of about 120 acres.

Hufford (*Eng.*) One who came from Ufford (Uffa's homestead), in Northamptonshire.

Huffsmith (*Ger.*) One who made horseshoes.

Hufnagel, Hufnagl (*Ger.*) One who made horseshoe nails; or who nailed shoes to horses' hoofs.

Hufschmidt (*Ger.*) The smith who made horseshoes.

Hug (*Ger., Fr., Eng.*) Descendant of Hug or Haug, pet forms of Hugo (spirit; mind); or of Ugga, a pet form of Uhtraed (dawn, counsel).

Hugel (*Ger.*) Variant of Huegel, q.v.

Hugger (*Ger.*) Descendant of Hucger (spirit, spear).

Huggins, Hugins (*Eng.*) Descendant of little Hug, a pet form of Hugh (spirit; mind).

Hughes, Hugh (*Wel., Eng.*) The son of Hugh (spirit; mind).

Hughey, Hughie (*Eng., Scot.*) Descendant of little Hugh (spirit; mind).

Hughley, Hugley (*Eng.*) One who came from Hughley (Hugh's grove), in Shropshire.

Hugo (*Ger.*) Descendant of Hugo (spirit; mind).

Huguelet (*Fr.*) Descendant of very little Hugue (spirit; mind).

Huhn (*Ger.*) Dweller at the sign of the hen or game bird; one who sneers or scoffs at others; descendant of

Huno, a pet form of names beginning with Hunne (young bear), as Hunold and Hunward.

Huie (*Scot.*) Descendant of little Hugh (spirit; mind); or of Huie, a shortened form of Macilghuie (son of the black lad).

Huizenga, Huizinga (*Du.*) Descendant of Huso (house); one who came from Huizinge, in Groningen.

Hujar (*Tur.*) One who leaves the country for permanent residence in another country, an emigrant.

Hulbert (*Eng.*) Descendant of Huldiberht (grace, bright).

Hulchly (*Cz.-Sl.*) One who has become deaf.

Hulett, Hulet (*Eng.*) Descendant of little Hugh (spirit; mind).

Hulford (*Eng.*) One who came from Halford (river crossing in a narrow valley), the name of places in Devonshire and Warwickshire.

Hulka, Hulko (*Cz.-Sl.*) One with a bald head.

Hull (*Eng.*) An early spelling of Hill, q.v.; one who lived near the Hull (muddy river), a river in Yorkshire; one who came from Hull (hollow), in Cheshire.

Hulst (*Du.*) One who came from Hulst (a wood), in Holland.

Hultberg (*Sw.*) Copse mountain.

Hultgren (*Sw.*) Copse branch.

Hultman (*Sw.*) Copse man.

Hultmark (*Sw.*) Copse ground.

Hultquist (*Sw.*) Copse twig.

Hults, Hult (*Sw.*) Dweller in, or near, a grove; copse.

Human (*Eng.*) The servant of Hugh (spirit; mind).

Humanski (*Pol.*) One who came from Human, in Poland.

Humbert (*Eng.*) Descendant of Humbert (young bear, bright).

Humble (*Eng., Ger.*) Descendant of Humbold or Hunbald (bear cub, bold); one thought to have some characteristic of a bumblebee or humblebee.

Humboldt (*Ger.*) Descendant of Hunbeald (bear cub, bold).

Hume, Humes, Hum (*Eng.*) Dweller on a river island or plot of land enclosed by a bend in a stream; dweller near a holly tree.

Humeston, Humiston (*Eng.*) One who came from Humberstone (Hunbeorht's stone; the Humber river stone), the name of places in Leicestershire and Lincolnshire.

Huml (*Cz.*) Dweller near where bumblebees were found; the restless or fidgety person.

Hummel, Hummell (*Ger.*) A nickname for an excited person; one who came from Hummel (bumblebee), in Germany; descendant of Hummo or Humbold (bear cub, bold).

Hummer (*Ger.*) The overseer or head servant who occupies or farms a hide of land.

Humperdinck (*Ger.*) Dweller at Humpert's settlement.

Humphrey, Humphries, Humphreys, Humphry, Humphryes, Humphury (*Wel., Eng.*) Descendant of Humphrey (giant, peace).

Hundley (*Eng.*) One who came from Handley (high grove), in Northamptonshire; a softened form of Huntley, q.v.

Hundseth (*Nor.*) One who came from Hundset (Hundr's dwelling; Hunn's dwelling), in Norway.

Hundt, Hund (*Ger.*) Popular nickname for knights and cavaliers in the Middle Ages, signifying a dangerous man; one in charge of the hunting dogs.

Hung (*Chin.*) Very.

Hunger (*Eng.*) One who came from Ongar (grazing land), in Essex; descendant of Hungar (bear cub, army); one who came from Hungary.

Hungerford (*Eng.*) One who came from Hungerford (ford where people starved), in Berkshire.

Hunley (*Eng.*) One who came from Honley (stone grove), in the West Riding of Yorkshire.

Hunn (*Eng.*) One thought to have the characteristics of a young bear; dweller at the sign of the young bear.

Hunnewell (*Eng.*) Dweller near a spring or well where honey was found.

Hunnicutt (*Eng.*) Variant of Honeycutt, q.v.

Hunrieser (*Ger.*) One who came from Hundriesen, in Germany.

Hunsicker, Hunsaker, Hunsucker (*Swis.*) Variant of Hunziker, q.v.

Hunsinger (*Ger.*) Variant of Hunzinger, q.v.

Hunsley (*Eng.*) One who came from Hunsley (Hund's grove), in the East Riding of Yorkshire.

Hunt, Hunter, Hunte (*Eng.*) One who hunted game, a huntsman.

Huntington (*Eng.*) One who came from Huntington (hill or place where men hunted), the name of several places in England.

Huntley (*Eng.*) One who came from Huntley (wood of the huntsmen), in Gloucestershire.

Hunton (*Eng.*) One who came from Hunton (homestead where hounds were kept; homestead of the huntsman), the name of places in Hampshire and Kent.

Hunyady (*Hun.*) One who came from Hunyad, a county and village in Hungary.

Hunziker (*Swis.*) One who came from Hunzikon or Hunziken, the names of cantons in Switzerland.

Hunzinger (*Ger.*) One who came from Hintschingen, in Germany.

Hupfer (*Ger.*) One who leaped and danced at fair and festival, an entertainer.

Hupp (*Ger.*) Descendant of Hupp, a pet form of Hupprecht (spirit; bright); dweller at the sign of the grasshopper; one with the characteristics of a grasshopper.

Huppert (*Ger.*) Descendant of Huppert (spirit, bright), a variant of Hugubert.

Hurd, Hird (*Eng.*) One who tended domestic animals.

Hurford (*Eng.*) One who came from Hereford (river crossing where an army could pass), in Herefordshire.

Hurlburt, Hurlbert, Hurlbut, Hurlbutt (*Eng.*) Descendant of Hurlbert (army, bright); one proficient with a hurlebatte in the medieval game of hurling; one who used a hurlbat in combat.

Hurless (*Eng.*) Descendant of the earl, a nickname or pageant name.

Hurley (*Eng.*) One who came from Hurley (homestead in a corner), the name of places in Berkshire and Warwickshire.

Hurney (*Ir.*) Grandson of Urnaidhe.

Hursky (*Ukr.*) Dweller on, or near, a mountain.

Hurst (*Eng.*) One who lived by, or in, the wood or copse, or on the knoll or hillock.

Hurt (*Eng.*) Dweller at the sign of the hart or stag, the adult male of the red deer; one thought to have some characteristic of the hart or stag.

Hurtado (*Sp.*) One who was kidnapped and escaped; robber; Hurtado is a very old and honorable name in Spain.

Hurter (*Ger.*) One who came from Hurt (woven fence), in Germany.

Hurtig (*Ger.*) The quick, agile, lively person.

Hurwitz, Hurwich, Hurvitz (*Cz.-Sl.*) One who came from Horovice, Horice or Horitz (mountainous place), in Bohemia; the son of the mountaineer.

Hurwood (*Eng.*) One who came from Horwood (muddy wood; gray wood), the name of places in Buckinghamshire and Devonshire.

Husain, Hussain, Hussein (*Arab.*) Descendant of the good man.

Husak (*Cz.-Sl.*) One who lived at the sign of the gander; one with the characteristics of a gander.

Husband, Husbands (*Eng.*) One who owned and cultivated a husbandland (about 26 acres), a middle class of

English villagers who lived in a house instead of a cote; one who tilled the soil, a farmer.

Husby, Huseby (*Nor.*) Dweller on the house farm, a farm name; one who came from Husby (house farm), in Norway; dweller in a house on the farm probably apart from the main residence.

Huskins (*Eng.*) Variant of Hoskins, q.v.

Husman, Hussman (*Eng., Ger.*) Early variant of Houseman, q.v.

Huss, Hus, Husch, Huscher (*Ger.*) Dweller at the sign of the goose; one with the qualities of a goose; descendant of Huss, a pet form of Hugo (spirit; mind).

Hussey (*Eng., Scot.*) One who wore hose; one who came from Houssay (holly grove), in Normandy; or from Housay, in Scotland.

Hussion (*Ir.*) Grandson of little Os (wild animal).

Husted, Hustead, Hustad, Hustedt (*Dan., Nor.*) One who came from Hussted (house site), in Denmark; house site.

Huster (*Ger.*) One who came from Huste (swamp), in Germany.

Huston (*Scot.*) A variant of Houston, q.v.

Hutchins, Hutchings, Hutchens (*Eng.*) Descendant of little Hutch, a pet form of Hugh (spirit; mind).

Hutchinson, Hutchison, Hutcherson, Hutcheson (*Eng., Scot.*) The son of little Hutch, a pet form of Hugh (spirit; mind).

Huth (*Eng.*) Dweller at the landing place or harbor.

Hutmacher (*Ger.*) One who made hats or head coverings.

Hutsell (*Ger.*) One who deals in dried fruit; a shriveled, old man.

Hutson (*Eng.*) Sharpened form of Hudson, q.v.

Hutt (*Ger.*) Dweller at the sign of the hat or helmet.

Hutter, Huttner, Hutten, Huttel, Hutner, Huttmann, Huttman (*Ger.*) One who made and sold hats and caps, a hat-

ter; one who came from Hutten (small house), the name of many places in Germany; dweller in a cottage; one who occupied a cottage and worked on land without owning it; one who watched or tended cattle, a herdsman; one who built houses, a carpenter.

Hutton (*Eng.*) One who came from Hutton (village on the spur of a hill), the name of many places in England.

Huxhold (*Ger.*) One who came from Huxhall (swamp hole), in Germany.

Huxley (*Eng.*) One who came from Huxley (Hucc's grove), in Cheshire.

Huxtable (*Eng.*) Dweller at Hucc's post or market place.

Huygens (*Du.*) Descendant of little Huges, a pet form of Hugo (spirit; mind).

Hwang (*Kor., Chin.*) Yellow.

Hyams (*Eng.*) One who came from Higham (high homestead), the name of various places in England.

Hyatt (*Eng.*) Dweller at the high gate or gap in a chain of hills.

Hyde (*Eng.*) One who lived on a homestead consisting of one hide, i.e., as much land as could be tilled with one plow in one year; homestead adequate for the support of one free family.

Hyder (*Eng.*) One who prepared hides for tanning.

Hyland, Hylan (*Eng., Ir.*) Dweller at the high land or field; grandson of Faolan (little wolf).

Hyman, Hymen (*Heb.*) Descendant of Hyam (life).

Hynek (*Cz.-Sl.*) Descendant of Hynek, a pet form of Hinrich, Slovakian form of Henry (home, rule).

Hynes, Hyne, Hynds (*Eng.*) One who worked as a domestic servant.

Hysmith (*Eng.*) Variant of Highsmith, q.v.

Hyson (*Eng.*) The son of Hyse (warrior; young man).

Hyzy, Hyzny (*Sl.*) One in charge of the wine, a butler.

I (*Chin.*) The first Chinese syllable of a Manchu's name, which serves as the family name.

Iacobazzi (*It.*) Descendant of Iacobazzi, an Italian form of James (may God protect; the supplanter).

Iacono (*It.*) Descendant of Iaco, a pet form of Giacomo, Italian form of James (may God protect; the supplanter).

Iacopelli, Iacopetti, Iacovelli, Iacovetti (*It.*) Descendant of Iacopo, a pet form of Giacomo, Italian form of James (may God protect; the supplanter).

Iacullo (*It.*) Descendant of Iaco, a pet form of Giacomo, Italian form of James (may God protect; the supplanter).

Iannello, Iannelli, Iannella (*It.*) Descendant of little Ianni, a pet form of Giovanni, Italian form of John (gracious gift of Jehovah).

Iannotta, Ianotti (*It.*) Descendant of little Ian, a form of John (gracious gift of Jehovah).

Iannucci (*It.*) Descendant of Ianni, a pet form of Giovanni, Italian form of John (gracious gift of Jehovah).

Ianson (*Scot.*) The son of Ian, Gaelic form of John (gracious gift of Jehovah).

Iarussi (*It.*) Descendant of John with the red hair or complexion.

Iasillo (*It.*) Descendant of Giacinto, Italian form of Hyacinth (purple).

Ibanez (*Sp.*) The son of Iban, a Basque form of John (gracious gift of Jehovah).

Ibarra (*Sp.*) One who came from Ibarra (sand bank), in Spain.

Ibbotson (*Eng.*) The son of little Ibb, a pet form of Isabel (oath to Baal); or of Ilbert (battle, bright).

Iberle (*Eng.*) One who came from Ebberly (Eadburg's grove), in Devonshire.

Ibrahim (*Arab., Tur.*) Descendant of Ibrahim, Arabian and Turkish form of Abraham (father of a multitude).

Ibsen (*Dan., Nor.*) The son of Ib, a Danish pet form of Jacob (may God protect; the supplanter); or of Ibb, a pet form of Isabel (oath to Baal).

Ickes, Icke (*Ger., Eng.*) Descendant of Yco or Iko; or of Hick, a pet form of Richard (rule, hard).

Idaszak (*Pol.*) One who goes on foot, a walker.

Ide, Ides (*Eng., Jap.*) One who came from Ide, an old river name, in Devonshire; descendant of Ide (labor); well, hand.

Idell, Idelman (*Eng.*) One who came from Idle (idle or uncultivated land), in the West Riding of Yorkshire; one who was lazy or would not work; dweller on an island.

Iden (*Eng.*) One who came from Iden (pasture in a marsh), in Sussex.

Iding (*Eng.*) The son of Ida (rich).

Idleburg (*Ger.*) One who came from Idelberg, in Germany.

Idler (*Eng.*) One who came from Idle (shining bright; uncultivated land), the name of several villages in England.

Idris (*Wel.*) Descendant of Idris (ardent lord).

Idstein (*Ger.*) One who came from Idstein, in Germany.

Ige (*Jap.*) This, art.

Iggins (*Eng.*) Variant of Higgins, q.v.

Igielski (*Pol.*) One who made and sold needles; or who used needles in his work, a tailor.

Igle, Igler, Igel (*Ger.*) One who came from Igel (hedgehog), in Germany; dweller near thorny or prickly brush.

Iglehart, Igleheart (*Ger.*) One with a bristly, prickly skin.

Iglesias, Iglesia (*Sp.*) Dweller near a church; one who came from Iglesias (church), in Spain.

Iglow, Iglowitz (*Rus.*) The smart or able man.

Ignacio (*Sp.*) Descendant of Ignacio, Spanish form of Ignatius (fiery).

Ignatius (*Eng.*) Descendant of Ignatius (fiery), the name of two early saints.

Ignatoff (*Rus.*) The son of Ignat, Russian form of Ignace (fiery).

Ignatowski (*Pol.*) Descendant of Ignacy, Polish form of Ignatius (fiery).

Ignjatovic (*Yu.-Sl.*) Son of Ignjat, Serbo-Croatian form of Ignace (fiery).

Igoe, Igo (*Ir.*) Son of Jago or Iago, Spanish form of James (may God protect; the supplanter).

Ijams (*Eng.*) Variant of Hyams, q.v.; descendant of Iam, a pet form of William (resolution, helmet).

Ike (*Jap.*) Pond.

Iken, Ikin (*Eng.*) Descendant of little Ick, a pet form of Isaac (he who laughs; the laugher).

Iles (*Eng.*) Dweller on the small island.

Ilg (*Ger.*) Descendant of Ilg or Gilg, pet forms of Aegidius (shield of Zeus), the sixth century French saint.

Iliff (*Eng., Scot.*) Descendant of Aethelgifu (noble, gift); or of Eglaf (awe, relic).

Illes (*Hun.*) Descendant of Illes, Hungarian form of Elijah (Jehovah is my God).

Illingsworth, Illingworth (*Eng.*) One who came from Illingworth (homestead of Illa's people), in Yorkshire.

Illsley, Ilsley (*Eng.*) One who came from Ilsley (Hild's meadow), in Berkshire.

Illy, Illyes (*Eng.*) Dweller on the isle.

Ilves (*Est.*) Dweller at the sign of the lynx; one thought to possess the characteristics of a lynx.

Imai (*Jap.*) Now, well.

Imber (*Eng.*) One who came from Imber (Imma's homestead; Imma's lake), the name of places in Surrey and Wiltshire.

Imbrogno (*It.*) One who is confused or perplexed.

Imes (*Eng.*) The son of Emm, a pet form of Emma (nurse).

Imhof, Imhoff (*Ger.*) Dweller in the court.

Imlach, Imlack, Imlah (*Eng., Scot.*) Dweller at the lake or marshy river.

Imlay (*Hun.*) One who came from Imola, a town in North Italy.

Immel (*Ger.*) Descendant of Immel, a pet form of names beginning with Irmin (universal), as Irminhard and Ermengild.

Immenhausen (*Ger.*) One who came from Immenhausen, the name of two places in Germany.

Immergluck (*Ger.*) A nickname for the always happy, ever lucky man.

Impey (*Eng.*) Dweller at a hedge or enclosure made of young trees.

Imre (*Hun.*) Descendant of Imre, Hungarian form of Emery (work, rule).

Imrie (*Eng.*) Variant of Emery, q.v.

Inaba (*Jap.*) Rice plant, leaf.

Incardone, Incardona (*It.*) One who came from Cardona, in Spain.

Ince (*Eng.*) One who came from Ince (island), the name of places in Cheshire and Lancashire.

Inch (*Scot.*) One who came from Inch (island), the name of places in Angus and Perthshire.

Incura (*It.*) One who is in the care of another; perhaps an invalid.

Inda (*Fr., Sp.*) The strong, vigorous man.

Indelicato (*It.*) The indelicate, coarse, offensive man.

Indovina (*It.*) One who predicts or foresees events, a seer.

Indurante (*It.*) The irresolute, infirm, weak man.

Infante, Infanti, Infantino (*Sp., It.*) One who was a young monk or nun in a monastery; one who fought on foot, a foot soldier; the younger Spanish prince; sometimes a title given to the nephews of the king; nickname for one who acted like a child.

Infelise (*It.*) The poor, wretched, miserable man.

Ing, Inge (*Eng.*) Dweller at, or near, a swampy meadow.

Ingalls (*Eng.*) Descendant of Ingeld (Ing's tribute); one who came from Ingol (Inga's valley), in Lancashire.

Ingebrigtsen, Ingebretsen, Ingebritsen (*Nor., Dan.*) The son of Ingebrigt or Ingebret (angle, bright; angel, bright).

Ingels, Ingle (*Eng.*) Descendant of Ingulf (Ing's wolf); or of Ingald (Ing's tribute).

Ingers, Ingerson (*Eng.*) The son of Inger (Ing's army).

Ingersoll, Ingersol (*Eng.*) One who came from Inkersall (the monks' field), in Derbyshire.

Ingham (*Eng.*) One who came from Ingham (Inga's estate), the name of several places in England.

Inglefield (*Eng.*) One who came from Englefield (Ingweald's land which was free of trees).

Ingles (*Sp., Eng.*) One who came from England, an Englishman; descendant of Ingulf (Ing's wolf); or of Ingald (Ing's tribute).

Inglesby (*Eng.*) One who came from Ingoldsby (Ingialdr's homestead), in Lincolnshire.

Inglese (*It., Eng.*) One who came from England, an Englishman; descendant of Ingulf (Ing's wolf).

Ingley, Inglee (*Eng.*) Descendant of Ingelric (angel, rule); or of Ingrith.

Inglis, Inglish (*Scot., Eng.*) One who came from England, an Englishman.

Ingman (*Eng.*) Dweller at a meadow; descendant of Ingemund (Ing's protection).

Ingold (*Eng.*) One who came from Ingol (Inga's valley), in Lancashire; descendant of Ingald (Ing's tribute).

Ingoldby (*Eng.*) One who came from Ingoldsby (Ingialdr's homestead), in Lincolnshire.

Ingram, Ingraham (*Eng.*) Descendant of Ingram (Ing's raven—Ing was a mythical Scandinavian hero); one who came from Ingram (grassland enclosure), in Northumberland.

Ingsby (*Dan., Sw., Nor.*) Dweller at Ingi's farm.

Ingstad (*Nor.*) Dweller at Ingi's homestead.

Ingstrup (*Dan.*) Dweller in a meadow which was part of a dependent farm.

Ingwersen, Ingwer (*Nor.*) The son of Ingvar (Ing's army).

Inholz (*Ger.*) Dweller in, or at, the grove.

Iniguez (*Sp.*) The son of Inigo, a Spanish form of Ignatius (fiery).

Inlander (*Eng.*) One who dwelt by, or worked on, the land belonging to the lord of the manor; one who came from the interior to dwell by the sea.

Inman, Inmon (*Eng.*) One who kept a lodging house or inn.

Innamorato (*It.*) One who loves another, a lover.

Innes, Innis, Inness, Inniss (*Scot., Ir.*) One who came from the barony of Innes (island), in Moray; the son of Aonghus (one-choice); dweller on an island.

Innocenti (*It.*) The innocent, naïve or simple man; the foundling or child born out of wedlock, probably a baby left at the church door.

Inouye (*Jap.*) Well, upper.

Insalata, Insalato (*It.*) One who made and sold salads.

Inskip, Inskeep, Inkeep (*Eng.*) One who came from Inskip (island basket), in Lancashire.

Insley (*Eng.*) Dweller in, or near, Enna's grove.

Instone (*Eng.*) One who came from Enstone (Enna's stone), in Oxfordshire.

Ioannides (*Gr.*) The son of Ioannes, a Greek form of John (gracious gift of Jehovah).

Ion (*Eng.*) Descendant of Ion, a variant of John (gracious gift of Jehovah).

Ionescu (*Rom.*) The son of Ion, Romanian form of John (gracious gift of Jehovah).

Iovescu (*Rom.*) The son of Iovan, Romanian form of John (gracious gift of Jehovah).

Iovino (*It.*) Descendant of Iovino (one born on a Thursday).

Iozzo (*It.*) Dweller at the sign of the wood grouse.

Ippolito (*It.*) Descendant of Ippolito, Italian form of Hippolytus (he who sets horses free).

Iqbal (*Arab., Tur.*) One who wishes another good luck or prosperity.

Irby (*Eng.*) One who came from Irby (village of the Irish), the name of places in Cheshire, Lincolnshire, and the North Riding of Yorkshire.

Iredell, Iredale (*Eng.*) One who came from Airedale (valley of the Aire river), in Yorkshire.

Ireland (*Eng.*) One who came to England from Ireland.

Ireton (*Eng.*) One who came from Ireton (village of the Irish), in Derbyshire.

Irey (*Eng.*) Descendant of the heir, i.e., the person in whom the fee of real property of an intestate is vested at his death.

Irgang (*Ger.*) The restless man.

Irish (*Eng.*) One who came from Ireland.

Irizarry, Irizarri (*Sp.*) One who came from the old village.

Irk (*Eng.*) Dweller near the Irk river in Lancashire.

Irons (*Eng., Scot.*) One who came from Airaines (brass), in France.

Ironside (*Eng.*) Nickname for a brave, strong soldier. King Edmund Ironside was so called for his doughtiness according to the Anglo-Saxon Chronicle, A.D. 1057.

Irvin, Irving, Irvine (*Scot.*) One who came from Irvine or Irving (green river), the names of several villages in Scotland.

Irwin (*Eng., Scot.*) Descendant of Erewine (sea friend); one who came from Irvine (green river), in Ayrshire.

Isa (*Arab.*) Descendant of Isa, Arabian form of Jesus (Jehovah saves).

Isaacson, Isaac, Isaacs, Isacson (*Eng.*) The son of Isaac (he who laughs; the laugher).

Isakov (*Bulg.*) The son of Isak, Bulgarian form of Isaac (he who laughs; the laugher).

Isaksen, Isakson (*Nor., Sw.*) The son of Isak, Scandinavian form of Isaac (he who laughs; the laugher).

Isbell, Isabell, Isabel (*Eng.*) Descendant of Isabel (oath to Baal); an English variant of Elizabeth (oath of God).

Isenberg, Isenburg (*Ger.*) One who came from Eisenberg (iron mountain), the

name of two towns in Germany; or from Isenburg (iron fortress), the name of two places in Germany.

Isenhart (*Ger.*) Descendant of Isenhart or Eisenhart (iron, hard).

Isenstein (*Ger.*) Variant of Eisenstein, q.v.

Isett (*Eng.*) Descendant of Iseulte or Iseut (fair).

Isham (*Eng.*) One who came from Isham (village on the Ise river), in Northamptonshire.

Isherwood (*Eng.*) One who came from Isherwood (Ishere's wooded land), in Lancashire.

Ishii (*Jap.*) Stone, well.

Ishmael (*Heb., Eng.*) Descendant of Ishmael (God hears).

Isidor, Isidore (*Fr.*) Descendant of Isidore (gift of Isis).

Islam (*Arab.*) Descendant of Islam (submission to the will of God).

Island (*Eng.*) Dweller on an island.

Islas, Isles (*Eng.*) Dweller on an island.

Isley (*Scot.*) One who came from Islay (swollen place), in Scotland.

Ismael (*Tur.*) Descendant of Ismael, Turkish form of Ishmael (God hears).

Isom (*Eng.*) Variant of Isham, q.v.

Israel, Israelson (*Heb.*) Descendant of Israel (champion of God).

Israelstam (*Ger.*) Member of the Israel family.

Issel (*Ger.*) One who came from Issel (swampy stream), in Germany.

Isserles (*Ger.*) Descendant of little Israel (champion of God).

Istvan (*Hun.*) Descendant of Istvan, Hungarian form of Stephen (crown or garland).

Itkin (*Rus.*) Descendant of Ita, a pet form of Judith (praise; a Jewess).

Ito (*Jap.*) This, east.

Itzkowitz (*Heb.*) Descendant of Yitzhak, Hebrew form of Isaac (he who laughs).

Ivan (*Rus., Bulg., Ukr., Yu.-Sl.*) Descendant of Ivan, Slavic form of John (gracious gift of Jehovah).

Ivanauskas (*Lith.*) The son of Ivan,

Slavic form of John (gracious gift of Jehovah).

Ivanauski (*Rus.*) One who came from Ivanov (Ivan's settlement), in Russia.

Ivancich (*Yu.-Sl.*) Descendant of Ivance, a form of Ivan, Slavic form of John (gracious gift of Jehovah).

Ivanoff (*Rus., Bulg.*) The son of Ivan, Slavic form of John (gracious gift of Jehovah).

Ivanov, Ivanow (*Rus., Bulg., Cz.-Sl., Ukr., Yu.-Sl.*) Descendant, or son, of Ivan, Slavic form of John (gracious gift of Jehovah).

Ivers (*Eng.*) Descendant of Iver (archer).

Iversen, Iverson, Ivarson (*Dan., Sw., Nor.*) The son of Iver (archer).

Ivert (*Eng.*) One who came from Iver (edge or steep slope), in Buckinghamshire.

Ives (*Eng.*) The son of Ive (yew).

Ivey (*Eng.*) One who came from Ivoy in France; descendant of Ivo (yew).

Ivor (*Eng., Wel.*) Descendant of Ivor (yew, army).

Ivory, Ivery, Ivry (*Eng.*) One who came from Ivry or Ivory, in Normandy; descendant of Ivor or Ivory (archer; yew, army).

Ivy, Ivie, Ives (*Eng.*) Descendant of Ivo (yew); one who came from St. Ives, the name of several places in England.

Iwai (*Jap.*) Rock, well.

Iwan, Iwanaga, Iwanicki (*Pol.*) Descendant of Iwan, Polish form of Ivan, Slavic form of John (gracious gift of Jehovah).

Iwanenko (*Ukr.*) The son of Iwan, a Slavic form of John (gracious gift of Jehovah).

Iwaniec (*Pol.*) One who came from Iwaniec (Iwan's town), in Poland.

Iwanowicz, Iwanski (*Pol.*) The son of Iwan, Polish form of Ivan (gracious gift of Jehovah).

Iwata (*Jap.*) Rock, rice field.

Iwatiw (*Ukr.*) The son of Iwat.

Izard (*Fr., Eng.*) Dweller at the sign of the wild goat; the agile man; descendant of Isard (ice, hard).

Izenstark (*Ger.*) Descendant of Isenstark (iron, strong).

Izmirlian (*Arm.*) One who came from Izmir, in Turkey.

Izokaitis (*Lith.*) The son of Izaokas, Lithuanian form of Isaac (he who laughs; the laugher).

Izquierdo (*Sp.*) The left-handed man.

Izumi (*Jap.*) Fountain.

Izzo, Izzi (*It.*) A nickname given to one thought to possess some of the characteristics of a snail; dweller near a holm oak.

Jablon (*Cz.*) Dweller near the apple tree.

Jablonowski (*Pol.*) One who came from Jablonow (village of apple trees), in Poland.

Jablonski, Jablonsky (*Pol.*) One who lived near an apple tree.

Jachim (*Eng., Ger.*) Descendant of Jachim or Joachim (Jehovah will raise).

Jachimek, Jachimiak (*Pol., Cz.-Sl.*) Descendant of Joachim (Jehovah will raise).

Jacinto (*Sp.*) Descendant of Jacinto, a Spanish shortening of Hyacintha (purple).

Jack (*Scot., Eng.*) Descendant of Jack, a pet form of John (gracious gift of Jehovah).

Jacklin (*Eng.*) Descendant of very little Jack, a pet form of John (gracious gift of Jehovah).

Jackman (*Eng.*) The servant of Jack.

Jackowiak, Jackowski (*Pol.*) Descendant of Jacek, a pet form of Jacenty.

Jackson, Jaxon (*Eng.*) The son of Jack, a pet form of John (gracious gift of Jehovah).

Jacob (*Ger., Eng.*) Descendant of Jacob (may God protect; the supplanter).

Jacobazzi, Jacobucci (*It.*) Descendant of little Jacob (may God protect; the supplanter).

Jacobi, Jacoby (*Fr., Ger.*) Descendant of

Jacob (may God protect; the supplanter).

Jacobson, Jacobs, Jacobsen (*Eng., Wel., Dan., Nor., Sw.*) The son of Jacob (may God protect; the supplanter).

Jacques, Jaques (*Fr.*) Descendant of Jacques, French form of Jacob (may God protect; the supplanter).

Jaeckel (*Ger.*) Descendant of little Jaeck, a dialectal form of Jacob (may God protect; the supplanter).

Jaeger, Jager (*Ger., Fr.*) One who hunted for game, a huntsman.

Jaffe, Jaffee, Jaffey (*Heb.*) Descendant of Jaffe, a pet form of Japheth (increase); variants of Joffe, q.v.

Jaffray, Jaffrey (*Scot., Eng.*) Variant of Jeffrey, q.v.

Jager, Jagers (*Eng., Scot.*) Variant of Jaggers, q.v.

Jaggers, Jagger (*Eng., Scot.*) One who carries his goods for sale from place to place, a peddler.

Jago, Jagow (*Sp., Wel.*) Spanish form of Jacob (may God protect; the supplanter).

Jagodzinski (*Pol.*) Dweller where berries grew.

Jahn (*Ger., Sw.*) Descendant of Jahn, German and Swedish dialectal form of John (gracious gift of Jehovah).

Jahnke, Janicke (*Ger.*) Descendant of little Jahn, a pet form of Johannes (gracious gift of Jehovah).

Jahns (*Ger.*) The son of Jahn, a German dialectal form of John (gracious gift of Jehovah).

Jaime, Jaimes (*Sp.*) Variant of James, q.v.

Jain, Jaine (*Eng.*) Descendant of Jan, a form of John (gracious gift of Jehovah).

Jajko (*Pol.*) One who sold eggs.

Jakaitis (*Lith.*) Descendant of Jakas, a pet form of Jokimas, Lithuanian form of Joachim (Jehovah will raise); and of Jokubas, Lithuanian form of Jacob (may God protect; the supplanter).

Jakala (*Pol.*) One who stammered or had an impediment in his speech.

Jakob (*Ger.*) Descendant of Jakob, German form of Jacob (may God protect; the supplanter).

Jakobi, Jakoby (*Ger.*) Descendant of Jakob (may God protect; the supplanter). Scholars sometimes added the Latin ending, -*i*.

Jakobsen, Jakobson, Jakobzen (*Dan., Nor., Sw.*) The son of Jakob, Scandinavian form of Jacob (may God protect, the supplanter).

Jakubczak (*Pol.*) Descendant of little Jakub, Polish form of Jacob (may God protect; the supplanter).

Jakubek, Jakubiak, Jakubiec, Jakubik (*Pol.*) Descendant of little Jakub, Polish form of Jacob (may God protect; the supplanter).

Jakubowicz (*Pol.*) The son of Jakub, Polish form of Jacob (may God protect; the supplanter)

Jakubowski (*Pol.*) The son of Jakub, Polish form of Jacob (may God protect; the supplanter).

Jalbert (*Fr.*) Descendant of Jalibert (delight, bright).

Jalowiec (*Pol., Rus.*) One who was sterile or barren, dweller on infertile soil.

Jambor (*Pol.*) Dweller by a ditch in a pine forest.

James (*Wel., Eng.*) Descendant of James, Old French form of Jacob (may God protect; the supplanter).

Jamie (*Scot.*) Descendant of Jamie, Scottish pet form of James (may God protect; the supplanter).

Jamison, Jameson, Jamieson (*Scot.*) The son of Jamie, Scottish pet form of James (may God protect; the supplanter).

Jamrose, Jamrosz, Jamrozy (*Pol.*) Descendant of Ambrozy, Polish form of Ambrose (immortal).

Jana, Janas (*Cz.-Sl.*) Descendant of Jan, Czechoslovakian form of John (gracious gift of Jehovah).

Janczak (*Pol.*) Descendant of little Jan, Polish form of John (gracious gift of Jehovah).

Janczewski (*Pol.*) Descendant of Janusz,

a pet form of Jan, Polish form of John (gracious gift of Jehovah).

Janczy (*Hun.*) Descendant of Jancsi, a pet form of John (gracious gift of Jehovah).

Janda (*Cz.-Sl.*) Descendant of Jan (gracious gift of Jehovah).

Jane (*Eng.*) Descendant of Jan, a form of John (gracious gift of Jehovah).

Janecek, Janecko, Janeczko (*Pol.*) Descendant of Janeczek, pet form of Jan, Polish form of John (gracious gift of Jehovah).

Janes, Jaynes (*Eng.*) Descendant of Jan, a form of John (gracious gift of Jehovah).

Jania, Janiak, Janicek, Janick (*Pol.*) Descendant of Jan, Polish form of John (gracious gift of Jehovah).

Janicki, Janicke (*Pol.*) Descendant of Jan (gracious gift of Jehovah).

Janik (*Pol.*) Descendant of little Jan (gracious gift of Jehovah).

Janis (*Lith.*) Descendant of Jan (gracious gift of Jehovah).

Janisch, Janish, Janitch, Janush, Janusch (*Ger., Cz.-Sl.*) Descendant of little Jan, a pet form of Johannes (gracious gift of Jehovah).

Janiszewski (*Pol.*) One who came from Janiszew(o) (Jan's place), in Poland.

Jankauskas (*Lith.*) Descendant of Jonas, a Lithuanian form of John (gracious gift of Jehovah).

Janke, Jankel (*Ger.*) Descendant of little Jan, a pet form of Johannes (gracious gift of Jehovah).

Jankiewicz (*Pol.*) The son of little Jan, a Polish form of John (gracious gift of Jehovah).

Jankovic, Jankovich (*Yu.-Sl.*) The son of Jan, a form of John (gracious gift of Jehovah).

Jankowski, Janowski (*Pol.*) The son of Jan (gracious gift of Jehovah).

Jankus (*Lith.*) Descendant of little Jan, a form of John (gracious gift of Jehovah).

Jann, Jannes (*Ger.*) Descendant of Jann, a short form of Johannes (gracious gift of Jehovah).

Jannotta (*It.*) Descendant of little Jan, a form of John (gracious gift of Jehovah).

Janos (*Hun.*) Descendant of Janos, the Hungarian form of John (gracious gift of Jehovah).

Janosfi (*Hun.*) The son of Janos, Hungarian form of John (gracious gift of Jehovah).

Janovsky (*Ukr.*) Descendant of Jan, Ukrainian form of John (gracious gift of Jehovah).

Janowiak, Janowick (*Pol.*) One who came from Janow (Jan's homestead), the name of several places in Poland.

Janowitz, Janowitch, Janowicz, Janczyk, Janowiez (*Pol.*) The son of Jan, a Polish form of John (gracious gift of Jehovah).

Janowski (*Pol.*) Descendant of Jan, Polish form of John (gracious gift of Jehovah).

Jans (*Eng.*) The son of Jan, a form of John (gracious gift of Jehovah).

Jansen, Janson, Jansson, Janssen, Janse (*Du., Dan., Nor., Sw., Ger.*) The son of Jan, Dutch and Scandinavian form of John (gracious gift of Jehovah).

Jansky (*Ukr., Pol.*) Descendant of Jan, a Slavic form of John (gracious gift of Jehovah).

Jantz, Janz (*Ger.*) Descendant of Jan, a pet form of Johannes (gracious gift of Jehovah).

Jantzen, Janzen (*Du.*) The son of Jan, Dutch form of John (gracious gift of Jehovah).

January (*Ger.*) Descendant of Januarius (January), a fourth century Italian saint.

Janulis (*Lith.*) Descendant of Jan, Polish form of John (gracious gift of Jehovah).

Janus, Janusz (*Pol.*) A follower of Janus (the ancient Roman deity with two opposite faces).

Jaquith (*Fr., Eng.*) Descendant of Jacques (may God protect; the supplanter).

Jaramillo (*Sp.*) One who came from

Jaramillo (place where orach grew), in Spain.

Jarczyk (*Pol.*) Dweller in a small ravine.

Jardine, Jarden, Jardin, Jarding (*Scot., Fr.*) Dweller at, or near, a garden.

Jarecki (*Pol.*) The lord of the village of Jarek, in Poland; one who came from Jarek.

Jarka (*Pol.*) One who raised spring corn or grain.

Jarman, Jarmon (*Eng.*) One who came from Germany, a German; descendant of German (a German); or of Gereman (spear, man).

Jarmusz (*Pol.*) One who came from Jarmuszewo, in Poland.

Jaroch, Jarocki (*Pol.*) Descendant of Jaroch, a pet form of Jaroslav (strong, glorious).

Jaros, Jarosz (*Pol., Ukr.*) Descendant of Jaros (strong).

Jaroszewski (*Pol.*) One who came from Jaroszewo, the name of four places in Poland.

Jarr (*Ger.*) Descendant of Jarr, a pet form of names beginning with Ger (spear), as Gerhard and Gerwig.

Jarrell, Jarrells (*Eng.*) Descendant of Jarrold, a variant of Gerald (spear, firm).

Jarrett, Jarratt (*Eng.*) Descendant of Gerard (spear, firm).

Jarrow (*Eng.*) One who came from Jarrow (the place of the Gyrwe tribe), in Durham.

Jarva (*Est.*) One who came from Jarva (lake), a district in Estonia.

Jarvi, Jarvinen (*Finn.*) Dweller at, or near, a lake.

Jarvis (*Eng.*) Descendant of Gervais or Gervase (spear, servant).

Jarzembowski, Jarzembski (*Pol.*) Dweller near a sorb tree or mountain ash.

Jarzyna, Jarzynski (*Pol.*) One who raised and sold greens and vegetables.

Jasien (*Pol.*) One who came from Jasien (ash tree), the name of two places in Poland; dweller near an ash tree.

Jasinski (*Pol.*) Descendant of little Jas, a pet form of Jan, Polish form of John (gracious gift of Jehovah).

Jaske, Jasek, Jasik, Jasiczek (*Pol.*) Descendant of little Jas, a pet form of Jan, Polish form of John (gracious gift of Jehovah).

Jaskowiak (*Ukr.*) The son of Jasko, a pet form of Jakiv, Ukrainian form of Jacob (may God protect; the supplanter).

Jaskulski (*Pol.*) Dweller at the sign of the swallow.

Jason, Jasin (*Eng., Heb.*) Descendant of Jason (healer); Jewish conversion of Jonas (dove).

Jasper, Jasperson (*Eng.*) Descendant of Jasper (master of the treasure; horseman). See Kasper.

Jaster (*Eng.*) Variant of Jester, q.v.

Jastrzebski (*Pol.*) Dweller on Jastrzebia hill in Poland.

Jaszkowski (*Pol.*) Descendant of Jacob (may God protect; the supplanter).

Jauch (*Ger.*) Dweller on, or tiller of, a *jauch*, a field area of 1000 square fathoms; dweller on a mountain ridge; descendant of Joachim (Jehovah will raise).

Jauregui, Jaurigue (*Sp.*) Dweller near, or worker in, a castle or palace; one who came from Jauregui (castle), in Spain.

Javor, Javorski, Javorsky (*Cz.-Sl., Pol.*) Dweller by the maple tree.

Javorka (*Cz.-Sl.*) Dweller by the maple tree.

Jawor (*Pol.*) Variant of Javor, q.v.

Jaworski, Jaworowski (*Pol.*) One who came from Jaworow (maple tree), in Poland.

Jay, Jaye (*Eng.*) One who talked incessantly; or was gaily dressed, after the jay; dweller at the sign of the jay.

Jazwinski (*Pol.*) Dweller near the badger's lair.

Jean, Jeane, Jeanes, Jeans (*Fr., Eng.*) Descendant of Jean, a French form of John (gracious gift of Jehovah).

Jedd, Jed, Jeddy (*Heb., Arab.*) Descendant of Jed, a pet form of Jedidiah (beloved of Jehovah; peaceful); descendant of Jed (hand).

Jedlicka (*Cz.*) Dweller in, or near, the fir wood.

Jedlinski (*Pol.*) Dweller near a fir tree.

Jedlowski (*Pol.*) Dweller in, or near, the firwood.

Jedrysiak, Jedrzejak (*Pol.*) Descendant of Jedrzej, a form of Andrew (manly).

Jedynak (*Pol.*) One who was an only son.

Jefferson, Jeffers (*Eng.*) The son of Geoffrey or Jeffrey (God's peace; land, peace).

Jeffrey, Jeffery, Jeffray (*Eng.*) Descendant of Geoffrey or Jeffrey (God's peace; land, peace).

Jeffries, Jefferies (*Eng.*) The son of Geoffrey or Jeffrey (God's peace; land, peace).

Jelinek, Jelen, Jelonek, Jelinski (*Cz., Pol.*) Dweller at the sign of the stag deer; one who hunted deer.

Jelks, Jelke (*Ger.*) Descendant of little Gel, a pet form of Gelmar (exuberant, fame).

Jelley (*Eng.*) Descendant of Jelley, a form of Jill, or Gill, short forms of Jillian, Gillian and other names beginning with this element.

Jellison (*Eng.*) The son of Jelley, a form of Jill or Gill, short forms of Jillian, Gillian and other names beginning with this element.

Jemison (*Scot.*) Variant of Jamison, q.v.

Jendrzejewski (*Pol.*) Descendant of Jendrzej, a Polish form of Andrew (manly).

Jenkins, Jenkinson, Jenks (*Wel., Scot., Eng.*) The son of little Jen or Jenk, pet forms of John (gracious gift of Jehovah).

Jenner (*Scot.*) One who operated an engine of war (an aphetic form of "engineer").

Jennings (*Eng.*) Descendant of Jen, a pet variant of John (gracious gift of Jehovah).

Jennison, Jenison (*Eng.*) The son of Jenny, a pet form of the French Jean (gracious gift of Jehovah).

Jenny, Jenni (*Fr.*) Descendant of little Jean (gracious gift of Jehovah).

Jensby (*Dan.*) One who came from Jensby (Jens' settlement), in Denmark.

Jensen, Jenssen, Jenson, Jenzen (*Dan., Nor.*) The son of Jens, a variant of John (gracious gift of Jehovah).

Jentzen, Jenzen (*Du.*) The son of Jente, a Frisian pet form of Johannes (gracious gift of Jehovah).

Jepsen, Jeppesen, Jepson (*Dan., Nor.*) The son of Jep, a pet form of Jacob (may God protect; the supplanter).

Jeremiah (*Wel.*) Descendant of Jeremiah (exalted of Jehovah).

Jerger (*Ger.*) Descendant of Jeorg, a German form of George (farmer).

Jericho, Jerico (*Arab., Ger.*) One who came from Jericho (constant fragrance), in Palestine; or from Jericho, in Germany.

Jerkins (*Eng.*) The son of little Jer, a pet form of such names as Jeremy, Jeremiah, Jerome, and Gerald.

Jerman, Jermyn, Jermin (*Eng.*) One who came from Germany; descendant of German (a German); descendant of Gereman (spear, man).

Jernberg (*Sw., Nor.*) One who came from Jernberg (iron mountain), in Norway.

Jernigan, Jernegan (*Eng.*) Descendant of Iarnogon (iron, fame); or of French Gernigon; or Old Teutonic Gerwig (spear, warrior).

Jerome (*Eng.*) Descendant of Jerome (holy name).

Jerrems (*Eng.*) The son of Jerrem, a form of Jerome (holy name).

Jerrick, Jerricks (*Eng.*) One who came from Garrick (triangular piece of land forming a dairy farm), in Lincolnshire.

Jerry (*Eng., It.*) Descendant of Jerry, pet form of Jerrold (spear, firm); or Anglicized pet form of Girolamo (holy name).

Jersild (*Dan.*) One who came from Jersild, in Denmark.

Jerz (*Pol.*) Descendant of Jerz, a pet

form of Jerzy, Polish form of George (farmer).

Jerzyk (*Pol.*) Dweller at the sign of the black martin.

Jeske, Jeschke, Jeschek (*Ger., Cz.-Sl.*) Descendant of little Jesch, a pet form of Johannes (gracious gift of Jehovah); one with the characteristics of a hedgehog.

Jespersen, Jesperson (*Dan., Nor., Sw.*) The son of Jesper, Swedish form of Jasper (treasure; horseman).

Jesse, Jess, Jessee, Jessie (*Eng.*) Descendant of Jesse (Jehovah is).

Jesselson, Jessel (*Ger.*) Descendant of Jessel, a corruption of Joseph (He shall add).

Jessen (*Dan.*) The son of Jes, a form of Jens, Danish form of John (gracious gift of Jehovah).

Jessup, Jessop, Jessopp (*Eng.*) Descendant of Joseph (He shall add).

Jester (*Eng., Ger.*) One who recited romances or acted the buffoon at fair and festival; the professional fool in attendance at the king or baron; descendant of Gastharo (guest, army).

Jesuit (*Eng.*) One who was a member of the clerks regular of the Society of Jesus; a crafty person likened to a Jesuit.

Jeter, Jetter, Jetters (*Eng.*) One who assumes a haughty or pompous carriage; one who struts.

Jett, Jette (*Eng.*) Variant of Jeter, q.v.

Jewell (*Eng.*) Descendant of Jewell or Joel (Jehovah is God).

Jewett (*Eng.*) Descendant of little Jew, a pet form of Julian (downy-bearded or youthful).

Jez, Jezek, Jezak (*Pol.*) Dweller at the sign of the hedgehog.

Jezierski, Jeziorski (*Pol.*) Dweller by a lake.

Jezior (*Pol.*) Dweller near a lake.

Jezuit (*Eng.*) Variant of Jesuit, q.v.

Jilek (*Cz.*) Dweller in, or near, jilek, a kind of grass.

Jiles (*Eng.*) Descendant of Gile or Aegidius (kid), the seventh century Provencal hermit.

Jillson (*Eng.*) The son of Jill, a short form of Jillian (downy-bearded or youthful).

Jimbo (*Jap.*) God, keep.

Jimenez, Jiminez (*Sp.*) Descendant of the house or family of Simon (gracious hearing; hearkening; snub-nosed).

Jindra (*Cz.-Sl.*) Descendant of Jindrich, Czech form of Henry (home, rule).

Jinkins (*Eng.*) Variant of Jenkins, q.v.

Jirik (*Cz.-Sl.*) Descendant of little Jiri, the Czech form of George (farmer).

Joachim (*Heb.*) Descendant of Joachim or Jehoiakim (Jehovah will raise).

Job, Jobe (*Eng.*) Descendant of Job (persecuted; affliction).

Jobin, Joblin (*Eng.*) Descendant of little Job (persecuted; affliction).

Jobst (*Ger.*) The son of Job (afflicted); a mixture of Job and Jost (fighter); descendant of Jobst, a form of Jodocus (fighter).

Jocelin, Jocelyn (*Scot., Eng.*) Descendant of very little Josse (just).

Jochum, Jochem, Jochim (*Eng.*) Descendant of Jokim or Joachim (Jehovah will raise).

Jodlowski (*Pol.*) Dweller near a fir tree.

Joe (*Eng.*) Descendant of Joe, a pet form of Joseph (He shall add).

Joel, Joelson (*Eng.*) Descendant of Joel (Jehovah is God).

Joerger (*Ger.*) Descendant of Jorg, a German form of George (farmer).

Joffe, Joffee (*Heb.*) The handsome or beautiful person; variants of Jaffe, q.v.

Joffre, Joffrey, Jofre (*Fr.*) Descendant of Geoffray or Godefroi (God's peace), French forms of Godfrey (God's peace).

Johannes, Johann (*Ger.*) Descendant of Johannes or Johann, German forms of John (gracious gift of Jehovah).

Johanson, Johansen, Johannsen, Johansson (*Sw., Nor., Dan.*) The son of Johan (gracious gift of Jehovah).

Johnigan, Johnikin (*Eng.*) Descendant of little John (gracious gift of Jehovah).

Johns, John (*Wel., Eng., Ger.*) Descendant of John (gracious gift of Jehovah), a short form of Johannes.

Johnson, Johnsen, Johnsson (*Eng., Dan., Nor., Sw.*) The son of John (gracious gift of Jehovah).

Johnston, Johnstone (*Scot.*) One who came from Johnston (John's manor), in Dumfriesshire; also confused with Johnson, q.v.

Joiner (*Eng.*) One who worked with wood, a carpenter.

Jointer (*Eng.*) Sharp form of Joiner, q.v.

Joki (*Finn.*) Dweller near a river.

Jokisch (*Ger.*) Descendant of Jok, a pet form of Jakob (may God protect; the supplanter).

Joliet (*Fr.*) Descendant of little Joli (pretty; pleasant).

Jolivetti (*It.*) Dweller in, or near, what was once an olive grove.

Jolliff, Jolliffe (*Eng.*) One who was gay and lively.

Jolly, Jolley, Jolie, Joly, Jollie (*Fr.*) One who is gay and lively.

Jolson (*Eng.*) The son of Joel (Jehovah is God).

Jonaitis (*Lith.*) The son of Jonas, Lithuanian form of John (gracious gift of Jehovah).

Jonas (*Lith., Wel., Eng., Heb.*) Descendant of Jonas, a Lithuanian form of John (gracious gift of Jehovah); the son of Jone, the Welsh pronunciation of John; descendant of Jonas (dove).

Jones (*Wel., Eng.*) The son of Jone, the Welsh pronunciation of John (gracious gift of Jehovah).

Jonesku, Jonescue (*Rom.*) The son of Ioan, Romanian form of John (gracious gift of Jehovah).

Jong, Jongh (*Du.*) The young man, one who is younger than another with whom he is associated.

Joniak, Joniec (*Pol.*) Descendant of Joanna (gracious gift of Jehovah).

Jonikas (*Lith.*) Descendant of little Jon, a pet form of Jonas, Lithuanian form of John (gracious gift of Jehovah).

Jonker, Jonkers (*Du.*) The young nobleman, not yet become a knight.

Jonsson, Jonson (*Ice., Sw.*) The son of Jon (gracious gift of Jehovah).

Jonynas (*Lith.*) Descendant of Jonas, Lithuanian form of John (gracious gift of Jehovah).

Joos (*Ger.*) Descendant of Joos, a short form of Jodocus (fighter).

Joost (*Du.*) Descendant of Joost or Just (the just).

Joplin (*Eng.*) Descendant of very little Jop, a sharpened form of Job (persecuted; affliction).

Jordan, Jorden, Jourdain, Jordon (*Eng., Fr.*) Descendant of Jordan or Jourdain (flowing down), a personal name sometimes given to one who was baptized with holy water from the river Jordan.

Jorgensen, Jorgenson (*Dan., Nor.*) The son of Jorgen, Norse form of George (farmer).

Jorstad (*Sw., Nor.*) Dweller on farm with arable land.

Josefson (*Sw., Nor.*) The son of Josef, Scandinavian form of Joseph (He shall add).

Joselane, Joselyn (*Scot., Eng.*) Variants of Jocelin, q.v.

Josenhans (*Ger.*) The son of Jose, German pet form of Jodocus (fighter); descendant of Josenhans, a combination of Jose and Hans, a pet form of John (gracious gift of Jehovah).

Joseph, Josephson, Josephs (*Eng.*) Descendant, or son, of Joseph (He shall add).

Josey (*Eng.*) Descendant of little Jose, a pet form of Joseph (He shall add).

Josh (*Eng.*) Descendant of Josh, a short form of Joshua (Jehovah is salvation).

Joshua (*Eng.*) Descendant of Joshua (Jehovah is salvation).

Joslyn, Joslin, Joslun, Josslin, Josselyn (*Eng.*) Descendant of Joscelin or Joscelin (the just).

Joss, Josse (*Eng., Fr.*) Descendant of Josse (just); or of Josse, a form of

Jodoc or Jodocus (fighter); a shortened form of names beginning with the element *god*.

Jossel (*Ger.*) Jewish variant of Joseph, q.v.

Jossell, Josset (*Fr.*) Descendant of little Joss, q.v.

Jost (*Ger.*) Descendant of Jodocus (fighter); or of Justinus (the just).

Jouett (*Fr.*) Variant of Jowett, q.v.

Jousselin (*Fr.*) Variant of Jocelin, q.v.

Jovanovic, Jovanovich (*Yu.-Sl.*) The son of Jovan; or of Ivan, Slavic form of John (gracious gift of Jehovah); dweller near an alder tree.

Jowett (*Eng.*) Descendant of little Jowe, a pet form of Juliana (downy-bearded or youthful).

Joy, Joye (*Eng., Ir.*) Descendant of Joy (joyful); one given to exhibitions of happiness.

Joyce (*Eng., Ir.*) Descendant of Joyce (joyful), a masculine name in medieval times.

Joyner (*Eng.*) One who worked with wood, a carpenter.

Jozaitis (*Lith.*) The son of Juozas, pet form of Juozapas, Lithuanian form of Joseph (He shall add).

Jozefowicz (*Pol.*) The son of Jozef, Polish form of Joseph (He shall add).

Jozwiak (*Pol.*) The son of Jozwa, a Polish form of Joseph (He shall add).

Juarez, Juares (*Sp.*) Variant of Suarez, q.v.

Judd, Jude, Jud (*Eng.*) Descendant of Jude or Judah (confession); descendant of Jud, a pet form of Jordan (flowing down).

Judge (*Eng., Ir.*) One who occupied the office of judge; a translation of the Irish Brehon, with the same meaning.

Judkins (*Eng.*) The son of little Jud, a pet form of Jordan (flowing down), or of Jud or Jude (confession).

Judson (*Eng.*) The son of Jud. See Judd.

Juhasz (*Hun.*) One who tended sheep, a shepherd.

Juhl (*Dan., Ger.*) Variant of Juul, q.v.

Juillard (*Fr.*) Descendant of Juliard, a pejorative form of Julien, French form of Julian (downy-bearded or youthful); one who entertains by tricks at fair and festival.

Julian, Julien, Julius (*Eng., Fr.*) Descendant of Julian (downy-bearded or youthful).

Juliano (*It.*) Descendant of Juliano, Italian form of Julian (downy-bearded or youthful).

Jump (*Eng.*) Dweller near a steep cliff; one who came from the village of Jump (abrupt descent), in the West Riding of Yorkshire.

June (*Eng., Fr.*) Descendant of June (from one born in that month); the young person.

Juneau (*Fr.*) The little, young person.

Jung, Junge (*Ger., Chin.*) One who is younger than another with whom he is associated, such as a son (younger than his father); glory.

Jungblut, Jungbluth, Jungblud (*Ger.*) The young man or youth.

Junger, Jungers (*Ger.*) One younger than another with whom he is associated.

Jungjohann (*Ger.*) The young man named John (gracious gift of Jehovah).

Jungmann, Jungman (*Ger.*) The young servant; the younger servant.

Junius, Junious (*Eng.*) Descendant of Junius (youthful).

Junker (*Ger.*) The country squire or titled landowner; leading citizen or townsman; son of a manufacturer or merchant; merchant.

Junkins (*Eng.*) Variant of Jenkins, q.v.

Juodvalkis (*Lith.*) Dweller near a black pool.

Juozaitis (*Lith.*) The son of Juozas, Lithuanian form of Joseph (He shall add).

Juozapaitis (*Lith.*) The son of Juozapas, Lithuanian form of Joseph (He shall add).

Juozapavicius (*Lith.*) Descendant of

259

Juozapas, Lithuanian form of Joseph (He shall add).

Jurado (*Sp.*) A minor officer of a tribunal or court; a corporate officer.

Jurasek, Jurasik, Juraska (*Cz.-Sl.*) Descendant of little Juraj, a Slovakian form of George (farmer).

Jurczak, Jurczyk (*Ukr., Pol.*) Descendant of Juri, a Slavic form of George (farmer).

Jurek, Jurcio (*Pol.*) Descendant of little Jur, a Polish form of George (farmer); dweller at, or near, a hole or depression.

Jurewicz (*Pol.*) The son of Jurek, Polish form of George (farmer).

Jurgaitis (*Lith.*) The son of Jurgis, Lithuanian form of George (farmer).

Jurgens, Jurgen (*Du.*) Descendant of Jurgen, a Dutch form of George (farmer).

Jurgensen, Jurgenson (*Dan.*) The son of Jurgen, Danish form of George (farmer).

Jurgensmeyer (*Ger.*) A head servant or farmer named Georg (farmer); Jurgen's servant.

Jurgovan (*Pol.*) One who came from Jurgowo, in Poland.

Juric, Jurica, Juricek, Jurich, Jurik (*Cz.-Sl.*) Descendant of Juri or Jurik, Czechoslovakian forms of George (farmer).

Jurinek (*Cz.*) Descendant of little Juri, Czech form of George (farmer).

Juris (*Ger.*) Descendant of Juris, a pet form of Georg, German form of George (farmer).

Jurka (*Lat.*) Descendant of Jurka, Latvian form of George (farmer).

Jurkiewicz (*Pol.*) The son of little Jur, a Polish pet form of George (farmer).

Jurkovic (*Cz.-Sl.*) Descendant of Jurko, Slovakian form of George (farmer).

Jurkowski (*Ukr.*) Descendant of Jurko, Ukrainian form of George (farmer).

Just (*Eng.*) The fair-dealing or righteous person; descendant of Just, a pet form of Justus and Justin (the just).

Juster (*Eng.*) One who frequently entered the tournaments or jousts.

Justice, Justus, Justis (*Eng.*) Descendant of Justus (the just); one who performed the functions of a judicial officer, a judge.

Justin, Justen, Justyn (*Eng.*) Descendant of Justin (the just).

Juszczak, Juszczyk (*Ukr.*) Descendant of Justyn (just or upright).

Juul, Juull (*Nor., Sw., Dan.*) Descendant of Juul, Danish form of Julius (downy-bearded or youthful); or of Jul (Christmas), a name often given to a child born on that day.

Kaad (*Du.*) Dweller near, or worker on, the quay.

Kaage (*Du.*) One who came from Kaag (flat-bottomed boat), in Holland.

Kabak (*Ukr., Pol.*) Dweller near, or worker at, a tavern.

Kabat (*Pol.*) One who made and sold overcoats; one who wore an unusual overcoat.

Kaberlein, Kaberline (*Ger.*) One who made and sold little baskets or knapsacks.

Kac (*Lith.*) Priest of righteousness; variant of Katz, q.v.

Kachadurian, Kachadoorian, Kachaturian (*Arm.*) Dweller by the cross; believer in the cross.

Kachel (*Ger.*) One who made and sold Dutch tile.

Kaczmarek, Kaczmarski (*Pol.*) Descendant of the bartender.

Kaczor (*Pol.*) Dweller at the sign of the drake; one who hunted drakes.

Kaczynski (*Pol.*) One who came from Kaczyn (duck farm), in Poland.

Kadar (*Hun.*) One who made and sold casks, buckets, and tubs, a cooper.

Kaden, Kadens, Kadner (*Ger.*) One who came from Kaden (fen), the name of two places in Germany.

Kadish (*Tur.*) The saintly or holy man.

Kadlec (*Cz.-Sl.*) Descendant of Karlec, a pet form of Karl (man); a worker or day laborer; one who weaves cloth, a weaver.

Kadow (*Pol., Ukr., Rus.*) One who made and sold barrels, a cooper.

Kaebisch, Kabisch (*Ger.*) The feeble, languid man.

Kaehler (*Ger.*) One who made and sold leather armor or jackets.

Kafka (*Cz.-Sl.*) One who lived at the sign of the black daw.

Kagan, Kagen (*Pol., Rus.*) The rabbi or teacher.

Kaganovich, Kaganoff (*Rus.*) The son of the rabbi or priest.

Kagawa (*Jap.*) Fragrance, river.

Kagel (*Ger.*) One who came from Kagel, in Germany.

Kahl, Kahle, Kahler (*Ger.*) The bare or bald-headed man.

Kahn, Kahne, Kahan, Kahane (*Ger., Arab.*) Descendant of Cagano, a pet form of names commencing with Gegen (against), as Gaganhard and Geginheri; German variants of Cohen, q.v.; dweller at the sign of the boat; one who owned or operated a boat; dweller at or near a market.

Kahr, Kahre (*Ger.*) Descendant of Kero, a pet form of names beginning with Ger (spear), as Gerulf and Gerwig; one who made and sold dishes or bowls; dweller at a curve or bend.

Kain, Kaine (*Ir., Eng.*) Descendant of Cahan (warrior); one who came from Caen, in France; descendant of Cana (reed; of mature judgment).

Kainz (*Ger.*) Descendant of Kainz, a dialectal form of Kuenz, a pet form of Konrad (bold, counsel).

Kairis, Kairys (*Lith.*) One who is left-handed.

Kaiser (*Ger.*) Descendant of Caesar, i.e., emperor; one who took that part in the Purim plays.

Kala (*Est.*) One who caught and sold fish; dweller at the sign of the fish.

Kalas (*Gr., Pol.*) One who coated the inside of pots and pans; one who came from Kalisch, a city of Poland.

Kalata, Kaleta, Kalita (*Pol., Rus., Ukr.*) Dweller in a corner or pocket.

Kalb, Kalber (*Ger.*) One who cared for the calves; dweller at the sign of the calf or fawn.

Kalbfell (*Ger.*) One who skinned calves and cut and sold the meat, a butcher.

Kalbfleisch (*Ger.*) One who cut and sold calves' meat, a butcher.

Kalbfus (*Ger.*) One with a calf's or mis-shapen foot.

Kaley (*Mx., Scot., Eng.*) Descendant of Caoladh (slender); the slender man; one who came from Cailly (forest), in Normandy; dweller by a cabbage field.

Kalfas, Kalfus (*Ger.*) One with a deformed or club foot.

Kalhauge (*Nor.*) One who came from Kalvhaugen (calf hill), in Norway.

Kalil, Kalal (*Heb.*) Descendant of Kalil (a crown).

Kalina (*Rus., Pol., Ukr.*) Dweller at, or near, a guelder-rose or snowball tree.

Kalinowski (*Pol.*) One who came from Kalinow(o) (guelder-rose or snowball), in Poland.

Kalinsky, Kalinski, Kalin (*Rus., Pol.*) Dweller near where guelder-roses grew; one who came from Kalen, in Poland.

Kalish, Kalis, Kalisz (*Pol.*) One who came from Kalisz, the name of three places in Poland.

Kall (*Ger.*) One who came from Kall (muddy place), in Germany.

Kallas (*Est.*) Dweller on the shore or bank.

Kallen (*Ger.*) Dweller at the sign of the cock.

Kallenbach (*Ger.*) One who came from Kallenbach (quiet stream), in Germany.

Kallenberg (*Ger.*) One who came from Kallenberg (quiet mountain), in Germany.

Kallenborn (*Ger.*) One who came from Kalenborn (quiet spring), the name of four places in Germany.

Kallinen (*Finn.*) The son of Kalle, Finnish form of Charles (man).

Kallio (*Finn.*) Dweller near a rock or cliff.

Kallman, Kallmann, Kalman (*Ger.*) Descendant of Kalman, a form of Clement (merciful).

Kallos, Kalos (*Gr.*) One who raised grain.

Kallstrom (*Sw.*) One who came from Kallstrom (man's stream), in Sweden; cold stream.

Kalman (*Hun., Heb.*) Descendant of Kalman, Hungarian form of Colman (dove); or of Kalman (merciful).

Kalmar (*Hun.*) The merchant or tradesman.

Kalmikoff (*Rus.*) One who came from Kalmuk, in Russia.

Kalnins (*Lith.*) Dweller in the mountains.

Kalogeropoulos (*Gr.*) The son of the monk.

Kalogeros, Kalogeras (*Gr.*) The good, agreeable man; descendant of Kalogera (beautiful); one who was a male member of a religious order, a monk.

Kaltenbach (*Ger.*) One who came from Kaltenbach (cold brook; swampy stream), the name of many places in Germany.

Kaltenborn (*Ger.*) One who came from Kaltenborn (cold stream; swampy stream), the name of several places in Germany.

Kaltschmidt (*Ger.*) One who worked with copper, a coppersmith.

Kaluzny (*Pol.*) Dweller in a soft muddy or slushy place.

Kalvaitis (*Lith.*) The son of the smith, or worker in metals.

Kamberos, Kamberis (*Gr.*) One who interferes with things; the hunchback or deformed man.

Kamei (*Jap.*) Tortoise, well.

Kamen (*Pol., Rus., Ukr., Cz.-Sl., Yu.-Sl.*) Dweller at, or near, a stone, a boundary mark.

Kamerman (*Du.*) The servant who took care of the room or chamber.

Kamien, Kamienski (*Pol.*) One who came from Kamien (stone), the name of two villages in Poland; dweller near a stone.

Kamin (*Ukr., Rus.*) One who lived in a hut with a fireplace; dweller at, or near, a stone, a boundary mark.

Kaminskas (*Lith.*) One who cleans out chimneys, a chimney sweep.

Kaminski, Kaminsky (*Pol., Rus.*) Dweller near a stone or boundary mark.

Kamm (*Ger.*) Dweller on the ridge or crest of a mountain.

Kammer (*Ger.*) The officer in charge of the private household of a nobleman.

Kammerer, Kamerer (*Ger.*) A superintendent or overseer; one in charge of the private household of a nobleman.

Kammerling, Kamerling (*Ger.*) One who acted as personal servant to another, a valet; one who made clothing or shoes.

Kamp, Kampf, Kampe, Kamps (*Eng., Ger.*) The warrior or soldier; also an athlete or wrestler.

Kampenga (*Du.*) The son of Kampe (combat).

Kamper (*Ger.*) Dweller in a field or enclosure; one who engages in combat, a soldier or warrior.

Kampwirth (*Ger.*) Dweller in an enclosed homestead.

Kamradt, Kamrad, Kamrath (*Ger.*) One who made glass drinking vessels.

Kamys, Kamysz (*Pol.*) Dweller near a small stone.

Kanada (*Jap.*) Gold, rice field.

Kanak (*Pol.*) One who made and sold necklaces of pearls.

Kanatas (*Gr.*) One who made utensils of earthenware, a potter.

Kanda (*Jap.*) God, rice field.

Kandel, Kandell, Kandelman, Kandl, Kandle (*Ger.*) One who made and sold mugs and jugs, a potter. One who worked on gutters.

Kane, Kahane (*Ir.*) Descendant of the warrior; grandson of Cathan (warrior).

Kanealy (*Ir.*) Variant of Kennelly, q.v.

Kanellos, Kanelos (*Gr.*) One who produces and sells cinnamon.

Kang (*Chin., Kor.*) Ease; dweller near a bay or river.

Kangas (*Finn.*) Dweller in, or near, a heath or moor.

Kangur (*Est.*) One who wove cloth, a weaver.

Kania (*Pol., Ukr.*) Dweller at the sign of the hawk; one with the qualities of a hawk.

Kaniuk (*Ukr.*) Dweller at the sign of the bird; one who trapped and sold birds.

Kanka (*Pol.*) Dweller at the sign of the cock.

Kann, Kanne (*Ger.*) Dweller at the sign of the jug, sometimes carved on doors of homes of Levites since it is the duty of the Levites to pour water over the hands of the priests before they bless the congregation.

Kannally, Kannaly (*Ir.*) Son of the poor man; descendant of Ceannfaoladh (wolf head; learned man).

Kano (*Jap.*) Grant.

Kanow (*Jap.*) Add, accept.

Kansteiner (*Ger.*) One who came from Kanstein, in Germany.

Kant (*Ger.*) One who came from Kanth, in Schleswig; dweller at the boundary or corner.

Kanter, Kantor (*Ger.*) The soloist who sang liturgical music in the synagogue.

Kanzler (*Ger.*) One who held the office of chancellor, an official secretary.

Kapchinski (*Pol.*) One who came from Kapczyn (Kapca's settlement), in Poland.

Kapel (*Du.*) Dweller near the chapel.

Kapelanski, Kapelinski (*Pol.*) One employed by the chaplain, a servant.

Kapka (*Pol.*) Nickname for a small, insignificant man.

Kaplan, Kaplin, Kaplon (*Ger., Pol.*) Descendant of the chaplain or high priest.

Kapp, Kappe (*Ger.*) Descendant of Kapp, a pet form of Kaspar (treasure); one who made hooded cloaks or mantles; dweller at the sign of the cap.

Kappel, Kapell, Kappeler, Kappler (*Ger., Hun.*) One who came from Kapelle (chapel), in Germany; dweller near a chapel.

Kapral, Kaprall, Kapralski (*Pol.*) One with the rank of a petty officer in the army, a corporal.

Kapustka, Kapusta, Kapustiak (*Pol.*) The cabbage head, a term of contempt for a stupid person; one who grew and sold cabbages.

Kaput (*Ger.*) Metonymic for one who made soldiers' coats and capes.

Kara (*Gr., Tur.*) One with a dark or swarthy complexion.

Karabatsos, Karabetsos (*Gr.*) The dark or black man who took care of the sheep, a shepherd.

Karabin (*Pol.*) One who fought with a carbine or musket.

Karadimos, Karadimas (*Gr.*) Descendant of dark-complexioned or black Dimos, a pet form of Dimitrios, Greek form of Demitrius (of Demeter, the goddess of fertility and harvests).

Karageorge, Karageorgis (*Gr.*) Descendant of black George (farmer).

Karagiannis, Karagianis, Karagianes (*Gr.*) Descendant of dark-complexioned or black Giannis, Greek form of John (gracious gift of Jehovah).

Karahalios (*Gr.*) Descendant of black Chalios, a diminutive form of Michael (who is like God).

Karaitis (*Lith.*) Descendant of Karolis, Lithuanian form of Karl (man).

Karalis (*Lith.*) One connected in some way with a king's household; descendant of Karolis, Lithuanian form of Charles (man).

Karall (*Ger.*) Descendant of Karal, a German form of Charles (man).

Karambelas (*Tur.*) Black disaster.

Karamitsos (*Gr.*) The dark or black man called Mitsos, a pet form of Demetrios, Greek form of Demitrius (of Demeter, the goddess of fertility and harvests).

Karas, Karras (*Gr.*) One with a swarthy complexion.

Karasek, Karasik (*Pol.*) Dweller at the sign of the crucian (carp).

Karbach (*Ger.*) One who came from Karbach (stream in a cirque; muddy stream), the name of several places in Germany.

Karch, Karcher (*Ger.*) One who drove a cart, a carter or drayman.

Karczewski, Karcz (*Pol.*) Dweller at, or near, an unusual stump; or in a clearing in the forest where tree stumps remain.

Kardelis (*Lith.*) Descendant of Kardas (sword), a nickname.

Kardon (*Eng.*) One who came from Carden (rock enclosure), in Cheshire.

Kardos (*Hun.*) The soldier armed with a sword.

Karel, Karels (*Du.*) Descendant of Karel, Dutch form of Charles (man).

Karge, Karger, Karg (*Ger.*) The crafty, sly, cunning man; the mean, stingy man.

Karl, Karle (*Eng., Ger.*) The husbandman or rustic; descendant of Karl (man); one who came from Karl (man), in Germany.

Karlic (*Yu.-Sl., Cz.-Sl.*) The son of Karl (man).

Karlin, Karlinsky (*Rus.*) Descendant of little Karl (man).

Karlovitz (*Yu.-Sl.*) The son of Karl, the Serbo-Croatian form of Charles (man).

Karlovsky, Karlov (*Rus.*) The son of Karl or Charles (man).

Karlowicz (*Pol.*) The son of Karl, Polish form of Charles (man).

Karlson, Karlsen (*Sw.*) The son of Karl, Swedish form of Charles (man).

Karlsson (*Ice., Sw.*) The son of Karl (man).

Karman, Karmann (*Ger.*) Dweller in the pasture in the valley; one who made, and sold, bowls or baskets; descendant of Gereman (spear, man); one who drove a cart, a carter.

Karner (*Ger.*) One who drove a cart, a carter; dweller near a charnel house.

Karnes, Karns (*Pol.*) Dweller in, or near, a building with an unusual cornice.

Karol, Karoll, Karolczak, Karolewicz,

Karolewski (*Pol.*) Descendant, or son, of Karol, Polish form of Charles (man).

Karolyi, Karoly (*Hun.*) One who came from Karoly (Charles), in Hungary; descendant of Karoly, Hungarian form of Charles (man).

Karow, Karowski, Karowsky (*Ger., Pol.*) One who came from Karow, the name of five places in Germany.

Karp (*Du.*) Dweller at the sign of the carp.

Karpel, Karpell (*Ger.*) One who fished for small carp.

Karpen (*Bel.*) Descendant of Karpen, a pet form of Polycarpe, Belgian form of Polycarp (much fruit).

Karpenstein (*Swis.*) One who carves or chisels inscriptions on stone.

Karpinski (*Ukr., Pol.*) One who fishes for carp.

Karpowicz (*Ukr., Pol.*) The son of Karpo, a pet form of Polikarp, Slavic form of Polycarp (much fruit).

Karpus, Karpuska (*Rus., Ukr.*) Descendant of Karpus, a pet form of Polikarp, Russian and Ukrainian form of Polycarp (much fruit).

Karr, Karre (*Ir.*) Grandson of Carra (spear).

Karras (*Gr., Est.*) One with a dark or swarthy complexion; black.

Karsh (*Ger.*) The lively, brisk, vigorous, gay, cheerful man.

Karson (*Sw.*) The son of Karl (man).

Karsten, Karstens (*Ger.*) Descendant of Karsten, German form of Christian (follower of Christ).

Karstensen, Karstenson (*Du.*) The son of Karsten, a form of Christian (a follower of Christ).

Karstrand (*Sw.*) One who came from Karlstrand (Karl's shore), in Sweden.

Karstrom (*Nor., Sw.*) Dweller near a swampy stream; marsh stream.

Kartheiser (*Ger.*) One who came from Karthaus, in Germany.

Kartje (*Du.*) One who drove a small cart.

Karwoski, Karwowski (*Pol.*) Descendant of Karol, Polish form of Charles (man).

Kash (*Ger.*) The quick, lively man.

Kask, Kaske (*Est.*) Dweller near a birch tree.

Kasman (*Ger.*) One who made and sold cheese.

Kasminski (*Pol.*) One who came from Kazimierz (Kazimir's homestead), in Poland.

Kasparian (*Arm.*) The son of Kaspar (master of the treasure; horseman).

Kaspars (*Lat.*) Descendant of Kaspars, Latvian form of Kaspar (master of the treasure; horseman).

Kasper, Kaspar (*Ger.*) Descendant of Kaspar or Caspar (master of the treasure; horseman), the traditional name of one of the wise men who went to Bethlehem to worship the infant Jesus.

Kasperski, Kasprowicz, Kasprzak, Kasprzycki, Kasprzyk (*Pol.*) Descendant, or son, of Kasper (master of the treasure; horseman).

Kasprowicz (*Pol.*) The son of Kasper, Polish form of Kaspar (master of the treasure; horseman).

Kass, Kase, Kasch, Kaese (*Ger.*) Descendant of Kass, a pet form of Cazo; one with the characteristics of a blackbird; one who produced and sold cheese.

Kassabian, Kasabian (*Arm.*) Dweller in the town.

Kassebaum, Kassabaum (*Ger.*) Dweller near a cherry tree.

Kassel, Kassler (*Ger.*) One who came from Kassel, in Prussia.

Kast (*Ger.*) Descendant of Kast, a pet form of Christianus (follower of Christ).

Kastner, Kaster, Kasten, Kassner (*Ger., Du.*) The manager of a granary; one who made cabinets.

Kasza (*Pol.*) One who prepared and sold coarsely ground grain or grits.

Kaszuba, Kaszubski (*Pol.*) One who came from Kaszuby, a region in Poland.

Kaszynski (*Pol.*) One who produced and sold groats.

Kataoka (*Jap.*) Fix, hill.

Katauskas (*Lith.*) One who raised cats.

Kates (*Eng.*) Descendant of Kati or Kate, pet forms of Catherine (pure); one who was merry and gay.

Kathrein (*Ger.*) Descendant of Katherine, German form of Catherine (pure).

Katkus (*Lith.*) Dweller at the sign of the little cat.

Kato (*Jap.*) Add, wisteria.

Katona (*Hun.*) One in military service, a soldier.

Katsaros (*Gr.*) One with naturally curly hair.

Katula, Katulick (*Finn.*) Dweller on the street.

Katz (*Heb.*) An abbreviation of *kohen tzedek*, "priest of righteousness," therefore, a priest.

Katzbeck (*Ger.*) One who came from Katzbach (muddy brook), in Germany.

Katzel (*Ger.*) Dweller at the sign of the little cat or kitten.

Katzenberg, Katzenberger (*Ger.*) One who came from Katzenberg (cats' mountain), in Germany.

Katzenstein (*Ger.*) One who came from Katzenstein (cat's stone), the name of three places in Germany.

Katzman, Katzmann (*Ger.*) The servant of Cazo; the priest. See Katz.

Katzmark (*Ger.*) Dweller near the boundary of the priest's place.

Katzoff (*Ger.*) One who cut meat, a butcher.

Kaufman, Kaufmann, Kauffman, Kauffmann (*Ger.*) The merchant or tradesman.

Kaulfuss (*Ger.*) One with a club foot, a cripple.

Kaunas (*Lith.*) One who came from Kaunas, a district of Lithuania.

Kauppinen (*Finn.*) One who kept a shop, a merchant or tradesman.

Kauth, Kautt (*Ger.*) Dweller at the sign of the cock pigeon.

Kautz, Kautzman (*Ger.*) The queer fellow or eccentric man.

Kavalauskas, Kavaliauskas, Kavaliunas (*Lith.*) One who worked in metal, a smith.

Kavanaugh, Kavanagh (*Ir.*) Grandson of little Caomh (comely) or Caomhan, the names of fifteen Irish saints.

Kavka (*Cz.*) Dweller at the sign of the crow; one with the characteristics of a crow.

Kawa (*Pol., Ukr.*) One who dealt in coffee.

Kawaguchi (*Jap.*) River, mouth.

Kawakami (*Jap.*) River, upper.

Kawasaki (*Jap.*) River, headland.

Kawczynski (*Pol.*) Dweller at the sign of the jackdaw; one thought to possess the characteristics of a jackdaw.

Kawka (*Pol.*) One who dealt in coffee.

Kay, Kaye (*Eng., Scot.*) Descendant of Gaius (rejoice); dweller near the wharf or boat landing place; the left-handed or clumsy person; one with the characteristics of a jackdaw; an abbreviation sometimes adopted by a newcomer who has a difficult surname beginning with K.

Kaya (*Jap.*) Miscanthus (a genus from Japan of hardy grasses with ornamental foliage).

Kayser (*Eng., Ger.*) One who took the part of Caesar in play or pageant; variant of Kaiser, q.v.

Kayton (*Eng.*) One who came from Kayton (Caega's homestead), in the North Riding of Yorkshire.

Kaywood (*Eng.*) One who came from Cawood (jackdaw wood), the name of places in Lancashire and the West Riding of Yorkshire.

Kazak (*Rus.*) Nickname for a brave soldier.

Kazarian (*Arm.*) One who made and sold silk.

Kazazis (*Gr., Tur.*) One who made and sold silk.

Kazlauskas (*Lith.*) Dweller at the sign of the buck.

Kazmar (*Hun.*) Descendant of Kazmer, Hungarian form of Casimir (show forth peace).

Kazmarek (*Pol.*) One who dealt in cashmere wool.

Kazmierczak (*Pol.*) Descendant of little Kazimier (show forth peace).

Kazmierski (*Pol.*) One who dealt in cashmere; one who came from Kazimierz, in Poland.

Keadle (*Eng.*) Variant of Kiddle, q.v.

Keady (*Ir.*) Grandson of Ceodach (possessing hundreds).

Keag, Keagy (*Ir.*) The son of Tadhg (poet; philosopher).

Keal (*Eng.*) One who came from Keal (ridge), in Lincolnshire.

Kealy, Kealey (*Ir., Eng.*) Grandson of Caollaidhe; or of Cadhla (beautiful); one who came from Keighley (Cyhha's grove), in the West Riding of Yorkshire.

Keane, Kean (*Ir., Eng.*) Descendant of the warrior; variant of Keen, q.v.

Keaney, Keany (*Ir.*) Descendant of Cianach (keen).

Kearby (*Eng.*) One who came from Kearby (Kaerir's homestead), in the West Riding of Yorkshire.

Kearney (*Ir.*) Grandson of Carney (victorious in battle).

Kearns, Kerns, Kernes (*Ir.*) Descendant of the little black one.

Keath (*Scot.*) One who came from Keith (wood), in Banffshire.

Keathley (*Eng.*) Variant of Keighley, q.v.

Keating, Keatinge (*Ir.*) Descendant of the reasonable or urbane person; grandson of Ceatfhaidh (sense).

Keaton (*Eng.*) One who came from Ketton (estate of the Kesteven people), in Rutland.

Keats, Keets, Keate, Keates (*Eng.*) Descendant of Keat (lively); or of Ket, an abbreviation of one of the names beginning with Ketil (caldron); descendant of Kit, a pet form of Christopher (Christ-bearer).

Keaty (*Ir.*) Grandson of Ceatfhaidh (sense).

Keaveny, Keaveney (*Ir.*) Grandson of Geibheannach (prisoner).

Keay, Keays (*Eng., Scot.*) Variant of Kay, q.v.

Keck, Kecker (*Ger.*) One who is full of life; the brave, bold, daring man.

Keddy, Keddie, Keady (*Scot.*) The son of Adie, a pet form of Adam (red earth).

Kedge (*Eng.*) The brisk, lively man.

Kedzior, Kedzierski (*Pol.*) One who made locks, a locksmith.

Kee (*Scot.*) Descendant of Aedh or Aodh (fire).

Keebler, Keeble (*Eng.*) One who made and sold cudgels; the stout, heavy man.

Keech (*Eng.*) One who cut and sold meat, a butcher (from keech, a lump of fat).

Keefe, Keeffe (*Ir.*) Grandson of Caomh (comely).

Keefer (*Ger.*) One who made and sold vats, tubs and barrels, a cooper; one in charge of the wine cellar.

Keegan (*Ir.*) The son of little Aodh (fire).

Keehan (*Ir.*) Descendant of little Aodh (fire); the small, blind man.

Keehn (*Ger.*) Variant of Kuhn, q.v.

Keel, Keele (*Eng.*) One who came from Keele (cow hill), in Staffordshire.

Keeler (*Eng.*) One who worked on a keel or long boat, a seaman or bargeman.

Keeley, Keely (*Ir.*) Descendant of the slender man; grandson of Caollaidhe.

Keeling (*Eng.*) The son of Ceol (ship).

Keenan (*Ir.*) Grandson of little Cian (ancient).

Keene, Keen (*Eng., Ir.*) The quick, sharp person; grandson of Cathan, a pet form of some name commencing with Cath, as Cathair or Cathal.

Keener (*Ger.*) Variant of Kuehner, q.v.

Keeney (*Ir.*) Grandson of Cianach (ancient).

Keenley (*Eng.*) One who came from Kenley (Cena's grove), in Shropshire.

Keenleyside (*Eng.*) One who came from Kinniside (royal head), in Cumberland.

Keer, Keers (*Eng.*) Dweller on, or near, the Keer (dark) river, in Westmorland and Lancashire; one who made keys.

Kees, Keese (*Ger.*) One who made and sold cheese.

Kefauver (*Ger.*) One who made and sold vats.

Kegel, Kagel (*Ger.*) One born out of wedlock, an illegitimate child; an unrefined person.

Kegley (*Eng.*) Variant of Keighley, q.v.

Kehl, Kehle (*Ger.*) One who came from Kehl (channel), the name of two places in Germany.

Kehoe, Keho (*Ir.*) The horseman or jockey.

Keighley, Keightly, Keithley (*Eng.*) One who came from Keighley (Cyhha's grove), in the West Riding of Yorkshire.

Keigwin (*Eng.*) Dweller in, or near, the white field.

Keil (*Ger.*) One who is supercilious or wanton; dweller on, or near, a wedge-shaped piece of land.

Keim (*Ger.*) One who raised plants from seeds.

Keir (*Scot., Ir.*) One who came from Keir (fort), in Scotland; one with a dark complexion; descendant of Ciar (black).

Keirstead (*Nor.*) One who came from Kjaerstad, in Norway.

Keiser (*Ger.*) Variant of Kaiser, q.v.

Keith (*Scot.*) One who lived on the lands of Keith (wood), in East Lothian.

Kelber (*Ger.*) One who made clubs and maces; one in charge of the calves.

Kelburn (*Scot.*) One who came from Kelburn (hazel stream), in Scotland.

Kelby (*Eng.*) One who came from Kelby (homestead on a ridge), in Lincolnshire.

Kelderhouse (*Eng.*) Dweller, or worker, at or near the children's house or orphanage.

Kelemen (*Hun.*) Descendant of Keleman, Hungarian form of Clement (merciful).

Kell, Kells (*Scot.*) Dweller near a spring; one who came from Kells (church), in Scotland.

Kellam, Kellams, Kellems, Kellum (*Eng.*) One who came from Kelham (at the ridges), in Nottinghamshire.

Kellberg (*Sw., Nor.*) One who came from Kjellberg (spring mountain), in Sweden; or from Kjelberg (spring mountain), in Norway.

Kelleher, Kelliher, Keleher, Kellegher (*Ir.*) Grandson of Ceiteachar (spouse-loving; dear companion).

Kellen (*Ger.*) One who came from Kellen (swamp), the name of two places in Germany.

Keller, Kellar (*Fr., Eng., Ger.*) One employed in a storeroom, particularly a food storage place; one who made or sold cauls or kells, a cap or hairnet for women; one who came from Keller (wine cellar), the name of several places in Germany.

Kellerhals (*Ger.*) Dweller near the covered entrance to a wine cellar.

Kellerman, Kellermann (*Ger.*) Worker in, or dweller in, a wine cellar or tavern.

Kelley (*Ir., Scot., Eng.*) Variant of Kelly, q.v.

Kelling (*Eng.*) One who came from Kelling (place of Cylla's people), in Norfolk.

Kellis, Kellison (*Sw.*) The son of Kelle, a pet form of Ketil (caldron).

Kellman, Kellmann (*Ger.*) Dweller in, or near, a swamp or marsh.

Kellner, Kelner (*Ger., Du.*) One in charge of the wine cellar; one who waits on table, a waiter.

Kellogg, Kellock (*Eng.*) One who slaughtered hogs.

Kelly (*Ir., Scot., Eng.*) Grandson of Ceallach (contention); one who came from Kelly (holly; woods); dweller in a grove.

Kelm, Kelmer (*Ger.*) One who came from Kelm (swamp), in Germany.

Kelsall (*Eng.*) One who came from Kelsall (Cenel's corner), in Cheshire.

Kelsey, Kelsie (*Eng.*) One who came from Kelsey (Cenel's island; high land in a marsh), in Lincolnshire.

Kelshaw (*Eng.*) One who came from Kelshall (Cylli's corner), in Hertfordshire.

Kelso (*Scot.*) One who came from Kelso (chalk height), in Roxburghshire.

Kelson (*Sw.*) The son of Kjell (sacrificial caldron).

Kelstrom (*Sw.*) Caldron stream.

Kelter, Keltner (*Ger.*) One who operated a wine press.

Kelton (*Eng.*) One who came from Kelton (calf homestead), in Cumberland.

Kelty (*Scot.*) One who came from Kelty (wood), in Kinross.

Kelvin (*Scot.*) Dweller by the Kelvin (narrow stream), a river in Scotland.

Kemal (*Tur.*) Descendant of Kemal (perfection).

Kemble (*Eng.*) One who came from Kemble (from Camulos, the name of a Celtic god), in Gloucestershire.

Kemeny (*Hun.*) The hard or severe man.

Kemmer, Kemmerer, Kemmler (*Ger.*) The officer in charge of the private household of a king or noble; one who made combs; or who combed wool.

Kemnitz, Kemnitzer (*Ger.*) One who came from Kemnitz (stone), the name of various places in Germany.

Kemp, Kempf, Kempfer, Kemph (*Eng., Ger.*) The warrior or soldier; an athlete or wrestler; dweller in an enclosure belonging to one person.

Kempa, Kempe, Kempen (*Ger.*) One who came from Kempen (swampy meadow), the name of several places in Germany.

Kemper (*Eng.*) A soldier or warrior; one who combed wool or flax.

Kempner (*Ger.*) One who came from Kempen (swampy meadow), the name of five places in Germany.

Kempston (*Eng.*) One who came from

Kempston (Cymi's homestead), in Norfolk.

Kempton (*Eng.*) One who came from Kempton (Cempa's homestead), in Shropshire.

Kendall, Kendell, Kendle, Kendal (*Eng.*) One who came from Kendal (valley of the Kent river), in Westmorland.

Kendrick, Kendricks (*Eng.*) Descendant of Kenrick (royal, rule).

Kendrigan (*Ir.*) Descendant of little Ceanndearg (red head).

Kendzior, Kendziora, Kendzierski (*Pol.*) One who had curly hair.

Kenerson (*Eng.*) The son of Cyneweard (bold, guardian).

Kengott (*Ger.*) Descendant of Kunigunde (bold, combat).

Kenig, Kenick (*Ger.*) Variant of Koenig, q.v.

Kenion (*Eng.*) One who came from Kenyon (Einion's mound), in Lancashire.

Kenison, Kennison (*Scot.*) Variant of Kinnison, q.v.

Keniston (*Eng.*) One who came from Kenstone (Centwine's valley), in Shropshire.

Kenley (*Eng., Scot.*) One who came from Kenley (Cena's grove), the name of places in Shropshire and Surrey; variant of Kinley, q.v.

Kenn (*Eng.*) One who came from Kenn (a stream name), the name of places in Devonshire and Somerset.

Kenna (*Ir.*) Variant of Kenney, q.v.

Kennard (*Eng.*) Descendant of Cenhard (bold, strong), or of Cynehard (royal, strong).

Kennedy (*Scot., Ir.*) One with an ugly or misshapen head; descendant of Cinneididh (helmeted-head).

Kennelly, Kenneally, Kenealy (*Ir.*) Grandson of Ceannfhaoladh (wolf head; learned man).

Kennett, Kennet (*Eng., Scot.*) Dweller at the sign of the little dog; one who came from Kennet (head ford), in Clackmannan.

Kenney (*Ir.*) Grandson of Cionaodh (ardent love; fire sprung).

Kenngott (*Ger.*) Descendant of Kunigund (bold, war).

Kennicott (*Eng.*) One who came from Kencott (Cena's cottage), in Oxfordshire.

Kenning (*Ger.*) Descendant of Keno, a pet form of Konrad (bold, counsel).

Kenniston, Kennison (*Eng.*) One who came from Kynaston (Cynfrith's homestead), in Shropshire; or from Kensington (homestead of Cynesige's people), in Middlesex; the son of Kenny (ardent love; fire sprung).

Kennon (*Ir.*) The son of Finghin (fair offspring).

Kenny (*Ir.*) Variant of Kenney, q.v.

Kenrick (*Eng.*) Descendant of Cenric or Kenric (bold, rule); or of Cynric (royal, rule).

Kensey (*Eng.*) Dweller near the Kensey river, in Cornwall.

Kenston (*Eng.*) One who came from Kenstone (Centwine's valley), in Shrophire.

Kent (*Eng.*) One who came from the county of Kent (open country), in the southeast corner of England.

Kenton (*Eng.*) One who came from Kenton (homestead on Kenn river; Cempa's homestead; royal manor), the name of four places in England.

Kenward (*Eng.*) Descendant of Cenweard (bold, guardian).

Kenwood (*Eng.*) One who came from Ken Wood (an early spelling was Canewood), in Middlesex.

Kenworthy (*Eng.*) One who came from Kenworthy, in Cheshire; or from Kensworth (Caegin's homestead), in Bedfordshire.

Kenyon (*Eng., Ir.*) One who came from Kenyon (Einion's mound), in Lancashire; the son of Coinin (rabbit); or of Finghin (fair offspring).

Keohane (*Ir.*) Descendant of Eochain.

Keough, Keogh (*Ir.*) The son of Eochaidh (rich in cattle).

Keown (*Scot.*) Son of Owen (young warrior; well-born).

Kepford (*Eng.*) Dweller at the market by the river crossing.

Kepler, Keppler, Kepner, Keppner (*Ger.*) One who made and sold caps and hoods.

Kerber (*Ger.*) One who came from Korb (basket), in Germany.

Kerby (*Eng.*) Variant of Kirby, q.v.

Kercher (*Ger.*) One who drove a cart; one who takes care of church property.

Kerckhove, Kerckhoff (*Du.*) Dweller in, or near, the church yard.

Kerekes (*Hun.*) One who made wheels and wheeled vehicles.

Kerkendoll (*Nor.*) Variant of Kirkendall, q.v.

Kerkhof, Kerkhoff (*Du., Ger.*) Dweller in, or near, the church yard.

Kerkstra (*Du.*) Dweller near the church.

Kerley (*Ir.*) The son of Fearghal (supervalor).

Kerman (*Eng.*) Dweller at, or near, a pond or bog.

Kern, Kerns (*Ger., Ir.*) Descendant of Kern, a pet form of Gernwin (desire, friend); one who came from Kern (kernel), in Germany; grandson of Ceirin (little black one).

Kernan, Kiernan (*Ir.*) The son of the lord or owner of the village.

Kerner (*Ger.*) One who drives a cart, a carter; one who grinds grain, a miller; one who came from Kern (kernel), in Germany.

Kerney (*Ir.*) Grandson of Ceithearnaigh (foot soldier).

Kerouac (*Fr.*) Dweller in the house in the field.

Kerr (*Eng., Ir.*) Dweller at, or near, a marsh, especially one grown up with low bushes; dweller near a fort.

Kerrick, Kerrich (*Eng.*) Descendant of Cyneric (family, rule).

Kerridge (*Eng.*) One who came from Kerridge (wet ground between ridges), in Cheshire; variant of Kerrick, q.v.

Kerrigan (*Ir.*) Grandson of little Ciar (black).

Kerrison (*Eng.*) One who came from Kerdiston (Cenred's homestead), in Norfolk.

Kerry (*Eng., Ir.*) Descendant of Ceolric (ship, rule); descendant of Ciardha (black).

Kerschner, Kerscher (*Ger.*) One who prepared, or bought and sold, furs, a furrier.

Kersey (*Eng.*) One who came from Kersey (cress island), in Suffolk.

Kershaw (*Eng.*) Dweller at, or near, the copse on the marsh, i.e., a boggy wood; one who came from Kirkshaw (wood by the church), in Lancashire.

Kersten, Kerstein, Kersting (*Ger.*) Descendant of Christianus (follower of Christ).

Kertesz (*Hun.*) One who tended a garden, cultivating flowers and vegetables.

Kerwin (*Ir.*) Grandson of little Ciardubh (jet black); one with a dark complexion.

Keser (*Ger.*) One who made and sold cheese.

Kesner, Kessner (*Ger.*) One who collected taxes.

Kessel, Kessell, Kesselman (*Ger., Eng.*) One who made and sold kettles; dweller in, or near, a fort or castle; one who came from Kessel (castle), the name of many places in Germany.

Kessler, Kestler, Kesseler (*Ger.*) One who made kettles; one who came from Kessel (castle), the name of many places in Germany.

Kestenbaum, Kestnbaum (*Ger.*) Dweller near a chestnut tree.

Kester (*Du.*) One who came from Kester in Holland; one who made and sold boxes.

Ketchell (*Eng.*) One who made and sold the small cakes given as alms in the name of God.

Ketchen, Ketchian (*Eng.*) Variant of Kitchen, q.v.

Ketchum, Ketcham (*Eng.*) One who came from Caecca's homestead.

Ketelsen, Ketelson (*Sw., Nor.*) The son of Ketil (caldron).

Keto (*Finn.*) Dweller in, or near, a field.

Kettell, Kettelson (*Eng.*) Variant of Kittle, q.v.

Kettering (*Eng.*) One who came from Kettering (estate of Cytringas), in Northamptonshire.

Kettle, Kettles, Ketill (*Eng., Ice., Scot.*) Descendant of Old Norse Ketill (sacrificial caldron); shortened form of several village names in England commencing with this term; one who came from Kettle (private place), in Scotland.

Kettler (*Ger.*) One who mended pots and kettles, a tinker; or who made and sold kettles.

Kettner, Ketner (*Cz., Ger.*) One who makes and sells chains and necklaces; one who came from Ketten, in Germany.

Kettrick, Kettridge (*Eng.*) Descendant of Cytelric (caldron, rule).

Kettunen (*Finn.*) One who lived at the sign of the fox; one with fox-like qualities.

Kevin, Kevane (*Ir.*) Grandson of little Caomh (comely).

Kew (*Eng., Scot.*) One who came from Kew (projecting piece of land at a bend), in Surrey; contraction of McHugh, q.v.; one who prepared food, a cook.

Kewley (*Eng., Mx.*) One who came from Quilly (Cullius' farm), in France; Manx contraction of Macaulay, q.v.

Key, Keyer (*Eng.*) The maker of keys and locks.

Keyes, Keys (*Scot.*) Dweller near the wharf or boat landing place.

Keyser (*Ger.*) Variant of Kaiser, q.v.

Khalaf (*Arab.*) One who inherits property from another.

Khalil, Khalili (*Arab.*) One who was a friend.

Khan (*Pers., Tur., Arab.*) One who kept a public place, the landlord of an inn; descendant of a lord; one who aped the manners of a lord or prince.

Khokhlov (*Rus.*) The man from Ukraine, a slightly contemptuous term.

Khoury, Khouri (*Arab.*) One who performed sacerdotal functions, a priest.

Khrushchev (*Rus.*) The son of the cockchafer, a large beetle; one with some characteristic of a large beetle.

Kibbee, Kibbe, Kibby (*Eng.*) One who came from Keadby (Keti's homestead), in Lincolnshire; or from Kearby (Kaeri's homestead), in Yorkshire.

Kibble (*Eng.*) Descendant of Cybbel (cudgel); one who made and sold cudgels.

Kibler (*Eng.*) One who made and sold cudgels.

Kidd, Kidde (*Eng., Scot.*) Dweller at the sign of the young goat; descendant of Kid, a pet form of Christopher (Christ-bearer).

Kiddall, Kiddell, Kiddle (*Eng.*) Dweller near a kiddle, a weir or fence of stakes, twigs, or nets at the mouth of a stream for catching fish; one in charge of a kiddle; one who came from Kiddal (cow valley), in the West Riding of Yorkshire.

Kidder (*Eng.*) One who tends or trains hawks for hunting.

Kiddie (*Scot.*) Descendant of Addie, a pet or double diminutive of Adam (red earth).

Kidwell (*Eng.*) Dweller near Cydda's spring; variant of Kiddall, q.v.

Kiefer, Keefer, Kieffer (*Ger.*) One who made and sold casks, a cooper; one who had charge of the wine cellar.

Kiehl (*Ger.*) One who came from Kiel (area of standing water), the name of several places in Germany.

Kiehn (*Ger.*) The bold, brave, audacious man.

Kiel (*Ger.*) One who came from Kiel (flood), the name of several places in Germany.

Kielbasa (*Pol.*) One who made and sold small sausages.

Kielczynski (*Pol.*) One who came from Kielce, the capital of the department of Kielce, in Poland.

Kiely (*Ir.*) Grandson of Cadhla (beautiful or graceful).

Kienzle (*Ger.*) Descendant of Kienzle, a pet form of Konrad (bold, counsel).

Kier (*Ger.*) Descendant of Kier, a pet form of names beginning with Ger (javelin), as Germund, Gerwin, and Gerulf.

Kieran, Kearon (*Ir.*) Grandson of Kieran (little black one), the name of fifteen Irish saints.

Kiernan (*Ir.*) Grandson of little Ciar (black).

Kierzek (*Pol.*) Dweller near a bush or shrub.

Kies (*Du.*) One with a prominent tooth.

Kiesel, Kiesler (*Ger.*) Dweller on a gravelly place.

Kiesling, Kiessling (*Ger.*) One who came from Kiesling (pebble place), the name of two villages in Germany.

Kight (*Eng.*) Dweller near a hut or shed for cattle or sheep; one who took care of animals, a herdsman; descendant of Keat (lively), or of Kit, a pet form of Christopher (Christbearer).

Kijak, Kijek, Kijewski (*Pol.*) One who used a walking-stick.

Kikkebusch (*Ger.*) One who came from Kieckebusch (peek in the bush), in Germany.

Kilborn, Kilbourn, Kilbourne, Kilborne (*Eng.*) One who came from Kilbourne or Kilburn (stream by a kiln), the names of several places in England.

Kilboy (*Eng.*) One who came from Kilby (the children's village), in Leicestershire.

Kilbride (*Scot., Ir.*) One who came from Kilbride (church of St. Brigit), in Lanarkshire; the son of the servant or devotee of St. Bridgid.

Kilburg (*Sw.*) One who came from Kilberg (wedge mountain), the name of several places in Sweden.

Kilburn (*Eng.*) One who came from Kilburn (kiln by a stream), the name of places in Middlesex and the North Riding of Yorkshire.

Kilby (*Eng.*) One who came from Kilby (Cilda's homestead), in Leicestershire.

Kilchrist, Kilcrest, Kilchreest (*Ir.*) The son of the servant of Christ.

Kilcommons (*Ir.*) The son of the servant of St. Coman.

Kilcourse (*Ir., Scot.*) The son of the rough youth; corruption of Kilgore, q.v.

Kilcoyne (*Ir.*) The son of the gentle youth.

Kilcullen (*Ir.*) The son of the devotee of St. Caillin.

Kildare, Kildaire (*Ir.*) One who came from Kildare (cell of the oak), in Ireland; variant of Kilderry, q.v.

Kilday, Kildea (*Scot., Ir.*) One who came from Keldall, in Orkney; the son of the servant of God.

Kilderry (*Ir.*) The son of the dark youth.

Kilduff (*Ir.*) The son of the black youth.

Kile (*Scot., Dan.*) One who came from the district of Kyle (a strait), in Ayrshire; dweller on a gore or wedge-shaped piece of land.

Kiley (*Ir.*) Grandson of Cadhla (beautiful; graceful).

Kilfeather (*Scot.*) One who came from Kilfeather (church of St. Peter), in Scotland.

Kilfoyle, Kilfoil (*Ir.*) Variant of Gilfoyle, q.v.

Kilgallen, Kilgallon (*Ir.*) The son of the devotee of St. Caillin.

Kilgannon (*Ir.*) The son of the servant of Gannan.

Kilgarriff, Kilgariff (*Ir.*) The son of the rough youth.

Kilgore, Kilgour, Killgore (*Ir., Scot.*) Dweller in the wood where goats are kept; one who tended goats; one who came from Kilgour, in Fife.

Kilham, Killam, Killham (*Eng.*) One who came from Kilham (kiln for drying brick), the name of places in Northumberland and Yorkshire.

Kilheeney, Kilhenney (*Ir.*) Variant of Kilkenny, q.v.

Kilian (*Ir.*) Descendant of Cillin or Cillean, pet forms of Ceallach (war).

Kilkenny (*Ir.*) The son of the devotee of St. Canice.

Kill (*Eng.*) Descendant of Killi or Kill, an old Scandinavian personal name.

Killacky, Killackey (*Ir.*) The son of the servant of Aithche; or of Eochaidh (rich in cattle).

Killebrew (*Eng.*) Variant of Killigrew, q.v.

Killeen, Killen (*Ir.*) Grandson of Cillin, a pet form of Ceallach (war or strife).

Killelea, Killilea (*Ir.*) The son of the gray youth.

Killgrove (*Ir.*) The son of the rough youth.

Killian, Killion (*Ir.*) Grandson of Cillin or Cillean, pet forms of Ceallach (war or strife).

Killigrew (*Eng.*) One who came from Killigrew (crane grove), in Cornwall.

Killingham (*Eng.*) One who came from Killingholme (island of Cynwulf's people), in Lincolnshire.

Killingsworth (*Eng.*) One who came from Killingworth (homestead of Cylla's people), in Northumberland.

Killion (*Scot., Ir.*) One who came from Killin (white church), in Scotland; variant of Killian, q.v.

Killkelly (*Ir.*) The son of the devotee of St. Ceallach (war or strife), the name of three Irish saints.

Kilmartin (*Scot., Ir.*) One who came from Kilmartin (church of St. Martin of Tours), in Scotland; the son of the servant of St. Martin (belonging to the god Mars).

Kilmer (*Ger.*) Descendant of Gisalmar (pledge, fame).

Kilpatrick (*Ir.*) The son of the servant of St. Patrick (noble or patrician).

Kilroy (*Ir.*) The son of the red-haired man.

Kilson (*Sw.*) The son of Kil, a pet form of Ketil or Kjell (caldron).

Kilstrom (*Sw.*) Caldron stream.

Kilty (*Ir.*) Grandson of Caoilte (hardness).

Kim (*Kor.*) Gold.

Kimball, Kimble, Kimbel, Kimbell (*Eng.*) One who came from Kimble (royal hill), in Buckinghamshire.

Kimber (*Eng.*) Descendant of Cyneburh (royal stronghold); one who combs wool or flax.

Kimberley, Kimberly (*Eng.*) One who came from Kimberley (Cyneburg's, Cynemaer's, or Cynebald's grove), the name of places in Norfolk, Nottinghamshire, and Warwickshire.

Kimbrew (*Eng.*) Variant of Kimbrough, q.v.

Kimbrough (*Eng.*) Descendant of Cyneburh (royal stronghold).

Kimmel, Kimmich, Kimmell (*Ger.*) One who produced and sold caraway seeds.

Kimmerle (*Ger.*) Descendant of little Khunemar (race, famous); descendant of little Gundemar (war, famous).

Kimmey (*Scot.*) One who came from Kemnay (head of the plain), in Aberdeenshire.

Kimmons (*Ir.*) The son of little Cam (bent).

Kimura (*Jap.*) Tree, village.

Kinane (*Ir.*) Grandson of Cuinean or Conan (high).

Kinard, Kinnard (*Eng.*) Descendant of Cenweard (bold, guardian).

Kincaid, Kincade, Kinkaid, Kinkade, Kinkead, Kincaide (*Scot.*) One who came from Kincaid (head of the pass), in Stirlingshire.

Kincannon, Kincanon (*Ir.*) Variant of Concannon, q.v.

Kind (*Ger.*) One with the characteristics of a child, the youngest in a family.

Kindahl, Kindall, Kindell (*Eng.*) Variant of Kendall, q.v.

Kinder (*Eng.*) One who came from Kinder (hill), in Derbyshire.

Kindle (*Eng.*) Variant of Kendall, q.v.

Kindred (*Eng.*) One related to another, sometimes only by marriage; descendant of Cenered (bold, counsel).

Kindrick, Kindredge (*Eng.*) Descendant of Cynwrig (chief man); or of Cyneric (family, rule).

Kindt (*Du.*) One with the characteristics of a child.

King (*Eng.*) One who played the part of the king in a play or pageant; one connected in some way with the king's household; one with a royal appearance or kingly qualities.

Kingdom, Kingdon (*Eng.*) Dweller at the royal hill.

Kingma (*Du.*) The son of Kinge, a Frisian pet form of names beginning with Ragin (counsel).

Kingsbury, Kingsberry, Kingsbery (*Eng.*) One who came from Kingsbury (the king's fort), the name of several places in England.

Kingsland (*Eng.*) One who came from Kingsland (the part of the land belonging to the king), in Herefordshire.

Kingsley, Kinsley (*Eng.*) One who came from Kingsley (the king's wood), the name of several places in England.

Kingsmill (*Eng.*) Dweller near, or worker at, the mill belonging to the king.

Kingsmith (*Eng.*) The smith who worked for the king, the king's smith.

Kingston (*Eng.*) One who came from Kingston (the king's manor), the name of many places in England.

Kinicutt (*Eng.*) Variant of Kennicott, q.v.

Kinlaw (*Scot.*) Variant of Kinloch, q.v.

Kinley, Kinlay (*Mx., Eng., Scot.*) The son of Cinfaoladh (wolf head); one who came from Kenley (Cena's grove), in Shropshire; the son of Finlay (fair hero).

Kinloch (*Scot.*) One who came from Kinloch (head of the lake), the name of many places in Scotland.

Kinnally (*Ir.*) Variant of Kennelly, q.v.

Kinnear, Kinneir (*Scot.*) One who came from Kinneir (the western head), in Fife.

Kinney, Kinnie (*Ir.*) Grandson of Cionaodh (fire sprung).

Kinnison (*Scot.*) The son of Conan (high).

Kinross (*Scot.*) One who came from the parish of Kinross (head of the moor), in Kinrossshire.

Kinsella (*Ir.*) Descendant of the Cinnsealaigh (head stained), a clan in Wexford, Ireland.

Kinsey (*Eng.*) Descendant of Cynesige (royal victory); one who came from Kilnsey (Cynel's island), in Yorkshire, or from Kingsley (the king's wood), the name of several places in England.

Kinsley (*Eng.*) One who came from Kinsley (Cyne's meadow), in the West Riding of Yorkshire.

Kinslow, Kinsloe (*Eng.*) One who came from Kingslow (the king's seat), in Shropshire.

Kinsman (*Eng.*) One who is related by blood or marriage; in parts of England the name refers to a first cousin; and in other parts, a nephew.

Kintzel, Kinzel, Kinzle (*Ger.*) Descendant of little Kuno, a pet form of names beginning with Kuhn (bold), as Konrad and Khunemar.

Kinzie (*Eng.*) Variant of Kinsey, q.v.

Kiolbasa, Kiobassa (*Pol.*) One who ground and sold sausages.

Kiphart (*Eng.*) Variant of Gebhardt, q.v.

Kipke (*Ger.*) Descendant of little Kippo, a pet form of names beginning with Geben (gift), as Gebahard, Giperich, and Gebald.

Kipling (*Eng.*) One who came from Kipling (Cybbel's people), in the East Riding of Yorkshire; or from Kiplin (Cyppel's people), in the North Riding of Yorkshire.

Kipp, Kippes (*Ger.*) Dweller at the peak of the hill or mountain; descendant of Kippo, a pet form of names beginning with Geben (gift), as Gebahard, Giperich, and Gebald.

Kiraly (*Hun.*) One connected in some way with a king's household; one who played the part of the king in play and pageant.

Kirby, Kirkby (*Eng.*) One who came from Kirby or Kirkby (village with a church), the name of various places in England.

Kirch, Kirchen (*Ger.*) One who lived by the church.

Kirchheimer (*Ger.*) One who came from Kirchheim (church home), the name of several places in Germany.

Kirchhoff, Kirchoff (*Ger.*) Dweller at, or near, a church yard or cemetery; one who came from Kirchhofen (church yard), in Germany.

Kirchner, Kircher (*Ger.*) A minor official of a church who had charge of the sacristy and its contents.

Kirchwehm (*Ger.*) One who endowed a church or cloister; dweller near church property.

Kirk, Kirke (*Scot.*) Dweller near a church.

Kirkbride (*Eng.*) One who came from Kirkbride (church of St. Bride), in Cumberland.

Kirkeby (*Scot., Eng.*) One who came from Kirkaby (church place), in Scotland; or from Kirkby (village with a church), the name of many places in England.

Kirkegaard (*Dan.*) Dweller near the church yard.

Kirkendall, Kirkendoll, Kirkendahl (*Dan., Nor.*) Dweller near the church in the valley.

Kirkham (*Eng.*) One who came from Kirkham (church village), the name of places in Lancashire and the East Riding of Yorkshire.

Kirkland (*Scot., Eng.*) Dweller on, or near, the land of the church, usually the land surrounding the church where burials were located; one who came from Kirkland (church land), the name of several places in England and Scotland.

Kirkley (*Eng.*) One who came from Kirkley, a place originally called *Cruc,* meaning "hill," but when the meaning of the word was lost they added *hyll,* meaning "hill," and later when the compound became obscured they added *hlaw* meaning "hill." The place now really means "hill hill hill."

Kirkman (*Eng., Scot.*) The person who took care of the church.

Kirkpatrick (*Scot.*) One who came from Kirkpatrick (church of St. Patrick), the name of several places in Scotland.

Kirksey (*Eng.*) One who came from Kersey (cress island), in Suffolk.

Kirkwood (*Scot.*) Dweller in, or near, the wood belonging to the church.

Kirn, Kirner (*Ger.*) One who came from Kirn (swamp), the name of two places in Germany.

Kirnbauer (*Ger.*) The farmer who operated a mill.

Kirsch, Kirsh (*Ger.*) One who grew and sold cherries; dweller at the sign of the cherry; one who came from Kirsch (cherry place), in Germany.

Kirschbaum, Kirschenbaum, Kirshenbaum, Kirshbaum (*Ger.*) Dweller at, or near, a cherry tree.

Kirschner, Kirshner (*Ger.*) One who prepared skins, a furrier.

Kirstein, Kirsten (*Ger.*) Descendant of Kirsten, a form of Kristin, a German form of Christianus (follower of Christ).

Kirtley (*Eng.*) Variant of Kirkley, q.v.

Kirwan, Kirwen, Kirwin (*Ir.*) Grandson of little Ciardubh (jet black).

Kisby (*Eng.*) One who came from Keisby (Kisi's homestead), in Lincolnshire.

Kiser (*Eng.*) One who made and sold leg armor; variant of Kaiser, q.v.

Kishi (*Jap.*) Coast.

Kishkunas (*Lith.*) One who raised or hunted hares; one thought to have the characteristics of a hare.

Kisiel (*Pol.*) One who prepared gruel with leaven.

Kiss (*Hun., Sl.*) The small man.

Kissack (*Mx.*) A condensation of Mac-Isaac, q.v.

Kissane (*Ir.*) Grandson of Casan (little curly one).

Kissel (*Ger.*) Descendant of little Giso, a pet form of names beginning with Geisel (staff), as Gisher, Gisemar, and Gisulf.

Kisseloff (*Rus.*) One who made and sold puddings.

Kisser (*Eng.*) One who made and sold leg armor.

Kissinger, Kissing (*Ger.*) One who came from Kissing (swamp), in Germany.

Kissner, Kisner (*Ger.*) One who made cushions, pillows and quilts; or who dealt in furs.

Kist, Kister (*Ger.*) One who came from Kist (box), in Germany. See also Kistler.

Kistler, Kistner (*Ger.*) One who made and sold boxes, chests, or coffers.

Kitahara (*Jap.*) North, field.

Kitch (*Ger.*) One who drove a coach.

Kitchell (*Eng.*) One who made and sold small cakes, called kichels, given as alms in the name of, or for the sake of, God.

Kitchen, Kitching, Kitchener (*Eng.*) One employed in a kitchen, especially one in charge of the kitchen in a monastery.

Kitchenman (*Eng.*) The servant who worked in the kitchen in a religious, or great noble's, house.

Kite (*Eng.*) Dweller at the sign of the kite or hawk.

Kitely (*Eng.*) One who came from Kitley (kite grove), in Devonshire.

Kitson, Kitt (*Eng., Scot.*) The son of Kit, a pet form of Christian (follower of Christ) and Christopher (Christ-bearer).

Kitterman (*Ger.*) One who came from Gitter (railing), in Germany; one who cemented things.

Kittle, Kittel, Kittell, Kittleson, Kittles (*Eng.*) Descendant of Ketill or Kitel (sacrificial caldron).

Kittler, Kittleman, Kittner (*Ger.*) One who made smocks or frocks; descendant of Kitto, a pet form of Christianus (follower of Christ).

Kittner, Kittnar (*Ger.*) One who came from Kutten, in Saxony.

Kitto, Kittoe (*Ir., Ger., Eng.*) Descendant of Kit, a pet form of Christopher (Christ-bearer); the left-handed man; descendant of Kitto, a

pet form of Christianus (follower of Christ).

Kittrell (*Eng.*) One who came from Kettlewell (spring in a narrow valley), in the West Riding of Yorkshire.

Kittridge, Kittredge (*Scot.*) The son of Sitreac or Sitrig (true victory).

Kitty (*Eng.*) Descendant of little Kitt, a pet form of Christopher (Christ-bearer); and of Katherine (pure).

Kitz (*Ger.*) Dweller at the sign of the young goat or roe deer.

Kitzing, Kitzinger (*Ger.*) One who came from Kitzing, in Germany.

Kitzman (*Ger.*) One who tended young goats.

Kivi (*Finn.*) Dweller near a stone.

Kizenberger (*Ger.*) One who came from Kitzeberg or Kinzenberg, in Germany.

Kizer (*Ger.*) Variant of Keiser, q.v.

Kjeldsen (*Nor.*) The son of Kjeld (kettle; caldron).

Kjelgren (*Nor., Sw.*) Spring, branch.

Kjellberg (*Nor., Sw.*) One who came from Kjelberget (spring hill), in Norway; or from Kallberget (spring hill), in Sweden; caldron, mountain.

Kjellstrom (*Nor.*) Dweller by a stream with a sacrificial caldron.

Kjelstad (*Nor., Sw.*) One who came from Kjelstad (Ketill's dwelling), the name of eight places in Norway; or from Kallstad (Ketill's dwelling), the name of eight places in Sweden.

Kjos, Kjoss (*Nor.*) Dweller in a narrow valley; or at a narrow creek.

Klaas (*Du.*) Descendant of Klaas, a pet form of Niklaas, Dutch form of Nicholas (people's victory).

Klages (*Ger.*) Descendant of Klawes, a pet form of Nikolaus, German form of Nicholas (people's victory).

Klappauf (*Ger.*) One given to idle or empty talk.

Klapper (*Ger.*) One who chatters and babbles, a gossip.

Klarkowski (*Pol.*) Descendant of Klara, Polish form of Clara (bright; clear).

Klasen (*Dan., Du.*) The son of Klas, a

Dutch pet form of Nicholas (people's victory).

Klass, Klaas (*Du.*) Descendant of Klaas, pet form of Nicolaas (people's victory).

Klatt (*Ger.*) One with tangled or disheveled hair.

Klauber (*Ger.*) Variant of Kluber, q.v.

Klauck, Klauke (*Ger.*) The clever, smart, cunning man.

Klaus (*Ger.*) Descendant of Klaus, pet form of Nicolaus, a German form of Nicholas (people's victory).

Klausner, Klauser (*Ger.*) One who came from Klaus, in Germany; dweller near a sluice or flood-gate; one who served as rabbi of a conventicle.

Klawitter (*Ger.*) Dweller near a maple or sycamore tree.

Kleban, Klebansky (*Pol.*) The parson or curate.

Klecka (*Pol., Rus.*) One who came from Kleck (house), in Byelorussia; or from Klecko (house), in Poland; dweller near the Kleca river in Byelorussia.

Klee, Klees (*Ger.*) Dweller in, or near, a meadow where clover grew; one who raised clover.

Kleehammer (*Ger.*) One who came from Kleeham (clover meadow), in Germany.

Kleeman (*Ger.*) Descendant of Klemens, German form of Clement (merciful); dweller in, or near, a meadow of clover.

Klegerman (*Swis.*) One who accuses or complains against another, a public prosecutor.

Kleiber (*Ger.*) One who constructed buildings with mud walls.

Kleiman, Kleimann (*Ger.*) Dweller on clay ground; one who came from Klei (clay), the name of various places in Germany.

Klein, Kleine (*Ger.*) The small man; the neat, nice man.

Kleinberg (*Ger.*) Dweller on, or near, a small hill.

Kleindienst (*Ger.*) One who occupies a minor post or office; the young servant.

Kleiner, Kleinert (*Ger.*) The small man; the younger man.

Kleinfeldt, Kleinfelder (*Ger.*) Dweller in, or near, a small field.

Kleinhammer (*Ger.*) The smith who made small metal objects, such as locks and nails.

Kleinhans, Kleinhenz (*Ger.*) The little man named Hans or Henz, pet forms of Johannes (gracious gift of Jehovah); and of names beginning with Hagin (hedged place), as Haganrich and Haginold.

Kleinke (*Ger.*) The little short man.

Kleinkopf (*Ger.*) One with a small head.

Kleinman (*Ger.*) The little man.

Kleinpeter (*Ger.*) Nickname for little Peter (rock).

Kleinschmidt (*Ger.*) The worker in metals who was small in stature; one who made small metal objects such as nails, locks, keys, etc.

Kleinsmith (*Ger.*) Partial Anglicization of Kleinschmidt, q.v.

Kleinstein (*Ger.*) Dweller near a small rock or boundary stone.

Kleist, Kleis (*Ger.*) Descendant of Kleist or Kleis, pet forms of Nikolaus, German form of Nicholas (people's victory).

Klemchuk (*Ukr.*) Descendant of Klem, a pet form of Kliment, Ukrainian form of Clement (merciful).

Klemens, Klement, Klemenz (*Ger.*) Descendant of Klemens, German form of Clement (merciful).

Klemm, Klemme, Klemmer (*Ger.*) Descendant of Klem, a pet form of Klemens (merciful); dweller at, or near, a narrow passage or steep slope.

Klemptner, Klempner, Klemperer, Klemp (*Ger.*) One who worked or dealt in lead; the sheet metal worker; one who mended kettles, pans, etc.

Klemz, Klems, Klem (*Ger.*) Descendant of Klemz, a pet form of Klemens, German form of Clement (merciful).

Klepper (*Ger.*) One who chatters and gossips.

277

Kletter (*Ice.*) Dweller near a rock or stone.

Klewer, Klever (*Ger.*) One who came from Kleve (bog), the name of three places in Germany.

Klima (*Pol., Ukr., Cz.-Sl.*) Descendant of Klim, a pet form of Klemens, Slavic form of Clement (merciful).

Klimala (*Cz.*) One who oversleeps.

Klimas (*Lith.*) Descendant of little Kliment, Lithuanian form of Clement (merciful).

Klimczak, Klimkiewicz (*Pol.*) The son of Klemens, Slavic form of Clement (merciful).

Klimek (*Pol., Cz.-Sl.*) Descendant of little Klim, a pet form of Klemens (merciful).

Kline (*Ger.*) Variant of Klein, q.v.

Klinenberg (*Ger.*) One who came from Kleinenberg (small hill), in Germany.

Kling, Klinge, Klingen (*Ger., Du.*) Dweller at, or near, a mountain stream; one who came from Kling, Klinge or Klingen (rushing stream), the names of many places in Germany.

Klingbeil (*Ger.*) Nickname for a woodcutter or carpenter, from sound of the ax.

Klingelhofer, Klingelhoffer (*Ger.*) Dweller on a farm or manor in a mountain ravine or gully through which flowed a brook.

Klingelsmith, Klingelschmidt (*Ger.*) One who made and sold bells.

Klingenberg (*Ger.*) One who came from Klingenberg (ravine mountain), the name of two places in Germany.

Klingensmith (*Ger.*) One who made blades, swords, and tools.

Klinger, Klingler, Klingner (*Ger.*) One who made and sold blades or swords.

Klink, Klinke, Klinck (*Du., Ger.*) Dweller near a rushing stream or ravine; dweller near a field gate; dweller near a corner; dweller on, or near, a low hill.

Klinsky (*Ukr., Pol.*) Dweller on a small plot of land.

Klintworth (*Eng.*) Dweller in, or near, the homestead on a hill.

Klipp (*Ger.*) Dweller on a rocky bank or shore.

Klippel (*Ger.*) Dweller near a small cliff.

Klish, Klisch (*Ger.*) Descendant of Klisch, a pet form of Klemens, German form of Clement (merciful).

Klobucar, Klobuchar (*Yu.-Sl.*) One who made and sold hats, a hatter.

Kloc, Klocek (*Pol.*) Dweller near a block or trunk of tree.

Klocke, Klock (*Ger.*) Variant of Klauck, q.v.; dweller at the sign of the bell.

Klockowski, Klockow (*Pol.*) Dweller near a stump.

Klodzinski (*Pol.*) Dweller near a tree stump.

Kloess, Kloese (*Ger.*) Descendant of Klaus, pet form of Nikolaus, German form of Nicholas (people's victory).

Kloiber (*Ger.*) One who gathers or picks up things.

Klonowski (*Pol.*) Dweller near a maple tree.

Kloos (*Du.*) Descendant of Kloot (ball).

Klooster (*Du.*) Dweller near, or worker in, a monastery.

Klopp (*Du., Ger.*) Descendant of Klopp, a pet form of names beginning with Lut (loud or distinct), as Chlodbald and Chlodobert; shortened form of Kloppman, q.v.

Kloppman, Klopper (*Du.*) The official who attached seals or marks of approval to pieces of cloth, by stamping them.

Klos, Klose (*Cz., Pol.*) One who raised grain.

Kloss, Klos, Klose (*Ger.*) Descendant of Nicholas (people's victory).

Kloster, Klostermann (*Dan., Sw., Ger.*) Tenant of a monastery; one employed by a monastery or convent; a male member of a religious order.

Klotz (*Ger.*) One with no manners; the awkward, clumsy fellow; the squat, dumpy man.

Klowden (*Eng.*) One who came from

Cloughton (homestead in a ravine), in the North Riding of Yorkshire.

Kluber (*Ger.*) One who cuts up and splits logs; one who makes shingles or slats; one who splits stones, a mason.

Kluch, Kluck (*Ger.*) One who handles brood hens, a poultry man.

Klucznik (*Pol.*) One who stood guard at a door, a door-keeper.

Kluczynski (*Ukr., Pol.*) Dweller near a spring.

Klug, Kluge, Klugman (*Ger.*) The wise or learned man; the intelligent, clever, smart man.

Kluk, Kluka (*Pol.*) One with a large or prominent nose.

Klump, Klumpp (*Ger.*) The big, coarse, clumsy man; the fat man.

Klunder, Klund (*Ger.*) One who made a lot of noise or uproar.

Klus, Kluss (*Ger.*) Descendant of Klus, a pet form of Nikolaus, German form of Nicholas (people's victory).

Kluth, Klut (*Ger.*) The clod, a nickname for a coarse, clumsy fellow.

Klutz (*Ger.*) One who came from Klutz (hot, bubbling spring), in Germany.

Kmet, Kmetz (*Sl., Yu.-Sl., Ukr.*) One who tilled the soil, a peasant.

Kmiec (*Pol.*) One who tills the soil; a peasant possessing a hide of land.

Kmiecik (*Pol.*) The little farmer.

Knaack, Knaak, Knach, Knack (*Ger.*) One who cut up, cooked, or sold bony meat.

Knabe, Knabb (*Ger.*) The boy or young man.

Knabel (*Du.*) One with the characteristics of a little boy.

Knaphurst (*Eng.*) Dweller by, or in, the wood or copse on the top of the hill or mountain.

Knapik (*Cz.*) Descendant of the young nobleman.

Knapp (*Eng.*) Dweller at the top of the hill; one who came from Knapp (hilltop), in Hampshire.

Knapton (*Eng.*) One who came from Knipton (homestead in a narrow valley), in Leicestershire.

Knatchbull (*Eng.*) One who cut up and sold meat, a butcher.

Knauer (*Ger.*) The coarse, crude, uncouth fellow.

Knauerhaze (*Ger.*) The crude, cowardly fellow.

Knauf, Knauff (*Ger.*) The little stout fellow.

Knaus, Knauss (*Ger.*) The bold, haughty man.

Knebel (*Ger.*) The coarse, rude, boorish fellow.

Knecht (*Ger.*) One employed to perform menial tasks, a servant.

Knee (*Eng.*) One with a crippled or peculiar knee.

Kneeland (*Nor.*) Dweller on a land or field at a bend.

Knees (*Ger.*) One who came from Kneese, the name of several places in Germany.

Kneezle (*Eng.*) One who came from Kneesall (Cyneheah's corner), in Nottinghamshire.

Kneip (*Ger.*) One who works with a knife on leather articles.

Knell, Kneller (*Eng., Ger.*) Dweller near a knoll or mound; one who sounded the alarm, a watchman.

Knezevich, Knezevic (*Rus., Ukr., Yu.-Sl.*) One who acted the part of a prince in play or pageant; member of a prince's entourage; descendant of a duke or leader.

Knickerbocker (*Du.*) An American surname, not found in Holland, possibly a nickname for a military man, meaning "clay marble baker."

Knierim (*Ger.*) One who makes or repairs shoes, a cobbler or shoemaker.

Knies (*Ger., Cz.*) One of superior rank, a lord or prince; one who performs sacerdotal functions, a priest.

Knifesmith (*Eng.*) One who made and sold knives or swords.

Knight (*Eng., Wel.*) A military servant of the king; one who held land in exchange for military service to be rendered to king or lord; descendant of Cniht (youth or servant).

Knightly, Knightley (*Eng.*) One who

279

came from Knightley (the servant's grove), in Staffordshire; dweller in, or near, the servant's or retainer's open place in a wood.

Knighton, Knighten (*Eng.*) One who came from Knighton (the servant's or knight's homestead), the name of many villages in England.

Knill (*Eng., Ger.*) One who came from Knill (knoll), in Herefordshire; variant of Knell, q.v.

Knipe (*Eng.*) Dweller on a peak or at the top of the hill.

Knipp, Knipper (*Ger.*) One who works with pointed scissors.

Knitter (*Eng.*) One who fashions materials by knots or forms fabric by interlacing.

Knivesmith (*Eng.*) Variant of Knifesmith, q.v.

Knobloch, Knoblauch, Knoblock (*Ger.*) One who raised and sold garlic.

Knoch, Knock (*Eng.*) One who came from Knock (hillock), in Westmorland.

Knoebel, Knobel (*Ger.*) Dweller on, or near, a small round elevation or hill; the fat or plump man; the little companion.

Knoll (*Eng., Ger.*) Dweller at the top of the hill; the big, thick, bulky man.

Knollmueller (*Ger.*) The big, coarse, bulky grinder of grain.

Knop, Knoop (*Du., Ger., Eng.*) Dweller on, or near, a knob or small hill; the short, chubby man; one who came from Knoop, in Germany; dweller on a peak or on top of the hill.

Knopf (*Ger.*) One who made and sold buttons; the short chubby man.

Knopp (*Eng.*) Dweller near a knob or small round hill.

Knorr, Knor (*Ger.*) Dweller near a knot or protuberance, or small hump or hill.

Knoth (*Ger.*) A boorish, rude, coarse man.

Knott, Knot (*Eng.*) Dweller at a rocky hilltop; descendant of Knut (hill;

white-haired); one who is fat or thickset.

Knotter (*Eng.*) Dweller on the hill.

Knotwell (*Eng.*) Dweller near a spring by a hill.

Knowlan (*Ir.*) Descendant of little Nuall (noble; famous).

Knowland (*Eng.*) Dweller at the knoll, or hill-top land.

Knowles (*Eng., Scot.*) Dweller near a small round hill.

Knowlton (*Eng.*) One who came from Knowlton (homestead by a knoll), the name of places in Dorset and Kent.

Knox, Knows (*Scot.*) One who lived on the lands of Knock (hill), in Renfrewshire and in various other places in Scotland; one who lived on, or near, a hill or prominence.

Knuckey (*Eng.*) Dweller in, or near, the boggy place.

Knudsen, Knudson (*Dan., Nor.*) The son of Knud or Canute (hill; white-haired).

Knudtson, Knudtzon, Knudtsen (*Dan.*) The son of Canute or Knut (hill; white-haired).

Knuth (*Dan., Sw., Nor., Pol.*) Descendant of Knut or Canute (hill; white-haired); dweller at, or on, a hill; one with an aggressive nature.

Knutson, Knutsen (*Sw., Nor., Dan., Eng.*) The son of Knut or Canute (hill; white-haired).

Knysmith (*Eng.*) Variant of Knifesmith, q.v.

Ko (*Chin., Kor.*) Go-between; yellow.

Kobayashi (*Jap.*) Little, forest.

Kober, Koeber (*Ger.*) One who made knapsacks or baskets; variant of Kovar, q.v.

Koblenz, Koblens, Koblentz (*Ger.*) One who came from Koblenz (confluence of two streams), a city in Germany.

Kobler (*Ger.*) One who lives in a hut and works for others by the day.

Kobs, Kob (*Ger.*) Descendant of Kob, a pet form of Jakob or Jacob (may God protect; the supplanter).

Kobus, Kobusch (*Du.*) Descendant of

Kobus, a pet form of Jacobus (may God protect; the supplanter).

Kobylecky, Kobylinski (*Ukr., Pol.*) The man in charge of the mares.

Koch, Koche (*Ger., Dan.*) One who prepared food, a cook.

Kochan (*Pol., Ukr.*) Descendant of Kochan (beloved); dweller near the Kochan, a small river in Ukraine.

Kochanski (*Pol.*) The dear, beloved person.

Kocher (*Ger.*) One who prepared food, a cook; one who made and sold receptacles or containers; one who came from Koch (swamp), in Germany.

Kochman (*Ger.*) One who prepared food, a cook.

Kocinski (*Pol.*) Dweller at the sign of the cat; one who raised cats.

Koclanis, Koclanes (*Lith.*) One who made or sold tiles; or who covered buildings with tiles, a roofer.

Kocol, Kocolowski (*Pol.*) Dweller at the sign of the caldron; one who worked at a caldron.

Kocsis (*Hun.*) One who drove a cart, a carter or coachman.

Kocur, Kocurek, Kocourek (*Sl.*) Dweller at the sign of the tomcat; one with the characteristics of a tomcat.

Kodama (*Jap.*) Child, gem.

Kodis (*Lith.*) One with a heavy tuft of hair.

Koegel, Koegler (*Ger.*) One who played at skittles or ninepins.

Koehler, Koeller, Koller, Kohler (*Ger.*) The charcoal-burner or coal worker.

Koek (*Du.*) One who bakes and sells cakes.

Koelling (*Ger.*) Descendant of Kohl, a pet form of names beginning with Kol (helmet), as Colobert and Colmar.

Koeln (*Ger.*) One who came from Koln (Cologne—dwelling of Agrippina), in Germany.

Koen (*Du.*) Descendant of Koen (bold); the bold, daring man.

Koenig, Konig (*Ger.*) One who played the part of the king in plays; a servant of the king; one with a royal appearance or kingly qualities.

Koenigsberg (*Ger.*) One who came from Konigsberg (king's hill), the name of three places in Germany.

Koepke (*Ger.*) Descendant of little Kob, a pet form of Jacobus (may God protect; the supplanter).

Koepp, Koeppe (*Ger.*) Descendant of Kob, a pet form of Jacobus (may God protect; the supplanter).

Koeppel, Koeppl (*Ger.*) One with a small head.

Koerber (*Ger.*) One who made and sold baskets.

Koerner, Korner (*Ger.*) Dweller near a mill; one who dealt in grain; one who came from Korner (place where corn or grain grew), in Germany.

Koestner, Koester (*Ger.*) One who was an under-officer of a church and had charge of the sacristy and its contents; one who came from Koesten, in Germany.

Koff (*Du.*) One who sells merchandise, a shopkeeper.

Koffman (*Ger.*) Variant of Kaufman, q.v.

Kofoed (*Dan.*) One with a cow's foot or clubfoot.

Koga (*Jap.*) Old, joy.

Kogan, Kogen (*Pol., Rus., Ukr.*) One who performed sacerdotal functions, a priest.

Koger (*Ger.*) One who buys worn-out horses and sells the meat for dog food.

Kogut (*Pol.*) Dweller at the sign of the cock; one who strutted like a cock.

Kohen (*Ger.*) Variant of Cohen, q.v.

Kohl, Kohlman, Kohlmann (*Ger.*) One who grew and sold cabbage.

Kohler (*Ger.*) One who burned charcoal; one who came from Koehlen or Koehler, in Germany.

Kohn, Kohnen (*Ger.*) Descendant of Kuno, a pet form of names beginning with Kun (bold), as Chunrad and Kunimund; variants of Cohen, q.v.

Kohnke (*Ger.*) Descendant of little

281

Kuno, a pet form of names beginning with Kun (bold), as Konrad and Kunigund.

Kohout, Kohut (*Cz.-Sl., Ukr.*) Dweller at the sign of the rooster.

Koivumaki (*Finn.*) Dweller on, or near, a hill covered by birch trees.

Kojima (*Jap.*) Little, island.

Kok (*Du.*) One who prepared food, a cook.

Kokinis, Kokinos, Kokkines (*Lat.*) Dweller in the woods or forest.

Kokoszka (*Pol., Cz.-Sl.*) One who raised and sold hens and eggs.

Kokot (*Pol.*) Dweller at the sign of the cock.

Kolak (*Pol.*) Dweller near where thorns grew.

Kolanko (*Pol.*) One with a small knee.

Kolanowski (*Pol.*) One with a crippled leg or unusual knee.

Kolar, Kolarz, Kollar (*Cz.-Sl.*) The wheel maker or wheelwright.

Kolasa, Kolassa (*Pol.*) One who made chaises, i.e., two-wheeled carriages drawn by one horse.

Kolb, Kolbe (*Ger.*) Descendant of Kolb, a pet form of names beginning with Kol (helmet), as Kolbert and Kohlhardt; one who had hair cut short; variant of Kalb, q.v.

Kolber (*Ger.*) One who made clubs and maces.

Kolberg (*Ger.*) One who came from Kolberg, in Germany.

Kole (*Eng., Pol.*) Variant of Cole, q.v. Often, however, a shortened form of a Polish surname.

Koleno (*Yu.-Sl.*) One with an unusual or crippled knee.

Kolinski, Kolinsky (*Pol., Ukr.*) One who gathered and sold cranberries.

Koll, Kolle (*Ger.*) Descendant of Koll, a pet form of names beginning with Kol (helmet), as Colmar and Colobert.

Koller (*Ger.*) One who made leather harness; a variant of Kohler, q.v.

Kolling (*Ger.*) One who came from Cologne (Agrippina's colony), in Germany.

Kollman, Kollmann, Kolman (*Ger.*) Descendant of Koloman, a German form of Coleman (little dove).

Kolmar, Kollmar (*Ger.*) One who came from Kollmar, in Germany.

Kolodenko (*Ukr.*) One who worked with logs.

Kolodny (*Ukr.*) The cool, calm man.

Kolody (*Ukr.*) One who makes wheels, a wheelwright.

Kolodziej (*Pol.*) One who made wheels and wheeled vehicles.

Kolosh (*Pol.*) The very large or fat man.

Kolpak, Kolpek (*Pol.*) One who usually wore a bearskin cap; one who made and sold bearskin caps.

Kolton, Koltonski, Koltun (*Pol.*) One who had plica polonica, a disease of the hair in which it becomes twisted and matted together.

Komaniecki (*Pol., Ukr.*) Dweller on a mountain.

Komar, Komarek (*Pol., Ukr.*) One with the size or other characteristic of a gnat.

Kominsky (*Pol., Rus.*) Variant of Kaminski, q.v.; dweller near a building with an unusual chimney.

Komoll (*Ger.*) The scuffling, brawling man.

Komorowski (*Pol.*) One who came from Komarow, in Poland.

Koncevic (*Yu.-Sl.*) One who took care of the horses.

Konczyk (*Pol.*) Dweller at the sharp end.

Kondor (*Pol.*) Dweller at the sign of the condor.

Kondrat (*Rus.*) Descendant of Konrat, Russian form of Conrad (bold, counsel).

Kondratuk (*Ukr.*) Descendant of Kondrat, Ukrainian form of Conrad (bold, counsel).

Konen (*Rus.*) One who was in charge of the horses.

Kong (*Kor., Chin.*) Hole.

Konicki, Konieczka (*Pol.*) Dweller at the sign of the horse; one who used a horse in his work.

Konieczny (*Pol.*) Dweller at the end, or outskirts, of the village.

Konikowski (*Pol.*) One who took care of ponies.

Konjevich (*Yu.-Sl.*) One who dealt with horses.

Konkel (*Ger.*) Variant of Kunkel, q.v.

Kono (*Jap.*) Little, field.

Konopka, Konopa (*Pol.*) Dweller at the sign of the linnet, a small finch; one who snared and sold small finches or linnets.

Konovsky (*Rus.*) Dweller at the sign of the horse; one who used a horse in his work.

Konrad, Konrath (*Ger.*) Descendant of Conrad (bold, counsel).

Konstantopoulos (*Gr.*) The son of Konstantinos, Greek form of Constantine (constant or firm of purpose).

Konstanty (*Pol.*) Descendant of Konstanty, Polish form of Constantine (constant or firm of purpose).

Kontos (*Gr.*) The little, short man.

Konz, Konzer, Konzen (*Ger.*) One who came from Konz or Konzen, the names of places in Germany.

Kooistra (*Du.*) One who made, or employed, cages used for trapping ducks.

Koonce, Koontz (*Ger.*) Variant of Kuntz, q.v.

Koons (*Ger.*) Variant of Kuhn, q.v.

Koop (*Ger.*) Descendant of Koop, a pet form of Jakob or Jacob (may God protect; the supplanter).

Kooper, Kooperman (*Eng.*) Variant of Cooper, q.v. and of Cooperman, q.v.

Koopersmith (*Ger.*) Variant of Kupersmith, q.v.

Koopman, Koopmann (*Du.*) The merchant or tradesman; a peddler.

Kopack, Kopach, Kopacki (*Pol.*) Variant of Kopacz, q.v.

Kopacz (*Pol., Cz.-Sl.*) One who digs in the ground, a digger.

Kopan, Kopanski (*Pol.*) One who digs holes or trenches.

Kopca (*Pol.*) Dweller on the mound; or near a grave.

Kopczyk (*Pol.*) Dweller at the sign of the hawk; one who used a hawk in hunting.

Kopec, Kopiec (*Ukr., Pol.*) Dweller near a boundary hill.

Kopecky, Kopeck (*Cz.-Sl.*) Dweller on, or near, a hill.

Kopera, Kopernik, Koperny (*Pol.*) Dweller near where fennel grew; one who cultivated and sold dill and fennel.

Kopf, Kopff (*Ger.*) Generally a shortened form of a name with this element meaning head; one whose head was unusual or distinctive in some manner.

Kopfer (*Ger.*) One who worked in copper, a coppersmith.

Kopp, Koppe (*Ger., Fr.*) One with a large or peculiar head; descendant of Kob, a pet form of Jacobus (may God protect; the supplanter); dweller at the head or uppermost part of some topographical feature; descendant of Gobbo (God), a pet form of such names as Godabald (God, bold), and Godaberht (God, bright).

Koppel, Kopple (*Ger.*) Variant of Koeppel, q.v.; descendant of Koppel, a pet form of Jacob (may God protect; the supplanter).

Koppelman, Koppelmann (*Ger.*) Servant of little Kob, a pet form of Jacobus (may God protect; the supplanter).

Kopper (*Ger.*) Variant of Kopfer, q.v.

Koppersmith (*Ger.*) Variant of Coppersmith, q.v.

Koprowski (*Pol.*) One who worked in copper, a coppersmith.

Koprulu (*Tur.*) Dweller at the bridge.

Korach (*Heb.*) One without hair, bald.

Koral, Koralik (*Pol.*) One who dealt in coral.

Koranda (*Cz.-Sl.*) One who operated a raft or flat boat; one who stripped bark from trees.

Korb (*Ger.*) One who made and sold baskets; one who came from Korb (basket), in Germany.

Korbas (*Gr.*) Dweller at the sign of the black goat; one who took care of black goats.

Korczyk (*Ukr.*) Dweller near low shrubbery.

Korda (*Pol.*) One who fought with a sabre.

Kordek, Kordik (*Pol.*) Nickname for one armed with a little sword.

Korelev (*Rus.*) One connected in some way with a king's household.

Koren (*Du.*) Dweller in, or near, a field of corn or grain.

Koretz, Koretzky (*Ukr.*) One who dealt in bark.

Korff, Korf (*Ger.*) One who made and sold baskets.

Korink (*Du.*) Descendant of Kors, a pet form of Christiaan, Dutch form of Christian (follower of Christ), and of Cornelis, Dutch form of Cornelius (cornel tree; hornlike).

Korman, Kormann (*Ger.*) One who grew, or dealt in, grain.

Korn, Korner (*Ger.*) One who raised and sold corn or grain.

Kornacker (*Ger.*) One who produced and sold animal fodder, usually acorns and beechnuts.

Kornblum (*Ger.*) Dweller near where corn-flower grew. •

Kornfeld, Kornfield (*Ger.*) Dweller at, or near, a grain field.

Korol, Korolenko (*Ukr.*) One who played the part of the king in play or pageant; one connected in some way with a king's household.

Koronakis, Koronis (*Gr.*) Descendant of Korona (crown).

Koronkowski (*Pol.*) One who made and sold lace.

Korotenko, Korotcenko (*Ukr.*) The son of the small or short man.

Korper (*Ger.*) One who made and sold baskets.

Korshak, Korsak (*Ukr.*) Dweller at the sign of the korshak, a bird of the eagle family.

Kort, Korte (*Du., Ger.*) The short, stubby man; descendant of Kort, a pet form of Konrad (bold, counsel).

Kortenhoeven (*Ger.*) Dweller near a short or small garden.

Korth, Korten (*Ger.*) Descendant of Chunrad, old form of Konrad (bold, counsel).

Korus (*Lith.*) Dweller near the ramparts of the castle.

Kos (*Du., Cz.-Sl.*) Descendant of Kos, a pet form of Cornelius (cornel tree; hornlike); one who lived at the sign of the blackbird; shortened form of various other names of which this is the root; one who made and sold baskets.

Kosak, Kosach, Kosacz (*Pol.*) One who reaps or harvests crops.

Kosche, Kosch, Koscher (*Pol.*) Descendant of Kosch, a pet form of Mikusch, Slavic form of Nicholas (people's victory).

Koschnitzki (*Pol.*) One who made and sold baskets.

Koscielniak (*Pol.*) Dweller near the small church.

Koscielny (*Pol.*) One in charge of church property, a sexton; dweller near the church.

Koscielski, Koscielniak (*Pol.*) One who worked in, or for, the church.

Kosciuszko (*Pol.*) Descendant of Koscia, a pet form of Konstanty, Polish form of Constantine (constant or firm of purpose).

Kosek (*Pol.*) Dweller at the sign of the little blackbird.

Kosiba, Kosiara (*Pol., Cz.*) One who cuts grass or grain with a scythe, a mower.

Kosiek (*Pol.*) Descendant of little Kos (blackbird); dweller at the sign of the little horse.

Kosinski (*Pol.*) One who came from Kosin(o) (scythe), in Poland.

Kosjacenko (*Ukr.*) Son of a squint-eyed man.

Koskela, Koska (*Finn.*) Dweller near a waterfall.

Koski, Koskinen (*Finn.*) Dweller at the rapids or near a waterfall.

Koskimaki (*Finn.*) Dweller near a waterfall in the mountains.

Kosla, Koslenko (*Ukr.*) One who raised and sold male goats; dweller at the sign of the goat.

Kosloff (*Rus.*) One with the characteristics of a billy-goat.

Koslowski, Koslowsky (*Pol.*) One who came from Kozlow (Koziol's settlement), in Poland.

Kosmas, Kosmopolis, Kosmos (*Gr.*) Descendant of Kosmas (world order).

Kosowski (*Pol.*) One who came from Kosow (scythe), in Poland.

Koss, Kosse (*Ger.*) Descendant of Koss, a pet form of Godizo (God).

Kossack, Kossak (*Pol.*) One who came from the Russian steppes, skilled as a horseman, a Cossack.

Kossoff, Kossow (*Ukr.*) One who came from Kosiv, in the Ukraine; the son of Kosa (scythe).

Kossuth (*Hun.*) One with unusual body hair.

Kost (*Rus., Nor.*) Descendant of Kost, a pet form of Konstantine, Russian form of Constantine (constant, or firm of purpose); descendant of Kostr.

Kostakes, Kostakis, Kostakos (*Gr.*) The son of Kostas, a pet form of Konstantinos, Greek form of Constantine (constant or firm of purpose).

Kostal (*Cz.*) Dweller in a field where cabbages have been cut.

Kostecki (*Pol., Ukr.*) One who came from Kostki (bone), the name of many places in Poland; dweller near the Kostka, a little river in Ukraine.

Kostelny (*Ukr., Cz.*) One employed to take care of a church, a sexton.

Kostenko, Kostiuk (*Ukr.*) The son of Kost, a pet form of Kostantin, a Slavic form of Constantine (constant or firm of purpose).

Koster, Kostner (*Ger., Du.*) An underofficer of a church who had charge of the sacristy and its contents; one who sold fruits and vegetables.

Kostka (*Pol.*) The crippled man, one with an unusual hipbone or anklebone.

Kostoff (*Bulg., Rus.*) The son of Kosta, a pet form of Konstantin, Slavic form of Constantine (constant or firm of purpose).

Kostopoulos (*Gr.*) The son of Kosta, a Greek form of Constance (constant or firm of purpose).

Kosygin (*Rus.*) The reaper; the squinteyed man.

Koszyk (*Pol.*) One who made and sold baskets or hampers.

Kot, Kotek, Kotecki (*Pol., Rus.*) Dweller at the sign of the cat or kitten; descendant of Kot, pet form of Konstantine, Russian form of Constantine (constant or firm of purpose).

Kotlarz (*Pol.*) One who worked in copper and brass, a coppersmith or brazier.

Kotler (*Ger.*) Dweller in a small house or hut.

Kotowski (*Pol.*) Dweller at the sign of the cat.

Kotrba, Kotrbaty (*Cz.-Sl.*) One with a big head.

Kotsakis (*Gr.*) Variant of Kotsiakos, q.v.

Kotsiakos, Kotsiopoulos (*Gr.*) The brave man.

Kotsis (*Hun.*) Variant of Kocsis, q.v.

Kotsos, Kotsopoulos (*Gr.*) Descendant, or son, of Kotsos, a pet form of Kostantinos, Greek form of Constantine (constant or firm of purpose).

Kott, Kot, Kotte (*Ger.*) Descendant of Godo, a pet form of names commencing with Gott (God), as Gotahard, Godowin, and Godeman; dweller in the little house or cottage.

Kotula, Kotulski (*Yu.-Sl.*) One who made skirts.

Kotz (*Ger.*) Descendant of Gutz, a pet form of Godizo (God); one who came from Kotz, in Germany.

Kouba, Kuha (*Cz.-Sl.*) Descendant of Kuba, a pet form of Jakub, Slavic form of Jacob (may God protect; the supplanter).

Koules, Koulias, Koulis (*Gr.*) The little man who belongs to the Lord; a follower of the Lord.

Koulogeorge (*Gr.*) The one-armed person named George (farmer).

Kountz (*Ger.*) Descendant of Kountz, a pet form of Chunizo (bold).

Koutavas (*Gr.*) One who sold newborn pups.

Koutsogiannis (*Gr.*) Descendant of lame Giannis, Greek form of John (gracious gift of Jehovah).

Kouwenhoven (*Du.*) Dweller in, or near, a cool garden or court.

Kovacevich, Kovacevic, Kovacic (*Yu.-Sl.*) The son of the smith or worker in metal.

Kovacs, Kovac, Kovatch, Kovach, Kovats (*Hun.*) The worker in metals, a smith.

Koval, Kovalcik (*Rus.*) One who worked in metals, a smith.

Kovalenko (*Ukr.*) The son of the smith.

Kovalik (*Pol., Rus.*) The little worker in metals.

Kovalsky (*Rus.*) One who worked in metals, a smith.

Kovar (*Cz.-Sl.*) The worker in metals, a smith.

Kovarik (*Cz.-Sl.*) The little smith or worker in metals.

Kovarsky (*Cz.-Sl.*) One who worked in metals, a smith.

Koven (*Ger.*) One who came from Koven, in Germany.

Kowalchuk, Kowalchick (*Ukr.*) The son of the smith or worker in metals.

Kowalczyk (*Pol.*) The son of the smith.

Kowalski Kowalewski, Kowal (*Pol.*) The worker in metals, a smith.

Kowalsky (*Rus.*) The worker in metals, a smith.

Kowalyszyn, Kowalyshen (*Ukr.*) The son of the smith's wife.

Kownacki (*Pol.*) One who came from Kowno, the capital of Lithuania.

Kowsky, Kowske (*Rus., Bulg., Pol.*) Descendant of Kowsky, a pet form of names ending in -kowsky, as Stankowsky, Berkowsky, and Jankowsky.

Koyama (*Jap.*) Little, mountain.

Koza, Koziol (*Cz.-Sl., Pol.*) One who takes care of goats; one who is like a goat in some respect.

Kozak (*Pol., Ukr.*) One of a warlike pastoral people, skillful as horsemen, a Cossack; a Ukrainian freedom fighter.

Kozar (*Yu.-Sl.*) One who took care of goats, a goatherd.

Kozel, Kozelka (*Ukr., Cz.*) One who took care of goats; one thought to possess the characteristics of a billygoat.

Kozeluh (*Cz.*) One who made or sold leather, a tanner; one who took care of goats.

Koziarz, Koziarski (*Pol.*) One who took care of goats, a goatherd.

Kozica, Kozicki (*Pol.*) Dweller at the sign of the chamois, a small goatlike antelope; one with the qualities of a chamois.

Koziel, Kozielski (*Pol.*) Dweller at the sign of the male goat.

Kozielec (*Pol.*) One in charge of the goats, a goatherd.

Kozik, Kozikowski (*Pol.*) One who used a weeding-knife in his work.

Kozin, Kozinski (*Bulg., Rus., Pol.*) One who took care of goats.

Kozlik (*Pol., Ukr.*) One who raised or took care of goats.

Kozloff, Kozlovich (*Rus.*) Descendant of one who took care of the goats.

Kozlowski, Kozlowsky (*Pol., Rus.*) One who took care of the goats.

Kozsis (*Hun.*) One who drove a cart, a carter.

Kozuch (*Ukr.*) One who took care of goats, a goatherd.

Krach (*Ger.*) The noisy man; the old, decrepit man.

Cracke, Krack (*Ger.*) Dweller at the sign of the raven or crow; one thought to possess the characteristics of a crow; dweller at the sign of the wretched horse; one who came from Krakow (the town of Duke Krak); dweller in the brushwood.

Kraemer, Kraehmer (*Ger.*) Same as Kramer, q.v.

Kraft, Krafft (*Ger., Sw.*) The strong or powerful man; strong, a Swedish soldier name.

Krahe, Kray, Krah (*Ger.*) Dweller at the sign of the crow; one thought to possess the characteristics of a crow.

Krahn (*Ger.*) One who operated a hoisting winch; dweller at the sign of the crane.

Kraig (*Eng.*) Variant of Craig, q.v.

Krainer, Krain (*Ger.*) One who came from Krain, in Germany.

Krajci (*Cz.*) One who made outer garments, a tailor.

Krajewski (*Pol.*) Dweller at the outskirts of the town.

Krakau, Krakauer (*Ger.*) One who came from Cracow (the town of Duke Krak), in southern Poland.

Krakow, Krakowski, Krakover (*Pol.*) One who came from Cracow or Krakow (the town of Duke Krak), in southern Poland.

Kral, Krall (*Cz.-Sl.*) One connected in some way with a king's household; one who played the part of a king in pageants and plays.

Kralik (*Cz.-Sl., Ger.*) One who hunted, raised, or sold rabbits; dweller at the sign of the rabbit; the little man who played the part of a king in the pageants; one who served the king.

Kram (*Du.*) One who sold small wares, odds and ends.

Kramarczyk, Kramarski, Kramarz (*Pol.*) One who kept a shop, a tradesman.

Kramer, Krammer (*Du., Ger.*) The shopkeeper or tradesman; one who traveled through the country buying butter, hens and eggs which he carried to the market in a cram or pack on his back.

Kramp, Kramper (*Ger.*) One who came from Kramp (edge); dweller at the brim or edge.

Kranich (*Ger.*) Dweller at the sign of the crane; one who conducts himself in an arrogant or haughty manner.

Kranick, Kranicke (*Pol.*) Dweller near the border or boundary line.

Krankheit (*Ger.*) One who was ill, an invalid.

Kranz, Krantz, Krantzler (*Ger.*) One who came from Kranz or Krantz (wreath), in Germany; one with a prominent nose.

Krapf (*Ger.*) One who cooked doughnuts or fritters.

Krapp (*Ger.*) Dweller at the sign of the raven.

Krappman, Krappmann (*Ger.*) One who prepared and sold madder, used in dyeing.

Krasauskas (*Lith.*) One who supplies transportation for passengers for the lord of the manor; one who makes and sells chairs.

Krasinski (*Pol.*) The beautiful or handsome person.

Krasner, Krasney (*Pol.*) The fat man; the handsome man.

Krasnoshtanov (*Rus.*) One known for wearing red pants.

Krasnow, Krasnowski (*Pol.*) One who came from Krasnik (place of beauty), in Poland.

Krasny (*Pol.*) The fat man; the handsome or beautiful person.

Kratky (*Cz.*) The little man, one of low stature.

Kratochvil, Kratovil (*Cz.-Sl.*) One who amuses others; one who conducts amusement places; the merry fellow, a merrymaker; one who moves with great haste.

Kratz (*Ger.*) Descendant of Kratz, a pet form of Pancratius (ruler of all), a fourth century saint.

Kratzer (*Ger.*) One who cards wool; one who cuts beards, a barber; one who made carders, an instrument for raising a nap on cloth.

Krauchunas (*Lith.*) Descendant of the tailor or maker of outer clothing.

Kraujalis (*Lith.*) One concerned in some way with a little blood, a bloodletter.

Krause, Kraus, Krauss (*Ger.*) Descendant of the curly-headed man.

Kraushaar (*Ger.*) One with curly hair.

Kraut, Krauth (*Ger.*) One who raised and sold vegetables.

Kravchuk (*Ukr.*) The son of the tailor.

Kravitz, Kravetz, Kravets, Kravits (*Cz.-Sl., Pol., Ukr.*) One who made outer garments, a tailor.

Krawczak (*Pol.*) One employed as a journeyman tailor.

Krawczyk (*Pol.*) The son of the tailor.

Krawiec, Krawitz, Krawetz (*Pol.*) Variant of Kravitz, q.v.

Kray (*Ger.*) Dweller at the sign of the crow; one thought to possess the characteristics of a crow; one who came from Kray (crow), in Germany.

Krc, Krch (*Cz.-Sl.*) One suffering from cramps; one who brushes and cleans; the stimulating person.

Krebs (*Ger.*) Dweller at the sign of the crab; one who came from Krebes, in Germany.

Krech (*Ger.*) Dweller at the sign of the jug; the weak, infirm man.

Kreczmer (*Ger.*) Variant of Kretschmer, q.v.

Kreft, Krefft (*Ger.*) The lively, vigorous man; dweller at the sign of the crab.

Kreger (*Ger.*) The warrior or champion; one who kept an inn, a publican.

Kreher (*Ger.*) Dweller at the sign of the crow; one who screeches or squawks like a crow.

Kreider, Kreidler (*Ger.*) One who dealt in chalk; or in cloves.

Kreienheder (*Ger.*) Dweller on, or near, a heath frequented by crows.

Kreienkamp (*Ger.*) Dweller in, or near, a field frequented by crows.

Krein, Kreiner (*Ger.*) One who came from Krein or Kreina, the names of towns in Germany.

Kreisler (*Ger.*) One who made utensils of earthenware, a potter; one who produced and sold groats; one who had curly hair.

Kreiter (*Ger.*) The quarrelsome, argumentative man; dweller at a clearing, that is, land cleared for cultivation.

Kreith (*Ger.*) One who came from Kreith (cleared land), the name of two places in Germany.

Kreitzer, Kreitzman (*Ger.*) One who came from Kreitz, in Germany.

Krejci (*Cz.-Sl.*) One who made outer garments, a tailor.

Krekel, Krekeler (*Ger., Du.*) One who came from Krekel (stagnant water), in Germany; a nickname for one with the characteristics of a cricket.

Krell, Krelle (*Ger.*) The irritable, cross, quick-tempered man.

Krema (*Yu.-Sl.*) Dweller near, or worker in, an inn or tavern.

Kremen (*Ger., Yu.-Sl.*) One who came from Kremmen (muddy water), in Germany; dweller near where flint was found.

Kremer (*Ger.*) Same as Kramer, q.v.

Krenkel (*Ger.*) Dweller at the sign of the small crane.

Krenz, Krentz (*Ger.*) A variant of Kranz, q.v.

Krepshaw (*Eng.*) Dweller in a small wood or thicket frequented by crows.

Kresge (*Ger.*) The eager, greedy man.

Kress, Kresse (*Ger.*) Descendant of Kress, a pet form of Erasmus (amiable).

Kressman, Kressmann (*Ger.*) One who caught and sold gudgeons, a fisher.

Kretschmer, Kretchmer, Kretchmar, Kretzschmar (*Ger.*) One who sold ale and wine, a tavern keeper.

Kretz (*Ger.*) Variant of Kratz, q.v.; one who came from Kretz (muddy place), in Germany.

Kretzer (*Ger.*) One who collected legal fines; one who made and sold baskets; one who came from Kretz (muddy place), in Germany.

Kreuser (*Ger.*) One who had curly hair.

Kreutz, Kreutzer, Kreuz, Kreuzer (*Ger.*) One who came from Kreuz (cross), the name of several places in Germany; dweller near a market cross or boundary mark.

Kreutzman (*Ger.*) Dweller at the cross or boundary mark; one who sold crucifixes.

Krey (*Ger.*) Dweller at the sign of the crow; one thought to possess the characteristics of a crow.

Krichbaum, Kriechbaum (*Ger.*) Dweller near the wild plum tree.

Krick (*Ger.*) One who came from Krickau (watery meadow), in Germany.

Krickhahn (*Ger.*) Dweller at the sign of the cock raven.

Krieger, Krieg (*Ger., Du.*) The warrior or champion; descendant of Gregorius (watchman); one who made and sold drinking vessels.

Kriegler (*Ger.*) One who made and sold jugs and mugs.

Krieter (*Ger.*) The quarrelsome, argumentative person.

Krikorian (*Arm.*) The son of Krikor, Armenian form of Gregory (watchful).

Kriloff (*Rus.*) The son of Krylo (wing).

Krimstock (*Eng.*) One who came from Crimscote (Cynemaer's cottage), in Warwickshire.

Krinsky (*Ukr.*) One who cultivated flowers; or who dwelt among flowers.

Krischke, Krischak (*Ger., Pol.*) Descendant of little Krisch, a pet form of Christian (follower of Christ).

Krischunas (*Lith.*) Descendant of Kriscius, a pet form of Kristinas, Lithuanian form of Christian (follower of Christ); and of Kristupas, Lithuanian form of Christopher (Christbearer).

Krisciunas (*Lith.*) One who attends at baptisms.

Krisolofsky (*Rus., Pol.*) One who caught rats, a ratcatcher.

Krispin (*Eng.*) Variant of Crispin, q.v.

Kriss, Krist (*Ger.*) Follower of Christ; descendant of Kriss or Krist, pet forms of Christopher (Christ-bearer) and of Christian (follower of Christ).

Kristal (*Ger.*) Descendant of little Krist, pet form of Christopher (Christbearer) and of Christian (follower of Christ).

Kristensen (*Dan., Nor.*) The son of Kristen, a Scandinavian form of Christian (follower of Christ).

Kristiansen (*Nor., Sw.*) The son of Kristian (follower of Christ).

Kristin (*Ger.*) Descendant of Christian (follower of Christ).

Kristof, Kristofek (*Cz.-Sl.*) Descendant of Kristof, Slovakian form of Christopher (Christ-bearer).

Kristofferson (*Sw.*) The son of Kristoffer, Swedish form of Christopher (Christbearer).

Kristovic, Kristufek (*Yu.-Sl.*) The son of Krist, a pet form of Kristofer, Serbo-Croatian form of Christopher (Christ-bearer).

Krit (*Ukr.*) One who trapped moles; one with the characteristics of a mole.

Kritchevsky (*Ukr.*) One who worked with steel.

Kritikos, Kretekos, Kriticos (*Gr.*) One who came from Crete, a Cretan.

Krivit, Krivitsky (*Rus.*) One who came from the region of the Krivici tribe.

Kriz, Kritz (*Ger.*) Dweller at, or near, a cross; one who proclaimed the orders or messages of a court.

Kroch (*Ger.*) One who came from Groch (pea), in Germany.

Krochmal (*Pol.*) One who produced and sold starch.

Krock (*Ger.*) One who came from Cracow (the town of Duke Krak), in southern Poland.

Kroeger, Kroger (*Du.*) A publican or innkeeper.

Kroening (*Ger.*) Descendant of Grun, a pet form of names beginning with Grun (green), as Grombert and Gronwald.

Krogh (*Dan., Nor., Du.*) Dweller in a corner or nook; dweller near, or worker at, an inn.

Krogman (*Ger.*) One who worked at an inn, an innkeeper.

Krogstad (*Nor., Sw.*) One who came from Krokstad (Krokr's dwelling), the name of several places in Norway; or from Krokstad (Krokr's dwelling), in Sweden.

Krohn (*Ger.*) Descendant of Grun (green), a pet form of names beginning with Grun, as Gruonrik and Gronwald; dweller at the sign of the crane.

Krolczyk (*Pol.*) The little man who played the part of the king in play or pageant.

Krolik (*Pol., Rus.*) One who hunted, raised, or sold rabbits.

Kroll, Krol (*Pol.*) One connected in some way with a king's household; one who played the part of a king in play and pageant.

Krom (*Du.*) The cripple.

Kromer (*Ger.*) Variant of Kramer, q.v.

Krone, Kron, Kroner (*Ger.*) Dweller at the sign of the Kron (crest); descendant of Krone (green), a pet form of Cruanhart and Gronhari (green, army).

Kronenberg, Kronenberger (*Ger.*) One who came from Kronenberg or Cronenberg (crown mountain), in West Germany.

Kronengold, Kronegold (*Ger.*) Eighteen carat gold; crown gold.

Kronmiller, Kronmueller (*Ger.*) The head miller.

Kronquist (*Sw.*) Crown, twig.

Kronschnabel (*Ger.*) One with a nose like that of a crane.

Kroon (*Du.*) Dweller at the sign of the crown.

Kropp, Kropf, Kropfel, Kropfl (*Ger.*) Descendant of Kropp, a pet form of names beginning with the element *hrod* (fame), as Hrodobert, Hrodgaer, Rotbrand, etc.; one who came from Kropp, in Germany; one who had a prominent goiter.

Kross (*Scot., Ger.*) One who came from Cross (a cross), formerly spelled Kross, in the Orkney Islands; the curly-headed man.

Kroulaidis (*Lith.*) One who bleeds others, a bloodletter.

Kroupa (*Pol., Ukr.*) Variant of Krupa, q.v.

Krowa (*Pol.*) One who took care of cows, a cowherd.

Krska, Krsak, Krsek (*Sl.*) One with big or broad shoulders.

Kruczek (*Pol.*) Dweller at the sign of the small raven; one engaged in trickery or sharp practice.

Krueger, Kruger (*Ger.*) A publican or innkeeper.

Krug, Krugman (*Ger.*) A publican or innkeeper; one who worked in the inn.

Kruizenga (*Du.*) The son of Kruis (cross).

Kruk (*Pol.*) Dweller at the sign of the raven.

Krukowski (*Pol.*) Dweller in a place frequented by ravens.

Krull (*Ger.*) The curly-haired man.

Krumbein (*Ger.*) One with bowed or crooked legs.

Krumhaar (*Ger.*) The man with crooked, i.e., curly, hair.

Krumholz (*Ger.*) One who made carts or wheels, a cartwright or wheelwright; one who made things of wood; dweller in a wood of dwarf mountain pine.

Krumm, Krumme (*Ger.*) Variant of Krump, q.v.

Krummel (*Ger.*) One who came from Krummel (pool), in Germany.

Krummer (*Ger.*) Dweller on a bend or curve.

Krump (*Ger.*) One with a bent or deformed body.

Krumrey, Krumroy (*Ger.*) Dweller near a field boundary mark, or near a ridge; descendant of Rumerich (fame, rule).

Krupa (*Pol., Ukr.*) One with some real or fancied resemblance to a grain of barley; one who is coarse or uncouth; one who dealt in groats and barley; dweller near where barley grew.

Krupinski (*Pol.*) One who made and sold groats; one who came from Krupina, in Slovakia.

Krupnik, Krupnick (*Pol.*) One who made soup of peeled barley.

Krupp (*Ger.*) Descendant of Krupp or Ruppo, pet forms of names beginning with Hrod (fame); variant of Kropp, q.v.

Kruse (*Ger.*) The curly-haired man.

Krushchev (*Rus.*) The son of cockchafer, a large beetle; one with some characteristic of a large beetle.

Kruskopf (*Ger.*) One with curly hair on his head.

Kruszynski (*Pol.*) One who came from Kruszyn, in Poland.

Krutz, Krutzler, Kruzel (*Ger.*) Dweller at the cross; or at the sign of the cross; one who made and sold crucifixes.

Krych (*Pol., Ukr.*) Nickname for a person of no consequence, a crumb.

Krydynski (*Pol.*) One who came from Krydyn (chalk place), in Poland.

Krygowski (*Pol.*) One who affected airs.

Kryvenko (*Ukr.*) The son of the lame man.

Krzak (*Pol.*) Dweller near a bush or shrub.

Krzemien, Krzeminski (*Pol.*) One who dealt with flint, a stonecutter.

Krzesinski (*Pol.*) Dweller near a cross.

Krzywicki (*Pol.*) Dweller at the bow or bend.

Krzyzak (*Pol.*) One who fought to recover the Holy Land from the Moslems, a Crusader; one who came from Krzyz (cross), the name of several places in Poland; dweller near a cross.

Krzyzanowski (*Pol.*) One who came from Krzyzanowo (place of the cross), in Poland.

Ksiazek, Ksiazkiewicz (*Pol.*) Descendant of the little prince.

Kuan (*Chin.*) To govern; to close.

Kubacki (*Pol., Rus.*) One who made cups and goblets.

Kubel, Kubelsky (*Ukr.*) Dweller in a small corner or little nest.

Kubiak, Kubic, Kubica, Kubicz, Kuban, Kubanek, Kubicki (*Pol.*) Descendant of Kuba, a pet form of Jacob (may God protect; the supplanter).

Kubik (*Pol., Rus., Ukr.*) Descendant of Kubik, a Slavic pet form of Jacob (may God protect; the supplanter).

Kubilius (*Lith.*) One who made tubs, a cooper.

Kubilunas (*Lith.*) The son of the tub maker.

Kubo (*Jap.*) Long, keep.

Kubota (*Jap.*) Hollow, rice field.

Kubowicz, Kubow (*Pol.*) Descendant of Kuba, pet form of Jakub, Polish form of Jacob (may God protect; the supplanter).

Kuby, Kubycheck (*Cz.-Sl.*) Descendant of Kuby, a pet form of Jakub, Slavic form of Jacob (may God protect; the supplanter).

Kuc, Kuca, Kucaba, Kucala (*Pol.*) One who forges or hammers material.

Kucera (*Cz.-Sl.*) One with curly hair.

Kuch (*Ukr.*) The small or short man.

Kuchar, Kucharski (*Pol.*) One who prepared food, a cook.

Kucharczyk (*Pol.*) Descendant of the little cook.

Kucharenko (*Ukr.*) The son of the cook.

Kuchel (*Ger.*) One who baked and sold small cakes.

Kuchenbecker (*Ger.*) One who baked cakes.

Kuchta (*Pol.*) Young boy who worked in the kitchen.

Kucia, Kuciak, Kucik (*Pol.*) One who made and sold sweet porridge, a Christmas dish.

Kuck (*Ger.*) Dweller in, or near, a bog or muddy swamp.

Kuczerenko (*Ukr.*) The son of the man with curly hair.

Kuczynski, Kucinski (*Pol.*) Dweller near a pile or mound.

Kuebler (*Ger.*) One who made and sold casks, buckets and tubs, a cooper.

Kuecker (*Ger.*) One who came from Kuchen (bog), in Germany.

Kuehl (*Ger.*) One with a cold personality; variant of Kuhl, q.v.

Kuehne, Kuehner, Kuehnle (*Ger.*) Descendant of Kuno, a pet form of names beginning with Kuhn (bold), as Konrad and Kuniald.

Kuenster (*Ger.*) Descendant of Kuno, a pet form of names beginning with Kuhn (bold), such as Konrad.

Kuester (*Ger.*) An under-officer of a church who had charge of the sacristy and its contents.

Kugel, Kugelman, Kugler (*Ger.*) One who made hoods or cowls; one who made bullets.

Kuh (*Ger.*) Dweller at the sign of the

cow or female animal; one in charge of the cows, a cowherd.

Kuhar (*Cz.-Sl.*) One who prepared and cooked food, a cook.

Kuhfuss (*Ger.*) One with a club foot or cow's foot, a deformed foot; nickname for one who cared for cows, a cowherd.

Kuhl, Kuhle (*Ger.*) One who came from Kuhle (pit; excavation), the name of three places in Germany; dweller near a mine or pit; descendant of Kuhl or Kuhle, pet forms of names beginning with Kol (helmet), as Colobert and Colohart.

Kuhlman, Kuhlmann (*Ger.*) Dweller near, or worker in, a mine or excavation; the man who lived at, or near, the pool.

Kuhlmey, Kuhlmeyer (*Ger.*) The farmer living near, or working in, the pit or mine.

Kuhn, Kuhne, Kuehn, Kuhns (*Ger.*) One who was bold or keen; descendant of Kuhn, a pet form of Kunrat, German form of Conrad (bold, counsel).

Kuhrt (*Ger.*) One of low stature, a little man; descendant of Konrad (bold, counsel).

Kuiken (*Du.*) One who raised and sold chicks; dweller at the sign of the chick.

Kuipers, Kuiper (*Du.*) One who made and sold casks, buckets, and tubs, a cooper.

Kujawa, Kujawski (*Pol.*) One who came from Kujawy, a province in Poland.

Kukielka (*Pol.*) One who made and sold small loaves or rolls.

Kukla (*Ukr., Rus.*) One who had some real or fancied resemblance to a puppet; one who operated a puppet show.

Kuklinski (*Pol.*) One who made and sold dolls or images.

Kukula (*Pol.*) Dweller at the sign of the cuckoo.

Kukulka (*Pol.*) Dweller at the sign of the cuckoo; one thought to have the characteristics of a cuckoo.

Kula (*Pol., Ukr.*) Dweller at the sign of the ball, or at some natural feature shaped like a ball.

Kulak (*Rus.*) A rich farmer.

Kulas (*Ger.*) Dweller at the sign of the ball.

Kulczycki, Kulczycky, Kulczyk (*Ukr.*) One who came from Kulczyci, in Western Ukraine.

Kulesza, Kulesa (*Ukr., Pol.*) One who made and sold a thin porridge made of corn or grain.

Kulick (*Ger.*) Dweller at the sign of the ball; the short, fat man.

Kulig (*Pol.*) Dweller at the sign of the sea gull; one with the characteristics of a sea gull.

Kulik (*Rus.*) Dweller at the sign of the snipe or stilt bird; one with some quality of a snipe.

Kulikowski (*Pol.*) One who came from Kulikow(o) (Kulik's settlement), the name of many places in Poland.

Kulinski, Kulinsky (*Pol.*) One who was bent over or deformed.

Kulis, Kulish (*Ukr.*) One who makes and sells gruel.

Kulka (*Pol.*) Dweller at the sign of the small ball.

Kulma, Kulmala (*Finn.*) Dweller near the edge or boundary.

Kulp (*Ger.*) One who made clubs and maces.

Kumamoto (*Jap.*) Bear, base.

Kumar (*Yu.-Sl.*) One who raises and sells cucumbers.

Kummer (*Ger.*) Descendant of Khunemar (race, famous), or of Gundemar (war, famous); one who came from Kummer (distress; need), the name of several places in Germany; one who is in need or afflicted; the sorrowful or miserable man.

Kummerer (*Ger.*) One who came from Kummer (distress; need), the name of two places in Germany.

Kuna (*Ger., Pol.*) Dweller at the sign of the pine marten.

Kunc (*Yu.-Sl.*) Dweller at the sign of the hare; one who hunts hares.

Kundrat (*Rus.*) Descendant of Kundrat, a Russian form of Conrad (bold, counsel).

Kung (*Chin.*) Dragon.

Kunhart (*Ger.*) Descendant of Kuhnhart (bold, hard).

Kunis (*Ger.*) Descendant of Kunath, a Wendish form of Conrad (bold, counsel).

Kunka, Kunke (*Cz.*) Dweller at the sign of the marten; one who trapped pine martens.

Kunkel, Kunkle (*Ger.*) Dweller at, or near, deep water; one from the distaff side, perhaps an effeminate man; descendant of Kuno, a pet form of names beginning with Kuhn (bold), as Kuniald and Chunrad.

Kunstadter, Kunstadt (*Cz.-Sl., Ger.*) One who came from Kunstat, in Czechoslovakia.

Kunstler, Kunzler (*Ger.*) The skillful artisan; the learned man.

Kuntz, Kunz, Kunze, Kunst (*Ger.*) Descendant of Kuno, a pet form of names beginning with Kuhn (bold), as Kunigund, Chunrad, and Konrad.

Kuntzman (*Ger.*) The servant of Kuntz, German short form of Conrad (bold, counsel).

Kuo (*Chin.*) Outer wall of fortifications.

Kupczyk (*Pol.*) One employed as a commercial clerk.

Kuper, Kuperman (*Ger.*) One who made and sold casks, buckets and tubs, a cooper.

Kupersmith (*Ger.*) Variant of Coppersmith, q.v.; the smith who made and sold casks, buckets, and tubs.

Kupfer, Kupferer (*Ger.*) One who worked in copper, a coppersmith.

Kupferberg (*Ger.*) One who came from Kupferberg (copper mountain), the name of two places in Germany.

Kupferschmidt (*Ger.*) The smith who worked with copper and brass.

Kupiainen (*Finn.*) One who supervised the farm workers, a foreman.

Kupiec (*Pol., Ukr.*) One who purchased merchandise to sell to others, a buyer.

Kupka, Kupke (*Ger.*) Descendant of little Kup, a pet form of Jacob (may God protect; the supplanter).

Kupper, Kupperman, Kuppermann (*Ger.*) Variant of Kuper, q.v.

Kuppinger (*Ger.*) One who came from Kuppingen, in Germany.

Kupsik, Kupski, Kupsky (*Pol.*) One who buys and sells, a merchant.

Kuraitis (*Lith.*) The son of the Curonian.

Kurath (*Ger.*) Descendant of Chuonrad, a German form of Conrad (bold, counsel).

Kurcz (*Pol.*) One subject to convulsions or cramps.

Kurczak (*Pol.*) One who raised and sold young hens.

Kurek (*Pol., Cz.-Sl.*) Dweller at the sign of the cock; one thought to possess some characteristic of a cock.

Kurfess (*Ger.*) One with a scabby face or defective eyesight.

Kurihara (*Jap.*) Post, field.

Kurinsky (*Ukr., Pol.*) One who raised and sold hens or chickens.

Kurk, Kurka (*Pol.*) One who raised and sold small hens or chicks.

Kurland, Kurlander (*Ger.*) One who came from Kurland or Courland (country of the Cours), in Latvia.

Kuroda (*Jap.*) Black, rice field.

Kurowski (*Pol.*) One who came from Kurowo (cock), the name of many places in Poland.

Kurth (*Ger.*) Descendant of Kurth, a pet form of Kunrath, a German form of Conrad (bold, counsel).

Kurtz (*Ger.*) The short man.

Kurtzeborn (*Ger.*) Dweller near a small spring or fountain.

Kurtzman (*Ger.*) One of low stature, a small man.

Kurylo (*Ukr.*) One who smokes a great deal.

Kurz (*Pol., Ger.*) Dweller in a dry, dusty place; the short man.

Kurzawski (*Pol.*) Dweller in a dirty, dusty place.

Kus (*Ger., Pol.*) The small person.

Kusaki (*Jap.*) Grass, tree.

293

Kusch, Kush (*Ger.*) Descendant of Godizo (God).

Kusek, Kusak (*Pol.*) Descendant of little Kus or Kusy, a nickname meaning "short tail," probably referring to a dog.

Kushner, Kushnir, Kushmar (*Pol., Cz.-Sl., Ukr.*) One who made fur coats, a furrier.

Kusnierz (*Pol.*) One who skinned animals and sold furs, a furrier.

Kuss, Kusse (*Ger.*) Descendant of Kus, a pet form of Marcus (belonging to Mars, the god of war), and of Dominicus (the Lord's day).

Kussmann, Kussman (*Ger.*) One who made and sold cheese.

Kussworm, Kusswurm (*Ger.*) Nickname for one who made cheese.

Kuster, Kusterer (*Ger.*) Variant of Koster, q.v.

Kuta (*Pol., Ukr.*) One who came from Kuta (corner), in Poland; dweller in a corner or angle of land.

Kutchinsky, Kutchinski, Kutchin (*Ukr., Rus., Pol.*) Dweller in a hut; or at a corner.

Kutner (*Pol.*) The man with shaggy hair.

Kutt (*Est.*) One who hunted game, a hunter.

Kuttner (*Ger., Pol.*) One who was a member of a religious order, devoted primarily to contemplation, a monk; one who came from Kutten, in Saxony; one with rough hair or bristles, a shaggy man.

Kutz (*Ger.*) Descendant of Gutz, a pet form of Godizo (God).

Kuusik (*Est.*) Dweller in a spruce forest.

Kuykendall, Kuykendoll (*Du.*) Dweller in the valley where chickens were raised.

Kuypers, Kuyper (*Du.*) Variant of Kuipers, q.v.

Kuzma (*Ukr.*) Descendant of Kuzma.

Kuznecov (*Rus.*) The son of the smith.

Kuznetsov (*Rus.*) The worker in metals, a smith.

Kuzniar (*Cz.-Sl.*) One who prepared skins or furs, a furrier.

Kuznicki (*Pol.*) Dweller near, or worker in, a smith's shop.

Kuznitsky (*Ukr., Pol.*) Dweller near, or worker at, a smithy.

Kvistad (*Nor.*) One who came from Kvistad (dwelling enclosed by a fence with movable parts), the name of three places in Norway.

Kwak (*Kor., Chin.*) Rampart.

Kwan (*Kor., Chin.*) To close.

Kwasiborski (*Pol.*) One who made beet soup.

Kwasigroch (*Pol.*) One who marinates peas.

Kwasniak, Kwasinski (*Pol.*) One who made and sold a sour drink or sour cabbage soup.

Kwasniewski, Kwasny (*Pol.*) The sour, peevish, morose man.

Kwerneland (*Nor.*) One who came from Kverneland (field with a mill), in Norway.

Kwiatek (*Pol.*) Dweller near the sign of the small flower; one who cultivated flowerets.

Kwiatkowski (*Pol.*) One who came from Kwiatkow(o) (flower place), in Poland.

Kwidzinski (*Pol.*) One who came from Kwidzyn, in Poland.

Kwiecien (*Pol.*) Descendant of Kwiecien (April).

Kwiecinski (*Pol.*) One who raises flowers.

Kwit, Kwitek, Kwitka (*Ukr.*) Dweller at the sign of the flower; one who grew flowers.

Kyle, Kyles (*Eng., Scot.*) Dweller near the Kyle (narrow), a river in Yorkshire; one who came from Kyle (narrow strait), in Ayrshire.

Kyllingstad (*Nor.*) One who came from Kyllingstad, in Norway.

Kyriakopoulos, Kyriac (*Gr.*) Descendant of Kyriaki, a female saint.

Kyriakos (*Gr.*) One who follows God; the Lord's servant.

Kyriazes, Kyriazis, Kyriazopoulos (*Gr.*) Descendant of the lord or master.

Kyros (*Gr.*) Short form of Kyriakos, q.v.

Kyrychenko (*Ukr.*) The son of the disorderly person.

Kyrylenko (*Ukr.*) The son of Kyrylo, Ukrainian form of Cyril (lordly).

Kyser (*Ger.*) Variant of Kaiser, q.v.

Kyst (*Nor., Dan.*) Dweller on the coast.

Laarkamp (*Du.*) Dweller in, or near, an empty or deserted field, one no longer cultivated.

Labadie (*Fr.*) Dweller near, or worker in, the abbey or monastery.

Laban (*Heb.*) The white-haired man; descendant of Laban (white).

Labarbera (*It.*) Descendant of Barbera (the stranger).

Labate, La Bate, Labatt (*Fr.*) Dweller in the valley or depression between the hills or mountains.

Labbe, Labbee (*Fr.*) A member of an abbot's entourage; sometimes the lay abbot of a monastery who inherited the office.

Label (*Fr.*) Variant of La Bell, q.v.

La Bell, La Bella, La Belle (*Fr.*) The handsome, good-looking person.

Labno (*Pol.*) The light-complexioned or white person.

Labrador (*Sp.*) One who cultivated the land, a farmer.

La Brecque, La Breck (*Fr.*) Dweller at, or near, the gap or opening in the wall or hedge; the gap-toothed man.

Labrencis (*Lat.*) Descendant of Labrencis, Latvian form of Lawrence (laurel, symbol of victory).

Labriola (*It.*) One who traps or poaches on a noble's land.

La Buda (*It.*) One who came from Buda (Buda's town), in Hungary.

Lacey (*Eng.*) One who came from Lassy or Lessay (Latius' estate), the names of places in France.

Lach (*Ger.*) Dweller at, or in, the bushes or small wood; dweller near a small pool.

La Chance (*Fr.*) One who came from Chance (Cantius' estate), in France.

Lachman, Lachmann (*Ger.*) Dweller at, or near, a pool or lake; a nickname

given to one who is continually laughing; dweller near a small wood or underbrush.

Lachowicz (*Rus., Pol.*) The son of the man from Poland.

Lack (*Eng.*) Dweller by the water.

Lackey, Lackie (*Eng., Ir.*) One who attended another, a footman; dweller at a stony or rocky place.

Lackland (*Eng., Scot.*) One who did not possess land at a time when land was practically the only source of wealth. King John of England was nicknamed Lackland because he received no grant when Henry assigned his lands to his sons. One who came from Lochlann, i.e., Norway.

Lackman (*Eng.*) Dweller at the lake.

La Combe, Lacombe (*Fr.*) One who came from LaCombe or Combe (dale), the names of places in France.

La Corte (*Fr.*) One who comes from the farm, homestead, village, or fortified place.

Lacount, La Counte (*Fr.*) The nobleman, corresponding in rank to an earl; attendant of the emperor.

Lacour, Lacourt, La Courte (*Fr.*) The short or small man; dweller near the courtyard or house; one who came from Lacour (estate or town), the name of numerous places in France.

La Croix (*Fr.*) Dweller at, or near, a cross; one who carried the cross in a procession. See Cross.

La Crosse (*Fr.*) A partially Englished form of La Croix, q.v.

Lacy (*Eng., Ir.*) One who came from Lassy (Lascius' estate), in Calvados.

Ladbury (*Eng.*) One who came from Ledbury (fort on the Leadon river), in Herefordshire.

Ladd (*Eng.*) A serving-man or attendant.

Laden, Ladenson (*Ger.*) One who operates a small shop or stall, a shopkeeper.

Ladendorf (*Ger.*) One who came from Latendorf, in Germany.

Laderman, Lader (*Ger.*) One who harvests crops; one who loads or packs merchandise.

Ladley (*Eng.*) Dweller at the stream in the grove; dweller at the servant's open place in the wood.

Ladner (*Ger.*) One who kept a shop or store; one who made and sold shutters.

Ladson (*Eng.*) The son of the servant.

Ladwig (*Ger.*) Variant of Ludwig, q.v.

Laennec (*Fr.*) The educated, well-read man.

Lafair, La Fair (*Eng., Fr.*) The handsome or beautiful person; one who came from LaFare (family homestead), in France.

La Fayette (*Fr.*) Dweller at, or near, a small beech grove.

Lafferty (*Ir.*) Variant of Laverty, q.v.

Laffey (*Ir.*) Descendant of Flaitheamh (lord; ruler).

Laffite, Laffitte (*Fr.*) Dweller at a boundary stone or marker.

Lafontant, Lafont (*Fr.*) Dweller at the the spring or fountain.

La Forge (*Fr.*) One who worked at the forge, a smith; dweller near the forge.

La Francois (*Fr.*) The free man; descendant of Francois, French form of Francis (free).

Laganella (*Fr.*) One who declared the law, a lawyer.

Lagerlof (*Sw.*) Laurel leaf.

La Grange (*Fr.*) One who paid rent for the land he farmed, a tenant farmer; one who came from Lagrange, in France.

La Greca, La Greco (*Fr.*) One who came from Greece, the Greek.

La Grossa (*It.*) The large, fleshy man.

La Guardia (*It., Sp.*) Dweller near an outpost; the guard; one who came from LaGuardia (outpost), in Italy.

Lahey (*Ir.*) Grandson of Flaitheamh (lord; ruler).

Lahr (*Ger.*) One who came from Lahr (empty; deserted), in Germany; descendant of Lahr, a pet form of Hilarius (cheerful).

Lahti (*Finn.*) Dweller near the bay.

Laib, Laibe (*Ger.*) One who baked and sold loaves of bread.

Laidlaw (*Scot.*) Dweller at the watercourse hill.

Laidley (*Scot., Eng.*) Variant of Laidlaw, q.v.; variant of Ladley, q.v.

Lain, Laine, Layne (*Eng.*) Dweller by certain tracts of arable land at the foot of the Sussex Downs; dweller in, or by, the lane. See Lane.

Laing (*Scot.*) The tall man.

Laino (*It.*) One who came from Laino, the name of three places in Italy.

Laird (*Scot.*) An owner of land or houses, a landlord.

Laity (*Eng.*) Dweller near the milk house.

La Jeunesse (*Fr.*) The young man or youthful person.

Lakatos (*Gr.*) Descendant of Loukas, Greek form of Luke (light).

Lake (*Eng.*) Dweller at a stream or brook; dweller in a dried-up watercourse in the moors.

Lakemacher (*Ger.*) One who made cloth or other fabric.

Laker (*Eng.*) Dweller by a stream or watercourse.

Lakin (*Rus.*) Descendant of Lakeh (the weary one), a woman's name.

Lal (*Hindi*) The cherished one.

Lala (*Cz.*) Descendant of Lala, a pet form of Ladislav (rule, glorious).

Lally, Lalley (*Fr.*) One who came from Lalley (Lallius' estate), in France; or from Alley (Allius' homestead), in France.

La Macchia (*It.*) Dweller in, or near, the thicket.

La Manna, La Manno (*It.*) One who came from La Manna, in Italy.

Lamantia (*It.*) One who came from Amantea, in Italy.

Lamar, La Mar (*Fr.*) Dweller near the pool.

Lamb, Lambe (*Eng.*) Descendant of Lamb (lamb); dweller at the sign of the lamb; one with some characteristic of a lamb.

Lambert, Lambart, Lamberty, Lamberts,

Lambertson (*Eng., Du.*) Descendant of Lambert (land, bright).

Lambeth (*Eng.*) One who came from Lambeth (harbor from where lambs were shipped), in Surrey.

Lambie, Lamby (*Scot.*) Descendant of little Lamb (lamb); or of little Lam, a pet form of Lambert (land, bright).

Lambrecht, Lambrechts, Lambright (*Ger.*) Descendant of Lambrecht (land, bright).

Lamkin, Lampkin, Lampkins (*Eng.*) Descendant of little Lamb, a pet form of Lambert (land, bright).

Lamm (*Ger.*) Dweller at the sign of the lamb; one considered to be gentle as a lamb.

Lammers (*Ger.*) Descendant of Lambert (land, bright).

Lammersfeld (*Ger.*) One who came from Lammersfelde (lambs' field), in Germany.

Lammey, Lammie (*Scot.*) Variants of Lambie, q.v.

La Monica (*Fr.*) The adviser; one who counsels others.

Lamont, Lamond, Limont (*Scot.*) The lawman or lawyer.

Lamoureaux (*Fr.*) The loving man, a lover or sweetheart.

Lampert (*Eng.*) One who came from Lamport (long market-place), the name of several places in England; a variant of Lambert, q.v.

Lamplough (*Eng.*) One who came from Lamplugh (the church of the parish), in Cumberland. The name is from the Welsh *llan plwy*.

Lamprecht, Lampright (*Ger.*) Variant of Lambrecht, q.v.

Lampshire (*Eng.*) One who came from Lancashire (Roman fort on the Lune river), a county in England.

Lampton (*Eng.*) One who came from Lambton (homestead where lambs were kept), in Durham.

Lamson, Lampson (*Eng.*) The son of Lam, a pet form of Lambert (land, bright).

Lanagan, Lanahan (*Ir.*) Descendant of little Lon (blackbird).

Lancaster (*Eng.*) One who came from Lancaster (Roman camp on the Lune river; long Roman camp), the county town of Lancashire.

Lance (*Eng.*) Descendant of Lance (land); also a pet form of Lancelot (very little Lance).

Land, Lande (*Eng., Nor.*) Dweller in, or near, the glade or grassy plain; or on Land, a farm name.

Landau, Landauer (*Ger.*) One who came from Landau (meadow land), the name of three towns in Germany.

Landenberger (*Ger.*) One who came from Landensberg, in Germany.

Landers, Lander, Landor (*Eng.*) One who washed and bleached flax, wool, cloth, etc.; dweller near the church yard; one who came from London (place of Londinos, or from a tribal name).

Landes (*Fr.*) One who came from Landes (swampy place), in France.

Landesman (*Scot.*) One who took care of the *launde* or open wood.

Landfair, Lanfair, Lanfar (*Wel., Eng.*) One who came from Llanfair (St. Mary's church); dweller near the great church; the tall companion.

Landgraf (*Ger.*) A nobleman with the rank of a count; a civil administrator; one connected in some way with a count's household.

Landgrebe (*Ger.*) Variant of Landgraf, q.v.

Landherr (*Ger.*) One who was a feudal lord; lord of a manor.

Landi (*It.*) Descendant of Lando, a pet form of names terminating in -lando (land), as Rollando and Orlando.

Landis, Landise (*Fr.*) Variant of Landes, q.v. See also Land.

Landman (*Eng.*) One who took care of the *launde* or open wood.

Landolfi (*It.*) Descendant of Landolfo (land, wolf).

Landon (*Eng., Fr.*) One who came from Langdon (long hill), the name of several places in England; descendant of Lando (land).

Landow, Landowski (*Ger., Pol.*) One who came from Landau or Landow (meadow land), the names of places in Germany.

Landreth (*Eng., Scot.*) One who came from Lanreath (court of justice), in Cornwall.

Landreville (*Fr.*) One who came from Landreville (Landerich's dwelling), in France.

Landry, Landrey, Landro (*Fr.*) Descendant of Landry (country, powerful).

Landsburg, Landsberg (*Ger.*) One who came from Landsberg (hill with arable land), in Germany.

Landsman (*Scot.*) One who tended the open wood or *launde*.

Landwehr (*Ger.*) Citizen enrolled as a soldier but not on active duty.

Landy (*Fr.*) One who came from Landy, in France.

Lane (*Eng.*) One who lived near the rural road, or narrow way between fences or hedges.

Laney (*Ir.*) Descendant of Dubslaine (black of the Slaney).

Lanfair (*Wel., Eng.*) One who came from Llanfair (St. Mary's church), in Wales.

Lang, Lange (*Ger., Eng., Scot.*) The tall man.

Langan (*Ir.*) Grandson of little Long (long or tall).

Langbauer (*Ger.*) The tall farmer or tiller of the soil.

Langdon (*Eng.*) One who came from Langdon (long hill), the name of several places in England.

Langemore (*Eng.*) Dweller in, or near, the large or extensive moor.

Langendorf (*Ger.*) One who came from Langendorf (long village), in Alsace-Lorraine.

Langer (*Ger., Fr.*) The tall man; one who tilled the soil, a farmer.

Langford (*Eng.*) One who came from Langford (long ford), the name of several places in England.

Langham (*Eng.*) One who came from Langham (long homestead; village

of Lawa's people), the name of several places in England.

Langhans (*Ger.*) The long or tall man named Hans, a pet form of Johannes (gracious gift of Jehovah).

Langhorne, Langhorn (*Eng.*) Dweller at the long horn; the trumpeter with the long horn; dweller at the big corner.

Langille, Langill (*Scot., Eng.*) One who came from Langwell (long field), the name of places in Caithness and in Ross and Cromarty; or from Langhale (long flat land), in Norfolk.

Langjahr (*Ger.*) Descendant of Langjahr (leap year), a name given to one born on the extra day.

Langland (*Eng.*) Dweller on the long narrow land.

Langley, Langlie (*Eng.*) One who came from Langley (long wood or clearing), the name of many places in England; an Englishman, from a corruption of the French *l'Anglais*.

Langlois, Langlais (*Fr.*) The Englishman or man from England.

Langman (*Eng.*) The tall man.

Langmuir (*Scot.*) Dweller in, or near, the long moor, or waste upland.

Langner (*Ger.*) One who came from Langen (long place), in Germany.

Langrock (*Eng., Fr.*) Dweller near a large rock or stone.

Langshaw (*Eng.*) Dweller in, or near, the long or extensive wood or thicket.

Langston (*Eng.*) One who came from Langstone (long stone), the name of places in Devonshire and Hampshire.

Langton (*Eng.*) One who came from Langton (long homestead; big hill), the name of several places in England.

Langtry, Langtree (*Eng.*) One who came from Langtree (tall tree), in Devonshire.

Langworthy (*Eng.*) One who came from Langworth (long ford), in Lincolnshire.

Lanham (*Eng.*) One who came from

Lenham (Leana's homestead), in Kent; or from Lanham (homestead at the lanes), in Nottinghamshire; variant of Langham, q.v.

Lanier (*Fr.*) One who dressed, wove or sold wool.

Lanigan, Lannigan (*Ir.*) Descendant of Lonagan (little blackbird).

Lankford (*Eng.*) Variant of Langford, q.v.

Lankin (*Eng.*) Descendant of little Lan, a pet form of Lancelot (very little Lance).

Lannon, Lannan, Lannen (*Ir.*) Grandson of little Leann (cloak or mantle).

Lanphear, Lanpher, Lanphier (*Wel.*) Dweller near the large church.

Lansden (*Eng.*) Variant of Lansdowne, q.v.

Lansdowne, Lansdown (*Eng.*) One who came from Lansdown (neck of land), in Somerset.

Lansford (*Eng.*) One who came from Landford (lane ford), in Wiltshire; or from Langford (Landa's ford), in Nottinghamshire.

Lansing (*Eng.*) One who came from Lancing (people of Wlenca), in Sussex.

Lanthier (*Fr.*) Descendant of Landhari (land, army).

Lantz, Lanz (*Ger.*) Descendant of Lanzo or Lando (land).

Lanyon (*Eng.*) Dweller near John's church, or church of St. Jona; or by the pool.

Lanza, Lanzi, Lanzo (*It.*) A mercenary German soldier; one who fought with a lance; descendant of Lanza, a pet form of Lancillotto (man servant).

La Pergola (*It.*) Dweller near the vine trellis.

Lapetina, Lapetino (*It.*) One who made and sold combs.

Lapham (*Eng.*) One who came from Lopham (Loppa's homestead), in Norfolk.

Lapidus (*Fr.*) One who dealt in precious stones.

Lapierre (*Fr.*) Dweller near the stone; one who came from La Pierre (the stone), in France.

Lapin (*Fr., Rus.*) One who hunted, raised, or sold rabbits; one who had big feet.

Lapinski (*Pol.*) One who came from Lapy (claws), a city in Poland.

La Plante (*Fr.*) Dweller near the place where bushes and young trees are started for transplanting.

La Pointe (*Fr.*) The fighting man, a soldier—from point (especially of a lance).

La Porta (*It.*) Dweller near the gate, probably the entrance to a walled town.

La Porte (*Fr.*) Dweller near a city gate or other large gate.

Lapp, Lappe (*Ger.*) A foolish person.

Lapsley (*Eng., Scot.*) One who came from Lapley (Laeppa's grove), in Staffordshire.

Lapworth (*Eng.*) One who came from Lapworth (Hlappa's homestead), in Warwickshire.

Laquintano (*Sp.*) Dweller in the country house; one who came from Quintana (country house), the name of many places in Spain.

Lara (*Sp.*) One who came from Lara (fernery; pagan household god), in Spain.

Laramie (*Fr.*) One who came from Aramits, in France.

Larcom, Larcome, Larcombe (*Eng.*) Dweller in Lar's valley.

Lardner, Lardiner, Larder (*Eng.*) The keeper of the larder, the place where provisions were stored.

Lareau (*Fr.*) The royal or noble man.

Large, Largman (*Eng.*) The big, fat man; the generous man.

Larimer (*Eng.*) Variant of Lorimer, q.v.

Lark, Larke (*Eng.*) One with some characteristic of a lark; dweller at the sign of the lark; descendant of little Lar, a pet form of Lawrence (laurel, symbol of victory).

Larkin, Larkins (*Eng.*) Descendant of little Lar, a pet form of Lawrence (laurel, symbol of victory).

Larmer, Larmore, Larmour (*Eng.*) One who made armor, an armorer.

La Rocco, La Rocca (*It.*) Dweller near, or worker at, a fortress; dweller near a cliff.

Larock, Larocque, La Roche (*Fr.*) Dweller near a rock or stone.

La Rosa (*It.*) Dweller at the sign of the Rose.

La Rose (*Fr.*) One who came from La Rose (place of wild roses), the name of several places in France; one who raised roses.

Larousse (*Fr.*) The red-haired or ruddy man.

Larrabee, Larabee (*Fr.*) Dweller on the shore of a lake or the bank of a river.

Larrier (*Fr.*) Dweller in the rear; or in a house behind another.

Larrimore, Larimore (*Eng.*) Enlarged variant of Larmer, q.v.

Larrington (*Eng.*) One who came from Lartington (village of Lyrti's people), in the North Riding of Yorkshire.

Larry (*Eng.*) Descendant of Larry, a pet form of Lawrence (laurel, symbol of victory).

Larson, Larsen, Larsson (*Sw., Dan., Nor., Eng.*) The son of Lars or Lawrence (laurel, symbol of victory).

La Rue (*Fr.*) Dweller on an important street.

La Salle (*Fr.*) One who lived, or worked, in the hall or large room; one who came from LaSalle, the name of several places in France.

La Salvia (*It.*) Dweller near, or grower of, salvia or sage.

La Scala (*It.*) Dweller near the steep incline, or stairs.

Lash, Lasch (*Ger.*) Descendant of Lash, a pet form of Lazarus (help of God).

Lasham (*Eng.*) One who came from Leasam (Leofel's enclosure), in Sussex.

Lashinsky (*Pol., Ukr.*) One who came from Laszyn in Pomerania.

Lashley (*Eng.*) Dweller near a bog in a low-lying meadow.

Laskin (*Rus.*) Dweller at the sign of the weasel.

Lasko (*Pol.*) Dweller in, or near, the forest; worker in the forest.

Laskowski (*Pol.*) Dweller in, or near, a forest; one who came from Laskow(o), in Poland.

Lasky, Laskey, Laski, Laske (*Ger., Pol.*) One who came from Lask, in Poland; dweller on cleared land.

La Smith, Lasmith (*Eng.*) The worker in metals, "the smith."

La Sota, Lasota (*Sp.*) One who came from Sota (low place), the name of many places in Spain.

La Spina (*It.*) Dweller at the sign of the porcupine; one thought to possess the characteristics of a porcupine.

Lassen (*Ger.*) Descendant of Las, a pet form of Nikolaus (people's victory), or of Lars, a pet form of Laurentius (laurel, symbol of victory); the lazy or indolent man.

Lasser, Lassers, Laser, Lassar (*Ger.*) One who bled people, a bloodletter; descendant of Lazarus (help of God).

Lassiter (*Eng.*) A variant of Lester, q.v.

Lasson (*Fr.*) One who came from Lasson (Lassius' estate), in France.

Laster (*Eng.*) One who made wooden molds of the foot for shoemakers.

Laszlo (*Hun.*) Descendant of Ladislaus (glorious lord), eleventh century king of Hungary who was later canonized.

Latch (*Eng.*) One who came from Lach Dennis (Dennis' stream in a bog); or from Lache (stream in a bog), both in Cheshire; dweller at a stream in a boggy area.

Latcham (*Eng.*) One who came from Lackham (Lacock's meadow), in Wiltshire.

Latchford (*Eng.*) One who came from Latchford (ford over a stream), the name of villages in Cheshire and Oxfordshire.

Latham (*Eng.*) One who came from Latham or Laytham, both in Yorkshire; or Lathom in Lancashire, all three meaning barn enclosure.

Lathrop, Lathrope (*Eng.*) One who came from Lowthorpe (Logi's farm), in the East Riding of Yorkshire.

Latimer, Latimore, Lattimore, Latturner, Lattner (*Eng.*) The Latiner or translator of Latin, an interpreter.

La Torre (*Sp.*) One who came from La Torre (the tower), the name of several places in Spain; dweller near the tower or spire.

Latour (*Fr.*) One who came from La Tour (the tower), the name of several places in France; dweller in a house by, or with, a tower.

Latrobe (*Fr.*) One who invents things, an inventor.

Latta (*Scot.*) One who came from the lands of Laithis, in Ayrshire.

Lattari (*It.*) One who sells milk, a milkman.

Lau, Laue (*Ger.*) Dweller at the sign of the lion; one who came from Laue or Lauen (lion), in Germany.

Laub, Lauber (*Ger.*) One who came from Laub (foliage), the name of various places in Germany.

Laudenslager (*Ger.*) One who plays the lute.

Lauder (*Scot.*) One who came from Lauder (trench), in Berwickshire.

Lauderbach (*Ger.*) Variant of Lauterbach, q.v.

Lauderdale (*Scot.*) One who came from Lauderdale (valley trench), the name of the western district of Berwickshire.

Lauer (*Ger.*) One who tans skins; one who fights by ambushing another; one who came from Laue or Lauen or Lauer (lion), the names of places in Germany.

Laughead (*Eng.*) Dweller at the head or upper end of the ridge.

Laughlin (*Ir.*) Variant of Loughlin, q.v.

Laughton (*Eng.*) One who came from Laughton (homestead where leeks were grown; enclosed homestead), the name of several places in England.

Lauletta (*It.*) Dweller at the sign of the little lark.

Laurence (*Wel.*) Descendant of Lawrence (laurel, symbol of victory).

Laurent (*Fr.*) Descendant of Laurent (laurel, symbol of victory); one who came from Lorraine, a medieval kingdom and duchy in Europe.

Lauria (*Sp., It.*) Descendant of the laureled one; dweller near where laurel grew.

Laurie (*Scot.*) Descendant of little Laurence (laurel, symbol of victory).

Laurito (*It.*) Descendant of little Laura (laurel, symbol of victory).

Lausche, Lausch, Lauch (*Ger.*) Dweller near quicksand.

Lautenschlager (*Ger.*) One who played the lute; one who made, and sold, lutes.

Lauterbach, Lauterback (*Ger.*) Dweller near the clear or pure brook; one who came from Lauterbach (clear brook), the name of many places in Germany.

Laux (*Ger.*) Descendant of Laux, a shortened form of Lukas, German form of Luke (light).

Lauzon (*Fr., Swis.*) One who covers roofs, a slater; one who came from Lausanne, in Switzerland.

La Valle, Laval (*Fr.*) Dweller in the valley.

Lavan, La Van (*Ir., Heb.*) Descendant of little Flaitheamh (lord; ruler); variant of Laban, q.v.

La Vecchia, La Vecchio (*It.*) One of an advanced age; the old man.

La Velle (*Fr.*) Dweller in, or one from, the town.

Lavender (*Eng.*) One who washed or bleached flax, wool, cloth, etc.

Laver (*Eng.*) One who came from Laver (sea; flood), in Essex; dweller near the Laver (babbling brook), in the West Riding of Yorkshire; one who washes, the washer.

Laverty (*Ir.*) Descendant of Flaithbheartach (rich hero).

Lavery (*Ir.*) Descendant of the speaker or spokesman.

Laveson (*Sw.*) The son of Lave (companion).

La Vigne, Lavigne (*Fr.*) Dweller at, or near, the vineyard.

Laville (*Fr.*) One who came from La Ville (the town), the name of numerous places in France.

Lavin, Lavine, La Vine (*Ir.*) Grandson of Flaitheamhan (little ruler).

Law, Lawe (*Eng.*) Dweller at a burial-mound or hillock.

Lawder, Lawter, Lawther (*Scot.*) Variant of Lauder, q.v.

Lawford (*Eng.*) One who came from Lawford (Lealla's river crossing), the name of places in Essex and Warwickshire.

Lawhead (*Eng.*) Variant of Laughead, q.v.

Lawhorn (*Eng.*) One who came from Laughern (fox), in Worcestershire.

Lawler, Lawlor (*Ir.*) One who mumbled or was unable to speak plainly.

Lawless (*Eng.*) One deprived of the protection of the law, an outlaw.

Lawley (*Eng.*) One who came from Lawley (Lafa's grove), in Shropshire.

Lawn, Laun (*Eng.*) Dweller at a glade or grassy plain.

Lawrence (*Eng.*) Descendant of Lawrence (laurel, symbol of victory). This is the usual English spelling of the name.

Lawson, Laws (*Eng.*) The son of Law, a pet form of Lawrence (laurel, symbol of victory).

Lawton (*Eng.*) One who came from Lawton (enclosure on a hill), the name of villages in Cheshire and Herefordshire.

Lawyer, Lawman (*Eng.*) One who followed the legal profession, a lawyer.

Lax (*Eng., Ger.*) Dweller near the water; dweller at the sign of the salmon; one who fished for salmon.

Lay (*Eng.*) Dweller at a meadow or open place in a wood.

Laybourn, Layburn (*Eng.*) One who came from Leyburn (shelter by the stream), in the North Riding of Yorkshire.

Laycock (*Eng.*) One who came from Laycock (small stream), in the West Riding of Yorkshire.

Layfield (*Eng.*) One who came from Leafield (the open country), in Oxfordshire.

Layman (*Eng.*) An official declarer of the law, a lawyer; dweller by the wood or clearing in a wood.

Layne (*Eng.*) Dweller in an open tract of arable land sown in regular succession to prevent the ground from being too much exhausted.

Layton (*Eng.*) One who came from Layton (village on a stream; homestead where leeks are grown), the name of several villages in England.

Lazaar (*Syr.*) Descendant of Lazarus (help of God).

Lazar, Lazare, Lazarus (*Heb., Rus., Ukr., Fr.*) Descendant of Lazarus (help of God); or of Lazar, Slavic form of Lazarus; one who has leprosy, a leper.

Lazard (*Fr.*) Variant of Lazar, q.v.

Lazaro (*Sp.*) Descendant of Lazarus (help of God).

Lazaroff, Lazarov (*Bulg., Rus.*) The son of Lazar, Slavic form of Lazarus (help of God).

Lazauskas (*Lith.*) Dweller near the willow trees.

Lazenbury, Lazenby (*Eng.*) One who came from Lazenby (the freedman's village), in the North Riding of Yorkshire.

Lazzara, Lazzaro, Lazzari (*It.*) Descendant of Lazzaro, Italian form of Lazarus (help of God); one who begs, a beggar.

Le (*Chin.*) Pear tree.

Lea (*Eng.*) One who came from Lea (wood or clearing), the name of several places in England; dweller at, or near, the Lea (light), an English river.

Leabourne (*Eng.*) One who came from Leybourne (Lylla's stream), in Kent.

Leace (*Eng.*) One who heals others, a physician.

Leach, Leech (*Eng.*) Dweller at, or near, the Leach (stream), a river in

Gloucestershire; a bloodletter or physician.

Leacock (*Eng.*) Variant of Laycock, q.v.

Leadbetter (*Scot., Eng.*) One who beat and flattened lead for roofs, a lead beater; or who made and sold leaden vessels.

Leader (*Eng.*) One who drove a vehicle, a carter.

Leadley (*Eng.*) One who came from Leathley (grove on the slope), in the West Riding of Yorkshire.

Leaf, Leef, Leafe (*Eng.*) The beloved person.

Leahy, Leahey (*Ir.*) Grandson of Laochdha (heroic).

Leake, Leak, Leek (*Eng.*) One who came from Leake (stream), the name of several places, all on streams, in England; dweller near a stream or pool.

Leal (*Port.*) The loyal man.

Leaman, Leamon (*Eng.*) Dweller at an open place in the wood; the dear beloved man.

Leaming (*Eng.*) One who came from Leeming Beck (shining stream), in the North Riding of Yorkshire.

Leamy (*Ir.*) Descendant of Laomdha (bowed).

Lean (*Eng.*) Dweller by the pool; the thin, undeveloped person.

Leander (*Eng., Fr.*) Descendant of Leander (lion man).

Leaness, Leanes (*Eng.*) Dweller in the meadow on the cape or headland.

Leaper (*Eng.*) Variant of Leeper, q.v.; one who jumps or leaps around, a dancer; a courier or messenger.

Leaphart (*Ger.*) Descendant of Liebhart (dear, hard).

Lear, Leare (*Ir., Eng.*) Dweller by the sea; one who came from Lier (public pasture), in France.

Learmouth (*Eng.*) One who came from Learmouth (the mouth of the Lever river), in Northumberland.

Learned, Learnard (*Eng.*) Descendant of Leonard (lion, bold).

Leary (*Ir.*) Grandson of the keeper of calves.

Leas, Lease (*Eng.*) Dweller by the wood or clearing.

Leasure (*Eng.*) Dweller in, or near, the pasture; corruption of Lazar (help of God).

Leath, Leathe (*Eng.*) One who came from Leath (hillside), in Cumberland; dweller on the hillside.

Leather (*Eng.*) Descendant of Hleothor (melody; song); one who worked with leather.

Leatherbarrow, Leatherbury (*Eng.*) One who came from Leatherbarrow (Hleothor's hill), in Westmorland.

Leathers (*Eng.*) Descendant of Leodhere (people, army); one who worked with leather.

Leatherwood (*Eng.*) Dweller in, or near, a wood on the slope.

Leaventon (*Eng.*) One who came from Leavington (village on the Leven river), in the North Riding of Yorkshire.

Leavenworth (*Eng.*) Dweller at Leofwine's homestead.

Leavitt (*Eng.*) Variant of Levitt, q.v.

Leavy, Leavey (*Eng.*) Descendant of Leofwig (dear, battle).

Le Beau (*Fr.*) The handsome man.

Lebedenko (*Ukr.*) Son of the dweller at the sign of the swan.

Lebedev (*Rus.*) Dweller at the sign of the swan.

Lebenson, Lebensohn (*Ger., Heb.*) A literal translation of ben Hayyim, the son of Hayyim (life).

Leber (*Ger.*) Nickname for a butcher, a seller of liver.

Le Blanc (*Fr.*) The white-haired or light-complexioned man.

Le Blang (*Fr.*) Variant of Le Blanc, q.v.

Le Blond (*Fr.*) The person with fair or flaxen hair or complexion.

Lebovitz (*Cz.-Sl., Yu.-Sl.*) The son of Leyba (life).

Lebowitz (*Ger.*) Variant of Liebowitz, q.v.

Lebron (*Sp.*) One who raised large hares.

Le Brun (*Fr.*) One with brown hair or a dark complexion.

Lech (*Cz.-Sl.*) One of high birth or exalted rank, a noble.

Le Chien (*Fr.*) Dweller at the sign of the dog; one who raised and sold dogs.

Lechner (*Ger.*) Variant of Lehner, q.v.

Leckey, Leckie (*Scot.*) One who came from the barony of Leckie, in Stirlingshire.

Le Clair, Leclaire (*Fr.*) One who is very quick to act; one with a clear complexion.

Leclerc (*Fr.*) The clergyman; the learned man or scholar.

Le Compte, Le Comte (*Fr.*) The appointed employee of the Count; an advocate.

Le Corbusier (*Swis.*) One who made and sold baskets without handles or covers.

Ledbetter, Ledbeater (*Scot., Eng.*) One who beat and flattened lead for roofs, a lead beater; or who made and sold leaden vessels.

Leddy (*Ir.*) Grandson of Lideadha.

Lederer (*Eng., Ger.*) One who drove a vehicle, a carter; one who tanned leather, a tanner.

Lederhandler (*Ger.*) One who bought and sold leather goods.

Lederman, Ledermann (*Ger.*) One who tanned leather, a tanner.

Ledford, Leadford (*Eng.*) One who came from Lydford (ford at the Lyd; ford at the torrent), the name of places in Somerset and Shropshire; or from Leckford (grove by a river crossing), in Hampshire; dweller on a path leading across a stream.

Ledger (*Eng.*) Descendant of Leodegar (people, spear). St. Leger was a popular seventh century saint.

Ledgerwood (*Scot.*) One who came from Legerwood (Loedgar's wood), in Scotland.

Ledingham (*Eng.*) One who came from Leadenham (Leoda's homestead), in Lincolnshire.

Le Donne (*Fr.*) The given, a short form of Dieudonne (God given).

Le Doux (*Fr.*) One who came from Doux (spring; ravine), the name of several places in France; one with a sweet, pleasant disposition.

Ledsmyth (*Eng.*) One who worked in lead.

Le Duc (*Fr.*) One who aped the ways of a noble; one with the characteristics of an owl.

Ledwell (*Eng.*) One who came from Ledwell (swift stream), in Oxfordshire.

Ledwidge (*Eng.*) One who came from Ledwyche (Leoda's dairy farm), in Shropshire.

Ledwith (*Eng.*) Softening of Ledwidge, q.v.

Lee, Ley (*Eng., Chin.*) Dweller at the meadow, or open place in a wood; one who came from Lee, the name of various places in England; plums.

Leecan (*Eng.*) Dweller near an irrigation channel.

Leech (*Eng.*) One skilled in physic or in the art of healing, a physician.

Leedom (*Eng.*) One who came from Leadenham (Leoda's homestead), in Lincolnshire.

Leeds (*Eng.*) One who came from Leeds (district on the river), in Yorkshire.

Leemhuis (*Du.*) Dweller in a mud or clay house.

Leeming (*Eng.*) One who came from Leeming (radiant stream), a place on Leeming Beck in the North Riding of Yorkshire.

Leemon, Leman (*Eng.*) Dweller at, or in, a meadow or pasture; descendant of Leofman (dear, man).

Leeper (*Eng.*) One who made or sold baskets.

Leese, Lees, Leece, Leeser (*Eng.*) Dweller in the wood or clearing.

Leet (*Est.*) Dweller on, or near, a sandbank.

Leetch (*Eng.*) Sharpened form of Leech, q.v.

Leeuwen (*Du.*) One who came from Leeuwen (lions), the name of two places in Holland.

Le Fevre, Le Febvre, Le Febre, Le Febure, Le Feber (*Fr.*) The worker in metals, a smith. Also found with the F not capitalized.

Leff (*Pol., Rus., Ukr.*) Descendant of Leff, a pet form of Leon (lion).

Lefferts, Leffert (*Du.*) The son of Leffert (dear, hard).

Lefkowitz, Lefkovitz, Lefko, Lefkow (*Heb.*) Descendant of Lefko, Hebrew form of Levi (united).

Lefton (*Eng.*) One who came from Lifton (homestead on the Lew river), in Devonshire.

Leftridge (*Eng.*) Variant of Leftwich, q.v.; or of Liversidge, q.v.

Leftwich (*Eng.*) One who came from Leftwich (Leoftaet's dairy farm), in Cheshire.

Legacki (*Pol.*) One who came from Legawka, in Poland.

Le Gall (*Fr.*) The French immigrant from Gaul.

Legault (*Fr.*) Dweller by the woods.

Legendre (*Fr.*) One who married a man's daughter, a son-in-law; variant of Gendreau, q.v.

Leger (*Fr., Eng.*) Descendant of Leger (people, spear), a popular seventh century French saint.

Legg, Legge (*Eng., Nor.*) Dweller in, or near, the meadow; one who had unusual legs; descendant of Leggr (leg).

Leggett, Leggitt (*Eng.*) One who represented a state as ambassador or legate. See also Liggett.

Leggins (*Eng.*) Descendant of little Leggr (leg).

Le Gower (*Fr.*) One who came from Gohier (Godehar's estate), in France.

Le Grand, Legrand (*Fr.*) The large or fat man; the tall man.

Legree, Le Gree (*Fr.*) One who came from Gree (gravelly spot), in France; dweller in a gravelly place.

Legris (*Fr.*) One with gray hair or grizzled complexion.

Lehane, Lehan (*Ir.*) Grandson of little Liath (gray).

Lehmann, Lehman (*Ger.*) One who held land on feudal tenure, a vassal or villein.

Lehner, Lehn (*Ger.*) One who worked for a lord in a feudal estate.

Lehr (*Ger.*) Descendant of Lehr, a pet form of Hilarius (cheerful); dweller in a swampy place.

Lehrer (*Ger.*) One who came from Lehr (swampy waters), in Germany; one who taught others, a teacher.

Lehrfeld (*Ger.*) Dweller in a swampy area.

Leib, Leeb (*Ger.*) Dweller at the sign of the lion; descendant of Leib, a variant of Laybo (life).

Leiber (*Ger.*) One who flatters others; descendant of Leiber, a variant of Liudberct (people, bright).

Leibfried (*Ger.*) Descendant of Leibfried (lion, peace).

Leibowitz, Leibovitz (*Ger.*) Variant of Liebowitz, q.v.

Leibrand, Leibrandt (*Ger.*) Descendant of Leibbrand (lion, firebrand).

Leicht (*Ger.*) The thoughtless, careless, inconsiderate man.

Leichter, Leichner (*Ger.*) One who castrated swine, a gelder.

Leider (*Ger.*) One who tans leather, a tanner.

Leidner (*Ger.*) Dweller on the slope of a hill or mountain; one who came from Leiten (slope), the name of several places in Germany.

Leier (*Ger.*) One who made and sold lyres or other musical instruments.

Leifholt, Leifholtz (*Ger.*) Descendant of Levold (dear, rule).

Leigh (*Eng.*) A variant of Lee, q.v.

Leighly (*Ger.*) Dweller at, or near, a small clump of low trees or bushes; dweller on ground recently cleared.

Leighton (*Eng.*) One who came from Leighton (homestead where leeks were grown), the name of several places in England.

Leimberg (*Ger.*) One who came from Leimberg, in Germany.

Leimkuhler (*Ger.*) Worker in, or dweller by, the loam or clay pit.

Leinhauser (*Ger.*) One who made and sold linen shorts or hose; one who came from Leinhausen (place where

305

linen or hemp was produced; or where flax was stored), in Germany.

Leinheiser (*Ger.*) One who came from Leinhausen (place where linen or hemp was produced; or where flax was stored), in Germany.

Leininger (*Ger.*) One who came from Leiningen, in Germany.

Leinweber, Leineweber, Leinenweber (*Ger.*) One who wove linen cloth.

Leipert (*Ger.*) Variant of Leppert, q.v.

Leipziger (*Ger.*) One who came from Leipzig (linden wood), in Saxony.

Leis, Leiser, Leiss (*Ger.*) One who came from Leis (swamp), in Germany.

Leisner (*Ger.*) One who came from Leisenau (swampy meadow), in Germany.

Leister (*Ger., Eng.*) One who came from Leist (ridge), in Germany; one who came from Leicester (place on the Legra river), in Leicestershire.

Leitch (*Eng.*) Variant of Leech, q.v.

Leiter, Leiterman (*Ger.*) Dweller on a mountain slope or hillside.

Leith (*Scot.*) One who formerly resided in the town or territory of Leith (overflow), in Midlothian.

Leithead (*Eng.*) One with a small head.

Leitner (*Ger.*) Dweller on the hillside; one who came from Leiten (slope), the name of several places in Germany.

Leitz (*Ger.*) Descendant of Leitz, a pet form of Luizo (people).

Lejeune (*Fr.*) One who was younger than another with whom he was associated.

Leland (*Eng.*) One who came from Leyland (fallow land), in Lancashire; dweller at, or near, the fallow or untilled field.

Le Luna (*Sp.*) Descendant of Luna (moon).

Lemaitre (*Fr.*) The master or overseer.

Leman (*Eng.*) Variant of Leaman, q.v.

Lemar, Le Mar (*Fr.*) Dweller near the pool.

Le May (*Fr.*) One who sets up the maypole.

Lemberg, Lemberger (*Ger.*) One who came from Lemberg (lion mountain), the name of two places in Germany; or from Lemberg, in Austria.

Lemke (*Ger.*) Descendant of little Lem, a pet form of Lambico (land); descendant of little Lampo, a pet form of names beginning with Land (land), as Landbald and Landebert; one who came from Lemke, in Germany.

Lemoine (*Fr.*) One who was a male member of a religious order, a monk; nickname for one who acted like a monk.

Lemon, Lemmon, Lemond, Lemons (*Eng.*) Dweller at, or near, the Lemon (elm), a river in Devonshire; the lover or sweetheart.

Le Monnier (*Fr.*) The grinder of grain, a miller.

Lempert (*Ger.*) Variant of Lambert, q.v.

Lempriere (*Fr., Eng.*) One nicknamed The Emperor, probably from part taken in play or pageant.

Lemuell (*Eng.*) Descendant of Lemuel (dedicated to God).

Lenard, Lennard (*Eng.*) Descendant of Leonard (lion, bold).

Lenart, Lenartowicz (*Pol.*) Descendant of Leonard (lion, hard).

Lenet, Lenetsky (*Pol.*) Descendant of little Lena, a pet form of Helena (light).

L'Enfant (*Fr.*) Nickname for a small man, the child; attendant at a house for children.

Lengel, Lengl, Lengle (*Fr., Du.*) One who came from England, an Englishman; one who came from Lengel, in Holland.

Lengyel (*Hun.*) One who came from Poland, a Pole.

Lenhart, Lenhardt, Lenhard (*Ger.*) Variant of Leonhardt, q.v.

Lenihan, Lenehan, Lenahan (*Ir.*) Grandson of little Leannach (cloaked).

Lenk, Lenke (*Ger.*) Descendant of Lenk, a shortening of Lendeke, i.e., little Lando (land); the tall man.

Lennon, Lenon (*Ir.*) Grandson of Lennane (small coat).

Lennox, Lenox (*Scot.*) One who came from the district of Lennox (place of elms), in Dumbarton.

Lenoir, Le Noir (*Fr.*) One with a dark or swarthy complexion.

Lenormand (*Fr.*) The Norman or man from Normandy.

Lentine, Lentini, Lentino (*It.*) One who came from Lentini, in Italy; descendant of Lentino, pet form of Valentino (valorous or healthy).

Lento (*It.*) The slender, lean man; the slow man.

Lenton, Lentin (*Eng.*) One who came from Lenton (Leofa's homestead; settlement on the Leen river), the name of places in Lincolnshire and Nottinghamshire.

Lentsch (*Ger.*) Descendant of little Lanzo, a pet form of Lando (land).

Lenz, Lentz (*Ger.*) Descendant of little Lanzo, a pet form of Lando (land).

Leo (*Eng.*) Descendant of Leo (lion).

Leon, Leone (*Gr., Sp.*) Dweller at the sign of the lion; nickname for a brave person; one who came from Leon (lion), an ancient kingdom and region in Spain.

Leonard (*Eng., Ger.*) Descendant of Leonard (lion, bold).

Leonardi, Leonardo (*It.*) Descendant of Leonardo (lion, bold).

Leonhardt, Leonhard (*Ger.*) Descendant of Leonhard (lion, bold).

Leopardo, Leopardi (*It.*) Dweller at the sign of the leopard; the cruel, fierce man.

Leopold, Liepold (*Ger.*) Descendant of Leudbald or Leopold (people, bold); one who came from Leopolis, Latin name of Lvov, in Poland.

Le Page (*Eng.*) The male servant, the attendant.

Lepchuk, Lepczyk (*Ukr.*) The handsome or beautiful man.

Le Pera, Lepera (*It.*) One who raised and sold pears.

Lepoff, Lepofsky (*Rus.*) One who works with glue.

Lepore (*It.*) Dweller at the sign of the hare; nickname for one who is fleet-footed or vigilant.

Leppanen (*Finn.*) Dweller near an alder tree.

Lepper (*It.*) One who had leprosy, a leper.

Leppert (*Ger.*) Descendant of Liebrecht (people, pride); dweller at the sign of the leopard.

Lerario (*It.*) One charged with management of the exchequer.

Lerch, Lerche (*Ger.*) One with some characteristic of a lark; dweller at the sign of the lark; one who came from Lerche, in Germany.

Lerman (*Ger.*) One who came from Leer in Germany; one who taught others, a teacher.

Lerner (*Ger.*) One who came from Lern (to learn), in Germany; one learned in the Jewish Talmud.

Leroux (*Fr.*) One with red or reddish-brown hair or complexion.

Leroy (*Fr.*) One connected in some way with the king's household; one who played the part of a king in plays and pageants.

Lerro (*It.*) Badger, an epithet for a sound sleeper.

Le Sage, Lesage (*Fr.*) The wise or learned man.

Lesar (*Ger.*) Variant of Lazar, q.v.

Lesko (*Ukr., Rus.*) Descendant of little Les, a pet form of Oles, Ukrainian form of Alexander (helper of mankind).

Leslie, Lesley, Lessley, Lesslie (*Scot.*) One who came from Leslie (garden of hollies), in Aberdeenshire; descendant of Leslie (from the gray fort).

Lesniak (*Pol.*) Dweller in, or near, a forest.

Lesnick (*Pol.*) Custodian of a forest, a gamekeeper.

Lesniewski (*Pol.*) One who came from Lesniew(o) (forest), the name of places in Poland and Ukraine.

Lesnik (*Cz.*) A forest warden or gamekeeper.

Lesse, Less (*Eng.*) The smaller man, perhaps the younger man.

Lesseps (*Fr.*) Dweller at the hedge around the estate.

Lesser (*Heb.*) Descendant of Eliezer (my God has helped), or of Elazar, a form of Lazarus (help of God).

Lessing (*Ger.*) Custodian of a forest, a gamekeeper.

Lester (*Eng.*) One who came from Leicester (dwellers on Legra river), a town and county in England.

Le Strange (*Fr.*) One who was strange, a foreigner.

Lesueur, Le Sueur (*Fr.*) One who made shoes, a shoemaker.

Leszczynski (*Pol.*) Dweller near hazel bushes.

Letchworth (*Eng.*) One who came from Letchworth (homestead enclosure), in Hertfordshire.

Letford (*Eng.*) Variant of Ledford, q.v.

Letizia, Letizio (*It.*) Descendant of Letizio (joy or gladness).

Leto (*It.*) Descendant of Leto (happy).

Letourneau (*Fr.*) One thought to possess the qualities of a starling, such as being lively and quick.

Le Tourneur, Letourneux (*Fr.*) One who fashioned objects on a lathe, the turner.

Letson (*Eng.*) The son of Lett, a pet form of Letitia (joy or gladness).

Lett, Letts (*Eng.*) Descendant of Lett, a pet form of Letitia (joy or gladness).

Lettenberger (*Ger.*) Dweller on, or near, a clay hill; or on the Lettenberg, the name of two mountains in Germany.

Lev (*Pol., Cz.*) Dweller at the sign of the lion; one with lionlike qualities; a shortened form of Levi, q.v.

Leva (*Fr.*) One who collected taxes.

Levan (*Heb.*) Variant of Levin, q.v.

Levandowski, Levandoski (*Pol.*) Dweller in, or near, a meadow.

Levant (*Fr., It., Du.*) Dweller in the eastern house; one who came from the east, particularly the lands in the Eastern Mediterranean.

Leven (*Eng.*) One who came from Leven

(smooth), on the Leven river in the East Riding of Yorkshire; dweller near the Leven river.

Levenberg (*Ger.*) One who came from Lowenberg (lion mountain), in Germany.

Levengood (*Du.*) One who lives well.

Levens (*Eng.*) One who came from Levens (Leofa's headland), in Westmorland.

Levenson, Levensohn (*Ger.*) The son of Levy, indicating attachment to the tribe of the Levites.

Leventhal (*Heb.*) An artificial name from Leven, a variant of the Hebrew Levi (united) plus suffix denoting "valley."

Leventon (*Eng.*) One who came from Lavendon (Lafa's valley), in Buckinghamshire.

Lever, Levere (*Eng.*) One who came from Lever (bed of rushes), in Lancashire.

Leverenz, Leverence, Leverentz (*Ger.*) Descendant of Leverenz, a variant of Laurentius (laurel, symbol of victory).

Leverett, Leveritt (*Eng.*) Dweller at the sign of the young hare; one who hunted hares; nickname for one who was timid or fleet of foot.

Leverick (*Eng.*) Descendant of Leofric (dear, rule).

Leverington (*Eng.*) One who came from Leverington (village of Leofhere's people), in Cambridgeshire.

Levi (*Heb., Eng.*) Descendant of Levi (united).

Levick (*Eng.*) Descendant of Leofeca, a pet form of Leofa (dear).

Levin, Levine (*Heb., Fr.*) Descendant of little Levi (united); dweller at the vine or vineyard; one who sold wine.

Levinson (*Eng., Ger.*) The son of Leofwin (dear, friend); the son of little Levi (united).

Levinthal (*Heb., Ger.*) Little Levi, valley. See Leventhal.

Levito, Levitsky (*Ukr.*) Dweller at the sign of the lion.

Leviton, Levitan (*Heb.*) The large or

heavy man; dweller at the sign of the
leviathan.

Levitt, Levit (*Eng.*) One who came from
Livet (wolf cub), in Normandy; descendant of little Levi (united);
dweller at the sign of the wolf cub.

Levy, Levey, Levee (*Heb., Eng.*) Descendant of Levi (united).

Lew, Lewe (*Eng., Pol.*) Dweller on, or
by, a hill; or at the sign of the wolf;
or at the sign of the lion.

Lewandowski, Lewan (*Pol.*) One who
came from Lewandow (Lewand's settlement), in Poland near Warsaw.

Lewellen, Lewellyn (*Wel.*) Variant of
Llewellyn, q.v.

Lewin, Lewinski (*Pol., Heb.*) One who
came from Lewin (lion place), the
name of two places in Poland; variant of Levin, q.v.

Lewis (*Wel., Eng.*) Descendant of Lewis
(glory, battle; hear, fight; hale,
wide).

Lewitt (*Fr.*) The light-haired or light-
complexioned man.

Lewkowicz, Lewkowitz (*Heb.*) Descendant of Levi (united).

Lewy, Lewi (*Heb.*) Variant of Levy, q.v.

Lex (*Ger.*) Descendant of Lex, a pet
form of Alexius, in its turn a pet
form of Alexandros (helper of mankind).

Leyden, Leydon (*Eng., Du., Ger.*)
Dweller at the meadow valley; a
variant of Lydon, q.v.; one who
came from Leiden (people), in Holland; descendant of Liuto (people).

Leyer (*Ger.*) Variant of Leier, q.v.

Leyland (*Eng.*) One who came from
Leyland (untilled ground), in Lancashire.

Leypoldt (*Ger.*) Descendant of Leudbald
or Leopold (people, bold).

Leyrer (*Ger.*) One who played the lyre,
a minstrel.

Leys (*Eng.*) Dweller by the wood or
clearing.

L'Hommedieu (*Fr.*) The man God, probably referring to a servant of God,
a clergyman.

Li (*Chin., Kor.*) Plums; black.

Libby, Libbey, Libbe (*Scot., Ger.*) Descendant of Ibb, a pet form of Isobel
(oath to Baal); or of a form of
Elizabeth (oath of God); the beloved person.

Liberati, Liberato (*It.*) Descendant of
Liberato (deliverance).

Liberatore (*It.*) One who has been freed
or rescued.

Liberi, Liberio (*It.*) Descendant of
Liberio (free).

Liberman (*Ger.*) Variant of Lieberman,
q.v.

Liberto (*It.*) One who has been freed of
duty to the lord of the manor.

Libman (*Heb.*) Variant of Liebman, q.v.

Lichfield, Lickfield (*Eng.*) One who
came from Lichfield (gray wood
open country), in Staffordshire.

Lichtenberg, Lichtenberger (*Ger.*) One
who came from Lichtenberg (hill
free of trees), the name of several
places in Germany.

Lichtenstein (*Ger.*) One who came from
Lichtenstein (light stone), in Germany; or from Liechtenstein, the
principality between Switzerland
and Austria.

Lichter, Licht, Lichten, Lichte (*Ger., Du.*)
The light-complexioned, or blond
man.

Lichterman (*Du., Ger.*) One who lit
lamps, a lamplighter.

Lichtman (*Ger.*) The light complexioned
man; one who made and sold candles.

Lickstein (*Ger.*) One who came from
Lichtenstein, in Germany.

Licorish (*Eng.*) One who is eager for or
craves enjoyment of food; a dainty
man.

Liddell, Liddle (*Eng., Scot.*) One who
came from Liddel (Hlyde, that is,
loud, river valley), in Cumberland;
or from Liddel, in Roxburghshire.

Liddicoat (*Eng.*) One who came from
Littlecote (small cottage), the name
of places in Buckinghamshire and
Wiltshire.

Liddington (*Eng.*) One who came from
Liddington (homestead on the Hlyde

river), the name of places in Wiltshire and Rutlandshire.

Liddy, Lidie (*Ir.*) Descendant of Lideadh.

Lidstone (*Eng.*) One who came from Lidstone (Leofede's homestead), in Devonshire.

Lie (*Nor.*) Dweller near a shrine, holy place, altar of stones, a place set apart for the practice of pagan rites.

Lieb (*Ger.*) The dear, beloved person; descendant of Lieb, a pet form of Liubwin (dear, friend).

Liebel (*Ger.*) Descendant of Liebel, a pet form of Liebhard (beloved, hard).

Lieber (*Ger.*) Descendant of Lieber, a variant of Liubheri (dear, army); one who came from Liebau, in Germany; one who flatters others.

Liebergot, Libergott, Liebgott (*Ger.*) Descendant of Liebgott (loved, God; dear, God; beloved of God); one who habitually exclaimed "dear God."

Lieberman, Liebermann (*Ger.*) The beloved servant; the servant of Lieber (beloved, army); sometimes employed by Jews as a synonym for Eliezer (God has helped).

Lieberson (*Ger.*) The son of Lieber, a softened form of Liebert (people, bright).

Liebert (*Ger.*) Descendant of Liebert, a form of Liudberct (people, bright).

Liebetruth (*Ger.*) Descendant of Liubdrut (beloved, strength).

Liebl (*Ger.*) Descendant of Liebl, a pet form of Liebhard (beloved, hard).

Liebman, Liebmann (*Heb.*) Descendant of Liebman, an endearing form of Levi (united).

Liebowitz, Liebovitz (*Ger.*) Descendant of Lieb, a pet form of names beginning with Lieb (beloved), as Liupram and Liubwin.

Liebrecht (*Ger.*) Descendant of Liebrecht, a form of Liudberct (people, bright).

Liebtag (*Ger.*) Descendant of Liebtag, a form of Liopdag (beloved, day).

Lietz (*Ger.*) Descendant of Liuzo, a pet form of Liuto (people).

Lifschutz, Lifschultz, Lifschitz (*Ger., Cz.-Sl.*) One who came from Liebschutz, in Germany; or from Liebeschutz, in Czechoslovakia.

Liggett (*Eng.*) One who came from Lidgate (swing-gate), in Suffolk; dweller at a swinging gate; a variant of Leggett, q.v.

Liggins, Liggon, Liggons, Liggin (*Eng.*) Descendant of little Lig, a pet form of Ligulf (spear-shaft, wolf).

Light, Licht (*Eng., Ger.*) One who lived at the light place or clearing in the forest.

Lightbody (*Eng.*) A light, active person.

Lightbourne, Lightbown, Lightburn (*Eng.*) Dweller at the clear stream.

Lightfoot (*Eng.*) One who was fleet of foot; a speedy runner or messenger.

Lightford (*Eng.*) Variant of Lightfoot, q.v.

Lightner (*Ger.*) One who came from Lichtenau (light meadow), the name of several places in Germany; variant of Leitner, q.v.

Lightsey, Lightsy (*Ger.*) One who came from Lichtensee (swampy water), in Germany.

Lightstone (*Ger.*) One who came from Lichtenstein (castle), in Germany.

Lightwine (*Ger.*) Descendant of Liutwin (people, friend).

Ligon, Ligons (*Fr.*) One who came from Ligonne (Licunnus' place), in France.

Liland (*Nor.*) Dweller at the field where flax was grown.

Liles (*Eng.*) Dweller on the isle.

Lilienfeld (*Ger.*) Lily field.

Lilienstein (*Ger.*) Dweller on Lilienstein (lily stone), a hill in Germany.

Lilienthal (*Ger.*) Lily valley; one who came from Lilienthal (lily valley), the name of two places in Germany.

Lillard (*Eng.*) Descendant of Lillard, a pejorative form of Lily or Liley, pet forms of Elizabeth (oath of God).

Lille, Lill (*Dan., Est., Fr.*) The short or small man; one who cultivated flowers; dweller near where flowers grew; dweller on the island; one who came from Lille (the island), in France.

Lilleston (*Eng.*) One who came from Lillesdon (Lill's hill), in Somerset.

Lilly, Lillie, Lilley (*Eng.*) One who came from Lilley (meadow where flax was grown), in Hertfordshire; dweller where lilies grew.

Lilywhite, Lillywhite (*Eng.*) Dweller in, or near, a little meadow; one thought to be white as a lily; a name sometimes applied ironically to a chimney sweep.

Lima (*Sp.*) One who came from Lima (place of lime trees), in Spain.

Limbach (*Ger.*) One who came from Limbach (lime tree brook), the name of many places in Germany.

Limberg (*Ger.*) One who came from Limburg (Linden castle), in Germany.

Limeburner (*Eng.*) One who produces lime by burning limestone.

Limehouse (*Eng.*) One who came from Limehouse (lime kilns), in Middlesex.

Limerick (*Ir.*) One who came from Limerick (barren site), in Munster.

Limper (*Ger.*) Descendant of Limper, a softened form of Limpert, that is, Lintbrecht (serpent, bright).

Lin (*Chin.*) Forest.

Lincoln (*Eng.*) One who came from Lincoln (lake colony), in Lincolnshire.

Lind, Linde (*Eng., Sw., Est.*) Dweller by the lime tree; linden-tree; dweller at the sign of the bird.

Lindahl (*Sw.*) Linden tree valley.

Lindauer (*Ger., Swis.*) One who came from Lindau (lime tree meadow), the name of several places in Germany and Switzerland.

Lindberg, Lindbergh (*Sw.*) Linden tree mountain.

Lindblad (*Sw., Nor.*) Linden tree leaf.

Lindblom (*Sw.*) Linden tree flower.

Lindell (*Eng.*) One who came from Lindal (lime tree valley), in Lancashire.

Lindemann, Lindeman (*Ger.*) Dweller at, or near, the linden tree; dweller at, or near, the open court or assembly place.

Lindemuth (*Ger.*) The mild, gentle-mannered man.

Linden (*Sw.*) Dweller near the linden tree.

Lindenbaum (*Ger.*) Dweller near the linden tree.

Lindenberg (*Sw.*) Linden tree mountain.

Lindenheim (*Ger.*) One who came from Lindheim (homestead where linden trees grew), in Germany.

Lindenmeyer (*Ger.*) The farmer near the linden tree.

Lindensmith, Lindesmith (*Ger.*) The smith who lived or had his smithy by a linden tree.

Linder (*Eng.*) Dweller at, or near, a lime tree or linden tree.

Lindfors (*Sw.*) Linden tree waterfall.

Lindgren (*Sw., Nor.*) Linden tree branch.

Lindh (*Sw.*) Linden tree.

Lindholm (*Sw.*) Linden tree island.

Lindhorst (*Ger.*) Dweller in, or near, a thicket of linden trees.

Lindinger (*Ger.*) One who came from Linding (swamp), the name of two places in Germany.

Lindley (*Eng.*) One who came from Lindley (glade where flax was grown), the name of several places in England.

Lindner (*Sw., Ger.*) Dweller near the linden tree; one who came from Lindenau (meadow with linden trees), in Germany.

Lindo (*Sp.*) The gentle, gracious, handsome man.

Lindquist, Linquist (*Sw.*) Linden tree twig.

Lindsey, Lindsay (*Scot., Ir.*) The man from Limesay or Lindesey (lime tree; linden isle), in Normandy; grandson of the sailor.

Lindsley (*Eng.*) One who came from Lindley (lime wood), in the West Riding of Yorkshire.

Lindstrom (*Sw.*) Linden tree river.

Lindvall, Lindwall (*Sw., Nor.*) Linden tree mound.

Linehan, Linnehan (*Ir.*) Grandson of little Leannach (cloaked).

Lineman (*Eng.*) One who dresses and sells flax.

Linenberg (*Ger.*) One who came from Lindenberg (hill where linden trees grew), in Germany.

Linett, Linette, Linet (*Eng.*) Dweller at the sign of the linnet, a small finch; descendant of little Lina, a pet form of names so ending, as Adelina, Emelina, and Carolina.

Ling (*Chin.*) Forest.

Lingen (*Eng.*) One who came from Lingen (clear water brook), in Herefordshire.

Lingham (*Eng.*) One who came from Lingen (clear water brook), in Herefordshire. Lingham was an early spelling of the village name.

Lingle, Lingley (*Eng.*) One who came from Linley (grove where flax was grown), in Shropshire.

Linley (*Eng.*) One who came from Linley (meadow where flax was grown), in Shropshire.

Lingwood (*Eng.*) One who came from Lingwood (wood by a hill), in Norfolk.

Linham (*Eng.*) One who came from Lenham (Leana's manor), in Kent.

Link, Linke (*Eng., Du.*) Dweller at a ridge or bank separating strips of arable land on rising ground; one who was left-handed.

Linker (*Ger., Du.*) One who came from Linken (wet place), in Germany; one who was left-handed.

Linklater, Linkletter (*Scot.*) One who came from Linklater (heather-covered cliff), the name of several places in Orkney.

Linn, Linne (*Eng.*) Dweller at, or near, a pool or lake; dweller near a linden tree.

Linnaeus (*Sw.*) Latinized form of Linne, q.v.

Linnane, Linane (*Ir.*) Descendant of the young tall man.

Linne (*Sw.*) One who dealt in linen.

Linnell (*Eng.*) Descendant of Lionel (little Leon or lion).

Linsalata (*It.*) One who made and sold salads.

Linscott (*Eng.*) Dweller in the cottage by the linden trees.

Linsey (*Eng.*) Variant of Lindsey, q.v.

Linsk, Linsky (*Ukr.*) Descendant of Lina, a pet form of Lilian (lily).

Linthwaite (*Eng.*) One who came from Linthwaite (flax clearing), in the West Riding of Yorkshire.

Linton (*Eng.*) One who came from Linton (homestead of flax or lime trees), the name of various places in England.

Linvill, Linville (*Fr.*) One who came from Linivilla (Lennius' estate), now Ninville, in France.

Lion (*Fr., Eng.*) One who came from Lion (Lion's homestead), the name of several places in France; dweller at the sign of the lion.

Lionel (*Eng.*) Dweller at the sign of the little lion. See also Lyons.

Lionheart (*Eng.*) Nickname given to a bold, brave man. There was Richard the Lion-Hearted, King of England.

Lipford (*Eng.*) Dweller near a ford crossed by leaping.

Lipinski (*Pol.*) One who came from Lipno (place where linden trees grew), in Poland; dweller near linden trees.

Lipkin, Lipkins, Lipkind (*Heb.*) Descendant of Eliezer (the help of my God); or of Lipske, a pet form of Ahuvah (love).

Lipman, Lippman, Lippmann (*Ger.*) The servant of Lipp, a pet form of Philip (lover of horses).

Lipoff, Lipow (*Rus.*) Dweller near a linden tree.

Lipp, Lippe (*Ger.*) Descendant of Lipp, a pet form of Philippus (lover of horses); one who came from Lipp or Lippe (muddy place; bank of a river), the names of places in Germany.

Lipper (*Ger.*) One who came from Lippe or Lipp (muddy place; bank of a river), the names of several places in Germany.

Lippert (*Ger.*) Descendant of Liutperaht

(people, pride); dweller in a clay and straw hut.

Lippi, Lippo (*It.*) Descendant of Lippo, a pet form of Filippo, Italian form of Philip (lover of horses).

Lippincott (*Eng.*) Dweller in the cottage at the edge, or bank, or shore; one who lived in Lippa's cottage; one who came from Luffincott (cottage of Luhha's people), in Devonshire.

Lips, Lipps (*Du., Ger.*) Descendant of Lip, a pet form of Philip (lover of horses).

Lipscher (*Cz.-Sl.*) One who came from Libous (named after Queen Libousa), in Czechoslovakia.

Lipschitz (*Ger.*) Dweller near the shelter of the linden or lime trees.

Lipschultz, Lipschutz, Lipshultz (*Ger.*) One who came from Leobschutz, in Silesia.

Lipscomb, Lipscombe (*Eng.*) One who came from Letcombe (ledge in the valley), in Berkshire; or from Liscombe (enclosed hollow), in Buckinghamshire; dweller in Lipp's valley.

Lipsey (*Eng.*) Descendant of Lepsi, a variant of Leofsige (dear, victory).

Lipsitz (*Ger.*) One who came from Lipsitz, in Germany.

Lipsius (*Du.*) Latinized form of Lips, q.v.

Lipsky, Lipski, Lipske (*Rus., Pol.*) One who came from Lipsk (place of the lime trees), in Poland; dweller near a linden tree.

Lipson (*Ger.*) The son of Lip, a pet form of Philippus (lover of horses); Americanized version of Lipschultz, q.v.

Lipton (*Eng.*) One who came from Lepton (homestead in an abyss), in Yorkshire.

Liquori (*It.*) One who sold liquors.

Lis (*Pol.*) Dweller at the sign of the fox; one with the characteristics of a fox.

Lisa (*Eng., Ger.*) Descendant of Lisa, a pet form of Elisabeth (oath of God).

Lisbon, Lisboa (*Eng., Port.*) One who

came from Lisbon (fortress), the capital of Portugal.

Lisicki, Lisiecki (*Pol.*) One with foxlike characteristics.

Liska, Lisak (*Cz.-Sl.*) One who dwelt at the sign of the fox; one with some of the qualities of a fox.

Lisle (*Fr.*) One who came from Ile or Isle (island), the names of many places in France.

Lisowski (*Pol.*) One who came from Lisow(o) (fox), in Poland.

Liss, Lisse (*Pol.*) One who lived at the sign of the fox; one with some foxlike characteristic.

Lissner (*Ger.*) One who came from Lissa, the name of several places in Germany.

List (*Ger.*) Descendant of List, a pet form of Listhard (clever, strong).

Lista (*Pol.*) One who walked with a list or rolling gait.

Lister (*Eng., Ger.*) One who dyed cloth; one who came from Liste, in Germany.

Listman (*Ger., Eng.*) One versed in the magic arts, cunning and crafty; the prudent, sensible man; one who dyes or colors cloth.

Liston (*Eng.*) One who came from Liston (Leofsige's homestead), in Essex.

Liszewski (*Pol.*) The miserable, poor, wretched man.

Liszt (*Hun.*) One who dealt in flour, probably a producer of flour.

Litchfield (*Eng.*) One who came from Litchfield (hill slope), in Hampshire; sharpened form of Lichfield, q.v.

Lithgow (*Scot.*) One who came from Linlithgow (dear broad lake), former name of West Lothian, also capital city of West Lothian, in Scotland.

Litka (*Ukr.*) Metonymic for one who took care of calves.

Litt, Lit (*Eng.*) The small or short man.

Little, Littell (*Eng.*) The small or short man.

Littlefield (*Eng.*) Dweller in, or near, the small field or open place in a wood.

Littlejohn (*Eng.*) The small man named

John (gracious gift of Jehovah), used to distinguish him from other Johns.

Littlepage, Littlepaige (*Eng.*) The small male servant or attendant.

Littleton (*Eng.*) One who came from Littleton (small homestead), the name of various places in England.

Littlewood (*Scot., Eng.*) One who came from Littlewood (small wood), in Lanarkshire; dweller by the little wood or grove; one who came from Littleworth (small homestead), in Berkshire.

Littman, Littmann, Litman (*Ger., Eng.*) Descendant of Lit, a pet form of names beginning with Lito (unruly), as Litomir and Litoslav; the small or little man.

Litto (*It.*) One who made beds, a domestic servant.

Litton, Litten (*Eng.*) One who came from Litton (homestead on a torrent or turbulent river; burial ground), the name of several places in England.

Litwin, Litvin (*Pol., Eng.*) One who came from Lithuania; descendant of Leohtwin (bright, friend).

Litz (*Ger.*) Descendant of Litz, a pet form of names beginning with Leute (people), as Liutwin and Ludwig; dweller near a fence or hedge.

Litzau (*Ger.*) One who came from Litzau, in Germany.

Liu (*Chin.*) Willow; battle-ax.

Livanos (*Gr.*) The gray-haired or old man.

Lively, Liveley (*Eng.*) The active or lively man.

Livengood, Livergood (*Ger., Du.*) Americanization of German nickname for one who lived well; variant of Levengood, q.v.

Livermore (*Eng.*) One who came from Livermere (pool with thick water), in Suffolk.

Liverpool (*Eng.*) One who came from Liverpool (pool with thick water), in Lancashire.

Liversidge (*Eng.*) One who came from

Liversedge (Leofhere's ridge), in the West Riding of Yorkshire.

Livesay, Livesey, Livsey (*Eng.*) One who came from Livesey (island with a shelter), in Lancashire.

Livingood (*Ger.*) One who lives well.

Livingston, Livingstone (*Scot.*) One who came from the lands, now parish, of Livingston (abode of Leofwine), in West Lothian.

Lizzi, Lizzo (*It.*) One who fished for, and sold, mackerel.

Ljungquist (*Sw.*) Heather twig.

Llamas (*Sp.*) One who came from Llamas (tongues of fire; flame), the name of several places in Spain.

Llanas, Llanes (*Sp.*) One who came from Llanas or Llanes (prairies), the names of towns in Spain.

Llewellyn, Llewellin (*Wel.*) Descendant of Llewellyn (lion-like).

Llorens (*Sp.*) Descendant of Llorente, Spanish form of Lawrence (laurel, symbol of victory); one who came from Llorens (laurel), in Spain.

Lloyd, Lloyds (*Wel.*) From *llwyd* meaning both brown and gray, referring to the complexion or hair.

Loacker (*Nor.*) Dweller in, or near, the meadow; or cultivated field.

Loane (*Ir., Eng.*) Grandson of Luan (warrior; champion); variant of Lane, q.v.

Lobb (*Eng.*) The squat, clumsy fellow; one who came from Lobb (spider), the name of places in Devonshire and Oxfordshire.

Lobdell (*Eng.*) Dweller in the deep hollow infested by spiders.

Lobel, Lobell (*Fr.*) One who flatters or deceives another; dweller at the sign of the wolf cub.

Lo Bello (*It.*) One with an attractive physique, handsome.

Lo Bianco, Lobianco (*It.*) The light-complexioned or white-haired man.

Lo Biondo (*It.*) One with white hair or very light complexion.

Lobley (*Eng.*) One who came from Lobley (wood where the branches were low), in the West Riding of Yorkshire.

Lo Casale (*It.*) One who came from the hamlet or group of houses.

Locascio, Locashio (*It.*) One who made and sold cheese; descendant of Cassius (vain).

Loch (*Scot.*) Dweller by a lake.

Lochhead (*Scot.*) One who came from Lochhead (head of the lake), the name of several places in Scotland.

Lochman (*Eng.*) Dweller near the lake; variant of Lockman, q.v.

Lochner (*Ger.*) One who came from Lochen (gap), the name of five places in Germany.

Lockard (*Eng.*) Variant of Lockhart, q.v.

Locke, Lock, Locks (*Eng.*) One who lived by an enclosure of some kind; one who had charge of a barrier in a river.

Lockerbie, Lockerby (*Scot.*) One who came from Lockerbie (Locard's homestead), in Dumfriesshire.

Lockett (*Eng.*) Dweller by, or in, a small enclosure.

Lockhart (*Scot.*) Descendant of Locard (enclosure, small); one in charge of domestic animals, a herdsman.

Lockhead, Lockheed (*Scot.*) Dweller at the head of the lake.

Lockie (*Eng.*) Descendant of little Loc (stronghold); or of little Loc, a pet form of Locard (enclosure, small).

Lockings (*Eng.*) One who came from Locking (Locc's people), in Somerset.

Lockley (*Eng.*) One who came from Lockerley (the shepherd's grove), in Hampshire.

Lockman (*Eng.*) One who made and sold locks; the servant of Loc (stronghold).

Locksmith (*Eng.*) One who made and sold locks.

Lockwood (*Eng.*) One who came from Lockwood (enclosed wood), in Yorkshire.

Lockyer (*Eng.*) One who made and sold locks, a locksmith.

Loden (*Eng.*) Dweller near the Lodden river in Dorset.

Loder, Loader (*Eng.*) Dweller by the road, or watercourse; one who loads or unloads a vessel in port, a stevedore.

Lodge (*Eng.*) Dweller in the cottage or hut.

Loeb, Loebl (*Ger.*) One who came from Lobau (dear meadow), in Germany; dweller at the sign of the lion.

Loeffler (*Ger.*) One who made and sold spoons.

Loesch, Loesche (*Ger.*) One who made charcoal.

Loeschhorn (*Ger.*) One who cleaned lamps; one who made and sold leather horns used as drinking utensils.

Loewe, Loew (*Ger.*) Variants of Lowe, q.v.

Loewenstein (*Ger.*) One who came from Lowenstein (lions stronghold), the name of several places in Germany.

Loewenstern (*Ger.*) Lions, star.

Loewy, Loevy (*Ger.*) Dweller at the sign of the lion; one with lion-like characteristics; descendant of Levi (united).

Lofton (*Eng.*) One who came from Lufton (Luca's homestead), in Somerset.

Loftsson (*Ice.*) The son of Loftur.

Loftus, Lofthouse, Loftis (*Eng.*) One who came from Lofthouse or Loftus (house with an upper floor), both places in Yorkshire; one who lived in a house with an upper story.

Logan, Login (*Scot., Ir.*) One who came from Logan (little hollow), in Ayrshire; grandson of the little weak person.

Loggia (*It.*) Dweller near an open-columned structure, an archway or balcony.

Loggins, Loggin (*Scot.*) One who came from Logan (little hollow), in Scotland; dweller near a small ravine.

Logie, Loggie (*Scot.*) One who came from Logie (hollow), the name of many places in Scotland.

315

Lo Giudice (*It.*) One who acted as the judge.

Logsdon, Logsden (*Eng.*) One who came from Longsdon (long ridge), in Staffordshire.

Logue (*Ir.*) Grandson of little Laogh (calf); descendant of the servant of St. Aedh.

Lohman, Lohmann (*Ger.*) One who came from Lohe (place of tan bark), the name of numerous places in Germany; dweller in a woodland, thicket or near brushwood; or on land cleared of trees.

Lohmeyer (*Ger.*) The farmer who lived in the woods; one who tanned leather; one who operated a dairy farm.

Lohmiller, Lohmuller (*Ger.*) One who operates a tanning mill for crushing tan bark.

Lohr (*Ger.*) One who made leather, a tanner; one who came from Lohr (tannery), the name of several places in Germany.

Lohwasser (*Ger.*) Dweller near the swampy water; or near the water operating the tanning mill.

Loiseau (*Fr.*) Dweller at the sign of the bird; one with birdlike characteristics.

Loizzo, Loizzi (*It.*) One with the characteristics of a snail.

Loman (*Eng.*) Dweller near the Loman (smooth) river, in Devonshire.

Lomax, Lomas (*Eng.*) One who came from Lomax (flat alluvial land by a pool), in Lancashire.

Lombard (*Eng.*) One who came from Lombardy (country of the long-bearded men), in Italy.

Lombardo, Lombardi (*It.*) One who came from Lombardia (country of the Lombardi), a province in Italy; a shopkeeper, from the fact that many from Lombardia set up shop in Sicily.

Lomberg (*Ger.*) Dweller on the Lomberg, a ridge in Germany.

Lombo (*It.*) One with large hips or haunch.

Lo Monaco (*It.*) The nun, a nickname applied because of resemblance to a nun.

Londergan (*Ir.*) Variant of Lonergan, q.v.

London (*Eng., Heb.*) One who came from London (place of Londinos; or from a tribal name), in England; one who was learned in Talmudic matters.

Lonergan (*Ir.*) The little, strong, fierce man.

Loney (*Ir.*) Variant of Looney, q.v.

Long (*Eng., Fr.*) The tall man.

Longacre, Longaker (*Eng.*) Dweller near a large acre, that is, a measure of land which a yoke of oxen could plow in a day.

Longbine (*Ger.*) One with long legs.

Longbotham, Longbottom (*Eng.*) Dweller in the large valley.

Longbrook (*Eng.*) Dweller near the large stream.

Longchamps (*Fr.*) One who came from Longchamps (large field), the name of several places in France.

Longden (*Eng.*) One who came from Longden (big hill), in Shropshire.

Longenecker (*Ger., Swis.*) One who formerly resided in Longenegg, in Switzerland.

Longfellow (*Eng., Fr.*) The tall partner or companion; one who came from Longueville (great town), in France.

Longfield (*Eng.*) One who came from Longfield (long field), in Kent; one who lived at, or in, the long, narrow field.

Longley (*Eng.*) Dweller in, or near, the extensive meadow or open place in a wood; variant of Langley, q.v.

Longmire (*Ger., Eng.*) The tall overseer or head servant; dweller at the large marsh.

Longmore (*Eng.*) Dweller on, or near, the extensive wet wasteland.

Longo, Longi (*It., Sp.*) The tall man.

Longsdorf (*Ger.*) One who came from Langsdorf (long village), in Germany.

Longshaw (*Eng.*) Dweller in, or near, the large copse or grove; one who came from Longshaw (large wood), in Derbyshire.

Longshore (*Eng.*) Dweller on the river shore.

Longsmith (*Eng.*) The smith who was tall, probably taller than another with whom he was associated.

Longstaff (*Eng.*) Nickname for the bailiff or other official who carried a long staff.

Longstreet (*Eng.*) Dweller on a long paved road, especially an ancient Roman road.

Longstreth (*Eng.*) One who came from Langstroth (big marsh), in the West Riding of Yorkshire.

Longwell, Longwill (*Eng.*) Dweller near the large spring or stream.

Longwith (*Eng.*) One who came from Langwith (big ford), the name of places in Derbyshire, Nottinghamshire, and the East Riding of Yorkshire.

Longwood (*Eng.*) Dweller in, or near, the big wood or forest.

Longworth (*Eng.*) One who came from Longworth (large homestead), the name of places in Berkshire and Lancashire.

Lonsdale (*Eng.*) One who came from Lonsdale (valley of the Lune, health-giving, river), in Lancashire.

Looby (*Ir.*) Grandson of Lubach (crooked; deceitful).

Look (*Du., Eng.*) Dweller in, or near, a field where leeks were grown; descendant of Luke (light).

Looker (*Eng.*) One who looks after something, a watcher or herdsman.

Loomis, Lomas (*Eng.*) One who came from Lomax (flat alluvial land by a pool), in Lancashire.

Looney (*Ir.*) A warrior or soldier; grandson of Luineach (merry or jovial; champion).

Loonstyn (*Du.*) Dweller near a leaden stone.

Loos, Loose, Loosen, Looser (*Ger., Fr., Du.*) One who came from Loose,

Loosen, Loos, or Lohsa, in Germany; descendant of Laus, a pet form of Nicolaus (people's victory); one who came from Loos, in France; the crafty or cunning person.

Lopata, Lopatin, Lopat (*Pol., Ukr.*) One who worked with a shovel or spade.

Lopatin (*Rus.*) Metonymic for one who works with a shovel.

Lopatka (*Pol.*) One who made and sold shovels.

Lopatynskyj (*Ukr.*) One who worked with a shovel.

Loper (*Ger.*) One who carried communications, a messenger; one who came from Loop (mire), in Germany.

Lopes (*Port., Sp.*) The son of Lope or Lupe (wolf).

Lopez, Lopaz (*Sp.*) The son of Lope or Lupe (wolf).

Lo Piccolo (*It.*) The small man.

Lo Presti, Lo Presto (*It.*) The priest.

Lorber (*Ger.*) One who sold foodstuffs, a grocer.

Lorch (*Ger.*) One who came from Lorch, in Wurttemberg.

Lord (*Eng.*) One who was master or head of the household; the lord's servant; nickname given to one assuming superior rank.

Lordan, Lorden (*Eng.*) The lazy person or vagabond.

Lore (*Fr.*) One who came from Lore (Laurius' estate), in France.

Lorel (*Eng.*) A worthless person, a rogue.

Lorenc (*Hun.*) Descendant of Lorencz, Hungarian form of Lawrence (laurel, symbol of victory).

Lorenz, Lorentz (*Ger.*) Descendant of Lorenz, German form of Lawrence (laurel, symbol of victory).

Lorenzen, Lorentzen (*Ger.*) One who came from Lorenzen, in Schleswig; descendant of Lorenzen, a variant of Laurentius (laurel, symbol of victory).

Lorenzo, Lorenzi (*Sp., It.*) Descendant of Lorenzo, Spanish and Italian form of Lawrence (laurel, symbol of victory).

317

Lorillard (*Fr.*) One with big ears.

Lorimer (*Eng.*) One who made bridle bits and spurs.

Loring (*Eng.*) One who came from Lorraine (dominion of King Lothar II), in France; dweller near a laurel tree; descendant of Loren, a pet form of Lawrence (laurel, symbol of victory).

Loro (*Sp.*) The tawny or dark brown-complexioned man.

Lorry, Lory (*Eng.*) Descendant of little Lar or Lor, pet forms of Lawrence (laurel, symbol of victory).

Lo Russo (*It.*) The man with red hair or ruddy complexion.

Lo Sasso (*It.*) One who came from Lo Sasso (the rock), a province of Rome.

Losch, Losche (*Ger.*) Variant of Loesch, q.v.

Loschiavo (*It.*) The slave.

Lose, Loseman, Losemann (*Ger.*) Descendant of Lose, a pet form of Ludwig (glory, battle; hear, fight; hale, wide).

Loth (*Fr.*) Descendant of Loth, French form of Lot (covering; protection).

Lothian (*Scot., Eng.*) One who came from Lothian, a district in South Scotland and Northern England.

Lothrop, Lowthorp (*Eng.*) One who came from Lowthorpe (Logi's farm), in Yorkshire.

Lotman (*Ger.*) Variant of Lottmann, q.v.

Lotridge (*Eng.*) One who came from Latteridge (ridge with road or stream), in Gloucestershire.

Lott, Lotts (*Eng.*) Dweller on the apportioned share of land, i.e., the allotted land.

Lotter (*Ger.*) A ne'er-do-well or one good-for-nothing; a juggler, tumbler, or buffoon; descendant of Lothar (fame, people).

Lottmann, Lottman (*Ger.*) One who came from Lotte (muddy water), in Germany.

Lotz (*Ger.*) Descendant of Lotze, a pet form of Hludizo (clear, plain).

Loucks (*Eng.*) Dweller near an enclosure

or bridge; descendant of Luke (light).

Loud (*Eng.*) Dweller near the Loud (the loud one), a river in Lancashire.

Louden, Loudon (*Scot.*) One who came from Loudoun (flame hill), in Ayrshire.

Loudenslager (*Ger.*) One who played the lute.

Louderback (*Ger.*) Dweller near the clear or pure brook; one who came from Lauterbach (clear brook), the name of many places in Germany.

Lougee (*Fr.*) One who came from Louge (Laudus' estate), in France.

Lough (*Scot.*) Dweller by a lake.

Loughead, Lougheed (*Scot.*) Dweller by the head or end of the lake.

Loughlin (*Ir.*) The grandson of Lochlainn (lake land); dweller near a lake or sea-inlet; grandson of Lachtna (gray); grandson of the servant of St. Secundinus.

Loughnane (*Ir.*) Descendant of Lachtnan (little gray one).

Loughney (*Ir.*) Descendant of Lachtna (gray).

Loughran (*Ir.*) Grandson of Luchairean (little bright one).

Loughrey, Loughry, Loughery (*Eng.*) Descendant of Lowrie, a pet form of Lawrence (laurel, symbol of victory).

Loughridge (*Eng.*) One who came from Loughrigg (ridge where leeks grew), in Westmorland.

Louie (*Chin.*) Thunder.

Louis (*Fr.*) Descendant of Louis (glory, battle; hear, fight; hale, wide).

Lounsbury, Lounsbery (*Eng.*) One who came from Londesborough (Lothen's fort), in Yorkshire.

Loup, Loupe (*Fr.*) Dweller at the sign of the wolf.

Lourie (*Eng., Scot.*) Descendant of Laurie, a pet form of Lawrence (laurel, symbol of victory); variant of Lowery, q.v.

Loux (*Ger.*) Variant of Lux, q.v.

Lovatt, Lovat (*Eng.*) Dweller near the

Lovat (gliding), a river in Buckinghamshire and Bedfordshire.

Love (*Eng.*) Descendant of Love or Lufa, an Early English given name; dweller at the sign of the wolf; one with the characteristics of a wolf.

Lovecchio (*It.*) The old man.

Loveday (*Eng.*) Descendant of Loveday (a name given to a child born on a loveday, i.e., a day appointed for reconciliations).

Lovejoy (*Eng.*) One who craved pleasure.

Lovelace (*Eng.*) Descendant of Lovelace (love token); nickname for an unfriendly person.

Lovelady (*Eng.*) One who makes love to, or flirts with, several women; a woman of easy virtue.

Loveland (*Eng.*) One who came from Leaveland (Leofa's land), in Kent.

Loveless (*Eng.*) One who is void of love; or is unlovable; one who loves a lass.

Lovell, Lovel (*Eng.*) Descendant of little Love (wolf; love).

Lovely (*Eng.*) The lovable person; one who came from Leathley (grove on the slope), in the West Riding of Yorkshire; dweller at, or near, Lufa's clearing or wood.

Loveman (*Eng.*) The servant of Love; the dear man or sweetheart; descendant of Leofman (beloved man).

Lovemore (*Eng.*) Dweller in a moor infested by wolves.

Lovenstein (*Heb.*) An artificial name from Lowi, a variant of Levi (united), plus suffix denoting "stone."

Lo Verde, Loverde, Loverdi (*It.*) Dweller at the green place; the young man.

Lovering (*Fr., Eng.*) One who came from Louvergny (Lovernios' estate), or from Auvergny (Arvernus' homestead), the names of places in France; descendant of Leofhere (beloved, army).

Lovett, Lovitt (*Eng.*) Descendant of little Love (love; wolf).

Lovgren (*Sw.*) Leaf, branch.

Loving, Lovinger (*Eng.*) One who came from Louvain (lions), in Belgium.

Lowden (*Scot.*) One who came from Loudoun (flame hill), in Ayrshire.

Lowder (*Eng.*) Variant of Lowther, q.v.

Lowe, Low (*Ger., Eng.*) One with lion-like characteristics, bold; dweller at the sign of the lion; dweller at the mound, or burial mound, or heap of stones; dweller at the sign of the wolf; descendant of Low, a pet form of Lawrence (laurel, symbol of victory).

Lowell (*Eng.*) Dweller at the sign of the little wolf.

Lowenberg (*Ger.*) One who came from Lowenberg (lion mountain), in Germany.

Lowenstein, Lowenstine (*Ger.*) Variant of Loewenstein, q.v.

Lowenthal (*Ger.*) One who came from Lowenthal (lion valley), in Germany.

Lower (*Eng.*) Dweller at the small hill or burial mound.

Lowery (*Scot.*) Descendant of Laurie, pet form of Lawrence (laurel, symbol of victory).

Lowes, Lowis (*Scot.*) One who came from Lowes (lake), in Selkirkshire.

Lowman (*Eng.*) Dweller at the small hill or burial mound; descendant of Leofmann (dear man).

Lownes, Lowndes (*Eng.*) Dweller in the glade or on a grassy plain.

Lowney (*Ir.*) Grandson of Luanach (warrior).

Lownsbury (*Eng.*) One who came from Londesborough (Lothen's fort), in the East Riding of Yorkshire.

Lowry, Lowrey, Lowrie (*Scot., Eng.*) Descendant of Lowry, a pet form of Lawrence (laurel, symbol of victory).

Lowther (*Eng., Scot.*) One who came from Lowther (foaming river), in Westmorland; one who came from Lowther (canal), in Dumfriesshire.

Lowy, Lowey (*Mx.*) The son of the devotee of St. Dhubhthaigh.

Loy (*Ger.*) Descendant of Loy, a short form of Eloy, popular form of Elegius (the chosen), patron saint of

319

metalworkers; one who came from Loy, in Germany.

Loyd (*Wel.*) The gray man, from Welsh *llwyd* (gray; brown).

Loyola (*Sp.*) One who came from the castle of Loyola, in Spain.

Lozowski (*Pol.*) Dweller near the willow trees.

Lubar, Lubaroff, Lubarsky (*Rus.*) Descendant of Lubar (lover).

Lubeck (*Ger.*) One who came from Lubeck (Liuby's estate), in Germany.

Lubell, Lubel (*Pol.*) One who came from Lubow or Lublin, in Poland.

Lubert, Lubart, Luber (*Ger.*) Descendant of Lubert (people, bright).

Lubin, Lubinski, Lubinsky (*Pol., Rus.*) One who came from Lubin (place where lupine grew), in Poland; dweller near where lupine (herbs of the pea family) was grown for fertilizer.

Lublin, Lubliner (*Pol., Ger.*) One who came from Lublin, in Poland.

Luboff, Lubow (*Rus.*) Descendant of the loved one.

Luby (*Pol., Rus., Ukr.*) The dear or beloved man.

Luca (*It.*) Descendant of Luca, Italian form of Luke (light).

Lucarini (*It.*) Dweller at the sign of the bramble finch; descendant of little Luca; Italian form of Luke (light).

Lucas, Lukas (*Eng., Pol., Fr.*) Descendant of Lucas or Luke (light).

Lucca, Lucci (*It.*) Descendant of Luca, Italian form of Luke (light).

Lucchesi, Lucchese (*It.*) One who came from Lucca, in Italy.

Luce (*Fr.*) Descendant of Luce, a pet form of Lucius (light); or of Louis (glory, battle; hear, fight; hale, wide).

Lucenko, Luchanko (*Ukr.*) The son of Luc, a form of Lucius (light).

Lucente, Lucenti (*It.*) Descendant of Lucenti, a name given to a child born on Epiphany, that is, January 6th, the anniversary of the coming of the wise men to Christ at Bethlehem, Twelfth day.

Lucero (*Sp.*) Descendant of Lucero (light; star; the morning star). Lucero is a name of the planet Venus.

Lucey, Lucie, Lucy (*Fr.*) Descendant of little Luc, a pet form of Lucas (light).

Luchs (*Ger.*) Dweller at the sign of the lynx; one with sharp eyesight.

Lucia (*It.*) Descendant of Lucia (light).

Luciano, Luciani (*It.*) Descendant of Luciano, Italian form of Lucian (light), the name of a fourth century saint.

Lucido (*Sp.*) Descendant of Lucidio (clear).

Lucifero (*It.*) One who played the part of the devil in play or pageant.

Luck, Lucke (*Eng.*) Descendant of Luck or Luke (light).

Luckenbach (*Ger.*) One who came from Luckenbach (marshy stream), in Germany.

Lucker (*Eng.*) One who came from Lucker (marsh where sandpipers were found), in Northumberland.

Luckett (*Eng.*) Descendant of little Luck, an English variant of Luke (light).

Luckey, Lucky, Lukey (*Eng.*) Descendant of little Luck or Luke (light).

Luczak (*Pol.*) One who fought with a bow and arrow, a bowman.

Luddington, Ludington (*Eng.*) One who came from Luddington (village of Luda's people; or of Lulla's people), the name of places in Lincolnshire, Northamptonshire, and Warwickshire.

Ludlow (*Eng.*) One who came from Ludlow (hill by the rapid), in Shropshire.

Ludolph, Ludolf (*Ger.*) Descendant of Ludolf (fame, wolf).

Ludwig (*Ger.*) Descendant of Ludwig (fame, warrior).

Ludwin (*Ger.*) Descendant of Liutwin (people, friend).

Luebke (*Ger.*) Descendant of little Luppo (people), a pet form of names beginning with Leute (people), as Liudberct and Liutbrand.

Lueck, Luecke (*Ger.*) Descendant of Luecke, a pet form of names begin-

ning with Leute (people), as Liudman, Liuderich, and Liutwin; or of
Liudiko (little people).

Leuders (*Ger.*) Descendant of Liuthari
(people, army).

Luedtke, Ludtke (*Ger.*) Descendant of
Liudiko (little people), a pet form of
Liuto (people).

Luff (*Wel.*) Descendant of Luff, a variant of Love or Lufa (love; wolf).

Lufkin (*Eng.*) Descendant of little Luf,
a pet form of Love or Lufa (love;
wolf).

Lugo (*Sp.*) One who came from Lugo
(light place), a province in Spain.

Luis (*Port., Sp.*) Descendant of Luis,
Portuguese and Spanish form of
Louis (glory, battle; hear, fight; hale,
wide).

Lukacs (*Hun.*) Descendant of Lukacs,
Hungarian form of Luke (light).

Lukas (*Pol.*) Descendant of Luke (light).

Lukasik, Lukasek (*Pol.*) Descendant of
little Lukasz, Polish form of Luke
(light).

Lukaszewski, Lukasiewicz (*Pol.*) The son
of Lukasz (light).

Lukens, Luken (*Eng., Ger.*) Descendant
of little Luke (light).

Lukes, Luke (*Eng.*) Descendant of Luke
(light).

Lukin, Lukins (*Eng.*) Descendant of little Luke (light); or of little Love
(love; wolf).

Lukoff (*Rus.*) Descendant of Luke
(light).

Lull (*Ger.*) One who lulls others to
sleep; the simple, foolish man.

Lum, Lumb (*Eng.*) Dweller near the
deep pool; one who came from
Lumb (pool), in Lancashire; dweller
at the sign of the lamb.

Lumley (*Eng.*) One who came from
Lumley (pool by the grove), in
Durham.

Lummis, Lummas (*Eng.*) Variant of
Loomis, q.v.

Lumpkin, Lumpkins (*Eng.*) Descendant
of little Lam or Lump, pet forms of
Lambert (land, bright).

Lumpp, Lump, Lumpe (*Eng.*) Dweller

at, or near, a deep pool or wooded
valley; descendant of Lump, a pet
form of Lambert (land, bright).

Lumsden (*Scot.*) One who came from
Lumsden (Lumm's valley), in Berwickshire.

Luna (*It.*) Dweller at the sign of the
moon; a nickname for a bald head.

Lund, Lunde (*Dan., Nor., Sw., Eng.*)
Grove; one who came from Lund
(grove), the name of several places
in England, and of a city in Sweden;
dweller in a grove.

Lundberg, Lundborg, Lundeberg (*Sw.*)
Grove mountain.

Lundell (*Sw.*) Grove valley.

Lundgren, Lundgreen, Lungren (*Sw.*)
Grove branch.

Lundin, Lundeen, Lundine (*Sw.*) One
who came from Lund (grove), the
name of a city and several villages
in Sweden.

Lundmark (*Sw.*) Grove field.

Lundquist (*Sw.*) Grove twig.

Lundstrom (*Sw.*) Grove river.

Lundy, Lundie (*Eng.*) One who came
from Lundy (puffin), an island in
Devonshire.

Lung (*Fr.*) One who butchered animals
and sold lights; one who sold tripe.

Luning (*Ger.*) Dweller at the sign of the
sparrow; one thought to have the
characteristics of a sparrow.

Lunn (*Eng., Scot.*) The strong, fierce
man; dweller at a marsh; dweller at
the sign of the blackbird; a corruption of Lund, q.v.

Lunney (*Ir.*) Grandson of Luineach
(champion).

Lunnon (*Eng.*) Variant of London, q.v.

Lunsford (*Eng.*) Dweller near the crossing of the river Lune, in England.

Lunsk, Lunsky (*Rus.*) Dweller at the
sign of the moon.

Lunt (*Eng.*) One who came from Lunt
(grove), in Lancashire.

Luongo (*It.*) The tall man.

Lupe (*Eng.*) Dweller on a steep slope or
place to jump over.

Lupescu (*Rom.*) The son of Lup, Romanian form of Lupe (wolf).

Lupinacci (*It.*) Dweller near where honeysuckle grew.

Lupino, Lupina, Luppino (*It.*) Dweller at the sign of the little wolf.

Lupo, Lupa, Lupi, Luppo (*It.*) A nickname, referring to the wolf, given to one who was voracious or fraudulent; dweller at the sign of the wolf.

Lupowitz (*Pol.*) The son of Lupus (wolf).

Lupton (*Eng.*) One who came from Lupton (Lubba's homestead), in Westmorland.

Lurch (*Ger.*) Variant of Lerch, q.v.

Lurie, Luria (*It.*) One who came from Luria (sorrowful), in Italy.

Lurton (*Eng.*) One who came from Larton (village on clayey soil), in Cheshire.

Lusby (*Eng.*) One who came from Lusby (Lutr's homestead), in Lincolnshire.

Lusch, Luscher (*Ger.*) Dweller where sedge grew.

Luscombe (*Eng.*) One who came from Loscombe (pigsty in the valley), in Dorset; or from Lyscombe (reed valley), in Dorset.

Lush, Luss (*Ir., Eng., Scot., Ger.*) One who came from Lusk (cave), in Ireland; descendant of Hlossa; one who came from Luss (herb), in Dumbartonshire; dweller in, or near, a marsh.

Lusk (*Pol., Ukr., Scot.*) One who came from Luck, a city in medieval Volhynia, in Western Ukraine; or from Lusk (cave), in Dublin.

Lustbader (*Ger.*) Pleasure baths.

Luster, Lust (*Nor., Ger.*) One who came from Luster, in Norway; or from Lust (pleasure), in Germany.

Lustgarten (*Ger.*) One who came from Lustgarten (pleasure garden), in Germany.

Lustig (*Ger.*) The jolly, merry, or gay man; one who came from Lustig, in Germany.

Luter, Lutter, Luterman (*Eng.*) One who played the lute.

Lutes (*Fr.*) One who came from Lutz (Lucius' homestead), in France.

Lutey (*Eng.*) Dweller by the calf house.

Luther (*Ger., Eng.*) Descendant of Lothair (famous, warrior); one who played the lute.

Luthi, Luthy, Luthin (*Swis.*) Descendant of Luthi, a Swiss form of Leuthold (people, rule).

Luthran (*Ir.*) Variant of Loughran, q.v.

Lutley (*Eng.*) One who came from Lutley (small grove), in Staffordshire.

Lutman (*Ger.*) Descendant of Liudman (people, man).

Luton (*Eng.*) One who came from Luton (homestead on the Lea river), in Bedfordshire.

Lutterbeck (*Ger.*) One who came from Lutterbeck (dirty stream), in Germany.

Luttrell (*Eng.*) Descendant of little Luther (hear, people; famous, battle); the little lute player.

Lutz, Lutze, Lutzer (*Ger.*) Descendant of Luizo, a pet form of names beginning with Leute (people), as Liutbald, Liutgard and Liutwin; one who came from Lutz (small place), in Germany.

Lux (*Ger.*) Descendant of Luks, a pet form of Lucas (light).

Lyall, Lyell, Lyells (*Eng., Scot.*) Descendant of Lionel (little lion).

Lyburn (*Eng.*) One who came from Leyburn (shelter by the stream), in the North Riding of Yorkshire; or from Leybourne (Lylla's stream), in Kent.

Lycett (*Ir.*) Variant of Lysaght, q.v.

Lycos (*Gr.*) Dweller at the sign of the wolf; one thought to possess the qualities of a wolf.

Lydon, Lyden, Lyddon (*Eng.*) One who came from Lydden (pasture with a shelter), in Kent.

Lydy, Lyddy (*Ir.*) Grandson of Lideadh.

Lyeth (*Eng.*) One who came from Lythe (slope), in the North Riding of Yorkshire.

Lyford (*Eng.*) One who came from Lyford (ford where flax grew), in Berkshire.

Lyles, Lyle (*Fr.*) Dweller on the small island.

Lyman, Lynan, Lymon (*Eng., Ir.*) One who came from Lyham (homestead by a wood), in Northumberland; grandson of Laidghnean (snow birth).

Lynam (*Eng.*) One who came from Lyneham (enclosure where flax was grown), in Oxfordshire.

Lynch, Lynk (*Eng.*) Dweller at the ridge or bank which separated strips of arable land often on a slope or rising ground.

Lynd, Lynde (*Eng., Sw.*) Variant of Lind, q.v.

Lyndall, Lyndell (*Eng.*) One who came from Lindal (lime tree valley), in Lancashire.

Lyng, Lynge (*Eng.*) One who came from Lyng (hill), the name of places in Norfolk and Somerset.

Lynn, Lyne, Lynne (*Eng.*) Dweller at, or near, a pool or lake.

Lyons, Lyon (*Eng., Scot.*) Descendant of Leon (lion); dweller at the sign of the lion. Jacob's reference to Judah as a lion (Gen. 49:9) has caused this name to be adopted by many Jews.

Lys, Lyss (*Rus., Ukr.*) Dweller at the sign of the fox; one with some of the qualities of a fox.

Lysaght, Lysaught (*Ir.*) The son of the strange youth; or of the loaned or adopted youth.

Lysenko (*Ukr.*) The son of the bald-headed man.

Lyster (*Eng.*) Variant of Lister, q.v.

Lythgoe, Lythgow (*Scot.*) Variant of Lithgow, q.v.

Lytle, Lyte, Lyttle, Lytell (*Eng.*) The small or short man.

Lytton (*Eng.*) One who came from Litton (village on a roaring stream; burial ground), the name of several places in England.

Lytvynenko (*Ukr.*) The son of the Lithuanian.

Lytwyn (*Ukr.*) One who came from Lithuania.

Lytwynenko (*Ukr.*) The son of the Lithuanian.

Ma (*Chin.*) Horse.

Maag (*Du.*) One with a prominent stomach, a fat man; one who was a kinsman to another.

Maar (*Du.*) One who brought news; one habitually hesitant, continually saying "but," "yet."

Maas (*Du., Bel.*) Dweller at, or near, the Meuse river in Western Europe; one who made chain mail used as defensive armor.

Mabie, Mabey (*Eng., Scot.*) Descendant of little Mab, a pet form of Mabel or Amabel (lovable); one who came from Mabie, in Kirkcudbrightshire.

Mabin, Maben, Mabon (*Eng., Scot.*) Descendant of little Mab, a pet form of Mabel or Amabel (lovable); or of Maban (son).

Mable, Mably, Mabley (*Eng.*) Descendant of Mabel or Amabel (lovable).

Mabrey, Mabry (*Fr.*) Descendant of my daughter-in-law.

Mabson (*Eng.*) The son of Mab, a pet form of Mabel or Amabel (lovable).

McAdams, McAdam, Macadams, Macadam (*Scot., Ir.*) The son of Adam (red earth).

McAdoo, McAddo (*Ir.*) The son of Cudabh (black hound).

McAfee, McAffee, Macaffee (*Ir.*) The son of Dubhshithe (black man of peace).

McAleer (*Ir., Scot.*) The son of Giollaodhar (the pale youth); variant of McClure, q.v.

McAleese (*Ir., Scot.*) The son of the servant of Jesus.

McAllister, Macallister, Macalister (*Scot.*) The son of Allister or Alistair, Scottish forms of Alexander (helper of mankind).

Macalpine, Macalpin (*Scot.*) The son of Ailpean (elf).

Macaluso (*It.*) One who came from Macala, in Italy.

McAnally, Macannally (*Scot., Ir.*) The son of the chief bard or physician; or of the poor man.

McAnany, McAneny, McAnneny, Mc-

Aneney (*Ir.*) The son of Cuaonaigh (hound of the fair).

McAndrew, McAndrews (*Ir., Scot.*) The son of Andrew (manly).

McAnulty (*Ir.*) The son of the Ulidian (native of East Ulster).

McArdle (*Ir.*) The son of Ardghal (high valor).

Macarthur, McArthur (*Ir., Scot.*) The son of Arthur (valorous; noble; bear man; Thor's eagle).

Macas (*Lith.*) One who prepared unleavened bread.

McAtee (*Ir.*) The son of the scholar.

McAteer (*Scot., Ir.*) Variant of McIntyre, q.v.

Macaulay, Macauley, Macalley, McAuley, McAulay (*Ir., Scot.*) The son of Amalghaidh (relic of the gods); or of Amhlaoibh, an Irish form of Olaf (ancestor's relic).

McAuliffe (*Ir.*) The son of Olaf (ancestor's relic).

McAvoy (*Ir.*) The son of the yellow-haired lad.

Macbain (*Scot.*) The son of Bheatha (life).

Macbeth, Macbean (*Scot.*) Descendant of Macbeatha (son of life; a religious person), a personal name.

McBrady (*Ir.*) The son of Bradach (spirited).

McBrearty (*Ir.*) The son of Muircheartach (navigator).

McBride, Macbride (*Ir.*) The son of the servant of St. Brigid.

McBryan, McBrien (*Ir.*) The son of Brian (hill).

McCabe, Maccabe (*Ir.*) The son of the hooded one.

McCafferty (*Ir.*) The son of Eachmharcach (horse rider).

McCaffrey, Maccaffray, McCaffrie (*Ir.*) The son of Godfrey (God's peace); the son of Eachmharcach (horse rider).

McCahey (*Ir.*) The son of the horseman or cavalry man.

McCain (*Ir.*) The son of Eoin, an Irish form of John (gracious gift of Jehovah).

McCall, Maccall, McColl (*Ir.*) The son of Cathal (battle mighty); or of Cathmhaol (battle chief).

McCalley (*Ir.*) Variant of McAuley, q.v.

McCallion (*Scot.*) The son of Cailin, the Scottish form of Colin (people's victory).

McCallum, Maccallum, Maccollom (*Ir., Scot.*) The son of the tender one, i.e., one who was like a dove.

McCambridge, Maccambridge (*Scot.*) The son of Ambrois (immortal).

McCandless, McCandlis (*Ir.*) The son of Cuindleas.

McCann (*Ir.*) The son of Annadh (a storm).

McCardell, McCardle (*Scot.*) The son of Ardghal (super valor).

McCarney (*Scot.*) The son of Cearnach (victorious).

McCarrick (*Scot., Ir.*) The son of Cucharraige (hound of the rock).

McCarron, McCarren (*Ir.*) The son of little Ciar (black).

McCarry, McCarrie (*Ir.*) The son of Fearadhach (manly).

McCarter (*Ir., Scot.*) Variant of MacArthur, q.v.

McCarthy, Maccarthy, McCarty (*Ir.*) The son of Carthach (loving).

McCartney (*Ir.*) The son of little Art (stone; bear).

McCaskill, Maccaskell (*Scot.*) The son of Askell (sacrificial caldron).

McCaughey (*Ir.*) The son of Eachaidh (rich in cattle).

McCauley, McCawley, Maccauly, Macallay (*Scot., Ir.*) The son of Amlaib, a Scottish form of Olaf (ancestor's relic); the son of Amhalghaidh, an ancient Irish personal name.

McCausland (*Scot.*) The son of Absalom (father's peace).

McCaw (*Scot., Ir.*) The son of Adhamh, Gaelic form of Adam (red earth).

McCay (*Scot.*) Variant of McKay, q.v.

McChesney (*Scot., Ir.*) The son of Cheyne; or of Jean, the Norman-French form of John (gracious gift of Jehovah).

Macchi (*It.*) Dweller in, or near, a thicket.

Macchiavelli (*It.*) One who stains vellum.

McClafferty (*Ir.*) The son of Flaithbheartach (bright lord).

McClain (*Ir.*) The son of the servant of St. John.

Macclamroch (*Scot.*) The son of the ready-handed or dexterous man; also, possibly, son of the ruddy-handed, or bloody-handed, person.

McClarren, McLauren (*Scot.*) Variant of McLaren, q.v.

McClary (*Ir.*) The son of the clerk.

Macclay (*Scot., Ir.*) The son of Donnshleibhe (Brown of the hill); the son of the physician.

McClean (*Scot.*) Variant of MacLean, q.v.

McCleary, McCleery, McClery (*Scot.*) The son of the clerk.

MacClellan, McClellan, MacClelland, Macleland (*Scot.*) The son of the servant of St. Faolan, Fillan, or Felan (little wolf).

McClenaghan, McClenahan (*Ir., Scot.*) The son of the servant of Onchu (mighty hound), an Irish saint; the son of little Leannach (cloaked; mantled).

McClendon, McClenton (*Ir.*) The son of little Leannach (cloaked; mantled).

McClennen, McClennon (*Ir., Scot.*) The son of the servant of Finnan, an Irish saint; variant of McClenaghan, q.v.

McClernan, McClernon (*Ir., Scot.*) The son of the servant of St. Ernan.

McClintock (*Scot.*) The son of the follower or servant of Findan (little fair one), a Scottish saint.

McClinton, McClenton (*Scot.*) Variant of McClintock, q.v.

McCloskey, McClosky (*Ir.*) The son of Bloscadh.

McCloud (*Scot.*) Variant of McLeod, q.v.

McCloy (*Scot.*) The son of Lewie, a pet form of Lewis (glory, battle; hear, fight; hale, wide).

McClung (*Scot.*) The son of the ship, a seaman.

McClure, Macclure, McCleur (*Scot.*) The son of the servant of Odhar.

McClurg (*Scot.*) The son of Lurg; or of Cleireach (clerk).

McCluskey, McClusky (*Ir.*) The son of Bloscadh.

McCole (*Scot., Ir.*) The son of Coll; the son of the servant of St. Comgall or Comhghaill.

McColgan (*Ir.*) The son of Colga.

McCollough (*Scot.*) Variant of McCullough, q.v.

McCollum, McCollom, McCollam (*Ir., Scot.*) The son of the tender one, i.e., one who was like a dove.

McComb, McCombe, McCombes, McCombs (*Scot.*) The son of Tom, a short form of Thomas (a twin).

McConaghy (*Scot., Ir.*) The son of Donnchadh (brown warrior).

McCone (*Scot., Ir.*) The son of Eoghan (well-born).

McConnell, Macconnell (*Ir.*) The son of Domhnall (world mighty).

McConomy (*Ir.*) The son of Cumidhe (hound of Meath).

McConville (*Ir.*) The son of Conmhaol (high chief).

McCook (*Ir., Scot.*) The son of Hugh (spirit; mind); the son of the cook.

McCool (*Scot., Ir.*) Variant of McCole, q.v.; the son of Dhubgall (black stranger).

McCoombe (*Scot.*) Variant of McComb, q.v.

McCord (*Ir., Scot.*) The son of Muircheartach (navigator).

McCorkle, McCorkel, McCorkell (*Scot.*) The son of Thorcull or Thorketill (Thor's kettle).

McCormick, McCormack, Maccormack, Maccormick, McCormac (*Ir.*) The son of Cormac (charioteer; son of Corb), the name of eight saints.

McCourt, McCort (*Scot.*) The son of Muircheartach (navigator).

McCoy, Maccoy (*Ir.*) The son of Aodh (fire).

McCracken, McCrackin (*Ir.*) The son of Neachtan (the pure one).

McCray, McCrea, Maccrea, McCree (*Ir., Scot.*) Descendant of MacRaith (a given name, meaning son of grace or prosperity).

McCready, McCreedy (*Ir.*) The son of Riada.

McCreary, McCreery (*Ir.*) The son of Hrothrekr, Norse form of Roderick (fame, rule).

McCreavy (*Ir.*) The son of Riabhach (grayish).

McCrory (*Ir., Scot.*) The son of Ruaidhri (red king).

McCrossen, McCrossin, McCrosson, Mc-Crossan (*Ir., Scot.*) The son of the rhymer.

McCrudden (*Ir.*) The son of Rodan (spirited).

McCue (*Ir.*) The son of Aodh (fire).

McCullen, McCullan (*Scot., Ir.*) The son of Coilin, a pet form of Nicholas (people's victory).

McCulley (*Scot.*) Softened form of Mc-Culloch, q.v.

McCullough, McCulloch, McCullock, McCullagh (*Scot.*) The son of Cullach (boar).

McCullum (*Ir.*) The son of Colum (dove).

McCune (*Ir.*) The son of Eoghan (well-born).

McCunney, McCunny (*Ir.*) The son of Connadh.

McCurdy, Maccurdy (*Ir.*) The son of the navigator.

McCusker, McCosker (*Ir.*) The son of Oscar (Os, spear); the son of the champion.

McCutcheon, Maccutcheon, McCutchan, McCutchen (*Scot.*) The son of Hutcheon, diminutive pet form of Hugh (spirit; mind).

McDade, McDaid (*Ir., Scot.*) The son of little David (commander; beloved; friend).

McDaniel, McDaniels, Macdaniel, Macdaniels (*Ir.*) The son of Domhnall (world mighty).

Macdavid (*Ir.*) The son of David (commander; beloved; friend).

McDermott, Macdermott, McDermut, Macdermid (*Ir.*) The son of Diarmaid (the freeman; common man); the son of Diarmuit or Dermot (free from envy).

McDevitt (*Ir.*) The son of David (commander; beloved; friend).

McDonald, Macdonald, McDonnell, McDonell, Macdonell (*Scot., Ir.*) The son of Donald (dark or brown-haired stranger); the son of Domhnall (world mighty).

McDonough, Macdonough, McDonagh (*Ir.*) The son of Donnchadh (brown warrior; strong warrior).

MacDougall, McDougall, Macdougal, McDougal, McDougald (*Scot., Ir.*) The son of Dougal (black stranger).

McDowell, MacDowell, McDowall, Macdowall (*Ir.*) The son of the dark foreigner.

MacDuff (*Scot.*) The son of Dubh (dark).

McDuffie, McDuffy (*Scot.*) The son of Dubhshithe (black man of peace).

Mace (*Fr.*) One who came from Mace or Macey (Macius' estate), the names of places in France.

McEachern, McEachin (*Scot.*) The son of the house lord.

McElfrish, McElfresh (*Scot.*) The son of the servant of Bricius, a Gaulish saint.

McElhatton (*Ir.*) The son of the servant of St. Catan.

McElhenney, McElhinney (*Ir.*) The son of the servant of Kenneth (comely; handsome).

McElligott (*Ir.*) The son of little Ulick, a pet form of William (resolution, helmet).

McElroy, MacElroy (*Ir.*) The son of the red youth.

McElwee (*Ir., Scot.*) The son of Giollabuidhe (yellow lad).

McEntee (*Ir.*) The son of the scholar.

McEntire, McEntyre (*Scot.*) Variant of McIntyre, q.v.

Macerato, Macera (*It.*) Dweller in, or near, a bowl-like depression.

McErlain, McErlane, McErlean (*Scot., Ir.*) The son of the lector or reader.

Macevicius (*Lith.*) One who prepared unleavened bread.

McEvoy (*Ir.*) The son of the yellow-haired lad.

McEwen, McEwan, MacEwan (*Scot., Ir.*) The son of Eoghan (well-born).

Macey (*Fr., Eng.*) One who came from Macey (Macius' estate), in France.

McFadden, MacFadden, McFaden, McFayden, McFadyen (*Scot., Ir.*) The son of little Pad, a pet form of Patrick (noble or patrician).

MacFall, McFalls (*Scot.*) Variant of MacPhail, q.v.

MacFarland, MacFarlane, MacFarlan (*Scot., Ir.*) The son of Parlan or Partholon (sea waves).

Macfee, Macfie (*Scot.*) The son of Dubhshithe (the black man of peace).

McFeeley, McFeely (*Ir.*) The son of Fithcheallach (chess player).

McFeeters (*Ir.*) The son of Peter (a rock).

McFetridge (*Scot.*) The son of Peadrus, a Gaelic form of Peter (a rock).

McGann, McGan (*Ir.*) The son of Annadh (a storm).

McGarrigle (*Ir.*) The son of Fearghal (super valor).

McGarrity (*Ir.*) The son of Aireachtach (member of a court or assembly).

McGarry, McGary (*Ir.*) The son of Fearadhach (manly).

McGarvey (*Ir.*) The son of Gairbhith.

McGeary (*Ir.*) The son of Gadhra; or of Pearadhach (manly).

MacGee, McGee, Magee (*Ir.*) The son of Aodh (fire).

McGeehan, McGehean, McGehan (*Ir.*) The son of Gaoithin, a pet form of Maolghaoithe (chief of the wind).

McGettigan (*Ir.*) The son of Eitigein.

McGhee, McGhie (*Scot.*) The son of Aodh (fire).

MacGibbon (*Scot.*) The son of little Gib, a pet form of Gilbert (pledge, bright).

McGill (*Ir.*) The son of the foreigner; a shortened form of some surname commencing with MacGiolla (son of the servant of . . .).

Macgillicuddy, Macgillycuddy (*Ir.*) The son of the servant, or devotee, of Mochuda, an early Irish saint of Lismore.

Macgillivray, McGillvray, McGilvray, Macgilvra, McGilvery (*Scot.*) The son of Gillebhrath (servant of judgment or doom).

McGinley (*Ir.*) The son of Fionnghal (fair valor).

McGinn, Macgenn (*Ir.*) The son of Fionn (fair).

McGinnis, Macginnis (*Ir.*) The son of Aonghus (one-choice).

McGinty (*Ir.*) The son of Fionnachta (fair snow).

McGirl, McGerl (*Ir.*) The son of Fhearghail (man of valor).

McGlade (*Scot.*) The son of Leod (ugly).

McGlinchey, McGlinchy (*Ir.*) The son of Loingseach (belonging to a fleet).

McGlinn, McGlynne (*Ir.*) The son of Flann (ruddy; red).

McGlone, McGloin (*Ir.*) The son of the servant of St. John (gracious gift of Jehovah).

McGoldrick, Macgoldrick (*Ir., Scot.*) The son of Ualgharg (proud and fierce; hot-tempered).

McGonagle, McGonigle (*Ir.*) The son of Congail.

McGorry, Macgorrie (*Scot.*) The son of Goraidh, Scottish form of Godfrey (God's peace).

McGough (*Ir.*) The son of Eochaidh (rich in cattle).

McGovern, Macgovern (*Ir.*) The son of little Samhradh (summer).

McGowan, Macgowan, McGowen (*Ir., Scot.*) The son of the smith or worker in metals.

Macgrady (*Ir.*) The son of Bradach (spirited).

McGrail (*Ir.*) The son of Niall (champion).

McGrane, McGrann (*Scot.*) The son of

Rayny, a pet form of Reginald (counsel, power; might, power).

McGrath, Macgrath (*Ir.*) Descendant of MacRaith (son of grace or prosperity, the full form being a given name).

McGraw (*Ir.*) Variant of McGrath, q.v.

McGreal (*Scot., Ir.*) Variant of McNeil, q.v.

MacGregor, McGregor, McGregory (*Scot.*) The son of Gregory (watchful).

McGrew (*Scot.*) The son of the brewer.

McGriff (*Ir.*) The son of Griff, a pet form of Griffin (fierce lord).

McGrogan (*Ir.*) The son of Gruagan, a pet form of Gruag (hair of the head); or of Grug (fierceness).

McGrory (*Ir.*) The son of Ruadhri (red king).

McGruder, Macgrudder (*Scot.*) The son of the brewer.

McGuckin (*Scot.*) Variant of McGugan, q.v.

McGuffey, McGuffie (*Scot., Ir.*) The son of Cobhthaigh (victorious).

McGugan, McGuigan (*Scot.*) The son of Eogan (well-born).

McGuinn (*Ir.*) The son of Conn (reason; freeman).

McGuinness, McGuiness (*Ir.*) The son of Aonghus (one-choice).

McGuire, Macguire (*Ir.*) The son of the pale, or light-complexioned, man.

McGurk (*Scot.*) The son of Corc (heart).

Machado (*Sp., Port.*) One who made and sold hatchets; or who used a hatchet in his work.

McHale, Machale (*Wel., Ir.*) The son of Howel (eminent).

McHenry (*Ir.*) The son of Henry (home rule).

Machugh, McHugh (*Ir., Scot.*) The son of Aodh (fire).

MacHutchin (*Scot.*) The son of little Hutch, a pet form of Hugh (spirit; mind).

McHutchison (*Scot.*) The son of the son of Hutch, a pet form of Hugh (spirit; mind).

MacIan (*Scot.*) The son of Ian, a Scottish form of John (gracious gift of Jehovah).

Macias (*Lith.*) Variant of Macas, q.v.

Maciejewski (*Pol.*) Descendant of Maciej, a pet form of Mateusz, Polish form of Matthew (gift of Jehovah).

McIlhenny, McIlhinney (*Ir.*) The son of the servant of St. Canice.

Macilroy (*Scot., Ir.*) Variant of McElroy, q.v.

McIlvaine, McIlvain, McIlwain (*Scot.*) The son of the servant of St. Beathan.

Macindoe (*Scot.*) The son of black John (gracious gift of Jehovah).

McInerney, McInerny (*Ir.*) The son of the steward of church lands.

Macinnis, McInnis, Macinnes, McInnes, Maginnis (*Scot.*) The son of Innes (islet), q.v.; the son of Angus (one-choice).

Macintaylor (*Scot.*) The son of the tailor.

McIntosh, Macintosh, Mackintosh (*Scot.*) The son of the chief or leader.

Macinturner (*Scot.*) The son of the turner.

McIntyre, MacIntyre, McIntire (*Scot., Ir.*) The son of the carpenter or worker in wood; one who was free, a freeman.

MacIsaac, McIsaac, Macisaacs (*Scot.*) The son of Isaac (he who laughs; the laugher).

Maciulis (*Lith.*) Descendant of little Matas, Lithuanian form of Matthew (gift of Jehovah).

MacIver, McIver, Macivor (*Scot.*) The son of Ivar or Iver (archer).

Mack, Mac (*Scot., Ir., Ger.*) Descendant of Mack or Mac (son), an abbreviation of one or another of the numerous Gaelic Mac- names, especially Macnamara; or of Mack, an Irish pet form of Magnus (great); one who acts as a border guard or frontier watchman.

McKain, McKane (*Scot.*) Variant of MacIan, q.v.

McKay, Mackay (*Scot.*) The son of Aoidh or Aodh (fire).

McKean (*Scot.*) Variant of MacIan, q.v.

McKee (*Scot.*) Variant of McKay, q.v.

McKeever (*Scot.*) Variant of MacIver, q.v.

Mackell, Mackel (*Scot.*) The son of Cathal (battle mighty).

McKelvey, McKelvie (*Scot.*) The son of Burdhe (yellow lad).

McKendrick, McKendry (*Scot.*) The son of Henry (home, rule).

McKenna, Mackenna, McKenney, Mc-Kenny (*Ir.*) The son of the man beloved by Aodh (fire), the fire god.

MacKenzie, McKenzie (*Scot.*) The son of Coinneach (fair one).

McKeogh, McKeough (*Ir.*) The son of Eochaidh (rich in cattle).

McKeon, McKeown, McKeone (*Ir.*) The son of Eoghan (well-born), or of Eoin, an Irish form of John (gracious gift of Jehovah).

Mackerell, Mackrell (*Scot.*) The son of Fearghal (super choice).

McKernan (*Ir.*) The son of little Tighearna (a lord).

McKesson, Mackessan (*Scot.*) The son of Kessan (spear).

MacKettrick (*Scot.*) The son of Sitric (true victory).

MacKey, McKee, Mackey, Mackie (*Ir.*) The son of Aodh (fire); or of Macdha (manly or virile).

Macki (*Finn.*) Variant of Maki, q.v.

McKibben, McKibbin (*Scot.*) Variant of MacGibbon, q.v.

McKiernan (*Ir.*) Variant of McKernan, q.v.

Mackiewicz (*Pol.*) The son of Maciej, a Polish form of Matthew (gift of Jehovah).

McKim (*Scot.*) The son of Sim, a pet form of Simon or Simeon (gracious hearing; hearkening; snub-nosed).

Mackin (*Ir.*) Grandson of Macin (little son; youth).

McKinley, Mackinley, McKinlay, Mackindlay (*Scot.*) The son of Finlay (fair hero).

McKinney, Mackinney, McKinnie, Mc-Kinny (*Ir.*) The son of Cionaodh (fire sprung).

Mackinnon, McKinnon (*Scot.*) The son of Findgaine (fair-born).

McKinsey (*Scot.*) Variant of MacKenzie, q.v.

McKinstry (*Scot., Ir.*) The son of the traveler.

Mackirdie (*Scot.*) The son of the sea ruler.

McKissick, McKissock (*Ir., Scot.*) The son of Iosaig, Gaelic form of Isaac (he who laughs; the laugher).

McKittrick (*Scot.*) Variant of Mac-Kettrick, q.v.

Mackle (*Ir.*) Variant of Magill, q.v.

Mackler (*Ger.*) Variant of Meckler, q.v.

Macklin, Mackling (*Ir.*) The son of Flann (the red; ruddy).

McKnight, Macknight (*Ir.*) The son of the knight.

Macko (*Pol.*) Descendant of Macko, a pet form of Maciej, Polish form of Matthew (gift of Jehovah).

Mackowiak (*Pol.*) One who came from Mackow(o) (Maciek's farm), the name of several places in Poland.

McKoy (*Ir.*) The son of Aodh (fire).

Mackristie (*Scot.*) The son of Kristie, a pet form of Christian (a follower of Christ); or of Christopher (Christbearer).

McLachlan (*Scot.*) The son of Lachlan (warlike).

McLain, McLane (*Ir.*) The son of the servant of St. John.

McLaren, McLaurin (*Scot.*) The son of Laurin or Laurence (laurel, symbol of victory).

McLaughlin, Maclaughlin, Maclachlan, McLaughlan (*Ir.*) The son of Lochlainn or Lochlann (Norway); the son of one who came from Norway.

McLaverty (*Scot.*) The son of the ruler.

Maclean, McLean, McLain, McLane (*Scot.*) The son of the servant of St. John (gracious gift of God).

McLeer (*Ir., Scot.*) The son of the pale youth.

Macleish, McLeish, Maclish (*Scot.*) The son of the servant of Jesus.

McLellan, Maclellan, McLelland (*Scot.*,

Ir.) The son of the servant of St. Faolan (little wolf).

Maclennan, McLennan (*Scot.*) The son of the servant of St. Finnian.

Macleod, McLeod, McLoud (*Scot.*) The son of Leod (ugly).

Maclese, Maclees (*Scot.*) The son of the servant of Jesus.

McLoughlin (*Ir.*) The son of Lochlainn; Anglicized form of O Maoilsheachlainn (servant of St. Secundinus, second).

McMahon, McMahan, Macmahon, McMahin (*Ir.*) The son of Mathghamhain (bear).

McMann (*Ir.*) Shortened form of McMahon, q.v.

McManus, Macmanus (*Ir.*) The son of Maghnuis (great).

McMaster, McMasters (*Scot.*) The son of the Master, i.e., a cleric.

McMenamin (*Ir., Scot.*) The son of Meanma (courage).

McMichael, McMichaels (*Scot.*) The son of the servant of St. Michael (who is like God).

Macmillan, McMillan, McMillen, McMillin (*Scot.*) The son of the bald, or tonsured, one.

McMonagle, McMonigle (*Ir.*) The son of Maonghal (wealth, valor).

McMorrow, McMurrough (*Ir.*) The son of Murchadh (sea warrior).

McMullen, Macmullen, McMullan, McMullin (*Ir.*) The son of little Maolan (little bald man).

Macmunn (*Scot.*) The son of the servant of St. Mundu.

McMurdo (*Scot.*) The son of Muiredachus (mariner); or of Murchadh (sea fighter).

McMurray, McMurry (*Ir., Scot.*) The son of Muireadhach (belonging to the sea; a lord).

Macmurtrie (*Ir., Scot.*) The son of Muircheartach (navigator).

McNabb, Macnabb, McNab (*Scot.*) The son of the Abbot.

McNair (*Scot., Ir.*) The son of dark, brown John (gracious gift of Jehovah); the son of the heir; or of the

steward; or of the smith; or of the stranger.

McNally, Macnally (*Ir.*) The son of the poor man.

McNamara, Macnamara (*Ir.*) The son of the hound of the sea, a name applied to a daring seaman.

McNamee, Macnamee (*Ir.*) The son of Cumidhe (hound of Meath).

McNaughton, Macnaught (*Scot., Ir.*) The son of Neachdain or Neachtan (the pure one).

McNeal (*Scot.*) The son of Neal or Neil (champion).

McNeely, McNealy (*Ir.*) The son of Conghal (high valor); or of the poet.

McNeil, Macneill, McNeill, Macneil (*Scot.*) The son of Niall or Neil (champion).

McNelis, McNellis (*Ir.*) The son of Niallghus (champion choice).

McNerney (*Ir.*) The son of the steward of church lands.

McNevin (*Scot.*) Variant of MacNivin, q.v.

McNicholas, McNichols, McNichol, Macnichol (*Ir.*) The son of Nicholas (people's victory).

McNiff (*Ir.*) The son of Cu-dubh (black hound).

McNish, McNeish (*Scot.*) The son of Aonghus or Angus (one-choice).

MacNivin (*Scot.*) The son of the holy one.

McNulty, Macnulty (*Ir.*) The son of the Ulidian (native of East Ulster).

McNutt (*Ir., Scot.*) The son of Nuadha (an ancient sea divinity); the son of Neachtan (the pure one).

Macomber, McComb, McCombs (*Scot.*) The son of Tom, a pet form of Thomas (a twin).

Macon (*Fr.*) One who built with stone or brick; one who came from Macon in France; descendant of Masson, a pet form of Thomasson (a twin); descendant of Macon (force, hard).

McParland (*Scot., Ir.*) Variant of MacFarland, q.v.

Macpartland (*Scot., Ir.*) The son of

Parthalon; the son of Bartholomew (son of Talmai, furrow).

McPeak, McPeake (*Ir.*) The son of Peic (point).

Macphail, McPhail (*Scot.*) The son of Paul (small).

McPhee, Macphee (*Scot.*) The son of Dubhshithe (the black man of peace).

Macpherson, McPherson (*Scot.*) The son of the parson.

McPhillips (*Scot., Ir.*) The son of Philip (lover of horses).

McPoyle (*Ir.*) The son of Paul (small).

McQuade, McQuaid, McQuaide (*Ir.*) The son of Wat, a pet form of Walter (rule, army).

Macquarrie, McQuarrie, McQuire (*Scot.*) The son of Guaire (proud, noble).

McQue, Macquay, Macquie (*Ir., Scot.*) The son of Aodh (fire).

McQueen, Macqueen, McQueyn (*Scot., Ir.*) The son of Suibhne (good going); the son of the peaceful or quiet man.

McQuiggan (*Ir.*) The son of little Eochaidh (rich in cattle).

McQuillan, McQuillen (*Ir.*) The son of Coilin (young dog; a youth).

McQuinn, McQuin (*Ir.*) The son of Conn (reason; freeman).

McQuiston, Macquistan, McQuistan (*Scot.*) The son of Hutchin, a pet form of Hugh (spirit; mind).

McRae, McRay, Macrae (*Scot.*) Descendant of Macrath (son of grace, the full form being a given name).

McReynolds (*Ir.*) The son of Reginald (powerful, force).

Macri, Macrina, Macrino (*It.*) The tall man.

McRory, Macrorie (*Scot.*) The son of Ruadhri (red king).

McShain, McShane (*Ir.*) The son of Jean, the Norman-French form of John; or of Seon or Sean, Irish forms of John (gracious gift of Jehovah).

McShea (*Ir.*) The son of Seaghdha (majestic; learned).

McSherry (*Ir., Scot.*) The son of Sear-

rach (foal; flighty); or of Sigfrid (victory, peace).

McSloy (*Ir.*) The son of Sluaghadhach (member of a hosting expedition).

McSmith (*Scot.*) The son of the smith.

McSorley (*Scot., Ir.*) The son of Somhairle (viking; sailor; summer wanderer).

McSwain, McSwan (*Scot.*) The son of Swan (youthful servant).

McSweeney, Macsweeney, McSwiney, McSweeny (*Ir.*) The son of Suibhne (good going).

McTague (*Ir.*) Variant of McTeague, q.v.

McTamany, McTamney (*Ir.*) The son of the tympanist.

Mactavish (*Scot.*) The son of Tammas, the Lowland Scots form of Thomas (a twin).

McTeague (*Ir.*) The son of the poet.

McTigue (*Ir.*) The son of Tadhg (poet; philosopher).

Macturk (*Scot.*) The son of Torc (boar).

Macvay, Macvaugh (*Scot.*) Variant of McVey, q.v.

McVey, McVeigh, McVeagh, McVea (*Ir.*) Descendant of Mac an Bheathadh (son of life), the full form being a given name.

McVicker, Macvicar (*Scot.*) The son of the vicar.

McWeeney (*Ir.*) The son of Maonach (wealthy; dumb).

McWilliams, Macwilliams, McWilliam, Macwilliam (*Scot., Ir.*) The son of William (resolution, helmet).

Macy (*Eng.*) One who came from Macy, Macey or Mace, all in France; descendant of Maci, a pet form of Mathiu (gift of Jehovah).

Maday (*Pol.*) Descendant of Madey, the name of a Polish legendary hero.

Maddaloni (*It.*) Descendant of Maddalena, Italian form of Magdalene (elevated; magnificent).

Madden, Maddin (*Eng., Ir.*) Descendant of little Matthew (gift of Jehovah); grandson of little Madadh (dog).

Maddern (*Eng.*) One who came from

Madron (church of St. Madernus), in Cornwall.

Maddox, Maddock, Maddocks (*Eng., Wel.*) Descendant, or son, of Madog or Madoc (fortunate).

Maddrey (*Pol.*) The wise, learned man.

Madej (*Pol.*) One who came from Madej (Madey's settlement), in Poland; dweller near the Madej river in Poland.

Mader, Madar, Madder (*Eng., Ger.*) One who dyes with, or sells, red dye-stuff; one who came from Maden, in Germany; one who mows or harvests grain; descendant of Matheri (court, army).

Madera (*Sp.*) One who came from Madera (place constructed with timber), in Spain.

Madewell (*Eng.*) Dweller at the meadow spring.

Madigan (*Ir.*) Grandson of little Madadh (dog).

Madison (*Eng.*) The son of Mad, a pet form of Matthew (gift of Jehovah).

Madjar (*Yu.-Sl.*) One who came from Hungary, a Hungarian.

Madley (*Eng.*) One who came from Madley (good grove), in Herefordshire.

Madoc, Madog (*Wel.*) Descendant of Madog or Madoc (fortunate).

Madon (*Fr.*) Descendant of Madon, a pet form of Madeleine (elevated; magnificent).

Madrid (*Sp.*) One who came from Madrid (town; small wood), the capital of Spain.

Madrigal (*Sp.*) One who came from Madrigal (pear orchard), the name of several places in Spain.

Madsen, Madson (*Dan., Nor.*) The son of Mad, a pet form of Mathies (gift of Jehovah).

Madura (*Pol.*) The wise or learned man.

Madway (*Eng.*) Variant of Medway, q.v.

Maeda (*Jap.*) Front, rice field.

Maeder (*Ger.*) One who cut grass or grain, a mower.

Maen (*Du.*) Descendant of Maen, a pet

form of Emanuel (God is with us); nickname for the moon-faced man.

Maerten, Maertens (*Ger.*) German variant of Martin, q.v.

Maeterlinck (*Bel.*) One who came from Maeterlinck, in Belgium.

Maffei, Maffeo (*It.*) Descendant of Maffeo, an Italian form of Matthew (gift of Jehovah) .

Magazino, Magazine, Magazzu (*It.*) Dweller near a warehouse; one who worked in a warehouse.

Magda (*Ger., Eng.*) Descendant of Magda, pet form of Magdalene (elevated; magnificent).

Magee (*Ir.*) Variant of MacKey, q.v.

Magenta (*It.*) One who came from Magenta, in Italy.

Mager, Magerr (*Du.*) The slender, gaunt person.

Maggi (*Swis., Fr., It.*) Descendant of Maggi, a pet form of Marguerite (a pearl); or of Maggi (May, the month).

Maggio, Maggini (*It.*) Descendant of Maggio (one born in the month of May).

Maggioncalda (*It.*) Dweller in a warm mansion.

Maggiore (*It.*) Descendant of the eldest son.

Maggot (*Eng.*) Descendant of little Magg, a pet form of Margaret (a pearl).

Maggs, Mag, Magg (*Ger., Eng.*) Descendant of Magg, a pet form of names beginning with Mag (blood relationship), as Magafrid and Magbald; descendant of Magg, a pet form of Margaret (pearl).

Magi (*Est.*) Dweller on a mountain.

Magid, Magidson (*Heb.*) Descendant of the announcer or preacher.

Magill (*Ir.*) The son of the foreigner.

Maginn (*Ir.*) The son of Fionn (fair).

Maginnis (*Ir.*) The son of Aonghus (one-choice).

Maglio, Magliocco, Maglione (*It.*) One who made coats of mail, an armorer.

Magnani (*It.*) One who made and sold locks, a locksmith.

Magnatta, Magnati (*It.*) Descendant of little Magno, Italian form of Magnus (great).

Magner (*Ir.*) Descendant of little Magnus (great).

Magness (*Sw.*) Descendant of Magnus (great).

Magnifico (*It.*) Dweller at the sign of the lark; the chubby man.

Magnin, Magnan (*Fr.*) The itinerant worker in brass or tin.

Magnuson, Magnus (*Sw.*) The son of Magnus (great).

Magor (*Eng.*) Dweller by the old walls or ruins.

Magoun, Magoon, Magowan (*Ir.*) The son of the smith or worker in metals.

Magri, Magro (*It., Sp.*) One who came from Magro in Spain; the thin, lean man.

Magruder (*Ir.*) The son of Bruadar.

Maguire (*Ir.*) The son of the pale, or light-complexioned, man.

Magyar (*Hun.*) One who came from Hungary, a Hungarian. Possibly the name was acquired while outside of Hungary and brought back.

Mahan (*Ir.*) Descendant of Mochain.

Mahdi (*Arab.*) Descendant of Mahdi (the guided one).

Maher (*Ir.*) Grandson of Meachar (hospitable).

Mahler (*Ger.*) One who paints buildings and ships, a painter; one who came from Mahlau, in Germany.

Mahmud, Mahmoud (*Tur., Arab.*) Variant of Muhammed, q.v.

Mahon, Mahan, Mahone (*Ir.*) Grandson of little Moch, a pet form of some early name commencing with Moch; the son of one with bearlike characteristics.

Mahoney, Mahony (*Ir.*) Grandson of Mathghamhain (bear).

Mahood (*Eng.*) Descendant of Maud, an English contraction of Matilda (might, battle).

Maiale, Maialetti (*It.*) One who raised and sold pigs; the fat, dirty man.

Maida (*Eng.*) Descendant of Maida or Mayda (maiden).

Maiden (*Eng.*) A derogatory nickname for an effeminate man.

Maidman (*Eng.*) Dweller in the meadow; the girls' or maidens' servant.

Maier (*Ger., Du.*) An overseer or head servant; later, a farmer; one who cut and gathered grain; a reaper.

Mailer, Mailler (*Eng., Wel., Scot.*) One who coats with enamel; descendant of Meilyr; one who came from the lands of Mailer, in Perthshire.

Mailey (*Ir.*) Variant of Malley, q.v.

Mailman (*Eng., Scot.*) The servant of the one who enamels or coats metal, glass or pottery; one who cultivated land, paying rent, a tenant farmer.

Maimon, Maimone (*Fr.*) Descendant, or follower, of Maximus (the greatest), the name of several saints.

Main, Maine (*Eng., Fr.*) Descendant of Magino (strength); one who came from Maine, in France; the strong man.

Mainardi (*It.*) Descendant of Mainardi, Italian form of Maynard (strength, hard).

Maines, Mains (*Eng., Scot.*) The man with unusual hands; the great man; descendant of Magnus (great); one who came from Maine (district), an old French province; one who came from Mains (group of houses), the name of several places in Scotland.

Mainwaring (*Eng.*) One who came from Mesnilwarin (manor of Warin), in France.

Maio (*It.*) Dweller near a laburnum tree; descendant of Maio (one born in May).

Maiorano (*It.*) One who grew and sold marjoram.

Mair, Maire (*Scot.*) The official who executed summons and other official writs; the king's sergeant or herald; a common term denoting any delegated office.

Maisenhelder (*Ger.*) One who came from Maisenhalden, in Germany.

Maison (*Fr.*) Dweller in the house, usually designating a house of some importance; one who came from Maison, the name of many places in France.

Maisonet, Maisonette (*Fr.*) Dweller in the small house or cottage.

Maisonneuve, Maisoneuve (*Fr.*) Dweller in, or near, the new house.

Maisus (*Lith.*) One who made and sold sacks.

Maitland (*Scot., Eng.*) Dweller at, or on, the meadow or pasture land.

Majewski (*Pol.*) One born in the month of May.

Majka (*Yu.-Sl., Bulg.*) The mother's son, probably referring to a widow's son.

Major (*Eng.*) The larger man.

Mak (*Pol.*) Dweller where poppies grew.

Makadon, Makadonsky (*Pol., Ukr., Rus.*) One who came from Macedonia.

Makarchuk, Makarchuck (*Ukr.*) Descendant of Makar (blessed).

Makarenko (*Ukr.*) The son of Makar (blessed).

Makarewicz, Makarczyk (*Pol.*) The son of Makar (blessed).

Makepeace (*Eng.*) One who acted as a peacemaker or mediator.

Maker, Makers (*Eng.*) One who came from Maker (ruins of an old building), in Cornwall.

Maki (*Finn.*) One who lived on, or near, a hill.

Makin, Makinson (*Eng.*) Descendant of little May, a pet form of Matthew (gift of Jehovah).

Makiver (*Scot.*) Variant of MacIver, q.v.

Makler (*Ger.*) One who acted as a broker, middleman, agent or negotiator; one regarded as a petty faultfinder.

Maklin (*Ir.*) Variant of Macklin, q.v.

Makonnen, Makkonen (*Ir.*) The son of little Fionn (fair).

Makowski (*Pol.*) Dweller where poppies grew; one who came from Makow(o) (poppy), in Poland.

Makris (*Gr.*) The large or tall man.

Maksimovic, Maksimovich (*Yu.-Sl.*) The son of Maksim, Yugoslavian form of Maximus (the greatest).

Maksym, Maksymuk (*Ukr.*) Descendant of Maksym, Ukrainian form of Maximus (the greatest).

Malachi (*Heb.*) Descendant of Malachi (messenger of Jehovah).

Malamed, Malamud, Malamut (*Tur.*) One who was envious or jealous.

Malandra, Malandrino, Malandro (*It.*) The blustering, browbeating man, a bully; a scamp or rascal.

Malarkey, Malarky (*Ir.*) Descendant of the devotee of St. Earc.

Malatesta (*It.*) One with a bad or misshapen head; one who is stubborn.

Malcolm, Malcom, Malcomb (*Scot.*) Descendant of Malcolm (devotee of St. Columba, dove).

Malcontento (*It.*) The discontented or dissatisfied man.

Malden, Maldon (*Eng.*) One who came from Malden (hill with a cross or mark), in Surrey; or from Maldon (hill with a cross or mark), in Essex.

Maldonado (*Sp.*) Descendant of Donald (dark or brown-haired stranger; world-ruler); or of Domhnall (world mighty); a name sometimes applied to a Scotsman, a corruption of McDonald, q.v.

Maldonato (*Sp.*) One who was deformed or hunchbacked.

Malecki, Malec (*Pol.*) The little man.

Malek, Malik (*Rus., Pol., Arab., Tur.*) The small man; descendant of Malik (king).

Malen (*Eng., Ir.*) Descendant of little Mal, a pet form of Mary (bitterness; wished-for child; rebellion); descendant of the little monk or disciple.

Malenki (*Rus.*) The short or small man.

Malenkov (*Rus.*) The son of the little man.

Maletta (*It.*) Dweller near an apple tree; one who sold apples.

Maley (*Ir.*) Descendant of Maille (noble or chief).

Malfatto (*It.*) The crippled or deformed man; one who made and sold macaroni.

Malia (*It.*) One who casts spells or practices witchcraft.

Malik (*Arab., Pers., Hindi, Rus.*) The prince, little king, or chief of the tribe; one who owns land; the small man.

Malin, Malina, Malinowski (*Pol.*) Dweller where raspberries grew; one who came from Malinowo, in Poland.

Malis, Malish (*Ir.*) The son of Maol Iosa (servant of Jesus).

Maliszewski (*Pol.*) The little man.

Malitsky (*Ukr.*) Descendant of the small man.

Malkiel, Malchiel (*Heb.*) Descendant of Malchiel (God is king).

Malkin, Malkinson (*Eng.*) Descendant of Malkin, a pet form of Mary (bitterness; wished-for child; rebellion); also of little Mal, a pet form of Matilda (might, battle).

Malkovsky (*Ukr.*) Descendant of the little one.

Malkowski (*Pol.*) One who came from Malkowo (little), in Poland.

Mallace, Mallis (*Scot.*) One who came from the lands of Mallis (mills), in Scotland.

Mallah (*Arab.*) One who dealt in pepper and other condiments.

Mallard (*Eng.*) Dweller at the sign of the wild drake, or common wild duck.

Mallett, Mallette, Mallet, Malet (*Eng., Fr.*) Descendant of little Mal, a pet form of names like Malcolm, Malculf, and Maldred; descendant of little Malo or Maclou, a saint of the seventh century.

Malley, Mally (*Ir.*) Grandson of Maille (chief); or of Meallach (pleasant).

Mallin, Mallen, Mallinson (*Eng.*) Descendant of little Mall, a pet form of Mary (bitterness; wished-for child; rebellion); or of Matilda (might, battle).

Mallis (*Eng.*) One who came from Mellis (the mills), in Suffolk.

Mallon (*Ir.*) Grandson of little Meall (pleasant).

Mallory, Malory, Mallery (*Eng.*) The unhappy or unfortunate man.

Mallough, Mallow (*Ir.*) Variant of Malloy, q.v.

Malloy (*Ir.*) Grandson of Maolaodha (servant of St. Aedh, fire).

Malm (*Sw.*) Ore.

Malmberg (*Sw.*) Ore mountain.

Malmborg (*Sw.*) Ore castle.

Malmed, Malmud (*Tur.*) One who was envious or jealous.

Malmgren (*Sw.*) Ore branch.

Malmquist (*Sw.*) Ore twig.

Malmrose (*Sw.*) Ore rose.

Malmstrom (*Sw.*) Ore stream.

Malone (*Ir.*) Grandson of the servant or devotee of St. John.

Maloney (*Ir.*) Grandson of Maoldomhnaigh (devoted to Sunday, or to the Church).

Malonson, Malanson (*Fr.*) The sick, or infirm, man.

Maloof, Malouf (*Arab.*) The well-known or famous man.

Malpass, Malpas (*Eng.*) One who came from Malpas (difficult passage), in Cheshire.

Malpede (*It.*) One with a crippled or deformed foot.

Maltby, Maltbie (*Eng.*) One who came from Maltby (Malti's homestead), the name of places in Lincolnshire and Yorkshire.

Maltese (*It.*) One who came from Malta (isle of honey; refuge).

Malthus (*Eng.*) Dweller at a house in which malt is prepared and stored.

Malvern (*Eng.*) One who came from Malvern (bare), in Worcestershire.

Malvestuto, Malvestito (*It.*) One dressed poorly or shabbily.

Maly, Maley (*Cz.-Sl., Pol.*) The small person.

Malyshev (*Rus.*) The small man, little boy.

Mamet, Mamett (*Bel., Fr.*) One who came from Mametz (Mamo's farm), in France; descendant of little Mame, a pet form of Mammes, the name of an obscure third century saint.

Manahan (*Ir.*) Variant of Monahan, q.v.

Manasse (*Fr.*) Descendant of Manasseh (forgetting).

Manceau, Manceaux (*Fr.*) Variant of Mansel, q.v.

Manchester (*Eng.*) One who came from Manchester (place of skins fortification; stone fortification), in Lancashire.

Mancini, Mancinelli (*It.*) One who is left-handed.

Mancoff (*Rus.*) The son of Manko, a Russian form of Mary (bitterness; wished-for child; rebellion).

Mancuso (*It.*) The left-handed person.

Mand (*Est.*) Dweller near a pine tree.

Mandel, Mandell, Mandl, Mandle (*Ger.*) Descendant of little Manto (pleasure; joy); one who came from Mandel (place of almonds), in Germany.

Mandelbaum (*Ger.*) Dweller near an almond tree.

Mandelblatt (*Sw.*) Almond tree leaf.

Mander (*Ger., Eng.*) One who came from Mandern (swamp), the name of two places in Germany; one who made and sold baskets.

Manderfield, Manderfeld (*Ger.*) Dweller in the swampy open country.

Mandeville (*Eng., Fr.*) One who came from Magneville (large estate), in France; or from Mandeville (Mando's estate), in France.

Maneely (*Ir.*) Variant of McNeely, q.v.

Manes (*Sp.*) Possibly one who played the part of the ghost of the dead in play or pageant.

Manet (*Fr.*) Descendant of little Man (man).

Manfred (*Eng.*) Descendant of Manfred (man, peace).

Manfredi, Manfredo (*It.*) Descendant of Manfredi, Italian form of Manfred (man, peace).

Manfredini (*It.*) Descendant of little Manfredi (man, peace).

Mangan, Mangin (*Ir.*) Grandson of Mongan (little hairy one).

Mangano (*It.*) One who fought with the crossbow.

Mangelsdorf (*Ger.*) One who came from

Mangelsdorf (Mangold's village), in Germany.

Mangini, Mangino (*It.*) The left-handed man.

Mangner (*Ir.*) Descendant of little Magnus (great).

Mango, Manco (*It.*) One who is left-handed.

Mangold, Mangel (*Eng., Ger.*) One who worked a mangonel, an engine for throwing stones; descendant of Mangold (one who governs over many); one who raises mangel-wurzel, a coarse variety of beet grown as food for cattle.

Mangrum (*Ger.*) Descendant of Maginrannus (might, counsel).

Mangum (*Eng., Fr.*) One who came from Manaccan, in Cornwall; one who cut and sold meat, a butcher.

Manheim, Manheimer (*Ger.*) Variant of Mannheim, q.v.

Manhoff (*Ger.*) One who came from Mannhof (marshy farm), the name of two places in Germany.

Maniaci (*It.*) The foolish, crazy man.

Maniates, Maniatis (*Gr.*) One who came from Mane, an indefinite district in Greece.

Manin (*Fr.*) Descendant of little Man, a pet form of names beginning with Man (man), as Mande and Manfroy.

Maniscalco (*It.*) One who shod horses, a farrier.

Manke (*Ger., Du.*) Descendant of Manke, a short form of Mangold (ruler over many); one who was crippled or lame.

Mankin (*Eng.*) Descendant of little Man (man).

Manko, Mankowski (*Pol.*) One who was left-handed.

Manley, Manly (*Eng.*) One who came from Manley (common wood), in Cheshire.

Manlove (*Eng.*) The philanthropic man, from Early English *mannlufe* "philanthropy."

Mann, Man, Manne, Manns (*Ger., Eng.*) The vassal or servant; one who came from the Isle of Man, a Manxman;

descendant of Mann (man); dweller at the sign of the happy man, a Frankfort house sign.

Mannal (*Ger.*) One with a small frame or low stature.

Mannasmith (*Eng.*) Dweller near a smithy.

Mannering (*Eng.*) Variant of Mainwaring, q.v.

Manners (*Eng.*) One who came from Mesnieres (fortified castle), in France; dweller in, or near, the manor; a servant in the manor.

Mannersmith (*Eng.*) The worker in metals in the manor or village.

Manney (*Ir.*) Descendant of Maonach (wealthy).

Mannheim, Mannheimer (*Ger.*) One who came from Mannheim (servant's home; swampy home), in Germany; or from Monheim, in Germany.

Mannik (*Est.*) Dweller in a pine forest.

Manning (*Eng.*) The son of the servant; descendant of Manning (little person).

Mannino (*It.*) Small sheaf or bundle, perhaps designating a little man.

Mannion, Manion (*Ir.*) Grandson of Mainnin or Maincin (little monk).

Manno (*It.*) Descendant of Manno, pet form of Alamanno (the German).

Manolatos (*Gr.*) The son of Manolis (God is with us).

Manos (*Gr.*) Descendant of Manos, a pet form of Manolis (God is with us).

Mansel, Mansell (*Eng., Fr.*) One who came from Maine or Le Mans (district), in France; a feudal tenant who occupied a manse, sufficient land to support a family.

Manser (*Eng., Heb.*) One who made handles and knives; one who came from Mansergh (shepherd's hut belonging to Man), in Westmorland; descendant of Manasseh (forgetting).

Mansfield (*Eng.*) One who came from Mansfield (open land by the hill named Mam), in Nottinghamshire.

Manship (*Eng.*) One who came from

Minskip (community of goods), in the West Riding of Yorkshire.

Mansky (*Ukr.*) Descendant of Manja, a pet form of Marija, Ukrainian form of Mary (bitterness; wished-for child; rebellion).

Mansley (*Eng.*) One who came from Minley (Myndel's grove), in Hampshire.

Mansmann (*Ger.*) The serf or unfree peasant; one subject to some kind of service.

Manson, Mansen (*Sw., Nor., Dan., Scot., Eng.*) The son of Man, a pet form of Magnus (great); the son of the servant.

Mansuroghu (*Tur.*) The son of Mansur (divinely aided).

Mantell, Mantel (*Eng.*) One who made and sold cloaks or mantles.

Manthey, Manthei, Manthie, Manthy (*Ger.*) One who came from Mantel, formerly Manthey (swamp); descendant of Mantheo.

Manthorpe (*Eng.*) One who came from Manthorpe (Manni's farm), in Lincolnshire.

Manton (*Eng.*) One who came from Manton (sandy homestead; Manna's homestead), the name of four places in England.

Mantz (*Ger.*) Descendant of Manz, pet form of Mangold (one who governs over many).

Manuel, Manual (*Eng., Scot.*) Descendant of Emmanuel (God with us); one who came from Manuel, in Stirlingshire.

Manus (*Ir.*) The son of Maghnuis (great).

Manville (*Fr.*) One who came from Mannville (Manni's domain), in France.

Manwaring (*Eng.*) Variant of Mainwaring, q.v.

Manypenny (*Eng.*) The man with much money; a wealthy man, or ironically, a nickname for a poor man.

Manz, Manze (*Ger.*) Descendant of Manz, a pet form of Manto (pleasure; joy).

Manzi, Manzo (*It.*) Dweller at the sign of the heifer or bullock; one in charge of the heifers and bullocks.

Mapes (*Wel., Eng.*) The son of Map (son), or of Mab, a pet form of Mabel (amiable).

Maple, Maples, Mapel, Maypole (*Eng.*) Dweller at, or near, a maple tree; or at the sign of the maypole.

Maplesden (*Eng.*) Dweller on a hill; or in a valley where maples grew.

Mapp, Mapps (*Eng., Wel.*) Descendant of Map (son); descendant of Mabb, a pet form of Mabel or Amabel (amiable).

Mar (*Scot.*) One who came from Mar (a tribe name), in Aberdeenshire.

Marais (*Fr.*) One who lived near a marsh.

Marangopoulos (*Gr.*) The son of the carpenter.

Marasco (*It.*) Dweller near a cherry tree.

Maratea (*It.*) Nickname for one who loves God.

Marazzi, Marazzo (*It.*) One who used a handax in his work, a cask maker.

Marbach (*Ger.*) One who came from Marbach (marshy stream), the name of many places in Germany.

Marberger (*Ger.*) One who came from Marburg, in Germany.

Marble, Marbles (*Eng.*) One who came from Marple (hill by the boundary valley), in Cheshire.

Marbry (*Eng.*) Variant of Marbury, q.v.

Marbury (*Eng.*) One who came from Marbury (fortified place by a lake), in Cheshire.

Marc (*Fr.*) Descendant of Marc, French form of Mark (belonging to the god Mars).

Marcantonio (*It.*) The tall, heavy-set man; nickname for a fool; descendant of Marc (Mark) Antonio (Anthony).

Marceau (*Fr.*) Descendant of Marcel, French form of Marcellus (belonging to the god Mars), the name of two saints.

Marcello, Marcelli, Marcellino (*It.*) Descendant of little Marco, Italian form of Mark (belonging to Mars, the god of war).

March, Marche (*Eng.*) Dweller at the boundary mark; the same as Marsh, q.v.; one who came from March (boundary), in Cambridgeshire.

Marchand, Marchant, Marcand, Marquand (*Fr.*) The tradesman or merchant.

Marchesani, Marchesano (*It.*) Descendant of a nobleman of hereditary rank, a marquis; one connected in some way with a marquis' household.

Marchese (*It.*) One with the title of marquis; one connected in some manner with a marquis' household.

Marchetti (*It.*) Descendant of little Marco (belonging to the god Mars).

Marchiano (*It.*) The very great man.

Marchione, Marchionne (*It.*) Descendant of Marchionne, a dialectal form of Melchior (king of light).

Marchuk (*Ukr.*) Descendant of Marko, Ukrainian form of Mark (belonging to the god Mars).

Marciano (*It.*) One who likes to march or advance in regular formation.

Marcinek, Marciniak (*Pol.*) Descendant of little Marcin, Polish form of Martin (belonging to the god Mars).

Marckwardt, Markwardt, Markvart, Markwart (*Ger.*) The warden of the marches; frontier watchman or guard; descendant of Marcward (border, guard).

Marco, Marcos (*It., Sp.*) Descendant of Marco (belonging to the god Mars).

Marconi (*It.*) Descendant of Marco, Italian form of Mark (belonging to the god Mars).

Marcum (*Eng.*) Variant of Markham, q.v.

Marcus (*Eng.*) Descendant of Marcus, the Latin form of Mark (belonging to the god Mars, the god of war).

Marden (*Eng.*) One who came from Marden (pasture for mares; boundary hill), the name of places in Kent and Sussex.

Marder (*Ger.*) Dweller at the sign of the

marten; dweller in a place infested by martens.

Mare (*Fr.*) Dweller by the sea.

Marek (*Pol.*) Descendant of Marek, Polish form of Mark (belonging to the god Mars).

Marengo (*It.*) One who came from Marengo in Italy; dweller at the sign of the partridge.

Mares (*Cz.-Sl.*) Dweller at, or near, a marsh.

Margerison (*Eng.*) The son of Margery, a pet form of Margaret (pearl).

Margerum (*Eng.*) Dweller near where marjoram grew.

Margeson (*Eng.*) The son of Marge, a pet form of Margaret (pearl).

Margolin (*Heb.*) Descendant of Margolin, Hebrew form of Margaret (pearl).

Margolis, Margolies, Margoles (*Heb., Ukr., Rus.*) Descendant of Margolis, a form of Margaret (pearl).

Margraff, Margraf, Margrave (*Ger.*) Variant of Markgraf, q.v.

Margulis, Margullis, Margulies (*Ukr., Rus., Heb.*) Variant of Margolis, q.v.

Mariani, Marianni, Mariano (*It.*) Descendant of Mariano, an Italian masculine form of Mary (bitterness; wished-for child; rebellion).

Marin (*Sp.*) One who came from Marin in Spain; descendant of Marino (of the sea).

Marinari, Marinaro (*It.*) One who worked on a ship, a sailor.

Marine, Marini (*It.*) Descendant of Marino or Marin (of the sea).

Marinello, Marinelli, Marinella (*It.*) A nickname given to one thought to possess some quality of the ladybug; dweller at the sign of the ladybug.

Mariner, Marner (*Eng.*) One who worked on a ship, a sailor.

Marinez, Marines (*Sp.*) The son of Marino (of the sea).

Marino, Marini, Marina (*It.*) Descendant of Marino or Marinus (of the sea).

Marinoff (*Rus.*) The son of Marina, Russian form of Mary (bitterness; wished-for child; rebellion).

Mario (*It., Sp.*) Descendant of Mario, an Italian and Spanish masculine form of Mary (bitterness; wished-for child; rebellion).

Marion, Marian (*Fr.*) Descendant of little Mary (bitterness; wished-for child; rebellion).

Marison (*Eng.*) The son of Mary (bitterness; wished-for child; rebellion).

Marker, Markers (*Eng., Ger.*) One who marks game, i.e., notes the spot to which it has retired, for the hunter; dweller at, or near, a landmark or boundary.

Markert (*Ger.*) Descendant of Marchart (boundary or horse, hard).

Markevicius (*Lith.*) Descendant of Mark (belonging to the god Mars).

Markey (*Ir.*) The horseman or rider.

Markfield (*Eng.*) One who came from Markfield (the open land of the Mercians), in Leicestershire.

Markgraf (*Ger.*) Military keeper of the marches or borders.

Markham (*Eng.*) One who came from Markham (homestead at the boundary), in Nottinghamshire.

Markiewicz (*Pol., Rus.*) The son of Marek, Slavic form of Mark (belonging to Mars).

Markley, Markle (*Eng., Scot.*) Dweller in, or near, the wood on the boundary; one who came from the lands of Markle (hill where there are horses), in East Lothian.

Markman, Markmann (*Ger.*) Dweller at the boundary mark; one who took care of horses.

Marko, Markoe, Markow (*Ukr.*) Descendant of Marko, Ukrainian form of Mark (belonging to the god Mars).

Markopoulos (*Gr.*) The son of Marinos, Greek form of Mark (belonging to the god Mars).

Markowitz, Markovitz (*Cz.-Sl., Yu.-Sl.*) The son of Mark (belonging to Mars).

Markowski (*Pol.*) One who came from

Markowo (Marek's place), in Poland.

Marks, Mark (*Eng.*) Dweller at the boundary or boundary mark; descendant of Mark (belonging to the god Mars); one who came from Marck (frontier district), in France; one who came from Mark (boundary house), in Somerset.

Markson (*Eng.*) The son of Mark (belonging to the god Mars).

Markus (*Ger.*) Descendant of Mark (belonging to Mars, the god of war).

Markward (*Ger.*) Variant of Marquardt, q.v.

Markwell (*Eng.*) One who came from Marwell (boundary stream), in Hampshire.

Markwick (*Eng.*) Dweller at the dairy farm at the boundary.

Marland, Marlan (*Eng.*) One who came from Marland (land on a lake), in Devonshire; dweller on the land by the lake.

Marlborough, Marlboro (*Eng.*) One who came from Marlborough (hill where gentian grew), in Wiltshire.

Marley (*Eng.*) One who came from Marley (boundary or pleasant wood), villages in Devonshire and Kent.

Marlin (*Eng.*) Variant of Marland, q.v.

Marlowe, Marlow (*Eng.*) One who came from Marlow (lake remains), in Buckinghamshire; dweller at the hill by the lake.

Marmaduke (*Eng.*) Descendant of Marmaduke (sea leader; steward).

Marmelstein (*Fr., Ger.*) One who dealt in, or worked with, marble.

Marmer (*Du.*) One who worked with marble, a mason.

Marmion, Marmon (*Fr.*) Dweller at the sign of the marmot, child, or little monkey; nickname for one thought to have the characteristics of a small child or urchin.

Marmol, Marmole (*Sp.*) One who came from Marmol (marble), in Spain.

Marmor (*Fr.*) One who dealt in, or worked with, marble.

Marnie, Marney (*Eng.*) One who came from Marigni (Marinius' estate), in LaManche.

Maroney, Marone (*Ir.*) Variants of Moroney, q.v.

Marotta (*It.*) The sick or invalid man; one in chronic ill health.

Marple, Marples (*Eng.*) One who came from Marple (boundary valley hill), in Cheshire.

Marquardt, Marquard, Marquart (*Ger.*) The warden of the marches; frontier watchman or guard; one who came from Marquard (border guard), in Germany; descendant of Marcward (border, guard).

Marques (*Port., Sp.*) Descendant of Marcos, Portuguese and Spanish form of Marcus (belonging to Mars).

Marquette, Marquet (*Fr.*) Descendant of little Marc, French form of Mark (belonging to the god Mars).

Marquez (*Sp.*) The son of Marcos, Spanish form of Mark (belonging to the god Mars).

Marquis, Marquiss (*Eng., Fr.*) Descendant of Marcus (belonging to Mars); one connected in some manner with a marquis' household.

Marr (*Eng., Scot.*) One who came from Marr (marsh), in the West Riding of Yorkshire; or from Mar, in Aberdeenshire.

Marra, Marro (*It.*) One who taught school; one who was a master of his trade; one who worked with a hoe.

Marren, Marrin (*Eng.*) Descendant of Marinus (of the sea), the name of several saints.

Marrero (*It.*) One who made and sold hoes.

Marriott (*Eng.*) Descendant of little Mary (bitterness; wished-for child; rebellion).

Marron, Marrone (*Eng.*) Dweller near the Marron (pool) river, in Cumberland.

Marrow (*Eng.*) The companion, friend, or sweetheart.

Mars, Marrs (*Scot., Eng.*) One who came from the parish of Mar (a tribal name), in Aberdeenshire; or from Marr (marsh), in Yorkshire; dweller at, or near, a marsh.

Marsala (*It.*) One who came from Marsala, in Sicily.

Marsden (*Eng.*) One who came from Marsden (boundary valley), the name of villages in Lancashire and Yorkshire.

Marsh, Mersh (*Eng.*) One who lived on, or near, the swamp or tract of soft, wet land.

Marshall, Marschall, Marshell (*Eng., Ger.*) One who cared for horses, especially one who treated their diseases; a shoeing smith; later, an official in a king's, or high noble's, household having charge of military affairs.

Marshbank, Marshbanks (*Scot.*) One who came from the lands of Majoribankis (Marjorie's slopes), in Renfrewshire; dweller near a marsh on the banks of a stream.

Marshburn (*Eng.*) Dweller by a stream flowing to or from a marsh.

Marshfield (*Eng.*) One who came from Marshfield (open country by a marsh), in Gloucestershire.

Marshman (*Eng.*) Dweller in a marsh or wet place.

Marshner (*Ger.*) Dweller in, or near, the marsh.

Marsters (*Eng.*) Variant, due to pronunciation, of Masters, q.v.

Marston (*Eng.*) One who came from Marston (homestead by a marsh), the name of many places in England.

Marszalek (*Pol.*) The officer in the household of a medieval king, prince, or noble having charge of military affairs.

Martell, Martel (*Eng., Fr.*) The worker who used a hammer in a smithy; a nickname for a warrior.

Martella, Martelli, Martello (*It.*) One who used a hammer in his work, a carpenter; dweller near a box tree; contraction of Martinelli, q.v.; descendant of little Marta, Italian form of Martha (mistress).

Martensen (*Nor., Dan.*) The son of Marten (belonging to Mars, the god of war).

Marti, Marta, Marte (*Swis., Sp., It.*) Descendant of Marti (belonging to the god Mars); descendant of Marti (Tuesday), a name sometimes given to one born on Tuesday.

Martikke (*Ukr.*) Descendant of Martycki (belonging to Mars, the god of war).

Martin, Marten, Martens, Martyn (*Fr., Sp., Eng.*) Descendant of Martinus (belonging to the god Mars, the god of war); one who came from Martin, the name of places in Spain and France. The popularity of the name in Western Europe is due to St. Martin of Tours, the fourth century French saint.

Martindale, Martindell (*Eng.*) One who came from Martindale (Martin's valley), in Westmorland.

Martinek (*Cz.-Sl.*) Descendant of little Martin (belonging to Mars).

Martinelli (*Fr., It.*) Descendant of little Martin (belonging to Mars, the god of war).

Martinet, Martineau, Martenet (*Fr.*) Descendant of little Martin (belonging to the god Mars).

Martinez (*Sp.*) The son of Martin (belonging to Mars, the god of war).

Martini, Martino (*It.*) Descendant of Martini (name sometimes given to one born on Tuesday).

Martinson, Martinsen (*Eng., Sw., Nor.*) The son of Martin (belonging to Mars, the god of war).

Marton, Martone (*Hun., Eng.*) Descendant of Marton, Hungarian form of Martin (belonging to the god Mars); one who came from Marton (homestead by a lake), the name of fourteen places in England.

Martorana, Martorano (*It.*) Dweller at the sign of the marten; one who trapped martens.

Martyniuk (*Ukr.*) The son of Martyn, Ukrainian form of Martin (belonging to the god Mars).

Marucci (*It.*) One who took care of the

calves; dweller at the sign of the calf or heifer.

Maruyama (*Jap.*) Round, mountain.

Marvel, Marvill, Marvele (*Eng.*) One who came from Marvell (pleasant open country), in Wight; or from Mereville (Merila's estate), in France; the marvelous or wonderful man.

Marvin (*Eng.*) Descendant of Marvin (sea, friend); or of Marwin (sea, friend).

Marx (*Ger., Eng.*) Descendant of Mark or Marcus (belonging to Mars, the god of war); dweller at a mark or boundary stone; one who came from Marx in Germany.

Marxen, Marxsen (*Ger.*) The son of Mark or Marcus (belonging to Mars, the god of war).

Maryanski (*Pol.*) Descendant of Marian (bitterness; wished-for child; rebellion).

Marzano (*It.*) Descendant of Marzano or Marzia (belonging to Mars).

Marzec (*Pol.*) Descendant of one born in the month of March.

Marzullo, Marzulli (*It.*) Descendant of Marzullo (name sometimes given to one born in March).

Masada (*Jap.*) Right, rice field.

Masaryk (*Cz.-Sl.*) The little man who cut and sold meat; the little butcher.

Mascaro (*It.*) Nickname for one with a large head.

Mascio (*It.*) The manly, vigorous fellow.

Masefield (*Eng.*) Dweller in the open country frequented by titmice.

Masek (*Cz.-Sl.*) One who sold meat, a butcher; descendant of Masek, a pet form of Mathes (gift of Jehovah).

Masello, Masella, Maselo (*It.*) Descendant of little Maso, a pet form of Tommaso, Italian form of Thomas (a twin).

Maser (*Eng.*) One who made masers, bowls made of maple-wood.

Mash, Mashman (*Eng.*) Dweller near a marsh.

Masi, Maso (*It.*) Descendant of Maso, a pet form of Tommaso, Italian form of Thomas (a twin).

Maslanka (*Ukr.*) One who had some characteristic of buttermilk; one who sold buttermilk.

Maslankowski (*Pol.*) One who came from Maslankow(o) (buttermilk).

Maslin, Maslen (*Fr., Eng.*) Descendant of very little Mass, a pet form of Thomas (a twin); or of little Mazo, another pet form of Thomas.

Maslowski, Maslowsky, Maslow (*Pol., Ukr.*) One who churned and sold butter.

Masny (*Cz.*) The large, fleshy man.

Mason (*Eng.*) The builder with stone or brick.

Mass (*Ger.*) Descendant of Mass, a pet form of Thomas (a twin).

Massa (*It.*) Dweller in, or near, a bowl-like depression; descendant of Masso, a pet form of Tommaso, Italian form of Thomas (a twin).

Massara (*It.*) One who wove cloth, a weaver.

Massaro, Massare (*Sp., It.*) One who managed a household or estate, a steward; one who worked in a church, a church porter; one who farmed land as a tenant.

Masse (*Fr.*) One who carries a mace, a heavy spiked staff used for breaking armor in the Middle Ages.

Massenberg (*Ger.*) Dweller on the Massenberg, a hill in Germany.

Massey, Massie (*Eng., Fr.*) One who came from Massy or Macey (Macius' estate), in Normandy; descendant of Massey, a pet form of Thomas (a twin).

Massi, Masso (*It.*) Dweller near a cliff or precipice; descendant of Masso, pet form of Tommaso, Italian form of Thomas (a twin).

Masson, Massot (*Fr.*) Descendant of little Mass, a pet form of Thomas (a twin).

Master, Masters (*Eng.*) One who taught school, a schoolmaster; one skilled in a craft, possibly as associated with an apprentice; dweller in the master's house.

Masterson (*Eng.*) The son of the leader or teacher.

Mastrangelo (*It.*) A master named Angelo (messenger). See Mastro.

Mastro (*It.*) A craftsman who was a master of his trade; one who was head of a workshop; one who taught in a school, a teacher; often this name is a shortened form of other names beginning with this term.

Mastrocola (*It.*) A master named Cola, a pet form of Nicola, Italian form of Nicholas (people's victory). See Mastro.

Mastrogiovanni (*It.*) A master named Giovanni, Italian form of John (gracious gift of Jehovah). See Mastro.

Mastronardo (*It.*) A master named Nardo (pet form of Bernardo and Leonardo). See Mastro.

Mastropaolo (*It.*) A master named Paolo, Italian form of Paul (small). See Mastro.

Mastropietro (*It.*) A master named Pietro, Italian form of Peter (a rock). See Mastro.

Mastrosante (*It.*) A master named Sante (saint). See Mastro.

Mastrovito (*It.*) A master named Vito (life). See Mastro.

Masuda (*Jap.*) Increase, rice field.

Matarazzo (*It.*) One who made and sold mattresses; by extension, the large, fat man.

Matczak (*Pol.*) Descendant of little Mat, a pet form of Matyas, Polish form of Mathias (gift of Jehovah).

Mateo, Mateos (*Sp.*) Descendant of Mateo, Spanish form of Matthew (gift of Jehovah).

Mathason (*Eng.*) The son of Math, a pet form of Matthew (gift of Jehovah).

Matheny (*Fr.*) One who came from Mathenay (Matto's estate), in France.

Mather, Mathers (*Eng.*) One who cut grass, a mower; descendant of Mathere (power, army).

Mathes (*Ger.*) Variant of Mathis, q.v.

Matheson, Mathisen, Mathison, Mathewson (*Scot., Dan.*) Son of Matthew (gift of Jehovah); descendant of Matgamna (bear).

Mathews, Mathew (*Wel., Eng.*) Variant of Matthews, q.v.

Mathias (*Eng.*) Variant of Matthies, q.v.

Mathiesen, Matthiesen (*Nor., Dan.*) The son of Mathies (gift of Jehovah).

Mathieu (*Fr.*) Descendant of Mathieu, French form of Matthew (gift of Jehovah).

Mathis (*Ger.*) Descendant of Mathe, German form of Mathias (gift of Jehovah).

Mathisen (*Nor.*) The son of Mathis (gift of Jehovah).

Matisse (*Fr.*) Descendant of Mathieu, French form of Matthew (gift of Jehovah).

Matkovich, Matkovic (*Rus., Yu.-Sl.*) The son of Matko, a pet form of Matfei, Russian form of Matthew (gift of Jehovah).

Matlock (*Eng.*) One who came from Matlock (oak where a meeting was held).

Matos (*Sp.*) Dweller near a place overgrown with briars.

Matson (*Eng.*) One who came from Matson (Matre's hill), in Gloucestershire; the son of Mat or Matt, pet forms of Matthew (gift of Jehovah).

Matsuda (*Jap.*) Pine, rice field.

Matsumoto (*Jap.*) Pine, base; one who came from Matsumoto (pine, base), a town in Japan.

Matt, Matte (*Eng., Ger.*) Descendant of Matt, a pet form of Matthew (gift of Jehovah); dweller on the meadow.

Matta (*Eng.*) Descendant of Matta, an Old English personal name.

Mattenson (*Eng.*) The son of little Matt, a pet form of Matthew (gift of Jehovah).

Matteo, Mattei (*It.*) Descendant of Matteo, Italian form of Mathias (gift of Jehovah).

Matter, Mattar (*Eng.*) One who made mats by weaving or plaiting rushes, straw, or other material, a most useful object in the cottages of the peasants.

Mattern (*Ger.*) Descendant of Maternus (the motherly).

Matters, Matterson (*Eng.*) The son of Maethhere (power, army).

Mattes, Matteson (*Eng., Ger., Sw.*) Descendant of Matt, a pet form of Matthew (gift of Jehovah).

Matthews, Matthew (*Wel., Eng.*) The son of Matthew (gift of Jehovah).

Matthies, Matthias (*Ger., Eng.*) Descendant of Matthies or Matthias (gift of Jehovah).

Matthis, Matthes (*Ger.*) Descendant of Matthes (gift of Jehovah).

Mattia, Mattiaci, Mattiace (*It.*) Descendant of Mattia, a form of Matthew (gift of Jehovah).

Mattinen (*Finn.*) The son of Matti, Finnish form of Matthew (gift of Jehovah).

Mattingley, Mattingly (*Eng.*) One who came from Mattingley (grove of Matta's people), in Hampshire.

Mattis, Mattison (*Sw.*) Descendant, or son, of Mattis, a Swedish form of Matthew (gift of Jehovah).

Mattmann (*Ger.*) Dweller on a sloping meadow.

Mattox, Mattocks, Mattock (*Eng., Wel.*) Descendant, or son, of Madog or Madoc (fortunate).

Mattson, Mattsson (*Eng., Sw.*) The son of Matt, a pet form of Matthew (gift of Jehovah).

Matty (*Eng.*) Descendant of little Matt, a pet form of Matthew (gift of Jehovah).

Matulevicius (*Lith.*) Descendant of Matas, Lithuanian form of Matthew (gift of Jehovah).

Matulis (*Lith.*) Descendant of little Matas, Lithuanian form of Matthew (gift of Jehovah).

Maturo, Matura (*Sp.*) Descendant of Maturo (mature; intellectual; ethical).

Matus, Matous (*Cz.-Sl., Pol., Lith.*) Descendant of Matas, a Slavic form of Matthew (gift of Jehovah).

Matusoff (*Rus.*) The son of Matus, a pet form of Matfei, Russian form of Matthew (gift of Jehovah).

Matusow (*Cz.-Sl.*) Descendant of Matus, Czechoslovakian form of Matthew (gift of Jehovah).

Matuszak, Matousek, Matushek (*Cz.-Sl., Pol.*) Descendant of Matus, Czechoslovakian form of Matthew; or of Mateusz, Polish form of Matthew (gift of Jehovah).

Matuszkiewicz (*Pol.*) The son of Mateoszek, a Polish form of Matthew (gift of Jehovah).

Matyas (*Hun.*) Descendant of Matyas, Hungarian form of Matthew (gift of Jehovah).

Matz (*Ger.*) Descendant of Mazo, a pet form of Math (assembly place); or of Matz, a pet form of Matthaus (gift of Jehovah).

Matzkin (*Ger.*) Descendant of little Matz, a pet form of Matthaus (gift of Jehovah).

Mau (*Ger.*) One who came from Maua, in Germany.

Mauch (*Ger.*) One who overeats, a glutton; or who enjoys fine food, a gourmet.

Maude, Maud (*Eng.*) Descendant of Maud, an English contraction of Matilda (might, battle).

Mauer (*Ger.*) Dweller near the wall.

Mauger (*Fr., Eng.*) Descendant of Malger (council, spear).

Maul, Maule, Maull (*Ger., Eng.*) One with a large, or animal-like, mouth; one who came from Maule (mouth), in France; descendant of Mall, a pet form of Matilda (might, battle).

Mauldin, Maulden (*Eng.*) One who came from Maulden (hill with a monument), in Bedfordshire.

Maurer (*Ger.*) One who builds with stone, a mason.

Mauriac (*Fr.*) One who came from Mauriac (Maurius' estate), in France; dweller in, or near, Maurus' homestead.

Maurizio (*It.*) Descendant of Maurizio, Italian form of Maurice (Moorish or dark).

Mauro, Mauri (*It.*) Descendant of Mauro (a Moor).

Maury (*Fr.*) Descendant of little Maurin (moorish or dark).

Maus, Mauser (*Ger.*) One who catches mice.

Mauskopf (*Ger.*) Nickname for one thought to have a head like a mouse.

Mavros (*Gr.*) One with a dark or swarthy complexion.

Mawhinney, Mawhiney (*Scot.*) The son of Suibhne (well-going).

Mawson (*Eng.*) The son of Maw, a pet form of Maud (might, battle).

Max (*Ger.*) Descendant of Max, a pet form of Maximilian (the greatest).

Maxey (*Eng.*) One who came from Maxey (Maccu's island), in Northamptonshire.

Maxfield (*Eng.*) One who came from Macclesfield (Malbert's farm), in Lincolnshire.

Maxim, Maxime (*Eng., Fr.*) The greatest, a nickname; descendant of Maxime (greatest).

Maximo (*It.*) The greatest, sometimes an ironical nickname.

Maxson (*Ger., Eng.*) The son of Max, a pet form of Maximilian (the greatest).

Maxwell (*Eng., Scot.*) Dweller by the big spring; one who came from Maccusville (Maccus' pool), in Scotland.

May (*Eng., Fr.*) Descendant of May, a pet form of Matthew (gift of Jehovah); a nickname for one who resembled a young lad or girl.

Maybaum (*Ger.*) Dweller at the sign of the maypole, a tree bedecked with flowers for the May dance.

Mayberry (*Eng.*) Dweller at, or near, the tribal hill.

Maybury (*Eng.*) One who came from Maesbury (Maerec's fort), in Somerset.

Maycock, Mayock (*Eng.*) Descendant of little May, a pet form of Matthew

(gift of Jehovah); the effeminate man, a coward.

Maydew (*Pol., Ukr.*) Dweller near a square or open place near a town, a parade ground or market place.

Maydole (*Scot.*) One who came from Maybole, in Ayrshire.

Mayeda (*Jap.*) Front, rice field.

Mayer (*Ger.*) An overseer or head servant; later, a farmer. See Meyer.

Mayes (*Eng.*) The son of May, a pet form of Matthew (gift of Jehovah).

Mayfield (*Eng.*) One who came from Mayfield (field where madder or mayweed grew), the name of places in Staffordshire and Sussex.

Mayhew (*Eng.*) Descendant of Mayheu, an old French form of Matthew (gift of Jehovah).

Mayhugh (*Eng.*) Variant of Mayhew, q.v.

Maynard (*Eng.*) Descendant of Maynard (strength, hard).

Maynes, Mayne (*Eng., Scot.*) Variant of Maines, q.v.; one who came from Mayne (stone), in Dorset.

Maynor, Mayner (*Eng.*) Descendant of Maginhari (might, army).

Mayo (*Eng., Ir.*) Descendant of Mayo, a pet form of Matthew (gift of Jehovah).

Mayor (*Eng., Ger.*) The mayor or chief official of a borough; variant of Mayer, q.v.

Mays (*Eng.*) The son of May, a pet form of Matthew (gift of Jehovah).

Maza (*Sp.*) Dweller at the sign of the wooden hammer; or at the sign of the bundle; one who fought with a wooden club or mace.

Mazeika (*Lith.*) The small man.

Mazor, Mazer (*Ger.*) One who came from Masuria, now a region in Poland.

Mazur, Mazurek, Mazursky, Mazurski (*Pol.*) One who came from Mazury or Masuria, a former East Prussian province, now a part of Poland; or from Mazowsze, a province in Poland.

Mazurkiewicz (*Pol., Ukr.*) The son of

345

Mazur (one who came from the province of Mazowsze, in Poland).

Mazza, Mazzei, Mazzio, Mazzeo (*It.*) Descendant of Mazzo, a pet form of Giacomazzo, an Italian form of James (may God protect; the supplanter).

Mazzarella (*It.*) Descendant of little Giacomazzo, an Italian form of James (may God protect; the supplanter); nickname for one overly fond of lamb lights.

Mazzino (*It.*) The fat, corpulent fellow.

Mazzola, Mazzoli (*It.*) Variant of Mazza, q.v.

Mazzone, Mazzoni (*It.*) Dweller at the sign of the fish; descendant of big Mazzo, a pet form of Giacomazzo (may God protect; the supplanter); the slow moving man; dweller at, or near, a field or meadow.

Mazzuca, Mazzucca (*It.*) Descendant of Mazzo, a pet form of Giacomazzo (may God protect; the supplanter).

Mc. See Mac. All *Mc* names are listed as if spelled *Mac*. Mc is just a shortened form of Mac.

Meacham, Meachem, Meachum (*Eng.*) One who came from Measham (homestead on the Mease river), in Leicestershire.

Mead, Meade (*Eng., Ir.*) Dweller at the grassland or meadow; the man from Meath (middle).

Meadowcroft (*Eng.*) One who came from Meadowcroft (enclosure in a field where grass is grown), in Lancashire; dweller in an enclosure in a field where grass is grown.

Meadows, Medow, Meadow (*Eng.*) Dweller at, or near, the field where grass is grown for hay.

Meagher (*Ir.*) Grandson of Meachar (hospitable).

Mealey, Mealy (*Ir.*) Grandson of Maille (chief).

Mealmaker (*Scot.*) One who ground grain, a miller.

Means, Mean, Menes (*Eng.*) Dweller near the common or unenclosed land.

Meanwell (*Eng.*) Dweller near the stony spring; or stone work.

Meany, Meaney (*Scot.*) One who came from the lands of Mennie, in Aberdeenshire.

Mearns (*Scot.*) One who came from Mearns (plain of Eire), in Renfrewshire; or from Mearns (plain of Earn), in Glasgow.

Mears, Meers, Mear, Meares (*Eng.*) Dweller at, or near, the lake or pond; dweller at the boundary line.

Mease (*Eng.*) Dweller near the Mease (moss), a river in England.

Mechanic, Mechanick (*Eng.*) A skilled worker with tools; a maker or inventor of machines or contrivances.

Meck, Mecke (*Ger.*) Dweller at the sign of the goat; metonym for one who took care of the goats, a goatherd.

Mecklenburg (*Ger.*) One who came from Mecklenburg (great castle), in Germany.

Meckler (*Ger.*) One who acted as a broker or middleman.

Medeiros, Medearis (*Port.*) One who came from Medeiros (wood), in Portugal.

Medford (*Eng.*) One who came from Meaford (ford at the junction of streams), in Staffordshire.

Medici, Medica (*It.*) One who practices medicine, a doctor.

Medill (*Eng.*) Dweller in, or near, the meadow on the hill.

Medina (*Sp.*) Dweller at, or near, the market; one who had returned from Medina (market), the holy city of Islam, in Arabia; one who came from Medina, the name of several places in Spain.

Medley (*Eng.*) One who came from Medley (middle island), in Oxfordshire.

Medlicott (*Eng.*) One who came from Medlicott (middle cottage), in Shropshire.

Medlock (*Eng.*) Dweller near the Medlock (meadow stream), a river in Lancashire.

Mednick, Mednik (*Rus.*) One who worked in copper, a coppersmith.

Medoff (*Bulg., Rus.*) The son of Med (honey).

Medora, Medori, Medoro (*It.*) Descendant of Medoro (might, hard).

Medved (*Yu.-Sl., Rus.*) Dweller at the sign of the honey bear.

Medway (*Eng.*) Dweller by the Medway (river with sweet water), a river in England.

Mee, Mey, Meye (*Scot., Eng.*) One who came from Mey (a plain), in Caithness; one with the appearance of a young lad or girl; descendant of May, a pet form of Matthew (gift of Jehovah).

Meecham (*Eng.*) Variant of Meacham, q.v.

Meehan, Mehan (*Ir.*) Grandson of Miadhachan (dim. of Miadhach, honorable).

Meeker (*Ger.*) One who came from Mucke (muddy place), in Germany.

Meekins (*Eng.*) Descendant of little May, a pet form of Matthew (gift of Jehovah).

Meeks, Meek (*Eng.*) The mild, or humble, person.

Meenan (*Ir.*) Grandson of little Mian (goodwill).

Meer (*Ger., Du.*) Dweller near a lake; or on the seacoast.

Meggett, Meggitt (*Scot., Eng.*) One who came from the lands of Megget, in Selkirkshire; variant of Maggot, q.v.

Meginley (*Ir.*) Son of Fionnghal (fair valor).

Mehaffey (*Scot., Ir.*) The son of Dubhshithe (black man of peace).

Mehl (*Ger.*) One who sold flour or meal; variant of Mehler, q.v.

Mehler, Mehlman, Mehlmann (*Ger.*) One who paints, a painter.

Mehmed, Mehmet (*Tur., Arab.*) Variant of Muhammed, q.v.

Mehr (*Ger.*) One who came from Meer (sea), in Germany.

Meier (*Ger.*) An overseer, or head servant; later, a farmer. See Meyer.

Meighan (*Ir.*) Variant form of Meehan, q.v.

Meicklejohn (*Eng.*) Descendant of big John (gracious gift of Jehovah).

Meinel (*Ger.*) Descendant of little Mein, a pet form of Meinhardt (might, hard).

Meiners, Meinert (*Ger.*) Variant of Meinhardt, q.v.

Meinhardt, Meinhart (*Ger.*) Descendant of Maginhard (power, hard).

Meinholtz, Meinhold (*Ger.*) Descendant of Maginold (power, rule); one who came from Meinholz, the name of two places in Germany.

Meinz (*Ger.*) Descendant of Meinz, a pet form of names beginning with Magan (power), as Maginhard and Maginolf.

Meir (*Heb.*) The erudite, scholarly, learned man.

Meisel (*Ger.*) Dweller at the sign of the little mouse; or at the sign of the titmouse.

Meisenzahl (*Ger.*) The bird's tail; one who buys and sells songbirds.

Meisler (*Ger.*) One who cut wood or stone.

Meissner, Meisner (*Ger.*) One who came from Meissen (place on the river Meissa), in Saxony; dweller near a swampy place.

Meister, Mester (*Ger.*) One who was master of a trade; a learned person or teacher; an artist.

Melady, Melody (*Eng.*) Descendant of Melodia (a song).

Melamed (*Heb.*) One who taught Talmudic and related subjects; the master or teacher.

Melanson, Melancon, Melonson (*Fr.*) The sick, or infirm, man.

Melaragni (*It.*) One who cultivated and sold oranges; dweller near an orange tree.

Melas (*Gr.*) The swarthy man, black.

Melbourne (*Eng.*) One who came from Melbourne (mill stream; middle stream), the name of places in Derbyshire and the East Riding of Yorkshire.

347

Melby (*Nor.*) One who came from Melby (sandy place), the name of several places in Norway.

Melcher, Melker (*Ger., Eng.*) One who milked cows or goats; a seller of milk; descendant of Melchior (king of the light).

Melchert (*Ger.*) Descendant of Melchert, a short form of Melchior (king of light).

Melchior, Melchiore, Melchiorre, Melchor (*Fr., Ger., It., Sp.*) Descendant of Melchior (king of light).

Meldrum (*Eng.*) Dweller by the bare ridge.

Mele (*Pol., Ukr., Rus.*) The pleasant or charming person.

Melendez, Melindez, Melendro (*Sp.*) Descendant of Melendro, a pet form of Hermenegildo (distributor to the soldiers; cattle, value), the sixth century Spanish saint.

Melin, Melind, Meline (*Fr., Sw.*) Descendant of Amelin (labor, bright).

Melish (*Eng.*) Dweller near the mill on the hide of land, a plot sufficient to support one family.

Mellace (*Eng.*) Variant of Mellish, q.v.

Mellen, Melling (*Eng., Wel.*) One who came from Melling (the people of Malla), the name of two places in Lancashire; one with yellow hair or light complexion.

Mellett (*Ir.*) Descendant of little Milo (soldier; merciful).

Mellinger (*Ger.*) One who came from Mehlingen (muddy water), in Germany.

Mellish, Mellis (*Eng.*) One who came from Mellis (the mills), in Suffolk.

Mellman (*Eng.*) Variant of Millman, q.v.

Mello, Melo (*Port.*) One who came from Mello, in Portugal.

Mellon (*Ir.*) Variant of Malone, q.v.; variant of Mellen, q.v.

Mellor, Meller (*Eng.*) One who came from Mellor (bare hill), in Derbyshire.

Melnick (*Cz.-Sl., Ukr.*) One who ground grain, a miller.

Melnicoff, Melnikov (*Rus.*) The son of the miller.

Melnyczenko (*Ukr.*) The son of the miller.

Melnyk, Melnychuk (*Ukr.*) One who grinds grain, a miller.

Melograna, Melograno (*It.*) Dweller near a pomegranate tree.

Melone, Meloni, Mellone (*It.*) Descendant of Melone, a pet form of Giacomelli (may God protect; the supplanter); one who grew and sold melons.

Melrose (*Scot.*) One who came from Melrose (bare wasteland), in Roxburghshire.

Melsby (*Eng.*) One who came from Melsonby (Maelsuithan's homestead), in the North Riding of Yorkshire.

Melton (*Eng.*) One who came from Melton (mill homestead), the name of several places in England.

Meltzer, Melzer, Meltzner (*Ger.*) One who brews, a brewer; one who came from Meltz, in Germany.

Melville (*Scot.*) One who came from Melville in Scotland or Maleville (bad town), in Normandy.

Melvin (*Scot.*) A variant of Melville, q.v.

Menaker, Menacker (*Ger.*) Dweller near the Menach river, in Germany.

Menard (*Fr.*) Descendant of Menard, a French form of Maynard (strength, hard).

Menarde, Menardi (*It.*) Descendant of Maynard (strength, hard).

Mench (*Ger.*) One who was a male member of a religious order, a monk.

Mencken, Menken (*Ger.*) One who lived in a monastery.

Mendel, Mendell (*Ger.*) Descendant of Mendel (knowledge; wisdom), a dim. of Menahem.

Mendeleev (*Rus.*) The son of Mendel (knowledge; wisdom).

Mendelsohn, Mendelson, Mendelssohn (*Ger.*) The son of Mendel (knowledge; wisdom).

Mendenhall (*Eng.*) One who came from Mildenhall (middle nook; Milda's nook), the name of places in Suffolk and Wiltshire.

Mendez, Mendes (*Sp., Port.*) Descendant of Mendel (knowledge; wisdom).

Mendoza (*Port., Sp.*) One who came from Mendoza (cold or high mountains).

Menear, Minear (*Eng.*) Dweller by the long stone or menhir.

Menefee (*Eng.*) One who came from Menefes (stone enclosure).

Menendez (*Sp.*) The son of Menende, a derivation from Hermenegildo (distributor to the soldiers; cattle, value), the sixth century Spanish saint.

Meneses (*Sp.*) Variant of Menendez, q.v.

Menhennet (*Eng.*) One who came from Menheniot (Huniat's stone), in Cornwall.

Menin (*Bel.*) One who came from Menin, in Belgium.

Menke, Menk (*Ger.*) Descendant of Menk, a pet form of Meinhardt (might, hard).

Menna (*It.*) One with a prominent breast; descendant of Menna, a pet form of Iakmen, a form of Iacabo, Italian form of Jacob (may God protect; the supplanter).

Menninger (*Ger.*) One who came from Menningen (the fens), the name of several places in Germany.

Mensch (*Ger.*) Descendant of Mensch, a pet form of Meinhardt (might, hard); the serving man or attendant at the table.

Menta, Mento (*It.*) One who raised and sold mint.

Mentzer (*Ger.*) One who came from Mainz (swamp), in Germany.

Menzel, Menzl (*Ger.*) Descendant of Manzo, a pet form of Hermann (army, man); one who came from Menzel (boggy lowland), in Germany.

Menzies, Menees (*Scot.*) One who came from Meyners in Normandy.

Meo (*It.*) Descendant of Meo, a pet form of Matteo, Italian form of Mathias (gift of Jehovah); or of Meo, a pet form of Bartolomeo,

Italian form of Bartholomew (son of Talmai, furrow).

Mercado (*Sp.*) One who came from Mercado (market place); dweller near the market place; bought child (Jewish).

Mercer, Mercier (*Eng., Fr.*) One who dealt in silks, velvets and other costly materials; a peddler or merchant of small wares.

Merchant (*Eng.*) The tradesman.

Mercurio (*Sp.*) Descendant of Mercurio (from the god, Mercury).

Meredith, Meridith, Merideth (*Wel.*) Descendant of Maredudd (sea lord).

Mereness (*Eng.*) Dweller near a lake on a headland or cape.

Merfield (*Eng.*) One who came from Marefield (open land frequented by martens), in Leicestershire.

Mergenthaler, Mergenthal, Merganthaler (*Ger.*) One who came from Mergenthal (muddy valley), in Germany.

Meriweather (*Eng.*) Variant of Merriweather, q.v.

Merkel, Merkle, Merkell, Merkl (*Ger.*) Descendant of little Merk or Mark (belonging to Mars, the god of war).

Merker, Merk, Merke (*Ger.*) One who came from Merke (boundary), in Germany; descendant of Marchari (boundary, army).

Merle (*Ger.*) Dweller at the sign of the blackbird.

Merlin (*Ger., Fr., Eng.*) Descendant of little Merl, a pet form of names beginning with Mar (horse), as Marbald and Merhart; dweller at the sign of the little blackbird; or of the falcon.

Merlino (*It.*) Dweller at the sign of the blackbird; the dark-complexioned or swarthy man; descendant of Merlino, Italian form of Merlin (falcon).

Mermelstein (*Ger.*) Nickname for one fond of marmelstein, the German game of marbles.

Merriam (*Eng.*) The gay or merry man.

Merrick, Merick, Merricks (*Eng., Scot.*) Descendant of Merick or Almeric (work, rule); one who came from

349

Merrick (pronged or branching place), in Kirkcudbright.

Merridith (*Wel.*) Variant of Meredith, q.v.

Merrifield, Merryfield (*Eng.*) One who came from Merevale (pleasant valley), in Warwickshire.

Merrigan (*Ir.*) Descendant of little Muir, a pet form of names commencing with this element.

Merrill, Merrell (*Eng.*) Descendant of Muriel, Miriel or Merel (sea, bright).

Merriman, Merryman, Merrymon (*Eng.*) A gay or pleasant man; one who followed a knight or outlaw.

Merritt (*Fr.*) One who tills the soil for which he pays rent, a tenant farmer; the small leader of the village.

Merriweather, Merryweather, Merriwether (*Eng.*) A gay, blithe or agreeable person.

Mersch (*Ger., Fr.*) One who came from Mersch (damp meadow), the name of places in Germany and Luxembourg.

Mertens (*Du., Fr.*) Descendant of Maarten, Dutch form of Martin; or of Martin (belonging to Mars, the god of war).

Mertes (*Ger.*) Descendant of Mertin or Martinus (from Mars, the god of war).

Mertz, Merz (*Ger.*) Descendant of Mertz, a pet form of Mertens (from Mars, the god of war); or of Maro, a pet form of names beginning with Mar (famous), as Maruin and Maroald; one who came from Mertz, in Germany; one who sold small articles.

Mescall (*Ir.*) Grandson of Meisceall.

Meserve, Meservey (*Fr.*) One who measured land, a surveyor.

Mesirow, Meserow (*Pol., Rus., Ukr.*) Dweller on a row, or strip, of land between ditches.

Meskell, Meskill (*Ir.*) Grandson of Meisceall.

Messer (*Eng., Ger.*) One who had charge of the fields, especially one appointed to oversee the reapers or mowers; one who made and sold knives.

Messersmith (*Ger.*) The smith who made knives.

Messina (*It.*) One who came from Messina (the sickle), in Italy.

Messing (*Ger.*) One who made articles of brass.

Messinger, Messenger (*Eng., Ger.*) One who carries communications; one who made and sold articles of brass.

Messmer, Messner (*Ger.*) The church officer who had charge of the sacristy and its contents, a sexton; one who took care of the interior of the church.

Meszaros (*Hun.*) One who cut and sold meat, a butcher.

Metaxas (*Gr.*) One who dealt in silk.

Metcalf, Metcalfe, Metcoff (*Eng.*) Dweller at, or near, the meadow where calves were kept.

Meth, Methe (*Eng.*) Dweller at the middle or center of some place.

Metheny (*Fr.*) Variant of Matheny, q.v.

Methven (*Scot.*) One who came from Methven (mead stone), in Perthshire.

Mets (*Est.*) Dweller in a forest.

Metsala (*Finn.*) Dweller in, or near, the forest.

Metz (*Ger.*) One who came from Metz (in the middle; swamp), in Lorraine; descendant of Metz, a pet form of Matthias (gift of Jehovah); or of Mark (belonging to Mars); or of names beginning with Macht (might), as Mahtfrid and Mahtulf.

Metzer (*Ger.*) One who came from Metz (in the middle; swamp), in Lorraine.

Metzger, Metzler (*Ger.*) One who sold or handled meat, a butcher.

Metzinger (*Ger.*) One who came from Metzingen, the name of several places in Germany.

Metzner (*Ger.*) The miller's helper who used the metze, a small dry measure, to ascertain the meal recompense due the miller; descendant of Metze, a pet form of Mechthild, German form of Matilda (might, battle).

Meunier (*Fr.*) One who grinds grain, a miller.

Meusborn (*Eng.*) Variant of Mewborn, q.v.

Meuser (*Ger.*) Variant of Maus, q.v.

Mew, Mewes (*Eng.*) Dweller at a mew, i.e., a range of stables, with coach houses around an open space.

Mewborn, Mewbourn (*Eng.*) Dweller near a stream frequented by gulls.

Meyer, Meyers (*Ger., Heb.*) An overseer, steward, or head servant; later a farmer or hereditary tenant; derived from the Hebrew *me'ir* (light); learned man.

Meyerson (*Heb., Ger.*) The son of Meir (light); or of the overseer or head servant.

Meyner, Meiner (*Ger.*) Descendant of Maganhar (strength, army); one who came from Meyn, in Germany.

Micek (*Pol.*) One who made and sold caps.

Miceli, Micelli, Micele (*It.*) Descendant of Michele, Italian form of Michael (who is like God).

Michaelis (*Ger.*) Descendant of Michael (who is like God).

Michaels, Michael (*Eng.*) Descendant of Michael (who is like God).

Michaelson, Michaelsen (*Eng., Dan.*) The son of Michael (who is like God).

Michal, Mical (*Pol., Cz.-Sl.*) Descendant of Michal, the Polish and Slovakian form of Michael (who is like God).

Michalak, Michalek, Michalik, Michalec (*Pol.*) Descendant of little Michal, Polish form of Michael (who is like God).

Michalowski, Michalski (*Pol.*) Descendant of Michal (who is like God).

Michaud, Michaux (*Fr.*) Descendant of little Michel, French form of Michael (who is like God).

Michelangelo (*It.*) Descendant of Michelangelo, that is, Michael (who is like God) and Angelus (messenger; angelic).

Michelbach, Michelbacher (*Ger.*) One who came from Michelbach (mud brook), the name of many places in Germany.

Michels, Michel (*Eng., Fr.*) Descendant of Michel, French form of Michael (who is like God).

Michelson, Michelsen (*Nor.*) The son of Michel (who is like God).

Michet (*Fr.*) Descendant of little Michel (who is like God).

Michetti (*It.*) Descendant of Michetti, a shortened form of Domenico (the Lord's day).

Michini (*It.*) Descendant of little Michele, Italian form of Michael (who is like God).

Mickel, Mickels (*Eng.*) Descendant of Michael (who is like God).

Mickelberg, Micklberg (*Ger.*) One who came from Michelsberg, in Germany.

Mickens (*Eng.*) The son of little Mick, a pet form of Michael (who is like God).

Mickey, Mickie (*Scot.*) Descendant of little Mick, a pet form of Michael (who is like God).

Mickle, Mickles (*Eng.*) The big, fat man.

Mickley (*Eng.*) One who came from Mickleby (large village), in the North Riding of Yorkshire.

Micklin (*Eng.*) Descendant of little Mick, a pet form of Michael (who is like God).

Micklos (*Hun.*) Descendant of Miklos, Hungarian form of Nicholas (people's victory).

Mickus (*Lith.*) Descendant of Miczko, a pet form of Demitrius (of Demeter, the goddess of fertility and harvests).

Middendorf (*Ger.*) One who came from Middendorf (middle village; muddy village), in Germany; dweller in the middle of the village.

Middleberg (*Eng.*) One who came from Middlesborough (the middle fort), in the North Riding of Yorkshire.

Middlebrook, Middlebrooks (*Eng.*) Dweller at the middle stream.

Middleman (*Eng.*) One who acts as an intermediary between others; one who buys merchandise in bulk and sells it in smaller quantities to retail dealers.

Middlemas, Midlemas (*Scot.*) Variant of Middlemiss, q.v.

Middlemiss, Middlemist (*Scot.*) One who occupied the Middlemest lands in and around Kelso, in Roxburghshire.

Middleton (*Eng.*) One who came from Middleton (the middle homestead or village), the name of many villages in England.

Midgett, Midgette, Midget (*Fr.*) Descendant of Miget, a pet form of Michel (who is like God).

Midgley (*Eng.*) One who came from Midgley (midge-infested grove), the name of two places in the West Riding of Yorkshire.

Miele (*It.*) One who gathered and sold honey.

Mielke (*Ger.*) Descendant of little Miel, a pet form of Aemilius (industrious); descendant of little Milan (beloved), a pet form of names beginning with Mil (beloved), as Miloslaw and Milobrat.

Mies (*Du.*) Descendant of Mies, a pet form of Bartholomaeus, Dutch form of Bartholomew (son of Talmai, furrow); or of Maria (bitterness; wished-for child; rebellion).

Migliaccio (*It.*) One who made black pudding; descendant of Miliaccio, a shortened form of Emiliaccio (little worker).

Miglio, Migliore (*It.*) Dweller near where millet grew; one who cultivated and sold millet; descendant of Miglio, a pet form of Emilio (work).

Mihalovich, Mihailovich (*Rus.*) The son of Mihal, Slavic form of Michael (who is like God).

Mihaly (*Hun.*) Descendant of Mihaly, Hungarian form of Michael (who is like God).

Mika (*Pol.*) Descendant of Mika, a pet form of Marika, variant of Mary (bitterness; wished-for child; rebellion).

Mike (*Eng.*) Descendant of Mike, a pet form of Michael (who is like God).

Mikelberg (*Ger.*) Variant of Mickelberg, q.v.

Mikkelsen (*Dan., Nor.*) The son of Mikkel, Scandinavian form of Michael (who is like God).

Mikkonen (*Finn.*) The son of Mikko, Finnish form of Michael (who is like God).

Miklos (*Hun.*) Descendant of Miklos, Hungarian form of Nicholas (people's victory).

Mikolajczyk (*Pol.*) Descendant of little Mikolaj, Polish form of Nicholas (people's victory).

Mikos (*Gr.*) Descendant of Michos, a pet form of Mihail, Greek form of Michael (who is like God).

Mikrut (*Pol.*) The little one; descendant of Mikolaj, Polish form of Nicholas (people's victory).

Mikula (*Pol., Rus., Ukr.*) Descendant of Mikolai, Slavic form of Nicholas (people's victory).

Mikulas (*Hun.*) Descendant of Mikulas, Hungarian form of Nicholas (people's victory).

Mikulich (*Yu.-Sl.*) Descendant of Mihailo, a Slavic form of Michael (who is like God).

Mikus (*Lith.*) Descendant of Mikus, a short form of Mykolas, Lithuanian form of Michael (who is like God).

Mikutis (*Lith., Lat.*) Descendant of Mikas, Slavic form of Michael (who is like God).

Milaknis (*Lith.*) Descendant of Milaknis.

Milam (*Eng.*) One who came from Mileham (village with a mill), in Norfolk.

Milan (*Eng., Fr.*) One who came from Milan (middle of the plain), in Italy.

Milano, Milani, Milanesi (*It.*) One who came from Milano (middle of the plain), in Italy.

Milazzo (*It.*) One who came from Milazzo, in Italy.

Milburn, Milbourn, Milbourne (*Eng.*) One who came from Milburn, Milbourne or Milborne (mill stream), the names of various places in England.

Milby (*Eng.*) One who came from Milby (Mildi's homestead), in the North Riding of Yorkshire.

Mileham (*Eng.*) One who came from Mileham (village with a mill), in Norfolk.

Miles (*Wel.*) Descendant of Mile or Miles (soldier).

Milestone (*Eng.*) One who came from Milston (middlemost homestead), in Wiltshire.

Miletto (*It.*) The small one who came from Milo, Italian form of Melos, a Grecian island in the Aegean Sea.

Milewski (*Pol.*) One who came from Milew(o) (dear), in Poland.

Miley (*Eng.*) Descendant of little Milo or Mile (soldier).

Milford (*Eng.*) One who came from Milford (ford by a mill), the name of several places in England.

Milgram, Milgroom, Milgrim (*Eng.*) One who came from Malham (stony place), in Yorkshire; descendant of Milegrim (Grimr with the big mouth).

Milham (*Eng.*) One who came from Mileham (village with a mill), in Norfolk.

Milhaud (*Fr.*) One who came from Milhaud (Aemilius' estate), in France.

Milhouse, Millhouse (*Eng.*) Dweller at the millhouse, a miller.

Milke, Milker (*Eng.*) One who sold milk; or habitually drank milk.

Milkman (*Eng.*) One who sold milk.

Mill (*Eng.*) Dweller at, or near, a mill.

Millan (*Fr., Ir.*) Descendant of Milian, short form of Emilian (industrious); or of Maolan (little bald man).

Millard (*Fr., Eng.*) Dweller at, or near, a field of millet; descendant of Milhard (dear, strong); the keeper of a mill, a miller.

Millberry (*Eng.*) One who came from Melbury (multicolored hill), in Dorset.

Millbourne, Millbourn (*Eng.*) One who came from Melbourne (mill stream; middle stream), the name of places in Derbyshire and the East Riding of Yorkshire; or from Milborne (mill stream), the name of several places in England.

Milledge, Millidge (*Eng.*) One who came from Milwich (mill dwelling), in Staffordshire.

Miller, Millar (*Eng.*) One who grinds grain.

Millet (*Fr.*) One who raised and sold millet; descendant of little Mile, a pet form of Emile, French form of Emil (work).

Milligan, Milliken, Millikin, Millican, Millikan (*Ir.*) Grandson of Maolagan (little bald one).

Milliner, Millner (*Eng.*) One who grinds grain, a miller.

Millington (*Eng.*) One who came from Millington (enclosure with a mill), the name of places in Cheshire and the East Riding of Yorkshire.

Million (*Fr.*) Dweller at, or near, a small field of millet; descendant of little Milo (soldier), or of little Emile (industrious).

Millman (*Eng.*) One who operates a mill, a miller.

Mills, Milles (*Eng.*) Dweller at, or near, a mill.

Millstein, Milstein (*Ger.*) Millstone.

Milman (*Eng.*) One who operated a mill, a miller.

Milmore (*Eng.*) Dweller at the mill on the moor or wet wasteland.

Milne, Miln (*Eng.*) Dweller near, or worker at, the mill.

Milner, Milnor (*Eng.*) One who grinds grain, a miller.

Milos (*Cz.-Sl., Yu.-Sl.*) Descendant of Milos (pleasant).

Milton (*Eng.*) One who came from Milton (middle homestead; mill homestead), the name of many places in England.

Mims, Mimms (*Eng.*) One who came from Mimms, the name of places in Hertfordshire and Middlesex.

Minami (*Jap.*) South.

Minard (*Scot., Fr.*) One who came from Minard (small bay), in Argyll; variant of Menard, q.v.

Minardi, Minardo (*It.*) Descendant of Minardo, Italian form of Maynard (strength, hard).

Minassian (*Arm.*) The son of Manasseh (he made to forget).

Minchener, Minchiner (*Ger.*) One who came from Munich (monk), in Bavaria.

Mindel, Mindell (*Ger.*) Descendant of little Minne, a pet form of Wilhelmina (resolution, helmet); the affectionate person; variant of Mendel, q.v.

Minden (*Eng.*) One who came from Minsden (Myndel's valley), in Hertfordshire.

Mindenhall (*Eng.*) One who came from Mildenhall (Milda's corner; middle place), the name of places in Suffolk and Wiltshire.

Minder, Minderman (*Ger.*) One who came from Minden (swampy area), the name of two places in Germany; the younger son.

Miner (*Eng.*) One who dug coal or mined for other minerals.

Mines, Miness (*Ger.*) Descendant of Mine (warrior).

Minet (*Fr.*) Descendant of Minet, a hypocoristic form of Jaminet, shortened from Benjamin (son of my right hand); or of Thominet, shortened from Thomas (a twin); one who measures; the small, delicate person.

Ming (*Chin.*) Bright.

Mingo (*Sp.*) Descendant of Mingo, a pet form of Domingo, Spanish form of Dominick (the Lord's day).

Minich, Minick (*Ger.*) One who was a male member of a religious order, a monk; variant of Minnick, q.v.

Minicozzi (*It.*) Descendant of Minicozzi, a corrupted form of Domenico, Italian form of Dominick (the Lord's day).

Minifie, Menefee (*Eng.*) One who came from Menefes (stone enclosure).

Miniscalco (*It.*) Superintendent of feats and domestic ceremonies for the nobility.

Minister (*Eng.*) One who acted as an attendant or assistant; variant of Minster, q.v.

Mink (*Ger.*) Variant of Menke, q.v.

Minkus (*Lith.*) Descendant of Minkus, a pet form of Minkantas (remember, suffer).

Minnick, Minnich (*Ger.*) Descendant of Minnich, a contracted form of Dominicus (Sunday's child); or of Minnich, a pet form of Meinhardt (might, bold).

Minogue (*Ir.*) Grandson of Muineog (little monk).

Minor (*Eng.*) One who worked in a mine; a soldier who undermines a fortress.

Minot, Minott (*Fr.*) One who measured goods.

Minshall, Minshull (*Eng.*) One who came from Minshull (Monn's ledge), in Cheshire.

Minsky (*Rus.*) One who came from Minsk, in Byelorussia.

Minson (*Eng., Ir.*) The son of Minn or Minna (love); or of Meann (famous).

Minster (*Eng.*) One who came from Minster (monastery), the name of places in Kent and Oxfordshire; dweller near a monastery; variant of Minister, q.v.

Minter (*Eng.*) One who coined money.

Minton (*Eng.*) One who came from Minton (village by a mountain), in Shropshire.

Minturn, Mintern (*Eng.*) One who came from Minterne (house where mint was stored), in Dorset.

Mintz, Mintzer (*Ger.*) Descendant of Magino, pet form of names beginning with Magan (strength), as Maginbald, Maginhard and Maganrad; one who came from Mainz (great water), the name of two places in Germany.

Minyard (*Fr.*) Descendant of Mingard, a shortened form of Ermengarde (universal, protection); or of Mignard (strong love).

Mir (*Arab.*) Descendant of Mir (prince), a title sometimes granted by the Shah.

Mirabella, Mirabelli (*It.*) Dweller near a beautiful sight.

Mirabile (*It.*) The admired, adored, wonderful man.

Miraglia, Miraglio (*It.*) One who made and sold mirrors.

Miranda, Mirando (*Port., Sp.*) One who came from Miranda (admired place), the name of places in Spain and Portugal.

Miriello (*It.*) Descendant of Mirella (marvel).

Mirkin (*Rus.*) Descendant of Mirke, a diminutive of Miryam (bitterness; wished-for child; rebellion).

Mirra (*It.*) One who produces and sells myrrh; blackbird, an epithet applied to dark-complexioned people, or to one dressed in black.

Mirsch (*Ger.*) Descendant of Mirek, a pet form of Miroslaw (honor, glory).

Mirth (*Eng.*) Dweller near a moor or marsh.

Mirza (*Pers.*) Descendant of Mirza (prince).

Mishkin, Mishkind (*Rus.*) Descendant of Misha, a pet form of Michail, Russian form of Michael (who is like God).

Mitani (*Jap.*) Three, valley.

Mitcham, Mitchum, Mitchem (*Eng.*) One who came from Mitcham (great homestead; swamp homestead), in Surrey.

Mitchell, Mitchel (*Eng., Scot.*) Descendant of Michael (who is like God); the large man.

Mitchner (*Eng.*) One who baked mitches, that is, small loaves of bread or biscuits.

Mitropoulos (*Gr.*) The son of Mitros, a pet form of Demetrius (of Demeter, the goddess of fertility and harvests).

Mitros (*Gr.*) Descendant, or son, of Mitros, a pet form of Dimitros, Greek form of Demetrius (vowed to Demeter, the goddess of fertility and harvests).

Mittelberg (*Ger.*) Dweller on the middle hill; one who came from Mittelberg (middle hill), the name of several places in Germany.

Mitteldorf, Mitteldorfer (*Ger.*) One who came from Mitteldorf (the middle hamlet), the name of several places in Germany.

Mittelman, Mittelmann, Mittleman (*Eng., Ger.*) Variant of Middleman, q.v.; one who acted as a broker or middleman, an agent or go-between.

Mitten, Mittin, Mitton (*Eng.*) One who came from Mitton (homestead at the juncture of two streams), the name of places in Lancashire, Worcestershire, and the West Riding of Yorkshire.

Mittenthal (*Ger.*) Dweller in the middle valley.

Mittman (*Ger.*) One who worked by the day, a day-laborer.

Mittnacht (*Ger.*) Nickname for one who performed some act at midnight.

Mix (*Eng.*) The son of Mick, a pet form of Michael (who is like God); one who came from Mix, in France.

Mixon, Mixson (*Eng.*) The son of Mick, a pet form of Michael (who is like God); one who came from Mixon (dunghill), in Staffordshire.

Miyagishima (*Jap.*) Shrine, castle, island.

Miyake (*Jap.*) Three, house.

Miyako (*Jap.*) Capital.

Miyashiro (*Jap.*) Shrine, castle.

Mizukami (*Jap.*) Water, upper.

Mlakar (*Yu.-Sl.*) Dweller in, or near, the swamp.

Mlynar (*Cz.-Sl.*) One who ground grain, a miller.

Mlynek, Mlejnek (*Cz.-Sl.*) The little miller or grinder of grain.

Moat, Moates, Moats (*Eng.*) Dweller near the moat or stream surrounding the castle.

355

Moberg, Moburg (*Sw.*) Heath, mountain.

Mobley, Moberly (*Eng.*) One who came from Mobberley (glade with an assembly mound), in Cheshire.

Moccia, Moccio (*It.*) Descendant of Moccia, a pet form of Giacomo, Italian form of James (may God protect; the supplanter).

Mock (*Ger.*) The plump or fat man; the clumsy or awkward man.

Mockler (*Ger., Ir.*) The plump or fat man; the bad clerk or clergyman.

Mockus (*Eng.*) One who came from Moccas (moor where pigs were raised), in Herefordshire.

Modell (*Ger.*) One who made and sold patterns or models of some sort.

Moder (*Ger.*) Variant of Maeder, q.v.

Moderski (*Pol.*) The wise, learned man.

Modley (*Eng.*) One who came from Madeley (Mada's grove), the name of places in Shropshire and Staffordshire.

Moe, Moen (*Nor.*) Dweller on the heath or low land.

Moebius (*Ger.*) Descendant of Mebes or Mewes, pet forms of Bartholomaus, German form of Bartholomew (son of Talmai, furrow).

Moeckel (*Ger.*) The little, heavy, bulky man.

Moeller (*Ger.*) One who grinds grain, a miller.

Moffa, Moffo (*It.*) The disagreeable person, a skunk.

Moffet, Moffett, Moffatt, Moffitt, Moffit (*Scot.*) One who came from Moffatt (long plain), in Dumfriesshire.

Mogan (*Ir.*) Descendant of Mochan, a pet form of some name beginning with Moc- (early).

Mogell, Mogel (*Eng.*) One who came from Maghull (corner where mayweed grew), in Lancashire.

Mogge, Mogg (*Eng.*) Descendant of Mogg, a pet form of Margaret (pearl).

Mogilefsky (*Rus.*) Dweller near a tomb or grave.

Mohammed, Mohammad, Mohamed (*Arab.*) Descendant of Mohammed (the praised one).

Mohan (*Ir.*) Grandson of Mochan.

Mohl (*Ger.*) Dweller, or worker, at the mill; descendant of Motilo, a pet form of names beginning with Mut (spirit), as Muotfrid and Modulf; dweller at the sign of the salamander.

Mohler (*Ger.*) Variant of Mehler, q.v.; or of Mueller, q.v.

Mohn (*Ger.*) Descendant of Mon, a pet form of Monrad (thought, counsel).

Mohr (*Ger., Fr.*) One who came from Morocco, a Moor; a dark or black man; descendant of Mohr, a pet form of names beginning with Mor (importance), as Morfrid and Morhart; dweller on the moor or wasteland.

Moir (*Scot.*) The big man; the great man.

Moise (*Fr.*) Descendant of Moise, French form of Moses (child; drawer of water; saved from the water).

Moldenhauer, Mollenhauer (*Ger.*) One who made wooden bowls and molds, especially oblong baking and meat troughs.

Mole (*Eng.*) One disfigured by a prominent mole; descendant of Mold, a contracted form of Matilda (might, battle).

Molesworth (*Eng.*) One who came from Molesworth (Mul's homestead), in Huntingdonshire.

Moliere (*Fr.*) One who lived near the quarry from which millstones were obtained.

Molina, Molino (*Sp., It.*) One who came from Molina (mill), the name of various towns in Spain; dweller near a mill.

Molinari, Molinaro (*It.*) One who grinds grain, a miller.

Moline (*Fr.*) One who came from Moline (mill), in France.

Molineaux (*Fr.*) Variant of Molyneaux, q.v.

Molinero (*Sp.*) One who ground grain, a miller.

Molinier, Moliner (*Fr.*) Variant of Moulinier, q.v.

Moll (*Eng., Ger.*) One who paid a money rent to the lord of the manor in return for the land he held and worked for the lord only on special occasions; descendant of Moll (the foolish one); or of Mall, a pet form of Mary (bitterness; wished-for child; rebellion); variant of Mohl, q.v.

Moller (*Sw., Nor., Ger.*) One who grinds grain, a miller; variant of Muller, q.v.

Molloy (*Ir.*) Grandson of Maolmuadh (noble chief).

Molnar, Molner, Molnor (*Hun.*) One who ground grain, a miller.

Moloney, Molony (*Ir.*) Grandson of Maoldomhnaigh (devoted to Sunday, or to the Church).

Molotov (*Rus.*) Hammer, an adopted name.

Molotsky (*Rus.*) One who ground grain, a miller; one who worked with a large hammer.

Molter (*Ger.*) One who prepares malt to brew or distill liquor.

Moltke (*Ger.*) Dweller at the sign of the little hammer; one who prepares malt.

Molyneaux, Molyneux (*Fr.*) One who grinds grain, a miller.

Molz, Moltz, Molzahn (*Ger.*) One who came from Molzen, in Germany.

Moman (*Du.*) Descendant of Momme, a pet form of Mombert (thought, bright).

Monaco (*Fr.*) One who came from Monaco (monk house), an independent principality on the Mediterranean Sea near the French-Italian border.

Monahan, Monaghan (*Ir.*) Descendant of the little monk, i.e., a tenant of ecclesiastical lands; grandson of Manachan (diminutive of manach, a monk).

Monckton (*Eng.*) One who came from Monkton (the village of the monks), the name of nine places in England.

Moncrief, Moncrieff, Moncreiffe (*Scot.*) One who came from Moncrieff (hill with trees), in Perthshire.

Monday (*Eng.*) One who occupied land in an English manor for which he worked for the lord one day a week, on Mondays; descendant of Monday (one born on Monday).

Mondillo, Mondello (*It.*) The little, cute, clean man.

Mondragon (*Fr.*) One who came from Mondragon (dragon mountain), in France.

Mondscheim, Mondschein, Mondshein (*Ger.*) Nickname for one who worked by moonlight; dweller at the sign of moonlight.

Monesmith (*Eng.*) One who made money, a minter.

Monet (*Fr.*) Descendant of little Mon, a pet form of names ending in -mon (protection), as Aymon and Emon.

Money, Monnie (*Eng., Ir.*) One who came from Monnaie (mint), in France; descendant of Maonach (wealthy).

Moneyhun (*Ir.*) Variant of Monahan, q.v.

Moneypenny (*Eng.*) One with much money, a wealthy man; or ironically, a nickname for a poor man.

Mongan (*Ir.*) Descendant of little Mongach (hairy).

Monger, Mounger (*Eng.*) One who sells merchandise, a dealer.

Moniz (*Sp.*) Variant of Nunez, q.v.

Monk, Monks (*Eng.*) One who was a male member of a religious order.

Monkhouse (*Eng.*) Dweller near, or worker in, the house where the monks lived.

Monkman (*Eng.*) The monk's servant.

Monks (*Eng.*) One who worked for the monks; the descendant of the monk.

Monkton (*Eng.*) One who came from Monkton (place where the monks resided), the name of various places in England.

Monnier (*Fr.*) Variant of Meunier, q.v.

Monnik (*Du.*) One who was a male member of a religious order, a monk.

357

Monreal (*Sp.*) One who came from Monreal (royal mountain), the name of several places in Spain.

Monroe, Monro (*Scot.*) One who came from near the Roe river in Derry, Ireland; dweller near a red swamp.

Monson, Monsen (*Sw., Dan.*) The son of Mon, a pet form of Magnus (great).

Montagna, Montegna (*It.*) One who came from Montagna (mountain), in Italy; dweller on the mountain.

Montagne (*Fr.*) Dweller on the mountain.

Montagnon (*Fr.*) Dweller in the mountains or high lands.

Montague, Montagu (*Fr., Eng.*) One who came from Montacute or Mont Aigu (peaked hill), in Normandy; dweller on a pointed mountain or hill.

Montaigne (*Fr.*) Early spelling of Montagne, q.v.

Montalbano (*It.*) One who came from Montalbano (white grape mountain), in Italy.

Montalto (*It., Sp.*) One who came from Montalto (high mountain), in Italy; or from Montalto (high mountain), in Spain.

Montalvo (*Port., Sp.*) One who came from Montalvo (white mountain), the name of places in Portugal and Spain.

Montana (*Sp.*) Dweller on the mountain.

Montanez (*Sp.*) Variant of Montana, q.v.

Montano (*Sp., It.*) Dweller in the mountains, or in a hilly district.

Montcalm (*Fr.*) One who came from Montcalm, in France.

Monte (*It., Sp., Port.*) Dweller on a mountain or large hill; one who came from Monte (mountain), the name of several places in Spain.

Montebello (*It., Fr.*) One who came from Montebello (beautiful mountain), in Italy; or from Montebello (beautiful mountain), now called Montbel, in France.

Montefiore (*It.*) One who came from Montefiore (flower mountain), in Italy.

Monteiro (*Port.*) One in charge of a forest, a gamekeeper.

Monteith, Monteath (*Scot.*) One who came from Monteith (moss wasteland), in Perthshire.

Monteleone (*It.*) One who came from Monteleone (lion mountain), in Italy.

Montemayor (*Sp.*) One who came from Montemayor (great mountain), in Spain.

Montenegro (*It., Sp.*) One who came from Montenegro (black mountain), in Italy; or from Montenegro (black mountain), in Spain; or from Montenegro (black mountain), a former kingdom in Southwest Europe.

Montes (*Sp.*) Dweller in the mountains.

Montessori (*It.*) One who came from Montessori, in Tuscany.

Monteux (*Fr.*) One who came from Monteux, originally Montilio (mountain), in France.

Monteverdi (*It.*) Dweller on, or near, the green hill.

Montez (*Sp.*) Dweller in the mountains.

Montgomery (*Wel.*) One who came from Montgomery (hill of Gomeric), in Wales; or from Sainte-Foy-de-Montgomery, in Normandy, or Saint-Germain-de-Montgomery, in Calvados.

Monti (*It.*) Dweller on the hill or mountain.

Montone (*It.*) Dweller on a large mound; dweller at the sign of the ram.

Montoya (*Sp.*) One who came from Montoya (horse pasture; mountain fort), in Spain; dweller on the hilly land.

Montroy (*Sp.*) One who came from Montroy (red mountain), in Spain.

Moock (*Du.*) One who came from Moock, in Holland.

Moody, Moodie, Mudie (*Eng.*) The bold, impetuous, brave man.

Moon, Moone (*Eng.*) One who came from Mohon, in France; dweller at the sign of the moon; variant of Munn, q.v.

Mooney (*Ir.*) Grandson of Maonach (wealthy).

Moonlight (*Scot.*) One who came from Munlochy (plain of the black place; foot of the loch), in Scotland.

Moonshine (*Ger.*) Translation from German Monschein (moonshine). The Germans also have names referring to the new moon, half moon, full moon and good moon.

Moore, Moor, Moors, More (*Eng., Scot.*) Dweller in, or near, the marsh or high wasteland; descendant of More, a form of Maur (Moorish or dark); nickname for one dark as a Moor.

Moorehead, Moorhead (*Eng., Scot.*) Dweller at the upper end of the moor or high wasteland. See Muirhead.

Moorer (*Eng.*) Dweller near the moor or high wasteland.

Moorhouse, Moorehouse (*Eng.*) Dweller in the house on the moor or high wasteland.

Moorman (*Scot.*) The official in charge of the cattle on the marsh or waste ground.

Moos, Moose (*Ger.*) Dweller near a peat bog.

Mora (*Sp., Ir.*) One who came from Mora (black mulberry tree), the name of two places in Spain; dweller at the moor or heath.

Morabito (*It.*) One who lives in solitude, a hermit.

Morais (*Port.*) Descendant of Moral (right and proper).

Morales, Moralez (*Sp.*) The son of Moral (right and proper); one who came from Morales (mulberry tree), the name of two towns in Spain.

Moran, Morane, Moraine (*Ir.*) Grandson of Moran (little great man); grandson of Mughron (slave-seal).

Morano (*It.*) One with a rather dark complexion.

Morantz, Moranz (*Pol.*) Descendant of Morana (goddess of winter and death in Slavic mythology).

Moravec, Moravek (*Cz.-Sl.*) One who came from Moravia (district of the marshy river), a former province in Czechoslovakia.

Morawski, Moravsky (*Pol., Cz.-Sl.*) One who came from Moravia (plain of the river Morava), in Czechoslovakia; dweller on a grassy plain.

Mordecai (*Wel.*) Descendant of Mordecai (taught of God); follower of Marduk, the state god of Babylon.

Moreau (*Fr.*) One who came from Moreau, the name of three places in France; the brown-skinned man, perhaps a Moor.

Morehead, Moorhead (*Scot.*) Variant of Muirhead, q.v.

Morehouse (*Eng.*) Dweller in the house by the swamp or wasteland.

Moreira (*Port.*) One who came from Moreira (mulberry tree), in Portugal; dweller near a mulberry tree.

Moreland (*Eng.*) One who came from Morland (grove by a moor), in Westmorland; dweller near a swamp.

Morell, Morel (*Sp., Fr.*) Descendant of little Mauro (a Moor); one who came from Morell, in Spain; one who had brown skin.

Morelli, Morello (*It.*) Descendant of little More, a pet form of Amore (love); or of Mauro (a Moor); the small, dark-complexioned man.

Moreno (*Sp., It., Heb.*) The dark-complexioned man; descendant of Moreno (black); a Hebrew title—Master.

Moretti, Moretta (*It.*) Same as Morelli, q.v.

Morey (*Ir.*) Grandson of Mordha (majestic).

Morff, Morf (*Swis., Ger.*) Descendant of Morolf (moor, wolf).

Morford (*Eng.*) Dweller by the river crossing at the moor or fen.

Morgan (*Wel.*) Descendant of Morgan (great, bright).

Morgenroth (*Ger.*) One who was active in some way at sunrise or dawn; one who commenced work at sunrise.

Morgenstein, Morganstein (*Ger.*) Dweller near the Morgenstein (morning rock), in Germany.

Morgenstern, Morganstern (*Ger.*) One who came from Morgenstern (morning star), the name of two places in Germany; the warrior who used a morgenstern, a medieval cudgel; dweller at the sign of the morning star.

Morgenthaler (*Ger.*) One who came from Mergenthal (muddy valley), in Germany.

Morgenthau (*Ger.*) Morning valley.

Mori (*Jap.*) Forest.

Moriarty (*Ir.*) Grandson of Muircheartach (expert navigator).

Morici (*It.*) Descendant of little Mauro, Italian form of Maurice (moorish or dark).

Morin (*Fr.*) One who had a dark complexion; a Moor.

Morita (*Jap.*) Forest, rice field.

Moritz, Morritz (*Ger.*) Descendant of Moritz, a variant of Mauritius (a Moor; dark).

Mork (*Nor.*) Dweller near the mork, or unenclosed land owned jointly by the surrounding landowners.

Morley (*Eng.*) One who came from Morley (wood by a marsh), the name of several places in England.

Morlock (*Eng.*) Dweller at the lake by the wasteland.

Morman, Mormon (*Scot.*) Variant of Moorman, q.v.

Mornar (*Yu.-Sl.*) One who worked on a ship, a sailor.

Moro (*Sp.*) One who came from Africa, a Moor; one who came from Moro (Moor's place), in Spain.

Morocco (*Sp.*) One who came from Morocco (the adorned city), in North Africa.

Moron (*Sp., Fr.*) Descendant of little Mor (swarthy); one who came from Moron, in Spain; one with a dark skin.

Moroney (*Ir.*) Grandson of Maolruanaidh (follower of Ruanaidh, hero).

Moroz, Moroze (*Ukr.*) Descendant of Moroz, possibly one born at time of frost.

Morphew, Morphie, Morfey (*Scot.*) One who came from Morphie (marsh; sea plain), in Kincardineshire.

Morreale (*It.*) One who came from Morreale (royal mountain), in Italy.

Morrill, Morrell, Morrall (*Eng.*) The little dark-complexioned man; descendant of Morel (dark-complexioned).

Morris, Morice (*Wel., Fr.*) Descendant of Maurice (Moorish, or dark-skinned).

Morrison, Morison (*Eng., Scot.*) The son of Morris (Moorish, or dark-skinned).

Morrissey, Morrisey (*Ir.*) Grandson of Muirgheas (sea prophet).

Morrone (*It.*) Dweller near a cliff or precipice; one with a dark or swarthy complexion.

Morroney (*Ir.*) Grandson of the follower of Ruanaidh (hero).

Morrow (*Eng.*) Dweller in the row of houses by the moor, i.e., marsh or wasteland.

Morse (*Eng.*) Dweller at, or near, a moor or marshy wasteland; the son of Moor (dark-complexioned man); one who came from North Africa.

Mort (*Fr., Eng.*) One with a brown skin or dark complexion, a Moor; descendant of Maur (dark); or of Mort, a pet form of Mortimer (sea warrior; stagnant water).

Mortensen, Mortenson (*Dan., Nor., Sw.*) The son of Morten (from Mars, the god of war).

Mortimer, Mortimore (*Eng.*) One who came from Mortemer (stagnant water), in Normandy.

Morton (*Eng.*) One who came from Morton (homestead by a marsh), the name of many places in England.

Mosby (*Nor.*) One who came from Mosby (place where malt is crushed), the name of several places in Norway.

Mosca, Moscone (*It.*) Nickname for a small, unimportant person, a fly; one with a pointed tuft of hair on the chin, an imperial.

Moscato (*It.*) Dweller near a vineyard; one with a dapple gray appearance.

Moseby (*Nor.*) One who came from Moseby (place where moss grew), in Norway.

Moseley, Mosley, Mosely (*Eng.*) One from Moseley (Moll's wood or clearing; clearing infested by mice), the name of villages in Staffordshire and Worcestershire.

Moser (*Fr., Ger.*) One who grew and sold vegetables; dweller in a marsh or swamp.

Moses, Moseson (*Wel., Eng.*) Descendant of Moses (child; drawer of water; saved from the water).

Mosher, Moshier (*Ger.*) Dweller on, or near, the moor or swamp.

Moshinsky (*Ukr.*) Dweller near where moss grew.

Mosier (*Fr.*) One who grew and sold vegetables.

Moskal (*Pol., Ukr.*) A Russian soldier who came from Muscovy, a principality in West Central Russia.

Moskovitz, Moskowitz (*Cz.-Sl., Yu.-Sl.*) The son of Mosko (child; drawer of water; saved from the water).

Moskovsky (*Rus.*) One who came from Moscow (mossy water), in Russia.

Moskvin (*Rus.*) One who came from Moscow (mossy water), in Russia.

Moskwa (*Pol.*) One who came from Moscow (mossy water), in Russia.

Moss, Mosse (*Fr., Eng.*) Descendant of Moss, a pet form of Moses (child; saved from the water; drawer of water); one who came from Moss (morass), in the West Riding of Yorkshire.

Most (*Ger., Pol., Bulg., Rus.*) One who prepared and sold new wine; dweller near, or keeper of, a bridge.

Mostovoy (*Rus.*) Dweller near a bridge.

Mostyn, Moston (*Wel.*) One who came from Mostyn (field fortress), in Wales.

Motel (*Pol., Fr.*) Dweller at the sign of the butterfly; one thought to possess some characteristic of a butterfly; dweller near a small fortification.

Motley, Mottley (*Eng.*) One who made cloth of a mixed color.

Moton (*Eng.*) One who took care of sheep, a shepherd; dweller at the sign of the sheep.

Motrenko (*Ukr.*) The son of Motrja, a mother's name, Motrona.

Mott, Mote (*Eng.*) Dweller near a moat; or near a mound or embankment.

Mottershead (*Eng.*) One who came from Mottershead (Modhere's headland), in Cheshire.

Motto, Mottola, Mottolo (*It.*) Descendant of Motto, a pet form of Giacomo, Italian form of James (may God protect; the supplanter).

Moul, Moule (*Eng.*) Variant of Mole, q.v.

Moulder (*Eng.*) One who made moulds or patterns.

Moulin (*Fr.*) Dweller near, or worker at, a mill.

Moulinier (*Fr.*) One who ground grain, a miller.

Moulton (*Eng.*) One who came from Moulton (Mula's homestead), the name of various places in England.

Moultrie (*Scot.*) One who came from Multreve, in Scotland.

Mounce (*Eng.*) Dweller on, or near, a small hill.

Mounday (*Eng.*) Variant of Monday, q.v.

Mounsey, Mouncey (*Eng.*) Variant of Munsey, q.v.

Mount (*Eng.*) Dweller on a hill or mound.

Mountain (*Eng.*) Dweller on a mountain or in a mountainous district.

Mountney, Mounteney (*Eng.*) One who came from Montigny (hilly district), in Normandy.

Mounts (*Eng.*) Dweller on a hill.

Mousley (*Eng.*) Variant of Moseley, q.v.

Mouton (*Fr.*) Dweller at the sign of the sheep; one who raised sheep.

Mouzon (*Fr.*) One who came from Mouzon (market on Meuse river), the name of several places in France.

Mowbray (*Eng.*) One who came from Montbrai (hill of wet spongy earth), in Normandy.

Mower, Mowery, Mowrey, Mowry (*Eng.*) One who cuts or mows grass and harvests crops; dweller at the moor or high wasteland.

Mowrer (*Ger.*) Americanized form of Maurer, q.v.

Moxley (*Eng.*) Dweller in, or near, Maccos's pasture; one who came from Mowsley (mouse-infested wood), in Leicestershire.

Moy (*Chin.*) Plum flower.

Moye (*Scot.*) One who came from Moy (plain or level field), in Inverness.

Moyer, Moyers (*Ir.*) The son of the steward.

Moylan (*Ir.*) Descendant of Maolan (little bald one).

Moyle, Moyles (*Eng.*) The bald-headed man.

Moynahan, Moynihan (*Ir.*) Descendant of Muimhneachain (Munsterman).

Moyse, Moyses (*Eng., Fr.*) Descendant of Moses (child; saved from the water; drawer of water).

Mozart (*Ger.*) Descendant of Muothart (spirit, strong).

Mozer (*Fr., Ger.*) Variant of Moser, q.v.

Mozitis (*Lith.*) The very small person.

Mraz (*Cz.-Sl., Yu.-Sl.*) Descendant of Mraz (frost).

Mrazek (*Cz.-Sl.*) Descendant of little Mraz (frost).

Mroz, Mrozek (*Cz.-Sl.*) One with the qualities of a walrus, for example, fat or mustached; one who lived at the sign of the walrus, or little walrus.

Mucci (*It.*) Descendant of Mucci, a pet form of Giacomo, Italian form of James (may God protect; the supplanter).

Much (*Eng.*) The large man.

Mucha, Muchnick (*Pol., Ukr., Cz.-Sl., Rus.*) One with the characteristics of a fly, perhaps a small insignificant man; dweller at the sign of the fly.

Muchmore (*Eng.*) Dweller in the large marsh or extensive high wasteland.

Muckenfuss (*Ger.*) Nickname for one with a gnat's foot, possibly a small foot.

Muckey (*Eng.*) Dweller on Mucca's island.

Muckle (*Eng.*) The big man; descendant of Mucel (large).

Muckley (*Eng., Ir.*) One who came from Mudgley (muddy grove), in Somerset; dweller at the dirty grove; descendant of Maolchluiche (gamester).

Mudd (*Eng.*) Dweller at the muddy place.

Mudge (*Eng.*) Dweller in, or near, a swamp.

Mudgett (*Eng.*) Dweller in, or near, the little swamp.

Mudie (*Eng.*) The bold, impetuous, brave man.

Mudrick, Mudry (*Ukr.*) Descendant of Mudryk, a pet form of Mudryj (wise).

Mueller (*Ger.*) One who ground grain, a miller.

Muench, Munch (*Ger.*) One who was a member of a religious order.

Muenzer (*Ger.*) Variant of Munzer, q.v.

Muffler (*Ger.*) The surly, disgruntled, bad-tempered man.

Mugford (*Eng.*) One who came from Mudford (muddy river crossing), in Somerset; dweller by the wide river crossing.

Muggeridge (*Eng.*) One who came from Mogridge (Muca's range of hills), in Devonshire.

Muggleworth (*Eng.*) One who came from Muggleswick (village of Mucel's people), in Durham.

Muhammed, Muhammad (*Arab., Pers., Tur.*) Descendant of Muhammed (praised one).

Muhl, Muhle (*Ger.*) Dweller near the mill.

Muhlberger (*Ger.*) One who came from Muhlberg (mountain stream), in Germany.

Muhlenberg (*Ger.*) One who came from Muhlenberg (mountain stream), the name of three places in Germany.

Muhler (*Ger.*) One who operated a mill, a miller.

Muhly (*Ger.*) The troublesome, irksome

man; dweller near, or worker at, the mill.

Muhr (*Ger.*) Dweller at the marsh land or moor; dweller near a wall.

Muir (*Scot.*) Dweller at, or near, a moor or heath.

Muirhead (*Scot.*) One who came from Muirhead (upper end of the moor), the name of several places in Scotland; dweller at the upper end of the marsh.

Mulcahy (*Ir.*) Grandson of Maolchatha (battle chief); or of Maolcathach (warlike chief); or of Maolchathaigh (follower of Cathach; warlike).

Mulder, Mulders (*Du.*) One who grinds grain, a miller.

Muldoon, Muldon (*Ir.*) Grandson of Maolduin (commander of the garrison).

Muldowney (*Ir.*) Grandson of Maoldomhnaigh (devoted to Sunday; or to the Church).

Muldrow, Muldrew (*Ir.*) Grandson of Maolruadh (red chief); the son of the little disciple.

Mule, Mula (*It., Ger.*) Dweller at the sign of the mule; one thought to be stubborn as a mule; the illegitimate child; dweller near the mill.

Mulford (*Eng.*) Dweller near the mill by the ford; dweller near the river crossing used by mules.

Mulgrew (*Ir.*) Descendant of Maolchraoibhe (chief of Craobh).

Mulhall (*Ir.*) Descendant of Maolchathail (devotee of St. Cathal).

Mulhern, Mulkearn (*Ir.*) Descendant of Maolchiarain (servant of St. Ciaran).

Mulholland (*Ir.*) Grandson of Maolchallann (chief of the calends); devotee of St. Calann.

Mulkin (*Ir.*) Descendant of Maolcaoim (gentle chief).

Mull (*Eng., Scot.*) One who lived, or worked, at the mill; one who came from Mull (bare rock), the name of several places in Scotland.

Mullane (*Ir.*) The little bald man.

Mullaney, Mullany (*Ir.*) Grandson of the follower or devotee of St. Senan

(old, wise), the name of various Irish saints.

Mullarkey (*Ir.*) Variant of Malarkey, q.v.

Mullee (*Ir.*) Descendant of Maolaodha (devotee of St. Aodh, fire).

Mullen, Mullon, Mullan (*Ir.*) Grandson of Maolan (diminutive of *maol*, bald); the son of the little bald man.

Muller (*Ger., Swis.*) One who ground grain, a miller.

Mulligan, Mulliken, Mullikin (*Ir.*) Grandson of Maolagan (little bald one).

Mullins, Mullin (*Ir., Fr.*) Grandson of Maolan (diminutive of *maol*, bald); one who came from Moulins or Moulines (mills), the names of several places in France; one who ground grain, a miller.

Mulroy (*Ir.*) Grandson of Maolruadh (red chief).

Mulvaney, Mulvany, Mulvanny, Mulvenny (*Ir.*) Grandson of one overly concerned with minor details, a fussy person; grandson of Maolmheana (follower of Meana).

Mulvey (*Ir.*) Grandson of Maolmiadhach (honorable chief).

Mulvihill (*Ir.*) Grandson of Maolmhichil (servant of St. Michael).

Mumby (*Eng.*) One who came from Mumby (Mundi's homestead), in Lincolnshire.

Mumford (*Eng.*) One who came from Mundford (Munda's river crossing), the name of several places in England.

Munch (*Ger., Nor.*) One previously resident in a monastery; a member of a religious order, a monk.

Munchen (*Ger.*) One who came from Munchen (monk), English form, Munich, a city in Bavaria.

Mundell (*Scot.*) One who came from Mandeville (great town; Mando's estate), in Normandy.

Mundt, Mund, Muntz, Munz (*Ger.*) Descendant of Mundo, a pet form of names beginning with Munt (protection), as Mundhart and Munderich; one who came from Muntz, in Germany.

Mundy, Munday (*Eng.*) Descendant of Monday, a name given to children in the Middle Ages born on a Monday; variant of Monday, q.v.

Munford (*Eng.*) One who came from Mundford (Munda's river crossing), in Norfolk.

Mungall, Mungal, Mungle (*Scot.*) One who came from Mungal (moss wall), in Stirlingshire.

Munger (*Eng.*) One who sold things, a merchant.

Munich (*Eng.*) One who came from Munich (monk), in Bavaria.

Munk (*Eng.*) One who resided in a monastic establishment, a monk.

Munn, Munns (*Eng.*) One who resided in a monastic establishment, a monk.

Munoz, Muniz (*Sp.*) The son of Muno (hill), or of Nuno (ninth).

Munro, Munroe (*Scot.*) One who came from near the Roe river in Derry, Ireland; dweller near a red swamp.

Munsey, Muncey, Munce (*Eng.*) One who came from Monceaux (little hill), in Calvados.

Munson, Munsen (*Sw., Eng., Nor.*) The son of Mans, a pet form of Magnus (great); the son of Mun, a pet form of Edmund (rich protector).

Munster (*Ir.*) One who came from Munster (Munhan's district), an Irish province.

Munzer (*Ger.*) One authorized to coin money, a minter.

Murakami (*Jap.*) Village, upper.

Muraresku (*Rom.*) The son of the miller.

Muratore (*Fr., It.*) One who worked with stone or brick, a mason.

Murawski (*Pol.*) One who lived near an outstanding lawn.

Murayama (*Jap.*) Village, mountain.

Murch, Murche, Murchie (*Ir., Eng.*) Descendant of Murchadh (sea warrior); or of the dwarf.

Murchison (*Eng.*) The son of the dwarf.

Murdock, Murdoch (*Eng., Ir., Scot.*) Descendant of Murdoch (seaman).

Murff, Murph (*Swis., Ger.*) American variant of Morff, q.v.

Murfield (*Eng.*) Dweller at a marsh or fen in open country.

Murgatroyd, Murgitroyde (*Eng.*) Dweller at Margaret's clearing.

Murillo (*Sp.*) One who came from Murillo de Rio de Leza, in Spain.

Murk (*Est.*) One who worked with steel.

Murnane (*Ir.*) Grandson of Manannan (the name of an ancient Irish sea-god).

Murphy, Murphey (*Ir.*) Descendant of Murchadh (sea warrior).

Murray, Murry, Murrie (*Scot.*) One who came from Moray (beside the sea), in Scotland.

Murre (*Est.*) One who worked in a quarry.

Murrell (*Eng.*) A variant of Morrill, q.v.

Murtaugh, Murtagh (*Ir.*) Grandson of Muircheartach (expert navigator).

Murtha (*Ir.*) Son of the sea-director or navigator.

Murzyn (*Pol.*) The black or dark-complexioned man; a Negro; a Moor.

Musa (*Arab.*) Descendant of Musa, Arabian form of Moses (child; saved from the water; drawer of water).

Muscarello, Muscarella (*It.*) One who cultivated the muscat or muscatel grape; one thought to possess the characteristics of a gnat.

Muschamp (*Scot.*) Dweller in, or near, the field of flies. The name is probably of Norman origin.

Muschek, Muschick (*Rus.*) The peasant or small landholder.

Muse, Muhs (*Eng.*) Dweller near the hawk's cage; dweller at a mew, i.e., a range of stables with coach houses around an open space.

Musgrave, Musgrove (*Eng.*) One who came from Musgrave (grove overrun with mice), in Westmorland.

Musial (*Pol.*) Descendant of Musial (he was forced to).

Musick, Music (*Pol.*) The peasant or vassal.

Muskett (*Eng.*) Dweller at the sign of the sparrowhawk.

Muskie (*Cz.-Sl.*) The strong or masculine person.

Musselman (*Eng.*) One who gathered and sold mussels.

Musser (*Ger.*) One who came from Mussen (swamp), the name of two places in Germany.

Musset (*Fr.*) The little reticent, secretive man; dweller near the hidden place.

Mussey (*Fr.*) One who came from Mussey (Mucius' estate), in France.

Musslewhite (*Eng.*) Dweller at a low meadow near where mussels were found.

Musso (*It.*) One with a large mouth and lips; descendant of Musso, a pet form of Giacomo, Italian form of James (may God protect; the supplanter).

Mussolini (*It.*) A nickname, from some supposed resemblance to a gnat.

Must (*Est., Finn.*) The dark, swarthy man, black.

Mustafa (*Tur., Arab.*) Descendant of Mustafa (the chosen one).

Mustanen (*Finn.*) Descendant of the swarthy or dark-complexioned man.

Mustin, Muston (*Eng.*) One who came from Muston (Musi's homestead; enclosure infested by mice), the name of places in Leicestershire and the East Riding of Yorkshire.

Mustoe, Musto (*Eng.*) Dweller near the moot stow, the meeting place of the hundred.

Muszynski (*Pol.*) One who came from Muszyn (fly), in Poland.

Mutch (*Eng.*) Sharpened form of Much, q.v.

Mutchler (*Ger.*) Variant of Mutschler, q.v.

Mutchnick (*Rus.*) One who grinds grain and sells flour.

Muth (*Ger.*) Descendant of Muth, a pet form of Helmuth (helmet, courage); the brave or courageous man; descendant of Muth, a pet form of names beginning with Mut (courage), as Muotfrid and Mothar.

Muto (*Jap.*) Brave, wisteria.

Mutschler (*Ger.*) One who baked bread, a baker.

Mutter (*Ger.*) The mother's son or mother's boy; dweller at, or near, a morass.

Mutz, Mutzer (*Ger.*) One who baked white bread, a baker; descendant of Mutz, a pet form of names beginning with Mut (courage), as Muothart and Modulf.

Mutziger (*Ger.*) One who came from Mutzig (swampy place), in Germany.

Muzyka (*Pol., Ukr.*) One with the characteristics of a little fly; one skilled in music, a musician.

Muzzey, Muzzy (*Fr.*) One who came from Mussey or Mussy (Mucius' estate), the names of several places in France.

Myatt (*Eng.*) Descendant of little My, a pet form of Michael (who is like God).

Myers, Myer (*Ger.*) An overseer, or head servant; later, a farmer.

Myerson (*Heb.*) The son of Meir (light).

Myles (*Eng.*) Descendant of Miles (soldier).

Myrick (*Eng.*) Descendant of Merick, a pet form of Almeric (work, rule).

Mysliwiec (*Pol.*) One who hunted game, a hunter.

Myszak, Myszka, Myszczak (*Pol.*) One with the characteristics of a little mouse.

Naal (*Du.*) One who worked with a needle, a tailor.

Nabb, Nabbe (*Eng.*) Descendant of Nabb, a pet form of Robert (fame, bright).

Naber, Nabor, Nabors (*Eng., Ger.*) The nearby farmer, the neighboring resident.

Naccarato (*It.*) Dweller near a wild fig grove.

Nachbar (*Ger.*) The neighbor or nearby resident.

Nachman, Nachmann (*Heb., Ger.*) Descendant of Nachman (comforter); or of Nehemiah (consolation of Jehovah). Nachman is an endearing form of Nachum and Nahum (comfort). The pleasant, agreeable man.

Nachmansohn (*Ger.*) The son of Nachman (comforter).

Nachtigall, Nachtigal (*Ger.*) Dweller at the sign of the nightingale, a thrush; one with the characteristics of a nightingale, such as a musical voice.

Nachtmann (*Ger.*) One who worked as a night watchman.

Nadeau (*Fr.*) Descendant of Noel (Christmas; birthday of Christ).

Nadel, Nadell (*Ger.*) One who worked with a needle.

Nader (*Ger.*) One who sews or stitches materials, a tailor, furrier, shoemaker, leather worker, in some cases a lace maker.

Nadler (*Eng., Ger.*) One who made needles.

Naesmith, Naysmith, Nasmith (*Scot.*) The smith who made nails.

Nafziger, Nafzger (*Ger.*) One who sleeps or dozes off.

Nagano (*Jap.*) Long, field.

Nagel, Nagle, Nagler, Nagl, Naegele, Nagele, Naegel (*Ger.*) One who made nails; one who came from Nagel (nail), the name of two places in Germany.

Nagelberg (*Ger.*) One who came from Nagelsberg, the name of two places in Germany; or from Nagelberg, the name of two hills in Germany.

Nagelsmith (*Ger.*) One who made nails.

Naggar (*Arab.*) One who worked with wood, a carpenter.

Nagy (*Hun.*) The big man.

Nahill (*Ir.*) Grandson of Nigel (champion).

Nahon (*Fr., Bel.*) The young bird, a nickname for a small man; one who hunts bird nests for the eggs.

Nahrstadt (*Ger.*) One who came from Nahrstedt (water settlement), in Germany.

Naidoff (*Rus.*) One who came from Najdy, in Lithuania.

Naik (*Hindi*) A leader.

Nailsmith (*Eng.*) One who made nails.

Nair (*Hindi*) Village leader.

Nairn, Nairne (*Scot.*) One who came from Nairn (alder trees), in Nairnshire.

Naisby (*Eng.*) One who came from Naseby (Hnaef's fort), in Northamptonshire.

Naismith (*Eng., Scot.*) Variant of Neasmith, q.v.

Nakada (*Jap.*) Middle, rice field.

Nakagawa (*Jap.*) Middle, river.

Nakamura (*Jap.*) Middle, village.

Nakano (*Jap.*) Middle, field.

Nakashima (*Jap.*) Middle, island.

Nakayama (*Jap.*) Middle, mountain.

Nalbandian (*Arm.*) The son of the man who shod horses.

Nall, Nalle (*Eng.*) Dweller, or worker, at the hall; or at the corner.

Nally, Nalley (*Ir.*) The son of the poor man.

Nalty (*Ir.*) Variant of Naulty, q.v.

Nameroff (*Ukr.*) One who came from Nemyriv (not peaceful), in Ukraine.

Nancarrow (*Eng.*) Dweller in the valley where stags were found.

Nance (*Eng.*) One who came from Nance (valley), in Cornwall; dweller in a valley.

Nangle (*Eng.*) Dweller at an angle, nook, or corner.

Nankivell (*Eng.*) Dweller in the valley where horses were raised.

Nanni (*It.*) Descendant of Nanni, a pet form of Giovanni, Italian form of John (gracious gift of Jehovah).

Nansen (*Dan., Nor.*) The son of Nanne, a pet word meaning father; or of Nanni.

Naparstek, Naprstek (*Rus., Pol., Cz.-Sl.*) One who sewed with a thimble, a tailor.

Napier, Naper (*Eng.*) One who had charge of the napery, or table linen, in a large household.

Napierkowski (*Pol.*) One who presses forward, or asserts himself.

Naples, Naple (*Eng., It.*) One who came from Naples (new city), in Italy.

Napoleon, Napoleone (*It.*) One who came from Neapolis (new city); descendant of Napoleon (lion of the forest).

Napoli, Napolitano (*It.*) One who came from Napoli (Naples, new city), in Italy.

Napp, Nappe (*Eng.*) Descendant of Napp, a pet form of Robert (fame, bright).

Napper (*Eng.*) One who had charge of the napery or table linen in a large household.

Narcisi, Narciso (*It.*) Dweller near where narcissus, daffodil, or jonquil grew.

Nardella, Nardelli, Nardello, Nardini, Nardulli, Narducci (*It.*) Descendant of little Nardo, a pet form of Leonardo and Bernardo.

Nardi, Nardo, Nardone (*It.*) Descendant of Nardi, a pet form of Leonardo (lion, firm), or Bernardo (bear, firm); dweller near a spindle tree; dweller near where lavender grew.

Nasby (*Eng.*) One who came from Naseby (Hnaef's fort), in Northamptonshire.

Nase (*Ger., Eng.*) One with a small or unusual nose; one who came from Nass (cape), in Gloucestershire.

Nash (*Eng.*) Dweller "atten ashe," which by wrong division became "atte Nashe," i.e., at the ash tree; one who came from Nash (the ash trees), in Buckinghamshire.

Nason (*Fr.*) One who had a small nose.

Nass (*Eng., Ger.*) One who came from Nass (cape), in Gloucestershire; or from Nassau (wet meadow), the name of two places in Germany.

Nassau, Nassauer (*Ger.*) One who came from Nassau (wet meadow), the name of two places in Germany.

Nast (*Ger.*) One who cut trees.

Nasuti (*It.*) One with a large or prominent nose.

Natale, Natali (*Fr., It.*) Descendant of Natalie (birthday of Christ).

Nathan, Nathanson, Nathans (*Eng.*) Descendant of Nathan (gift).

Nathaniel (*Eng.*) Descendant of Nathanael (gift of God).

Natson (*Eng.*) The son of Nat, a pet form of Nathan (gift).

Natterer, Natter (*Ger.*) One who caught and exhibited snakes; one who came from Natters, in Tirol.

Naughton, Naughten (*Ir.*) Grandson of Neachtan (the pure one).

Naulty (*Ir.*) The son of Cuallaidh (wild dog); the son of the Ulidian (native of East Ulster).

Naumann, Nauman (*Ger.*) Variant of Neumann, q.v.

Naumburg (*Ger.*) One who came from Neuburg (new stronghold), the name of several places in Germany.

Navarro, Navarra (*Sp., It.*) One who came from Navarre (plain among hills), an ancient kingdom in Spain.

Nave (*Eng.*) One who was a male servant to another; a boy attendant. The word is now spelled knave.

Nawrocki (*Pol.*) One who came from Nawra or Nawry (converted), the names of places in Poland.

Naybors (*Eng.*) The nearby farmer.

Naylor, Nayler (*Eng.*) One who made nails.

Nazworth (*Eng.*) Dweller at the homestead on the headland or cape.

Neal, Neale, Neel (*Eng.*) Descendant of Nigel or Neil (champion).

Nealy, Nealey (*Ir.*) The son of Conghal (high valor).

Neander (*Gr., Ger.*) The recent arrival or newcomer, translated from Neumann.

Nearing (*Ger.*) One who supports or maintains another.

Neary (*Ir.*) Grandson of Naradhach (good; noble).

Neasmith (*Eng., Scot.*) The smith who made nails.

Neat, Neate (*Eng.*) One who cultivated a yardland (about 30 acres), or half a yardland, the middle class of English villages; one who took care of the cows, a cowherd.

Neave, Neef (*Ger., Eng., Bel.*) A nephew; nickname for a parasite.

Nebel (*Ger.*) One who came from Nebel (night mist), the name of two places in Germany.

Necker (*Ger.*) One who teases or irritates others; dweller near the Neckar, a river in Germany.

Nedbal, Nedbalski (*Pol.*) One who is careless or heedless.

Nedby (*Sw., Nor., Dan.*) Dweller at the lower farm.

Nedd, Nedds (*Scot., Eng.*) One who came from Nedd (nest), in Sutherland; descendant of Ned, a pet form of Edward (rich, guardian).

Nedley (*Eng.*) One who came from Netley (grove where nettles grew), in Shropshire.

Nedwards (*Eng.*) One who came from Needwood (wood used by outlaws as a refuge), in Staffordshire.

Nee (*Fr.*) One who came from Nee (swamp), in France; one who worked on a ship, a sailor.

Neebe, Neeb (*Ger.*) The nephew, uncle or relative of another.

Needham (*Eng.*) One who came from Needham (needy or poor homestead), the name of several places in England.

Needle, Needleman, Needelman (*Eng.*) One who made and sold needles; or who used a needle in his work.

Neeld, Neels (*Eng.*) Variant of Neil, q.v.

Neely, Neeley (*Ir.*) The son of Conghal (high valor).

Neff (*Ger.*) A nephew.

Negrete (*Sp.*) One who came from Negrete (small black place), in Spain; one who has a dark or swarthy complexion.

Negro, Negri (*Sp., It.*) One with a dark or swarthy complexion; one who came from Africa.

Negron (*Sp.*) The very black man; this is the masculine augmentative of *negro* "black."

Neher (*Ger.*) One who operated a ferry, a ferryman.

Nehring, Nehrig (*Ger.*) One who furnished food or support to another; descendant of Narwald (food, power).

Neiburg (*Ger.*) One who came from Neuburg (new castle), the name of seven places in Germany.

Neider (*Ger.*) One who came from Neida (flowing stream), in Germany.

Neidert (*Ger.*) One who came from Neida (flowing stream), in Germany; descendant of Neidhard (hostility, hard).

Neidhardt, Neidhart (*Ger.*) Descendant of Nidhart (hatred, hard); one with a hostile disposition.

Neidorf (*Ger.*) One who came from Neudorf (new village), the name of several places in Germany.

Neighbors (*Eng.*) The nearby farmer.

Neil, Neill (*Scot., Ir., Eng.*) Descendant of Neil or Njal (champion).

Neiman (*Ger.*) One who has but recently arrived in the locality, a stranger.

Neis (*Ger.*) Descendant of Nys, pet form of Denys, a form of Dionysus (Grecian god of wine; judge of men).

Neithercott (*Eng.*) Dweller at the lower cottage.

Nell (*Eng.*) Variant of Neil, q.v.

Nelligan, Neligan (*Ir.*) Descendant of little Niall (champion).

Nellinger (*Ger.*) One who came from Nellingen, the name of two places in Germany.

Nellis, Nelis (*Ir.*) The son of Niallghus (champion, choice).

Nelms (*Eng.*) Dweller at, or near, the elm trees.

Nelson, Neilson, Nelsen, Neilsen (*Sw., Nor., Dan., Eng.*) The son of Nel or Neil (champion).

Nemec (*Cz.-Sl.*) Word meaning dumb, applied to one who came from Germany, because he did not understand the Slavic tongue.

Nemecek (*Cz.-Sl.*) A diminutive form of Nemec, q.v.

Nemeroff, Nemerofsky, Nemiroff, Nemirofsky (*Ukr.*) One who came from Nemyriv (place of a revolution), in Ukraine.

Nemes (*Hun.*) An illustrious or famous person, one of noble rank.

Nemeth (*Hun.*) One who came from Germany, a German.

Nemitz, Nemetz (*Pol., Cz.-Sl., Rus.*) One who came from Germany, a German. Literally one who could not speak, i.e., a mute.

Neri, Nero (*It.*) Descendant of Neri, a pet form of names with this termination, as Raineri and Maineri; the dark-complexioned or black-haired man.

Nesbitt, Nesbit, Nesbet, Nisbet (*Scot.*) One who came from the old barony of Nesbit in the parish of Edrom, Berwickshire.

Nesmith (*Eng.*) Variant of Neasmith, q.v.

Ness, Nesse (*Eng., Scot.*) Dweller at a promontory or headland; or on low marshy ground.

Nesson (*Sw.*) The son of Nisse, a pet form of Nils (champion).

Nestel, Nestle, Nestler (*Ger.*) One who makes string or thread.

Nestor, Nester (*Ir.*) The son of the short man of the halter.

Neth, Nether (*Ger.*) One who came from Nethen (muddy water), in Germany.

Nethercott, Nethercut (*Eng.*) Dweller at the lower cottage.

Netherton (*Eng.*) One who came from Netherton (lower homestead), the name of places in Northamptonshire and Worcestershire.

Netsch, Netscher (*Ger.*) One who came from Netsch (muddy water), in Germany.

Netsky (*Ukr.*) One who works with a kneading trough, a baker.

Netter (*Eng.*) One who made and sold nets.

Nettler (*Ger.*) One who gathered nettles; one who made needles or nails.

Nettles (*Eng.*) Dweller near where nettles grew.

Nettleton (*Eng.*) One who came from Nettleton (homestead where nettles grew), the name of places in Lincolnshire and Wiltshire.

Netzel (*Ger.*) Descendant of Nato, a pet form of names beginning with Nad (grace), as Nadhere and Nadold.

Neu (*Ger.*) Descendant of Neu (new), a pet form of names like Neubert, Neufred, and Neuhardt; the young person.

Neubauer (*Ger.*) The recently settled villager or new farmer.

Neuber (*Ger.*) Variant of Neubauer, q.v.

Neuberg, Neuberger (*Ger.*) One who came from Neuberg (new town), the name of two places in Germany.

Neudorf (*Ger.*) One who came from Neudorf (new village), the name of many places in Germany.

Neufeld (*Ger.*) One who came from Neufeld (newly opened field), the name of two places in Germany.

Neuffer (*Ger.*) One who came from Neuffen (bog), in Germany.

Neuhauser, Neuhaus (*Ger.*) One who came from Neuhausen or Neuhauser (new houses), the names of several places in Germany; dweller in, or near, the recently constructed house.

Neumann, Neuman (*Ger., Heb.*) The recent arrival or newcomer; one who performed as a notary.

Neumark (*Ger.*) Dweller at the new boundary or boundary mark; one who came from Neumark (new boundary mark), the name of three places in Germany.

Neumayer (*Ger.*) The newly installed overseer or head servant.

Neuville (*Fr.*) One who came from Neuville (new town), the name of several places in France.

Neuwirth, Neuvirth, Neuwerth (*Ger.*) Descendant of Neubert (new, bright); landlord; master of the house.

Neva (*Finn.*) Dweller at, or near, a swamp or marsh.

Neveil (*Eng.*) Variant of Neville, q.v.

Neville, Nevill, Nevil (*Eng.*) One who came from Neville (new town), in Normandy, or Neuville (new town), a common place name in France.

Nevins, Nevin, Nevens, Neven (*Ir.*)

Grandson of Cnaimhin (little bone); the son of Naoimhin (little saint).

Nevison (*Scot.*) The son of Niven (saint).

New (*Eng.*) The recent arrival or newcomer; dweller near a yew tree.

Newall (*Eng.*) Variant of Newhall, q.v.

Newberg (*Eng., Ger.*) One who lived in, or dwelt near, the new castle.

Newberger, Newburger (*Ger.*) One who came from Neuburg (new town), the name of two places in Germany.

Newberry (*Eng.*) Variant of Newbury, q.v.

Newbold (*Eng.*) One who came from Newbald (new building), in the East Riding of Yorkshire.

Newborn (*Eng.*) One who came from Newbourn (stream which changed its course), in Suffolk.

Newburn (*Eng.*) One who came from Newburn (stream which changed its course), in Northumberland.

Newbury, Newbry (*Eng.*) One who came from Newbury (recently built stronghold), in Berkshire.

Newby (*Eng.*) One who came from Newby (the new or recently founded settlement), the name of various places in England.

Newcomb, Newcombe, Newcom, Newcomer, Newcome (*Eng.*) The newly settled stranger, a newcomer.

Newell (*Eng.*) A variant of Newhall, q.v.

Newhall (*Eng.*) Dweller, or worker in, the newly-built hall or principal dwelling in the village.

Newhouse (*Eng.*) One who dwelt in the newly-built house.

Newkirk (*Scot.*) Dweller near the recently built church.

Newland, Newlander, Newlands (*Eng.*) One who dwelt on, or near, the newly cleared or newly acquired land; one who came from Newland (newly cleared land), the name of various places in England.

Newlin (*Eng.*) Variant of Newland, q.v.

Newman, Newmann (*Eng.*) The recent arrival or newcomer.

Newmark (*Sw., Eng.*) New field; dweller

at the new boundary or boundary mark.

Newmiller (*Eng.*) The grinder of grain recently installed in the mill; one who took the place of the previous miller.

Newnham, Newnam (*Eng.*) One who came from Newnham (the recently constructed homestead), the name of twelve places in England.

Newsham (*Eng.*) One who came from Newsham (new houses), the name of eleven places in England.

Newsome, Newsom (*Eng.*) One who came from places now called Newsham, Newhouse, Newsam, and Newsholme, all formerly spelled Neusum, or a similar spelling, and meaning "new houses," all in England.

Newson, Newsone (*Eng.*) Dweller at the new house; the son of the newcomer.

Newton (*Eng., Scot.*) One who came from Newton (the recently founded homestead), probably the most common English place name, also the name of several places in Scotland.

Ney (*Eng., Fr.*) Variant of Nye, q.v.; the new man, the recent arrival.

Ng (*Chin.*) Crow; one who came from the province of Kiangsu.

Niarchos (*Gr.*) Descendant of Nearchos (new ruler).

Nice (*Eng., Fr.*) One who came from Nice (victory), in France; the simple, foolish man.

Nicely (*Ger.*) American variant of Nissley, q.v.

Nicholas, Nichol, Nicol, Nicholl, Nicoll (*Wel., Eng.*) Descendant of Nicholas (people's victory).

Nichols, Nicholson, Nicholls (*Eng.*) The son of Nichol (people's victory).

Nickel, Nickells, Nickels, Nickerson, Nickell (*Eng.*) Descendant of Nickel (people's victory).

Nickelson, Nickelsen (*Sw., Nor.*) The son of Nicklas, Scandinavian form of Nicholas (people's victory).

Nickens, Nickinson (*Eng.*) The son of little Nick, a pet form of Nicholas (people's victory).

Nickerson (*Eng.*) The son of Nicker, a form of Nicholas (people's victory).

Nicklas, Nickless, Nicklous (*Eng.*) Variants of Nicholas, q.v.

Nicodemus, Nicodemo (*Eng., It.*) Descendant of Nicodemus (conquerer of the people).

Nicol, Nicoll (*Scot.*) Descendant of Nicol, a Scottish form of Nicholas (people's victory).

Nicolai (*Nor.*) Descendant of Nicolai, Norwegian form of Nicholas (people's victory).

Nicolas (*Fr.*) Descendant of Nicolas, French form of Nicholas (people's victory).

Nicolaysen (*Nor.*) The son of Nicolai, Norwegian form of Nicholas (people's victory).

Nicolella, Nicoletti (*It.*) Descendant of little Nicola, Italian form of Nicholas (people's victory).

Nicolo, Nicolosi, Nicolai (*It.*) Descendant of Nicola, Italian form of Nicholas (people's victory).

Nicolopoulos, Nicolopulos (*Gr.*) The son of Nicolo, a pet form of Nicolaos, Greek form of Nicholas (people's victory).

Nicosia (*It.*) One who came from Nicosia, the capital of Cyprus.

Niebuhr (*Ger.*) The newcomer or new peasant.

Nieder, Niederer, Niederman (*Ger.*) The peasant who dwelt below the boundary.

Niederberger (*Ger.*) One who came from Niederberg (mountain stream), in Germany.

Niedermayer (*Ger.*) The overseer or head servant below another.

Niedosik (*Pol.*) Nickname for one who is always saying "not enough."

Niehaus (*Ger.*) Dweller in the recently constructed house.

Nield, Nields (*Eng.*) Descendant of Niel (champion).

Nielsen, Nielson (*Dan., Nor.*) The son of Niel (champion).

Niemann, Nieman (*Ger.*) One who has but recently arrived in the locality, a stranger.

Niemeyer (*Ger.*) The peasant who has only recently been allotted a tract of land.

Niemi (*Finn.*) Dweller on a cape or headland.

Niemiec (*Pol.*) One who came from Germany, a German.

Nierman, Niermann (*Ger.*) Dweller in the lower location, such as farther down the hill.

Niess (*Ger.*) Descendant of Niess, a pet form of Dionysus (the Grecian god of wine; judge of men).

Niessen (*Du.*) The son of Nies, a pet form of Dionysus (the Grecian god of wine; judge of men).

Nietzsche (*Ger.*) Descendant of little Neid, a pet form of Niedhardt (envy, strong).

Nieves (*Sp.*) One who came from Nieves (snowy place), in Spain; descendant of Maria Nieves (Mary of the Snows), a name adopted because of religious devotion; the white-haired man.

Nieweg (*Du.*) Dweller by the new way or road.

Niewodowski (*Pol.*) One who used a trammel or drag-net in catching fish.

Nigh (*Eng.*) Variant of Nye, q.v.

Nightingale, Nightengale (*Eng.*) One who came from Nightingale, a village in Monmouthshire; dweller at the sign of the nightingale, a thrush.

Nigro (*It., Sp.*) One with a dark or swarthy complexion.

Nihill (*Eng.*) Variant of Neal, q.v.

Nii (*Jap.*) Two, well.

Nikolaou (*Gr.*) The son of Nikola, a shortened form of Nikolaos, Greek form of Nicholas (people's victory).

Nikolich, Nikolic (*Yu.-Sl.*) Son of Nikola, Serbo-Croatian form of Nicholas (people's victory).

Niland, Nilan (*Ir.*) Grandson of little Niall (champion).

Niles, Nilles (*Ger., Eng.*) Descendant of Nils, a pet form of Nicholas (people's victory); descendant of Nilles, a pet form of Cornelius (cornel tree); dweller "atten iles," i.e., at the islands.

Nilson, Nilsen, Nilsson (*Dan., Nor., Sw.*) The son of Nils (champion).

Nimczenko (*Ukr.*) The son of the man from Germany.

Nimitz (*Pol., Cz.-Sl., Rus.*) Variant of Nemitz, q.v.

Nino (*It.*) Descendant of Nino, a pet form of Zannino, an Italian form of John (gracious gift of Jehovah).

Nippes (*Ger.*) One who came from Nippes, in Germany.

Nipson (*Ger.*) The son of Nip, a pet form of Nippert.

Nirenberg (*Ger.*) One who came from Nurnberg (the fortress of the Noricii), in Germany.

Nise (*Ger.*) Variant of Neis, q.v.

Nishi (*Jap.*) West.

Nishimura (*Jap.*) West, village.

Niskanen (*Finn.*) Dweller at the bend of the river.

Nissan (*Heb.*) Descendant of one born during Nissan (the month of flowers), the seventh month in the Hebrew calendar.

Nissen, Nisson (*Dan.*) The son of Nis, a pet form of Nils (champion); or Nicolaus (people's victory).

Nissenbaum (*Ger.*) Dweller near a walnut tree.

Nissim (*Heb.*) Descendant of Nissim (wonders; miracles), an ancient Hebrew given name.

Nissley (*Ger.*) Descendant of Niess, a pet form of Dionysus (the Grecian god of wine; judge of men); one who dealt in nuts.

Nissman (*Ger.*) One who collected and sold nuts; the lousy, mean man.

Niszczak (*Pol., Ukr., Rus.*) One without goods, a very poor person.

Nitka (*Pol.*) One who made and sold thread.

Nitti (*It.*) Descendant of Nitti, a pet form of Giovanitti, an Italian form of John (gracious gift of Jehovah).

Nitz, Nitsche, Nitsch (*Ger.*) Descendant of Nizo or Nitho, pet forms of names

beginning with Neid (envy), as Nidolf and Nidmar; descendant of Nitz, a pet form of Nikolaus, German form of Nicolas (people's victory).

Nitzberg, Nitzburg (*Ger.*) Dweller on the Nitze-berg, a hill in Germany.

Nitzky (*Ukr.*) The unimportant man, a nothing.

Niven, Nivens (*Scot.*) Descendant of Niven (saint).

Nix (*Eng., Ger.*) The son of Nick, a pet form of Nicholas (people's victory).

Nixon, Nickson (*Eng.*) The son of Nick, a pet form of Nicholas (people's victory).

Niziolek (*Pol.*) One who was short in stature.

Noakes, Noak (*Eng.*) One who lived "atten oak," which by wrong division became "atte Noak," i.e., at the oak tree.

Nobel (*Eng., Ger.*) Variant of Noble, q.v.; one who came from Nobold (new building), in Northamptonshire; one who came from Nobeln, in Germany.

Nobile (*It.*) The noble, illustrious, worthy person; a nobleman, one of high birth.

Noble (*Eng.*) An illustrious or famous person; or one possessing dignity; or of high birth or exalted rank, a name sometimes given ironically.

Noce, Nocella (*It.*) Dweller near a walnut tree.

Nocito (*It.*) Dweller in, or near, a nut grove.

Nock (*Eng.*) One who came from Knock (a hillock), in Westmorland; dweller at an oak tree.

Noda (*Jap.*) Field, rice field.

Nodler (*Ger.*) Variant of Nadler, q.v.

Noe, Noy (*Scot., Eng., It., Sp.*) Descendant of Noah (rest; long-lived); one who played the part of Noah in the medieval drama; descendant of Noe, Italian and Spanish form of Noah.

Noecker (*Ger.*) Descendant of Notker or Notger (combat, spear).

Noel, Noell, Noelle (*Fr., Eng.*) Descendant of Noel, a name given to a child born on Christmas Day.

Noga (*Pol.*) One with an unusual or misshapen foot or leg.

Nogales (*Sp.*) One who came from Nogales (walnut tree), in Spain.

Noguchi (*Jap.*) Field, mouth.

Noie (*Rom.*) Descendant of Noah (rest; long-lived).

Noisette (*Fr.*) One who gathered and sold hazelnuts.

Nokes, Noke (*Eng.*) Dweller at an oak tree or grove of oak trees; one who came from Noke (the oaks), in Oxfordshire.

Nolan, Nolen, Noland (*Ir.*) Grandson of little Nuall (noble, famous).

Noll, Nolle (*Eng., Ger.*) Descendant of Noll, an old pet form of Oliver (elf host; the olive); one who came from Noll or Nolle (hill), the names of places in Germany.

Nolley (*Eng.*) Descendant of little Noll, a pet form of Oliver (elf host; the olive).

Nolte (*Ger.*) Descendant of Nolte, a pet form of Arnold (eagle, rule).

Nolting (*Ger.*) The son of Nolte, a pet form of Arnold (eagle, rule).

Nolton (*Eng.*) One who came from Knowlton (homestead by a knoll), the name of places in Dorset and Kent.

Nonemacker, Nonemaker, Nonnamaker, Nonnemacher (*Ger.*) One who castrated hogs.

Noon, Noone (*Ir.*) Grandson of Nuadha (an ancient sea divinity); dweller on the moor.

Noonan (*Ir.*) Descendant of the little beloved one.

Norbeck (*Nor.*) Dweller at the north brook.

Norberg (*Sw.*) North mountain.

Norbert (*Ger.*) Descendant of Norbert (north, bright; Njord's brightness).

Norbury (*Eng.*) One who came from Norbury (northern fort), the name of several places in England.

Norbut, Norbot (*Ger.*) Descendant of Norbert (north, bright).

Norby (*Ger.*) One who came from Norby (north village), the name of two places in Germany.

Norcott, Northcott, Northcutt (*Eng.*) Dweller at the northern cottage.

Norcross, Northcross (*Eng.*) One who lived near, or by, the north cross.

Nord (*Sw.*) North.

Nordberg (*Sw.*) North, mountain.

Nordby (*Nor.*) North, village; northern homestead or farm.

Norden, Nordan, Nordin (*Sw., Nor., Dan., Du.*) One who came from the Scandinavian north, a Scandinavian; dweller at the north farm; one who came from Norden, in Holland.

Nordgren (*Sw.*) North, branch.

Nordquist (*Sw.*) North, twig.

Nordstrom (*Sw.*) North, river.

Noren (*Sw., Nor.*) North; narrow strait.

Norenberg (*Ger.*) One who came from Norenberg (north mountain; swamp water mountain), in Germany.

Norfleet, Norflett (*Eng.*) Dweller at the north stream, or estuary.

Norgard, Norgaard (*Nor., Dan.*) Dweller at, or near, the north yard; or on the north farm.

Norkus (*Lith.*) Descendant of Norkus, a pet form of Norkantas (wish, suffer).

Norman, Normand (*Eng., Sw.*) Descendant of Norman (the northman); one who came from Normandy.

Normoyle, Normile (*Ir.*) Descendant of Cu Fhormaoile (hound of Formoyle, in County Clare).

Noronha, Norona (*Port., Sp.*) One who came from Norona, in Spain.

Norrington (*Eng.*) One who came from Norrington (northern part of the village), in Westmorland.

Norris (*Eng.*) One who came from the north country, a northman; one who took care of another, a nurse.

Norstrom (*Sw., Nor.*) North stream.

Norsworthy (*Eng.*) Variant of Noseworthy, q.v.

North (*Eng.*) One who came from the north.

Northam (*Eng.*) One who came from Northam (northern enclosure or meadow), the name of places in Devonshire and Hampshire.

Northbrook (*Eng.*) One who lived at the stream to the north.

Northcote, Northcott (*Eng.*) One who came from Northcote (north cottage), in Devonshire; or from Northcott, in Staffordshire.

Northcutt (*Eng.*) Variant of Northcote, q.v.

Northern, Northen, Northan (*Eng.*) One who came from the north.

Northey (*Eng.*) Dweller on the north island; or on the north enclosure.

Northgate (*Eng.*) Dweller near the north gate to the walled town.

Northime (*Eng.*) One who came from Northiam (northern homestead where hay was obtained), in Sussex.

Northington (*Eng.*) One who came from Northington (the village of the northern dwellers), in Hampshire.

Northlake (*Eng.*) One who lived at the stream or brook to the north.

Northrop, Northrup, Northrip (*Eng.*) One who came from Northorpe (the northern farm), in Lincolnshire.

Northway (*Eng.*) One who lived by the path or road leading to the north or located north of another.

Norton (*Eng.*) One who came from Norton (the homestead or village north of another), the name of several villages in England.

Norville (*Fr.*) One who came from Norville (Nordo's domain), in France.

Norwich, Norwick, Norwish (*Eng.*) One who came from Norwich (north town), in Cheshire.

Norwood (*Eng.*) One who came from Norwood (north of the wood), in Middlesex.

Noseworthy (*Eng.*) Dweller at a homestead on a neck of land.

Nossbaum (*Ger.*) Variant of Nussbaum, q.v.

Notardonato (*It.*) The shorthand writer or notary named Donato (gift).

Notarfrancesco (*It.*) The shorthand writer or notary named Francesco, Italian form of Francis (free).

Notaro, Notari (*It.*) The shorthand writer or notary.

Noteboom (*Du.*) Dweller near a walnut tree.

Nothacker (*Eng.*) Dweller in, or near, the north acre or field.

Nothnagel (*Ger.*) Emergency nail, that is, an emergency helper.

Notley (*Eng.*) One who came from Notley (nut grove), the name of places in Buckinghamshire and Essex.

Noto, Noti, Notto (*It.*) Descendant of Noto, a pet form of Giovannotti (gracious gift of Jehovah); one who came from Noto, a town in Sicily.

Nott, Notte (*Eng.*) The man with the bald or closely-cropped head.

Nottage (*Eng.*) Dweller at the sign of the nuthatch; one thought to possess the characteristics of a nuthatch.

Nottingham (*Eng.*) One who came from Nottingham (the village of Snot's people), in Nottinghamshire.

Nourse, Nurse (*Eng.*) One who attended, or took care of, sick people.

Novak, Novack, Novacek (*Cz.-Sl.*) The stranger or newcomer.

Novek (*Cz.-Sl., Pol.*) Variant of Novick, q.v.

Novelli, Novello (*It.*) The younger man or younger son.

Novgorodcev (*Rus.*) One who came from Novgorod (new village), a city and a principality in Russia.

Novick (*Cz.-Sl., Pol.*) One who had but recently arrived in the vicinity, a newcomer.

Novotny, Novy (*Cz.-Sl.*) One who had but recently arrived in the vicinity, a newcomer.

Nowak (*Pol., Ukr.*) One who came from Nowaki (new), the name of places in Poland and Ukraine; dweller on new, or virgin, land.

Nowakowski (*Pol., Rus.*) One who came from Nowakowo (new), the name of places in Poland and Byelorussia.

Nowell, Nowill (*Eng.*) Descendant of Noel (birthday of Christ).

Nowicki (*Pol., Ukr.*) One who had but

recently arrived in the vicinity, a newcomer.

Nowlin, Nowlan (*Ir.*) Variant of Nolan, q.v.

Noyes, Noyce (*Eng.*) Dweller at, or near, a walnut tree; descendant of Noah (rest; long-lived).

Nozawa (*Jap.*) Field, swamp.

Nuccio, Nucci (*It.*) Descendant of Nucci, a pet form of Giovannucci (gracious gift of Jehovah); and of other names terminating in -no, as Stefano and Marino.

Nuckles, Nuckols, Nuckolls (*Ger.*) One who came from Nuckel (steep slope), in Germany.

Nudelman, Nudleman (*Ger.*) One who made and sold needles.

Nugent (*Ir.*) One who came from Nogent (fair wet meadow), the name of several places in France.

Null (*Ger.*) Dweller on, or near, a hill.

Nulty (*Ir.*) Variant of Naulty, q.v.

Nunally, Nunnally (*Eng.*) Dweller at, or near, the nun's grove or meadow.

Nunamaker, Nunnamaker, Nunemaker (*Ger.*) One who castrates hogs.

Nunez, Nunes (*Sp., Port.*) The son of Nuno (ninth).

Nunn, Nunne (*Eng.*) Descendant of a nun; descendant of Nunna (monk); a nickname given to a demure man.

Nurnberg, Nurnberger (*Ger.*) One who came from Nurnberg (the fortress of the Noricii), in Germany.

Nurse (*Eng.*) One who nourishes or takes care of incapacitated persons.

Nussbaum, Nusbaum (*Ger.*) One who came from Nusbaum or Nussbaum (walnut tree), the names of several places in Germany; dweller at, or near, the nut or walnut tree; or at the sign of the walnut tree.

Nutt, Nute (*Eng.*) Descendant of Nute, a pet form of Canute or Knut (hill; white-haired).

Nuttall, Nutall (*Eng.*) One who came from Nuthall (corner where nuts grew), in Nottinghamshire.

Nutter (*Eng.*) One who collected and sold nuts; one who wrote notes, a scribe or public writer.

Nutting (*Eng.*) The son of Knut (hill; white-haired).

Nuzzi, Nuzzo (*It.*) Descendant of Nuzzi, a pet form of Giovanni, Italian form of John (gracious gift of Jehovah).

Nyberg (*Sw.*) New, mountain.

Nyborg (*Nor., Dan.*) One who came from Nyborg (new fortress), the name of places in Norway and Denmark.

Nyby (*Nor., Sw.*) One who came from Nyby (new town), the name of villages in Norway and Sweden.

Nyce (*Bel.*) Variant of Nice, q.v.

Nydick (*Du.*) One who came from Nieuwedijk (recently built dike), the name of two places in Holland.

Nye (*Eng.*) Dweller at the island.

Nygaard, Nygard (*Nor., Dan.*) One who came from Nygaard (new farm), the name of several places in Norway and Denmark; dweller at the new farm or farmstead.

Nygren (*Sw.*) New, branch.

Nyholm (*Dan.*) Dweller at the new river island.

Nyhus (*Nor., Sw.*) Dweller in, or near, the new house.

Nyland, Nylan (*Eng., Nor., Sw.*) One who came from Nyland (island), the name of places in Dorset and Somerset; dweller on an island; dweller on the new or recently cleared land, or on the new farm.

Nylund (*Sw.*) New, grove.

Nyman (*Sw., Nor.*) New, man; the recent arrival or newcomer.

Nystrom (*Sw.*) New, stream.

Oakes, Oaks (*Eng.*) Dweller at, or near, an oak tree.

Oakey (*Eng.*) Dweller on the island where oaks grew.

Oakley (*Eng.*) Dweller in, or near, the wood or grove where oak trees grew.

Oakman (*Eng.*) Dweller at the oak tree.

375

Oaksmith (*Eng.*) The smith who lived or had his anvil near, or under, the oak tree.

Oakwood (*Eng.*) One who came from Oakworth (homestead where oaks grew), in the West Riding of Yorkshire; dweller in, or near, a wood of oak trees.

Oates, Oatis, Oats (*Eng.*) Descendant of Odo (rich).

Oatman (*Eng.*) The servant of Ode (rich).

Oatney (*Eng.*) Dweller on the island where oats grew.

Obadia, Obadiah (*Heb.*) Descendant of Obadiah (servant of God; worshiper of God).

O'Bannon (*Ir.*) Grandson of Banan (little white one).

O'Beirne (*Ir.*) Grandson of Biorn (bear).

Ober (*Ger.*) Dweller on the upper or higher place.

Oberdorf, Oberdorfer (*Ger., Swis.*) One who came from Oberdorf (upper village), the name of several villages in Switzerland.

Oberfeld, Oberfield (*Ger.*) Dweller in the upper or higher field; one who came from Oberfeld (upper field), in Germany.

Oberg (*Sw.*) Island, mountain.

Oberholtzer, Oberholz, Oberholzer (*Ger.*) One who came from Oberholz (upper wood), the name of two places in Germany; dweller in, or near, the upper wood.

Oberlander (*Swis.*) One who came from Oberland (high land), the name of several districts in Switzerland; dweller in the high lands or mountains.

Oberlin (*Ger.*) One who came from Oberlind (upper linden tree), in Germany; descendant of little Adelbert (noble, bright).

Oberman, Obermann (*Ger.*) One who acted as a foreman or supervisor.

Obermayer, Obermeier, Obermeyer (*Ger.*) Dweller near the overseer or head servant's place; the overseer or head servant.

Oberst (*Ger.*) Dweller at the topmost or highest place.

Obert (*Ger.*) Descendant of Audoberht (possession, bright).

O'Boyle (*Ir.*) Grandson of Baoigheall (vain pledge).

O'Brien, O'Bryan, O'Brion (*Ir.*) Grandson of Bryan or Brian (hill).

O'Bryant (*Ir.*) Grandson of Brian (hill).

Obst (*Ger.*) One who sold fruit, a fruiterer.

Oby, Obey, Obie (*Eng.*) One who came from Oby (Authi's homestead), in Norfolk.

O'Byrne (*Ir.*) Grandson of Bran (raven).

O'Callaghan, O'Callahan (*Ir.*) Grandson of little Ceallach (war or strife).

Ochman, Ochmann (*Ger.*) One who took care of the oxen; or who worked with oxen.

Ochs (*Ger.*) Dweller at the sign of the ox; one thought to possess the qualities of an ox; one who took care of oxen.

O'Connell (*Ir.*) Grandson of Conall (high-powerful).

O'Connor, O'Conner, O'Conchor (*Ir.*) Grandson of Concobair (meddlesome); or of Conchor (high-will or desire).

Oczkowski (*Pol.*) One who came from Oczkow, in Poland.

Oda (*Jap.*) Little, rice field.

Odam (*Eng.*) Variant of Odom, q.v.

Odarczenko (*Ukr.*) The son of Odarka, a woman's name.

O'Day, O'Dea (*Ir.*) Grandson of Deaghadh (good luck).

Odegard, Odegaard (*Nor.*) Dweller on, or near, the deserted or abandoned farm; or on an uncultivated farm.

Odell, O'Dell, Odel (*Eng.*) One who came from Odell (woad hill), in Bedfordshire. The place was also called Woodhill.

Odessey, Odoseey (*Eng.*) One who came from Odsey (Odda's pond), in Cambridgeshire.

Odgers (*Eng.*) The son of Odger (rich, spear).

Odland (*Nor., Sw.*) Dweller on alodial

land; or on waste, uncultivated ground.

Odom, Odem (*Eng., Heb.*) One who came from Odeham (Ode's homestead), in Devonshire; descendant of Adam, this being the Hebrew pronunciation of Adam; the son-in-law; one with red hair or ruddy complexion.

O'Donnell, O'Donill (*Ir.*) Grandson of Domnall (world mighty).

O'Dowd (*Ir.*) Grandson of Dubhda (black).

O'Driscoll (*Ir.*) Grandson of the interpreter.

Odum, Odums (*Eng.*) Variant of Odom, q.v.

O'Dwyer, O'Duire (*Ir.*) Descendant of Duibhidhir (black Odhar).

Oechsle, Oechslin (*Ger.*) One who plows with oxen; or who cares for the cattle.

Oehler (*Ger.*) One who sells oil; or who presses or produces oil; one who boils soap.

Oehlert (*Ger.*) Descendant of Ohlbrecht (wolf, bright).

Oelbaum (*Ger.*) Dweller near an olive tree.

Oelschlager, Oelschlegel (*Ger.*) One who processed oil by pressing.

Oestreich, Oestricher, Oestreichner (*Ger.*) Descendant of Austericus (east, rule); one who came from Austria, an Austrian.

Oetinger, Oettinger (*Ger.*) One who came from Ottingen, in Germany.

Oetzel (*Ger.*) Descendant of Otzel, a pet form of names beginning with Od (possession), as Audoberht and Autfrid.

Ofenloch, Ofenlock (*Ger.*) Stove vent, probably a nickname for one who repaired stove or oven vents.

Off, Offen (*Ger.*) Descendant of Offo or Offe (inheritance).

Offenbacher, Offenbach, Offenback (*Ger.*) One who came from Offenbach (swampy stream), the name of several places in Germany.

Officer (*Ger.*) Americanization of the German Offizier (the senior official).

Offley (*Eng.*) One who came from Offley (Offa's grove), the name of places in Hertfordshire and Staffordshire.

Offner (*Ger.*) One who installed stoves, a stovefitter; one who made bread, a baker.

Offord (*Eng.*) One who came from Offord (upper ford), in Huntingdonshire.

O'Flynn (*Ir.*) Grandson of Flann (red).

O'Gara (*Ir.*) Grandson of Gadhar (dog).

Ogawa (*Jap.*) Little, river.

Ogborn, Ogborne, Ogburn (*Eng.*) One who came from Ogbourne (Occa's stream), in Wiltshire.

Ogden, Ogdon (*Eng.*) Dweller in the oak valley.

Ogg (*Scot.*) One younger than another with whom he was associated.

Ogilvie, Ogilvy, Ogilby (*Scot., Mx.*) One who came from the barony of Ogilvie (high plain or hill), in Angus; descendant of the yellow lad.

Ogle (*Eng.*) One who came from Ogle (Ocga's hill), in Northumberland.

Oglesby, Oglesbee (*Scot.*) Dweller at Odkell's or Egel's homestead; variants of Ogilvie, q.v.

Oglethorpe (*Eng.*) One who came from Ogletharpe (Odkell's farm), in the West Riding of Yorkshire.

Ogletree (*Eng.*) Dweller near Odkell's tree.

O'Gorman (*Ir.*) Grandson of the little blue one.

O'Grady (*Ir.*) Grandson of Grada (noble; illustrious).

Ogston (*Eng.*) One who came from Ogston (Oggod's homestead), in Derbyshire.

Oh (*Chin.*) Recklessly.

O'Hagan (*Ir.*) Grandson of the little young one.

O'Halloran, O'Hallaren, O'Holleran, O'Halloren (*Ir.*) Grandson of Allmhuran (stranger from beyond the sea).

O'Hanlan, O'Hanlon (*Ir.*) Grandson of Anluan (great hero).

O'Hara (*Ir.*) Grandson of Eaghra (bitter; sharp).

Ohara (*Jap.*) Large, field.

O'Hare (*Ir.*) Grandson of Ir; grandson of Aichear (bitter, angry).

O'Hart (*Ir.*) Grandson of Art (bear; stone; noble).

O'Hearn, O'Hearne (*Ir.*) Grandson of Eachthighearn (horse lord); or of Earadh (little fear); or of Odhar (little pale one).

O'Hern (*Ir.*) Variant of O'Hearn, q.v.

O'Higgins (*Ir.*) Grandson of Uige (knowledge; skill).

Ohler (*Ger.*) Variant of Oehler, q.v.

Ohlman (*Ger.*) One who sold oil.

Ohlson, Ohlsen (*Sw., Nor.*) The son of Olof or Olaf (ancestor's relic).

Ohlwein (*Ger.*) Descendant of Odalwin (noble, friend).

Ohm, Ohms (*Ger.*) Descendant of the mother's brother, the uncle.

Ohman (*Ger.*) One who came from Ohe (water meadow; swamp); descendant of Audman (rich, man).

Oishi (*Jap.*) Large, stone.

Ojeda (*Sp.*) One who came from the village, as opposed to one from the open country.

Okamoto (*Jap.*) Hill, base.

O'Kane (*Ir.*) Grandson of Cathan, a pet form of some name beginning with Cath, as Cathaoir and Cathbharr.

O'Keefe, O'Keeffe (*Ir.*) Grandson of Caomh (beautiful; noble).

O'Kelley, O'Kelly (*Ir.*) Grandson of Cellach (contention).

Okenquist (*Sw.*) Field, twig.

Okerstrom (*Sw.*) Field, stream.

Oki (*Jap.*) Offing.

Okie, Okey (*Eng.*) Dweller on the island where oaks grew.

Okon, Okonski (*Pol.*) One who trapped perch, a fisherman.

Okun (*Pol., Rus., Ger.*) One who fished for, or sold, perch.

Olander (*Sw.*) Islander.

Olbert (*Ger.*) Descendant of Odalbert (fatherland, bright).

Olcott (*Eng.*) Dweller in, or near, the old cottage.

Oldach (*Ger.*) Descendant of Oldach, a nickname for Adaldag (noble, day).

Oldacre, Oldaker (*Eng.*) Dweller on, or by, the old plowed field.

Olden (*Eng.*) Descendant of Ealdwine (old, friend).

Oldenburg, Oldenburger (*Ger.*) One who came from Oldenburg (old fortification), the name of four places in Germany.

Older (*Eng.*) Dweller by the alder tree.

Oldfield (*Eng.*) Dweller near the old field, a designation given to a field after another has been cleared; one who came from Aldfield (old field), in Yorkshire.

Oldham, Oldam (*Eng.*) One who came from Oldham (old island), in Lancashire.

Oldroyd (*Eng.*) Dweller in the old forest clearing.

Olds, Oldis (*Eng.*) Dweller at the old house.

O'Leary (*Ir.*) Grandson of Laoghaire (calf keeper).

Olejniczak (*Pol.*) The son of one who made oil from sunflower seeds or linseeds for food purposes.

Oleksandrenko (*Ukr.*) The son of Oleksandr, Ukrainian form of Alexander (helper of mankind).

Oleksiak (*Ukr., Rus.*) Descendant of Oleksa, a Slavic form of Alexander (helper of mankind).

Oleksy (*Ukr.*) Descendant of Oleksiy, Ukrainian form of Alexis (helper of mankind).

Olenberg (*Ger.*) One who came from Ohlenburg (swamp fortress), in Germany.

Oleson, Olesen (*Nor., Dan.*) The son of Ole, a pet form of Olaf (ancestor).

Oliff, Olliff (*Eng.*) Descendant of Olaf (ancestor).

Olimpo (*It.*) Descendant of Olimpio (from Mount Olympus in Greece); dweller on the height or eminence.

Olin (*Sw.*) Descendant of Olin from the

Latinized Olinus derived from Olaf (ancestor).

Oliphant, Olivant (*Fr., Eng.*) One who dealt in ivory; one who played a horn, a trumpeter; dweller at the sign of the elephant; a corruption of Olifard or Holifard; nickname for a large, heavy man.

Oliva, Olive, Olivia, Olivo (*Sp., It.*) One who grew and sold olives; descendant of Olivo (olive); one with an olive complexion.

Oliveira (*Port.*) One who came from Oliveira (olive tree), in Portugal; dweller near an olive tree.

Oliver, Olivar (*Eng., Fr.*) Descendant of Oliver or Olivier (elf, host; an olive tree); one who cultivated olive trees.

Olivera (*Sp.*) Variant of Oliva, q.v.; dweller near an olive tree.

Oliveri, Olivero, Olivere (*It.*) Dweller near olive trees; one who raised and sold olives.

Olivier, Ollivier (*Fr.*) One who possessed an olive grove; descendant of Olivier (the olive).

Olivieri, Oliviero (*It.*) Descendant of Oliviero, Italian form of Oliver (the olive).

Olkowski (*Pol.*) One who came from Olkow, in Poland.

Oller (*Ger.*) One who processed oil.

Olley, Ollie (*Scot., Eng.*) One who came from Ouilly (Olius' farm), the name of five places in Normandy; descendant of Ollie, a pet form of Olive and Oliver (the olive).

Olliff, Olliffe (*Eng.*) Descendant of Olaf (ancestor).

Ollis, Ollison (*Eng.*) The son of Olley, a pet form of Oliver (the olive).

Olmsted, Olmstead (*Du.*) Dweller at the homestead where elms grew.

Olney (*Eng.*) One who came from Olney (Olla's island; lonely grove), the name of places in Buckinghamshire and Northamptonshire.

Olofson (*Sw.*) The son of Olof (ancestor).

O'Loughlin, O'Loughlan (*Ir.*) Grandson of Lochlainn (lake land); or of

Lachtna (gray); or of the devotee of St. Secundinus.

Olson, Olsen, Olsson (*Nor., Sw.*) The son of Ole or Olaf (ancestor).

Olszewski (*Pol.*) Dweller at, or near, the alder tree.

Oltman, Oltmann (*Ger.*) The old, experienced man; descendant of Oltman (old, man).

O'Mahoney (*Ir.*) Grandson of Mathghamhain (bear).

O'Malley (*Ir.*) Grandson of Maille (noble; chief).

Oman (*Sw.*) Island, man.

O'Mara, O'Meara (*Ir.*) Grandson of Meadhair (mirth).

Onassis (*Gr.*) The useful, serviceable man.

Onderdonk (*Du.*) One who lived, or came from, below Donk (knoll in a swamp), in Brabant.

Ondrus (*Cz.-Sl.*) Descendant of Andrew (manly).

O'Neal (*Ir.*) Grandson of Niall (champion; military hero).

O'Neill, O'Neil (*Ir.*) Grandson of Niall (champion; military hero).

Onesti (*It.*) The honorable, honest man.

Onion (*Wel.*) Descendant of Einion or Annion (anvil; upright).

Onley, Only, Onely (*Eng.*) One who came from Onley (lonely grove), in Northamptonshire.

Ono (*Jap.*) Little, field.

Onorato (*It.*) The noble, illustrious, honorable man.

Onyshkevych (*Ukr.*) The son of Onysko.

Ooms (*Du.*) The son of the uncle.

Oosterbaan (*Du.*) Dweller on the east road.

Oosterhout (*Du.*) One who came from Oosterhout (east wood), in Holland.

Opalka, Opalko (*Cz.-Sl.*) Burning, conflagration; one connected in some way with fire.

Opdahl (*Nor.*) Dweller in the upper valley.

Opdyck (*Du.*) One who lived on the dike.

Openshaw (*Eng.*) One who came from

Openshaw (unenclosed wood), in Lancashire.

Opfer (*Ger.*) One who takes the money offering in the church.

Opie (*Eng.*) Descendant of little Oppa; descendant of Oby, a pet form of Obadiah (servant of Jehovah).

Oppegard, Oppegaard (*Nor.*) Dweller on the upper farm.

Oppenheimer, Oppenheim (*Ger.*) One who came from Oppenheim (Oppo's place), in Germany.

Oppermann, Opperman (*Ger.*) The church officer who takes the collection.

Oquendo (*Sp.*) One who came from Oquendo (side of the pasture), in Spain.

Oram (*Eng.*) Dweller at the homestead on the river bank; one who came from Owram (ridge), in Yorkshire; variant of Orme, q.v.

Orange (*Eng., Fr.*) One who came from Orange (town on the river Araise), in France.

Orchard, Orchart (*Eng., Scot.*) Dweller at a fruit garden; corruption of Urquhart, q.v., from its early pronunciation; one who came from Orchard, the name of several places in England and one in Scotland.

Orcutt (*Eng.*) Dweller in a hillside, or river bank, cottage.

Ord (*Eng.*) One who came from Ord (point; sword), in Northumberland.

Ordway (*Eng.*) Descendant of Ordwig (spear, warrior).

O'Regan (*Ir.*) Grandson of Riagan (little king).

O'Reilly, O'Reyly, O'Reely, O'Riley (*Ir.*) Grandson of Raghallach (the sportive one).

Oren (*Sw.*) Variant of Orne, q.v.

Orenstein (*Ger.*) One who came from Arnstein, the name of three places in Germany.

Orf (*Ger.*) Descendant of Orf, a shortened form of Aurifrid (bright, peace).

Orfevre (*Fr.*) One who made and sold gold articles, a goldsmith.

Organ, Organe (*Eng., Wel.*) Usually metonymic for Organer, that is, one who made and sold organs or who played them; variant of Morgan, q.v.

Oriente (*It.*) One who came from the East, the Levant.

O'Riordan (*Ir.*) Grandson of Rioghbhardan (royal bard).

Orlando, Orlandi (*It.*) Descendant of Orlando (fame, land).

Orlich (*Eng.*) One who made and sold clocks.

Orloff, Orlov, Orlof, Orlow (*Rus.*) One with eaglelike characteristics; dweller at the sign of the eagle.

Orlowski (*Pol.*) Descendant of one with eaglelike characteristics.

Orman, Ormond, Ormand (*Wel.*) One who came from Ormond, in Ireland.

Ormandy (*Eng.*) One who came from Osmotherley (Asmund's hill or grove), the name of places in Lancashire and the North Riding of Yorkshire.

Orme, Ormes (*Eng., Fr.*) Descendant of Orm (serpent); dweller near an elm tree.

Ormerod, Ormrod (*Eng.*) One who came from Ormerod (Orm's clearing), in Lancashire.

Ormsby, Ormsbee (*Eng.*) One who came from Ormesby (Orm's homestead), the name of places in Norfolk, Lincolnshire, and the North Riding of Yorkshire.

Orne, Orn (*Sw.*) Eagle.

Orner (*Ger.*) One who harvests, reaps, or mows.

Ornstein (*Du.*) One who came from Arnstein, the name of three places in Germany.

O'Rourke (*Ir.*) Grandson of Ruarc (Norse Hrothrekr); descendant of the restless man.

Orr (*Eng., Ir.*) One who lived near the border, bank, shore, hill or ridge; the pale person.

Orrell (*Eng.*) One who came from Orrell (ore hill), in Lancashire.

Orrick (*Scot.*) One who came from Orrock, in Fife.

Orsi, Orsini, Orsino (*It.*) Descendant of Orso (bear).

Orsley (*Eng.*) One who came from Horsley (pasture for horses), the name of several places in England.

Ortega, Ortego (*Sp.*) Dweller at the sign of the grouse; one with the characteristics of a grouse.

Orth, Ort (*Ger.*) One who came from Orth (the place), in Germany; descendant of Ort, a pet form of names beginning with Ort (point), as Ortgis and Ordwig.

Ortiz (*Sp.*) The son of Ordono (the fortunate).

Ortlieb, Ortlip (*Ger.*) Descendant of Ortlieb (sharp, dear).

Ortmann, Ortman (*Ger.*) Descendant of Ortman (point, man); one who acted as an arbitrator or referee.

Orton (*Eng.*) One who came from Orton (homestead on a slope or upper homestead), the name of various places in England.

Orwell (*Eng., Scot.*) One who came from Orwell (stream by the shore), in Suffolk; one who came from Orwell, in Kinross.

O'Ryan, O'Rian (*Ir.*) Descendant of the servant of the queen; grandson of Rian or Riaghan; or of a follower of Rian or Riaghan.

Orzechowski (*Pol.*) One who came from Orzechow(o); dweller near hazel bushes.

Osaki (*Jap.*) Large, headland.

Osako (*Jap.*) Large, press.

Osborne, Osborn, Osburn, Osbourne (*Eng.*) Descendant of Osborn (god, man); one who came from Osborne (Aust's stream), in Wight.

Osby, Osbey (*Eng.*) One who came from Oseby (Aswith's homestead), in Lincolnshire.

Oscarson (*Eng.*) The son of Oscar (god, spear).

Oschmann, Oschman (*Ger.*) Dweller near an ash tree.

Oser (*Ger.*) One who came from Osc (ring); or from Oos (swampy water), the names of places in Germany; descendant of Oser, a form of Ansher (half-god, army); one who made sewing needles.

Osgood (*Eng.*) Descendant of Osgood (divine, goodness).

O'Shaughnessy (*Ir.*) Grandson of Seachnasach (elusive).

O'Shea, O'Shay (*Ir.*) Grandson of Seaghdha (majestic or learned).

Oshiro (*Jap.*) Large, castle.

Osiecki (*Pol.*) One who operated a hop kiln.

Osinski (*Pol.*) Dweller near an aspen tree.

Osis (*Lat.*) Descendant of Osis, Latvian pet form of Oscar (Os, a god, spear), and Oswald (Os, a god, power).

Oskarsson (*Sw.*) The son of Oskar, Swedish form of Oscar (Os, a god, spear).

Osler (*Eng.*) Variant of Ostler, q.v.

Osman, Osmon, Osmun (*Eng.*) Descendant of Osmund (divine protection).

Osmanski (*Pol.*) One who came from Turkey.

Osmond, Osmund (*Eng.*) Descendant of Osmund (divine, protection).

Osowski (*Pol.*) Dweller near the aspen tree; one who came from Osow, in Poland.

Ost (*Ger.*) One who came from the east.

Ostberg (*Ger., Nor., Sw.*) One who came from Ostberge (east mountain), in Germany; east, hill.

Osten (*Ger.*) One who came from Osten (east), the name of several places in Germany.

Ostendorf (*Ger.*) One who came from Ostendorf (eastern village), the name of several places in Germany.

Oster, Ost (*Sw.*) East.

Osterberg, Osterberger (*Sw.*) East, mountain.

Osterman, Ostermann (*Ger.*) One who sold oysters; one who came from the east.

Ostermeyer (*Ger.*) The meyer situated toward the east. See Meyer.

Ostertag (*Ger.*) Easterday; descendant of one born on Easter.

Ostheimer (*Ger.*) Dweller at the east dwelling.

Ostler (*Eng.*) One who lodges or entertains guests, especially in a monastery; one who keeps a hostelry or inn.

Ostlund (*Sw.*) East, grove.

Ostrand, Ostrander (*Sw.*) Island, shore.

Ostroff, Ostrofsky (*Rus.*) Dweller on a small island in a river.

Ostrom (*Sw.*) Island, stream.

Ostrow (*Pol.*) Dweller on a small island in a river.

Ostrowski (*Pol.*) Dweller on a river island; one who came from Ostrov (river island), in Poland.

O'Sullivan (*Ir.*) Grandson of Suileabhan (black-eyed).

Oswald, Oswaldt, Oswalt (*Eng., Fr.*) Descendant of Oswald (divine power); dweller in, or near, the eastern forest.

Ota (*Jap.*) Thick, rice field.

Otero (*Sp.*) One who came from Otero (height), the name of several places in Spain.

Otis (*Eng.*) Descendant of Otis or Otes, forms of Odo (rich).

Otley, Ottley (*Eng.*) One who came from Oteley (grove where oats were grown), in Shropshire; or from Otley (Otta's grove), the name of places in Suffolk and the West Riding of Yorkshire.

O'Toole (*Ir.*) Grandson of Tuothal (people mighty).

Ott, Otte (*Eng., Ger.*) Descendant of Otta or Otto (rich).

Ottaviano (*It.*) The eighth-born child.

Ottenberg (*Ger.*) One who came from Ottenberg, the name of several places in Germany.

Otter (*Nor., Eng.*) Dweller at the sign of the otter; descendant of Otthar (terrible, army); dweller at the Otter (otter stream), a river in England.

Ottesen, Otteson (*Nor.*) The son of Otte, a pet form of Otto (rich).

Ottinger (*Ger.*) One who came from Otting or Ottingen, the names of several places in Germany.

Otto (*Ger.*) Descendant of Otto or Odo (rich).

Ottoson, Ottosen (*Sw., Nor.*) The son of Otto (rich).

Ouderkirk (*Du.*) Dweller by, or worker in, the older church.

Oudheusden (*Du.*) One who came from the village of Oud-Heusden (old Heusden or inn), in North Brabant.

Ouellette, Ouellet (*Fr.*) Dweller at the eye, or source, of the little stream or fountain.

Ouimet, Ouimette (*Fr.*) One who came from Omet (place of elm trees), in France.

Oursler (*Eng.*) Variant of Ostler, q.v.

Oury (*Fr.*) Descendant of Oury, a pet form of Othalric (fatherland, rule).

Ousey (*Eng.*) Dweller on an island in the Ouse (water), a British river.

Ousley, Ouseley, Owsley (*Eng.*) Dweller at, or in, the wood or meadow by the Ouse (water), the name of several streams in England.

Outerbridge, Otterbridge (*Eng.*) One who came from Oughtibridge (Uhtred's bridge), in Yorkshire.

Outhous (*Eng.*) Dweller in the house beyond the limits of the village.

Outlaw, Outlow (*Eng.*) Descendant of the outlaw, one who contemptuously fails to appear in court when summoned, and is deprived of the protection and benefit of the law. In early times it was lawful for anyone to kill such a person.

Outwater (*Eng.*) Dweller near the pool or stream outside of the village.

Ovcik (*Cz.-Sl.*) One who took care of a flock, a shepherd.

Over (*Eng.*) One who came from Over (river bank; place at the foot of the hill), the name of several places in England; dweller on a river bank or steep slope.

Overacker (*Eng.*) Dweller at the cultivated field on the river bank or slope.

Overall (*Eng.*) One who came from Overhall (the upper corner), in Essex; dweller in, or near, the upper hall.

Overbeck (*Eng.*) Dweller beyond the stream.

Overby, Overbey, Overbee (*Nor., Eng.*) Dweller at Overby, a farm name; one who came from Overbury (upper earthwork or fort), in Worcestershire.

Overend (*Eng.*) Dweller at the upper end of some natural feature such as a lake, ridge or perhaps a row of houses.

Overfield (*Eng.*) Dweller on the open place on the river bank or hill slope.

Overholt, Overholtz (*Eng.*) Dweller at the edge of the woods; or at the upper or further woods.

Overington (*Eng.*) One who came from Ovington (village of Ufa's people; or of Wulfa's people), the name of places in Essex, Hampshire, and the North Riding of Yorkshire.

Overland (*Swis., Nor.*) One who came from Oberland (high land), the name of several districts in Switzerland; dweller in the high lands or mountains; one who came from Overland, the name of several places in Norway.

Overley, Overly, Overlee (*Eng.*) Dweller in a grove by the river bank.

Overman (*Eng.*) Dweller on the bank of a river; one in charge in a coal mine.

Overstreet (*Eng.*) Dweller at a Roman road by a river bank.

Overton (*Eng.*) One who came from Overton (homestead on a river bank or ridge), the name of several places in England.

Overy (*Eng.*) One who came from Overy (across the stream), in Oxfordshire.

Ovington (*Eng.*) One who came from Ovington (the village of Ufa's people), the name of places in Essex, Hampshire, and Oxfordshire.

Owens, Owen (*Wel.*) The son of Owen (well-born).

Owings (*Wel.*) Variant of Owens, q.v.

Ownbey, Owmby (*Eng.*) One who came from Ovmby (Aun's homestead), in Lincolnshire.

Owsley (*Eng.*) One who came from Oversley (grove by a river bank), in Warwickshire.

Owston (*Eng.*) One who came from Ouston (Ulfkell's homestead), the name of places in Durham and Northumberland.

Oxenberg (*Dan.*) One who came from Oxenberg, in Denmark.

Oxenburg (*Eng.*) One who came from Oxborough (fortress where oxen were kept), in Norfolk.

Oxendine (*Eng.*) One who came from Oxendon (hill or hill pasture where oxen were kept), in Northamptonshire; dweller on the hill where oxen grazed.

Oxenford (*Eng.*) One who came from Oxford (ford used by oxen), the shortened form of the old town, now the county borough, of Oxfordshire.

Oxenreider (*Ger.*) One who cut and sold ox meat, a butcher.

Oxford (*Eng.*) One who came from Oxford (ford for oxen), in Oxfordshire.

Oxley (*Eng.*) One who came from Oxley (grassy enclosure for oxen), in Staffordshire.

Oxman (*Eng.*) One who had charge of the oxen, an oxherd.

Oxnam (*Scot.*) One who came from Oxnam (oxen homestead), in Scotland.

Oxnard (*Eng.*) The oxherd who took care of the oxen.

Oxton (*Eng.*) One who came from Oxton (farm where oxen were kept), the name of places in Cheshire, Nottinghamshire, and the West Riding of Yorkshire.

Ozawa (*Jap.*) Little, swamp.

Ozga (*Pol.*) One who came from Ozga, in Poland.

Ozman, Ozmun (*Eng.*) Variant of Osman, q.v.

Paar (*Ger.*) Dweller near swampy water.

Pablo (*Sp.*) Descendant of Pablo, Spanish form of Paul (small).

Pabon (*Sp.*) Dweller at the sign of the peacock; one unduly ostentatious in dress or manner.

Pabst, Papst (*Ger.*) One who performed sacerdotal functions; one whose function, behavior, spirit or appearance resembled that of a priest.

Pace (*Eng., It.*) Descendant of Pace or Pash, a name given to one born during the Passover festival or at Easter; descendant of Pace (peace), or of Pace, a pet form of Bonapace (good peace).

Pacelli (*It.*) Descendant of little Pace, a pet form of Bonapace (good peace).

Pacheco (*Port., Sp.*) The slow or sluggish person; dweller in, or near, a country palace; descendant of Pacheco.

Pachman (*Eng.*) Variant of Packman, q.v.

Pacholski (*Pol.*) The boyish, or young, person.

Pacifico, Pacifici (*It.*) The easy-going man; descendant of Pacifico (the peaceful).

Pacini (*It.*) Descendant of little Pace, a pet form of Bonapace (good peace).

Pack, Packel (*Eng.*) Descendant of Pack or little Pack (suffering), name given to one born during the Jewish Passover or Christian Easter.

Packard (*Fr.*) Descendant of Bacard (combat, strong).

Packer (*Eng.*) One who packed wool.

Packett (*Eng.*) Descendant of little Pack (child born during the Passover festival or during Easter).

Packman (*Eng.*) A merchant who carried his wares in a pack on his back, a peddler.

Packwood (*Eng.*) One who came from Packwood (Pacca's wood), in Warwickshire.

Pacovsky, Pacak, Paca (*Cz.-Sl.*) One who came from Pacov, in Bohemia.

Padbury (*Eng.*) One who came from Padbury (Padda's fort), in Buckinghamshire.

Padden, Paden (*Ir.*) The son of Padin, a pet form of Patrick (noble or patrician).

Paddington (*Eng.*) One who came from Paddington (village of Padda's people; Padda's valley), the name of places in Middlesex and Surrey.

Paddock, Paddack (*Eng., Scot.*) One who came from Paddock (enclosure), now Paddock Wood, in Kent; dweller at the sign of the frog; one thought to possess some of the characteristics of a frog.

Paddy (*Eng., Scot.*) Descendant of little Pad, a pet form of Patrick (noble or patrician).

Pade (*Eng.*) Dweller by the path.

Paderewski (*Pol.*) The son of Patrick (noble or patrician).

Padgett, Padgitt, Padget (*Eng., Fr.*) The young male servant; descendant of Padge, a variant of Madge, pet form of Margaret (pearl).

Padilla, Padella (*Sp., It.*) One who came from Padilla (frying pan), in Spain; dweller at the sign of the frying pan; one who prepared food, a cook.

Padmore (*Eng.*) Dweller at the path to the moor or wasteland.

Padova (*It.*) One who came from Padua, in Italy.

Padron, Padro (*Sp.*) One who came from Padron (master's place), in Spain; the straw boss or master.

Padula (*It.*) Dweller at, or near, a swamp.

Paez (*Sp.*) The son of Pae, a pet form of Pelayo (man of the sea; mariner).

Paff (*Ger.*) American form of Pfaff, q.v.

Pafko (*Cz.-Sl.*) The son of Palko, a Czechoslovakian form of Paul (small).

Pagan (*Eng.*) Descendant of Payen (villager or rustic; later heathen); the rustic or countryman.

Pagano, Pagani, Paganini (*It.*) Nickname for a wicked, irreligious man; one who did not believe, a heathen; descendant of Pagano (pagan).

Page (*Eng.*) A male servant of the lowest grade, an attendant.

Pagel (*Eng.*) The small page; a boy servant or attendant.

Paget, Paggett, Pagett (*Eng.*) The small page or male attendant.

Paglia, Pagliaro (*It.*) Dweller in a hut or hovel.

Pagorek (*Pol.*) Dweller on, or near, the hill.

Pahl (*Ger.*) The bold, audacious man; descendant of Paulus (small); descendant of Baldo, a pet form of names beginning with Bald (bold), as Baldwig, Baldawin and Baldulf.

Paige (*Eng.*) Variant of Page, q.v.

Paine, Pain (*Eng.*) The rustic or countryman, a pagan; descendant of Payen (villager or rustic; later heathen).

Painter, Paynter (*Eng.*) One who covers buildings and ships with paint; or who makes or creates a picture; the official in charge of bread in a large household.

Paisley (*Scot.*) One who came from Paisley (pasture slope), in Renfrewshire.

Pajak (*Pol.*) One with spider-like characteristics; dweller at the sign of the spider.

Palacios, Palacio (*Sp.*) One who came from Palacios (royal residence), in Spain; dweller in, or near, a nobleman's house.

Paladino (*It.*) A palace official; nickname for a strong, brave man.

Palazzo, Palazzolo, Palazzi (*It.*) Dweller in, or near, a nobleman's country home; dweller at the sign of the boat.

Palermo (*It.*) One who came from Palermo (the spacious harbor), in Italy.

Palestini (*It.*) One who came from Palestine; one who had been to Palestine on a pilgrimage.

Paley (*Eng.*) Dweller at the grove set off by stakes or poles.

Palfrey (*Eng.*) Metonymic for one who had charge of the palfreys, the saddle-horse used by ladies.

Palfy (*Eng.*) Variant of Palfrey, q.v.

Palin, Pallin (*Sw.*) Dweller near the marsh or swamp.

Palka, Palko (*Cz.-Sl.*) One who walked with a cane.

Palladino (*It.*) Variant of Paladino, q.v.

Pallis, Palles (*Eng.*) Dweller at a fenced enclosure; or in a straw house; or in, or near, the palace; or near the fence or palisade.

Pallister, Palliser (*Eng.*) Dweller at a fenced enclosure; one who made palings or fences.

Palm (*Sw.*) Palm-tree.

Palma (*It., Sp., Port.*) Dweller near a palm tree; descendant of Palma (one born on Palm Sunday); one who came from Palma (place of palms), the name of places in Spain and Italy.

Palmeira (*Port.*) Dweller near a palm tree.

Palmer (*Eng.*) A palm-bearing pilgrim returned from the Holy Land.

Palmieri, Palmiero (*It.*) One who carries the palm in religious processions; one who granted or sold indulgences.

Palmisano (*It.*) One who came from Palma (palm tree), in Italy.

Palmquist (*Sw.*) Palm-tree, twig.

Palo (*Sp.*) Dweller near a tree; or near a stake or boundary marker.

Palombaro (*It.*) One who raised and sold doves; one who made his living under water, a diver.

Palombo, Palombi (*It.*) Dweller at the sign of the wood pigeon or ring dove; nickname for one with the characteristics of a butterfly, a flighty, frivolous fellow.

Paltin (*Rus.*) One who paid fifty kopecks in some way, possibly as rent for his land.

Paluch (*Pol.*) One with an unusual finger.

Palumbo (*It.*) Dweller at the sign of the dove.

Panas (*Ukr.*) Descendant of Panas, a pet form of Afanasiy or of Opanas.

Panasiuk (*Ukr.*) The son of Panas, q.v.

Pancake (*Eng., Ger.*) One who made and sold pancakes.

385

Pancoast (*Eng.*) Variant of Pentecost, q.v.

Pandazi, Pandazis (*Gr.*) Descendant of Pandazi (one who may always live).

Pandit (*Hindi*) One learned in Hindu scriptures.

Pandolfi (*It.*) Descendant of Pandolfo (flag, wolf).

Pandya (*Hindi*) One who acted as a priest at place of pilgrimage.

Pane (*Eng.*) Variant of Paine, q.v.

Panebianco (*It.*) One who baked and sold white bread.

Panek (*Pol.*) The little gentleman; one who assumed the prerogatives of a gentleman.

Panetta, Panetti (*It.*) One who baked and sold bread.

Panfil (*Eng.*) One who came from Panfield (open land on the Pant river), in Essex.

Pangborn, Pangborne, Pangburn (*Eng.*) One who came from Pangbourne (stream of Paega's people), in Berkshire.

Panico, Panici, Panicola (*It.*) Dweller in, or near, a field of millet; one who grew millet.

Pankey (*Eng., Ger.*) Dweller at the end of the hedge; a lordling or member of the minor nobility.

Pankhurst (*Eng.*) Dweller at a bridge near a wood.

Pankiewicz (*Pol.*) The son of the lordling or minor noble.

Pankowicz (*Pol.*) The son of the young gentleman.

Pannebakker, Pannebecker (*Ger.*) One who made tiles by hardening clay while moist in the sun or by fire.

Pannell (*Eng.*) Descendant of the little pagan, a rustic or countryman; or of little Paganus (villager, later heathen); metonymic for one who made the panels, that is, the pads or cushions that served as saddles.

Panos (*Gr.*) Descendant of Panos, a pet form of Panayotis (pertaining to Our Lady); or of Panos, a Greek form of Peter (a rock).

Panozzo (*It.*) A variant of Panico, q.v.

Pantaleo, Pantaleone (*It.*) Descendant of Pantaleone (all lion).

Pantano (*It.*) Dweller in, or near, a swamp.

Panter, Panther (*Eng., Scot.*) The official in charge of bread in a large household, a pantry-keeper.

Panton (*Eng.*) One who came from Panton (Pamp's homestead), in Lincolnshire.

Panunto (*It.*) One who prepared and sold panunto, that is, bread toasted and dipped in oil.

Panzer (*Ger.*) One who made armor.

Paoletti, Paoletto, Paolello (*It.*) Descendant of little Paolo, an Italian form of Paul (small).

Paoli (*It.*) Descendant of Paolo, Italian form of Paul (small).

Paolini, Paolino (*It.*) Nickname for one with the characteristics of a young peacock; variant of Paoletti, q.v.

Paone (*It.*) Dweller at the sign of the peacock; one who raised and sold peafowl.

Papa (*It.*) One who performed sacerdotal functions, a priest; one whose function, behavior, spirit or appearance resembled that of a priest.

Papadakis (*Gr.*) The son of the priest.

Papadopoulos, Papadopulos, Pappadopulos (*Gr.*) The son of the priest.

Papageorge, Papageorgiou (*Gr., It.*) Descendant of Priest George (earth worker or farmer); or of Uncle George.

Papajohn (*Gr., It.*) Descendant of Priest John (gracious gift of Jehovah); or of Uncle John.

Papaleo (*It.*) Descendant of the priest named Leo; nickname for one thought to have the characteristics of a beetle.

Paparo (*It.*) One who raised and sold geese; sometimes a nickname for a dull, awkward man.

Papathanasiou (*Gr.*) Descendant of Priest Athanasiou, Greek form of Athanasius (immortal); or of Uncle Athanasiou.

Papazian (*Arm.*) The son of the priest.

Pape (*Eng.*) A variant of Pope, q.v.

Papillon (*Fr.*) One thought to possess some characteristics of a butterfly.

Papp (*Hun., Ger.*) One who performed sacerdotal functions, a priest; one who prepared soft food for infants.

Pappalardo (*It.*) Nickname for a simpleton.

Pappas, Papas (*Gr.*) One who performed sacerdotal functions, a priest.

Paprocki (*Pol.*) Dweller near where ferns grew.

Paquette, Paquet (*Fr.*) Descendant of Paschase (Easter devotions); the itinerant seller of fagots.

Paquin (*Fr.*) One who gathered and sold fagots; one who cleaned streets, a scavenger.

Paradis, Paradise (*Fr.*) One who played the part of Paradise in the ancient mystery plays.

Paradiso (*It.*) Dweller in, or near, a fruit grove or flower garden.

Paramore (*Eng.*) Nickname for the lover or sweetheart.

Pardew, Pardue, Pardee (*Eng.*) Nickname for one frequently heard to exclaim *par Dieu* (in God's name; by God).

Pardo, Pardoe (*Sp., It.*) One who had gray hair; descendant of Pardo, a pet form of Leopardo (lion, hard).

Pardys (*Eng.*) Variant of Pardew, q.v.

Paredes, Paredez (*Sp.*) Dweller near the walls.

Parent, Parente, Parenteau (*Fr.*) The father, probably a nickname; descendant of a priest, or other dignitary of the church.

Parenti (*It.*) One who had a child, a parent; or who stood in the place of a parent; one who came from Parenti, a place in Calabrese.

Parham (*Eng.*) One who came from Parham (homestead where pears grew), the name of places in Suffolk and Sussex.

Paris, Parris (*Eng., Fr.*) One who came from Paris (the marshy land of the Parisii), in France; one of the tribe of the Parisii (valiant; well-placed);

descendant of Paris, a pet form of Patrice, French form of Patrick (noble or patrician).

Pariseau (*Fr.*) French diminutive of Paris, q.v.

Parish (*Eng.*) Variant of Parrish, q.v.

Parisi, Pariso, Parisio (*It.*) One who came from Paros, in Greece.

Park, Parke (*Eng.*) Dweller in, or near, a park or enclosure; often a metonym for a parker or gamekeeper.

Parker (*Eng., Wel.*) One in charge of a park for the lord of the manor; a gamekeeper.

Parkhill (*Scot., Eng.*) One who came from the lands of Parkhill (enclosed tract on a hillside), in Ayrshire; or from Parkhill in the West Riding of Yorkshire.

Parkhouse (*Eng.*) Dweller in the house by the enclosed space stocked with game for the hunt.

Parkhurst (*Eng.*) Dweller in an enclosure on a wooded hill.

Parkinson, Parkin, Parkins, Parkison (*Eng.*) Descendant, or son, of Parkin, a pet form of Peter (a rock).

Parkman (*Eng.*) One who had charge of a park for the lord of the manor; a gamekeeper.

Parks, Parkes (*Eng.*) Dweller near the enclosed spaced stocked with game for use of the king or great nobles; sometimes metonymic for one in charge of a park. Medieval parks were often enclosed by ditches and massive earthworks.

Parkton (*Eng.*) Dweller in the homestead in a park or enclosure.

Parlee, Parlea (*Eng.*) One who came from Parley (glade where pears grew), the name of places in Dorset and Hampshire.

Parler (*Ger., Eng.*) One who made glass pearls; one who embroidered cloth; the servant who attended the parlor, the conversation or interview room in a monastery.

Parlin (*Eng.*) Descendant of little Par, a pet form of Peter (a rock).

Parmelee, Parmele, Parmley (*Eng.*)
Dweller at the meadow belonging
to the palmer. See Palmer.

Parmenter, Parmentier (*Eng., Fr.*) One
who made outer garments, a tailor.

Parmer (*Eng.*) Variant of Palmer, q.v.;
the noisy man.

Parnell (*Eng.*) Descendant of Parnel,
a contraction of Petronella (little
rock); descendant of Pernell, a pet
form of Peter (a rock).

Parnes, Parness, Parns (*Heb.*) President
of the congregation.

Parr (*Eng.*) One who came from Parr
(enclosure or district), in Lancashire; dweller near an animal pen.

Parra (*It.*) Dweller at the sign of the
finch.

Parrilli, Parrillo, Parrilla (*It.*) Descendant
of little Parro, a pet form of
Gasparro (treasure).

Parriott (*Eng., Fr.*) Descendant of little
Parr or Pierre, the French form of
Peter (a rock).

Parrish (*Eng.*) One who resided within
the limits of the parish, a territorial
division originally in the care of a
single priest; one who had something
to do with the organization or government of the parish; variant of
Paris, q.v.

Parrott, Parrot (*Eng.*) Descendant of
little Perre (Peter); one thought to
have the characteristics of a parrot.

Parry (*Wel.*) The son of Harry, a pet
form of Henry (home rule).

Parsley, Parsly (*Eng.*) Dweller near
Parr's grove; dweller in a grove of
pear trees.

Parsons, Parson (*Wel., Eng.*) The son of
the parson; the son of Par, a pet
form of Peter (a rock).

Partelow (*Eng.*) One who came from
Pathlow (path by a tumulus or
barrow), in Warwickshire.

Partington (*Eng.*) One who came from
Partington (village of Pearta's people), in Cheshire.

Partipilo (*It.*) One who came from
Partipilo, in Italy.

Partlow, Partlowe (*Eng.*) One who came

from Pathlow (path by a sepulchral
mound), in Warwickshire.

Partridge, Partrick (*Eng.*) Dweller at the
sign of the partridge; one with some
characteristic of a partridge; one
who hunts or catches partridges.

Pasa (*Tur.*) One in the military services
above the rank of colonel.

Pascal, Paschal, Paschall (*Fr.*) Descendant of Pascal (sufferings).

Pascale (*It.*) Variant of Pasquale, q.v.

Paschke, Patschke (*Ger.*) Descendant of
little Paulus (small).

Pasco, Pascoe (*Eng.*) Descendant of
Pasco (Easter).

Pascual (*Sp.*) Descendant of Pascual,
Spanish form of Pascal (sufferings).

Pasha (*Tur.*) An honorary title placed
after the name given to officers of
high rank in Turkey.

Paske, Pask (*Eng., Ger.*) Descendant of
Pash, a name given to one born at
Easter.

Paskey (*Eng.*) Descendant of little Pash
(Easter).

Paskin, Paskings, Paskins (*Eng.*) Descendant, or son, of little Pash (Easter).

Pasley (*Scot.*) Variant of Paisley, q.v.

Pasquale, Pasquarella, Pasquarello (*It.*)
Descendant of Pasquale (one born
at the Easter time).

Pass (*Eng.*) Descendant of Pash, a name
given to one born during the Passover festival or at Easter.

Passalacqua (*It.*) One who came from
Passalacqua (pass water), in Italy;
nickname for one with the characteristics of a butterfly, a flighty,
frivolous fellow.

Passanante, Passananti (*It.*) One who
continues forward, or passes on.

Passaro (*It.*) Dweller at the sign of the
sparrow; the sharp, discerning,
shrewd man.

Passe (*Fr.*) Dweller near a pass or crossing of some sort.

Passenger (*Eng.*) The traveler, usually on
foot, a wayfarer.

Passic (*Yu.-Sl.*) Descendant of the pasha,
an honorary title for officers of
high rank.

Passley (*Scot.*) Variant of Paisley, q.v.

Passman (*Eng.*) Dweller near the path or passageway.

Passmore (*Eng.*) Dweller near the path through the moor.

Passon (*Eng.*) The son of Pash (Easter).

Pasternak, Pasternack (*Pol., Ukr., Rus.*) Dweller at the sign of the parsnip; one who grew and sold parsnips.

Pasteur (*Fr.*) The keeper of a flock, a shepherd.

Paston (*Eng.*) One who came from Paston (Palloc's homestead; homestead by a puddle), the name of places in Norfolk, Northamptonshire, and Northumberland.

Pastor, Paster (*Eng., Fr.*) One who took care of animals, a herdsman; one who baked bread, a baker.

Pastore (*It.*) One who performed sacerdotal functions, a priest, sometimes a bishop; one who tended sheep or other animals, a herdsman or shepherd.

Patch (*Eng.*) Descendant of Pache, a name given to one born during the Passover festival or at Easter.

Patchett (*Eng.*) Descendant of little Pash (Easter).

Pate, Patt, Pait (*Scot., Eng., Fr.*) Descendant of Pate or Pait, pet forms of Patrick (noble or patrician); one who sold meat or fish pies.

Patel (*Fr., Hindi*) One who sold cakes and tarts; headman in the village.

Pates (*Fr.*) One who sold meat or fish pies.

Pathe (*Eng., Fr.*) Dweller near an important path or footway; one who sold meat or fish pies.

Patience (*Eng.*) Descendant of Patience (long-suffering).

Patillo, Pattillo (*Scot.*) One who came from Pittilloch (croft by a lake), the name of places in Fife and Perthshire.

Patnode, Patenaude, Patenotre, Paternot (*Fr.*) One who sang or chanted, from the first word of the Lord's prayer in Latin.

Paton, Patonson (*Fr., Scot.*) Descendant

of little Pat, a pet form of Patrick (noble or patrician).

Patrick, Patricks (*Eng.*) Descendant of Patrick (noble or patrician).

Patrizio (*It.*) Descendant of Patrizio, Italian form of Patrick (noble or patrician).

Patterson, Pattison, Paterson (*Scot., Eng.*) The son of Patrick (noble or patrician).

Patti (*It.*) Descendant of Patti, a pet form of Patrizio, Italian form of Patrick (noble or patrician).

Patton, Patten, Pattin (*Eng.*) Descendant of little Pat, a pet form of Patrick (noble or patrician); one who came from Patton (village of Peatti's people; Patta's homestead), the name of places in Shropshire and Westmorland.

Paugh (*Wel.*) Variant of Pugh, q.v.

Pauker (*Ger.*) One who beats the kettledrum.

Paul, Paull, Paule, Pawl (*Scot., Eng., Fr.*) Descendant of Paul (small); one who came from Paull (pole marking a ferry), in Yorkshire; or from Paul (church of St. Paulinus), in Cornwall.

Paula, Paulo (*Sp.*) Descendant of Paulo, a Spanish form of Paul (small).

Pauley, Pauly, Pauli (*Eng., Ger.*) Descendant of Pauley, a pet form of Paul (small).

Paulin, Pauline, Pauling (*Eng.*) Descendant of little Paul (small).

Paulino, Paulini (*It.*) Descendant of little Paulo, Italian form of Paul (small).

Paulson, Paulsen, Poulson (*Sw., Nor., Dan., Eng.*) The son of Paul (small).

Paulsworth (*Eng.*) Dweller near Paul's homestead.

Paulus (*Ger.*) Descendant of Paulus (small).

Pav (*Cz.*) Dweller at the sign of the peacock; nickname given to a proud or gaudily dressed man.

Pavel, Pavell (*Bulg., Rom., Rus.*) Descendant of Pavel, a Slavic form of Paul (small).

Pavlatos (*Gr.*) Descendant of Pavlos, Greek form of Paul (small).

Pavlenko, Pavlinko (*Ukr.*) The son of Pavlo, Ukrainian form of Paul (small).

Pavlik (*Ukr.*) Descendant of little Pavlo (small).

Pavlov, Pavlow (*Cz.-Sl., Rus.*) The son of Pavel, Slavic form of Paul (small).

Pavlovich (*Yu.-Sl., Rus.*) The son of Pavle, Serbo-Croatian form of Paul (small).

Pavone, Pavoni (*It.*) One who raised and sold peafowl; the proud or conceited man.

Pawlak, Pawlik (*Pol.*) Descendant of little Pawell (small).

Pawlicki (*Pol.*) The son of Pawel, Polish form of Paul (small).

Pawling (*Eng.*) Variant of Paulin, q.v.

Pawlowski (*Pol.*) One who came from Pawlow, in Poland.

Pawluk (*Ukr.*) Descendant of Pawl, Slavic form of Paul (small).

Pawlyszyn, Pawlyshin (*Ukr., Rus.*) The son of Pawl's (Paul's) wife.

Paxson, Paxon (*Eng.*) The son of Pack (Easter).

Paxton (*Eng., Scot.*) One who came from Paxton (Pack's homestead), the name of places in Huntingdonshire and Berwickshire.

Payne, Paynes (*Eng.*) The rustic or countryman; a pagan; descendant of Payen (villager, later heathen).

Payson (*Eng.*) The son of Pash (Easter).

Payton (*Eng.*) One who came from Peyton (Paega's homestead), in Suffolk; descendant of little Pate, a pet form of Patrick (noble or patrician).

Paz (*Sp.*) One who came from Paz (peace), in Spain.

Peabody (*Eng.*) Nickname for a showily-dressed individual.

Peace (*Eng.*) Descendant of Pace, a name given to one born during the Passover festival or at Easter; or of Pace, a pet form of Bonapace (good peace); variant of Pease, q.v.

Peacher (*Eng.*) One who caught or sold fish.

Peachey (*Eng.*) Dweller on the small hill; nickname for one who sinned.

Peacock (*Eng.*) Dweller at the sign of the peacock; nickname given to a proud or gaudily dressed man.

Peak, Peake, Peaks (*Eng.*) One who lived at, or on, a pointed hill; one who came from Peak (hill), in Derbyshire.

Peaker (*Eng.*) Dweller by the peak or hill.

Peale, Peal (*Eng.*) Variant of Peele, q.v.

Pearce, Pearse (*Eng.*) Descendant of Piers (a rock).

Pearcy (*Eng.*) Variant of Percy, q.v.; descendant of little Piers, an early English form of Peter (a rock).

Pearl (*Eng.*) One who sold pearls.

Pearlman (*Ger.*) An Anglicized form of Perlman, q.v.

Pearlstein (*Ger.*) Variant of Perlstein, q.v.

Pearsall (*Eng.*) One who came from Pearshall or Pershill (Per's hill), in Staffordshire.

Pearson (*Eng.*) The son of Pears, an early form of Peter (a rock).

Peart (*Eng.*) The ready, skillful man.

Peartree (*Eng.*) Dweller near a pear tree.

Peary, Peery (*Eng.*) Descendant of little Pear, a pet form of Peter (a rock).

Pease (*Eng.*) Variant of Pace, q.v.; one who raised and sold peas.

Peasley, Peaslee (*Eng.*) Dweller at the field or grove where peas were grown.

Peavey, Peavy (*Eng.*) One who came from Pavie, in France.

Peberdy, Peberday (*Eng.*) Abbreviated form of Peabody, q.v.

Pebworth (*Eng.*) One who came from Pebworth (Pybba's homestead), in Gloucestershire.

Pecarsky (*Ukr.*) One who made bread, a baker.

Pech, Peach (*Eng.*) One who came from Pech or Peche (peach), in Normandy; dweller at, or on, a peaked hill.

Pechter (*Ger.*) One who leased and cultivated land, a farmer; one who collected tolls, rents, or taxes.

Pecic (*Yu.-Sl.*) One who came from Pec, in Yugoslavia.

Peck, Pec (*Eng.*) Dweller at, or on, a pointed hill.

Pecker, Peckar, Peckerman (*Eng.*) Dweller on the hill; one who made and sold peck measures.

Peckham (*Eng.*) One who came from Peckham (homestead by a hill), the name of several places in England.

Pecora (*It.*) One who raised and sold sheep.

Pecoraro (*It.*) One who took care of sheep, a shepherd.

Peddle (*Eng.*) One who carries goods about for sale, a peddler.

Pedersen, Pederson, Peddersen, Pedderson (*Nor., Dan.*) The son of Peder, Norse form of Peter (a rock).

Pedley (*Eng.*) One who came from Padley (Padda's grove), in Derbyshire.

Pedrick (*Eng.*) One who came from Petherick (church of St. Petroc), in Cornwall.

Peebles, Peeples (*Scot.*) One who came from Peebles (place of assembly), in Peeblesshire; dweller in a tent or pavilion.

Peek (*Eng.*) Dweller at, or on, a pointed hill.

Peele, Peel (*Eng.*) Dweller in, or near, a small fortress or fortified castle; one who came from Peel (fortress), on the Isle of Man.

Peer, Peers (*Eng., Fr.*) Descendant of Pierce or Piers, early English forms of Peter (a rock); descendant of Pier (a rock); dweller near a stone.

Peet, Peete (*Eng., Du., Scot.*) Descendant of Peet, a pet form of Pieter or Peter (a rock); dweller near a hole or steep hollow; one who was delicate or a pampered pet.

Pegg, Peggs (*Eng.*) Descendant of Peg, a pet form of Margaret (a pearl); metonymic for one who made and sold pegs.

Pegram (*Eng.*) Abbreviated form of Pilgrim, q.v.

Pegues (*Fr.*) One who produced and sold pitch or wax.

Pehkonen (*Finn.*) Dweller near a bush.

Pei (*It., Chin.*) Dweller near a pear tree; one who sold pears; shells.

Peiffer, Peifer (*Ger.*) Variant of Pfeiffer, q.v.

Peiper (*Ger.*) Variant of Pfeiffer, q.v.

Peirce (*Eng.*) A variant of Pierce, q.v.

Peitzman, Peitz (*Ger.*) One who came from Peitz, in Germany.

Pekarek, Pekarik, Pekar (*Yu.-Sl., Ukr., Pol.*) One who made bread, a baker.

Pelham (*Eng.*) One who came from Pelham (Peola's homestead), in Hertfordshire.

Pelikan, Pelican, Pellikan (*Ger.*) Dweller at the sign of the pelican; one thought to have some of the characteristics of a pelican. The pelican feeding its young was used as a symbol of Christ.

Pelkey, Pelkie (*Eng.*) Descendant of Pileca.

Pell, Pelle (*Eng.*) Dweller at, or near, a pool; descendant of Pell, a pet form of Peter (a rock).

Pellegrini, Pellegrino (*It.*) Descendant of Pellegrino (pilgrim).

Pelletier, Pelletiere, Pellettiere (*Fr.*) One who dressed or dealt in furs; a furrier; or who prepared skins, a skinner.

Pellettieri (*It.*) One who dressed or dealt in furs.

Pellicano, Pellicane (*It.*) One thought to possess the characteristics of a pelican.

Pellicciotti (*It.*) One who produced and sold fur coats; one who wore a small fur coat.

Pellow (*Eng.*) One who had a round head or figure.

Pelosi, Pelosy (*It.*) One with bristly, shaggy hair.

Peltier (*Fr.*) Contraction of Pelletier, q.v.

Pelton (*Eng.*) One who came from Pelton (Peola's homestead), in Durham.

Peltonen (*Finn.*) One who had many fields.

Peltz, Peltzer, Peltzman (*Ger.*) One who deals in furs, a furrier.

Pelz, Pelzer, Pelzmann (*Ger.*) One who made or sold fur coats, a furrier.

Pemberton, Pembleton (*Eng.*) One who came from Pemberton (barley enclosure by the hill), in Lancashire.

Pembridge (*Eng.*) One who came from Pembridge (bridge by the pens; Paegna's bridge), in Hertfordshire.

Pembroke, Pembrook (*Wel., Eng.*) One who came from Pembroke (head or end of the land), a county in Wales.

Pena (*Sp.*) One who came from Pena (large rock), the name of several places in Spain; dweller near a large stone.

Penberth, Penberthy (*Eng.*) Dweller at the green hilltop; or at the head of the cove; or at the end of the bushes.

Pence, Pentz, Penz (*Ger.*) Descendant of Benzo, a pet form of names beginning with Bar (bear), and Band (banner); one who came from Pentz, in Germany.

Pendarvis (*Eng.*) Dweller at the end of the oak trees.

Pendell, Pendle (*Eng.*) One who came from Pendle (both elements mean "hill"), in Lancashire.

Pender, Penders, Penter (*Eng., Scot.*) Variant of Pinder, q.v.; descendant of Pender (head, army).

Pendergast, Pendergrass (*Eng., Ir.*) Descendant of Pendegast (head stranger); one who came from Prendergast, a parish in Pembrokeshire.

Pendlebury (*Eng.*) One who came from Pendlebury (fort by Pen hill), in Lancashire.

Pendleton, Pendelton (*Eng.*) One who came from Pendleton (hilltop village), in Lancashire.

Penfil (*Eng.*) Variant of Penfold, q.v.

Penfold (*Eng.*) Dweller near the animal pound or enclosure; one in charge of the pound.

Pengelly, Pengilly (*Eng.*) One who came from Pengelly (head of the grove), in Cornwall; dweller at the end of the copse.

Pengler (*Ger.*) One who wandered from place to place; the coarse, uncouth man.

Penhallow (*Eng.*) One who came from Penhallow (head of the moor; hilltop with tumulus), in Cornwall.

Penley (*Eng.*) One who came from Pinley (pin, or narrow, grove), in Warwickshire.

Penn, Penna (*Eng.*) Dweller near a pen or sheepfold; one who came from Penn (enclosure; hill), the name of places in Buckinghamshire and Staffordshire; dweller on the hilltop.

Pennell (*Eng., Fr.*) Descendant of little Pinn (peg), or of little Pain or Pagan (rustic or countryman); one who wore ragged, tattered clothing.

Penner, Pender (*Eng.*) Dweller at the pen enclosure.

Pennick, Penick (*Eng., Scot.*) Dweller at the head of the creek; the man with the large head; one who came from Penick (spotted place), in Nairnshire.

Penniman (*Eng.*) The servant of Penny (a feather).

Penning (*Du.*) The son of Penne, a pet form of Penelope (weaver; duck).

Pennington (*Eng.*) One who came from Pennington (village that had to pay a penny tribute; the village of Pinna's people), the name of several villages in England.

Pennock (*Eng.*) One who came from Pinnock (little hill), in Gloucestershire; variant of Pennick, q.v.

Penny, Penney, Pennie (*Eng., Scot., Fr.*) Dweller at the sign of the feather; descendant of Penny (feather); or of little Penn (peg).

Pennycuick (*Scot.*) One who came from Penicuik (head of the cuckoo), in Midlothian.

Pennypacker (*Ger.*) Variant of Pannebakker, q.v.

Penrod (*Eng.*) Dweller near the enclosed rood or cross.

Penrose (*Eng., Wel.*) One who lived at the head, or upper end, of the heath.

Penry (*Wel.*) The son of Henry (home, rule).

Penta (*It.*) One who made and sold bottles.

Pentecost (*Eng.*) Descendant of Pentecost (fiftieth), a name given to children born on the fiftieth day after Easter.

Penton (*Eng.*) One who came from Penton (homestead that paid a penny tax or tribute), in Hampshire.

Penttinen (*Finn.*) Descendant of Pentti, Finnish form of Benedict (blessed).

Pentz (*Ger.*) One who came from Pentz, in Germany.

Penwarden (*Eng.*) The principal or head guard or watchman.

Penza (*It.*) One who thinks or reflects on his actions.

Penzur (*Pol.*) The thick, stout man.

Peoples (*Scot.*) One who came from Peebles (place of assembly), in Peeblesshire; descendant of little Pepin (chirper).

Pepe, Pepi (*It.*) One who dealt in pepper and other spices.

Pepin, Peppin (*Fr.*) Descendant of Pepin (trembler), an old French given name derived from the onomatopoetic word for the baby language of pips, chirps or squeaks.

Peplow (*Eng.*) One who came from Peplow (pebble hill), in Shropshire.

Pepper, Peppers (*Eng.*) One who dealt in pepper and other condiments.

Peppercorn (*Eng.*) One who held land for which he paid rent of a peppercorn; one who dealt in spices.

Pepperman (*Eng.*) One who dealt in pepper and other spices.

Pepys (*Eng.*) Descendant of Pepin (trembler). See Pepin.

Pera (*It.*) Dweller near a pear tree; one who sold pears.

Peralta (*Sp.*) Dweller near the high rock.

Percefull (*Eng.*) Variant of Percival, q.v.

Percell (*Eng.*) Variant of Purcell, q.v.

Perchick (*Ukr.*) One who dealt in pepper and other condiments.

Perchonock (*Rus.*) One who dealt in pepper and other condiments.

Percival, Perceval (*Eng.*) One who came from Percheval or Perceval (valley-piercer), in France; descendant of Percival (pierce valley); one who pierced the valley, that is, entered to poach; one notorious for breaking into places.

Percy, Piercy, Piercey (*Eng.*) One who came from Perci or Percy (Persius' estate), in Normandy.

Perdue (*Fr., Eng.*) Descendant of Perdu (lost), a name given to a foundling; a nickname given to one addicted to use of the oath, "By God," i.e., *par Dieu.*

Peregrine, Peregrin (*Eng.*) Descendant of Peregrine (wanderer); one who was a stranger in the community.

Pereira (*Port.*) One who came from Pereira (pear tree), in Portugal; dweller near a pear tree.

Perez (*Sp.*) The son of Pero, a pet form of Pedro, Spanish form of Peter (a rock).

Perfetti, Perfetto (*It.*) The faultless, perfect man, probably applied in an ironic vein.

Pergolini (*It.*) One who came from Pergola (vine-trellis), in Italy; dweller near a vine-trellis.

Perham (*Eng.*) One who came from Parham (homestead where pears grew), in Sussex.

Perillo, Perilli (*It.*) Descendant of little Peri, a pet form of Pedro, Italian form of Peter (a rock).

Perkins, Perkinson (*Wel.*) The son of little Pier, a pet form of Peter (a rock).

Perks (*Eng.*) The son of Pier, a form of Peter (a rock).

Perl, Perle (*Ger.*) Descendant of Perle (pearl); one who came from Perl (pearl), in Germany.

Perlberg, Perlberger (*Ger.*) One who came from Perleberg, in Germany.

393

Perlman, Perelman (*Ger.*) Pearl man; one who buys and sells pearls or beads; the husband of Perl (pearl).

Perlmutter (*Ger.*) Dealer in mother of pearl; possibly a name taken by one whose mother was named Perl.

Perloff (*Rus.*) One who sells pearls; the son of Perl (pearl).

Perlstein (*Ger.*) Descendant of Perlstein, an endearing form of Perl, German form of Pearl (pearl); pearl stone.

Permenter (*Eng.*) Variant of Parmenter, q.v.

Permer (*Eng., Ger.*) Variant of Palmer, q.v.; descendant of Bermar (bear, famous).

Perna, Perno (*It.*) One who dealt in pearls.

Pernell (*Eng.*) Descendant of Pernell, a pet form of Peter (a rock).

Pernsley (*Eng.*) Dweller in a grove where pears grew.

Pero (*Sp.*) Descendant of Pero, a pet form of Pedro (a rock).

Perot (*Fr.*) Descendant of little Pierre, French form of Peter (a rock).

Perpetua (*It.*) Descendant of Perpetua (the everlasting), a name given by Italian mothers honoring St. Vivia Perpetua to symbolize their faith in life everlasting.

Perreault, Perreau, Perreaud (*Fr.*) Descendant of Perreau, pet form of Pierre, French form of Peter (a rock).

Perri (*It.*) Descendant of Piero, Italian form of Peter (a rock).

Perrie (*Scot.*) Descendant of little Pier, a pet form of Peter (a rock).

Perrier (*Eng., Fr.*) One who cut or quarried stone; dweller by a pear tree.

Perrin, Perrine, Perron, Perret (*Fr.*) Descendant of little Pierre, French form of Peter (a rock).

Perrone, Perone (*It.*) Dweller at a cliff or steep incline; descendant of big Perro, an Italian form of Peter (a rock).

Perrotta (*It.*) Descendant of little Perro, an Italian form of Peter (a rock).

Perry (*Wel., Eng.*) The son of Harry, English pet form of Henry (home, rule); dweller by the pear tree; descendant of little Pier, a pet form of Peter (a rock); descendant of Perry, a pet form of Peregrine (wanderer).

Persefield (*Eng.*) One notorious for breaking into a field.

Pershing, Pfoersching (*Ger.*) One who lived at, or near, a peach tree.

Persichetti (*It.*) One who raised and sold peaches.

Persico (*It.*) One who fished for perch; one who raised and sold peaches.

Persky, Perski (*Ukr.*) One who came from Persia, a Persian.

Person, Persson, Persons (*Sw., Nor., Fr.*) The son of Per, Swedish form of Peter (a rock); descendant of little Pierre (a rock); the parish priest.

Pertschi (*Hun.*) One who came from Percs, in Hungary.

Perugini (*It.*) One who came from Perugia, a province in Italy.

Pescatore (*It.*) One who caught and sold fish, a fisherman.

Pesce (*It.*) Dweller at the sign of the fish; the good swimmer; a simpleton.

Pestalozzi (*Swis., It.*) One who cut bones, a bone-cutter.

Pester (*Eng.*) One who makes bread, a baker.

Petchon (*Eng.*) Dweller on a small hill.

Peter (*Ger., Eng.*) Descendant of Peter (a rock).

Peterfreund (*Ger.*) The friend or companion named Peter (a rock).

Peterkin, Peterkins (*Eng., Du.*) Descendant of little Peter (a rock).

Peterman, Petermann (*Eng., Ger.*) Servant to Peter.

Peters (*Wel., Eng.*) The son of Peter (a rock).

Peterson, Petersen (*Eng., Dan., Nor., Sw.*) The son of Peter (a rock).

Petersson (*Sw.*) The son of Peter (a rock).

Petherick, Pethick (*Eng.*) One who came from Petherick (church of St.

Petroc), in Cornwall; descendant of little Peter (a rock).

Petit, Pettit, Petiet (*Fr.*) The short or small man.

Petitjean (*Fr.*) The little man named Jean, the French form of John (gracious gift of Jehovah).

Petitperrin (*Fr.*) Descendant of short, little Pierre (a rock).

Petka (*Rus.*) Descendant of Petka, a pet form of Petr, Russian form of Peter (a rock).

Petkov (*Bulg.*) The son of Petko, a diminutive form of Peter (a rock).

Petkus (*Lith.*) Descendant of Petko, a pet form of Petras, Lithuanian form of Peter (a rock).

Petofi (*Hun.*) The son of Peter (a rock).

Petraitis, Petrusaitis (*Lith.*) The son of Petras, Lithuanian form of Peter (a rock).

Petrakos, Petrakis (*Gr.*) Descendant of little Petros, Greek form of Peter (a rock).

Petrauskas, Petrauskis (*Lith.*) Descendant of little Petras, Lithuanian form of Peter (a rock).

Petre (*Fr.*) One who made bread, a baker; descendant of Peter (a rock).

Petrella, Petrelli (*It.*) Descendant of little Petri, an Italian form of Peter (a rock).

Petrenko (*Ukr.*) The son of Petro, Ukrainian form of Peter (a rock).

Petrescu (*Rom.*) Descendant, or follower, of Petru, Romanian form of Peter (a rock).

Petri (*It.*) Descendant of Pietro, Italian form of Peter (a rock).

Petrick, Petrich (*Eng.*) Descendant of little Peter (a rock).

Petrie, Petry (*Scot.*) Descendant of little Peter (a rock); or of little Patrick (noble or patrician).

Petrillo, Petrilli (*It.*) Descendant of little Pietro, Italian form of Peter (a rock).

Petro (*Ukr.*) Descendant of Petro, Ukrainian form of Peter (a rock).

Petroff, Petrov, Petro (*Rus.*) The son of Petr, Russian form of Peter (a rock).

Petrone, Petroni, Petronio (*It.*) Descendant of big Pietro, Italian form of Peter (a rock).

Petronis (*Lith.*) The son of Petras, Lithuanian form of Peter (a rock).

Petropoulos (*Gr.*) The son of Petros, Greek form of Peter (a rock).

Petros (*Gr.*) Descendant of Petros, Greek form of Peter (a rock).

Petroski (*Pol.*) Descendant of Piotr, Polish form of Peter (a rock).

Petrov, Petroff (*Rus., Bulg.*) The son of Petr, Russian and Bulgarian form of Peter (a rock).

Petrovich, Petrovic (*Rus.*) The son of Petr, Russian form of Peter (a rock).

Petrowski (*Pol.*) Descendant of Piotr, Polish form of Peter (a rock).

Petrucci, Petruzzi, Petruzzo (*It.*) Descendant of little Pietro, Italian form of Peter (a rock).

Petruska (*Rus.*) Descendant of Petrusha, a pet form of Petr, Russian form of Peter (a rock).

Petryshyn (*Ukr.*) The son of Petro's (Peter's) wife.

Pettaway, Pettiway, Pettway (*Eng.*) Dweller at the way or path to the pit or hollow.

Pettengill, Pettingell, Pettengell (*Eng.*) One who came from Portugal (the harbor).

Petterson, Pettersen, Pettersson (*Sw., Nor.*) The son of Petter, Norwegian form of Peter (a rock).

Pettibone (*Eng., Fr.*) One of little worth or use.

Pettiford, Pettifer (*Eng.*) The iron-footed person, a nickname.

Pettigrew, Petticrew (*Scot., Eng.*) Dweller at a grove frequented by cranes; nickname for a small man or one of stunted growth.

Pettijohn (*Fr.*) Variant of Pettyjohn, q.v.

Pettinelli (*It.*) One who made and sold small combs.

Pettis, Pettes, Pettas, Pettus (*Eng.*) Dweller in the house by the pit or deep hollow.

Petty, Pettie, Pettee, Pettey (*Scot., Eng.*,

Fr.) One small in stature; one who came from Petty (piece), in Scotland; American variants of Petit, q.v.

Pettygrove (*Eng.*) Dweller at a small wood or shaw; variant of Pettigrew, q.v.

Pettyjohn (*Fr.*) The little man named John (gracious gift of Jehovah).

Petursson (*Ice.*) The son of Petur, Icelandic form of Peter (a rock).

Peugh (*Wel.*) Variant of Pugh, q.v.

Peurifoy (*Eng.*) Variant of Purifoy, q.v.

Peverill, Peverell, Peverall (*Eng.*) Descendant of Peverel (pepper); the small man with a peppery disposition; one with a small rounded shape.

Pew (*Wel.*) The son of Hew or Hugh (spirit; mind).

Pewtherer, Pewterer, Pewtrer (*Eng.*) One who made and sold pewter vessels.

Peyrot, Peyret (*Fr.*) Descendant of little Peyre, a form of Pierre, French form of Peter (a rock).

Peyser (*Ger., Cz.*) One who came from Peise, in Germany; one in charge of a hostel; a clerk or official scribe.

Peyton (*Eng.*) One who came from Peyton (Paega's homestead), in Suffolk; descendant of little Pate, a pet form of Patrick (noble or patrician).

Pfaff (*Ger.*) One who performed sacerdotal functions, a priest; one whose behavior, spirit or appearance resembled that of a priest.

Pfaller, Pfaler, Pfahler (*Ger.*) Dweller near Der Pfall, a place name for the ruins of the Roman fortifications in the Jura mountains in Bavaria. Pfall refers to posts or stakes driven into the ground as barriers.

Pfannebecker (*Ger.*) One who made roof tiles by hardening clay while moist in the sun or by fire.

Pfannkuche (*Ger.*) One who made pancakes.

Pfarrer (*Ger.*) The clergyman, minister, or priest.

Pfau (*Ger.*) Dweller at the sign of the peacock; one thought to possess the characteristics of a peacock; dweller near swamp grass.

Pfeffer (*Ger.*) One who dealt in pepper and other condiments; nickname for one who dealt in foodstuffs, a grocer.

Pfeiffer, Pfeifer (*Ger.*) One who played a fife or pipe, a piper; one engaged in music, a musician.

Pfeil (*Ger.*) One who made and sold arrows or darts.

Pfender, Pfendner (*Ger.*) One who guards the fields and impounds straying cattle; one who loans money on the security of personal property pledged in his keeping, a pawnbroker; a court official who attaches property.

Pfister, Pfisterer (*Ger.*) One who made bread, a baker.

Pfizenmaier, Pfizenmayer (*Ger.*) The overseer or head servant who dwelt by the pool.

Pflaum, Pflaumer (*Ger.*) One who sold plums.

Pflueger, Pfleger, Pfluger (*Ger.*) One who plowed the arable land, a plowman.

Pflugfelder (*Ger.*) One who came from Pflugfelden (plowed field), in Germany.

Pfoertner (*Ger.*) One who tended a gate or door, a doorkeeper, especially one who guarded a city or monastery gate.

Pfundt, Pfund (*Ger.*) One who weighed merchandise, especially for the wholesale merchant or for the assessment of tax.

Pharr (*Eng.*) Dweller at the sign of the bull or boar.

Phaup (*Scot.*) One who came from Fawhope (locally pronounced as Phaup), in Scotland.

Phelan, Phelon, Phalan, Phalon (*Ir.*) Grandson of little Faol (wolf).

Phelps, Philp (*Eng.*) Descendant of Philip (lover of horses).

Phifer (*Ger.*) Variant of Pfeiffer, q.v.

Philbin (*Eng.*) Descendant of little Philip (lover of horses).

Philbrick (*Eng.*) One who came from

Felbridge (bridge by a field), in Surrey; or from Felbrigg (plank bridge), in Norfolk.

Philbrook (*Eng.*) Dweller near a mountain stream.

Philhower (*Du.*) One who made files, a corruption of the original Villhouwer.

Phillips, Philipps, Phillip, Phillipp, Philipp, Philips (*Wel., Eng.*) The son of Philip (lover of horses).

Philmore, Phillimore (*Eng.*) Descendant of Filimar or Filomor (very famous).

Philo (*Eng.*) Descendant of Philo (love).

Philpott, Philpot, Philipot (*Eng.*) Descendant of little Philip (lover of horses).

Phinney, Phinnie (*Ir.*) Descendant of the soldier.

Phipps (*Eng.*) Descendant of Phip, a pet form of Philip (lover of horses).

Phyfe (*Scot.*) A variant of Fyfe, q.v.

Physick (*Eng.*) Metonymic for one who practiced medicine, a physician.

Pianka (*Pol.*) One who mines for meerschaum; or who is addicted to smoking meerschaum pipes.

Piano (*Sp., It., Fr.*) Dweller on a plain, flat, level ground; one who came from Piano (level ground), in Corsica.

Piasecki (*Pol.*) Dweller on sandy soil.

Piazza, Piazzi (*It.*) Dweller on, or near, the square.

Picard (*Fr.*) One who came from Picardy (district of the pike men), in France.

Picardi, Picardo (*It.*) One who came from Picardy (district of the pike men), in France.

Picasso (*Sp., It.*) One who uses a pick or pickax in his work; one with the characteristics of a magpie.

Piccard (*Fr.*) Variant of Picard, q.v.

Piccinini, Piccinni, Piccini (*It.*) One of low stature, a little man.

Piccolo, Piccoli (*It.*) Descendant of Piccolo, a pet name for a small child; one of low stature.

Pichardo (*Sp.*) One who came from Picardy (district of the pike men), in France.

Pichon (*Fr.*) One who worked with a small pick; dweller at the sign of the pigeon.

Pick (*Eng., Cz.-Sl., Ger.*) Dweller near a pointed hill; or on a highway; or at the sign of the pick (the bartailed godwit); or at the sign of the bull; a name sometimes adopted by people named Joseph because the Bible likened Joseph to a young bullock.

Pickard (*Eng.*) One who came from Picardy (district of the pike men), in France; descendant of Pichard (point, hard).

Pickell, Pickel, Pickle (*Eng.*) One who came from Pickhill (Pica's nook; nook by the hills), in Yorkshire; dweller in, or near, a pightle or enclosure.

Pickens, Picken (*Eng., Scot.*) Descendant of little Pic, or Picon (pike).

Picker (*Eng.*) One who made and sold picks, pikes, and pickaxes; dweller on the peak; one who caught and sold pike.

Pickering (*Eng.*) One who came from Pickering (people at the edge of the hill), in the North Riding of Yorkshire.

Pickersgill (*Eng., Scot.*) One who came from Pickersgill (robbers' ravine), in the West Riding of Yorkshire.

Pickett, Picket (*Eng.*) Descendant of little Pic, or Picot (pike).

Pickford (*Eng.*) One who came from Pitchford (ford near where pitch is found), in Shropshire; dweller at a ford near a pointed hill.

Picon (*Fr.*) One who worked with a pick; one who made or sold javelins or spears.

Picone (*It.*) Dweller at the sign of the woodpecker.

Picot, Picott (*Eng.*) Descendant of little Pic (point).

Pidcock (*Eng.*) Descendant of little Peot (a Pict).

Piddington (*Eng.*) One who came from Piddington (village of Pydda's people), in Northamptonshire.

Piddubnyj, Piddubnyi (*Ukr.*) Dweller near an oak tree.

Pidgeon, Pigeon (*Eng.*) Dweller at the sign of the pigeon; one thought to have some characteristic of a pigeon.

Piechocki, Piechoski (*Pol.*) One who travels on foot, a pedestrian.

Pieczynski (*Pol.*) One who prepares food, a baker.

Piehl, Piehler (*Ger.*) Dweller at, or near, a hill.

Piekarski (*Pol.*) One who made bread, a baker.

Piekarz (*Pol.*) One who prepared bread, a baker.

Piel (*Eng.*) Variant of Peele, q.v.

Pieper (*Ger.*) One who whistled or played a pipe or fife, a piper.

Pierce, Piers (*Wel., Eng.*) Descendant of Pierce or Piers, early English forms of Peter (a rock).

Pieri, Pierri (*It.*) Descendant of Pieri or Pierro, variants of Pietro, Italian form of Peter (a rock).

Piermattei, Piermatteo (*It.*) Descendant of Piero Matteo, Italian form of Peter (a rock), and Matthew (gift of Jehovah).

Pieroni (*It.*) Descendant of little Piero, an Italian form of Peter (a rock).

Pierpont (*Fr.*) Dweller at, or near, the stone bridge.

Pierre (*Fr.*) Descendant of Pierre, French form of Peter (a rock).

Pierro (*It.*) Descendant of Pierro, an Italian form of Peter (a rock).

Pierrot (*Fr.*) Descendant of little Pierre, French form of Peter (a rock).

Pierson (*Eng.*) The son of Piers, early English form of Peter (a rock).

Piet (*Du.*) Descendant of Piet, Dutch pet form of Peter (a rock).

Pieters (*Du.*) Descendant of Pieter, Dutch form of Peter (a rock).

Pietro (*It.*) Descendant of Pietro, an Italian form of Peter (a rock).

Pietrobono (*It.*) Descendant of good Pietro, Italian form of Peter (a rock).

Pietromartire (*It.*) Follower of St. Peter, the martyr.

Pietronigro (*It.*) Descendant of black Pietro, Italian form of Peter (a rock); dweller near a black stone.

Pietropaolo, Pietropaula (*It.*) Descendant of Pietropaolo (Peter Paul); follower of Saints Peter and Paul.

Pietrowski (*Pol.*) One who came from Pietrowa (Peter's place), in Poland.

Pietrzak (*Pol.*) Descendant of Piotr, Slavic form of Peter (a rock).

Piggott (*Eng.*) Variant of Pickett, q.v.

Pigman (*Eng.*) One who had charge of the pigs.

Pignatelli, Pignotti (*It.*) One who made boilers, or handled them in his work.

Pigott, Pigot (*Eng.*) One whose face was pitted or pockmarked; variant of Pickett, q.v.

Pike, Pikes (*Eng.*) Dweller at, or on, a pointed hill; one who fought with a pike; dweller at the sign of the pike.

Pilch, Pilcher (*Ger., Eng.*) Dweller at the sign of the dormouse; one who made and sold fur garments.

Pilgrim, Pilgram (*Eng.*) One who had visited a distant shrine.

Pilkerton (*Eng.*) One who came from Pillerton (village of Pilheard's people), in Warwickshire.

Pilkington (*Eng.*) One who came from Pilkington (village of Pileca's people), in Lancashire.

Pill, Pilles (*Eng.*) Dweller near the pointed object, such as a pointed stake, post or hill; or at the creek.

Piller, Pillar, Pillers, Pillars (*Ger.*) Descendant of Bilihar (sword, army).

Pilling (*Eng.*) Dweller at the estate of the Pil family; dweller at a stake by a pool.

Pillmore (*Eng.*) Variant of Philmore, q.v.

Pillow, Pellow (*Eng.*) One with a misshapen foot—like a wolf's foot.

Pillsbury, Pilsbury (*Eng.*) One who came from Pilsbury (Pil's fort), in Derbyshire.

Pillsworth (*Eng.*) One who came from Pilsworth (Pil's homestead), in Lancashire.

Pilny (*Cz.*) The hard-working, industrious man.

Pilson (*Eng.*) One who came from Pilson (Peofel's hill), in Shropshire.

Pilz (*Ger.*) One who gathers and sells mushrooms.

Pimentel (*Sp., Fr.*) One who sold pimentos.

Pimpinella, Pimpinelli, Pimpinello (*It.*) The little joyous, exuberant person.

Pina (*Sp.*) Dweller near a pine tree.

Pinch, Pinches (*Eng.*) Variant of Pink, q.v.

Pinchbeck, Pinchback (*Eng.*) One who came from Pinchbeck (stream frequented by finches; minnow stream), in Lincolnshire.

Pinchon (*Fr.*) Dweller at the sign of the finch; one with the characteristics of a finch, such as ability to sing.

Pinchot (*Fr.*) The little, gay, singing man.

Pinchuk, Pintzuk (*Ukr., Rus.*) One who came from Pinsk (foam), in Byelorussia.

Pinchum, Pincham (*Eng.*) Dweller in, or near, Pince's homestead; variant of Pinkham, q.v.

Pinckney (*Eng.*) One who came from Picquigny (Pinco's estate), in France.

Pincus, Pincuss (*Heb.*) Variant of Pinkus, q.v.

Pinder, Pindar (*Eng.*) The officer in a manor whose duty was to impound stray animals.

Pindle (*Eng.*) Variant of Penley, q.v.

Pine, Pines (*Eng.*) Dweller at, or near, a pine tree; dweller at the sign of the pine tree.

Pineda (*Sp., It.*) One who came from Pineda (place of pine trees), the name of several places in Spain and Italy; dweller near a pine tree.

Pinello (*It.*) Dweller near a small pine tree.

Pinger, Pingre (*Fr.*) One in the habit of playing the game of knuckle-bones.

Pingree (*Fr.*) One who played the old French game of cockles.

Pingue (*Fr.*) The large fat man.

Pinheiro, Pineiro (*Port.*) One who came from Pinheiro (pine tree), in Portugal; dweller near a pine tree.

Pinho (*Port.*) Dweller near a pine tree.

Pinion (*Wel.*) The son of Einion (anvil).

Pink (*Eng.*) One with some quality of a chaffinch; dweller at the sign of the chaffinch.

Pinkapank (*Ger.*) The smith who worked at the forge—from the sound made by his hammer.

Pinkerton (*Scot.*) One who came from the old barony of Pinkerton, in East Lothian.

Pinkett (*Eng.*) Dweller at the sign of the little chaffinch; variant of Pickett, q.v.

Pinkham (*Eng.*) Dweller at a homestead where chaffinches are found.

Pinkney (*Eng., Fr.*) One who came from Pinkney, in Norfolk; one who came from Picquigny (Pinco's estate), in France.

Pinkowitz (*Ukr.*) The son of Pinka (foam).

Pinkston, Pinkstone (*Eng.*) One who came from Pinxton (homestead by the end of the wood), in Derbyshire.

Pinkus (*Heb.*) Latinized form of Pinchas or Phineas (mouth of brass; dark complexion); one with a dark complexion.

Pinnell, Pinel, Pinell (*Eng.*) Dweller near a small pine tree.

Pinner (*Eng.*) Variant of Pinder, q.v.

Pinney (*Fr., Eng.*) One who came from Pinay (pines); dweller in, or near, the pine woods; variant of Penny, q.v.

Pinnock (*Eng.*) One who came from Pinnock (small hill), in Gloucestershire.

Pino (*It., Sp.*) Dweller near a pine tree.

Pinsky, Pinsker, Pinski (*Rus., Ukr., Pol.*) One who came from Pinsk (foam), in Byelorussia.

Pinsmith (*Eng.*) One who made pegs, pins, small needles, and other wire articles.

Pinson (*Fr.*) Dweller at the sign of the bird; one with birdlike characteristics.

Pinter (*Ger., Hun.*) One who made and sold casks, buckets, and tubs, a cooper.

Pinto, Pinta (*Sp., Port., It.*) One who painted; one who had a scar or blemish; nickname for a childish person; or for a devilish man; one who came from Pinto, in Spain.

Pintozzi (*It.*) Descendant of the little painted or colored one.

Pion (*Fr.*) One who goes on foot, a pedestrian; one who drinks, a toper.

Piotrowicz (*Pol.*) The son of Piotr, Polish form of Peter (a rock).

Piotrowski (*Pol.*) Descendant of Piotr, Polish form of Peter (a rock).

Pious (*Eng.*) One who manifested devotion to God; one who was dutiful and loyal to parents.

Piper (*Eng.*) One who played a pipe, especially a strolling musician.

Pippen, Pippens, Pippin, Pipping (*Fr., Eng.*) Variant of Pepin, q.v.

Piree (*Scot.*) Variant of Pirie, q.v.

Pires (*Port.*) The son of Pero, Portuguese form of Peter (a rock).

Pirie, Pirrie (*Scot., Eng.*) Descendant of little Pierre (a rock); dweller by the pear tree.

Pirman, Pirmann (*Ger.*) Descendant of Permann, a form of Berman, pet form of names beginning with Ber (bear), as Berold and Bernhard.

Piro (*Port.*) Descendant of Pero, Portuguese form of Peter (a rock).

Pirolli, Pirollo (*It.*) Descendant of little Piro, a pet form of Pietro, Italian form of Peter (a rock).

Pisacano, Pisacane (*It.*) Dweller near where dandelions grew.

Pisani, Pisano (*Fr., It.*) One who came from Pisa, in Italy.

Pisarek (*Pol.*) A scribe or clerk; a public writer.

Pisch (*Pol., Ukr.*) One who prepared food.

Pisciolo (*It.*) One who caught or sold fish, a fisherman.

Piscitelli, Piscitello (*It.*) Dweller at the sign of the little fish; nickname for a good swimmer.

Piselli, Pisellini (*It.*) One who cultivated and sold peas.

Pistilli (*It.*) Nickname for one with the qualities of a bat.

Pistorio (*It.*) One who made bread, a baker.

Pisz (*Pol.*) One who came from Pisz, in Poland.

Pitcher, Picher (*Eng.*) One who covered or caulked ships with pitch.

Pitchford, Pitchforth (*Eng.*) One who came from Pitchford (river crossing near where pitch was found), in Shropshire.

Pitchman (*Eng.*) One who covers or caulks with pitch.

Pitcock (*Eng.*) Variant of Pidcock, q.v.

Pitkin (*Eng.*) Descendant of little Pit, a pet form of Peter (a rock).

Pitkoff, Pitkow (*Rus.*) The son of Pitko, a pet form of Peter (a rock); one who drank too much, a drunkard.

Pitney (*Eng.*) One who came from Pitney (Pytta's island), in Somerset.

Pittman, Pitman, Pitmon (*Eng.*) Dweller at, or near, a pit or deep hollow.

Pittner (*Ger.*) One who made and sold casks, buckets, and tubs, a cooper.

Pitts, Pitt (*Eng.*) Dweller near a hole or steep hollow; one who came from Pitt (pit), in Hampshire.

Pixley (*Eng.*) One who came from Pixley (Peoht's grove), in Herefordshire.

Pizarro (*Sp.*) One who produces, or deals in, slate.

Pizza, Pizzi, Pizzo (*It.*) One who made and sold pizzas, a kind of cake; one with a goatee; dweller on a peak or pointed hill.

Pizzoferrato (*It.*) One who came from Pizzoferrato in Italy; one with a goatee.

Place, Plaice (*Eng., Fr.*) Dweller at a country mansion, near a market square; or on a plot of land; one who came from Place (town, or fortress), in France; one who came from Plash or Plaish (marshy pool), the names of places in Somerset and Shropshire.

Placek (*Pol.*) Pancake, probably designating one who cooked and sold them.

Plaisted (*Eng.*) Dweller near a playground, or place where sports are held.

Plamondon (*Fr.*) Dweller on the small piece of level ground on the mountain.

Plant, Plante (*Eng.*) Dweller at the place where bushes and young trees were started for transplanting.

Plaskett (*Eng.*) Dweller at a swampy meadow.

Plaskow (*Eng.*) One who came from Plaistow (playground), the name of several places in England.

Plasky (*Ukr.*) Dweller on smooth or flat land.

Plater (*Eng.*) One who made plates; or plate armor; one who coats or plates articles, usually with silver or gold.

Platesmith (*Eng.*) One who hammered the metal into plates or flat dishes; or who made armor plates.

Plath (*Ger.*) One who came from Plath (swamp), in Germany.

Platt (*Eng.*) One who lived on, or worked, a small piece of ground or patch; dweller near a small footbridge over a stream.

Plaut (*Ger.*) One who fought with a short, broad sword.

Player (*Eng.*) One who performed tricks to amuse others at fair and festival.

Playford (*Eng.*) One who came from Playford (river crossing where games were played), in Suffolk.

Pleasant (*Eng.*) An affable or agreeable person; descendant of Pleasant (pleasing).

Pleis, Pleiss (*Ger.*) One who came from Pleiss (swamp), in Germany.

Plenty, Plentty (*Eng.*) One who had an abundance of goods, a wealthy man.

Pless, Plesse, Plese (*Eng., Ger.*) Descendant of Plesa (plump); one who came from Pless or Plessa (swamp), the names of places in Germany.

Plesser (*Ger.*) One who came from Pless (swamp), in Germany.

Pletcher (*Eng.*) One who made and sold arrows, and sometimes bows as well.

Plews (*Wel.*) The son of Lewis (glory, battle; hear, fight; hale, wide).

Plieninger (*Ger.*) One who came from Plieningen (swampy place), in Germany.

Plimpton (*Eng.*) One who came from Plympton (homestead with plum trees), in Devonshire.

Pliszka (*Pol.*) Nickname for one with the characteristics of a wagtail; dweller at the sign of the wagtail.

Ploch, Plocher (*Ger.*) The stranger or foreigner; the square-built or stocky man; the plump or fat man.

Plocharski (*Pol.*) The simple or light-minded man.

Plotke (*Ger.*) Dweller near a small fence; dweller near quicksand.

Plotkin (*Rus.*) Dweller at the sign of the plotka (kind of fish).

Plotnick, Plotnik (*Rus.*) One who works with wood, a carpenter.

Plotts (*Eng.*) Dweller at the small plot of ground.

Ploughman, Plough (*Eng.*) One who follows and guides the plow.

Plover (*Eng.*) Dweller at the sign of the plover; one who hunted plovers for food.

Plowden (*Eng.*) One who came from Plowden (valley where games were played), in Shropshire.

Plowman, Plower (*Eng.*) One who follows and guides the plow.

Ployd (*Wel.*) The son of Lloyd (gray; dark complexion).

Plucinski (*Pol.*) One who came from Plucice (settlement of Plut's descendants), a village in Poland.

Plum, Plumb, Plumbe (*Eng.*) Dweller near a plum tree; one who works or deals in lead.

Plume (*Eng.*) Dweller at the sign of the feather; one who dealt in feathers.

Plumer, Plomer (*Eng.*) A dealer in plumes or feathers; variant of Plummer, q.v.

Plumley, Plumly, Plumlee, Plumleigh

(*Eng.*) One who came from Plumley (plum grove), in Cheshire.

Plummer, Plumber (*Eng.*) One who worked, or dealt in, lead.

Plumridge (*Eng.*) Dweller at the ridge where plum trees grew.

Plunkett, Plunket (*Eng.*) One who made and sold plunket, a coarse, white, woolen cloth.

Pluta (*Pol.*) One who came from Pluty (settlement of the Pluty family), in Poland.

Poate, Pote (*Scot.*) Descendant of Pote or Pate, pet forms of Patrick (noble or patrician).

Pociask (*Pol.*) Cannon fire.

Pocius (*Pol.*) The powerful one, perhaps a noble.

Pocock (*Eng.*) Variant of Peacock, q.v.

Podell, Podel (*Pol.*) One who came from Podell, in Poland.

Podesta (*It.*) The head of a village or commune; a governor or warden of a castle.

Podgorny (*Pol., Rus.*) Dweller at the foot of the mountain.

Podgorski, Podgwiski (*Pol.*) Dweller at the base of the mountain; one who came from Podgorz (foot of mountain), in Poland.

Podolsky (*Ukr.*) Dweller on the lowland.

Podraza (*Pol.*) An agitator, one who incited others to action.

Poe, Powe, Pow (*Eng.*) Dweller at the sign of the peacock; a nickname given to a proud or gaudily dressed man.

Poelstra (*Du.*) Dweller near a pool.

Pogach, Pogachefsky (*Ukr.*) Dweller at the sign of the horned owl; one who was wealthy, a rich man.

Poggi, Poggio (*It.*) Dweller on, or near, a hill.

Pogson (*Eng.*) The son of Pogg, a pet form of Margaret (a pearl).

Pogue (*Eng.*) Descendant of Pogg, a pet form of Margaret (a pearl).

Pohl, Poel, Pohle (*Ger., Du., Fr.*) The man who lived at, or near, the pool; descendant of Paul (small).

Pohlman, Pohlmann (*Ger., Du.*) Dweller near, or worker at, the pool.

Poincare (*Fr.*) Square fist, referring to the strong man; dweller at the sign of the square fist.

Poindexter (*Eng.*) Dweller at the sign of the poindexter (right fist).

Poinsett, Poinsette (*Fr.*) Descendant of little Pons, a pet form of St. Pontius (bridge).

Pointer, Poynter (*Eng.*) One who made laces for fastening clothes.

Poirier (*Fr.*) One who grew and sold pears.

Poisson (*Fr.*) One who sold fish.

Poitier (*Fr.*) One who came from Poitiers in France; one who made utensils of earthenware, a potter.

Poker, Poke (*Eng.*) One who made pokes, i.e., bags or small sacks.

Pokorny, Pokorney (*Cz.-Sl., Pol., Ukr.*) A humble or submissive man.

Pol (*Fr.*) Descendant of Pol, a French form of Paul (small).

Polacek (*Cz.-Sl.*) The little man from Poland (level land).

Polak, Polack (*Cz.-Sl., Ukr., Rus., Ger.*) One who came from Poland (level land).

Polakoff (*Rus.*) The son of the man from Poland.

Polanco (*Sp.*) One who raised and sold turkeys; or who came from Polanco, in Spain.

Poland, Polan, Polland (*Eng.*) Dweller at the homestead on which there was a pool; or through which a stream flowed; one who made and sold the long pointed shoes worn in the fourteenth century.

Polanski, Polansky (*Pol., Ukr.*) One who came from Poljana (log of wood), in the Ukraine.

Polaski (*Pol.*) One who came from Polazy (beaten track), in Poland.

Pole, Poles (*Eng.*) Dweller at a pool; descendant of Paul (small).

Polek (*Pol.*) Descendant of Polek, a pet form of Napoleon (lion of forest).

Poli (*It.*) One who came from Poli, in Italy; descendant of Poli, a pet form of names beginning with Poli (many), as Policarpo and Polidoro.

Polidor, Polidore, Polidoro, Polidori (*It.*) Descendant of Polidoro (abundant gift).

Polikoff, Polakoff, Polokoff (*Rus.*) One who came from Poland, a Pole.

Polin, Pollon (*Fr.*) Descendant of little Pol, a French form of Paul (small).

Poling (*Eng.*) One who came from Poling (people of Pal), in Sussex.

Polinski (*Pol.*) Dweller on, or owner of, a field.

Polis (*Gr.*) A shortened form of Polites, q.v.; variant of Poulos, q.v.

Polischuk, Polishuck, Polishook (*Ukr.*) One who came from Polissia (woody and marshy land), in the Ukraine.

Polites, Polite, Politis (*Fr., Gr.*) Descendant of Polytus, pet form of Hippolytus (horse destruction); one who lived in a town or city, a citizen.

Polito (*It., Sp.*) Descendant of Polito, pet form of Ippolito, Italian form of Hippolytus (horse destruction); or of Hipolito, Spanish form of Hippolytus.

Politz, Politzer (*Ger.*) One who came from Politz, in Germany.

Polizzi, Polizze (*It.*) Descendant of little Paolo, Italian form of Paul (small).

Poljak (*Ukr.*) One who came from Poland, a Pole.

Polk, Polke (*Scot.*) One who came from the lands of Pollock (little pool), in Renfrewshire.

Polka (*Ukr., Rus.*) Descendant of the Polish woman.

Polkinghorn, Polkinghorne (*Eng.*) Dweller at a pool of chalybeate water.

Poll, Polle (*Ger.*) One who came from Poll or Polle (a round hill), the name of places in Germany; dweller on, or near, a small hill; or near a pool.

Pollack, Pollak (*Ger., Fr.*) One who came from Poland (level land).

Pollard (*Eng.*) Dweller at, or near, the head or end of the pool; descendant

of little Paul (small); one who had his hair cropped short.

Pollen (*Eng.*) Variant of Paulin, q.v.

Poller (*Eng.*) Dweller near a small hill; a boisterous, blustering fellow.

Polley, Pollay, Polly, Polleys (*Fr., Eng.*) Descendant of little Paul (small); one who came from Poilley or Poilly (Polius' estate; Pavilius' estate), the names of several places in France.

Pollinger (*Fr.*) One who made bread, a baker.

Pollins (*Eng.*) Descendant of little Paul (small).

Pollitt, Pollett (*Fr.*) Descendant of little Paul (small).

Pollock, Pollok (*Scot., Ger.*) One who came from the lands of Pollock (little pool), in Renfrewshire; variant of Pollack, q.v.

Polo (*Sp.*) Descendant of Paulo, Spanish form of Paul (small).

Polonsky (*Ukr.*) One who was imprisoned, a captive.

Polsky (*Pol.*) One who came from Poland, a Pole, probably one who acquired the name outside of Poland.

Polsley (*Eng.*) Dweller in, or near, Paul's grove; or in the grove near a pool.

Polson (*Eng.*) The son of Pol, an early form of Paul (small); or of Poll, a pet form of Mary (bitterness; wished-for child; rebellion).

Polston (*Eng.*) One who came from Polesden (pasture fenced with poles), in Surrey.

Polwhele (*Eng.*) One who lived in, or near, the field containing a pool.

Polzin (*Rus.*) One who engaged in transactions for profit, a merchant.

Pomerantz, Pomerance, Pomeranz (*Fr.*) One who sold oranges.

Pomeroy, Pomroy (*Eng., Ir., Fr.*) Dweller at, or near, an apple orchard; one who came from La Pommeraye, (apple orchard), in France.

Pomfret (*Eng.*) Local pronunciation of Pontefract, q.v.

Pommer (*Ger.*) One who came from Pomerania (on the sea), a historical

403

region on the Baltic sea; the blusterer or scolder.

Pomper (*Ger.*) One who works in a mine or pit as a pumper.

Pompey, Pompei (*Rus., Bulg., Ukr.*) Descendant of Pompey (the fifth).

Pomykacz (*Pol.*) One who moves forward.

Ponce (*Sp., Fr.*) Descendant of Ponce, Spanish and French form of Pontius (belonging to the sea; sailor; the fifth).

Pond, Ponde (*Eng.*) Dweller near a small body of water; variant of Pound, q.v.

Ponder (*Eng.*) Dweller near a pool; or near the pound.

Pondexter (*Eng.*) Dweller at the sign of the right fist.

Ponds (*Eng.*) Dweller by the pond or pool.

Pons (*Fr.*) Descendant of Pons, French form of Pontius (belonging to the sea; sailor; the fifth).

Pontarelli (*It.*) One who built bridges.

Ponte, Pontes (*Sp., Port.*) One who came from Ponte (bridges), the name of many places; dweller near a bridge,

Pontefract (*Eng.*) One who came from Pontefract (broken bridge), in the West Riding of Yorkshire.

Ponton (*Eng.*) One who came from Ponton (homestead on a mound), in Lincolnshire.

Ponzio (*Fr., It.*) Variant of Pons, q.v.

Poole, Pool (*Eng.*) Dweller near the deep place in a river or stream; one who came from Pool (pool), the name of several places in England.

Pooler (*Eng.*) Dweller at the pool.

Pooley (*Eng.*) One who came from Pooley (small piece of land near a grove), in Warwickshire; dweller at the pool island.

Poor, Poore (*Eng.*) A poverty-stricken person; one who had taken a vow of poverty.

Poorman (*Eng.*) One with little of this world's goods, a poor man.

Poot (*Du.*) Descendant of Bote (lord; messenger).

Pope (*Eng.*) One who played the part of the Pope in pageants and plays; nickname for an austere, ascetic man.

Popenko (*Ukr.*) The son of the priest.

Popescu (*Rom.*) The son of the priest or minister.

Popham (*Eng.*) One who came from Popham (pebble homestead), in Hampshire.

Popjoy (*Eng., Fr.*) Nickname from the parrot; possibly a title of the winner each year in the shooting at the popingay or wooden parrot set up on top of a tree or high pole.

Popkin (*Wel.*) The son of Hopkin, a pet form of Robert (fame, bright).

Popov, Popoff (*Bulg., Rus.*) The son of the priest; one who performed sacerdotal functions, a priest.

Popovich, Popovic (*Yu.-Sl., Ukr.*) The son of the priest.

Popp, Poppe (*Ger.*) Descendant of Poppo, a pet form of Bodebert (messenger, bright); and of Jakob, German form of Jacob (may God protect; the supplanter).

Popper, Poppert (*Ger., Fr.*) A lall name; descendant of Bodberht (messenger, bright).

Popplewell (*Eng.*) Dweller at the spring near the poplar trees.

Porcaro (*It.*) One who raised and sold pigs.

Porcelli, Porcello, Porcellino, Porcella, Porcellini (*It.*) One who takes care of swine; nickname for the fat, dirty man; or for one who overeats, a glutton.

Porch, Porcher (*Eng.*) Dweller near the porch or covered entrance to some great house or public building.

Porges (*Fr.*) One who came from Porge, in France.

Porretta, Porretti, Porretto (*It.*) One who grew and sold leeks.

Porst, Porster (*Ger.*) One with bristly hair.

Port, Porte (*Eng.*) Dweller near the entrance or gate; one who acted as a gatekeeper.

Porten, Porton (*Eng.*) One who came from Porton, in Wiltshire.

Porteous (*Eng.*) One who carried the breviary out of doors.

Porter (*Eng.*) One who carried goods; one who tended a gate, a gatekeeper.

Porterfield (*Scot.*) One who came from Porterfield (field allocated to the porter), in Renfrew; some monasteries appropriated a portion of land to the porter, who was sometimes a layman, and thus took his name from his land.

Portington (*Eng.*) One who came from Portington (village of the townspeople), in the East Riding of Yorkshire.

Portley (*Eng.*) One who came from Portley (Porca's homestead), in Surrey.

Portlock (*Eng.*) One who came from Porlock (enclosure by the harbor), in Somerset.

Portman (*Eng.*) One in charge of the port or gate; a townsman or burgess; one of the body of citizens selected to administer the affairs of the borough.

Portner (*Ger.*) Variant of Pfoertner, q.v.

Portnoff (*Rus.*) The son of the tailor.

Portnoy (*Rus.*) One who made outer garments, a tailor.

Porto (*Port.*) One who came from Oporto (the port), in Portugal.

Portugal (*Eng.*) One who came from Portugal.

Portwood (*Eng.*) One who came from Portswood (wood belonging to the town); dweller in the wood belonging to the town.

Posen, Posener (*Ger.*) One who came from Posen (now Poznan), a province in Poland.

Posey (*Eng.*) One who came from Poce, in France; dweller near a post by the enclosure.

Posluszny, Posluszynyj (*Pol., Ukr.*) The obedient person.

Posnanski (*Pol.*) One who came from Posen (now Poznan), in Poland.

Posner, Posnan (*Ger.*) One who came from Posen (now Poznan), a province in Poland.

Pospiech (*Ger.*) One who was always in a hurry.

Pospisil (*Cz.*) One who was always in a hurry.

Post (*Eng., Ger.*) Dweller at, or near, an important or unusual post, stake, or marker; one who came from Post, in Germany.

Postell, Postill, Postol (*Eng.*) Variant of Postle, q.v.

Poster (*Ger.*) One who came from Post, Posta, or Postau, the names of places in Germany; descendant of Post, a pet form of Pozdimir (backward); or of Apostel (apostle).

Posternack, Posternock (*Pol., Ukr., Rus.*) Variant of Pasternak, q.v.

Posthumous, Posthuma (*Eng.*) Descendant of Posthumous, a name given to one born after the death of the father.

Postle, Postles (*Eng.*) One who played the part of one of the Saviour's apostles or the Pope in the religious plays or pageants.

Postlethwaite, Postlewaite, Postleweight (*Eng.*) One who came from Postlethwaite (Postol's clearing), in Cumberland.

Postman, Postmann (*Ger.*) One who came from Postau (swampy meadow), in Germany; the servant of Post, a pet form of Apostel (apostle); dweller near a post.

Poston (*Eng.*) One who came from Poston (village of the Pos tribe), in Herefordshire.

Potamkin (*Rus.*) The dark-complexioned or dusky man.

Potash, Pottash (*Ger.*) One who made potash, an ashburner.

Potemkin (*Rus.*) One who works after dark or at night.

Potempa (*Pol.*) One who played the part of a martyr in play or pageant; one who sacrificed something for the sake of principle.

Potier, Pothier (*Fr.*) One who made utensils of earthenware or metal, a potter.

Potocki, Potok (*Pol.*) Dweller near the brook.

Potokar, Potoker (*Yu.-Sl.*) Dweller near the brook.

Pototsky (*Pol., Ukr.*) Dweller near a stream.

Potter (*Eng.*) One who made utensils of earthenware or metal.

Potterton (*Eng.*) One who came from Potterton (the potters' village), in the West Riding of Yorkshire.

Pottier (*Fr.*) Variant of Potier, q.v.

Pottle, Potel (*Eng., Fr., Bel.*) Descendant of little Pott, a pet form of Philip (lover of horses); dweller near a post or pole; or near a pillory.

Potts, Pott (*Eng.*) Descendant of Pot or Pott, pet forms of Philpot (little lover of horses); one who made and sold pots; one who worked in the kitchen, cleaning utensils.

Pough (*Wel.*) Variant of Pugh, q.v.

Poulakidas (*Gr.*) One who raised and sold young chicks.

Poulos (*Gr.*) The son, a shortened form of a longer name with this ending.

Poulsen, Poulson (*Dan., Nor., Sw., Eng.*) The son of Poul, a Scandinavian form of Paul (small).

Poulshock (*Eng.*) One who came from Poulshot (Paul's wood), in Wiltshire.

Poulterer, Poulter (*Eng.*) One who dealt in chickens and other poultry.

Poulton (*Eng.*) One who came from Poulton (homestead near a pool), the name of eight places in England.

Pounden, Poundon (*Eng.*) One who came from Poundon (large hill), in Buckinghamshire.

Pounds, Pound, Pounder (*Eng.*) One who lived near, or had charge of, the pinfold or enclosure for animals.

Poundstone (*Eng.*) Dweller in an enclosure where animals were confined, as in a pinfold.

Poupard (*Fr.*) One with the expression or characteristics of a baby or small child.

Povey (*Eng.*) Dweller at the sign of the owl; one thought to have owlish characteristics.

Povilaitis (*Lith.*) The son of Povilas, Lithuanian form of Paul (small).

Powals (*Wel.*) Variant of Powell, q.v.

Powdermaker (*Eng.*) One who made gunpowder out of saltpetre, sulphur, and charcoal, used since the second half of the thirteenth century as an explosive.

Powders (*Eng.*) One who came from Powder (oaktree region), in Cornwall.

Powe (*Eng.*) Dweller at the sign of the peacock; one with some characteristic of a peacock.

Powell, Powel (*Wel., Eng.*) The son of Howell (eminent); descendant of Powel, an early English form of Paul (small); dweller at a pool.

Powers, Power (*Eng., Ir.*) The poor man, a pauper; one who had taken a vow of poverty.

Powis (*Wel.*) One who came from Powys, an ancient province in North Wales.

Powley, Powles (*Eng.*) One who came from Pooley, in Warwickshire.

Pownall (*Eng.*) One who came from Pownall (Pun's corner), in Cheshire.

Poynter (*Eng.*) Variant of Pointer, q.v.

Poynton (*Eng.*) One who came from Poynton (homestead of the Puningas; Peofa's homestead), the name of places in Cheshire and Shropshire.

Poznanski, Poznansky (*Pol., Rus.*) One who came from Poznan, Polish form of Posen, in Poland.

Pozza, Pozzi (*It.*) Descendant of Pazzo, a pet form of Giacomo, Italian form of James (may God protect; the supplanter).

Prado (*Sp.*) One who came from Prado (meadow), the name of several places in Spain; dweller in a meadow or in a pasture.

Prager, Prague, Praeger (*Ger., Fr.*) One who came from Prague (threshold), in Czechoslovakia.

Praissman (*Eng.*) Variant of Priestman, q.v.

Prater, Preater, Praytor (*Eng., Du.*) A manor official appointed by the lord of the manor to supervise the tenants' work; one who performed sacerdotal functions, a priest.

Prather (*Wel.*) The son of Rhydderch or Rhudderch (the reddish-brown one).

Prato (*It.*) One who came from Prato (meadow), in Italy.

Pratt, Prett (*Eng., Scot.*) Dweller on, or near, a meadow; one who employed wiles or stratagems in fighting; a cunning, astute person.

Pravitz (*Ukr., Rus.*) The son of the right one; or of the one who rules.

Pray (*Eng., Fr.*) Dweller at, or near, the grassy land or meadow.

Prayer, Prayor (*Eng.*) Dweller in, or near, a meadow; one who came from Presles (meadow), in Calvados.

Prazac (*Cz.-Sl.*) One who came from Prague (the threshold), in Czechoslovakia.

Preble, Prebble (*Eng.*) One who came from Prevelles, in France.

Preece (*Wel.*) The son of Rhys (ardor, a rush); variant of Priest, q.v.

Preedy (*Wel.*) The son of Reddie, a pet form of Redmond (counsel, protection).

Preiss, Preis, Preissman (*Ger.*) One who is praised or glorified; one who makes and sells lace; the proud, arrogant man.

Prell, Prelle (*Ger.*) One noted for his crying, bawling, or howling.

Preminger (*Ger.*) One who came from Preming (swampy shore), in Germany.

Prendergast (*Eng., Ir., Scot.*) Descendant of Pendegast (head stranger); one who came from Prendergast, a parish in Pembrokeshire; one who came from Prendergast (priest's deep glen), in Scotland.

Prentice, Prentiss (*Eng.*) One bound by agreement to serve another for the purpose of learning an art or craft, an apprentice.

Presbery, Presberry (*Eng.*) One who came from Prestbury (the priest's manor), the name of places in Cheshire and Gloucestershire.

Presby (*Nor.*) Dweller at Praestby (priest's farm).

Prescott (*Eng.*) One who came from Prescot (priest's cottage), the name of places in Lancashire and Oxfordshire; dweller near the priest's cottage.

Presley, Pressley (*Scot., Eng.*) One who came from Preslie or Presslie, the names of places in Aberdeen; dweller in, or near, the priest's wood.

Press (*Eng., Wel., Scot.*) One who came from Prees (brushwood), in Shropshire; or Preese (brushwood), in Lancashire; dweller at, or near, a thicket; the son of Rees (ardor, a rush); one who came from Press or Preas (thicket), in Scotland.

Presser (*Eng.*) One who performed sacerdotal functions, a priest.

Pressey (*Eng.*) Dweller near the priest's enclosure; or on the priest's island.

Pressler (*Ger.*) One who came from Breslau (named after King Vratislaw), the capital of Silesia.

Pressman (*Eng.*) Variant of Priestman, q.v.

Prest, Prester, Priester (*Eng., Fr.*) One who performed sacerdotal functions; one whose function, behavior, spirit or appearance resembled that of a priest.

Presto, Prestoe (*Eng.*) One who came from Prestall, in Lancashire.

Preston (*Eng., Scot.*) One who came from Preston (priest's homestead), the name of many places in England; or from the barony of Preston, in Midlothian.

Prestwood (*Eng.*) Dweller in, or by, the priest's wood.

Prete (*It.*) One who performed sacerdotal functions, a priest.

Pretty (*Eng.*) The crafty, cunning man.

Prettyman (*Eng.*) The cunning, crafty, sly person.

Previti, Previty, Previte (*It.*) One who performed sacerdotal functions, a priest.

Prevost, Prevot (*Fr., Scot.*) An officer of

a monastery; a keeper of a prison; a chief magistrate.

Prewitt, Prewett (*Eng.*) The little valiant, doughty man.

Price, Preece (*Wel., Eng.*) The son of Rhys (ardor, a rush); one who came from Prees (brushwood), in Shropshire or from Preese, in Lancashire.

Prickett, Prickitt (*Eng.*) Dweller at the sign of the buck in its second year; a nickname from some relation to a buck in its second year.

Priddy (*Eng.*) One who came from Priddy (earth or soil), in Somerset.

Pride, Pryde (*Eng.*) One who played the part of Pride in the early mystery plays or pageants; one who came from Priddy (earth or soil), in Somerset.

Pridgen, Pridgeon, Pridegon (*Fr.*) Gallant John, a nickname.

Priest, Priester, Priess, Pries (*Eng.*) One who performed sacerdotal functions; one whose function, behavior, spirit or appearance resembled that of a priest; one who played the part of the priest in play or pageant.

Priestley, Priestly (*Eng.*) Dweller in, or near, the priest's meadow or wood.

Priestman (*Eng.*) The priest's servant.

Prieto (*Sp.*) One with a dark or swarthy complexion; the close-fisted, narrow-minded, mean man.

Prigge, Prigg, Prigger (*Eng.*) One who made, or used, a pointed weapon.

Primavera (*It.*) Descendant of Primavera (Spring).

Prime, Prim, Primm (*Eng.*) The slender or small man.

Primeau, Primeaux (*Fr.*) One who is first or foremost; one with superior rank.

Primmer (*Eng.*) The priest or official who read at prime, the first canonical hour.

Primus, Primous (*Eng.*) Descendant of Primus (first-born), the name of several saints.

Prince, Printz (*Eng., Ger., Fr.*) Descendant of a prince or sovereign; or of one connected in some way with his household; sometimes an ironic nickname.

Principe (*It.*) A member of the nobility or aristocracy.

Prindiville, Prendiville, Prindeville (*Eng., Ir.*) One who came from Frendeville or Fermainville, in France.

Prindle (*Eng.*) Dweller in a small field or on a small farm.

Pringle (*Scot.*) One who came from Pringle, formerly Hopringle (narrow valley; peg valley), in Roxburghshire.

Prins (*Du.*) One who played the part of the prince in play or pageant; one connected in some way with a prince's household.

Prinscott (*Eng.*) Dweller near the cottage of the one who acted the part of the prince in play or pageant.

Prinz (*Ger.*) One who played the part of the prince in play or pageant; a governor.

Prioleau (*Fr.*) Nickname ironically applied to one who resembled or acted like a little prior.

Prior (*Eng.*) A member of a prior's entourage; one who was the head of a priory, a monastic official next in rank below an abbot; one who played the part of a prior in play or pageant.

Priore, Priori (*It.*) Italian version of Prior, q.v.

Pritchard, Prichard (*Wel.*) The son of Richard (rule, hard).

Pritchett (*Eng.*) Dweller at the sign of the pricket, a buck in his second year; a variant of Pritchard, q.v.

Pritikin (*Rus.*) One who dwelt adjacent to another, a neighbor.

Pritz (*Ger.*) Descendant of Pritz, a pet form of Pritzlaff (increase, glory); dweller near a birch tree.

Pritzker (*Ger.*) Descendant of Pritzlaff (increase, glory).

Privett, Privette, Privott (*Eng.*) One who came from Privett (copse of privet, an ornamental shrub), in Hampshire.

Prk, Prch (*Cz.-Sl.*) One with a goatish odor.

Probert (*Wel.*) The son of Robert (fame, bright).

Probst (*Ger.*) A provost, superintendent, or official head of an institution.

Procaccino (*It.*) One who carries letters, a postman.

Prochaska (*Cz.-Sl.*) One who traveled by foot, a walker.

Procopio (*It.*) Descendant of Procopius (progressive).

Proctor, Procter (*Eng.*) One who acted as an attorney in an ecclesiastical court.

Profeta, Profeto (*It.*) One who played the part of the Prophet in play or pageant.

Proffitt, Proffit (*Eng., Scot., Fr.*) One who enacted the part of the Prophet in medieval pageants; one who was wealthy or in comfortable circumstances.

Proietto, Proietti (*It.*) Descendant of Proietti (exposed), a name sometimes given to a foundling.

Prokofiev (*Rus.*) The son of Prokofiy, Russian form of Procopius (progressive).

Prokop (*Pol., Ukr., Rus.*) Descendant of Prokop, Slavic form of Procopius (progressive).

Prokopchuk, Prokopchuck (*Ukr.*) The son of Prokop, Slavic form of Procopius (progressive).

Pron, Pronchik (*Ukr.*) Descendant of Pron, a pet form of Prokip, Ukrainian form of Procopius (progressive).

Prophet (*Eng.*) One who played the part of a Prophet in play or pageant; a nickname for one who acted like a prophet.

Propper (*Ger.*) Nickname for a gardener, one who grafts plants and trees.

Prosperi, Prospero (*It.*) Descendant of Prospero (prosperous).

Prosser (*Wel.*) The son of Rosser (fame, spear).

Prost (*Eng.*) A variant of Priest, q.v.

Prothero, Protheroe, Prothro (*Wel.*) The son of Rhydderch (the reddish-brown one).

Proud, Proudman (*Eng.*) One who acted in a proud, arrogant manner.

Proudfoot, Proudfit (*Eng.*) One who walked with a haughty step or arrogant gait.

Prout, Prouty (*Eng.*) The proud, arrogant man.

Provence, Province (*Fr.*) One who came from Provence, a historical region of France.

Provenzano, Provenzale (*It.*) One who came from Provence, a historical region of France.

Provine, Provines (*Fr.*) One who came from Provin (Probus' estate), in France.

Provost, Proust (*Eng., Fr.*) A commander; the chief magistrate.

Prowse (*Eng., Wel.*) The valiant, doughty man; the son of Rosser, a Welsh form of Roger (fame, spear).

Proxmire (*Ger.*) One who came from Praxmar, in Tirol.

Prucil (*Cz.-Sl.*) The very learned person.

Prude, Pruden (*Eng.*) The proud, haughty man.

Prudente, Prudent (*It.*) Descendant of Prudenzio (the prudent); one who was careful and discreet.

Prudhomme, Prud'homme (*Eng., Fr.*) The upright, honest man, the greater folk; a man of experience and integrity.

Prue (*Eng.*) The valiant, doughty man.

Pruitt, Pruett, Prewitt (*Eng.*) The little gallant or valiant man.

Pruna (*It.*) One who raised and sold plums; dweller near a plum tree.

Prunier (*Fr.*) Dweller near a plum tree; one who raised and sold plums.

Prusa (*Sl.*) One who came from Prussia, a Prussian.

Prusek (*Cz.*) Dweller in a clearing in the forest.

Prusky, Pruski (*Pol.*) One who came from Prussia (neighbors), in Germany.

Pruszynski (*Pol.*) One who came from Pruszyn (Pruch's settlement), in Poland.

Prynn, Prynne (*Wel., Eng.*) The son of Rhun (grand); the small, thin man; the superior man.

Pryor (*Eng.*) A member of a prior's entourage; one who was the head of a priory, a monastic official next in rank below an abbot; one who played the part of a prior in a play or pageant.

Przyborski (*Pol.*) Dweller beside the forest.

Przybylski, Przybylo, Przybyla, Przybysz, Przybylowski (*Pol.*) One who has recently arrived, a stranger or newcomer.

Psiharis (*Gr.*) One who contributes for the good of his soul.

Psoras (*Gr.*) One with scabies, or the itch.

Ptacek (*Cz.-Sl.*) Dweller at the sign of the little bird; one with some characteristic of a small bird.

Ptak, Ptack (*Pol.*) Dweller at the sign of the bird; one with birdlike characteristics.

Ptashkin (*Rus.*) Dweller at the sign of the small bird; one who trapped and sold small birds.

Pucci, Puccini, Puccio (*It.*) Descendant of Pucci, a pet form of Iacopucci, an Italian variant of Jacob (the supplanter; may God protect).

Puchalski (*Pol.*) One who is fuzzy or fluffy.

Puckett (*Eng.*) Descendant of little Puca (goblin).

Puddifoot (*Eng.*) One with a large, protuberant stomach; the stumpy man; one with a club-foot.

Puddister, Puddester (*Eng.*) One, especially a woman, who is very busy doing what is of little or no practical value.

Pue (*Wel.*) The son of Hugh (spirit; mind).

Puetz (*Ger.*) One who came from Putz (pool or slough), in Germany; dweller near a pool.

Puffer (*Ger.*) Descendant of Bodefrit (messenger, peace).

Pugh (*Wel.*) The son of Hugh or Hu (spirit; mind).

Pugliese, Puglisi, Puglise (*It.*) One who came from Puglia, a region in Italy.

Pugsley (*Wel.*) The son of Hugsley, a pet form of Hugh (spirit; mind).

Puhl (*Ger.*) Dweller near a pool or slough; one who came from Puls (pool), in Germany.

Pulaski (*Pol.*) One who came from Pulawy, in Poland.

Pulcinella (*It.*) Dweller at the sign of the little chicken; one who raised and sold young chickens.

Puleo (*It.*) Dweller near where pennyroyal grew; one who came from Puglia, a region in Italy.

Puleston (*Eng.*) One who came from Pudleston (hill of the mousehawks), in Herefordshire.

Pulford (*Eng.*) One who came from Pulford (river crossing by the pool), in Cheshire.

Pulgram (*Ger.*) Descendant of the pilgrim, one who had visited a distant shrine.

Pulham (*Eng.*) One who came from Pulham (homestead by the pool), the name of places in Dorset and Norfolk.

Pulitzer (*Ger.*) One who dresses or deals in furs, a furrier.

Pullen, Pullin, Pullins (*Eng.*) Dweller at the sign of the colt; one thought to possess the characteristics of a colt.

Puller (*Eng.*) Dweller at the pool bank.

Pulley, Pullay (*Eng., Scot.*) Dweller near the pool in the grove; or near the pool enclosure; or on the pool island; one who came from Pulhay Burn (stream in a swamp), in Scotland.

Pulliam (*Wel.*) The son of William (resolution, helmet).

Pullinger (*Eng.*) An unvoiced form of Bullinger, q.v.

Pullman (*Eng.*) Dweller at, or near, a pool or lake.

Pullum (*Eng.*) Variant of Pulham, q.v.

Puls (*Ger.*) One who came from Puls (pool), in Germany; descendant of

Pul, a pet form of Boleslaw (great glory).

Pulson (*Eng.*) The son of Paul (small).

Pulver, Pulvermacher (*Ger.*) One who made potash, an ashburner; one who made gunpowder.

Pumphrey (*Wel.*) The son of Humphrey (supporter of peace).

Punch, Punches (*Eng.*) Dweller at, or near, a bridge.

Purcell, Pursell (*Eng.*) Dweller at the sign of the young pig; one with some quality of a young pig.

Purchase, Purchas (*Eng.*) One who acted as a messenger or courier; a nickname for one who obtained the booty or gain; one who pursued another.

Purdham (*Eng.*) Variant of Prudhomme, q.v.

Purdy, Purdie (*Eng.*) One given to blasphemy, from the French *par Dieu* ("by God").

Pure (*Fr.*) Dweller near the Pure (pure), a river in Ardennes.

Purifoy, Purefoy, Puriefoy (*Eng.*) One who habitually used the oath "by [my] faith."

Purinton, Purrington, Purington (*Eng.*) One who came from Puriton (pear tree enclosure), in Somerset.

Purnell (*Eng.*) Descendant of Pernel or Parnel, a contraction of Petronella, dim. of Peter (a rock). St. Petronella was thought to be a daughter of St. Peter.

Purpura (*It.*) The red-haired or ruddy-complexioned man.

Purse (*Eng.*) Metonymic for one who made and sold purses or bags.

Pursley (*Eng.*) Dweller in, or near, Pusa's grove.

Purtell, Purtle, Purtill (*Ir.*) One who came from Porthull, that is, Porthill; dweller at the sign of the little pig, an Irish variant of Purcell, q.v.

Purton (*Eng.*) One who came from Purton (homestead with pear tree), the name of places in Gloucestershire, Staffordshire, and Wiltshire.

Purvis, Purves (*Scot., Eng.*) Dweller, or frequenter at, or near, a porch (generally of a church).

Purvy, Purvey (*Eng.*) One who furnished or supplied merchandise.

Puryear, Puryer (*Eng., Fr.*) Variant of Perrier, q.v.

Pusateri, Pusatera (*It.*) One who kept a public inn, an innkeeper.

Pusey (*Eng.*) One who came from Pusey (pea island), in Berkshire.

Pushkin (*Rus.*) One who operated a cannon.

Putman (*Eng.*) Dweller near, or worker in, a pit.

Putnam (*Eng.*) One who came from Puttenham (Putta's homestead), the name of places in Hertfordshire and Surrey.

Putney (*Eng.*) One who came from Putney (Putta's harbor), in Surrey.

Putnick (*Rus.*) One who is on the road, a traveler.

Putt (*Du., Eng.*) Dweller near a well; dweller at a pit or pond.

Putter, Puttman (*Ger.*) Dweller by a pit or hollow; one who came from Putt or Putte, the names of places in Germany.

Puttkamer, Puttkammer (*Ger.*) One who cleaned rooms.

Putz (*Ger.*) One who came from Putz, in Germany; dweller at, or near, a well or spring.

Pye (*Eng., Wel.*) Dweller at the sign of the magpie; one with some characteristic of a magpie; the son of Hu, a spelling of Hugh (spirit; mind).

Pyle, Pyles (*Eng.*) One who came from Pylle (creek), in Somerset; dweller at a post; or small castle.

Pyne (*Eng.*) Dweller at, or near, the pine tree; dweller at the sign of the pine tree.

Pyott (*Scot.*) Dweller at the sign of the little magpie; one thought to have the characteristics of a magpie.

Pyper (*Eng.*) Variant of Piper, q.v.

Pyrrhos (*Gr.*) The red-haired or ruddy man.

Pytel, Pytell (*Pol., Eng.*) A babbler or senseless chatterer; dweller in a small field or enclosure.

Quackenbush (*Ger., Du.*) Dweller near the bridge across the bog; or at the swamp where bushes grew; or in, or near, the swampy wood frequented by frogs.

Quade, Quaide (*Ir., Ger.*) The son of Wat, a pet form of Walter (rule, army); the cross, ill-tempered man.

Quaglia, Quagliani (*It.*) Dweller at the sign of the quail.

Quail (*Mx.*) The son of Fhail, Manx form of Paul (small).

Quaile, Quill, Quale (*Ir.*) Dweller near the hazel tree.

Quain (*Ir.*) Grandson of Cuan, a pet form of Donnchuan (lord of harbors).

Quaintance (*Scot.*) One who is known, not a stranger.

Qualters, Qualter, Qualtier (*Mx., Eng.*) Descendant of Walter (rule, folk); one who made quilts.

Quam, Quamme (*Nor.*) Dweller in a narrow glen or valley.

Quan, Quann, Quane (*Ir.*) Grandson of Cuan, a pet form of Donnchuan (lord of harbors).

Quanstrom, Quanstrum (*Sw., Nor.*) One who came from Qvarnstrom (mill stream), in Sweden; dweller at the mill stream.

Quant, Quante (*Eng.*) The prudent, skillful, quaint, neat man; the cunning, crafty, clever, wise man.

Quaranta (*It.*) Dweller near a signboard indicating forty kilometers to some place.

Quarles, Qualls (*Eng.*) One who came from Quarles (circles), in Norfolk.

Quarrells, Quarrell, Quarell (*Eng.*) Metonymic for one who made short, heavy arrows or bolts for the crossbow; or for an arbalester; one who came from Quarles (circles), in Norfolk.

Quarrie, Quarry (*Eng., Mx.*) Dweller near a quarry, an open excavation for obtaining stone; metonymic for a stone cutter; the son of Guaire (noble).

Quarterman, Quartman, Quartermain (*Eng.*) The man with four hands, that is, mail-fisted, the extra hands being mailed; the dexterous man.

Quast, Quastler (*Ger.*) One who came from Quast (twig), the name of two places in Germany; the attendant at the baths who works with a bunch of twigs.

Quattrocchi, Quatrocci, Quattrochi, Quattrocki (*It.*) Four eyes, a nickname for one who wore spectacles; dweller at the sign of the plover.

Quay, Quaye (*Mx.*) The son of Aodh (fire).

Quayle (*Mx.*) The son of Paul (small).

Quealy, Queally (*Ir.*) Grandson of Caollaidhe.

Quearles (*Eng.*) Variant of Quarles, q.v.

Queen (*Eng.*) One who played the part of the queen in a play or pageant; one connected in some way with the queen's household.

Queeney (*Ir.*) The son of Maonach (wealthy; dumb).

Queer, Quear (*Ger.*) American corruption of Kreher, q.v.

Quell (*Ir., Mx.*) The grandson of Coll (hazel; head); the son of Coll.

Quellet, Quellette (*Fr.*) The agreeable, pleasant man.

Quentin (*Fr.*) Descendant of Quentin (fifth child).

Quesada, Quezada (*Sp.*) One who came from Quesada, in Spain.

Quick (*Du., Eng., Ir.*) The lively or bright person; dweller by an aspen tree; grandson of Corc (heart); one who came from Quickbury, formerly Cuwyk (cow farm), in Essex; dweller near quickset hedge.

Quickley, Quickle (*Eng.*) Dweller in the glade where quick grass grew.

Quieti (*It.*) The peaceful, quiet man.

Quigg (*Ir.*) Grandson of Cuaig.

Quigley, Quigly (*Ir.*) Grandson of the escort or companion.

Quiles, Quilez (*Sp.*) One who came from Quilez (place of ferns), in Spain.

Quilici (*It.*) One who performed sacerdotal functions, a priest; one whose appearance or actions resembled that of a clergyman.

Quill (*Ir.*) Grandson of Coll (hazel; head); the son of Coll.

Quillen, Quillin (*Mx.*) Grandson of Cuileann (holly).

Quilliam (*Mx.*) A condensation of Mac-William, the son of William (resolution, helmet).

Quilligan (*Ir.*) The son of the bearded man; variant of Culligan, q.v.

Quillinan (*Ir.*) Descendant of little Cuileann (holly).

Quilter (*Eng.*) One who made and sold quilts or mattresses.

Quilty (*Ir.*) Grandson of Caoilte (hardness).

Quimby, Quinby (*Eng.*) One who came from Quenby (queen's manor), in Leicestershire.

Quincy, Quinci, Quinsey (*Eng., Scot.*) One who came from Quincay, formerly Quinci (Quintus' estate), in Maine, France.

Quindlen (*Ir.*) Variant of Quinlan, q.v.

Quindry, Quintrie (*Fr.*) One who held land, a fifth of the produce of which went to the lord.

Quinlan, Quinlin (*Ir.*) Grandson of Caoindealbhan (gracefully shaped).

Quinlisk (*Ir.*) Descendant of Cuindleas.

Quinn, Quin (*Ir.*) Grandson of Conn (counsel).

Quinnell, Quennell (*Eng.*) Dweller near the little oak tree.

Quinney (*Mx., Ir.*) The son of Connaidh (crafty).

Quinones, Quinonez (*Sp.*) One who came from Quinones (allotted portions of land), in Spain; one who farmed land on shares.

Quinson (*Eng.*) The son of Quyn or Cuinn, forms of Conn (counsel).

Quint (*Ger., Eng.*) One who came from Quint (dirty water), in Germany; descendant of Quint, a short form of Quintius (fifth son).

Quintana, Quintano (*Sp.*) One who came from Quintana (country estate), in Spain; dweller in a country mansion; one who came from Quinta (village), in Spain.

Quintanilla (*Sp.*) One who came from Quintanilla (land held at a rental of one-fifth of the produce therefrom), in Spain; dweller in, or near, a small country mansion.

Quintard (*Fr.*) Descendant of Quentin (fifth child); the heavy, ungainly, lumbering man.

Quinter, Quintier (*Fr.*) One who administered the goods of a church or of a hospital, deducting in advance a fifth of the revenue.

Quintieri, Quintiero (*It., Port.*) Dweller in, or near, a country house; one who acted as a caretaker on a gentleman's farm.

Quintiliani (*It.*) Descendant of little Quintino (fifth child).

Quintin (*Fr.*) Descendant of Quentin (fifth child).

Quinto, Quintos (*It., Sp.*) Descendant of Quinto (fifth; the fifth-born child).

Quinton (*Eng., Fr.*) One who came from Quinton (the queen's manor), the name of places in Gloucestershire and Northamptonshire; variant of Quentin, q.v.

Quintus (*Du.*) Descendant of Quintus (fifth).

Quirk, Quirke (*Ir.*) Descendant of the bushy-haired man; grandson of Corc (heart).

Quiroz (*Sp.*) One who came from Quiros (rock; mountain), in Spain; dweller near where heather grew.

Quist (*Sw.*) Twig.

Quitman, Quitmon (*Ger.*) One who raised and sold quinces.

Quitt, Quitter, Quittner (*Ger.*) Dweller near a quince tree.

Quon (*Chin.*) To close.

Raab, Raabe (*Ger., Fr.*) Dweller at the sign of the crow; one thought to possess the characteristics of a crow.

Raban (*Eng.*) Dweller at the sign of the raven; one with the characteristics of a raven.

Rabb (*Eng.*) Descendant of Rabb, a pet form of Robert (fame, bright).

Rabbit, Rabbitt (*Eng.*) Descendant of little Rab, a short form of Raban (raven); or of little Rabb, a pet form of Robert (fame, bright); one with some characteristic of a rabbit, such as timidity.

Rabe (*Ger., Fr.*) Descendant of the rabbi or teacher; dweller at the sign of the crow.

Raber (*Ger.*) One who raised rape, a European herb of the mustard family grown as a forage crop for sheep and hogs.

Rabin (*Fr.*) Descendant of the rabbi, or teacher.

Rabinovich, Rabinovitch (*Rus.*) The son of the rabbi or Jewish teacher.

Rabinowitz, Rabinovitz (*Cz.-Sl., Yu.-Sl., Pol., Ukr., Rus.*) The son of the rabbi, or Jewish teacher.

Rabourn (*Eng.*) One who came from Radbourn (stream where reeds grew), in Warwickshire.

Raby (*Eng.*) One who came from Raby (homestead near a boundary mark), the name of places in Cheshire and Durham.

Race (*Wel.*) Variant of Rhys, q.v.

Rachlin (*Rus., Pol.*) Descendant of Rakhil, Russian form of Rachel (the ewe); one who came from Rachlin, in Poland.

Rachmaninov (*Rus.*) The son of Rakhman (happy one).

Racine (*Fr.*) One who grows and sells root vegetables such as turnips, carrots, etc.

Rack (*Ger.*) Descendant of Rack, a pet form of names beginning with Ragin (counsel), as Ragolf and Ragibald.

Racz (*Hun.*) One who came from Serbia, a Serbian.

Radcliffe, Radcliff (*Eng.*) One who came from Radcliffe (red cliff), in Lancashire.

Raddatz (*Yu.-Sl.*) Descendant of Radac, a pet form of Rad (happy).

Radel, Radell (*Eng.*) Variant of Radwell, q.v.

Rademacher, Rademaker (*Ger.*) Variant of Radermacher, q.v.

Rademan (*Ger., Eng.*) One who occupied the office of alderman or town councillor; one who was a thatcher or cutter of reeds.

Rader (*Ger.*) One who made wheels, a wheelwright; one who occupied the office of alderman or town councillor; one who came from Raden (moor; reedy place), in Germany; descendant of Radheri (counsel, army); one who thatched with reed.

Radermacher (*Ger.*) One who made wheels, a wheelwright.

Radetsky (*Ukr.*) One who counseled others or gave advice.

Radford (*Eng.*) One who came from Radford (red ford), the name of several places in England.

Radick (*Cz.-Sl.*) The benevolent, charitable man.

Radin (*Rus., Pol.*) The son of Rad, a pet form of names beginning with Rad (counsel), as Radomir and Radislav; one who came from Radin (council), in Poland.

Radley (*Eng.*) One who came from Radley (red wood), in Berkshire.

Radoff (*Rus.*) The son of Rad, a pet form of names beginning with or ending with Rad (counsel), as Radomir, Radislav, Milorad, and Donnarad.

Radomski (*Pol.*) One who came from Radom or Radomsko in Poland.

Radtke, Radke (*Ger.*) Descendant of little Rado (counsel); descendant of little Rad, a pet form of Konrad (bold, counsel).

Radwell, Radwill (*Eng.*) One who came from Radwell (red spring), in Bedfordshire.

Rae, Ree (*Scot., Eng.*) Variants of Ray, q.v.

Raebuck (*Scot.*) Dweller at the sign of

the male roe deer; metonym for a hunter of deer.

Raeder (*Ger.*) Variant of Rader, q.v.

Rafael (*Sp.*) Descendant of Rafael, Spanish form of Raphael (healed by God; medicine of God).

Rafes, Rafe (*Eng.*) Descendant of Rafe, a pet form of Ralph (counsel, wolf).

Raff, Raffe (*Eng., Heb.*) Descendant of Raff, a variant of Ralph (counsel, wolf); a Jewish teacher or doctor of the law.

Raffaele, Raffaelli (*It.*) Descendant of Raffaele, Italian form of Raphael (healed by God; medicine of God).

Raffel, Raffle, Raffles, Raffl (*Eng.*) Descendant of Raphael (healed by God; medicine of God).

Rafferty (*Ir.*) Grandson of Robhartach.

Raffield (*Eng.*) Descendant of Raphael (healed by God; medicine of God).

Rafford, Raford (*Eng.*) One who came from Rufford (rough river crossing), the name of places in Lancashire, Nottinghamshire, and the West Riding of Yorkshire; or from Rofford (Hroppa's ford), in Oxfordshire.

Raftery, Rafter (*Ir.*) Descendant of Reachtabhra (law border).

Rafu (*Jap.*) Net, urban prefecture.

Ragan, Ragen, Ragin (*Ger.*) Descendant of Ragin, a short form of names beginning with Ragin (counsel), as Raganfrid, Ragingar and Raginald.

Ragg (*Eng., Scot.*) Descendant of Rag, a short form of names beginning with Ragn such as Ragnar and Ragnuald; one who had shaggy hair; descendant of Wraghi.

Ragland, Raglan, Raglin (*Eng., Wel.*) One who came from Raglan, in Monmouthshire.

Rago (*It.*) One thought to possess some of the qualities of a frog, such as a croaking voice or a short fat body; dweller at the sign of the green frog.

Ragsdale (*Eng.*) One who came from Ragdale (valley at the pass), in Leicestershire; dweller in the valley where lichen grew.

Ragusa, Ragusi, Raguso (*It.*) One who came from Ragusa, in Sicily.

Rahilly (*Ir.*) Grandson of Raithile.

Rahm (*Ger.*) One who came from Rahm (cream), the name of several places in Germany.

Rahn (*Ger.*) The slender, or thin, man.

Raich, Raiche (*Ger.*) One who came from Raich (swamp), in Germany.

Raiford (*Eng.*) Dweller near the river crossing where rye was grown.

Raikes (*Eng.*) One who came from Raikes (narrow valley), in the West Riding of Yorkshire; dweller in a pass or narrow valley.

Railey (*Eng.*) Variant of Raleigh, q.v.

Raimo (*Ger.*) Descendant of Raimo, a pet form of names beginning with Ragin (counsel), as Raginman and Raginmund.

Raimondi, Raimondo (*It.*) Descendant of Raimondo, Italian form of Raymond (counsel, protection).

Rainbird (*Eng.*) A corruption of Rambert (raven, bright).

Rainbow (*Eng.*) Descendant of Reginbald (might, bold).

Rainer (*Ger.*) One who came from Rainen (ridge), in Germany; dweller at the edge of a field or on a slope; descendant of Reiner (counsel, army).

Raines, Raine, Raynes, Rains (*Eng., Scot.*) Descendant of Rain, a pet form of one of the old names beginning with Regen or Ragin (counsel); or of Rayner (might, army); dweller at a boundary line; or at the sign of the frog; one with frog-like characteristics; one who came from Rayne (division), in Aberdeenshire.

Rainey, Raining (*Scot.*) Descendant of little Ren, a pet form of Reginald (counsel, power; might, power).

Rainsford (*Eng.*) One who came from Rainford (Regna's ford), in Lancashire.

Rainwater, Rainwaters (*Eng.*) Dweller near where rain forms a pool of water not quickly drained away.

415

Raiser (*Ger.*) Dweller in, or near, brush-wood; one who fought on horseback; a knight.

Raish, Raisch, Raisher (*Ger.*) Dweller near where rushes grew.

Rait, Raitt, Raite (*Scot.*) One who came from Rait (fort), the name of several places in Scotland.

Raith (*Scot.*) One who came from Raith (fort; fern), in Ayrshire.

Raja, Rajah (*Hindi*) Title of an Indian king, prince, or chief.

Rajca (*Pol.*) One who served as a Common Councilman.

Rak (*Pol., Ukr., Cz.*) Descendant of Rak, a pet form of Rochus, a fourteenth century French saint; dweller at the sign of the crab; one who fished for and sold crabs.

Rakauskas (*Lith.*) Descendant of Rak, a pet form of Rochus, a fourteenth century French saint.

Rake, Rakes, Raker (*Eng., Ger.*) One who came from Rake (throat; pass), in Sussex; dweller in a pass or narrow valley; dweller at a muddy place.

Rakestraw (*Eng., Ger.*) Sentence name or nickname for one who raked or gathered straw into piles or bundles; or for a stoker; later in a transferred sense, an agitator or mischief maker.

Rakowski (*Pol.*) Dweller at the sign of the crab; one who fished for crabs.

Raleigh, Raley, Ralley (*Eng.*) One who came from Raleigh (red meadow), in Devonshire.

Ralis (*Lith.*) Descendant of Ralys, pet form of Laurynas, Lithuanian form of Lawrence (the laurel, symbol of victory).

Rall (*Fr.*) Corruption of Raoul, q.v.

Ralls (*Eng.*) Descendant of Rall, a pet form of Ralph (counsel, wolf).

Ralph (*Eng.*) Descendant of Ralph (counsel, wolf).

Ralston (*Eng., Scot.*) One who came from Rolleston (Hrolf's homestead), the name of several places in England; one who came from the lands of Ralston, in Renfrewshire.

Ramage, Rammage (*Scot.*) The wild one who lived in the forest.

Rambow, Rambo (*Ger., Pol., Rus., Bel.*) One who came from Rambow, the name of four places in Germany; one who came from Rebowo, in Pomerania, a village which no longer exists; descendant of Raimbaud (counsel, bold).

Ramby (*Eng.*) One who came from Ranby (Randi's or Hrani's homestead), the name of places in Lincolnshire and Nottinghamshire.

Rameau (*Fr.*) Dweller at the sign of the small branch or palm branch.

Rameaux (*Fr.*) Descendant of the child born, baptized, or found on Palm Sunday.

Ramesbottom (*Eng.*) Variant of Ramsbottom, q.v.

Ramey (*Fr.*) Dweller in a wooded area; a pilgrim who returned from Jerusalem with palm branches; descendant of Remy or Remigius (protector), a French saint of the fifth century.

Ramirez (*Sp.*) The son of Ramon (wise protector).

Ramkins (*Eng.*) Descendant of little Ram or Rem, pet forms of Rambaud and Rambald (counsel, bold).

Ramm, Ram (*Eng.*) Dweller at the sign of the ram; or raven; or wild garlic.

Ramos (*Sp., Port.*) Descendant of Ramos (palms), a name given to one born during the religious fiesta of Palm Sunday; one who came from Ramos (branch), in Spain.

Ramsbottom (*Eng.*) One who came from Ramsbottom (low land where wild garlic grew), in Lancashire.

Ramsdell, Ramsdill (*Eng.*) One who came from Ramsdale (ram valley), in Hampshire.

Ramsden (*Eng.*) One who came from Ramsden (ram valley), the name of several places in England.

Ramsey, Ramsay (*Scot., Eng.*) One who came from Ramsay (ram's isle), in Scotland; or from Ramsey (wild garlic island), the name of places in Essex and Huntingdonshire.

Ranallo, Ranalli (*It.*) Descendant of Rinaldo, Italian form of Reginald (counsel, force).

Rand (*Eng., Ger., Est.*) Descendant of Rand, a pet form of Randal or Randolph (shield, wolf); or of German names beginning with Rand (shield), as Ranthar and Randulf; one who came from Rand (marshy edge), the name of places in Lincolnshire and Yorkshire; dweller near the rim or edge; dweller on the beach or shore.

Randall, Randle, Randale, Randel, Randell (*Eng.*) Descendant of Randal or Randwulf (shield, wolf).

Randazzo (*It.*) One who came from Randazzo, in Italy.

Randolph (*Eng.*) Descendant of Randwulf (shield, wolf).

Raney, Ranney (*Scot.*) Variants of Rainey, q.v.

Range (*Ger.*) The bad boy or rogue, a young scamp.

Ranger (*Ger., Eng.*) One who came from Rangen (slope or hill), the name of two places in Germany; one in charge of a forest or park.

Ranieri, Raniere (*It.*) Descendant of Ranieri (counsel, army).

Rank, Ranke (*Ger.*) Descendant of Rank, a pet form of Randolf (shield, wolf).

Rankin, Rankine, Ranken (*Eng.*) Descendant of little Rand, pet form of Randal or Randolph (shield, wolf).

Ransdell (*Eng.*) One who came from Ranskill (hill frequented by ravens), in Nottinghamshire.

Ransford (*Eng.*) Dweller near the river crossing frequented by ravens.

Ranshaw (*Eng.*) Dweller in a thicket frequented by ravens.

Ransom, Ranson, Ransome (*Eng.*) The son of Rand, pet form of Randolph or Randal (shield, wolf).

Rao (*Hindi*) A Hindi title.

Raoul (*Fr.*) Descendant of Raoul, a French form of Ralph (counsel, wolf).

Raphael, Raphel (*Eng., Fr.*) Descendant

of Raphael (healed by God; medicine of God).

Raposo, Raposa (*Port., Sp.*) Nickname, the fox, for a cunning, clever man.

Rapp (*Ger.*) Dweller at the sign of the black horse or raven; descendant of Rapp, a pet form of names beginning with Rabe (raven), as Ramfrid and Hrabanolt.

Rappaport, Rapoport, Rappeport, Rapaport, Rappoport (*It.*) The physician who came from Porto (gate), in Italy.

Rasch, Rascher (*Ger.*) The quick, lively person; one who came from Rasch, in Germany.

Raschke (*Ger.*) Descendant of little Rado (counsel).

Rascoe (*Eng.*) Dweller in the forest frequented by deer.

Rash (*Eng.*) Dweller at the ash tree.

Rashbaum (*Ger.*) Dweller near an elm tree.

Rashid (*Tur.*) Descendant of Rashid (the rightly guided).

Rasin, Rasinski, Rasinsky (*Rus.*) One of the same race or blood, a kinsman.

Raske, Rask (*Sw.*) Daring, a soldier name.

Raskin, Raskind (*Rus., Pol.*) Descendant, or son, of Rashe, a pet form of Rachel (the ewe).

Rasmus (*Eng.*) Descendant of Rasmus, pet form of Erasmus (lovable).

Rasmussen, Rasmusson, Rasmusen, Rasmuson (*Dan., Nor.*) The son of Rasmus, a pet form of Erasmus (lovable).

Raspberry, Raspburry (*Eng.*) Dweller near where raspberries grew.

Ratchford (*Eng.*) One who came from Rochford (ford of the hunting dog), the name of places in Essex and Worcestershire.

Ratcliff, Ratcliffe (*Eng.*) One who came from Ratcliff (red cliff), the name of several places in England.

Rateau (*Fr.*) One who made and sold rakes for use by farmers; the man who used the rake.

Rath, Rathe (*Ger., Ir.*) One who came

from Rath (counsel), in Rheinland; descendant of Rath, a form of Rado, a pet form of names beginning with Rat (counsel), as Radulf, Ratward, and Radoald; one who counseled or gave advice; one who came from Rath (fort), in Ireland.

Rathaus (*Ger.*) Dweller near the town hall or guild hall.

Rathbun, Rathbone, Rathburn (*Eng., Wel.*) One who came from Radbourn (stream where reeds grew), in Warwickshire; or from Radbourne, with the same meaning, in Derbyshire; dweller in a stumpy clearing.

Rathgeb, Rathgeber (*Ger.*) One who advises or gives counsel to others.

Rathmann, Rathman (*Ger.*) A city officer or alderman.

Rathsmill, Rathmill, Rathmell (*Eng.*) One who came from Rathmell (red sandbank), in the West Riding of Yorkshire.

Ratinaud (*Fr.*) The little rat, a nickname applied to one agile in gliding or sliding.

Ratliff, Ratliffe (*Eng.*) A variant of Ratcliff, q.v.

Ratner, Rattner (*Eng.*) One who caught rats.

Ratsep (*Est.*) One who made outer garments, a tailor.

Ratti (*It.*) Dweller on, or near, a steep incline.

Rattray (*Scot.*) One who came from Rattray (fort or mound dwelling), in Perthshire.

Rau, Rauh (*Nor., Ger.*) One who carried himself in a graceful manner; one with unusual body hair; a rough, boorish person.

Raub (*Ger.*) Descendant of Raub, a pet form of names beginning with Hrod (fame), as Hrodobert and Hrodbald.

Raubfogel (*Ger.*) One who robbed birds' nests; nickname, bird of prey, for one who robbed others.

Rauch, Raucher (*Ger.*) One who smoked meats; the hairy man.

Raudenbush (*Ger.*) Nickname for a gardener who produces rhomboidal bushes; dweller near where rue bushes grew; one who raised and sold rue.

Raudsepp (*Est.*) One who worked in iron, a smith.

Rauen, Rauh, Rauhe (*Ger.*) The hairy man, one with unusual body hair.

Rauer (*Ger.*) One who came from Rauen, in Germany; one with rough, coarse hair.

Raughley (*Eng.*) Variant of Raleigh, q.v.

Raum, Raumer (*Ger.*) One who came from Raum (room; place), the name of two places in Germany.

Raup, Raupp (*Ger.*) Descendant of Ruppo, a pet form of names beginning with Hrod (fame), as Hrotbald, Hrodobert, and Rotbrand.

Rausch (*Ger.*) The excitable or hurried man; dweller near rushes.

Rauschenbach (*Ger.*) One who came from Rauschenbach (stream by rushes), in Germany.

Rauschenberg (*Ger.*) One who came from Rauschenberg (hill covered by rushes), in Germany.

Rauscher (*Ger.*) One who came from Rausch (place where sedge grew), in Germany; the turbulent, blustering man.

Ravanell, Ravanel, Ravenel (*Eng.*) One who came from Ravenhill (hill frequented by ravens), in the North Riding of Yorkshire.

Ravel (*Fr.*) One who came from Ravel (rebellious house), in France; one who cultivated rape and produced rape oil.

Raven (*Eng.*) Dweller at the sign of the raven; one thought to exhibit some characteristic of the bird; descendant of Raven (raven).

Ravenfeld (*Eng.*) One who came from Ravenfield (open country frequented by ravens), in the West Riding of Yorkshire.

Ravenna (*It.*) One who came from Ravenna, in Italy.

Ravenscroft (*Eng.*) One who came from Ravenscroft (Hraefn's enclosed arable land), in Cheshire.

Ravetz (*Pol., Ger.*) One who came from Rawicz, in Poland.

Ravitch, Ravitz, Ravin (*Rus., Ukr., Cz.-Sl., Pol.*) One who came from Rava (black creek), in Ukraine; dweller near a dark stream.

Rawleigh, Rawley (*Eng.*) One who came from Rayleigh (meadow where rye was grown), in Essex; or from Rowley (rough wood), the name of several places in England; variant of Raleigh, q.v.

Rawlings, Rawlins, Rawlinson (*Eng.*) Descendant of little Raoul or little Raw, pet forms of Ralph (counsel, wolf).

Rawls, Rawl, Rawle (*Eng.*) Descendant of Raoul, a French form of Ralph (counsel, wolf).

Rawski (*Pol., Ukr., Rus.*) Variant of Ravitch, q.v.

Rawson (*Eng.*) The son of Raw, a pet form of Ralph (counsel, wolf).

Ray, Raye (*Eng.*) Descendant of Ray, a pet form of Raymond (wise, protector); dweller at the sign of the roe deer; one with some of the qualities of the roe deer; one who played the part of the king in play or pageant; one who was connected in some way with a king's household.

Raybold (*Eng.*) Descendant of Reginbald (might, bold).

Rayburn, Raybourn, Raybourne, Rayborn, Raeburn (*Eng., Scot.*) One who came from Ripponden, early form, Ryburn (fierce stream), in Yorkshire; one who came from the old lands of Ryburn, in Ayrshire.

Rayca (*Pol.*) Variant of Rajca, q.v.

Rayfield (*Eng.*) Dweller at, or near, the river field.

Rayford (*Eng.*) Dweller at, or near, the ford across the river.

Raymond, Reymond (*Eng.*) Descendant of Raymond (wise, protector).

Raynaud (*Fr.*) Variant of Renaud, q.v.

Rayner, Raynor, Rainer (*Eng.*) Descendant of Rayner, a form of Reginhari (counsel, army).

Razzi, Razza (*It.*) Descendant of Razza, a pet form of Pietro, Italian form of Peter (a rock); dweller near where smilax grew; or near where blackberries grew.

Rea (*Eng.*) Dweller at, or near, the Rea (river), the name of several rivers in England.

Read, Reade (*Eng.*) The ruddy or red-haired man; one who came from Read (roe headland), in Lancashire.

Reader (*Eng.*) A variant of Reeder, q.v.

Reading (*Eng.*) One who came from Reading (the people of Read, red), in Berkshire.

Ready, Readey, Readdy, Readie (*Eng., Scot.*) Descendant of little Read (red), a nickname given to one with red hair; descendant of little Read or Red, pet forms of Redmond (counsel, protection); one who came from Reedie, in Angus; descendant of Riada (trained).

Reagan, Reagen, Reagin (*Ir.*) Grandson of Riagan (little king).

Real (*Fr.*) The royal or noble man.

Reale, Reali (*It.*) Dweller at the sign of the royal eagle.

Ream (*Ger.*) Americanization of Rehm, q.v.

Reamer (*Ger.*) Americanization of Riemer, q.v.

Reaney (*Eng.*) One who came from Ranah Stones (raven hill stones), in the West Riding of Yorkshire; variant of Rainey, q.v.

Reaper, Reape, Reap (*Eng.*) One who cuts grain with a scythe or sickle.

Reardon, Rearden (*Ir.*) Grandson of Rioghbhardan (royal poet).

Reason (*Eng.*) The son of Rea (gray); or of the reeve.

Reaves, Reavis (*Eng.*) Variant of Reeves, q.v.

Reavley (*Eng.*) One who came from Reaveley (the reeve's grove), in Northumberland.

Rebane (*Est.*) Nickname for one thought to possess the characteristics of a fox.

Reber, Rebmann (*Ger.*) One who produced wine.

Rebstock (*Ger.*) Nickname for one who worked in a vineyard; dweller at the sign of the vine.

Reck, Recke, Recker (*Ger.*) One who came from Recke (swamp), in Germany; dweller in, or near, a swamp.

Reckard (*Eng.*) Variant of Rickard, q.v.

Recknagel (*Ger.*) Worker with nails, literally, stretch or extend nail; sometimes an obscene nickname referring to a little staff or penis.

Recktenwald (*Ger.*) One who came from Recktenwald, in Germany.

Rector (*Eng.*) The official who had charge of a church or parish.

Redburn (*Eng.*) One who came from Redbourn (stream with reeds), in Hertfordshire.

Redcross (*Eng.*) Dweller near a cross where reeds grew.

Redd (*Eng.*) The red-haired or ruddy person.

Reddall, Reddell (*Eng.*) Variant of Radwell, q.v.

Redden, Reddin (*Scot.*) One who came from Redden (raven dell), in Roxburghshire.

Reddick, Riddick, Reddicks (*Eng.*) One who came from Redditch (red or reedy ditch), in Worcestershire.

Redding (*Scot., Eng.*) One who came from Redding (clearing), the name of several places in Scotland; dweller in, or near, a clearing; or in, or near, a red meadow; one who came from Reading (Read's people), in Berkshire.

Reddington, Redington (*Eng.*) Dweller at the homestead in the clearing, that is, place cleared of trees; one who came from Rodington (homestead on the Roden river), in Shropshire.

Reddish (*Eng.*) One who came from Reddish (reed ditch), in Lancashire.

Reddix (*Eng.*) Dweller at the red dike; one who came from Redditch (reedy ditch), in Worcestershire.

Reddy (*Scot., Eng.*) One who came from Reedy, in Angus. See also Ready.

Reder (*Eng.*) One who covered roofs with reeds, a thatcher.

Redesmith (*Eng.*) One who worked in gold; the smith with red hair or ruddy complexion.

Redfern, Redfearn (*Eng.*) Dweller at, or near, a place where red ferns grew.

Redfield (*Eng.*) One who lived on, or by, the cleared land.

Redford (*Scot., Eng.*) One who came from Redford (red river crossing), the name of three places in Scotland; or from Radford (red ford), the name of eight places in England; or from Retford (red ford), in Nottinghamshire; dweller by the red river crossing.

Redhouse (*Eng.*) Dweller in the red house.

Rediker (*Ger.*) One who made wheels for wagons.

Reding (*Eng.*) Variant of Reading, q.v.

Redlich (*Ger.*) The honest, sincere man.

Redman, Redmon (*Eng.*) The red-haired or ruddy man; descendant of Redmond (counsel, protection); one who came from Redmain (red stones), in Cumberland.

Redmond (*Eng.*) Descendant of Redmond (counsel, protection).

Redpath (*Scot.*) One who came from Redpath (reedy passage), in Berwickshire.

Redshaw (*Eng.*) Dweller in the red wood; or in the thicket where reeds grew.

Redstone (*Eng.*) One who came from Radstone (stone cross), in Northamptonshire; dweller near a red stone.

Ree (*Eng.*) Dweller near a stream or channel; or on an island.

Reece (*Wel.*) The son of Rhys (ardor, a rush).

Reed (*Eng.*) The red-haired or ruddy person; one who came from Reed (reedy or rough growth), in Hertfordshire.

Reeder (*Eng.*) One who covered roofs with reeds, a thatcher.

Reedy (*Eng., Scot.*) A variant of Ready, q.v. Reed was an early spelling of red.

Reese, Rees (*Wel.*) The son of Rhys (ardor, a rush).

Reeves, Reeve (*Eng.*) A minor official appointed by the lord of the manor to supervise his tenants' work.

Refsin, Refsen (*Dan.*) Descendant of Ref, a pet form of Rafael (healed by God; medicine of God).

Regan (*Ir.*) Descendant of the impulsive man; grandson of Riagan (little king).

Regenstein, Regensteiner (*Ger.*) One who came from Regenstein, in Germany.

Register (*Eng.*) One who keeps a register or record of names.

Regnier, Regner (*Fr.*) Descendant of Raginhari (counsel, army).

Rego (*Port.*) One who came from Rego (irrigated place), the name of many small places in Portugal.

Rehfuss (*Ger.*) Nickname for one fleet of foot.

Rehm (*Ger.*) Descendant of Raimo, a pet form of Reginmund (counsel, protection); one who came from Rehm, in Schleswig; one who made and sold straps and bolts.

Rehnquist (*Sw.*) Reindeer, twig.

Rehr, Rehrer (*Ger.*) One who came from Rehren (swamp; place of reeds), the name of two places in Germany.

Reiber (*Ger.*) One who worked at the baths, giving patrons a rubdown.

Reich, Reiche (*Ger.*) Descendant of Rico, a pet form of Riculf (powerful, wolf).

Reichel (*Ger.*) Descendant of little Rico, a pet form of Riculf (powerful, wolf).

Reichenbach, Reichenback (*Ger.*) One who came from Reichenbach (muddy stream), the name of many places in Germany.

Reicher (*Ger.*) One who came from Reich (kingdom), the name of two places in Germany; descendant of Richari (rule, army).

Reichert, Reichard, Reichardt, Reichart (*Ger.*) Descendant of Ricohard (rule, hard).

Reichman, Reichmann (*Ger.*) Descendant of Ricman (powerful, man).

Reichner (*Ger.*) One who came from Reichenau (muddy meadow), the name of several places in Germany.

Reid (*Scot.*) Variant of Reed, q.v.

Reidy (*Eng., Scot.*) A variant of Ready, q.v. Reid was an early spelling of red.

Reif, Reiff, Riff (*Ger.*) Descendant of Rifo, a pet form of Ricfrid (rule, peace).

Reifsnyder, Reifsneider (*Ger.*) One who made barrel hoops.

Reigle, Reigel (*Ger.*) Dweller at the sign of the heron.

Reilly, Reilley, Reiley (*Ir.*) Variant of Riley, q.v.

Reim (*Ger.*) Descendant of Reim, a pet form of names beginning with Rim (mature), as Rimhart and Rimher; or of names beginning with Ragin (counsel), as Raginmar and Raginmund.

Reimann, Reiman (*Ger.*) Descendant of Raginman (counsel, man); dweller near the Rhine river.

Reimer, Reimers (*Ger.*) Descendant of Raginmar (counsel, famous); or of Ricmer (power, famous); or of Rimher (mature, army).

Rein (*Ger.*) Descendant of Ragino, a pet form of names beginning with Ragin (counsel), as Raganfrid, Ragingar, and Raginhart.

Reinach (*Swis.*) One who came from Reinach, in Switzerland.

Reinard (*Eng.*) Variant of Reinert, q.v.

Reinecke, Reinicke, Reineck, Reinick (*Ger.*) Descendant of little Ragino, a pet form of names beginning with Ragin (counsel), as Raginrich, Raginscalc, and Raginulf.

Reiner (*Ger.*) Descendant of Raginhari (counsel, army).

Reinert (*Ger.*) Descendant of Raginhart (counsel, strong).

Reingold (*Ger.*) Descendant of Ringold (national assembly, wood).

Reinhardt, Reinhart, Reinhard (*Ger.*)

Descendant of Reinhardt or Raginhart (counsel, hard).

Reinheimer (*Ger.*) One who came from Reinheim (swampy homestead), the name of two places in Germany.

Reinhold, Reinholtz (*Ger.*) Descendant of Reinold (counsel, force).

Reiniger, Reininger (*Ger.*) One who came from Reiningen (Raginger's place), in Germany.

Reinish, Reinisch (*Ger.*) Descendant of Reinhold (counsel, force); or of Reinhard (counsel, hard).

Reinke (*Ger.*) Descendant of little Ragino, a pet form of Raginulf (counsel, wolf).

Reinwald, Reinwall (*Ger.*) Descendant of Reinwald (counsel, govern).

Reisch, Reische (*Ger.*) Dweller among rushes, reeds, or sedge.

Reiser, Reisser (*Ger.*) One who left to go to war; one who came from Reiser, in Germany.

Reisman, Reismann (*Ger.*) One who went to war, a warrior.

Reiss, Reis (*Ger.*) Descendant of Riso (giant); dweller among shrubbery or in, or near, a thicket.

Reiter (*Ger.*) One who rode a horse, a cavalryman; one who cleared land for tilling.

Reith, Reath (*Ger.*) One who came from Reith (cleared forest place; courtyard), the name of many places in Germany.

Reitman (*Ger.*) Dweller in, or near, a cleared forest area; or among reeds or bulrushes.

Reitz (*Ger.*) Descendant of Ragizo, a pet form of names beginning with Ragan (counsel), as Raginhari and Reginmund; one who came from Ragizo, in Germany.

Rembert (*Eng.*) Descendant of Reginbert (counsel, bright).

Rembrandt (*Ger., Du.*) Descendant of Raginbrand (counsel, sword).

Remer (*Eng.*) Variant of Rimer, q.v.

Remington (*Eng.*) One who came from Rimington (homestead on the rim or border), in the West Riding of Yorkshire.

Remmer, Remmers (*Eng.*) Variant of Rimer, q.v.

Rempert (*Eng.*) Descendant of Reimbert (power, bright).

Remus (*Eng.*) Descendant of Remus (protector).

Remy (*Fr.*) Descendant of Remy, French form of Remigius (protector), fifth century French saint.

Renard (*Fr., Eng.*) Descendant of Raginhard (counsel, hard); dweller at the sign of the fox; one with foxlike characteristics.

Renaud, Renaut, Renault (*Fr., Bel.*) Descendant of Raginwald (counsel, govern); one who came from Renaix, in Belgium.

Rendon, Rendone (*Sp.*) Dweller at the border or boundary line.

Rene (*Fr.*) Descendant of Rene, French form of Renatus (reborn).

Renfro, Renfroe, Renfrow, Rentfro, Rentfrew (*Scot.*) One who came from Renfrew (flowing brook), in Renfrewshire.

Renick (*Eng.*) Shortened form of Renwick, q.v.

Renn, Renne (*Ger.*) Descendant of Renn, a pet form of names beginning with Ragin (counsel), as Raganbert and Raginulf.

Renner (*Eng., Du.*) One who carried messages on foot or horseback, a runner.

Rennert (*Ger.*) One who served a king or noble as an armed groom or riding messenger.

Rennick (*Eng.*) Variant of Renwick, q.v.

Rennie (*Scot.*) Variant of Rainey, q.v.

Renninger (*Ger.*) One who came from Renningen, in Germany.

Reno (*Sp.*) Dweller at the sign of the reindeer.

Renoir (*Fr.*) Descendant of Raginwulf (counsel, wolf); or of Raginward (counsel, guardian).

Renshaw (*Eng.*) Dweller in the wood frequented by ravens; dweller in the circular wood.

Rentner (*Ger.*) One who had charge of the treasure; or who managed a household or estate.

Renton (*Eng.*) One who came from Ranton (homestead on a bank), in Staffordshire.

Rentschler (*Ger.*) The lazy, indolent man who follows the old routine way.

Rentz, Renz, Rentsch (*Ger.*) Descendant of Renz, a pet form of Laurentius, German form of Lawrence (the laurel, symbol of victory).

Renwick (*Eng.*) One who came from Renwick (Hrafn's dwelling; farm frequented by ravens), in Cumberland.

Renzi, Renzulli (*It.*) Descendant of Renzi, pet form of Lorenzo, Italian form of Lawrence (the laurel, symbol of victory).

Repa (*Cz.*) Metonymic for one who raised and sold beets.

Repholz (*Eng.*) Dweller in, or near, a strip of wooded land.

Reppert (*Eng.*) Descendant of Ruprecht, a variant of Robert (fame, bright).

Repsch (*Ger.*) Variant of Rapp, q.v.

Requa (*Ger.*) Descendant of Ricward (rule, guardian).

Rescigno (*It.*) One who came from Rescigno, in Italy.

Resnick, Resnik (*Pol., Rus., Ukr.*) One who sold meat, a butcher; one who slaughtered animals for meat according to Jewish ritual.

Resnikoff (*Rus.*) The son of the meat seller.

Ressler (*Ger.*) One who raised and sold flowers.

Restall, Restell (*Eng.*) Descendant of Restold; dweller at the sign of the rake.

Restarick (*Eng.*) Dweller at the watery place.

Retallick (*Eng.*) Dweller at the steep hill spur.

Retherford (*Scot.*) Variant of Rutherford, q.v.

Retter (*Eng.*) One who made and sold nets.

Rettig (*Ger.*) Nickname for one who grows and sells vegetables.

Reuben, Reubens (*Eng.*) Descendant of Reuben (behold a son; renewer).

Reuss, Reusser (*Ger.*) One who repaired shoes; one who came from Russia.

Reutenauer (*Ger.*) One who came from Rudenau (muddy meadow), in Germany.

Reuter, Reuther (*Du., Ger.*) One who cleared land for tilling; one who fought on horseback.

Reutlinger (*Ger.*) One who came from Reutlingen, in Germany.

Revak (*Ukr.*) One who roars or bellows.

Reveley (*Eng.*) Variant of Reavley, q.v.

Revell, Revel, Revels (*Eng.*) Descendant of Revel (rebel); metonymic for one who makes merry in a noisy manner; one who came from Ravel (brook), in France.

Revencroft (*Eng.*) Variant of Ravenscroft, q.v.

Revere (*Eng., Fr.*) The robber; dweller on, or near, the bank or shore; one who came from Riviere, a village in Belgium.

Revesz (*Hun.*) One who operated a ferry, a ferryman.

Revis (*Eng.*) Variant of Rivers, q.v.

Rew (*Eng.*) One who came from Rew (row of houses), in Wight.

Rex (*Eng.*) Latin for King, q.v.; the son of Rick, a pet form of Richard (rule, hard).

Rexford (*Eng.*) Dweller at the king's river crossing.

Reyburn (*Eng., Scot.*) Variant of Rayburn, q.v.

Reyes, Rey (*Eng., Sp.*) One who played the part of the king in a play or pageant; one connected in some way with the king's household; a variant of Ray, q.v.; dweller near a stream; or on an island; one who came from Reyes or Rey (king), the names of places in Spain.

Reyna (*Sp.*) One who came from Reina (queen's place), in Spain.

Reynard (*Fr.*) Variant of Renard, q.v.

Reynaud (*Fr.*) Variant of Renaud, q.v.

Reynolds (*Eng.*) Descendant of Reginald or Regenweald (counsel, govern).

Reznick, Reznik (*Ger., Pol., Rus., Ukr., Cz.-Sl.*) One who cut and sold meat, a butcher; one who slaughtered animals for meat according to Jewish ritual.

Rhea, Rhay (*Wel.*) Dweller near the rapids; dweller near the river Rea (river), in Wales.

Rhein (*Ger.*) Dweller at the river Rhine (flow); one who came from Rhein, the name of three places in Germany.

Rheiner (*Ger.*) One who came from Rheinen or Rheine (flowing), the names of places in Germany.

Rheinlander (*Ger.*) One who came from West of the Rhine river in Germany.

Rheinstadter (*Ger.*) One who came from Reinstadt (muddy stream place) or Reinstedt, the names of towns in Germany.

Rhine (*Ger.*) Variant of Rhein, q.v.

Rhodes, Rhoades, Rhoads, Rhode (*Eng.*) Dweller at a clearing in the woods; one who lived at the roadside.

Rhodeside (*Eng.*) Dweller by the side of the road; or near the clearing.

Rhody (*Ger.*) One with red hair or red beard; dweller in, or near, a clearing.

Rhomberg (*Ger., Swis.*) Variant of Romberg, q.v.

Rhone (*Fr.*) One who came from Rhone (fens), the name of two places in France.

Rhyme (*Ger.*) Variant of Rhein, q.v.

Rhys (*Wel.*) Descendant of Rhys (ardor, a rush).

Ribar (*Yu.-Sl.*) One who caught or sold fish.

Ribaudo (*It.*) Descendant of Ribaudo (debauched; vagabond).

Ribeiro (*Port.*) One who came from Ribeiro (brook), in Portugal; dweller near a brook or small stream.

Ricardo (*Port., Sp.*) Descendant of Ricardo, Portuguese and Spanish form of Richard (rule, hard).

Riccardi, Riccardo (*It.*) Descendant of Riccardo, Italian form of Richard (rule, hard).

Ricchetti, Ricchini (*It.*) Descendant of little Ricca, a pet form of Riccardo, Italian form of Richard (rule, hard).

Ricci, Ricca (*It.*) Descendant of Ricci, a pet form of Enrico, Italian form of Henry (home, rule); and of Ricca, a pet form of Riccardo, Italian form of Richard (rule, hard).

Ricciardi (*It.*) Variant of Riccardi, q.v.

Riccio, Ricciuti (*It.*) One who had wavy or curly hair.

Riccobono (*It.*) Descendant of good Ricca, a pet form of Riccardo, Italian form of Richard (rule, hard).

Rice (*Wel.*) Descendant of Rhys (ardor, a rush).

Rich, Riche (*Eng.*) Descendant of Rich, a pet form of Richard (rule, hard); dweller near a ditch or small stream.

Richards, Richard (*Eng., Wel.*) Descendant of Richard (rule, hard).

Richardson (*Eng.*) The son of Richard (rule, hard).

Richburg (*Eng.*) One who came from Richborough, in Kent.

Richelieu (*Fr.*) One who came from Richelieu (wealthy place), in France.

Richelson, Richel (*Eng.*) The son of little Rich, a pet form of Richard (rule, hard).

Richer, Richerson (*Eng.*) Descendant of Richer (rule, army).

Richert, Richart (*Eng., Bel.*) Descendant of Richert, Flemish form of Richard (rule, hard).

Richie, Richey (*Eng., Scot.*) Descendant of little Rich, a pet form of Richard (rule, hard).

Richman (*Eng.*) The servant of Rich, a pet form of Richard (rule, hard); variant of Richmond, q.v.

Richmond (*Eng.*) One who came from Richemont (lofty mountain), in Normandy; or from Richmond, in Yorkshire, which was named after one of the Richemonts in France.

Richter, Richters (*Ger.*) One who held the office of judge or magistrate.

Rick (*Eng.*) Descendant of Rick, a pet form of Richard (rule, hard).

Rickard, Rickards, Rickart (*Eng.*) Descendant of Rickard or Ricard, variants of Richard (rule, hard).

Rickenbacker (*Ger.*) One who came from Rickenbach (muddy stream), the name of several places in Germany.

Ricker, Rickerson (*Eng.*) Descendant of Richere (might, army).

Rickert (*Eng.*) An Anglicization of the Dutch Rijkert, a variant of Richard (rule, hard).

Ricketts, Rickett (*Eng.*) Descendant of little Rick, a pet form of Richard (rule, hard).

Rickles, Rickells (*Eng.*) Descendant of Ricoald (rule, power); or of Richild (rule, war).

Rickman (*Eng.*) The servant of Rick, a pet form of Richard (rule, hard).

Rickover (*Ger.*) One who came from Reichau (mighty stream), in Germany.

Ricks (*Eng.*) Dweller by the rushes; descendant of Rick, a pet form of Richard (rule, hard).

Rico (*It., Ger.*) Descendant of Rico, a pet form of Enrico, Italian form of Henry (home, rule); or of Rico (strong).

Riddell, Riddle, Riddel, Ridell, Riddles (*Eng.*) Descendant of little Rad, a pet form of names beginning with Rad (counsel), as Radbald and Radulf; dweller at the red hill; or red well; or red hall; one who came from Rydal or Rydale (valley where rye was grown), in Westmorland and Yorkshire, respectively.

Riddick (*Eng.*) Dweller at the sign of the robin.

Riddiford (*Eng.*) One who came from Radford (red river crossing), the name of several places in England.

Ridenour (*Ger.*) One who came from Rietenau (meadow with reeds growing), in Germany.

Rideout (*Fr., Eng.*) Descendant of Ridwulf (horseman, wolf); or Ridald (horseman, bold); dweller near a fortification; nickname for one who rides out on an errand.

Rider (*Eng.*) The rider or trooper; a mounted guardian of a forest.

Ridewood (*Eng.*) Dweller in, or near, a wood where reeds grew.

Ridge, Ridges (*Eng.*) One who came from Ridge (ridge), in Hertfordshire; dweller at, or near, a range of hills.

Ridgley (*Eng.*) Dweller on the ridge by the grove.

Ridgway, Ridgeway (*Eng.*) Dweller at the way or road along a ridge.

Riding, Ridings (*Eng.*) One who came from Riding (clearing), in Northumberland.

Ridley (*Eng.*) One who came from Ridley (cleared, or reedy, meadow), the name of several places in England.

Ridolfi, Ridolfo (*It.*) Variant of Rodolfo, q.v.

Ridout (*Fr., Eng.*) Variant of Rideout, q.v.

Ridpath (*Scot.*) Variant of Redpath, q.v.

Riebel (*Ger.*) One who raised and sold turnips.

Rieben, Rieber (*Ger.*) Descendant of little Ribo, a pet form of names beginning with Reich (might), as Rigobert and Ricbald.

Rieck, Riecke (*Ger.*) Descendant of Rieck, a pet form of Rieckert (rule, hard).

Riedel, Riedl, Riedle, Riedell (*Ger.*) Descendant of Riedel, a pet form of names beginning with Hrod (fame), as Hrotfrid, Rothhari, and Hrodmar.

Rieder, Riederer (*Ger.*) One who came from Rieder (land overgrown with sedge), the name of several places in Germany.

Riegel (*Ger.*) Dweller at the town fence; descendant of Ricoald (rule, power).

Rieger (*Ger.*) Descendant of Hrodgaer (fame, spear); the magistrate who censored people.

Riehl, Riehle (*Ger.*) Descendant of Rico, a pet form of names beginning with Rich (rule), as Riculf and Richowin.

Riemer (*Ger.*) One who made and sold

harness; descendant of Rimher (mature, army).

Rienzi (*It.*) Variant of Renzi, q.v.

Ries, Riess, Riese (*Ger.*) The large man; descendant of Riso (giant); one who came from Riess, in Germany.

Riesel (*Ger.*) Dweller in a swampy lowland.

Riesenbeck, Riesenbach (*Ger.*) One who came from Riesenbeck (swampy stream), in Germany; dweller near a swampy stream.

Rieser (*Ger.*) One who came from Riesen (place overgrown with bushes and shrubs), the name of several places in Germany.

Rife, Riff (*Fr.*) Dweller near a brook.

Rifkin (*Rus., Ukr.*) The son of Rifka (a snare); descendant of Rivke, a diminutive of Rebecca (heifer; binding).

Rigal (*Fr.*) Descendant of Ricwald (might, rule).

Rigas (*Gr.*) One who played the part of a king in play or pageant.

Rigberg (*Sw.*) One who came from Rigberg, in Sweden.

Rigby (*Eng.*) One who came from Ribby (formerly Rigbi, homestead on a ridge), in Lancashire.

Rigdale (*Eng.*) Dweller in the valley by the ridge.

Riggins, Riggin (*Eng.*) Descendant of little Riggs or Ricks, pet forms of Richard (rule, hard).

Riggio (*It.*) One who came from Reggio, in Italy.

Riggs, Rigg (*Eng., Scot.*) Dweller at a ridge or range of hills; one who came from the lands of Rigg, in East Lothian.

Righter (*Eng., Ger.*) One who adjusts or redresses wrongs; Americanization of Richter, q.v.

Rightley, Rightly (*Eng.*) Dweller on a homestead on the Rye river; or on a homestead where rye was grown.

Rigler (*Ger.*) One who came from Riegel (bolt), in Germany; one who made bolts and cross-bars.

Rigney (*Fr.*) One who came from Rigney (Renius' or Renos' estate), the name of several places in France.

Rigoni (*It.*) Descendant of big Rigo, a pet form of Arrigo or Enrico (home, rule).

Rigsby, Rigsbey (*Eng.*) One who came from Rigsby (settlement on a ridge), in Lincolnshire.

Riha (*Cz.-Sl.*) The belching, vomiting person.

Rihl (*Ger.*) One who came from Ruhle (watery area), the name of two places in Germany; descendant of Ruhl, a pet form of Rudolf (fame, wolf).

Riis (*Dan., Sw., Nor.*) Dweller near dead brushwood.

Rile, Riles (*Eng.*) Dweller on the hill where rye was grown.

Riley (*Ir.*) Grandson of Raghallach (sportive).

Rill (*Ger.*) Descendant of Rido, a pet form of names beginning with Reiten (rider), as Ridperht, Ridhart, and Ridher.

Rilley (*Eng., Ir.*) Dweller near the rye field; variant of Riley, q.v.

Rimas (*Lith.*) Descendant of Rim or Rimas, pet forms of Rimvydas and such names as Gaudrimas and Mantrimas.

Rimer, Rimerman, Rimes (*Eng.*) One who produced rhymed verse, a poet.

Rimkevicius (*Lith.*) The son of Rimkus, a pet form of Rimkantas (peaceful, suffer; quiet).

Rimkus (*Lith.*) Descendant of Rimkus, a pet form of Rimkantas (peaceful, suffer; quiet); the quiet man.

Rimmer, Rimmerman (*Eng.*) Variant of Rimer, q.v.

Rimshaw (*Eng.*) Variant of Renshaw, q.v.

Rimsky (*Rus.*) One who came from Rim, Russian form of Rome (four crossroads), in Italy.

Rinaldi, Rinaldo (*It.*) Descendant of Rinaldo, Italian form of Reynold or Reginald (counsel, power).

Rinck (*Ger.*) Variant of Rink, q.v.

Rindskopf (*Ger.*) Dweller at the sign of the ox head.

Rinehart (*Ger.*) Variant of Reinhardt, q.v.

Rinella (*It.*) Descendant of little Rina, a pet form of Catrina, or Caterina (pure).

Ring, Ringe (*Eng.*) Dweller at a stone circle or circular entrenchment; descendant of Ring, a pet form of Hringwulf or Ringulfus (ring, wolf).

Ringel (*Ger.*) One who made and sold small rings.

Ringer, Ringman (*Eng.*) A bell or change ringer; one whose business it was to ring a church or town bell at stated times; one who wrings or presses cheese.

Ringgold, Ringold (*Ger.*) Descendant of Ringolt (circle, gold); or of Ringold (national assembly, wood).

Ringland (*Eng.*) One who came from Ringland (border people), in Norfolk.

Ringler (*Ger.*) One who made and sold rings.

Ringrose (*Eng.*) Dweller near a circular hedge or row of houses.

Ringsby (*Eng.*) One who came from Rigsby (Hrygg's village), in Lincolnshire.

Ringsted (*Eng.*) One who came from Ringstead (circular place), in Dorset.

Ringstrom (*Nor.*) Dweller near a winding stream.

Ringwald (*Ger.*) Descendant of Reinald (counsel, force); one who came from Ringenwalde, in Germany.

Ringwood (*Eng.*) One who came from Ringwood (boundary wood), in Hampshire.

Rink, Rinke, Rinker (*Ger.*) One who made and sold buckles and clasps.

Rinkevicius (*Lith.*) Variant of Rimkevicius, q.v.

Rinkus (*Lith.*) Variant of Rimkus, q.v.

Riordan (*Ir.*) Grandson of Rioghbhardan (royal poet).

Rios, Rio (*Sp.*) Dweller near the river; one who came from Rios (rivers), in Spain.

Riou (*Fr.*) Dweller near a brook or small stream; descendant of Riou—there existed a St. Riou.

Rioux (*Fr.*) Descendant of Ridwulf (rider, wolf).

Ripka (*Ukr.*) One who raises and sells small turnips.

Ripley (*Eng.*) One who came from Ripley (long, narrow wood or meadow), the name of several places in England.

Ripp, Rippe (*Ger.*) Descendant of Ripp, a pet form of names beginning with Reich (might), as Ricbald and Rigobert.

Rippert (*Ger.*) Descendant of Rigobert (might, bright).

Risby (*Eng.*) One who came from Risby (village in brushwood; or in a clearing), the name of four places in England.

Rise (*Eng., Wel., Ger.*) One who came from Rise (brushwood), in the East Riding of Yorkshire; dweller near brushwood; variant of Rhys, q.v.; and of Reiss, q.v.

Risher (*Ger.*) One who came from Rischen (rushes), in Germany.

Risler, Rissler (*Fr.*) One who works by tearing or rending material; descendant of Risler, a pet form of Rico (strong).

Risley (*Eng.*) One who came from Risley (brushwood grove), the name of places in Derbyshire and Lancashire.

Ritchie, Ritchey (*Scot., Eng.*) Descendant of little Rich, a pet form of Richard (rule, hard).

Ritrovato (*It.*) One born out of wedlock.

Ritt (*Ger.*) Dweller among reeds, rushes, or sedge.

Rittenberg (*Ger.*) One who came from Rittenburg (stronghold among reeds), in Germany.

Rittenhouse (*Ger.*) Dweller in the house on the slope where reeds or sedge grew.

Ritter (*Ger.*) A military servant, a knight.

Rittmaster (*Ger.*) A cavalry captain.

Ritz, Ritzer (*Ger.*) One who came from Ritze (reedy place), in Germany; descendant of Ritz, a pet form of Richard (rule, hard).

Rivard (*Fr.*) Dweller near a small stream.

Rivas (*Sp.*) One who came from Rivas, in Spain.

Rivera, Rivero (*Sp.*) Dweller near a brook or stream.

Rivers, River (*Eng.*) One who came from River (river), in Kent; or from River (brow of a hill), in Sussex; dweller by the river; one who came from Rivieres (shore), in France; one who came from Rievoulx (valley of the Rye), pronounced rivers, in the North Riding of Yorkshire.

Riviere, Rivier (*Fr.*) Dweller on the bank of a river, or shore of a lake; or at the edge of a wood; one who came from Riviere (bank; shore), the name of several places in France.

Rivkin, Rivkind (*Rus.*) Descendant of Rivke, a diminutive of Rebecca (heifer; binding).

Rivoir, Rivoire (*Fr.*) Variant of Riviere, q.v.

Rix, Rixe (*Eng.*) The son of Rick, a pet form of Richard (rule, hard); dweller near, or in, the rushes.

Rixford (*Eng.*) Dweller at the river crossing near where rushes grew.

Rizzo, Rizza, Rizzi, Rizzuto (*It.*) One who had wavy or curly hair.

Roach, Roache (*Ir.*) Dweller at, or near, a rock. See also Roche.

Roak (*Eng.*) Dweller at, or near, a rock.

Roane, Roan (*Eng.*) One who came from Rouen, in Normandy.

Roantree (*Eng., Scot.*) Variant of Rountree, q.v.

Roark (*Eng.*) Dweller near a rock.

Roback, Robeck (*Ger.*) One who worked for another, without pay, a vassal.

Robards, Robard (*Fr.*) Descendant of Robard, a French variant of Robert (fame, bright).

Robb (*Eng.*) Descendant of Rob, a pet form of Robert (fame, bright).

Robbie, Robie (*Scot.*) Descendant of little Rob, a pet form of Robert (fame, bright).

Robbins (*Eng.*) The son of little Rob, a pet form of Robert (fame, bright).

Roberson (*Eng.*) The son of Robert (fame, bright).

Roberts, Robert, Robart (*Wel., Eng.*) The son of Robert (fame, bright).

Robertson (*Scot., Eng.*) The son of Robert (fame, bright).

Robespierre (*Fr.*) Descendant of Robert Pierre, French form of Robert Peter (fame, bright/a rock).

Robey, Roby (*Eng.*) One who came from Robey or Roby (homestead near a boundary mark), in Derbyshire and Lancashire, respectively; variant of Robbie, q.v.

Robins, Robin, Robyn (*Eng.*) Descendant of little Rob, a pet form of Robert (fame, bright).

Robinson, Robison (*Eng., Scot.*) The son of little Rob, a pet form of Robert (fame, bright).

Robles (*Sp.*) One who came from Robles (oak tree grove), in Spain.

Robson, Robeson (*Eng., Scot.*) The son of Rob, a pet form of Robert (fame, bright).

Rocca, Roccia (*It.*) Dweller near a cliff; or near a fortress.

Rocco (*It.*) Descendant of Rocco (to crow or roar).

Roche, Roch, Rocher, Rochet (*Fr., Eng.*) Dweller near a rock; one who came from Roche (rock), in Cornwall; or from Roche (rock), the name of many places in France.

Rochelle (*Fr.*) Dweller near a small rock or stone.

Rochester (*Eng.*) One who came from Rochester (bridges of the stronghold), the name of places in Kent and Northumberland.

Rochford (*Eng.*) One who came from Rochford (hunting dog's ford), the name of places in Essex and Worcestershire.

Rock, Rocke, Rocks (*Eng.*) Dweller near some prominent boulder, probably a boundary marker; one who came from Rock (rock), in Northumberland; or from Rock (the oak), in Worcestershire.

Rockefeller, Rockenfeller (*Ger.*) Dweller in, or near, the rye field.

Rocker (*Eng.*) Dweller by a rock; one who made distaffs.

Rockett (*Eng.*) One who came from LaRoquette (the little rock), in Normandy.

Rockey (*Eng.*) Dweller near a small rock.

Rockeymore (*Eng.*) One who came from Rockmoor (lake with trestles for the support of a bridge), in Hampshire; dweller on a rocky moor or waste land.

Rockhill (*Eng.*) Dweller on, or near, the rocky hill.

Rockingham (*Eng.*) One who came from Rockingham (village of Hroc's people), in Northamptonshire.

Rockley (*Eng.*) One who came from Rockley (grove frequented by rooks), in Wiltshire.

Rockmore (*Eng.*) One who came from Rockmoor (lake with supports for a bridge), in Hampshire.

Rockne (*Nor.*) An ancient farm name said to be older than written history.

Rockower (*Ger.*) One who came from Rockow (swampy lowland), in Germany.

Rockstroh (*Ger.*) Rye straw, a nickname for the rye farmer.

Rockwell (*Eng.*) Dweller at, or near, the stony spring or stream.

Rockwood (*Eng.*) Dweller in, or near, a rocky wood or grove, or in, or near, a wood frequented by rooks.

Rodden (*Eng.*) One who came from Rodden (valley where roes were found), in Somerset.

Roddis (*Eng.*) Shortened form of Roodhouse, q.v.

Roddy (*Eng.*) Descendant of little Rod, a pet form of Roderick (fame, rule).

Rode, Rodd, Rodde, Rod (*Eng.*) Dweller in the clearing or place where the trees have been removed; descendant of Rod, a pet form of Roderick (fame, rule).

Rodebaugh (*Ger.*) One who came from Rodebach, in Germany.

Roden (*Ger., Eng.*) One who came from Roden (cleared land), the name of two places in Germany; or from Roden (swift river), in Shropshire.

Rodenbaugh (*Ger.*) One who came from Rodenbach, the name of many places in Germany.

Roder (*Ger.*) One who came from Roder, in Germany; descendant of Hrodhari (fame, army).

Roderick, Rodrick (*Eng.*) Descendant of Roderick (fame, rule).

Rodesmith (*Eng.*) The smith at the clearing or open space in the forest; or who lived by the road; one who made roods or wayside crosses; variant of Redesmith, q.v.

Rodgers, Rodger (*Wel., Eng.*) Variant of Rogers, q.v.

Rodham (*Eng.*) One who came from Roddam (homestead at a cross), in Northumberland.

Rodin (*Fr.*) Descendant of little Rod, a pet form of Gerard (spear, firm).

Rodman (*Eng.*) Descendant of Rodmund (fame, protection); dweller near a cross; servant of Rod, a pet form of Roderick (fame, rule).

Rodney (*Eng.*) One who came from Rodney (Hroda's island), in Somerset.

Rodolfo (*It.*) Descendant of Rodolfo, Italian form of Rudolph (fame, wolf).

Rodrian (*Ger.*) The red-haired or ruddy man named John (gracious gift of Jehovah).

Rodriguez, Rodrigues (*Sp., Port.*) The son of Rodrigo, Spanish and Portuguese form of Roderick (fame, rule).

Rodriquez, Rodiquez (*Sp.*) The son of Rodrigo, Spanish form of Roderick (fame, rule).

Rodvill, Rodville (*Eng.*) Variant of Rodwell, q.v.

Rodway (*Eng.*) One who came from Rodway (roadway), in Somerset.

Rodwell (*Eng.*) Dweller at the spring, or well, by the road, or cross; one who came from Rodwell (red spring, or stream), the name of places in Bedfordshire and Hertfordshire.

Roe (*Eng.*) Dweller at the sign of the roe deer; dweller at the row or hedgerow.

Roebuck, Robuck (*Eng.*) Dweller at the sign of the male roe deer.

Roedell, Roedel (*Ger.*) The official who kept the scroll, register or tax roll.

Roeder, Roedder, Roeters (*Ger.*) Descendant of Rothari (fame, army); dweller on land recently cleared for tilling.

Roelandts, Roeland, Roelant (*Du., Bel.*) Descendant of Roeland (fame, land).

Roemer (*Ger.*) One who came from Rome (four crossroads), a Roman; one who had made a pilgrimage to Rome, sometimes in expiation for attempted murder.

Roemhild (*Ger.*) One who came from Romhild (spongy earth), in Germany.

Roentgen (*Ger.*) Descendant of little Ron (secret magic writing), a pet form of such names as Runger and Runuald, also Hieronymus.

Roesler, Roessler (*Ger.*) One who tended a rose garden; or who sold roses.

Roffe, Roff (*Heb.*) The medical man or doctor.

Rog (*Pol.*) Dweller in the nook or corner.

Rogalla, Rogala (*Pol., Ger.*) Dweller where sedge or bulrushes grew.

Rogalski (*Pol.*) Dweller near the Rogalskie (place frequented by animals with horns), a lake in Poland; a betrayed husband.

Rogan (*Ir.*) One with red hair or ruddy complexion.

Roger (*Fr., Eng.*) Descendant of Roger (fame, spear).

Rogers, Rogerson (*Wel., Eng.*) The son of Roger (fame, spear).

Roget (*Fr.*) Descendant of little Rog, a pet form of Roger (fame, spear).

Rogge, Rogg (*Du.*) Dweller in, or near, a rye field; descendant of Rogge.

Roggen (*Ger.*) One who cultivated rye.

Rogowski, Rogow (*Pol.*) One who came from Rogowo (corner village; horn), the name of two places in Poland.

Rogozinski (*Pol.*) Dweller among rushes.

Rohde (*Ger.*) Descendant of Hrodo, a pet form of names beginning with Hrod (fame), as Hrodulf, Hrodric, and Hrodowald.

Rohn, Rohne, Rohner (*Ger.*) One who came from Rohn or Rohne (muddy place), the names of places in Germany.

Rohr (*Ger.*) One who came from Rohr (reeds), the name of many small places in Germany; dweller at a place where reeds grew in abundance.

Rohrbacher, Rohrbach, Rohrback, Rohrbacker (*Ger.*) One who came from Rohrbach (reedy stream), the name of places in Austria and Germany; dweller near the Rohrbach, the name of thirteen rivers in Germany.

Rohrbaugh (*Ger.*) One who came from Rohrbach (reedy stream), the name of many places in Germany.

Rohrer (*Ger.*) One who came from Rohr (reeds), the name of many small places in Germany; or from Rohrau (reedy place), in Austria.

Rojahn (*Ger.*) The man named Johann (gracious gift of Jehovah), who had red hair.

Rojas (*Sp.*) One with red or rust-colored hair.

Rojewski (*Pol.*) One who came from Rojewo, the name of three places in Poland.

Rokeach (*Ger., Heb.*) One who sold drugs, a druggist; a dealer in spices.

Roker (*Eng.*) One who made and sold distaffs.

Roland, Rolland (*Eng., Fr.*) Descendant of Roland (fame, land).

Roldan (*Sp.*) Descendant of Roldan, Spanish form of Roland (fame, land).

Rolek (*Pol.*) Descendant of Rolek, a pet form of Roland (fame, land).

Rolfe, Rolf, Rolff, Rolph (*Eng.*) Descendant of Rolf (counsel, wolf).

Roll, Rolle (*Eng.*) Descendant of Roll, a pet form of Rolf (counsel, wolf); and of Roland (fame, land).

Roller (*Eng.*) One who made and sold parchment rolls for manuscripts.

Rollerson, Rollason (*Eng.*) The son of Rolla, a shortened form of Roland (fame, land).

Rolleston (*Eng.*) One who came from Rolleston (Hrolf's homestead; Hroald's homestead), the name of places in Leicestershire, Staffordshire, and Nottinghamshire.

Rollings, Rolling (*Eng.*) Descendant of little Roll, a pet form of Rolf (counsel, wolf); and of Roland (fame, land).

Rollins, Rollin (*Eng., Fr.*) The son of little Roll, a pet form of Raoul or Ralph (counsel, wolf); descendant of Roland (fame, land).

Rollinson, Rollison (*Eng.*) The son of little Roll, a pet form of Rolf (counsel, wolf) and of Roland (fame, land).

Rollo, Rolla (*Eng., Scot.*) Descendant of Rollo, a pet form of Rolf (counsel, wolf); and of Roland (fame, land).

Rolnick, Rolnik (*Pol., Cz.*) One who tilled the land, a farmer.

Rolph (*Eng.*) Variant of Rolfe, q.v.

Rolston, Rolleston (*Eng., Scot.*) Variant of Ralston, q.v.

Rom (*Ger., Heb.*) A Jewish acronymic name shaped out of the initials of the words *Reish Mesivos* (chief of the Yeshivah, religious institute of higher learning); one who came from Rome (four crossroads), in Italy; or from Rom (swamp), the name of places in Germany; dweller on a height.

Roma (*It.*) One who came from Rome (four crossroads), in Italy.

Romain (*Eng.*) Variant of Roman, q.v.

Roman, Romans (*Eng., Scot.*) One who had made a pilgrimage to Rome (four crossroads); one who came from Rome, a Roman; one who

came from Romanno (circle of the monk), in Peeblesshire.

Romanchek, Romanchak, Romanchik (*Ukr.*) Descendant of Roman (one from Rome).

Romanelli (*It.*) Descendant of little Romano (one from Rome).

Romanenko (*Ukr.*) The son of Roman (one from Rome).

Romano, Romani (*It.*) One who came from Rome (four crossroads), or from within Rome's political sphere; one who had visited Rome.

Romanowski (*Pol.*) The son of Roman (one from Rome).

Romanski, Romansky (*Ukr.*) One who came from Rome, a Roman.

Rombeau (*Fr.*) Descendant of Rumbeald (noble, bold).

Romberg (*Ger., Swis.*) One who came from Romberg, the name of places in Germany and Switzerland.

Rome (*Eng.*) One who had made a pilgrimage to Rome (four crossroads); one who came from Rome; variant of Rom, q.v.; descendant of Rome, a pet form of Jerome (holy name).

Romeo (*It.*) One who has made a pilgrimage to Rome.

Romer (*Eng.*) One who had made a pilgrimage to Rome; one who wandered from place to place.

Romero (*Sp.*) One who has visited a shrine, a pilgrim.

Romisher (*Ger.*) One who came from Rome, a Roman.

Romm (*Ger.*) One who came from Rome, a Roman; or from Roumania (the Romans).

Rommel (*Ger., Du.*) Descendant of Ruhm, a pet form of names beginning with Ruhm (fame), as Hrumheri, Rumerich, and Rumuald; the messy or untidy man; the blustering or noisy man.

Romney (*Eng.*) One who came from Romney (spacious river; island in a marsh), in Kent.

Romsey (*Eng.*) One who came from Romsey (Rum's island; large island), in Hampshire.

Ronald (*Scot.*) Descendant of Ronald (counsel, power; might, power).

Ronan, Ronayne (*Ir.*) Grandson of Ronan (little seal).

Rondell, Rondel (*Eng., Fr.*) The plump, round man.

Roney (*Ir.*) Grandson of Ruanaidh (hero).

Ronquist (*Sw.*) Rowan-tree, twig.

Ronson (*Eng.*) The son of Ron, a pet form of Ronald (counsel, power; might, power).

Rood, Roode (*Eng., Du.*) Dweller near a roadside cross; one with red hair or a ruddy complexion; variant of Rode, q.v.

Roodhouse (*Eng.*) Dweller in the house in the clearing.

Roof, Roofe (*Eng.*) The famous, renowned man; the red-haired or ruddy-complexioned man; variant of Rolfe, q.v.

Rook, Rooks, Rooke (*Eng.*) Dweller at the sign of the rook; nickname given to one with black hair and dark complexion.

Rooker, Roker (*Eng.*) Dweller by a rock; one who made distaffs.

Roomberg (*Ger., Swis.*) Variant of Romberg, q.v.

Rooney (*Ir.*) Grandson of Ruanaidh (hero).

Roop, Roope (*Eng.*) Metonymic for one who made rope, a ropemaker.

Roos, Roose (*Eng., Ger.*) A variant of Rose, q.v.; one who came from Roos (moor; heath), in the East Riding of Yorkshire.

Roosevelt (*Du.*) One who lived at, or near, the rose farm or field.

Root, Rote, Rot (*Eng.*) The gay or cheerful man.

Rooth (*Ger., Eng.*) Variant of Roth, q.v.; and of Ruth, q.v.

Rooz (*Du.*) Dweller at the sign of the rose.

Roozeboom, Rooseboom (*Du.*) One who cultivated rose bushes; dweller at the sign of the rose bush.

Roper (*Eng.*) One who made and sold rope.

Roque (*Fr.*) One who came from Roque (rock), in France; dweller near a rock.

Rorer (*Ger.*) Variant of Rohrer, q.v.

Rorie (*Scot.*) Descendant of Ruairidh (red king).

Rorke (*Ir.*) Variant of O'Rourke, q.v.

Ros (*Sw.*) Rose.

Rosa (*Sp., It.*) One who cultivated roses; dweller near where roses grew; dweller at the sign of the rose.

Rosado (*Sp.*) Descendant of Rosado (rose).

Rosario (*It., Sp.*) One who made and sold rosaries; descendant of Rosario (rosary).

Rosati, Rosato (*It.*) One who made and sold stammel, a coarse woolen cloth usually dyed red.

Rosberg (*Ger.*) One who came from Rosberg, in Germany.

Rosborough (*Scot.*) Variant of Roxburgh, q.v.

Rosbottom (*Eng.*) Dweller in the valley where roes were found; or in the horse vale.

Roscoe (*Eng.*) Dweller in, or near, a wood frequented by roes; one who came from Roscoe, in Yorkshire.

Rose, Rosa (*Eng., Scot., Ger.*) Dweller at the sign of the rose, a not uncommon inn sign; dweller at the sign of the horse.

Roseberry (*Eng., Scot.*) One who came from Roseberry (Othinn's hill), in the North Riding of Yorkshire; or from Roseberry (Roe's stronghold), in Midlothian; dweller on, or near, a hill where roses grew.

Roseboro, Roseborough, Rosebourgh (*Scot.*) Variant of Roxburgh, q.v.

Rosecranz (*Ger.*) Dweller at the sign of the rose wreath.

Rosedale (*Eng.*) One who came from Rosedale (horse valley), in the North Riding of Yorkshire.

Rosella, Roselli, Roselle, Rosetti (*It.*) Dweller at the sign of the rose.

Rosellini (*It.*) Descendant of little Rossello, Italian form of Russell (red).

Rosemann, Roseman (*Ger., Eng.*) Man

in charge of the roses; descendant of Rosmund (horse or rose, protection).

Rosemond (*Eng.*) Descendant of Rosemunda (horse, protection), a woman's name.

Rosen (*Ger., Sw.*) Roses; descendant of Rose (horse or rose).

Rosenauer, Rosenau (*Ger.*) One who came from Rosenau (meadow where roses grew), the name of several places in Germany.

Rosenbach, Rosenbacher (*Ger.*) One who came from Rosenbach (rose brook), the name of many places in Germany and in Austria.

Rosenband (*Ger.*) Rose token.

Rosenbaum (*Ger.*) Rose tree; dweller near a rose bush.

Rosenberg, Rosenberger (*Ger., Sw.*) One who came from Rosenberg (rose mountain), the name of many places in Germany; rose mountain.

Rosenblatt, Rosenblat (*Ger.*) Rose leaf.

Rosenblum, Rosenbloom (*Ger., Sw.*) Rose flower.

Rosenbluth (*Ger.*) Rose blossom.

Rosenbusch (*Ger.*) Rose bush.

Rosencranz (*Ger.*) Variant of Rosenkranz, q.v.

Rosendahl (*Ger., Sw.*) One who came from Rosendahl (rose valley), the name of two places in Germany; rose, valley.

Rosendale (*Eng.*) Dweller in the valley where roses grew.

Rosenfeld, Rosenfield, Rosenfelder, Rosenfelt (*Ger.*) One who came from Rosenfeld (rose field), the name of four places in Germany.

Rosengarten, Rosengarden, Rosengart, Rosengard (*Ger., Sw.*) One who came from Rosengarten (rose garden), the name of four places in Germany; rose, hedge.

Rosengren (*Sw.*) Rose, branch.

Rosenhaus (*Ger.*) Dweller in a house surrounded by roses.

Rosenheim (*Ger.*) One who came from Rosenheim (home with roses growing), in Germany.

Rosenholtz (*Ger.*) Rose wood.

Rosenkoetter (*Ger.*) Dweller in a rose covered cottage.

Rosenkranz, Rosenkrantz, Rosenkrans (*Ger.*) One who came from Rosenkranz (rose wreath), in Germany.

Rosenmayer (*Ger.*) The farmer who raised roses.

Rosenow (*Ger.*) One who came from Rosenau (rose meadow), the name of four places in Germany.

Rosenquist (*Sw.*) Rose, twig.

Rosenschmidt (*Ger.*) The smith who dwelt, or worked, at the sign of the rose.

Rosenstadt (*Ger.*) Rose city.

Rosenstein (*Ger.*) Rose stone.

Rosenstock (*Ger.*) Rose tree.

Rosensweig (*Ger.*) Rose branch.

Rosenthal (*Ger.*) One who came from Rosenthal (rose valley), the name of six places in Germany.

Rosenwald, Rosewald, Rosewall (*Ger.*) One who came from Rosenwald (rose forest), in Germany.

Rosenwasser (*Ger.*) Rose water.

Rosenzweig (*Ger.*) Rose branch.

Rosetti (*It.*) Dweller at the sign of the rose; or near where small roses grew.

Rosevear (*Eng.*) Dweller in the big heath or moor.

Rosewarne (*Eng.*) Dweller at the swampy heath.

Rosier (*Fr.*) One who cultivated roses; dweller on land overgrown with reeds; one who came from Rosier (rose; reed), in France.

Rosin (*Fr., Ger.*) Descendant of little Rose; one who came from Rosien, in Germany.

Rosinski (*Pol.*) One who came from Rosiho (dew), in Poland; or from Rosinski, in Byelorussia.

Rosler (*Ger.*) One who raised and sold flowers; one who came from Rossla or Rosslau, the names of places in Germany.

Rosner, Rossner (*Ger.*) One who rode a horse; one who came from Rosna, Rossen, or Roessen, the names of places in Germany; descendant of Rozzo, a pet form of names beginning with Hrod (famous), as Hrod-mund, Rothari, and Hrotfrid.

Rosoff, Rosov, Rosowski (*Rus.*) The son of Roza (rose).

Ross, Rosse (*Scot.*) Dweller at the promontory or peninsula; one who came from Ross (promontory), in Scotland.

Rossbach, Rossbacher (*Ger.*) One who came from Rossbach (swampy stream), the name of many places in Germany.

Rosseau (*Fr.*) Dweller among reeds.

Rosselli, Rossello (*Fr., It.*) One who raised and sold small horses; dweller near where roses grew.

Rosser (*Wel.*) Descendant of Rosser, Welsh form of Roger (fame, spear).

Rossetti, Rossetto (*It.*) One who had ruddy cheeks or red hair.

Rossi, Rossini, Rossa, Rosso (*It.*) The red-haired or ruddy-complexioned man; a miniaturist who used red minium in his work.

Rossiter (*Eng.*) One who came from Wroxeter (Virconion's Roman fort), in Shropshire.

Rossman (*Eng.*) Dweller at a promontory or peninsula.

Rossow, Rosso (*Pol.*) One who came from Russia (derived from the Rossi, a tribe of Norsemen flourishing in the ninth century), a Russian.

Rost (*Ger.*) Dweller at the sign of the gridiron or fire grate.

Rostick (*Pol.*) Descendant of Rostick, a pet form of Roshslav (who grows famous).

Roston (*Eng.*) One who came from Roston (village of Hrothsige's people), in Derbyshire.

Roswell (*Scot.*) One who came from Rosewell, in Midlothian; dweller near a spring in a marsh.

Rota (*It.*) Descendant of Rota, a pet form of Pierro, an Italian form of Peter (a rock).

Rotblatt, Rotblat (*Ger.*) Red leaf.

Rotella (*It.*) Descendant of Rotella, a pet form of Pierro, Italian form of

Peter (a rock); one who fought with a round shield.

Rotenberg, Rottenberg, Rottenberk (*Ger.*) One who came from Rotenberg or Rottenberg or Rotenburg (all meaning "red mountain"), the names of several places in Germany.

Roth, Rothe (*Ger., Eng.*) The red-haired or ruddy-complexioned man; one who came from Roth (red), the name of several places in Germany; descendant of Ruodo, a pet form of names beginning with Hrod (fame), as Hrodric, Hrodulf, and Hrodowin; dweller at the clearing.

Rothaus, Rothhauser (*Ger.*) One who came from Rothaus (red house), the name of two places in Germany.

Rothbart (*Ger.*) The man with the red beard.

Rothberg (*Ger.*) Dweller on the red hill.

Rothblatt (*Ger.*) Red leaf.

Rothblum (*Ger.*) Red flower.

Rothchild (*Ger.*) Variant of Rothschild, q.v.

Rothenbach (*Ger.*) One who came from Rothenbach (red stream), the name of several places in Germany.

Rothenberg, Rothenberger (*Ger.*) One who came from Rothenberg (red fortress), the name of several places in Germany.

Rothenbuhler (*Ger.*) One who came from Rothenbuhl (red hill), in Germany.

Rother (*Eng.*) One who came from Rother (oxen), the name of places in Hampshire and Sussex.

Rotherham (*Eng.*) One who came from Rotherham (village on the Rother, chief river), in the West Riding of Yorkshire.

Rothermel, Rothmel (*Ger.*) One clad in bright or colorful clothing; one attired in a fashionable manner.

Rothfeld, Rothfield (*Ger.*) Dweller in, or near, the red field.

Rothfuss (*Ger.*) Dweller at the sign of the red fox.

Rothgeb (*Ger.*) One who advises or counsels others.

Rothkopf (*Ger.*) One with a red head, i.e., red-haired.

Rothkugel (*Ger.*) One who made and sold red hoods or cowled coats; nickname for one who wore a red cowl.

Rothman, Rothmann (*Ger.*) One who had red hair; descendant of Hrodman (fame, man).

Rothrauff (*Ger.*) Descendant of Hrodulfr (fame, wolf; red wolf).

Rothrock (*Ger.*) One dressed in a red coat.

Rothschild (*Ger.*) The great banking family drew its name from the red shield which swung before the shop door in Frankfurt.

Rothstein (*Ger.*) Dweller at, or near, a red stone.

Rothwein (*Ger.*) One who made and sold red wine.

Rothwell (*Eng.*) One who came from Rothwell (spring or stream by a clearing), the name of several places in England; dweller near a red spring or stream.

Rotman (*Ger.*) The town councillor.

Rotolo (*It.*) One who made, or wrote on, scrolls.

Rotondo, Rotondi (*It.*) The fat, fleshy man; dweller near a circular building.

Rotter, Roter (*Eng., Ger.*) One who played a rote, a musical instrument of the violin class; one with red hair or a ruddy complexion; one who came from Roth (red), the name of several places in Germany.

Rough (*Eng.*) Dweller on, or near, the rough, uncultivated ground.

Roughton (*Eng.*) One who came from Roughton (rough ground homestead; rye farm), the name of places in Lincolnshire, Norfolk, and Shropshire.

Rouillard (*Fr.*) One who made and sold barrels and casks; dweller at the sign of the barrel.

Roulston (*Eng.*) One who came from Rowlston (Hrolf's homestead), in the East Riding of Yorkshire.

Rounds, Round (*Eng.*) The rotund, or plump, man; a variant of Rowan, q.v.

Rountree, Roundtree, Rowantree, Rowntree (*Eng., Scot.*) Dweller at, or near, a rowan tree (mountain ash); one who came from Rowantree, in Scotland.

Rouse, Roux, Rous (*Fr., Eng.*) The red-haired man; or one with a ruddy complexion.

Rousseau (*Fr.*) One with a ruddy complexion or with red hair.

Roussel (*Eng.*) Descendant of Russel (red); the little red-headed or ruddy-complexioned man.

Routledge (*Eng.*) One who came from Routledge (red pool), in Cumberland.

Roux (*Fr.*) One with red or reddish-brown hair or complexion.

Rover (*Ger.*) One who robbed on the highway, sometimes a robber knight.

Rovere (*It.*) Dweller near the English oak tree.

Rovin, Rovine, Rovins, Rovinsky (*Rus., Pol.*) Dweller at the canal or ditch.

Rovner (*Pol.*) One who came from Rover, in Poland.

Rowan, Rowen (*Eng., Ir.*) Dweller at, or near, a rowan tree (mountain ash); the little red-haired man.

Rowbotham, Rowbottom (*Eng.*) Dweller in the rough valley.

Rowbury (*Eng.*) One who came from Rowberrow (rough hill), the name of places in Somerset and Wight.

Rowden, Rowdon (*Eng.*) One who came from Rowden (rough hill), in Herefordshire.

Rowe, Row (*Eng.*) Dweller at the rough or uncultivated land; one who lived at the hedge-row; dweller in the row of houses.

Rowell, Rowells, Rowels, Rowel (*Eng.*) One who came from Rowell (roe stream), in Gloucestershire; dweller at a spring frequented by roes; descendant of little Rowland (fame, land).

Rowland, Rowlands (*Wel., Eng.*) Descen-

435

dant of Roland (fame, land); one who came from Rowland (roe wood), in Derbyshire.

Rowles (*Eng.*) Descendant of Roul or Roulf, contracted forms of Hrodwulf (fame, wolf).

Rowley, Rowlee (*Eng.*) One who came from Rowley (rough meadow), the name of several places in England.

Rowling, Rowlings (*Eng.*) Descendant of Roll, a pet form of Rolf (fame, wolf), and of Roland (fame, land).

Roxburgh, Roxbury, Roxbourgh (*Scot.*) One who came from Roxburgh (Hroc's castle), in Roxburghshire.

Roxby (*Eng.*) One who came from Roxby (Hrok's cowhouse; Rauth's village), the name of places in Lincolnshire and the North Riding of Yorkshire.

Roy, Roye (*Fr., Eng., Scot.*) One connected in some way with the king's household; one who played the part of a king in tournaments; the red-haired or ruddy man.

Royal, Royall, Royals (*Eng.*) One who came from Ryal (hill where rye grew), in Northumberland; descendant of Riulf (rule, wolf).

Royce, Royse (*Eng.*) Dweller at the sign of the rose; one who lived at the sign of the horse.

Royle (*Eng.*) Variant of Ryle, q.v.; descendant of Roll, a pet form of Rolf (fame, wolf), and of Roland (fame, land).

Royster (*Eng.*) A blustering, swaggering person, a roisterer, a bully.

Royston (*Eng.*) One who came from Royston (Roese's stone; Hror's homestead), the name of places in Hertfordshire and the West Riding of Yorkshire.

Rozanski (*Pol.*) One who came from Rozana, in Byelorussia.

Rozier (*Fr.*) Dweller near a rose bush.

Ruane, Ruan (*Ir.*) Descendant of little Ruadh (red); the red-haired or ruddy man.

Ruback, Rubach (*Ger.*) One who works with stone, a mason.

Rubel, Rubell (*Ger.*) One who raised and sold rape, a forage crop for sheep and hogs; one who raised and sold turnips.

Ruben, Rubens (*Eng., Ger.*) Descendant of Ruben (behold a son; renewer); one who came from Ruben, the name of two places in Germany.

Rubenfeld (*Ger.*) Dweller in, or near, a field of turnips.

Rubenstein, Rubinstein (*Ger.*) Ruby, or red precious stone; one who came from Rubenstein, in Germany.

Rubenstone (*Ger.*) Partially Englished form of Rubenstein, q.v.

Ruberg (*Ger.*) Dweller on the Ruberg, a mountain in Germany.

Rubin, Rubins (*Ger.*) One who came from Rubyn or Ruben (ruby stone), in Germany; descendant of Ruben (behold, a son; renewer).

Rubincam, Rubicam, Rubenkamp (*Ger.*) Dweller in, or near, a turnip field.

Rubino, Rubini (*It.*) Descendant of Rubino, a pet form of Cherubini (cherub); one with red hair or a ruddy complexion; one who dealt in rubies.

Rubinson, Rubinsohn (*Ger.*) The son of Rubin (precious stone).

Rubio (*Sp.*) One with red hair or a ruddy complexion; the fair, golden-haired person; one who came from Rubio (red) in Spain.

Ruby, Rubey (*Eng.*) One who came from Roubaix, in France; descendant of Ruby, a pet form of Reuben (behold, a son; renewer); red precious stone.

Rucci (*It.*) Descendant of Rucci, a pet form of Perucca, a variant of Pierro, an Italian form of Peter (a rock).

Ruch, Ruche (*Ger.*) The rough-haired man.

Rucinski (*Pol.*) Dweller at a place where rue (a medicinal herb) grew.

Ruck (*Ger.*) Descendant of Rocco, a pet form of names beginning with Hrok (to crow), as Rochold and Hroculf.

Rucker (*Ger.*) Descendant of Hrodgaer (fame, spear).

Ruczynski (*Pol., Rus., Ukr.*) Dweller near a brook or small stream.

Rudd, Ruud, Rude, Rud, Rudde (*Eng., Nor.*) One with a ruddy complexion; descendant of Rud, a pet form of Rudolf (fame, wolf); variant of Rood, q.v.; dweller in, or near, the clearing in the forest.

Ruddell, Ruddle (*Eng.*) Variant of Rudhall, q.v.

Ruddick, Ruddock, Rudduck (*Eng.*) Dweller at the sign of the robin.

Ruddy, Ruddie (*Eng.*) One with a red, or ruddy complexion; variant of Rudy, q.v.

Ruder, Ruderman (*Ger.*) Nickname for a sailor.

Rudge (*Eng.*) Dweller at, or near, a ridge or range of hills; one who came from Rudge (ridge), the name of places in Gloucestershire and Shropshire.

Rudhall (*Eng.*) One who came from Rudhall (red hall), in Gloucestershire; dweller in the red corner.

Rudi (*Ger.*) Descendant of Rudi, a pet form of Rudolph (fame, wolf), and Ralph (counsel, wolf).

Rudick (*Eng.*) Variant of Ruddick, q.v.

Rudin (*Rus.*) One with red hair.

Rudkin (*Ger.*) Descendant of little Rud, a pet form of such names as Rudolf (fame, wolf), and Rudger (fame, spear).

Rudley (*Eng.*) One who came from Rodley (grove where reeds grew), the name of places in Gloucestershire and the West Riding of Yorkshire.

Rudloff (*Ger.*) Descendant of Rudolf (fame, wolf), a dialectal form.

Rudman, Rudmann (*Ger.*) Descendant of Hrodman (fame, man); dweller in, or near, the swamp.

Rudney (*Eng.*) Variant of Rodney, q.v.

Rudnick, Rudnicki, Rudnik (*Pol.*) One who worked in a mine; dweller near a mine; one who came from Rudnik (red), the name of many places in Poland and Ukraine.

Rudnitsky, Rudnitzky, Rudnytzky (*Ukr.*) Variants of Rudnyckyj, q.v.

Rudnyckyj (*Ukr.*) One who came from Rudnyk, Rudnyky, or Rudnyca (red), in Ukraine; or who was the owner of these places.

Rudolph, Rudolf (*Eng., Ger.*) Descendant of Rudolf (fame, wolf).

Rudy (*Eng., Ger.*) Descendant of little Rud, a pet form of Rudolf (fame, wolf).

Rudyard (*Eng.*) One who came from Rudyard (garden where rue was grown), in Staffordshire.

Rudzinski (*Pol.*) Dweller near a mine where ore was obtained; one who had red hair or a ruddy complexion.

Rue (*Eng.*) Variant of Rew, q.v.; dweller near where rue grew.

Ruegg (*Ger.*) Descendant of Ruegg, a pet form of Rudiger (glory, spear).

Rueter (*Ger.*) Variant of Reuter, q.v.

Ruff, Ruf (*Eng., Fr.*) The red-haired, or ruddy, man.

Ruffin, Ruffing, Ruffins (*Eng., Fr.*) The little red-haired or ruddy-complexioned man; descendant of Ruffin or Rufinus (red), the name of several saints.

Ruffo, Rufo (*Sp.*) One with red hair or ruddy complexion; one with frizzed or curly hair.

Ruffolo, Ruffulo, Rufolo (*It.*) Descendant of Ruffuli (fame, wolf); one thought to possess the qualities of a horned owl.

Rufus (*Eng.*) Descendant of Rufus (red-haired).

Ruge, Rugg (*Eng., Du.*) Dweller at, or on, the ridge or range of hills; one who came from Rudge (ridge), the name of places in Gloucestershire and Shropshire.

Ruger (*Eng.*) Descendant of Roger (fame, spear).

Ruggeri, Ruggero (*It.*) Descendant of Ruggero, Italian form of Roger (fame, spear).

Ruggiero, Ruggieri (*It.*) Descendant of Ruggiero, Italian form of Roger (fame, spear).

Ruggles (*Eng.*) One who came from

Rugley (woodcock glade), in Northumberland.

Ruh (*Eng.*) Dweller on rough or uncultivated ground.

Ruhl, Ruhle (*Ger.*) Descendant of Ruhl, a pet form of Rudolf (fame, wolf).

Ruhland, Ruhlander (*Ger.*) One who came from Ruhland (boggy land), in Germany; descendant of Hrodlant (fame, land).

Ruiz (*Sp., Fr.*) The son of Ruy, a pet form of Rodrigo, Spanish form of Roderick (fame, rule); one who came from Ruiz, in Spain; dweller near a stream.

Rule (*Eng.*) One who came from Rule (hedgerow spring), in Staffordshire; descendant of Raoul (counsel, wolf).

Rulis (*Lat.*) Descendant of Rauls, Latvian form of Ralph (counsel, wolf).

Rullo (*Eng.*) Variant of Rollo, q.v.

Rumbaugh (*Ger.*) One who came from Rumbach, in Germany.

Rumble (*Eng.*) Descendant of Rumbeald (fame, bold).

Rumford (*Eng.*) One who came from Romford (wide river crossing), in Essex. Romford was pronounced "Rumford."

Ruml (*Cz., Rus.*) One who did not drink, a teetotaler.

Rumley (*Eng.*) One who came from Romiley (spacious river), in Kent.

Rummell, Rummel, Rummele (*Ger.*) Variant of Rommel, q.v.

Rummonds (*Eng.*) Descendant, or son, of Hruodmund (fame, protection).

Rumpf, Rumph (*Ger.*) The short fat man; the clumsy, coarse, uncouth person.

Rumsey (*Eng.*) Variant of Romsey, q.v.

Rund, Runde (*Ger.*) The round, or fat, man.

Rundle, Rundall, Rundell, Rundel (*Eng.*) One who came from Rundale (round valley), in Kent.

Rundlett (*Fr.*) The little rotund, or fat, man.

Runge, Rung (*Ger.*) Descendant of Runico (secret wisdom).

Runner (*Eng.*) One who carried messages, usually by foot.

Runyon, Runyan (*Eng.*) A mangy, scurvy person.

Rupp (*Ger.*) Descendant of Rupp (fame), a pet form of names beginning with Hrod (fame), as Hrotbald and Hrodobert.

Ruppel (*Eng.*) Descendant of little Rupp, a pet form of Ruppert (fame, bright); dweller near where rypel (a kind of grass) grew.

Ruppert, Rupert (*Eng.*) Descendant of Rupert, a variant of Robert (fame, bright).

Ruprecht (*Ger.*) Descendant of Ruprecht, a German variant of Robert (fame, bright).

Rusch (*Ger., Swis.*) Dweller in, or near, rushes or bent grass; dweller near an elm tree; an excitable person.

Ruscomb, Ruscombe (*Eng.*) One who came from Ruscombe (Rot's pasture), in Berkshire.

Rusden (*Eng.*) One who came from Roseden (valley where rushes grew), in Northumberland.

Rush (*Eng., Ger., Swis.*) Dweller near a clump of rushes; dweller near an elm tree; an excitable person.

Rushford (*Eng.*) One who came from Rushford (homestead where rushes grew), in Norfolk.

Rushforth (*Eng.*) One who came from Rushford (homestead overgrown with rushes), in Norfolk.

Rushing (*Ger.*) The son of Rusch (rose); dweller near an elm tree or pear tree.

Rushmore (*Eng.*) One who came from Rushmere (lake with rushes), the name of two places in Suffolk.

Rushton (*Eng.*) One who came from Rushton (homestead with rushes), the name of several places in England.

Rushworth (*Eng.*) Dweller at the homestead where rushes grew.

Rusin (*Pol.*) One who came from Rus, now Ukraine.

Rusk (*Sw., Dan.*) The valiant, brave, active man.

Ruskin (*Eng.*) Descendant of little Rous (red); or of Rus, a diminutive of Ruth (beauty; compassionate).

Rusnak (*Ukr.*) One who came from Rus, now Ukraine.

Russ (*Eng.*) The red-haired or ruddy-complexioned man; descendant of Russ, a pet form of Russell (diminutive of red).

Russakoff, Russakov (*Rus., Bulg.*) The son of the Russian; or of Russak (gray horse).

Russaw (*Rus.*) One who came from Russia, a Russian.

Russell (*Eng.*) The little red-haired man.

Russo, Russow (*Pol.*) One who came from Russia (from Rossi, a tribe of Norsemen in the ninth century).

Russock (*Eng.*) One who came from Rushock (clump of rushes), the name of places in Worcestershire and Herefordshire.

Russum (*Eng.*) One who came from Rusholme (rushes), in Lancashire.

Rust (*Eng., Scot.*) Shortened form of Russet (red-haired).

Rustin, Ruston (*Eng.*) One who came from Ruston (homestead in brushwood; Hror's homestead; roof rafters), the name of places in Norfolk and both the East Riding and the North Riding of Yorkshire.

Rutberg (*Sw.*) One who came from Rutberg, in Sweden.

Rutecki (*Ukr., Pol.*) Dweller near where rue was grown.

Rutenberg (*Ger.*) One who came from Rutenberg, in Germany.

Rutgers (*Du.*) The son of Rutger, Dutch form of Roger (fame, spear).

Ruth (*Ger.*) Descendant of Ruodo, a pet form of names beginning with Hrod (fame), as Hrotfrid, Rothhari, and Hrodmar.

Rutherford (*Scot.*) One who came from Rutherford (river crossing used by cattle), in Scotland.

Ruthven (*Scot.*) One who came from Ruthven (red place), the name of several places in Scotland.

Rutkowski (*Pol.*) Dweller at a place where rue grew.

Rutland (*Eng.*) One who came from Rutland (Rota's land), a county in England.

Rutledge (*Eng.*) Dweller at, or near, a red lake or pool; variant of Routledge, q.v.

Rutley (*Eng.*) Dweller in the red grove.

Rutsen (*Du.*) The son of Rut, or Ruut (fame).

Ruttenberg (*Ger., Pol.*) One who came from Rothenberg (red mountain), also called Rostarzewo, in Poland; or from Rutenberg or Rothenberg, the names of places in Germany.

Rutter (*Eng., Du., Ger.*) One who played the rote, a kind of fiddle; the trooper or horseman; variant of Reuter, q.v.

Ruud (*Nor.*) Dweller in the clearing.

Ruus (*Est.*) Dweller on gravelly land.

Ruusu (*Finn.*) Dweller at the sign of the rose; one who resided near a rose bush.

Ruxton (*Eng.*) Dweller in, or near, Hroc's homestead.

Ruzicka (*Cz.-Sl.*) Dweller at the sign of the little rose.

Ryall, Ryalls, Ryal, Ryals (*Eng.*) One who came from Ryal (rye hill), in Northumberland.

Ryan (*Ir.*) Grandson of Rian (little king).

Ryba (*Cz.-Sl., Pol.*) Dweller at the sign of the fish; one who sold fish.

Rybak, Ryback (*Pol.*) One who caught and sold fish, a fisherman.

Rybar (*Cz.-Sl.*) One who caught and sold fish, a fisherman.

Rybarczyk (*Pol.*) The son of the fisherman.

Rybicki (*Pol.*) Dweller at, or near, a fish pond.

Rychlak (*Pol.*) One who was always early or ahead of time.

Ryder (*Wel., Eng.*) The rider or trooper; a mounted guardian of a forest.

Rydzewski (*Pol.*) One who gathers and sells the meadow or common edible mushroom.

Rye (*Eng.*) One who came from Rye (at the island), in Sussex; dweller at the island or low-lying ground.

Ryerson, Ryersen (*Du.*) The son of Reyer or Reijer (rider).

Ryhal, Ryhall (*Eng.*) One who came from Ryhall (corner where rye was grown), in Rutland.

Rykaczewski (*Pol.*) One who roars or bellows.

Rykard (*Eng.*) Descendant of Ricard, an early English form of Richard (rule, hard).

Rylander, Ryland (*Eng.*) Dweller at, or on, the land where rye was grown.

Ryle, Ryles (*Eng.*) One who came from Ryle (rye hill), in Northumberland; dweller on a hill where rye was grown.

Ryman (*Eng.*) One who raised and sold rye.

Rymer (*Ger.*) Americanization of Reimer, q.v.

Rymshaw (*Eng.*) Dweller near the boundary thicket.

Rynkiewicz (*Pol.*) The son of the man who made utensils of earthenware, a potter.

Rynne, Rynn (*Eng.*) Dweller at a large drain or channel on the moor.

Rys (*Eng.*) Dweller near rushes; or in the brushwood.

Ryzinski (*Pol.*) One who had charge of the vestments in a church, a sexton; one who had red hair or a ruddy complexion.

Rzepka, Rzepski (*Pol.*) One who grew turnips; dweller near where turnips grew.

Rzymski (*Pol.*) One who came from Rome, a Roman.

Saal (*Ger.*) One who came from Saal (mud), the name of several places in Germany.

Saar (*Est., Ger.*) Dweller on an island; or near an ash tree; one who came from Saar, in Germany.

Saari (*Finn.*) Dweller on an island; dweller on, or near, a ridge.

Sabath, Sabbath (*Heb.*) Descendant of Sabath or Sabbatai, names given to boys born on the Sabbath; dweller near, or worker at, a Saturday market.

Sabatino, Sabatini (*It.*) Descendant of Sabbatino (name given to a child born on the Sabbath).

Sabato (*It.*) Descendant of Sabato (Saturday, a name given to one born on the Sabbath).

Sabb (*Eng.*) Descendant of Sabb, a pet form of Sabina (a Sabine, an ancient Italian tribe).

Saber (*Fr.*) The learned or scholarly man.

Sabin, Sabine (*Eng.*) Descendant of Sabin, a name from the ancient Italian tribe of the Sabines.

Sabino (*It.*) Descendant of Sabino, a name from the ancient Italian tribe of the Sabines.

Sable, Sabel, Sabol (*Ger., Fr., Rus.*) One who trapped sables for the fur; dweller at the sign of the sable; one who came from Sabel, the name of two places in Germany and one in France.

Sablosky (*Pol.*) Variant of Szablewski, q.v.

Sabo (*Hun.*) One who made outer garments, a tailor.

Sacca, Sacchetti (*It.*) Variant of Sacco, q.v.

Sacco (*It., Ger.*) Descendant of Sacco, a pet form of Isacco or Isaak (he who laughs); descendant of Sacco, a pet form of names beginning with Sache (legal action), such as Sacbert and Saghart; one who made and sold sackcloth; one who made and sold purses or pouches.

Sacerdote (*Fr.*) One who performed sacerdotal functions, a priest.

Sacher, Sachar (*Ger., Heb.*) The peddler or itinerant dealer; descendant of Sacher, a form of Zacharias (whom Jehovah remembers); or of Sacher, a shortened form of Issachar (reward).

Sacheverell (*Eng.*) One who came from

Sault-Chevreuil (roebuck forest), in Normandy.

Sachs (*Ger.*) One who came from Saxony; a name taken by the Jewish refugees from Stendal, in memory of the martyrdom of their companions, from the Hebrew initials for "The Holy Seed of Stendal."

Sack (*Eng., Fr., Ger.*) One who made and sold sacks and bags; one who came from Le Sacq, in France; descendant of Sak or Saak, pet forms of Isaac (he who laughs).

Sacker (*Eng.*) One who made and sold sacks and bags.

Sackerson (*Eng.*) The son of Zachary (whom Jehovah remembers; pure).

Sackett, Sacket, Sackette (*Eng.*) Descendant of little Sacq (adversary).

Sackley (*Fr., Eng.*) One who came from Saclay, in France.

Sackman, Sackmann (*Ger.*) The man in charge of baggage for the camp; one who robs or takes by force, a plunderer.

Sacknoff (*Rus.*) The son of little Sakhon.

Sacks, Sack (*Fr.*) One who made, or sold, sackcloth or bags; descendant of Sack, a pet form of Isaac (the laugher); one who came from Sacq, in France.

Sackson (*Eng.*) Variant of Saxon, q.v.

Sackville (*Eng.*) One who came from Sacquenville (Sachano's estate), in Eure.

Sacwright (*Eng.*) One who made and sold sacks.

Saddington (*Eng.*) One who came from Saddington (village of Saegeat's people), in Leicestershire.

Sadek, Sadecki (*Pol.*) Dweller in, or near, a small orchard.

Sadler, Saddler, Sadtler (*Eng.*) One who made, or dealt in, saddles.

Sadoff (*Rus.*) Dweller near a garden or orchard.

Sadowski (*Pol.*) Dweller at, or near, an orchard.

Sadowy (*Pol.*) One who tended a garden.

Saenz, Sainz (*Sp.*) The saintly or holy person; the son of Sancho (sanctified).

Saez (*Sp.*) Variant of Saenz, q.v.

Safer, Saffer, Safar, Saffir (*Eng., Fr.*) One who ate to excess; descendant of Sabaric (mind, rule).

Saffold (*Eng.*) Dweller near, or worker at, a fold or pen for sheep; dweller at the sign of a sea fowl such as a cormorant.

Safford (*Eng.*) One who came from Salford (ford where sallows or willow trees grew; river crossing over which salt was carried), the name of places in Bedfordshire, Lancashire, and Oxfordshire; or from Seaford (ford by the sea), in Sussex; dweller at the ford where willows grew.

Saffran, Saffren, Saffern (*Ger.*) One who deals in saffron, a dyestuff obtained from the crocus.

Safran, Safren, Safrin, Safron (*Ger., Cz.*) One who produced and sold saffron.

Safstrom (*Sw.*) Bulrush, stream.

Saft (*Ger.*) The gentle, soft, mild man.

Sagan (*Fr.*) A commoner from the Southeast clothed in a soldier's coat; the titled stranger.

Sage (*Eng., Fr.*) The wise or learned person.

Sager (*Eng.*) Descendant of Sagar (sea, spear); one who sawed timber into boards.

Saget, Sagett, Sagel (*Fr.*) The little erudite, scholarly man.

Sagot (*Fr.*) One who habitually wore a small soldier's coat.

Sahagian, Sahakian (*Arm.*) The son of Sahag or Sahak.

Sahl (*Ger.*) Dweller in a swampy place.

Sahlman, Sahlmann (*Ger.*) Dweller on, or near, a tract of swampy land.

Sahm (*Ger.*) Descendant of Sahm, a pet form of Samobor; one who sold seed and grain.

Saia (*It.*) Descendant of Saia, pet form of Isaia, Italian form of Isaiah (salvation of Jah); and of Osaia, Italian form of Oshea (He has saved); one who wove and sold a twilled worsted fabric, serge, often used in doublets; or who sold or wore doublets.

Said (*Tur.*) Descendant of Said (lucky).

Saile, Sails (*Eng.*) Variant of Sale, q.v.

Sailer, Sailor (*Eng.*) One who danced at fair and festival; one who worked on a ship, a seaman.

Sailsbery (*Eng.*) One who came from Salesbury (fort where sallows grew), in Lancashire.

Sain, Saine (*Fr.*) The large, fat man; one who is sound and healthy; one who butchered and sold pork.

Saindon (*Eng.*) Variant of Sandon, q.v.

Sainsbury, Saintsbury (*Eng.*) One who came from Saintbury (Saewine's fort), in Gloucestershire.

St. Amant, St. Amand (*Fr.*) One who came from St. Amand, the name of several villages in France.

St. Clair, St. Claire, St. Clare (*Eng.*) One who came from St. Clair (bright), the name of several villages in France.

Saint-Gaudens (*Fr.*) Descendant of Gaudentius (rejoicing), the name of five different saints revered by the Catholic Church.

St. George (*Fr.*) One who came from St. Georges in France.

St. Germain, St. Germaine (*Fr.*) One who came from St. Germain, the name of many places in France.

St. James (*Fr.*) One who came from St. James, in France.

St. John (*Eng.*) One who came from St. Jean, a common French place name.

St. Lawrence (*Fr.*) One who came from St. Laurent, in France.

St. Leger (*Fr.*) One who came from St. Leger, in France.

St. Louis (*Fr.*) One who came from St. Louis, the name of several places in France.

St. Martin (*Fr., Scot.*) One who came from St. Martin, the name of many places in France.

St. Pierre (*Fr.*) One who came from St. Pierre, the name of many places in France.

Saint-Saens (*Fr.*) One who came from Saint-Saens (Sidonius), in France.

Saintsbury (*Eng.*) One who came from Saintsbury (Swein's camp), in Gloucestershire.

Sainz (*Sp.*) Variant of Saenz, q.v.

Saito (*Jap.*) Festival, wisteria.

Saiz, Saez (*Sp.*) Variant of Saenz, q.v.

Sajdak (*Ukr., Pol.*) One who made and sold quivers, that is, cases for carrying arrows.

Sak (*Ger.*) Descendant of Sak, a pet form of Isaak, German form of Isaac (he who laughs).

Sakamoto (*Jap.*) Slope, base.

Sakata (*Jap.*) Slope, rice field.

Sakowicz, Sakowitz (*Pol.*) One who used a drag net to catch fish; the son of Sak, a pet form of Isaac (he who laughs).

Saks (*Ger.*) A name taken from the Hebrew initials for "Seed of the Holy Martyrs of Spire"; variant of Sax, q.v.; descendant of Sak, a pet form of Isaak, German form of Isaac (he who laughs).

Sakuma (*Jap.*) Help, long, space.

Sala (*Fr., It.*) Dweller, or worker, in a manor or country house.

Salaman, Salamon, Salamone (*Eng., Fr.*) Descendant of Salomon, Old French form of Solomon (peaceful; worshiper of the god Shalman).

Salandra, Salandria (*It.*) Dweller at the sign of the salamander; one thought to have the characteristics of a salamander.

Salas (*Sp.*) One who came from Salas (dwelling places; halls), in Spain.

Salazar (*Sp.*) One who came from Salazar (corral; manor house), in Spain; dweller in, or near, the house or palace; dweller near the place sacred to St. Lazar.

Salberg (*Nor.*) One who came from Salberg (saddle-shaped mountain), in Norway.

Salcedo (*Sp.*) Dweller in, or near, a damp spot overgrown with trees; one who came from Salcedo (grove of willow trees), in Spain.

Saldan, Salden (*Eng.*) One who came from Salden (hill with a ledge), in Buckinghamshire.

Saldana (*Sp.*) One who came from Saldana, in Spain.

Sale, Salle, Sales (*Eng., Fr.*) Dweller in, or near, the manor house; servant in the principal room of the manor house; one who came from Sale (sallow), in Cheshire.

Salemi (*It.*) One who came from Salemi, in Sicily.

Salerno (*It.*) One who came from Salerno, a province and city in Italy.

Salesky (*Pol.*) Variant of Zaleski, q.v.

Salgado (*Sp.*) Dweller near where mountain spinach grew.

Salinas (*Sp.*) Worker in a salt mine; one who came from Salinas in Spain.

Salinger (*Ger.*) One who came from Salingen (wet place), in Germany; corruption of Solomon, q.v.

Salis (*Fr., Eng.*) Dweller at a place where salt is produced; dweller near, or worker at, the manor house.

Salisbury (*Eng.*) One who came from Salisbury (Searu's stronghold; armor fort), in Wiltshire.

Salk (*Ger., Du.*) Dweller near a willow tree.

Salkeld (*Eng.*) One who came from Salkeld (sallow wood), in Cumberland.

Salkin, Salkind (*Heb.*) Descendant of Salkin, an endearing form of Shlomo, Hebrew form of Solomon (peaceful); or of little Sal, a pet form of Salaman (peace).

Sall (*Eng.*) One who came from Sall (sallow wood), in Norfolk; the servant at the hall; descendant of Sall, a pet form of Solomon (peaceful; worshiper of the god Shalman); or of Saul (desire; asked for).

Sallard (*Fr.*) One who dealt in salt.

Saller (*Ger.*) Dweller near, or among, willow trees.

Salley, Sally, Sallee, Sallie (*Eng.*) Dweller in, or by, a grove where sallow grew; or on an island where sallow grew; or near the willow trees.

Salm (*Est.*) Dweller near a strait or narrow waterway.

Salmon, Salomon, Salman, Salomone (*Eng., Fr.*) Descendant of Solomon (peaceful; worshiper of the god Shalman).

Salon (*Fr.*) One who came from Salon (little chamber), the name of two places in France.

Salsberg, Salsburg (*Ger.*) Variant of Salzberg, q.v.

Salsbury (*Eng.*) Variant of Salisbury, q.v.

Salt (*Eng.*) One who came from Salt (salt-works), in Staffordshire.

Saltarelli (*It.*) Nickname for one with the characteristics of a grasshopper.

Salter, Saltman, Salzer (*Eng.*) One who processed or sold salt; one who came from Salter (salt hut), in Cumberland; one who played the psaltery.

Saltiel (*Fr.*) One employed as a forest ranger.

Salton (*Eng.*) One who came from Salton (homestead where sallow grew), in the North Riding of Yorkshire.

Saltonstall (*Eng.*) One who came from Salternstall (salt works place), in Kent.

Saltz, Saltzman, Saltzmann (*Ger., Heb.*) One who processed and sold salt.

Saltzberg, Saltsberg (*Ger.*) One who came from Saltzberg (salt fortress), in Germany.

Saltzer (*Ger.*) Variant of Salzer, q.v.

Salvador (*Sp., Port.*) Descendant of Salvador (Savior, referring to Christ Jesus); one who came from Salvador (Savior), in Portugal; or from Salvador, the name of several places in Spain.

Salvage (*Eng.*) The old French form of Savage, q.v.

Salvaggio, Salvagio (*It.*) Nickname for one who frightens others.

Salvato, Salvati (*It.*) One who has been saved from some mishap.

Salvatore, Salvatori (*It.*) Descendant of

Salvatore (Savior, referring to Christ Jesus).

Salvi, Salvo (*It.*) One who frequently employed the phrases Diotisalvi and Salvidio (God save you).

Salvin (*Eng.*) Descendant of Silvanus, (woods; god of the forests); or of Salvius, an obscure seventh century French saint.

Salz (*Ger.*) One who dealt in salt.

Salzberg, Salzburg (*Ger.*) One who came from Salzberg or Salzburg (salt hill), the names of places in Germany; or from Salzburg, in Austria.

Salzer (*Ger.*) One who came from Salz (salt), the name of several places in Germany; one who processed and sold salt; one who processed and sold salt fish.

Salzman, Salzmann (*Ger.*) One who processed, or sold, salt.

Samanns, Samans (*Eng.*) Variant of Sammons, q.v.

Sambuca, Sambuco (*It.*) Dweller near an elder tree.

Samet, Samit, Samitz (*Ger.*) One who weaves and sells velvet.

Sammartino (*It.*) One who came from Sammartino (place of St. Martin), in Italy.

Sammons, Sammon, Sammonds (*Eng.*) Descendant of Solomon (peaceful; worshiper of the god Shalman).

Samojla (*Rom.*) Descendant of Samoila, Romanian form of Samuel (God hath heard; name of God; Shem is God).

Samp (*Eng.*) A contraction of Sampson, q.v.

Sample, Samples (*Fr.*) One who came from St. Paul (small), the name of several places in France.

Sampson (*Eng., Fr.*) The son of Sam, a pet form of Samuel (God hath heard; name of God; Shem is God); one who came from St. Samson, the name of several places in France.

Samson (*Eng., Fr.*) The son of Sam, a short form of Samuel (God hath heard; name of God; Shem is God);

descendant of Samson (splendid sun).

Samuels, Samuelson, Samuel (*Eng., Sw.*) The son of Samuel (God hath heard; name of God; Shem is God);

Sanabria (*Sp.*) One who came from La Sanabria, a region in Spain.

Sanborn (*Eng.*) One who came from Sambourn (sandy stream), in Warwickshire.

Sanchez (*Sp.*) The son of Sancho (sanctified).

Sandaker (*Eng.*) Dweller on, or near, a sandy field.

Sandall (*Eng.*) One who came from Sandal (sandy corner or enclosure), in the West Riding of Yorkshire.

Sandberg, Sandburg (*Ger., Sw.*) Dweller on a sandy hill; one who came from Sandberg (sandy hill), in Germany; dweller on a fortified place; sand, mountain.

Sandell, Sandle (*Eng.*) Variant of Sandall, q.v.

Sanderlin (*Eng., Ger.*) Descendant of little Sander, a pet form of Alexander (helper of mankind).

Sanders, Sander (*Scot., Eng., Ger.*) The son of Sander, an abbreviation of Alexander (helper of mankind).

Sanderson (*Scot., Eng.*) The son of Sander, a pet form of Alexander (helper of mankind).

Sandford (*Eng.*) One who came from Sandford (sandy river crossing), the name of seven places in England.

Sandidge (*Eng.*) One who came from Sandridge (sandy ridge), in Devonshire.

Sandifer, Sandefur (*Eng., Nor.*) Dweller at the sandy bay; or at the sandy ford.

Sandilands (*Scot.*) One who came from Sandilands (sandy land), in Scotland).

Sandler (*Eng., Heb.*) One who carts sand or gravel; one who repaired shoes, a cobbler.

Sandman, Sandmann (*Ger.*) Dweller on a sandy place.

Sandon, Sandone (*Eng.*) One who came

from Sandown (sandy enclosure), in Wight; or from Sandon (sand hill), the name of several places in England.

Sandor (*Sl., Hun.*) Descendant of Sandor, a Slovakian and Hungarian form of Alexander (helper of mankind).

Sandos (*Sp.*) The saintly or holy man.

Sandoval (*Sp.*) One who came from Sandoval, in Spain.

Sandquist (*Sw.*) Sand, twig.

Sands, Sand, Sande (*Eng.*) One who came from Send (sandy place), in Surrey.

Sandstead (*Eng.*) One who came from Sanderstead (sandy homestead), in Surrey.

Sandstrom (*Sw.*) Sand, stream.

Sandy (*Eng.*) One who came from Sandy (sandy island), in Bedfordshire.

Sanfilippo, San Filippo, Sanfillippo (*It.*) Follower of St. Philip; dweller near a church dedicated to St. Philip (lover of horses).

Sanford (*Eng.*) One who came from Sandford (sandy ford), the name of several places in England.

Sanger, Sangster (*Eng.*) One who sang in church; a chorister.

Sankey (*Eng.*) One who came from Sankey (holy), in Lancashire; dweller near the Sankey, a brook in Lancashire.

San Martin (*Sp.*) One who came from San Martin (St. Martin), the name of several places in Spain.

Sansburn (*Eng.*) Variant of Sanborn, q.v.

Sansbury (*Eng.*) Variant of Saintsbury, q.v.

Sanschagrin (*Fr.*) One who is without trouble, worry, or care.

Sanson (*Eng., Fr.*) Variant of Samson, q.v.

Sansone (*It.*) Descendant of Sansone (splendid sun).

Santacaterina (*It.*) Dweller near the church dedicated to Saint Catherine.

Santacroce (*It.*) Dweller near the church of the Holy Cross.

Santamaria (*Fr.*) One who came from Santa-Maria (St. Mary), in France.

Santana (*Sp.*) One who came from Santana (Saint Ana), in Spain.

Santangelo (*It.*) One who came from Sant'Angelo (saint angel), in Italy.

Santarelli, Santarella (*It.*) The saintly or devout person.

Santarone (*It.*) One who made saintly images.

Santella, Santelli (*It.*) The saintly, devout person.

Santerre (*Fr.*) One who owned no land.

Santiago (*Sp.*) One who came from Santiago (St. James), in Spain.

Santini, Santino, Santina (*It.*) Descendant of Santino (sacred).

Santo (*It.*) One with a saintly nature; descendant of Santo (saint).

Santoro, Santore, Santori, Santora (*It.*) One who made and sold saintly images.

Santos (*Port., Sp.*) One who came from Dos Santos or Los Santos (of the saints), the names of places in Portugal and Spain.

Santry (*Eng.*) One who has taken sanctuary in a church or religious house; dweller near a shrine.

Santucci, Santelli, Santilli, Santillo (*It.*) The saintly or devout person; descendant of little Santo (saint).

Sanville (*Fr.*) One who came from Sainville (Sagin's domain), in France.

Saper, Sapir (*Ger.*) Variant of Shapiro, q.v.

Sapienza (*It.*) One with great learning or wisdom.

Saponara, Saponari, Saponaro (*It.*) One who made and sold soap.

Saporito (*It.*) The joyful, happy, pleased man.

Sapoznik, Saposnik, Sapoznick (*Rus.*) One who made and sold shoes, a shoemaker.

Sapp, Sappe (*Ger.*) Descendant of Sabbe, a short form of names beginning with Sache (legal action), such as Sacbert and Sagebrecht.

Sappenfield (*Ger.*) One who came from Sappenfeld, in Germany.

Sapper (*Ger.*) The heavy, cumbersome,

bulky, unwieldy man; one quick to seize things, greedy.

Sappington (*Eng.*) One who came from Sapperton (village of the soap-makers), the name of four places in England.

Saracco (*It.*) One who fished for herring.

Saraceno, Saraceni, Saracino (*It.*) One who came from the Near East; the cruel, wicked, or irreligious man; descendant of Saraceno (the Saracen).

Sard (*Eng.*) One who came from Sardinia, an island in the Mediterranean Sea.

Sardou (*Fr.*) One who came from Sardinia, an island in the Mediterranean Sea.

Sarg, Sarge (*Ger.*) One who made coffins.

Sargent, Sargeant, Sergeant (*Eng.*) One who worked as a servant; a tenant by military service under the rank of a knight; a court officer.

Sargis (*Lith.*) The guard or watchman.

Sarkauskas (*Lith.*) One who came from Sarkauskas (place of magpies), in Lithuania.

Sarkioglu (*Tur.*) The son of the singer.

Sarkisian, Sarkessian (*Arm.*) The son of the saint.

Sarle (*Eng.*) Variant of Serle, q.v.

Sarna (*Pol.*) Dweller at the sign of the roe deer; one thought to possess some of the qualities of a roe deer; one who came from Sarnay (place where deer were found), in Poland.

Sarne (*Wel.*) Dweller near the road.

Sarno (*It., Sp.*) One who came from Sarno, in Italy; one with an itch; the scabrous man.

Sarnoff (*Ukr.*) The son of Sarna (deer).

Sarnow, Sarnowski (*Pol.*) One who came from Sarnowa (place where roe deer were found).

Saroyan (*Arm.*) A corruption of the Armenian *Saro Khan* (mountain prince).

Sarro (*Sp.*) One with yellow or discolored teeth.

Sarsfield (*Eng.*) Dweller in, or near, the open country belonging to Sare.

Sartori, Sartore, Sarto (*It.*) One who made outer garments, a tailor.

Sarzynski (*Cz.-Sl., Pol.*) One who dealt in raw silk or other fabric.

Sasaki (*Jap.*) Help, help, tree.

Sass, Sasse, Sasser (*Eng., Du.*) Dweller at, or near, a willow tree; or at a lock in a river.

Sasseville (*Fr.*) One who came from Sasseville (farming lease place), in France.

Sasso, Sassa, Sassi (*It.*) One who came from Lo Sasso (stone), a province of Rome; dweller near a rock or stone.

Sasson (*Fr.*) Descendant of little Sahso (Saxon).

Satchell, Satchel (*Eng.*) Descendant of little Sacq (adversary); metonymic for a maker of small bags.

Saterlund (*Nor.*) Dweller at the farm grove, a farm name.

Sather (*Nor.*) Dweller on the mountain pasture.

Satin (*Fr.*) One who produced and sold a fabric with a satin weave.

Satinsky (*Pol.*) Dweller beyond the fence.

Sato (*Jap.*) Help, wisteria.

Sattelmacher (*Ger.*) One who made and sold saddles.

Satterfield (*Eng.*) Dweller in a hut in open country; or in, or near, the hill pasture; or in, or near, the field where robbers gathered.

Satterlee, Satterley (*Eng.*) One who came from Satterleigh (robbers' wood), in Devonshire.

Satterthwaite, Satterwhite (*Eng.*) One who came from Satterthwaite (clearing by a hut), in Lancashire.

Sattler (*Ger.*) One who made and sold saddles.

Saturday (*Eng.*) One who came from Satterleigh (robber's grove), in Devonshire.

Satz (*Ger.*) One who settled or commenced to reside on the land; the newcomer or recent settler.

Sauber (*Ger.*) The clean, neat man.

Sauceman (*Eng.*) One who makes and sells sauces and condiments; or is in charge of the saucery in a large household.

Saucerman (*Eng.*) One who makes and sells saucers and other shallow dishes.

Saucier, Saucer, Sauser, Sausser (*Fr., Eng.*) One who made and sold sauces, mustard, etc.; one in charge of that department of the kitchen where sauces were made in large households.

Sauer (*Ger.*) The sour or morose person; the sower.

Sauerbaum (*Ger.*) One who came from Sauerbrunn (south or swampy stream), in Germany.

Sauerbier (*Ger., Du.*) One who brews and sells sour beer or ale.

Sauerbrey (*Ger.*) One who prepared beer and ale from malt and hops, a brewer.

Sauerwein (*Ger.*) One who pressed and sold the juice of green fruit; one who sold vinegar.

Saul, Saull, Sauls (*Eng.*) Descendant of Saul (desire; asked for); one who came from Saul (sallow wood), in Gloucestershire; or from Sall (sallow wood), in Norfolk.

Saulnier (*Fr.*) One who gathered, processed, or sold, salt.

Saulsberry, Saulsbury, Saulsburry (*Eng.*) Variant of Salisbury, q.v.

Sault (*Eng.*) Variant of Salt, q.v.

Saunders, Saunder (*Scot., Eng.*) The son of Saunder, an abbreviation of Alexander (helper of mankind).

Sauter, Sautner (*Ger., Eng.*) One who sewed shoes, a shoemaker; one who cuts and sews cloth, a tailor; variant of Salter, q.v.

Sautier (*Fr.*) One who guarded the forest, a forest keeper; one who played on the psaltery.

Sautter (*Ger.*) One who made or repaired shoes.

Sauvage (*Fr.*) French form of Savage, q.v.

Sauvageau, Sauvageot (*Fr.*) The little, uncivilized, unsociable man.

Savage (*Eng., Ir.*) The wild or fierce

man; one who had rough or uncouth manners.

Savarin, Saverin (*Fr.*) Variant of Severin, q.v.

Savidge (*Eng.*) Variant of Savage, q.v.

Saville, Savill (*Eng.*) One who came from Saville or Sauville (willow estate), the names of places in France.

Savin (*Fr.*) Descendant of Savin, French form of Sabinus (Sabine tribe), a fourth century saint.

Savini, Savino (*It.*) Descendant of Savino, a name from the ancient Italian tribe of the Sabines.

Savio (*It.*) The wise, learned man, a sage.

Savoy, Savoye (*Fr.*) One who came from Savoy or Sauvoy, the names of places in France.

Sawa (*Pol.*) Descendant of Sawa (desire).

Sawdon (*Eng.*) One who came from Sawdon (valley where sallows or willows grew), in the North Riding of Yorkshire.

Sawhill (*Eng.*) Dweller on the hill where sallows or willow trees grew.

Sawicki (*Pol., Ukr.*) The son of Sawa (desire).

Sawin, Sawinski (*Pol., Ukr., Rus.*) Descendant of Sawa (desire).

Sawka (*Pol.*) Descendant of Sawka, a pet form of Sawa (desire).

Sawrey (*Eng.*) One who came from Sawrey (muddy place), in Lancashire.

Sawyer, Sawier, Sawyier (*Eng.*) One who cut timber into boards or slats.

Sax, Saxon, Saxe (*Eng.*) One who came from Saxony (place of the men who were armed with the short sword), now Holstein; descendant of Saxa, Saxo or Seaxa (short sword). See also Sacks.

Saxelby (*Eng.*) One who came from Saxelby (Saxulf's homestead), in Leicestershire.

Saxer (*Swis.*) One who came from Sax (craig), in Switzerland.

Saxinger (*Ger.*) One who came from Saxing, in Germany.

Saxon (*Eng.*) One who came from Sax-

ton (village of the Saxons), the name
of places in Cambridgeshire and the
West Riding of Yorkshire; descendant of Saxa, a pet form of names
beginning with Sax or Seax (sword),
as Seaxbald and Seaxbeorht.

Saxton (*Eng.*) One who came from Saxton (village of the Saxons), the name
of places in Cambridgeshire and the
West Riding of Yorkshire.

Sayce, Sayse (*Wel.*) The foreigner; the
Englishman.

Sayers, Sayre, Sayres, Sayer (*Eng.*) One
who sold silk or serge; one who
assayed or tested metals, or tasted
food; descendant of Saer or Sayer
(victory, people).

Sayles, Sayle (*Eng.*) Dweller in, or near,
a hall; one who worked in the din-
ing hall; one who came from Sale
(sallow), in Cheshire; dweller near
a mire or pool.

Saylor, Saylors (*Eng., Ger.*) Variant of
Sailer, q.v.; Americanization of Seiler,
q.v.

Sayward (*Eng.*) The sea warden or coast
guard; descendant of Saeward (sea,
protection).

Sbarbaro, Sbarboro (*It.*) Descendant of
Barbaro (the stranger); the foreigner,
one in a rude, uncivilized state.

Sbraccia (*It.*) One who habitually brags
or boasts.

Scala, Scalea, Scali (*It.*) One who came
from Scala (stairs), in Italy; descendant of Scala, a pet form of Pasquale (suffering); dweller on a stair-
like path or road.

Scales (*Eng.*) One who came from Scales
(hut or temporary shelter), the name
of several places in England; dweller
in the hut or shed.

Scaletta (*It.*) Descendant of little Scala,
a pet form of Pasquale (suffering);
one who came from Scaletta, in
Sicily.

Scally (*Eng.*) One who came from
Scalby (Skalli's homestead), in the
East Riding of Yorkshire.

Scaltrito (*It.*) The clever, skilful, intel-

ligent man, but applied sometimes
in a derogatory sense.

Scalzitti (*It.*) One who was in the habit
of going barefoot.

Scalzo (*It.*) The unshod or barefoot man;
one who went on a pilgrimage barefoot.

Scampton (*Eng.*) One who came
from Scampton (short homestead;
Skammi's homestead), in Lincolnshire.

Scanlan, Scanlon (*Ir.*) Grandson of little
Scannal (scandal).

Scannapieco (*It.*) One who cut meat, a
butcher.

Scannell, Scannel (*Ir.*) Grandson of
Scannal (scandal).

Scantling, Scantlin (*Eng.*) One who
builds houses using scantlings, a
carpenter.

Scarborough, Scarbrough, Scarbro (*Eng.*)
One who came from Scarborough
(Skarthi's fortified place), in the
North Riding of Yorkshire.

Scardina, Scardino, Scardine (*It.*) Descendant of Cardo, a pet form of
Riccardo, Italian form of Richard
(rule, hard).

Scargill, Scargle (*Eng.*) One who came
from Scargill (valley frequented by
mergansers, that is, fish-eating ducks),
in the North Riding of Yorkshire.

Scarlata, Scarlati (*It.*) One usually
dressed in scarlet cloth.

Scarlett (*Scot., Eng.*) One with yellow-
ish-red complexion or dress.

Scarpelli, Scarpetti, Scarpa (*It.*) One
who made and sold shoes; one with
unduly large or small feet; one who
chiseled stone.

Scattergood (*Eng.*) One who scatters his
goods, a nickname for either a phi-
lanthropist or a prodigal.

Scavo (*It.*) Dweller near a hollow, ditch,
or pit.

Scavuzzo (*It.*) Dweller near where wheat
was grown; one with the characteristics of a snail.

Schaaf, Schaaff (*Du.*) Dweller at the sign
of the carpenter's plane, probably a
carpenter.

Schaafsma (*Du.*) The son of the carpenter.

Schaal (*Ger.*) One who came from Schaala (muddy water), in Germany; one who made and sold basins and bowls.

Schaap (*Du.*) Dweller at the sign of the sheep; one who took care of sheep.

Schacht (*Ger., Du.*) Dweller at, or near, a mine; dweller on a ridge or tongue of land.

Schachter, Schachtman (*Ger.*) One who slaughtered cattle and sold meat in accordance with Jewish ritual.

Schad, Schade (*Ger.*) One who destroyed property; or who robbed or plundered; dweller in, or near, a moor or fen.

Schaefer, Schaffer, Schafer, Schaeffer (*Ger.*) One who took care of sheep, a shepherd.

Schaffner (*Ger.*) The manager, or steward, of a household.

Schaible (*Ger.*) Dweller at the sign of the sheaf.

Schairer (*Ger.*) Dweller near a barn or granary.

Schalk (*Ger.*) One who worked for another, a servant.

Schall, Schaller (*Ger.*) One who boasts, but does not produce; a talkative or garrulous person; dweller near a stone slab; one who worked for another, a servant.

Schanbacher (*Ger.*) One who came from Schanbach (swamp plants), in Germany.

Schank, Schanker (*Ger.*) One who sold liquor, a publican.

Schantz, Schanz (*Ger.*) One who made and sold peasants' smocks.

Schapiro (*Ger.*) Variant of Shapiro, q.v.

Scharf, Scharff (*Ger.*) An acute, keen-witted, or sharp person.

Schattner (*Ger.*) One who came from Schattin (shady place), in Germany.

Schatz (*Ger., Heb.*) One who acted as representative of the congregation; a leader in congregational prayers; the dear or beloved person; contraction of Sheliah Tzibbur (minister of the congregation).

Schatzmann (*Ger.*) One who had charge of the treasury.

Schaub (*Ger.*) Dweller at the sign of the sheaf.

Schauer (*Ger.*) One who came from Schauen, in Germany; descendant of Scuro (storm of battle); one related in some way to a storm or bad weather.

Schauffele (*Ger.*) One who made and sold shovels.

Schaum (*Ger.*) Nickname for a cook or gossiper.

Schechter, Schechtman, Schecter, Schectman (*Ger.*) Variant of Schachter, q.v.

Scheck (*Ger.*) Dweller at the sign of the roan horse; one who made and sold certain quilted, tight-fitting coats.

Scheel, Scheele (*Ger., Du.*) One who was crooked or bent, a cripple; one who was cross-eyed; one who came from Scheel (bend), in Germany.

Scheer (*Ger., Du.*) Dweller at the sign of the shears, probably a tailor; one who cut hair or cloth.

Scheffler (*Ger.*) One who made casks and barrels, a cooper.

Scheibel, Scheible, Scheibe, Scheib (*Ger.*) Dweller on a round plain or field; or near some round or ball-like object; dweller at the sign of the bundle of straw.

Scheid, Scheider (*Ger.*) One who came from Scheid (border), the name of several places in Germany.

Scheidle, Scheidl, Scheidel, Scheidell (*Ger.*) Dweller near the border; one who acted as a mediator or go-between.

Scheidt, Scheiter (*Ger.*) One who came from Scheidt (border), the name of several places in Germany.

Scheier, Scheiee (*Ger.*) One who came from Scheie (forest place), in Germany; one who made and sold scarves or kerchiefs worn on the head.

Schein, Scheiner (*Ger.*) The distinguished, handsome, or outstanding man; the fine, well-bred, polite man; one who came from Schonau (beautiful meadow), the name of many places in Germany.

Scheinberg (*Ger.*) Dweller on the Scheinberg (bright mountain), a mountain in Germany.

Scheinblum (*Ger.*) Dweller where bright flowers grew.

Scheinfeld, Scheinfeldt, Scheinfield (*Ger.*) Dweller in the bright, blooming field.

Schell, Schelle (*Ger.*) One who is easily irritated; the wild or noisy man; variant of Scheel, q.v.; dweller at the sign of the stallion; one with the qualities of a steed or stallion.

Schellenberg, Schellenberger (*Ger.*) One who came from Schellenberg (bell mountain), the name of several places in Germany.

Scheller (*Ger.*) The loud, noisy, unruly man.

Schelling (*Ger.*) Variant of Schilling, q.v.

Schellinger (*Ger.*) One who came from Schelingen, in Germany.

Schellsmith (*Ger.*) One who made bells.

Schemm (*Ger.*) One with a masklike face.

Schempp (*Ger.*) Variant of Schimpf, q.v.

Schenk, Schenke, Schenck (*Du., Ger.*) The servant who pours, a cupbearer or butler; one who sold wine; or who kept an inn, an innkeeper.

Schenkel (*Ger.*) One with an unusual or deformed leg.

Schenker (*Ger.*) One who kept a public house, a publican.

Schepp (*Ger.*) Descendant of Schepp, a pet form of Stephen (crown or garland); one selected to serve on a jury.

Scher, Schere (*Ger.*) One who caught moles; a contraction of Scherer, q.v.

Scherer, Scherrer (*Ger.*) One who shaved another, a barber; one who caught moles.

Scherf, Scherff (*Ger.*) A person of no importance or of little worth.

Schermer (*Ger.*) One who protects others; a musical entertainer or minstrel.

Schernecke, Scherneck (*Ukr.*) One with a dark complexion.

Scherr (*Ger.*) One who shaves or trims the beard or hair, a barber.

Scherzer (*Ger.*) The joker, clown, or buffoon.

Schettler (*Ger.*) One who came from Schuttlau (dirt; debris), in Germany.

Scheuer, Scheuerle, Scheuerman, Scheuermann (*Ger.*) Dweller near a barn or granary.

Scheurer (*Ger.*) One who had charge of the barn or granary.

Scheyer (*Ger.*) One who came from Scheyern (boggy water), in Germany.

Schiavo, Schiavino (*It.*) One who came from a Slavic country, a Slav; one who labored for another without pay, a slave.

Schiavone, Schiavoni, Schiavon (*It.*) Guard of the Doge of Venice who was armed with a schiavone, a broadsword.

Schick, Schicker (*Ger.*) One who organizes or directs others; the smart, stylish, well-dressed person; descendant of Schiko (order).

Schieber (*Ger.*) One who made window sashes; one who came from Schieben, in Germany.

Schiele, Schieler (*Ger.*) The squint or cross-eyed man; occasionally the one-eyed man.

Schiff, Schiffer, Schiffman, Schiffmann (*Ger.*) One who worked on a ship, a sailor; dweller at the sign of the ship.

Schifferdecker (*Ger.*) One who lays slates, a slater.

Schild (*Ger.*) Descendant of Schild, a pet form of names beginning with Schild (shield), as Scildfrid and Scildwald; dweller at the sign of the shield.

Schildhorn (*Ger.*) One who came from Schildhorn, a point or peak in Germany.

Schildhouse (*Ger.*) Dweller in, or near, the house with the shield.

Schildknecht (*Ger.*) One who took care of the shield or armor of a knight, a squire or personal attendant.

Schildkraut (*Ger.*) One who hunted or raised tortoises or turtles.

Schill (*Ger.*) Dweller near a muddy place.

Schiller (*Ger., Du.*) One having the habit of squinting his eyes, a squinter; one who prepared skins.

Schilling (*Ger.*) A serf who had paid money to his lord for his freedom; descendant of Schilling, a pet form of Scildwin (shield, friend).

Schillinger (*Ger.*) One who came from Schillingen (swampy place), in Germany.

Schimmel, Schimel (*Ger., Du.*) Dweller at the sign of the gray, or white, horse; one with gray hair or beard.

Schimmelpfennig (*Ger.*) The greedy or covetous man, a miser.

Schimpf (*Ger.*) One fond of joking, jesting, playing tricks, and ridiculing others.

Schina (*It.*) Descendant of Schina, pet form of Franceschina, an Italian form of Francis (free).

Schindeldecker (*Ger.*) One who covered roofs with shingles.

Schindler (*Ger.*) One who made, or lays, shingles.

Schirmer (*Ger.*) Variant of Schermer, q.v.

Schirra (*Ir., Ger.*) The son of Seartha, an Irish equivalent of Geoffrey (God's peace); descendant of Gerard (spear, hard).

Schissler, Schisler (*Ger.*) One who made dishes or bowls; one who fashioned objects on a lathe, a turner.

Schlacter, Schlachter, Schlachterman (*Ger.*) One who cut and sold meat, a butcher.

Schlaff, Schlaffman (*Ger.*) The sleepy, indolent man.

Schlager (*Ger.*) One who cleans or cards wool.

Schlanger (*Ger.*) One who came from Schlangen (swamp), in Germany; or from Schonlanke, in Poland.

Schlater, Schlatter, Schlattman, Schlattmann (*Ger.*) One who came from Schlat or Schlatt (place where reeds grew), the names of several places in Germany; dweller in, or near, a swampy meadow.

Schlecht, Schlechter (*Ger.*) The simple, plain straightforward man.

Schlegel, Schlegl (*Ger.*) One who was a guard or watchman in a prison; one who came from Schlegel (smith's shop; slaughterhouse), the name of several places in Germany.

Schleicher, Schleich (*Ger.*) One who came from Schleich or Schleicher (muddy place), the names of places in Germany; one who walks smoothly and quietly.

Schleifer, Schleiffer (*Ger.*) The possesser or occupant of a grinding mill; one who cut or polished glass.

Schlemmer (*Ger.*) One who engages in drinking and carousing; a gormandiser.

Schlesinger (*Ger.*) One who came from Schleusingen, in Thuringia.

Schless, Schlesser (*Ger.*) One who came from Schlesen (swampy place), in Germany; dweller in the castle or manor house; one who made small tools and locks.

Schlett, Schletter (*Ger.*) One who came from Schlettau (wet meadow), the name of several places in Germany.

Schleusener (*Ger.*) The administrator or manager of a sluice or lock.

Schley, Schleyer (*Ger.*) One who caught and sold tench, a European fresh-water fish of the carp family.

Schlie (*Ger.*) One who sold fish, especially tench, a fresh-water fish of the carp family.

Schliefer, Schlief (*Ger.*) One who made wooden spoons or ladles.

Schliemann (*Ger.*) One who caught and sold tench, a kind of fish.

Schlitt (*Ger.*) Dweller near a landslide.

Schlittler (*Ger.*) One who drove a cart, a carter.

451

Schlitzer, Schlitz (*Ger.*) One who came from Schlitz (arable land; notch), in Germany; dweller near a slippery, slimy place.

Schloesser (*Ger.*) One who made and sold locks.

Schlossberg (*Ger.*) One who came from Schlossberg (mountain castle), the name of four places in Germany.

Schlosser, Schloss (*Ger.*) One who made locks, a locksmith; dweller in, or near, the manor house or castle; dweller at the sign of the castle.

Schlotterback, Schlotterbeck (*Ger.*) Dweller near a muddy stream; one who baked using sour milk.

Schlueter, Schluter (*Ger.*) One who worked as doorkeeper of a prison, a turnkey; one who came from Schluete, in Germany.

Schlussman (*Ger.*) One in charge of a sluice or lock in a stream.

Schmalbach, Schmalenbach (*Ger.*) One who came from Schmalbach or Schmalenbach (narrow brook), the names of places in Germany.

Schmalz, Schmaltz (*Ger.*) One who had a fat stomach; one who rendered lard; an old-fashioned, sloppy, sentimental person.

Schmeer (*Ger.*) Nickname for one who sold grease, lard, or tallow.

Schmeisser (*Ger.*) One who hits, punches, or beats, probably in his work.

Schmelzer, Schmeltzer (*Ger.*) One who came from Schmelz, the name of several places in Germany; one who melts or fuses metal.

Schmidt, Schmitt, Schmid, Schmit (*Ger.*) The worker in metals, a smith.

Schmidtke, Schmidtlein (*Ger.*) Descendant of the little smith.

Schmied (*Ger.*) One who worked in metal.

Schmith (*Ger.*) Partial Anglicization of Schmidt, q.v.

Schmitz (*Ger.*) One who worked in metal, a smith.

Schmuck (*Ger.*) The elegant, neat man.

Schmucker, Schmuckler, Schmukler (*Ger.*) One who decorates, embellishes, or ornaments things.

Schmutz, Schmutzler (*Ger.*) Dweller near a dirty place.

Schnabel, Schnabele, Schnabl, Schnable (*Ger.*) Nickname for the talkative, garrulous man; one with an unusual or prominent nose thought to resemble a beak.

Schneck, Schnecke (*Ger.*) Nickname for one thought to possess the characteristics of a snail.

Schnee (*Ger.*) One with snow-white hair or very light complexion.

Schneeberger, Schneberger, Schneberg (*Ger.*) One who came from Schneeberg (snow mountain), the name of several places in Germany.

Schneemann, Schneeman (*Ger.*) One who came from Schnee (damp place), in Germany.

Schneeweiss, Schneeweis (*Ger.*) One with snow-white hair, usually designating an old man.

Schneider, Schnieder (*Ger.*) One who made outer garments, a tailor.

Schneiderman (*Ger.*) The servant of the one who made outer garments, i.e., a tailor.

Schneier (*Ger.*) One who came from Schney, in Germany; one who made outer garments, a tailor.

Schnell (*Ger.*) The quick, lively person.

Schneller (*Ger.*) One who carried messages, a messenger.

Schnepp, Schneppe (*Ger.*) Dweller at the sign of the snipe or woodcock.

Schneyer (*Ger.*) One who came from Schney, in Germany; one who made outer garments, a tailor.

Schnitzer, Schnitzler (*Ger.*) One who carved things of wood, a wood carver.

Schnoll (*Ger.*) The quick, eager, brave man.

Schnur, Schnurr (*Ger.*) One who made cord or rope; the buffoon or jester; the droll, quaint man.

Schnyder (*Swis.*) One who made outer garments, a tailor.

Schober (*Ger.*) One who works in the barn or at the haystack.

Schoch (*Ger.*) Dweller near a haystack, or the barn where hay is stored.

Schochet (*Ger.*) Jewish ritual slaughterer of animals for meat.

Schock (*Ger.*) Dweller near a haystack or barn; or near a heap or pile.

Schoell (*Ger.*) Variant of Schell, q.v.

Schoemaker (*Du.*) One who made and sold shoes.

Schoeman, Schoemann (*Ger.*) The polite, handsome, friendly man.

Schoen (*Ger.*) Beautiful, the handsome person; one who came from Schon (beautiful), in Germany.

Schoenbacher, Schoenbach (*Ger.*) One who came from Schonbach (beautiful stream), the name of seven places in Germany.

Schoenberg, Schoenberger (*Ger.*) One who came from Schonberg (beautiful mountain), the name of many places in Germany.

Schoenenberger (*Ger.*) One who came from Schonenberg (beautiful hill), the name of several places in Germany.

Schoener (*Ger.*) One who came from Schonau (beautiful meadow), the name of many places in Germany.

Schoenfeld, Schoenfeldt, Schoenfelder (*Ger.*) One who came from Schonfeld (beautiful field), the name of numerous places in Germany.

Schoenherr (*Ger.*) The handsome lord or gentleman.

Schoenijahn (*Ger.*) The handsome man named John (gracious gift of Jehovah).

Schoening (*Ger.*) The fine, handsome, well-bred man; variant of Schoeninger, q.v.

Schoeninger (*Ger.*) One who came from Schoningen, the name of two places in Germany.

Schoenleber, Schonleber (*Ger.*) One who leads a pleasant, agreeable life.

Schoenthal (*Ger.*) One who came from Schonthal (beautiful valley), the name of three places in Germany.

Schoenwetter, Schonwetter (*Ger.*) Nickname for one who habitually refers to the beautiful weather.

Schoettler (*Ger.*) One who makes wooden bowls or dishes.

Schofield (*Eng.*) Dweller at the hut or shed in the field; one who came from Scrafield (landslip field), in Lincolnshire.

Scholar, Schollar (*Ger., Eng.*) One who attends a school, usually for advanced study.

Scholes (*Eng.*) One who came from Scholes (hut or temporary building), in the West Riding of Yorkshire.

Scholl, Scholle (*Ger.*) One who is indebted to another, a debtor.

Scholler, Scholer (*Eng.*) Dweller in a hut or temporary building; one who attended a school, a scholar.

Scholz, Scholtz, Scholtes (*Ger.*) Variants of Schultz, q.v.

Schomberg (*Ger.*) One who came from Schomberg, the name of several places in Germany.

Schommer, Schomer (*Heb.*) The watchman; one who supervises the ritual preparation of the food.

Schon (*Ger.*) Variant of Schoen, q.v.

Schonberg, Schonberger (*Ger.*) Variant of Schoenberg, q.v.

Schonbrun, Schonbrunn (*Ger.*) Dweller near a beautiful spring; one who came from Schonbrunn (beautiful spring), the name of several places in Germany.

Schonfeld (*Ger.*) Variant of Schoenfeld, q.v.

Schonwald (*Ger.*) Dweller in, or near, a beautiful woodland; one who came from Schonwald (beautiful woods), the name of two places in Germany.

Schoolcraft (*Eng.*) Dweller in a hut or temporary building in a small field or enclosure.

Schooley, Scholey (*Eng.*) Dweller in a hut or temporary building in a grove.

Schoolfield (*Eng.*) Dweller in a hut or temporary building in the open country.

Schoolman (*Eng.*) One who worked in a school, a teacher.

Schools, Schooles (*Eng.*) Variant of Scholes, q.v.

Schoonhoven (*Du.*) One who came from Schoonhoven (beautiful court), in Holland.

Schoonmaker (*Du.*) One who made and sold shoes, a shoemaker; one who sweeps and cleans.

Schoonover (*Du.*) One who came from Schoonhoven (beautiful court), in Holland.

Schoonveld (*Du.*) Dweller in, or near, a beautiful field.

Schoot (*Du.*) One who came from Schoot (womb; bosom), in Holland.

Schopenhauer (*Ger.*) One who hewed scoops; one who made things from wood.

Schopp, Schoppe (*Ger.*) Variant of Schepp, q.v.

Schori (*Du.*) One who shears sheep.

Schorpp (*Ger.*) Dweller at the sign of the tortoise or turtle.

Schorr, Schor, Schore, Schorle (*Ger.*) Dweller near a rocky peak; or near a spring.

Schott, Schotte (*Ger., Du.*) One who carried goods for sale, a peddler; dweller near a sluice or floodgate; one who came from Scotland.

Schotz (*Ger.*) Variant of Schutz, q.v.

Schrader, Schraeder (*Ger.*) One who made outer garments, a tailor.

Schrage, Schrag (*Ger.*) One who made the stand or rack for the market place; nickname for a wheelwright or carpenter.

Schrager (*Ger.*) One who made trestles or frames for market tables; nickname for a cabinet maker; nickname for a thin man.

Schram, Schramm (*Ger.*) One deformed in body, a cripple; dweller near a rock cleft.

Schrank (*Ger.*) Dweller near a barrier or fence.

Schranz, Schrantz (*Ger.*) One in attendance at the court of a prince; a hanger-on at a court.

Schraut (*Ger.*) Dweller near a pillory or whipping post.

Schreck, Schrecke (*Ger., Pol.*) One who instills fright or horror in others by springing or jumping; one who is timid, easily frightened or startled; dweller at the broad place.

Schreiber, Schreibman (*Ger.*) An official, or public, writer, a clerk.

Schreier (*Ger.*) The town crier; official who made announcements.

Schreiner (*Ger.*) One who worked with wood, a cabinet maker.

Schrenk (*Ger.*) The sly, cunning, crafty man.

Schrey (*Ger.*) One who screams and shrieks.

Schriver (*Ger.*) An official, or public, writer, a scribe.

Schrock, Schrocker (*Ger.*) One who came from Schrock (slippery place), the name of two places in Germany; one who jumps or leaps around.

Schroeder, Schroder, Schroter (*Ger.*) One who made garments, a tailor; one who drove a dray, a drayman.

Schroth, Schrot, Schrott (*Ger.*) One who cuts wood or metal; one who handles coarsely ground grain.

Schubert, Schuberth (*Ger.*) One who made and sold shoes.

Schuch, Schuh, Schuck, Schug (*Ger.*) Dweller at the sign of the shoe; one who made and sold shoes.

Schuchard, Schuchardt (*Ger.*) One who made shoes, a shoemaker.

Schuchmann, Schuchman (*Ger.*) One who made boots and shoes.

Schuckmann (*Ger.*) Variant of Schuchmann, q.v.

Schuessler, Schussler (*Ger.*) One who made wooden dishes.

Schuette (*Ger.*) Dweller near a heap or pile.

Schuetz, Schutz, Schuetze, Schutze (*Ger.*) One who hunted and killed game; a watchman; one who came from Schutz, in Germany; one who fought with bow and arrow, an archer.

Schuler, Schuller, Schueler, Schueller (*Ger.*) One who taught school, a schoolmaster; a man who studied, a scholar.

Schulgasser (*Ger.*) Dweller on the school or synagogue alley.

Schull (*Ger.*) A ruffian, boor, or hooligan.

Schulman (*Ger., Pol.*) One who taught in a school, a schoolmaster; an important functionary of the synagogue in the early Jewish communities of Poland.

Schultheis, Schultheiss, Schulthess (*Ger.*) One who administers the rural parish and collects taxes; one who acts as a judge.

Schultz, Schulz, Schulze, Schulte, Schultze (*Ger.*) The magistrate or sheriff; a steward or overseer.

Schumacher, Schumaker (*Ger.*) One who made and sold shoes.

Schuman, Schumann (*Ger.*) One who made and sold shoes.

Schummer, Schumer, Schumm (*Ger.*) The ne'er-do-well, a tramp or vagrant; one who came from Schumm, in Germany.

Schupak (*Pol., Ukr.*) One who caught and sold pickerel, a fisher.

Schupp, Schuppe (*Ger.*) One who caught and sold fish.

Schurr, Schur (*Ger.*) Dweller in, or near, a rubble or gravelly place.

Schurz (*Ger.*) One who wore, or made and sold, aprons, or short articles of clothing.

Schussel (*Ger.*) One who had charge of the keys.

Schuster, Shuster (*Ger.*) One who made and repaired shoes, a cobbler.

Schutt, Schuett, Schuette (*Du.*) Dweller at, or near, the fence or hedge.

Schutter, Schutters (*Du.*) The marksman or militiaman.

Schuttloeffel (*Ger.*) A sentence name "to shake a spoon," probably referring to a cook.

Schutz, Schutze (*Ger.*) The watchman, protector, or guard.

Schuur (*Du.*) Dweller near the barn.

Schuurman (*Du.*) One in charge of the barn.

Schuyler (*Du.*) One who taught school, a schoolmaster; one who protected refugees.

Schwab, Schwabe (*Ger.*) One who came from Swabia (freemen), a duchy in medieval Germany.

Schwager (*Ger.*) One related to another by marriage, father-in-law or son-in-law.

Schwalb, Schwalbe (*Ger.*) One thought to possess some of the characteristics of a swallow.

Schwamm, Schwam (*Ger.*) One who gathered and sold mushrooms; dweller near where mushrooms grew.

Schwan, Schwaan (*Ger.*) Dweller at the sign of the swan; one with the characteristics of a swan. The Germans considered the swan to be a holy bird.

Schwanke, Schwank (*Ger.*) Descendant of little Schwan (swan); dweller at the sign of the little swan; the thin, supple man.

Schwartz, Schwarz (*Ger.*) One with a dark or swarthy complexion, black.

Schwartzberg, Schwarzberg (*Ger.*) One who came from Schwarzburg (black mountain), in Germany; dweller on a black hill.

Schwartzman, Schwarzman, Schwarzmann (*Ger.*) Same as Schwartz, q.v.

Schwarzkopf, Schwartzkopf (*Ger.*) The dark or black-haired, man.

Schwarzschild (*Ger.*) Dweller at the sign of the black shield.

Schwegel, Schwegler (*Ger.*) One who plays the flute or pipe.

Schweiger, Schweigerdt, Schweigert (*Ger.*) The silent, quiet, taciturn man; one who tended cows.

Schweikert, Schweiker (*Ger.*) Descendant of Swidiger (strong, spear).

Schweitzer, Schweizer (*Ger.*) One who came from Switzerland, a Swiss.

Schwemmer (*Ger.*) One who was a spendthrift; one who operated a raft.

Schwendeman, Schwender (*Ger.*) Dweller in a cleared place in a forest.

Schwenk (*Ger.*) Dweller at the sign of the swan; descendant of Schwenk, a pet form of Schwan (swan).

Schwerdtfeger, Schwertfager (*Ger.*) One who made swords, an armorer or weaponsmith.

Schwerin, Schweriner (*Ger.*) One who came from Schwerin, the name of three places in Germany.

Schwering (*Ger.*) One who came from Schweringen (standing water), in Germany.

Schwimmer, Schwimer (*Ger.*) One who reels or staggers, of unsteady gait.

Schwind (*Ger.*) Descendant of Schwind (strong), a pet form of such names as Schwindberct, Swindhelm, and Swindheri.

Schwing, Schwinger (*Ger.*) One who came from Schwinge or Schwingen (marshland river), the names of places in Germany.

Schwinn (*Ger.*) One who cared for the swine; one who raised and sold swine.

Schwitzer (*Swis.*) One who came from Switzerland, a Swiss.

Sciarra, Sciarretta (*It.*) One who came from Sciara (uncultivated volcanic ground), in Sicily.

Scimeca (*It.*) One who came from Scimeca, in Italy.

Scioli, Sciola (*It.*) Dweller near where grape hyacinth grew; or where onions grew.

Scofield (*Eng.*) Variant of Schofield, q.v.

Scoggins, Scoggin (*Eng.*) The son of the little idler or fool; or of the fop or flatterer.

Scola, Scoleri (*It.*) Dweller near a school or college; metonymic for a teacher.

Scolaro (*It.*) The student or scholar.

Scolnick, Scolnik (*Cz.-Sl., Ukr.*) Variant of Skolnik, q.v.

Scopa (*It.*) Dweller at the sign of the broom; one who made and sold brooms.

Scotland (*Scot.*) One who came from Scotland (cut place), a village in Scotland.

Scott, Scotch (*Eng.*) One who came from Scotland; originally the word also included the Irish, i.e., one who came from Ireland.

Scotti (*It.*) Descendant of Scotto, a pet form of Francescotto, Italian form of Francis (free).

Scotton (*Eng.*) One who came from Scotton (village of the Scots), the name of places in Lincolnshire and in the North and West Ridings of Yorkshire.

Scottsmith (*Eng.*) One who made and sold darts or small javelins.

Scoville, Scovill, Scovil, Scovell (*Eng.*) One who came from Escoville (Scot's estate), in Normandy.

Scowcroft (*Eng.*) One who came from Scarcroft (Skarthi's enclosure), in the West Riding of Yorkshire.

Scrafield (*Eng.*) One who came from Scrafield (landslip in open country), in Lincolnshire.

Scrafton (*Eng.*) One who came from Scrafton (homestead in a ravine), in the North Riding of Yorkshire.

Scragg (*Eng.*) The thin, bony man.

Scranton (*Du.*) Descendant of Schrantsen (tear, break).

Scribe (*Fr.*) One who served as clerk in a court; or as a public letter-writer.

Scribner, Scriber (*Eng.*) One who copied books and manuscripts.

Scrimgeour (*Scot.*) One who taught fencing, a fencing-master.

Scrimpsher (*Scot.*) Variant of Scrimgeour, q.v.

Scripps (*Eng.*) One with curly hair, from *cryps* with prefixed S.

Scriven, Scrivens (*Eng.*) One who came from Scriven (hollow), in the West Riding of Yorkshire; one who writes or copies books and manuscripts, a clerk.

Scrivener, Scrivenor (*Eng.*) An official, or public, writer, a scribe.

Scroggie (*Eng.*) Dweller on land covered by a stunted undergrowth, a scraggy place; the lean, scrawny man.

Scroggins, Scroggin (*Eng.*) Dweller at a thicket or stunted undergrowth or brushwood.

Scruggs, Scroggs (*Eng.*) The thin, scraggy person; dweller by, or among, stunted bushes.

Scudder (*Eng., Du.*) One who fought

with bow and arrow, an archer; one who constantly shook or trembled, from disease.

Scull (*Eng.*) Descendant of Skuli (shelter).

Scullion, Scullin (*Ir.*) Descendant of Sceallan (kernel).

Scully, Scally, Sculley (*Ir.*) Descendant of the scholar or schoolman; variant of Scullion, q.v.

Scurlock, Scurlark (*Ir.*) One with short or shorn hair.

Scurry (*Eng.*) Descendant of Skorri (notch).

Seaberg, Seeberg, Seabergh (*Sw.*) Sea, mountain.

Seaborg (*Sw.*) Americanized form of Sjoberg, q.v.

Seaborn, Seaborne (*Eng.*) Descendant of Saebjorn (sea, bear).

Seaborough (*Eng.*) One who came from Seaborough (seven hills), in Dorset.

Seabright (*Eng.*) Descendant of Saebeorht (sea, bright).

Seabrook, Seabrooke, Seabrooks (*Eng.*) One who came from Seabrook (slow-moving stream), in Buckinghamshire.

Seabury, Seaberry (*Eng.*) One who came from Seaborough (seven hills), in Dorset.

Seagraves, Seagrave (*Eng.*) One who came from Seagrave (pool by a ditch; fold in a grove) in Leicestershire.

Seagrist (*Ger.*) Variant of Siegrist, q.v.

Seagull (*Ger.*) Variant of Siegel, q.v.

Sealock (*Eng.*) Dweller near the lake or lock surrounded by sedge.

Seals, Seale, Seales, Seal (*Eng.*) Dweller in, or near, a hall; one who came from Seal (hall; small wood), the name of places in Kent and Derbyshire; or from Seale (hall), in Surrey.

Sealy, Sealey (*Eng.*) Variant of Seeley, q.v.

Seaman, Seamans, Seamon (*Eng.*) One who worked on a ship, a sailor; descendant of Siemond (victory, protector); or of Saemann (victory, man).

Seaner (*Eng.*) Variant of Senior, q.v.

Searcy, Searcie (*Eng.*) One who came from Cerisy or Cercy (Cercious' estate), in France.

Searles, Searls, Searle (*Eng.*) Descendant of Serle (armor).

Sears, Sear (*Eng., Ir.*) Descendant of Segar (sea, warrior); or of Sigehere (victorious, army).

Seashore (*Sw.*) An American translation of Swedish Sjostrand (sea, shore).

Seasongood (*Ger.*) Americanization of the German *sussengut* (meadow property); dweller in a meadow.

Seaton (*Eng.*) One who came from Seaton (farm by the sea or lake), the name of several places in England.

Seaver, Sever, Seavers (*Eng.*) One with a grave and austere demeanor.

Seaverns (*Eng.*) Variant of Severns, q.v.

Seavey (*Eng.*) Descendant of Saewig (sea, war).

Seaward (*Eng.*) Descendant of Sigeweard (victory, protection); or of Saeweard (sea, protection).

Seawood (*Eng.*) Variant of Seward, q.v.

Seawright, Searight (*Eng.*) Descendant or Saeric (sea, rule).

Seay, Say, Saye (*Eng.*) Dweller near the sea; one who came from Sai (Saius' estate), in Normandy; the wise or prudent man.

Sebastian, Sebastiano (*Sp.*) Descendant of Sebastian (venerable).

Sebold (*Eng.*) Descendant of Saebeald (sea, bold).

Sebzda (*Pol.*) One in the habit of expelling a flatus through the anus, a farter.

Sechrist, Secrest, Secrist (*Ger.*) Variant of Siegrist, q.v.

Seckinger (*Ger.*) One who came from Sackingen (dirty brook), in Germany.

Secor, Secore (*Sp.*) Dweller on the dry, barren land.

Secord (*Fr.*) Descendant of Sicard (victory, hard).

Seda (*Sp.*) One who dealt in silk.

Sedbrook (*Eng.*) One who came from

Sedgebrook (stream where sedge grew), in Lincolnshire.

Seddon, Sedden, Seddons (*Eng.*) Dweller in a hut or shed on a hill; one who came from Sabden (valley where spruce grew), in Lancashire.

Seder, Sedar, Sedor (*Nor.*) Dweller by a cedar tree.

Sederholm (*Sw.*) Cedar, river island.

Sedgley (*Eng.*) One who came from Sedgley (Secg's grove), in Staffordshire.

Sedgwick (*Eng.*) One who came from Sedgwick (Siggi's dairy farm), in Westmorland.

Sedivy, Sediwy (*Cz.-Sl.*) The old, or gray-haired, man.

Sedlacek, Sedlak, Sedlack (*Cz.-Sl.*) One who tilled the soil, a farmer.

Sedwick (*Eng.*) One who came from Sedgwick (Siggi's dairy farm), in Westmorland.

Sedwin (*Eng.*) Descendant of Siduwine (custom, friend).

See, Sea (*Eng.*) Dweller by the seacoast; dweller by a lake or pool.

Seeber (*Ger.*) One who came from Seeb, Seeba, or Seeben (lake or body of water), the names of places in Germany.

Seeburger, Seeberger (*Ger.*) One who came from Seeburg (lake stronghold) or Seebergen (mountain lake), the names of places in Germany.

Seed, Seedes, Seeds (*Eng.*) Metonymic for a dealer in seeds; descendant of Sida, a short form of such names as Siduwine and Siduwulf.

Seefried (*Ger.*) Descendant of Siegfried (victory, peace).

Seeger, Seegers (*Ger.*) Descendant of Sigiheri (victory, army).

Seehousen, Seehusen (*Ger.*) One who came from Seehausen (houses by the water), the name of three places in Germany.

Seekford (*Eng.*) One who came from Sedgeford (river crossing where sedge grass grew), in Norfolk.

Seelenfreund (*Ger.*) One who was a bosom friend to another.

Seeler (*Eng.*) One who made seals; one who made saddles.

Seeley, Seely, Seelye (*Eng.*) The happy or prosperous person; the good, simple man.

Seelig, Seeliger (*Ger.*) One who came from Seelig (prosperous place), in Germany; the happy, lucky or fortunate man.

Seeling (*Eng.*) One who came from Selling (residence), in Kent.

Seeman, Seemann (*Ger.*) One who worked on a ship, a sailor; descendant of Simon (gracious hearing; hearkening; snub-nosed); or of Sigiman (victory, man).

Seemiller (*Ger.*) One who operated a sawmill.

Seersma (*Du.*) Descendant of Seer or Sear, pet forms of Seger (victory).

Seery (*Ir.*) The laborer or earner; one who worked with wood, a carpenter.

Seeton (*Eng.*) Variant of Seaton, q.v.

Seff (*Ger.*) Descendant of Seff, a pet form of names beginning with Sieg (victory), as Sigibald and Sigifrith.

Sefton (*Eng.*) One who came from Sefton (homestead where rushes grew), in Lancashire.

Segal, Segall, Segel, Segale, Seegal (*Fr., Ger.*) One who cultivated rye; contraction of *segan leviyyah,* literally, assistant priest or rabbi, a name often adopted by Levites.

Segarra (*Sp.*) Dweller near an apple tree.

Segars, Segar, Segear (*Eng.*) Descendant of Saeger (sea, spear); or of Sigegar (victory, spear).

Seger, Segers (*Eng., Ger.*) Variant of Segars, q.v.

Segraves (*Eng.*) Variant of Seagraves, q.v.

Segures (*Fr.*) One who came from Segur (safe; secure), in France.

Seibel, Seib (*Ger.*) Descendant of little Seib, a pet form of Seibert (victory, bright).

Seiberlich (*Ger.*) The clean, careful man.

Seibert (*Ger.*) Descendant of Sigiperaht (victory, bright).

Seibold (*Ger.*) Descendant of Sigibald (victory, bold).

Seidel, Seidl (*Ger.*) Descendant of Sitto, a pet form of Sigebert (victory, bright); one who came from Seidel, in Germany; dweller at the sign of the beer mug.

Seidelmann, Seidelman (*Ger.*) One who worked with, or dealt in, silks; one who came from Seidel, in Germany.

Seiden, Seidenman (*Ger.*) One who dealt in silk.

Seidenberg, Seidenburg (*Ger.*) One who came from Seidenberg, in Silesia.

Seidensticker (*Ger.*) One who embroiders in silk.

Seidler (*Ger., Fr.*) One who made and sold beer mugs and tankards; one who kept bees, a beekeeper.

Seidman, Seidmon, Seideman, Seidemann (*Ger.*) Descendant of Sitto, a pet form of Sigebert (victory, bright). See also Seidelmann.

Seif (*Ger.*) Descendant of Seif, a pet form of Sigifrith (victory, peace).

Seifer (*Ger.*) Descendant of Siegfried (victory, peace).

Seifert, Seiferth, Seiffert, Seifferth (*Ger.*) Descendant of Sigifrith (victory, peace).

Seigel, Seigle (*Ger.*) Variant of Siegel, q.v.

Seiger (*Ger.*) One who tested or inspected scales and meters to assay standards.

Seiler (*Ger.*) One who made and sold rope and cord.

Seim (*Nor.*) Dweller on the seaside farm, a farm name; one who came from Seim, the name of several places in Norway.

Seitchik, Seitchick (*Ukr.*) Dweller at the sign of the little hare; one with some of the characteristics of a small hare.

Seitter, Seiter (*Ger.*) One who made or repaired shoes, a shoemaker or cobbler.

Seitz (*Ger.*) Descendant of Sigizo, a pet form of names beginning with Sieg

(victory), as Sigibald, Sigiheri, and Sigismund.

Selber, Selb (*Ger.*) One who came from Selb, in Germany.

Selbst (*Ger.*) The self-willed man.

Selby (*Eng.*) One who came from Selby (sallow copse), in Yorkshire.

Selden, Seldon, Seldom (*Eng.*) Dweller in a valley where willow trees grew; one who came from Salden (hill with a ledge), in Buckinghamshire; one who tended a booth or shop.

Self (*Eng.*) Dweller near a rock, or ledge, such as a river bank; descendant of Saewulf (sea, wolf).

Selfridge (*Eng.*) Dweller on, or near, the rocky ridge.

Selig (*Ger.*) Descendant of Selig (fortunate); the lucky, successful man; the blessed man.

Seligman, Seligmann, Selig (*Ger.*) The happy, lucky, or fortunate man; a variant of Salomon (peaceful).

Seligsohn, Seligson (*Ger.*) The son of Selig (fortunate).

Selinger (*Du.*) One who came from Sellingen, in Holland.

Selkirk (*Scot.*) One who came from Selkirk (church in the hall), in Selkirkshire.

Sell, Selle, Sells (*Eng.*) Dweller at the shelter for animals; or in the herdsman's hut.

Sellars (*Eng.*) One who worked in the cellar of the inn where wine was stored.

Sellers, Seller (*Eng.*) One who made saddles; one who had charge of the cellar or storeroom; one who dealt in commodities, a merchant.

Sellinger, Selinger (*Eng., Ger.*) One who came from St. Leger, in France; one who came from Soellingen, in Germany; or from Selling in Germany.

Sellstrom (*Sw.*) Dweller at a stretch of quiet water in a river.

Selm (*Eng.*) Descendant of Selm, a pet form of Anselm (divine, helmet).

Selman, Sellman (*Eng.*) Variant of Sillman, q.v.

Selmer (*Ger.*) One who came from Selm

459

(swamp), in Germany; the servant in charge of the hall.

Selsky (*Ukr.*) Dweller in the village.

Seltner (*Ger.*) One who worked for daily wages, a day laborer; dweller in a peasant's hut.

Selvaggio, Selvaggi (*It.*) Descendant of Selvaggia (forest dweller).

Selwyn, Selwin (*Eng.*) Descendant of Selwyn (hall friend).

Selzer, Seltzer, Selz (*Ger.*) One who came from Selzen (swamp), in Germany; one who salted or pickled foods.

Selznick (*Ukr.*) One who was thought to resemble a drake or dragon.

Semans, Semon (*Eng.*) Variant of Seaman, q.v.

Semberg (*Sw., Nor.*) Dweller on the hill by the lake or seaside.

Semmel, Semmler (*Ger.*) One who bakes and sells white bread or breakfast rolls.

Semmens (*Eng.*) Variant of Simmons, q.v.

Semola (*It.*) One who sifts the bran from wheat or other grain; nickname for one with freckles.

Semper (*Eng.*) One who came from St. Pierre (rock), the name of many places in France.

Semple (*Eng.*) One who came from St. Paul (small), the name of many places in France.

Semprevivo (*It.*) One who grew and sold house-leeks.

Sena (*Sp.*) One who came from Sena (passing place), in Spain.

Senatore (*It.*) One who was the head of a village, a mayor; a member of the senate.

Sender, Sendor (*Ger., Eng.*) Descendant of Sender, a pet form of Alexander (helper of mankind); one who came from Sende in Germany.

Senechal, Senecal, Senechalle (*Fr.*) The steward or senior servant, a seneschal.

Sener (*Swis.*) One who tended a flock, a herdsman.

Senescu (*Rom.*) The son of Sena, a pet form of Auxinie.

Senese (*It.*) One who came from Senise, in Lucania.

Senf, Senft (*Ger.*) One who prepared and sold mustard.

Senick (*Eng.*) One who came from Sevenoaks (seven oaks), in Kent, an old pronunciation of the name.

Senior, Seniour (*Eng.*) The older person; the seignior or lord of the manor; nickname for one who aped the ways of the lord.

Senker (*Ger.*) One who fished with nets and plummet or sounding lead.

Senn, Senner (*Swis.*) The head man of an Alpine dairy farm.

Sennott, Sennett, Sennet (*Eng., Fr.*) The old, wise, or sage person; descendant of Senet, a pet form of Sene (sensible); variants of Sinnett, q.v.

Sepp (*Ger., Est.*) Descendant of Sepp, a pet form of Joseph (He shall add); one who worked in metal, a smith.

Seppanen, Seppa (*Finn.*) One who worked in metals, a smith.

Sepulveda (*Sp.*) One who came from Sepulveda (place of burials), in Spain.

Serad (*Tur.*) The brave man.

Serafin (*Sp., Pol.*) Descendant of Serafin (ardent of God).

Serafini, Serafino, Serafine (*It.*) Descendant of Serafino, Italian form of Serafin (ardent of God).

Seraydarian (*Arm.*) The son of the palace guard.

Sereda (*Ukr.*) Wednesday, probably a nickname for one who habitually performed some act on that day.

Serena (*It.*) Descendant of Serena (bright; clear).

Sergejev (*Rus.*) The son of Sergej, Russian form of Sergius (to serve).

Serinsky (*Rus.*) The gray-haired man.

Serio (*It.*) The serious or solemn person.

Serle, Serles (*Eng.*) Descendant of Serle or Serlo (armor).

Serlin (*Eng., Fr.*) Descendant of little Serle (armor); descendant of Saturnin (of, or belonging to, Saturn, the earliest king of Latium, afterwards the god of agriculture).

Serna (*Sp.*) One who came from Serna (cultivated field), the name of several places in Spain; dweller in a cultivated field.

Serody (*Hun.*) One who came from Serod or Sered, in Hungary.

Serota (*Pol., It.*) Descendant of the orphan; one who is usually late.

Serra (*Fr., It.*) One who came from Serra (mountain range), the name of many places in France; dweller in a narrow passage or gorge; one who used a saw in his work.

Serrano (*Sp.*) One who came from Serrano (saw-shaped mountain), in Spain; dweller on, or near, a mountain ridge.

Serrantino (*It.*) One who came from Sorrento, in the province of Napoli in Italy.

Serravalle (*Fr.*) Dweller in a narrow valley; one who came from Serraval (closed valley), in France.

Serritella, Serritelli, Serritello (*It.*) Dweller in, or by, a narrow valley or ravine.

Serrurier, Serruel (*Fr.*) One who made locks, a locksmith.

Service (*Eng., Fr.*) One who sold ale or other beverages, a taverner.

Servin (*Fr.*) Dweller at the sign of the lynx.

Servis, Serviss (*Eng.*) One who sold ale, a taverner.

Serwaitis (*Lith.*) The son of Sirvydas or Sirvydis.

Sessa, Sesso (*It.*) One who gathered the crop with a scythe or sickle.

Sessions, Session (*Eng.*) One who came from Soissons, a district in France.

Sessoms, Sessom (*Ger.*) Dweller on a swampy, reedy homestead.

Setchell (*Eng.*) Variant of Satchell, q.v.

Setchfield (*Eng.*) One who came from Secqueville (dry valley), the name of two places in Normandy.

Seth (*Heb.*) Descendant of Seth (the appointed; substitute).

Seto (*Jap.*) Rapids, door.

Seton (*Scot.*) One who came from the village of Sai, in Normandy.

Settimio (*It.*) Descendant of Settimio (seven); the seventh born child. In Sicily such a person is thought to have the power to cure fevers.

Settles, Settle (*Eng.*) One who came from Settle (dwelling), in Yorkshire; one who lived in a dwelling in the manor, but had no rights in the cultivated fields.

Setzer, Setzman (*Ger.*) One who sets type, a compositor; the official inspector.

Seufert, Seuffert (*Ger.*) Descendant of Sigifrith (victory, peace).

Seurat (*Fr.*) Descendant of little Seurin, a contracted form of Severin (respected; grave).

Sevcik (*Cz., Ukr.*) One who made and sold shoes, a shoemaker, a diminutive form.

Sevenko (*Ukr.*) The son of the shoemaker.

Severance (*Fr.*) Descendant of Severian (severe), the name of several saints.

Severin, Seurin (*Fr.*) Descendant of Severin (severe), a sixth century French saint.

Severino, Severini (*It.*) Descendant of Severino (stern; severe).

Severns, Severn (*Eng.*) Dweller by the Severn, a river in England.

Severs, Severson (*Eng.*) The son of Saefaru (sea, passage).

Seville (*Eng.*) Variant of Saville, q.v.

Seward, Sewards, Sewart (*Eng.*) Descendant of Siward or Sigeweard (victory, protection); or of Saeweard (sea, protection).

Sewell, Sewall (*Eng., Scot.*) Descendant of Sewal (victory, strength); one who came from Sewell (seven wells), the name of places in Bedfordshire and Oxfordshire.

Sexauer, Sexaur (*Ger.*) One who came from Sexau, in Germany.

Sexson (*Eng.*) Variant of Sexton, q.v.

Sexton (*Eng.*) One who acted as an under-officer of a church and who had charge of the sacristy and its contents, a sacristan; variant of Saxton, q.v.

Seybert (*Eng.*) Descendant of Saebeorht (sea, bright).

Seybold (*Eng.*) Descendant of Saebeald (sea, bold).

Seyfarth, Seyferth (*Ger.*) Variant of Seifert, q.v.

Seyfert, Seyffert (*Ger.*) Variant of Seifert, q.v.

Seyfried (*Ger.*) Descendant of Siegfried (victory, peace).

Seyler (*Ger.*) Variant of Seiler, q.v.

Seymour, Seymore, Seymoure (*Eng.*) Descendant of Seamer (sea, famous); one who came from Seamer (lake, sea), in Yorkshire; one who came from St. Maur (black), in France.

Seys (*Wel.*) The foreigner; the Englishman.

Sforza (*It.*) The fierce man.

Sgro (*It.*) One with wavy or curly hair.

Shachter (*Ger.*) Variant of Schachter, q.v.

Shackelford, Shackleford (*Eng.*) One who came from Shackleford (Shackel's ford), in Surrey.

Shackford (*Eng.*) One who came from Shadforth (shallow ford), in Durham; a contraction of Shackelford, q.v.

Shacklady (*Eng.*) One who came from Shackerley (robber's wood), in Lancashire; nickname for a fickle, capricious man.

Shackles (*Eng.*) One who came from Shackerley (robber's wood), in Lancashire; descendant of Skakul (pole of carriage).

Shackleton (*Eng.*) Dweller in, or near, Scacel's homestead.

Shackley (*Eng.*) One who came from Shackerley (wood of the robbers), in Lancashire.

Shacklock (*Eng.*) Metonymic for a jailer who shackles or puts fetters on prisoners; nickname for one who shakes his long hair.

Shackmaster (*Ger.*) One who supervises unskilled labor.

Shaddon (*Eng.*) One who came from Shebdon (Sceobba's hill), in Staffordshire.

Shade, Shadd (*Eng.*) One who caught and sold shad; dweller by the boundary.

Shadford (*Eng.*) One who came from Shadforth (shallow ford), in Durham.

Shadley, Shadle, Shadel (*Eng.*) Dweller at the grove by the boundary.

Shadwell (*Eng.*) One who came from Shadwell (shallow spring; boundary stream), the name of places in Middlesex and Norfolk.

Shadwick (*Eng.*) Dweller in the dairy farm by the boundary.

Shaffer, Shafer, Shaeffer (*Ger.*) One who took care of sheep, a shepherd. Shaffer is the most common spelling in the United States of this common name.

Shaffstall, Shafstall (*Ger.*) Dweller near a sheepfold.

Shafran (*Ger., Heb.*) One who prepared and sold saffron; descendant of Shifre or Shifra (beautiful).

Shafton (*Eng.*) One who came from Shafton (homestead by a pole or boundary mark), in the West Riding of Yorkshire.

Shagren (*Sw.*) Lake, branch.

Shah (*Pers., Tur., Hindi*) One connected in some manner with a king's household. In Nepal Shah is the family name of members of the royal family.

Shahinian (*Arm.*) The son of the shah or king.

Shain, Shaine, Shaines (*Ger.*) The beautiful or handsome person.

Shakespeare, Shakespere (*Eng.*) One who lived on the peasant's farm; nickname for a soldier, one who wielded a spear.

Shaklee (*Eng.*) Variant of Shackley, q.v.

Shall (*Ger.*) Variant of Schall, q.v.

Shallberg (*Ger.*) One who came from Schallenberg, in Germany.

Shallcross (*Eng.*) One who came from Shackelcross (Skakel's cross), in Derbyshire.

Shallow, Shalloo (*Ir.*) Grandson of Sealbhach (possessor; proprietor).

Shamash (*Heb.*) The minor official who acted as the beadle in the synagogue.

Shambaugh (*Ger.*) One who came from Schambach (swampy brook; reedy stream), the name of five places in Germany.

Shamberg, Shamberger (*Ger.*) One who came from, or dwelt on, the Schammberg, a ridge in Germany.

Shambourger (*Ger.*) One who came from Schaumburg, the name of two places in Germany.

Shamis, Shames (*Heb.*) Yiddish form of Shamash, q.v.

Shamley (*Eng.*) Dweller on a ledge or shelf; one who came from Shamley (grove with bench or table), in Surrey.

Shanahan (*Ir.*) Grandson of little Seanach (old; wise).

Shand, Shands (*Eng., Scot.*) One who came from Chandai (Candius' estate), in France.

Shander (*Ger.*) Englished form of Schander, that is, one who came from Schandau (wet meadow), in Germany.

Shandlay, Shandley (*Ir.*) Variant of Shanley, q.v.

Shane (*Ir.*) Descendant of Eoin or Seon, Irish forms of John (gracious gift of Jehovah).

Shanefield, Shanfield (*Eng.*) One who came from Shenfield (beautiful open country), in Essex.

Shank, Shanks, Shanke (*Eng., Scot.*) A nickname given because of some peculiarity of the legs; one who came from the lands of Shank, in Midlothian.

Shanker (*Ger.*) Variant of Schank, q.v.

Shanklin (*Eng.*) One who came from Shanklin (leg hill), in Wight.

Shanley (*Ir.*) The son of Seanlaoch (old hero).

Shannon (*Ir.*) Grandson of little Seanach (old; wise).

Shantz (*Ger.*) Variant of Schantz, q.v.

Shanzer (*Ger.*) One who came from Schanz or Schanze (slag heap), the names of several places in Germany; dweller near a bulwark.

Shapcott (*Eng.*) Dweller near the sheep shelter.

Shapelow (*Eng.*) Dweller near the mound or hill where sheep were kept.

Shapey (*Eng.*) Dweller on the island where sheep were raised; one who came from the Isle of Sheppey (island where sheep were kept).

Shapiro, Shapira, Shapero, Shapera (*Ger.*) One who came from Speyer (in the Middle Ages, spelled Spira, and by Jews spelled Shapira), in Bavaria.

Shapley, Shapleigh (*Eng.*) One who came from Shipley (pasture for sheep), the name of several places in England.

Shapowal, Shapowalenko (*Ukr.*) One who made and sold caps.

Shappell (*Eng.*) One who came from Shephall (corner where sheep were raised).

Sharer, Share (*Ger.*) One who cuts cloth and makes garments, a tailor.

Sharesmith (*Eng., Ger.*) One who made shares, the iron blade in a plow which cuts the ground, now better known as a plowshare.

Sharf, Sharff (*Ger.*) Variant of Scharf, q.v.

Shariff, Sharif (*Pers., Arab.*) Descendant or Sharif (noble; honorable); descendant of the Prophet through Hasan who administered Holy Places in Mecca.

Sharkey (*Ir.*) Grandson of Searcach (loving).

Sharlip (*Ger.*) One who came from Scharlibbe, in Germany.

Sharman (*Eng.*) Variant of Sherman, q.v.

Sharp, Sharpe (*Eng.*) An acute, keen-witted or quick person.

Sharples, Sharpless (*Eng.*) One who came from Sharples (steep place), in Lancashire.

Sharrett, Sharratt (*Eng.*) Descendant of Scirheard (bright, hard); dweller at the steep gate.

Sharrock (*Eng.*) Dweller near Shorrock Green, in Lancashire; dweller at the split rock.

Sharrow (*Eng.*) One who came from Sharow (boundary hill), in the West Riding of Yorkshire.

Shassian (*Arm.*) The son of the cross-eyed man.

Shattuck, Shaddick, Shattock (*Eng.*) Dweller at the sign of the little shad (fish); one who caught and sold shad.

Shatz (*Ger., Heb.*) Variant of Schatz, q.v.

Shaub (*Ger.*) Variant of Schaub, q.v.

Shaughnessy, Shannessy, Shaunnessey, Shanesy (*Ir.*) Grandson of Seachnasach; descendant of the elusive person.

Shaver, Shavers (*Ger.*) An Anglicization of Shaffer, q.v.

Shaw, Shawe (*Scot., Eng.*) Dweller at the small wood or thicket; descendant of Sithech (wolf); one who came from Shaw (small wood), the name of several places in England.

Shawcross (*Eng.*) Dweller by the cross in the grove; variant of Shallcross, q.v.

Shay (*Ir.*) A variant of Shea, q.v.

Shayne (*Ir.*) Variant of Shane, q.v.

Shea (*Ir.*) Grandson of Seaghdha (majestic; learned).

Shead (*Eng.*) Dweller at the top of a ridge; or in a shed or hut.

Sheaff (*Eng.*) Dweller at the sign of the bundle of the stalks and ears of grain, a sheaf; descendant of Sceafa; dweller by the Sheaf (boundary), a river in England; or by a boundary.

Sheaffer (*Ger.*) Variant of Shaffer, q.v.

Shealey, Shealy (*Ir.*) Grandson of Sealbhach (proprietor; possessor).

Shear (*Eng.*) Variant of Shere, q.v.

Shearburn (*Eng.*) Variant of Sherbourne, q.v.

Sheard, Sheared (*Eng.*) Contraction of Sherrod, q.v.

Shearer, Shearier, Sheerer (*Eng.*) One who reaped standing crops; one who removed the fleece from animals.

Shearin (*Eng.*) Variant of Sherwin, q.v.

Shearman (*Eng.*) Variant of Sherman, q.v.

Shearn (*Ir.*) Variant of Sheeran, q.v.

Shearon (*Ir.*) Variant of Sheeran, q.v.

Shears, Shearson (*Eng.*) Descendant of Scira (bright).

Shearsmith (*Eng.*) Variant of Sharesmith, q.v.

Shearston (*Eng.*) One who came from Sharstone (stone with a notch), in Cheshire.

Sheats (*Eng.*) One who came from Sheat (park), in Wight; or from Sheet (park), in Hampshire.

Shechter, Shechtman, Sheckter, Shecter, Shectman (*Ger.*) Variant of Schachter, q.v.

Shedd, Shed, Shedis (*Eng.*) Dweller at the ridge or division separating lands sloping in different directions; dweller at, or near, a hut or shed.

Sheed (*Eng.*) Variant of Shead, q.v.

Sheedy (*Ir.*) Grandson of Sioda (silk).

Sheehan, Sheahan (*Ir.*) Grandson of little Siodhach (peaceful).

Sheehy, Sheehey (*Ir.*) The son of Sitheach (peaceful; eerie).

Sheel, Sheeler (*Eng.*) Dweller in a hut or shed.

Sheen (*Eng., Ir.*) One who came from Sheen (shelter), in Staffordshire; abbreviated form of Sheehan, q.v.

Sheer, Sheerr (*Eng.*) Variant of Shere, q.v.

Sheeran, Sheerin, Sheeren (*Ir.*) Grandson of Sirin.

Sheersmith (*Eng.*) One who made shears; variant of Sharesmith, q.v.

Sheets, Sheetz (*Eng., Ger.*) Dweller at, or near, a corner or projection; or on, or near, a steep hill; one who came from Sheat or Sheet (park), in Wight and Hampshire respectively; a field guard.

Sheffield (*Eng.*) One who came from Sheffield (sheep field), the name of several towns in England.

Sheffler (*Ger.*) Variant of Scheffler, q.v.

Sheinfeld (*Ger.*) Variant of Scheinfeld, q.v.

Shelansky, Shelanski (*Ukr.*) One who came from Selansky, in the Ukraine.

Shelbourn, Shelbourne (*Eng.*) One who

came from Shalbourne (shallow stream), in Wiltshire.

Shelby (*Eng.*) One who came from Selby (village where willows grew), in Yorkshire.

Sheldon, Shelden (*Eng.*) One who came from Sheldon (valley with steep sides; hill with a flat top), the name of three places in England.

Sheldrake (*Eng.*) Dweller at the sign of the sheldrake, a duck remarkable for its bright and variegated coloring; one thought to have some of the characteristics of a sheldrake.

Sheley (*Eng.*) Variant of Shelley, q.v.

Shell (*Eng.*) One who came from Shell (bank), in Worcestershire; dweller near a bank or ridge.

Shellenberger (*Ger.*) Variant of Schellenberg, q.v.

Sheller (*Ger.*) Variant of Scheller, q.v.

Shelley, Shelly (*Eng.*) One who came from Shelley (wood on a slope), in Essex.

Shelmerdine (*Eng.*) One who came from, or dwelt in, Hjalmar's valley.

Shelton (*Eng.*) One who came from Shelton (homestead on a bank or ledge), the name of several places in England.

Shender (*Ger.*) One who came from Schandau (muddy meadow), in Germany; one who prepared skins, a skinner.

Shenk (*Ger.*) Variant of Schenk, q.v.

Shenker, Shenkman (*Ger.*) Variant of Schenker, q.v.

Shenton (*Eng.*) One who came from Shenton (homestead on the Sence River), in Leicestershire.

Shepard, Sheppard, Shepherd, Shephard (*Eng.*) One who tended sheep.

Shepherdson (*Eng.*) The son of the man who tended the sheep.

Shepley (*Eng.*) Variant of Shipley, q.v.

Shepp (*Ger.*) Variant of Schepp, q.v.

Sher, Sherr (*Ger.*) Variant of Scher, q.v.

Sherbourne, Sherburne, Sherborne (*Eng.*) One who came from Sherbourne, Sherborne, or Sherburn (bright

stream), the names of several places in England.

Shere (*Eng.*) One who came from Shere (bright), in Surrey.

Sheresmyth (*Eng.*) An early spelling of Sheersmith, q.v.

Sheridan, Sherridan (*Ir.*) Grandson of Siridean (peaceful).

Sherif (*Arab.*) The prince or chief.

Sheriff, Sheriffs (*Eng.*) Descendant of the shire-reeve, the chief executive officer of a shire or county.

Sherin (*Ir.*) Grandson of Sirin.

Sherlock (*Eng.*) One who had white hair; dweller at the bright, or clear, stream or pool.

Sherman (*Eng.*) The shearman or cutter of wool or cloth.

Shermer (*Ger.*) Variant of Schermer, q.v.

Shernoff (*Rus.*) The son of the man with black hair or swarthy complexion.

Sherrick (*Scot.*) One who came from Sherraig (clear bay), in Scotland.

Sherriff (*Eng.*) Variant of Sheriff, q.v.

Sherrill, Shirrell (*Eng.*) One who came from Shirwell (clear spring), in Devonshire.

Sherrod, Sherrard, Sherard, Sherred (*Eng.*) Descendant of Scirheard (bright, hard); variants of Sherwood, q.v.

Sherry (*Ir.*) The son of Searrach (colt, flighty).

Sherwin (*Eng.*) Descendant of Scirwine (bright, friend); a nickname for a fast runner, "shear wind"; descendant of Sharvin (bitter).

Sherwood (*Eng.*) One who came from Sherwood (the wood belonging to the shire or county), in Nottinghamshire.

Sherzer (*Ger.*) Variant of Scherzer, q.v.

Shestack, Shestakov (*Rus., Ukr.*) The sixth one, probably the sixth born in the family.

Shetler (*Ger.*) Variant of Schettler, q.v.

Shevchuk, Shevchenko (*Ukr.*) The son of the shoemaker.

Sheward (*Eng.*) Variant of Seward, q.v.

Shewbrooks (*Eng.*) One who came from

Shobrooke (goblin stream), in Devonshire.

Shewell (*Eng.*) Descendant of Sjouald (sea, rule).

Shewsmith (*Eng.*) Variant of Shoesmith, q.v.

Shick, Shickman (*Ger.*) Variant of Schick, q.v.

Shields, Shield (*Eng.*) One who came from Shields (shepherd's summer hut), the name of places in Durham and Northumberland.

Shiff, Shiffman, Shifman (*Ger.*) Variant of Schiff, q.v.

Shifrin, Shiffrin (*Heb.*) Descendant of Shifre or Shifra (beautiful).

Shiller (*Ger.*) Variant of Schiller, q.v.

Shilliday (*Scot.*) Dweller at a shelter path.

Shilling (*Eng., Ger.*) Descendant of Scilling (shilling); variant of Schilling, q.v.

Shillingford (*Eng.*) One who came from Shillingford (river crossing of the Scillingas tribe), the name of places in Devonshire and Oxfordshire.

Shillitoe (*Eng.*) Dweller on the path or sheepwalk leading to a shed on a mountain pasture.

Shilton (*Eng.*) One who came from Shilton (homestead on a bank or ledge), the name of places in Berkshire, Leicestershire, and Oxfordshire.

Shimada (*Jap.*) Island, rice field.

Shimizu (*Jap.*) Pure, water.

Shimkonas (*Lith.*) Descendant of Simkus from Polish Szymek, endearing form of Szymon, Polish form of Simon (gracious hearing; hearkening; snubnosed).

Shimkus (*Lith.*) Descendant of Simkus or Shimko, pet forms of Szymon (gracious hearing; hearkening; snubnosed).

Shindler, Shindel, Shindell (*Ger.*) Variant of Schindler, q.v.

Shine (*Ir.*) Grandson of Seighin (wild ox).

Shinefeld, Shinefield, Shinfeld, Shinfield (*Eng.*) One who came from Shinfield (Scene's open country), in Berkshire.

Shingle, Shingles (*Eng.*) Metonymic for one who covered roofs with wooden tiles; one who came from Shingle Hall (manor house covered with wood laths), in Essex.

Shingler (*Eng.*) One who covered a roof with shingles or wood laths, a roofer.

Shinn (*Eng.*) Metonymic for one who prepared skins, a skinner.

Shinner, Shinners (*Eng.*) One who prepared skins, a skinner.

Shinnick (*Ir.*) Grandson of Seanach (wise; old).

Shintani (*Jap.*) New, valley.

Shiozaki (*Jap.*) Salt, headland.

Shipley (*Eng.*) One who came from Shipley (pasture for sheep), the name of several places in England.

Shipman (*Eng.*) One who worked on a ship, a seaman or sailor; one who had the care of sheep, a shepherd.

Shipp (*Eng.*) Dweller at the sign of the ship; one who worked on a ship, a sailor.

Shippen (*Eng.*) One who came from Shippen (cow shed), in the West Riding of Yorkshire.

Shippey (*Eng.*) One who came from the Isle of Sheppey (island where sheep were raised), in Kent.

Shippley (*Eng.*) Variant of Shipley, q.v.

Shipton (*Eng.*) One who came from Shipton (valley where sheep were kept), in Buckinghamshire.

Shire, Shires (*Eng.*) Dweller in the shire or county; one who came from Shere (bright), in Surrey.

Shireman (*Eng.*) The official or steward of a shire, a sheriff.

Shirey (*Eng.*) Dweller on the shire island, that is, the island belonging to the shire or county.

Shirk (*Ger.*) Descendant of Schirk, a Wendish form of George (farmer).

Shirley (*Eng.*) One who came from Shirley (wood belonging to the shire), the name of several places in England.

Shiroff (*Rus.*) The son of the big or wide man.

Shishido (*Jap.*) Flesh, door.

Shisler, Shissler (*Ger.*) Variant of Schissler, q.v.

Shively (*Ger.*) Dweller on a round, level piece of land; one who made and sold shovels.

Shivers, Shiver, Shivver (*Fr.*) One who tended goats, a goatherd.

Shlifer (*Ger.*) Variant of Schleifer, q.v.

Shlosser (*Ger.*) Variant of Schlosser, q.v.

Shmid (*Ger.*) A shortened form of the German Schmidt, q.v.

Shmukler, Shmuckler, Shmookler (*Ger.*) Variant of Schmucker, q.v.

Shober (*Ger.*) Variant of Schober, q.v.

Shock, Shocker (*Eng.*) One who gathers sheaves of grain into piles in the field.

Shockett, Shocket, Shochet (*Fr.*) One who collected taxes on wine; dweller at, or on, cleared land with stumps.

Shockey (*Eng.*) Dweller on an island where goblins roamed.

Shockley (*Eng.*) One who came from Shocklach (goblin stream), in Cheshire.

Shoemaker (*Eng.*) One who made and sold shoes and boots.

Shoenfeld (*Ger.*) Variant of Schoenfeld, q.v.

Shoesmith (*Eng.*) One who made horseshoes, a farrier.

Shogren (*Sw.*) Sea, branch.

Sholl, Sholler (*Ger.*) Variant of Scholl, q.v.

Shomo (*Sw.*) Sea, sandy plain.

Shone (*Ir., Ger.*) Descendant of Shone, an Irish form of John (gracious gift of Jehovah); one who came from Schon (beautiful) in Germany.

Shook (*Ger.*) Descendant of Cak (expectation); a corruption of Zschacke, q.v.

Shoosmith, Shoowsmith (*Eng.*) Variant of Shoesmith, q.v.

Shooter (*Eng.*) The fighting man armed with a bow and arrows, an archer.

Shore, Shor, Shorr, Shores (*Eng., Heb., Ger.*) Dweller at the shore; dweller at the sign of the bullock; a name adopted by people named Joseph in response to Deut. 33:17 where Joseph is likened to a young bullock.

Shorey (*Eng.*) Dweller on the island near the shore.

Shorrock (*Eng.*) One who came from Shorrock (precipitous rock), in Lancashire.

Short (*Eng.*) One of low stature, a little man.

Shortall, Shortell (*Eng.*) Dweller at the small nook or corner.

Shortridge, Shortrig (*Scot.*) One who came from Shortrig (small ridge), in Dumphriesshire.

Shostak (*Ukr.*) One born the sixth child in the family.

Shostakovitch (*Rus., Ukr.*) The son of Shostak (the sixth male child); one who has six fingers.

Shott (*Eng.*) Dweller at, or near, the shot, an area designation; the same as Furlong, q.v.

Shotwell (*Eng.*) One who came from Shotteswell (Scott's spring), in Warwickshire.

Shotz (*Ger.*) Variant of Schuetz, q.v.

Showalter (*Ger.*) Dweller in the woods; the schoolmaster.

Showell (*Eng.*) One who came from Showell (seven springs), in Bedfordshire.

Showers (*Eng.*) One who pushes or shoves his way, a man of violent habits.

Shpikula (*Ukr.*) The sixth-born in the family.

Shrader (*Ger.*) A variant of Schrader, q.v.

Shrank (*Ger.*) Variant of Schrank, q.v.

Shreck (*Ger.*) Variant of Schreck, q.v.

Shreeves (*Eng.*) Variant of Sheriff, q.v.

Shreffler (*Ger.*) Dweller at the fissured, rugged rock wall.

Shreibman (*Ger.*) A man expert in writing, employed in the service of clerics or lay gentlemen.

Shreiner (*Ger.*) Variant of Schreiner, q.v.

Shreve (*Eng.*) The shire-reeve, the chief

civil officer of the crown in the county, a sheriff.

Shrewsbury, Shrewsberry (*Eng.*) One who came from Shrewsbury (Scrobb's fort), in Shropshire.

Shriber (*Ger.*) Variant of Schreiber, q.v.

Shrier (*Ger.*) Variant of Schreier, q.v.

Shrieves (*Eng.*) Variant of Sheriff, q.v.

Shriner, Shreiner (*Ger.*) Variants of Schreiner, q.v.

Shriver, Shriber (*Ger.*) An official or public writer, a scribe.

Shropshire, Shropshear (*Eng.*) One who came from Shropshire (the shire with Shrewsbury as its head), a county in England.

Shryock (*Eng.*) One who came from Shireoaks (oak trees at the shire meeting place), in Nottinghamshire.

Shub, Shube (*Heb.*) One who slaughtered and examined meat under Jewish dietary laws.

Shubert, Shubart, Shubat (*Ger.*) One who made and sold shoes.

Shubrick, Shubrook (*Eng.*) One who came from Shobrooke (goblin stream), in Devonshire.

Shucker, Shuck (*Ger.*) One who made and sold shoes.

Shuford, Shufro (*Eng.*) One who came from Shifford (sheep ford), in Oxfordshire.

Shugar (*Ger.*) Variant of Shucker, q.v.

Shughsmith (*Eng.*) Variant of Shoesmith, q.v.

Shugrue (*Ir.*) Descendant of Slocfhraidh (victory, peace).

Shuhwerk (*Ger.*) One who made footwear, boots and shoes.

Shuler (*Ger.*) Variant of Schuler, q.v.

Shull (*Ger.*) Variant of Schull, q.v.

Shulman (*Ger.*) A variant of Schulman, q.v.

Shultz, Shultze (*Ger.*) Variant of Schultz, q.v.

Shuman, Shumaker, Shumacher (*Ger.*) One who made and sold shoes, a shoemaker.

Shumsky (*Ukr.*) One who made a lot of noise.

Shunk (*Ger.*) One with an unusual leg; metonym for one who took care of young pigs.

Shupp (*Ger.*) Variant of Schupp, q.v.

Shure, Shur (*Ger.*) One who sheared sheep; the cunning or crafty man; variant of Schauer, q.v.

Shurtleff (*Eng.*) Dweller near the short cliff; or the bright or white cliff.

Shuster, Shusterman (*Ger.*) Variant of Schuster, q.v.

Shute (*Eng., Wel.*) One who came from Shute (park), in Devonshire; dweller at a narrow lane; the tall, erect, straight man.

Shutt, Shutts (*Eng.*) Metonymic for an archer, a fighting man armed with a bow and arrows; dweller at a shoot or archery range.

Shutter, Shuter (*Eng.*) Variant of Shooter, q.v.

Shuttie (*Ger.*) One who guarded the fields, a hayward.

Shuttleworth (*Eng.*) One who came from Shuttleworth (enclosure made of bars), the name of several places in England.

Shvetz (*Ukr.*) One who made and sold shoes.

Shy (*Du., Ger.*) One who dwelt in, or near, the brushwood; one who came from Scheie (forest place), in Germany.

Shyer (*Ger.*) Variant of Scheier, q.v.

Siarczynski (*Pol.*) One who works with sulfate.

Sibbald (*Eng., Scot.*) Descendant of Saebeald (sea, bold).

Sibert (*Eng.*) Descendant of Saebeorht (sea, bright).

Sibilla, Sibila (*It.*) Descendant of Sibilla, Italian form of Sibyl (prophetess).

Sibley (*Eng.*) Descendant of Sibley, an English pet form of Sibyl (prophetess).

Sibson (*Eng.*) The son of Sib, a pet form of Sibyl (prophetess); or of Sibba (peace).

Sichel, Sichelman (*Fr., Ger.*) Dweller at the sign of the sickle or reaping hook, a sign sometimes chosen because of the resemblance of the word to

Sickl, a nickname for Isaac (he who laughs); one who works or harvests with a sickle; descendant of little Sich, a pet form of Isaac.

Siciliano, Sicilia (*It.*) One who came from Sicily (island of the Siculi tribe), an island in the Mediterranean Sea.

Sick (*Ger.*) Descendant of Sicco, a short form of names beginning with Sieg (victory), as Sigibold, Sigifrith, and Sigismund.

Sickafoose (*Ger.*) Variant of Sigafoos, q.v.

Sickel, Sickels, Sickles (*Ger., Eng.*) Dweller at the sign of the sickle, a sign sometimes chosen because of the resemblance of the word to Sickl, a nickname for Isaac (he who laughs); one who works or harvests with a sickle.

Sickelsmith (*Eng., Ger.*) Variant of Sicklesmith, q.v.

Sickenberger (*Ger.*) One who came from Sickenberg (hill by a swamp), in Germany.

Sickinger (*Ger.*) One who came from Sicking (Sica's people), the name of two places in Germany.

Sicklesmith (*Eng.*) One who made sickles, a crescent-shaped, agricultural implement similar to a reaping-hook except that it is provided with a serrated cutting-edge.

Sickman (*Eng.*) Descendant of Sigmund (victory, protection).

Sidberry, Sidbury (*Eng.*) One who came from Sidbury (southern fort), in Shropshire; dweller near the large stronghold.

Siddall, Siddell (*Eng.*) Dweller at the wide valley.

Siddons, Siddon (*Eng.*) Dweller at the broad hill.

Sidebotham, Sidebottom (*Eng.*) Dweller in the wide valley.

Sidel, Sidell (*Ger., Eng.*) Variant of Seidel, q.v.; descendant of Sidel (broad).

Sides, Side (*Eng., Ger.*) Dweller by the slope; one who came from Syde

(slope), in Gloucestershire; Americanization of Seitz, q.v.

Sidley (*Eng.*) Dweller at the broad, spacious grove.

Sidney (*Eng.*) Dweller on the wide, well-watered land.

Sidor, Sider (*Pol., Cz.-Sl., Ukr.*) Descendant of Sidor or Sydor (gift of Isis).

Sidwell (*Eng.*) One who came from Sidwell (broad stream), the name of places in Hampshire and Devonshire.

Sieber (*Ger.*) One who made and sold sieves.

Siebert, Sibert, Seebert (*Eng.*) Descendant of Sigibert (victory, bright).

Siefert (*Ger.*) Descendant of Siegfried (victory, peace).

Sieff (*Heb.*) Dweller at the sign of the wolf.

Siegel, Siegal, Siegl, Siegle (*Ger.*) Descendant of little Sigo, a pet form of names beginning with Sieg (victory), as Sigivald, Sigiwart, and Sigiwolf; variants of Segal, q.v.

Siegmann, Siegman (*Ger.*) Descendant of Sigimund (victory, protection).

Siegner (*Ger.*) One who came from Siegen (damp place), in Germany.

Siegrist (*Ger.*) An underofficer of a church who had charge of the sacristy and its contents, a sexton.

Siemer, Siemers (*Ger.*) Descendant of Sigimar (victory, fame).

Siems, Siemms (*Eng.*) Variant of Sims, q.v.

Sienkiewicz (*Pol., Rus.*) The son of Sienko, a pet form of Szymon, Slavic form of Simon (gracious hearing; hearkening; snub-nosed).

Sienko (*Pol.*) Descendant of Sienko, a pet form of Szymon, Polish form of Simon (gracious hearing; hearkening; snub-nosed).

Sieracki (*Pol.*) One who came from Sieradz, in Poland.

Sierocinski (*Pol.*) Descendant of the orphan.

Sierra (*Sp.*) Dweller among saw-shaped mountains; one who came from

Sierra (saw-toothed mountain), the name of several places in Spain.

Sievers, Siever (*Ger., Nor.*) Descendant of Sigiwart (victory, worthy); or of Syver, a short form of Sigvarthr (victory, guardian).

Sievert, Siewert, Siewerth (*Ger.*) Descendant of Sigiwart (victory, worthy).

Siewell (*Eng.*) Variant of Sewell, q.v.

Sifford (*Eng.*) Variant of Seifert, q.v.

Sigafoos, Sigafoose (*Ger.*) Americanized form of Sigafuss, q.v.

Sigafuss (*Ger.*) One who worked with a crowbar; one who had a foot like a goat; descendant of Sigifuns (victory, quick).

Sigal, Sigall, Sigel (*Ger.*) Variant of Siegel, q.v.

Sigg (*Eng., Ger.*) Descendant of Sig, a pet form of names beginning with Sieg (victory), such as Sigibrand, Sigiwolf, and Sigilbert.

Siggson (*Eng.*) The son of Sigga (victory).

Sigismondi (*It.*) Descendant of Sigismondo, Italian form of Sigmund (victory, protection).

Sigler (*Ger.*) One who made and sold seals for documents; one who made rubber stamps.

Sigman, Sigmann (*Ger.*) Variant of Siegmann, q.v.

Sigmond, Sigmund (*Eng.*) Descendant of Sigmund (victory, protection).

Signore, Signorelli, Signorello, Signoretti, Signora (*It.*) The master or head of the household; a man of superior rank, a lord.

Sigovich (*Rus.*) The son of Sig, a pet form of Siegfried (victory, peace).

Sigrist (*Ger.*) Variant of Siegrist, q.v.

Sikora (*Pol., Ukr.*) One with some real or fancied resemblance to a titmouse; one who came from Sikora, in Poland.

Sikorski (*Pol., Ukr.*) One who came from Sikora or Sikory (titmouse), the names of places in Poland.

Sikorsky (*Rus.*) Dweller at the sign of the titmouse.

Silas (*Eng.*) Descendant of Silas, a contraction of Silvanus, the god of trees.

Silber (*Ger.*) Descendant of Silber, a pet form of Sigilbert (victory, bright); one who came from Silber (silver), the name of various places in Germany; one with gray or silvery hair.

Silberberg, Silberberger (*Ger.*) One who came from Silberberg (silver mountain), the name of two places in Germany.

Silberg (*Ger.*) One who came from Silberg, the name of two places in Germany.

Silberman, Silbermann (*Ger.*) One who made and sold silver articles, a silversmith.

Silberstein (*Ger.*) Silver stone.

Silbert (*Ger.*) Descendant of Sigilbert (victory, bright).

Silby (*Eng.*) One who came from Sileby (Sighulf's homestead), in Leicestershire.

Silcox, Silcott (*Eng.*) Descendant of little Sil, a pet form of Silvester (forest dweller).

Siler (*Ger.*) Variant of Seiler, q.v.

Silk, Silkes (*Eng.*) One who dealt in silk; variant of Sills, q.v.

Siller, Sillers, Sillars (*Eng.*) One in charge of the cellar or storeroom; one who made, or dealt in, saddles.

Sillito, Sillitoe (*Eng.*) Variant of Shillitoe, q.v.

Sillman, Silliman (*Eng.*) The happy, blessed, simple man.

Sills, Sill (*Eng.*) Descendant of Sill, a pet form of Silvester (forest dweller); or of Silvanus (woods); or of Cecil (blind).

Silva (*Sp., Port.*) One who came from Silva (thicket of briers; woods), the name of several places in Spain and Portugal; dweller in, or by, the woods.

Silvan (*Eng.*) Descendant of Silvan or Silvanus (the woods).

Silvano, Silvanio (*It.*) Descendant of Silvanus (the woods).

Silveira (*Port.*) Dweller in, or near, a

wood, especially a wood of brier trees.

Silver, Silvers (*Eng., Ger.*) One who came from a locality of that name; dweller near one of various streams in England with that name because of their clear and sparkling water; an Anglicization of Silber, q.v.

Silverberg (*Ger.*) Englished form of Silberberg, q.v.

Silverman (*Ger.*) An Anglicization of Silberman, q.v.

Silversmith (*Eng.*) One who made or sold silver articles.

Silverstein, Silverstine (*Ger.*) Silver stone.

Silverstone (*Eng.*) One who came from Silverstone (Saewulf's homestead), in Northamptonshire.

Silverthorn, Silverthorne (*Eng.*) Dweller near the silver or white thorn tree.

Silvester, Silvestre (*Eng., Fr.*) Descendant of Silvester (forest dweller).

Silvestri, Silvestro (*It.*) Descendant of Silvestro (forest dweller).

Silvey (*Fr.*) Descendant of Silvius (forest).

Sim (*Eng.*) Descendant of Sim, a pet form of Simeon (gracious hearing; hearkening; snub-nosed).

Sima (*Sp.*) Dweller near a hole or pit in the ground; or at the top of the hill.

Simaitis (*Lith.*) The son of Simonas, Lithuanian form of Simon (gracious hearing; hearkening; snub-nosed).

Simcock, Simcox (*Eng.*) Descendant of little Sim, a pet form of Simon or Simeon (gracious hearing; hearkening; snub-nosed).

Simek (*Pol.*) Descendant of little Sim, a pet form of Szymon, Polish form of Simon (gracious hearing; hearkening; snub-nosed).

Simeon, Simeone (*Eng., Fr., Rus.*) Descendant of Simeon (gracious hearing; hearkening; snub-nosed).

Simkin, Simkins (*Eng.*) Descendant of little Sim, a pet form of Simon (gracious hearing; hearkening; snub-nosed).

Simko (*Eng.*) Descendant of little Sim, a pet form of Simon (gracious hearing; hearkening; snub-nosed).

Simkus (*Lith.*) Descendant of Simkus (possibly meaning hundred).

Simmelink (*Du.*) Son of Simon (gracious hearing; hearkening; snub-nosed).

Simmens (*Eng.*) Variant of Simmons, q.v.

Simmer, Simmers (*Scot.*) Scottish variant of Summers, q.v.

Simmons, Simmonds (*Eng.*) The son of Simon or Simeon (gracious hearing; hearkening; snub-nosed).

Simms (*Eng.*) Variant of Sims, q.v.

Simoes (*Port.*) The son of Simao, Portuguese form of Simon (gracious hearing; hearkening; snub-nosed).

Simokaitis (*Lith.*) The son of Simonas, a Lithuanian form of Simon (gracious hearing; hearkening; snub-nosed).

Simon (*Eng., Fr.*) Descendant of Simon (gracious hearing; hearkening; snub-nosed).

Simonds, Simond, Simund (*Eng.*) Descendant of Simon (gracious hearing; hearkening; snub-nosed).

Simone, Simoni (*Eng., It., Fr.*) Variant of Simon, q.v.

Simoneaux (*Fr.*) Descendant of little Simon (gracious hearing; hearkening; snub-nosed).

Simonetti (*It.*) Descendant of little Simon (gracious hearing; hearkening; snub-nosed).

Simonian (*Arm.*) The son of Simon (gracious hearing; hearkening; snub-nosed).

Simons (*Eng., Fr.*) Variant of Simmons, q.v.

Simonsen, Simonson (*Dan., Sw., Nor.*) The son of Simon (gracious hearing; hearkening; snub-nosed).

Simonton (*Eng.*) Dweller in, or near, Sigemund's homestead.

Simpkins, Simkins, Simkin (*Eng.*) Descendant of little Sim, a pet form of Simon or Simeon (gracious hearing; hearkening; snub-nosed).

Simpkinson (*Eng.*) The son of little Sim, a pet form of Simon or Simeon (gracious hearing; hearkening; snub-nosed).

Simpson, Simson (*Eng.*) The son of Sim, pet form of Simon or Simeon (gracious hearing; hearkening; snub-nosed); one who came from Simpson (Sigewine's homestead), in Buckinghamshire.

Sims (*Eng.*) Descendant of Sim, a pet form of Simon or Simeon (gracious hearing; hearkening; snub-nosed).

Sinclair (*Scot., Eng.*) One who came from St. Clair (bright), the name of several places in Normandy; follower of St. Clare.

Sindelar (*Cz.-Sl.*) One who made shingles.

Sing (*Chin.*) To vanquish.

Singer, Singerman (*Eng.*) One who sang, especially a church-singer; the soloist in the synagogue; one who came from Singen, in Germany.

Singh, Sinha (*Hindi*) Descendant of Singh (lion).

Single (*Eng.*) Dweller in, or near, the burnt clearing.

Singler (*Eng.*) One who lived alone.

Singletary, Singletarry, Singleterry (*Eng.*) One who came from St. Gaultier, in France.

Singleton (*Eng.*) One who came from Singleton (homestead with shingled roof; or on shingly soil), the name of places in Lancashire and Sussex.

Sink, Sinke (*Ger.*) Descendant of Sink, a Frisian form of Signand (victory, venture).

Sinkinson (*Eng., Ger.*) Variant of Simpkinson, q.v.; the son of little Sink, a Frisian form of Signand (victory, venture).

Sinkler (*Eng.*) Variant of Singler, q.v.

Sinn, Sinner (*Ger.*) One who came from Sinn (swamp), in Germany.

Sinnett, Sinnott (*Eng.*) Dweller at the sign of the little swan; variant of Sennott, q.v.

Sinton (*Eng., Scot.*) One who came from Sinton (south in the village), in Worcestershire; or from the barony of Sinton in Selkirkshire.

Sion, Sions (*Eng.*) One who came from Syon House (named from the Biblical Sion), in Middlesex.

Sippel, Sipple (*Ger.*) Descendant of Sigibald (victory, bold); one who made soup or gravies.

Sippy (*Ger.*) Descendant of Sippe, a pet form of names beginning with Sieg (victory), as Sigiberht and Sigibrand.

Siracusa (*It.*) One who came from Siracusa, in Sicily.

Sire (*Fr.*) The master or head of the household, a lord.

Sirianni (*It.*) Descendant of Father Anni, or one connected in some way with his household.

Sirkin, Sirken (*Ukr., Rus.*) Descendant of Sirka or Sirke, pet forms of Sarah (princess).

Siroky (*Cz.*) The large, broad-shouldered man.

Sirota (*Pol.*) Descendant of the orphan.

Sisco, Sisca (*It.*) Descendant of Sisca, a pet form of Francesco, Italian form of Francis (free).

Siskind, Siskin (*Ger.*) Sweet child.

Sisson, Sison, Sissen, Sissons (*Eng.*) The son of Siss, a pet form of Cecil (blind).

Sisto (*It.*) Descendant of Sisto (sixth).

Sites (*Ger.*) Descendant of Seitz, a short form of Siegfried (victory, peace).

Sitko (*Pol.*) One who works with a small sieve.

Sitnick (*Pol.*) Dweller in, or near, bullrushes.

Siwek (*Pol.*) Dweller at the sign of the gray horse; one who rode a gray horse.

Six (*Fr.*) Descendant of Sixte (sixth); one who came from Sixte (sixth), in France.

Sixsmith, Sexsmith (*Eng.*) The smith who made small swords or daggers.

Sizemore (*Eng.*) Descendant of Sigmar (victory, great); dweller on the Saxon's wasteland.

Sjoberg (*Sw.*) Sea, mountain.

Sjoblad (*Sw.*) Sea, leaf.

Sjogren (*Sw.*) Sea, branch.

Sjostrom (*Sw.*) Sea, stream.

Skaggs (*Eng., Sw.*) One with rough, shaggy hair or beard; one who came from Skaggs on the island of Gotland, Sweden.

Skala (*Cz.-Sl., Pol.*) Dweller near the rock.

Skalski, Skalsky (*Pol.*) Dweller near a rock.

Skarbek (*Eng.*) One who came from Skirbeck (bright stream), in Lincolnshire.

Skeels, Skeeles (*Dan., Ice.*) Variant of Skyles, q.v.

Skeen, Skeens (*Scot.*) One who came from Skene (a bush), in Aberdeenshire.

Skeete, Skeet, Skeeter (*Eng.*) One who moved quickly; descendant of Skeet (swift).

Skeffington (*Eng.*) One who came from Skeffington (homestead of Sceaft's people), in Leicestershire.

Skeggs (*Eng.*) One with a rough, shaggy beard.

Skeldon (*Eng.*) Variant of Sheldon, q.v.

Skelly, Skelley (*Ir.*) The son of Scalaighe (crier).

Skelton (*Eng.*) One who came from Skelton (the hill, or bank, manor), the name of parishes in Yorkshire and Cumberland.

Skene, Skeene (*Scot.*) One who came from the lands of Skene (a bush), in Aberdeenshire.

Skepton (*Eng.*) Variant of Shipton, q.v.

Skerry (*Eng.*) Dweller on a rocky isle.

Sketchley (*Eng.*) One who came from Sketchley (Shakk's grove), in Leicestershire.

Skiba (*Pol., Ukr.*) Single strip of soil thrown up by a plow, probably designating a plowman.

Skidmore (*Eng.*) Dweller at, or near, the dirty wasteland; or Skyti's wasteland.

Skiffington (*Eng.*) One who came from Skeffington (homestead of Sceaft's people), in Leicestershire.

Skillings, Skilling (*Eng.*) Descendant of Scilling (sonorous or shrill).

Skillman (*Eng.*) One thought to be trustworthy.

Skilton (*Eng.*) Variant of Skelton, q.v.

Skinner, Skynner (*Eng.*) One who prepared skins.

Skipp (*Eng.*) Variant of Shipp, q.v.

Skipper (*Eng.*) One in charge of a ship, a captain or shipmaster.

Skipwith, Skipworth (*Eng.*) One who came from Skipwith (sheep farm), in the East Riding of Yorkshire.

Sklar, Sklare (*Cz.-Sl., Ukr., Heb.*) One who made and sold glass and glassware, a glazier.

Sklaroff, Sklarow (*Rus.*) The son of the glazier.

Skloff (*Rus.*) One who dealt in glass.

Skoczylas (*Pol.*) One who leaps or jumps about.

Skog, Skogh (*Sw.*) Forest.

Skoglund, Skooglund (*Sw.*) Forest grove.

Skogsberg, Skogsbergh (*Nor., Sw.*) Dweller on a wooded hill or mountain; forest mountain.

Skolnik, Skolnick (*Cz.-Sl., Ukr.*) The student, or one connected in some way with a school; an important functionary of the synagogue in the early Jewish communities.

Skoog (*Nor., Sw.*) Dweller in, or near, the woods; forest.

Skora (*Pol.*) One who prepared skins, a skinner.

Skotarczak (*Pol.*) One who took care of domestic animals, a herdsman.

Skowronek (*Pol.*) Dweller at the sign of the lark; one who trapped larks.

Skowronski, Skowron (*Pol.*) Dweller at the sign of the lark; one with the qualities of a lark.

Skulsky, Skulski, Skulskyj (*Ukr., Rus.*) One with a prominent cheek bone.

Skversky (*Pol.*) Dweller on the square.

Skyles, Skiles (*Dan., Ice.*) Descendant of Skyli (protector, king).

Slack (*Eng.*) Dweller at a hollow or pass between hills.

Slackway (*Eng.*) Dweller at the path or road across the valley.

Slade (*Eng.*) Dweller in the valley or dell.

Sladek (*Pol.*) Footprint, possibly one who made a large footprint.

Slager (*Ger., Du.*) One who chopped wood and cleared land; one who cut meat, a butcher.

Slane (*Ir.*) One who came from Slaine or Slane, in County Meath.

Slansky (*Cz.*) One who came from Slane (salty place), in Czechoslovakia.

Slap (*Eng.*) Dweller near a wet, miry place.

Slappy, Slappey (*Eng.*) Dweller on a miry island; or on an island with a portage, a place where boats are dragged.

Slatcher (*Eng.*) Variant of Slater, q.v.

Slater, Slayter (*Eng.*) One who roofed buildings with flat rock or slate; variant of Slaughter, q.v.

Slattery (*Ir.*) Grandson of Slatra (bold; strong).

Slaughter (*Eng.*) Dweller at, or near, a slough or muddy place; one who came from Slaughter (muddy place), in Gloucestershire; one who killed animals, a butcher.

Slaven, Slavin (*Ir., Rus.*) Descendant of Sleibhin (little mountain), a pet form of Donnsleidhe; the son of Slav, a pet form of Jaroslav (strong, glorious).

Slavinski, Slavinsky (*Pol., Ukr.*) Descendant of Slawa, a short form of names terminating in slawa (glory), as Jaroslav and Stanislaw.

Slavutych (*Ukr.*) Dweller near the Slavuta, poetic name for the Dnieper river.

Slaw, Slawe, Slawsky (*Pol.*) Descendant of Slaw (glory).

Slawter (*Eng.*) Variant of Slaughter, q.v.

Slay (*Eng.*) Variant of Sleigh, q.v.; metonymic for one who made slays, an instrument used in weaving.

Slaymaker (*Eng.*) One who made slays for use in weaving to beat up the weft.

Slayman, Slaysman (*Eng.*) One who made slays for use in weaving to beat up the weft; dweller at the grassy slope.

Slayton (*Eng.*) Dweller in the homestead on a grassy slope.

Sleath (*Eng.*) Variant of Slay, q.v.

Sledge (*Eng.*) One who used a large, heavy hammer in his work.

Sleep (*Eng.*) One who came from Sleep, in Hertfordshire; dweller at the slip or boatlanding place; or at the slope or side of the hill.

Sleeper (*Eng.*) One who made scabbards for swords; one who polished or sharpened swords.

Sleeter (*Eng.*) One who slaughtered animals and cut and sold meat, a butcher.

Sleigh (*Eng.*) One who was dexterous or skilled.

Slemp (*Ger.*) One who habitually engages in drinking and revelry.

Slevin, Sleven (*Ir.*) Descendant of Sliabhin (small mountain).

Slezak (*Cz.-Sl.*) One who came from Silesia (the bad land), for centuries a part of Poland.

Slicer (*Eng.*) One who cuts broad thin pieces of wood, probably in shipbuilding.

Slick (*Eng.*) The sleek, smooth man.

Slifkin (*Rus.*) One who sold and delivered fresh cream.

Sligh (*Eng.*) Variant of Sleigh, q.v.

Slimm (*Du.*) The clever man.

Slingbaum (*Ger.*) Dweller near a hedge.

Slingsby (*Eng.*) One who came from Slingsby (Sleng's homestead), in the North Riding of Yorkshire.

Slipakoff (*Rus., Ukr.*) The son of the blind man.

Sliva (*Cz.*) Dweller near the plum tree.

Slivka (*Cz.*) One who grows and sells small plums.

Sliwa (*Pol., Ukr.*) Dweller near a plum tree.

Sliwinski (*Pol.*) Dweller near a plum tree.

Sloan, Sloane, Slown, Sloyne (*Ir.*) Grandson of Sluaghan (soldier or warrior).

Sloate, Sloat (*Ger.*) Variant of Slote, q.v.

Sloboda (*Rus.*) One who came from a large village.

Slobodian (*Ukr.*) One who lived in suburbs or village on the main road; the villager.

Slobotkin (*Rus.*) One who came from Slobodka (village), in Russia.

Slocum, Slocomb, Slocombe, Slocumb (*Eng.*) Dweller in a valley where blackthorn or sloe trees flourished.

Sloman, Slomon (*Eng., Heb.*) Jewish variant of Solomon, q.v.

Slosberg (*Ger.*) Dweller near, or worker in, the castle on the mountain.

Slosser, Sloss (*Ger.*) Americanized form of Schlosser, q.v.

Slote (*Ger.*) Dweller near a reedy ditch or quagmire.

Slotnick, Slotnik (*Cz.-Sl., Rus., Pol.*) One who made, or sold, gold articles, a goldsmith.

Slott, Slotter (*Eng., Nor., Dan.*) Dweller in, or near, or worker in, the castle or stronghold.

Slough (*Eng.*) Dweller near the deep muddy place; one who came from Slough (mire), in Buckinghamshire.

Slovak (*Cz.-Sl., Yu.-Sl.*) One who came from Slovakia (speakers of the word).

Slow, Slowe (*Eng.*) Dweller by the slough or marshy place.

Slowey (*Ir.*) Grandson of Sluaghadhach (belonging to a host).

Slowik, Slowick (*Pol.*) Dweller at the sign of the nightingale; one with some quality of a nightingale.

Slowinski (*Pol.*) One who came from Slovenia, a territory now in Yugoslavia.

Sloyne, Sloyan (*Ir.*) Grandson of Sluaighhin (belonging to a host).

Slusarski (*Pol.*) One who made and sold locks, a locksmith.

Slutsky (*Rus.*) One who came from Slutsk, in Byelorussia.

Sly, Slye (*Eng.*) One who was dexterous or skilled.

Slygh (*Eng.*) Variant of Sleigh, q.v.

Slyne (*Eng.*) One who came from Slyne (slope), in Lancashire.

Smail (*Scot.*) A variant of Small, q.v.

Small, Smale, Smalls (*Eng.*) The little or slender person.

Smalley (*Eng.*) One who came from Smalley (narrow wood), in Derbyshire.

Smallwood (*Eng., Scot.*) Dweller in, or near, the little wood or small group of trees.

Smart, Smert (*Eng.*) The quick, sharp person.

Smathers (*Eng.*) Dweller on the smooth or level ground.

Smaw (*Eng.*) Variant of Small, q.v.

Smeath (*Eng.*) Dweller at the smooth or level field; one who came from Smeeth (smithy), in Kent.

Smeaton (*Eng.*) One who came from Smeaton (the smith's homestead), the name of places in the North and West Ridings of Yorkshire.

Smeedy (*Eng.*) Variant of Smiddy, q.v.

Smedley (*Eng.*) Dweller at the smooth, or flat, meadow.

Smeed (*Eng.*) One who came from Smeeth (smithy), in Kent; dweller on the smooth, level ground.

Smelley, Smellie (*Eng.*) One who came from Smalley (narrow wood), in Derbyshire.

Smeltzer (*Ger.*) Variant of Schmelzer, q.v.

Smerilson (*Eng.*) The son of Smerel, a pet form of Smerius.

Smet (*Du.*) Variant of Smit, q.v.

Smetana (*Cz.-Sl., Pol., Ukr.*) Sour cream, a nickname given to one in recognition of some quality, probably mental.

Smeth (*Eng.*) Variant of Smeath, q.v.

Smethills (*Eng.*) One who came from Smithills (smooth hill), in Lancashire.

Smethurst (*Eng.*) Dweller at the wood on the smooth or level land; variant of Smithurst, q.v.

Smey (*Eng.*) Dweller on smooth, level ground; colloquial pronunciation of Smeth or Smith, q.v.

Smiddy, Smiddie (*Eng., Scot.*) One who worked in the smithy; dweller near the smith's workshop.

Smidl (*Eng., Ger.*) The little smith.

Smietana (*Cz.-Sl., Pol., Ukr.*) Variant of Smetana, q.v.

Smijth, Smijtt (*Eng.*) Variation in the spelling of Smyth caused by the *y* being dotted.

Smiles (*Eng.*) One who came from Smales (the narrow one), in Northumberland.

Smiley, Smilie, Smillie (*Eng., Scot.*) One who came from Semilly or Semily, in France; variant of Smalley, q.v.

Smilowitz (*Ukr.*) The son of the bold man.

Smit, Smid, Smidt (*Du.*) The worker in metals.

Smith, Smithe (*Eng., Scot., Ir.*) The worker in metals.

Smitham (*Eng.*) Dweller at the smith's homestead; or at the smooth, level enclosure.

Smithard (*Eng.*) The worker in metal who lived by the height or hill.

Smithausler (*Ger.*) The worker in metal who was the owner of a cottage with little land around it.

Smithbaker (*Eng.*) The smith whose father was a baker; the smith who became a baker.

Smithdale (*Eng.*) The worker in metal who dwelt or had his forge in the meadow or valley.

Smitheal (*Eng.*) Dweller in the smith's valley.

Smithers, Smither (*Eng.*) One who plies the trade of a smith, or worker in metals; dweller near the workshop of a smith.

Smithgall (*Eng.*) The worker in metals who lived or worked in the ravine or narrow lane.

Smithheimer (*Ger.*) Dweller in the home of a smith.

Smithies (*Eng.*) Dweller near, or worker in, the workshop of the smith.

Smithke, Smithkey, Smithka (*Ger.*) The smith who was small in stature.

Smithline, Smithlin (*Eng.*) The smith who lived or worked by a deep pool or lake.

Smithmeyer, Smithmier (*Ger.*) The worker in metal who was also a farmer.

Smithson, Smithsonne, Smithsome (*Eng.*) The son of the worker in metal, probably one who failed to follow his father's trade.

Smithurst (*Eng.*) Dweller in the smith's wood; variant of Smethurst, q.v.

Smithus (*Eng.*) Dweller in, or near, the smith's house.

Smithwaite, Smithwhite (*Eng.*) Dweller at the smith's clearing; or at the small clearing; or at the smooth clearing or meadow.

Smithweeke (*Eng.*) Variant of Smithwick, q.v.

Smithwick, Smithwich (*Eng.*) One who came from Smethwick (smith's dwelling), the name of places in Cheshire and Staffordshire.

Smithy (*Eng.*) Dweller near the workshop of a smith; one who worked in a smithy.

Smitz (*Ger.*) One who worked in metal.

Smock (*Eng.*) Metonymic for one who made and sold smocks.

Smoker (*Eng.*) One who made and sold smocks, formerly a woman's undergarment; one who cured fish or meat by means of smoke.

Smolen, Smolens, Smolin, Smolenski, Smolensky (*Pol., Rus.*) Dweller in, or near, a pine wood.

Smolinski (*Pol.*) One who came from Smolensk (pitch), in Russia.

Smollett (*Eng., Scot.*) One who had a small head.

Smolow, Smolowitz (*Rus., Ukr.*) One who dealt in, or worked with, pitch or tar.

Smoluk (*Ukr.*) One who produced and sold tar.

Smookler (*Du.*) One who smokes.

Smoot (*Du.*) One who renders lard.

Smotherman, Smothermon (*Eng.*) One who plies the trade of a smith or worker in metals.

Smothers (*Eng.*) Variant of Smithers, q.v.

Smucker, Smuckler, Smukler (*Ger.*) Variant of Schmucker, q.v.

Smullen (*Ir.*) Grandson of Spealain (little scythe).

Smulyan (*Arm.*) The son of Smul, Armenian form of Samuel (God hath heard; name of God; Shem is God).

Smurthwaite (*Eng.*) Dweller in a small clearing; or in a clearing where butter was produced.

Smutnik (*Rus.*) One who created a disturbance.

Smutny, Smutney (*Cz.-Sl.*) The moody or sad, sorrowful man.

Smylie, Smyly (*Eng., Scot.*) Variant of Smiley, q.v.

Smyrl (*Cz.-Sl.*) The quiet, peaceful man.

Smyser (*Ger.*) Americanization of Schmeisser, q.v.

Smyth, Smythe (*Eng.*) The worker in metals. This is the common, old spelling of the name.

Snaith (*Eng.*) One who came from Snaith (piece of land), in the West Riding of Yorkshire.

Snape (*Eng.*) One who came from Snape (pasture), in Suffolk.

Snapp, (*Eng., Mx.*) One who came from Snape (pasture), in Suffolk; dweller on land with scanty grass or poor grazing for sheep; dweller on boggy ground.

Snavely (*Eng., Ger.*) Dweller in a grove on a narrow strip of land; American variant of Schnabele, q.v.

Sneath (*Eng.*) Variant of Snaith, q.v.

Snedaker, Snedeker (*Eng.*) Dweller on the hillside field.

Sneddon (*Eng.*) One who came from Sneaton (homestead on woodland), in the North Riding of Yorkshire.

Snee (*Ger., Du., Dan., Nor.*) One with snow-white clothing; variant of Schnee, q.v.

Sneed, Snead, Sneyd (*Eng.*) Dweller at a clearing or piece of woodland; one who came from Snaith (piece of land), in Yorkshire.

Sneider (*Du.*) Variant of Snyder, q.v.

Sneith (*Eng.*) Variant of Snaith, q.v.

Snelgrove, Snelgro, Snellgrove (*Eng.*) Dweller in a grove or wood infested by snails.

Snell (*Ger., Eng., Scot.*) The quick agile person; descendant of Snell (strong; smart).

Snellbaker, Snelbaker (*Eng.*) The quick cooker of bread or biscuits.

Snellenberg, Snellenburg (*Du.*) One who came from Snellenberg, in Holland.

Snelling, Snellings (*Eng.*) The son of Snell (strong; smart).

Snelson (*Eng.*) One who came from Snelson (Snell's homestead), in Cheshire; the son of Snel (strong; smart).

Snesmyth (*Eng.*) Dweller in, or near, the smith's clearing.

Snider, Sneider (*Du.*) Variant of Snyder, q.v.

Snipes, Snipe (*Eng.*) One who came from Snipe (swamp land), in Northumberland; dweller on a boggy patch of ground.

Snitcher (*Ger.*) Americanized form of Schnitzer, q.v.

Snite (*Eng.*) Dweller at the sign of the snipe; one with some characteristic of a snipe.

Snitzer (*Ger.*) Variant of Schnitzer, q.v.

Snively (*Eng., Ger.*) Variant of Snavely, q.v.

Snoddy (*Scot.*) The neat, smooth man.

Snodell (*Eng.*) One who came from Snodhill (snowy hill), in Herefordshire.

Snoden, Snodon (*Eng.*) Variant of Snowden, q.v.

Snodgrass (*Eng., Scot.*) Dweller at the smooth, trim, grassy place; one who came from Snodgrasse, in Ayrshire.

Snooks, Snook (*Eng.*) One who came from Sevenoaks (seven oaks), in Kent; dweller on, or near, a projecting point or piece of land.

Snow (*Eng.*) Descendant of Snow, a name given to one born in the time of snow; a white-haired or very light-complexioned person.

Snowden, Snowdon (*Eng.*) Dweller near a snow hill; one who came from Snowden (snow hill), the name of several small places in England.

Snowhite (*Eng.*) One with snow-white hair; nickname for an old man.

Snowman (*Ger.*) Americanized form of Schneemann, q.v.; one who had snow-white hair.

Snyder (*Du.*) One who made outer garments, a tailor.

Snyderman, Snydman (*Du.*) An extension of Snyder, q.v.

Soares, Soars (*Eng.*) One with reddish-brown or yellowish-brown hair.

Soave (*It.*) The calm, gentle man.

Sobczak (*Pol.*) Descendant of the egotist.

Sobel, Soble, Sobol, Sobelman (*Pol., Rus.*) Dweller at the sign of the sable; one who trapped and sold sables.

Sobieski (*Pol.*) One who came from Sobieski, Sobieszki or Sobieszyn (Sobiech's settlement), the names of villages in Poland.

Soboleff (*Rus.*) Dweller at the sign of the sable; one who hunted sables; one who wore spotted clothing.

Sobolewski (*Pol.*) One who trapped sables for the fur.

Sobota, Sobotka (*Pol.*) Saturday, probably a nickname for one who habitually did something on that day.

Socha (*Pol., Rus., Ukr., Cz.-Sl.*) One who used the wooden plow.

Socksmith (*Eng.*) The worker in metal who held land in socage, that is, money rent rather than by work service; one who made socks, an old word for a plowshare.

Soden (*Eng.*) Variant of Sowden, q.v.

Soder (*Sw.*) One who came from the south; descendant of Sauthr (sheep).

Soderberg (*Sw.*) South, mountain.

Sodergren (*Sw.*) South, branch.

Soderlind (*Sw.*) Dweller by the south linden tree.

Soderlund (*Sw.*) South, grove.

Soderquist (*Sw.*) South, twig.

Soderstrom (*Sw.*) South, stream.

Soffer, Sofer (*Heb.*) One who copied books and manuscripts, a scribe.

Sofia (*It.*) Descendant of Sofia, Italian form of Sophia (wisdom).

Softly, Softley (*Eng.*) One who came from Softley (grove on spongy soil), in Durham.

Sohn (*Ger.*) The son, usually a shortened form of names with this termination.

Soifer, Soiffer (*Heb.*) Variant of Soffer, q.v.

Sojourner (*Eng.*) One who established a temporary residence; a stranger.

Sokol, Sokolowski, Sokolski (*Cz.-Sl., Pol.*) One with the qualities of a falcon or hawk; dweller at the sign of the falcon.

Sokoloff, Sokolove, Sokolow, Sokolsky (*Rus.*) The son of one who hunted with a hawk or falcon; dweller at the sign of the falcon.

Sokolovsky (*Rus.*) One who came from Sokolovo (town where falcons were found), in Russia.

Sol, Soll (*Eng., Fr.*) Descendant of Sol, a pet form of Solomon (peaceful; worshipper of the god Shalman); dweller on, or near, the ground used for beating grain.

Sola (*Finn.*) Dweller at the pass or gorge.

Solakzade (*Pers.*) Descendant of Solak (left).

Solar (*Sp.*) Dweller on, or near, the place on which stands the original mansion of a noble family.

Solari, Solaro (*It.*) Dweller in an attic; or in a house with an attic.

Solarz (*Pol.*) One who prepared and sold salt.

Solberg (*Nor., Sw., Dan.*) One who came from Solberg (sunny hill), the name of places in Norway, Sweden, and Denmark; sun mountain.

Solecki (*Pol.*) One who came from Solec (salt), in Poland.

Solis (*Sp.*) One who came from Solis (sunny place), in Spain.

Solliway, Soloway (*Eng.*) One who came from Solway (sunny ford), in Cumberland.

Solly, Solley (*Eng.*) Descendant of little Sol, a pet form of Solomon (peaceful; worshiper of the god Shalman).

Solnick (*Pol.*) One who dealt in salt.

Soloff (*Rus.*) Dweller at the sign of the

nightingale; one thought to possess the qualities of a nightingale.

Solomon, Soloman (*Eng.*) Descendant of Solomon (peaceful; worshiper of the god Shalman).

Solow (*Rus.*) Descendant of the singer.

Soltis, Soltys (*Pol.*) The official who performed the duties of a magistrate or mayor of a village.

Solway (*Eng.*) One who came from Solway (sunny ford), in Cumberland.

Somerman (*Eng.*) One who worked in the summer, a seasonal worker.

Somersall (*Eng.*) One who came from Somersall (Sumor's corner), in Derbyshire.

Somerset (*Eng.*) One who came from Somerset (people of Somerset), the name of a county in England.

Somerson (*Eng.*) The son of Somer (summer).

Somerville, Sommerville (*Eng., Ir.*) One who came from Sommerville (Sumar's estate), in Normandy; grandson of Somachan (soft, innocent person).

Sommer, Sommers, Somers (*Eng.*) Descendant of Sumer or Somer (summer); variant of Summers, q.v.

Sommerfeld, Sommerfield (*Ger.*) One who came from Sommerfeld (summer field), the name of several places in Germany; dweller at, or near, the place used in summer.

Somogyi (*Hun.*) One who came from the county of Somogy, in Hungary.

Sonaband, Sonabend (*Ger.*) Descendant of Sonnabend (Saturday); one who habitually did some act on Saturday.

Sondberg (*Sw.*) Sound, mountain.

Sonder (*Ger.*) Dweller in a swampy area.

Song (*Chin.*) To dwell (a dynasty name).

Sonne, Sonn, Son (*Eng.*) The son of another; possibly one who was younger than another with whom he was associated.

Sonneborn (*Ger.*) One who came from Sonneborn (sunny spring), in Germany.

Sonnenberg (*Ger.*) One who came from

Sonnenberg, the name of numerous places in Germany.

Sonnenschein, Sonenshein (*Ger.*) Dweller near a sunny place; the sunny, radiant man; sunshine.

Sonnheim (*Ger.*) One who came from Sondheim (home in a swampy place), the name of two places in Germany.

Sonntag, Sontag (*Ger.*) Descendant of Sonntag, a name sometimes given to one born on Sunday.

Soo (*Chin.*) To revive.

Sookasian (*Arm.*) The son of the martyr.

Soop (*Est.*) Dweller on low, easily flooded land.

Soos (*Hun.*) One who processed and sold salt.

Soper, Sopster (*Eng.*) One who made, or sold, soap.

Sophocles (*Gr.*) Descendant of Sophocles (wisdom).

Sopp, Sop (*Ger.*) Dweller in, or near, a swamp.

Sorber (*Ger.*) One who sold sour beer.

Sorensen, Sorenson, Soren (*Dan., Nor.*) The son of Soren (severe or strict), from Severinus, the name of several saints. Soren has also been used as a term for the devil.

Sorge, Sorg, Sorger (*Ger.*) One who came from Sorge (sorrow), the name of many places in Germany.

Soriano (*Sp.*) One who came from the province of Soria (brown place), in Spain.

Sorkin (*Rus.*) Descendant of Sorkeh, a pet form of Sarah (princess).

Soroka (*Ukr., Rus.*) Dweller at the sign of the magpie; one with the characteristics of a magpie.

Sorokin (*Rus.*) Dweller at the sign of the magpie; one thought to have the characteristics of a magpie; variant of Sorkin, q.v.

Sorrell, Sorrells, Sorrels (*Eng.*) The man with the reddish-brown complexion.

Sorrentino, Sorrento, Sorrenti (*It.*) One who came from Sorrento, in Napoli.

Sosa (*Sp.*) Spanish form of Sousa, q.v.

Sosna (*Pol.*) Dweller near a pine tree.

Sosnovec (*Yu.-Sl.*) Dweller near a pine tree.

Sosnow, Sosnov, Sosnowski (*Pol.*) Dweller near a pine tree; one who came from Sosnowica (place of pine trees).

Sostmann (*Ger.*) One who sold sweet beer; nickname for a brewer.

Soto (*Sp.*) One who came from Soto (wooded place on the bank of a river), the name of numerous places in Spain.

Souch, Souche (*Fr.*) One who came from Souche (Soppius' estate), in France; dweller near a tree stump.

Souder, Souders (*Fr.*) One who repairs by welding or soldering.

Soukup (*Pol.*) One who was a business partner of another.

Soulberry (*Eng.*) One who came from Soulbury (fort by a gully), in Buckinghamshire.

Soule, Soul, Soules (*Eng.*) Dweller at, or near, a muddy pond.

Soulsby (*Eng.*) One who came from Soulby (homestead with a gully), the name of places in Cumberland and Westmorland.

Sours (*Eng.*) Variant of Sowers, q.v.

Sourwine (*Ger., Fr.*) One who pressed green fruits and produced and sold verjuice; sour wine.

Sousa (*Port., Sp.*) One who came from Sousa (salty place), in Portugal; dweller near the Sousa, a river in Portugal.

Souter, Soutar (*Eng.*) One who made and sold shoes, a shoemaker.

South, Southe (*Eng.*) One who came from the south.

Southall (*Eng.*) One who came from Southall (the southern corner), in Middlesex.

Southard (*Eng.*) Dweller at the south wood; one who came from Southworth (southern homestead), in Lancashire.

Southcott (*Eng.*) Dweller in the cottage to the south; one who came from Southcot (southern cottage), in Berkshire.

Southerland (*Scot.*) One who came from Sutherland (the southern land), the name of a county in Scotland.

Southern, Souther, Southerne (*Eng.*) One who came from the south.

Southey (*Eng.*) Dweller on the south island; or near the south stream.

Southgate (*Eng.*) Dweller near the southern gate to the town.

Southrey (*Eng.*) One who came from Southery (the southern island), in Norfolk.

Southward (*Eng.*) One who came from Southwark (southern fort), in Surrey.

Southwell (*Eng.*) One who came from Southwell (the southern spring), in Nottinghamshire.

Southwick (*Eng.*) One who came from Southwick (southern dwelling), the name of several places in England.

Southwood (*Eng.*) One who came from Southwood (the southern wood), in Norfolk.

Southworth (*Eng.*) One who came from Southworth (southern homestead), in Lancashire.

Souza (*Port., Sp.*) One who came from Souza (salty place), in Portugal.

Sowa (*Pol.*) One with owlish qualities; dweller at the sign of the owl.

Sowden (*Eng., Scot.*) Dweller in the valley where sows were kept; or in the south valley; one who played the part of a sultan in the pageants; one who came from Southdean (southern pasture), in Roxburghshire.

Sowder (*Eng.*) Variant of Souter, q.v.

Sowell (*Eng.*) Variant of Southwell, q.v.

Sowers, Sower (*Eng.*) One who scatters the seeds, the planter.

Sowinski (*Pol.*) One who came from Sowa or Sowin (owl), the name of places in Ukraine and Byelorussia.

Sowle, Sowles, Sowl (*Eng.*) Variant of Soule, q.v.

Spada, Spadoni (*It.*) One who made swords.

Spadafora (*It.*) One who came from Spadafora (drawn sword), in Sicily.

Spadaro (*It.*) Soldier armed with a sword; one who made swords.

Spadavecchia, Spadavecchio (*It.*) One armed with an old sword.

Spaeth, Spath (*Ger.*) One in the habit of being late or tardy.

Spagna (*It.*) One who came from Spain, a Spaniard.

Spagnola, Spagnolo, Spagnuolo, Spagnolia (*It.*) One who came from Spain, a Spaniard; nickname for one who had been to Spain and returned; the haughty or elegantly attired man.

Spahn (*Ger.*) One who came from Spahn (moor or bog), in Germany.

Spahr (*Ger.*) Dweller at the sign of the sparrow.

Spain (*Eng., Scot.*) One who came from Spain, or who returned after having resided in Spain.

Spalding (*Eng.*) One who came from Spalding (the Spaldas tribe), in Lincolnshire.

Spang (*Ger.*) One who came from Spang (bog).

Spangemacher (*Ger.*) One who made clasps, buckles, brooches, and bracelets.

Spangenberg (*Ger.*) One who came from Spangenberg (moor on the hill), in Germany.

Spangler (*Ger.*) One who mended pots and kettles, a tinker, one who worked with, or dealt in, lead.

Spanier, Spanjer (*Ger.*) One who came from Spain, a Spaniard.

Spann, Span (*Ger.*) One who came from Spann, the name of two farms in Germany; or from Spahn (moor or bog), a town in Germany.

Spano (*It.*) One who came from Spain, a Spaniard; the man with a sparse beard; the bald man.

Spanos (*Gr.*) The clean-shaven man, that is, beardless.

Spargo, Spargue (*Eng.*) Dweller in, or near, the thicket of thorns.

Sparhawk (*Eng.*) Shortened form of Sparrowhawk, q.v.

Sparkman (*Eng.*) The gay, lively man.

Sparks, Sparkes, Spark (*Eng.*) Dweller at the sign of the sparrow hawk; one with some characteristic of a sparrow hawk.

Sparling (*Eng.*) One with some characteristic of a little sparrow.

Sparnall (*Eng.*) One who came from Spernall (chalk bank), in Warwickshire.

Sparrow, Sparr (*Eng.*) One thought to possess some quality of a sparrow, such as a homey, chirpy disposition; dweller at the sign of the sparrow.

Sparrowhawk (*Eng.*) Dweller at the sign of the sparrow hawk; descendant of Sparrowhawk, an early personal name.

Sparta (*Sp.*) One who came from Sparta, in Greece.

Spatola (*It.*) Dweller near where iris grew; or near a century plant.

Spatz (*Ger.*) Dweller at the sign of the sparrow; one with some characteristic of a little sparrow.

Spaulding (*Eng.*) One who came from Spalding (tribe of Spaldas), in Lincolnshire.

Speach, Speech (*Eng.*) One who came from Speke (brushwood), in Lancashire; dweller at the sign of the woodpecker.

Speak, Speakes, Speaks (*Eng.*) One who came from Speke (brushwood), in Lancashire; dweller at the sign of the woodpecker; one thought to possess some characteristic of a woodpecker.

Speaker, Speakman (*Eng.*) One who acted as a spokesman for others.

Spearing (*Eng.*) Variant of Spering, q.v.

Spearman (*Eng.*) A soldier or warrior armed with a spear.

Spears, Spear, Spiers (*Eng.*) The watchman or lookout man.

Specht (*Ger.*) Dweller at the sign of the woodpecker; one with the qualities of a woodpecker.

Speck, Speight (*Eng.*) One who came from Speke (brushwood), in Lancashire; one thought to possess some characteristic of a woodpecker; dweller at the sign of the woodpecker.

Specker (*Ger.*) One who came from Speck (bacon) or Specken (swampy area), the names of several places in Germany; one who cut blubber; or who dealt in bacon.

Spector, Specter (*Rus.*) A title meaning "inspector," used by Hebrew teachers in old Russia, which, when registered with the police, enabled them to live in areas forbidden to Jews.

Spedding (*Eng.*) The son of Sped (prosperity).

Speechley (*Eng.*) One who came from Spetchley (grove where men spoke to the people, a meeting place), in Worcestershire.

Speed (*Eng.*) Descendant of Sped (prosperity).

Speer, Speers (*Eng.*) The watchman or lookout man.

Spees, Speese (*Du.*) One who raised and sold pears.

Speidel (*Ger.*) One who made pegs, plugs, or dowels; a rude or uncouth man.

Speier (*Eng.*) One who acted as a spy or watchman.

Speight, Speights (*Eng.*) Dweller at the sign of the woodpecker; one thought to possess some characteristic of a woodpecker.

Speirs, Speir (*Eng.*) One who acted as a spy or watchman; the son of Spere (spear).

Speiser (*Ger.*) The official in charge of the food in a castle or monastery.

Spellberg (*Ger.*) Variant of Spielberg, q.v.

Speller, Spellar (*Ger., Eng.*) One who came from Spelle or Spellen (wet mud), the names of places in Germany; one who made and sold pins; the speaker, preacher, or professional storyteller.

Spellman, Spelman, Spellmann (*Eng., Ger., Ir.*) A preacher or orator; one who entertained by stories, songs, buffoonery or juggling; grandson of Spealan (small scythe).

Spence, Spens (*Eng., Scot.*) Custodian of a storage room for provisions; dweller near the place where provisions were stored.

Spencer, Spenser (*Eng.*) One who dispensed, or had charge of, the provisions in a household.

Spengler (*Ger.*) One who worked with tin, a tinsmith; or who mended pots and kettles, a tinker.

Sperber (*Ger.*) Dweller at the sign of the sparrow hawk.

Spereson, Sperison (*Eng.*) The son of Spere (spear).

Spering, Sperring (*Eng.*) The son of Spere (spear).

Sperling (*Ger., Eng.*) One with some characteristic of a sparrow; dweller at the sign of the sparrow; descendant of Sperling (twig).

Spero, Spera (*Ger.*) One who came from Spira, now spelled Speyer, in Bavaria.

Sperr (*Eng.*) Descendant of Spere (spear).

Sperry (*Eng.*) Descendant of Sperri (spear).

Spevack, Spevak (*Ukr.*) Variant of Spivak, q.v.

Speyer (*Ger.*) One who came from Speyer, in Bavaria.

Speziale (*It.*) One who prepares drugs and dispenses medicines, a pharmacist; one who deals in spices.

Spicely (*Eng.*) One who came from Spetchley (grove where speeches were made, a meeting place), in Worcestershire.

Spicer (*Eng.*) One who dealt in spices, a druggist or apothecary.

Spicka (*Cz.*) Dweller near a point of land.

Spidell, Spidle (*Ger.*) Variant of Speidel, q.v.

Spiegel, Spiegl (*Ger.*) Dweller at, or near, a watch tower; one who made and sold tools; dweller at the sign of the mirror.

Spielberg, Spielberger (*Ger.*) One who came from Spielberg (muddy hill), the name of many places in Germany.

Spielman, Spielmann (*Ger.*) One who

manned a watch tower, a watchman; one who made and sold toys; a player.

Spies, Spiess, Spietz (*Ger.*) One who fashioned objects on a lathe, a turner; one who came from Spies, in Germany.

Spiewak (*Pol.*) The singer, one who is continually singing.

Spigler (*Ger.*) One who made and sold mirrors.

Spikes, Spiker, Spike (*Eng.*) One who made and sold spikes or nails.

Spilker, Spilkes (*Ger.*) One who made and sold spindles.

Spillane (*Ir.*) Grandson of Spealan (little scythe).

Spiller (*Eng.*) One who preached, a preacher; one who entertained others.

Spillman (*Eng., Ir.*) Servant of Spil (player); variant of Spellman, q.v.

Spilsbury (*Eng.*) One who came from Spelsbury (watchful fort), in Oxfordshire.

Spina, Spino (*It.*) Descendant of Spino, a pet form of Crispino (curly-haired); dweller near a thorn tree; the gloomy, morose, sullen man; dweller at the sign of the porcupine.

Spindel, Spindell (*Bel.*) One who made and sold bobbins and spools used in weaving.

Spindler, Spindle (*Eng., Ger.*) One who made spindles for use in spinning.

Spinelli, Spinello, Spinella (*It.*) Descendant of little Spino, a pet form of Crispino (curly-haired).

Spingler (*Eng.*) Variant of Spindler, q.v.

Spink, Spinks (*Eng.*) Dweller at the sign of the finch, probably a chaffinch; trapper of finches.

Spinnato (*It.*) One without hair, bald.

Spinner (*Eng.*) One who spun wool or yarn.

Spinney (*Eng.*) One who came from Spinney (thicket), in Cambridgeshire.

Spinosa, Spinosi (*It.*) The crabby, ill-natured man.

Spinoza (*Sp.*) One who came from Espinosa (thorny place), in Spain.

Spires (*Eng.*) One who acted as a spy or watchman.

Spiro, Spira (*Ger.*) Variant of Spero, q.v.

Spirt (*Eng.*) Descendant of the tall, thin man; or of Spirhard (spear, brave).

Spitalli, Spitali, Spitale (*It.*) Dweller near, or worker in, a guest house,

Spitalny (*Pol.*) Dweller near, or worker in, a hospital.

Spitler (*Ger.*) One who came from Spittel (hospital), the name of two places in Germany; one in charge of a hospital.

Spittal, Spital, Spittle, Spittall, Spittell (*Eng., Scot.*) Dweller in, or near, a hospital, a house for travelers, generally a religious house, later a home for the needy and infirm; one who came from Spittal (house), the name of many places in Scotland.

Spitzer, Spitz (*Ger.*) Dweller on, or near, a peak or pointed hill; one who came from Spitzen (peak), the name of places in Germany.

Spitzkopf (*Ger.*) Dweller at the top of the peak or hill.

Spivak, Spivack (*Pol., Ukr., Cz.-Sl.*) One who sang in church or synagogue, especially a solo singer.

Spivey (*Scot.*) The crippled or deformed man.

Spock (*Ger.*) One who came from Spock (swamp water), the name of several places in Germany.

Spodobalski (*Pol.*) One who is pleasant and agreeable.

Spoerl (*Ger.*) Dweller at the sign of the sparrow.

Spofford (*Eng.*) One who came from Spofforth (plot of land by a ford), in Yorkshire.

Spohn (*Ger.*) Variant of Spahn, q.v.

Spohrer, Spohr (*Ger.*) One who made spurs; nickname for a knight.

Sponheimer (*Ger.*) One who came from Sponheim (homestead on the moor), in Germany.

Sponner, Sponder, Spooner (*Eng.*) One who made shingles or spoons.

483

Spoon (*Eng.*) Metonymic for one who made or installed roofing shingles; or who made spoons.

Sporkin (*Rus.*) One who offers much.

Sporrer, Sporrier (*Eng.*) Variant of Spurrier, q.v.

Spotwood, Spotswood, Spottiswood (*Scot.*) One who came from Spottiswood (Spot's wood), in Berwickshire.

Spradley (*Eng.*) Variant of Spratley, q.v.

Spraggins, Spracklin, Spracklen (*Eng.*) The little, lively, talkative person.

Sprague, Spragg (*Eng.*) The alert, lively, intelligent man.

Sprang (*Du.*) One who came from Sprang, in Holland.

Spranger (*Ger.*) Variant of Springer, q.v.

Spratley (*Eng.*) One who came from Sproatley (grove of young trees), in the East Riding of Yorkshire.

Spratt, Sprott, Sprotte, Spratte (*Eng.*) Descendant of Sprot (twig or small branch); one thought to possess some characteristic of a sprat (fish); dweller at the sign of the sprat.

Sprecher (*Ger.*) The babbler or chatterer; one who uses rhymes in speech; the speaker.

Spreckels (*Ger.*) One who came from Spreckel (crumbling place), in Germany.

Spreng, Sprenger (*Eng., Ger.*) Variant of Springer, q.v.; one who came from Sprenge, in Germany.

Spriggs, Sprigg (*Eng.*) A small, slender person, one so called from some resemblance to a stick or twig; dweller at the sign of the twigs.

Springall, Springel, Springle (*Eng.*) The active, nimble man; dweller at the hall by the spring.

Springer, Springs, Spring (*Eng., Ger.*) Dweller at, or near, the spring or well; dweller near a thicket or group of young trees; the juggler, tumbler, dancer at fair and festival.

Springfield (*Eng.*) One who came from Springfield (spring or stream in open country), in Essex.

Springston (*Eng.*) Dweller in a homestead by a spring or stream.

Sprinkle, Sprinkel (*Eng.*) The soldier in charge of the springalde, a bow or catapult used in medieval warfare for throwing heavy missiles.

Sproat, Sprout (*Scot.*) Descendant of Sprota (twig).

Sprott, Sprotte (*Eng.*) Descendant of Sprota (twig).

Sproul, Sproule, Sprowl, Sprowles (*Eng.*) One who spoke in a slow, drawling voice.

Spruill, Spruille, Spruell, Spruel (*Eng.*) The quick, agile man.

Spry, Spray (*Eng.*) The lively, alert person.

Spurgeon, Spurgin (*Eng.*) Descendant of Sprigin (small twig).

Spurill (*Eng.*) Dweller at the sign of the little sparrow; dweller on a hill where sparrows congregated.

Spurley (*Eng.*) Dweller in a grove infested by sparrows.

Spurlock (*Eng.*) Dweller near a lake infested with sparrows.

Spurr, Spurlin, Spurling (*Eng.*) One with some characteristic of a sparrow; dweller near a beam or pole; dweller at the sign of the sparrow.

Spurrier (*Eng.*) One who made and sold spurs.

Squall, Squalls (*Eng.*) The quick, agile man; the thrifty, frugal man.

Square, Squares (*Eng.*) The short, fat man.

Squarrel (*Eng.*) Variant of Squirrel, q.v.

Squibb, Squibbs (*Eng.*) Nickname applied to a mean, insignificant, or paltry fellow.

Squillante (*It.*) One who made and sold cowbells; dweller at the sign of the cowbell.

Squires, Squire, Squier (*Eng.*) A young man of gentle birth attendant upon a knight.

Squirrel (*Eng.*) Dweller at the sign of the squirrel; the agile or thrifty man.

Srednick (*Pol.*) One who came from the middle place.

Sremac (*Yu.-Sl.*) One who came from Srem, in Yugoslavia.

Sroka (*Pol.*) One who had some characteristic of a magpie; dweller at the sign of the magpie.

Staab (*Ger.*) The official who carried the mace or acted as a sergeant-at-arms.

Staats (*Du.*) Descendant of Staas, a pet form of Eustachius (steadfast).

Stabilito, Stabile (*It.*) An important court or military officer, a constable.

Stable, Stabler, Stables (*Eng.*) One in charge of a stable; dweller near a stable; one who was sound, steadfast, trustworthy.

Stacey, Stacy (*Eng.*) Descendant of Stacy, a pet form of Anastasius (one who shall rise again; resurrection); and of Eustace (steadfast); descendant of Stacius (stability).

Stach (*Pol.*) Descendant of big Stanislaw (camp, glorious); or of Stach, a pet form of Eustachy, Polish form of Eustace (steadfast).

Stachnik (*Pol.*) Descendant of Stachnik, a pet form of Stanislaw (camp, glorious).

Stachowicz (*Pol.*) The son of Stach, a pet form of Eustachy, Polish form of Eustace (steadfast); or of Stacho (star).

Stack (*Eng., Scot.*) Dweller at a cliff or steep rock; one who came from Stack (cliff, isolated rock) in Caithness.

Stackhouse (*Eng.*) One who came from Stackhouse (habitation by a steep rock or hill), a hamlet in Yorkshire.

Stackpole, Stackpool (*Wel., Eng.*) One who came from Stackpole (pool by a cliff), in Pembrokeshire; dweller near a pool by a steep hill or cliff.

Stadel, Stadell, Stadl (*Ger.*) Dweller near the barn or shed; one who was overseer of the barn for the lord of the manor; one who came from Stadel (barn), in Germany.

Stadham (*Eng.*) One who came from Stedham (the stallion's enclosure), in Sussex.

Stadler (*Eng., Ger.*) Dweller near a barn; one who came from Stadel (barn), in Germany.

Staff (*Eng.*) The thin, lean man.

Staffieri, Staffiere (*It.*) A servant who attends the door or table, a footman or groom.

Stafford (*Eng.*) One who came from Stafford (stony ford; ford by a landing place), the name of several places, besides the county with that name, in England.

Stagg, Staggs (*Eng.*) Dweller at the sign of the stag, a word also used for male birds and other animals.

Stahl, Staehle (*Ger.*) One who worked with steel.

Stahler (*Ger.*) One who sold steel; one who worked in a stable, a groom.

Stahlschmidt (*Ger.*) One who worked in steel.

Staib (*Ger.*) One who raises dust, creates a disturbance.

Staiger (*Ger.*) Dweller at a steep mound; or near a precipice or declivity.

Stailey (*Ger.*) One who worked with steel hardened iron, a steelsmith.

Stainer (*Eng.*) One who stains, paints or decorates rooms; descendant of Steinarr (stone, army).

Staines, Stains (*Eng.*) One who came from Staines (stone), in Middlesex.

Stair (*Scot.*) One who came from Stair (stepping stones over a bog), in Ayrshire.

Staley (*Eng.*) One who came from Staveley (wood where staves were obtained), the name of several places in England.

Stalin (*Rus.*) Steel (an adopted name).

Stalker (*Eng.*) One who hunted game by stealthy approach.

Stall, Stalle, Stalls (*Eng., Du.*) Dweller near, or worker in, a stable.

Stallard (*Eng.*) One who had charge of the stable.

Staller (*Eng.*) One in charge of the horses for the king or important noble.

Stallings, Stalling (*Eng.*) One who came

485

from Stalling (stallion), in York-shire.

Stallsmith (*Ger.*) English respelling of Stahlschmidt, q.v.

Stallworth, Stallsworth (*Eng.*) The strong, stalwart man.

Stambaugh (*Ger.*) One who came from Stambach, in Germany.

Stambul (*Ger.*) One who came from Istanbul (at the city), in Turkey.

Stamler, Stammler (*Ger.*) One who stammers or stutters.

Stamm (*Ger.*) Dweller near an unusual tree-trunk.

Stamos (*Gr.*) Descendant of Stamos, a Greek form of Stephen (a crown or garland).

Stampar (*Yu.-Sl.*) A printer.

Stamper, Stamp (*Eng.*) One who stamps, prints, or pounds.

Stamps (*Eng.*) One who came from Estampes, in Normandy.

Stanberry, Stanbery, Stanbury (*Eng.*) One who came from Stanbury (stone fort), in the West Riding of Yorkshire.

Stancil, Stancel, Stancill (*Ger., Pol.*) Variant of Stenzel, q.v.

Stanczak, Stanczyk (*Pol.*) Descendant of little Stan, a pet form of Stanislaw (camp, glorious).

Standberry (*Eng.*) One who came from Stanbury (stone fort), in the West Riding of Yorkshire.

Standen (*Eng.*) One who came from Standen (stone valley; stony hill), the name of places in Berkshire, Lancashire, and Wight.

Stander (*Ger.*) One who made barrels of staves wherein three are length-ened to serve as feet or supports.

Standfield (*Eng.*) One who came from Stanfield (stony land), in Norfolk.

Standfuss (*Ger.*) Variant of Stander, q.v.

Standifer (*Eng.*) Dweller at the stony ford.

Standish (*Eng.*) One who came from Standish (stony pasture), the name of places in Gloucestershire and Lancashire.

Stanek (*Pol.*) Descendant of Stanek, a

pet form of Stanislaw (camp, glori-ous).

Stanfield, Stanfel, Stanfill (*Eng.*) One who came from Stanfield (stony field), in Norfolk; dweller on, or near, stony land.

Stanford, Stamford, Stanforth (*Eng.*) One who came from Stanford (stony ford), the name of several places in England.

Stange, Stang, Stanger (*Eng., Ger.*) Dweller at, or near, a stagnant pool; dweller near a pole; a tall, or thin, man.

Stanger (*Eng.*) One who came from Stanghow (boundary mark hill), in the North Riding of Yorkshire.

Stanhope (*Eng.*) One who came from Stanhope (stony valley), in Durham.

Staniforth (*Eng.*) Dweller at the paved ford; or at the stony ford.

Stanish (*Eng.*) Variant of Standish, q.v.

Stanistreet (*Eng.*) Dweller by the Roman road paved with stone.

Stank, Stanke (*Eng., Ger.*) Dweller by the pool; descendant of Stanke, a pet form of Stanislaw (camp, glori-ous).

Stankey, Stanky (*Ger.*) Descendant of little Stanke, a pet form of Stanislaw (camp, glorious).

Stankiewicz (*Pol.*) The son of Stankie, a pet form of Stanislaus (camp, glori-ous).

Stanko (*Cz.-Sl., Pol., Yu.-Sl.*) Descendant of Stanko, a pet form of Stanislaw (camp, glorious).

Stankovich, Stankovic (*Yu.-Sl.*) The son of Stanko, a pet form of Stanislaus (camp, glorious).

Stankowski (*Pol.*) One who came from Stankowo (Stanko's village), in Po-land.

Stankus (*Pol.*) Descendant of Stankus, a pet form of Stanislaw (camp, glori-ous).

Stanlake (*Eng.*) One who came from Standlake (stony stream), in Ox-fordshire.

Stanley, Standley (*Eng.*) One who came from Stanley (stony meadow), the name of several places in England; dweller at a rocky meadow.

Stanmore (*Eng.*) One who came from Stanmore (stony lake), in Middlesex.

Stannard, Stankard (*Eng.*) Descendant of Stanard (stone, firm).

Stanovich (*Rus.*) The son of Stan, a pet form of Stanislav, Russian form of Stanislaus (camp, glorious).

Stansberry, Stansbury (*Eng.*) Variant of Stanberry, q.v.

Stansfield (*Eng.*) One who came from Stansfield (stone field), the name of places in Suffolk and the West Riding of Yorkshire.

Stanton (*Eng.*) One who came from Stanton (homestead on stony ground), the name of many places in England.

Stanwick (*Eng.*) One who came from Stanwick (wiggling stone), in Northamptonshire.

Stanwood (*Eng.*) Dweller in, or near, a stony wood.

Stape, Stapp (*Eng.*) Dweller by the stepping stones.

Stapleford (*Eng.*) One who came from Stapleford (river crossing designated by a post), the name of seven places in England.

Stapler (*Eng.*) One who bought and sold goods at a market.

Staples, Staple (*Eng.*) One who came from Staple (post or pillar), in Kent; dweller at a post.

Stapleton (*Eng.*) One who came from Stapleton (homestead by a post), the name of several places in England.

Stappen (*Ger.*) Dweller on the lane or road.

Starbird (*Eng.*) Descendant of Storbeorht (strong, bright).

Starbuck, Starbeck (*Eng.*) One who came from Starbeck (brook near where sedge grew), in Yorkshire; dweller at, or near, a stream where sedge or swamp grass grew.

Starcevich (*Rus.*) The son of the old man.

Starck, Stark, Starke, Starch (*Ger.*) De-

scendant of Starco, a pet form of Starculf (strong, wolf).

Stark, Starkes, Starke, Starkman (*Eng.*) The strong, severe man.

Starkey, Starkie (*Eng., Ir.*) Descendant of Starkie, a pet form of names beginning with Starc (strong), such as Starcbeorht, Starcfrith or Starcwulf; the little strong man.

Starkman (*Eng.*) The strong, stern, severe man.

Starkweather (*Eng.*) One who worked in severe weather.

Starling (*Eng.*) Dweller at the sign of the starling; one who trapped starlings for food.

Starnes (*Eng.*) The severe, austere man; dweller at the sign of the stars.

Starr, Star (*Eng.*) Dweller at the sign of the star; descendant of Sterre (star).

Starrett, Starratt (*Scot., Ir.*) One who came from Stairaird, now Stirie (path over a bog), in Ayrshire; variant of Stewart, q.v.

Start, Startt (*Eng.*) Dweller on, or near, a promontory or tongue of land.

Startifant (*Eng.*) A nickname for a messenger or pursuivant ready to start forward.

Startup (*Eng.*) Dweller on a promontory with a hope, i.e., dry land in a fen; nickname for one who commences a task by leaping up; nickname for one suddenly sprung up, now known as an upstart.

Starzyk (*Pol.*) The gray-haired man.

Stasiak, Stasiek (*Pol.*) Descendant of Stasiek, a pet form of Stanislaw (camp, glorious).

Stasinskas (*Lith.*) One who is like Stasys, a pet form of Stanislovas, Lithuanian form of Stanislaus (camp, glorious).

Stassen (*Nor.*) The son of Stass, a pet form of Anastasius (resurrection).

Stastny (*Cz.*) The happy, lucky, joyful man.

Staszak (*Pol.*) Descendant of Staszek, a pet form of Stanislaw (camp, glorious).

Staten, Staton (*Eng.*) Dweller on the

homestead where there was a wharf or boat-landing place.

Statler (*Ger.*) Variant of Stettler, q.v.

Statura (*Sp.*) The tall man.

Staub, Stauber, Stauble (*Ger.*) One who ground grain, a miller.

Staudenmaier, Staudenmayer, Staudenmeyer (*Ger.*) One who took care of the shrubs or bushes, a horticulturist or forester.

Staufenberg, Stauffenberg (*Ger.*) One who came from Staufenberg (towering crag), the name of two places in Germany.

Stauffer, Staufer (*Ger.*) One who came from Staufen (towering cliff), the name of several places in Germany; dweller at the top of the mountain, or at the sign of the goblet or cup, a tavern sign.

Staunton (*Eng.*) One who came from Staunton (homestead on stony ground), the name of seven places in England.

Stauss (*Ger.*) One with a prominent rump or buttocks.

Stave (*Eng.*) Dweller by the stake, probably a marker of some sort.

Staveley, Stavely (*Eng.*) One who came from Staveley (wood where staves were obtained), the name of places in Derbyshire, Lancashire, and the West Riding of Yorkshire.

Stavropoulos, Stavropulos (*Gr.*) The son of Stavros, Greek form of Stephen (a crown or garland).

Stead (*Eng., Wel.*) Dweller at a dairy farm; one who worked on a farm.

Steadley (*Eng.*) Dweller in a grove where stallions were kept.

Steadman (*Eng.*) Dweller on a farmstead, a farm-worker; one responsible for the care of war-horses.

Stearne (*Eng.*) The austere, severe man; dweller at the sign of the star.

Stearns (*Eng.*) Variant of Starnes, q.v.

Stears, Stear (*Eng.*) Variants of Steer, q.v.

Steave (*Eng.*) Descendant of Steve, a pet form of Stephen (a crown or garland).

Stebbins, Stebbing (*Eng.*) One who came from Stebbing (clearing), in Essex.

Stebly (*Eng.*) Dweller in a wood where tree stumps were found.

Stec (*Ukr.*) Descendant of Stecko, a pet form of Stepan, Ukrainian form of Stephen (a crown or garland).

Stecher, Stechman (*Ger.*) One who came from Stechau (pool meadow), in Germany.

Steck (*Ger.*) Dweller on, or near, a steep incline.

Stedman (*Eng.*) One who had charge of horses; one who tilled the soil, a farmer.

Steed (*Eng.*) Dweller at the sign of the stallion; or at the farmstead, a farm worker.

Steedley (*Eng.*) Variant of Steadley, q.v.

Steege, Steeg (*Du.*) Dweller on the alley or lane.

Steele, Steel (*Eng.*) One who came from Steel (stile or place where one has to climb), the name of places in Northumberland and Shropshire.

Steelman (*Eng.*) The servant of Steel (steel); dweller at the stile.

Steen, Steens (*Du., Nor., Scot.*) Dweller near a stone; descendant of Stephen (a crown or garland).

Steenson (*Eng.*) The son of Steen, a syncopated form of Stephen (a crown or garland).

Steere, Steer (*Eng.*) Dweller at the sign of the ox; one with ox-like qualities; one in charge of the oxen.

Steerman (*Eng.*) The man in charge of the steers or oxen; the servant of Styr (star).

Steeves, Steeve (*Eng.*) Descendant of Steeve, a pet form of Stephen (a crown or garland).

Stefan, Stefanski (*Pol.*) Descendant of Stefan, Polish form of Stephen (a crown or garland).

Stefani (*It.*) Descendant of Stefano, Italian form of Stephen (a crown or garland).

Stefanik, Stefanek (*Sl.*) Descendant of little Stefan, Slavic form of Stephen (a crown or garland).

Stefankiewicz (*Pol.*) The son of Stefan, Polish form of Stephen (a crown or garland).

Stefano (*It.*) Descendant of Stefano, Italian form of Stephen (a crown or garland).

Stefanovich, Stefanovic (*Rus., Yu.-Sl.*) The son of Stefan, Slavic form of Stephen (a crown or garland).

Stefanowicz (*Pol.*) The son of Stefan, Polish form of Stephen (a crown or garland).

Stefansson (*Ice.*) The son of Stefan, Icelandic form of Stephen (a crown or garland).

Steff, Steffe (*Eng.*) Descendant of Steff, a contracted form of Stephen (a crown or garland).

Steffens, Steffen, Steffan (*Eng.*) Descendant of Steffen, a variant of Stephen (a crown or garland).

Stegall, Steggal, Steggalls (*Eng., Ger.*) Dweller at the stile or steep path up a hill.

Steger (*Ger.*) Dweller near a narrow bridge; one who came from Stegen, in Germany.

Stegman (*Ger.*) Dweller at, or near, a narrow way or small bridge.

Steiger, Stiger (*Du.*) Dweller on, or near, the pier or boat-landing place.

Steigerwald, Steigerwalt (*Ger.*) One who came from the Steigerwald, the forested mountain chains in Franconia.

Steiman (*Ger.*) Variant of Steinman, q.v.

Stein (*Ger., Du., Swis.*) Dweller near a stone or rock, often a boundary mark; one who came from Stein, the name of numerous villages in Germany and Switzerland; descendant of Staino or Stein, pet forms of names beginning with Stein (stone), as Steinher and Stainold; dweller in, or near, the stone castle.

Steinbach, Steinback, Steinbeck (*Ger.*) One who came from Steinbach (stony brook), the name of many places in Germany.

Steinberg, Steinberger (*Ger.*) One who came from Steinberg (stone moun-tain), the name of many places in Germany.

Steinbrecher, Steinbrecker (*Ger.*) One who worked in a stone quarry; one who crushed stone.

Steinbronn (*Ger.*) Dweller near a stone fountain; one who came from Steinbronnen (stony spring), in Germany.

Steinbrueck, Steinbruck (*Ger.*) One who came from Steinbruck (stone bridge), the name of several places in Germany.

Steinbruegge (*Ger.*) Dweller near a stone bridge.

Steiner (*Ger., Du., Swis.*) Dweller near a stone or rock, often a boundary mark; one who came from Stein (stone), the name of numerous villages in Germany and Switzerland; one who worked with stone, a stonemason.

Steinfeld, Steinfeldt (*Ger.*) One who came from Steinfeld (stony country), the name of several places in Germany; dweller in, or near, a stony field.

Steingard, Steingart (*Ger.*) Dweller in, or near, a rock garden.

Steinhart (*Ger.*) Descendant of Steinhard (stone, hard).

Steinhauer (*Ger.*) One who cuts and builds with stone.

Steinhaus, Steinhauser (*Ger.*) One who came from Steinhaus (stone homestead or castle), the name of many places in Germany.

Steinhoff (*Ger.*) One who came from Steinhofel (stone hill), in Germany; dweller near a stone courtyard.

Steinhouse (*Ger.*) Anglicized form of Steinhaus, q.v.

Steinig (*Ger.*) Dweller at a stony place.

Steininger (*Ger.*) One who came from Steining or Steiningen (Stein's homestead), the names of places in Germany.

Steinkamp (*Ger.*) One who came from Steinkamp (stone enclosure), the name of two places in Germany.

Steinke, Steinicke, Steinken (*Ger.*) Descendant of little Staino, a pet form of names beginning with Stein (stone), such as Stenulf, Stainold, and Steinwart.

Steinman, Steinmann (*Ger.*) One who worked with stone, a mason.

Steinmetz (*Ger.*) The stone cutter, or builder with stone.

Steinmeyer (*Ger.*) The farmer who came from Stein (stone), the name of many places in Germany.

Steinweg, Steinway (*Ger.*) Dweller near the stony path or road; one who came from Steinweg (stony way), in Germany.

Steitz (*Ger.*) One who cleaned and thickened cloth, a fuller.

Stella, Stello (*It., Eng.*) Dweller at the sign of the star; descendant of Stella (star); descendant of Stella, a pet form of Battisstella; one who came from Stella (pasture with a cattle shed), in Durham.

Stelmach, Stelmack, Stellmach (*Ger.*) One who made and sold carriages.

Stelzer, Stelzner (*Ger.*) One who walked on stilts, to entertain, as at a carnival; one who came from Stelzen, in Germany; dweller in a narrow field.

Stelzfuss (*Ger.*) The cripple, one with a wooden leg.

Stem (*Du.*) One with an unusual voice.

Stembridge (*Eng.*) Dweller by the stone bridge.

Stenberg (*Nor., Sw., Finn.*) Stone, mountain; dweller on the stony mountain.

Stengel, Stengele (*Ger.*) Dweller near a small pole or stake.

Stenger (*Ger., Fr.*) The tall, thin man.

Stenhouse (*Eng., Sw., Dan.*) Dweller in, or near, the stone house.

Stenlund (*Sw.*) Stone, grove.

Stenn, Sten (*Eng.*) Descendant of Sten, a pet form of Stephen (a crown or garland).

Stennett, Stinnette (*Eng.*) Descendant of little Sten, a pet form of Stephen (a crown or garland).

Stensland (*Nor.*) Dweller on the stony field.

Stenson (*Eng.*) One who came from Stenson (Stein's homestead), in Der-

byshire; the son of Stean (stone); or of Sten, a pet form of Stephen (a crown or garland).

Stensrud (*Nor.*) Dweller in the stony clearing.

Stenstrom (*Sw.*) Stone, stream.

Stenzel, Stencel (*Ger., Pol.*) Descendant of Stenzel, a pet form of Stanislaus (camp, glorious).

Stepan (*Ukr.*) Descendant of Stepan, a Russian form of Stephen (a crown or garland).

Stepanek (*Pol.*) Descendant of little Stepan, Slavic form of Stephen (a crown or garland).

Stepanian (*Arm.*) The son of Stepan, Armenian form of Stephen (a crown or garland).

Stephan (*Ger., Eng.*) Descendant of Stephen (a crown or garland).

Stephani, Stephano (*It.*) Variant of Stefani, q.v.

Stephanos (*Gr.*) Descendant of Stephanos, Greek form of Stephen (a crown or garland).

Stephens, Stephenson, Stephen (*Wel., Eng.*) The son of Stephen (a crown or garland).

Stepney (*Eng.*) One who came from Stepney (Stybba's landing-place), in Middlesex.

Stepnowski (*Pol.*) Descendant of Stefan, Slavic form of Stephen (a crown or garland).

Stepp, Steppe (*Eng.*) Descendant of Stepp, a pet form of Stephen (a crown or garland).

Steptoe (*Eng.*) Nickname for one who walks on his toes.

Sterling (*Scot., Eng.*) One who came from Stirling (dwelling of Velyn), in Scotland; descendant of Starling; one thought to possess the characteristics of a starling.

Stern, Sterne (*Eng., Ger.*) The severe, austere man; dweller at the sign of the star; the star, alluding to the star of David.

Sternberg, Sternberger (*Ger.*) One who came from Sternberg (star mountain), the name of ten places in Germany.

Sterner (*Ger.*) One who came from Stern (star), the name of two places in Germany.

Sternfeld, Sternfield (*Eng.*) One who came from Sternfield (Sterne's open land), in Suffolk.

Sterrett, Sterritt (*Scot.*) Variant of Starrett, q.v.

Stetson, Stutson (*Eng.*) The son of the stupid, clumsy fellow; the son of Stedda or Stith; descendant of the stepson.

Stetter, Stettner, Stettin, Stettinius (*Ger.*) One who came from Stetten (place of green grain), the name of many small places in Germany.

Stettler, Stetler (*Ger.*) One in charge of the grain storage; one who came from Stetten (place of green grain), the name of many places in Germany.

Steuer, Steur, Steuerman (*Ger.*) One who collected taxes; the helmsman or man at the wheel of a ship.

Stevens, Stevenson, Steven (*Eng.*) The son of Stephen (a crown or garland).

Stever, Steverson (*Eng.*) Descendant, or son, of Stever, a pet form of Stephen (a crown or garland).

Stewart, Steward (*Eng., Scot.*) Keeper of the sty, pen, or hall, later manager of a household or estate; one who had charge of a king's, or important noble's, household.

Stickel, Stickle, Stickles (*Eng.*) Dweller near the stile or steep ascent.

Stickler (*Ger.*) Dweller on a steep path or incline.

Stickley (*Eng.*) Dweller in the grove fenced in with sticks or stakes.

Stickney (*Eng.*) One who came from Stickney (stick island), in Lincolnshire.

Stidham, Stidem (*Eng.*) One who came from Stedham (enclosure where stallions grazed), in Sussex.

Stieber (*Ger.*) One who works in a hot room, a bath attendant.

Stief (*Ger.*) The stubborn, obstinate man.

Stiefel (*Ger., Fr.*) One who made and sold boots.

Stiegel (*Ger.*) Dweller near the stile or steps over the town fence.

Stier (*Ger.*) Metonym for one who took care of bulls.

Stiff (*Eng.*) The stiff, firm, proud man.

Stiffel, Stiffler, Stifel (*Ger.*) Variant of Stiefel, q.v.

Stigale, Stigall (*Eng.*) Variant of Stegall, q.v.

Stiles (*Eng.*) Dweller at the steps leading over a fence or wall; or at a steep path up a hill.

Stille, Still (*Eng.*) Dweller at a place where fish were caught; the calm, quiet person; variant of Stiles, q.v.

Stiller (*Eng., Ger.*) Dweller at a stile; or at a place where fish were caught; the calm, quiet man; one who came from Stille or Still (quiet), the names of places in Germany.

Stilley (*Eng.*) Dweller on an island where fish were caught or trapped.

Stillings, Stilling, Stelling (*Eng.*) One who came from Stelling (Stealla's people), in Kent.

Stillman (*Eng.*) Dweller at the stile, or steep path up a hill.

Stillwell, Stilwell (*Eng.*) Dweller at the spring where the water flowed continuously.

Stine, Stiner (*Ger.*) An Anglicization of Stein and Steiner, q.v.

Stinnett, Stinnette (*Eng.*) Variant of Stennett, q.v.

Stinson, Stimpson, Stimson (*Eng.*) The son of Stin, a pet form of Stephen (a crown or garland).

Stirewalt (*Ger.*) The forceful or brutal man.

Stirk (*Eng.*) Metonymic for one who took care of bullocks and heifers; dweller at the sign of the bullock.

Stirling (*Scot.*) One who came from Stirling (dwelling of Velyn), in Stirlingshire.

Stitely (*Eng.*) One who came from Steetley (stump grove), in Derbyshire.

Stith (*Eng.*) One who came from Stathe (landing place), in Somerset; the strong, hard man.

Stitsworth (*Eng.*) Dweller in a homestead infested by gnats.

Stitt, Stitts (*Eng.*) The strong, hard man.

Stiver, Stiverson (*Eng.*) Variant of Stever, q.v.

Stoakes (*Eng.*) Variant of Stocks, q.v.

Stock, Stocker (*Eng., Ger.*) Dweller near a tree stump; dweller near a foot bridge; one employed in grubbing up trees; one who came from Stock, Stockau, or Stocken (tree stumps), the names of many places in Germany.

Stockberger, Stockburger (*Ger.*) One who came from Stockberg or Stockburg (tree stump mountain or stronghold), the names of places in Germany.

Stockbridge (*Eng.*) One who came from Stockbridge (bridge made of trunks of trees; monastery cell at the bridge), in Hampshire.

Stockdale (*Eng.*) One who came from Stockdale (valley with tree stumps), the name of several places in England.

Stockham (*Eng.*) One who came from Stockham (homestead with tree stumps), in Cheshire.

Stockholm (*Sw.*) One who came from Stockholm (island in the sound), the capital of Sweden.

Stocking (*Scot., Ger., Eng.*) One who came from Stocking (enclosed), in Scotland; or from Stocking, in Germany; dweller on a plot of land cleared of stumps; or at the tree stump.

Stockler (*Ger.*) Dweller near, or among, tree stumps—newly cleared land.

Stockley (*Eng.*) One who came from Stockleigh (grove belonging to a monastery), the name of four places in England.

Stocklin (*Eng.*) One who came from Stockland (land belonging to a monastery), the name of places in Devonshire and Somerset.

Stockmann, Stockman (*Ger., Eng.*) Dweller in, or near, a recently cleared space where tree stumps are evident.

Stockridge (*Eng.*) One who came from Stockbridge (bridge made of trunks of trees; monastery cell at the bridge), in Hampshire.

Stocks (*Eng.*) Dweller near a monastery or holy place.

Stockton (*Eng.*) One who came from Stockton (village belonging to a monastery, or some outlying place), the name of various places in England.

Stockwell (*Eng.*) One who came from Stockwell (stream with a footbridge), in Surrey.

Stockwood (*Eng.*) One who came from Stockwood (monastery by a wood), in Dorset.

Stoddard, Stoddart (*Eng.*) One who had the care of the horses or oxen.

Stofer, Stoffer (*Eng.*) Descendant of Stopher, a pet form of Christopher (Christ-bearer).

Stoffel, Stoffle (*Ger., Fr.*) Descendant of Stoffel, a pet form of Christoforus, German form of Christopher (Christ-bearer).

Stoffer (*Sw., Nor.*) Descendant of Stoffer, a pet form of Kristoffer, Scandinavian form of Christopher (Christ-bearer).

Stogsdill (*Eng.*) One who came from Stockdale (tree stump valley), the name of several places in England.

Stojak, Stojek (*Ukr., Pol.*) One who used a stick, possibly in walking.

Stokely, Stokley (*Eng.*) Variant of Stockley, q.v.

Stokes, Stoke, Stoker (*Eng.*) One who came from Stoke or Stokes (monastery; cell; place; outlying farm), very common place names in England.

Stolar (*Yu.-Sl.*) One who worked with wood, a carpenter.

Stolarz (*Pol.*) One who worked with wood, a carpenter.

Stoll, Stoller, Stolle (*Ger.*) Dweller near

a post or pole; dweller near a mine shaft.

Stollstorff (*Ger.*) One who came from Stollsdorf (hamlet with posts or stakes as protection), in Germany.

Stoloff (*Rus.*) The son of Stol (table).

Stolp, Stolpe, Stolper (*Ger.*) One who came from Stolpe, the name of two places in Germany.

Stoltz, Stolz, Stolzer (*Ger.*) The proud, arrogant, haughty man.

Stoltzfus (*Ger.*) The man with the proud or haughty step; one with an awkward gait; one who limps.

Stone (*Eng.*) Dweller near some remarkable stone or rock, often a boundary mark; one who came from Stone (the stone; or stones), the name of various places in England.

Stonebridge (*Eng.*) Dweller near a bridge built of stone.

Stonehill (*Eng.*) Dweller on, or near, a stony or rocky hill.

Stonehouse (*Eng.*) One who came from Stonehouse (house built of stones), the name of places in Devonshire and Gloucestershire.

Stonelake (*Eng.*) Dweller near a lake surrounded by stones or rocks.

Stonely, Stoneley (*Eng.*) One who came from Stonely (grove with stones), in Huntingdonshire.

Stoner (*Eng.*) One who hewed stones, a mason; dweller near an outstanding stone.

Stonesifer, Stonecifer (*Ger.*) One who polishes semiprecious stones.

Stoney (*Eng.*) Dweller on the stony or rocky island.

Stoodley (*Eng.*) One who came from Stoodleigh (horse pasture), in Devonshire.

Stookesberry, Stooksbury (*Eng.*) One who came from Stockbury (swine pasture of the people at Stoke), in Kent.

Stoops, Stoop (*Eng.*) Dweller by a post or pillar.

Stoots (*Eng.*) Variant of Stott, q.v.

Stopford (*Eng.*) One who came from Stockport (monastery town), in Cheshire, the local pronunciation of which is Stopford.

Stopka (*Pol., Rus., Ukr.*) One who drank large glasses of vodka.

Stopper (*Ger.*) One who mends or repairs things.

Storck, Storch (*Eng., Ger.*) Variant of Stork, q.v.

Storer (*Eng.*) The keeper, or overseer, of the provisions for a large household.

Storey, Story, Storie (*Eng.*) Descendant of little Store or Stori (strong; powerful).

Stork (*Eng.*) Dweller at the sign of the stork; nickname for one with long legs.

Storm, Storms (*Eng.*) Descendant of Storm (storm); variants of Sturm, q.v.

Storr (*Eng.*) The big man; the strong, powerful man.

Storz, Stortz, Storts (*Ger.*) Dweller among tree stumps, or among cabbage stalks.

Stotesbury, Stotesberry (*Eng.*) Dweller near the fortified place where stots, that is, stallions, horses, bullocks and oxen, grazed.

Stotland (*Eng.*) Dweller on the land where stots grazed.

Stott, Stotts (*Eng.*) Dweller at the sign of the stot, that is, a stallion, horse, bullock, ox, etc.; the fat or stout man.

Stotz (*Ger.*) The thick-set, stocky man.

Stoudemire, Stoudenmire, Stoudmire (*Ger.*) One who took care of the shrubs or bushes, a horticulturist or forester.

Stoudt (*Eng.*) Variant of Stout, q.v.

Stouffer (*Eng., Ger.*) Variant of Stofer, q.v.; or of Stauffer, q.v.

Stough (*Eng.*) Dweller near a holy place, a hermitage or monastery.

Stoughton (*Eng.*) One who came from Stoughton (monastery settlement), the name of places in Leicestershire, Surrey, and Sussex.

Stout, Stoute (*Eng.*) The bold, strong and valiant man; the proud man.

Stovall (*Eng.*) One who came from Esteville (east settlement), in France.

Stover (*Ger.*) One who came from Stove, in Mecklenburg; one who conducted a public bathhouse; variant of Stauffer, q.v.

Stowe, Stow (*Eng.*) Dweller near a holy place, probably a monastery or church; one who came from Stow (holy place), the name of many places in England.

Stowell (*Eng.*) One who came from Stowell (stony stream), in Gloucestershire.

Stowers (*Eng.*) Dweller near the Stour (strong river), the name of several rivers in England; one who had charge of the flocks or herd; or was an overseer of the provisions for a household.

Stoyle (*Eng.*) Dweller at the sign of the star; or near a stile or sharp ascent.

Strachan (*Scot., Ir.*) One who came from Strachan (valley field), in Kincardineshire; grandson of Struthan (poet).

Strack, Stracke (*Ger.*) The stiff, stubborn, obstinate man.

Stradford (*Eng.*) Variant of Stratford, q.v.

Stradley (*Eng.*) One who came from Straddle (valley of the Dore), an old name of the Golden Valley, in Herefordshire.

Stradling (*Eng.*) Nickname for a straddle-legged man; also a cant term for a wandering beggar.

Strahan (*Ir., Scot.*) Grandson of Struthan (poet); variant of Strachan, q.v.

Strahl, Strahle (*Ger.*) One who made and sold arrows and shafts.

Straight (*Eng.*) The upright, erect man of good posture.

Strain, Straine (*Ir.*) Anglicized form of Strahan, q.v.

Strait (*Eng.*) Variant of Straight, q.v.; dweller near a Roman road.

Straley (*Eng.*) One who came from Strelley (wood on a Roman road), in Nottinghamshire.

Strand, Strande (*Eng., Sw.*) Dweller on the bank of a river; shore.

Strandberg (*Sw.*) Shore mountain.

Strang, Stranger (*Ger., Eng., Scot.*) One with great physical power, a strong man; one who came from a distance, a stranger.

Strange, Strangeman (*Eng.*) The stranger, one who came from a distance.

Strangeways (*Eng.*) One who came from Strangeways (strong current), in Lancashire.

Strano (*It.*) The stranger or foreigner.

Strass (*Ger.*) Dweller near a country road.

Strassburger, Strassberger (*Ger.*) One who came from Strassburg (fortified place on a road), a German city now within the French border.

Strasser (*Ger.*) Dweller on, or near, a country road.

Strassman, Strassmann, Strassner (*Ger.*) Dweller at the road or street.

Stratford (*Eng.*) One who came from Stratford (ford at a Roman road), the name of various places in England.

Stratton (*Eng.*) One who came from Stratton (homestead on a Roman road), the name of various places in England.

Stratz (*Ger.*) The haughty or arrogant man.

Straub, Straube (*Ger.*) One with bushy or bristly hair; one who came from Straube, in Germany; descendant of Strubo, a pet form of names beginning with Strud (destroy, rob), as Strudbalt and Strudolf.

Straubinger (*Ger.*) One who came from Straubing (place of Strubo's people), in Bavaria.

Strauch (*Ger.*) Dweller near a bush, underbrush or copse; one who came from Strauchau (swamp with low bushes), in Germany.

Straughn (*Scot.*) Variant of Strachan, q.v.

Strauman (*Ger.*) One who dealt in straw.

Strausfogel (*Ger.*) Dweller at the sign of the ostrich; one with ostrich-like characteristics.

Strauss, Straus, Strausser (*Ger.*) Dweller at the sign of the ostrich; one with ostrich-like characteristics; bouquet of flowers; dweller among shrubbery.

Strawn (*Scot., Ir.*) One who came from Strachan, pronounced Strawn (valley of the little horse), in Kincardineshire; or from Strowan (little stream), in Scotland; variant of Strahan, q.v.

Strayhorn, Strayhon (*Scot.*) One who came from Strawarrane, in Ayrshire.

Streadbeck (*Sw.*) Dweller near a violent, or rapid, brook.

Streams, Stream (*Eng.*) Dweller by the flowing water.

Streat, Streater (*Eng.*) Variant of Streeter, q.v.; one who came from Streat (Roman road), in Sussex.

Strecker (*Ger.*) One who came from Streckau (tract of land), in Germany; the torturer.

Streckfuss (*Ger.*) One who inflicts severe pain, a torturer.

Streep (*Du.*) One who measures or ascertains quantity, size, or weight.

Streeter, Street, Streets (*Eng.*) Dweller on a paved road, especially an ancient Roman road; one who came from Street or Strete (Roman road), the names of several places in England.

Strehle (*Ger.*) One who came from Strehla, the name of two places in Germany.

Streich (*Ger.*) Descendant of Stregus (refuge, protection).

Streicher (*Ger.*) The official inspector or assayer; one who measured grain or examined cloth.

Streit (*Ger.*) Descendant of Streit (battle), a short form of names beginning with Streit, as Stridbert, Striter, and Stritmar.

Streitfeld (*Ger.*) One who came from Streitfeld (field of strife or contest), in Germany.

Streng, Strenge (*Ger.*) One with great physical power, a strong man; the brave man; descendant of Streng (strong).

Stretch (*Eng.*) The strong, violent man.

Stretton (*Eng.*) One who came from

Stretton (homestead with heifers), in Cheshire.

Stribling (*Eng.*) Voiced form of Stripling, q.v.

Strick, Stricker (*Ger.*) One who made rope or cord.

Stricker, Strickler (*Eng., Ger.*) One who stretched, or smoothed, fabrics; one who poached or killed game unlawfully; one who came from Streich, in Germany.

Strickland (*Eng.*) One who came from Strickland (pasture for cattle), the name of several places in England.

Striker (*Eng.*) One who measured grain by passing a flat stick over a heaped bushel to reduce it to a striked bushel.

Strindberg (*Sw.*) Stretch of shore land, hill; stone, mountain.

Stringer (*Eng.*) One who made strings for bows.

Stringfellow (*Eng.*) The strong, powerful man; the severe partner.

Stringfield (*Eng.*) The long, narrow field.

Stringham (*Eng.*) One who came from Strensham (Strenge's homestead), in Worcestershire.

Stringman (*Eng.*) The strong man.

Stripling, Striplin (*Eng.*) Nickname for a youthful-appearing man.

Stritch (*Ir.*) Dweller at the street or paved road.

Strite (*Ger.*) One addicted to disputes and quarrels.

Strittmatter (*Ger.*) One who came from Strittmatt (pasture where fights were held), in Germany.

Strobel, Strobl (*Ger.*) One with bushy or bristly hair; descendant of Strubo, a pet form of names beginning with Strud (destroy; rob), as Strudbalt and Strudolf; one who came from Strobel, in Germany.

Strode, Stroder (*Eng.*) Dweller at, or near, a marshy place overgrown with brushwood.

Stroh (*Ger.*) One who sold thatch for roofs.

Strohecker, Strohaker, Strohacker, Stro-

heker (*Ger.*) One who cuts straw, that is, threshes grain.

Strohm (*Ger.*) Dweller at, or near, a stream; one who came from Strohm (stream), in Germany.

Strohmeyer, Strohmeier (*Ger.*) One who collects the tithes of straw, the straw steward.

Strom (*Sw.*) Stream.

Stromberg (*Sw.*) Stream, mountain.

Stromquist (*Sw.*) Stream, twig.

Stronach (*Scot.*) One with a large or prominent nose.

Strong, Strongs (*Eng.*) One with great physical power, a strong man.

Stroot (*Du.*) Dweller near the street.

Strother, Strothers, Stroter, Strotter, Strothman (*Eng.*) Dweller on, or near, marshy land overgrown with brushwood; one who came from Strother (marshy meadow), in Northumberland.

Stroud, Strode, Strout (*Eng., Ger.*) Dweller at a marshy place overgrown with brushwood; one who came from Stroud (marshy land), in Gloucestershire; descendant of Strut, a pet form of Strudmar (ravage, famous), or Strudolf (ravage, wolf).

Stroup, Stroupe (*Ger.*) One with stiff, bristly hair; or with shaggy, unkempt hair.

Strube, Strub, Strubbe (*Ger.*) One who had bristled or tousled hair.

Strubel, Struble (*Ger.*) One with rough, bristly hair.

Struck (*Ger.*) Dweller near a bush, underbrush, or copse.

Strudwick (*Eng.*) Dweller on a dairy farm on marshy land overgrown with brushwood.

Struempf, Struempfler (*Ger.*) Dweller near, or among, tree stumps—newly cleared land.

Strum, Strumm (*Sw.*) Dweller near a stream.

Strumpf (*Ger.*) Variant of Struempf, q.v.

Strunk (*Ger.*) Dweller near, or among, tree stumps.

Struthers (*Scot.*) Dweller in, or near, a marsh or swamp; one who came from Struthers (marsh), in Fife.

Stryker (*Eng.*) Variant of Striker, q.v.

Strzelecki (*Pol.*) One who handled a bow or rifle in battle; a sharpshooter or marksman; one who hunted game, a hunter.

Stuart (*Eng., Scot.*) Keeper of the sty, pen, or hall, later manager of a household.

Stubblefield (*Eng.*) Dweller in a recently cleared field where the stumps of the trees were still evident.

Stubbs, Stubbe (*Eng.*) Dweller near a tree stump; or on recently cleared land where the stumps were still evident; nickname given to one of a short, stumpy stature; one who came from Stubbs (tree stumps), in Yorkshire.

Stuber (*Ger.*) The proprietor of a public bath facility.

Stuck, Stucker, Stucke (*Ger.*) One who came from Stuck (plot of land), in Mecklenburg; dweller on a piece of land; or near a tree stump.

Stuckey, Stockey, Stocky (*Eng.*) The short, thick, or stocky man.

Stuckmeyer (*Ger.*) The farmer who lived among tree stumps.

Studebaker (*Ger.*) One who prepared and sold pastries.

Studer (*Ger., Swis.*) Dweller among shrubbery or in a bushy place; one who came from Stude (shrubs), in Germany.

Studivant (*Eng.*) Variant of Sturtevant, q.v.

Studley (*Eng.*) One who came from Studley (pasture for horses), the name of several places in England.

Studt (*Ger.*) One who prepared wheat bread or pastry.

Stuhl, Stuhlman, Stuhlmann (*Ger.*) Dweller at the sign of the chair or stool; one who made stools.

Stull (*Ger.*) Variant of Stoll, q.v.

Stumpf, Stump (*Ger.*) Dweller near a tree stump; one who was short and fat.

Sturdivant, Sturdavant, Sturdevant (*Eng.*) Variant of Sturtevant, q.v.

Sturgeon (*Eng.*) Dweller at the sign of the sturgeon; one who caught and sold sturgeon.

Sturgis, Sturges (*Eng.*) Descendant of Turgis (hostage of Thor, god of thunder).

Sturm, Sturmer (*Ger.*) One who was stormy and excitable; one who engaged in combat.

Sturman (*Du.*) One who worked on a boat, a sailor or navigator.

Sturrock (*Eng., Scot.*) Dweller by the high rock; one who raised sheep.

Sturt, Sturts (*Eng.*) Dweller on a promontory or tongue of land; one who came from Stert (promontory), the name of places in Somerset and Wiltshire.

Sturtevant (*Eng.*) A nickname given to a messenger or pursuivant, the surname literally meaning "start forward."

Stutman (*Eng.*) The man in charge of the cattle; the bold strong man.

Stutt, Stutts (*Eng.*) The bold, strong, valiant man; the stout man.

Stutuvaunt (*Eng.*) Variant of Sturtevant, q.v.

Stutz, Stutzke (*Ger.*) The short, or little, man.

Stuyvesant (*Du.*) One who came from Stuvesant (quicksand), in Zeeland.

Styer (*Eng.*) The man in charge of the sties or animal pens.

Styles (*Eng.*) Dweller at the steps leading over a fence or wall; or at a steep path up a hill.

Su (*Chin.*) Chestnut tree; to revive.

Suarez, Suares (*Sp.*) The son of Suero (south army); one who came from Suarez (south army), in Spain; descendant of the maker or seller of cheese.

Suber, Subers (*Ger.*) Variant of Schubert, q.v.

Such (*Eng.*) Dweller by a tree stump; one who came from Souche (Soppius' estate), in France.

Sucharski (*Pol.*) One who baked bread or biscuits, a baker.

Suchodolski (*Rus., Pol.*) Dweller in a dry valley.

Suckle (*Eng.*) One who came from Suckley (wood frequented by hedge sparrows), in Worcestershire.

Sudbo (*Nor.*) Dweller on the south farm, a farm name.

Sudbury (*Eng.*) One who came from Sudbury (southern fort), in Derbyshire.

Sudell (*Eng.*) Dweller in the south dale or valley.

Suder (*Ger.*) One who made or repaired shoes; one who came from the south.

Sudhalter, Sudalter (*Ger.*) Dweller on the south slope, or side of the hill.

Sudhoff (*Ger.*) Dweller, or worker, at the south farm; one who came from Sudhof, in Germany.

Sudhop (*Ger.*) Dweller, or worker, at the south farm.

Sudler (*Ger.*) One who prepares dirty food for soldiers, a messy cook.

Sudlow (*Eng.*) Dweller at the south hill or mound.

Suess (*Ger.*) The dear, or beloved, person; the kind, amiable man.

Suesskind (*Ger.*) Variant of Suskind, q.v.

Suevo (*Sp.*) One who came from Swabia, the medieval German duchy.

Suffield (*Eng.*) One who came from Suffield (southern plain), the name of places in Norfolk and the North Riding of Yorkshire.

Sugar, Sugarman, Sugerman (*Eng.*) One who shoes horses; descendant of Sigar or Sigegar (victory, spear).

Sugden (*Eng.*) Dweller in the valley where sows were kept.

Suggs, Sugg (*Eng.*) Dweller at the sign of the sow; one with some characteristic of a female hog.

Sugimoto (*Jap.*) Cedar, base.

Sugrue, Sughrue (*Ir.*) Grandson of Siocfhraidh (victory, peace).

Suiter, Suitor (*Eng.*) Variant of Souter, q.v.

497

Suk (*Tur.*) Dweller near, or worker in, the bazaar or market.

Sukonick, Sukonik, Sukoneck (*Rus.*) One who dealt in broadcloth.

Sulaiman (*Heb.*) Descendant of Sulaiman, Hebrew form of Solomon (peaceful; worshiper of the god Shalman).

Sulby (*Eng., Mx.*) One who came from Sulby (village or homestead by a gully or gorge), in Northamptonshire; or from Sulby (Solvi's farm), in the Isle of Man.

Suleiman (*Arab.*) Descendant of Suleiman, Arabian form of Solomon (peaceful; worshiper of the god Shalman).

Sulgrove (*Eng.*) One who came from Sulgrave (grove by a gully), in Northamptonshire.

Sullinger (*Ger.*) One who came from Sulingen (swamp), in Germany.

Sullivan (*Ir.*) Grandson of Suileabhan (black-eyed).

Sully (*Eng.*) One who came from Sully (Sulla's estate), in Normandy; or from Sudeley (southern grove), in Gloucestershire.

Sultan (*Eng., Tur.*) Variant of Sowden, q.v.; nickname for one who aped the ways of the Sultan.

Sulzbach, Sulzbacher (*Ger.*) One who came from Sulzbach (muddy brook), the name of many places in Germany.

Sulzberger (*Ger.*) One who came from Sulzberg (quagmire hill), in Germany.

Sumerson (*Eng.*) The son of Sumar (summer).

Sumi (*Jap.*) Corner.

Summerell, Summerill (*Eng.*) One who came from Semerville (Sicmar's domain), in Loire-et-Cher.

Summerfield, Summerfelt (*Eng., Ger.*) Dweller in, or near, Summer's field; or in, or near, a field used by sheep or cattle in the summer.

Summerford (*Eng.*) One who came from Somerford (ford usable only in the summer), the name of places in Cheshire, Gloucestershire, and Wiltshire.

Summers, Sumner, Summer (*Eng.*) The summoner, i.e., the petty officer who warns people to appear in court; descendant of Sumer (summer).

Summerville, Summerbell (*Eng.*) Variants of Somerville, q.v.

Summerwell (*Eng.*) Variant of Summerell, q.v.; or of Somerville, q.v.

Sumner (*Eng.*) The petty officer who cites and warns people to appear in court.

Sumpter, Sumter (*Eng.*) One who had the care of the packhorses.

Sunbery (*Eng.*) One who came from Sunbury (Sunna's fort), in Middlesex.

Sunday (*Eng., Ger.*) Descendant of Sunday (one born on Sunday; translation of the German Sonntag).

Sundberg (*Sw.*) Sound (i.e., a narrow water course), mountain.

Sunde, Sund (*Sw., Dan., Nor.*) Dweller near the sound or narrow water passage; dweller near the ferry landing.

Sundel, Sundell, Sundelius (*Sw., Nor.*) Narrow channel; one who came from Sundell, the name of several Scandinavian places.

Sunderhauf (*Ger.*) One who came from Sinderhauf (cinder heap), in Germany.

Sunderland (*Eng., Nor.*) One who came from Sunderland (separate land; private land; southern land), the name of places in Cumberland, Durham, and Northumberland; dweller on the private or reserved land.

Sundermann, Sunderman (*Ger.*) One who came from Sundern (muddy terrain), the name of various places in Germany.

Sundermeier, Sundermeyer (*Ger.*) The farmer who dwelt at the swampy, muddy place.

Sundheim (*Nor.*) Dweller at the south homestead.

Sundheimer (*Ger.*) One who came from

Sundheim (home on the sound), in Germany.

Sundin (*Sw.*) Dweller near a sound or strait.

Sundquist, Sundkvist (*Sw., Nor.*) Sound, twig.

Sundstrom (*Sw.*) Sound (i.e., a narrow water course), stream.

Sunners (*Eng.*) A variant of Summers, q.v.

Sunshine (*Ger.*) Translation of Sonnenschein, q.v.

Superfine (*Eng.*) One who surpassed others in elegant qualities, possibly a proud, haughty individual.

Supper (*Ger.*) Dweller in the swamp; one who came from Suppo, in Germany.

Supple, Supplee, Supplice (*Fr.*) Descendant of Sulpicius (red-spotted face).

Surden, Surdan (*Eng.*) Dweller in the south pasture or valley.

Surette, Surrette (*Fr.*) Descendant of Suret, a pet form of Sureau (elder tree); one who was stable, steady, or sure.

Surfleet (*Eng.*) One who came from Surfleet (sour stream), in Lincolnshire.

Surgener, Surgenor, Surginer, Surgner (*Eng.*) A temporary resident, a sojourner; a medical man who performs manual operations on a patient; a medical practitioner who visits his patients at home.

Surkin (*Rus.*) Variant of Sirkin, q.v.

Surles (*Eng.*) The son of Serle (armor).

Surman, Surmin (*Eng.*) The sour or surly man.

Surrell (*Fr., Eng.*) One who came from Sourdeval (dark valley), in Manche; dweller near an elder tree.

Surrey (*Eng.*) One who came from Surrey (southern district), a county in England.

Surrick (*Eng.*) Dweller on the south farm.

Surridge, Surrage (*Eng.*) One who came from Surridge (south ridge), in Devonshire.

Surtees (*Eng.*) Dweller on the Tees (hot, surging), a river in England.

Susann, Susan (*Heb.*) Descendant of Susan (lily), the Biblical Shushannah.

Susi (*Est.*) Dweller at the sign of the wolf; one thought to possess the characteristics of a wolf.

Suski, Suskey (*Pol., Cz.-Sl.*) Dweller near, or worker at, the grain bin.

Suskind, Suskin, Susskind (*Ger.*) The mealy-mouthed, smooth-tongued man; the dear, sweet, cherished person; sweet child.

Suslov (*Rus.*) One with some resemblance to a gopher; dweller at the sign of the gopher.

Sussenbach (*Ger.*) One who came from Sussenbach (meadow stream), the name of two places in Germany.

Sussewell, Suswell (*Eng.*) Dweller near the south spring.

Sussland (*Eng.*) Dweller on the south estate or district.

Sussman, Susman (*Ger.*) Sweet man, an affectionate person.

Susson (*Eng.*) Descendant of Susan (a lily); variant of Sisson, q.v.

Sutch (*Eng.*) Variant of Such, q.v.

Sutcliffe, Sutcliff (*Eng.*) Dweller by the south cliff or slope.

Suter, Sutor (*Eng., Ger.*) Variant of Souter, q.v.; variant of Suder, q.v.

Sutfin (*Eng., Du.*) Dweller on, or near, the south fen or marsh; variant of Sutphen, q.v.

Sutherland, Sutherlan, Sutherlin (*Scot.*) One who came from the county of Sutherland (southern land), in Scotland.

Sutley (*Eng.*) Dweller in, or near, the southern grove; one who came from Sotterley (south grove), in Suffolk.

Sutliff (*Eng.*) Dweller near the rock or steep descent.

Sutor (*Eng.*) One who made and sold shoes, a shoemaker.

Sutphen, Sutphin (*Du.*) One who came from Zutphen, in Holland.

Sutter (*Eng.*) One who made shoes, a shoemaker.

Suttles (*Eng.*) Dweller at the south hill; the clever, cunning man.

Sutton (*Eng.*) One who came from Sutton (southern village or homestead), the name of many places in England.

Suwala, Suwalski (*Pol.*) One who shuffles his feet, or who wanders from place to place.

Suzuki (*Jap.*) Bell, tree.

Svec, Sveck (*Cz.-Sl., Ukr.*) One who made shoes and boots, a shoemaker.

Svedas (*Lith.*) One who came from Sweden, a Swede; one who was like a Swede.

Svendsen, Svensen (*Dan., Nor.*) The son of Svend or Sven (young boy; servant).

Svenson (*Sw.*) The son of Sven (young boy; servant).

Svilar (*Yu.-Sl.*) One who weaves silk, a silkweaver.

Svizzero (*It.*) One who came from Switzerland, a Swiss.

Svoboda (*Cz.-Sl., Pol., Ukr.*) Liberty or freedom, a name suggesting a free man, not a serf.

Swaby, Swabey (*Eng.*) One who came from Swaby (Svafi's homestead), in Lincolnshire.

Swafford (*Eng.*) Dweller at the river crossing of the Swaefas, an early English tribe.

Swain, Swaine, Swayne (*Eng.*) The man who acted as a servant or attendant; one who tended swine; descendant of Swain (young man; boy servant).

Swainson (*Eng.*) The son of Swain (young man; boy servant).

Swallow (*Eng.*) One who came from Swallow (rushing river), in Lincolnshire; dweller at a deep hollow.

Swan, Swann, Swane (*Eng., Sw.*) Dweller at the sign of the swan; the swain, a servant; descendant of Sveinn or Swan (knight's attendant); one who kept swans.

Swanberg (*Nor., Ger.*) Dweller on the hill used by swineherds; one who came from Schwanberg, in Austria.

Swanborn (*Eng.*) One who came from Swanbourne (stream frequented by swans), in Buckinghamshire.

Swank, Swanke (*Ger.*) Descendant of little Schwan (swan); dweller at the sign of the little swan; the thin, supple man.

Swanson, Swansen (*Sw.*) The son of Swan (servant).

Swanston (*Eng.*) Variant of Swanton, q.v.

Swanstrom (*Sw.*) Swan, stream.

Swanton (*Eng.*) One who came from Swanton (village of the swineherds), the name of places in Kent and Norfolk.

Sward (*Sw.*) Sword, a soldier name.

Swarthout (*Du.*) Dweller in, or near, the black wood.

Swartley (*Eng.*) Dweller at the black or dark homestead.

Swartz, Swarts, Swart, Swarz (*Ger., Du.*) One with a dark or swarthy complexion, black.

Swayze (*Eng.*) One who came from Swavesey (Swaef's landing place), in Cambridgeshire.

Swearer (*Eng.*) Dweller by a neck of land; one with some peculiarity of the neck.

Swearingen, Swearingin (*Ger.*) One who came from Schweringen (swamp water), in Germany.

Sweat, Sweatt (*Eng.*) The dear or beloved person; descendant of Sweta (agreeable).

Sweatman (*Eng.*) Variant of Sweetman, q.v.

Swedberg (*Sw.*) Burnt over clearing mountain; contraction of Swedenborg, q.v.

Swedenborg, Swedenburg (*Sw.*) Sweden, stronghold.

Swedloff (*Rus.*) Descendant of the man from Sweden.

Sweeney, Sweeny (*Ir., Eng.*) Descendant of Suibhne (little hero); dweller on the island where pigs were kept; or at the meadow where pigs were raised; descendant of the peaceful or quiet man.

Sweet, Sweete (*Eng.*) The dear, or beloved person; descendant of Swet or Sweta (agreeable).

Sweeting, Sweeten, Sweetin (*Eng.*) The son of Sweet (sweet); dweller at the sweet meadow.

Sweetman, Sweetnam (*Eng.*) One who was pleasant and agreeable; the servant of Swet (sweet); one who came from Swettenham (Sweta's homestead), in Cheshire; descendant of Sweetmann (agreeable man).

Sweetser, Sweetsir (*Eng.*) One who came from Switzerland; an agreeable, elderly person.

Sweetwood (*Eng.*) Dweller in the sweet or pleasant wood.

Sweigart, Sweigert (*Swis., Ger.*) One who took care of cattle in the mountains, an Alpine herdsman; a taciturn person.

Sweitzer, Switzer (*Ger., Ir.*) One who came from Switzerland, a Swiss.

Swem, Swaim (*Du.*) Dweller at the sign of the swan.

Sweney (*Ir.*) Variant of Sweeney, q.v.

Swenson, Swensen (*Sw., Dan.*) The son of Swen (young boy; servant).

Swerdloff, Swerdlow, Swertloff (*Rus.*) The son of the driller.

Swetland (*Eng.*) One who came from Sweetlands (denoting lands of great fertility), in Devonshire.

Swetnam (*Eng.*) One who came from Swettenham (Sweta's homestead), in Cheshire; variant of Sweetman, q.v.

Swett, Swetts, Swets, Swetz (*Eng., Rus., Du.*) Descendant of Swet (agreeable); the light-complexioned man.

Swiatek (*Pol.*) One who came from the demimonde.

Swiatkowski (*Pol.*) One who came from Swiatkowka, a city, or from Swiatkowo, a village (both meaning world), in Poland.

Swiderski, Swider (*Pol.*) One who bored or drilled holes.

Swier (*Eng.*) Variant of Swire, q.v.

Swierczynski (*Pol.*) Dweller near a fir tree.

Swift (*Eng.*) One who was fleet of foot, probably a messenger.

Swinburne, Swinbourn (*Eng.*) One who came from Swinburn (brook near where pigs were kept), in Northumberland.

Swindell, Swindells, Swindle, Swindall (*Eng.*) Dweller in the valley where swine were bred.

Swindlehurst (*Eng.*) Dweller in the wooded valley where swine were bred.

Swindler (*Eng.*) One who beat and dressed flax.

Swineford (*Eng.*) One who came from Swinford (place where pigs crossed), in Berkshire.

Swinehart (*Eng.*) One who came from Swineshead (pig hill; source of the creek), the name of places in Bedfordshire and Lincolnshire.

Swinford (*Eng.*) One who came from Swinford (pig ford), in Berkshire.

Swingler, Swinger, Swingle (*Eng.*) One who beats and cleans flax using a swingle, a knife-like wooden instrument.

Swiniuch (*Pol.*) Nickname for a dirty man, a pig; one who raised and sold pigs.

Swinney, Swiney (*Ir., Eng.*) Variant of Sweeney, q.v.

Swinson (*Eng.*) Variant of Swainson, q.v.

Swinton (*Eng., Scot.*) One who came from Swinton (pig farm), the name of places in Lancashire and the North and West Ridings of Yorkshire, and in Scotland.

Swire (*Eng.*) Dweller on, or by, a neck of land; one with some peculiarity of the neck; one who came from Swyre (neck; pass between mountain peaks), in Dorset; dweller at a hollow near the top of the hill.

Swisher, Swiss (*Eng.*) One who came from Switzerland, a Swiss.

Swoboda (*Cz.-Sl., Pol., Ukr.*) Variant of Svoboda, q.v.

Swope, Swopes (*Ger.*) American variant of Schwab, q.v.

Sycamore (*Eng.*) Dweller near a sycamore tree.

Syckelmoore (*Eng.*) Dweller on, or near, Sicel's wasteland.

Sydenham (*Eng.*) One who came from Sydenham (wide homestead; Cippa's homestead), the name of four places in England.

Sydlow (*Eng.*) One who came from Sidlow Bridge (Sidelufu's bridge), in Surrey.

Sydney (*Eng.*) Variant of Sidney, q.v.

Sydor (*Cz.-Sl., Ukr.*) Descendant of Sydor (gift of Isis).

Sydoruk (*Ukr.*) The son of Sydor (gift of Isis).

Sykes (*Eng.*) Dweller by a mountain stream or ditch.

Sylk (*Eng.*) Dweller in a narrow valley; or on plowed land; metonymic for a worker or dealer in silk.

Sylvester (*Eng.*) Descendant of Silvester (forest dweller).

Syme, Symes (*Eng.*) Descendant of Sime, a pet form of Simon or Simeon (gracious hearing; hearkening; snub-nosed).

Symington (*Scot.*) One who came from Symington (Symond's stone), the name of places in Ayrshire and Lanarkshire.

Symmes, Symms, Syms (*Eng.*) Descendant of Sim, a pet form of Simon or Simeon (gracious hearing; hearkening; snub-nosed).

Symons, Symmons, Symonds, Symon, Symond (*Eng.*) The son of Simon or Simeon (gracious hearing; hearkening; snub-nosed).

Synnott (*Eng.*) Variant of Sinnett, q.v.; and of Sennott, q.v.

Sypniewski (*Pol.*) One who came from Sypniewo (Sypien's settlement), in Poland.

Syre, Syres (*Eng.*) The lord or master; descendant of Sigehere (victory, army).

Szablewski (*Pol.*) One who made swords.

Szabo (*Hun.*) One who made outer garments, a tailor.

Szafran (*Pol.*) One who grew and sold saffron, a plant used in dyeing.

Szafranski (*Pol.*) Dweller at a place where saffron or crocus grew.

Szanto (*Hun.*) Dweller on arable land.

Szarek (*Pol.*) A nobleman with little wealth.

Szasz (*Hun.*) One who came from Saxony, a Saxon.

Szczepaniak, Szczepanik, Szczepanek (*Pol.*) Descendant of little Szczepan, Polish form of Stephen (a crown or garland).

Szczepanski (*Pol.*) The son of Szczepan, Polish form of Stephen (a crown or garland).

Szczesny (*Pol.*) The fortunate person.

Szczurek (*Pol.*) Dweller at the sign of the small rat; one with the characteristics of a small rat.

Szekely (*Hun.*) A Szekely, a Hungarian of Eastern Transylvania, a tribal name.

Szewc (*Pol.*) One who made and repaired shoes, a shoemaker or cobbler.

Szewczyk, Szewczak (*Pol.*) One who was learning the craft of making shoes and boots; a journeyman shoemaker.

Szigeti (*Hun.*) One who came from one of the many towns or villages in Hungary ending in -sziget (island of . . .); dweller on an island.

Szilagyi (*Hun.*) One who came from the county of Szilagy, in Hungary.

Szlachta (*Pol.*) A member of the gentry, a man of gentle birth.

Szmulewitz (*Rus.*) Descendant of Szmule, a Slavic form of Samuel (God hath heard; name of God; Shem is God).

Szpak (*Pol.*) Dweller at the sign of the starling; a cunning fellow.

Szucs (*Hun.*) One who dressed or dealt in furs, a furrier.

Szymanski (*Pol.*) Descendant of Szymon, Polish form of Simon (gracious hearing; hearkening; snub-nosed).

Szymczak (*Pol.*) The son of Szymon, Polish form of Simon (gracious hearing; hearkening; snub-nosed).

Tabak, Taback, Tabachnick (*Pol.*) One who prepared and sold snuff.

Tabb (*Ger.*) Descendant of Tabb, a pet form of Tabbert (people, bright).

Tabbert (*Ger.*) Descendant of Tabbert (people, bright); one who habitually wore a tabard or long overcoat.

Tabbey, Tabby (*Eng., Ger.*) One who made and sold tabby, a fabric in plain or taffeta weave; one who wore tabby; descendant of little Tabb, a pet form of Tabbert (people, bright).

Tabor, Taber, Tabour (*Eng.*) One who performed on the tabor, a small drum.

Taborn, Taborne, Tabourn, Tabourne (*Eng.*) Metonymic for one who played the taborin, a small tabor.

Tacey (*Eng.*) Descendant of little Tace, a pet form of Eustace (steadfast).

Tackbary (*Eng.*) Dweller near a grove where ewes were kept.

Taddei (*Rus.*) Descendant of Taddei, a Slavic form of Thaddeus (praising God).

Tadley (*Eng.*) One who came from Tadley (grove where toads were found), in Hampshire.

Taft, Taff, Taffe (*Eng., Ir.*) Dweller at a toft, a yard enclosing a residence; descendant of Taff, a pet form of David (commander; beloved; friend); or of Theophilus (loved by God).

Tagawa (*Jap.*) Rice field, river.

Taggart, Taggert (*Scot.*) The son of the priest.

Taglia (*It.*) One who cuts or slaughters animals, a butcher; often a first part of a longer name.

Tagliaferro (*It.*) One who cut, or otherwise worked with, iron.

Tague (*Ir.*) Grandson of Tadhg (poet).

Taillandier (*Fr.*) One who made and sold iron articles.

Tailleur (*Fr.*) One who made outer garments, a tailor.

Taine (*Fr.*) Dweller near the den or burrow of wild animals.

Taintor, Tainter (*Eng.*) One who dyes or tints cloth, a dyer.

Tait, Taitt (*Eng.*) One with a large or peculiar head; a gay or cheerful person; dweller at the top of the hill.

Takacs, Takach (*Hun.*) One who wove cloth, a weaver.

Takahashi (*Jap.*) High, bridge.

Takai (*Jap.*) High, well.

Takata (*Jap.*) High, rice field.

Takeda (*Jap.*) Brave, rice field.

Takeuchi (*Jap.*) Bamboo, inside.

Talbot, Talbert, Talbott (*Eng.*) Descendant of Talbot (to cut faggots); the pillager or bandit; dweller at the sign of the talbot, a white sporting dog.

Talcott (*Eng.*) Dweller in front of, or opposite, the cottage, or in the cottage in the dale.

Taliaferro (*It.*) One who cut iron, an ironworker.

Talis (*Eng.*) Dweller in, or near, a copse or small thicket.

Talkington (*Eng.*) One who came from Tallington (village of Tala's people), in Lincolnshire.

Talley, Tally (*Ir.*) Grandson of Taithleach (quiet, peaceful).

Tallick (*Eng.*) Dweller at the steep place.

Tallman, Talman (*Eng.*) The able, obedient servant.

Talmadge, Talmage (*Eng.*) One who carried a knapsack.

Tamashiro (*Jap.*) Gem, castle.

Tamblyn, Tamblin (*Eng., Scot.*) Descendant of little Tam, a Scottish pet form of Thomas (a twin).

Tamburri, Tamburro, Tamburino (*It.*) One who beats the drum in band or drum corps; one who made and sold drums.

Tames (*Eng.*) Dweller by the Thames (dark), a river in England; or by the Tame (dark), the name of several streams in England.

Tamkin, Tamlyn (*Scot.*) Descendant of little Tam, a pet form of Thomas (a twin).

Tamm (*Est.*) Dweller near an oak tree.

Tammaro (*It.*) The uncouth person, a rustic.

Tamony, Tamney (*Ir.*) The son of the tympanist.

Tamp (*Scot.*) Descendant of Tamp, a Scottish form of Tom, the short form of Thomas (a twin).

Tamton (*Eng.*) Dweller at the homestead on the Tame (dark), the name of several streams in England.

Tanabe (*Jap.*) Rice field, side.

Tanaka (*Jap.*) Rice field, middle.

Tancredi (*It.*) Descendant of Tancredi, Italian form of Tancred (thought, counsel).

Tandy (*Scot.*) Descendant of Dandy, a pet form of Andrew (manly).

Taney (*Eng.*) One who came from Saint-Aubin-du-Thenney or Saint-Jean-du-Thenney, in France.

Tangney (*Ir.*) Grandson of Teangana.

Tanguay, Tanguy (*Eng., Fr.*) Descendant of Tanguy (fire, dog).

Taniguchi (*Jap.*) Valley, mouth.

Tanis (*Lith.*) Descendant of Tanis, a pet form of Athanasius (immortal).

Tank, Tanke (*Ger.*). Descendant of Tanko, a pet form of Thankmar or Tancmar (thought, fame).

Tankard, Tankerd (*Eng.*) Descendant of Tancard (thought, hard); metonymic for one who made tankards.

Tankersley, Tanksley (*Eng.*) One who came from Tankersley (Thancred's grove), in the West Riding of Yorkshire.

Tankins (*Du.*) Descendant of Tanneke, a pet form of Tane (thought).

Tann (*Eng.*) Dweller at the scrub, that is, land covered by rough vegetation.

Tannahill, Tannehill (*Eng., Scot.*) Dweller on a hill covered by scrub; one who came from Tannahill (narrow place), in Scotland.

Tannenbaum, Tanenbaum, Tannebaum (*Ger.*) Dweller at, or near, a fir tree; one who came from Tannenbaum (fir tree), the name of two places in Germany.

Tanner (*Eng., Ger.*) One who made or sold leather; one who came from Tann (fir trees), the name of several places in Germany.

Tanney (*Eng.*) Dweller on the island covered by scrub.

Tansey (*Eng.*) One who came from Tansey (island in the branch of a river), in Somerset.

Tantillo (*It.*) One of low stature, the small man.

Tanton (*Eng.*) One who came from Tanton (homestead on the Tame river), in the North Riding of Yorkshire.

Tanz, Tanzer, Tanzler (*Ger.*) One who entertains by tricks, a juggler or conjurer; or by leading in dancing.

Tapley (*Eng.*) One who came from Tapeley (wood where pegs were obtained), in Devonshire.

Taplin (*Eng.*) Descendant of little Tam, a pet form of Thomas (a twin).

Tapp, Tappe (*Eng., Scot.*) Descendant of Taeppa (peg); dweller at the top of the hill.

Tappan, Tappen (*Du.*) One who drew wine or beer.

Tapper (*Eng., Sw.*) One who tapped casks, or drew liquor, a tavern-keeper; brave.

Tarantelli, Tarantella (*It.*) The lively dancing man; one who dances the tarantella, a dance supposed to cure the bite of the tarantula.

Tarantino (*It.*) One who came from Taranto, in Italy.

Tarasenko (*Ukr.*) The son of Taras.

Tarbell (*Fr.*) One who came from Tarabel (auger), in France.

Tarbert (*Scot., Nor.*) One who came from Tarbert (isthmus), in Ross and Cromarty; descendant of Thorbiartr (Thor, bright).

Tarbox, Tarbuck, Tarbock (*Eng.*) One who came from Tarbock (thorn brook), in Lancashire.

Tarby (*Sw.*) One who came from Tarby, the name of two places in Sweden.

Tarde (*Fr.*) One who came from Tardes (Tardus' homestead), in France.

Targ, Targe (*Eng.*) Dweller at the sign of the shield.

Tarin (*Fr.*) One who changed money, a moneychanger; one who came from Tarentaise (rocky place), in France.

Tarkenton (*Eng.*) One who came from

Torkington (village of Turec's people), in Cheshire.

Tarkington (*Eng.*) Variant of Torkington, q.v.

Tarleton (*Eng.*) One who came from Tarleton (homestead where thorn bushes grew; Tharald's homestead), the name of places in Gloucestershire and Lancashire.

Tarlow, Tarlowe (*Pol.*) One who came from Tarlow, in Poland.

Tarmey, Tarmy (*Ir.*) Grandson of Tormaigh.

Tarnow, Tarnowski, Tarnoff (*Pol.*) Dweller near a blackthorn or sloe tree; one who came from Tarnow (blackthorn or sloe), in Poland.

Tarpey, Tarpy (*Ir.*) Descendant of Tarpach (sturdy).

Tarpley (*Eng.*) One who came from Tarporley (pear wood on the rocky hill), in Cheshire.

Tarr, Tarre, Tar (*Eng.*) Dweller in, or near, a tower; or near a tower-like rock or hill.

Tarrance (*Eng.*) Variant of Tarrant, q.v.

Tarrant (*Eng.*) One who came from Tarrant (trespasser), the name of several places in England; or who dwelt at the Tarrant river, in Dorset.

Tarshish, Tarshis (*Heb.*) Descendant of Tarshish (precious stone; yellow jasper).

Tart, Tartt (*Eng.*) Nickname for one who was sharp or caustic in his speech; one who came from Tarrant, the name of several places on the Tarrant (trespasser), a river in England.

Tartaglia, Tartaglione (*It.*) One who stammers or stutters.

Tartar, Tarter (*Fr.*) One who came from Tatary (robbers); one with a dark skin.

Tartarsky (*Ukr.*) One who came from Tatary (robbers), an indefinite region in Asia and Europe.

Tartt, Tart (*Eng., Bel.*) The sharp, severe man; one who prepared and sold slices of bread with butter or jam.

Tarver (*Eng.*) One who came from

Torver (hut made of sods), in Lancashire.

Tasch, Taschner, Taschler (*Ger.*) One who made and sold purses and handbags.

Tash (*Eng.*) Dweller at the ash tree.

Tashjian (*Arm.*) The son of Tash (stone); dweller near a stone.

Tasker (*Eng.*) One who worked, or was paid, by the task or piece.

Tassone, Tassoni, Tasso (*It.*) Dweller near a yew tree; dweller at the sign of the badger.

Tatar (*Ger.*) One who came from Tatary, an indefinite region in Asia and Europe; a Tatar, a member of a tribe mostly of Turkic origin.

Tatcher (*Eng.*) Variant of Thatcher, q.v.

Tate (*Eng.*) One who had a large, or peculiar, head; a gay or cheerful person; dweller at the top of the hill.

Tatelbaum, Tattlebaum (*Hun.*) Variant of Teitelbaum, q.v.

Tatham, Tathum (*Eng.*) One who came from Tatham (Tate's homestead), in Lancashire.

Tatlow (*Eng.*) Variant of Tetlow, q.v.

Tatnall (*Eng.*) One who came from Tatenhill (Tata's hill), in Staffordshire.

Tator (*Fr.*) Variant of Tartar, q.v.

Tatten (*Eng.*) One who came from Tatton (Tata's homestead), the name of places in Cheshire and Dorset.

Tattersall (*Eng.*) One who came from Tattershall (Tathere's valley), in Lincolnshire.

Tattersfield (*Eng.*) One who came from Tatsfield (Tatel's open country), in Surrey.

Tatterson (*Eng.*) The son of Tathere (beloved, army).

Tatton (*Eng.*) One who came from Tatton (Tata's homestead), the name of places in Cheshire and Dorset.

Tatum, Tatem, Tatam, Tatom (*Eng.*) One who came from Tatham (Tata's homestead), in Lancashire.

Tauber, Taube, Taub (*Ger.*) Dweller at the sign of the dove; one with the qualities of a dove; descendant of

505

Tabo, a pet form of names beginning with Diet, as Theudobald, Theudobert, and Theudobrand.

Taussig, Tausig, Tauss (*Ger.*) One who came from Tauss, in Bohemia.

Tavarez, Tavares (*Sp.*) Descendant of the hermit or retired man.

Tavenner (*Eng.*) One who sold ale and wine, a tavernkeeper.

Taverna (*It.*) Dweller near the wineshop.

Tawber (*Ger.*) Variant of Tauber, q.v.

Tawell (*Eng.*) Dweller by the silent spring or river.

Taws (*Scot.*) Corruption of Tamhas, a Gaelic form of Thomas (a twin).

Taxter (*Eng.*) Variant of Textor, q.v.

Taylor, Tayler, Taylour (*Eng.*) One who made outer garments, a tailor.

Taymore, Taymor (*Heb.*) Descendant of Tamar or Tawmawr (palm tree).

Tayyarzade (*Pers.*) The son of Tayyar.

Tazelaar (*Eng.*) One who teasels cloth to raise a nap on it.

Tazwell, Tazewell (*Eng.*) Dweller at the ash tree spring.

Tchaikovsky (*Rus., Pol.*) Variant of Tschaikovsky, q.v.

Teacher (*Eng.*) One who instructs others.

Teachout (*Fr.*) Descendant of little Tache (spot or blemish).

Tead (*Eng.*) Descendant of Tead, a pet form of names beginning with Theod (people), as Theodberht, Theodred, and Theodric.

Teagle (*Eng.*) Dweller by, or in, an enclosure in a grove.

Teague (*Wel., Ir., Eng.*) One with a fair complexion; grandson of Tadhg (poet); dweller in an enclosure or near a common pasture.

Tearle (*Eng.*) The stern, strict man.

Teasdale, Teesdale (*Eng.*) One who came from Teesdale (surging river valley).

Teasley (*Eng.*) Dweller in the homestead on the Tees (heat), an English river; one who came from Tasley (homestead overgrown with teasels), in Shropshire.

Tebbetts, Tebbets (*Eng.*) Descendant of little Tebb, a pet form of Theobald (people, bold).

Tedesco, Tedeschi (*It.*) One who came from Germany, a German.

Tedrick (*Eng.*) Descendant of Theodric (people, rule); one who came from Todrick (Tata's dairy farm), in the West Riding of Yorkshire.

Tee (*Eng.*) Dweller by a stream.

Teed (*Eng.*) Descendant of Teed, a pet form of names beginning with Theod (people), such as Theodbald, Theodric, and Theodred.

Teehan, Teahan (*Ir.*) Grandson of Teitheachan (fugitive; runaway).

Teele, Teel, Teal (*Eng.*) Dweller at the sign of the teal (a small duck).

Tees (*Eng.*) Dweller by the Tees (heat), a river in England.

Tegge (*Wel., Ir., Eng.*) Variant of Teague, q.v.; metonymic for one who took care of young sheep.

Tegtmeyer, Tegmeyer, Tegtmeier (*Ger.*) One who collected the farm rent equal to a tenth of the income.

Teich, Teicher (*Ger.*) One who came from Teich (low ground), in Germany.

Teichert (*Ger.*) Descendant of Tagahard (light, hard); descendant of Dihart (thrive, firm).

Teichman, Teichmann (*Ger.*) Dweller near a pond or depression in the ground; same as Teich, q.v.

Teitelbaum (*Hun.*) The date palm tree, a name selected from Psalm 92:12, where it is written, "The righteous shall flourish like the palm tree."

Teitelman (*Ger.*) Date palm man.

Teixeira (*Port.*) One who came from Teixeira (place of yew trees), the name of several places in Portugal.

Telfer, Telfair (*Eng.*) One who cut or otherwise worked with iron.

Telford (*Eng.*) One who came from Tilford (convenient river crossing), in Surrey.

Teller (*Eng.*) One who made or sold linen cloth.

Tellier (*Fr.*) One who wove linen cloth.

Tellison (*Eng.*) The son of Tella (swift; ready).

Telliver (*Scot., Fr.*) Scottish corruption of Taylor; one who cut iron.

Temkin, Tempkin (*Eng.*) Descendant of little Tim, a pet form of Timothy (honoring God).

Temme, Temm (*Ger.*) Descendant of Temme, a pet form of Theudemar or Dietmar (folk, fame).

Temperley (*Eng.*) One who came from Timperleigh (timber wood), in Cheshire.

Tempest (*Eng.*) Nickname for a violent, agitated man.

Temple, Tempel (*Eng.*) Dweller in, or near, a religious house of the Knights Templars; descendant of Temple, a name sometimes given a foundling abandoned in a temple.

Templeman (*Eng.*) The man who acted as servant to the Templars; or who dwelt in one of the houses of the Knights Templars.

Templeton (*Eng.*) One who came from Templeton (manor belonging to the Knights Templars), the name of places in Berkshire and Devonshire.

Templin (*Eng.*) Descendant of little Tim, a pet form of Timothy (honoring God).

Tempson (*Eng.*) The son of Timm, a pet form of Timothy (honoring God).

Tenaglia (*It.*) One who used pincers in his work, a blacksmith.

Tenant (*Eng.*) One who rented land of another; the holder of a tenement.

Tenbroeck, Ten Broek, Ten Brook (*Du.*) Dweller at, or near, the marsh.

Tendler (*Ger.*) One who dealt in worn or second-hand clothing.

Tenenbaum (*Ger.*) Variant of Tannenbaum, q.v.

Ten Eyck (*Du.*) One who lived near an oak tree.

Teng (*Chin.*) Mound.

Tennant (*Eng.*) One who rented land of another, a tenant.

Tennenbaum (*Ger.*) Variant of Tannenbaum, q.v.

Tenner, Tener (*Eng., Ger.*) Variant of Tenant, q.v.; dweller near the Tann or Thann, a river in Germany.

Tennett (*Eng.*) Variant of Tenant, q.v.

Tenney, Tenny (*Eng.*) Descendant of Tenney, a pet form of Dennis (belonging to Dionysus, Grecian god of wine).

Tennyson, Tennison (*Eng.*) The son of Tenny, a pet form of Dennis (belonging to Dionysus, Grecian god of wine).

Tenuto, Tenuta (*It.*) The dear, beloved person.

Teplick (*Cz.-Sl., Rus.*) One who came from Teplitsa (warmth), in Czechoslovakia.

Teplitsky, Teplitz, Teplitzky (*Rus., Cz.-Sl.*) Dweller near, or worker in, a greenhouse; one who came from Teplitsa (warmth), in Czechoslovakia.

Tepper, Tipper (*Eng.*) One who furnished articles, particularly arrows, with metal tips.

Teraji (*Jap.*) Temple, land.

Terhune (*Du.*) Dweller at the hedge.

Terkeltaub, Terkeltoub (*Ger.*) Dweller at the sign of the turtledove.

Termini, Termine (*It.*) Dweller near the boundary.

Terpeluk (*Ukr.*) The son of the patient man.

Terpstra (*Du.*) Dweller on, or near, a hill or mound.

Terracina, Terracino (*It.*) One who came from Terracina, in Italy.

Terranova (*It.*) One who came from Terranova (new land), in Sardinia; dweller on the newly cleared land.

Terrell, Terrill (*Eng.*) Descendant of Turold or Thorold (Thor, strong); one who came from Tirril (wooden hut), in Westmorland.

Terrence (*Eng.*) Descendant of Terrence (soft or tender).

Terry (*Eng., Ir.*) Descendant of Terry, a pet form of Terrence (soft or tender); or of Toirdhealbhach (shaped like Thor).

Terwilliger (*Du.*) One who came from Willige (Wille's settlement), in Holland.

Tesar (*Cz.-Sl.*) One who worked in wood, a carpenter.

Teske, Teska, Teschke (*Ger.*) Descendant of Tech (consolation).

Tesla (*Yu.-Sl., Ukr.*) One who worked with an adz, a carpenter.

Teslenko (*Ukr.*) The son of the carpenter.

Tesluk (*Ukr.*) One who worked in wood, a carpenter.

Tesmond (*Eng.*) Descendant of Teosmund (evil, protection).

Tessaro, Tessari (*It.*) One who wove cloth, a weaver.

Tessier (*Fr.*) One who wove cloth, a weaver.

Tessler, Tesler (*Eng.*) One who scratches, teases, or teasels cloth to raise a nap on it.

Tessmer, Tesmer (*Ger.*) Descendant of Tesmar (comfort, fame).

Test (*Fr.*) One with a large or unusual head.

Testa (*Sp., It.*) One who had a large or unusual head; descendant of Testa, a pet form of Battista, Italian form of Baptist (a baptizer).

Tester (*Fr.*) One with a big head, from Old French, Testard.

Tete (*Fr.*) More modern form of Test, q.v.

Tetlow (*Eng.*) One who came from Tetlow (Tette's mound), in Lancashire.

Tett (*Eng.*) Descendant of Tetta (merry).

Tetzlaff (*Ger.*) Descendant of Tetzlaff (consolation, fame).

Teufel (*Ger.*) Descendant of Tiefel, a pet form of Theudobald (people, bold), and Theudofrid (people, peace); descendant of one nicknamed, the devil.

Tevell, Tevelson (*Eng.*) Descendant of Tevel, a name derived from David (commander; beloved; friend).

Tew (*Eng.*) One who came from Tew (long row), in Oxfordshire; the fat, plump man.

Tewdwr (*Wel.*) Descendant of Tudor (gift of God); or of Tudyr (country; tribe).

Tewksbury, Tewkesbury (*Eng.*) One who came from Tewkesbury (Teodec's fort), in Gloucestershire.

Tews (*Ger.*) Descendant of Tews, a pet form of Matheus (gift of Jehovah).

Texidor (*Port.*) One who weaves cloth, a weaver.

Textor, Texter (*Eng.*) One who wove cloth, a weaver.

Thacker, Thacher (*Eng.*) Variant of Thatcher, q.v.

Thackeray, Thackery, Thackrey, Thackray, Thackrah (*Eng.*) Dweller at the corner where the thatch was grown or stored.

Thain, Thaine (*Eng.*) One who was a tenant by military service.

Thal, Thaler (*Ger.*) One who came from Thal (valley), the name of many small places in Germany.

Thalheimer (*Ger.*) One who came from Thalheim (valley home), the name of several places in Germany.

Thane (*Eng.*) One who was a tenant by military service.

Thanhauser (*Ger.*) One who came from Thanhausen (forest settlement), the name of several places in Germany.

Thanos (*Gr.*) Descendant of Thanos, a pet form of Athanasios, Greek form of Athanasius (immortal).

Tharp, Tharpe (*Eng.*) Variant of Thorpe, q.v.

Thatcher, Thaxter (*Eng.*) One who covered roofs with straw, rushes, reeds or the like.

Thawley (*Eng.*) One who came from Thorley (thorny grove), the name of places in Hertfordshire and Wight.

Thaxton (*Eng.*) Dweller in a homestead where thatch was obtained.

Thayer (*Eng.*) Descendant of Thaider (people, army).

Theil, Theile (*Fr.*) Dweller near a lime tree or linden tree.

Theis, Theiss, Theise (*Ger.*) Descendant of Theis, a pet form of Matthias (gift of Jehovah); descendant of Theis, a form of Dago, a pet form of names beginning with Dag (light), as Tagibod and Tagamar.

Theisen (*Ger.*) The son of Theis, a pet form of Matthias (gift of Jehovah).

Thelen, Thelin (*Ger.*) Descendant of Thilo, a form of Tiuto, or Theuda, short forms of names beginning with Thiud (people), as Theudobald, Theudoricus and Theudoald.

Then (*Ger.*) Descendant of Degen (young fighter or attendant).

Theobald, Theobold (*Eng.*) Descendant of Theobald (people, bold).

Theodore (*Eng.*) Descendant of Theodoric (people, rule); rarely of Theodore (gift of God).

Theodoropoulos (*Gr.*) The son of Theodoros, Greek form of Theodore (gift of God).

Theodorou (*Gr.*) Descendant of Theodora, a Greek form of Theodore (gift of God).

Theodos (*Gr.*) Descendant of Theodos, a pet form of Theodoros, a Greek form of Theodore (gift of God).

Theriault, Theriot (*Fr.*) Descendant of little Thierry, a pet form of Theodore (gift of God).

Thetford, Thedford (*Eng.*) One who came from Thetford (people's river crossing), the name of places in Cambridgeshire and Norfolk.

Theurer (*Ger.*) One who assesses or values for tax purposes; one who came from Theuern (flowing), in Germany.

Thew (*Eng.*) The servant, bondsman, or slave.

Thibault, Thibeault, Thibeau (*Fr.*) Descendant of Theudbald, Thibaut, or Thibaud (people, bold).

Thibodeau, Thibedeau, Thibideau (*Fr.*) Descendant of Theudbald, Thibaut, or Thibaud (people, bold).

Thiel, Thiele, Thielen, Thiell (*Ger.*) Same as Thelen, q.v.

Thierry, Thiery (*Fr.*) Descendant of Thierry, French form of Theodoric (people, rule).

Thies, Thiese (*Swis.*) Descendant of Thies, a pet form of Mathies, a Swiss form of Matthew (gift of Jehovah).

Thigpen (*Ger.*) Descendant of Thigfuns (thrive, swift); one who begged for coins; dweller at, or near, Thyga's enclosure or hill.

Thill (*Fr.*) One who came from Thil (lime tree); dweller near a lime tree or linden tree.

Thimbleby (*Eng.*) One who came from Thimbleby (Thymli's village), in Lincolnshire.

Thin (*Scot.*) Dweller at "the inn"; the tall slim man.

Thirsk (*Eng.*) One who came from Thirsk (lake), in the North Riding of Yorkshire.

Thistle, Thissel (*Eng.*) Dweller near thistles or prickly plants.

Thistlethwaite (*Eng.*) Dweller in the clearing infested with thistles.

Thistlewood (*Eng.*) Dweller in the wood where thistles abounded.

Thom, Thoms (*Eng.*) Descendant of Thom, the abbreviated form of Thomas (a twin).

Thoma (*Ger.*) Descendant of Thoma, a German form of Thomas (a twin).

Thomas (*Wel.*) Descendant of Thomas (a twin).

Thomason, Thomasson (*Eng.*) The son of Thomas (a twin).

Thome (*Eng.*) Descendant of Thome, a pet form of Thomas (a twin).

Thompkins (*Eng.*) The son of little Thom, a pet form of Thomas (a twin).

Thompson, Thompsen (*Eng., Scot., Sw., Nor.*) The son of Thom, a pet form of Thomas (a twin); one who came from Thompson (Tumi's homestead), in Norfolk.

Thomson, Thomsen (*Sw., Dan., Nor.*) The son of Thom, a pet form of Thomas (a twin).

Thore (*Nor., Fr.*) Descendant of Thor, the god of thunder, often a short form for one of the many names beginning with this element, as Thorstan, Thoraldr, and Thorbjorn; one who came from Thore (Taurius' estate), in France.

Thoreau (*Fr.*) One who is strong as a bull; descendant of little Thore, a pet form of Mathore, a French form of Matthew (gift of Jehovah).

Thoresen, Thoreson (*Nor., Sw.*) The son of Thor (the old Norse god of thunder).

Thorgren (*Sw.*) Thor, branch.

Thorington (*Eng.*) One who came from Thorington (homestead where thorn brushes grew), in Suffolk.

Thorley (*Eng.*) One who came from Thorley (thorny wood), the name of places in Hertfordshire and Wight.

Thornberry (*Eng.*) One who came from Thornbury (fort where thorns grew), in Devonshire.

Thornborrow, Thornborough (*Eng.*) One who came from Thornborough (thorn hill), the name of places in Buckinghamshire and the North Riding of Yorkshire.

Thornburg (*Eng.*) Dweller near a fort where thorns grew; one who came from Thornbrough (fort protected by a thorn hedge), the name of several places in England.

Thornburn (*Eng., Scot.*) Dweller near a stream where thorn-bushes grew.

Thorndike, Thorndyke (*Eng.*) Dweller on, or near, a dike where thorn-bushes grew.

Thorne, Thorn, Thornes (*Eng.*) Dweller near a thorn-bush; one who came from Thorne (thorn-bush), the name of several places in England.

Thornehill, Thornell, Thornhill (*Eng.*) One who came from Thornhill (hill overgrown with thorn-bushes), the name of several places in England.

Thorner (*Eng.*) Dweller at, or near, a thorn-bush.

Thornley (*Eng.*) One who came from Thornley (thorny glade), the name of places in Durham and Lancashire.

Thornquist, Thornqvist (*Sw.*) Thorn, twig.

Thornton (*Eng.*) One who came from Thornton (place where thorn-bushes grew), the name of many places in England.

Thoroughgood (*Eng.*) The very good man.

Thorpe, Thorp (*Eng.*) One who came from Thorpe (farm), the name of many places in England; dweller at a farmstead.

Thorsen, Thorson (*Nor.*) The son of Thor (the old Norse god of thunder).

Thorvaldsen (*Nor.*) The son of Thorvaldr (Thor, ruler).

Thrall, Thrale (*Eng.*) The serf, servant, peasant, bondsman.

Thrasher, Thresher (*Eng.*) One who beat out grain by striking with a flail.

Threadgill (*Eng.*) One who threads gold or ornaments with needlework, an embroiderer.

Threatt, Threat, Threats (*Eng.*) Dweller in a clearing or enclosed piece of land; one who came from Thwaite (meadow; wood; piece of land; forest clearing), the name of three places in England.

Threlfall (*Eng.*) One who came from Threlfall (the thrall's hill), in Lancashire.

Threlkeld (*Nor., Sw.*) The thrall's spring, probably designating one who resided nearby.

Threston (*Eng.*) One who came from Threxton (dirty homestead), in Norfolk.

Thrift (*Eng.*) One who managed his affairs in an economical, frugal manner.

Thring (*Eng.*) One who came from Tring (tree-covered slope), in Hertfordshire.

Throckmorton (*Eng.*) One who came from Throckmorton (lake with trestles supporting a table, probably for use in washing), in Worcestershire.

Thronebury (*Eng.*) One who came from Thornbury (fort where thorns grew), in Devonshire.

Thrower (*Eng.*) A thread-thrower, that is, one who produces silk thread from raw silk. The name may, in some cases, refer to the potter's wheel or the turner's lathe, both called a throw.

Thrush (*Eng.*) Metonymic for one who trapped thrushes for food.

Thulin, Thullen, Thull (*Ger.*) Same as Thelin, q.v.

Thum, Thumm (*Eng.*) One who had a peculiar thumb, or who had lost a thumb.

Thummel (*Ger.*) The noisy, restless, tumultuous man.

Thurber (*Eng.*) Descendant of Thurgar or Thorgeirr (Thor's spear); dweller at Thor's grove.

Thurgood (*Eng.*) Descendant of Thorgautr (Thor, the god, man from Gautland); contraction of Thoroughgood, q.v.

Thurlow (*Eng.*) One who came from Thurlow (assembly hill), in Suffolk.

Thurman, Thurmond (*Eng.*) Descendant of Thurmund (Thor's protection).

Thurston (*Eng.*) Descendant of Thurstan (the stone of Thor, Norse god of thunder); one who came from Thurston (Thori's homestead), in Suffolk.

Thwaites, Thweatt, Thwaite (*Eng.*) One who came from Thwaite (meadow), in Norfolk; dweller in a forest clearing or enclosure.

Thyne, Thynne (*Eng.*) The slim, thin, man; dweller at "the inn."

Tiano (*It.*) Descendant of Tiano, a pet form of Sabastiano, Italian form of Sebastian (venerable); one who made and sold pots or bowls.

Tibbetts, Tibbits, Tibbitts, Tibbett (*Eng.*) Descendant of little Tib, a pet form of Theobald (people, bold).

Tibbs, Tebbe (*Eng.*) Descendant of Tibb or Tebb, pet forms of Theobald (people, bold).

Tibon, Tibbon (*Sp.*) The son of Tibbon (generous, noble or wolf), from the Arabic *ibn Tibbon;* the straw merchant.

Tice (*Eng., Ger.*) Descendant of Tica (pleasant); Americanization of Theis, q.v.

Tichenor (*Eng.*) Variant of Ticknor, q.v.

Tickle (*Eng.*) One who came from Tick-hill (Tica's hill), in the West Riding of Yorkshire.

Ticknor, Tichnor, Tickner (*Eng.*) One who came from Tichnor (Tyca's shore), in Kent.

Tidd (*Eng.*) Descendant of Tidda or Tida (festival); one who came from Tidd in Cambridgeshire.

Tideman, Tidman (*Eng.*) The chief man of a tithing, an administrative division consisting originally of ten householders.

Tidwell (*Eng.*) One who came from Tideswell (Tidi's stream), in Derbyshire.

Tidy (*Eng.*) The prompt, honest man.

Tiefenbach (*Ger.*) One who came from Tiefenbach (deep brook), the name of many places in Germany; dweller near the deep brook.

Tiernan (*Ir.*) Grandson of Tighearnan (little lord).

Tierney (*Ir.*) Grandson of Tighearnach (lordly).

Tietz, Tietze (*Ger.*) Descendant of Teuzo (people).

Tiffany, Tiffin (*Eng.*) Descendant of Tiffany (name given to child born on Epiphany Day, January 6); or a pet form of Theophania (manifestation of God).

Tiger, Tigar (*Eng.*) Descendant of Tigier (people, spear).

Tiggett (*Eng.*) Dweller at the sign of the little yearling sheep; metonymic for one who had charge of the yearling sheep.

Tiggle (*Eng.*) Metonymic for one who made tiles, usually for roofs.

Tighe, Tigue, Tige (*Ir.*) Grandson of Tadhg (poet).

Tilbrook (*Eng.*) One who came from Tilbrook (Tila's stream), in Huntingdonshire.

Tilden (*Eng.*) One who came from Tillingdown (Tilmund's hill), in Surrey; or from Tilden (Tila's valley), in Kent.

Tildsley (*Eng.*) One who came from Tyldesley (Tilwald's meadow), in Lancashire.

511

Tiley (*Eng.*) Variant of Tilley, q.v.

Tilford (*Eng.*) One who came from Tilford (convenient ford), in Surrey.

Till (*Eng.*) Descendant of Tilla, Tilli, or Tila (good; brave); or of Till, a pet form of Matilda (might, battle); or of Till, a pet form of such names as Tilli, Tilbeorht, and Tilfrid; dweller near the Till (stream), a river in Lincolnshire.

Tiller (*Eng.*) One who cultivates the soil, a husbandman, farmer or farm worker; one who made tiles; or who roofed buildings with tiles.

Tillery (*Scot.*) One who came from Tillery, in Kinross.

Tillett (*Eng.*) Descendant of little Till, a pet form of Matilda (might, battle); descendant of Tilla, Tilli, or Tila (good; brave).

Tilley, Tilly (*Eng.*) One who came from Tilley (branch or bough) in Shropshire; one who came from Tilly (lime tree), the name of two places in France; descendant of little Till, a pet form of Matilda (might, battle).

Tillinghast (*Eng.*) Dweller near a place where auctions were held.

Tillison (*Eng.*) The son of Tilli (good, brave).

Tillman, Tillmann, Tillmon (*Eng.*) One who was employed in tilling the soil; the brave man.

Tillotson (*Eng.*) The son of little Till, a pet form of names so beginning, as Tilli, Tilbeorht, and Tilfrid, as well as of Mathilda.

Tilney (*Eng.*) Dweller at Tila's river or island.

Tilsley (*Eng.*) One who came from Tyldesley (Tilwald's grove), in Lancashire.

Tilson, Tillson (*Eng.*) The son of Til or Till. See Tillotson.

Tilton (*Eng.*) One who came from Tilton (Tila's homestead), in Leicestershire.

Timberlake, Timblake, Timperlake (*Eng.*) One who came from Timberlake (wooded stream), in Worcestershire.

Timbers (*Eng.*) Dweller in the wood where timber was obtained; or in the timbered house.

Timble, Timbel (*Eng.*) One who came from Timble (fort on the bare hill), in the West Riding of Yorkshire.

Timlin, Timblin (*Eng.*) Descendant of very little Tim, a pet form of Timothy (honoring God).

Timm, Timms, Tims, Timme (*Ger., Eng.*) Descendant of Thim or Tim, pet forms of Thiemo, a short form of Theudemar (people, famous); descendant of Tim, a pet form of Timothy or Timotheus (honoring God).

Timmerman, Timmermann (*Ger., Du.*) One who worked in wood, a carpenter.

Timmons, Timmins (*Eng.*) Descendant of little Timm, a pet form of Timothy (honoring God).

Timothy (*Eng.*) Descendant of Timothy (honoring God).

Timperley (*Eng.*) One who came from Timperleigh (timber grove), in Cheshire.

Timson (*Eng.*) The son of Tim, a pet form of Timothy (honoring God).

Tincher, Tincker (*Eng.*) Variant of Tinker, q.v.

Tindall, Tindal, Tindill, Tindle (*Eng., Scot.*) One who came from Tindale (fort in fertile upland region; Tyne valley), in Cumberland.

Tingley, Tingle (*Eng.*) Dweller at, or near, the meeting place or court.

Tinker, Tinkler (*Eng.*) One who mended pots and kettles.

Tinkham (*Eng.*) One who came from Tyneham (homestead where goats were bred), in Dorset.

Tinkle (*Eng.*) Variant of Tingley, q.v.

Tinsley (*Eng.*) One who came from Tinsley (Tynne's hill), in Yorkshire.

Tint, Tintner (*Ger.*) One who made and sold ink.

Tippett, Tippet, Tippetts, Tippitt (*Eng.*)

Descendant of little Tibb, a pet form of Theobald (people, bold).

Tipping (*Eng.*) The son of Tibba, pet forms of Theobald (people bold); the son of Tippa (to tap).

Tipple (*Eng.*) Descendant of little Tipp, a pet form of Theobald (folk, bold).

Tippy (*Eng.*) Descendant of little Tip, a variant of Tibb, a pet form of Theobald (folk, bold).

Tipton (*Eng.*) One who came from Tipton (Tibba's homestead), in Staffordshire.

Tirado (*Sp.*) The sharp-shooter or marksman.

Tirrell (*Eng.*) One who came from Tirril (wooden hut), in Westmorland; descendant of Tirrell, a variant of Turold or Thorold (Thor, strong).

Tisby (*Sw.*) One who came from Tisby, in Sweden.

Tischler, Tishler, Tischer (*Ger.*) One who made and sold tables and cabinets, a joiner or carpenter.

Tisdale, Tisdell, Tisdel (*Eng.*) One who came from Teesdale (surging river valley), in Durham.

Tishman (*Ger.*) One who served at the table, a waiter.

Tison (*Fr.*) One who came from Tison (piece of wood), in France.

Tissier (*Fr.*) Variant of Tessier, q.v.

Tissot, Tisot (*Fr.*) One who wove cloth, a weaver.

Titcomb (*Eng.*) One who came from Tidcombe (Titta's valley), in Wiltshire.

Tither (*Eng.*) Descendant of Tidhere (festival, spear).

Titlow (*Eng.*) Variant of Tetlow, q.v.

Titsworth (*Eng.*) One who came from Tetsworth (Taetel's homestead), in Oxfordshire.

Tittle, Tittel (*Eng.*) One who came from Titley (Titta's wood), in Herefordshire.

Titus (*Eng.*) Descendant of Titus (safe).

Tivnan (*Ir.*) Grandson of little Teimhean (dark; gray).

Tkach, Tkacz (*Rus., Ukr.*) One who wove cloth, a weaver.

Tkachenko, Tkacenko (*Ukr.*) The son of the weaver.

Tkachuk, Tkaczuk, Tkaczyk (*Ukr.*) Descendant of the young weaver; one who wove cloth, a weaver.

Toal (*Ir.*) Descendant of Tuathal (people, mighty).

Toatley (*Eng.*) One who came from Totley (grove of Tota's people), in Derbyshire.

Tobias, Tobiason (*Eng.*) Descendant of Tobias (Jehovah is good).

Tobin (*Eng.*) Descendant of little Tob, a pet form of Tobias (Jehovah is good).

Tobler (*Ger.*) Dweller in the forest valley or ravine.

Toby, Tobey, Tobie (*Eng.*) Descendant of Toby, a pet form of Tobias (Jehovah is good).

Tochterman, Tochtermann (*Ger.*) The son-in-law.

Tocqueville (*Fr.*) One who came from Tocqueville (Toki's estate), the name of several places in France.

Todd (*Eng.*) Dweller at the sign of the fox; one with some of the qualities of a fox.

Todesca, Todesco, Todisco (*It.*) One who came from Germany, a German.

Todhunter (*Eng.*) One who hunted foxes.

Todorovich (*Yu.-Sl.*) The son of Teodor, Yugoslavian form of Theodore (gift of God).

Tofani (*It.*) Descendant of Tofano, a pet form of Cristofano, a variant of Cristoforo, Italian form of Christopher (Christ-bearer).

Toffard (*Fr.*) One with a tuft of hair.

Toft, Toff (*Eng.*) Dweller at a toft, a yard enclosing a residence; one who came from Toft, the name of several places in England.

Tokarz, Tokarski (*Pol.*) One who fashioned objects on a lathe, a turner.

Tokunaga (*Jap.*) Virtue, long.

Toland, Tolan, Tolland (*Eng.*) One who came from Tolland (land on Tone river), in Somerset.

Tolbert, Tolbart (*Eng.*) Variants of Talbot, q.v.

Told (*Ger.*) Descendant of Told, a pet form of Berthold (bright, ruler).

Tole, Toles (*Eng.*) Descendant of Tole, a pet form of Bartholomew (son of Talmai, furrow).

Toledo (*Sp.*) One who came from Toledo, the capital of Gothic Spain.

Toler, Toller (*Eng.*) One who collected tolls at a toll gate, a tax collector.

Tolhurst (*Eng.*) Dweller near the clump of trees on the small hill.

Toliver, Tolliver (*It.*) One who cut iron; a worker in iron.

Tolk (*Du.*) One who interprets for others.

Toll, Tolson (*Eng.*) Descendant of Toll, a pet form of Bartholomew (son of Talmai, furrow); dweller, or collector, at a toll house.

Tolman, Tollman (*Eng.*) The man who collected tolls, the keeper of a toll gate.

Tolomeo (*It.*) Descendant of Tolomeo, short form of Bartolomeo, Italian form of Bartholomew (son of Talmai, furrow).

Tolson (*Eng.*) The son of little Tom, the abbreviated form of Thomas (a twin); or of Toll, a pet form of Bartholomew (son of Talmai, furrow).

Tolstoy (*Rus.*) The thick or fat man.

Toman, Tomas (*Cz.-Sl.*) Descendant of little Tomas, Czechoslovakian form of Thomas (a twin).

Tomasek (*Cz.*) Descendant of little Tomas (a twin).

Tomaselli, Tomasetti (*It.*) Descendant of little Tomas, Italian form of Thomas (a twin).

Tomasevich (*Rus.*) The son of Tomas, Russian form of Thomas (a twin).

Tomasian (*Arm.*) Descendant of Tomas, Armenian form of Thomas (a twin).

Tomaszewski (*Pol.*) One who came from Tomaszow ('Thomas' homestead), the name of several places in Poland; descendant of Tomasz, Polish form of Thomas (a twin).

Tombleson (*Eng.*) The son of little Tom, a pet form of Thomas (a twin).

Tomblin (*Eng.*) Descendant of very little Tom, a pet form of Thomas (a twin).

Tomczak (*Pol.*) The son of Tom, a pet form of Tomasz, Polish form of Thomas (a twin).

Tomicic (*Yu.-Sl.*) Descendant of Toma, Serbo-Croatian form of Thomas (a twin).

Tomita (*Jap.*) Wealth, rice field.

Tomlinson, Tomlin (*Eng.*) The son of little Tom, a pet form of Thomas (a twin).

Tompkins, Tomkins, Tomkin (*Eng.*) Descendant of little Tom, a pet form of Thomas (a twin).

Toms, Tomes (*Eng.*) The son of Tom, a pet form of Thomas (a twin).

Tomsett (*Eng.*) Descendant of little Toms, a pet form of Thomas (a twin).

Ton (*Eng.*) Dweller in the village.

Tonelli (*It.*) Descendant of Tonello, a pet form of Antonello, a hypocoristic form of Antonio, Italian form of Anthony (inestimable).

Toner (*Ir.*) Grandson of Tomhrar.

Tonetti (*It.*) Descendant of little Ton, a pet form of Antonio, Italian form of Anthony (inestimable).

Toney, Tony (*Eng.*) Descendant of Tony, a pet form of Anthony (inestimable).

Tong, Tonge (*Eng., Chin.*) One who came from Tong (fork of river), the name of five places in England; or from Tonge (tongue of land), in Leicestershire; to correct.

Tongue (*Scot., Eng.*) One who came from Tongue (spit of land), in Sutherland; nickname for a talkative person.

Tonkin, Tonkins, Tonkinson (*Eng.*) Descendant, or son, of little Tony, pet form of Anthony (inestimable).

Tonnellier (*Fr.*) One who made and sold casks, buckets, and tubs, a cooper.

Toogood (*Eng.*) An ironic nickname for one thought to be too good; descendant of Turgod (Thor, god).

514

Toohey, Toohy, Tooey (*Ir.*) Variant of Touhy, q.v.

Tooker (*Eng.*) Variant of Tucker, q.v.

Tookes, Tooks (*Nor., Eng.*) Descendant of Toke, a pet contraction of Tiodgeir (people, spear); descendant of Toka.

Tookey (*Eng.*) Descendant of Tokig, Toky, or Toki, pet contractions of Tiodgeir (people, spear).

Toole (*Ir.*) Descendant of Tuathal (people, mighty).

Tooley (*Eng., Ir.*) One who came from Tooley (lookout hill), in Leicestershire; descendant of Tuathal (people, mighty).

Toombs, Tomb (*Eng.*) Descendant of Tom, a pet form of Thomas (a twin).

Toomepuu (*Est.*) Dweller near a wild cherry tree.

Toomer (*Eng.*) One who came from St. Omer (Audomar: rich, fame), in Calvados.

Toomey, Tomey (*Ir.*) Grandson of Tuaim (a sound).

Toon (*Eng.*) Variant of Towne, q.v.

Toothaker (*Eng.*) Dweller at, or in, the lookout field.

Toothill (*Eng.*) Dweller on, or near, the lookout hill; variant of Tothill, q.v.

Tootle (*Eng.*) Variant of Toothill, q.v.

Topel, Toppel (*Ger., Pol.*) Dweller near a poplar tree.

Topf, Topfer (*Ger.*) One who made and sold utensils of earthenware or metal, a potter.

Topham (*Eng.*) Dweller at the upper, or highest, homestead; one who came from Topsham (Topp's enclosure), in Devonshire.

Topley (*Eng.*) Dweller in the upper grove or wood.

Topliff (*Eng.*) One who came from Topcliffe (Toppa's river bank), in the North Riding of Yorkshire.

Topol, Topolski (*Pol.*) Dweller near a poplar tree.

Topp, Topps (*Eng., Ger.*) Descendant of Topp; one with a tuft or pigtail; variant of Topf, q.v.

Topper (*Eng.*) One who put the flax on the distaff; one with an unusual tuft of hair; dweller at the top or summit.

Topping (*Eng.*) Dweller at the upper meadow.

Toran, Toren (*Eng.*) Dweller at a knoll or hillock.

Torbert (*Eng.*) Descendant of Thorbiart (Thor, bright).

Torchon (*Fr.*) One who cleans by wiping or dusting.

Tori (*It.*) Variant of Toro, q.v.

Torkelson, Torkilsen, Torkildsen (*Nor.*) The son of Torkel or Torkil (thunder, kettle; Thor's sacrificial caldron).

Torkington (*Eng.*) One who came from Torkington (village of Torec's people), in Cheshire.

Torme, Tormey (*Ir.*) Grandson of Tormaigh (increase); or of Thormodr.

Tornay, Torney (*Ir.*) Grandson of Torna.

Tornheim (*Sw.*) Tower, homestead; thorn home.

Tornquist (*Sw.*) Thorn, twig; tower, twig.

Toro, Torelli (*It., Sp.*) Dweller at the sign of the bull; descendant of Toro, a pet form of names terminating in -tore, as Salvatore and Vittore; one who came from Toro (bull), the name of several villages in Spain.

Torok (*Hun.*) One who came from Turkey, a Turk.

Torp (*Nor.*) Dweller on the outlying farm, that is, one farm dependent on another farm.

Torpey (*Ir.*) Variant of Tarpey, q.v.

Torre, Torr (*Eng.*) Dweller on the rocky peak or hill.

Torrence, Torrance (*Scot.*) One who came from Torrance (little hills), the name of places in Lanarkshire and Stirlingshire.

Torres, Torre (*Sp., Port.*) Dweller at, or near, a tower or spire; one who came from Torres, the name of many places in Spain and Portugal.

Torresdale (*Eng.*) Dweller near Thorald's valley.

Torrey, Torry (*Scot., Eng.*) One who came from Torrie (hill), the name of places in Kincardineshire and Fife; or from Torry, in Aberdeen; descendant of Torry, a pet form of Theodoric (gift of God).

Tortora, Tortorella (*It.*) Dweller at the sign of the dove; nickname for the innocent, inexperienced person.

Toscano, Toscanini, Toscani, Toscana (*It.*) One who came from Tuscany (land of the Etrusci).

Tosi, Toso (*It.*) One with closely clipped hair.

Toson (*Eng.*) One who came from Tosson (lookout stone), in Northumberland.

Toth (*Hun.*) One who came from Slovakia, a Slovak.

Tothill (*Eng.*) One who came from Tothill (lookout hill), the name of places in Lincolnshire and Middlesex.

Totten, Toton (*Eng.*) One who came from Toton (Tofi's homestead), in Nottinghamshire.

Tough (*Eng.*) The stubborn, tenacious man.

Touhill (*Ir.*) Grandson of Tuathal (people mighty).

Touhy, Touhey (*Ir.*) Descendant of the sturdy man; grandson of Tuathach (rustic; a lord).

Tousley (*Eng.*) One who came from Tasley (grove where teasels grew), in Shropshire.

Toussaint (*Fr.*) Descendant of Toussaint (all saints).

Tovar (*Sp.*) One who came from Tovar (quarry of soft, sandy stone), in Spain.

Towe, Tow (*Eng.*) The steadfast, stubborn man.

Towell, Towall, Towel (*Ir.*) Variant of Towle, q.v.

Tower, Towers (*Eng.*) Dweller in, or near, a high building; one who processed leather.

Towey, Towie (*Scot.*) One who came from Towie (hole), in Aberdeenshire.

Towle, Towles (*Ir., Eng.*) Descendant of Tuathal (people, mighty); or of Toll, q.v.

Towne, Towner, Town, Towns (*Eng.*) Dweller at the enclosure, homestead, or manor.

Townley (*Eng.*) One who came from Towneley (grove belonging to the homestead or village), in Lancashire.

Townseed (*Eng.*) Variant of Townsend, q.v.

Townsend (*Eng.*) Dweller at the outskirts of the village.

Townsley, Townsle (*Eng.*) One who came from Towneley (grove belonging to the town), in Lancashire.

Townson (*Eng.*) The son of little Tom, the abbreviated form of Thomas (a twin); variant of Townsend, q.v.

Towsey (*Eng.*) One who came from Towersey (the island of Turs), in Buckinghamshire.

Towson (*Eng.*) Variant of Townsend, q.v.; or of Townson, q.v.

Toy, Toye (*Chin.*) Tortoise.

Toyama (*Jap.*) Wealth, mountain.

Toynbee (*Eng.*) Dweller at Teoda's homestead.

Toyota (*Jap.*) Plentiful, rice field.

Tozar, Tozer (*Eng.*) One who teased or carded wool.

Tozzi (*It.*) The short, squat man.

Trachtenberg, Tractenberg (*Ger.*) One who came from Trachenberge, in Germany.

Trachtman, Trachte (*Ger.*) One who came from Tracht (fish haul), in Germany.

Tracton (*Eng.*) One who came from Treeton (homestead with trees), in the West Riding of Yorkshire.

Tracy, Tracey (*Eng., Fr., Ir.*) One who came from Tracy (Thracius' estate), in France; descendant of Treasach (battler).

Trader (*Eng.*) One who buys and sells goods, a merchant.

Trafford (*Eng.*) One who came from Trafford (ford on Roman road; ford by a trap), the name of places in Lancashire and Northamptonshire.

Trager (*Ger.*) One who carried burdens, a carrier or porter; one who carries goods for sale in a bag, a peddler.

Trahey (*Ir.*) Grandson of Troightheach (foot soldier).

Train (*Eng.*) Metonymic for one who trapped wild animals.

Trainham (*Eng.*) One who came from Trentham (homestead on the Trent), in Staffordshire.

Trainor, Treanor, Trainer (*Ir., Eng.*) The son of Treanfhear (strong man or champion); one who sets traps, a trapper.

Tralies (*Eng.*) One who came from Treales (village court), in Lancashire.

Trambley (*Scot.*) Variant of Tremblay, q.v.

Tramontina (*It.*) One who came from beyond the mountains; or from the north.

Tranfield (*Eng.*) Dweller in the open country where cranes abounded.

Tranquillo (*It.*) The quiet or peaceful man.

Trant (*Eng.*) Variant of Trent, q.v.

Tranter (*Eng.*) One who peddled or carried goods.

Trantham (*Eng.*) One who came from Trentham (homestead on the Trent river), in Staffordshire.

Trapnell (*Eng.*) The little squat, stumpy person; the too quick man.

Trapp, Trappe (*Eng., Ger.*) The short, stocky man; dweller near a footbridge; the simpleton.

Trarbach, Traubach (*Ger., Fr.*) One who came from Traubach (muddy brook), in Mosel.

Trask, Traske (*Eng.*) Dweller on, or near, a bog or marsh.

Tratton (*Eng.*) One who came from Trotton (village of Trott's people), in Sussex.

Traub, Traube (*Ger.*) Dweller near where grapes are grown; descendant of Trubo, a pet form of names beginning with Drud (power), as Drudbald and Drudpraht.

Traubel (*Ger.*) Dweller at the sign of the bunch of grapes; one who tended a vineyard.

Trautman, Traut, Trautmann (*Ger.*) The dear, beloved servant.

Trautwein (*Ger.*) The dear, beloved friend.

Travers, Traver, Traverse (*Eng., Fr.*) Dweller at a crossroad.

Travia (*It.*) Dweller at a crossroad.

Travillian (*Eng.*) Variant of Trevelyan, q.v.

Travis, Travise, Traviss (*Eng., Fr.*) Variants of Travers, q.v.

Trawick (*Eng.*) One who came from Trewick (tree farm), in Northumberland.

Traxler, Trachsler (*Ger.*) One who fashioned objects on a lathe, a turner.

Traylor (*Eng.*) One who constructed trellis work; one who travels on foot, sometimes with long trailing garments.

Traynham (*Eng.*) Variant of Trantham, q.v.

Traynor (*Ir., Eng.*) The son of Treanfhear (strong man or champion); one who sets traps, a trapper.

Treacy (*Eng., Ir.*) Variant of Tracy, q.v.

Treadway (*Eng.*) Descendant of Thrythwig (strength, battle).

Treadwell, Tredwell (*Eng.*) Dweller at a path, or road, by a spring or stream.

Treat (*Eng.*) The dear, beloved person.

Tredinnick (*Eng.*) Dweller near the little fort; or in the bracken.

Tredway (*Eng.*) Variant of Treadway, q.v.

Trees, Tree (*Eng.*) One who dwelt near a tree or trees.

Trefil (*Eng.*) Dweller near the rustic's place.

Trefry, Trefrey (*Eng.*) Dweller on the hillside.

Treftz, Trefz (*Ger.*) Dweller among weeds; a mean miserable fellow.

Treganowan (*Eng.*) Dweller in, or near, the hollow.

Tregaskes (*Eng.*) Dweller in the sheltered place.

517

Tregea, Tregay (*Eng.*) Dweller by the bank or hedge.

Tregear, Tregeir (*Eng.*) Dweller by the earthwork or embankment; one who came from Tregear (hamlet of the fort), in Cornwall.

Treherne (*Wel.*) The very strong or super-iron man.

Treichel (*Ger.*) Dweller at the sign of the cowbell; one who made cowbells.

Trelawny (*Eng.*) One who came from Trelawny (church village), in Cornwall.

Trelease (*Eng.*) Dweller in the court homestead.

Treleaven, Treleven (*Eng.*) Dweller in the homestead where elm trees grew.

Treloar (*Eng.*) Dweller in the homestead with a garden.

Tremaine, Tremain (*Eng.*) One who came from Tremaine (hamlet of the stone), in Cornwall; dweller near the place of the monolith.

Tremayne (*Eng.*) Variant of Tremaine, q.v.

Trembath (*Eng.*) Dweller in the homestead in the corner.

Tremberth (*Eng.*) Dweller in the homestead by the bush.

Trembeth (*Eng.*) Dweller in the homestead by the burial mound.

Tremblay, Trembly, Trembley (*Eng., Scot., Fr.*) One who came from Trimley (Trymma's wood), in Suffolk; dweller in, or near, Trympa's grove; dweller in, or near, an aspen wood; one who came from Tremblay (aspen trees), in France.

Tremble (*Eng., Fr.*) Descendant of Trumbold (strong, bold); dweller near an aspen tree.

Trench, Trencher (*Eng.*) Dweller at a cutting or alley.

Trenchard (*Eng.*) One who cut, possibly a butcher.

Trendell, Trendel, Trendle (*Eng.*) Dweller by the circle, such as a circle of stones, earthworks, bushes, etc.

Trendler (*Eng.*) One who made wheels, a wheelwright.

Trengove (*Eng.*) Dweller near, or in, the smith's homestead.

Trenholm, Trenholme (*Eng.*) One who came from Trenholme (crane island), in the North Riding of Yorkshire.

Trent (*Eng.*) One who came from Trent (trespasser), in Dorset; one who lived on, or near, the Trent river in England.

Trenter (*Eng.*) Variant of Tranter, q.v.

Trerice (*Eng.*) Dweller in the homestead by the ford.

Trescott (*Eng.*) One who came from Trescott (labor cottage), in Staffordshire.

Tressel, Tress, Tressler (*Eng.*) One who made, or used, trussels, a mold used in stamping coins.

Treston (*Eng.*) One who came from Troston (village of Trost's people), in Suffolk.

Tresville (*Eng.*) One who came from Treswell (Tir's spring), in Nottinghamshire.

Trethaway (*Eng.*) Dweller in, or near, David's homestead.

Tretter (*Ger.*) One who treads pedals of an organ, an organ-blower; one who dances.

Trevelyan (*Eng.*) Dweller at the mill homestead; or at Milian's homestead.

Trevena (*Eng.*) Dweller in the little homestead.

Trevenen, Treven (*Eng.*) Dweller in the homestead by the white stone.

Trevethan, Treveathan (*Eng.*) Dweller in the homestead by the meadow.

Trevino (*Sp.*) Dweller near a boundary stone touching three districts.

Trevitt, Trevett (*Eng.*) Variant of Trippett, q.v.; dweller at the sign of the little colt.

Trevor, Trevore (*Eng.*) One who came from Trevor (big village), the name of several places in Cornwall.

Trevost (*Eng.*) Dweller in the homestead by the trench or wall.

Trew (*Eng.*) Variant of True, q.v.; dweller by a prominent tree.

Trewhella (*Eng.*) Dweller in the homestead by the stream.

Trexler (*Ger.*) Variant of Traxler, q.v.

Tribbett, Tribbitt, Tribit (*Eng.*) Variant of Trippett, q.v.

Tribble (*Eng.*) Descendant of Thrythbald (might, bold).

Trice, Triche (*Ger.*) One who made and sold little bells; dweller on, or near, a fallow field.

Trick (*Eng.*) The trusty, true man, from Old Norse Tryggui "trusty"; metonymic for one who cheats or deceives.

Tricker (*Eng.*) One who cheats or deceives; descendant of Tryggeir (true, spear).

Trickett (*Fr.*) Descendant of little Trigg (true); one who carried a little cudgel.

Trickey (*Eng.*) One who came from Trickey in Devonshire.

Trier (*Ger.*) One who came from Trier, in Germany.

Trifilio (*It.*) The third-born son.

Triggs, Trigg (*Eng.*) Descendant of Trigg (true); one who was faithful and trustworthy; one who came from Trigg (those with three armies), an old district in Cornwall.

Triller (*Ger.*) One who fashioned objects on a lathe, a turner; one who entertained by juggling.

Trilling (*Ger.*) One of three born at one birth, a triplet.

Trimarco, Trimarchi (*It.*) One who came from Trimarco, in Italy.

Trimble (*Eng.*) Dweller near an aspen tree.

Trindle (*Eng.*) Variant of Trendell, q.v.

Trinkaus, Trinkhaus (*Ger.*) Dweller near, or worker in, the building where drinks were imbibed.

Trinkle, Trinkl (*Ger.*) The gay, jovial drinker.

Triplett, Triplet, Triplette, Tripplett (*Eng.*) One of three born at one birth, a triplet.

Tripmaker (*Ger.*) One who made wooden shoes or clogs, sometimes stilts for crossing muddy, unpaved streets.

Tripp, Trippe (*Eng.*) One who took care of a flock of sheep or a herd of swine or goats; metonymic for a tripe-seller.

Trippett, Trippet (*Eng.*) One with the reputation of playing malicious tricks on others.

Trippetti, Trippetta (*It.*) One with a prominent stomach.

Trobough (*Ger., Fr.*) Variant of Trarbach, q.v.

Trodden (*Eng.*) Dweller near the path up the hill or in the valley.

Trogden, Trogdon (*Eng.*) Dweller in, or near, a trough or hollow on a hill.

Troike, Troik (*Pol.*) One of a group of three.

Trois (*Fr.*) One of a group of three.

Trojan (*Ger., Bel., Pol.*) Descendant of Trojan (from Troy, the settlement of the Tricasses); one who came from Trojan, in Germany; descendant of Trojan (one of three sons).

Trojanowski (*Pol.*) One who came from Trojano(w) (settlement of three brothers), in Poland.

Troland, Trouland (*Nor.*) One who came from Troland (place where cattle graze), in Norway.

Trollope (*Eng.*) Dweller in, or near, the elf hollow; the untidy, slovenly person.

Trombetta (*It.*) One who plays the trumpet; one who carries messages, a messenger.

Trombley, Trombly, Tromblay (*Eng.*) Variants of Tremblay, q.v.

Trommer (*Ger.*) One who beat on a drum, a drummer.

Trompetter (*Ger.*) One who played a trumpet.

Troop (*Eng.*) Variant of Thorpe, q.v.

Trost (*Ger., Yu.-Sl.*) Descendant of Traostilo (helper); the helpful or expectant man.

Trotman (*Eng.*) One who carried messages, a messenger.

Trott, Trotty (*Eng.*) Descendant of Trott (defiance); the dear, beloved friend.

Trotter, Trottier, Troter, Trotier (*Eng., Scot., Fr.*) One who acted as a runner or messenger.

Trottnow (*Eng.*) The messenger set to start right away. Compare Sturtevant.

Troughton (*Eng.*) One who came from Troughton (farmstead in the hollow), in Lancashire.

Troup, Troupe (*Eng.*) Variant of Thorpe, q.v.

Trousdale (*Eng.*) One who came from Trouts Dale (trout pool), in the North Riding of Yorkshire.

Trout, Troutt, Trouts (*Eng.*) Metonymic for one who fished for trout; variant of Trott, q.v.

Troutman (*Eng.*) Variant of Trotman, q.v.

Trovato (*It.*) An infant found after its unknown parents deserted it, a foundling.

Trowbridge (*Eng.*) One who came from Trowbridge (wooden bridge), in Wiltshire.

Trowell (*Eng.*) One who came from Trowell (tree stream), in Nottinghamshire.

Trower (*Eng.*) Variant of Thrower, q.v.

Troxell, Troxel (*Ger.*) One who fashioned objects on a lathe, a turner.

Troy (*Eng.*) One who came from Troyes (from Gaulish tribe, the Tricassii), in France.

Trudeau (*Fr.*) Descendant of little Troude, a pet form of Gertrude (spear, strength).

Trudel, Trudell, Trudelle (*Fr.*) Variant of Trudeau, q.v.

True (*Eng.*) The faithful, loyal man.

Trueblood (*Eng.*) The true or loyal man.

Truehart, Trueheart (*Eng.*) Nickname for the true, faithful friend.

Truelove (*Eng.*) The true, faithful lover or sweetheart.

Truesdale, Truesdell, Trusdell (*Eng.*) One who came from Trouts Dale (earlier spelling Trucedale, trout pool), in Yorkshire.

Truhlar (*Cz.-Sl.*) One who worked in wood, a carpenter.

Truitt, Truitte, Truett (*Eng.*) The dear, beloved friend; one who came from Trewhitt (dry resinous meadow), in Northumberland.

Trujillo, Trujilo (*Sp.*) One who came from Trujillo (citadel of Julian), in Spain.

Trukenbrod (*Ger.*) One who made and sold dry bread.

Trull (*Eng.*) One who came from Trull (ring), in Somerset.

Trulli (*It.*) Descendant of Trulli, a pet form of Pietrulli, an Italian form of Peter (a rock).

Trulson (*Nor.*) The son of Truls (Thor's hammer).

Truman, Trueman (*Eng.*) The faithful or loyal servant.

Trumbull, Trumble (*Eng.*) Descendant of Trumbald (strong, bold).

Trump, Trumpp (*Eng.*) Descendant of Trum (strong), a pet form of names beginning with Trum, such as Trumbald, Trumbeorht, and Trumwine; metonymic for a trumpeter.

Trumpler (*Ger.*) Variant of Trommer, q.v.

Truncer (*Eng.*) One who made and sold clubs and cudgels.

Trunk (*Ger.*) One often intoxicated with strong drink, a drunkard.

Truscott (*Eng.*) Variant of Trescott, q.v.

Trussell, Trusselle (*Eng., Fr.*) One who came from Trusley (wood with fallen leaves), in Derbyshire; the short, fat man.

Truxton (*Eng.*) One who came from Troston (the home of Trosta's people), in Suffolk.

Trybula (*Pol.*) One who raised and sold chervil, a herb of the carrot family used in soups and salads.

Tryder (*Eng., Du.*) Dweller in the oak hamlet; one who traveled.

Trzaska (*Pol.*) One who splits wood into laths or splinters; or works by cracking materials.

Tschaikowsky (*Rus.*) One who came from Czajkowo, the name of many places in Poland and Russia; or from Tschaykovo in Russia (place frequented by lapwings).

Tschudi (*Swis.*) One who sat in judgment, a judge.

Tsuji (*Jap.*) Crossroads.

Tubbs (*Eng.*) One who made tubs, a cooper.

Tubelis (*Lith.*) Descendant of little Tobiosius or Tobijas, Lithuanian forms of Tobias (goodness of Jehovah).

Tuch (*Fr.*) One who came from Touque or Touche, in France.

Tuchman, Tuchmann (*Ger.*) One who deals in cloth.

Tuck (*Eng.*) Descendant of Tucca (to draw), or of Toke (people).

Tucker (*Eng.*) One who cleaned and thickened cloth.

Tuckerman, Tuckman (*Eng.*) One who assisted in cleaning and thickening cloth, the tucker's servant.

Tuddenham (*Eng.*) One who came from Tuddenham (Tudda's homestead), the name of places in Norfolk and Suffolk.

Tudor, Tudyr (*Wel.*) Descendant of Tudor (gift of God); or of Tudyr (country; tribe).

Tue (*Nor.*) Dweller near a knoll or little hillock.

Tuffield (*Eng.*) One who came from Touville (Teald's domain), in Normandy.

Tufo (*It.*) Dweller on lava, the fluid material issued from volcanoes.

Tufts, Tuff, Tuffs, Tuft, Tufte (*Eng.*) Dweller at a toft, a yard enclosing a residence.

Tuggle, Tuggles (*Eng.*) One who came from Tughall (Tucga's corner), in Northumberland.

Tull, Tuller (*Ger.*) One who came from Tullau, in Germany; dweller by the fence or hedge.

Tulloch, Tullock (*Scot.*) One who came from Tulloch (hillock), in Scotland.

Tully, Tulley (*Scot., Ir.*) One who came from Tullo, in Scotland; or Tully (small hill), in Ireland.

Tuman, Tumman (*Ir.*) Grandson of little Tuaim (a sound).

Tumas, Tumasonis (*Lith.*) Descendant of Tomas, Lithuanian form of Thomas (a twin).

Tumbridge (*Eng.*) One who came from Tonbridge (Tunna's bridge), in Kent.

Tumulty, Tumelty (*Ir.*) The son, or grandson, of Tomaltach (large; bulky).

Tung (*Chin.*) To correct.

Tunnell (*Eng.*) Metonymic for one who made barrels, casks, and tubs, a cooper.

Tunney, Tunny (*Ir.*) Grandson of Tonnach (glittering).

Tunstall (*Eng.*) One who came from Tunstall (site of a farm), the name of eleven places in England.

Tunstead (*Eng.*) One who came from Tunstead (farmstead), the name of places in Derbyshire and Norfolk.

Tuohy (*Ir.*) Variant of Touhy, q.v.

Tuppeny (*Eng.*) Nickname for one who paid two pence rent.

Tupper (*Eng.*) One who bred tups or rams; one who made and sold tubs.

Tupponce (*Eng.*) One who cultivated land on which he paid a rent of two pence.

Turbitt, Turbett (*Eng.*) Descendant of Thorbiart (Thor, bright).

Turcenko (*Ukr.*) The son of the Turk; one from Turkey.

Turco (*It.*) One who came from Turkey, a Turk.

Turcotte (*Fr.*) The little Turk, a medieval nickname applied to a crusader.

Turcyn (*Ukr.*) One who came from Turkey, a Turk.

Turek (*Pol., Cz.-Sl.*) One who came from Turkey, a Turk.

Turk (*Eng., Cz.-Sl., Yu.-Sl.*) One who came from Turkmen, now a Soviet Socialist Republic; one who came from Turkey, a Turk.

Turkington (*Eng.*) Variant of Torkington, q.v.

Turkovich, Turkovic (*Yu.-Sl.*) The son of one who came from Turkey.

Turley (*Ir.*) The son of Toirdhealbhach (handsome).

Turlington (*Eng.*) Variant of Torkington, q.v.

Turman (*Eng.*) One who came from Turnham (thorn tree enclosure), the name of several places in England.

Turnbull (*Scot.*) Descendant of Trumbald (strong, bold); nickname from an act, "turn bull," indicative of strength or bravery.

Turner (*Eng.*) One who fashioned objects on a lathe.

Turney (*Ir., Eng.*) Grandson of Torna (a lord); one who came from Tournai, Tournay or Tourny (Tornus' estate), the names of places in Normandy.

Turnipseed (*Ger.*) English form of the German nickname for the rape farmer, that is, one who grew and sold turnips, carrots and beets.

Turnquist (*Sw.*) Thorn, twig.

Turoff (*Ukr.*) One who came from Turov, now Turiv (place frequented by aurochs, a European bison now nearly extinct), in Ukraine.

Turpin, Turping (*Fr., Eng.*) Descendant of Turpinus (depraved); or of Thorfinnr (Thor, the god, and ethnic name, Finnr). Through humility early Christians sometimes took injurious names.

Turtle (*Eng.*) One with some characteristic of the European wild dove, such as an affectionate disposition; the deformed or crippled man; descendant of Torquil (Thor's kettle).

Turtletaub, Turteltaube (*Ger.*) Dweller at the sign of the turtle dove.

Turton (*Eng.*) One who came from Turton (Thori's homestead), in Lancashire.

Turvey (*Eng.*) One who came from Turvey (island with good turf), in Bedfordshire.

Tustin (*Eng.*) Descendant of Thurstan (Thor's stone).

Tuton, Tutin (*Eng.*) Descendant of Thurstan (Thor's stone).

Tutt (*Eng.*) Descendant of Tutta (people).

Tuttle, Tuthill, Tutle (*Eng.*) Dweller at a toot-hill, i.e., a hill with a good outlook to detect an enemy's approach; one who came from Tothill (lookout hill), the name of places in Lincolnshire and Middlesex.

Tveit, Tvedt (*Nor.*) Dweller on a grassy plot; one who lived or worked on a farm so named.

Tveter (*Nor.*) One who came from Tveter, the name of two places in Norway.

Twaddle, Twaddell, Twadell (*Eng.*) Variant of Tweedale, q.v.

Tweed (*Eng., Scot.*) Dweller by the Tweed (powerful), a river forming part of the boundary between England and Scotland.

Tweedale, Tweddle, Tweedle (*Scot.*) One who lived in, or near, the pasture dale; dweller in the valley of the Tweed (powerful), a British river; one who came from Tweedle (pasture dale), in Scotland.

Tweedie, Tweedy (*Scot.*) One who came from the lands of Tweedie (hemming in), in the parish of Stonehouse, Lanarkshire.

Tweet (*Nor.*) Dweller on the grassy plot, an Americanization of Norwegian *tveit*.

Twells, Twell (*Eng.*) Dweller at a spring or stream.

Twelves (*Eng.*) Variant of Twells, q.v.

Twelvetrees (*Eng.*) Dweller in, or near, a clump of trees.

Twersky (*Rus.*) One who came from Tver, in Russia.

Twesten (*Eng.*) One who came from Twisden (twin valley), in Kent.

Twiddy (*Scot.*) Variant of Tweedie, q.v.

Twiford (*Eng.*) Variant of Twyford, q.v.

Twigg, Twiggs, Twigge (*Eng.*) Descendant of Twicga (twig).

Twine, Twinn (*Eng.*) One born the same time as his sibling; metonymic for one who made thread or twine.

Twineham (*Eng.*) One who came from Twineham (place between streams), in Sussex.

Twining (*Eng.*) One who came from Twyning (between streams), in Gloucestershire.

Twisdale (*Eng.*) Dweller in the valley located in the fork of a stream.

Twiss (*Eng.*) One born at the same time as his sibling, a twin.

Twist (*Eng.*) Dweller near the fork of a river; or on the land in such a fork; variant of Twiss, q.v.

Twitchell, Twichell (*Eng.*) Dweller at an alley, or narrow passage, between houses; dweller at a bend in the road.

Twitty (*Eng., Scot.*) One who came from Thwaite (forest clearing), the name of places in Norfolk and Suffolk; variant of Tweedie, q.v.

Twohey (*Ir.*) Variant of Touhy, q.v.

Twohig (*Ir.*) Grandson of Tuathach (rustic; a lord).

Twombly (*Eng.*) One who came from Twemlow (by the two hills), in Cheshire.

Twomey, Tuomey (*Ir.*) Grandson of Tuaim (a sound).

Twyford (*Eng.*) One who came from Twyford (double river crossing), the name of eight places in England.

Twyman (*Eng.*) One who came from Twineham (between the streams), in Sussex; or from Twinham (between the streams), the old name of Christchurch, in Hampshire.

Twyne (*Eng.*) Variant of Twine, q.v.

Tyas, Tyes (*Eng.*) One who came from Germany, a German.

Tye (*Eng.*) Dweller near the large common pasture or enclosure.

Tygh (*Ir.*) One who wrote poetry, a poet.

Tyler (*Eng.*) One who made, or sold, tiles; or who covered buildings with tiles.

Tyminski (*Pol.*) Descendant of Tymon, Polish form of Timothy (honoring God).

Tymoszenko (*Ukr.*) The son of Tymish, Ukrainian form of Timothy (honoring God).

Tynan (*Ir.*) Grandson of Teimhnean (cover).

Tyndall, Tyndale (*Eng.*) One who came from Tindale (the Tyne valley), in Cumberland.

Tyne, Tynes (*Eng., Scot.*) Dweller near the Tyne (river), the name of rivers in England and Scotland.

Tyner (*Ger.*) One who came from Tinnen, in Germany.

Tyre, Tyer (*Eng.*) One who covers buildings, a tiler.

Tyree, Tyrey (*Scot.*) One who came from Tyrie (land), in Perthshire.

Tyrrell, Tyrell (*Eng.*) Variants of Terrell, q.v.

Tyson (*Eng., Du.*) The son of Ty, a variant of Dye, a pet form of Dionysus (the Grecian god of wine); the son of Tys, a pet form of Matthias (gift of Jehovah); one who kindles strife or mischief.

Uber (*Ger.*) The active, industrious, enterprising man.

Uberti (*It.*) The son of Uberto, Italian form of Hubert (spirit, bright).

Uchida (*Jap.*) Inside, rice field.

Uchison (*Eng.*) The son of Huch, a pet form of Hugh (spirit; mind).

Udell, Udall (*Eng.*) One who came from Yewdale (yew valley), in Lancashire.

Uebele, Uebel (*Ger.*) Descendant of Oppo or Ubo, pet forms of Audoberht (possession, bright).

Ueda (*Jap.*) Upper, rice field.

Uff, Uffe (*Eng.*) Descendant of Uffa (owl); or of Ulfr (wolf).

Uher (*Cz.*) One who came from Hungary.

Uhl, Uhle (*Ger.*) Descendant of Uhl, a pet form of Ulrich (wolf, rule).

Uhlig (*Ger.*) Descendant of Uodalrich (ancestral estate, rule) or Ulrich (wolf, rule).

Uhlir (*Cz.*) One who dug and sold coal.

Uhr (*Ger.*) Dweller at the sign of the

523

aurochs, a nearly extinct European bison.

Ulan (*Pol.*) One with the characteristics of a youth, a lad.

Ulander (*Sw.*) Variant of Olander, q.v.

Ulitsky (*Rus.*) One who accuses others.

Ullman, Ullmann, Ulman (*Ger.*) One who owned land in fee, i.e., without paying rent or acknowledging any superior; one who came from Ulm (bog), in Germany.

Ulmer (*Ger., Fr., Eng.*) One who came from Ulm (bog), the name of several places in Germany; dweller near marshy water; descendant of Othalmar (native country, fame); or of Ulmar (owl, fame).

Ulrich, Ullrich, Ulreich, Ulrick (*Ger., Eng.*) Descendant of Ulrich (wolf, rule).

Umansky (*Rus., Ukr.*) One who came from Uman (the wise one's settlement), in Ukraine.

Umbreit, Umbright (*Ger.*) The awkward, clumsy man.

Umland (*Nor.*) Dweller in, or about, the land or field.

Umlauf (*Ger.*) Nickname for a town policeman who runs here and there in his duties.

Umnov (*Rus.*) The son of the wise man.

Umphrey, Umphries (*Eng.*) Variant of Humphrey, q.v.

Umpleby (*Eng.*) One who came from Anlaby (Anlaf's homestead), in the East Riding of Yorkshire.

Unbegaun (*Ger.*) The unknown man from the Baltic States.

Underdown (*Eng.*) Dweller at the foot of the downs or hill.

Underhill (*Eng.*) Dweller under, or at the foot of, the hill.

Underland (*Nor.*) Dweller on the lower land, a farm name.

Underwood (*Eng.*) One who came from Underwood (within a forest), the name of places in Derbyshire and Nottinghamshire; dweller within a wood.

Ungaro, Ungaretti (*It.*) One who came from Hungary (country of the Huns).

Unger, Ungar, Ungerer (*Ger.*) One who came from Hungary (country of the Huns).

Unitas (*Lith.*) The son of Jonas, Lithuanian form of John (gracious gift of Jehovah).

Uno (*Jap.*) Universe, field.

Unrath (*Ger.*) The distressed or troubled man.

Unrein (*Ger.*) The faithless, unchaste, lecherous man.

Unruh (*Ger.*) An agitator or trouble maker; one who was careless, restless, or indolent; one who came from Unruh, in Germany.

Unsworth (*Eng.*) One who came from Unsworth (Hund's homestead), in Lancashire.

Unterberger, Unterberg (*Ger.*) One who came from Unterberg (below the mountain), in Germany.

Unterkoefler (*Ger.*) Dweller under the knoll; or below the summit of the hill.

Unthank (*Eng., Scot.*) One who came from Unthank (place settled without leave of the lord), the name of several places in England; one who came from Unthank (barren soil), a common farm name in Scotland.

Unwin (*Eng.*) Descendant of Hunwine (young bear, friend); one who was not a friend, an enemy.

Upchurch (*Eng.*) One who came from Upchurch (the higher or farther inland church), in Kent.

Updegrave, Updegrove, Updegraff (*Du.*) Dweller at the tomb.

Updyck, Updike (*Du.*) Dweller on the dike.

Upgreen (*Eng.*) Dweller at the upper or higher green.

Upham (*Eng.*) Dweller at the homestead which was higher than another neighboring one.

Uphouse (*Eng.*) Dweller in the upper or higher house.

Upjohn (*Wel.*) The son of John (gracious gift of Jehovah).

Uppinghouse (*Eng.*) Dweller near the habitation of the Uppingas.

Uppstrom (*Sw.*) Up stream; one who came from the upper or higher stream.

Uprichard (*Wel.*) The son of Richard (rule, hard).

Upright (*Eng.*) The straight, erect man.

Upsal, Upsall (*Eng.*) One who came from Upsall (higher dwelling), in the North Riding of Yorkshire.

Upshaw (*Eng.*) Dweller at a grove or thicket above another; or up a stream.

Upshire, Upsher, Upshur (*Eng.*) One who came from Upshire (the upper district), in Essex.

Upson (*Eng.*) Dweller at the upper or high rock or stone.

Upthegrove (*Eng.*) Dweller further in the grove or wood.

Upton (*Eng.*) One who came from Upton (higher homestead or village), the name of many places in England.

Urba (*Cz.-Sl.*) Dweller at, or near, a willow tree.

Urbach (*Ger.*) One who came from Urbach (aurochs stream), in Germany.

Urban, Urbain (*Eng., Cz.-Sl.*) Descendant of Urban (town dweller).

Urbanczyk (*Pol.*) Descendant of little Urban (town dweller).

Urbanek (*Pol., Cz.-Sl.*) Descendant of little Urban (town dweller).

Urbano, Urbani (*Sp., It.*) Descendant of Urbano, Spanish and Italian form of Urban (town dweller).

Urbanowicz (*Pol.*) The son of Urban (town dweller).

Urbanski (*Pol.*) Descendant of Urban (town dweller).

Ure (*Eng.*) Dweller near the Ure, a river in the North Riding of Yorkshire.

Urena (*Sp.*) One who came from Urena (place where oats are grown), in Spain.

Urenson (*Eng.*) The son of Uren (town-born; impure).

Urey, Urie (*Scot.*) One who came from Urie (abounding in yews), in Scotland.

Uribe (*Sp.*) One who came from Uribe (town or city), in Spain.

Urick, Urich (*Ger.*) Descendant of Urich, a shortened form of Uodalrich (ancestral estate, rule).

Urkov (*Rus.*) The son of the hooligan.

Urmson (*Eng.*) The son of Orm (serpent).

Urquhart (*Scot.*) One who came from Urquhart (on a wood), the name of several places in Scotland.

Urso (*It.*) Dweller at the sign of the bear; one thought to possess some of the qualities of a bear, such as uncouthness, surliness, hirsuteness, and dullness.

Ury (*Heb.*) Fire, light.

Useller (*Eng.*) One who kept an inn, an innkeeper.

Usenko (*Ukr.*) The son of the man with the long mustache.

Usher (*Eng., Scot.*) A door-keeper, one who kept the door of the king's apartment.

Ushler (*Eng., Scot.*) Variant of Usher, q.v.

Utley (*Eng.*) One who came from Utley (outer wood or meadow), in Yorkshire; dweller at the outer meadow or wood.

Utter (*Sw.*) Otter.

Utterback (*Ger.*) One who came from Otterbach (stream frequented by otters), the name of four places in Germany.

Uttley (*Eng.*) Variant of Utley, q.v.

Uyeda (*Jap.*) Plant, rice field.

Uyeno (*Jap.*) Upper, field.

Uzzell, Uzzle (*Eng.*) Metonymic for one who caught and sold birds.

Vaccaro, Vaccari, Vaccarello (*It.*) One who tended cows.

Vacco, Vacca (*It.*) Descendant of Vacca, a pet form of Giacomo, Italian form of James (may God protect; the supplanter); dweller at the sign of the cow.

Vache, Vach (*Fr.*) One who took care of cows, a cowherd.

Vaden (*Sw.*) Dweller near a ford.

Vaher (*Est.*) Dweller near a maple tree.

Vahey (*Ir.*) Descendant of Mac an Bheathadh (son of life); variant of Fahey, q.v.

Vail, Vale (*Eng., Scot.*) Dweller in the valley.

Vaillant (*Fr.*) The courageous man.

Vain (*Eng.*) One who came from Vains, in France.

Vajda (*Hun.*) One who acted as a military governor in Slavic countries.

Valadez, Valades (*Sp.*) Variant of Valdez, q.v.

Valdez, Valdes (*Sp.*) One who came from Valdes (tableland), in Spain; the son of Baldo, a shortened form of Baldomero (prince, fame).

Valencia (*Sp.*) One who came from Valencia (strength of the Edetani), in Spain.

Valente, Valenti (*It.*) The valiant or brave man; descendant of Valente (valiant).

Valentine, Vallentyne, Valentin (*Eng., Sp., Fr.*) Descendant of Valentine (vigorous or healthy).

Valentino, Valentini (*It.*) Descendant of Valentino (vigorous or healthy).

Valera, Valere, Valero (*Sp.*) One who came from Valero (fortified place), in Spain.

Valerio (*It., Sp.*) Descendant of Valerio, Italian form of Valerian (the strong).

Valinsky (*Rus.*) One who came from Volynia, in Russia.

Valkoinen (*Finn.*) The son of the light-complexioned man.

Vallance, Vallence (*Eng.*) One who came from Valence (stronghold), the name of several places in France.

Valle (*Sp., Fr., It.*) Dweller in a dale or small valley; one who came from Valle (valley), the name of many small places.

Vallee, Valley (*Fr.*) Dweller in a depression between ranges of hills or mountains, a valley.

Vallejo (*Sp.*) One who came from Vallejo (small valley), in Spain.

Valleto, Valleta, Vallette (*It.*) One who acted as a personal servant to another, a valet.

Vallone, Vallon (*It., Sw.*) Dweller in the wide valley; one who came from southern Belgium, a Walloon.

Valosky (*Pol., Ukr.*) One who uses a protective wall or shield in battle.

Valverde (*It.*) Dweller in a green vale.

Vana (*Rus.*) Descendant of Vanya, a pet form of Ivan, Russian form of John (gracious gift of Jehovah).

Van Acker (*Du.*) Dweller in, or near, the field.

Van Aken (*Du., Bel.*) One who came from Aachen in Germany; or from Aken in Belgium.

Van Allen, Van Alen (*Du.*) One who came from Allan (Alanus' homestead), in France.

Van Beuren (*Du.*) One who came from Beuren, in Germany.

Van Boskirk (*Du.*) Dweller near the church in the wood.

Van Brugge, Vanbrugh (*Du.*) One who lived at, or near, the bridge; one who came from Bruggen, in Holland; or from Bruges, in Belgium.

Van Buren (*Du.*) One who came from the neighborhood; or from Buren (neighborhood), the name of two places in Holland.

Van Buskirk (*Du.*) One who came from Boskerck (church in the wood), in Holland.

Van Camp (*Du.*) Dweller at, or in, the field.

Vance (*Eng., Du.*) Dweller near a small hill or burial mound; the son of Van.

Van Cleave, Van Cleve, Van Cleef, Van Clief (*Du.*) One who came from the city or duchy of Cleve (cliff), in West Germany; dweller near the cliff.

Van Cortlandt (*Du.*) One who came from Cortlandt, a local district in Holland.

Van Dam, Van Damm, Van Damme

(*Du.*) Dweller on, or near, the dam or dike.

Vandenberg, Van Den Bergh (*Du.*) Dweller on, or near, the hill; one who came from Berg (hill), the name of two places in Holland.

Vander (*Du.*) Shortened form of names beginning with Vander (of the).

Van Der Aa, Vanderaa (*Du.*) Dweller near the Aa (river), a river in Holland.

Vanderbilt (*Du.*) Dweller at, or near, the heap or mound.

Vandergrift, Vandergriff, Vandegrift (*Du.*) Dweller near the canal or moat.

Vanderhorst (*Du.*) Dweller in, or near, a small thickly grown wood.

Van Der Jagt (*Du.*) One having to do with the hunt.

Vanderlinden (*Du.*) Dweller near the linden tree; one who came from Linden (lime tree), in Belgium.

Vandermark (*Du.*) Dweller near the border or boundary; one who came from Mark (borderland), in Holland.

Vandermeer (*Du.*) Dweller at, or near, the lake.

Vanderploeg, Vanderplow (*Du.*) One who was formerly a plowman.

Vander Poel (*Du.*) Dweller in, or near, the polder, a field reclaimed from the sea.

Vanderpool (*Du.*) Dweller near a pond.

Vanderslice (*Du.*) Dweller near the sluice.

Vandersteen (*Du.*) Dweller at, or near, the rock or stone, usually a boundary marker.

Vanderveen (*Du.*) Dweller near the peat bog.

Vanderwoude (*Du.*) Dweller in, or near, a wood.

Van Devanter (*Du.*) One who came from Deventer, in Holland.

Van De Veer, Vanderveer (*Du.*) Dweller near the ferry; one who operated a ferry.

Vandevender, Vandeventer (*Du.*) One

who came from Deventer, in Holland.

Vandiver (*Du.*) One who came from Vere, in Holland.

Van Dorn (*Du.*) One who came from Doorn (thorn), the name of two places in Holland.

Vandross (*Du.*) One who came from Rossum, in Holland.

Van Dusen, Van Deusen (*Du.*) One who came from Doezum, in Holland.

Van Dyke, Vandyck, Van Dyk (*Du.*) Dweller on, or near, the dike.

Vanek (*Cz.-Sl.*) Descendant of Vanek, or little Van, pet forms of Ivan (gracious gift of Jehovah).

Van Fossen (*Du.*) One who came from Vossem, in Belgium.

Van Gelder (*Du.*) One who came from the province of Gelder, in Holland.

Van Gogh (*Du.*) One who came from Goch, in Germany.

Van Hoek (*Du.*) Dweller in, or near, the spur, river bend, or corner, referring to some natural feature.

Van Hook (*Du.*) One who came from the Hook of Holland, in Holland.

Van Horn, Van Horne, Van Hoorn (*Du.*) One who came from Hoorn (the promontory), in Holland.

Van Houten (*Du.*) One who came from Houten (wooden), in Holland; dweller in the woods.

Vaniver (*Du.*) American contraction of Van De Veer, q.v.

Van Kirk (*Du.*) One who came from Kerk (church), in Holland.

Vanko (*Rus., Ukr.*) Descendant of Vanko, a Slavic form of John (gracious gift of Jehovah).

Van Leer (*Du.*) One who came from Leer, in Germany.

Van Leeuwen (*Du.*) One who came from Leeuwen (lion), in Holland.

Van Loon (*Du.*) One who came from Loon, the name of places in Belgium and Holland.

Van Meter (*Du.*) One who came from Meteren, the name of places in Holland and France.

Vann, Van (*Eng.*) Dweller near the place where grain was threshed.

Van Ness, Van Nes, Van Ess (*Bel., Du.*) Dweller near, or on, the cape or headland; one who came from Nes (headland), the name of several villages in Holland; dweller near an ash tree.

Van Nostrand (*Du.*) Variant of Van Ostrand, q.v.

Van Osten (*Du.*) One who came from Ostend (east end), in Belgium.

Van Ostrand (*Du.*) Dweller on the east shore.

Van Parys (*Du.*) One who came from Paris (place of the Parisii), in France.

Van Patten (*Du.*) One who came from Putten (well or pool), in Holland.

Van Pelt (*Du.*) One who came from Pelt (the marshy place), in Holland.

Van Praag (*Du.*) One who came from Prague (threshold), in Czechoslovakia.

Van Rensselaer (*Du.*) One who came from Renselaer in Gelderland; dweller near a place frequented by deer.

Van Rijn, Van Ryn (*Du.*) Dweller near the Rhine river.

Van Sant, Van Sandt (*Du.*) Variant of Van Zandt, q.v.

Van Schaack, Van Schaick (*Du.*) One who came from Schaijk, in Holland.

Van Sickle, Van Sickel, Van Syckel (*Du.*) Dweller on, or near, a sickle- or crescent-shaped plot of land.

Vansittart (*Du.*) The man from Sittard, a town in Holland.

Van Steen (*Du., Bel.*) Dweller near the stone; one who came from Steene (stone), in Belgium.

Van Stone (*Du., Bel.*) Englished form of Van Steen, q.v.

Vanterpool (*Du.*) Variant of Vanderpool, q.v.

Van Valkenburg (*Du.*) One who came from Valkenburg (falcon hill), the name of two places in Holland.

Van Voorhees (*Du.*) One who came from

in front of Hees, the name of four places in Holland.

Van Winkle, Van Winkel (*Du.*) One who worked, or lived, in a shop or store; one who came from Winkel (shop), in Holland.

Van Wyck, Van Wyk (*Du.*) One who came from Wijk (district), the name of five places in Holland.

Van Zandt, Van Zant (*Du.*) One who came from Xanten, in Germany.

Vapaa (*Finn.*) The free man, i.e., one not owing allegiance to a lord.

Varden, Vardon (*Eng.*) Variant of Verdon, q.v.

Varg (*Sw.*) Wolf, a soldier name.

Varga (*Hun.*) One who made or repaired shoes, a shoemaker or cobbler.

Vargas (*Sp., Port.*) One who came from Vargas (steep hill), the name of several places in Spain and Portugal.

Varley, Verley (*Eng., Ir.*) One who came from Verly, in France; the son of the sharp-eyed man.

Varner (*Fr., Ger.*) Descendant of Warner (protection, warrior); dweller in, or near, a bog or swamp.

Varney, Verney (*Eng.*) One who came from Vernay or Verney (alder grove), in France.

Varnum (*Eng.*) One who came from Farnham (homestead where ferns grew; thorn bushes), the name of several places in England.

Vartanian, Vardanian (*Arm.*) Descendant of Vartan (savior).

Vasey (*Eng.*) One who came from Vassy (Waso's estate), in Calvados; variant of Veasey, q.v.

Vasilakos (*Gr.*) Descendant of Vasilis, a Greek form of Basil (kingly).

Vasilauskas (*Lith.*) Descendant of Vasil, Slavic form of Basil (kingly).

Vasilescu (*Rom.*) The son of Vasil, a Romanian form of Basil (kingly).

Vasilevich, Vasilenko (*Rus., Ukr.*) The son of Vasil, a Slavic form of Basil (kingly).

Vasilevsky (*Rus.*) One who came from Vasilevo (Vasili's estate), in Russia.

Vasquez (*Sp.*) One who came from the

Basque country; one who tended ewes, a shepherd; dweller at the sign of the raven.

Vass (*Eng.*) One who was a servant or vassal of another.

Vassall, Vassell, Vassal, Vassel (*Eng.*) One who was a dependant, subject, or servant of another.

Vassallo (*It.*) One who has placed himself under the protection of another as his lord; a feudal tenant.

Vassar, Vasser (*Eng.*) One who was an underservant; one who ranked immediately below a baron.

Vasylenko, Vasylenak (*Ukr., Rus.*) The son of Vasyl, a Slavic form of Basil (kingly).

Vath (*Ger.*) One who made barrels and tubs, a cooper; a minor government official.

Vaughn, Vaughan (*Wel.*) Descendant of Vaughan (little).

Vautier, Vauthier (*Fr.*) Variant of Gautier, q.v.

Vavra (*Ukr., Rus.*) Descendant of Vavra, short form of Vavara, Ukrainian and Russian form of Barbara (the stranger).

Vazquez (*Sp.*) One who came from the Basque country; one who tended ewes, a shepherd; dweller at the sign of the raven.

Veach (*Eng.*) Variant of Veitch, q.v.

Veacock (*Eng.*) Dweller at the sign of the woodcock; one thought to possess the characteristics of a woodcock.

Veal, Veale (*Eng.*) Dweller at the sign of the calf; or in the valley; descendant of Viel (pertaining to life).

Veasey, Veasy, Veazey (*Eng.*) Variant of Vessey, q.v.; nickname for a playful person.

Veatch (*Eng.*) Variant of Veitch, q.v.

Veblen (*Nor.*) One who came from Veblen, an island off Norway.

Vecchio, Vecchiolli, Vecchione (*It.*) The old or aged man; the older man.

Vedder (*Ger.*) The father's brother; one related to another; later, a male cousin.

Vedmedenko (*Ukr.*) Dweller at the sign of the bear.

Veen (*Du.*) Dweller in, or near, the peat bog.

Vega, Vegas (*Sp.*) Dweller in the meadow.

Veil, Veill (*Eng.*) One who worked as a watchman.

Veit, Veith (*Ger.*) Descendant of Veit, German form of Vitus (life; wood).

Veitch (*Eng.*) One who came from Vic (estate; hamlet), the name of many places in France.

Vela (*Sp.*) One who took care of sheep, a shepherd; one who came from Vela (raven), in Spain.

Velardo, Velarde, Velardi (*Sp., It.*) Descendant of Velardo, a variant of Abelardo (noble, hard).

Velasco (*Sp.*) One who came from Velasco (raven), in Spain; or from the Basque country; descendant of Velasco (raven); one who took care of sheep.

Velasquez, Velazquez (*Sp.*) The sluggish, slow or weak person; descendant of Bela (raven or crow).

Velez (*Sp.*) The son of Velio (elevated place); one who took care of sheep, a shepherd; descendant of Bela (raven or crow); dweller at the sign of the crow.

Veljkovich, Veljkovic (*Yu.-Sl.*) One who came from Veljkov, in Yugoslavia.

Vellenoweth (*Eng.*) Dweller near the new mill.

Venables, Venable (*Wel.*) One who came from Venables or Vignoles (vineyard), in France.

Vender (*Eng.*) One who sold goods, a dealer.

Vendetti, Vendetta (*It.*) The spiteful, vindictive, vengeful man.

Venezia, Veneziani, Veneziano (*It.*) One who came from Venezia (Venice), in Italy.

Vennard (*Fr.*) Descendant of Wanhard (hope, firm).

Vennell, Vennel, Vennall (*Eng., Scot.*) Dweller in a small street or alley.

Venner (*Eng.*) One who hunted game, a huntsman.

Venneri (*It.*) Descendant of one born on a Friday.

Venning (*Eng.*) Variant of Fenning, q.v.

Venson (*Fr.*) One who came from Vence (Vencius' estate), in France.

Venters (*Eng.*) One who came from La Ventrouse (red market), in France.

Ventham (*Eng.*) One who came from Fenham (meadow by a fen), in Northumberland.

Ventre (*Fr.*) The man with a large abdomen.

Ventresca (*It.*) One who prepared and sold salt pork.

Ventris (*Eng.*) The venturesome man, one willing to take chances.

Ventura, Venturini (*It.*) Descendant of Ventura, a pet form of Buonaventura (good luck); or of Ventura, a name sometimes given to a deserted baby.

Venus (*Eng.*) One who came from Venoix, in France, or from Venice, in Italy.

Venuti, Venuto (*It.*) Descendant of Venuto, pet form of Benvenuto (welcome).

Vera (*Sp.*) One who came from Vera (border), in Spain.

Verbrugge, Verbrughe, Verbrugghen, Verbruggen (*Du.*) Dweller at, or near, the bridge.

Verdejo, Verdeja (*Sp.*) One who raised and sold green gage plums.

Verdell (*Du.*) Dweller in the valley.

Verdi (*It.*) One who wore green clothing; dweller in a green place.

Verdier (*Fr.*) One who came from Verdier (orchard), the name of several places in France; one who had charge of a forest for the lord, a gamekeeper.

Verdon, Verden, Verdin, Verdone (*Eng., Fr.*) One who came from Verdun (moor hill; moor fort), the name of several places in France; descendant of little Ver, the name of an obscure saint.

Vergara (*Sp.*) One who tended animals, a herdsman.

Verge (*Eng., Fr.*) One who tilled a verge or yardland (from fifteen to thirty acres); one who had sworn fealty to his lord; dweller near a boundary.

Vermeer (*Du.*) Dweller near the lake.

Vermeulen (*Du.*) One who worked in, or resided near, the mill.

Verna, Verni (*It.*) Descendant of Berna, a pet form of Bernardo, Italian form of Bernard (bear, hard).

Verne (*Fr.*) Dweller in, or near, a grove of alders.

Vernekoff (*Rus.*) Nickname for one thought to be right.

Verner, Vernier, Verniere (*Fr., Eng.*) Descendant of Warinhari (protection, army).

Vernick, Vernik (*Yu.-Sl.*) The faithful man.

Vernon (*Fr., Eng.*) One who came from Vernon (the alder grove), the name of several places in France.

Verrall, Verrell, Verrelle, Verrill (*Eng.*) Descendant of Verelle (true).

Verry, Very, Verrey (*Eng.*) One who came from Verrey, Very or Verry (glass works), the names of several places in France.

Vesci, Vescio (*It.*) Dweller near where corn cockle grew.

Vesely, Vessely, Vesley (*Rus., Ukr., Pol., Cz.-Sl., Eng.*) Descendant of Vasily, a pet form of Vasyl, Slavic form of Basil (kingly); one who came from Vesly (Verilus' estate); or Vezelay (Vitellius' estate), in France; the joyous or happy fellow.

Vesey, Vessey (*Eng.*) One who came from Vessey (estate of Vitius), the name of places in Normandy and Burgundy.

Vessels (*Eng.*) One who made and sold household utensils or vessels.

Vest, Veste (*Ger., Eng.*) Descendant of Fest (firm); or of Vest, a pet form of Silvester (forest dweller).

Veto (*Sp.*) Descendant of Veto, a pet form of Roberto, Spanish form of Robert (fame, bright).

Vetri, Vetro, Vetrone (*It.*) One who made glass.

Vetter (*Ger.*) The father's brother; one related to another; later, a male cousin.

Vey (*Ir., Fr., Eng.*) Descendant of Mac Bhuidhe (yellow); one who came from Le Vey in Calvados; dweller at the ford.

Vial, Viale, Viall (*Eng., Fr.*) Descendant of Viel, the French form of Vitalis (pertaining to life), the name of various saints.

Viana (*Port.*) One who came from Viana do Castelo in Portugal.

Viaud, Viault (*Fr.*) Variant of Vial, q.v.

Vicari, Vicario (*It.*) One in charge of provisions; an ecclesiastic who acts as substitute for another, a vicar.

Vicars (*Eng.*) Descendant of the vicar, an incumbent of a parish. See Vickery.

Vicente (*Sp.*) Descendant of Vicente, Spanish form of Vincent (conquering).

Vick, Vicks (*Eng., Wel.*) One who came from Vicq (village), the name of various places in France; the small man.

Vickers (*Eng.*) Variant of Vicars, q.v.

Vickery (*Eng.*) The priest of a parish who receives only the smaller tithes or a salary.

Victor (*Eng., Fr.*) Descendant of Victor (the victorious; conqueror).

Victors, Victorson (*Eng.*) The son of Victor (the victorious; conqueror).

Vidal (*Fr., Sp.*) Variant of Vial, q.v.; life.

Vidor (*Hun.*) Descendant of Vidor (gay; joyful).

Vieira (*Port.*) One who came from Vieira, in Portugal.

Vieu (*Fr.*) One who came from Vieu, the name of two places in France.

Vieux (*Fr.*) One who came from Vieux (old place), the name of several places in France; the elderly or old man.

Vig, Viig (*Nor.*) Dweller near the bay or cove.

Vigars, Vigar (*Eng.*) The active vigorous man; variant of Vicars, q.v.

Vigil (*Sp.*) Descendant of Vigil (watchful); one born on the feast of the nativity.

Vigilante (*It.*) The sharp, alert man.

Vigilio (*Sp.*) Descendant of Vigil, a name given to commemorate the watch the night before the birth (of our Lord).

Vigneau, Vignaux (*Fr.*) One who owned or managed a vineyard; one who came from Vignaux or Vigneaux (vineyard), the names of places in France.

Vigneron (*Fr.*) One who owned a vineyard.

Vik (*Nor.*) Dweller near the bay; one who lived, or worked, on a farm so named.

Viles (*Eng.*) Variant of Files, q.v.; the old man.

Villa, Vila (*Sp.*) Dweller on a large estate; one who came from Villa (free town), the name of many places in Spain.

Villalobos (*Sp.*) One who came from Villalobos (village of the wolf), in Spain.

Villani (*It.*) One who farmed the land, a farmer.

Villano (*It.*) The crude or uncouth man.

Villanova (*Sp.*) One who came from Vilanova (village of the nobleman), in Spain.

Villanueva (*Sp.*) One who came from Villanueva (the recently founded settlement), the name of several places in Spain.

Villar, Villars (*Fr.*) One who came from Villar or Villars (country house; settlement), the names of several places in France.

Villard (*Fr.*) One who came from Villard or Villars (small suburban residence), the names of several places in France.

Villari (*It.*) Resident of a town; a peasant.

Villarreal, Villareal (*Sp.*) One who came from Villareal (the royal estate), the name of several places in Spain.

Villemaire (*Fr.*) The headman in a village; one who came from Villemer (homestead with a pond), the name of two places in France.

Villeneuve (*Fr.*) One who came from Villeneuve (new village), the name of several places in France.

Villiers (*Fr.*) One who came from Villiers (village), the name of many places in France.

Vince (*Eng.*) Descendant of Vince, a pet form of Vincent (conquering).

Vincent (*Eng.*) Descendant of Vincent (conquering).

Vinci (*It.*) One who came from Vinci (enclosed place), in Italy.

Vinegar (*Eng.*) Descendant of Winegar (friend, spear).

Vines, Vine (*Eng.*) Dweller at a vine; or in, or near, a vineyard.

Vining, Vinning (*Eng.*) The son of Wine (friend); descendant of Wynning (pleasure).

Vinje (*Nor.*) Dweller on Vinje (farm), a farm name.

Vinnacombe, Vinicombe (*Eng.*) Dweller in the stony valley; or marshy valley.

Vinson, Vincson, Vincon (*Eng., Fr.*) The son of Vin, a pet form of Vincent (conquering); descendant of Vincent.

Vinter (*Eng.*) One who sold wines, a vintner or wine merchant.

Vinton (*Eng.*) One who came from Feniton (village by a boundary stream), in Devonshire.

Vinyard (*Eng.*) Dweller in, or near, the vineyard or place where grapes were grown.

Viola (*It.*) Descendant of Viola (violet); one who played a viol.

Violante (*It., Sp.*) Descendant of Violante, Italian and Spanish form of Violet (violet).

Virchow (*Rus.*) Dweller on the high land.

Virgil (*Eng.*) Descendant of Virgil (flourishing; green bough).

Virgilio (*It.*) Descendant of Virgilio, Italian form of Virgil (flourishing; green bough).

Virgin (*Eng.*) Dweller at, or near, a medieval image of the Virgin Mary;

one who played the part of the Virgin in a play or pageant.

Virtu, Virtue (*Eng.*) One noted for his moral excellence.

Visack (*Eng.*) Dweller near the promontory or finger of land.

Vischer (*Du.*) One who caught or sold fish.

Visco (*It.*) Dweller near where mistletoe grew; member of a bishop's entourage; descendant of a bishop.

Visconti, Visconto (*It.*) A nobleman ranking just below a count; one connected with a viscount's household.

Vishton (*Eng.*) Dweller in a homestead on a damp meadow.

Visser (*Du.*) One who caught or sold, fish.

Vita (*Sp.*) Nickname of the type reminding Christians of immortality and the resurrection of Christ.

Vitale, Vitalo (*It.*) Descendant of Vitalis (relative to life), the name of ten martyrs in the early Church.

Vitello, Vitelli (*It.*) Dweller at the sign of the calf, heifer or bullock; one who cared for calves and heifers; one who sold veal.

Vito (*Sp., It., Yu.-Sl.*) One who came from Vito, in Spain; descendant of Vito (life); descendant of Vito, a Yugoslavian form of Victor (the victorious; conqueror).

Vitullo, Vitallo, Vitacco (*It.*) Descendant of little Vito (life).

Vivian (*Eng.*) Descendant of Vivian (animated).

Viviano (*It.*) Descendant of Viviano, Italian form of Vivian (animated).

Vizard, Vizzard (*Fr., Eng.*) Descendant of Wishard (wise, hard).

Vizer (*Eng.*) One who observes or oversees matters.

Vlach (*Cz.*) One who came from Italy, an Italian.

Vlachos, Vlahos (*Gr., Cz.-Sl.*) One who took care of sheep, a shepherd; one who came from Italy (land of cattle), an Italian.

Vladescu (*Rom.*) The son of Vlad, a pet form of Vladislaus.

Vladimir (*Rus., Yu.-Sl.*) Descendant of Vladimir, Russian form of Walter (rule, folk or army).

Vlahos (*Gr.*) One who tended sheep, a shepherd.

Vlk (*Cz.-Sl.*) Dweller at the sign of the wolf; one with the qualities of a wolf.

Voak (*Eng.*) Descendant of Foake or Fulke (people).

Voce (*Du., Ger.*) Anglicized form of Voss or Vos, q.v.

Vodicka (*Cz.*) Dweller near the water.

Voelker (*Ger.*) Descendant of Fulchar or Volker (people, army); one who came from Volken or Volkers (people), the names of places in Germany.

Vogel, Vogl (*Ger., Du.*) Dweller at the sign of the bird; one with birdlike characteristics.

Vogelman (*Ger.*) One who hunted or trapped birds.

Vogelsanger, Voglsanger (*Ger.*) One who lived on a farm where birds sang. This is a common field name.

Vogler (*Ger.*) The birdcatcher or fowler.

Vogt, Voight, Voigt, Voit, Voigts (*Ger.*) The overseer or manager of a household, a steward.

Voisin (*Fr.*) One who came from Voisines (hamlet; common land), in France; the nearby resident, the neighbor.

Voke, Vokey, Vokes (*Eng.*) Descendant of Foulk or Fulko (people).

Volf (*Lith.*) Dweller at the sign of the wolf.

Volk, Volke (*Ger.*) Descendant of Volk, a short form of names commencing with Volk (people), as Volkold, Folcmar and Fulculf.

Volker, Volkers (*Ger.*) Variant of Voelker, q.v.

Volkman, Volkmann (*Ger.*) Descendant of Folcman (people, servant).

Volkov (*Rus.*) Dweller at the sign of the wolf.

Volkow (*Pol.*) Dweller at the sign of the wolf.

Vollmer, Vollmar, Volmar, Volkmar (*Ger.*) Descendant of Folcmar (people, famous).

Vollrath (*Ger.*) Descendant of Fulchrad (people, counsel).

Voloscenko (*Ukr.*) The son of the Italian.

Volpe, Volpi (*It.*) Dweller at the sign of the fox; a cunning person; one with fox-like characteristics.

Volz, Voltz (*Ger.*) Descendant of Volz, a pet form of names beginning with Volk (people), as Volmar and Fulculf.

Von Bergen (*Ger.*) One who came from Bergen (mountain; hill), the name of many places in Germany.

Vonder Haar, Vonderhaar (*Ger.*) One who came from Haar (moor; eminence), the name of many places in Germany.

Von der Tann (*Ger.*) Dweller near a pine tree.

Von Feilitzen (*Ger.*) One who came from Feilitzsch, in Bavaria.

Voorhees, Voorhies, Voorheis (*Du.*) One who lived in front of Hees, the name of four places in Holland.

Vormittag (*Ger.*) Nickname for one whose work or other action was before midday.

Vorona (*Rus.*) Dweller at the sign of the crow; one thought to have the characteristics of a crow.

Voros (*Hun.*) The red-haired or ruddy man.

Voroshilov (*Rus.*) One who stirs or tosses, a restless person.

Vorst (*Du.*) Dweller in, or near, the forest.

Vose (*Eng.*) Dweller at, or near, a ditch.

Voss, Vos (*Du., Ger.*) One with fox-like characteristics; dweller at the sign of the fox; one with red hair or a ruddy complexion.

Vovcenko (*Ukr.*) Dweller at the sign of the wolf.

Vowell, Vowells (*Eng.*) Dweller at the sign of the bird or fowl.

Vozzella, Vozella (*It.*) Descendant of little Vozzo, a pet form of Iacovozzo, an Italian form of Jacob (may God protect; the supplanter).

Vratny (*Cz.*) One who had charge of the door or gate, a doorkeeper.

Vrba (*Cz., Pol.*) Dweller near a willow tree.

Vrchota (*Cz.*) Dweller on the mountain.

Vreeland (*Du.*) One who came from Vreeland (land of peace), in Holland.

Vries (*Du.*) One who came from Friesland, a Frisian.

Vrooman, Vroman, Vromans, Vroom (*Du.*) The pious, devout man.

Vyvyan (*Eng.*) Variant of Vivian, q.v.

Waage, Waag (*Ger.*) Dweller at the sign of the scales.

Waber (*Ger.*) Dialectal variant of Weber, q.v.

Wachowski (*Pol.*) One who came from Wachow(e) (guard), in Poland.

Wachs, Wachsman, Wachsmann (*Ger.*) One who made and sold wax candles.

Wachtel (*Ger.*) One who caught and sold quail; dweller at the sign of the quail.

Wachter, Wachtler (*Ger., Du.*) The watchman or guard, especially a night watchman.

Wacker (*Ger., Eng.*) Descendant of Wacar (vigilant); the active and energetic man.

Wackerle (*Eng.*) One who came from Wakerley (grove with willows), in Northamptonshire.

Wackerman (*Ger.*) The lively, active, energetic man.

Wackley (*Eng.*) One who came from Walkley (Walca's grove), in the West Riding of Yorkshire.

Waclawski, Waclawik (*Cz.-Sl., Pol.*) Descendant of Waclaw, Slavic form of Wenceslaus (great, glory).

Wada (*Jap.*) Peace, rice field.

Waddell, Waddill (*Scot., Eng.*) Dweller in the valley where woad grew; one who came from the parish of Waddel (valley where woad grows), in Midlothian; one who came from

Wadley (Wada's wood or meadow), in Berkshire.

Waddingham (*Eng.*) One who came from Waddingham (village of Wada's people), in Lincolnshire.

Waddington, Waddleton (*Eng.*) One who came from Waddington (homestead of Wada's people), in the West Riding of Yorkshire; or from Waddington (wheat hill), in Surrey.

Waddle, Waddles (*Scot., Eng.*) One who came from Waddel (valley where woad grows), in Midlothian; one who came from Wadley (Wada's wood or meadow), in Berkshire.

Waddy, Wadda, Wadd (*Eng., Scot.*) Descendant of little Wada (advance); or of little Wad, a pet form of Waldtheof (power, serf; foreign, thief).

Wade, Waide, Waid (*Eng.*) Dweller at the shallow river crossing or ford; descendant of Wada (to advance).

Wadkins (*Eng.*) The son of little Wada (advance); variant of Watkins, q.v.

Wadley, Wadleigh (*Eng.*) One who came from Wadley (Wada's wood or meadow), in Berkshire.

Wadlington (*Eng.*) One who came from Waddington (wheat hill; village of the Wada's people), the name of places in Surrey and the West Riding of Yorkshire.

Wadstrom (*Sw.*) Ford, stream; dweller by the ford across the stream.

Wadsworth (*Eng.*) One who came from Wadsworth (Wadda's homestead), in the West Riding of Yorkshire.

Wafer (*Eng.*) Metonymic for the maker or seller of thin, crisp cakes. They often sold their wares from house to house.

Waffensmith (*Ger.*) The smith who made weapons.

Wagener (*Ger.*) Variant of Wagner, q.v.

Wagenhoffer (*Ger.*) One who came from Wagenhoff (cart yard), in Germany.

Wagenknecht (*Ger.*) The wagon, or cart, driver or coachman.

Wager (*Eng.*) The official in charge of a

weighbridge, or inspector of weights and measures.

Wagg, Wagge (*Eng.*) Dweller near the quaking bog or marsh.

Wagman (*Ger.*) One who had charge of the town scales.

Wagner, Waggoner, Wagoner (*Eng., Ger.*) Driver of a wagon; one who made wagons, a cartwright.

Wagstaff (*Eng.*) Nickname given to an official who carried a wand or staff, such as the parish beadle.

Wahl (*Ger., Sw., Eng.*) Dweller at, or near, a wall; one who lived at, or near, a well or spring; one who lived at, or near, the pool or bog; dweller in a field.

Wahlgren (*Sw.*) Field, branch.

Wahlstrom (*Sw.*) Field, stream.

Waibel (*Ger.*) Court official or beadle.

Waine, Wain (*Eng.*) Metonymic for a wagoner or carter.

Wainer, Wayner (*Eng.*) One who drove a wagon or cart, a carter.

Wainhouse (*Eng.*) Dweller at, or near, the house where wagons were made or stored.

Wainscott (*Eng.*) One who made wainscot, the best kind of oak wood used in carts.

Wainwright (*Eng.*) One who made wagons and carts.

Wais (*Ger.*) One who baked and sold white bread.

Waite, Wait, Wayt (*Eng.*) The watchman or lookout, especially a watchman in a castle or fortified place.

Waiters, Waiter (*Eng.*) One who watches or guards, a watchman.

Waites (*Eng.*) The son of the watchman or guard.

Wake (*Eng.*) The watchful or alert man.

Wakefield (*Eng.*) One who came from Wakefield (field where the festival plays were held), the name of several places in England.

Wakelam (*Eng.*) Descendant of very little Walho or Walico (foreigner).

Wakeley, Wakelee (*Eng.*) One who came from Wakerley (willow grove), in

Northamptonshire; dweller at the soft or wet meadow.

Wakeling, Wakelin (*Eng.*) Descendant of Walcelin (little foreigner).

Wakeman (*Eng.*) The watchman for a village, castle or fortified place; the chief magistrate of a borough.

Walborn (*Eng.*) One who came from Walburn (steam of the Welsh), in the North Riding of Yorkshire.

Walbridge (*Eng.*) Dweller at the bridge near the Roman wall; one who came from Waldridge (ridge by a wall), in Durham.

Walburn (*Eng.*) One who came from Walburn (stream of the Welsh), in the North Riding of Yorkshire.

Walch (*Eng.*) Variant of Walsh, q.v.

Walcoff (*Rus.*) Descendant of Valya, a pet form of Valentyna (vigorous or healthy); or of Valeria (strong).

Walcott (*Eng.*) One who came from Walcot (cottage of the serfs), the name of various places in England.

Walczak, Walczyk (*Pol.*) Descendant of little Wal, a pet form of Walenty (valorous).

Wald, Walder (*Eng., Ger.*) Dweller near, or in, a forest; one who came from Wald (forest), the name of many places in Germany.

Waldbaum (*Ger.*) Dweller near a woodland tree; or near a walnut tree.

Waldeck, Waldecker (*Ger.*) One who came from Waldeck (swampy place), the name of several places in Germany.

Walden, Waldon (*Eng.*) One who came from Walden (the valley of the Britons), the name of several places in England; dweller in a forested valley; descendant of Walden (power, little).

Walder (*Ger., Eng.*) Dweller in the forest. One who came from Wald (forest), in Germany; dweller near, or in, a forest.

Waldman, Waldmann (*Ger., Eng.*) One who took care of a forest for the lord; a gamekeeper; dweller in the forest.

Waldo (*Ger., Eng.*) Descendant of Waldo, a pet form of names beginning with Wald (forest), as Waldomar and Waldorad; descendant of Waldo, a pet form of Waltheof (power, thief).

Waldorf (*Ger.*) One who came from Waldorf (swampy village), the name of several places in Germany.

Waldron (*Eng.*) One who came from Waldron (house in a wood), in Sussex.

Waldschmidt, Waldsmith (*Ger.*) The smith who worked, or lived, in the forest where ample fuel was near at hand.

Waldstein (*Ger.*) Forest stone.

Walek (*Pol.*) Descendant of Walek, a pet form of Walenty (valorous).

Wales (*Eng.*) One who came from Wales (the Welsh), the country, or from Wales, in the West Riding of Yorkshire.

Walesby (*Eng.*) One who came from Walesby (Val's homestead), the name of places in Lincolnshire and Nottinghamshire.

Walford (*Eng.*) One who came from Walford (unsteady ford; ford of the Welsh), the name of places in Dorset and Herefordshire.

Walgren, Walgreen, Wallgren (*Sw.*) Variant of Wahlgren, q.v.

Walheim (*Ger.*) One who came from Walheim (swampy settlement), the name of two places in Germany.

Walk, Walke (*Ger., Pol.*) Dweller at the sign of the wolf; one with the characteristics of a wolf; descendant of Walek, a pet form of Walerian (healthy).

Walker (*Eng.*) One who cleaned and thickened cloth, a fuller; one who came from Walker (marsh by the Roman wall), in Northumberland.

Walkinshaw (*Scot.*) One who came from the lands of Walkinshaw, in Renfrewshire.

Walkley (*Eng.*) One who came from Walkley (Walca's grove), in the West Riding of Yorkshire.

Walkowiak (*Pol.*) One who came from Walkow (battle place), in Poland.

Walkup (*Eng.*) One who came from Wallop (valley of the stream), in Hampshire; or from Warcop (beacon hill), in Westmorland.

Wall, Walle (*Eng.*) Dweller at, or near, a wall such as the old Roman wall; dweller at, or near, a spring or stream; one who came from Wall (on the Roman wall; spring), the name of several places in England; dweller at, or near, a pool or bog. During surname times many towns still had walls for protection.

Wallace, Wallis (*Scot.*) The foreigner or stranger; one who came from Wales.

Wallach, Wallack (*Ger.*) One who came from Wallach in Germany; the stranger or foreigner.

Waller (*Eng., Ger.*) One who built walls; dweller at, or near, a wall, such as the old Roman wall; the stranger or foreigner; one who has visited a distant shrine, a pilgrim.

Walley (*Eng.*) A variant of Whaley, q.v.

Wallin, Wallen, Wallins (*Sw.*) Dweller on, or near, a fallow field.

Walling (*Eng.*) The son of Wealh (foreigner).

Wallingford (*Eng.*) One who came from Wallingford (ford of Wealh's people), in Berkshire.

Wallner (*Ger.*) One who came from Wallen (forest), in Germany.

Wallop (*Eng.*) One who came from Wallop (valley with the stream), in Hampshire.

Walls (*Eng.*) Variant of Wall, q.v.

Walmsley (*Eng.*) One who came from Walmersley (lake by the wood), in Lancashire.

Walpole (*Eng.*) One who came from Walpole (pool by the wall; pool of the Welsh), the name of places in Norfolk and Suffolk.

Walsh, Walshe (*Eng., Ir.*) One who came from Wales, a Welshman; one who came from a distance, a foreigner.

Walsmith (*Eng., Ger.*) The smith who worked, or lived, in the forest.

Walston (*Eng.*) One who came from Walsden (Walsa's valley), in Lancashire.

Walters, Walter (*Wel.*) Descendant of Walter (rule, folk or army).

Walther, Walthers (*Ger.*) Descendant of Walthari (rule, folk or army).

Walton (*Eng.*) One who came from Walton (homestead by a wall; homestead in a wood; the serf's homestead), the name of many places in England.

Waltonen (*Finn.*) Descendant of Valtari, Finnish form of Walter (rule, folk or army); one who was single, that is, not married.

Waltzer, Walzer (*Ger.*) One who worked in a rolling mill; one who rolls out dough, a baker.

Walz, Waltz (*Ger.*) Descendant of Walzo (to rule or manage).

Wambach, Wambaugh (*Ger.*) One who came from Wambach (marshy pool), the name of several places in Germany.

Wambold, Wamboldt, Wamble (*Ger.*) Descendant of Wanbald (hope, bold).

Wampler (*Ger.*) One with a prominent stomach; one who came from Wampen, in Germany.

Wampole (*Eng.*) Dweller near the Wampool, a river in Cumberland.

Wamser (*Ger.*) One who made, and sold, jackets and doublets.

Wamsley (*Eng.*) Variant of Walmsley, q.v.; dweller in the boundary field.

Wanamaker, Wannamaker, Wannemacher (*Du.*) One who made baskets, particularly certain broad, shallow baskets.

Wandell, Wandel (*Ger.*) Variant of Wendell, q.v.

Wander (*Ger.*) Dweller by a rock wall.

Wandrer, Wanderer (*Eng.*) One who traps moles.

Wang (*Chin.*) The prince; yellow.

Wanger (*Ger.*) Descendant of Wanger (hope, spear); one who came from Wang or Wangen (grassy plain),

the names of numerous places in Germany.

Wann (*Eng.*) One with a wan, pale complexion.

Wanner (*Ger.*) Dweller in a basin-shaped valley; one who winnows grain; one who came from Wanne, the name of two places in Germany.

Wannop (*Eng.*) Dweller in, or by, a dark hollow.

Wansley (*Eng.*) One who came from Wansley (Want's grove), in Devonshire.

Wantenaer (*Du.*) One who made and sold gloves.

Wantman (*Eng.*) One who trapped moles; dweller by the crossroad.

Wanzer (*Ger.*) One who came from Wansen, in Germany; one who made garments or cut cloth.

Waples (*Eng.*) Variant of Walpole, q.v.

Warboys (*Eng.*) One who came from Warboys (beacon in the bushes), in Huntingdonshire.

Warburton (*Eng.*) One who came from Warburton (Waerburg's homestead), in Cheshire.

Warchol, Warchal (*Pol.*) One who wrangles or brawls with others.

Ward, Warden, Warder (*Eng.*) The guard, keeper, or watchman; dweller near a marsh.

Wardell, Wardle (*Eng.*) One who came from Wardle (watch hill), the name of places in Cheshire and Lancashire.

Warden (*Eng.*) Variant of Worden, q.v.

Wardlow, Wardlaw (*Eng., Scot.*) One who came from Wardlow (watch hill or slope), in Derbyshire; or from Wardlaw (hill where guard was kept), the name of several places in Scotland.

Wardsworth (*Eng.*) One who came from Wardleworth (Wuerdle's homestead), in Lancashire.

Wardwell (*Eng.*) One who came from Wordwell (winding brook), in Suffolk.

Ware (*Eng.*) One who came from Ware

(dam or fish trap), in Hertfordshire; dweller near a dam or fish trap.

Wareham (*Eng.*) One who came from Wareham (homestead by a dam or fish trap), in Dorset.

Warfield (*Eng.*) One who came from Warfield (cleared land on the Wearne river), in Berkshire.

Warford (*Eng.*) One who came from Warford (weir by a ford), in Cheshire.

Waring, Wareing (*Eng.*) Descendant of Warin or Guarin (protection).

Wark (*Eng., Scot.*) One who came from Wark (fort), in Northumberland; one who constructed, or was in charge of a fortification; shortened form of Warwick, q.v.

Warley (*Eng.*) One who came from Warley (grove by a weir; pasture for cattle), the name of places in Essex and Worcestershire.

Warlow (*Eng.*) Variant of Wardlow, q.v.

Warman (*Eng.*) The merchant or tradesman; descendant of Waermund (faith, protection).

Warmflash (*Ger.*) One who sold warm or hot meat; or belly meat.

Warmington (*Eng.*) One who came from Warmington (village of Waermund's people), in Warwickshire.

Warne (*Eng.*) One who came from Wawne (quaking bog), in the East Riding of Yorkshire; contraction of Warin (protection); dweller at, or keeper of, a game preserve; dweller in, or near, a swamp.

Warneke, Warnecke, Warneck, Warnicke (*Ger.*) Descendant of little Waro (protection), a pet form of names beginning with Warin, as Warinbold, Warengar, and Werinhart.

Warner (*Eng.*) Descendant of Warner (protecting warrior); an officer employed to watch over the game in a park.

Warnock (*Eng.*) Descendant of little Warn or Warin (protection).

Warr (*Eng.*) Variant of Ware, q.v.; one who engaged in combat, a warrior.

Warren, Warrin (*Eng.*) Dweller at, or keeper of, a game preserve; descendant of Warren, from Old French, Warin (protection); dweller near the hutch where rabbits were kept.

Warrender (*Eng.*) Variant of Warriner, q.v.

Warrick (*Eng., Scot.*) Variant of Warwick, q.v.

Warriner, Warrener (*Eng.*) One who had charge of a warren or game preserve.

Warrington (*Eng.*) One who came from Warrington (homestead at a dam or fish trap), in Lancashire.

Warsaw, Warsawsky (*Pol., Rus.*) One who came from Warsaw (the fortified place), the capital of Poland.

Warshaw, Warshauer, Warshawsky, Warshawer (*Pol., Rus.*) One who came from Warszawa (the fortified place), the capital of Poland.

Wartell (*Eng.*) One who came from Warthill (watch hill), in the North Riding of Yorkshire.

Wartenberg, Wartenburg (*Ger.*) One who came from Wartenberg, the name of two places in Germany.

Warwick (*Eng., Scot.*) One who came from Warwick (farm by a dam or fish trap; or on the bank), the name of places in Warwickshire and Cumberland; descendent of Warrack.

Was (*Pol.*) One who wore a mustache.

Wasco (*Eng.*) Descendant of Wazo (sharp).

Washam (*Eng.*) Variant of Worsham, q.v.

Washburn, Washburne (*Eng.*) One who came from Washburn (fuller's stream), in Yorkshire; or from Washbourne (stream where washing was done; the Wash river), in Devonshire and Gloucestershire.

Washer, Wascher (*Eng., Ger.*) One who washed, especially one who washed or bleached flax and wool fibers, and finished cloth.

Washington (*Eng.*) One who came from Washington (the homestead of Wassa's people; the manor of the Wessyng family), the name of places in Durham and Sussex.

Wasielewski *(Pol.)* The son of Basyl or Wasyl (kingly).

Wasik *(Pol.)* One who had a small mustache.

Wasilewski *(Ukr., Rus., Pol.)* Descendant of Wasyl, Slavic form of Basil (kingly).

Waskey *(Ukr.)* The heavy, or fat, man.

Waskiewicz *(Pol.)* The son of Waska, a pet form of Wasyl, Slavic form of Basil (kingly).

Wasko *(Ukr.)* Descendant of Wasko, a pet form of Vasyl, Slavic form of Basil (kingly).

Wasner *(Ger.)* Dweller on the grassy land; or on the marshy ground.

Wass, Was *(Eng., Ger.)* One who came from Wass (swamp), in Yorkshire; dweller in, or near, a swamp; descendant of Was (sharp); or of Vad (strife).

Wasser *(Ger.)* Dweller near the water; one who came from Wasser (water), the name of three places in Germany.

Wasserleben *(Ger.)* One who lived by the water.

Wasserman, Wassermann *(Ger.)* One who worked on the water, a seaman; one who came from Wasser (water), the name of three places in Germany.

Wasson, Wason *(Eng., Sw., Ger.)* Descendant of little Waso, or Wasso (sharp); or of little Wace (watchful); the son of Waso or Wace; the son of one who came from Wasa, a province in Finland; descendant of Waso, a pet form of names commencing with Was (sharp), as Hwasmot.

Watanabe *(Jap.)* Cross, side.

Watchorn *(Eng.)* Dweller at a lookout hill shaped like a horn.

Waterbury *(Eng.)* One who came from Waterperry (pear tree by a stream), in Oxfordshire.

Waterfield *(Eng.)* Dweller on wet, watery, open country; one who came from Vatierville (Vatheri's domain), in France.

Waterford *(Eng.)* One who came from

Watford (ford where woad grew), the name of places in Hertfordshire and Northamptonshire.

Waterhouse *(Eng.)* Dweller in the house by the lake or stream.

Waterloo *(Bel.)* One who came from Waterloo (settlement near water), in Belgium.

Waterman *(Eng.)* One who operated a boat, especially a ferryman; the servant of Wat or Walter (rule, folk or army).

Waterous, Watrous *(Eng.)* Dweller in the house by the water.

Waters, Water *(Wel., Eng.)* Descendant of Walter (rule, folk or army), the early pronunciation of the name; dweller near the stream or lake.

Waterworth *(Eng.)* Dweller at the homestead by the water.

Watford *(Eng.)* One who came from Watford (ford used in hunting; Old Scandinavian vath, "ford," to which was later added the explanatory word "ford"), the name of places in Hertfordshire and Northamptonshire.

Wathen *(Eng.)* Dweller near a ford or river crossing.

Watkins, Watkin *(Wel., Eng.)* Descendant of little Wat, a pet form of Walter (rule, folk or army).

Watkinson *(Eng.)* The son of little Wat, a pet form of Walter (rule, folk or army).

Watland *(Nor.)* Dweller on land near the water.

Watley *(Eng.)* Variant of Whatley, q.v.

Watling *(Eng.)* The son of Waetla (bandage); or of little Hwaet (bold).

Watlington *(Eng.)* One who came from Watlington (village of Wacol's people), the name of places in Norfolk and Oxfordshire.

Watlow *(Eng.)* Dweller near Watt's mound.

Watman *(Eng.)* Descendant of Hwatman (bold, man); the servant of Wat, the pet form of Walter (rule, folk or army).

Watmough *(Eng.)* The brother-in-law of

Wat, a pet form of Walter (rule, folk or army).

Watney (*Eng.*) One who came from Wata's island.

Watson (*Eng.*) The son of Wat, a pet form of Walter (rule, folk or army).

Watteau (*Fr.*) Descendant of Watteau, a regional pet form of Vatier or Gadier, French forms of Wadhari (pledge, army).

Wattenmaker (*Ger.*) One who made nets and rough woven fabric.

Watters, Watterson (*Wel., Eng.*) Variant of Waters, q.v.

Wattis (*Eng.*) The son of Watt, a pet form of Walter (rule, folk or army).

Watton (*Eng.*) One who came from Watton (homestead where woad grew; Wada's homestead; wet hill), the name of places in Hertfordshire, Norfolk, and the East Riding of Yorkshire.

Watts, Watt, Watte (*Eng.*) Descendant of Wat, a pet form of Walter (rule, folk or army).

Waugh (*Scot.*) Dweller at, or near, the wall.

Wavell (*Eng.*) One who came from Vauville (Valr's village), in France.

Wawrzyniak (*Pol.*) The son of Wawrzyn or Wawrzyniec, Polish forms of Lawrence (laurel, symbol of victory).

Wax, Wacks, Wachs (*Ger.*) One who dealt with wax; descendant of Waccho, a pet form of names beginning with Wachen (watch), as Wachari and Wacald; descendant of Waso (sharp).

Waxler (*Eng.*) One who produces and sells wax.

Waxman (*Eng.*) One who gathered and sold wax.

Way, Weye, Wayer (*Eng.*) Dweller at the path or road.

Wayes, Ways (*Eng.*) The servant or vassal.

Wayland (*Eng.*) One who came from Wayland (land by the path), in Norfolk; descendant of Weland (foreign land).

Wayman, Waymon (*Eng.*) One who hunted game, a huntsman; variant of Wyman, q.v.

Wayne (*Eng.*) Dweller at the sign of the wagon; metonymic for a maker of wagons.

Weakley, Weakly (*Eng.*) Variant of Weekley, q.v.

Weams (*Scot.*) Variant of Weems, q.v.

Weaner (*Ger.*) Variant of Wiener, q.v.

Wear, Weare (*Eng.*) Dweller at a weir, dam, or fish trap; one in charge of a fishing weir; one who came from Weare (weir), in Somerset.

Wearing (*Eng.*) Variant of Waring, q.v.

Wearne, Wearn (*Eng.*) Dweller in, or near, the swamp.

Weary, Wearry (*Eng.*) Descendant of Werric (man, rule).

Weatherall (*Eng.*) One who came from Wetheral (enclosure where sheep were kept), in Cumberland.

Weatherby, Weatherbee (*Eng.*) One who came from Wetherby (the wether farm), in the West Riding of Yorkshire.

Weatherford (*Eng.*) Dweller at, or near, a stream crossing used by wethers, i.e., castrated rams or sheep.

Weatherley (*Eng.*) Dweller near the meadow, or wood where sheep were kept.

Weathers, Wethers (*Eng.*) One who tended wethers or sheep, a shepherd.

Weathersby (*Eng.*) One who came from Wetherby (the wether farm), in the West Riding of Yorkshire; dweller on a farm where wethers were bred.

Weatherspoon (*Scot., Eng.*) Variant of Wetherspoon, q.v.

Weatherstone (*Eng.*) One who came from Witherstone (Withere's rock or monument), in Dorset.

Weaver (*Eng.*) One who wove cloth; dweller near the Weaver (winding river), a river in Cheshire.

Webb, Webbe (*Eng.*) One who wove cloth, either a male or a female.

Weber, Webber (*Eng., Ger.*) One who wove cloth.

Webster (*Eng.*) A female weaver, one

who wove cloth. The term was later used to designate a male weaver generally.

Wechsler (*Ger.*) One who changed money, a banker or money changer.

Wecht, Wechter (*Ger.*) Variant of Wachter, q.v.

Weckerly (*Eng.*) One who came from Wickersley (steward's grove), in the West Riding of Yorkshire.

Weckesser (*Ger.*) One in the habit of eating breakfast rolls; or who made or sold breakfast rolls.

Wedderburn (*Scot.*) One who came from Wedderburn (rams' stream), in Scotland.

Wedderspoon (*Scot., Eng.*) Variant of Wetherspoon, q.v.

Wedding (*Ger.*) One who came from Weddingen (swampy place), in Germany.

Weddingfield (*Eng.*) Dweller on Waeta's open country.

Weddington (*Eng.*) One who came from Weddington (wet homestead), in Warwickshire.

Weddleton (*Eng.*) One who came from Widdington (homestead by the wood), in Yorkshire.

Wedel, Wedell, Weddle (*Eng.*) Descendant of Wedel (to move); dweller at Wada's hill; one who came from Wadley (Wada's wood or meadow), in Berkshire.

Wedemeyer (*Ger.*) The farmer or head servant who lived in, or near, the wood; variant of Widmeyer, q.v.

Wedge (*Eng.*) One who acted as pledge or surety for another.

Wedgewood, Wedgwood (*Eng.*) One who came from Wedgwood (guarded wood), in Staffordshire.

Wedlock, Wedlake (*Eng.*) One who gave a gift in pledge of marriage.

Weed (*Ger., Eng.*) Descendant of Wido, a pet form of names beginning with Wid (forest), as Widwalt and Widulf; dweller in, or near, a weedy place.

Weeden, Weedon (*Eng.*) One who came

from Weedon (temple on a hill), in Buckinghamshire.

Weedman (*Eng.*) One in charge of a heathen temple.

Weekley (*Eng.*) One who came from Weekley (wych elm wood), in Northamptonshire.

Weeks, Weaks, Weekes, Weeke (*Eng.*) Dweller at the dairy farm; one who came from Week (dairy farm), the name of several places in England.

Weems (*Scot.*) One who came from the lands of Wemyss (caves), pronounced Weems, in Fifeshire.

Weger (*Ger.*) Variant of Wager, q.v.

Weglarz (*Pol.*) One who dealt with coal.

Wegman, Wegmann (*Ger.*) Dweller at the way or path.

Wegner, Wegener (*Ger.*) One who made wagons, a cartwright; dweller near a path.

Wegrzyn (*Pol.*) One who came from Wegry, i.e., a Hungarian.

Wehr (*Ger.*) Descendant of Wehr, a pet form of Widher (wood, army).

Wehrle (*Ger.*) Descendant of Wehrle, a pet form of Warinhari (protection, army).

Weick (*Ger.*) Descendant of Weick, a pet form of names beginning with Wig (battle), as Wigirich and Wigwart.

Weidemann, Weideman (*Ger.*) One who hunts and fishes; one who came from Weiden (meadow), the name of many places in Germany; dweller by, or among, willow trees.

Weidenbach (*Ger.*) One who came from Weidenbach (meadow brook), the name of four places in Germany.

Weidinger (*Ger.*) One who came from Weiding or Weidingen (the meadow), the names of several places in Germany.

Weidman, Weidmann (*Ger.*) One who hunted game, a huntsman.

Weidner (*Ger.*) One who came from Weiden (meadow), the name of many places in Germany; one who hunted game, a huntsman; dweller

541

on, or near, a pasture; or by, or among, willow trees.

Weigand (*Ger.*) Descendant of Wigant (warrior).

Weightman (*Eng.*) Descendant of Wihtmann (elf, man); the brave, strong man.

Weigle, Weigel (*Ger.*) Descendant of Weigle, a pet form of Weigand (warrior).

Weik (*Ger.*) Descendant of Wigo (battle), a short form of names beginning with Wig (battle), such as Wigberht and Wigheri.

Weikert, Weikart (*Ger.*) Descendant of Wighard (battle, hard).

Weil, Weiler, Weill, Weiller (*Ger.*) One who came from Weil (house), in Wurttemberg.

Weiland (*Ger., Du.*) One who came from Weilen (hamlet), in Germany; a variant of Wieland, q.v.; dweller in the meadow.

Weiman, Weimann (*Ger.*) Variant of Weinman, q.v.

Weimer, Weimar (*Ger.*) One who came from Weimar (soft swamp), in Thuringia; descendant of Wigmar (fight or sanctify, famous); dweller on, or near, church property.

Wein (*Ger.*) One who made and sold wine.

Weinbaum (*Ger.*) Dweller near a grape vine.

Weinberg, Weinberger (*Ger., Swis.*) One who came from Weinberg or Weinberge (grape mountain), the name of many places in Germany and Switzerland; dweller at, or near, a vineyard.

Weindorfer, Weindorf (*Ger.*) One who came from Weindorf (wine village), in Germany.

Weiner (*Ger.*) Descendant of Winiheri (friend, army); one who made and sold wine; one who came from Weine, in Germany; one who made and sold wagons or carts.

Weinerman (*Ger.*) One who made and sold wagons and carts.

Weinert (*Ger.*) Descendant of Winihart

(friend, strong); one who made and sold wagons or carts.

Weinfeld (*Ger.*) Dweller in, or near, a field where grapes were grown.

Weingart, Weingard, Weingarten, Weingartner (*Ger.*) One who came from Weingarten (vineyard), the name of many places in Germany; one who lived in, or near, a vineyard.

Weinhardt (*Ger.*) Descendant of Winehart (friend, hard).

Weinman, Weinmann (*Ger.*) One who sold, or dispensed, wine; one who made and sold wagons or carts.

Weinrich, Weinreich (*Ger.*) Descendant of Winirich (friend, rule).

Weinstein (*Ger.*) Dweller on the Weinstein, a mountain in Germany; nickname for the shopkeeper who sold weinstein, that is, cream of tartar.

Weinstock (*Ger.*) Dweller near a large or unusual grapevine.

Weintraub, Weintrob, Weintroub (*Ger.*) One who grew, or handled, grapes.

Weinworm (*Ger.*) One who caroused, a tippler.

Weir (*Eng., Wel.*) Dweller near a dam or fish trap; one who came from Vere (place), the name of several places in France.

Weis (*Ger.*) The wise, prudent, or judicious man; variant of Weiss, q.v.

Weisbart, Weisbard (*Ger.*) One with a white beard.

Weisberg, Weissberg, Weisberger (*Ger., Cz.-Sl.*) One who came from Weisserberg (white mountain), the name of places in Germany and Czechoslovakia; dweller on, or near, a white hill.

Weisblatt (*Ger.*) White leaf.

Weisbord (*Ger.*) Variant of Weisbrod, q.v.

Weisbrod, Weisbrot (*Ger.*) One who made and sold white bread, a baker.

Weise (*Ger.*) Descendant of Weise (wisdom); the learned person; one who had no parents, an orphan; descendant of Wigo, a pet form of names beginning with Wid (forest), as Witbald and Wittimar.

Weiser (*Ger.*) One who came from Weis (white), in Germany; descendant of Wisheri (wise, army); a learned man; one who whitewashed walls.

Weisfeld (*Ger.*) White field; dweller on, or near, a white field.

Weisgrau (*Ger.*) One with light gray hair.

Weishaar, Weishar (*Ger.*) One who had white hair, usually designating an old man.

Weiskopf, Weisskopf, Weishaupt (*Ger.*) One with a white head, i.e., white hair.

Weisman, Weismann, Weiseman (*Ger.*) The wise or learned man; descendant of Wisman (wise, man).

Weiss (*Ger.*) One who came from Weis (white), in Germany; the light-complexioned or white-haired man; variant of Weitz, q.v.; one who came from Weiss, the name of two places in Germany.

Weissinger (*Ger.*) One who came from Wiessingen (wet grassland), in Germany.

Weissman, Weissmann (*Ger.*) The light-complexioned or white-haired man.

Weiswasser (*Ger.*) One who came from Weisswasser (white water), in Germany.

Weisz (*Hun.*) White; the light or fair-complexioned man; one with white hair.

Weitz, Weitzel (*Ger.*) Descendant of Wizo, a pet form of names beginning with Wid (forest), as Witbald and Wittimar, or with Wig (battle), as Wigibald and Wigbrand.

Weitzman, Weitzmann (*Ger.*) Same as Weitz, q.v.; one who dealt in corn and grain.

Welborn, Welburn, Welbourn (*Eng.*) One who came from Welborne (stream from a spring), in Norfolk; or from Welbourn, in Lincolnshire; or from Welburn, in the North Riding of Yorkshire.

Welby (*Eng.*) One who came from Welby (Ali's homestead; homestead by a spring), the name of places in Leicestershire and Lincolnshire.

Welch (*Eng.*) One who came from Wales, a Welshman.

Welcome (*Eng.*) One who came from Welcombe (valley with a stream), in Devonshire.

Weld (*Eng.*) One who came from Weald (woodland), the name of several places in England; dweller at a woodland.

Welding (*Eng.*) Descendant of Waldin (forest); dweller in a forest.

Weldon, Weldin (*Eng.*) One who came from Weldon (hill by a stream), in Northamptonshire.

Welfare (*Eng.*) One who wished others welfare; literally, a good journey; one who was well faring.

Welham (*Eng.*) One who came from Welham (homestead by the water; spring), the name of places in Leicestershire, Nottinghamshire, and the East Riding of Yorkshire.

Welke, Welk (*Cz.*) Dweller at the sign of the wolf; one with the characteristics of a wolf.

Welker (*Ger.*) One who cleaned and thickened cloth, a fuller.

Wellborn (*Eng.*) Variant of Welborn, q.v.

Weller (*Eng., Ger.*) One who boils, probably a saltboiler; one who casts metal; dweller at the spring or well; one who came from Well, in Germany.

Welling, Wellings (*Eng.*) One who came from Welwyn (willow), in Hertfordshire.

Wellington (*Eng.*) One who came from Wellington (village of the heathen temple in a glade), the name of several places in England.

Wellman (*Eng.*) Dweller at the spring or well.

Wellock (*Eng.*) One who came from Wheelock (turning river), in Cheshire.

Wells, Welles, Well, Welle (*Eng.*) Dweller at, or near, the spring or stream; one who came from Well (spring or stream), the name of several places in England.

Welp (*Ger.*) One in charge of young animals.

Welpton (*Eng.*) One who came from Whelpington (village of Hwelp's people), in Northumberland; dweller in a homestead where cubs were raised.

Welsby (*Eng.*) Variant of Welby, q.v.

Welsh, Welsch (*Eng.*) One who came from Wales, a Welshman.

Welter, Welther (*Ger.*) Variants of Walter, q.v.; one who came from Welte (fen), in Germany.

Welton (*Eng.*) One who came from Welton (homestead by a stream or on the Welve river), the name of various places in England.

Welty, Welte, Welti, Weltin (*Ger., Swis.*) Descendant of Welte, a pet form of names beginning with Walten (rule), as Walthari and Walhart; one who came from Welte (fen), in Germany.

Wembley (*Eng.*) One who came from Wembley (Wemba's grove), in Middlesex.

Wemyss (*Scot.*) One who came from Wemyss (caves), in Fifeshire.

Wendell, Wendel (*Ger.*) Descendant of little Wendimar (wander, famous).

Wendler (*Ger.*) One who travels about, a wanderer; one who makes a pilgrimage; descendant of Wendel (wandering).

Wendling (*Eng.*) One who came from Wendling (Wendel's people), in Norfolk.

Wendorf, Wendorff (*Ger.*) One who came from Wendorf (village of the Wends), the name of many places in Germany.

Wendt (*Ger.*) One who came from the Wends, a Slavic tribe of eastern Germany.

Wendy (*Eng.*) One who came from Wendy (island at the bend), in Cambridgeshire.

Wenger (*Ger.*) One who came from Weng or Wengen (sloping meadow),

the names of numerous places in Germany.

Wenick (*Eng.*) One who came from Winwick (Wina's farm; Wineca's farm), the name of places in Huntingdonshire, Northamptonshire, and Lancashire.

Wenig, Weniger (*Ger.*) The short, or small, man.

Wenitsky (*Ukr.*) One who came from Vinnytsja, in the Ukraine.

Wenk, Wenke, Wenkel, Wenkle (*Ger.*) Descendant of Wenk, a pet form of names beginning with Wahn (hope), as Wanger and Wanheri.

Wenner (*Ger.*) One who made and sold tubs and vats.

Wenograd (*Rus.*) Dweller in, or near, the grape vines or vineyard.

Wentworth (*Eng.*) One who came from Wentworth (Wintra's homestead), the name of places in Cambridgeshire and the West Riding of Yorkshire.

Wentz (*Ger.*) Descendant of Wentz, a pet form of Warinhari (protection, army).

Wenzel, Wentzel (*Ger.*) Descendant of Wenzel, a pet form of Wenzeslaus (garland, glory).

Werkley (*Eng.*) Dweller in, or near, Wirc's grove.

Werkman (*Eng.*) One who worked so many days a week for the lord of the manor in return for the land he held.

Werkmeister (*Ger.*) One who supervises the work of others, a foreman.

Wermer (*Ger.*) Descendant of Werimer (protection, fame).

Wermuth (*Ger.*) Dweller near where wormwood grew; descendant of Warmut (valiant, protection).

Werner (*Ger.*) Descendant of Warinhari (protection, army).

Wernick, Wernicke, Wernecke (*Ger.*) Variants of Warneke, q.v.

Werth, Wert (*Ger.*) Descendant of Wirth, a pet form of names beginning with Wert (worth), as Werdheri and Werdmann.

Wertheimer, Wertheim, Werthimer (*Ger.*) One who came from Wertheim (river island place), the name of several towns in Germany.

Werts, Wertz, Werz (*Ger.*) Descendant of Wero, a pet form of names beginning with War (guardian), as Warfrid, Warhart, and Warulf.

Wesby (*Eng.*) Variant of Westby, q.v.

Wescott, Wescoat, Wescoatt (*Eng.*) Variant of Westcott, q.v.

Wesebaum (*Ger.*) Dweller at, or near, the meadow tree.

Wesemann, Weseman (*Ger.*) Dweller on damp grassland or meadow.

Weslager (*Ger.*) American corruption of Wohlschlager, q.v.

Wesley (*Eng.*) One who came from Westleigh or Westley (western glade), the name of several places in England.

Wesolowski (*Pol.*) One who came from Wesolow (gay), in Poland.

Wessel, Wessels, Wessells, Wessell (*Ger.*) One who came from Wesel in Germany; descendant of little Varin, a pet form of names beginning with Warin (protector), as Warinbert and Warinhari.

Wessler (*Ger.*) Variant of Wechsler, q.v.

West (*Eng.*) One who came from the West, a west countryman.

Westberg (*Eng.*) One who came from Westborough (western fort), in Lincolnshire.

Westberry, Westbury (*Eng.*) One who came from Westbury (western fort), the name of seven places in England.

Westbrook (*Eng.*) One who came from Westbrook (western brook), the name of several places in England.

Westby (*Eng.*) One who came from Westby (western village), the name of places in Lancashire, Lincolnshire, and the West Riding of Yorkshire.

Westcott, Wescott, Westcot (*Eng.*) One who came from Westcot (western cottage), the name of several places in England; dweller at the western cottage.

Westdyke (*Eng.*) Dweller at the western embankment or ditch.

Westenberger, Westenberg (*Ger.*) One who came from Westenberg (the west mountain), in Germany.

Wester (*Du.*) One who came from the West.

Westerberg (*Sw.*) Western mountain.

Westerfield (*Eng.*) One who came from Westerfield (the westerly field), in Suffolk.

Westergaard (*Dan.*) Dweller at the western farm.

Westerhausen, Westerhouse (*Ger.*) One who came from Westerhausen (western house), the name of several places in Germany.

Westerlund (*Sw.*) West grove.

Westerman, Westermann (*Eng.*) The man who came from the West.

Westerveld, Westervelt (*Du.*) Dweller in, or near, the western open land or field.

Westfall, Westfal (*Ger., Nor.*) One who came from Westphalia (western plain), a province of Prussia; dweller at the western clearing.

Westfield (*Eng.*) One who came from Westfield (western plain), the name of places in Norfolk and Sussex.

Westgate (*Eng.*) One who came from Westgate (west gate), the name of several places in England.

Westinghouse (*Ger.*) Dweller in the house to the west.

Westlake (*Eng.*) Dweller at, or near, the west stream or pool.

Westley (*Eng.*) One who came from Westley (western grove), the name of places in Cambridgeshire and Suffolk.

Westlund (*Sw.*) West grove.

Westman (*Eng.*) The man who came from the west.

Weston (*Eng., Scot.*) One who lived in the western homestead; one who came from Weston (the western homestead; the homestead west of another), the name of many places in England, and in Lanarkshire and Peebleshire.

Westover (*Eng.*) One who came from Westover (western bank or shore), the name of places in Somerset and Wight.

Westphal, Westphalen (*Ger.*) One who came from Westphalen (western plain), in Germany.

Westwood (*Eng., Scot.*) One who came from Westwood (west of the wood; western wood), the name of four places in England; one who came from Westwood, the name of places in Fife and Perthshire.

Wetherby, Wetherbee (*Eng.*) One who came from Wetherby (sheep farm), in the West Riding of Yorkshire.

Wetherell, Wetherill, Wetherall, Wetherald (*Eng.*) One who came from Wetheral (enclosure where sheep were kept), in Cumberland; dweller near an enclosure where sheep were kept.

Wetherspoon (*Scot., Eng.*) Dweller at, or near, the wether or sheep enclosure.

Wetmore (*Eng.*) One who came from Wetmoor (lake by a river bend), in Staffordshire.

Wetter, Wetters (*Eng.*) Dweller by the water.

Wetzel, Wetzell (*Ger.*) Descendant of little Varin, a pet form of names beginning with Warin (protector), as Warinbert and Warinhari.

Wexler (*Ger.*) Variant of Wechsler, q.v.

Weyand (*Eng.*) Variant of Wyant, q.v.

Weyer (*Ger.*) Dweller near the swampy pool; one who came from Weyer (swampy pool), the name of several places in Germany.

Weyerhaeuser (*Ger.*) One who came from Weiershausen (swamp house), in Germany.

Weyland (*Eng.*) Variant of Wayland, q.v.

Weyman, Weymann (*Eng., Ger.*) Variant of Wayman, q.v.; variant of Weinman, q.v.

Weymouth (*Eng.*) One who came from Weymouth (mouth of the Wey river), in Dorset.

Whalen, Whalin, Whalon (*Ir.*) Grandson of Faolan (little wolf).

Whaley, Whalley (*Eng.*) One who came from Whaley (meadow by a road or hill), the name of places in Cheshire and Derbyshire.

Wham, Whan (*Eng., Scot.*) Dweller at a corner; or at a morass; one who came from Wham (cave), in Scotland.

Wharfield (*Eng.*) Variant of Warfield, q.v.

Wharton (*Eng.*) One who came from Wharton (homestead on Weaver river; or on an embankment), the name of several places in England.

Whatley, Whateley (*Eng.*) One who came from Whatley (grove where wheat was grown), in Somerset.

Whealton (*Eng.*) One who came from Wheelton (water wheel or circle homestead), in Lancashire.

Wheat (*Eng.*) The light-complexioned or white-haired man; a variant of Waite, q.v.

Wheatcroft, Wheatcraft (*Eng.*) Dweller in an enclosure where wheat was grown.

Wheatley (*Eng.*) One who came from Wheatley (open place where wheat was grown), the name of several places in England.

Wheaton (*Eng.*) One who came from Wheaton (homestead where wheat was grown), in Staffordshire.

Whedon (*Eng.*) One who came from Wheddon (wheat hill or valley), in Somerset.

Wheeler, Wheler (*Eng.*) One who made wheels and wheeled vehicles.

Wheelhouse (*Eng.*) Dweller near, or worker in, the house or shed covering a wheel turned by a stream.

Wheelock (*Eng.*) One who came from Wheelock (winding), in Cheshire; dweller near the Wheelock river.

Wheels, Wheel (*Eng.*) Dweller near, or worker at, a water wheel.

Wheelwright (*Eng.*) One who made wheels and wheeled vehicles.

Whelan, Wheland (*Ir.*) Grandson of Faolan (little wolf).

Whelpley (*Eng.*) Dweller in the wood frequented by cubs or young animals.

Whelton (*Eng.*) Variant of Whealton, q.v.

Wherrity (*Ir.*) Descendant of Faghartach (noisy).

Wherry (*Scot.*) The son of Guaire (proud); the beloved person.

Whertley (*Eng.*) One who came from Wortley (grove with plants), in the West Riding of Yorkshire.

Whetstone (*Eng.*) One who came from Whitstone (white rock), in Cornwall.

Whetts (*Eng.*) One who whets or sharpens tools.

Whidbee (*Eng.*) Variant of Whitby, q.v.

Whidden, Whiddon (*Eng.*) One who came from Wheddon (wheat hill or valley), in Somerset.

Whigham (*Eng.*) One who came from Whickham (homestead with quickset hedge), in Durham; one who worked on a dairy farm.

Whilby (*Eng.*) One who came from Wilby (village among willows), in Norfolk.

Whilden (*Eng.*) One who came from Wilden (willow valley), in Bedfordshire.

Whinney, Whinny, Whiney (*Eng.*) Dweller on the plain or hill covered by whin, a spiny evergreen shrub.

Whipple (*Eng.*) One who came from Whimple (white stream), in Devonshire.

Whipps, Whips (*Eng.*) Descendant of Wippa (swing).

Whisby (*Eng.*) One who came from Whisby (Hvit's homestead), in Lincolnshire.

Whisker (*Eng.*) Descendant of Wiscard (wise, hard); or of Wisgar (wise, spear).

Whisler (*Eng.*) Dweller near the fork of a river, from Old English *twisla* (fork of a river).

Whisman (*Eng.*) One with white hair or very light complexion.

Whissel, Whissell (*Eng.*) Metonymic for

a whistler, one who whistled or piped at fair and festival.

Whisted (*Sw., Nor., Dan.*) Holy place; pagan temple farm; one who came from Vista, the name of three places in Sweden.

Whistler (*Eng.*) One who whistled or piped at fair and festival.

Whiston (*Eng.*) One who came from Whiston (white stone; Hwit's homestead), the name of several places in England.

Whitacre (*Eng.*) One who came from Whitacre (white field), in Warwickshire; dweller at the white field.

Whitaker, Whiteaker (*Eng.*) Dweller at, or in, the white field; variant of Whitacre, q.v.

Whitall (*Eng.*) One who came from Whittle (white hill), the name of places in Lancashire and Northumberland; dweller near, or in, a white hall or manor house; or in a white corner or nook.

Whitcomb (*Eng.*) One who came from Whitbeck (white stream), in Cumberland.

Whitby (*Eng.*) One who came from Whitby (white village), the name of places in Cheshire and the North Riding of Yorkshire.

Whitcher (*Eng.*) One who made whitches, i.e., chests and coffers.

Whitcomb (*Eng.*) One who came from Whitcombe (wide valley), the name of places in Dorset and Wiltshire.

Whitcraft (*Eng.*) Dweller near enclosed land where wheat was grown.

White (*Eng.*) The light or fair-complexioned person; one with white hair; descendant of Hwita (white); variant of Waite, q.v.; dweller by a bend or curve in a river or road; dweller near a look-out post.

Whitecotton (*Eng.*) Dweller at the white cottages.

Whited, Whitted (*Eng.*) Contracted form of Whitehead, q.v.

Whitefield (*Eng., Scot.*) One who came from Whitefield (white open country), the name of places in Gloucestershire and Lancashire; or from Whitefield, the name of several places in Scotland.

Whitehair (*Eng.*) The white or fair-haired man.

Whitehall (*Eng.*) Dweller near, or worker in, the white hall or manor house; dweller near a white corner or nook.

Whitehead (*Eng.*) One with a white head, i.e., white hair; one who wore a white hood; dweller at the light head of a field or top of the hill.

Whitehill (*Eng., Scot.*) One who came from Whitehill (white hill; hill with a hollow), the name of places in Durham and Oxfordshire; or from Whitehill, the name of several places in Scotland.

Whitehouse (*Eng.*) Dweller in, or near, a white house.

Whitehurst (*Eng.*) Dweller in or near a white copse or wooded hill.

Whitelaw (*Scot.*) One who came from Whitelaw (white hill), the name of places in Scotland.

Whiteley, Whitely (*Eng.*) Variant of Whitley, q.v.

Whitemarsh (*Eng.*) Dweller near the white marsh or swamp.

Whitemore (*Eng.*) Dweller on a white wasteland; or near a white lake; one who came from Whitmoor (white wasteland), in Staffordshire.

Whiten (*Eng.*) Variant of Whitten, q.v.

Whitenack (*Eng.*) Dweller near the white oak tree.

Whitener (*Eng.*) One who bleaches or whitens cloth.

Whiteoak (*Eng.*) Dweller near the white oak tree, a British species of oak.

Whiters (*Eng.*) One who whitewashes; or who bleaches or whitens wool.

Whitesell (*Ger.*) American respelling of Witzel, q.v.

Whiteside (*Eng.*) Dweller on the white side (of a hill, valley, etc.).

Whitesmith (*Eng.*) One who worked in tin.

Whitestone (*Eng.*) One who came from Whitestone (white rock), in Devonshire.

Whiteway (*Eng.*) Dweller at the white road; one who came from Whiteway (white clay way), in Devonshire.

Whitfield (*Eng.*) One who came from Whitfield (white field), the name of several places in England.

Whitford (*Eng.*) One who came from Whitford (white ford), in Devonshire.

Whitham (*Eng.*) Dweller at the white homestead; one who came from Whitwham (white valley or corner), in Northumberland.

Whithead (*Eng.*) Variant of Whitehead, q.v.

Whithorn (*Scot.*) One who came from Whithorn (white house), in Wigtown.

Whiting (*Eng.*) Descendant of Whiting (Hwita's son); dweller at the white meadow.

Whitledge (*Eng.*) Dweller on the white ledge or shelf.

Whitley (*Eng.*) One who came from Whitleigh (white wood), the name of several places in England.

Whitlock, Whitelock (*Eng.*) One who had white hair; dweller at, or near, the white enclosure.

Whitlow (*Eng.*) Dweller on, or at, the white hill or burial mound.

Whitman, Whiteman (*Eng.*) The light-complexioned or white-haired man; descendant of Hwitman (white man).

Whitmarsh (*Eng.*) Dweller in, or near, the white marsh or bog.

Whitmire, Whitmer (*Eng.*) Dweller near the white lake.

Whitmore, Whittemore (*Eng.*) One who came from Whitmore (white moor), in Staffordshire.

Whitner (*Eng.*) Variant of Whitener, q.v.

Whitney (*Eng.*) One who came from Whitney (Hwita's island; white island), in Herefordshire.

Whitridge (*Eng.*) Dweller at the white ridge; one who came from Whitridge (white ridge), in Northumberland.

Whitson (*Eng.*) The son of Hwita (white); variant of Whitestone, q.v.

Whitt (*Eng.*) Variant of White, q.v.

Whittaker (*Eng.*) Variant of Whitaker, q.v.

Whittall (*Eng.*) Variant of Whitehall, q.v.; one who came from Whittle (white hill), the name of places in Lancashire and Northumberland.

Whittel, Whittell (*Eng.*) Variant of Whittle, q.v.

Whittelsey (*Eng.*) Variant of Whittlesey, q.v.

Whittemore (*Eng.*) Variant of Whitemore, q.v.

Whitten (*Eng.*) One who came from Whitton (Hwita's homestead; white homestead), the name of several places in England.

Whittier (*Eng.*) One who prepared white leather; one who came from Whitacre (white field), in Warwickshire.

Whittill (*Eng.*) Variant of Whittle, q.v.

Whittington (*Eng.*) One who came from Whittington (homestead of Hwita's people), the name of several places in England.

Whittle (*Eng.*) One who came from Whittle (white hill), the name of places in Lancashire and Northumberland.

Whittlesey (*Eng.*) One who came from Whittlesey (little Witta's island), in Cambridgeshire.

Whittmer (*Eng.*) Variant of Whitmire, q.v.

Whittock, Whittick (*Eng.*) Variants of Whiteoak, q.v.

Whitton (*Eng.*) One who came from Whitton (Hwita's homestead; the white homestead), the name of various places in England.

Whittredge, Whittridge (*Eng.*) Dweller at, or near, a white ridge or range of hills.

Whitty, Whitey (*Eng.*) Dweller at the white enclosure; one with white eyes.

Whitwell (*Eng.*) One who came from Whitwell (white stream or spring), the name of nine places in England.

Whitworth (*Eng.*) One who came from Whitworth (Hwita's homestead), the name of places in Durham and Lancashire.

Wholey, Wholley, Wholly, Whooley (*Ir.*) Grandson of Uallach (proud; boastful); the boastful man.

Whomsley (*Eng.*) Variant of Wamsley, q.v.

Whoriskey, Whorisky (*Ukr.*) One who gathered and sold nuts.

Why, Whye (*Eng.*) Descendant of Guy (wood).

Whyatt (*Eng.*) Variant of Wyatt, q.v.

Whybrow (*Eng.*) Descendant of Wigburh (battle, fortress); one who came from Wigborough (Wicga's mound), in Essex.

Whynot, Whynott, Whynaught (*Fr.*) Descendant of little Guyon (little wood).

Whyte (*Eng.*) Variant of White, q.v.

Wiberg (*Ger.*) One who came from Weiberg, the name of two places in Germany.

Wiborg (*Dan.*) One who came from Viborg, in Denmark.

Wich, Wiche (*Eng.*) Dweller by the wych-elm tree; dweller at, or near, a salt spring.

Wichman, Wichmann (*Ger.*) Descendant of Wigman (battle, man).

Wichterman, Wichtermann (*Ger.*) The little man, dwarf, midget or elf.

Wick, Wicker, Wicke (*Eng.*) Dweller at the dairy farm; one who came from Wick (dairy farm), the name of several places in England.

Wickersham (*Eng.*) Dweller in, or near, the estate belonging to the steward.

Wickett (*Eng.*) Dweller by a small gate.

Wickham, Wickum, Wickhem (*Eng.*) One who came from Wickham (manor or dwelling place; homestead with a dairy farm), the name of various places in England.

Wicklund (*Sw.*) Variant of Wiklund, q.v.

Wickman (*Eng.*) One who worked on a dairy farm.

Wicks, Wickes, Wix (*Eng.*) The son of little Wilk, a pet form of William (resolution, helmet); variants of

549

Wick, q.v.; one who came from Wix (dairy farms), in Essex.

Wickstrom (*Sw.*) Variant of Wikstrom, q.v.

Widamen, Widaman (*Ger.*) Variant of Wideman, q.v.

Widder (*Eng., Ger.*) Descendant of Widhere (great, army); dweller at the sign of the ram.

Widdicomb, Widdicombe (*Eng.*) One who came from Widdicombe (willow valley), in Devonshire.

Widdifield (*Eng.*) Dweller in, or near, an open space where willows grew.

Widdop (*Eng.*) Dweller on wide, dry land in a fen.

Widdows, Widdowson (*Eng.*) The son of the widow, the woman who has lost her husband by death, and did not remarry.

Wideman, Widman, Widmann (*Ger.*) Descendant of Widiman (forest, man); one who hunts game, a hunter; dweller at the place where willows grew; one who took care of church property.

Widen, Widden (*Eng.*) Dweller in the broad valley; one who came from Weedon (hill with a temple), the name of several places in England.

Widener (*Ger.*) Variant of Weidner, q.v.

Widger, Widgar (*Eng.*) Descendant of Wihtgar (elf, spear).

Widmaier, Widmayer (*Ger.*) Variant of Widmeyer, q.v.

Widmer (*Ger.*) One in charge of the parish church or other parochial property.

Widmeyer, Witmeyer (*Ger.*) One who worked a farm, the products of which went to the support of a church.

Wieczorek, Wieczerak (*Pol.*) One who engaged in some activity in the early evening.

Wiedemann, Wiedeman (*Ger.*) Dweller at the willow thicket; one who hunts and fishes.

Wiedemer (*Ger.*) Variant of Widmer, q.v.

Wiedenmann, Wiedenman (*Ger.*) One who hunts game, a hunter.

Wiedman, Wiedmann (*Ger.*) Variant of Wideman, q.v.

Wiedmayer (*Ger.*) Variant of Widmeyer, q.v.

Wiegand (*Ger.*) Descendant of Wigant (warrior).

Wiegel, Wiegele (*Ger.*) Descendant of Wigilo, a pet form of names beginning with Wig (fight; sanctify), as Wigold, Wigland, and Wigheri.

Wieland (*Ger.*) Descendant of Wieland or Wayland (work by hand), the fabled smith.

Wielgus (*Pol.*) The large, husky man.

Wien, Wiens (*Ger.*) One who came from Wien (town of the Wends), in Austria. The English name is Vienna.

Wiencek (*Pol.*) Descendant of Wiencek, a pet form of Wiencyslaw (more glorious than his parents).

Wieneke (*Ger.*) Descendant of little Wien, a pet form of Wienand or Wignand (friend, brave).

Wiener, Wieners (*Ger.*) One who came from Wien (Vienna), in Austria.

Wiercinsky (*Pol.*) One who bores or drills; one who fashions objects on a lathe, a turner.

Wierzbicki, Wierzba (*Pol.*) Dweller near a willow tree.

Wiese (*Ger.*) Dweller in, or near, a meadow.

Wiesen, Wieser, Wiesner (*Ger.*) One who came from Wiesen (meadow), the name of various places in Germany; dweller in the meadow.

Wiest, Wiestner (*Ger.*) Dweller on, or near, the uncultivated land; or on the rough wasteland.

Wigand (*Eng.*) Descendant of Wigand (warrior).

Wigfall (*Eng.*) Dweller on the hill where a battle was fought.

Wiggins, Wiggin (*Eng.*) Descendant of little Wicga (warrior); or of Wigan or Wygan (warrior); one who came from Wigan (Wigan's homestead), in Lancashire; dweller by a mountain ash.

Wigginton (*Eng.*) One who came from Wigginton (Wicga's village), the name of several places in England.

Wiggle (*Eng., Ger.*) One who came from Wighill (corner with a dairy farm); descendant of Wincel (child); or of Wiggo, a short form of names beginning with Wig (fight), such as Wigberht, Wigbrand, Wighard, and Wigheri.

Wigglesworth (*Eng.*) One who came from Wigglesworth (Wincel's homestead), in Yorkshire.

Wiggs, Wigg (*Eng.*) Descendant of Wig (battle); or Wiga (warrior).

Wight (*Eng.*) One who came from the Isle of Wight (that which has been raised), part of the former county of Hampshire.

Wightman (*Scot., Eng.*) The agile, or strong, man; the man from Wight, q.v.

Wighton (*Eng.*) One who came from Wighton (dwelling place), in Norfolk.

Wigman (*Eng.*) One engaged in military service, a warrior; one who worked on a dairy farm.

Wigmore (*Eng.*) One who came from Wigmore (Wicga's wasteland), in Herefordshire.

Wigton (*Eng.*) One who came from Wigton (Wicga's homestead), in Cumberland.

Wiig, Wiigh, Wieg (*Nor.*) Dweller near the bay or cove; one who worked, or lived, on a farm so named.

Wike (*Eng., Ger.*) One who came from Wick (dairy farm), in Gloucestershire; one who came from Wike (dairy farm), in the West Riding of Yorkshire; descendant of Wigo, a short form of names beginning with Wig (battle), such as Wigberht and Wigheri.

Wiklund (*Sw.*) Cove, grove.

Wikstrom (*Sw.*) Cove, stream.

Wilberforce (*Eng.*) One who came from Wilberfoss (Wilburg's ditch), in the East Riding of Yorkshire.

Wilberg (*Nor.*) One who came from Vil-

berg, the name of six places in Norway.

Wilbert, Wilber (*Eng.*) Descendant of Wilbeorht (will, bright); or of Wilburh (will, stronghold).

Wilborn, Wilbon (*Eng.*) One who came from Welborne (brook from a spring), in Norfolk.

Wilbraham (*Eng.*) One who came from Wilbraham (Wilburg's estate), in Cambridgeshire.

Wilbur (*Eng.*) Descendant of Wilburh or Wilburg (beloved, stronghold), a woman's name.

Wilburn, Wilborn, Wilbourn, Wilborne (*Eng.*) One who came from Welborne (brook coming from a spring), the name of several places in England; dweller at the stream where willows grew.

Wilby, Wilbee (*Eng.*) One who came from Wilby (homestead among willows; Willa's homestead), the name of places in Norfolk, Northamptonshire, and Suffolk.

Wilcher (*Eng.*) One who came from Wilpshire (lisping manor), in Lancashire; variant of Wiltshire, q.v.

Wilcock (*Eng.*) Descendant of little Will, a pet form of William (resolution; helmet); one who came from Wilcott (Winela's cottage), in Shropshire.

Wilcots, Wilcutts (*Eng.*) One who came from Wilcot (cottage by a spring), in Wiltshire; or from Wilcott (Winela's cottage), in Shropshire.

Wilcox, Willcox (*Eng.*) Descendant of little Will, a pet form of William (resolution, helmet).

Wilcoxon, Wilcoxson (*Eng.*) The son of little Will, a pet form of William (resolution, helmet).

Wilczak, Wilczek (*Pol.*) Dweller at the sign of the little wolf; one thought to have some characteristic of a wolf cub.

Wilczynski (*Pol.*) Dweller at the sign of the wolf cub.

Wildberger (*Ger.*) One who came from

551

Wildberg (jungle hill), the name of four places in Germany.

Wilde, Wild (*Eng.*) One who came from Wild or Wyld (trick), in Berkshire; dweller on a wasteland.

Wildemore (*Eng.*) One who came from Wildmore (waste moor), in Lincolnshire.

Wilder (*Eng.*) Dweller in a forest; descendant of Wealdhere (powerful, army); dweller at the sign of the wild animal.

Wilderman (*Eng.*) The servant of Wealdhere (might, army).

Wildermuth (*Ger.*) Descendant of Wildermut (unrestrained spirit); the joyous, gay spirited man; one who exhibits unpredictable behavior.

Wildey (*Eng.*) Descendant of Waltheof (foreign, serf).

Wildgust (*Eng.*) Dweller at the sign of the wild goose; one thought to possess the characteristics of a wild goose.

Wilding (*Eng., Ger.*) The son of Wild (wild); dweller on the uncultivated land or wasteland.

Wildman (*Eng.*) The savage, fierce man.

Wilds, Wildes (*Eng.*) One who came from Wild (trick), in Berkshire.

Wildsmith (*Ger., Eng.*) The smith, the worker in metals, who lived and worked in the forest; one who made wheels, a wheelwright.

Wilensky (*Pol., Rus., Ukr.*) One who came from Vilnas in Lithuania.

Wiles, Wile (*Eng.*) Dweller on the waste or uncultivated land; softening of Wilds, q.v.

Wiley (*Eng.*) Dweller near a trap or mill; dweller near the Wylye or Wiley (tricky river), a river in Wiltshire; one who came from Wylye, in Wiltshire.

Wilford (*Eng.*) One who came from Wilford (ford near where willows grew), in Nottinghamshire.

Wilhelm (*Ger.*) Descendant of Wilhelm, German form of William (resolution, helmet).

Wilk (*Pol., Eng.*) Polish form of Wolf, q.v.; shortened form of Wilkins, q.v.

Wilken, Wilkin (*Eng., Du.*) Descendant of little Will, a pet form of William (resolution, helmet).

Wilkerson, Wilker (*Eng.*) Variant of Wilkinson, q.v.

Wilkes, Wilke, Wilks (*Eng.*) Shortened form of Wilkins or Wilkinson, q.v.

Wilkie, Wilkey (*Scot., Eng.*) Descendant of little Wilk, a shortened form of Wilkins or Wilkinson, q.v.

Wilkinson, Wilkins, Wilkens (*Eng., Du.*) The son of little Will, a pet form of William (resolution, helmet).

Will (*Eng.*) Descendant of Will, a pet form of William (resolution, helmet); or of Willa (will); dweller at, or near, a spring or stream.

Willard (*Eng.*) Descendant of Wilhead (resolution, brave).

Wille (*Ger., Eng.*) Descendant of Wille (resolution), or of Willo, a pet form of names beginning with Wille, as Willifrid, Willibrand, and Willimod.

Willeke, Willecke (*Ger.*) Descendant of little Willo, a pet form of names beginning with Wille (resolution), as Willifrid, Williger, and Willamar.

Willem, Willems, Willemsen (*Du.*) Descendant of Willem, Dutch form of William (resolution, helmet).

Willer, Willers (*Eng., Ger.*) Descendant of Wilhere (desire, army); or of Williheri (resolution, army); one who made baskets; dweller at, or near, a spring or stream.

Willett, Willet, Willette (*Eng.*) Descendant of little Will, a pet form of William (resolution, helmet); dweller near the Willett (stream), a river in Somerset; one who came from Willet (stream), a village in Somerset.

Willey (*Eng.*) Descendant of little Will, a pet form of William (resolution, helmet); one who came from Willey (willow wood; heathen temple in a wood), the name of six places in England.

Willgoos, Willgoss (*Eng.*) Dweller at the

sign of the wild goose; one thought to possess the characteristics of a wild goose; metonymic for one who hunted wild geese.

Willi (*Ger.*) Descendant of Willi, a pet from of Wilhelm, German form of William (resolution, helmet).

William (*Eng.*) Descendant of William (resolution, helmet).

Williams, Williamson (*Wel., Eng.*) The son of William (resolution, helmet).

Williamston (*Eng.*) Dweller at William's homestead.

Williard (*Eng.*) Descendant of Willard or Wilhead (resolution, brave).

Willie (*Eng.*) Descendant of little Will, a pet form of William (resolution, helmet).

Williford (*Eng.*) One who came from Wilford (willow ford), the name of places in Nottinghamshire and Suffolk; dweller at a river crossing where willows grew.

Willig (*Ger.*) Descendant of Willi, a pet form of Wilhelm, German form of William (resolution, helmet).

Williman (*Eng., Fr.*) Descendant of Guillemin, a pet form of Guillaume, French form of William (resolution, helmet).

Willing, Willin, Willings (*Eng.*) Descendant of little Will, a pet form of William (resolution, helmet).

Willingham (*Eng.*) One who came from Willingham (village of Wifel's people; or of Willa's people), the name of several places in England.

Willington (*Eng.*) One who came from Willington (homestead among willows; Winflaed's homestead; homestead of Wifel's people; homestead of Wiglaf's people), the name of four places in England, all with different derivations.

Willis, Willison (*Eng.*) The son of Will, a pet form of William (resolution, helmet).

Williston (*Eng.*) One who came from Willaston (Wiglaf's homestead), in Cheshire.

Willits (*Eng.*) Variant of Willett, q.v.

Willkie (*Scot., Eng.*) Variant of Wilkie, q.v.

Willner (*Ger.*) One who came from Wildenau, the name of two places in Germany.

Willoughby (*Eng.*) One who came from Willoughby (homestead among willows), the name of various places in England.

Wills (*Eng.*) The son of Will, a pet form of William (resolution, helmet).

Wilmer, Willmer (*Eng.*) Descendant of Wilmer (resolution, fame).

Wilmington (*Eng.*) One who came from Wilmington (village of Wilhelm's people; Willa's meadow hill), the name of five places in England.

Wilmore (*Eng.*) Variant of Wilmer, q.v.

Wilmot, Wilmoth (*Fr.*) Contraction of Willemotte, a regional form of Guillemotte (resolution, helmet), a woman's name.

Wilms, Wilmsen, Wilmes, Wilm (*Dan., Ger.*) Descendant of Wilm, a shortened form of Wilhelm or William (resolution, helmet).

Wilner (*Ger.*) Variant of Willner, q.v.

Wilsey, Willsey (*Eng.*) Descendant of little Will, a pet form of William (resolution, helmet); one who came from the island belonging to Will.

Wilshaw, Wilsher, Willsher (*Eng.*) Same as Wiltshire, q.v.

Wilson, Willson (*Eng., Scot.*) The son of Will, pet form of William (resolution, helmet).

Wilt, Wiltz (*Ger.*) Descendant of Willihard (resolution, brave).

Wilton (*Eng.*) One who came from Wilton (homestead among willows; or by a well), the name of several places in England.

Wiltshire (*Eng.*) One who came from Wiltshire (district dependent on Wilton), a county in England.

Wimberly, Wimberley, Wimbley (*Eng.*) One who came from Wimboldsley (Wynbald's wood), in Cheshire.

Wimble (*Eng.*) Descendant of Winebald (friend, bold); metonymic for one who made and sold wimples, a woman's head covering.

Wimbush (*Eng.*) One who came from Wimbush (vine bush), in Essex.

Wimer (*Eng.*) Descendant of Wigmaer (battle, fame).

Wimmer (*Ger.*) One who came from Wimm or Wimmer (tree stumps), the names of several places in Germany; dweller among tree stumps; one who tended the vines in a vineyard; one who took care of church property; descendant of Winimar (friend, fame).

Winandy, Winand (*Ger., Du.*) Descendant of Wignand (combat, venture).

Winberg (*Nor., Sw.*) Dweller in, or near, a vineyard.

Winbish, Winbush (*Eng.*) Variant of Wimbush, q.v.

Winborne, Winborn, Winburn (*Eng.*) One who came from Wimborne (meadow stream), in Dorset; dweller near the Wimborne, the name of a river in Dorset.

Winch (*Eng.*) Dweller at a bend or corner; or at a well from which water was drawn by means of a rope and pulley.

Winchell, Winchel (*Eng.*) Descendant of Wincel (child); dweller by a corner or nook.

Winchester (*Eng.*) One who came from Winchester (Roman fort of Wintan), in Hampshire.

Wind, Winde (*Eng.*) Dweller on the narrow street or passage turning off from the main thoroughfare.

Winder, Winders (*Eng.*) One who came from Winder (shelter from the wind), the name of places in Cumberland and Westmorland; one engaged in winding, probably a winder of wool; dweller by a bend.

Winderman (*Eng.*) One engaged in winding, usually a winder of wool.

Windham (*Eng.*) One who came from Wenham (meadow homestead), in Suffolk; variant of Wyndham, q.v.

Windisch (*Ger.*) One from the Wends, a Slavic people living in Northern Germany.

Windle (*Eng.*) One who came from Windle (winding hill; windy hill), in Lancashire; descendant of little Wenda (boundary).

Windley (*Eng.*) One who came from Windley (meadow grove), in Derbyshire.

Windmiller, Windmueller (*Ger.*) One who owned, or dwelt by, a windmill.

Windsor (*Eng.*) One who came from Windsor or Winsor (landing place with a windlass), the names of several places in England.

Wine (*Eng.*) Descendant of Wine, a pet form of names beginning with Wine (friend), as Winebald and Winegod; an esteemed person, a friend.

Winegrad, Winegred (*Pol.*) One who worked in the vineyard; dweller by the vineyard; variant of Winograd, q.v.

Winer (*Ger.*) One who came from Wien (Vienna), in Austria; one who dealt in wines.

Winfield (*Eng.*) One who came from Wingfield (grazing ground), in Derbyshire.

Winfree, Winfrey (*Eng.*) One who came from Winfrith (white stream), in Dorset.

Wing, Winge (*Chin., Eng.*) Warm; one who came from Wing (Weohthun's people, or field), the name of places in Buckinghamshire and Rutland; descendant of Winge (protector).

Wingard (*Eng.*) Dweller at, or near, a vineyard.

Wingate (*Eng.*) One who came from Wingate (pass where wind rushes through), in Durham.

Winger, Wingar (*Eng.*) Descendant of Winegar (friend, spear).

Wingert, Wingerter (*Ger.*) Dweller in, or near, a vineyard.

Wingfield (*Eng.*) One who came from Wingfield (grazing ground; field of Wiga's people), the name of various places in England.

Winiarski (*Pol.*) One who sold wine, a wine-merchant.

Winitz (*Cz.-Sl., Pol.*) Dweller in, or near, a vineyard.

Wink (*Eng.*) Variant of Winch, q.v.; descendant of Wineca, a pet form of Wine (friend).

Winkler, Winkelman, Winkel, Winkle, Winkleman, Winkelmann (*Ger., Du.*) Dweller on land enclosed by mountains or woods; one who came from Winkel (corner); one who operated a small shop.

Winn, Winne (*Eng.*) Dweller at a meadow or pasture.

Winner (*Eng., Ger.*) Dweller in, or near, a meadow or pasture; descendant of Wynhere (joy, army); one who came from Winn or Winnen, the names of several places in Germany.

Winning (*Eng.*) The son of Wine, a pet form of names beginning with Wine (friend), as Winebald and Winegod.

Winograd (*Pol.*) One who came from Winograd (vine branch; vineyard), in Poland.

Winpenny (*Eng.*) Nickname for a miser; a covetous, grasping person.

Winrow (*Eng.*) One who came from Whinneray (bent grass corner), in Cumberland; dweller at the corner where whin grew.

Winscom, Winscombe (*Eng.*) One who came from Winscombe (Wine's valley), in Somerset.

Winship (*Eng.*) One who played the part of Friendship in the medieval pageants.

Winslow, Winsloe (*Eng.*) One who came from Winslow (Wine's burial mound), in Buckinghamshire.

Winsor (*Eng.*) One who came from Winsor (landing place with a windlass), the name of places in Devonshire and Hampshire; variant of Windsor, q.v.

Winstanley (*Eng.*) One who came from Winstanley (Wynstan's grove), in Lancashire.

Winstead (*Eng.*) One who came from Winestead (wife's place), in the East Riding of Yorkshire.

Winston (*Eng.*) One who came from Winston (Wine's or Winec's homestead), the name of several places in England.

Wint (*Du.*) The windy man or braggart.

Winterborne (*Eng.*) One who came from Winterborne (stream dry except in winter), the name of several places in England.

Winterbottom, Winterbotham (*Eng.*) Dweller at the valley or hollow used by shepherds for shelter in the winter.

Winterer (*Eng.*) One who sold wines, a wine merchant.

Winters, Winter (*Eng., Ger.*) Descendant of Winter (name given to one born during the winter); dweller at the white water; descendant of Winidhari (wind, army); one who dealt in wine.

Wintersmith (*Eng.*) The smith who worked in a different place in the winter.

Winthrop (*Eng.*) One who came from Winthorpe (Wina's, or Wigmund's, dairy farm), the name of places in Lincolnshire and Nottinghamshire.

Winton (*Eng.*) One who came from Winton (grazing farm; Wina's homestead; homestead with willows), the name of several places in England.

Wintz (*Ger.*) Descendant of Wintz, a short form of names beginning with Win (friend), as Winihart, Winimar, and Winulf.

Winward (*Eng.*) One who worked in, or lived near, a vineyard.

Winzer (*Ger.*) One who cultivates a vineyard and makes wine, a vintager.

Wipplinger (*Ger.*) One who came from Wippling (mire), in Germany.

Wirth, Wirt (*Eng., Ger.*) One who came from Worth (enclosure), the name of several places in England; one who acted as host in a tavern or inn.

Wirtschafter, Wirtshafter (*Ger.*) One who entertains; the steward or manager in a large household.

Wirtz, Wirz (*Ger.*) One who acted as host in a tavern or inn.

Wisdom (*Eng., Ir.*) One noted for his wisdom and learning, but sometimes a nickname ironically applied; descendant of Wisdom (knowledge; learning); one who came from Wisdom in Devonshire; grandson of Ceile (servant; friend).

Wise (*Eng., Scot., Ger.*) The sage or learned man; dweller by a stream or marshy meadow.

Wiseley, Wisely, Wisley (*Eng.*) One who came from Wisley (meadow grove), in Surrey.

Wiseman, Wisman (*Eng., Scot.*) A learned man; one who practiced magic arts; one who played the part of one of the "wise men" of the East in the Candlemas pageant; a nickname sometimes ironically applied to a fool.

Wish, Wisher (*Eng.*) Dweller at, or near, a marsh.

Wisham (*Eng.*) One who came from Wesham (western dwellings), in Lancashire.

Wishard, Wishart (*Eng.*) The wise, sagacious man; descendant of Guiscard (wise, hard).

Wishnov, Wishnow (*Pol., Rus.*) Dweller near a cherry tree.

Wisler (*Eng.*) Softened form of Whistler, q.v.

Wismer (*Ger.*) One who came from Wismer, the name of several places in Germany.

Wisner, Wissner (*Ger.*) One who came from Wissen (white sand), in Germany; dweller on, or near, a meadow.

Wisneski, Wisnesky (*Pol.*) Dweller near a cherry tree; one who raised and sold cherries.

Wisniewski (*Pol.*) One who came from Wisznia (cherry tree), in Poland.

Wissman, Wissmann (*Ger.*) Dweller in the meadow.

Wister (*Ger.*) One who came from Wust (deserted), the name of two places in Germany.

Wiswall, Wiswell (*Eng.*) One who came from Wiswell (Wissey river), in Lancashire.

Witalec (*Ukr.*) One who welcomes or greets others.

Witcher, Wicher (*Eng.*) Dweller by the wych-elm tree; dweller at, or near, a salt spring.

Witek (*Pol.*) Descendant of Witek, a pet form of Witosz or Witold (with, rule).

Witham (*Eng.*) One who came from Witham (Wita's homestead), the name of several places in England; dweller near the Witham (forest river), a river in England.

Withee, Withey (*Eng.*) Dweller at a willow tree.

Witherell (*Eng.*) A variant of Wetherell, q.v.

Witherow (*Eng.*) Dweller on a lane or row where willows grew.

Withers (*Eng., Wel.*) Dweller at the sign of the ram; the son of Gwythyr (victor).

Witherspoon (*Eng.*) A variant of Weatherspoon, q.v.

Withington (*Eng.*) One who came from Withington (homestead among willows), the name of several places in England.

Withrow (*Eng.*) Dweller at a lane through the willow trees.

Withycombe (*Eng.*) One who came from Withycombe (willow valley), the name of places in Devonshire and Somerset.

Witkin, Witkind (*Rus.*) Descendant of Vitke, a diminutive of Vitka (life).

Witkowski (*Pol.*) The son of Witek, a pet form of Witold (with, rule).

Witney (*Eng.*) One who came from Witney (Witta's island), in Oxfordshire.

Witt, Witte, Witty, Witts (*Du., Ger., Eng., Fr.*) The light-haired or light-complexioned man; variant of White, q.v.

Witten, Witton (*Eng.*) One who came from Witton (homestead by a village or wood), the name of many places in England.

Wittenberg, Wittenberger (*Ger.*) One

who came from Wittenberg (white mountain), in Germany.

Wittick (*Eng.*) One who came from Whitwick (white farm), pronounced Wittick, in Leicestershire.

Wittig (*Ger.*) Descendant of Wittig, a pet form of names beginning with Wid (wood), as Widulf and Widwalt.

Wittmaier (*Ger.*) The steward or farmer who lives in the woodland.

Wittman, Wittmann (*Eng., Ger.*) Descendant of Hwitman (white, man); the white or white-haired man.

Wittmer (*Ger.*) One who came from Wittmar, in Germany; descendant of Wittimar (forest, fame).

Wittrock (*Ger.*) One who wore a white coat.

Wittwer, Witwer (*Ger.*) One whose wife has died, a widower.

Witz, Witzel (*Ger.*) Descendant of Witzel, a pet form of names beginning with Wig (battle), or Wid (wood), as Wignand and Widfrid.

Wixted (*Eng.*) One who came from Wicksted (dairy-farm site), in Wiltshire.

Wlock (*Pol.*) The foreigner or stranger.

Wlodarczyk, Wlodarski (*Pol.*) Descendant of the steward.

Wlotko (*Pol.*) Descendant of Wlotko, a pet form of Wlodzimierz, Polish form of Vladimir (glory of princes).

Wnek (*Cz.-Sl.*) Grandson, probably a shortened form of a longer name; one associated with his grandfather.

Wode (*Eng.*) Early form of Wood, q.v.

Wodrich, Wodrick (*Ger.*) Descendant of Wodrich or Wodaricus (battle rage, king).

Woehr (*Ger.*) Dweller on an elevated spot in a wet area or marsh.

Woehrle (*Ger.*) Descendant of Woehrle, a pet form of Warinhari (protection, army).

Woerner, Woern (*Ger.*) Variant of Werner, q.v.

Woertz (*Ger.*) Variant of Werts, q.v.

Woffenden (*Eng.*) Variant of Wolfenden, q.v.

Wofford (*Eng.*) One who came from Wolford (enclosure for protection against wolves), in Warwickshire.

Wogan (*Eng.*) One who scowls or frowns.

Wohl (*Ger.*) Descendant of Wohl, a pet form of Wolter (rule, folk or army).

Wohlfarth (*Ger.*) Descendant of Wolfhart (wolf, hard).

Wohlgelernter (*Ger.*) One well versed in the Talmud, the body of Jewish civil and canonical law.

Wohlgemuth, Wohlmuth (*Ger.*) The cheerful, gay person.

Wohlleben, Wohleb (*Ger.*) One who leads a good, beautiful life.

Wohlschlager, Wohlschlaeger (*Ger.*) One who beats wool for the purpose of cleaning it.

Wojciech (*Pol.*) Descendant of Wojciech (noble, bright). The name is common due to Voitech, a popular Czech missionary who converted Poland to Christianity.

Wojciechowicz (*Pol.*) The son of Wojciech, q.v.

Wojciechowski (*Pol.*) One who came from Wojciechow (Wojciech's place), in Poland.

Wojcik (*Pol.*) Descendant of little Wojciech (noble, bright).

Wojeck (*Ukr.*) One in military service, a soldier.

Wojnar, Wojnarowicz (*Pol.*) One eager to make war or quarrel.

Wojtas (*Pol., Lith.*) Descendant of large Wojciek (noble, bright).

Wojtowicz (*Pol., Ukr.*) The son of the mayor (of a village).

Wolcott (*Eng.*) One who came from Woolscott (Wulfsige's cottage), in Warwickshire.

Wold (*Eng.*) Dweller at, or in, the wold or forest.

Wolder (*Eng.*) Variant of Walder, q.v.

Wolf, Wolff, Wolfe (*Eng., Ger.*) Dweller at the sign of the wolf; one with the characteristics of a wolf; descendant of Vulf, a pet form of names beginning with Wolf (wolf), as Wolfbrand, Wolfgang and Wolfgard; used by Jews as a symbol for Benjamin (Gen. 49:27).

Wolfenden (*Eng.*) One who came from Wolfenden (wolf valley), in Lancashire.

Wolfert (*Ger.*) Descendant of Wolfhar (wolf, army); or of Wolfhart (wolf, hard).

Wolfeschlegelsteinhausenbergerdorff (*Ger.*) An assumed name meaning "a descendant of Wolfeschlegelstein (one who prepared wool for manufacture on a stone), of the house of Bergerdorf (mountain village)." (Found in a Philadelphia telephone directory.)

Wolfgang (*Ger.*) Descendant of Wolfgang (wolf, combat route); one who came from Wolfgang, in Germany.

Wolfinger (*Ger.*) One who came from Wolfing, the name of two places in Germany.

Wolfington (*Eng.*) One who came from Wolverton (village of Wulfhere's people), in Worcestershire.

Wolfman (*Ger., Eng.*) Descendant of Wulfman (wolf, man); one who dealt in wool, a wool merchant.

Wolford (*Eng.*) One who came from Wolford (enclosure protected from wolves), in Warwickshire.

Wolfram, Wolfrom, Wolfrum (*Ger.*) Descendant of Wolfraban (wolf, raven).

Wolfsberger, Wolfsberg (*Ger.*) One who came from Wolfsberg (wolf mountain), the name of several places in Germany.

Wolfsmith (*Ger.*) One who worked with lumps of malleable iron obtained direct from the furnace.

Wolfson, Wolfsohn (*Eng., Ger.*) The son of Wolf (wolf); or of Wolf, a pet form of one of the many names beginning with Wolf.

Wolin (*Pol.*) One who came from Volhynia (the plain), in Poland.

Wolk, Wolke (*Ger.*) Dweller at the sign of the wolf; one with the characteristics of a wolf.

Wolkowicz (*Pol.*) The son of Wolf, a short form of many longer names.

Woll, Woller (*Eng.*) Dweller at, or near, a wall.

Wollack, Wollak (*Rom.*) One who came from Wallachia (the stranger's land), a district in Romania.

Wollard, Wolard (*Eng.*) Variant of Woollard, q.v.

Wollenschlager (*Ger.*) Variant of Wohlschlager, q.v.

Wollman, Wolman (*Eng.*) Variant of Woolman, q.v.

Wollschlaeger, Wollschlager (*Ger.*) Variant of Wohlschlager, q.v.

Wolov (*Rus.*) The son of Wol (ox).

Wolpert (*Ger.*) Descendant of Waldobert (rule, bright).

Wolsey (*Eng.*) One who came from Wolseley (Wulfsige's grove), in Staffordshire.

Wolski (*Pol.*) One who came from Wola (liberty), in Poland.

Wolson (*Eng.*) Variant of Wolfson, q.v.

Wolsoncroft (*Eng.*) Variant of Wolstencroft, q.v.

Wolstencroft (*Eng.*) One who came from Wolstancroft (Wolfstan's enclosed land), in Lancashire.

Wolstenholme (*Eng.*) One who came from Wolstenholme (Wulfstan's manor), in Staffordshire.

Wolter, Wolters (*Eng.*) Descendant of Walter (rule, folk or army).

Wolverton (*Eng.*) One who came from Wolverton (village of Wulfhere's people), the name of four places in England.

Womack (*Eng.*) Dweller near the hollow oak; or crooked oak.

Womble (*Eng.*) Variant of Wombwell, q.v.

Wombwell (*Eng.*) One who came from Wombwell (Wamba's spring), in the West Riding of Yorkshire.

Womelsdorf (*Ger.*) One who came from Womelsdorf (Womele's village), in Germany.

Won (*Chin.*) Warm; literature.

Wong (*Chin., Eng.*) Wide (sea or ocean);

a variant of Wang, q.v.; dweller in, or near, a field or meadow.

Wood (*Eng.*) Dweller in, or near, a grove or dense growth of trees; the wild or frenzied man. Much of England was still thickly wooded even in districts that had long been settled during surname times.

Woodall (*Eng.*) One who came from Woodale (wolves' valley), in Yorkshire; dweller at the hall by, or in, the wood.

Woodard (*Eng.*) Variant of Woodward, q.v.; descendant of Wodard (wood, hard).

Woodbridge (*Eng.*) One who came from Woodbridge (wooden bridge), in Suffolk; dweller at, or near, a wooden bridge.

Woodburn (*Eng.*) One who came from Woodburn (stream in the wood), in Northumberland.

Woodbury, Woodberry (*Eng.*) One who came from Woodbury or Woodborough (fort built of wood; or in a wood), the names of several places in England.

Woodcock (*Eng.*) One who came from Woodcote (cottage in the wood), the name of six places in England; dweller at the sign of the woodcock; nickname for a fool or simpleton.

Woodend (*Eng.*) One who came from Woodend (end of the wood), in Northamptonshire.

Woodens, Wooden (*Eng.*) One who came from Wooden (wolves' valley), in Northumberland; dweller at the end of the wood.

Woodfall (*Eng.*) One who came from Woodfall (wood where trees are down), in Lancashire.

Woodford (*Eng.*) One who came from Woodford (ford by a wood), the name of various places in England.

Woodfork, Woodforks (*Eng.*) Variant of Woodford, q.v.

Woodham (*Eng.*) One who came from Woodham (woods; homestead in a wood), the name of several places in England.

Woodhead (*Eng.*) Dweller at the head or upper end of the wood; one who came from Woodhead, the name of places in Devonshire and the West Riding of Yorkshire.

Woodhouse (*Eng.*) Dweller in the house in, or by, a wood; or in the house made of wood.

Woodhull (*Eng.*) Variant of Woodill, q.v.

Woodill, Woodell (*Eng.*) One who came from Woodhill (hill where woad grew), in Bedfordshire.

Wooding, Woodin (*Eng.*) Dweller at a clearing or place where wood has been cut.

Woodington (*Eng.*) One who came from Waddington (wheat hill; village of Wada's people), the name of places in Surrey and the West Riding of Yorkshire.

Woodland (*Eng.*) One who came from Woodland (wooded land), the name of several places in England.

Woodley, Woodle (*Eng.*) One who came from Woodleigh (glade in a wood), in Devonshire.

Woodlock (*Eng.*) Dweller at the enclosure in, or by, the wood.

Woodman (*Eng.*) One who cut and sold timber in a wood or forest; one who hunted game in a wood; one who dyed with woad; descendant of Wudeman (woodman).

Woodrick, Woodrich, Woodridge (*Eng.*) Dweller in, or near, the wood on a ridge or range of hills.

Woodrow (*Eng.*) One who came from Woodrow (row of trees), the name of places in Wiltshire and Worcestershire.

Woodruff, Woodroffe, Woodroofe (*Eng.*) A wood or forest keeper for the lord of the manor.

Woods (*Eng.*) Dweller in, or near, a grove or dense growth of trees.

Woodside (*Eng., Scot.*) Dweller at the side of the wood; one who came from Woodside (side of the wood), in Ayrshire.

Woodson, Woodsum, Woodsome (*Eng.*) One who came from Woodsome (houses in a wood), in Yorkshire; the son of Wuda (wood).

Woodward (*Eng.*) The officer who had charge of the wood, a forester.

Woodworth (*Eng.*) Dweller at the homestead in, or by, a wood.

Woody, Woodie, Woodey (*Eng.*) One who came from Woodhay (enclosure in the wood), the name of places in Berkshire and Hampshire; dweller at the enclosure in the wood; the wild man.

Woodyard (*Eng.*) Dweller at the yard by the wood; variant of Woodard, q.v.

Wooke, Wookey (*Eng.*) One who came from Wookey (trap), in Somerset.

Wool (*Eng.*) One who came from Wool (springs), in Dorset.

Woolard (*Eng.*) Variant of Woollard, q.v.

Wooldridge, Wooldredge (*Eng.*) Descendant of Wulfric (wolf, rule).

Wooler, Wooller (*Eng.*) One who came from Wooler (bank of the stream), in Northumberland.

Wooley, Woolley (*Eng.*) One who came from Woolley (wolves' meadow), in Yorkshire.

Woolf (*Ger.*) Variant of Wolf, q.v.

Woolfolk, Woolfork (*Eng.*) The people who worked with wool; descendant of Woolfolk (wolf, people).

Woolford (*Eng.*) Variant of Wolford, q.v.

Woollard (*Eng.*) Descendant of Wulfweard (wolf, ward); or of Wulfheard (wolf, hard).

Woollcott (*Eng.*) One who came from Woolcot (Wulfa's cottage), in Somerset.

Woolley (*Eng.*) One who came from Woolley (wolves' wood; grove by a stream), the name of five places in England.

Woolman (*Eng.*) One who dealt in wool, a wool merchant.

Woolmington (*Eng.*) Variant of Wilmington, q.v.

Woolner (*Ger.*) One who prepared wool for manufacture.

Woolridge, Woolrich (*Eng.*) Descendant of Ulrich (wolf, rule).

Woolsey (*Eng.*) Descendant of Wulfsige (wolf, victory); one who came from Wolseley (Wulfsige's grove), in Staffordshire.

Woolslager, Woolslayer (*Ger.*) Variant of Wohlschlager, q.v.

Woolson (*Eng.*) Variant of Wolfson, q.v.

Woolston (*Eng.*) One who came from Woolston (Wulfsige's or Wulfheah's or Wulfweard's or Wulf's homestead), the name of five places in England.

Woolverton (*Eng.*) One who came from Woolverton (village of Wulfhere's people; Wulfrun's homestead), in Somerset.

Woolworth (*Eng.*) Dweller at the homestead where wool was produced.

Woosley (*Eng.*) Variant of Worsley, q.v.

Wooten, Wootton, Wootten (*Eng.*) One who came from Wootton (homestead in, or by, a wood), the name of many places in England.

Worcester, Wooster, Wurster, Worster (*Eng.*) One who came from Worcester (Roman fort of the Wigoran tribe), in Worcestershire.

Word (*Eng., Ger.*) Dweller near a thicket or a winding brook; descendant of Werdo, a pet form of names commencing with Wert (worthy), as Werdheri and Werdmann; dweller at an open place in a village.

Worden, Werden (*Eng.*) One who came from Worden (valley with a weir or dam), in Lancashire.

Wordsworth (*Eng.*) Dweller at, or near, Wada's homestead.

Work, Worker, Works (*Eng.*) Dweller, or worker, in, or near, the fortification; variant of Wark, q.v.

Workman (*Eng.*) One who worked so many days a week for the lord of the manor in return for the land he held.

Worley (*Eng.*) One who came from Worle (woodgrouse wood), in Somerset.

Wormack, Wormick (*Eng.*) Variant of Womack, q.v.

Wormer, Worm (*Ger.*) One who came from Worm, in Germany.

Wormley (*Eng.*) One who came from Wormley or Warmley (wood infested by reptiles), in Hertfordshire and Gloucestershire respectively.

Worms, Wormser (*Ger.*) One who came from Worms (high plain), in Germany.

Wornum (*Eng.*) One who came from Warnham (homestead where stallions were raised), in Sussex.

Worrell (*Eng.*) One who came from Worrall (bog myrtle on a river lowland), in Yorkshire.

Worren (*Eng.*) Variant of Warren, q.v.

Worrick (*Eng.*) One who came from Warwick (village by a dam or shore), the name of places in Cumberland and Warwickshire.

Worsham (*Eng.*) One who came from Worsham (Wyrtel's homestead), in Sussex.

Worsley, Worssley (*Eng.*) One who came from Worsley (Weorchaeth's grove; pasture for cattle), the name of places in Lancashire and Worcestershire.

Worst (*Ger.*) Metonymic for a maker or seller of sausages.

Worstall, Worstell (*Eng.*) One who came from Worsall (Weorc's corner), in the North Riding of Yorkshire.

Worswick (*Eng.*) One who came from Urswick (farm of wild cattle), in Lancashire.

Worth (*Eng.*) Dweller in, or near, an enclosure or on a dependent farm; one who came from Worth (enclosure), the name of several places in England.

Wortham, Worthem (*Eng.*) One who came from Wortham (enclosed homestead), in Suffolk.

Worthen (*Eng.*) One who came from Worthen (open place in the village), in Shropshire.

Worthington (*Eng.*) One who came from Worthington (village of the Wurthingas), in Lancashire.

Worthy, Worthey (*Eng.*) One who came from Worthy (enclosed homestead), in Hampshire.

Worton (*Eng.*) One who came from Worton (homestead with garden; homestead on a bank or slope), the name of places in Oxfordshire, Wiltshire, and the North Riding of Yorkshire.

Wotten (*Eng.*) One who came from Wootton (homestead in, or by, a wood), the name of many places in England.

Woulfe (*Ir.*) Irish form of Wolf, q.v.

Wozniak (*Pol., Ukr.*) The son of the messenger.

Wozny (*Pol.*) One who summoned people to a court of law.

Wragg (*Eng.*) Descendant of Ragg (the gods), the shortened form of names beginning with Ragn, such as Ragnhar and Ragnuald.

Wraight (*Eng.*) Variant of Wright, q.v.

Wray (*Eng.*) One who came from Wray (isolated place), the name of several places in England.

Wren, Wrenn (*Eng., Ir.*) One with some characteristic of the wren; grandson of Reann (spear).

Wright (*Eng.*) One who worked in wood, or other hard material, a carpenter.

Wrightman (*Eng.*) The servant of Wright; one who worked in wood or other hard material.

Wrightson (*Eng.*) The son of the worker in wood.

Wrigley (*Eng.*) Dweller at the ridge meadow.

Wrobel (*Pol.*) One with some real or fancied quality of a sparrow; dweller at the sign of the sparrow.

Wroblewski (*Pol.*) One who came from Wroblewsk (sparrow village), in Poland.

Wrona (*Pol.*) Dweller at the sign of the

crow; one with the qualities of a crow.

Wroten, Wrotten (*Eng.*) One who came from Wroughton (homestead on a winding river), in Wiltshire.

Wrzyszcz (*Pol.*) One who cries or bawls loud.

Wu (*Chin.*) Company; warlike; province of Kiangsu.

Wuennenberg (*Ger.*) One who came from Wunnenberg, in Germany.

Wuertz (*Ger.*) One who sold condiments and vegetables.

Wuest, Wuester, Wuestner, Wuesteman (*Ger.*) Dweller on the wild, un-cultivated, wasteland.

Wulf, Wulff (*Ger.*) Descendant of Vulf, a pet form of names beginning with Wolf (wolf), as Wolfbrand, Wolf-gang, and Wolfgard; dweller at the sign of the wolf; one with the qualities of a wolf.

Wunderle (*Ger.*) One who works mira-cles.

Wunderlich, Wunder (*Ger.*) The odd, or moody, man; one who was curious or nosey.

Wunsch (*Ger.*) One who came from Wunscha, in Germany.

Wuori (*Finn.*) Dweller on a mountain.

Wurm (*Ger.*) Descendant of Wurm (worm), a short form of names beginning with Wurm, as Wurm-hari and Wurmprant.

Wurster, Wurst (*Ger.*) One who made and sold sausage. See also Worces-ter.

Wurth (*Eng.*) Variant of Worth, q.v.

Wurtz, Wurts, Wurz (*Ger.*) Variant of Wuertz, q.v.

Wust, Wuster (*Ger.*) Dweller on the barren, uncultivated land; one who came from Wust (deserted), the name of two places in Germany.

Wyant, Wyand, Wyands (*Eng.*) Descen-dant of Weigand or Wygan (war-rior).

Wyatt, Wyott (*Eng.*) Descendant of little Guy (wood; sensible; life).

Wybar (*Eng.*) Descendant of Wigburh (battle, fortress).

Wyburn, Wyburne (*Eng.*) Descendant of Wigbeorn (battle, bear).

Wyche, Wych (*Eng.*) Variant of Wich, q.v.

Wydra, Wydro (*Pol.*) Dweller at the sign of the otter; one with some quality of an otter; one who trapped otters for the fur.

Wye (*Eng.*) One who came from Wye (heathen temple), in Kent; dweller at, or near, the Wye (running water), or Wey, the names of several British rivers.

Wyer (*Eng.*) Dweller at, or near, a dam or fish trap; dweller near one of the Rivers Wye (running water), in En-gland.

Wyeth, Wythe (*Wel., Scot.*) The brave man; dweller near a ford or wood; dweller near a willow tree.

Wygand, Wygant (*Eng., Ger.*) Descen-dant of Wigant (warrior).

Wygoda (*Pol.*) The comfortable man.

Wyke (*Eng.*) Variant of Wich, q.v.

Wyker (*Eng.*) Dweller or worker at a dairy farm.

Wyld, Wylde (*Eng.*) Variant of Wilde, q.v.

Wylie, Wyllie, Wyllys, Wyly (*Eng.*) Variant of Wiley, q.v.

Wyman (*Eng.*) The warrior or soldier; descendant of Wigmund (war, pro-tection).

Wymard, Wymark (*Eng.*) Descendant of Wigmearc (battle, mark).

Wymer (*Eng.*) Descendant of Wigmaer (battle, fame).

Wynder (*Eng.*) Variant of Winder, q.v.

Wyndham (*Eng.*) Dweller at a home-stead approached by a winding ascent or path; one who came from Wynd-ham, in Sussex.

Wyness, Wynes (*Eng.*) Descendant of Wine (friend).

Wynhym (*Eng.*) One who came from Wenham (pasture homestead), in Suffolk.

Wynkoop, Wynekoop (*Du.*) One who sold wine, a wine merchant; one who came from Wijnkoop (place where wine was sold), a small local district in Holland.

Wynn, Wynne (*Scot., Wel.*) Dweller on a wynd, a narrow street in a town; descendant of Gwynn (fair).

Wynnfield (*Eng.*) One who came from Wingfield (grazing ground), in Derbyshire; dweller in, or near, Wine's open country.

Wynot, Wynott (*Fr.*) Descendant of little Guyon (little wood; sensible; life).

Wynter, Wynters (*Eng.*) Variant of Winters, q.v.

Wyse (*Eng., Scot., Ger.*) Variant of Wise, q.v.

Wysocki, Wysocky (*Pol.*) One who came from Wysock (high), in Poland; the tall man.

Wyss (*Swis.*) One with white hair or very light complexion.

Wyszynski (*Ukr.*) One who came from Wyshnya (place where sour cherries grew), in Ukraine; dweller where sour cherries grew.

Xander, Xanders (*Gr.*) Descendant of Xander, a shortened form of Alexander (helper of mankind).

Xanthopoulos (*Gr.*) The son of Ksanthos (blond).

Xanthos (*Gr.*) The golden, or yellow-haired, man.

Xaverius (*Ger.*) Descendant of Xaverius (brilliant).

Xavier (*Sp.*) One who came from Xaberri or Xaverri, abbreviated forms of Etchaberri (new house), the name of numerous places in Spain.

Xenakes, Xenakis (*Gr.*) Descendant of the stranger or foreigner.

Xenophon (*Eng.*) Descendant of Xenophon (strange voice).

Xenos (*Gr.*) The stranger.

Ximena (*Sp.*) One who came from Ximena (place of Jimena or Simon), in Spain.

Yablon, Yablonski, Yablonsky (*Pol.*) Dweller near an apple tree.

Yacker (*Heb.*) Descendant of Yakir (dear; beloved).

Yaeger, Yager (*Ger.*) One who hunted game, a huntsman.

Yaffe, Yaffee (*Heb.*) Descendant of Yaffe, a pet form of Japheth (increase).

Yahya (*Arab.*) Descendant of Yahya, Arabian form of John (gracious gift of Jehovah).

Yale (*Eng.*) Dweller at a corner, nook or secret place, or at the side of a hill.

Yalman (*Tur.*) Modern name meaning "the highest summit of a mountain."

Yalowitz (*Ukr.*) Dweller near a green bush or juniper tree.

Yamada (*Jap.*) Mountain, rice field.

Yamaguchi (*Jap.*) Mountain, mouth.

Yamamoto (*Jap.*) Mountain, base.

Yamashita (*Jap.*) Mountain, below.

Yampolsky (*Pol., Rus., Ukr.*) One who came from Yampol, in the Ukraine.

Yanaitis (*Lith.*) Variant of Jonaitis, q.v.

Yancey, Yancy (*Fr.*) One who came from England, an Englishman.

Yanke, Yankee (*Du.*) Descendant of little Yan, a variant form of Jan, Dutch form of John (gracious gift of Jehovah); one who came from Holland, a name sometimes applied to a stranger.

Yano (*Jap.*) Arrow, field.

Yanoff, Yanofsky (*Rus.*) The son of Yan, a Russian form of John (gracious gift of Jehovah).

Yap (*Chin.*) Leaf.

Yarbrough, Yarborough (*Eng.*) One who came from Yarborough or Yarburgh (earth fortification), the names of places in Lincolnshire.

Yard, Yarde (*Eng.*) One who tilled a yard or yardland (about thirty acres).

Yardley (*Eng.*) One who came from Yardley (wood where spars were obtained), the name of several places in England.

Yarnell, Yarnall (*Eng.*) Dweller at the slope where eagles were seen; descendant of Arnold (eagle, rule).

Yaros, Yarosh (*Ukr.*) Descendant of Yarosh, a Ukrainian form of Russian Yerofey.

Yarrell (*Eng.*) One who came from Yarwell (stream with fish trap), in Northamptonshire.

Yarrington (*Eng.*) One who came from Yarnton (dwelling place of Earda's people), in Oxfordshire.

Yarrow (*Eng., Scot.*) Dweller at the Yarrow (rough stream), a river in Lancashire; one who came from Yarrow (rough stream), in Selkirk.

Yarwood (*Eng.*) Dweller in, or near, the wood where hares were found.

Yashar (*Heb.*) Descendant of Yashar or Yesher (honest).

Yates, Yate (*Eng.*) One who lived in, or near, the gate; or gap in a chain of hills; a gatekeeper.

Yaworski, Yaworsky (*Pol., Ukr.*) One who came from Yavorov (place of sycamore trees), in the Ukraine; dweller near a sycamore tree.

Ybarra (*Sp.*) Variant of Ibarra, q.v.

Yeager (*Ger.*) One who hunted game, a huntsman.

Yeamans, Yeaman (*Eng.*) Variant of Yeomans, q.v.

Yearby (*Eng.*) One who came from Yearby (upper village), in the North Riding of Yorkshire.

Yearsley, Yearly (*Eng.*) One who came from Yearsley (boar's grove), in the North Riding of Yorkshire.

Yeater, Yeatman (*Eng.*) Dweller near a gate; or gap in a chain of hills; a gatekeeper.

Yeaton (*Eng.*) One who came from Yeaton (homestead on a river), in Shropshire.

Yeats, Yeates (*Eng., Ir.*) Dweller by the gate; or gap in a chain of hills; a gatekeeper.

Yee (*Chin.*) First person singular pronoun, I.

Yehuda, Yehouda (*Heb.*) The Jew; descendant of Judah (praised).

Yeldham (*Eng.*) One who came from Yeldham (village which paid tribute or tax), in Essex.

Yell (*Scot.*) One who came from Yell (barren), an island in the Shetland Islands.

Yelland (*Eng.*) Dweller on sloping land; one who came from Yealand (high land), in Lancashire; the old or long-cultivated land.

Yellin (*Eng., Ger.*) One who came from Yelling (scream), in Huntingdonshire; variant of Yelland, q.v.; dweller at the sign of the red deer.

Yellock (*Eng.*) Dweller near the oak tree where a tribute or tax was collected.

Yelverton (*Eng.*) One who came from Yelverton (Geldfrith's homestead), in Norfolk.

Yemm (*Eng.*) One who was an uncle to another.

Yen (*Chin.*) Stern; words; village gate; color.

Yeo (*Eng.*) Dweller near the river; or on the Yeo (river), a river name in Devonshire and Somerset.

Yeomans, Yeoman (*Eng.*) One owning a small landed property, a freeholder; one who acted as a retainer or gentleman attendant in a royal or noble household.

Yergey (*Rus.*) Descendant of Sergey, Russian form of Sergius (to serve).

Yerkes, Yerke (*Ger.*) Descendant of Jeorg, a German form of George (farmer).

Yerusalim (*Eng.*) One who had been to Jerusalem on a pilgrimage.

Yetke (*Ger.*) Descendant of Gattke (little pond); one who came from Jatzke, in Pomerania.

Yetter (*Ger.*) American variant of Gotter, q.v.

Yewdall (*Eng.*) One who came from Yewdale (yew valley), in Lancashire.

Yinger (*Ger.*) Americanization of German pronunciation of Junger, q.v.

Yniquez (*Sp.*) The son of Inigo, a Spanish form of Ignatius (fiery).

Yoast (*Eng.*) Variant of Yost, q.v.

Yoblick (*Rus.*) Descendant of little Yob, Russian form of Job (persecuted; affliction).

Yocum, Yocom, Yokum, Yoakum (*Du.*)

Descendant of Jojakim (Yah makes to stand still).

Yoder (*Ger.*) Descendant of Joder, a variant of Theodor (gift of God); or of Jodocus (the just).

Yohanan, Yohanna, Yohana (*Ger., Heb.*) Descendant of Johannes (gracious gift of Jehovah); descendant of Yohanan, the Hebrew form of John.

Yohn (*Ger.*) Americanization of German pronunciation of John (gracious gift of Jehovah).

Yokoyama (*Jap.*) Side, mountain.

Yollin (*Eng.*) Dweller on the old or long-cultivated land.

Yomtob, Yomtoob (*Heb.*) One who wished others a good day or good holiday.

Yonaitis (*Lith.*) Variant of Jonaitis, q.v.

Yonan (*Ger.*) Descendant of Johann (gracious gift of Jehovah).

Yonker, Yonkers, Younker (*Du.*) The young nobleman or squire.

Yoos (*Ger.*) Phonetic respelling of Joos, q.v.

Yore (*Eng.*) Dweller near the Yare (babbling river), a river in Norfolk; or near the Yar or Yare, a river in Wight.

York, Yorke, Yorks (*Eng.*) One who came from York (estate of Eburos; place of yew trees), in Yorkshire.

Yorkdale (*Eng.*) One who came from Yordale (valley of the Ure river), in the North Riding of Yorkshire.

Yorker, Yorkman (*Eng.*) One who came from York (place of yew trees), in Yorkshire; or from Yorkshire (district of yew trees), a county in England.

Yoshida (*Jap.*) Fortune, rice field.

Yoshino (*Jap.*) Fortune, field.

Yost (*Ger.*) Descendant of Yost, a pet form of Jodocus and Justinius (the just).

Youell, Youel, Youle (*Eng.*) Descendant of Yule (Christmas).

Youlton (*Eng.*) One who came from Youlton (Ioli's homestead), in the North Riding of Yorkshire.

Youmans, Youman, Yomans (*Eng.*) Variants of Yeomans, q.v.

Young, Younger, Younge (*Eng., Ger.*) One younger than another with whom he was associated; or of two bearing the same Christian name; the younger son.

Youngberg (*Sw.*) Heather, mountain. The name is an Anglicization of Ljungberg.

Youngblood (*Sw., Ger.*) Heather, leaf; a translation of German Jungblut, q.v.

Youngblut (*Ger.*) Partial Anglicization of Jungblut, q.v.

Youngdahl (*Sw.*) Heather, valley.

Younghusband (*Eng.*) The farmer who was younger than another with whom he was associated.

Youngjohns (*Eng.*) The younger man named John (gracious gift of Jehovah).

Younglove (*Eng., Sw.*) Dweller at the sign of the young wolf or cub; heather, leaf.

Youngman, Youngmann, Youngerman (*Eng., Ger.*) The young servant. Sometimes this is a translation of the German Jungmann, q.v.; one younger than another with whom he was associated.

Youngquist (*Sw.*) Heather, twig.

Youngson (*Eng.*) The younger son.

Youngstrom (*Sw.*) Heather, stream.

Yousef, Youssef (*Ger.*) Descendant of Yousef, a Yiddish form of Joseph (He shall add).

Yowell (*Eng.*) Variant of Youell, q.v.

Yoxall (*Eng.*) One who came from Yoxall (corner with a yoke of oxen), in Staffordshire.

Yu (*Chin.*) Still more; to float; to oppose; yes; elegant.

Yucel (*Tur.*) Dweller in the higher place.

Yudel, Yudell (*Ger.*) Descendant of Yehudah (praised); or of Yudel (Jew).

Yudelson (*Eng.*) The son of Yudel, a name derived from Yehudah (praised); or of the Jew.

Yudenfriend, Yudenfreund (*Ger.*) The Jewish friend.

Yuen (*Chin.*) Appearance.

Yuengling (*Chin.*) The willow tingling of gem pendants.

Yule, Yuill (*Eng.*) Dweller near a yew tree; descendant of Yule (Christmas).

Yung, Yunger (*Ger.*) Respelling of Jung, q.v.

Yunker (*Du.*) Variant of Yonker, q.v.

Yurko (*Rus.*) Descendant of Yurko, a Russian form of George (farmer).

Yurkovich (*Rus.*) The son of Yurko, a Russian form of George (farmer).

Yust (*Du.*) Descendant of Joost (the just).

Yusuf (*Arab.*) Descendant of Yusuf, Arabian form of Joseph (He shall add).

Zabel (*Pol., Cz.-Sl.*) Dweller at the sign of the sable; one with the qualities of a sable; one who trapped and sold sables.

Zabinski (*Pol.*) Dweller at the sign of the frog; one thought to resemble a frog.

Zablin (*Rus.*) Dweller at the sign of the frog; one with the characteristics of a frog.

Zabludoff (*Ukr.*) One who came from Zabludov, in the Ukraine.

Zaborowski (*Pol.*) One who came from Zaborow (Zabor's settlement).

Zaccaria, Zaccario (*It.*) Descendant of Zaccaria, Italian form of Zachary (whom Jehovah remembers; pure).

Zaccone (*It.*) Descendant of Zacco, a pet form of Giacomo, Italian form of James (may God protect; the supplanter).

Zacharias, Zachary (*Eng.*) Descendant of Zacharias or Zachary (whom Jehovah remembers; pure).

Zachman, Zachmann (*Ger.*) The servant of Zach, a pet form of Zacharias (whom Jehovah remembers; pure).

Zacierka (*Pol.*) One who prepared zacierka, a kind of gruel.

Zack, Zach (*Ger.*) Descendant of Zacco or Zach, pet forms of Zacharias (whom Jehovah remembers; pure).

Zadel (*Du.*) Dweller at the sign of the saddle.

Zadlo (*Pol.*) One who goads or stings others.

Zadroga (*Pol.*) Dweller behind or beyond the road.

Zafran (*Ger.*) Variant of Safran, q.v.

Zagacki (*Pol.*) Dweller near a weir or fence of stakes across a stream.

Zagar, Zager (*Du.*) One who cut timber into boards, a sawyer.

Zagorski (*Pol.*) One who came from Zagorz (behind the hill), in Poland; dweller beyond the hill or mountain.

Zagursky (*Pol.*) Dweller beyond the hill.

Zahara (*Sp.*) One who came from Zahara (desert; bright), a town in Spain.

Zaharias (*Gr.*) Descendant of Zaharias, Greek form of Zachariah (whom Jehovah remembers; pure).

Zahn (*Ger.*) Dweller near a pointed rock; one who had a prominent tooth.

Zahradnik (*Cz.*) One who tended a garden, cultivating flowers and vegetables.

Zajac, Zajic (*Pol., Ukr.*) One with some characteristic of a rabbit; dweller at the sign of the rabbit.

Zajicek (*Cz.*) Dweller at the sign of the hare; one who hunts hares.

Zajicka, Zajic (*Cz.-Sl.*) One with some characteristic of a rabbit; dweller at the sign of the rabbit.

Zak (*Cz.-Sl., Heb.*) One who attended school, a schoolboy; abbreviation of *zera kedoshim* (the seed of martyrs).

Zakhar (*Ukr.*) Descendant of Zakhar, Ukrainian form of Zachary (whom Jehovah remembers; pure).

Zakrzewski (*Pol.*) Dweller behind the bushes or shrubs.

Zal (*Rus.*) Dweller in, or near, a hall.

Zaleski (*Pol.*) Dweller beyond the forest.

Zaleskyj (*Ukr.*) Dweller behind the woods.

Zalewski (*Pol.*) Dweller near a flooded place.

Zalkind, Zalkin (*Heb.*) Variant of Salkin, q.v.

Zalman (*Ger.*) Descendant of Zalman, a Yiddish form of Solomon (peaceful; worshiper of the god Shalman).

Zalsman (*Du.*) One who refines or sells salt.

Zambrano (*Sp.*) One who came from Zambrano (place of the Moorish festival; sailor's place), in Spain.

Zander (*Ger.*) Descendant of Zander, a pet form of Alexander (helper of mankind); one who came from Zandt, the name of several places in Germany.

Zangari, Zangaro (*It.*) Dweller on mire or on a swampy place.

Zanger, Zangerle (*Du., Ger.*) One who sang in church or synagogue; the lively, gay vigorous man.

Zangwill (*Ger., Fr.*) Descendant of Zangwill, Jewish pet form for Samuel (God hath heard; name of God; Shem is God).

Zanis (*Lat.*) Descendant of Zanis, a Latvian form of John (gracious gift of Jehovah).

Zapata (*Sp.*) One who made and sold boots and shoes.

Zapf, Zappe (*Ger.*) One who sold liquor, a publican.

Zaremba (*Pol.*) A warrior who fought with a sword.

Zarenkiewicz, Zaren (*Pol.*) One who warrants or answers for others.

Zaretsky, Zaritsky (*Rus.*) Dweller beyond the river.

Zaroff (*Rus.*) The son of the tsar (probably short for the tsar's servant).

Zarzecki, Zarzycki (*Pol.*) Dweller on the other side of the river.

Zatz (*Heb.*) Acronymic combination of *zera tzadikim* (the seed of righteous men).

Zaun (*Ger.*) Dweller near a hedge or fenced enclosure.

Zavodnick (*Ukr.*) One who winds up or starts things.

Zavorski (*Pol.*) Dweller in, or near, the Zawory, a mountain pass in the Tatra mountains.

Zawacki (*Pol.*) One who came from Zawada (troublemaker), a village in Poland; one who hinders or stands in the way of others.

Zayas (*Sp.*) One who came from Zayas, in Spain.

Zazzara, Zazzaro (*It.*) One with long hanging hair.

Zbarsky (*Ukr.*) One who came from Zbarazh, in Ukraine.

Zbik (*Pol.*) Dweller at the sign of the wild cat; one with the characteristics of a wild cat.

Zdanowicz (*Pol.*) The son of Zdan (enchantress).

Zdravkovich (*Yu.-Sl.*) The son of Zdravko (good health).

Zebrowski (*Pol.*) Dweller at the sign of the zebra.

Zecca (*It.*) Dweller near, or worker in, a mint or place where money is coined.

Zechman (*Ger.*) One who came from Zechau (mine meadow), in Germany.

Zeff (*Ger.*) Variant of Seff, q.v.

Zeh (*Ger.*) One with an unusual toe.

Zehnder, Zehner (*Ger.*) One who levies or collects the tithe or tenth for the lord of the manor, a peasant's tribute of cattle, grain, or harvest portion.

Zeidler (*Ger.*) One engaged in bee culture, a beekeeper; dweller in a forest region where bees were raised.

Zeidman, Zeid (*Ger.*) Variant of Seidman, q.v.; one who worked with, or dealt in, silks.

Zeigenfuss (*Ger.*) Variant of Ziegenfuss, q.v.

Zeiger (*Ger.*) Dweller near a signboard.

Zeigler (*Ger.*) A variant of Ziegler, q.v.

Zeiser (*Ger.*) One who picks wool; one addicted to fighting.

Zeiss (*Ger.*) The charming, pleasant, gracious man.

Zeitenberg (*Ger.*) One who came from Seitenberg (side of the hill), in Germany.

Zeitlin (*Rus.*) Descendant of Tseytl, a female name.

Zeitz, Zeitzer (*Ger.*) One who came from Zeitz, in Germany.

Zelazny (*Pol.*) One who was as strong as iron.

Zelenka (*Cz.-Sl.*) The little green one; one not acquainted with the ways of man, a greenhorn.

Zeleny (*Cz.-Sl.*) One who wore green garments.

Zelig (*Heb.*) Descendant of Zelig (blessed; blessed soul).

Zelinski, Zelinsky (*Rus.*) One who wore green clothing; dweller in a green place.

Zelkovitz (*Ger., Pol.*) One who came from Zelkow, in Poland.

Zeller, Zell (*Ger., Swis.*) One who came from Zell (church), the name of many places in Germany and of a village in Switzerland.

Zelman, Zellman (*Ger.*) Dweller near, or worker in, a church; one who occupied a cell.

Zeman (*Cz.-Sl.*) One who acted as a gentleman; one who aped the manner of a gentleman; one who was a landowner or landlord.

Zender (*Ger.*) One who collected rents; descendant of Zender, a pet form of Alexander (helper of mankind).

Zenker (*Ger.*) The quarrelsome man.

Zenner (*Ger.*) One who worked in pewter; an officer of a hundred, a district in the Middle Ages chiefly important for its court of justice.

Zeno (*It.*) Descendant of Zeno (of Zeus).

Zentner (*Ger.*) Variant of Zehnder, q.v.; one who is a judge in a hundred, a small political division.

Zepp, Zepf (*Ger.*) Variant of Zapf, q.v.

Zerbe (*Ger.*) One who came from Zerben, in Germany; a Serb, one of a Slavic tribe living in Germany.

Zerfass, Zerfoss (*Ger.*) Descendant of Servatius (saving), a fourth century saint.

Zerkowski (*Pol.*) One who came from Zerkowo (the town of the Greek church), in Poland.

Zerr, Zerrer (*Ger.*) A blustering, browbeating person, a bully.

Zervos (*Gr.*) One who was left-handed.

Zev (*Heb.*) Descendant of Zev (wolf). See Wolf.

Zhukov (*Rus.*) Dweller at the sign of the beetle or scarab.

Zick (*Ger.*) Descendant of Sigo, a pet form of names beginning with Sieg (victory), as Sigimar, Sigibrand, and Sigivald.

Zidek (*Pol.*) The little Jew, a contemptuous term.

Ziebell, Zibell (*Ger.*) One who raised and sold onions; one who came from Zibelle (place where onions grew), in Germany.

Ziegenfuss, Ziegenfus (*Ger.*) Nickname, goat's foot.

Zieger (*Ger.*) One who prepared and sold curds or cream cheese.

Ziegfeld (*Ger.*) Dweller in, or near, the field where goats were kept.

Ziegler (*Ger.*) One who built with, or made, bricks or roof tiles.

Zielinski (*Pol., Ukr.*) One who came from Zielinsk or Zielen (green place), the names of places in Poland and Ukraine.

Zielke, Ziehlke (*Ger.*) One who raised and sold cabbages.

Ziemann, Zieman (*Ger.*) Descendant of Sigiman (victory, man).

Ziemba (*Pol.*) Dweller at the sign of the bullfinch or grosbeak; one thought to possess the characteristics of a bullfinch.

Ziemer (*Ger.*) Descendant of Sigimar (victory, famous).

Ziff, Zipf (*Ger.*) Dweller near the point or corner.

Zigler (*Ger.*) Variant of Ziegler, q.v.

Zilch, Zillich, Zillig (*Ger.*) Descendant of Ziv (alive).

Zima (*Cz.-Sl., Pol., Ger.*) One who worked in the winter.

Zimbalist (*Ger.*) One who plays the cymbals.

Zimmerman, Zimmer, Zimmermann (*Ger.*) One who worked in wood, a carpenter.

Zinberg (*Ger.*) One who came from Zinnberg (tin mountain), the name of two places in Germany.

Zindell, Zindel (*Ger.*) One who dealt in silk.

Zink, Zinke (*Ger.*) One with a large or prominent nose; one who played the medieval cornet, the zinke.

Zinn, Zinner (*Ger.*) One who came from Zinna (tin foundry), the name of two places in Germany.

Zinsser, Zinser (*Ger.*) The tenant farmer who paid taxes.

Ziolko (*Pol.*) One who grew and sold herbs; dweller at a place where herbs grew; in figurative speech, a smart man.

Ziolkowski (*Pol.*) One who came from Ziolkow(o) (herbs), in Poland.

Zion (*Heb.*) One who came from Zion (monument raised up), a hill in Jerusalem; one who had made a pilgrimage to Zion, a religious name for the Holy Land of Palestine.

Zipfel (*Ger.*) Dweller on a tip or point of land; the simple, plain man; one who wore a pointed hood or cape.

Zipin (*Rus.*) Descendant of Zippe, a pet form of Zipporah (bird).

Zipp (*Ger.*) Dweller at the sign of the song thrush.

Zipper (*Heb., Ger.*) Dweller at the sign of the bird; one who came from Cyprus (tree); one who beats out grain, a thresher.

Ziskind, Ziskin (*Ger.*) Variant of Siskind, q.v.

Zisook (*Pol.*) Descendant of Isaac (he who laughs).

Zito (*Cz.-Sl.*) Dweller near the rye field.

Ziv, Zivin, Ziven (*Pol., Cz.-Sl., Rus.*) The vigorous, alive person.

Zivy, Zivi (*Heb.*) Dweller at the sign of the hind.

Zizzo, Zizza (*It.*) One who gave undue attention to dress, a dandy.

Zlaty (*Cz.-Sl.*) One who had a golden complexion, or golden-colored hair.

Zlotnick, Zlotnik (*Pol.*) One who made or sold gold articles, a goldsmith.

Zmich (*Ukr.*) The pleasant, smiling person.

Zmuda (*Pol., Ukr.*) One who bothers or annoys others; the inactive or lazy person.

Zobel (*Ger.*) One who trapped sables and sold the fur; dweller at the sign of the sable.

Zola, Zolla (*It.*) Dweller on, or near, a hill or mound; descendant of Zola, a pet form of names so ending, as Franzola, Renzola, and Anzola.

Zoll (*Ger.*) Descendant of Zollo; a variant of Zoller, q.v.

Zoller, Zollner (*Ger.*) One who collected duty on goods coming into the country, perhaps one who had purchased the concession.

Zollo, Zolla (*It.*) Descendant of Zolla, a pet form of Francesco, Italian form of Francis (free).

Zoltowski (*Pol.*) One with yellow hair or light complexion.

Zona (*It.*) Descendant of Zona, a pet form of Franzona (the free).

Zook (*Pol., Ukr., Rus., Swis., Ger.*) Descendant of Zuk (beetle); American respelling of Zug, q.v.

Zoolalian (*Arm.*) Dweller near clear water.

Zorich (*Ukr.*) The son of Zorya (star).

Zorin (*Rus.*) Dweller at the sign of the star.

Zorn, Zorner (*Ger.*) One who came from Zorn (anger), in Germany.

Zschacke (*Ger.*) Descendant of Zschacke (anticipation).

Zsoldos (*Hun.*) One hired for service in the army, a mercenary soldier.

Zuber (*Ger., Swis.*) Dweller by the little stream.

Zuccarelli, Zuccarello (*It.*) One who cultivated and sold almonds; or who grew small gourds.

Zuccaro (*It.*) One who raised and sold pumpkins.

Zuckerman, Zucker (*Ger.*) The robber; one who dealt in sugar.

Zuelke (*Pol.*) One who gathered herbs; the smart or clever man.

Zuercher (*Swis.*) One who came from Zurich (people of the hills), in Switzerland.

Zug (*Swis., Ger.*) One who came from

569

Zug (from the tribe of the Tugeni), a canton in Switzerland.

Zugsmith (*Ger.*) One who worked with fibrous iron.

Zuk (*Pol., Ukr.*) One thought to have the characteristics of a beetle.

Zukauskas, Zukas (*Lith.*) Descendant of Zukas (insect); one thought to have the characteristics of a beetle; dweller at the sign of the beetle.

Zukerman, Zuker (*Ger.*) The robber; one who dealt in sugar.

Zukor, Zuker (*Hun.*) One who dealt in sugar.

Zukov (*Rus.*) One with some characteristic of a beetle; son of Zuk (beetle).

Zukovich (*Yu.-Sl., Rus.*) The son of Zuk (beetle).

Zukowski (*Pol.*) One who came from Zukow(o) (place infested by beetles), in Poland.

Zulalian (*Arm.*) Dweller near clear water.

Zulawski (*Pol.*) Dweller on low, marshy ground.

Zullo (*It.*) Descendant of Zullo, a pet form of Ignazio, Italian form of Ignatius (fiery).

Zumoff (*Ukr.*) One who came from Izum or Izyum, in the Ukraine.

Zumstein (*Ger.*) Dweller near, or at, the stone.

Zumwalt (*Ger.*) Dweller in, or near, the forest.

Zunz (*Ger.*) One who came from Zonz on the Rhine, in Germany.

Zupan (*Yu.-Sl.*) The mayor or head man in a village; descendant of the priest.

Zurawski (*Pol.*) One who came from Zuraw (place where cranes abound), in Poland.

Zurcher (*Swis., Fr.*) One who came from Zurich (people of the hills), in Switzerland.

Zurek (*Pol.*) One who made sour meal pap.

Zurich, Zurick (*Swis.*) One who came from Zurich (people of the hills), in Switzerland.

Zuschmidt (*Ger.*) Dweller at the smith's place.

Zussman, Zusman (*Ger., Heb.*) Descendant of Zussman (beloved); variant of Sussman, q.v.

Zver (*Rus.*) Dweller at the sign of the beast.

Zwadzki (*Pol.*) One who came from Zawada (obstacle), in Poland.

Zwart, Zwartz (*Du.*) One with a dark or swarthy complexion.

Zweig (*Ger.*) Branch (of a plant).

Zweigler (*Ger.*) Dweller on the side road; or branch of the stream.

Zwick, Zwickel (*Ger.*) Dweller on a wedge-shaped piece of land; one who dealt in nails; descendant of Cvik (crafty man).

Zwicker (*Ger.*) One who came from Zwickau (market town), a city and district in Saxony; one who made and sold nails; descendant of Swidiger (strong, spear).

Zwolak (*Pol.*) One who calls others together in meetings.

Zych (*Pol.*) Descendant of Zych, a pet form of Zyla (vein).

Zygmunt, Zygmund, Zygmont (*Pol.*) Descendant of Zygmunt, Polish form of Sigmund (victory, protection)

Zyla (*Ukr.*) One with prominent veins; descendant of Zyla (vein).

Zylstra (*Du.*) Dweller near the lock, the enclosure for raising and lowering the water level in a canal or sluice; or near a drainage sluice.

Zysk (*Ukr., Pol.*) One who buys and sells for gain or profit.

Zzzu, Zzzpt, Zzyn Manufactured names adopted in order to be last in the telephone directory.

74 75 10 9 8 7 6 5 4 3